THE D.H.4/D.H.9 FILE

by Ray Sturtivant and Gordon Page

AN AIR-BRITAIN PUBLICATION

Published in the United Kingdom by

Air-Britain (Historians) Ltd,
12 Lonsdale Gardens
Tunbridge Wells, Kent TN1 1PA

Sales Dept:
19 Kent Road, Grays, Essex RM17 6DE
[E-mail: mike@absales.demon.co.uk]

Correspondence to:

R.C.Sturtivant, 26 Monks Horton Way,
St.Albans, Herts, AL1 4HA
and not to the Tunbridge Wells address

ISBN 0 85130 274 2

Printed by
Unwin Brothers Ltd
The Gresham Press
Old Woking
Surrey, GU22 9LH

Front cover painting by Dugald Cameron
depicts two D.H.9As and an Avro 504K
of No.602 (City of Glasgow) Squadron.

Back cover drawing by Dave Howley.

CONTENTS

A parachutist leaving an American-built USD-9 during tests in 1925. According to the official caption he jumped clear, then was dragged off his feet when the parachute opened and carried him clear. (via Philip Jarrett)

CREDITS

The authors wish to acknowledge the generous help given by numerous individuals and organisations in providing information and photographs for this book. The following have given help in respect of specific gaps, but the help is equally appreciated of many others who have given assistance over the years.

Lennart Andersson, Chris Ashworth, Dave Birch, Trevor Boughton, Chaz Bowyer, Jack Bruce, Edvins Bruvelis, Mosha Bukhman, Mick Burrow, Byron B.Calomiris (of AAHS), Bob Casari, Gerard Casius, Frank Cheesman, Patrick J Cummins, Pat Dempsey, Ted and Dianne Darcy, Mick Davis, Herman Dekker, Carlos Dufriche, Major John M.Elliott USMC (Ret), Malcolm Fillmore, Santiago A.Flores, Norman Franks, Jim Freidhoff (via AAHS), Frits Gerdessen, Jennifer M.Gradidge, Peter Green, John A.Griffin, Daniel P.Hagedorn Snr, Jim Halley, John Havers, Peter Hillman, John Hopton, Phil Jarrett, Derek A.King, Paul Leaman, Stuart Leslie, Wojtek Matusiak, Mike O'Connor, David W.Ostrowski, Bruce Robertson, Mike Schoeman, Ken Smy, Stewart Taylor, Terry Treadwell, Victor Turon, Joe Warne, Colin Waugh and Larry Webster.

Also the staffs of the Fleet Air Arm Museum, Imperial War Museum, Liddle Archive (Brotherton Library, Leeds University), Public Record Office, the Royal Air Force Museum and the Belgian National Air Museum.

The authors are especially grateful to Dave Howley for providing the colour drawings, Dugald Cameron for the front cover painting and Frank Cheesman for his assistance in checking the manuscript.

We are also extremely grateful to Ted Darcy of the WFI Research Group for his considerable help in providing information on American accidents. Members of this American-based group, whose activities are probably little known in the UK, has the motto is "Bringing closure to long unanswered questions...". They have for the past thirty years been involved with various aspects of military research, and in 1984, following the advent of affordable PCs, they decided to consolidate their various efforts into a centralised a database system. With the Internet boom of the early 1990s, the communication speed provided by greatly enhanced e-mail permitted a higher volume of traffic in a timely manner, allowing costs to be kept to a minimum and the quality standards high. The group is also active in the recovery of historical artifacts as well as manuscript preparation on selected topics. They may be contacted at PO Box 231, Fall River, MA 02724, USA, Fax 508-675-5956 or http://www.cntn.net/wfirg/.

BIBLIOGRAPHY

Aah! de Havilland-ski! (Andre Alexandrov & Gannady Petrov - Air Enthusiast 1998)
Aircraft of the Royal Air Force since 1918. (Owen Thetford, Putnam)
Aircraft of the Spanish Civil War. (Howson, Putnam)
American Aviation Historical Society Journal (various issues)
Aviones de la Guerra Civil Espanola. (Miranda, Silex)
Aviones en Espana. (Rello, San Martin)
Boeing Aircraft. (Peter M Bowers, Putnam)
Canadian Military Aircraft. (J.A.Griffin)
de Havilland DH-4, From Flaming Coffin to Living Legend. (Walter J.Boyne)
Enciclopedia de la Aviacion. (Editorial Planeta)
For Your Tomorrow. (Errol W.Martyn)
Historia de la Aviacion Espanola. (several authors, for IHCA - Instituto de Historia y Cultura Aerea)
Marine Corps Aviation: The Early Years. (Lt Col Edward C.Johnson USMC)
RCAF Squadrons and Aircraft. (S.Kostenuk and J.Griffin)
Royal Air Force Squadrons. (Wg Cdr C.G.Jefford MBE, Airlife)
Soviet Aircraft and Aviation 1917 - 1941. (Lennart Andersson, Putnam)
The Imperial Gift - British Aeroplanes Which Formed the RAAF in 1921. (John Bennett, Banner Books)
The Measure of America's World War Aeronautical Effort. (Col Edgar S.Gorell)
The Sky Their Battlefield. (Trevor Henshaw, Grub Street)
The Squadrons of the Royal Air Force and Commonwealth 1918 - 1988. (James J. Halley, Air-Britain)
United States Military Aircraft since 1908. (Gordon Swanborough & Peter M Bowers, Putnam)
United States Navy Aircraft since 1911. (Gordon Swanborough & Peter M Bowers, Putnam)
Windsock Datafile 72 - Airco D.H.9. (J.M.Bruce, Windsock Publications)
World War II Combat Squadrons of the United States Air Force. (Maurer Maurer, Platinum Press)

GLOSSARY OF TERMS AND ABBREVIATIONS

A/	Acting
AA	Anti Aircraft
AAM	Acting Air Mechanic
AAP	Aircraft Acceptance Park
A/B	Able seaman
AC	Aircraftman
A/c	Aircraft
ACIS	Air Council Inspection Squadron
ACMM	Aviation Chief Machinist Mate
ACR	Aviation Chief Radioman
AD	Aircraft Depot/ Acceptance Depot/ Air Department (Admiralty)
Adv	Advanced
AES	Aeroplane Experimental Station
AFC	Australian Flying Corps
A/F/Cdr	Acting Flight Commander
A/G	Air Gunner
AG&FS	Aerial Gunnery and Fighting School
AGL	Acting Gunlayer
AGP	Anti-Gotha patrol
AI	Air Issues (otherwise Issues Section)
AID	Aeronautical Inspection Department
Airco	Aircraft Manufacturing Co Ltd
AL	Alabama
AM	Air Mechanic
AMM	Aviation Machinist Mate
AMM1	Aviation Machinist Mate First Class
AP	Aircraft Park/ Air Pilotage/ Aviation Pilot
AR	Arkansas
ARD	Aircraft Repair Depot
AR&ED	Aeroplane Repair and Engine Depot [at Pizzone]
Arr	Arrived
ARS	Aircraft Repair Section
A.S.	Armament Supplies (contracts)
A/S	Anti-submarine
ASD	Aircraft Supply Depot
ASIPOS	Anti-Submarine Inshore Patrol Observers School
Assd	Assembled
Asst Payr	Assistant Paymaster
ASU	Aeroplane Storage Unit
Aux	Auxiliary
AZ	Arizona
AZP	Anti-Zeppelin Patrol [intruder identified as Zeppelin]
Bboc	Brought back on charge
Bde	Brigade
BO	Burnt out
BR	British Requisition/Beyond repair
BU	Broken up/broke up
C	German two-seat aeroplane
CA	California
CAAD	Coastal Area Aircraft Depot
CAF	Canadian Air Force
Capt	Captain
Cdr	Commander
Cdt	Cadet
CFS	Central Flying School (Upavon)
Cld	Cancelled
CofA	Certificate of Airworthiness
CofR	Certificate of Registration
COL	Crashed on landing
Comm(s)	Communication(s)
Cont	Contract
Conv	Converted
Corpn	Corporation
CPW	Coventry Ordance Works
C.P.	Contract & Purchase Branch (contracts)
CPO	Chief Petty Officer
Cpl	Corporal
CSD	Central Supply Depot
CT	Connecticut
CTD	Controller Technical Development
CW	Completely wrecked
D	German single-seat scout
Dbf	Destroyed by fire
DBR	Damaged beyond repair
DC	Dual control/District of Columbia
DCM	Distinguished Conduct Medal
DD	Driven down (not necessarily crashed)
Deld	Delivered
Dest	Destroyed
Dett	Detachment
Devt	Development
DFC	Distinguished Flying Cross
DFM	Distinguished Flying Medal
DFW	Deutsche Flugzeug-Werke
DH	de Havilland
DL	Deck landing
DLG	Day Landing Ground
DoI	Died of Injuries
DoW	Died of Wounds
DR	Daily Report
DofR	Directorate of Research
DRO	Daily Routine Orders
DSC	Distinguished Service Cross
DSM	Distinguished Service Medal
DSO	Distinguished Service Order
E.1c	Department or section responsible for storage units
EA	Enemy aircraft
EAD	Experimental Armament Department
(E)ARD	(Eastern) Aircraft Repair Depot
EC&AD	Experimental Constructive & Armament Department
ECD	Experimental Constructive Department
EF	Engine failure/Expeditionary Force
Elec	Electrician
Eng Lt	Engineer Lieutenant
Ens	Ensign (US Navy)
ERA	Engine Room Artificer
Exptl	Experimental(ly)
FB	Flying boat
F/Cdr	Flight Commander
F/Cdt	Flight Cadet
FF	First flew
FIS	Flying Instructors School
FL	Force landed/Florida
F/L	Flight Lieutenant
Fl.Abt	Flieger Abteilung (German reconnaissance unit) [or FLA]
Fl.Abt(A)	Flieger Abteilung (German artillery spotting unit)
Flgm	Flugmaat (German Naval Flying Mate)
FlgObm	FlugObermaat (German Naval Flying 1st Mate)
Flt	Flight
F/Sgt	Flight Sergeant
FM	First mention
F/O	Flight Officer
FS	Fighting School/Flying School
FSL	Flight Sub-Lieutenant
ft	Foot/feet
FTR	Failed to return
Fw	Feldwebel (German sergeant)
FwLt	FeldwebelLeutnant (German Master Sergeant)
FW&T	Fair wear and tear
G	German multi-engined aircraft
GA	Georgia
Gen	General
GHQ	General Headquarters
GI	Ground instructional (airframe)
G/L	Gunlayer
Gnr	Gunner
Govt	Government
Grp	Group
GS	Gunnery School
Gy Sgt	Gunnery Sergeant
HACP	Hostile Aircraft Patrol [enemy intruder of unknown type]
HAPP	Hostile Aeroplane Patrol [enemy intruder identified as aeroplane]
Haupt	Hauptmann (German Captain)
HD	Home defence
HI	Hawaii
HMS	His Majesty's Ship
HP	Handley Page
hp	Horsepower
HQ	Headquarters
HSMP	Hostile Submarine Patrol [reported U-boat]

Unidentified D.H.4 and pilot of No.25 Squadron. The significance of the lettering 'RAA' forward of the fuselage roundel unknown. (MAP)

HSPP	Hostile Seaplane Patrol [enemy intruder identified as seaplane]
HT	High tension [wire]
IAAD	Inland Area Aircraft Depot
IF	Independent Force
IL	Illinois
IN	Indiana
IS	Issues Section (otherwise Air Issues)
Jasta	Jagdstaffel (German scout unit)
KB	Kite balloon
KNIL	Kon. Nederlands Indisch Leger [Royal Netherlands Indies Army]
KS	Kansas
LVA	Luchtvaart Afdeling [the acronym for the Army Air Branch in the Netherlands (Europe)]
LAM	Leading Air Mechanic
lb	Pound weight
L/Col	Lieutenant Colonel
LFG	Luftfahrzeug Gesellschaft
LG	Landing Ground
LM	Leading Mechanic/Last mention
Lt	Lieutenant
2/Lt	Second Lieutenant
L/Tel	Leading Telegraphist
Ltn	Leutnant (German 2nd Lieutenant)
LtzS	Leutnant zur See (German Naval Lieutenant)
L/Tel	Leading Telegraphist
LV	Light vessel
LVG	Luft-Verkehrs Gesellschaft
M	Miles
MA	Massachusetts
MAD	Marine Aeroplane Depot
MAEE	Marine Aircraft Experimental Establishment
MAES	Marine Aircraft Experimental Section
MB	Motor boat
MC	Military Cross
MD	Maryland
M/c	Machine
Mech	Mechanic
m/g	Machine gun
MI	Michigan
Mid	Midshipman
Min	Minute
Misc	Miscellaneous
Mjr	Major
Mk	Mark
ML	Motor Launch
MM	Military Medal
MN	Minnesota
MO	Missouri
Mob	Mobilising
Mod	Modified
Mods	Modifications
MOS	Marine Operators School
MPK	Missing presumed killed
M/Sgt	Master Sergeant
MT	Motor transport/Mechanical transport
MU	Maintenance Unit
N	Naval
NAD	Naval Aeroplane Depot/ Naval Air Division
NADD	Naval Aeroplane Depot Dunkirk
NAP	Naval Aeroplane Park
NARD	Naval Aeroplane Repair Depot
(N)ARD	Naval Aircraft Repair Depot
NC	North Carolina
NE	New England
NFS	Naval Flying School
NFT	No further trace
NJ	New Jersey
NLG	Night Landing Ground
NM	New Mexico
(N)MAD	(Northern) Marine Aeroplane Depot
No	Number
NPL	National Physical Laboratory
nr	Near
NTU	Not taken up
NV	Nevada
NWF	North West Frontier [of India]
NWR	Not worth repair
NY	New York
NZPAF	New Zealand Permanent Air Force
(O)	(Observers)
Oblt	Oberleutnant (German 1st Lieutenant)
Obs	Observer

Offstlvtr Offizier Stellvertreter (German Warrant Officer)
OH Ohio
OK Oklahoma
O/L Observer Lieutenant
OOC Out of control
OD Operator
OR Oregon
OS Observers School
OSL Observer Sub-Lieutenant
OSR&AP Observers School of Reconnaissance and Aerial Photography
o/t Overturned
OUAS Oxford University Air Squadron
PA Pennsylvania
PD Packing Depot
Pdr Pounder
PFO Probationary Flying Officer
PFSL Probationary Flight Sub-Lieutenant
PoW Prisoner of War
PRO Public Record Office
Pte Private
Pty Proprietary
PVRD Port Victoria Repair Depot (Grain)
PVRS Port Victoria Repair Station (Grain)
Pwfu Presumed withdrawn from use
QANTAS Queensland and Northern Territories Aerial Services Ltd
Q/M Quartermaster
RAE Royal Aircraft Establishment
RAF Royal Air Force/Royal Aircraft Factory
RAF(R) Royal Air Force (Russia)
RCNAS Royal Canadian Naval Air Service
RD Repair Depot
Rec Pk Reception Park
Recond Reconditioned
Refd Reformed
Regd Registered
Rep Pk Repair Park
Retd Returned
RFA Royal Fleet Auxiliary/Royal Field Artillery
RFC Royal Flying Corps (Military Wing)
RHNAS Royal Hellenic Naval Air Service
RI Rhode Island
Rittm Rittmeister (German Cavalry Captain)
RKKVF Raboche-Krest'Yanskii Krasny Voenno Vozdusyhnyi Floi (Workers' and Peasants' Red Military Air Fleet)
Rly Railway
RM Royal Marines
RMA Royal Marines Artillery
RMLI Royal Marines Light Infantry
RN Royal Navy
RNAS Royal Naval Air Service/Royal Naval Air Station
RNASTE Royal Navy Aircraft Service Training Establishment
RNR Royal Naval Reserve
RNVR Royal Naval Volunteer Reserve
RR Rolls-Royce
RS Reserve Squadron
RTP Reduced to produce
SAAC South African Air Corps
SABCA Société Anonyme Belge de Constructions Aéronautiques
SABENA Societe Anonyme Belge pour l'Exploitation de la Navigation Aerienne
Salv Salvage
(S)ARD (Southern) Aircraft Repair Depot
SC South Carolina

S/Cdr Squadron Commander
SD Special Duties/ Stores Depot
Sgt Sergeant
Slg Signalman/Signaller
S/L Sub-Lieutenant
S/Ldr Squadron Leader
(S)MAD (Southern) Marine Aeroplane Depot
SMOP School for Marine Operational Pilots
SNETA Société Nationale pour l'Etude des Transports Aériens
SoAF&G School of Aerial Fighting and Gunnery
SOC Struck off charge
SoN&BD School of Navigation and Bomb Dropping
SOS Struck off strength
Spec Specification
Sqn Squadron
SS Steam ship/Salvage Section
SSF School of Special Flying
Staffel [German flying unit]
Stn Station
T/ Temporary
TB Torpedo boat
TBD Torpedo boat destroyer
TD Test Depot
TDS Training Depot Station
TFSL Temporary Flight Sub-Lieutenant
TL Total loss
TO Take-off [and T/O]
TOC Taken on charge
TPFO Temporary Probationary Flight Officer
TPFSL Temporary Probationary Flight Sub-Lieutenant
TS Training Squadron
T/S/L Temporary Sub-Lieutenant
TW Totally wrecked
TX Texas
U-boat Unterseeboot (German submarine)
u/c Undercarriage
Uffz Unteroffizier (German corporal)
u/s Unserviceable
US United States
USAS United States Air Service
USMC United States Marine Corps
USMCR United States Marine Corps Reserve
USN United States Navy
UT Utah
VA Virginia
VC Victoria Cross
Vzfm Vizeflugmeister (German Sergeant Pilot)
Vzfw Vizefeldwebel (German Sergeant Major)
W Wasser [= water] (German water aeroplanes)
WA Washington
(W)ARD (Western) Aircraft Repair Depot
W/Capt Wing Captain
W/Cdr Wing Commander
W/E Week ending
WEE Wireless Experimental Establishment
Wfu Withdrawn from use
WR Weekly Report
W/T Wireless Telegraphy (equipment/ operator)
W&T Wear and tear
WO Written off/ Warrant Officer
WOC Written off charge
WY Wyoming
Yds Yards

D.H.4s of No.2 Squadron RNAS lined up at Bergues in early 1918. (MAP)

D.H.4, D.H.9 & D.H.9A PRODUCTION

Serials	Contractor	Quantity
D.H.4		
3696 - 3697	Airco	2
A2125 - A2174	Airco	50
A7401 - A8090	Airco	690 (1 cancelled)
B1482	Airco	1
B2051 - B2150	Berwick	100
B5451 - B5550	Vulcan	100
B9476 - B9500	Westland	25
C1051 - C1150	Vulcan	100 (all cancelled)
C4501 - C4550	Airco	50 (10 cancelled)
D1751 - D1775	Westland	25
D8351 - D8430	Airco	80
D9231 - D9280	Airco	50
E4624 - E4228	Airco	5
F1551 - F1552	Airco	2
F2633 - F2732	Airco	100
F5699 - F5798	Palladium	100
F7597 - F7598	Airco	2
H5290	Glendower	1
H5894 - H5939	Waring & Gillow	46
H8263	Palladium	1
N5960 - N6009	Westland	50
N6380 - N6429	Westland	50
D.H.9		
A7559	Airco	1 (D.H.4 conv)
B7581 - B7680	Westland	100
B9331 - B9430	Vulcan	100
C1151 - C1450	Weir	300
C2151 - C2230	Berwick	80
C6051 - C6121	Airco	71
C6123 - C6349	Airco	227
D451 - D950	NAF.1 (Cubitt)	500 (254 cancelled)
D1001 - D1500	NAF.2 (Crossley)	500 (50 cancelled)
D1651 - D1750	Mann Egerton	100
D2776 - D2875	Short Brothers	100
D2876 - D3275	Airco	400
D4011 - D4210	Weir	200 (all cancelled)
D5551 - D5850	Waring & Gillow	300
D7201 - D7300	Westland	100 (50 cancelled)
D7301 - D7400	Berwick	100 (70 cancelled)
D7331 - D7380	Berwick	50
D9800 - D9899	Weir	100 (15 cancelled)
E601 - E700	Whitehead	100
E5435 - E5436	Airco	2
E8857 - E9056	Airco	200
F1 - F300	NAF.1 (Cubitt)	300 (all cancelled)
F1101 - F1300	Waring & Gillow	200
F1767 - F1866	Westland	100 (all cancelled?)
H3196 - H3395	NAF.1 (Cubitt)	200 (all cancelled)
H4216 - H4315	Airco	100
H4316	Airco	1 (cancelled)
H4320 - H4369	Berwick	50
H5541 - H5890	Waring & Gillow	350
H7563 - H7612	Weir	50 (all cancelled)
H7913 - H8112	NAF.2 (Crossley)	200 (all cancelled)
H8113 - H8412	Unknown	300 (cancelled)
H9113 - H9412	Airco	300 (39 cancelled)

Serials	Contractor	Quantity
D.H.9A		
C6122 & C6350	Westland	2
E701 - E1100	Whitehead	400 (60 cancelled)
E8407 - E8806	Airco	400
E9657 - E9756	Mann Egerton	100
E9857 - E9956	Vulcan	100
F951 - F1100	Westland	150
F1603 - F1652	Westland	50
F2733 - F2902	Berwick	170 (30 cancelled)
H1 - H200	Airco	200 (25 cancelled)
H3396 - H3545	Westland	150
H3546 - H3795	Vulcan	250 (125 cancelled)
J401 - J450	Westland	50 (all cancelled)
J551 - J600	Mann Egerton	50
J5192 - J5491	Airco	300 (all cancelled)
J6957 - J6962	Westland	6 (rebuilds)
J6963 - J6968	Handley Page	6 (rebuilds)
J7008 - J7017	de Havilland	10 (rebuilds)
J7018 - J7032	Handley Page	15 (rebuilds)
J7033 - J7072	Westland	40 (rebuilds)
J7073 - J7084	Gloster	15 (rebuilds)
J7088 - J7102	Hawker	15 (rebuilds)
J7103 - J7127	PD Ascot	25 (rebuilds)
J7249 - J7258	Gloster	10
J7302 - J7309	de Havilland	8 (rebuilds)
J7310 - J7321	Hawker	12 (rebuilds)
J7347 - J7356	Gloster	10 (rebuilds)
J7604 - J7615	Hawker	12 (rebuilds)
J7700	de Havilland	1
J7799 - J7819	Westland	21
J7823 - J7834	Short	12
J7835 - J7854	Hawker	20
J7855 - J7866	Westland	12
J7867 - J7876	Hawker	10
J7877 - J7883	de Havilland	7
J7884 - J7890	Short	7
J8096 - J8128	Westland	33
J8129 - J8153	de Havilland	25
J8154 - J8171	Short	18
J8172 - J8189	Parnall	18
J8190 - J8207	Saunders	18
J8208 - J8225	Blackburn	18
J8460 - J8482	Westland	23 (dual control)
J8483 - J8494	Parnall	12 (dual control)

A D.H.9, possibly coded '110', of No.1 Fighting School, Turnberry. (via Frank Cheesman)

A D.H.4 fitted experimentally with a 360hp Rolls-Royce Eagle VIII engine and four-bladed propeller. (via Philip Jarrett)

THE D.H.4, D.H.9 & D.H.9A SERIES

D.H.4

The Aircraft Manufacturing Co Ltd, which was based at Hendon and generally referred to as Airco, produced a number of aircraft types to the designs of Geoffrey de Havilland. Designations commenced at D.H.1, which was a two-seat fighter reconnaissance pusher biplane. Next came the D.H.2, a single-seat fighting scout, also of a pusher layout. These two were moderately successful, but were followed the unsuccessful D.H.3, a twin-engine long-range bomber.

The D.H.4 bomber and fighter-reconnaissance tractor biplane, which followed, represented a considerable technological advance on its predecessors, and was destined to become one of the most successful aircraft of the First World War. It was designed to take a 160hp Beardmore engine, but in the event the new 200hp water-cooled six-cylinder upright in-line B.H.P. (Beardmore-Halford-Pullinger) engine had become available by the time of completion of the first of two prototypes. 3696 made its first flight at Hendon in mid-August 1916 piloted by Geoffrey de Havilland, its designer. After successful trials with the Central Flying School Testing Flight at Upavon, it was flown to France to spend three days at No.2 Aircraft Depot, Candas. The second prototype, 3697, flew two months later, powered by a 250-hp Rolls-Royce engine (later named the Eagle) and incorporating a number of modifications. The engine position had been lowered by three inches to improve forward view, and various alterations had been made to the mainplanes and undercarriage.

In the meantime the first production order had been placed, on 13 July for 50 aircraft to be numbered A2125 to A2174, followed in October by the Royal Flying Corps' largest order up until that time, for 600 aircraft to be serialled A7401 to A8090. A number of other orders followed, some for the Royal Naval Air Service until it was amalgamated on 1 April 1918 with the Royal Flying Corps to form the Royal Air Force.

With the aircraft quantities involved, engine supply became a problem, especially as officialdom was uncooperative in respect of efforts being made to increase production of the preferred Rolls-Royce engine. This had originally been designed for the Admiralty Air Department, for use in float seaplanes and flying boats, but had attracted the attention of the War Office, who secured some for fitting in the F.E.2d. Enough were available by early 1917 for the D.H.4s of No.55 Squadron, then mobilising at Lilbourne, though these had not been fitted with bomb racks on the assumption that they would only be used for fighter-reconnaissance work. The bomber variant was intended to be fitted with either the B.H.P or the R.A.F.3a engine. However, the B.H.P. was not yet available in quantity, and in any case development had so altered its dimensions that it would not fit into the existing D.H.4 airframe. Instead, therefore a number of Rolls-Royce engines intended for the F.E.2d was supplied in order to maintain D.H.4 production. The various marks of Eagle were of different rotation, some being left-handed and some right-handed, according to their originally intended use, but by June 1917 the D.H.4 fuselage had been modified by Airco so as to be able to accommodate any version of this highly successful engine. A7446 was the first aircraft to be so modified, and was specially fitted with the uprated 375hp Eagle VIII.

Meanwhile, in the spring of 1917 it was agreed to supply the Russians with fifty D.H.4 airframes, to be with Fiat A.12s to be provided by the Russians. By October 1917 it was evident that with winter so close at hand these aircraft could not be then delivered. The Russians were therefore asked to relinquish the 50 aircraft on the understanding that 75 would be supplied in the spring of 1918, to which the Russians agreed. Serials C4501 to C4550 were given to the ex-Russian order, of which forty were completed and the balance of ten delivered as spares. No.49 Sqn was the only user of this variant on the Western Front and then only between January and April 1918 when they were replaced by D.H.9s. By the spring of 1918 the Bolsheviks were in power, and by the Treaty of Brest-Litovsk in March 1918 had taken Russia out of the war, so the 75 aircraft promised never materialised.

In October 1917 the 41st Wing RFC was set up at Bainville-sur-Madon to carry out bombing raids over Germany in retaliation for enemy night bombing attacks which had begun on London on 2 September, its initial equipment including the D.H.4s of No.55 Squadron. In June 1918 the wing became part of a newly-formed Independent Force.

It was not until late January 1918 that the deliveries began of Eagle VIII-engined D.H.4s. This was partly due to this more powerful engine being earmarked for RNAS use in Felixstowe flying boats and Handley Page bombers, but also the lack of suitable radiators. It was also intended that the D.H.4 would be superseded by the D.H.9, but the latter was beset by difficulties with the Siddeley Puma engine and therefore lacked the necessary performance for the operational needs of the last year of the war.

On the Western Front, D.H.4s were flown by Nos.18, 25, 27, 49, 55 and 57 Squadrons, whilst in Mesopotamia it was issued to Nos.30 and 72 Squadrons. A few were used for Home Defence duties, and quite a number served in the training role and with test and experimental units. A small number were fitted after the Armistice with cabins, designated D.H.4A, for use by No.1 (Communications) Squadron at Kenley.

In addition to Airco, production was also entrusted to F.W.Berwick, Glendower Aircraft, Palladium Autocars, Vulcan Motor & Engineering, Waring & Gillow and Westland. The last named company was able to put this wartime experience to good use in the post-war period with designs of its own. A total of 1,461 aircraft was built. The type was finally declared obsolete by the RAF in August 1919.

Postwar, quite a number of D.H.4s were sold for civil use, both at home and overseas, with various modifications being made for this purpose. Others went to overseas air force, but by far the biggest foreign user was the United States, which put an Americanised version into mass production as the DH-4, details of which are given elsewhere.

A mixed bag of D.H.4s and D.H.9s of No.98 Squadron in the Spring of 1918.
(via Frank Cheesman)

D.H.9

In July 1917 the British Government agreed to an increase, from 108 to 200, of the number of operational squadrons in service with the RFC. The majority of these squadrons were to be bomber units, many of which would be equipped with a new long-range aircraft developed from the D.H.4.

Airco had initiated design work and development of this new bomber, under the designation D.H.9. The pilot's cockpit was moved several feet further back than in the D.H.4, with consequent improvement to communication, but at the expense of a reduction in the pilot's visibility due to the relative position of the wings to his cockpit. The bomber was to have been powered by a 300hp Siddeley Puma piston engine, this being a development of the 230hp B.H.P. engine, modified for large scale production by the Siddeley Deasy Motor Car Co. However, due to the unreliability of the Puma engine, caused by production problems, the engine had to be de-rated to 230hp for installation in the D.H.9.

Powered by a 230hp Galloway Adriatic engine, a modified D.H.4 (A7559) underwent performance and handling trials in July 1917, as the prototype D.H.9. In November 1917 the first production D.H.9 (C6051), powered by a 230hp Puma engine, and with two 250lb. bombs in the internal bomb-bay, was extensively tested, but its performance was found to be inferior to that of the D.H.4. Tests were also carried out fitted with various other types of engine.

The D.H.9 had meanwhile been ordered into large-scale production, replacing orders for the D.H.4. Geoffrey de Havilland warned Major General H.M.Trenchard that the aircraft performance would be unsatisfactory with the Puma engine, and Trenchard tried to stop introduction of the type. However, he was told by Sir William Weir, Controller of Supplies in the Ministry of Munitions, that all the contractual and production arrangements had been completed, and it was therefore a case of proceeding with the D.H.9 or nothing at all. Production continued throughout 1918 and well over 3,000 were eventually constructed by Airco and various other British aircraft manufacturers.

Deliveries of the D.H.9 commenced in December 1917 and the bomber first entered service with Nos.6 and 11 Squadrons, RNAS, in February 1918. It started service with No.98 Squadron, RAF, in April 1918 and went on to equip eleven other RAF bomber squadrons on the Western Front in France. These sustained heavy losses in combat operations over the Western Front, due to the unreliability of the Puma engine and the bomber's poor performance above 13,000 feet, with a full load of bombs and fuel, though in the right hands it could give a good account of itself. The D.H.9 also equipped RAF squadrons in the Middle East in addition to being used for coastal defence patrols, flying training and other duties in the United Kingdom.

When the First World War ended in November 1918 the D.H.9 was rapidly withdrawn from service with RAF bomber squadrons, except for some overseas units. These included activities in support of the White Russians by Nos.47 and 221 Squadrons, and also with 'Z' Force in Somaliland, where one was converted to become an air ambulance.

A large number of the D.H.9s constructed in 1918, which had not entered service with the RAF, were surplus to requirements and were acquired by ADC for disposal. Many of these were purchased for foreign air forces, and the type was also constructed under licence in Belgium and Spain, in the post-war years.

Front view of an early D.H.9 photographed in March 1918. (via Philip Jarrett)

Dual control D.H.9A E8673 'E' of No.27 Squadron in India around 1923. (via Philip Jarrett)

D.H.9A

The D.H.9A, which became referred to colloquially as the 'Ninak', was based on the less than successful D.H.9, and was initially for use mainly by squadrons of the Independent Force in France, but had increased wing area and various other modifications The prototype was C6350, which had been intended as the last aircraft in a batch of D.H.9s, and was fitted with an Eagle VIII engine, this being sent to Martlesham Heath for testing in February 1918. Shortly after this, large deliveries were promised of the 400-hp American-built Liberty engine for arrival from June onwards. This was of similar power and configuration to the Eagle, which was in short supply, but the small Airco drawing office could not cope with the necessary adaptation, so the task was entrusted to Westland Aircraft Works at Yeovil, who also subsequently undertook production of the type, thus laying the foundations of that firm's post-war success.

No.110 Squadron was the first to receive the type, which reached France less than three months before the Armistice. In that time it proved itself to be very effective, flying in close formation at 17,000ft in daylight raids on German towns within its range. Quite a number of squadrons received the D.H.9A during the latter part of 1918, but many of these were still mobilising in the UK at the time of the Armistice, and consequently never went to France. When the war ended, a total of 885 had been delivered to the RAF.

Although more than 1,000 Liberty engines were delivered from America, their supply was stopped in July 1918 due to the U.S. Navy being given priority for them. Consequently B7664 was fitted with an Eagle VIII, the wings being given a 4-inch stagger, this latter modification being introduced as standard shortly afterwards. In the event, stocks of Liberty engines proved sufficient for reduced post-war needs, and the D.H.9A never needed to switch to the Eagle.

During 1919-20 the D.H.9A served with Nos.47 and 221 Squadrons in Russia, then went on to become the mainstay of the day bomber squadrons, both at home and overseas, as well as being issued to Auxiliary Air Force squadrons. It remained in production until 1927, being finally withdrawn from service four years later.

A ground crew member handing up equipment to a well-wrapped D.H.4 observer.

EXPLANATION

This book largely follows the format adopted by the authors for their previous joint WW1 works, 'Royal Navy Aircraft Serials and Units 1911 - 1919', 'The Camel File' and 'The S.E.5 File'. Much of what follows will therefore of necessity be a repetition of the wording used in those books.

Dates

Wherever possible, exact dates are given. If a date has no qualification, it will be the actual date of the event in question - such as initial delivery; movement between units; operations; struck off charge or an incident.

In the absence of a precise date, especially in relation to movements, the first known date with that particular unit is prefixed "by" (e.g. "by 28.7.18") and the last known date is prefixed '@' (e.g. "@28.7.18"). In some instances it is possible to be more precise than that, even where the exact date is unknown. This is especially the case, for instance, where the source is a series of regular returns, and the change could only have taken place within a few days either way. In such cases the date may be marked either "FM" (first mention) or "LM" (last mention); very often these dates have turned out to be the actual date of a movement or incident when further information has been found in contemporary records. Alternatively, the date of a movement or event may be prefixed "W/E" (e.g. W/E 29.7.18) indicating that the change took place in the week ending the date given, but the precise date has not been traced. Where a date is incomplete, because no surviving record has been found which can pinpoint the actual date, it will be expressed as, for instance, "6.18" or occasionally just ".18".

A word of caution on dates. Daily returns were generally made up in the early evening, very often effectively at 16.00 hours. In many instances this is not clear on individual returns, so the earliest events listed on a particular day may actually have occurred late the previous day, but not noted as such.

Times

If time is considered important, this is given, if known, usually immediately before the relevant date, the 24-hour clock system being used. Times can be useful in relation to aerial combats since, taken in conjunction with

A D.H.9 of No.555/556 Flight, No.219 Squadron at Manston in 1918. (via Frank Cheesman)

locations, they may help to identify the enemy pilot(s) involved from German records. They have also been found useful in discounting published information, such as where the supposed enemy opponent was actually involved in an incident at a quite different time on the same date.

Care has to be exercised over times quoted in official documents. These might give only the time of departure or overall patrol times, with no indication of actual combat times. Where actual combat times were recorded, these are given, but they were often very approximate, and may only relate to the commencement of the fight, which could have lasted some time, especially in general combat. Where an aircraft was seen to crash, the time is more likely to be accurate, though not always so if noted by someone who was busy with his own combat.

Locations

Locations are given wherever available, using contemporary spelling. The location of an accident is given where away from base, but to save space the aerodrome name is not given in the many instances, especially at training establishments, where it occurred on or around the aerodrome. In the ,case of a squadron or other titled unit, the base at the time of the accident can be found from the lists of units near the end of this book.

With regard to combats or losses, it should be borne in mind that in many cases the location can only be approximate. A combat, particularly a general one involving numbers of aircraft on both sides, could drift some distance. It is therefore quite possible for two reports to give different locations for the same combat. Similarly an aircraft may be seen to go down, or may have been last seen, in one location, but to have crashed some distance away. Place names were often misspelt, or hyphens or accents omitted, but the majority of such errors have been identified and corrected. Where an aircraft crashed in enemy territory, any location quoted in surviving German records is likely to be the more accurate.

Names and Ranks

Names are given wherever possible in relation to specific activities or incidents, though many documents do not record these. Where relevant names are recorded, it is quite common for these to consist only of rank and surname, especially in the case of other ranks, and often the names are wrongly spelt or initials given incorrectly or omitted altogether especially in case of other ranks. We have tried to correct such errors in our own lists, including tracing missing initials in most cases. Ranks and decorations are generally as given in the record from which the information was obtained. The name index, however gives the highest rank relevant to all entries listed. Where a pilot is promoted during a series of incidents, both ranks are usually given, for instance 'Lt/Capt Z.Z.Smith', in the relevant entry.

Casualties

All known casualties are listed against the relevant or likely serial. Where no serial has been traced, the incident involved is included in the appendix 'Unidentified Incidents'. The records for some squadrons are particularly troublesome in this respect, or have not survived at all, and lists are therefore given for relevant unidentified incidents.

It will usually be apparent from the entry whether the casualty was sustained in combat or an accident. In the case of a non-fatal casualty, this is referred to as "injured" in the case of an accident and "wounded" if in combat. Where the man concerned subsequently died of his injuries, the actual date of death is also quoted if this is later than the incident concerned.

Contemporary records often failed to record the ultimate fate of aircrew who were posted as missing. As far as possible the authors have ascertained from later records whether each individual was killed, taken prisoner or interned in Holland. Where taken prisoner or interned, it is noted if the person concerned was known to have been wounded or injured.

Aircraft Histories

It has been possible to compile complete or near complete histories for the greater proportion of the aircraft listed. The main exceptions are aircraft which served with training or Home Defence units, or which remained in storage, for which very little official documentation has survived.

Where relevant records have been traced, the fate of each individual aircraft has been listed, and also the cause, if known. Such information has been derived from a variety of sources with consequent variation in the amount of detail. Very occasionally an aircraft would be rebuilt and brought back on charge even where striking off charge had been authorised.

During 1918, numerous RAF aircraft were completely rebuilt at depots in France, and given fresh serial numbers, even where, in some instances, such rebuilding was completed within only a few days. A hiatus occurred however, when batch F5801 to F6300 was exhausted, as numbers continued to be allocated up to F6513 before the error came to light. The offending aircraft were then retrospectively renumbered in the H6843 to H7293 range, though a few had already been in service using their incorrect numbers.

The phraseology relating to crashed aircraft was somewhat unsophisticated with none of the designated categories of later years. Terms such as "wrecked", "smashed", "completely wrecked", "totally wrecked", struck off strength" were used, and it was not until the 1920s that official damage categories were introduced. The latter were Cat U (undamaged), Cat M(u) (repairable on site by unit), Cat M(c) (repair beyond unit capacity), Cat.R (beyond repair on site) and Cat W (write-off)

Anomalies

Many anomalies have come to light during our researches, especially in relation to serial numbers. Omitted prefix letters and transposed digits were often found in official documentation, especially flying logbooks. A number of Combat Reports were found to contain typing and compilation errors, presumably due to the adverse conditions in which clerks had to work. If a pilot flew more than one sortie, especially if in different aircraft, the clerk would sometimes extract the wrong serial from the Daily Report when subsequently compiling the individual Combat Report. In the case of a Combat Report for a shared victory, the pilots' names were sometimes typed in a different sequence from those of the aircraft serials as shown in the relevant Daily Report. Times were also occasionally prone to typing error, and did not always distinguish between a.m. and p.m., leading, for example, to some researchers quoting times which would have been most unlikely, being during the hours of darkness.

Many Combat Reports have failed to survive, and a few years ago large number of aviation documents, including many WW I Combat Reports, were stolen from the Public Record Office, many of these being never recovered. To some extent it has been possible to reconstruct the essential details of such missing Combat Reports from other records. Often no serial is quoted, but in the majority of such cases it has been possible to trace or deduce this from Daily Reports where these exist.

It is not always apparent from surviving Combat Reports whether a claim has been allowed, many being officially recorded as indecisive on investigation by higher authority. Where squadron diaries or similar records are available we have regarded these as being most likely correct.

Where there is no such record we have used our own judgment based on such evidence as is available. We have also noted a number of instances where a Combat Report would lead one to believe that a shared victory was involved, but this was not necessarily supported by the squadron record, which might credit it to only one or sometime two of the pilots. Here we have generally followed the squadron's likely intentions as regards credit and made no reference to the other pilots involved.

Generally, we have not included "driven down" claims, as being indecisive, but we have made some exceptions to this rule where we feel it might be helpful.

It follows from the foregoing that our own findings will quite often differ from those of other researchers. Despite all our efforts, however, we are well aware that we have not always discovered the whole truth. Readers must form their own views as to whether our approach is a sensible one. Interpretation of surviving papers is an inexact science, made more difficult by the loss of relevant records over the years.

German Victors and Victims

In some instances it has been possible to give the names, ranks and units of German victors and victims. These are based mainly on German sources, including Den Toten zur Ehrung (Ehrentafel der gefallen Flieger), a list of German casualties produced shortly after the First World War by Major Wilhelm Haehnelt, and extracts from official German victory claims. [See Trevor Henshaw's book 'The Sky Their Battlefield (Grub Street 1995) for more detailed information]

Any conclusions we have drawn by comparisons between these German lists and contemporary British records are our own. In a small number of cases we tend to disagree with previously published identities of such victims or victors, since the place and/or times in respective records appear to us not to fit each other. Our knowledge of German aspects is, however, somewhat limited, and we are therefore open to correction.

German aircraft which fell on the British side of the lines were given G-numbers for record purposes. Most such aircraft were wrecks, but a few were reasonably intact and the G-number was painted on the fuselage of these. The original series of numbers, started in early in 1917, extended from G.1 to G.167, but later RAF Headquarters and the Brigades each had their own series (e.g. G/5Bde/8). Such numbers are given where known or deduced.

Units

The Royal Flying Corps (Military Wing), following Army practice, numbered its units in a straightforward aeroplane squadron numbering system, from No.1 onwards, this being continued to the present day by the Royal Air Force. Similarly, training units were generally numbered 1 onwards, these being by the summer of 1917 mainly Training Squadrons, most of which were grouped during 1918 as Training Depot Stations.

With the formation of the Royal Air Force on 1 April 1918, all naval squadrons had 200 added to their numbers and naval training stations were absorbed into the RFC system of Training Depot Stations, each station being allocated one or more numbers from 200 onwards, some of these being renumbered in the 50 series in July 1918, and the remainder restyled to more precisely reflect the particular role they had acquired.

Details of the majority of units having D.H.4s, D.H.9s or D.H.9As on strength appear in an appendix.

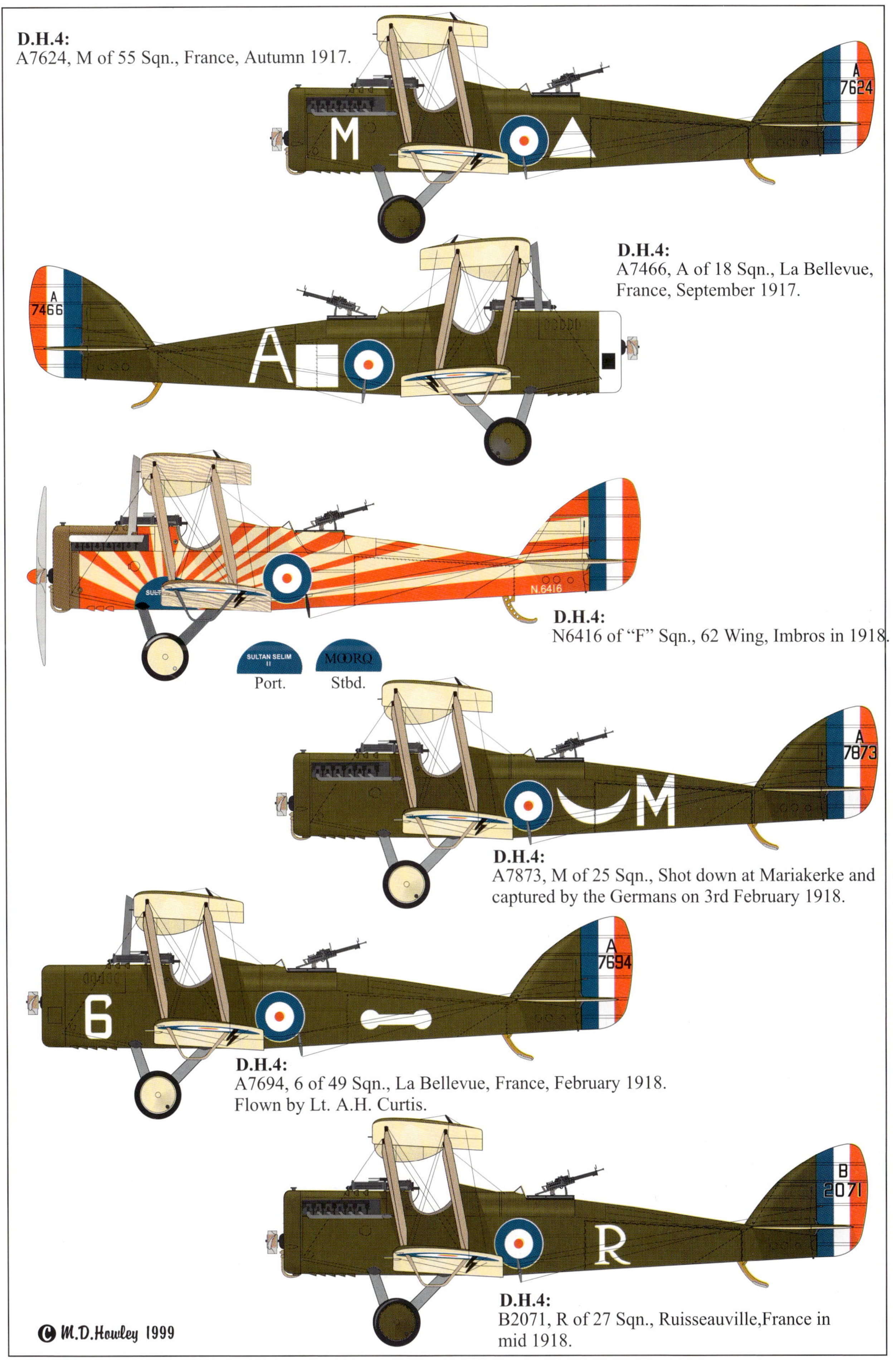

D.H.4:
A7624, M of 55 Sqn., France, Autumn 1917.

D.H.4:
A7466, A of 18 Sqn., La Bellevue, France, September 1917.

D.H.4:
N6416 of "F" Sqn., 62 Wing, Imbros in 1918.

D.H.4:
A7873, M of 25 Sqn., Shot down at Mariakerke and captured by the Germans on 3rd February 1918.

D.H.4:
A7694, 6 of 49 Sqn., La Bellevue, France, February 1918. Flown by Lt. A.H. Curtis.

D.H.4:
B2071, R of 27 Sqn., Ruisseauville,France in mid 1918.

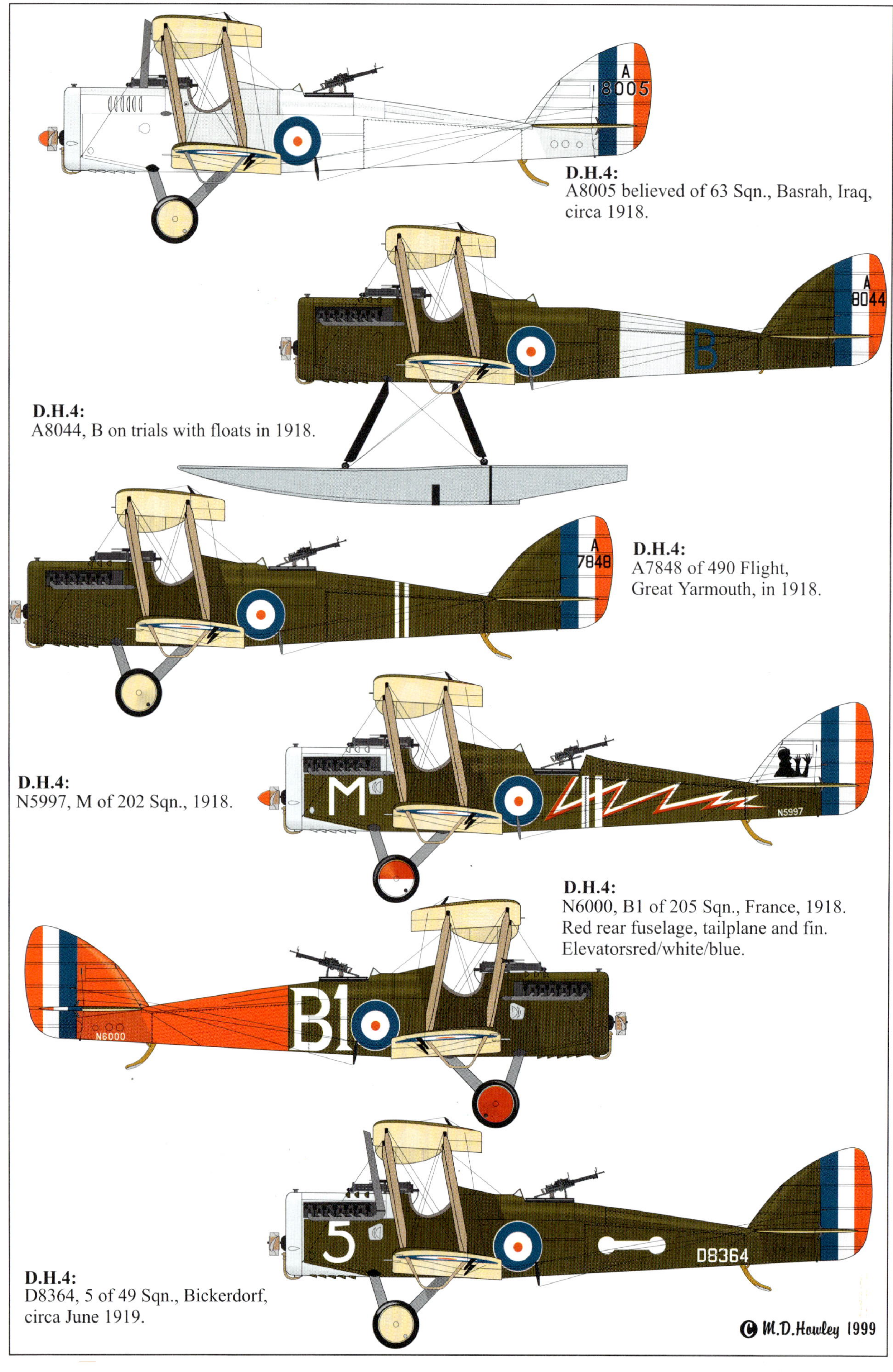

D.H.4:
A8005 believed of 63 Sqn., Basrah, Iraq, circa 1918.

D.H.4:
A8044, B on trials with floats in 1918.

D.H.4:
A7848 of 490 Flight, Great Yarmouth, in 1918.

D.H.4:
N5997, M of 202 Sqn., 1918.

D.H.4:
N6000, B1 of 205 Sqn., France, 1918. Red rear fuselage, tailplane and fin. Elevatorsred/white/blue.

D.H.4:
D8364, 5 of 49 Sqn., Bickerdorf, circa June 1919.

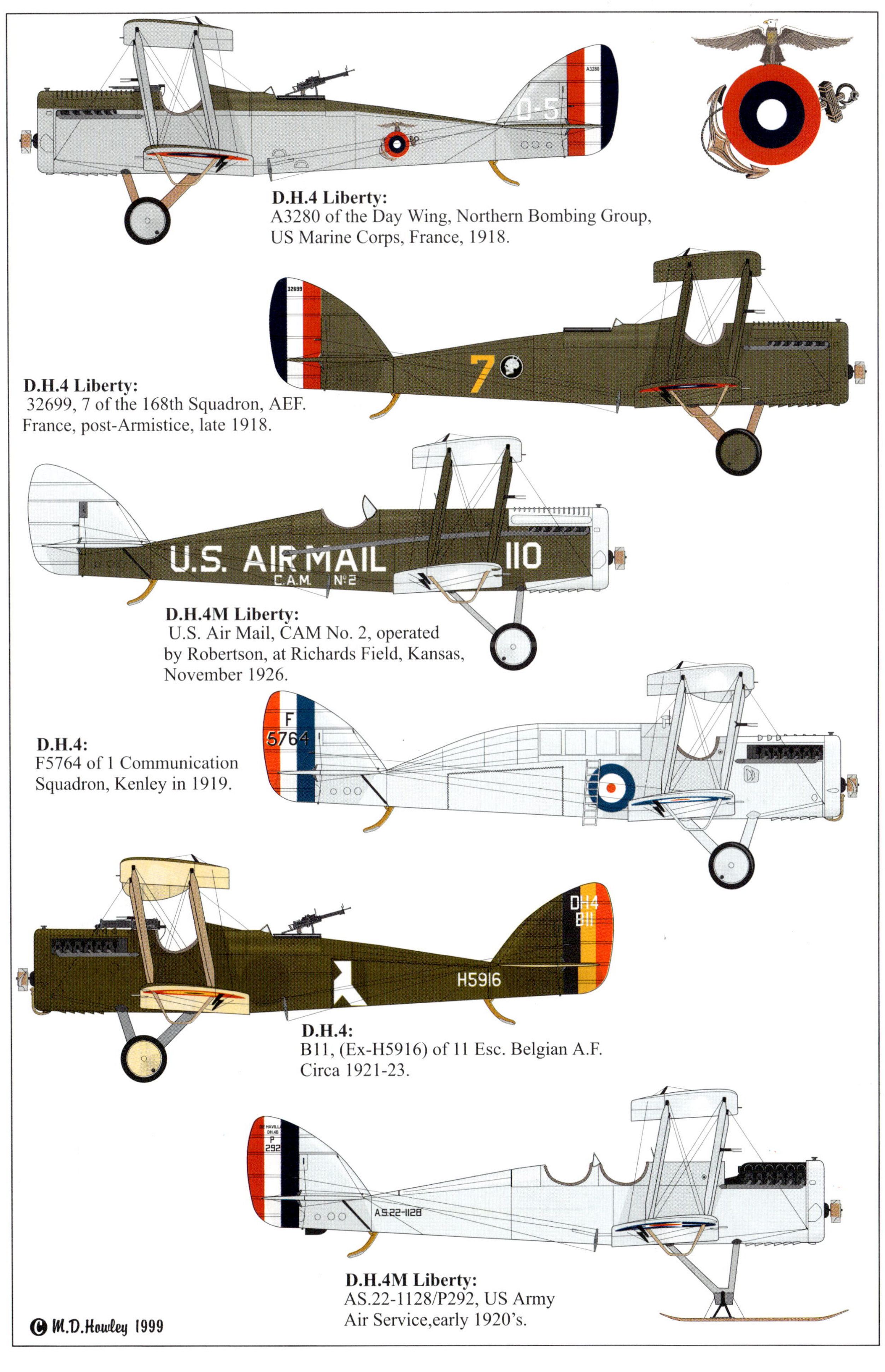

D.H.4 Liberty:
A3280 of the Day Wing, Northern Bombing Group, US Marine Corps, France, 1918.

D.H.4 Liberty:
32699, 7 of the 168th Squadron, AEF. France, post-Armistice, late 1918.

D.H.4M Liberty:
U.S. Air Mail, CAM No. 2, operated by Robertson, at Richards Field, Kansas, November 1926.

D.H.4:
F5764 of 1 Communication Squadron, Kenley in 1919.

D.H.4:
B11, (Ex-H5916) of 11 Esc. Belgian A.F. Circa 1921-23.

D.H.4M Liberty:
AS.22-1128/P292, US Army Air Service,early 1920's.

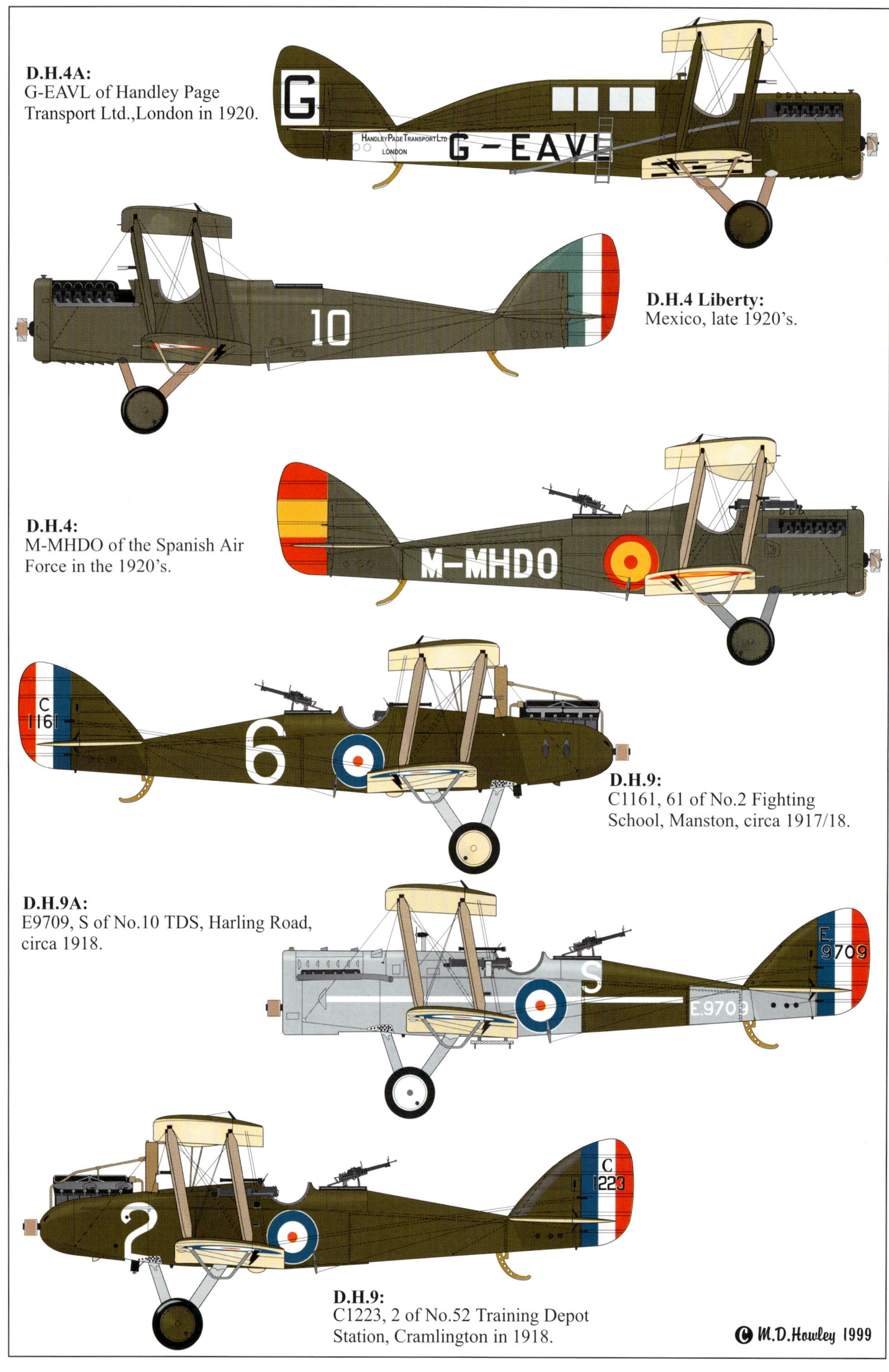

D.H.4A:
G-EAVL of Handley Page Transport Ltd.,London in 1920.

D.H.4 Liberty:
Mexico, late 1920's.

D.H.4:
M-MHDO of the Spanish Air Force in the 1920's.

D.H.9:
C1161, 61 of No.2 Fighting School, Manston, circa 1917/18.

D.H.9A:
E9709, S of No.10 TDS, Harling Road, circa 1918.

D.H.9:
C1223, 2 of No.52 Training Depot Station, Cramlington in 1918.

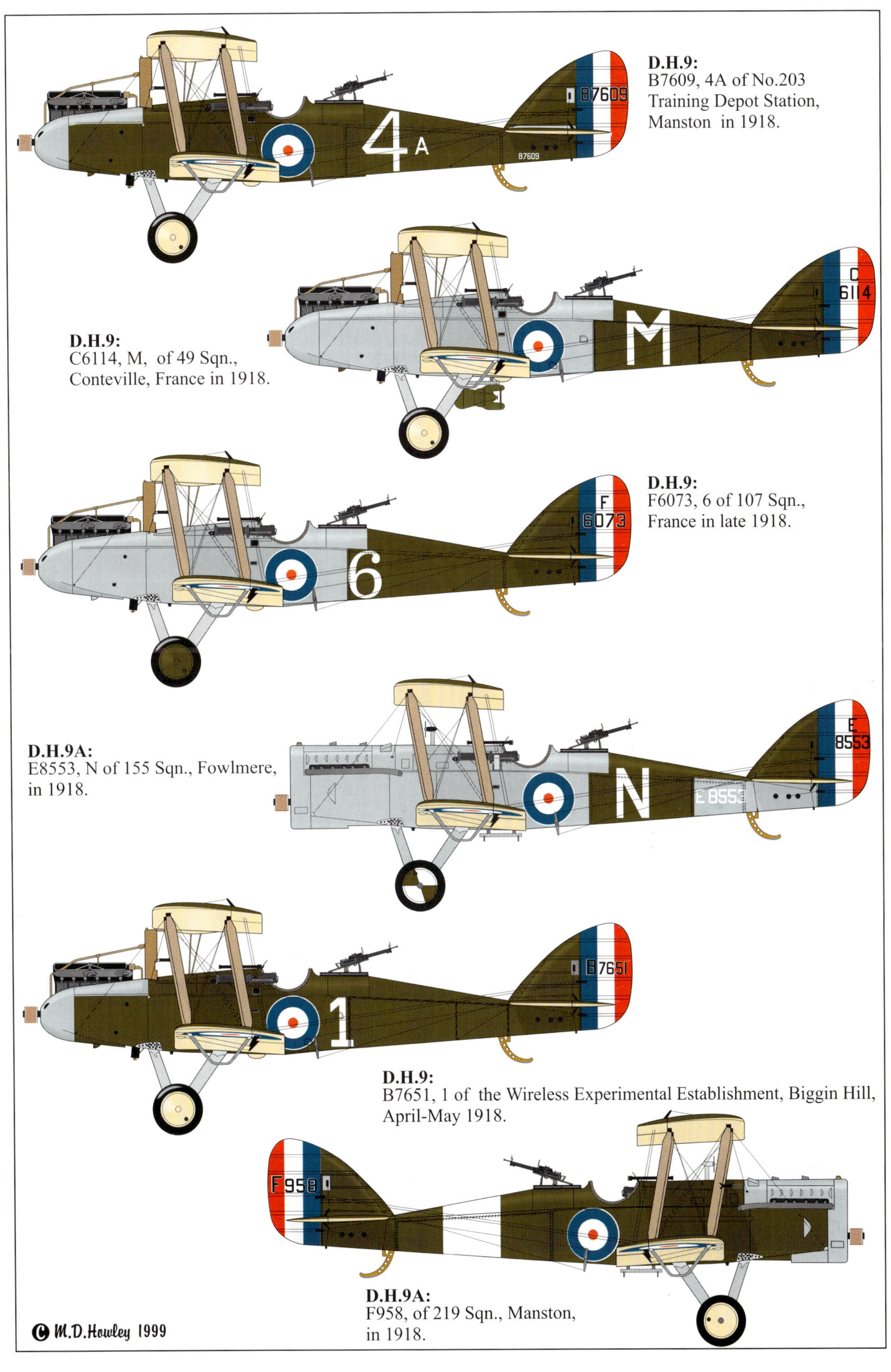

D.H.9:
B7609, 4A of No.203 Training Depot Station, Manston in 1918.

D.H.9:
C6114, M, of 49 Sqn., Conteville, France in 1918.

D.H.9:
F6073, 6 of 107 Sqn., France in late 1918.

D.H.9A:
E8553, N of 155 Sqn., Fowlmere, in 1918.

D.H.9:
B7651, 1 of the Wireless Experimental Establishment, Biggin Hill, April-May 1918.

D.H.9A:
F958, of 219 Sqn., Manston, in 1918.

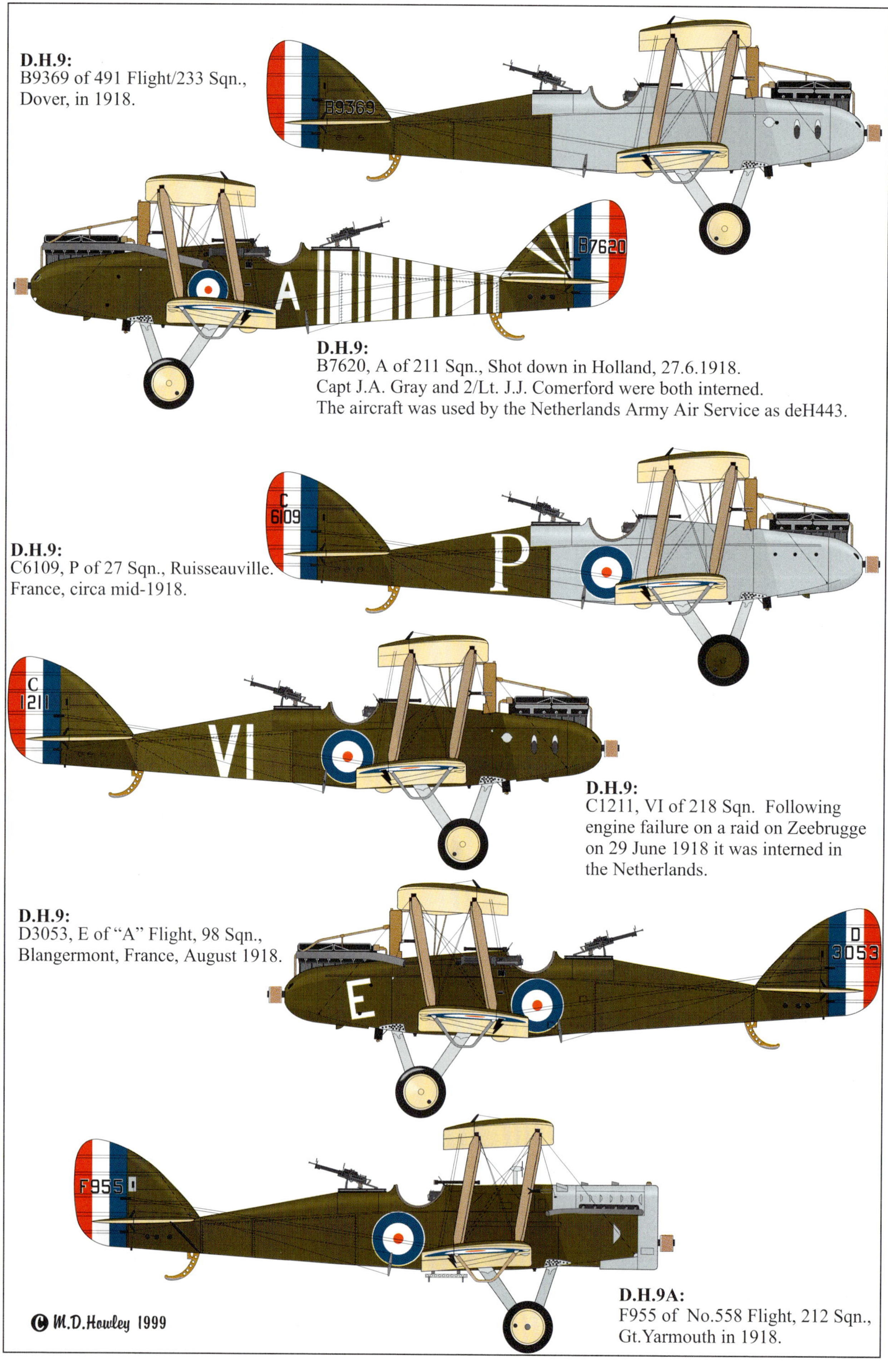

D.H.9:
B9369 of 491 Flight/233 Sqn., Dover, in 1918.

D.H.9:
B7620, A of 211 Sqn., Shot down in Holland, 27.6.1918. Capt J.A. Gray and 2/Lt. J.J. Comerford were both interned. The aircraft was used by the Netherlands Army Air Service as deH443.

D.H.9:
C6109, P of 27 Sqn., Ruisseauville. France, circa mid-1918.

D.H.9:
C1211, VI of 218 Sqn. Following engine failure on a raid on Zeebrugge on 29 June 1918 it was interned in the Netherlands.

D.H.9:
D3053, E of "A" Flight, 98 Sqn., Blangermont, France, August 1918.

D.H.9A:
F955 of No.558 Flight, 212 Sqn., Gt.Yarmouth in 1918.

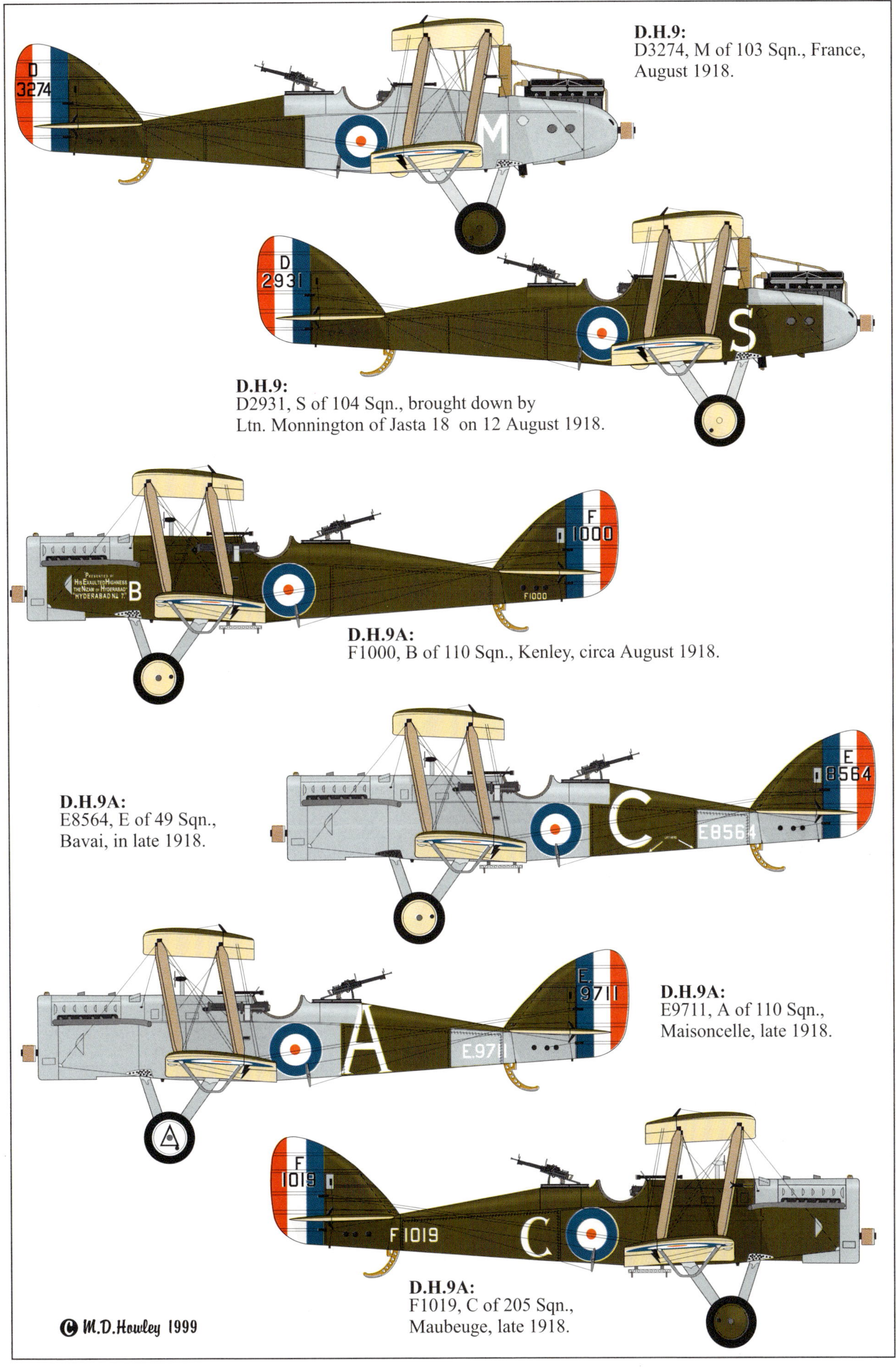

D.H.9:
D3274, M of 103 Sqn., France, August 1918.

D.H.9:
D2931, S of 104 Sqn., brought down by Ltn. Monnington of Jasta 18 on 12 August 1918.

D.H.9A:
F1000, B of 110 Sqn., Kenley, circa August 1918.

D.H.9A:
E8564, E of 49 Sqn., Bavai, in late 1918.

D.H.9A:
E9711, A of 110 Sqn., Maisoncelle, late 1918.

D.H.9A:
F1019, C of 205 Sqn., Maubeuge, late 1918.

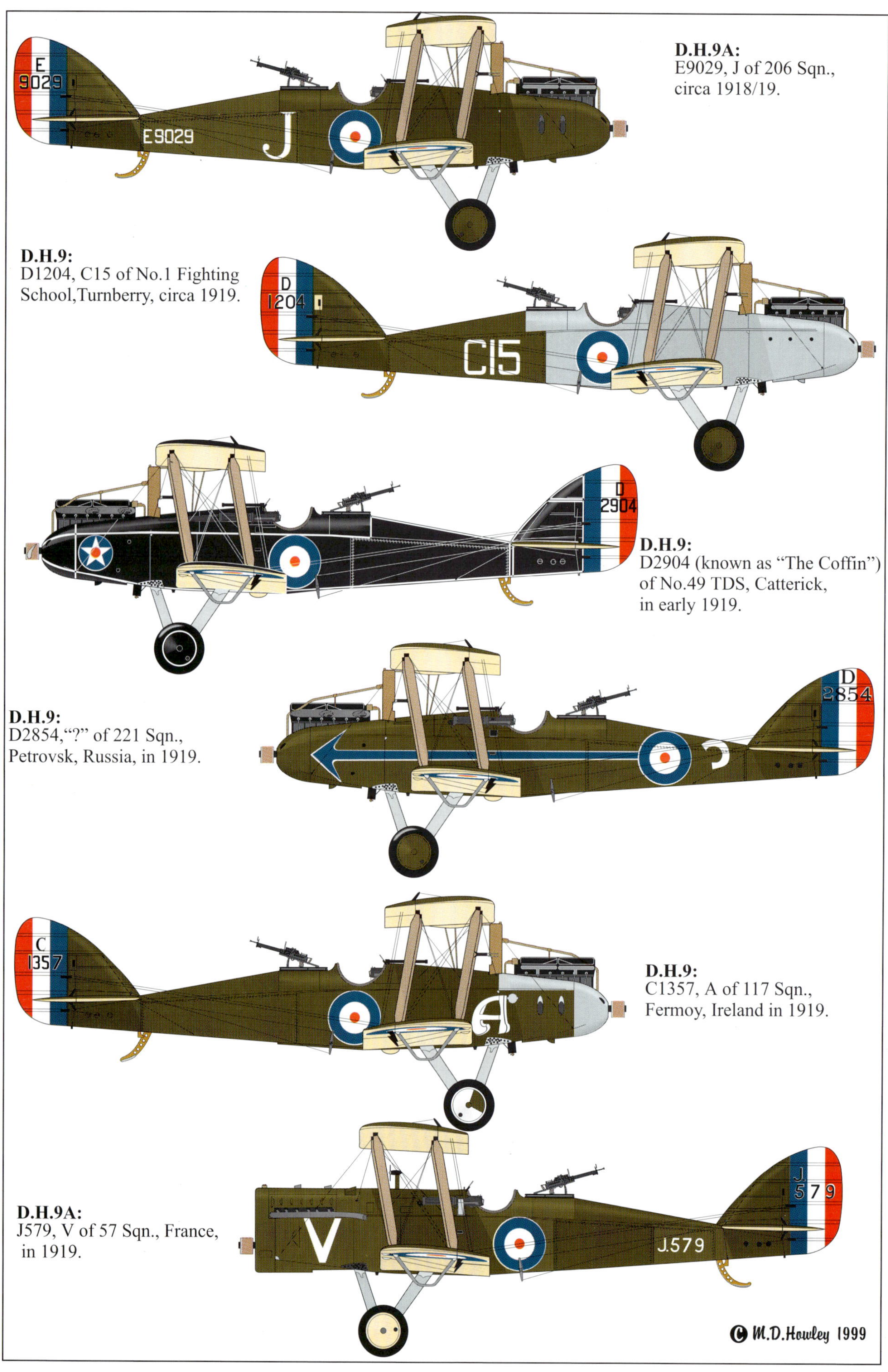

D.H.9A:
E9029, J of 206 Sqn., circa 1918/19.

D.H.9:
D1204, C15 of No.1 Fighting School,Turnberry, circa 1919.

D.H.9:
D2904 (known as "The Coffin") of No.49 TDS, Catterick, in early 1919.

D.H.9:
D2854,"?" of 221 Sqn., Petrovsk, Russia, in 1919.

D.H.9:
C1357, A of 117 Sqn., Fermoy, Ireland in 1919.

D.H.9A:
J579, V of 57 Sqn., France, in 1919.

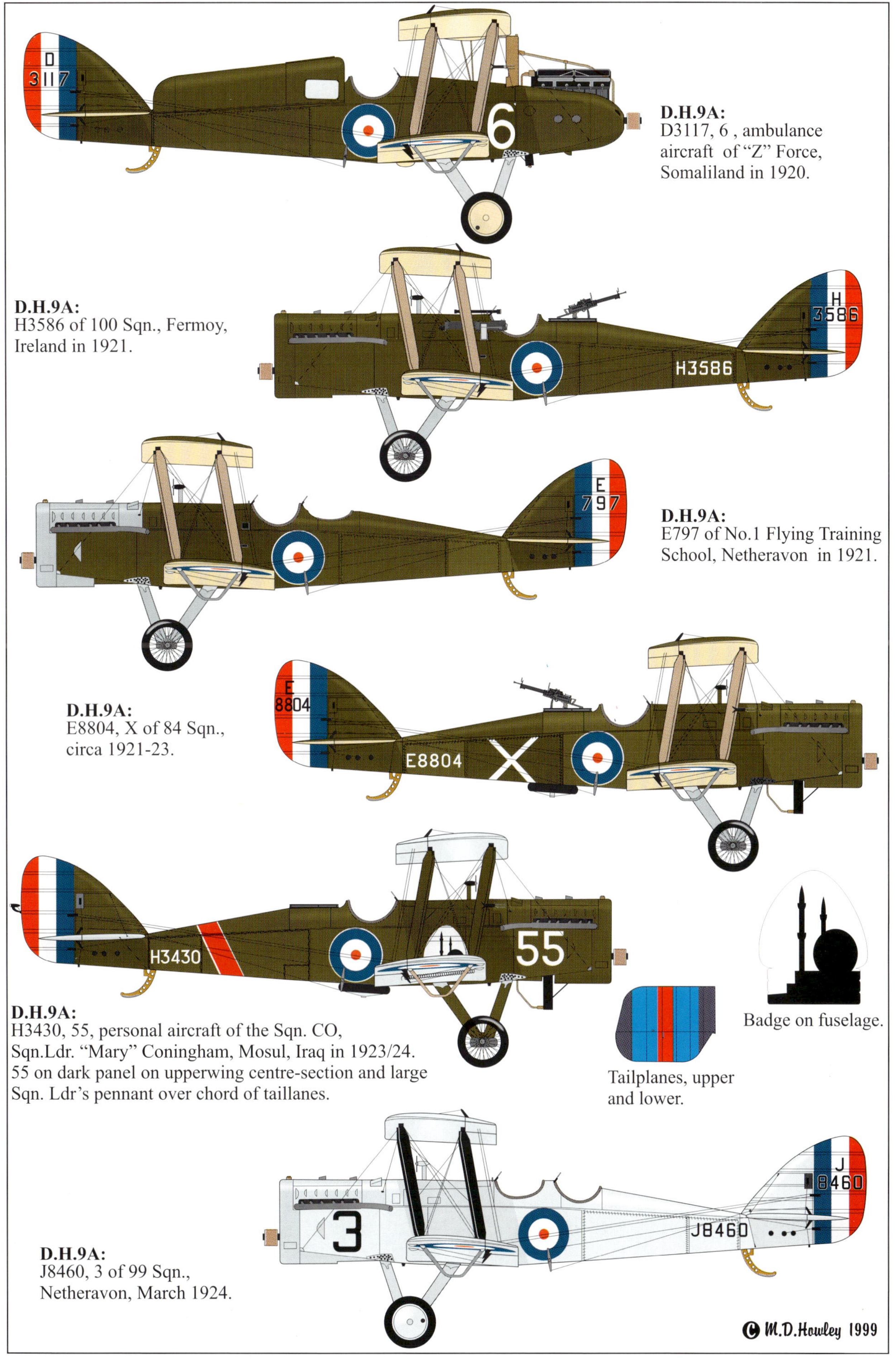
D.H.9A:
D3117, 6 , ambulance aircraft of "Z" Force, Somaliland in 1920.
D.H.9A:
H3586 of 100 Sqn., Fermoy, Ireland in 1921.
H3586
D.H.9A:
E797 of No.1 Flying Training School, Netheravon in 1921.
D.H.9A:
E8804, X of 84 Sqn., circa 1921-23.
E8804
D.H.9A:
H3430, 55, personal aircraft of the Sqn. CO, Sqn.Ldr. "Mary" Coningham, Mosul, Iraq in 1923/24. 55 on dark panel on upperwing centre-section and large Sqn. Ldr's pennant over chord of taillanes.
H3430
55
Badge on fuselage.
Tailplanes, upper and lower.
D.H.9A:
J8460, 3 of 99 Sqn., Netheravon, March 1924.
J8460
© M.D.Howley 1999

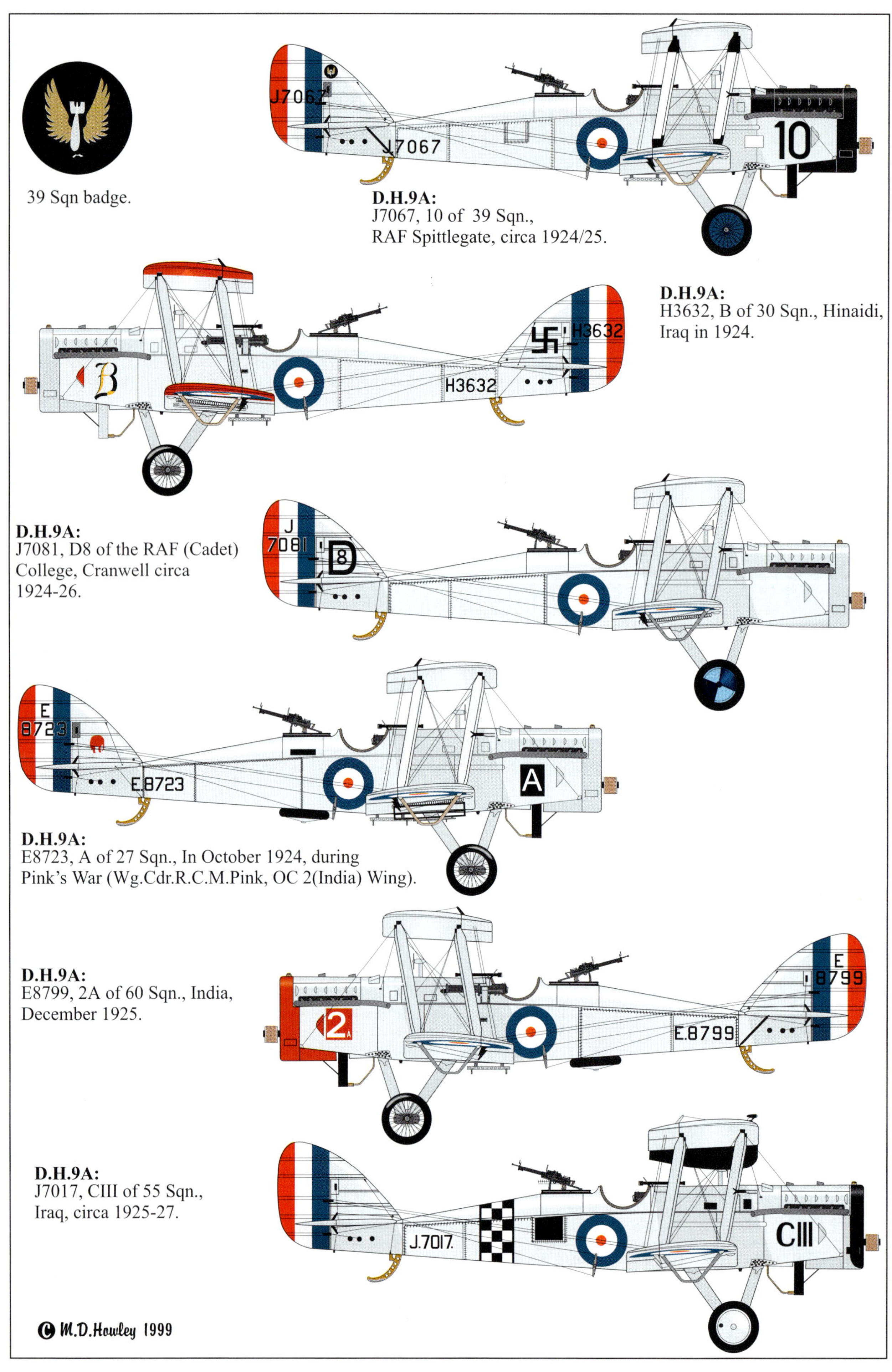

39 Sqn badge.

D.H.9A:
J7067, 10 of 39 Sqn.,
RAF Spittlegate, circa 1924/25.

D.H.9A:
H3632, B of 30 Sqn., Hinaidi,
Iraq in 1924.

D.H.9A:
J7081, D8 of the RAF (Cadet)
College, Cranwell circa
1924-26.

D.H.9A:
E8723, A of 27 Sqn., In October 1924, during
Pink's War (Wg.Cdr.R.C.M.Pink, OC 2(India) Wing).

D.H.9A:
E8799, 2A of 60 Sqn., India,
December 1925.

D.H.9A:
J7017, CIII of 55 Sqn.,
Iraq, circa 1925-27.

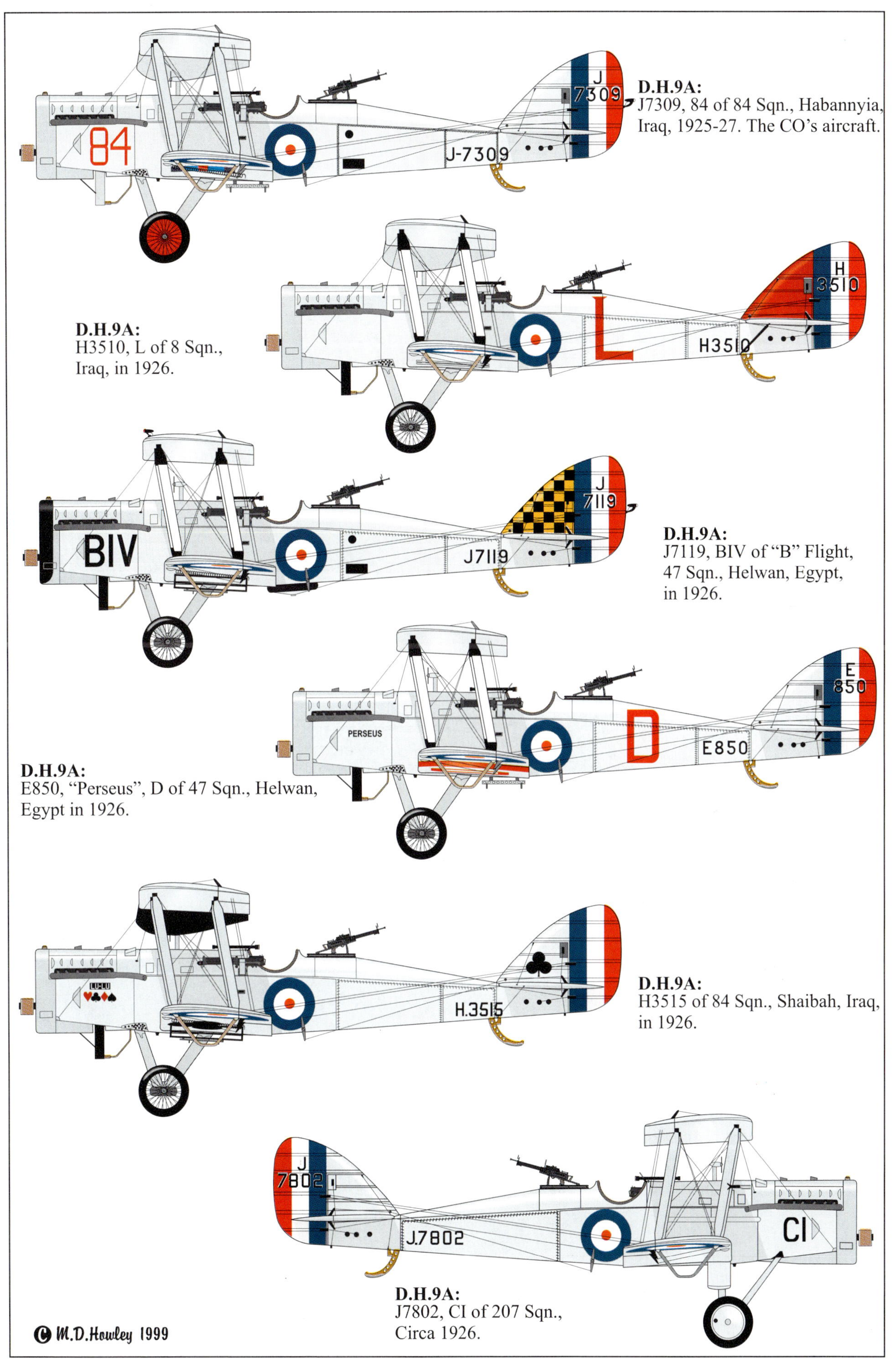

D.H.9A:
J7309, 84 of 84 Sqn., Habannyia, Iraq, 1925-27. The CO's aircraft.

D.H.9A:
H3510, L of 8 Sqn., Iraq, in 1926.

D.H.9A:
J7119, BIV of "B" Flight, 47 Sqn., Helwan, Egypt, in 1926.

D.H.9A:
E850, "Perseus", D of 47 Sqn., Helwan, Egypt in 1926.

D.H.9A:
H3515 of 84 Sqn., Shaibah, Iraq, in 1926.

D.H.9A:
J7802, CI of 207 Sqn., Circa 1926.

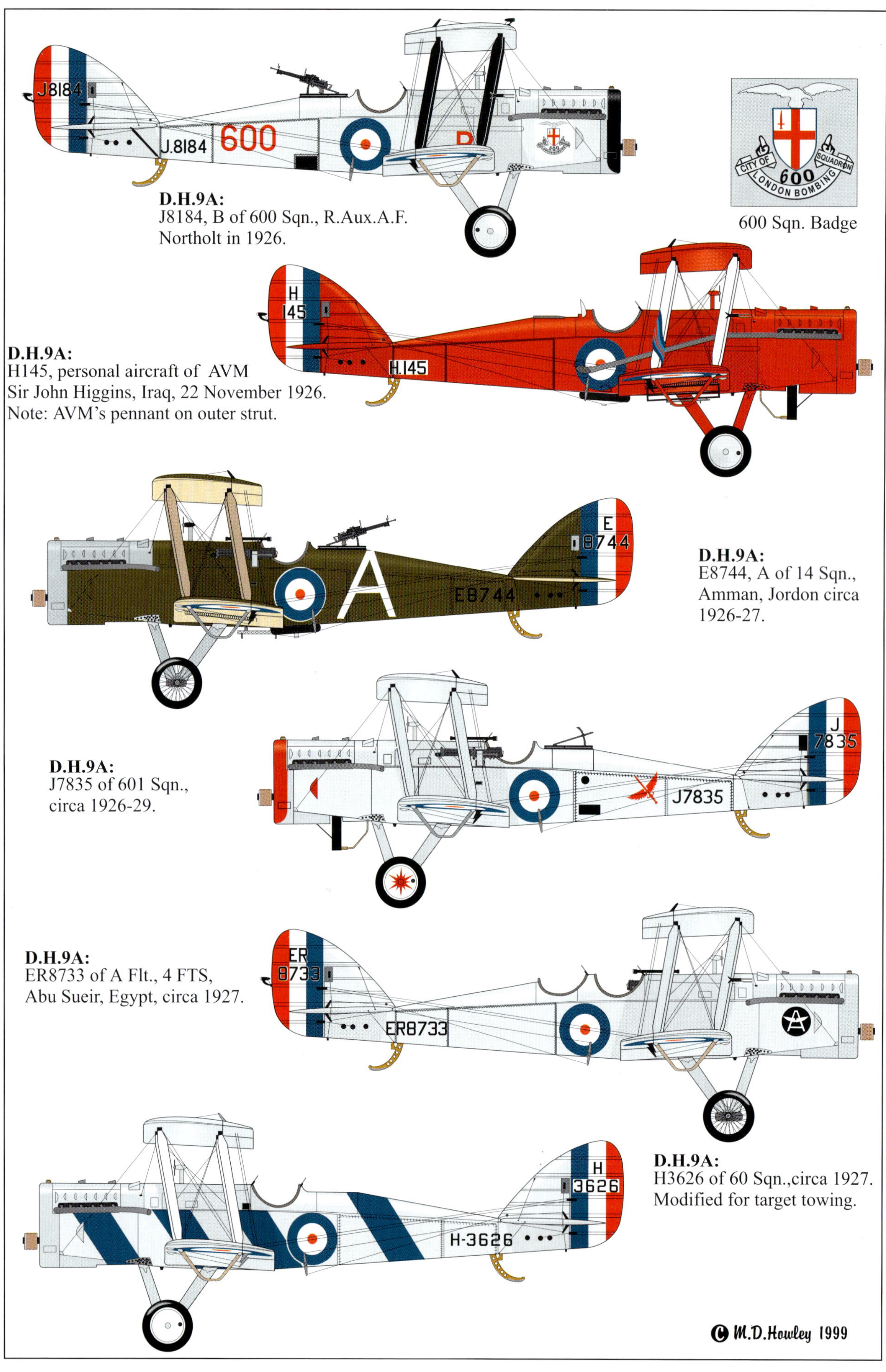

D.H.9A:
J8184, B of 600 Sqn., R.Aux.A.F.
Northolt in 1926.

600 Sqn. Badge

D.H.9A:
H145, personal aircraft of AVM Sir John Higgins, Iraq, 22 November 1926.
Note: AVM's pennant on outer strut.

D.H.9A:
E8744, A of 14 Sqn., Amman, Jordon circa 1926-27.

D.H.9A:
J7835 of 601 Sqn., circa 1926-29.

D.H.9A:
ER8733 of A Flt., 4 FTS, Abu Sueir, Egypt, circa 1927.

D.H.9A:
H3626 of 60 Sqn.,circa 1927.
Modified for target towing.

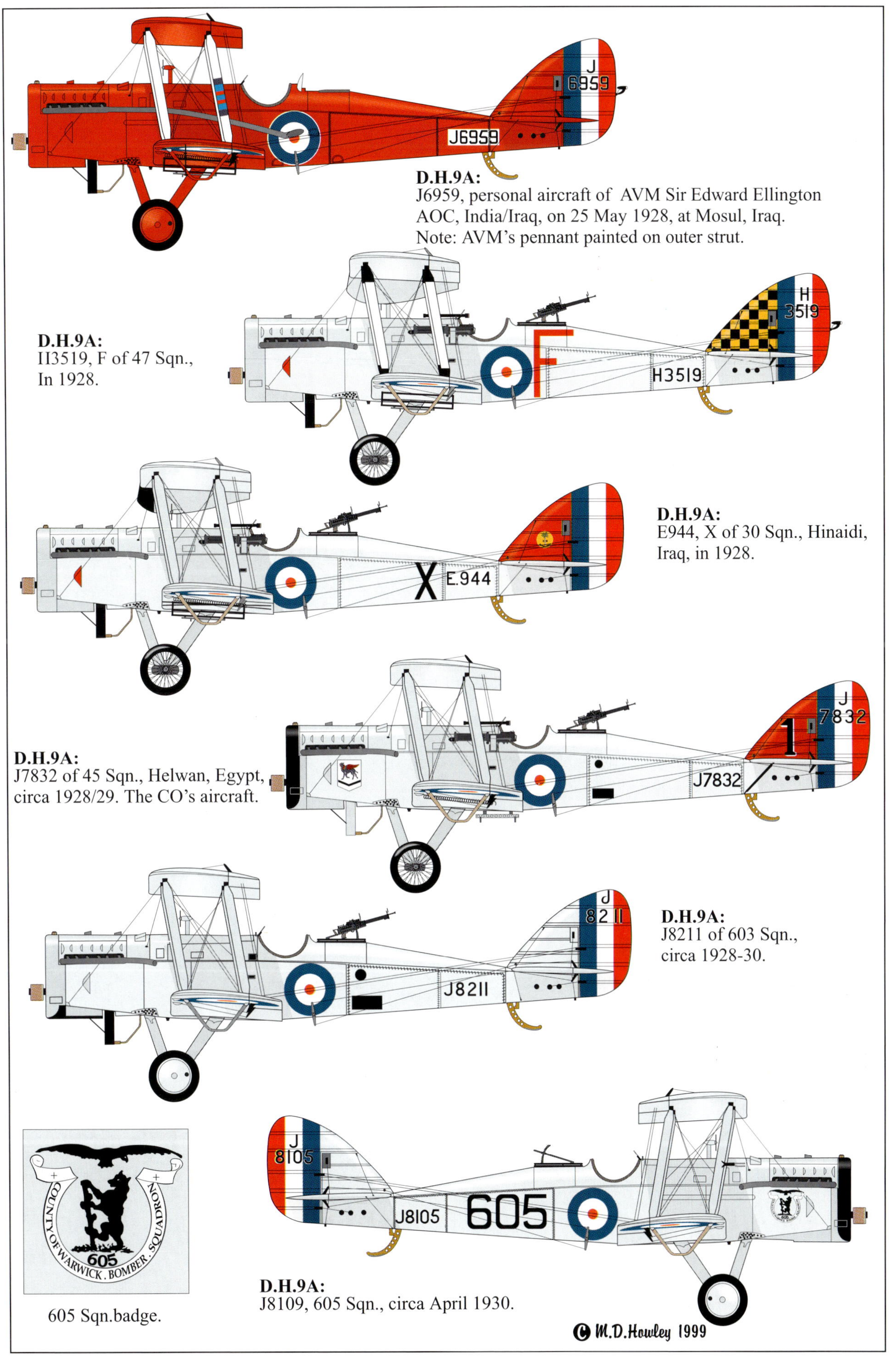

D.H.9A:
J6959, personal aircraft of AVM Sir Edward Ellington AOC, India/Iraq, on 25 May 1928, at Mosul, Iraq.
Note: AVM's pennant painted on outer strut.

D.H.9A:
H3519, F of 47 Sqn., In 1928.

D.H.9A:
E944, X of 30 Sqn., Hinaidi, Iraq, in 1928.

D.H.9A:
J7832 of 45 Sqn., Helwan, Egypt, circa 1928/29. The CO's aircraft.

D.H.9A:
J8211 of 603 Sqn., circa 1928-30.

605 Sqn.badge.

D.H.9A:
J8109, 605 Sqn., circa April 1930.

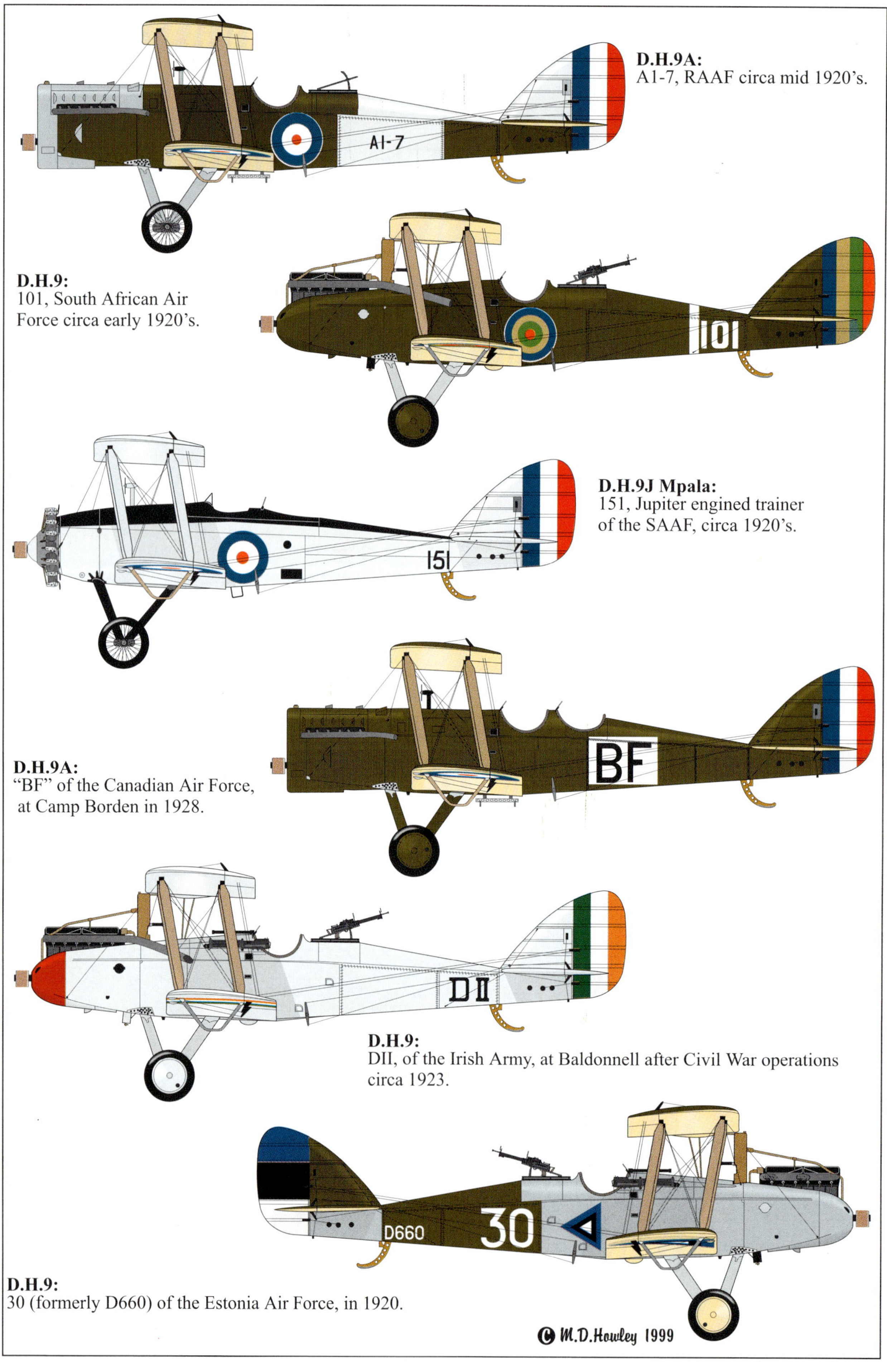

D.H.9A:
A1-7, RAAF circa mid 1920's.

D.H.9:
101, South African Air Force circa early 1920's.

D.H.9J Mpala:
151, Jupiter engined trainer of the SAAF, circa 1920's.

D.H.9A:
"BF" of the Canadian Air Force, at Camp Borden in 1928.

D.H.9:
DII, of the Irish Army, at Baldonnell after Civil War operations circa 1923.

D.H.9:
30 (formerly D660) of the Estonia Air Force, in 1920.

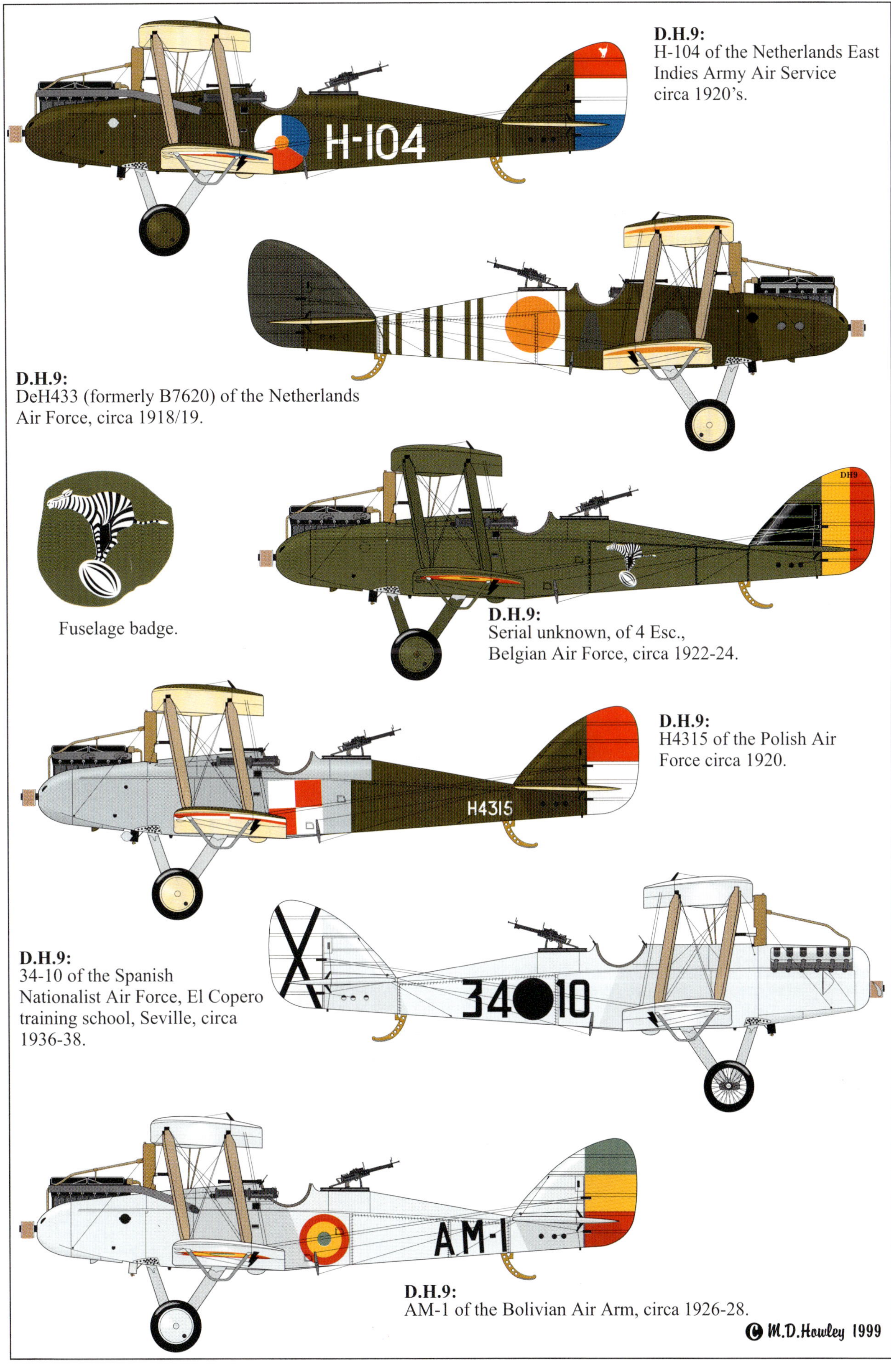

D.H.9:
H-104 of the Netherlands East Indies Army Air Service circa 1920's.

D.H.9:
DeH433 (formerly B7620) of the Netherlands Air Force, circa 1918/19.

Fuselage badge.

D.H.9:
Serial unknown, of 4 Esc., Belgian Air Force, circa 1922-24.

D.H.9:
H4315 of the Polish Air Force circa 1920.

D.H.9:
34-10 of the Spanish Nationalist Air Force, El Copero training school, Seville, circa 1936-38.

D.H.9:
AM-1 of the Bolivian Air Arm, circa 1926-28.

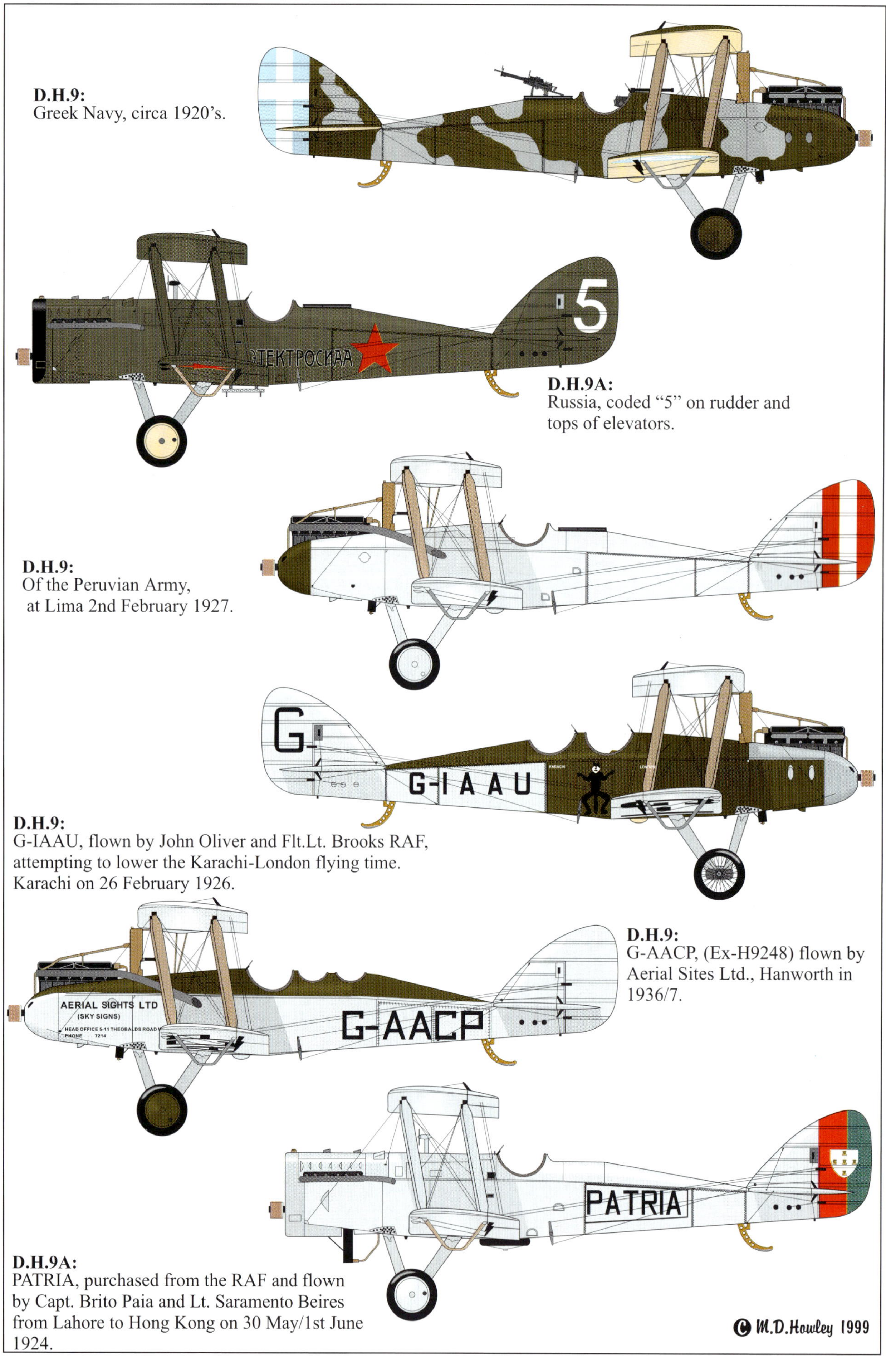

D.H.9:
Greek Navy, circa 1920's.

D.H.9A:
Russia, coded "5" on rudder and tops of elevators.

D.H.9:
Of the Peruvian Army, at Lima 2nd February 1927.

D.H.9:
G-IAAU, flown by John Oliver and Flt.Lt. Brooks RAF, attempting to lower the Karachi-London flying time. Karachi on 26 February 1926.

D.H.9:
G-AACP, (Ex-H9248) flown by Aerial Sites Ltd., Hanworth in 1936/7.

D.H.9A:
PATRIA, purchased from the RAF and flown by Capt. Brito Paia and Lt. Saramento Beires from Lahore to Hong Kong on 30 May/1st June 1924.

TECHNICAL DATA

D.H.4

Fitted 200-hp R.A.F.3a. 235-bhp at 1,800ft.
Speeds: 120mph at 6,500ft. 117mph at 10,000ft. 110.5 mph at 16,500ft.
Rates of climb: 8min to 6,500ft. 14.2min to 10,000ft. 29.3min to 15,000ft. 38min to 16,500ft.
Endurance: 4 hours. Service Ceiling: 19,500ft.
Weights: Empty 2,394lbs. Gross 3,340lbs.
Dimensions: Wing area 436 sq ft. Span 42ft 6in. Length 29ft 8in. Height 10ft 5in.

Fitted 250-hp Rolls-Royce. 285-bhp at 1,800ft.
Speeds: 117mph at 6,500ft. 113mph at 10,000ft. 102.5 mph at 16,500ft.
Rates of climb: 8.9min to 6,500ft. 16.4min to 10,000ft. 36.7min to 15,000ft. 46min to 16,500ft.
Endurance: 3.5 hours. Service Ceiling: 18,000ft.
Weights: Empty 2,303lbs. Gross 3,313lbs.
Dimensions: Wing area 436 sq ft. Span 42ft 6in. Length 30ft 8in. Height 10ft 5in.

Fitted 375-hp Rolls-Royce. 375-bhp at 2,000ft.
Speeds: 136.5mph at 6,500ft. 133.5 at 10,000ft. 126mph at 16,500ft. 122.5mph at 16,500ft.
Rates of climb: 5.2min to 6,500ft. 9min to 10,000ft. 16.5min to 15,000ft. 20min to 16,500ft.
Endurance: 3.75 hours. Service Ceiling: 23,000ft.
Weights: Empty 2,403lbs. Gross 3,472lbs.
Dimensions: Wing area 436 sq ft. Span 42ft 6in. Length 29ft 8in. Height 11ft.
[NB. Eagle engines were 250-hp Eagle I, II, III, IV; 275-hp Eagle V, VI, VI; 375-hp Eagle VIII]

D.H.9

Fitted 200-hp B.H.P. 240-bhp at 1,400ft.
Speeds with full bomb load: 111.5mph at 10,000ft. 97.5mph at 16,500ft. 91mph at 16,500ft.
Rates of climb: 10min to 6,500ft. 20min to 10,000ft. 45min to 15,000ft. 67min to 16,500ft.
Endurance: 4.5 hours. Service Ceiling: 17,500ft.
Weights: Empty 2,203lbs. Gross 3,669lbs.
Dimensions: Wing area 436 sq ft. Span 42ft 6in. Length 30ft 6in. Height 10ft.

D.H.9A

Fitted 350-hp Rolls-Royce VIII. 359-bhp at 1,800ft.
Speeds with full bomb load: 107mph at 10,000ft.
Rates of climb: 14.7min to 6,500ft. 27.1min to 10,000ft.
Endurance: 6 hours. Service Ceiling: 13,500ft.
Weights: Empty 2,732lbs. Gross 5,000lbs.
Dimensions: Wing area 488 sq ft. Span 46ft. Length 30ft. Height 10ft 9.5in.

Fitted 400-hp Liberty. 405-bhp at 1,650ft.
Speeds with full bomb load: 114mph at 10,000ft. 106mph at 15,000ft. 102mph at 16,500ft.
Rates of climb: 8.9min to 6,500ft. 15.8min to 10,000ft. 33min to 15,000ft. 43.8min to 16,500ft.
Endurance: 5.75 hours. Service Ceiling: 16,500ft.
Weights: Empty 2,695lbs. Gross 4,645lbs.
Dimensions: Wing area 493 sq ft. Span 46ft. Length 30ft. Height 11ft 4in.

[Data based on Table appended to Appendix XXVII to 'The War in the Air'. Other sources differ in some respects]

The first prototype D.H.4, fitted with a B.H.P.engine, photographed before receiving serial number 3696 (via Philip Jarrett)

D.H.4 - SERIAL LISTING

2 D.H.4 ordered on Cont No C.P.151348/16 from The Aircraft Manufacturing Co Ltd, Hendon and numbered 3696 and 3697

3696 (B.H.P later Eagle V) FF Hendon mid-8.16; CFS Testing Flight 21.9.16; Retd Hendon 12.10.16; 2 AD 15.10.16; Hendon 18.10.16; Almost ready 2.2.17; Tested Experimental Station Orfordness; AD Dunkirk by 1.3.17; 2N Sqn 6.3.17 (only mention); 2N Sqn St.Pol by 5.17; AD Dunkirk 25.10.17 - @1.11.17 (for 2N Sqn); NAD Dunkirk by 29.12.17; 2N Sqn 15.2.18; Fast landing, went into ditch, broke u/c & prop 17.2.18 (FSL LHN Langworthy OK); AD Dunkirk 22.2.18 - @21.3.18; Dover by 28.3.18; Became 491 Flt Dover by 25.5.18; 4 ASD Audembert 18.6.18; 202 Sqn Bergues by 6.18; 4 ASD 23.6.18; Pilots Pool; 4 ASD, deleted 31.8.18 general fatigue

3697 (250hp Eagle); FF late 10.16; At 2 AAP Hendon 13.3.17 allotted to EF, was to be B394 for the RFC, but this cancelled 16.3.17, a/c to be retained by the Admiralty; Deld 2N Sqn 24.3.17 - @29.7.17; AD Dunkirk by 2.8.17 (for service); Destroyed by fire on night of 1.10.17; Surveyed 17.10.17; Deleted 23.10.17 burnt

50 D.H.4 ordered 13.7.16 under Cont No 87/A/496 from The Aircraft Manufacturing Co Ltd, Hendon and numbered A2125 to A2174. (200hp RAF 3a or 250hp Eagle III).

A2125 44 RS Harlaxton by 3.17 - 4.17; Pilot walked into prop 13.3.17 (Lt L Murray killed)

A2126 (250hp Eagle) At 2 AAP Hendon 4.4.17, allotted to EF but reallotted to Training Bde 5.4.17; 44 RS Harlaxton by 4.17

A2127 44 RS Harlaxton by 2.17 - 4.17; 8 AAP Lympne by 8.17 (flew HD sorties inc 22.8.17); 52 TS Catterick by 6.18; Became 49 TDS Catterick 15.7.18 - 9.18

A2128 (Eagle III) 51 TS Waddington by 7.17 - 10.17; 75 TS Cramlington, forced landed 18.3.18 (Lt D de Wolfe Cunningham slightly injured)

A2129 Martlesham c.3.17; Orfordness 5.17 - 6.17 (flew HD sorties); Tested with 150hp Falcon (No WD 10071)

A2130 (250hp Eagle) Orfordness 5.17; 1 AD to 55 Sqn 3.6.17; Crashed at aerodrome 17.6.17 (Lt NB Harris & 2/Lt WD Mckeown); ARS 1 AD 20.6.17; 55 Sqn 21.7.17; FTR from 12.00 raid on Worteghem, last seen going down under control nr Lille 15.9.17 (Lt EEF Lloyd & Lt TG Deason both PoW)

A2131 44 TS Harlaxton by 2.17 - 21.9.17; (Eagle VI) At 1 (S)ARD 29.6.18 allotted to EF; Arr Rec Pk 3.8.18; 2 AI 6.8.18; 3 ASD 11.8.18; 55 Sqn 11.8.18; Hit by mg fire while bombing Luxembourg, FL, wrecked 25.8.18 (pilot OK & 2/Lt JA Lee killed); 3 ASD 30.8.18

A2132 (250hp Eagle) At 2 AAP Hendon 26.1.17 allotted to 55 Sqn (Mob) Lilbourne; Reallotted to EF 6.2.17; England to ARS 1 AD, wrecked on landing 15.2.17 (Lt JM Burd); 55 Sqn ('B6') 2.4.17; Damaged in bad landing 26.4.17 (2/Lt BW Pitt & Lt RW Langmaid both OK); ARS 2 AD 29.4.17; Altered to take 275hp Eagle; 57 Sqn 19.7.17; EA OOC Passchendaele by pilot and another BU by observer 17.45 27.7.17 (2/Lt ACS Irwin wounded & 2/Lt SJ Leete); Albatros D OOC E of Houthulst Forest 16.40 20.8.17 (Sgt EV Bousher & 1/AM W Harmston); 17.00 bombing raid on Ledeghem airfield and ammunition dump, one cwt bomb would not release after three runs, attacked by 6 EA ["Baron von Richtofen's Red Devils"], 1 shot down in flames and 1 apparently crippled, petrol tank shot through, FL nr Ypres, bomb did not explode 21.8.17 (Sgt EV Bousher wounded in leg & 1/AM W Harmston DoW); ARS 1 AD 24.8.17; SOC 26.8.17

A2133 55 Sqn Lilbourne by 2.17

A2134 51 RS Wye 3.17; 51 RS to Waddington 14.5.17; Became 51 TS Waddington 31.5.17 - 9.17; 44 TS Waddington 2.18

A2135 (250hp Eagle II) 55 Sqn, COL 20.4.17 (Lt WJ Tempest DSO & 2/Lt JS Holroyde); ARS 2 AD 26.4.17; 57 Sqn 4.6.17; Wrecked on landing 10.6.17 (2/Lt RW Howard & Lt TE Godwin OK); ARS 2 AD 10.6.17; 275hp Eagle

A close-up view of the B.H.P engine of the D.H.4 prototype. (J.M.Bruce/G.S.Leslie collection)

Second prototype D.H.4 at Orfordness, still without its serial number 3697, but marked on the rudder "GX" and below it "D4" (J.M.Bruce/G.S.Leslie collection)

fitted; ARS 1 AD 21.8.17; 57 Sqn 22.8.17; Attacked by EAs over Roulers, 2 OOC, 11.20 3.9.17 (pilot OK & observer Lt GM Guillon wounded); 2-str OOC Staden 17.10 2.10.17 (2/Lt GW Armstrong & 2/Lt H Pughe-Evans); FTR left 11.45 for raid on Roulers 12.10.17 (2/Lt GW Armstrong & 2/Lt H Pughe-Evans both PoW)

A2136 Allotted to 55 Sqn Lilbourne 24.1.17, at sqn by 3.2.17; 51 RS Wye 3.17; 51 RS to Waddington 14.5.17; Became 51 TS Waddington 31.5.17 - 8.17; 1 SoN&BD Stonehenge by 25.7.18

A2137 55 Sqn Lilbourne by 2.17

A2138 (250hp Eagle II) 51 RS Wye; 55 Sqn, COL 23.4.17 (Lt AP Matheson & Cpl PH Holland); ARS 2 AD 24.4.17; Altered to take 275hp Eagle; 57 Sqn ('C6') 19.7.17; EA OOC Courtrai 19.20 18.8.17; Albatros D OOC nr Houthulst Forest 11.30 20.8.17 (both 2/Lt AT Drinkwater & Lt FTS Menendez); Left 15.00 on raid on Oostnieuwkerke, last seen British side of lines on return journey 10.10.17 (Sgt FV Legge PoW & 1/AM JS Clarke killed)

A2139 No information

A2140 (250hp Eagle) In France with 55 Sqn ('2') by 11.3.17; FTR from raid on Château Hardenpont, last seen in steep dive after combat, shot down by Ltn Schaefer of Jasta 11 8.4.17 (Lt RA Logan & Lt FR Henry); Captured by Germans

A2141 (250hp Eagle) At 2 AAP Hendon, reallotted from 55 Sqn to EF but this cancelled 1.2.17; In France with Sqn by 17.3.17; FTR raid on Château Hardenpont, last seen in combat 8.4.17 (Lt B Evans & 2/Lt BW White killed)

A2142 At 2 AAP Hendon 30.1.17 reallotted from 55 Sqn to EF; (One of the two a/c for 55 Sqn which GHQ RFC asked in 1.17 be sent to France ie in advance of 55 Sqn); England to ARS 1 AD 9.2.17; ARS 2 AD 10.2.17; Sold to French Government; To Villacoublay (300hp Renault)

A2143 55 Sqn Lilbourne, flying accident (S/L WH Legge RNVR attd RFC DoI 11.2.17)

A2144 (Eagle IV) 55 Sqn Lilbourne by 2.17; 55 Sqn by 5.17; Bad landing, a/c turned turtle 7.7.17 (2/Lt RCW Morgan & Lt WR Cooke OK); ARS 1 AD 9.7.17; ARS 2 AD 20.7.17 for reconstruction, Eagle VI fitted; 25 Sqn 4.9.17; Misjudged landing, left wing struck ground 15.9.17 (2/Lt LG Bristowe OK); ARS 2 AD 17.9.17; 2 AI to Rec Pk 3.1.18; 1 AI 6.1.18; 25 Sqn 4.2.18; Overshot landing and crashed into road 26.3.18 (2/Lt AE Hulme & Cpl T Ramadaden OK); Rep Pk 2 ASD 1.4.18; Rebuilt as F6169 3.7.18

A2145 (250hp Eagle) 55 Sqn Lilbourne by 2.17; To France with 55 Sqn 6.3.17; Scout apparently OOC Le Cateau 13.50 10.5.17 (Capt EAB Rice & 2/Lt A Clarke); Damaged in bad landing 26.8.17 (2/Lt LdeG Godet); ARS 1 AD 28.8.17; 25 Sqn 15.10.17; On practice flight stalled on landing and crashed 4.12.17 (Lt N Braithwaite OK); Adv Salv to Rep Pk 1 ASD 5.12.17; 2 AI 25.3.18; Rep Pk 1 ASD 11.4.18; SOC 20.4.18

A2146 51 RS Wye by 4.17; 44 TS Harlaxton by 8.17 - 9.17

A2147 (250hp Eagle) 55 Sqn, left 15.30, combat damaged in raid on Boue 23.4.17 (Lt IV Pyott DSO OK & 2/Lt AD Taylor wounded); ARS 2 AD 28.4.17; 57 Sqn ('A6') 3.6.17; ARS 1 AD 12.8.17; To England 13.8.17; 61 TS South Carlton, wings came off at 1,500ft, crashed, Burton, nr Lincoln 27.8.17 (Capt C Butler & Cdt JL Baker killed)

A2148 Exptl, fitted 300hp Renault 12Fe; 51 RS Wye 3.17 (Eagle); Sideslipped in off turn at 100ft 23.4.17 (Lt AW Spence DoI 25.4.17)

A2149 (250hp Eagle) In France with 55 Sqn by 11.3.17; Left at 05.55 on raid, FL nr Doullens after combat, TW 24.4.17 (Lt AM de Lavison wounded & 2/AM K Oliver killed); ARS 2 AD 28.4.17; SOC 28.4.17

A2150 (250hp Eagle) In France with 55 Sqn 17.3.17; Albatros D OOC NW of Douai 14.45 4.5.17 (Lt CA Stevens & 2/Lt BF Sandy); Photo recce, shot up, damaged on landing 10.5.17 (Lt CA Stevens & Lt FL Oliver); At ARS 2 AD 1.6.17; 55 Sqn 14.7.17; On practice flight went into vertical dive, a/c completely wrecked 14.7.17 (2/Lt HE Macfarlane & Lt JC Hanson both killed); ARS 1 AD and SOC 17.7.17

A2151 No information

A2152 44 RS Harlaxton by 3.17; Became 44 TS Harlaxton 31.5.17 - 10.17; 24 Wing ARS Spittlegate, port wings collapsed pulling out of spin 5.9.17 (Sgt G Dunville killed)

A2153 (250hp Eagle) In France with 55 Sqn by 17.3.17; At ARS 2 AD 1.6.17, Altered to take 275hp Eagle; Eagle VII fitted; ARS 1 AD 15.8.17; 57 Sqn 17.8.17; Overturned on landing 2.4.18 (2/Lt R Willey & 2/Lt HSG Palmer OK); Adv Salvage Dump to Rep Pk 2 ASD 21.4.18; SOC 28.4.18

A2154 No information

A2155 (Eagle V) England to ARS 1 AD and on to 55 Sqn 4.4.17; Crashed at Routet on raid 30.4.17 (Lt EH Marshall & Lt JC Trulock); Wreckage collected by Port Depot Rouen for 2 AD; At ARS 2 AD 1.6.17, Eagle VII fitted; 25 Sqn 31.7.17; COL 16.9.17; ARS 2 AD 17.9.17; 1 ASD to 57 Sqn 10.12.17; Shot up by AA on photographic mission to Bapaume, FL 27.3.18 (Lt CM Powell & 2/Lt A Leach OK); Rep Pk 1 ASD 5.4.18; SOC 17.5.18 NWR

A2156 No information

A2157 (250hp Eagle) From England FL nr Boulogne 19.3.17 (Lt Wallace); ARS 1 AD 22.3.17; ARS 2 AD 22.4.17; 55 Sqn 25.4.17; Photo recce Valenciennes, shot up by EA, FL, damaged 4.5.17 (Lt BJ Silly MC OK & Lt RK Abram wounded); 2 AD; 57 Sqn 31.5.17; Damaged 2.6.17; ARS 2 AD 2.6.17, altered to take 275hp Eagle; ARS 1 AD 7.7.17; 55 Sqn 10.7.17; FTR from 06.33 raid on Ghent, attacked after dropping bombs, was seen to go down OOC nr Melle 13.8.17 (Lt PB McNally & 2/AM C Kelly both killed) [possibly shot down Schellebeke, E of Ghent 08.20 by Ltn Bockelmann of Jasta 11]

D.H.4 A2129 in mid-1917 at Orfordness, where it flew Home Defence sorties. (J.M.Bruce/G.S.Leslie collection)

D.H.4 A2140 '2' of No.55 Sqn being repainted with German markings after its capture on 8 April 1917. (via Frank Cheesman)

Rolls-Royce-engined D.H.4 A213? from the first production batch. (via J.J.Halley)

D.H.4 A2142 at Villacoublay with a 300hp Renault engine, after being transferred to the French Government. (via Frank Cheesman)

A pleasing shot of D.H.4 A2152 in pristine condition. (via Philip Jarrett)

D.H.4 A2168 at Orfordness, fitted with an RAF.3A engine and special exhausts and carrying a 30mm 1½-pounder C.O.W. gun for anti-Zeppelin attacks. (via Frank Cheesman)

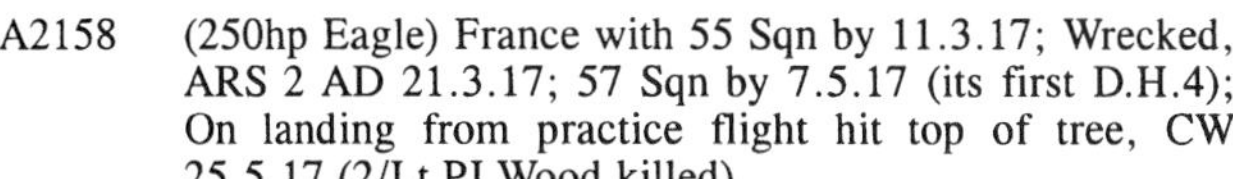

A D.H.4, possibly A2169, after a landing accident, maybe at 51 TS Waddington. It has 'WULLYPUG' and the number '1' painted on the nose, both in white. (J.M.Bruce/G.S.Leslie collection)

A2158 (250hp Eagle) France with 55 Sqn by 11.3.17; Wrecked, ARS 2 AD 21.3.17; 57 Sqn by 7.5.17 (its first D.H.4); On landing from practice flight hit top of tree, CW 25.5.17 (2/Lt PJ Wood killed)

A2159 (250hp Eagle) In France with 55 Sqn by 17.3.17; COL 19.3.17 (2/Lt A Lindley & 2/Lt FA Pattinson); Damaged in bad landing 14.4.17 (2/Lt RE Jeffries & Lt BF Sandy); ARS 2 AD 16.4.17; 55 Sqn; Scout crashed 3m E of Moorslede then Scout in spin smoking 13.30 4.6.17 (Lt CC Knight & Lt JC Trulock); Damaged by enemy fire in raid on Ramegnies Chin, COL 7.6.17 (2/Lt CC Knight & 2/Lt JC Trulock OK); ARS 1 AD 10.6.17; 25 Sqn 7.8.17; On 18.05 raid, attacked by EA, broke up in the air nr Wingles 19.35 14.8.17 (2/Lt PL McGavin & 2/Lt N Field both killed) [probably the claim 19.30 Pont-à-Vendin by Ltn E Udet, Jasta 37]

A2160 (250hp Eagle) 55 Sqn; Apparently hit by AA, brought down 2m SW of Amiens 8.4.17 (2/Lt AJ Hamar killed & 2/Lt JA Myburgh DoW 10.4.17); ARS 2 AD 11.4.17; SOC 13.4.17

A2161 (250hp Eagle) From England FL at Lynck 18.3.17 (Lt WJ Tempest), ARS 1 AD 19.3.17; 55 Sqn 23.3.17; Damaged landing 23.4.17 (Lt RE Jeffries & 1/AM Bradbeer); ARS 2 AD 26.4.17; 55 Sqn; Crashed at aerodrome 17.6.17 (Lt PW Battersby & Capt WW Fitzherbert); ARS 1 AD 20.6.17; 25 Sqn 27.7.17; FL due to engine failure and turned over 19.8.17 (2/Lt FA Watson & 2/Lt LE Bradshaw); ARS 2 AD 21.8.17; ARS 1 AD 23.9.17; 57 Sqn 14.10.17; Fokker Dr1 in flames and an Albatros D OOC NW of Roulers 11.30 24.1.18 (2/Lt WE Green & 2/Lt HS Gros); Left 14.20 for raid on Bapaume, FTR 31.3.18 (Lt ESC Pearce killed & 2/Lt CB Coleman PoW wounded)

A2162 No information

A2163 (250hp Eagle) 55 Sqn; FL nr Frevent 5.4.17 (Capt DAL Davidson MC slightly injured & 2/Lt JA Myburgh OK); ARS 2 AD 9.4.17; SOC 21.4.17, Dismantled for spares

A2164 (250hp Eagle) 44 RS Harlaxton, banked steeply at 1,000ft, spinning nose dive, BO 30.5.17 (2/Lt ATB Charlesworth killed)

A2165 44 RS Harlaxton by 4.17

A2166 (250hp Eagle) At AID Farnborough 13.4.17, allotted to EF; England to ARS 1 AD 15.4.17; ARS 2 AD 20.4.17; 55 Sqn 23.4.17; Recce of aerodrome Le Cateau, Sulinnes, Mailly, EF over lines, followed by 2 EA, crashed Mailly, landed in shell hole 1.5.17 (2/Lt CC Knight injured)

A2167 No information

A2168 (RAF 3a - the first installation of this engine) At 2 AAP Hendon 18.3.17, allotted to EF; Still at Hendon 6.4.17, reallotted to Controller of Technical Dept for test at Martlesham Heath; Tested CFS Upavon 10.4.17 (for Martlesham Heath); AES Orfordness 12.8.17; Fitted with COW gun at Orfordness 17.9.17, allotted to EF but this cancelled 18.9.17; RAF Farnborough 19.12.17; AES Orfordness 28.12.17; AES Grain 2.4.18 - @25.5.18 (fitted 1½-pdr COW gun firing upwards through centre section); Tested with 200hp RAF 3a with modified exhaust; Later to USA for evaluation

A2169 (250hp Eagle) At AID Farnborough 13.4.17, allotted to -EF but reallotted to Training Bde 27.4.17; 51 RS Wye 3.17; 51 RS to Waddington 14.5.17; Became 51 TS Waddington 31.5.17 - 9.17.

A2170 (250hp Eagle) At AID Farnborough 13.4.17, allotted to EF; England to ARS 1 AD 22.4.17; ARS 2 AD 24.4.17; 55 Sqn 25.4.17; Misjudged landing and struck bank 15.6.17 (Sgt Mitchell slightly injured & Pte Smith OK); ARS 1 AD 16.6.17; Altered to take 275hp Eagle; 55 Sqn 15.8.17; Damaged in combat with several EA 5.9.17 (Lt AG Whitehead & 2/Lt HB Macdonald both OK); ARS 1 AD 8.9.17; 25 Sqn ('L') 1.10.17; Raid on Somain, left at 10.15, last seen over Arras 23.11.17 (2/Lt R Main & 1/AM GP Leach both PoW)

A2171 (250hp Eagle) Allotted to EF, left Farnborough for Lympne, but engine trouble, FL Redhill 22.5.17 (Lt H Slingsby); ARS 1 AD to 57 Sqn 23.5.17; Left 07.25 for photo recce Steenbeck, hit by AA, COL Aire 21.6.17 (2/Lt JF Hillier & 2/Lt DRC Drury-Lowe OK); ARS 1 AD 23.6.17; 25 Sqn 9.8.17; Left at 09.10, FTR photographic mission to Maubeuge 18.3.18 (Lt JH Wensley & 2/Lt AW Matson both PoW)

A2172 (250hp Eagle) En route to EF via Lympne 22.5.17, allotted to EF; Farnborough to Lympne 27.5.17; 55 Sqn 5.17; Stalled and spun in 31.5.17 (2/Lt WF Sleeman & Lt G Inchbold both killed); ARS 1 AD 3.6.17; SOC 4.6.17

A2173 (275hp Eagle) Allotted to EF 29.5.17; ARS 1 AD; 57 Sqn 29.5.17; Albatros D destroyed c.12.40 17.6.17 (Lt WB Hutcheson & Sgt AT Rose); Wrecked landing 25.6.17 (Mjr LA Pattinson & 1/AM FH Towers OK); ARS 1 AD and SOC 29.6.17

A2174 (275hp Eagle) Allotted to EF 29.5.17, aircraft then in France; Tested at ARS 1 AD 1.6.17; 57 Sqn ('B5') 4.6.17; Practice flight, wrecked on landing 14.8.17 (Lt-Col FV Holt DSO OK); ARS 1 AD 17.8.17; 57 Sqn 3.10.17; Rep Pk 1 ASD 12.11.17; 57 Sqn by 1.18; Albatros D OOC Moorslede 12.55 28.1.18 (Sgt CW Noel & 2/Lt JN Stennett); Albatros D OOC Courtrai 10.00 26.2.18 (Sgt CW Noel & Cpl T Hodgson); Albatros D in vertical dive SW of Roulers 12.00 then Albatros D OOC 16.3.18 (Sgt CW Noel & 2/Lt LLT Sloot); Wrecked in FL 24.3.18 (2/Lt JMcC Lee OK & Cpl W Long injured); SOC 26.3.18; Rep Pk 1 ASD 27.3.18; Bboc; Rec Pk to 2 AI 28.6.18; 25 Sqn 29.6.18; EF, crashed nr aerodrome 24.7.18 (Lt LLK Straw & 2/Lt EF Boyce OK); To Depot 27.7.18; Rebuilt as F6236 10.8.19.

689 D.H.4 ordered 11.7.16 under running Cont No 87/A/496 from The Aircraft Manufacturing Co Ltd, Hendon for trials and numbered A7401 to A8090. (a variety of engines were fitted, these being indicated where known).

"A7142" (Eagle VI) Rep Pk 1 ASD to Rec Pk 4.5.18; 2 AI 14.5.18; 57 Sqn, on landing ran into partly filled shell hole, tyre burst, a/c wrecked 20.5.18 (Lt A Newman MC & Sgt PS Tidy) [rogue serial, possibly mis-painted]

A7401 (Eagle) At 55 Sqn 2.6.17; EF, FL in rough field 20.7.17 (2/Lt BJ Silly & Lt CH Sands OK); ARS 1 AD 23.7.17; 55 Sqn 9.9.17; Combat damaged returning from raid, FL nr Dickebusch 7.10.17 (Sgt MJC Weare wounded & 2/AM S Moreman OK); to 1 AD; Rep Pk 1 ASD to 1 AI 2.12.17; Rep Pk 1 ASD to 1 AI 3.12.17; Rep Pk 1 ASD 4.12.17 "From FL"; 57 Sqn 4.12.17; Loaned 6 Sqn (R.E.8) 1.18 to provide fighting experience; Retd 57 Sqn 18.1.18; FL and crashed 16.2.18 (pilot Lt LdeV Wiener slightly injured); Left for raid on Bapaume 07.30, last seen in combat with EA 1.4.18 (2/Lt E Whitfield & Lt WCF Nicol-Hart killed) (Eagle VI fitted by then)

A7402 (250hp Eagle) En route to EF via Lympne 25.5.17, allotted to EF; ARS 1 AD; 57 Sqn 29.5.17; Wrecked on landing from practice flight 12.7.17 (2/Lt AS Turner & Lt LS Brooke OK); ARS 1 AD 14.7.17; ARS 2 AD 19.7.17 for reconstruction; 275hp Eagle fitted; 25 Sqn 31.8.17; Overran aerodrome on landing and crashed into hedge 19.11.17 (2/Lt N Braithwaite & 2/Lt RW Nobbs both OK); Rep Pk 1 ASD 20.11.17; SOC 9.2.18

A7403 (275hp Eagle) En route to EF via Lympne 25.5.17, allotted to EF; At 57 Sqn by 28.5.17; Wrecked on landing 23.7.17 (Lt TS Roadley & 2/Lt CR Thomas); ARS 1 AD 26.7.17

A7404 (250hp Eagle) At Lympne 8 AAP 22.5.17, allotted to EF; ARS 1 AD, test 26.5.17; To 57 Sqn but crashed on arrival 4.6.17 (Lt WG Helpman & 2/Lt GG Barker); Dismantled at 1 AD and parts used to repair other a/c; SOC ARS 1 AD 20.6.17

A7405 (250hp Eagle) ARS 1 AD; 57 Sqn 24.5.17; On practice flight, COL 26.5.17 (Lt DM Goodyear & 2/Lt FR Martin OK); ARS 2 AD by 1.6.17, Eagle VII fitted; ARS 1 AD 23.7.17; 25 Sqn 26.7.17; In combat with 12 Albatros DIII over La Bassée, 1 down in flames shared 18.50 4.9.17 (Lt DGE Jardine & 2/Lt G Bliss); Crashed and CW nr Burbure, believed shot down 14.00 1.10.17 (2/Lt CO Rayner & Lt JL Hughes both killed); ARS 2 AD 2.10.17; SOC 3.10.17

A7406 (250hp Eagle) ARS 2 AD to 57 Sqn 28.5.17; COL 1.6.17; (2/Lt R Trattles & Lt PH Bigwood OK); ARS 2 AD 2.6.17; 275hp Eagle fitted; 57 Sqn 18.8.17; Lost in mist, made FL at 1 AD, landed cross wind and misjudged distance 9.9.17 (Sgt FV Legge & 2/AM JS Clarke), a/c to be retained by ARS 1 AD; 57 Sqn 22.10.17; Albatros D in flames Roulers 16.35 21.2.18 (2/Lt FA Martin & 2/Lt WC Venmore); FL nr St Pol 1.4.18 (m/c and pilot 2/Lt FA Martin OK but observer Cpl EC Lovelock DoW); Collided with wind gauge on take off, nose dived in, caught fire 20.5.18 (Lt R Willey killed & 2/Lt HSG Palmer injured); SOC Rep Pk 2 ASD 21.5.18

A7407 (250hp Eagle) At 2 AAP Hendon 15.3.17, allotted to EF; England to ARS 1 AD 27.3.17; 55 Sqn 28.3.17

A7408 (250hp Eagle) At 2 AAP Hendon 22.3.17, allotted to EF; England to ARS 1 AD and on to ARS 2 AD 7.4.17; 55 Sqn 4.17; Left 15.50 on raid on Boue, shot down Urvillers 23.4.17 (Capt AT Greg killed & 1/AM RW Robson DoW 18.5.17)

A7409 (250hp Eagle) At 2 AAP Hendon 6.4.17, Reallotted from Training Bde to EF; England to ARS 1 AD 7.4.17; To 55 Sqn 10.4.17, FL nr Bethune (Lt PJ Barnett); Bad landing 21.4.17 (Lt CC Knight & Lt JC Trulock both OK); ARS 2 AD 24.4.17; 55 Sqn; Left on raid 11.55 on Cantin, attacked by EA, dived, tail came off, a/c broke up nr Noyelles 25.5.17 (2/Lt RE Jeffery & 2/Lt PR Palmer both killed)

A7410 (250hp Eagle) At 2 AAP Hendon 22.3.17, allotted to EF; England to ARS 1 AD 12.4.17; ARS 2 AD 13.4.17; 55 Sqn 14.4.17; Left at 15.30 for raid on Boue, engine shot up by EA over Edgehill (sic), FL, crashed nr Buire 23.4.17 (Lt T Webb & 1/AM W Bond both OK); ARS 2 AD 26.4.17; Altered to take 275hp Eagle; ARS 1 AD 11.7.17; 55 Sqn 16.7.17; Scout OOC nr Ghent 08.25 13.8.17 (Lt AG Whitehead & 2/Lt HB Macdonald); Controls shot away on 16.05 raid on Abeelhoek airfield, FL, completely wrecked 14.8.17 (Lt AG Whitehead & 2/Lt HB Macdonald) [possibly shot down 16.40 Hollebeke by Ltn W Blume, Jasta 26]

A7411 (250hp Eagle) At 2 AAP Hendon 26.3.17, allotted to EF; England to ARS 1 AD 9.4.17; To 55 Sqn but FL and crashed nr Bethune, wrecked 10.4.17 (2/Lt A Lindley injured); ARS 1 AD 15.4.17; SOC 19.4.17

A7412 (250hp Eagle) At 2 AAP Hendon 22.3.17, allotted to EF; England to ARS 1 AD 12.4.17; 55 Sqn 12.4.17; On raid on Boue lost formation, landed at Rouen, on way to rejoin unit crashed at Evreux, totally destroyed by fire 23.4.17 (2/Lt DRG Mackay & 2/Lt AE Watkinson both injured)

A7413 (250hp Eagle) At 2 AAP Hendon 22.3.17, allotted to EF; England to ARS 1 AD and on to 55 Sqn 4.4.17; Photo recce Gouzeaucourt, hit by shellfire 10.5.17 (Capt N Senior wounded & Cpl PH Holland killed [he served under this name but his real name was Hubbard])

A7414 (250hp Eagle) At 2 AAP Hendon 22.3.17, allotted to EF; England to ARS 1 AD 24.4.17; ARS 2 AD 25.4.17; 55 Sqn 25.4.17; 57 Sqn; ARS 1 AD 12.8.17; To England 13.8.17

A7415 (250hp Eagle) At 2 AAP Hendon 22.3.17, allotted to EF; England to ARS 1 AD and on to ARS 2 AD 8.4.17; 55 Sqn 9.4.17; COL 2.6.17 (Lt PJ Barnett & 2/Lt T Durrant); ARS 1 AD 5.6.17; 57 Sqn 3.7.17; On take off for practice flight, sideslipped then nose dived in and caught fire 7.7.17 (2/Lt JHS Green & 2/Lt R Tardugno both killed); ARS 1 AD 8.7.17; SOC 9.7.17

A7416 (250hp Eagle) At 2 AAP Hendon 22.3.17, allotted to EF; England to ARS 1 AD 15.4.17; ARS 2 AD 20.4.17; 55 Sqn 23.4.17; Left 12.55 for Caudry-Neuvilly, shot down in flames over Le Cateau 10.5.17 (2/Lt BW Pitt & 2/Lt JS Holroyde both killed) [claimed 14.00 by Vzfw F Krebs, Jasta 6 N of Le Cateau, S of Solesmes]

A7417 (Eagle IV) At 2 AAP Hendon 5.4.17, allotted to EF; England to ARS 1 AD 20.4.17; ARS 2 AD 22.4.17; 55 Sqn 22.4.17; At ARS 2 AD 1.6.17; ARS 1 AD 26.6.17; 57 Sqn ('B4') 27.6.17; COL 12.7.17 (2/Lt HE Biederman & 2/Lt DRC Drury-Lowe OK); ARS 1 AD 13.7.17; ARS 2 AD 1.10.17; To 55 Sqn by rail 21.10.17; Collided with obstacle on landing, overturned 10.3.18 (2/Lt RB Brookes & Sgt H Gostling), by then Eagle VI fitted; Rep Pk 2 ASD 10.3.18; By rail to Rep Pk 1 ASD 1.4.18; Rebuilt as F5831 25.6.18

A7418 (250hp Eagle) At 2 AAP Hendon 5.4.17, allotted to EF; England to ARS 1 AD 20.4.17; ARS 2 AD 22.4.17; 55 Sqn 23.4.17; 2-str crashed nr Ypres 15.45 6.6.17 (Capt AB Adams & 2/Lt RW Langmaid); Bad landing 21.7.17 (2/Lt ES Guy & 2/AM Shaw OK); ARS 1 AD 23.7.17; 55 Sqn 30.8.17; Albatros D OOC Thielt 14.30 5.9.17 (2/Lt JB Fox & 2/AM SL Leyland); Albatros D OOC E of Thielt 10.15 30.9.17 (Lt MG Jones MC & 2/AM SL Leyland); Caught fire in air, crashed 10.3.18 (Capt JB Fox slightly burned & Lt SS Jones MC OK); By then Eagle VII fitted; Rep Pk 2 ASD 10.3.18; 55 Sqn 23.4.18; Rep Pk 2 ASD 28.4.18; SOC 18.6.18 NWR

A7419 (250hp Eagle) At 2 AAP Hendon 5.4.17, allotted to EF. England to ARS 1 AD 22.4.17; ARS 2 AD and on to 55 Sqn 24.4.17; Photo recce, hit by AA, BU over Le Cateau 10.5.17 (2/Lt T Webb & Sgt W Bond both killed)

A7420 (250hp Eagle) At 2 AAP Hendon 5.4.17, allotted to EF: England to ARS 1 AD 22.4.17; ARS 2 AD and on to 55 Sqn 24.4.17; Scout OOC Le Cateau, then FL 14.00 9.5.17 (2/Lt F McQuistan wounded & 2/AM FG Ellis OK); Shot down SW of Ingelmunster around 13.15 4.6.17 (2/Lt DJ Honer killed & Pte G Cluney PoW) [claimed 13.10 Moorslede by Ltn K Scaefer, Jasta 28]

A7421 (250hp Eagle) At 2 AAP Hendon 5.4.17, allotted to EF; At 55 Sqn 2.6.17; FTR from 13.30 raid, attacked by 6 EA W of Audenarde, last seen going down in steep spiral 13.7.17 (Lt AP Matheson & 2/Lt FL Oliver both killed)

A7422 (250hp Eagle) At 2 AAP Hendon 5.4.17, allotted to EF; At ARS 2 AD 1.6.17; 57 Sqn 3.6.17; Wrecked on landing 8.6.17 (2/Lt JHS Green & 2/Lt R Tardugno); ARS 2 AD 9.6.17; Altered to take 275hp Eagle; 57 Sqn 18.8.17; Capt AB Cook wounded by splinter 27.10.17; Albatros D OOC Hooglede 11.05 8.11.17 (Capt AB Cook & Lt E Drudge); FTR from 08.00 raid 2.12.17 (2/Lt D Miller wounded PoW & 2/Lt AHC Hoyles killed)

A7423 (250hp Eagle) At 2 AAP Hendon 5.4.17, allotted to EF; At (S)ARD 5.5.17, Allotment to EF cancelled, Now on charge E.1 Repair Section; At (S)ARD 27.6.17, Reallotted to EF but this again cancelled 24.7.17, A/c still at (S)ARD and on charge E 1 Repair Section; 44 TS

D.H.4 A7433 with a white 'club' motif on its nose, believed at Hounslow. (H.S.Clarke)

Harlaxton by 8.17 - 9.17

A7424 (250hp Eagle) Presentation Aircraft 'Punjab No.4'. At 2 AAP Hendon 5.4.17, allotted to EF; 55 Sqn; Crashed on return from raid 5.6.17 (Lt CC Knight & Lt JC Trulock OK); ARS 1 AD 8.6.17; 57 Sqn 20.7.17; Hit by explosive bullet on raid 16.8.17 (Lt AD Pryor OK & Sgt CR Goffe wounded in arm); Albatros D in flames 1 mile W of Roulers 14.00 2.10.17 (2/Lt FA Martin wounded in foot & Lt JD O'Neill OK); EA OOC SE of Houthulst Forest 11.45 12.11.17 (2/Lt AT Drinkwater & Lt FTS Menendez); Left on photographic mission 11.45 FTR 4.1.18 (Capt EEE Pope & Lt AF Wynne both PoW); SOS 57 Sqn 6.1.18

A7425 (275hp Eagle) At 2 AAP Hendon 3.5.17, allotted to EF; School of Instruction, Hendon, EF at 20ft, stalled attempting to reach aerodrome 7.5.17 (Lt FH Hambly & 2/Lt GRH Box both injured); At (S)ARD 9.5.17, Allotment to EF cancelled, now on charge AE 1 Repair Section

A7426 (275hp Eagle) Presentation Aircraft 'Gold Coast No.1', At 2 AAP Hendon 18.5.17, allotted to EF; ARS 1 AD; 57 Sqn 23.5.17; On practice flight COL 30.5.17 (2/Lt CL de Beer OK); ARS 2 AD 1.6.17; 25 Sqn 31.7.17; On line patrol engine lost power, overshot and crashed trying to land at 2 Sqn 20.00 12.8.17 (2/Lt D McLaurin & Lt JH Lark OK); ARS 2 AD; ARS 1 AD 29.9.17; 25 Sqn 2.10.17; FTR from 10.35 raid on Beythem 12.10.17 (Sgt AL Clear & 2/Lt FW Talbot both PoW; Talbot interned in Holland 9.4.18)

A7427 (275hp Eagle/ Eagle VIII) Presentation Aircraft 'Manitoba'. At 2 AAP Hendon 10.5.17, allotted to EF; At 55 Sqn 2.6.17; COL 16.8.17 (Capt FMcDC Turner & 2/Lt RdeR Brett); ARS 1 AD 19.8.17; ARS 2 AD 9.9.17 for reconstruction; 1 AI to 55 Sqn 1.4.18; EA crashed nr Baccarat then FL Rambervillers 20.7.18 (Lt AS Keep MC wounded & 2/Lt JF Pollock killed; 3 ASD 21.7.18; 55 Sqn ('J') 12.9.18; Fokker DVII crashed W of Strasburg 11.00 15.9.18 (Lt C Turner & 2/Lt JTL Attwood); Shortly after attacking Saarbrücken, Fokker DVII broke up and another OOC 14.30 6.11.18 (Capt JB Fox & Lt J Parke DFC); Engine trouble, COL 2.12.18 (Capt RW Rose & 2/Lt GE Little OK); SOC 6.12.18

D.H.4 A7466 'A' and others of No.18 Squadron at La Bellevue in September 1917. (via Frank Cheesman)

A7428 (250hp Eagle) Presentation Aircraft 'South Africa'. At 2 AAP Hendon 3.5.17, allotted to EF; 55 Sqn; Flying to new aerodrome ran into barbed wire fence 31.5.17 (Lt A Lindley & Lt LB Goodyear OK); ARS 1 AD 4.6.17; 57 Sqn 3.7.17; On 19.05 reconnaissance flight collided with another a/c W of Ypres and completely wrecked 12.7.17 (2/Lt FE Bishop & 2/Lt GS Ellis both killed); ARS 1 AD 15.7.17; SOC 16.7.17

A7429 (275hp Eagle) Presentation Aircraft 'British Subjects of all Races in Siam'. At 2 AAP Hendon 11.5.17, allotted to EF; At 55 Sqn 2.6.17; Bombing raid on Deynze, 2-str OOC smoking 08.25 between Thielt and the line, then FL 50 yards behind the Belgian front line with controls shot away 13.8.17 (Lt CW Davyes OK & Lt WR Cooke wounded); ARS 1 AD and SOC 22.8.17

A7430 to A7432 No information

A7433 Hounslow

A7434 No information

A7435 30 Wing ARS Turnhouse to 52 TS Catterick 31.10.17

A7436 (RAF 3a) Presentation Aircraft 'Zanzibar No.10'. At 2 AAP Hendon 25.4.17, allotted to EF but reallotted to Aircraft Manufacturing Company for experimental purposes 28.4.17; AES Martlesham 6.17 - 9.17; Anti-Gotha patrol, attacked centre of formation of 18 a/c at 14,000ft over Suffolk coast but front gun failed to work 4.7.17 (Capt J Palethorpe unhurt awarded MC & 1/AM JO Jessop killed by enemy bullet)

A7437 No information

A7438 52 TS Montrose, EF, turned back, stalled and dived in 16.10.17 (Lt WC Thompson killed)

The wreckage of D.H.4 A7439 of No.57 Squadron after being brought down by Ltn P.Schober of Jasta 18 on 11 September 1917. (J.M.Bruce/G.S.Leslie collection)

A7439 (275hp Eagle) Presentation Aircraft 'Gold Coast No.2'. At 2 AAP Hendon 11.5.17, allotted to EF; En route Lympne to (S)ARD 14.5.17, allocation to EF cancelled now on charge AE 1 Repair Section; (S)ARD 4.6.17, Reallotted to EF; England to ARS 1 AD 9.6.17; 57 Sqn 22.6.17; Damaged landing 29.6.17 (Lt WB Hutcheson & 2/Lt NM Pizey); ARS 1 AD 2.7.17; 57 Sqn 28.7.17; FTR from 10.45 raid on Courtrai sidings, crashed W of Courtrai, claimed by Ltn O Schober, Jasta 18 11.9.17 (Sgt SF Edgington & 2/Lt ETH Hearn both killed)

A7440 No information

A7441 (275hp Eagle) Presentation Aircraft 'River Plate'. At 2 AAP Hendon 15.5.17, allotted to EF; At 55 Sqn 2.6.17; Engine cut out on take off, FL in cornfield, a/c turned over 16.8.17 (Lt JM Burd & 2/Lt F Singleton); ARS 1 AD 17.8.17; ARS 2 AD 8.9.17 for reconstruction; At 2 AI, hit bank on landing after test flight 9.4.18 (Lt JES Gill OK); To Salvage 15.4.18; SOC 22.4.18

A7442 (275hp Eagle) Presentation Aircraft 'Presented by His Highness the Maharaja of Bikanir'; At 2 AAP Hendon 16.5.17, allotted to EF; 55 Sqn, damaged in bad landing 6.6.17 (2/Lt RCW Morgan slightly injured & Lt L Miller OK); ARS 1 AD 10.6.17; 25 Sqn ('B') 7.8.17; On practice flight stalled landing too slowly 24.10.17 (2/Lt JA Baker & Lt JH Kirk both OK); At Rep Pk 1 ASD by 11.11.17; Rep Pk 2 ASD 17.2.18; Rep Pk 1 ASD 2.4.18; Rec Pk to 2 ASD 2.6.18; Rebuilt as F5830 25.6.18

A7443 (275hp Eagle) At 2 AAP Hendon 21.5.17, allotted to EF; ARS 1 AD; 57 Sqn 25.5.17; Controls damaged in combat on 10.05 patrol Bixchoote-Houthem, struck telegraph pole swung and crashed nr Poperinghe 21.6.17 (2/Lt R Trattles slightly injured & Lt PH Bigwood killed); ARS 1 AD 24.6.17; SOC 25.6.17

A7444 (275hp Eagle) Presentation Aircraft 'Newfoundland No.1'. At 2 AAP Hendon 22.5.17, allotted to EF; England to ARS 1 AD 3.6.17; 57 Sqn 6.6.17; Wrecked on take off 16.6.17 (2/Lt CL de Beer & Sgt GA Broad OK); ARS 1 AD 18.6.17; SOC 20.6.17

A7445 (275hp Eagle) Presentation Aircraft 'Jamaica No.1'. At 2 AAP Hendon 18.5.17, allotted to EF; ARS 1 AD; 57 Sqn 25.5.17; Caught fire at 1,500ft, FL, bombs exploded, completely destroyed by fire 23.7.17 (Lt HNS Skeffington & Lt AC Malloch OK); ARS 1 AD 24.7.17; SOC 27.7.17

A7446 (275hp Eagle VIII) Makers alterations to water system by 7.7.17; At ARS 1 AD 21.7.17 "Capt De Havilland's m/c"; Testing Sqn Martlesham Heath 9.8.17 (performance with Eagle VIII); Makers 17.9.17; 5N Sqn 24.10.17; 2N Sqn 24.10.17; [Went to Dunkirk 24.10.17 and had been retained by the RNAS, this was recognised by reallotting it to RNAS 14.3.18; Became 202 Sqn 1.4.18; Pfalz DIII, wing came off, crashed N of Eessen 12.00 5.6.18; Fokker DVII OOC over Bruges 14.25 10.8.18; Fokker DVII in flames Dudzeele & Pfalz crashed Beukemaere Farm, Lisseweghe 11.05-11.25 16.9.18 (all Capt N Keeble DFC DSC & Capt EBC Betts DFC); COL Ghistelles 17.10.18 (Lt LF Pendred & Lt NH Jenkins); Salved; 4 ASD 22.10.18 - 25.10.18

A7447 (275hp Eagle) At 2 AAP Hendon 21.5.17, allotted to EF; ARS 1 AD; 57 Sqn 22.5.17; Struck horse drawn mowing machine on landing 2.6.17 (2/Lt AW Erlebach & Lt CH Trotter OK); SOC ARS 2 AD 3.6.17

A7448 (275hp Eagle) At 2 AAP Hendon 22.5.17, allotted to EF; ARS 1 AD; 57 Sqn ('A2') 24.5.17; EA OOC 11.40 21.6.17 (Lt CS Morice & Lt ACM Pym); Attacked over Houthulst by 7 Nieuport types with Belgian markings 11.30 13.7.17 (Lt WB Hutcheson OK & Lt ACM Pym wounded); FTR from 16.15 bombing raid on Ingelmunster, 28.7.17 (Lt HNS Skeffington killed & Lt AC Malloch PoW wounded) [probably shot down by Oblt E von Dostler, Jasta 6]

A7449 (275hp Eagle) At 2 AAP Hendon 21.5.17, allotted to EF; ARS 1 AD; 57 Sqn 25.5.17; FTR from 06.05 raid on Ingelmunster, engine cut then dropped out of formation, last seen W of line nr Ypres 12.7.17 (Sgt T Walker & 2/AM W Harris both PoW)

A7450 No information

A7451 (275hp Eagle) At 2 AAP Hendon 22.5.17, allotted to EF; At ARS 1 AD 1.6.17; 57 Sqn ('B3') 22.6.17; Left 16.45 for bombing raid on Abeele airfield, left aileron control shot away by Belgian Nieuport, elevator control practically severed, petrol tank and gun mounting also hit, FL in cornfield, overturned 21.7.17 (Sgt EV Bousher OK & Sgt AG Broad badly shocked); ARS 1 AD; 57 Sqn 24.9.17; Left at 11.45 for raid on Abeele aerodrome, last seen in combat over Roulers 2.10.17 (2/Lt CRB Halley & 1/AM TJ Barlow both killed)

A7452 (Eagle VII) Presentation Aircraft 'Malaya No.24. Penang'. At 2 AAP Hendon 23.5.17, allotted to EF; ARS 1 AD; 57 Sqn 25.5.17; On practice flight, COL 28.5.17 (2/Lt CL de Beer & Sgt AG Broad OK); ARS 2 AD by 1.6.17; ARS 1 AD 14.8.17; 55 Sqn 15.8.17; Raid on Hesdin l'Abbée, lagging behind on return, in combat with 11 EA, Albatros D OOC Ghent 15.30, own a/c damaged 27.9.17 (Capt D Owen OK & 2/AM WA Fraser wounded); To ARS 1 AD; Became Rep Pk 1 ASD 1.11.17; 1 AI 19.11.17; 25 Sqn 28.11.17; FL Thieville when petrol ran out 13.30 16.2.18 (2/Lt C Ross & 2/Lt JCO'R King); Rep Pk 2 ASD 27.2.18; Rep Pk 1 ASD 2.4.18; Rec Pk and on to 2AI 4.5.18; 57 Sqn 9.5.18; Tyre burst on landing 15.5.18 (Lt LL Brown & 1/AM O Shepstone OK); Rep Pk 2 ASD 17.5.18; Rebuilt as F6096 3.7.18

A7453 (275hp Eagle) At 2 AAP Hendon 29.5.17, allotted to EF; England to ARS 1 AD 3.6.17; 55 Sqn 5.6.17; Bad landing, wrecked 27.7.17 (Capt GW Frost & Lt H Dunstan OK); ARS 1 AD 30.7.17; 55 Sqn 30.9.17; Bad landing in fog 20.10.17 (2/Lt EF Van der Riet & Cpl Choate); 2 AD 20.10.17; SOC Rep Pk 2 ASD 11.11.17

A7454 (275hp Eagle) At 2 AAP Hendon 21.5.17, allotted to EF; ARS 1 AD; 57 Sqn 26.5.17; COL 3.6.17 (Lt DM Goodyear & 2/Lt FR Martin OK); ARS 2 AD 4.6.17; 57 Sqn 22.7.17; FTR from 05.45 raid on Courtrai, last seen NW of Roulers diving under control with 3 EA on tail 18.8.17 (Sgt CJ Comerford & 2/Lt N Bell both killed)

A7455 (275hp Eagle) ARS 1 AD; 57 Sqn 27.5.17; EA crashed S of Houthulst Forest 06.40 18.6.17 (Capt HR Harker & Lt WEB Barclay); Wrecked on take-off 18.6.17 (Lt DM Goodyear & 2/Lt FR Martin); ARS 1 AD and SOC 21.6.17

A7456 (BHP) Martlesham Heath c.6.17 (awaiting new engine 7.7.17); Retd Makers W/E 21.7.17; 2 TDS Stonehenge by 15.11.17

A7457 (RAF 3a) Deld Hendon for Special Service 12.6.17; Eastchurch 16.6.17; Flown Hendon 25.6.17; Bacton 9.8.17, AZP (named 'NON STARTER'); AZP, landed Bacton 22.8.17 (F/L GWR Fane); retd Yarmouth 26.8.17; Experimental Constructive Dept Grain 30.9.17 (air bag trials); later EC&AD; Test Dept Grain W/E 26.1.18 (flotation tests 28.1.18); EC&AD Grain by W/E 9.2.18; Test Dept Grain 3.18; EC&AD Grain W/E 9.3.18 - 25.5.18 (hydrovane and flotation gear experiments)

A7458 (RAF 3a) Presentation Aircraft 'Malaya No.26, The Malacca Chinese'. At 2 AAP Hendon 22.6.17, allotted to "R Replacement Sqn now with EF"; England to ARS 1 AD and on to 18 Sqn 3.7.17; COL due to tyre bursting 20.7.17 (2/Lt AV Pearman & 2/Lt LO Stocken OK); ARS 2 AD 23.7.17; 18 Sqn 18.10.17; Damaged landing due to very hard condition of ground 9.1.18 (Lt H Hudson & Lt TW Nicholson); Rep Pk 1 ASD 25.1.18

A7459 (RAF 3a) Deld Hendon for Special Service 12.6.17; Bacton 9.8.17 (named "Allo Lédeé Bird"); crashed in North Sea, BR 5.9.17; Surveyed 12.9.17; Deleted 24.9.17 total loss

A7460 Deld Old Sarum 15.11.17; 103 Sqn Old Sarum by 19-24.12.17

A7461 (275hp Eagle) Presentation Aircraft 'The Akyab'. At 2 AAP Hendon 29.5.17, allotted to EF; En route Lympne to (S)ARD 30.5.17, Allotment to EF cancelled, Now on charge E 1 Repair Section; Reallotted to EF 4.7.17; ARS 1 AD to 57 Sqn 29.7.17; FTR from 06.17 raid, last seen between Courtrai and Ledeghem in a steep dive 17.8.17 (Lt TS Roadley & 2/Lt CR Thomas both killed)

A7462 At Makers 28.7.17 (intended for AES Martlesham Heath to replace A7456, but apparently NTU); SoSF Gosport to 83 Sqn Wyton/Narborough 27.10.17 - 2.1.18

A7463 (275hp Eagle) Presentation Aircraft 'Zanzibar No.8'. At 2 AAP Hendon 2.6.17, allotted to EF; England to ARS 1 AD 8.6.17; 57 Sqn 9.6.17; Wrecked on landing at new aerodrome 12.6.17 (Capt NG McNaughton & 1/AM R Taggart OK); ARS 1 AD 16.6.17; 25 Sqn 26.7.17; Overran aerodrome on landing, tried to take off but wing hit tree and a/c overturned 28.7.17 (2/Lt HA Hope killed & 2/AM H Else injured); ARS 2 AD 29.7.17; SOC 30.7.17

A7464 (Eagle V) Presentation Aircraft 'Mauritius No.1'. At 2 AAP Hendon 31.5.17, allotted to EF; England to ARS 1 AD 2.6.17; 57 Sqn 11.6.17; Wrecked on landing 24.6.17 (Lt TS Roadley & 2/Lt LA Rushbrooke OK); ARS 1 AD 27.6.17; 25 Sqn 7.8.17; FL Clairmarais 28.11.17 (crew unhurt); Rep Pk 1 ASD 29.11.17; Rep Pk 2 ASD 17.2.18; 2 AI 30.5.18; 205 Sqn 3.6.18; COL 5.6.18 (Lt JG Kerr & 2/Lt HW Hopton); 2 ASD 7.6.18; Rebuilt as F6119 3.7.18

A7465 (Eagle VII) Presentation Aircraft 'Zanzibar No.6'. Deld 2 AAP Hendon 5.17, allotted to EF; 8 AAP Lympne to ARS 1 AD 28.5.17; 55 Sqn 1.6.17; Returning from raid, COL 12.8.17 (Lt HJ Forsaith & 2/AM S Moreman); ARS 1 AD; ARS 2 AD 5.9.17 for reconstruction; To 55 Sqn by rail 21.10.17; In combat during raid on Mannheim, last seen going down under control nr Speyer 24.12.17 (2/Lt GF Turner & 2/Lt AF Castle both PoW)

A7466 (RAF 3a) At 2 AAP Hendon 18.6.17, allotted to EF; Reallotted 20.6.17 to "R Replacement Sqn now with the EF"; England to ARS 1 AD 25.6.17; 18 Sqn ('A') 26.6.17 (this Sqn's first D.H.4); Wrecked 25.9.17; ARS 2 AD 28.9.17; Altered to take Eagle VII; At Rep Pk 2 ASD 31.12.17; 2 AI 3.2.18; Rep Pk 2 ASD 26.2.18; To 55 Sqn by rail ('P') 11.3.18, arrived 15.3.18; Bombing raid on Treves, under control over target, then combat with EAs, down in flames 13.6.18 (Lt W Legge & 2/Lt

D.H.4 A7457, nicknamed 'NON-STARTER', at Bacton in 1917. (J.M.Bruce/G.S.Leslie collection)

A close-up of the armament carried by D.H.4 A7457 at Bacton in 1917 for anti-Zeppelin work. (J.M.Bruce/G.S.Leslie collection)

A close-up view of the flotation gear and hydrovane fitted to D.H.4 A7457, at Grain on 28 January 1918. (via Frank Cheesman)

A front view view of the flotation gear and hydrovane fitted to D.H.4 A7457, at Grain on 28 January 1918. (via Frank Cheesman)

D.H.4 A7457 during the ditching experiment at Grain on 29 March 1918. (via J.M.Bruce/G.S.Leslie collection)

D.H.4 A7457 being hauled ashore. The wheels were blown off by compressed air before the ditching. (J.M.Bruce/G.S.Leslie)

D.H.4 A7459 at Bacton during 1917. A plate below the pilot's seat bears the nickname 'ALLO LÉDÉ BIRD'. (via J.M.Bruce/G.S.Leslie collection)

D.H.4 A7468 'H' of No.55 Squadron was shot down on 19 Febrary 1918, the crew being taken prisoner. (via Frank Cheesman)

A McKenzie both killed)

A7467 (275hp Eagle) At 2 AAP Hendon 7.6.17, allotted to EF; England to ARS 1 AD 11.6.17; 57 Sqn 23.6.17; FTR from 15.20 raid on Heule aerodrome, last seen over Houthulst Forest, later report said a/c down at "Farm de Coeninck" 27.7.17 (Lt AJL O'Beirne DoW 28.7.17 & 2/Lt NR Rayner killed); ARS 1 AD 30.7.17; SOC 1.8.17

A7468 (Eagle VII) At 2 AAP Hendon 30.5.17, allotted to EF; England to ARS 1 AD 5.7.17; 55 Sqn 7.7.17; Engine trouble, FL Beaumetz 12.7.17 (Lt JWF Neill slightly injured & 2/Lt TM Webster OK); ARS 1 AD 15.7.17; ARS 2 AD 1.10.17; To 55 Sqn ('H') by rail 11.10.17; FTR, last seen 15m from Treves turning back under control, shot down nr Metz-Frescaty 19.2.18 (Lt W Ross & 2/Lt HA Hewitt both PoW); A/c captured by Germans

A7469 (275hp Eagle) Presentation Aircraft 'Bombay No.1'. At 2 AAP Hendon 29.5.17, allotted to EF; ARS 1 AD to 55 Sqn 1.6.17; On photo reconnaissance, left at 14.30, attacked by EA, petrol tank holed, crashed 10.6.17 (Lt PJ Barnett & 2/Lt RM Dixon wounded); ARS 1 AD 11.6.17; SOC 14.6.17

A7470 (250hp Eagle) Presentation Aircraft 'Malaya No.27'. At 2 AAP Hendon 31.5.17, allotted to EF; England to ARS 1 AD 4.6.17; 55 Sqn 7.6.17; Bombing attack on Abeelhoek, combat damaged 14.8.17 (2/Lt CA Stevens OK & 2/Lt BF Sandy slightly wounded); ARS 1 AD 17.8.17; 25 Sqn 2.10.17; FL due to leaking radiator 11.10.17 (Lt JE Pugh & 2/Lt WJ Walsh both OK); ARS 1 AD 16.10.17; 1 AI 19.11.17; 25 Sqn 12.12.17 (by then 275hp Eagle fitted); Lost way in mist, FL, struck trees nr Recques 23.1.18 (Lt E Gordon severely bruised & Lt CM Sinclair shaken); Rep Pk 1 ASD 28.1.18; SOC 8.2.18

A7471 (275hp Eagle) At 2 AAP Hendon 29.5.17, allotted to EF; En route 8 AAP Lympne to (S)ARD 11.6.17, allotment to EF cancelled, now on charge E 1 Repair Section; At (S)ARD 12.7.17 reallotted to EF; England to ARS 1 AD 9.8.17; 55 Sqn 13.8.17; FTR from 06.17 raid on La Briquette aerodrome, on recrossing the lines nr Ocre hit by fire from AA & EA, BU in air 18.8.17 (Lt HJ Forsaith & 2/Lt H Dunstan both killed); ARS 1 AD and SOC 22.8.17

A7472 (275hp Eagle) Presentation Aircraft 'Baroda No.16'. At 2 AAP Hendon 2.6.17, allotted to EF; England to ARS 1 AD 3.6.17; 55 Sqn 7.6.17; Misjudged distance in landing, crashed into hangar at 57 Sqn 16.7.17 (2/Lt EGHC Williams OK); ARS 1 AD and SOC 19.7.17

A7473 (275hp Eagle) At 2 AAP Hendon 2.6.17, allotted to EF; England to ARS 1 AD 10.6.17; 57 Sqn 13.6.17; FTR from 07.40 photographic mission, last seen in a spin at 9,000 feet over Becelaere 24.6.17 (Capt NG McNaughton MC & Capt AH Mearns both killed) [Claimed 08.30 by Rittm M von Richtofen of JG1]

A7474 (RAF 3a) 8 AAP Lympne to ARS 1 AD 27.6.17; 18 Sqn 2.7.17; On camera gun practice flight believed to have pulled out of a dive too suddenly, crashed 6.7.17 (Lt WH Ryder & Lt EG Rowley both killed); ARS 2 AD 8.7.17; SOC 9.7.17

A7475 (275hp Eagle) At 2 AAP Hendon 8.6.17, allotted to EF; England to ARS 1 AD 11.6.17; 55 Sqn 15.6.17; Scout OOC W of Roulers 18.15 12.8.17 (Capt PG Kirk & 2/Lt GY Fullalove); Left 06.42 on bombing raid on Deynze, attacked by EA over Roulers and presumed shot down in flames, observer jumped out 13.8.17 (Capt PG Kirk & 2/Lt GY Fullalove both killed)

A7476 (275hp Eagle) Presentation Aircraft 'Malaya No.21'. At 2 AAP Hendon 2.6.17, allotted to EF; England to ARS 1 AD 3.6.17; 55 Sqn 5.6.17; Engine trouble, FL nr St Omer 13.7.17 (2/Lt ES Guy & 2/AM Shaw both slightly injured); ARS 1 AD 15.7.17; SOC 16.7.17

A7477 (Eagle VII) Deld 2 AAP Hendon 8.6.17, allotted to EF 8.6.17; England to ARS 1 AD 23.6.17; 25 Sqn 24.6.17; Landed badly in cross wind 5.9.17 (2/Lt GS Wood & 2/Lt DD Humphreys both OK); ARS 2 AD 7.9.17; Rep Pk 2 ASD to 55 Sqn by rail ('F') 31.12.17; Albatros D in vertical dive smoking Mannheim 12.00 24.3.18 (2/Lt RC Sansom OK and Sgt J Ryan killed); Shot down in flames over Saarbrücken in bombing raid 16.5.18 (Lt RC Sansom & 3/AM GC Smith both killed)

A7478 (RAF 3a) At 2 AAP Hendon 21.6.17, allotted to "R" Replacement Sqn now with EF; England to ARS 1 AD 24.6.17; Wrecked on landing (Lt Baker); 18 Sqn 22.7.17; Engine cut out, FL 28.7.17 (Lt GHS Dinsmore & 2/Lt EJ Detmold); SOC ARS 2 AD 31.7.17

A7479 (275hp Eagle) At 2 AAP Hendon 11.6.17, allotted to EF; England to ARS 1 AD 16.6.17; 25 Sqn 19.6.17; On photographic flight shot down and crashed Foufflin 16.15 27.7.17 (2/Lt WL Lovell & 2/Lt WW Fitzgerald both killed); ARS 2 AD and SOC 28.7.17

A7480 (275hp Eagle) At 2 AAP Hendon 11.6.17, allotted to EF; 8 AAP Lympne to ARS 1 AD 11.6.17; 57 Sqn 15.6.17; Overshot aerodrome, tipped up in ditch 26.6.17 (Lt TS Roadley & 2/Lt LA Rushbrooke); ARS 1 AD 29.6.17; 25 Sqn 31.8.17; Left 17.35, combat with 10 EA, shot down OOC nr La Bassée 19.00 4.9.17 (Lt CJ Pullen & 2/Lt EDS Robinson both killed)

A7481 (275hp Eagle) At 2 AAP Hendon 13.6.17, allotted to

EF; England to ARS 1 AD 13.6.17; 57 Sqn ('C4') 14.6.17; 2 Str OOC Westroosebeke 08.10 7.7.17 (Lt TS Roadley & Lt LA Rushbrooke wounded); On climbing test with two 112-lb bombs, ran into hole on TO, broke propeller, stalled, tried to turn, nose dived, caught fire, bombs exploded, completely destroyed 24.7.17 (2/Lt HAB Norris killed & 2/Lt H St.Clair Roy MC injured); ARS 1 AD 26.7.17

A7482 (Eagle VII) At 2 AAP Hendon 14.6.17, allotted to EF; England to ARS 1 AD 23.6.17; 25 Sqn (marked 'NUS') 24.6.17; Damaged landing in strong wind 8.10.17 (2/Lt ES Pfeiffer & Pte R Ireland); ARS 2 AD 10.10.17; Became Rep Pk 2 ASD 1.11.17; By rail to 55 Sqn ('B') 11.3.18, arr 16.3.18; Bombing raid, BU in dive nr Metz 1.6.18 (Lt LdeG Godet & 2/Lt A Haley both killed)

D.H.4 A7482 of No.25 Squadron, marked 'NUS', on its nose on 8 October 1917. (J.M.Bruce/G.S.Leslie collection)

A7483 (RAF 3a) Presentation Aircraft 'Australia No.5, N.S.W.No.4, The F.J.White, Saumarez and Baldblair'. At 2 AAP Hendon 23.6.17, allotted to "R Replacement Sqn now with EF" but this cancelled 18.7.17, a/c now on charge E.1 Repair Section and to be sent from Hendon to 1 (S)ARD; At 1 (S)ARD 26.10.17, reallotted to EF; Farnborough to Lympne for France but mist and engine trouble, landed Redhill 10.11.17; Arr 8 AAP Lympne 11.11.17; Rec Pk 11.11.17; FL en route to 2 ASD 16.11.17, a/c "cared for by 2 ASD"; 2 AI to 18 Sqn 19.1.18; 2 AI and on to Rep Pk 2 ASD 22.1.18; 2 AI 10.5.18; 1 AI 17.5.18; 18 Sqn 21.5.18; Heavy landing broke u/c and turned over 23.5.18 (2/Lt G Leitch & Capt D Gale OK); Rep Pk 1 ASD 26.5.18; Rebuilt as F5838 25.6.18

A7484 (275hp Eagle) Presentation Aircraft 'Shanghai Raceclub No.2'. At 2 AAP Hendon 22.6.17, allotted to EF; England to ARS 1 AD 25.6.17; 57 Sqn ('B2') 26.6.17; FTR from 17.00 raid, last seen spiralling down under control from 10,000ft nr Roulers 11.7.17 (2/Lt R Trattles & 2/Lt AJ Savory both PoW) [possibly "Sopwith" claimed 18.45 nr Ledeghem by Ltn O Creutzmann of Jasta 20]

A7485 (275hp Eagle) At 2 AAP Hendon 15.6.16, allotted to EF; England to ARS 1 AD 23.6.17; 57 Sqn 1.7.17; U/c struck side of road, pilot tried to gain height to release bombs, It was presumed that only one rack of bombs was dropped, u/c fell off and bombs exploded when fuselage touched the ground, crashed about 3 miles from aerodrome, A/c destroyed by fire 5.7.17 (2/Lt AW Erlebach killed & Lt CH Trotter badly shaken); ARS 1 AD 8.7.17; SOC 9.7.17

A7486 (Eagle V) At 2 AAP Hendon 13.6.17, allotted to EF; England to ARS 1 AD 15.6.17; 25 Sqn 17.6.17; On practice flight overshot on landing and touched ground with left wingtip 7.8.17 (2/Lt PL McGavin & 2/AM F Millington) ARS 2 AD 8.8.17; ARS 1 AD 24.9.17; 57 Sqn 25.9.17; On practice flight wrecked on landing 8.11.17 (2/Lt WE Green); Rep Pk 1 ASD 10.11.17 (Eagle IV); 2 AI 25.3.18; 5N Sqn 31.3.18, became 205 Sqn 1.4.18; Crashed returning from bombing raid, Dampiere 12.4.18 (Lt RC Day & Sgt SM MacKay); 2 ASD 13.4.18; SOC Rep Pk 1 ASD 19.4.18

D.H.4 A7486 served with of Nos.25, 57 and 205 Squadrons. (via Don Neate)

A7487 (Eagle VIII) Presentation Aircraft 'Gold Coast No.2'. At 2 AAP Hendon 18.6.17, allotted to EF; England to ARS 1 AD 23.6.17; 57 Sqn 25.6.17; FL Clairmarais due to engine trouble 12.7.17 (Lt AD Pryor & 1/AM W Harris); ARS 1 AD 13.7.17; 25 Sqn 23.8.17; In combat with 12 Albatros DIII over La Bassée, 1 down in flames shared 18.50 4.9.17 (Lt CA Pike OK & 2/Lt AT Williams DoW); Victory 27.10.17 (Lt JA McCudden & AM J Harris); Landed at 46 Sqn to refuel, engine cut out on take off, crashed 3.1.18 (Lt JH Wensley & Lt AW Matson unhurt); Rep Pk 1 ASD 12.1.18; 2 AI 2.4.18; Rep Pk 2 ASD 12.4.18; 2 AI 29.5.18; To 205 Sqn but FL en route at Sains-les-Pernes 3.6.18; arr 205 Sqn 4.6.18; COL 4.7.18 (Lt GC Matthews & Sgt L Murphy unhurt); Rep Pk 2 ASD 7.7.18; SOC 31.7.18 NWR
NOTE: Allocated 26.3.18 by E.1A for delivery to Islington [Plane Repair Unit?] for intended preservation and eventually delivered 6.9.18 (250hp Eagle).

A7488 (275hp Eagle) Presentation Aircraft 'Australia No.18, N.S.W. Government No.17, The Upper Hunter Battleplane'. At 2 AAP Hendon 18.6.17, allotted to EF; England to ARS 1 AD 24.6.17; 57 Sqn 25.6.17; Shot down by AA on 12.00 sortie 29.6.17 within 1,000 yards of the front line, A/c destroyed by fire (Lt DM Goodyear & 2/Lt FR Martin both killed)

A7489 (Eagle VII) Presentation Aircraft 'Zanzibar No.12'. At 2 AAP Hendon 22.6.17, allotted to EF; England to ARS 1 AD 25.6.17, FL Belgian aerodrome Calais en route; Arrived 29.6.17; 1 AD, tested 3.7.17; 25 Sqn 4.7.17; Misjudged landing on practice flight, caught u/c against bank at edge of a/f 19.8.17 (2/Lt LA Hacklett slightly injured & Lt VP Barbat unhurt); ARS 2 AD 20.8.17; By rail to 55 Sqn ('P') 11.10.17; FTR Freiburg raid 13.3.18 (2/Lt RB Brookes & Sgt H Gostling both killed)

A7490 (RAF 3a) At 2 AAP Hendon 29.6.17, allotted to "R Replacement Sqn now with EF"; England to ARS 1 AD 2.7.17; 18 Sqn 3.7.17; Left 16.05 to view the line, shot down by Ltn K Jacob, Jasta 31 17.20 15.7.17 (2/Lt VC Coombs-Taylor & 2/Lt HM Tayler both PoW wounded); A/c captured by Germans

A7491 (RAF 3a) Presentation Aircraft 'Punjab No.6, 7 Nabha'; At 2 AAP Hendon 28.6.17, allotted to "R Replacement Sqn now with EF"; At (S)ARD 24.7.17, Allotment cancelled, now on charge E 1 Repair Section; 9 TS Norwich by 28.10.17; 1 (S)ARD Farnborough to 2 TDS Stonehenge 27.11.17; 99 Sqn Old Sarum 8.12.17 - @21.1.18; 98 Sqn Old Sarum by 3.2.18; 108 Sqn Lake Down 16.2.18

A7492 (275hp Eagle) At 2 AAP Hendon 19.6.17, allotted to EF England to ARS 1 AD 23.6.17; 57 Sqn 25.6.17; Attacked by a Belgian Nieuport, Dixmude 13.00 7.7.17 (Capt HR Harker & Lt WEB Barclay MC); Scout crashed S of Courtrai 12.45 11.9.17 (2/Lt CRB Bailey & 2/AM TJ Barlow); FTR 17.9.17 (2/Lt CF Pritchard & 2/Lt T Grosvenor both killed)

A7493 (275hp Eagle) At 2 AAP Hendon 25.6.17, allotted to EF; England to ARS 1 AD 1.7.17; 55 Sqn 5.7.17; FTR from 08.50 raid on Ramegnies-Chi aerodrome, last seen going down under control over Lille 7.7.17 (Lt PW Battersby & Capt WW Fitzherbert both killed) [possibly

"Sopwith" claimed 11.00 SW of Warneton by Oblt E von Dostler, Jasta 6]

A7494 Flew Redcar to Stirling 15.8.17

A7495 (275hp Eagle) At 2 AAP Hendon 6.7.17, allotted to EF; England to ARS 1 AD 14.7.17; 55 Sqn 15.7.17; Scout OOC W of Roulers 18.15 12.8.17 (2/Lt PG Kirk & 2/Lt GY Fullalove); Albatros D tail broke off W of Deynze 08.15 13.8.17 (Lt CB Waters & 2/Lt GM Smith); FTR from 10.40 solo bombing and photographic mission to Lys Valley 16.8.17 (Lt CB Waters & 2/Lt GM Smith both PoW)

A7496 (275hp Eagle) 9 TS Norwich by 6.8.17

A7497 No information

A7498 (RAF 3a) At 2 AAP Hendon 2.7.17, allotted to EF; England to ARS 1 AD 27.7.17; 18 Sqn 28.7.17; Overran aerodrome into corn and ran into hidden shell hole 5.8.17 (Capt TFW Thomson & 2/Lt LO Stocken); ARS 2 AD 8.8.17; 2 ASD to 49 Sqn 23.11.17; 2 AI 11.2.18 (exchanged for Fiat-engined m/c); Rep Pk 2 ASD 22.2.18; 2 AI to 1 AI 1.4.18; 18 Sqn 14.4.18; Heavy landing u/c collapsed 30.5.18 (2/Lt JW Mellish & Lt BJ Blackett); Rep Pk 1 ASD 1.6.18; SOC 3.6.18 NWR

A7499 (RAF 3a) At 46 TS Catterick 11.17

A7500 (RAF 3a) Presentation Aircraft 'Britons in Chile'. At 2 AAP Hendon 29.6.17, allotted to EF; England to ARS 1 AD 25.7.17; 18 Sqn 13.8.17; U/c caught stones in old shell hole on take-off 7.9.17 (2/Lt AV Pearman & 2/AM W Jones OK); ARS 2 AD 11.9.17; Altered to take Eagle

A7501 (RAF 3a) At 2 AAP Hendon 29.6.17, allotted to EF; At (S)ARD 24.7.17, Allotment to EF cancelled, now on charge E.1 Repair Section; At 1 (S)ARD 25.10.17, Reallotted to EF; 1 ASD to 18 Sqn 9.11.17; Damaged by AA in cloud, landed to examine m/c but crashed 23.11.17 (2/Lt DA Stewart & Lt HWM Mackay OK); 2 ASD 26.11.17; Collected from Neuville by Rep Pk 1 ASD 15.4.18; Rep Pk 2 ASD; Adv Salvage Dump 2 ASD

A7502 (RAF 3a) 19 TS Hounslow, engine cut in circuit, dived in from 100ft 5.9.17 (2/Lt RV Cullinan injured)

A7503 (275hp Eagle) At 2 AAP Hendon 21.6.17, allotted to EF; England to ARS 1 AD 23.6.17; 25 Sqn 24.6.17; FL due to engine failure, On landing hit obstacle 2.7.17 (Lt A Roulstone & Lt N Field); ARS 2 AD 4.7.17; 25 Sqn 14.8.17; Left at 11.20 on photographic mission Lophem-Coolkerke, FTR 21.10.17 (2/Lt D McLaurin & 2/Lt OM Hills MC both PoW)

A7504 9 TS Norwich by 5.11.17

A7505 (Eagle IV) At 2 AAP Hendon 25.6.17, allotted to EF; England to ARS 1 AD 28.6.17; 25 Sqn 4.7.17; Albatros OOC Dorignies 13.00 7.7.17 (Capt J Fitz-Morris & Lt DL Burgess); Overshot aerodrome and in making a sharp turn broke u/c 27.1.18 (2/Lt RM Tate & Lt HA Lloyd); Rep Pk 1 ASD 30.1.18; SOC 8.2.18

A7506 (RAF 3a) At 2 AAP Hendon 19.7.17, allotted to EF but reallotted to Training 21.7.17; 9 TS Norwich by 7.9.17

A7507 (Eagle VII) At 2 AAP Hendon 27.6.17, allotted to EF; At (S)ARD 24.7.17, Allotment to EF cancelled, Now on charge E 1 Repair Section; Still at (S)ARD 4.10.17, Reallotted to EF; Farnborough to Lympne for France, but retd London and spent night at Whetstone 27.10.17; At 1 AI 3.12.17; 25 Sqn 5.12.17; On practice flight landed too slowly, partially pancaked 2.1.18 (2/Lt BL Lindley); Rep Pk 1 ASD 6.1.18; Rep Pk 2 ASD 17.2.18; Rec Pk to 2 AI 2.6.18; 25 Sqn 6.6.18; Standing on aerodrome damaged when bombs exploded on crashed 27 Sqn's B9338 7.7.18; Rebuilt as F6214 25.7.18

A7508 (275hp Eagle) At 2 AAP Hendon 2.7.17, allotted to EF; England to ARS 1 AD 13.7.17; 55 Sqn 14.7.17; Left 04.58, FTR bombing raid on Ghent, fired Very light and burnt a/c, Terneuzen, 22.7.17 (2/Lt CC Knight & 2/Lt JC Trulock both PoW)

A7509 (275hp Eagle) At 2 AAP Hendon 29.6.17, allotted to EF; England to ARS 1 AD 6.7.17; 55 Sqn 22.7.17; Shot down in raid on Gontrode, COL 27.7.17 (2/Lt RCW Morgan DoW 28.7.17 & Lt WR Clarke OK); ARS 1 AD 30.7.17; SOC 1.8.17

A7510 (275hp Eagle) At 2 AAP Hendon 27.6.17, allotted to EF; 8 AAP Lympne to ARS 1 AD 22.7.17; 57 Sqn 14.8.17; Twin engined m/c OOC Menin 12.30 16.8.17 (Lt J Hood & 2/Lt JR MacDaniel); FTR from 17.50 raid, last seen in a spin with EA on tail SW of Roulers 18.8.17 (Lt J Hood & 2/Lt JR MacDaniel both killed)

A7511 19 TS Hounslow, crashed 9.8.17 (2/Lt CR Waller killed)

A7512 (RAF 3a) At 2 AAP Hendon 31.7.17, allotted to EF; England to ARS 1 AD and on to 18 Sqn 22.8.17; Wrecked 19.9.17; ARS 2 AD 22.9.17

A7513 (275hp Eagle) At 2 AAP Hendon 27.6.17, allotted to EF; England to ARS 1 AD 3.7.17; 57 Sqn ('A4') 6.7.17; FTR from 17.30 photo reconnaissance 10.8.17 (2/Lt HE Biederman & Lt A Calder both killed)

A7514 (RAF 3a) At 2 AAP Hendon 21.7.17, allotted to EF; England to ARS 1 AD 10.8.17; 18 Sqn 11.8.17; Overturned landing after practice flight, then prop hit pilot on head 31.8.17 (2/Lt AW Harrison injured); On dismantling engine longeron found to be split, It was believed to have been damaged at the makers 5.9.17; ARS 2 AD 9.9.17; At Rep Pk 2 ASD 31.12.17; 2 AI to 27 Sqn 6.5.18; Left 05.05 on bombing raid, combat with 20-30 EA SW of Péronne, seen going down 10.5.18 (Capt GBS McBain & Lt W Spencer killed)

A7515 (Eagle VI) At 2 AAP Hendon 1.9.17 allotted to EF; England to ARS 1 AD 2.9.17; 57 Sqn 11.9.17; Left at 10.07, last seen at 10,000 feet S of Staden 12.10.17 (Lt SH Allen & Lt GCE Smithett both killed)

A7516 (RAF 3a) At 2 AAP Hendon 19.7.17, allotted to EF but reallotted to Training 21.7.17; 19 TS Hounslow, crashed 11.8.17 (2/Lt W McIlwraith & 2/Lt F Spalding both injured)

A7517 (RAF 3a) Presentation Aircraft 'Shanghai Raceclub No.2'. At 2 AAP Hendon 31.7.17, allotted to EF; England to ARS 1 AD 11.8.17; 18 Sqn 12.8.17; Last seen between Vitry-en-Artois and Henin Lietard 12.00 8.11.17 (2/Lt WC Pruden OK & 2/AM J Conlin wounded, both PoW)

A7518 (Eagle VI) At 2 AAP Hendon 29.6.17, allotted to EF; England to ARS 1 AD 3.7.17; 55 Sqn 6.7.17; Engine failure, FL in ploughed field 7.7.17 (Lt EH Marshall & 1/AM C Kelly OK); ARS 1 AD 9.7.17; 57 Sqn 22.8.17; Wrecked 10.9.17; ARS 1 AD; 55 Sqn 8.10.17; Collided with tender on landing 24.12.17 (2/Lt TS Wilson & 2/Lt L Cann unhurt); Rep Pk 2 ASD 24.12.17 (arr 5.1.18); Rep Pk 1 ASD 2.4.18; 2 AI 28.5.18; 205 Sqn 3.6.18; Direct hit by AA in raid on Barleux, FL, COL nr Villers-Bretonneux 23.8.18 (Lt EO Danger & 2/Lt AD Hollingsworth unhurt); SOC Rep Pk 2 ASD 26.8.18 NWR

A7519 (200hp BHP) At 1 (S)ARD 26.10.17, allotted to EF; Tested Farnborough 27.11.17; 8 AAP to Rec Pk 27.11.17; 27 Sqn 3.12.17; 1 AI 26.1.18; Rec Pk 29.1.18; To England 23.2.18

A7520 83 Sqn Wyton by 11.17

A7521 No information

A7522 (275hp Eagle) At 2 AAP Hendon 2.7.17, allotted to EF; England to ARS 1 AD 12.7.17; 55 Sqn 13.7.17; Bad landing, wrecked 16.7.17 (2/Lt ES Guy & 2/AM Shaw OK); ARS 1 AD and on to 2 AD 19.7.17 for reconstruction; ARS 1 AD and on to 55 Sqn 17.8.17; Raid on Farmars aerodrome, last seen going down under control in the direction of Brebières aerodrome 20.8.17 (2/Lt CP Adamson wounded PoW & 2/AM FJ Smith DoW)

A7523 (RAF 3a) At 2 AAP Hendon 23.7.17, allotted to EF; England to ARS 1 AD and on to 18 Sqn 28.7.17; ARS 2 AD 1.9.17; 18 Sqn by 11.10.17; Apparently stalled on climbing turn and spun in, burnt 31.10.17 (2/Lt GH Gallinger & 2/Lt AW McJannet both killed); Rep Pk 2 ASD 1.11.17; SOC 2.11.17

A7524 (RAF 3a) At 2 AAP Hendon 31.7.17, allotted to EF; England to ARS 1 AD 20.8.17; ARS 2 AD 21.8.17; 2 ASD to 18 Sqn 15.11.17; Shot up, longerons splitting 21.2.18; Rep Pk 1 ASD 23.2.18; SOC 1.3.18

A7525 (275hp Eagle) At 2 AAP Hendon 2.7.17, allotted to EF; England to ARS 1 AD 4.7.17, landed at Calais en route due to bad weather, arrived 5.7.17; 57 Sqn 7.7.17; Completely wrecked on take off returning from FL 21.7.17 (2/Lt AS Turner & Lt LS Brooke); ARS 1 AD 24.7.17; SOC 27.7.17

A7526 (Eagle VI) At 2 AAP Hendon 14.7.17, allotted to EF; England to ARS 1 AD 20.7.17; 55 Sqn 21.7.17; Albatros D in flames Ghent-Thielt 10.15 30.9.17 (2/Lt EF Van der Riet & 2/AM SA Groves); COL on return from raid 1.10.17 (Capt D Owen & Gnr WG Osborne both OK); ARS 1 AD 1.10.17; Became Rep Pk 1 ASD 1.11.17; 2 AI 12.11.17; Rep Pk 2 ASD 14.2.18; 25 Sqn 13.3.18; Engine and radiator shot through by mg Bapaume, FL Warfussee-Abancourt, m/c burnt, instruments and guns salved 26.3.18 (2/Lt CJ Fitzgibbon wounded & 2/Lt RW Hobbs MC OK)

A7527 (Eagle VI) At 2 AAP Hendon 6.7.17, allotted to EF; England to ARS 1 AD 26.7.17; 25 Sqn 28.7.17; After line patrol lost way and FL nr Hesdin, a/c turned over 21.8.17 (2/Lt GS Wood & 1/AM J Harris) ARS 2 AD 23.8.17; 25 Sqn ('P') 10.10.17; Engine cut on TO, crashed 4.1.18 (2/Lt JS Macaulay & 2/Lt AE Thornhill injured); Rep Pk 1 ASD 10.1.18; SOC

A7528 (RAF 3a) At 2 AAP Hendon 25.7.17, allotted to EF; England to ARS 1 AD 5.8.17; 18 Sqn 8.8.17; EF, hit by AA on glide back, crashed, wrecked 19.9.17 (2/Lt AC Atkey & 1/AM T McGrath both OK)

A7529 (275hp Eagle) At 2 AAP Hendon 19.7.17, allotted to EF; 8 AAP Lympne to ARS 1 AD 22.7.17; 57 Sqn 24.7.17; Left 18.05 for photo recce, last seen 19.30 at 14,000ft going west nr Houthulst Wood 10.8.17 (2/Lt AN Barlow PoW & Lt CD Hutchinson PoW DoW 12.8.17) [probably shot down Ingelmunster 19.30 by Ltn Müller of Jasta 28]

A7530 (275hp Eagle) At 2 AAP Hendon 13.7.17, allotted to EF; England to ARS 1 AD 20.7.17; 55 Sqn 21.7.17; Scout OOC nr Ghent 08.26 13.8.17 (Lt JWF Neill & 2/Lt TM Webster); FTR from 12.04 raid, combat with EA nr Melle, last seen going down in a spiral smoking nr Gitsberg 5.9.17 (Lt JWF Neill & 2/Lt TM Webster both wounded PoW)

A7531 Sold to American Government

A7532 First installation of 260hp Fiat A.12 engine; Arr Martlesham Heath 30.6.17; Arr Rec Pk 31.8.18 (Eagle VIII fitted); To 2 AI and on to 3 ASD 1.9.18; 55 Sqn ('D') 4.9.18; 3 ASD 21.9.18, wrecked

A7533 (275hp Eagle) At 2 AAP Hendon 19.7.17, allotted to EF; 8 AAP Lympne to ARS 1 AD 22.7.17; 57 Sqn 26.7.17; Albatros D crashed 4 miles SW of Roulers 09.35 3.10.17 (Sgt FV Legge & 1/AM JS Clarke); Bad landing at new aerodrome Le Quesnoy 29.3.18 (Lt A MacGregor & 1/AM WO Lochhead OK); At Rep Pk 2 ASD by 1.4.18; To UK; 28 TS(?) Castle Bromwich by 9.5.18

A7534 (275hp Eagle) At 2 AAP Hendon 9.7.17, allotted to EF; AES Orfordness by 21.7.17 (fit new bomb carriers); To Hounslow 9.8.17; At (S)ARD 24.7.17, allotment to EF cancelled, now on charge E 1 Repair Section

A7535 (Eagle VI) Presentation Aircraft 'Newfoundland No.1'. At 2 AAP Hendon 19.7.17, allotted to EF; England to ARS 1 AD 25.7.17; 57 Sqn 29.7.17; Damaged by AA on 05.45 raid on Courtrai, wrecked on landing nr Droglandt 18.8.17 (Lt DS Hall & Lt AF Brittan OK); ARS 1 AD 21.8.17; ARS 2 AD 9.9.17; ARS 1 AD 23.10.17; 25 Sqn ('H':'B') 24.10.17; Left for Bray 11.25, shell hit u/c axle which broke in two, crashed on landing 13.15 27.3.18 (2/Lt BL Lindley & Sgt A Remington OK); Rep Pk 2 ASD 1.4.18; SOC 28.4.18; Brought back on charge; 2 AI 25.5.18; 55 Sqn 30.5.18; Overturned on landing 13.6.18 (Sgt AW Mepsted & Sgt Brass OK); SOC Rep Pk 2 ASD 10.7.18 NWR (ex 6 AP)

A7536 (Eagle VI) At 2 AAP Hendon 24.7.17, allotted to EF; England to ARS 1 AD 27.7.17; 25 Sqn 9.8.17; On practice flight, landed too slowly, stalled and overturned 18.10.17 (2/Lt FV Bird OK & 2/Lt G Dixon cuts); ARS 1 AD 18.10.17; Became Rep Pk 1 ASD 1.11.17; 57 Sqn 4.12.17; Crashed into by A8068 while stationary 30.7.18; To Rep Pk 2 ASD; SOC 11.8.18 NWR

A7537 (Eagle VII) At 2 AAP Hendon 20.7.17, allotted to EF; England to ARS 1 AD 22.7.17; 57 Sqn 25.7.17; In combat with Albatros DVs in bombing raid on Ingelmunster 18.30 (Mjr EG Joy & Lt F Leathley OK); Broke a wheel on landing and turned on nose 5.8.17 (Mjr EG Joy & Lt F Leathley); ARS 1 AD 7.8.17; ARS 2 AD 19.8.17 for reconstruction; ARS 1 AD 23.9.17; 57 Sqn 24.9.17; 1 AD 17.10.17; Rep Pk 1 ASD to Rec Pk 1.5.18; 2 AI 4.5.18; 57 Sqn 9.5.18; Albatros D BU Bapaume 20.15 10.6.18 (Lt ADR Jones & Sgt JT Ward); Just after take off engine cut out, landed in field with stacks of alfalfa grass, m/c wrecked 1.7.18 (Lt WH Kilbourne & Sgt AC Lovesey); To 2 Adv Salvage Dump 3.7.18; SOC Rep Pk 2 ASD 23.7.18

D.H.4 A7532, seen here at Martlesham Heath with B.E.2e C7133 in the background, is fitted with the prototype FIAT A.12 engine installation. (via Frank Cheesman)

A7538 (275hp Eagle) At 2 AAP Hendon 19.7.17, allotted to EF; England to ARS 1 AD 21.7.17; 57 Sqn 23.7.17; FTR from 16.15 bombing raid on Ingelmunster 28.7.17 (2/Lt HWB Rickards & 2/Lt RH Corbishley both killed)

A7539 (275hp Eagle) At 2 AAP Hendon 19.7.17, allotted to EF but reallotted to Training 21.7.17; AES Martlesham Heath from W/E 25.8.17 (prop and consumption tests); Catterick 30.8.17; AES Martlesham Heath 5.10.17 until 18.10.17

A7540 (275hp Eagle) Presentation Aircraft 'Bombay No.1'. At 2 AAP Hendon 19.7.17, allotted to EF; England to ARS 1 AD 21.7.17; 57 Sqn 22.7.17; FTR from 16.15 bombing raid on Ingelmunster 28.7.17 (Capt L Minot & 2/Lt SJ Leete both killed)

A7541 83 Sqn Wyton, EF after TO, turned back, stalled on turn, crashed 9.11.17 (2/Lt LA Palmer killed)

A7542 (Eagle VII) At 2 AAP Hendon 19.7.17, allotted to EF; En route from 8 AAP Lympne to (S)ARD 23.7.17, allotment to EF cancelled, Now on charge E 1 Repair Section; Still at (S)ARD 4.10.17, Reallotted to EF; Rep Pk 1 ASD by 11.11.17; 57 Sqn 15.11.17; Crashed nr aerodrome, m/c completely burnt 20.11.17 (Capt AB Cook & 2/Lt SBH Coppard killed); SOC Rep Pk 1 ASD 23.11.17

A7543 (275hp Eagle) At 2 AAP Hendon 24.7.17, allotted to EF; England to ARS 1 AD 26.7.17; 25 Sqn 27.7.17; FL Compiègne, then returning attempted to land Le Crotoy, dived in from 100ft, wrecked 9.11.17 (2/Lt SB Cragg killed & 2/Lt G Dixon injured); Rep Pk 1 ASD 12.11.17; SOC 15.11.17

A7544 (R.A.F. 3a) At 2 AAP Hendon 3.8.17, allotted to EF; England to ARS 1 AD 19.8.17; ARS 2 AD 21.8.17; 18 Sqn 20.9.17; Landed rather fast, hit ridge, damaged 15.10.17 (2/Lt AC Atkey & 1/AM T McGrath OK); ARS 2AD 17.10.17; Became Rep Pk 2 ASD 1.11.17; BHP fitted; 2 AI 28.4.18; 27 Sqn 11.5.18; Landed in ploughed field 15.5.18 (Lt H Wild & 2/AM W Hilton OK); Rep Pk 2 ASD and SOC 16.5.18

A7545 (275hp Eagle) At 2 AAP Hendon 19.7.17, allotted to EF; England to ARS 1 AD 22.7.17; 57 Sqn 17.8.17; Misjudged landing on practice flight, hit cart in road 5.10.17 (2/Lt WL Sumsion OK); ARS 1 AD 6.10.17; Became Rep Pk 1 ASD 1.11.17; 1 AI 19.11.17; 57 Sqn 23.11.17; M/c caught fire in the air, struck tree on FL, completely destroyed by fire 2.12.17 (Sgt ES Fitzgerald injured & Sgt W Morris killed)

A7546 (Eagle VI) 51 TS Waddington by 8.17 - 9.17; 44 TS Waddington ('7', named 'IKANOPIT') by 11.17 - 12.17; At 1 (S)ARD 27.6.18, allotted to EF; Rec Pk to 2 AI 29.6.18; 3 ASD 1.7.18; 55 Sqn 8.7.18; Pfalz DIII OOC W of Oberndorf 07.30 20.7.18 (Lt EP Critchley & Sgt SE Lewis);3 ASD 23.8.18

A7547 (Eagle VI) At 2 AAP 23.7.17, allotted to EF; England to ARS 1 AD 25.7.17; 25 Sqn 27.7.17; On practice flight lost way, FL, Ran into ditch 6.12.17 (2/Lt J Anderson & 2/Lt AE Thornhill both OK); Rep Pk 1 ASD 9.12.17; 2 AI 17.4.18; 25 Sqn 21.4.18; Overshot on landing and ran into hedge 14.8.18 (Lt HC Bryant & 2/Lt J Skidmore OK); SOC Rep Pk 2 ASD 15.8.18 NWR

A7548 (RAF 3a) At 2 AAP Hendon 3.8.17, allotted to EF; England to ARS 1 AD 14.8.17; 18 Sqn 15.8.17; COL 7.10.17 (2/Lt DH Ogden & 2/Lt W Smith both OK); ARS 2 AD 8.10.17 (Altered to take Eagle, Eagle VI fitted); Became Rep Pk 2 ASD 1.11.17; 2 AI 16.2.18; 55 Sqn 11.3.18; Tail bracing wire shot through in raid on Mannheim, tailplane broke when engine opened up, FL nr aerodrome 18.3.18 (2/Lt RC Sansom & Sgt J Ryan OK); 2 ASD 18.3.18; 55 Sqn 23.4.18; Into spinning nose dive on practice flight 14.5.18 (2/Lt S Sephton & 2/Lt HA Nash both killed); SOC 18.5.18 wrecked

A7549 (Eagle VII) Presentation Aircraft 'South Africa'. At 2 AAP Hendon 27.7.17, allotted to EF; En route from Old Romney to (S)ARD 10.8.17, Allotment to EF cancelled, now on charge E1 Repair Section

A7550 (RAF 3a) At 2 AAP Hendon 10.8.17, allotted to EF; England to ARS 1 AD and on to 18 Sqn 16.8.17; Wrecked 21.9.17; ARS 2 AD 25.9.17; Altered to take Eagle

A7551 (RAF 3a) 8 AAP Lympne, on delivery, EF, FL in field, stalled in Wilmington, nr Dartford, Kent 24.9.17 (2/Lt FG Litchfield killed & 2/Lt H Nunn injured)

A7552 No information

A7553 (RAF 3a) Presentation Aircraft 'Zanzibar No.8'. At 2 AAP Hendon 13.8.17, allotted to EF; England to ARS 1 AD and on to 18 Sqn 19.8.17; Engine cut out at 500 feet, m/c bumped on landing and swung in cross wind 16.10.17 (Lt J Carling & Lt E Farncombe); ARS 2 AD 19.10.17 (altered to take Eagle, Eagle VII fitted); Became Rep Pk 2 ASD 1.11.17; 2 AI 2.2.18; 55 Sqn ('J') 11.3.18; FTR Luxembourg 5.4.18 (2/Lt PH O'Lieff & 2/Lt SR Wells both PoW)

A7554 (275hp Eagle) At 2 AAP Hendon 27.7.17, allotted to EF; England to ARS 1 AD 8.8.17; 57 Sqn ('C2') 12.8.17; Albatros D OOC SW of Houthulst Forest 10.30 then FL at Pitgam due to engine seizing up, Sideslipped and completely wrecked 17.8.17 (Sgt EV Bousher & 2/Lt PEG Heffer OK); ARS 1 AD 19.8.17; SOC 21.8.17

A7555 (275hp Eagle) Presentation Aircraft 'Malaya No.21'. At 2 AAP Hendon 31.7.17, allotted to EF; 8 AAP Lympne to ARS 1 AD 9.8.17; 57 Sqn 11.8.17; Two Albatros D OOC E of Ypres 11.20 20.8.17 (Lt WB Hutcheson & Lt TE Godwin); FTR from 17.00 raid on Ledeghem Dump, last seen OK at 3,000ft nr Menin 21.8.17 (Lt WB Hutcheson PoW & Lt TE Godwin killed)

A7556 (Eagle VII) At 2 AAP Hendon 28.7.17, allotted to EF; 8 AAP Lympne to ARS 1 AD 14.8.17; 55 Sqn 17.8.17; Raid on Stuttgart, combat with EA, main fuel tank shot through, FL Burnville-aux-Mirrois, wrecked 10.3.18 (2/Lt C Gavaghan OK & Lt JM Carroll wounded); 6 AP to Rep Pk 2 ASD 28.4.18; SOC 7.5.18

A7557 (RAF 3a) At 2 AAP Hendon 3.8.17, allotted to EF; England to ARS 1 AD and on to 18 Sqn ('2') 16.8.17; Casualty Report 24.10.17 says on examination top left and right hand longerons damaged; ARS 2 AD 26.10.17

A7558 No information

A7559 Convtd to prototype D.H.9 under Cont Nos A.S.17569 & A.S.21273/1/17 dated 23.1.17 (Galloway-built BHP); AAP Hendon to Testing Sqn, Martlesham Heath 5.10.17; AES Orfordness 18.10.17; Testing Sqn Martlesham Heath 24.10.17; AES Orfordness 28.11.17 - 2.18

A7560 (Eagle VI) At 2 AAP Hendon 31.7.17, allotted to EF; England to ARS 1 AD 10.8.17; 55 Sqn 13.8.17; Wrecked 11.10.17; ARS 2 AD 11.10.17; Became Rep Pk 2 ASD 1.11.17; 2 AI 12.2.18; Rep Pk 2 ASD 26.2.18; By rail to 55 Sqn 11.3.18, arrived 15.3.18; Crashed on take off 29.5.18 (2/Lt AC Hill & Sgt A Boocock); Rep Pk 2 ASD 29.5.18; SOC 14.7.18 NWR

A7561 (Eagle V) At 2 AAP Hendon 31.7.17, allotted to EF; England to ARS 1 AD 10.8.17; 57 Sqn 13.8.17; Albatros shot down 18.8.17 (2/Lt AB Cook & 2/Lt RN Bullock); COL 21.10.17 (2/Lt FA Martin & Lt JD O'Neill); ARS 1 AD 23.10.17; Became Rep Pk 1 ASD 1.11.17; 1 AI 1.12.17; 25 Sqn 25.1.18; On practice flight engine cut out, FL, u/c struck ditch and ac turned over 5.2.18 (2/Lt J Loupinsky & 2/Lt CA Sundy both OK); Rep Pk 1 ASD; 205 Sqn 10.4.18; EA OOC 23.4.18 (Lt W Elliott & 1/AM AGL G Smith); Pfalz DIII OOC Chaulnes 10.30 15.5.18 (Lt W Elliott unhurt & 2/Lt HP Bennett wounded); In action 17.5.18 (Lt W Elliott OK & 2/Lt JA Whalley wounded); Casualty Report 14.8.18 says time expired; SOC Rep Pk 1 ASD; 28.8.18 ex 6 Salvage; Rebuilt 28.8.18, numbered F6512 in error, changed to H7119

A7562 (Eagle VII) At 2 AAP Hendon 24.7.17, allotted to EF; 8 AAP Lympne to ARS 1 AD 5.8.17; 25 Sqn 9.8.17; Engine failed to pick up, FL, caught sheaves of corn and crashed 22.8.17 (Lt CJ Pullen & 2/Lt DD Humphreys OK); ARS 2 AD 30.8.17; By rail to 55 Sqn 11.10.17; FTR Mannheim Chemical Works raid, seen in combat with large formation of EA over target 24.3.18 (2/Lt CF Westing & Sgt H Hodge both PoW)

A7563 (Eagle VI) At 2 AAP Hendon 26.7.17, allotted to EF; England to ARS 1 AD 5.8.17; 57 Sqn ('C4') 7.8.17; Albatros D OOC Houthulst Forest 17.45 16.8.17; 05.50 raid on Courtrai-Menin, three Albatros Ds OOC Menin 07.30 then FL after engine badly shot up 17.8.17 (all Mjr EG Joy & Lt F Leathley, both OK); ARS 1 AD 19.8.17; ARS 2 AD 19.9.17 for reconstruction; 2 AI to 25 Sqn 10.3.18; FTR reconnaissance Valenciennes-

Busigny 21.4.18 (2/Lt CJ Fitzgibbon & 2/Lt W Rudman MC both killed)

A7564 (275hp Eagle/Eagle II) At 2 AAP Hendon 31.7.17, allotted to EF; England to ARS 1 AD 8.8.17; 57 Sqn 11.8.17; Albatros D OOC Ypres 11.15 20.8.17 (Mjr EG Joy & Lt F Leathley); Damaged in FL nr Arques due to storm 29.10.17 (2/Lt CM Powell & 2/Lt JH Behrens both injured); ARS 1 AD 31.10.17; Became Rep Pk 1 ASD 1.11.17; SOC 3.11.17

A7565 (Eagle V) At 2 AAP Hendon 2.8.17 allotted to EF; England to ARS 1 AD 9.8.17; 55 Sqn 13.8.17; FL due to engine trouble 12.9.17 (Lt MG Jones MC & 2/AM L Leyland); ARS 1 AD 13.9.17; 1 AI 19.11.17; Rep Pk 1 ASD to 1 AI 16.12.17; 25 Sqn 3.1.18; Cylinder burst, FL nr Bailleul 9.3.18 (2/Lt AWP Cumming & Sgt JR Wright OK); To Rep Pk 1 ASD; Rec Pk 6.5.18; 2 AI 16.5.18; 25 Sqn 20.5.18; Collided with 27 Sqn's B2083 on take-off 21.5.18 (Lt RP Bufton & Sgt WC Elliott OK); SOC Rep Pk 2 ASD 22.5.18 NWR

A7566 (275hp Eagle) At 2 AAP Hendon 31.7.17, allotted to EF; England to ARS 1 AD 11.8.17; 55 Sqn 12.8.17; FTR from 05.40 raid on Raismes ammunition factory, seen to go down under control over Valenciennes, apparently with engine trouble 21.8.17 (2/Lt CW Davies Aust wounded & 2/Lt JL Richardson killed)

A7567 (275hp Eagle) At 2 AAP Hendon 3.8.17, allotted to EF; England to ARS 1 AD 14.8.17; 57 Sqn 17.8.17; Controls shot away on 09.55 raid on Ledeghem Dump, wrecked on landing 20.8.17 (2/Lt AB Cook OK & 2/Lt RN Bullock wounded); ARS 1 AD 24.8.17; SOC 26.8.17

A7568 (275hp Eagle) At 2 AAP Hendon 24.7.17, allotted to EF; England to ARS 1 AD 28.7.17; 57 Sqn ('A6') 30.7.17; Albatros D OOC smoking Ledeghem-Menin 18.15 21.8.17 (Capt HR Harker & Capt WEB Barclay MC); Three Albatros D OOC, one in flames Roulers-Houthulst Forest 13.35 2.10.17 (Capt DS Hall & 2/Lt EP Hartigan); Left at 09.45 on weather test flight, crashed at Les Alleux 20.11.17 (Capt DS Hall & Lt EP Hartigan both killed); SOC Rep Pk 1 ASD 26.11.17

A7569 (Eagle VII) At 2 AAP Hendon 26.7.17, allotted to EF; England to ARS 1 AD 29.7.17; 25 Sqn 7.8.17; U/c collapsed on landing 20.8.17 (2/Lt MA Hancock & 2/Lt OM Hills OK); ARS 2 AD 21.8.17; ARS 1 AD 27.9.17; ARS 2 AD 1.10.17; 55 Sqn 16.10.17; ARS 2 AD 27.10.17; Became Rep Pk 2 ASD 1.11.17; Railed to 41 Wing 17.2.18; 6 AP to 55 Sqn 21.2.18; FTR, last seen going down under control nr Stuttgart after combat with EA SE of Oberkirch 10.3.18 (2/Lt R Caldecott & 2/Lt GPF Thomas both PoW)

A7570 No information

A7571 (RAF 3a) At 2 AAP Hendon 28.8.17, allotted to EF; but reallotted to 49 Sqn (Mob) Dover 30.10.17 (not taken to France by 49 Sqn 11.17)

A7572 (RAF 3a) At 2 AAP Hendon 22.8.17, allotted to EF; England to ARS 1 AD 30.8.17; 18 Sqn 1.9.17; U/c collapsed on landing 6.12.17 (Lt AG Graves & Lt W Smith both OK); Rec Pk to 1 AI 7.5.18; 18 Sqn 25.5.18; Casualty Report 21.6.18 says a/c unsatisfactory both in speed and climb and is unfit for further service in the field; Rec Pk 24.6.18; To England 24.6.18

A7573 (RAF 3a) At 2 AAP Hendon 20.8.17, allotted to EF; England to ARS 1 AD 9.9.17; ARS 2 AD 10.9.17; 18 Sqn 22.9.17; Landed rather fast, hit ridge, damaged 15.10.17 (2/Lt D Richardson & Lt CRH Ffolliott); ARS 2 AD 20.10.17 (altered to take Eagle); Became Rep Pk 2 ASD 1.11.17; 2 AI 16.2.18; 25 Sqn 9.3.18; Stalled on landing 11.3.18 (2/Lt CJ Fitzgibbon & 2/Lt CA Sundy OK); Rep Pk 2 ASD; Rep Pk 1 ASD 7.4.18; 2 AI 4.6.18; 205 Sqn 9.6.18 (Eagle VI); Fokker DVII OOC Chaulnes-Brie Bridge 15.40 10.8.18 (Lt WE Clarke & 2/Lt CN Witham); Left 05.12, shot down on photo reconnaissance 13.8.18 (Lt T Fattorini & 2/Lt SJ Parkes both killed); SOC in field 14.8.18

A7574 (RAF 3a) At 2 AAP Hendon 3.8.17, allotted to EF; Engine trouble on TO for (S)ARD, turned back, spun in, BO 14.8.17 (2/Lt MAE Cremetti killed & Cpl JH Bingham injured)

A7575 (Eagle VII) At 2 AAP Hendon 2.8.17, allotted to EF; England to ARS 1 AD 10.8.17; ARS 2 AD 19.8.17; ARS 1 AD 26.9.17; 55 Sqn ('E') 28.9.17; Stalled on turn, spun in 14.11.17 (2/Lt CC Morse killed & 2/Lt CD Palmer injured); SOC Rep Pk 2 ASD 23.11.17

A7576 (275hp Eagle) 46 TS Catterick, spinning nose-dive at low height, crashed before able to pull out, Bolton-on-Swale 10.9.17 (2/Lt TR Jarvie killed & 2/Lt SW Wilkins injured)
BUT 44 TS Harlaxton by 11.17 - 12.17

A7577 (275hp Eagle) At 2 AAP Hendon 9.8.17, allotted to EF; Makers in case to ARS 2 AD 15.8.17; ARS 1 AD and on to 57 Sqn 18.8.17; FTR from 05.30 reconnaissance flight to Roulers-Menin 21.8.17 (Lt C Barry & 2/Lt FEB Falkiner MC both killed)

A7578 (Eagle VI) Presentation Aircraft 'Baroda No.16'. At 2 AAP Hendon 13.8.17, allotted to EF; England to ARS 1 AD 17.8.17; 55 Sqn 18.8.17; Approaching aerodrome engine cut out, landed in cornfield 9.9.17 (Sgt MJC Weare & 2/AM S Moreman); ARS 1 AD 10.9.17; ARS 2 AD 1.10.17; By rail to 55 Sqn 21.10.17; Stalled on take off 20.4.18 (2/Lt HE Townsend & 2/AM WC Taylor); 6 AP to Rep Pk 2 ASD 28.4.18; SOC Rep Pk 2 ASD 7.5.18

A7579 (Eagle VII) At 2 AAP Hendon 17.8.17, allotted to EF; England to ARS 1 AD 19.8.17; 55 Sqn ('I') 21.8.17; Albatros D OOC nr Thielt 14.20 5.9.17 (2/Lt JH Hedding & Lt A Sattin); FTR from bombing raid Freiburg 13.3.18 (2/Lt TS Wilson PoW wounded & 2/Lt L Cann killed)

A7580 (200hp BHP) At 1 (S)ARD 16.11.17, allotted to EF; On flight from Rec Pk to 27 Sqn landed downwind at 1 AI Serny, hit hangar and then hut 5.12.17 (2/Lt GC Burnside shaken only)

A7581 (275hp Eagle) Presentation Aircraft 'Jamaica No.1'. At 2 AAP Hendon 13.8.17, allotted to EF; ARS 1 AD to 57 Sqn 20.8.17; 2 Albatros DV OOC Dadizeele 10.50 21.9.17 (2/Lt AT Drinkwater (Aust) & Lt FTS Menendez); FTR from raid on Abeele aerodrome, left at 11.45, last seen over Roulers 2.10.17 (2/Lt CGO MacAndrew & 2/Lt LP Sidney both killed)

A7582 (275hp Eagle) Presentation Aircraft 'Bombay No.1'. At 2 AAP Hendon 11.8.17, allotted to EF; England to ARS 1 AD 18.8.17; 57 Sqn 19.8.17; Observer Lt AF Britton wounded by stray shots from French Spad between Pilckem and Ypres 09.25 20.8.17 (pilot Lt DS Hall OK); FTR from 10.45 raid on Courtrai Sidings, shot down in combat with EA 11.9.17 (2/Lt JA Mackay & 2/Lt EJ Halliwell both killed)

D.H.4 A7583 of No.57 Squadron after being captured on 2 October 1917. (via Frank Cheesman)

A7583 (275hp. Eagle) At 2 AAP Hendon 15.8.17, allotted to EF; England to ARS 1 AD 30.8.17; 57 Sqn ('2') 10.9.17; Left at 11.45 for raid on Abeele aerodrome, last seen over Roulers, shot down by Ltn Kleffel of Jasta 18 2.10.17 (2/Lt CG Crane PoW & 2/Lt WL Inglis killed); A/c captured by Germans

A7584 No information

A7585 (275hp Eagle) 46 TS Catterick by 27.8.17; Engine trouble, tried to land in field, lost speed, stalled and dived in Kirkby Fleetham, Yorks, TW 30.8.17 (Sgt RJ Malone killed)

A7586 (275hp Eagle) At 2 AAP Hendon 17.8.17, allotted to EF; England to ARS 1 AD 19.8.17; 55 Sqn ('5')

20.8.17; Albatros D OOC then in flames Courtrai 08.00 7.10.17 (Capt D Owen & Gnr WG Osborne); Albatros D possibly OOC W of Freiburg 16.00 13.3.18 (2/Lt EJ Whyte & 2/Lt JEw Reynolds); Albatros D crashed centre of Mannheim 12.05 24.3.18 (2/Lt EJ Whyte & 2/Lt WG Robins); 3 ASD 15.8.18; Crashed on test at 3 ASD 23.10.18 (Lt HT Hunter & Sgt CJ Ross of 835th US Aero Sqn both killed)

A7587 (Eagle V) Presentation Aircraft 'Gold Coast No.2'. At 2 AAP Hendon 12.10.17, allotted to EF; Rec Pk to 2 AI 11.11.17; Rep Pk 2 ASD 1.2.18; 2 AI 12.2.18; 5N Sqn 10.3.18; EF, FL 16.3.18 (FSL GE Siedle & Sgt AGL WJH Middleton); Damaged when attacked by 3 triplanes, claimed EA shot down, then FL Estrees 18.3.18 (FSL CE Wodehouse wounded & AGL L James unhurt); Rep Pk 2 ASD by 1.4.18; Rep Pk 1 ASD 7.4.18; Rec Pk 26.5.18; 2 AI 28.5.18; 205 Sqn 3.6.18; Pfalz DIII on tail of D8412 sent down OOC nr Chaulnes 15.50 10.8.18; Pfalz DIII last seen in vertical dive c.08.00 11.8.18 (both Lt R Chalmers & 2/Lt SH Hamblin); Left on recce 08.30, FTR 7.9.18 (Lt DJT Mellor killed & 2/Lt JC Walker PoW); SOC in field 7.9.18

A7588 (Eagle) 46 TS Catterick by 27.8.17; Caught fire in air, suspected leaking oil pipe, hit tree landing, BO 10.3.18 (Lt ER Wheatley)

A7589 (275hp Eagle) At 2 AAP Hendon 18.8.17, allotted to EF; England to ARS 1 AD 21.8.17; 57 Sqn 22.8.17; Crashed at Wimeureux returning from FL 14.11.17 (2/Lt D Miller & 2/Lt AHC Hoyles both OK); Rep Pk 1 ASD 16.11.17; Rep Pk 2 ASD 9.2.18; Rep Pk 1 ASD to 2 AI 17.4.18; 57 Sqn 2.5.18; COL 9.5.18 (Lt LL Brown & Lt AM Shepstone); Rep Pk 2 ASD 10.5.18; 2 AI to 55 Sqn 26.6.18; FTR 30.8.18 (1/Lt WW Tanney USAS & 2/Lt AJC Gormley both PoW)

A7590 (200hp BHP) At 1 (S)ARD 16.11.17, allotted to EF; Rec Pk to 1 AI 6.1.18; Rec Pk 5.2.18; 8 AAP Lympne 18.2.18; 7 AAP Kenley 28.2.18; 5 TDS Easton-on-the-Hill 6.3.18; 69 TS Narborough by 7.18

A7591 UK to Baghdad for 31 Wing 19.11.17; 30 Sqn, bombing attack on Kifri aerodrome, direct hit by AA at 7,000ft, FTR 21.1.18 (Lt WS Bean & 3/AM RG Castor both killed)

A7592 (Eagle V) At 2 AAP Hendon 20.8.17, allotted to EF; England to ARS 1 AD 2.9.17; 55 Sqn ('M') 5.9.17; Scout OOC and Scout crashed Mannheim 12.45 24.3.18 (2/Lt PH O'Lieff & 2/Lt SR Wells); COL 15.5.18 (2/Lt AC Hill & 2/Lt JG Quinton OK); Rep Pk 2 ASD 15.5.18; SOC 14.6.18 NWR

A7593 (RAF 3a) At 2 AAP Hendon 15.8.17, allotted to EF; England to ARS 1 AD and on to 18 Sqn 22.8.17; Engine cut out, FL, ran over steep bank 18.10.17 (2/Lt AG Graves & Lt CC Claye); ARS 2 AD 21.10.17; Eagle VII fitted; At Rep Pk 2 ASD by 31.12.17; By rail to 55 Sqn 11.3.18, arr 55 Sqn ('O') 16.3.18 (Eagle VI); Shot up in bombing raid on Cologne, crashed nr aerodrome 18.5.18 (Lt CE Reynolds slightly injured & 2/Lt JE Reynolds killed)

A7594 (RAF 3a) At 2 AAP Hendon 20.8.17, allotted to EF; England to ARS 1 AD 30.8.17; 18 Sqn 1.9.17; 2-str believed to be Aviatik OOC S of Roubaix 10.15 31.10.17 (2/Lt BD Bate & 2/Lt DS Broadhurst); In combat with a 2-str SE of Béthune, observer in German m/c shot 13.10 26.11.17 (2/Lt DA Stewart & Lt HWM Mackay); Albatros C OOC Valenciennes 10.30 6.12.17 (2/Lt DA Stewart & Lt HWM Mackay); Casualty Report 11.3.18 says not fit for further service in the field; Rep Pk 1 ASD 15.3.18; SOC 31.5.18 NWR

A7595 (Eagle VI) At 2 AAP Hendon 18.9.17, allotted to EF; ARS 1 AD to 25 Sqn 19.10.17; FL in fog, crashed La Capelle on Calais road 13.11.17 (2/Lt JA Baker injured & Lt WA Miller seriously injured); Rec Pk to Rep Pk 1 ASD 17.11.17; SOC 21.11.17

A7596 (RAF 3a) At 2 AAP Hendon 22.8.17, allotted to EF; England to ARS 1 AD 26.8.17; ARS 2 AD and on to 18 Sqn 3.9.17; COL 27.10.17 (2/Lt RP Fenn & Capt HW Barwell MC); ARS 2 AD 30.10.17

A7597 (RAF 3a) At 2 AAP Hendon 30.8.17, allotted to EF; England to ARS 1 AD 2.9.17; ARS 2 AD 3.9.17; 18 Sqn 9.9.17; Albatros D crashed just S of Douai 11.30 23.11.17 (2/Lt C Evans & 1/AM KA Gellan); Heavy landing, damaged 26.11.17 (Lt WN Bussell & Lt EM Farncombe both OK); Rep Pk 2 ASD 28.11.17 (awaiting engine 31.12.17); 2 AI 16.5.18; 27 Sqn 19.5.18; Albatros D OOC W of Roye, shared B2086 11.20 7.6.18 (Lt CH Gannaway & Sgt WEA Brookes); Left 08.55 on bombing raid, in combat with EA 2m W of Roye, shot down in flames 16.6.18 (2/Lt CH Gannaway & Sgt WEA Brookes both killed)

A7598 (RAF 3a) At 2 AAP Hendon 28.8.17, allotted to EF; England to ARS 1 AD 31.8.17; ARS 2 AD 3.9.17; 18 Sqn 5.9.17; Casualty Report 4.3.18 says not fit for service in the field; 1 AI 6.3.18 (unfit); Rec Pk 10.3.18; 8 AAP Lympne 15.3.18

A7599 (Eagle VI) At 2 AAP Hendon 25.8.17, allotted to EF; England to ARS 1 AD 30.8.17; 25 Sqn 31.8.17; On practice flight stalled landing too slowly 19.10.17 (2/Lt FV Bird OK); ARS 1 AD 19.10.17; Became Rep Pk 1 ASD 1.11.17; 1 AI 25.1.18; 25 Sqn 27.2.18; Crashed into by A7823 in hangar 26.3.18; Rep Pk 2 ASD 1.4.18; SOC 22.4.18

A7600 (Eagle VI) Presentation Aircraft 'Australia No.18, New South Wales No.17'. At 2 AAP Hendon 1.9.17, allotted to EF; Rep Pk 1 ASD by 11.11.17; 1 AI 19.11.17; 25 Sqn 10.12.17; On photo recce, attacked by Fokke DrI & 4 Albatros Ds N of Cambrai 13.1.18 (Capt AG Whitehead OK Lt JH Haughan wounded); Left at 09.05 on photographic mission, FTR 29.1.18 (Capt AG Whitehead & Lt WJ Borthistle both killed)

A7601 UK to Baghdad for 31 Wing 19.11.17

A7602 (Eagle VII) At 2 AAP Hendon 1.9.17 allotted to EF; England to ARS 1 AD 4.9.17; 25 Sqn 5.9.17; Damaged in heavy landing on test flight 9.6.18 (Lt RG Dobeson & 1/AM FE Warren OK); SOC Rep Pk 2 ASD 18.6.18 NWR

A7603 No information

A7604 9 TS Norwich by 15.9.17

A7605 (275hp Eagle) Presentation Aircraft 'Mauritius No.2'. At 2 AAP Hendon 15.9.17, allotted to EF; At Rep Pk 1 ASD by 11.11.17; 1 AI 13.11.17; 25 Sqn 20.11.17; In combat on photographic mission, petrol tank shot through, FL, struck telephone wires crashed 14.30 8.12.17 (Capt CI Lally severely shaken & Lt JE Cole wounded); SOC Rep Pk 1 ASD 7.2.18

A7606 (RAF 3a) At 2 AAP Hendon 1.9.17 allotted to EF; England to ARS 1 AD 4.9.17; ARS 2 AD 9.9.17; ARS 1 AD and on to 18 Sqn 27.10.17; Engine trouble crashed in ploughed field nr aerodrome 13.11.17 (Lt WN Bussell & Lt EM Farncombe); 2 ASD 17.11.17

A7607 (Eagle VII) At 2 AAP Hendon 27.8.17, allotted to EF; England to ARS 1 AD 2.9.17; 55 Sqn 5.9.17; Engine cut on return from raid, FL in valley nr aerodrome 9.3.18 (2/Lt NH Thackrah & 2/Lt CL Rayment OK); Rep Pk 2 ASD; Rep Pk 1 ASD 7.4.18; SOC 8.4.18

A7608 (Eagle VII) At 2 AAP Hendon 31.8.17, allotted to EF; England to ARS 1 AD 4.9.17; 57 Sqn 9.9.17; ARS 1 AD 27.9.17; SOC 29.9.17

A7609 At 2 AAP Hendon 29.8.17, allotted to EF; England to ARS 1 AD and on to 25 Sqn 2.9.17; Attacked by 12 EA at 17,000ft Roulers-Ypres, 1 shot down by observer c.12.00 25.1.18 (Lt CA Pike & obs Hinson); Extra fuel tank fitted c.28.2.18-8.3.18; Casualty Report 4.4.18 says unfit for further service in the field; Rep Pk 2 ASD and on to 2 AI 19.4.18; Rec Pk and on to England 20.4.18

A7610 (Eagle VII) At 2 AAP Hendon 15.9.17, allotted to EF; At Rep Pk 1 ASD 12.11.17; 1 AI 19.11.17; 57 Sqn 5.12.17; On practice flight, FL with engine trouble, CW, 8.12.17 (2/Lt FA Jeppe injured & 2/Lt A Leach shaken)

A7611 46 TS Catterick by 14.10.17

A7612 No information

A7613 (275hp Eagle) At 8 AAP Lympne 17.9.17, allotted to EF; ARS 1 AD 28.9.17; 57 Sqn 3.10.17; Completely wrecked on FL 2.1.18 (Capt HB McKinnon & 2/Lt GH Halls); SOC Rep Pk 1 ASD 7.2.18

A7614 (RAF 3a) At 2 AAP Hendon 1.9.17 allotted to EF; England to ARS 1 AD 5.9.17; ARS 2 AD 11.9.17; 18 Sqn 17.10.17; Damaged landing on hard rough ground 6.1.18 (2/Lt JW Ritch & Lt V Scott); Rep Pk 1 ASD 25.1.18; SOC 4.2.18

A7615 No information

A7616 (RAF 3a) At 2 AAP Hendon 23.8.17, allotted to EF;

England to ARS 1 AD 2.9.17; ARS 2 AD and on to 18 Sqn 3.9.17; SOS 1.12.17 wrecked

A7617 (275hp Eagle) 46 TS Catterick by 10.10.17; Broke up in spinning nose dive 30.10.17 (2/Lt HP Stuttard killed)

A7618 At 2 AAP Hendon 20.9.17, allotted to EF; England to ARS 1 AD 25.9.17; 57 Sqn 14.10.17; Engine failed just after take-off on raid, FL nr aerodrome 21.4.18 (2/Lt H Erskine & Lt WAB Eastwood OK); SOC Rep Pk 2 ASD 7.5.18

A7619 (Eagle VI) At 1 (S)ARD 26.10.17, allotted to EF; 1 ASD to 57 Sqn 12.12.17; FL, wrecked 1.1.18 (2/Lt EH Piper & 2/Lt AS White); Rep Pk 1 ASD 6.1.18; 2 AI 26.3.18; Rep Pk 2 ASD to 205 Sqn 5.4.18; 2 ASD 3.6.18 (cracked longeron); Rebuilt as F6077 3.7.18

A7620 (Eagle VI) Ex RFC Ascot via CSD White City to Dover 25.9.17; Arrived and left Dover on/by 13.10.17; AD Dunkirk from W/E 7.12.17; 5N Sqn 11.1.18; Red Albatros DV with plain black crosses OOC Busigny aerodrome 10.45 18.3.18 (F/L E Dickson DSO wounded & OSL WH Scott); Pfalz DIII left wing folded, crashed Rainecourt 15.30 27.3.18; Pfalz DIII OOC Proyart-Foucaucourt 09.50 28.3.18 (both F/L E Dickson DSC & OSL W Stewart); EF, FL Bertangles 30.3.18; Became 205 Sqn 1.4.18; Left 15.14, FTR raid on La Motte aerodrome 6.4.18 (Lt GM Cartmel & 1/AM G/L AJ Lane both killed); SOC in field 7.4.18

A7621 UK to Baghdad for 31 Wing 19.11.17; 30 Sqn, engine hit on bombing raid, FL, m/c destroyed by fire 25.1.18 (Lt F Nuttall & Lt RBB Sievier both OK)

A7622 (200hp BHP) At 1 (S)ARD 16.11.17, allotted to EF; Rec Pk to 27 Sqn 12.12.17; Stationary on aerodrome, crashed into by B2145 25.4.18; SOC Rep Pk 1 ASD 28.4.18

A7623 UK to Baghdad for 31 Wing 19.11.17
BUT 46 TS Catterick by 23.12.17

A7624 (Eagle V) At 2 AAP Hendon 3.9.17, allotted to EF; England to ARS 1 AD 10.9.17; 55 Sqn ('M') 15.9.17; Stalled on take off, crashed, fuselage broke in half 14.11.17 (2/Lt AS White & 2/Lt AF Castle both OK); SOC Rep Pk 2 ASD 23.11.17

A7625 (200hp BHP) At 1 (S)ARD 16.11.17, allotted to EF; Rec Pk to Rep Pk 1 ASD 18.12.17; 1 AI 3.1.18; Rep Pk 1 ASD 29.1.18; 2 AI 6.3.18; 27 Sqn 11.3.18; Engine cut out on return from raid, crashed 25.3.18 (2/Lt EJ Smith & 2/Lt HE Gooding OK)

A7626 (Eagle VI) At 1 (S)ARD 26.10.17, allotted to EF; Rep Pk 1 ASD to 2 AI 11.11.17; 25 Sqn ('N') 3.12.17; U/c broke on landing 8.7.18 (Capt JF Gordon & Cpl H Emerson OK) - the Casualty Report says m/c has been rebuilt twice, fuselage is strained and woodwork is saturated with oil; Rep Pk 2 ASD; Rebuilt as F6215 25.7.18

A7627 (200hp BHP) At 1 (S)ARD 16.11.17, allotted to EF; 1 ASD to 27 Sqn ('D') 6.12.17; Returned from raid with engine trouble, COL 21.2.18 (2/Lt DTC Rundle-Woolcock & Sgt AJ Beavis OK); Rep Pk 1 ASD 23.2.18; SOC 7.3.18

A7628 No information

A7629 Deld 2 AAP Hendon for erection 28.8.17; For RNAS Dunkirke, but to RFC instead as fitted with Galloway BHP; 2 TDS Lake Down 9.9.17 - 10.17; 103 Sqn Old Sarum by 28.1.18 - 21.2.18; 99 Sqn Old Sarum by 21.2.18

A7630 (RAF 3a) At 2 AAP Hendon 8.9.17, allotted to EF; England to ARS 1 AD 12.9.17; ARS 2 AD 13.9.17; 18 Sqn 22.10.17; COL, CW 26.1.18 (Lt D Richardson & Capt C L'Estrange); Rep Pk 1 ASD: SOC 4.2.18

A7631 (200hp BHP) At 1 (S)ARD 16.11.17, allotted to EF; Rec Pk to 27 Sqn 15.12.17; COL 2.2.18 (2/Lt S Hewett & 2/Lt FB Ford both OK); Rep Pk 1 ASD 5.2.18; SOC 7.3.18

A7632 (Eagle VIII) Deld RFC Ascot via CSD White City to Dover 25.9.17; Hendon W/E 13.10.17; AP Dover W/E 1.12.17; 2N Sqn (via AD Dunkirk) 16.2.18; Became 202 Sqn 1.4.18; Hit by AA over Ostende 12.6.18 (Capt CF Brewerton unhurt & Lt MG English slightly wounded); Pfalz DIII OOC inland of Ostende 17.00 16.7.18 (Capt AV Bowater & 2/Lt E Darby DSM); Monoplane OOC over Nieuport 11.35 14.8.18 (Lt LH Pearson & 2/Lt E Darby); Pfalz DIII OOC 16.9.18 (Lt LH Pearson & 2/Lt E Darby DSM); FTR last seen at 16,500 ft over Ostende pursued by 5 EA 11.00 26.9.18 (Lt FAB Gasson & 2/Lt S King both killed); Deleted 15.10.18

A7633 (200hp BHP) Deld 2 AAP Hendon; 2 TDS Lake Down 10.9.17; At 2 AAP Hendon 20.9.17, reallotted from Training Division to EF; England to ARS 1 AD and on to 27 Sqn 14.10.17; On height test lost way and FL at Bailleul, m/c had suffered damage from mg fire 7.11.17 (2/Lt WJ Henney & 2/Lt PS Driver both OK); Rep Pk 1 ASD 8.11.17; 27 Sqn 28.11.17; 1 AI 26.1.18; Rec Pk 27.1.18; 8 AAP Lympne 2.2.18; New Romney 20.2.18 [3(Aux) SoAG?]

A7634 (RAF 3a) At 2 AAP Hendon 31.8.17, allotted to EF; England to ARS 1 AD 4.9.17; 2 AD 11.9.17; 18 Sqn 16.10.17; Damaged landing probably due to rough and hard frozen ground 21.12.17 (2/Lt HR Gould & 2/Lt JY Baird); To Rep Pk 1 ASD 18.1.18 (arr 25.1.18)

A7635 (RAF 3a) At 2 AAP Hendon 1.9.17 allotted to EF; England to ARS 1 AD 4.9.17; To 2 AD 10.9.17 but wrecked en route; ARS 1 AD 12.9.17; 2 AD 23.9.17; 18 Sqn 31.10.17; Engine lost revs, landing in thick mist ran into fence 12.11.17 (2/Lt F Jones & Pte H Sampson OK); 2 ASD 15.11.17

A7636 (Eagle) 46 TS Catterick, crashed 24.4.18 (Sgt JC Gillis slightly injured)

A7637 (Eagle VI) At 1 (S)ARD 26.10.17, allotted to EF; At Rep Pk 1 ASD 1.11.17; 1 AI 19.11.17; 57 Sqn 23.11.17; Albatros D OOC NE of Courtrai 12.00 6.1.18; Attacked by three Albatros D Dadizeele 11.15, 1 in flames BU 26.2.18 (all Sgt EA Clayton & 2/Lt LLT Sloot); Engine cut out, FL and crashed 19.3.18 (2/Lt W Whitfield & 2/Lt M a'B Boyd OK); Rep Pk 22.3.18; SOC 23.3.18 but from Salvage for reconstruction 27.3.18; Bboc 1 ASD 27.3.18; Rep Pk 1 ASD to Rec Pk and on to 2 AI 2.6.18; 25 Sqn 8.6.18; Photo recce, hit by AA Le Hameau, FL, damaged 15.00 14.10.18 (Lt LLK Straw & 2/Lt J Skidmore both unhurt)

A7638 Deld 2 AAP Hendon; 2 TDS Lake Down 15.9.17 - 26.11.17

A7639 (RAF 3a) At 2 AAP Hendon 17.9.17, allotted to EF but reallotted to Training 18.9.17; 29th Wing ARS Shawbury to 33rd Wing ARS 16.11.17 for repair (2 TDS a/c); 2 TDS Lake Down 23.11.17

A7640 (200hp BHP) At 2 AAP Hendon 10.9.17, allotted to EF; Reallotted to Training 11.9.17; 2 TDS Lake Down 13.9.17; Again allotted to EF 20.9.17; England to ARS 1 AD and on to 27 Sqn 21.9.17 (its first DH 4); ARS 1AD 8.10.17; 27 Sqn 15.10.17; Rep Pk 1 ASD 24.12.17; 2 AI 25.3.18; 27 Sqn 27.3.18; On test flight, landed too fast, overran aerodrome 3.4.18 (2/Lt EJ Smith & 1/AM J Faulkner); Adv Salvage to Rep Pk 1 ASD 7.4.18; SOC 10.4.18

A7641 (Eagle VII) Presentation Aircraft 'Overseas Club No.33, 'The Akyab'. At 2 AAP Hendon 15.9.17, allotted to EF; England to ARS 1 AD 21.9.17; 55 Sqn ('N') 24.9.17; 3 ASD 10.8.18; 55 Sqn 6.10.18; 3 ASD 29.10.18

A7642 (275hp Eagle) At 2 AAP Hendon 14.9.17, allotted to EF; England to ARS 1 AD and on to 55 Sqn 19.9.17; Left at 08.59 on raid on Marke, last seen recrossing the line nr Ypres 2.10.17 (2/Lt WR Bishop & Lt G Mathews both killed) [Mathews real name was Lt DF Mackintosh]

A7643 (Eagle VII) Presentation Aircraft 'South Africa'. At 2 AAP Hendon 15.9.17, allotted to EF; England to ARS 1 AD 20.9.17; 57 Sqn 22.9.17; Left 07.50 for raid on Hooglede, shot down by EA Roulers 08.30 23.9.17 (2/Lt SLJ Bramley & 2/Lt JM de Lacey both killed)

A7644 (Eagle VII) At 2 AAP Hendon by 9.17; AD Dunkirk 27.9.17; 5N Sqn 3.10.17; After raid on Guise dump landed Villers-Bretonneux 8.3.18 (FSL BR Carter wounded & AGL HF Watson unhurt); 2 EA shot down in raid on Busigny aerodrome & dump, shared N6009 09.44-11.48 16.3.18 (F/Cdr CPO Bartlett & AGL W Naylor); COL 18.3.18 (F/L E Dickson DSC & OSL WH Scott both unhurt); to 2 ASD; 4 ASD 25.3.18; For deletion by 25.5.18

A7645 (Eagle VII) At 2 AAP Hendon 22.9.17, allotted to EF; England to ARS 1 AD 27.9.17; ARS 2 AD 1.10.17; 1 AD 27.10.17; 57 Sqn 31.10.17; COL at new aerodrome 29.3.18 (2/Lt DP Trollip & Lt JD Moses OK); Left 09.50 on photographic mission, shot down in combat with EA W of lines, Bouzencourt nr Corbie 15.5.18 (Lt FL Mond & Lt EM Martyn both killed); Unsalvable

D.H.4 A76??, nicknamed 'EFFIE' and coded '8', believed with 44 TS Waddington. (via Frank Cheesman)

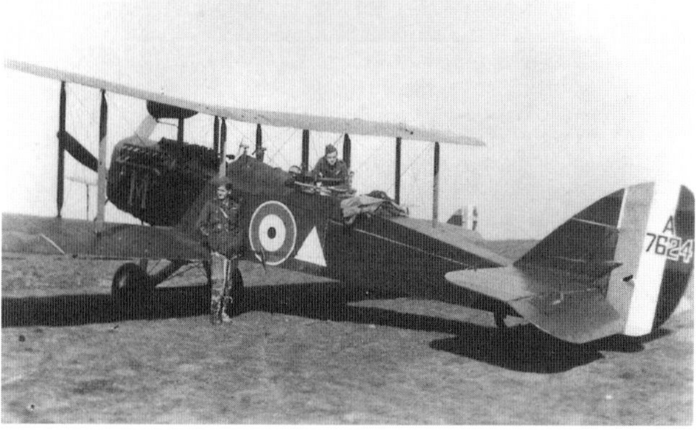

D.H.4 A7624 'M' of No.55 Squadron c.August-November 1918. (via R.L.Ward).

D.H.4 A7641 'N' of No.55 Squadron at Tantonville. (J.M.Bruce/G.S.Leslie collection)

D.H.4 A7661 of No.55 Squadron being examined by Germans after being shot down on 24 March 1918. (RAF Museum P.20946)

A7646 (RAF 3a, later Eagle VI) At 2 AAP Hendon 1.9.17, allotted to EF; England to ARS 1 AD 9.9.17; ARS 2 AD 10.9.17; 18 Sqn 10.10.17; Engine cut out, crashed on nose 21.10.17 (2/Lt JW Ritch & 1/AM T McGrath); ARS 2 AD 24.10.17 (altered to take Eagle VI); Became Rep Pk 2 ASD 1.11.17; 55 Sqn by rail 25.2.18; Slewed round on take off, banked to clear wood, sideslipped and crashed 10.3.18 (2/Lt IC Dick concussed & Lt G Bryer-Ash OK); Rep Pk 2 ASD; railed to Rep Pk 1 ASD 2.4.18; SOC 27.5.18

A7647 (Eagle VI by 12.17, Eagle VII by 1.18) Deld Dover (via Hendon) W/E 13.10.17; 5N Sqn 23.11.17; Crashed, CW Petite Synthe 11?.3.18; Deleted in squadron 18.3.18

A7648 No information

A7649 7th Wing to TS (which?) 5.11.17

A7650 (Eagle VII) At 2 AAP Hendon 10.9.17, allotted to EF; England to ARS 1 AD 12.9.17; 55 Sqn ('C') 13.9.17; Albatros DIII OOC Mannheim 12.10 and Albatros DIII in vertical dive apparently OOC 12.45 Germingen 24.3.18 (2/Lt W Legge & Sgt AS Allan); Caught on height test over Cheneurières, combat with EA west of lines, shot up, dived in 12.6.18 (Lt MG Jones & 2/Lt TE Brewer both killed)

A7651 No information

A7652 (Eagle VIII) To RNAS Hendon 24.10.17; Reallotted to EF but this cancelled 5.11.17 when reallotted to Inspector of Stores without engine; 44 TS Harlaxton by 10.17; 44 TS to Waddington 24.11.17; 51 TS Waddington 1.18; At 1 (S)ARD 29.6.18 reallotted to EF with Eagle VI; Rep Pk 1 ASD to 2 AI 12.8.18; 205 Sqn 14.8.18; 2 AI 26.9.18 exchanged for DH9A; 57 Sqn, in action 2.10.18 (Lt AE Bourns OK & Lt MG Robson MC wounded); In action 27.10.18 (Lt AE Bourns slightly wounded & Capt R Colville-Jones OK); Left 09.20 for photo recce, FTR 4.11.18 (Lt AE Bourns & Capt R Colville-Jones MC both killed)

A7653 (RAF 3a) Presentation Aircraft 'British Subjects of all Races in Siam'. At 2 AAP Hendon 15.9.17, allotted to EF; ARS 1 AD to ARS 2 AD 15.10.17; 18 Sqn 23.11.17; Albatros D OOC Valenciennes 12.05 6.1.18 (2/Lt DA Stewart & Lt HWM Mackay); EF, FL hit trees 25.1.18 (2/Lt GWF Darvill & Lt A Priestman OK); Rep Pk 1 ASD 31.1.18; SOC 1.2.18

A7654 (RAF 3a) 17 TS Yatesbury [19 TS Hounslow per casualty card], to Anglesey with five other DH.4s for anti U-boat work, stalled turning downwind to land in 40mph wind, Llangefni, Anglesey 7.11.17 (2/Lt BRH Carter killed & Cpl H Smith injured)

A7655 No information

A7656 19 TS Hounslow to 7th Wing 7.11.17

A7657 (Eagle VIII) RNAS Hendon 24.10.17; Reallotted to EF but this cancelled 5.11.17 when reallotted to Inspector of Stores without engine; At No 8 AAP Lympne 6.12.17 reallotted to EF (with Eagle VI); Rec Pk 21.1.18; 1 AI 28.2.18; 25 Sqn 1.3.18; FL in ploughed field, overturned 15.5.18 (Lt TR Hatton & Cpl H Edwards); Rebuilt as F6127 3.7.18

A7658 (RAF 3a) At 2 AAP Hendon 27.9.17, allotted to EF; ARS 1 AD to ARS 2 AD 15.10.17; 2 ASD to 18 Sqn 30.11.17; Badly damaged in combat 6.3.18 (2/Lt LJ Balderson & 2/Lt J Baird OK); Rep Pk 1 ASD 13.3.18; SOC 14.4.18

A7659 33 Wing ARS to 2 TDS Lake Down 22.11.17; Half ARS 2 TDS 27.11.17; 103 Sqn Old Sarum by 22.12.17

A7660 (Eagle VII) At No 8 AAP Lympne 6.12.17, allotted to EF; Rec Pk to 1 AI 6.1.18; 25 Sqn 28.1.18; Crashed on take off 29.1.18 (Lt GM Shaw & 1/AM L Jones); Rep Pk 1 ASD 31.1.18; SOC 6.2.18

A7661 (Eagle VI) Presentation Aircraft 'Malaya No.21'. At 2 AAP Hendon 17.9.17, allotted to EF; England to ARS 1 AD 21.9.17; 57 Sqn 22.9.17; Two Albatros Ds in flames NE of Houthulst Forest 15.20 2.10.17 (2/Lt JT Orrell & 1/AM CB Spicer); Completely wrecked on FL on practice flight 10.12.17 (Capt HB Mckinnon & 2/Lt GH Halls both slightly injured); To Rep Pk 1 ASD; 2 AI 12.3.18; 55 Sqn 15.3.18; FTR Mannheim raid, shot down Pirmasens by Ltn Ruckle, Jasta 33 24.3.18 (2/Lt NH Thackrah & Lt WG Fluke DSO both PoW)

A7662 (RAF 3a) Deld 2 AAP Hendon, FF 1.10.17; 9 TS Norwich, engine caught fire in air, attempted FL but

D.H.4 A7671, fitted with a B.H.P. engine, was used in 1918 at Martlesham Heath for tests with KLG sparking plugs. (via Frank Cheesman)

sideslipped in, BO 3.1.18 (2/Lt DWB Black killed)

A7663 (Eagle VII) Deld 2 AAP Hendon for erection 25.9.17; Allotted to EF but cancelled 27.9.17.; AP Dover 3.10.17; 5N Sqn 4.12.17; FTR raid on Busigny aerodrome, last seen diving nr Prémont 18.3.18 (FSL RB Ransford & 1/AM G/L G Smith DSM both killed); for deletion by 30.3.18

A7664 (Eagle VII) At No 8 AAP Lympne 22.12.17, Reallotted from Training to EF; Rec Pk to 1 AI 17.2.18; 25 Sqn 27.2.18; Left 07.00, shot down E of Albert 27.3.18 (2/Lt CG Pentecost & Lt A Rentoul both killed)

A7665 (Eagle VII) Deld Hendon W/E 6.10.17; AES Martlesham Heath 25.10.17 (tested with exptl u/c & larger propeller); Dunkirk 18.11.17; Hendon to Dover 23.11.17; 2N Sqn 4.12.18; Hit searchlight on landing 4.1.18 (FSL FS Russell & observer unhurt); AD Dunkirk 5.1.18; 2N Sqn 18.3.18; Shot down by AA fire nr Sassenbrug [?]/crashed Pervyse 16.00 22.3.18 (FSL FEA Bembridge seriously injured & 1/AM G/L HG Lovelock DSM killed); Recovered badly damaged; Deleted 17.4.18

A7666 2 ASD to Rep Pk 1 ASD 7.4.18; SOC 8.4.18.

A7667 10 TDS Harling Road by 6.18 - 10.18

A7668 No information

A7669 2 TDS Lake Down 10.17; ARS Lake Down to 2 TDS Lake Down 23.11.17

A7670 (Eagle VI) Allocated RNAS Dunkirk 10.9.17 (NTU); At No 8 AAP Lympne 20.12.17, allotted to EF; Rec Pk 18.2.18; 2 AI 5.3.18; 25 Sqn 7.3.18; Left 17.15 for photographic reconnaissance Landrecies, FTR 28.6.18 (Lt J Webster & 2/Lt CM Gray both PoW)

A7671 (230hp Adriatic) At 2 AAP Hendon 24.9.17 allotted to EF for "S" Replacement Sqn; Reallotted Controller Technical Dept for Martlesham Heath 28.9.17; FF 1.10.17; Testing Sqn (became AES 16.10.17), Martlesham Heath 3.10.17 (tests with bombs and modified Zenith carburettor); Engine borrowed and temporarily fitted to DH 9 prototype A7559; Airco Hendon 28.12.17 (Puma fitted); AES Martlesham Heath 25.2.18 (engine tests); Airco Hendon 7.3.18; Yeovil 23.3.18; Northolt to Experimental Sqn RAF/RAE Farnborough 26.3.18 (pressure tests on tailplane); Tailplane failed, broke up in the air, crashed Trimley 8.5.18 (Lt LFD Lutyens & Mr DH Pincent both killed); SOC 4.7.18

A7672 (Eagle VI) At 2 AAP Hendon 20.9.17, allotted to EF; England to ARS 1 AD 26.9.17; 25 Sqn 2.10.17; Bounced on landing 24.10.17 (2/Lt RP Pohlmann & 2/AM CN Harvey both OK); ARS 1 AD 24.10.17; Became Rep Pk 1 ASD 1.11.17; 1 AI 27.1.18; 25 Sqn 6.2.18; FL and crashed due it was believed to lack of petrol causing the engine to stop 26.2.18 (2/Lt EW Guest DoI & Lt HG Ashton injured); Rep Pk 1 ASD 28.2.18; SOC 1.3.18

A7673 No information

A7674 (275hp Eagle) At 2 AAP Hendon 20.9.17, allotted to EF; England to ARS 1 AD 27.9.17; 57 Sqn 3.10.17; Albatros D OOC Moorslede 11.50 12.10.17 (2/Lt FD Grant & Lt HF Attwater); EA in flames and another OOC Gheluwe 10.30 13.1.18 (Capt PD Robinson & Lt WC Venmore); Albatros D OOC Menin 12.45 3.2.18 (2/Lt WE Green & 2/Lt HS Gros); Left 12.50 on photographic mission, FTR 31.3.18 (Capt PD Robinson MC & Lt JQF Walker both killed)

A7675 (Eagle V) At 2 AAP Hendon 28.9.17, allotted to EF; ARS 1 AD to 57 Sqn 17.10.17; Swung and stalled on take off, hit tree 10.12.17 (2/Lt FAW Mann OK & 1/AM J Crowther cut about face)

A7676 S.T.B. (sic) to 2 TDS Lake Down 29.9.17; Engine choked slightly on TO, turned back, stalled avoiding trees, dived in 2.10.17 (2/Lt HI Mahaffy killed)

A7677 (200hp BHP) At 2 AAP Hendon 24.9.17, allotted to EF for "S" Replacement Sqn; England to ARS 1 AD and on to 27 Sqn 29.9.17; Rep Pk 1 ASD 13.1.18; 2 AI 11.3.18; Rep Pk 2 ASD 12.4.18; 2 AI to 27 Sqn ('G') 8.6.18; Left 18.50 on low strafing mission, fell in pieces nr Gourney 10.6.18 (2/Lt T Noad & Sgt E Sterling both killed)

A7678 S.T.B. (sic) to 2 TDS Lake Down 29.9.17; 49 Sqn Dover, wings broke off in spin 5.11.17 (Lt RS Leventon & Lt CA Jackson both drowned)

A7679 (Eagle VII) At 2 AAP Hendon 28.9.17, allotted to EF; 1 AD to 57 Sqn 6.10.17; In combat Clerken 09.40 17.10.17 (2/Lt FD Grant wounded & Lt HF Attwater OK); Left 10.10 on photographic mission, FTR 2.12.17 (2/Lt JT Orrell killed & 2/Lt JG Glendinning PoW DoW 16.12.17)

A7680 (Eagle V) At 2 AAP Hendon 1.10.17, allotted to EF; England to ARS 1 AD 14.10.17; 25 Sqn 15.10.17; Left at 13.00 on raid on Deynze railway station, attacked by EA, last seen gliding down under control 5.2.18 (2/Lt EO Cudmore & 1/AM LJW Bain both PoW)

A7681 No information

A7682 (RAF 3a) From Dover to France with 49 Sqn 8.11.17;

Fokker DrI OOC Cambrai 11.45 13.1.18 (2/Lt HL Rough & 2/Lt V Dreschfeld); Fokker DrI OOC E of Cambrai 14.55 2.2.18 (2/Lt GS Stewart & Lt DD Richardson); Albatros DV OOC 11.50 26.2.18 (Lt R Mitton & 2/Lt BSB Bayliss); 2 AI 13.3.18 exchanged for a Fiat-engined m/c; 1 AI 3.4.18; 18 Sqn 8.5.18; Albatros D and Fokker DrI OOC Carvin-Lens 11.30 25.5.18 (2/Lt LJ Balderson & Lt G Bullen); Landed crosswind, LH plane struck ground, u/c collapsed 26.5.18 (2/Lt L Balderson & 2/AM G Bridge); Rep Pk 1 ASD 31.5.18; SOC 2.6.18 NWR

A7683 (Eagle VII) At 2 AAP Hendon 2.10.17, allotted to EF; At Rep Pk 1 ASD by 11.11.17; 1 AI 23.11.17; 25 Sqn 28.11.17; Lost way, FL at Laigle 28.12.17, returning 31.12.17 crashed nr Rouen (2/Lt AWP Cumming & Sgt F Hopper both OK); Wreckage railed to 2 ASD; Rep Pk 2 ASD 10.1.18; SOC 15.1.18

A7684 (RAF 3a) From Dover to France with 49 Sqn 8.11.17; Landed too fast, wrecked 26.11.17 (2/Lt RA Curry & 2/Lt F Nightingale OK); Rep Pk 2 ASD 29.11.17; Engine cut out on take off 23.2.18 (Sgt Parke); Rep Pk 2 ASD to 2 AI 10.5.18; 1 AI 17.5.18; 18 Sqn 29.6.18; Struck ridge on landing which wrecked u/c 1.7.18 (Capt HR Gould MC & Sgt Mech LG Vredenburg OK); Rep Pk 1 ASD 3.7.18; Rebuilt as F5836 7.8.18

A7685 No information

A7686 (BHP) 2 TDS Stonehenge by 27.11.17; 99 Sqn, EF on TO, FL, hit tree Old Sarum, WO 8.12.17 (2/Lt WAE Pepler injured)

A7687 (Eagle V) At 2 AAP Hendon 3.10.17, allotted to EF; 1 AD to 57 Sqn 11.10.17; Albatros D OOC Menin-Comines 13.45 6.12.17; DFW C OOC smoking N of Roulers 11.45 10.12.17 (both Lt AFE Pitman & Lt CW Pearson); Photo recce, took off 10.50, FTR 3.1.18 (Capt AFE Pitman & Lt CW Pearson both killed)

A7688 (RAF 3a) From Dover to France with 49 Sqn 8.11.17; 2 AI 15.2.18 (exchanged for Fiat-engined m/c); 5N Sqn 6.3.18; 1 ASD SOC 8.4.18 NWR

A7689 WEE Biggin Hill by 17.5.18

A7690 WEE Biggin Hill by 16.5.18

A7691 No information

A7692 (250hp Eagle) 44 TS Harlaxton by 8.17; 44 TS to Waddington 24.11.17; Overbanked on climbing turn on TO, stalled, crashed 12.3.18 (Cdt GO Middleditch killed & Cdt CA Pudith DoI 30.4.18)

A7693 (RAF 3a) 49 Sqn (Mob) Dover, sideslipped in from vertical bank too near ground 27.10.17 (Lt JH Keeble & 2/Lt LS Hudson both killed)

A7694 (RAF 3a) From Dover to France with 49 Sqn ('6') 8.11.17; Advanced Salvage to Rep Pk 1 ASD, & SOC 12.4.18

A7695 72 Sqn Baghdad @31.3.18; SOC with squadron 20.8.18

A7696 46 TS Catterick by 18.10.17

A7697 (Eagle V) At 2 AAP Hendon 3.10.17, allotted to EF; ARS 1 AD to 25 Sqn 27.10.17; FTR from photographic mission Laon 26.2.18 (Lt GM Shaw wounded & Lt CHS Ackers both PoW)

A7698 (275hp Eagle) 51 TS Waddington, flat spin landing, crashed 10.11.17 (2/Lt JRH Liddell killed)

A7699 No information

A7700 (RAF 3a) From Dover to France with 49 Sqn 8.11.17; 1 AI 6.4.18 (exchanged for a D.H.9); 18 Sqn 20.4.18; Landed cross wind, bumped heavily on stbd wheel, u/c torn off 21.4.18 (2/Lt CW Snook & 2/Lt B Tussaud OK); Rep Pk 1 ASD 21.4.18; SOC 25.4.18

A7701 (RAF 3a) Tested CFS Upavon 10.11.17 (for AES Martlesham Heath); EC&AD Grain 11.1.18; ECD Grain by 25.5.18 (for deletion by 23.3.18)

A7702 (250hp Eagle IV) At 2 AAP Hendon 15.10.17, allotted to EF; Rep Pk 1 ASD to 2 ASD 12.11.17; 1 AI 15.12.17; 57 Sqn 6.1.18; FL in dark 6.1.18 (2/Lt H Erskine wounded & Lt J Howard-Brown injured); Rep Pk 1 ASD 9.1.18

A7703 (Eagle V) At 2 AAP Hendon 25.9.17, allotted to EF; 1 AD to 55 Sqn ('K') 3.10.17; Albatros D OOC Courtrai 08.00 7.10.17 (Sgt PH O'Lieff & A/Cpl A Walters); Hit by AA 19.2.18 (2/Lt EF Van der Riet OK & Lt JM Carroll wounded); In action 30.5.18 (Capt WA Pace OK & Lt LF Short wounded); Shot down by EA in raid on Thionville sidings 30.8.18 (2/Lt HH Doehler USA & 2/Lt AS Papworth both PoW)

Bombed-up D.H.4 A7703 'K' of No.55 Squadron. The pilot is Lt E.F. Van der Riet and the observer either Lt A.Sattin or Lt J.M.Carroll. (via Frank Cheesman)

A7704 (RAF 3a) Tested RAE Farnborough 18.10.17; 6th Wing ARS Dover 19.10.17; 49 Sqn (Mobilising) Dover 31.10.17; To France with 49 Sqn 8.11.17; Left at 09.00, seen to go down in flames Thun St.Martin 10.10 29.11.17 (2/Lt CB Campbell & 1/AM WAE Samways both killed)

A7705 (RAF 3a) From Dover to France with 49 Sqn 8.11.17; LVG C OOC Marquion Le Sains 14.00 10.3.18 (2/Lt G Fox-Rule & 2/Lt PT Holligan); Just after take off pilot decided to return as engine was running irregularly due to overheating, the m/c loaded with bombs overran the landing mark, the pilot attempted to cross road and land in field on opposite side but having insufficient speed hit ditch 11.3.18 (Capt TE Gorman & Lt DD Richardson OK); Rep Pk 2 ASD to Rep Pk 1 ASD by rail 1.4.18 (arr 4.4.18); SOC 8.4.18

A7706 (200hp BHP) Presentation Aircraft 'Bombay No.1'. At 2 AAP Hendon 8.10.17, allotted to EF; England to ARS 1 AD in case 15.10.17; 27 Sqn ('R') 16.10.17; On raid on Cambrai, FL nr Ames, burst into flames, bomb exploded 6.1.18 (2/Lt GR Vickers killed & Lt GS Rodmell injured); Rep Pk 1 ASD 8.1.18

A7707 (200hp BHP) At 2 AAP Hendon 8.10.17, allotted to EF; ARS 1 AD to 27 Sqn 19.10.17; Left 15.30 on compass course exercise, crashed nr Montreuil 13.11.17 (Lt FP Galloway & Lt FW Best both killed); SOC Rep Pk 1 ASD 17.11.17

A7708 (RAF 3a) From Dover to France with 49 Sqn 8.11.17; On raid crashed nr St Amand at 09.30 4.12.17 (2/Lt GH Whyte & 2/Lt CE Coddington both killed)

A7709 (RAF 3a) At No 8 AAP Lympne 21.11.17, Reallotted from Training to EF; Rec Pk to 1 AI 8.12.17; 2 AI to 18 Sqn 19.1.18; Water joint broke, engine over heated and seized at 500ft, landed on light railway and crashed 18.3.18 (2/Lt HR Gould & Lt J Bard OK): Rep Pk 1 ASD 19.3.18 SOC 14.4.18

A7710 (200hp BHP) Presentation Aircraft 'Elizabeth Campbell of Inverell Station'. At 2 AAP Hendon 15.10.17, allotted to EF; ARS 1 AD to 27 Sqn 1.11.17; Rep Pk 1 ASD 24.12.17; 2 AI 12.3.18; Rep Pk 2 ASD by 1.4.18; 27 Sqn 11.5.18; On take off engine revs dropped, crashed in cornfield and turned over 21.5.18 (Lt DB Robertson & Sgt SB Percival OK); SOC Rep Pk 2 ASD 23.5.18 NWR

A7711 44 TS Harlaxton, hit treetop landing, overturned, crashed 16.11.17 (Lt S Rutledge killed & 2/Lt JW Rhodes injured)

A7712 (RAF 3a) 49 Sqn (Mobilising) Dover 22.10.17; To France with 49 Sqn 8.11.17; FL Frevant due to storm and darkness, crashed 16.30 11.11.17 (Lt R Mitton & Capt GC Easton); At Rep Pk 2 ASD 21.11.17; 2 AI 20.2.18; 49 Sqn 12.3.18; 2 AI 17.3.18 exchanged for Fiat-engined m/c; 1 AI 12.4.18; 18 Sqn ('5') 13.4.18; Casualty Report 4.5.18 says unfit for war flying; Rec Pk and on to England 13.5.18

A7713 (Eagle VII) Presentation Aircraft 'Zanzibar No.10'. At 2 AAP Hendon 10.10.17, allotted to EF; ARS 1 AD to 25

Sqn 27.10.17; Left 08.30 on photographic mission, in combat with 6 EA over Le Cateau, shot up on return 11.15 6.3.18 (2/Lt C Ross & Lt HE Pohlmann both OK); 2 ASD to Rep Pk 1 ASD 15.3.18; Rec Pk to 2 AI 3.6.18; 57 Sqn 8.6.18; Hit by AA 15.6.18 (Capt H Liver OK & Sgt PS Tidy wounded in head); Returning from raid on landing to avoid A8070 which had just crashed turned and landed with drift on, m/c wrecked 1.7.18 (2/Lt PWJ Timson & Sgt EEAG Bridger OK); Rep Pk 2 ASD 3.7.18; Rebuilt as F6212 25.7.18

A7714 Deld 2 AAP Hendon; 19 TS 31.10.17 (TS Div Flt for Gen Longcroft); 10 TDS Harling Road 6.18

A7715 (RAF 3a) From Dover to France with 49 Sqn 8.11.17; 4 ASD Dunkirk and on to Rec Pk 3.4.18 (exchanged for D.H.9); To England 20.4.18.

A7716 (Eagle V) At 2 AAP Hendon 20.10.17, allotted to EF; Rep Pk 1 ASD to 2 ASD 11.11.17; Rec Pk 28.12.17; 1 AI 4.2.18; 25 Sqn 6.2.18; Stalled and crashed on landing after practice flight 1.4.18 (2/Lt LLK Straw OK); Adv Salvage to Rep Pk 1 ASD 9.4.18; Rebuilt as F5826 25.6.18

A7717 9 TS Sedgeford by 2.18; 10 TDS Harling Road by 7.18

A7718 (RAF 3a) 8 AAP Lympne to 2 TDS Lake Down 27.11.17; At No 8 AAP Lympne 30.11.17, Reallotted from Training to EF; Rec Pk to 2 AI 15.12.17; 1 AI 3.1.18; Rep Pk 1 ASD 2.2.18; SOC 5.2.18

A7719 (RAF 3a) 8 AAP Lympne to 2 TDS Lake Down 27.11.17; At No 8 AAP Lympne 30.11.17, Reallotted from Training to EF; Rec Pk to 2 AI 16.12.17; 18 Sqn 22.1.18; Last seen going down under control during combat at Orignies at 12.30, crashed Allienes 10.3.18 (2/Lt JNB McKim & Lt CRH Ffolliott both killed)

A7720 (RAF 3a) At No 8 AAP Lympne 14.11.17, allotted to EF; Rec Pk to 2 AI and on to 49 Sqn 5.12.17; Engine failure, landing on incline ran into barbed wire 17.3.18 (Capt TE Gorman & 2/Lt PT Holligan), m/c was being returned to 2 ASD for exchange; Rep Pk 2 ASD to Rep Pk 1 ASD by rail 1.4.18, arrived 4.4.18, SOC 8.4.18

A7721 121 Sqn Narborough by 5.18

A7722 (RAF 3a) From Dover to France with 49 Sqn 8.11.17; Just after take off, m/c sideslipped due to wind, crashed on nose and turned turtle 2.12.17 (2/Lt WH Valentine & Lt FC Aulagnier both OK); to Rep Pk 2 ASD

A7723 (Eagle VI) At 2 AAP Hendon 15.10.17, allotted to EF; Rep Pk 1 ASD by 11.11.17; 25 Sqn 12.11.17; Damaged landing 26.11.17; Rep Pk 1 ASD 26.11.17; Rep Pk 2 ASD 9.2.18; 2 AI 6.5.18; 57 Sqn 16.5.18; Longeron broke in the air, FL and crashed Treizennes 17.5.18 (Lt A Newman MC & Lt EG Pernet both injured); SOC Rep Pk 2 ASD 20.5.18

A7724 (RAF 3a) At 2 AAP Hendon 22.10.17, allotted to EF but reallotted to 49 Sqn (Mob) Dover 30.10.17; To France with 49 Sqn, landed badly on arrival at St.Omer 8.11.17 (2/Lt JC Robinson & observer); Rep Pk 1 ASD 8.11.17; 1 AI 6.1.18; 18 Sqn 22.1.18; Combat with 10 EA over Courrières, badly shot up, FL at 16 Sqn at 12.45 16.2.18 (Lt J Hudson OK & Lt TW Nicholson seriously wounded); Rep Pk 1 ASD 19.2.18;

A7725 (Eagle VII) At 2 AAP Hendon 18.10.17, allotted to EF; Rep Pk 1 ASD to 25 Sqn 15.11.17; FL but hit parapet of old trench 30.11.17 (2/Lt HG Milnes & Capt JH Graham shaken); Rep Pk 1 ASD 2.12.17; 2 AI 1.4.18; 57 Sqn 2.4.18; Left 09.50 on photographic mission, FTR 15.5.18 (Lt EH Piper & 2/Lt HLB Crabbe both killed)

A7726 (190hp Renault 8G) Deld RFC Ascot to Hendon W/E 3.11.17; RNASTE Cranwell by rail W/E 10.11.17; Became 201/2 TDS Cranwell 1.4.18

A7727 No information

A7728 (RAF 3a) At 2 AAP Hendon 29.10.17, allotted to EF but reallotted to 49 Sqn (Mob) Dover 6.11.17; To France with 49 Sqn 8.11.17; 2 AI 13.3.18, exchanged for Fiat-engined m/c; At Rep Pk 2 ASD by 1.4.18; SOC 7.5.18

A7729 46 TS Catterick by 27.1.18

A7730 (Eagle V) At 2 AAP Hendon 19.10.17, allotted to EF; Rep Pk 1 ASD to 2 AI 10.11.17; 55 Sqn 22.11.17; Rep Pk 2 ASD 19.2.18; SOC 21.2.18

A7731 No information

A7732 No information

A7733 (Eagle V) At 1 (S)ARD 16.11.17, allotted to EF; Farnborough to France 2.12.17; Rec Pk to 1 AI 8.12.17; 25 Sqn 28.12.17; FTR from height test and photographic practice, left at 14.45, shot down into sea 27.2.18 (Lt MW Dickens & Sgt FJ Swain both killed); Salvaged from sea 23.6.18

A7734 110 Sqn Sedgeford by 2.18

A7735 No information

A7736 44 TS Waddington by 11.17 - 15.3.18

A7737 (Eagle VII) Deld Hendon ex Gosport Works W/E 27.10.17; AP Dover W/E 24.11.17; 202 Sqn 8.4.18; 4 ASD 6.11.18

A7738 No information

A7739 (Eagle VII later VI) Deld Hendon ex Gosport Works W/E 27.10.17; AP Dover W/E 24.11.17; NAD Dunkirk 18.2.18; 5N Sqn W/E 7.3.18; Albatros DV crashed Busigny aerodrome 11.00 16.3.18 (F/L E Dickson DSC & OSL WH Scott); Became 205 Sqn 1.4.18; Attacked by 6 EA over Péronne, green & yellow Pfalz DIII OOC nr Villers-Bretonneux 2.4.18 (Capt E Dickson DSC & 2/Lt WH Scott); Attacked nr Abancourt by 3 triplanes and black Pfalz with crosses on white background, sent down the Pfalz DIII OOC 15.50 6.4.18 (Capt E Dickson DSC & 2/Lt WH Scott); Fokker DrI OOC Chaulnes 16.15 22.4.18 (Capt E Dickson DSC & AGL CV Robinson DSM); Fokker DrI OOC Chaulnes Rly Stn 19.30-19.40 23.4.18 (Capt E Dickson DSC & Sgt AGL CV Middleton); COL 8.6.18 (Lt JC Wilson & Sgt SM MacKay both unhurt); Rep Pk 2 ASD 11.6.18; SOC 21.6.18 NWR

A7740 (RAF 3a) From Dover to France with 49 Sqn 8.11.17; Raid on Cambrai, shot up by AA 29.11.17 (2/Lt GS Stewart & Lt DD Richardson OK); Rep Pk 2 ASD 29.11.17 (BHP fitted); 2 AI to 27 Sqn 23.4.18; Failed to flatten out on landing, crashed 3.5.18 (Lt HP Schoeman & 2/Lt W Spencer OK); To Rep Pk 2 ASD 5.5.18; SOC 28.5.18 NWR

A7741 Half ARS Old Sarum 8.1.18 from Ascot by rail; 98 Sqn Old Sarum 9.1.18; Half ARS 12.1.18; 98 Sqn 20.1.18; 103 Sqn 22.1.18

A7742 (Eagle VII) Deld Hendon by 2.12.17; AP Dover 8.12.17; 5N Sqn 15.12.17; Albatros DV, tailplane broke off nr Promour 10.55 18.3.18 (FSL GBS McBain & 1/AM AGL W Jones); In combat, lost wing on landing and crashed 27.3.18 (FSL GBS McBain & 1/AM AGL W Jones both injured); 2 ASD by 1.4.18; Railed from Rep Pk 2 ASD to Rep Pk 1 ASD 2.4.18, arrived 7.4.18; Rec Pk to 2 AI 2.6.18; 57 Sqn 7.6.18; Left 03.40 for bombing raid, driven down by Fokker DrI W of Montauban, last seen going south Bapaume 23.6.18 (2/Lt CW Peckham PoW & 2/Lt AJ Cobbin PoW DoW 14.7.18); SOC 23.6.18

A7743 44 TS Waddington by 13.3.18

A7744 (Eagle VII) Deld Hendon W/E 3.11.17; AP Dover W/E 1.12.17; Grain 12.17; AP Dover 13.12.17; 5N Sqn 19.12.17; EA OOC 30.1.18 (FSL JM Mason & AGL CV Robinson DSM); Became 205 Sqn 1.4.18; Rep Pk 2 ASD 4.6.18 (cracked longeron); Rebuilt as F6099 3.7.18

A7745 (RAF 3a) At 2 AAP Hendon 22.10.17, allotted to EF; At Rep Pk 1 ASD by 11.11.17; 1 AI 19.11.17; Rep Pk 1 ASD to 18 Sqn 6.2.18; Descended to ascertain whereabouts, landed heavily 25.3.18 (2/Lt WA Rochelle & Sgt C Lines); Rep Pk 1 ASD 2.4.18; SOC 8.4.18

A7746 10 TDS Harling Road 11.18; 46 TS Catterick by 24.1.18

A7747 (RAF 3a) At 8 AAP Lympne 14.11.17, allotted to EF; Rec Pk to 1 AI 2.1.18; 18 Sqn 30.1.18; On landing did a flat turn too low to get into the wind, touched the ground with a lot of drift sweeping u/c off 5.2.18 (2/Lt RA Mayne & Lt V Scott MC); Rep Pk 1 ASD 8.2.18; SOC 9.2.18

A7748 (Eagle) 46 TS Catterick by 28.1.18; Stalled and crashed after dive 7.2.18 (2/Lt J Pitt killed)

A7749 (Eagle VIII) Arr Rec Pk ex UK 22.8.18; to 2 AI and on to 3 ASD 23.8.18; 55 Sqn 23.8.18; On take off smashed propeller, lost flying speed and nose dived 20.12.18 (2/Lt DG Beaudry & 2/Lt W Ward OK); SOC by 28.12.18

A7750 (Eagle VIII) Farnborough to Rec Pk 13.9.18; 2 AI 13.9.18; 3 ASD 14.9.18 (arr 15.9.18); 55 Sqn 21.9.18; Shot about 10.11.18; 2 ASD 16.1.19

A7751 (190hp Renault 8G) Deld RFC Ascot to Hendon W/E 3.11.17; RNASTE Cranwell by rail W/E 10.11.17 - 30.3.18

A7752 52 TS Montrose from 1.11.17; 9 TS Sedgeford by 2.18;

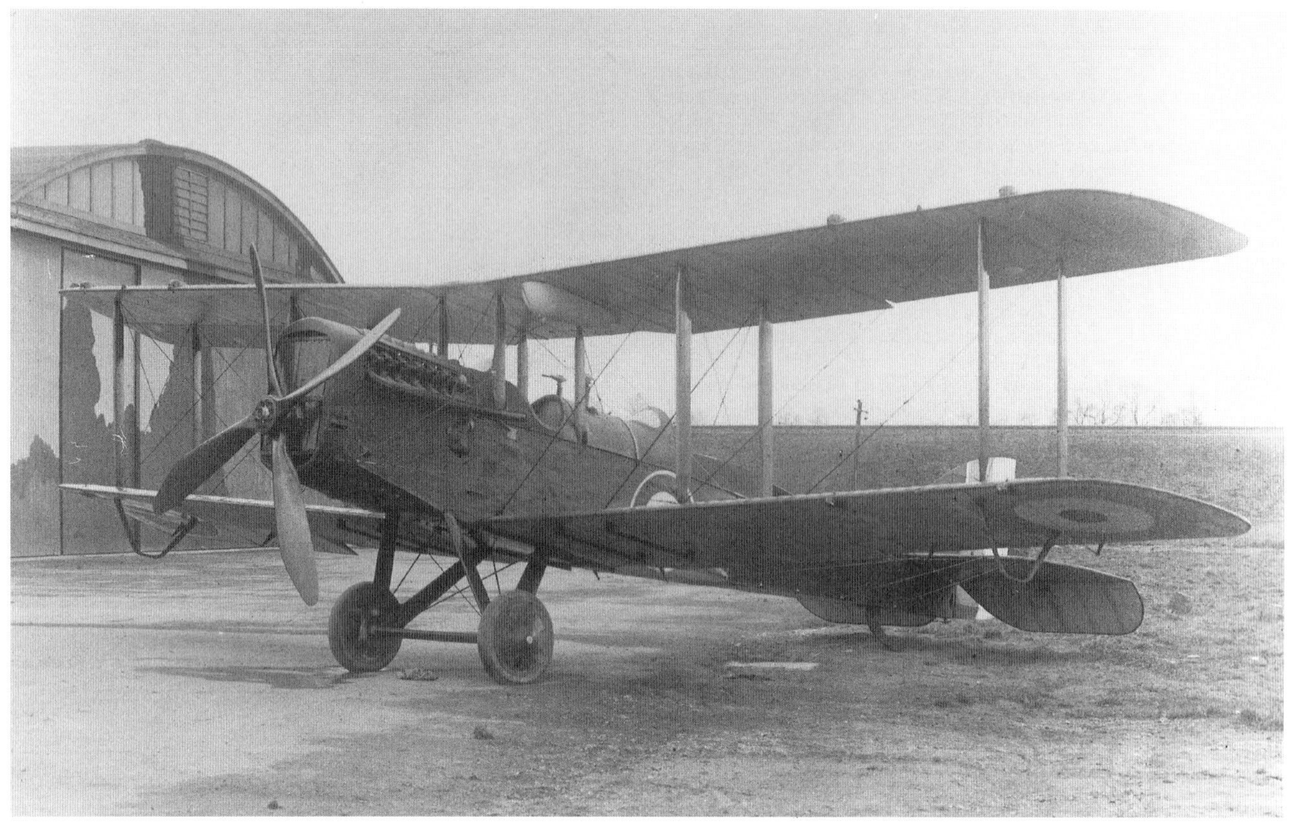

An unidentified D.H.4 at Hendon. (via Frank Cheesman)

10 TDS Harling Road by 6.18 - 10.18

A7753 10 TDS Harling Road 8.18 - 9.18; Prop accident 15.8.18 (3/AM E Hayward injured)

A7754 No information

A7755 (RAF 3a) 99 Sqn Old Sarum by 22.12.17; 103 Sqn Old Sarum, FL, crashed 14.1.18 (2/Lt LH Cunningham killed)

A7756 Presentation Aircraft 'Presented by His Highness the Maharaja of Jind'. 72 Sqn, SOC 19.6.18

A7757 Grain (ditching and hydrovane trials); WO at 31 Wing AP 10.6.19

A7758 49 Sqn (Mob) Dover from 31.10.17 but not to France with sqn 8.11.17; Plane Repair Unit, Islington to 2 TDS Lake Down 20.11.17

A7759 Rec Pk to 2 AI 24.10.18; 1 ASD to England 4.1.19

A7760 (Eagle VIII) Ex Lilbourne to Hendon, then Brooklands W/E 17.11.17; 1 (S)ARD Farnborough to EC&AD Grain W/E 2.3.18 (fit flotation gear); 217 Sqn 11.6.18; En route raid on Zeebrugge, EF, FL beach, Mardyck 29.7.18 (Lt GC Matthews & Sgt E Farley); Collided with A7772 on landing, badly damaged, Crochte 16.8.18 (1/Lt AL Grimme USA slightly injured & 2/Lt F Sutherland unhurt); to 4 ASD; 2 SS Richborough 15.9.18

A7761 RNAS Tregantle & Withnoe by 30.3.18; 7th (Training) Wing 6.18

A7762 (Eagle VIII) 1 (S)ARD Farnborough by 27.4.18 allocated Dunkirk; 491 Flt Dover by 25.5.18; 217 Sqn by 31.5.18; COL 7.6.18 (Lt JH Hardman & Sgt Mech G/L FW Shufflebotham); 4 ASD repair 8.6.18 - 27.10.18

A7763 (Eagle VIII) At 2 AAP Hendon 27.10.17, allotted to EF; 1 AD to ARS 2 AD 29.10.17; 6 AP to 55 Sqn 23.11.17; 3 ASD 20.8.18

A7764 (Eagle VIII) 1 (S)ARD Farnborough to East Fortune for erection W/E 9.3.18; Dunkirk 28.3.18; Turnhouse by 31.3.18; Deleted W/E 4.7.18

A7765 104 Sqn Andover to 105 Sqn Andover 17.2.18

A7766 No information

A7767 (RAF 3a) At 8 AAP Lympne 16.1.18, allotted to EF; England to Rec Pk 30.1.18; 1 AI 18.3.18; 18 Sqn 20.3.18; Left 09.25 FTR 27.3.18 (2/Lt RB Smith USA & 1/AM H Sinclair both PoW)

A7768 (Eagle VII later VI) Deld Hendon W/E 3.11.17; AP Dover W/E 24.11.17 - 4.18; To 202 Sqn by 27.4.18; Last seen between Ostende & Zeebrugge 14.5.18 (Lt F Titchener & Pte 1 G/L JG Waller both killed)

A7769 (RAF 3a) At 8 AAP Lympne 16.1.18, allotted to EF; Rec Pk to 1 AI 28.2.18; 18 Sqn 8.3.18; On landing ran into shell hole and overturned 28.3.18 (2/Lt J Gillanders & Lt JM Brisbane OK); Rep Pk 1 ASD 5.4.18; SOC 8.4.18

A7770 (RAF 3a) At No 8 AAP Lympne 14.11.17, allotted to EF; Reallotted to Training 21.11.17 but this cancelled 30.11.17 and again allotted to EF; 8 AAP to Rec Pk 21.1.18; 2 AI 6.2.18; 18 Sqn 17.2.18; Pfalz OOC Carvin-Fromelles 12.05-13.05 10.3.18 (Capt AG Waller & Sgt MV Kilroy); Made good landing but had to turn sharply to avoid other machines landing, own m/c badly strained 8.4.18 (2/Lt HR Gould & Capt MSE Archibald); Rep Pk 1 ASD 13.4.18; SOC 20.4.18

A7771 (Eagle VII) Presentation Aircraft 'Jamaica No.1'. At 2 AAP Hendon 31.10.17, allotted to EF; Rep Pk 1 ASD to 57 Sqn 9.11.17; Left 14.10, hit by AA Bapaume, FL 7.6.18 (Capt H Liver & Sgt PS Tidy OK); SOC Rep Pk 2 ASD 21.6.18 NWR

A7772 (Eagle VIII) 1 (S)ARD Farnborough to AAP Dover W/E 9.3.18 (erected in Repair Shops 13.3.18); NAD Dunkirk 21.3.18; Became 4 ASD Guines by 28.3.18; 217 Sqn 1.4.18; With A7935 dropped 2x230-lb bombs each on U-boat 25m NNE of Dunkirk 30.5.18; With A7846 dropped 2x230-lb bombs each on U-boat 3m N of Ostende 1.6.18; Taxied into bomb hole 7.6.18 (Lt H Rudd & AM HA Child unhurt); Repaired on Sqn; With A8050 dropped 4 bombs each on U-boat NNE of Middelkerke 12.8.18; Collided A7760 on landing, badly damaged, Crochte 16.8.18 (Lt HS Stidston injured & Pte1 G/L MC Day unhurt); To 4 ASD Guines; Deleted 31.8.18 general fatigue

A7773 (Eagle VIII) 1 (S)ARD Farnborough to AAP Dover 15.2.18; 17N Sqn 27.2.18; Became 217 Sqn 1.4.18; Damaged in enemy air raid 5/6.6.18; With A8059 attacked U-boat with 2x250-lb bombs each 12m N of Zeebrugge 23.4.18; With A8013 dropped 2x230-lb bombs on U-boat nr CI Buoy, East Dyke 29.6.18 (Lt GR Judge); Run into by A8067, Crochte 30.7.18; 4 ASD

30.7.18 - 25.10.18

A7774 (Eagle VI) Rec Pk to 2 AI 18.10.18; 57 Sqn 8.12.18, arrived at 12.55, hit and damaged by F6104 at 13.50; Flying again by 15.12.18; On mail flight when landing at Verviers nr Spa overshot, on take-off engine cut out, m/c crashed into a wood 10.2.19 (2/Lt FK Damant & 2/Lt WA Ford both OK)

A7775 (Eagle V) Presentation Aircraft 'Gold Coast No.1'. At 2 AAP Hendon 5.11.17, allotted to EF; 6 AP to 55 Sqn 23.11.17; Having to FL due to bad weather engine failed, landed in ploughed field 11.12.17 (Capt AG Walter & Lt LH Mackay); At Rep Pk 2 ASD by 31.12.17; 2 AI to 25 Sqn 29.3.18; Damaged in heavy landing 9.6.18 (Lt AE Hulme & 1/AM W Gray OK); SOC Rep Pk 2 ASD 19.6.18

A7776 (Eagle VI) At 2 AAP Hendon 16.11.17, allotted to EF; 1 ASD to 25 Sqn 5.12.17; Stalled and crashed on landing 3.5.18 (Lt TR Hatten & Cpl T Ramsden OK); To Rep Pk 2 ASD; Rebuilt as F6075 3.7.18

A7777 103 Sqn Old Sarum by 3-7.2.18; 109 Sqn Lake Down by 13.3.18

A7778 Redcar?

A7779 52 TS Catterick by 6.18; Became 49 TDS Catterick 15.7.18 - 9.18; Once coded 'X'

A7780 Presentation Aircraft 'South Africa'. No information

A7781 (Eagle V) Presentation Aircraft 'South Africa'. At 2 AAP Hendon 5.11.17, allotted to EF; 2 ASD to 55 Sqn ('H') 15.3.18; Started for Mannheim but retd, COL 30.6.18 (Lt AS Keep & Lt HA Patey); 2 ASD 30.6.18; 3 ASD to 55 Sqn 11.8.18; Bombing raid on Darmstadt, shot down in combat, crashed S of Mannheim 16.8.18 (Lt JB McIntyre & 2/Lt HH Bracker both killed)

A7782 44 TS Waddington by 3.12.17

A7783 (Eagle VI) 44 TS Waddington by 28.11.17; U/c collapsed landing, went on nose 3.2.18 (Capt [KT?] Dowding & Capt Senior); At 1 (S)ARD 29.6.18 allotted to EF; Rec Pk to 2 AI 28.7.18; 3 ASD 29.7.18; 55 Sqn 31.7.18; Returning from raid on Thionville sidings, combat damaged, attempting to land at 2nd Pursuit Group USAS Gengoult, nr Toul, stalled, crashed and burnt 11.05 30.8.18 (2/Lt PJ Cunningham killed & 2/Lt JG Quinton DoW)

D.H.4 A7783 of 44 TS Waddington after crashing on 3.2.18. The names of Captain Dowding and Captain Senior are painted in white just forward of the front cockpit. (via Terry Treadwell)

A7784 No information

A7785 (Eagle V) At 2 AAP Hendon 15.11.17, allotted to EF; England to Rec Pk 19.11.17; 1 AI 23.11.17; 25 Sqn 29.11.17; FL 10 minutes after take off, crashed 28.12.17 (2/Lt J Anderson OK & 2/AM R Ireland injured); Rep Pk 1 ASD 2.1.18; SOC 7.2.18

A7786 No information

A7787 61 TS South Carlton by 9.11.17; Attempted forced landing on very small field, sideslipped in avoiding church, crashed 16.11.17 (Lt JS Robertson killed)

A7788 (Eagle VIII) At 2 AAP Hendon 9.11.17, allotted to EF; England to Rec Pk 23.11.17; 2 AI to Rep Pk 2 ASD 25.5.18; 2 AI 30.5.18; 25 Sqn 11.7.18; Left 08.30 on photo recce 16.9.18 (Capt RL Whalley & 2/Lt EB Andrews both killed)

A7789 No information

A7790 (Eagle IV) At Makers 10.11.17, allotted to EF; 2 AI to Rep Pk 2 ASD 14.2.18; 2 AI 14.5.18; 205 Sqn 19.5.18; COL 31.5.18 (Lt BW Fletcher & Sgt FL Roberts both unhurt); SOC 2 Advanced Salvage Dump 4.6.18; Rebuilt as F5828 25.6.18

A7791 (Eagle VIII) At 2 AAP Hendon 12.11.17, allotted to EF; England to Rec Pk 19.11.17; 2 AI to 55 Sqn ('R') 24.12.17; Note dated 16.3.18 says to be re-rigged and fitted with 275hp Eagle VII; FTR bombing raid on Charleroi, last seen N of Verdun 21.5.18 (2/Lt HE Townsend & 1/AM J Greenway both PoW)

A7792 (250hp Eagle) 44 TS Waddington by 11.17; Caught by wind landing, stalled and dived in 3.4.18 (2/Lt SR Tipple injured & Boy JH Tunnicliffe unhurt)

A7793 (Eagle) 9 TS Sedgeford by 3.2.18; Stalled on turn at 500ft, dived in from 100ft 21.5.18 (Lt HH Cotton slightly injured & Pte SM Campbell DoI)

A7794 (200hp BHP) At 1 (S)ARD 16.11.17, allotted to EF; Still at 1 (S)ARD 30.1.18, reallotted to Training

A7795 (RAF 3a) Rec Pk to 1 AI 8.10.18; 18 Sqn 17.10.18; 2 AI 21.11.18, exchanged for D.H.9A

A7796 (RAF 3a) At 2 AAP Hendon 18.12.18 reallotted from EF to Store

A7797 (RAF 3a) At Makers 9.11.17, allotted to EF; At Rep Pk 2ASD by 22.12.17; 2AI by 31.12.17; 18 Sqn 3.1.18; Returning from raid on dump nr Carvin intercepted by 3 formations of EA mainly Pfalz and in total about 30 a/c, pilot two Pfalz OOC, observer Pfalz OOC then wounded in chest but continued to fire and sent another EA OOC, m/c badly shot up, 11.05 6.3.18 (2/Lt DA Stewart OK & Lt HWM Mackay DoW on way to hospital); Rep Pk 1 ASD, 11.3.18; SOC 14.4.18

A7798 (RAF 3a) At Makers 9.11.17, allotted to EF; At Rep Pk 2 ASD by 31.12.17; 2 AI 12.1.18; 18 Sqn 19.1.18; Two Siemens-Schuckert OOC Messines 11.15 4.2.18 (2/Lt AC Atkey & Lt CRH Ffolliott); Returning from raid saw one of the sqn's m/cs being attacked over Carvin dived and opened fire, two EAs OOC 11.15 6.3.18 (Capt AG Waller & Sgt MV Kilroy); Engine began to overheat, attempting to FL, stalled at about 20 feet, total wreck 28.3.18 (2/Lt D Robinson & 2/Lt J Baird); Rep Pk 1 ASD 1.4.18; SOC 3.4.18

A7799 (RAF 3a) At Makers 9.11.17, allotted to EF; 2 AI to 18 Sqn 2.2.18; Pfalz OOC Neuve Chapelle-Fromelles 12.45 10.3.18 (2/Lt DA Stewart & Sgt C Beardmore); Albatros D crashed SE of Bapaume 09.00 26.3.18 (2/Lt RV Irwin & Sgt C Beardmore); Albatros D crashed in flames Plouvain 14.40 27.3.18 (Sgt W McCleary & 2/Lt HR Gould); On reconnaissance with A8010, 17.6.18 attacked by six Pfalz DIII one of which was sent down OOC, Hulluch 20.45 17.6.18 (Lt A Pickin & Sgt WA Dyke DCM); Casualty Report 18.7.18 says unfit; Rec Pk and on to England 21.7.18

A7800 (RAF 3a) At Makers 9.11.17, allotted to EF; 2 ASD by 12.17; 2 AI to 18 Sqn 5.1.18; In combat in raid on Ascq 17.2.18 (2/Lt F Jones OK & Lt AC Morris killed); Fokker Drl crashed Albert 11.30 27.3.18 (2/Lt DA Stewart MC & Capt LI Collins); Damaged in combat with EA, 12.4.18 (2/Lt GN Wilton wounded & Lt W Miller OK); Adv Salv to Rep Pk 1 ASD 22.4.18; SOC 25.4.18

A7801 (RAF 3a) At Makers 9.11.17, allotted to EF; 2 AI to 49 Sqn 6.12.17; Rep Pk 2 ASD 29.3.18; SOC 15.4.18

A7802 No information

A7803 UK to 31 Wing AP Mesopotamia 28.9.18

A7804 (250hp Eagle IV) At Makers 10.11.17, allotted to EF; Rep Pk 1 ASD by 31.12.17; 1 AI 6.1.18; 57 Sqn 7.1.18; Photographic mission, indecisive combat with Albatros D, m/c undamaged, FL at 21 Sqn 19.1.18 (Capt FD Grant wounded & Lt GH Halls OK); Left 09.10 for raid on Courtrai, last seen going down W of Courtrai 26.2.18 (2/Lt JM Allen & Capt FR Sutcliffe both PoW)

A7805 (Eagle VIII) At 2 AAP Hendon 29.11.17, allotted to EF; Rec Pk to Rep Pk 1 ASD 13.12.17; 2 AI to 1 AI 2.4.18; 2 AI 10.7.18; 25 Sqn 24.7.18; Damaged 1.11.18 (2/Lt F Meenan & 2/Lt PE Olley OK); Rep Pk 2 ASD 1.11.18

A7806 UK to 31 Wing AP Mesopotamia 28.9.18; WO there 30.5.19

A7807 (RAF 3a) 8 AAP Lympne by 23.10.18

A7808 (RAF 3a) At 8 AAP Lympne 9.3.18, allotted to EF; England to Rec Pk 18.5.18; 1 AI 30.5.18; 18 Sqn 1.6.18; Casualty Report 31.8.18 says m/c unsafe to fly;

Rep Pk 1 ASD 31.8.18; SOC 4.9.18 NWR

A7809 No information

A7810 (RAF 3a) At 8 AAP Lympne 9.3.18, allotted to EF; England to Rec Pk 21.4.18; 18 Sqn 26.5.18; FL in cornfield, attempted to take off struck hedge and crashed 31.5.18 (Lt G Leitch & Capt D Gale OK); Rep Pk 1 ASD 2.6.18; SOC 4.6.18 NWR

A7811 (Eagle V later VI) At 2 AAP Hendon 22.11.17, allotted to EF; Rec Pk to 1 AI 8.12.17; 57 Sqn 12.12.17; Wrecked on landing 10.1.18 (Capt HB McKinnon & Lt LG Martin OK); Rep Pk 1 ASD 16.1.18; Rep Pk 2 ASD 9.2.18; Rep Pk 1 ASD 2.4.18; 2 AI 17.4.18; 205 Sqn 21.4.18; Pfalz DIII OOC Chaulnes 10.30 15.5.18 (Lt W Grossart & Sgt PL Richards); Damaged by flak then attacked by 2 Fokker DrI and a Fokker DVII, observer shot down the biplane, but rudder controls shot away, spun in from 200/300 ft on approach, TW 09.15 19.7.18 (Lt JC Wilson severely wounded & 2/Lt JB Leach unhurt); Remains to 2 Adv Salvage Dump and SOC 20.7.18

A7812 (RAF 3a) At 2 AAP Hendon 1.12.17, allotted to EF; Rec Pk to 2 AI 4.12.17; 49 Sqn 5.12.17; Engine cut out, attempting to land struck tree and crashed 11.3.18 (2/Lt WH Valentine slight injuries & Lt FC Aulagnier OK); SOC Rep Pk 2 ASD 13.3.18

A7813 61 TS South Carlton by 30.11.17 - @5.12.17; 83 Sqn Narborough by 2.1.18; Arr Rec Pk 29.7.18; 2 AI 4.8.18; 3ASD 11.8.18; 55 Sqn 12.8.18; Bombing raid on Darmstadt, shot down in combat, in control, crashed S of Mannheim 16.8.18 (2/Lt J Campbell PoW & 2/Lt JR Fox PoW DoW)

A7814 (250hp Eagle) 75 TS Cramlington, stalled at 5ft on turning back after TO 25.2.18 (2/Lt AE Cartland DoI & 2/Lt CE Halford OK)

A7815 (RAF 3a) At 8 AAP Lympne 8.3.18 allotted to EF; England to Rec Pk 8.5.18;1AI 29.5.18; 18 Sqn 1.6.18; Fokker DVII crashed Henin-Lietard-Courrières 08.30 8.7.18; Scout OOC Vitry 07.20 28.7.18 (both Lt GWF Darvill & Lt W Miller); Returning from raid on Aubigny formation attacked by about 15 Fokker DVII, pilot tried to engage but gun jammed, the observer shot one down in flames,was then wounded but sent another down OOC, with controls shot away crashed amid shell holes and trenches 07.50 4.9.18 (Capt GWF Darvill DFC & Lt W Miller wounded); Rep Pk 1ASD 9.9.18;SOC 12.9.18 NWR

A7816 (RAF 3a) At 8 AAP Lympne 9.3.18, allotted to EF; Rec Pk and on to 1 AI 7.4.18; 18 Sqn 10.4.18; Damaged landing on rough ground 6.5.18 (2/Lt H Leach & Lt J Fenwick); Rep Pk 1 ASD 9.5.18; SOC 11.5.18.

A7817 (RAF 3a) RFC Islington to RNAS Eastchurch by road W/E 8.3.18; Became 204 TDS Eastchurch 1.4.18 - 27.6.18

A7818 (RAF 3a) At Hendon 30.11.17, allotted to EF; Landed cross wind at Rec Pk, Broke propeller and turned over 1.12.17 (2/Lt G Walker OK); Rep Pk 1 ASD to 1 AI 1.4.18; 18 Sqn ('G') 11.4.18; Misjudged landing and crashed into hut 20.4.18 (2/Lt CW Snook & 2/Lt B Tussaud OK); Rep Pk 1 ASD 23.4.18; SOC 25.4.18

A7819 (Eagle VI) To AES Martlesham Heath 19.12.17 (petrol pump and consumption tests); Rep Pk 1 ASD 1.4.18; Damaged W/E 20.4.18; Reallotted from Controller Technical Department charge to EF 16.5.18; 2 AI to 57 Sqn 23.6.18; Misjudged landing, touched down in corn at edge of aerodrome and turned over 8.7.18 (Sgt DE Edgley & Sgt J Grant OK); SOC 2 Adv Salvage Dump 10.7.18

A7820 (Eagle VIII) At 2 AAP Hendon 28.11.17, allotted to EF; Rec Pk to 2 AI 24.12.17; Rep Pk 2 ASD to 2 AI 11.4.18; Rep Pk 2 ASD 22.5.18; 2 AI 25.5.18; 25 Sqn 26.5.18; Photo recce, in combat with EA Haute Avèsnes 10.30, shot up, FL 17.9.18 (Lt RG Dobeson OK & Lt AG Grant wounded); Rebuilt as H6882 23.10.18

A7821 (Eagle IV) At Makers 10.11.17, allotted to EF; At Rep Pk 2 ASD by 31.12.17; 2 AI 10.1.18; 57 Sqn 2.4.18; Misjudged distance on landing, flattened out too soon, came down on one wheel 30.6.18 (Lt WH Kilbourne & Sgt AC Lovesey OK); SOC Rep Pk 2 ASD 9.7.18 ex 2 Adv Salvage Dump

A7822 (Eagle VIII) At 2 AAP Hendon 26.11.17, allotted to EF; 2 AI to 1 AI 2.4.18; Rec Pk to 2 AI 10.7.18; 25 Sqn 11.7.18; FL and crashed due to mist 29.10.18 (Lt RP Bufton & 2/Lt HWH Argyle OK); Rep Pk 2 ASD 29.10.18

A7823 (Eagle IV) At Makers 10.11.17, allotted to EF; Rep Pk 1 ASD to 1 AI 9.1.18; 25 Sqn 2.2.18; On take off swung and crashed into hangar, 2 mechanics killed, 1 injured, A7599 damaged 26.3.18 (2/Lt AWP Cumming & 2/Lt JE Pulling OK); Rep Pk 2 ASD 1.4.18; SOC 22.4.18.

A7824 No information

A7825 (Eagle IV) At Makers 10.11.17, allotted to EF; Rep Pk 1 ASD by 18.1.18; 1 AI 27.1.18; 25 Sqn 20.3.18; Stalled on landing 27.3.18 (2/Lt CEH Allen & Sgt JR Wright OK); Rep Pk 2 ASD 1.4.18; 2 AI and on to 55 Sqn 19.5.18 (by then Eagle VI); Bombing raid, shot down in flames by EA over Karlsruhe 31.5.18 (Lt JCK Anderson PoW DoW & Sgt H Nelle killed)

A7826 52 TS Catterick by 6.18; Became 49 TDS Catterick 15.7.18 - 9.18

A7827 11 TDS Old Sarum by 5.18; Dived in off flat turn 15.7.18 (Lt HL Breakey killed)

A7828 (Eagle VIII) Rec Pk to 2 AI 16.7.18; 3 ASD 17.7.18; 55 Sqn ('H') 17.7.18; 3 ASD 12.8.18; 55 Sqn 27.10.18; On mail flight struck post landing at Valenciennes 24.12.18 (2/Lt GP Dymond OK); SOC 55 Sqn by 30.12.18

A7829 (Eagle VIII) Deld Hendon W/E 1.12.17; AAP Dover 15.12.17; 17N Sqn 17.2.18 [deld Bergues ex Calais 21.2.18]; Became 217 Sqn 1.4.18; Badly shot up 27.4.18; 4 ASD Guines 30.4.18 - 25.10.18

A7830 (Eagle VIII) Deld Hendon W/E 1.12.17; Yarmouth 8.12.17 (special service); Dropped 2x65-lb bombs on U-boat 6½m ESE of Lowestoft 21.3.18 (W/Cdr CR Samson DSO & AM Radcliffe); Became 490 Flt Yarmouth by 25.5.18; Martlesham Heath 16.7.18; Air Council Inspection Sqn by 8.19; Became 24 Sqn 1.2.20 - 11.20 (for Chief of Air Staff)

A7831 (RAF 3a) RFC Islington to RNAS Eastchurch by road W/E 8.3.18; Became 204 TDS Eastchurch 1.4.18; Manston W/E 27.6.18 - 8.18

A7832 (RAF 3a) RFC Islington to RNAS Eastchurch by road W/E 8.3.18; Became 204 TDS Eastchurch 1.4.18; Cranwell 29.5.18

A7833 (RAF 3a) At Makers 11.12.17, allotted to EF; At Rep Pk 2 ASD by 31.12.17; 2 AI 19.1.18; 18 Sqn 2.2.18; Attacked over Pont-à-Vendin, Albatros D and 2 Str OOC 11.15 6.3.18 (Sgt W McCleary & Sgt WA Dyke DCM); Pfalz crashed in flames then Albatros D OOC Bapaume 16.10 25.3.18 (2/Lt AC Atkey & Lt JM Brisbane); Returning from raid on Valenciennes, Albatros D OOC Douai, shared A8010 & A8021 12.00 19.5.18 (2/Lt A Green & Lt F Loly); Casualty Report 16.6.18 says in poor condition and overhaul needed; Rep Pk 1 ASD 21.6.18; SOC 10.8.18 NWR

A7834 (Eagle VIII) At 2 AAP Hendon 26.11.17, allotted to EF; Rec Pk to 2 AI 10.12.17; 1 AI 2.4.18; 25 Sqn 14.9.18; Left sqn 19.5.19.

A7835 (Eagle IV) At 2 AAP Hendon 27.11.17, allotted to EF; Rec Pk to 2 AI 10.12.17; 25 Sqn 10.1.18; Photographic reconnaissance, shot up Le Cateau, FL 10.30 6.3.18 (2/Lt RM Tate wounded & Sgt AH Muff OK); SOC Rep Pk 2 ASD 19.3.18

A7836 (Eagle VIII) At 2 AAP Hendon 28.11.17, allotted to EF; 2 AI to 55 Sqn 24.3.18 (Weekly Report has annotation "Not to be flown, surplus to establishment", but evidently stayed with sqn); 6 AP 8.10.18; 3 ASD 9.10.18

A7837 (Eagle VIII) At 2 AAP Hendon 28.11.17, allotted to EF; Rec Pk to 2 AI 5.12.17; Rep Pk 2 ASD to 55 Sqn by rail 11.3.18, arrived 15.3.18; Crashed La Neuve Ville Bayon 6.10.18 (2/Lt R Kelley & 2/Lt F Seddon both injured); 6 AP 11.10.18; 3 ASD 12.10.18

A7838 (Eagle IV) At 2 AAP Hendon 24.11.17, allotted to EF; 1 AI to 25 Sqn 30.1.18; Crashed 24.3.18; Rep Pk 2 ASD to Rep Pk 1 ASD by rail 2.4.18; Rebuilt as F5825 25.6.18

A7839 (RAF 3a) At Makers 11.12.17, allotted to EF; At Rep Pk 2 ASD by 31.12.17; 2 AI 17.2.18; 18 Sqn 23.2.18; Fokker Dr1 crashed nr Vaulx 09.20 26.3.18 (2/Lt RB Smith & Sgt AOA Pollard); Engine choked and cut out just after take off 14.5.18 (Lt RT Minors & Lt WH Lyall OK): Rep Pk 1 ASD 19.5.18; SOC 20.5.18 NWR

D.H.4 A7818 'G' of No.18 Squadron after crashing into a hut at Serny on 20.4.18. (via Mike O'Connor)

D.H.4 A7828 'H' of No.55 Squadron in late 1918. (J.M.Bruce/G.S.Leslie collection)

D.H.4 A7830 with what appears to be an early type of camouflage marking, probably whilst on anti-submarine duty at Yarmouth. (J.M.Bruce/G.S.Leslie collection)

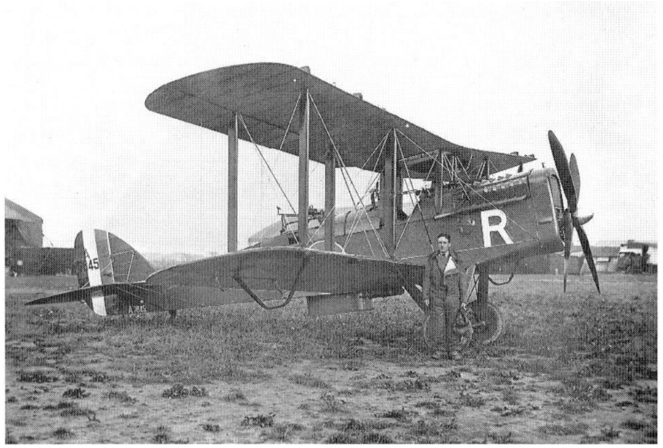

D.H.4 A7845 'R' of No.202 Squadron with a BIB container under the fuselage for a Michelin parachute flare. (J.M.Bruce/G.S.Leslie collection)

D.H.4 A7848 '11' of No.490 Flight at Yarmouth mid-1918 with pillar armament. (via J.M.Bruce/G.S.Leslie collection)

D.H.4 A7864 was a presentation aircraft named 'Felixstowe'. It was fitted experimentally with RAF.3a and RAF.4d engines. (J.M.Bruce/G.S.Leslie collection)

D.H.4 A7919 is believed to have been sent to North Russia. (J.M.Bruce/G.S.Leslie collection)

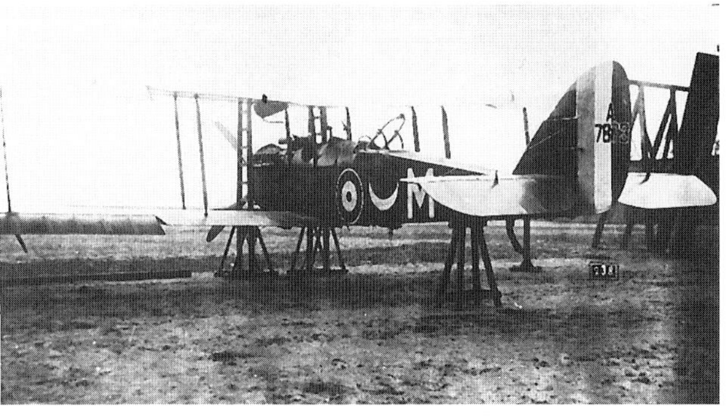

D.H.4 A7873 'M' of No.25 Squadron in German hands after being captured on 3.2.18. (via Frank Cheesman)

A7840 (RAF 3a) At 2 AAP Hendon 30.11.17, Reallotted from Training to EF; Rec Pk to 2 AI 4.12.17; 49 Sqn 5.12.17; Losing water from radiator, FL in bad visibility, crashed 10.12.17 (2/Lt WH Valentine & 2/Lt FC Aulagnier both OK); At Rep Pk 2 ASD by 31.12.17; BHP fitted; Rep Pk 2 ASD to 2 AI 23.4.18; 27 Sqn 6.5.18; EA OOC Bray 19.15 10.5.18 (Lt GE Ffrench & 2/Lt FA Gledhill); Pfalz DIII front half of fuselage red, remainder camouflaged, crashed S of Douai 10.45 20.5.18 (Capt AE Palfreyman & Lt WG Hurrell); Left 06.10 for raid on Thourout, in combat with EA, went into dive Maria Aeltre 23.5.18 (Capt AE Palfreyman killed & 2/Lt WI Crawford PoW wounded); SOC missing 24.5.18

A7841 (RAF 3a) RFC Islington to RNAS Eastchurch by road W/E 8.3.18; Became 204 TDS Eastchurch 1.4.18

A7842 (RAF 3a) At 2 AAP Hendon 1.12.17, allotted to EF; Rec Pk to 2 AI 4.12.17; 49 Sqn 6.12.17; Stalled on take off 28.1.18 (Lt WH Turner injured & 2/Lt PT Holligan OK); To Rep Pk 2 ASD

A7843 (190hp Renault 8G) RFC Islington to RNAS Eastchurch by road W/E 8.3.18; Became 204 TDS Eastchurch 1.4.18 - 22.5.18

A7844 (RAF 3a) RFC Islington to RNAS Eastchurch by road W/E 8.3.18; Became 204 TDS Eastchurch 1.4.18

A7845 (Eagle VIII) Deld Hendon for erection W/E 1.12.17; AAP Dover 15.12.17; NAD Dunkirk 29.12.17; 2N Sqn by 2.1.18; Became 202 Sqn ('R') 1.4.18; Lost u/c landing 25.5.18 (Capt CF Brewerton & Lt MG English both unhurt); to 4 ASD Guines; 202 Sqn 28.6.18; 98 Sqn 16.3.19; 1 ASD 18.3.19

A7846 (Eagle VIII) Deld Hendon for erection W/E 1.12.17; To AAP Dover but FL Twickenham, damaged, retd Hendon by road 29.12.17 (pilot unhurt); AAP Dover 16.2.18; 17N Sqn 28.2.18; Became 217 Sqn 1.4.18; With A7867 attacked U-boat, each dropped 2x230-lb bombs 8 miles NE of Dunkirk 3.4.18 (Lt G Dymore-Brown & AC1 G/L AS Harper); With A8065 dropped 2x230-lb bombs each on 4 destroyers 15m NNW Ostende 19.40 19.5.18; With A7772 dropped 2x230-lb bombs each on U-boat 3m N of Ostende 1.6.18; Damaged in enemy air raid 5/6.6.18; Albatros driven down OOC into sea 19.35 28.6.18 (Lt CW Bragg & 1/Pte G/L EE Hunnisett); Seaplane on water attacked last seen smoking 28.6.18 [possibly the same victory]; Claimed direct hit on trawler 24.7.18 (Lt AM Phillips & Lt NS Dougall); Hit by A7863 when standing on aerodrome, BO 22.8.18; Deleted 31.8.18

A7847 (RAF 3a) Rec Pk to 18 Sqn 21.9.18; 1 ASD 30.10.18 exchanged for D.H.9A

A7848 (Eagle VIII) Deld Hendon W/E 1.12.17; To Yarmouth but landed Northolt 28.12.17; retd Hendon 31.12.17; arr Yarmouth (special service); AZP 13.4.18 (Mjr V Nicholl DSC & 2/Lt HG Owen); Became 490 Flt Yarmouth ('11') by 25.5.18 - 25.9.18; 'B' Flt 1 Comm Sqn Kenley 6.19

A7849 (Eagle VIII, later VI) Deld Hendon W/E 1.12.17; AAP Dover 15.12.17; 2N Sqn 2.1.18; Became 202 Sqn 1.4.18 - 25.4.18 (LM); 4 ASD by 25.5.18; 4 ASD 202 Sqn 17.9.18; Left 13.35, shot down OOC in combat with 5 EA, crashed Engel Dump 28.9.18 (Lt AM Stevens & 2/Lt WHL Halford both killed); Deleted 15.10.18

A7850 (RAF 3a) Rec Pk to 18 Sqn 15.8.18; Con-rod broke causing heavy FL 25.8.18 (Lt WB Hogg & 2/Lt A Petersen); Rep Pk 1 ASD 30.8.18; SOC 1.9.18 NWR

A7851 (RAF 3a) Rec Pk to 1 AI 16.8.18; 18 Sqn 24.8.18; Fokker DVII in flames Marquion 17.15 24.9.18 (2/Lt B Champion & Sgt FL Flavell); 2 AI 21.11.18, exchanged for D.H.9A

A7852 (RAF 3a) Rec Pk to 1 AI 19.8.18; 18 Sqn 24.8.18; Fokker DVII OOC W of Péronne 18.30 25.8.18 (2/Lt B Champion & 2/Lt E Lay); Fokker Dr1 OOC S of Douai 18.40 3.9.18 (2/Lt H Cardwell & 2/Lt HPA O'Mant); 2 AI 21.11.18, exchanged for D.H.9A

A7853 (RAF 3a) Rec Pk to 1 AI 27.8.18; 18 Sqn 29.8.18; Returning from raid on Aubigny-au-Bac, formation attacked by about 15 Fokker DVII, shot down in flames 07.50 4.9.18 (Lt WB Hogg & 2/Lt AE Stock both killed)

A7854 (RAF 3a) Rec Pk to 2 AI 1.10.18; 1 AI 3.10.18; 18 Sqn 4.10.18; 2 ASD 1.11.18 exchanged for D.H.9A

A7855 (RAF 3a) Rec Pk to 18 Sqn 17.9.18; Crashed due to carburettor trouble 24.9.18 (Lt GF Lane & 2/Lt H Yates OK); To Rep Pk 1 ASD 25.9.18

A7856 (RAF 3a) At 2 AAP Hendon 14.6.18, allotted to EF; At Rec Pk by 16.7.18; 1 AI 30.7.18; 18 Sqn 5.8.18; Left on Marquion raid 17.35, hit by AA over La Bassée, left wing seen to fold up 14.8.18 (1/Lt TE Kearney USAS & Sgt Mech JH Hammond both killed)

A7857 (RAF 3a) At 2 AAP Hendon 6.6.18, allotted to EF; Rec Pk to 1 AI 8.7.18; 18 Sqn 28.7.18; Returning m/c to 2 ASD, misjudged landing at 8 Sqn, took off again, attempted second landing but at 400 feet banked steeply and nose dived in, total wreck 22.11.18 (2/Lt EF Wilkinson killed & 2/AM T Whitlock OK); W/O 29.11.18

A7858 (RAF 3a) Rec Pk to 1 AI 4.9.18; 18 Sqn 5.9.18; Camshaft broke, FL on rough ground 28.9.18 (2/Lt CQ Snook & 2/Lt A Lilley OK); Rep Pk 1 ASD 4.10.18

A7859 (RAF 3a) At Makers 11.12.17, allotted to EF; Rep Pk 2 ASD 7.1.18, From Makers in case; 2 AI to 1 AI 1.4.18; 18 Sqn 2.4.18; Scout in flames and another OOC Estaires, shared A7990, A7998, A8000 10.25 12.4.18 (2/Lt HR Gould & Capt MSE Archibald); Engine knocking badly, FL in ploughed field 13.4.18 (2/Lt AC Atkey MC & Sgt H Hammond OK); Rep Pk 1 ASD 15.4.18; SOC 23.4.18

A7860 Rec Pk to 1 AI 19.10.18

A7861 (RAF 3a) At 2 AAP Hendon 1.12.17, allotted to EF; 2 AI to 49 Sqn 4.12.17; Fokker Dr1 OOC 2.2.18 (2/Lt GS Stewart & Lt DD Richardson); Engine cut out just after take off, forced to bank steeply to avoid a clump of trees, m/c crashed before pilot could flatten out 6.3.18 (2/Lt GS Stewart & Lt DD Richardson OK); SOC Rep Pk 2 ASD 18.3.18

A7862 (RAF 3a) At 2 AAP Hendon 14.6.18, allotted to EF; 1 AI to 18 Sqn 15.7.18; Left on bombing raid 14.40, in combat NE of La Bassée, last seen going down in spin followed by EA 22.7.18 (2/Lt HC Tussaud & Sgt Mech LG Vredenburg both PoW)

A7863 (Eagle VIII) Deld Hendon for erection W/E 1.12.17; AP Dover 13.1.18; AD Dunkirk 16.2.18; 12N Sqn 2.18; 17N Sqn 17.2.18; Dropped 230-lb bomb on U-boat NE of Dunkirk 13.3.18 (FSL JN Rutter & LAC G/L AW Vidler); Crashed and damaged nr Bergues aerodrome 19.3.18 (FSL GD Brown & AC1 GL HG Groves); 4 ASD Guines 23.3.18; 217 Sqn 26.5.18; Damaged in enemy air raid 5/6.6.18; Anti-submarine patrol, combat with 8 enemy seaplanes nr Zeebrugge, Brandenburg W.29 seaplane crashed in sea, shared A7941 19.40 29.7.18 (Lt AM Phillips & Lt NS Dougall); Crashed on TO, BO 22.8.18 (Ens E Schoonmaker USNRF & Q/M2 GE Sprague USNRF both unhurt)

A7864 (RAF 4d) Presentation Aircraft 'Felixstowe' Deld AAP Dover W/E 22.12.17; Felixstowe (exptl engine fitting RAF 3a and RAF 4d)

A7865 (Eagle V) At 2 AAP Hendon 3.12.17, allotted to EF; Rec Pk to 1 AI 16.12.17; 25 Sqn 3.1.18; Left at 13.00, combat with 15 EA, shot down, believed in flames W of Deynze 5.2.18 (2/Lt RP Pohlmann & 2/AM R Ireland both killed)

A7866 (RAF 3a) Rec Pk to 1 AI and on to 18 Sqn 3.9.18; 1 ASD 30.10.18 exchanged for D.H.9A

A7867 (Eagle VIII) Deld Hendon W/E 7.12.17; AAP Dover W/E 7.1.18; 17N Sqn 3.2.18; AD Dunkirk 2.18; 17N Sqn 16.2.18; AD Dunkirk 2.18; 17N Sqn 28.2.18; Became 217 Sqn 1.4.18; With A7846 attacked U-boat, each dropped 2x230-lb bombs 8m NE of Dunkirk 3.4.18 (Capt HH Gonyou & Lt JF Reid); With A8022 dropped 2x230-lb bombs on U-boat 2m off Ostende Piers 27.6.18; Spun into sea 3m NE of Dunkirk 06.45 20.8.18 (Yeoman 1st Class ME O'Gorman USNRF & Ens TN McKinnon USNRF both drowned); Deleted 31.8.18

A7868 (Eagle VIII) Deld Hendon W/E 1.12.17; AAP Dover 18.12.17; 2N Sqn after FL Calais 4.1.18; Became 202 Sqn 1.4.18 (segmented circle marking on fin); Halberstadt 1-str OOC over Meetkerke aerodrome 11.10 18.5.18; Attacked 5 Albatros off Ostende, 1 shot down in flames and 1 OOC in sea 3m off Ostende 19.20 21.5.18 (all Lt LA Ashfield & G/L Cpl LA Allen); Attacked by 5 EA nr Middelkerke, landed safely 27.6.18 (Lt LA Ashfield unhurt & Lt NH Jenkins DSM seriously wounded); FTR photo recce, in combat with EA Ostende

16.7.18 (Lt LA Ashfield DFC & Lt MG English both killed) [credited Flgm Goerth, Marine Jasta 3 at Zevecote 18.10]; Deleted 31.8.18

A7869 (RAF 3a) Rec Pk to 1 AI 31.8.18; 18 Sqn 3.9.18; 1 ASD 30.10.18 exchanged for D.H.9A

A7870 (Eagle VIII) Deld Hendon W/E 22.12.17; Airco W/E 16.2.18 (expts); Hendon 2.18; AAP Dover 21.2.18; 17N Sqn (via AD Dunkirk) 5.3.18; Became 217 Sqn 1.4.18; FL on beach at Mardyck 22.4.18; Badly damaged after bombing raid 19.5.18 (Lt JH Hardman & A/G H Tallboys unhurt); 4 ASD 19.5.18; 217 Sqn 24.9.18; Crashed 23.10.18; 4 ASD 25.10.18; Deleted 31.10.18

A7871 1 SoN&BD Stonehenge by 7.18 - @2.8.18; Recd Rec Pk ex UK 16.10.18; Paris 17.10.18; 3 AD 17.10.18

A7872 (Eagle V) At Makers 8.12.17, allotted to EF; England to Rep Pk 1 ASD 6.1.18; 1 AI 27.1.18; 57 Sqn 27.2.18; Left 08.20 for raid on Bapaume, last seen nr target 1.4.18 (2/Lt DP Trollip & Lt JD Moses killed)

A7873 (Eagle V) At 2 AAP Hendon 1.12.17, allotted to EF; Rec Pk to 1 AI 4.1.18; 25 Sqn ('M') 6.1.18; Left at 07.40, FTR from raid on Melle sidings, shot down Mariakerke 09.40 3.2.18 (Lt EG Green MC & Lt PC Campbell-Martin both PoW); A/c captured by Germans

A7874 No information

A7875 1 (S)ARD Farnborough to 4 ASD 25.10.18; 217 Sqn by 2.11.18 (FM); COL 20.11.18 (2/Lt SJ Saunders & 2/Lt TC Tyers both unhurt); 11 AP 28.11.18; To be WOC 4.1.19

A7876 (Eagle VI) Presentation Aircraft 'Shanghai Raceclub No.2'. At 2 AAP Hendon 3.12.17, allotted to EF; Rec Pk to 1 AI and on to 57 Sqn 6.1.18; Albatros D OOC Courtrai 12.00 30.1.18; Albatros D OOC smoking nr Cortemarck 13.00 2.2.18 (both Sgt EA Gay & 2/Lt AC Flavell); Left 10.25 on photographic mission, shot up in combat with 5 EA Beaurevoir, FL 73 Sqn aerodrome 7.4.18 (2/Lt FAW Mann & 2/Lt JT White OK); Rep Pk 2 ASD from 2 Adv Salvage Dump 22.4.18; 2 AI to Rep Pk 2 ASD 21.6.18; 55 Sqn 27.6.18; FTR raid on Oberndorf, last seen NE of Colmar 20.7.18 (Sgt FE Nash PoW & Sgt WE Baker killed)

A7877 (Eagle VIII) At 2 AAP Hendon 15.12.17, allotted to EF; Rec Pk to 1 AI 7.1.18; Rec Pk to 2 AI 10.7.18; 25 Sqn 11.7.18; Excessive vibration, FL, crashed 30.7.18 (Capt JF Gordon & Lt GM Lawson MC both unhurt); To Rep Pk 2 ASD; SOC 8.8.18 NWR

A7878 (Eagle VIII) Deld Hendon W/E 7.12.17; AAP Dover 10.1.18; AD Dunkirk 16.2.18; 17N Sqn 18.2.18; Dover 8.3.18 (visit?); 17N Sqn 9.3.18; Became 217 Sqn 1.4.18; Ran into lorry on landing, badly damaged 12.6.18 (Lt HS Matthews & 1/Pte G/L E Farley both injured); 4 ASD 13.6.18; 2 SS Richborough 15.9.18

A7879 (Eagle III) At Grain 2.12.18 reallotted from EF to SE Area for CTD (fitted COW gun)

A7880 (RAF 3a) Rec Pk to 18 Sqn 10.9.18; 1 ASD 30.10.18 exchanged for D.H.9A

A7881 No information

A7882 (Eagle VII later VI) At Makers 8.12.17, allotted to EF; England to Rep Pk 6.1.18; 1 AI 16.2.18; 25 Sqn 21.2.18; Engine seized due to leaking radiator, FL 26.2.18 (2/Lt C Ross & Lt HE Pohlmann); to 2 ASD; Rep Pk 1 ASD to Rec Pk 25.5.18; 2 AI 26.5.18; 25 Sqn 30.5.18; Left 04.00 for bombing raid on Cambrai, EF, FL intact nr Cambrai, pilot seen to set fire to a/c 05.40 2.6.18 (Lt JR Zilman & 2/Lt H Tannenbaum both PoW)

A7883 44 TS Waddington by 11.17

A7884 44 TS Waddington by 11.17; Mid-air collision with Maurice Farman 7.2.18 (2/Lt GL Smart injured); 55 TDS Manston by 20.7.18

A7885 No information

A7886 44 TS Waddington by 11.17; Caught fire in air 16.3.18 (Lt GA Sweet)

A7887 (RAF 3a) At 2 AAP Hendon 7.6.18, allotted to EF; Rec Pk to 1 AI 24.7.18; 18 Sqn 28.7.18; Left 10.30 for raid on Dechy 25.8.18 (Lt J Smith OK & 2/Lt GA Duthie wounded; Left 10.40 for raid on Pailleul 2.9.18 (2/Lt CW Snook OK & Lt RL Aslin wounded); Left 10.25 for photo mission in First Army area, badly shot up in combat with EA, retd 13.25 27.9.18 (2/Lt JKS Smith & 2/Lt A Lilley both unhurt); Rep Pk 1 ASD 29.9.18

A7888 & A7889 No information

A7890 (Eagle VIII) 1 SoN&BD Stonehenge by 17.3.18; Arr Rec Pk 4.8.18; 2 AI 6.8.18; 25 Sqn 13.9.18; 6 AI 13.5.19; WEE Biggin Hill

A7891 (Eagle IV) 2 AAP Hendon to 98 Sqn Old Sarum 3.1.18; 107 Sqn Lake Down 16.2.18; (Now Eagle VI) At 1 (S)ARD 29.6.18 allotted to EF; Rec Pk to 2 AI 29.7.18; 25 Sqn 5.8.18; Left 05.00 on recce to Douai, FTR 15.8.18 (Lt TJ Arthur & 2/Lt AG Lawe both PoW)

A7892 No information

A7893 (Eagle VIII) To 1 (S)ARD Farnborough (for HMS *Argus*) W/E 16.1.19 - 30.1.19; Imperial Gift to New Zealand; To NZPAF Sockburn by 1921

A7894 (Eagle III) At Grain 2.12.18 reallotted from EF to SE Area for CTD (fitted COW gun)

A7895 (Eagle VI) At Makers 8.12.17, allotted to EF; Rep Pk 1 ASD by 14.1.18; 1 AI 25.1.18; 25 Sqn 12.2.18; Overturned on making FL in rough ground 6.3.18 (2/Lt FF Keen & 2/Lt BD Bennett OK); Railed from Rep Pk 2 ASD to Rep Pk 1 ASD 1.4.18, arr 4.4.18; SOC 14.4.18

A7896 No information

A7897 (RAF 3a) At 2 AAP Hendon 24.6.18, allotted to EF; Rec Pk to 1 AI 24.8.18; 18 Sqn 26.8.18; 2 AI 18.11.18, exchanged for D.H.9A; To England 11.3.19

A7898 (RAF 3a) At 2 AAP Hendon 27.6.18, allotted to EF; Rec Pk to 1 AI 14.8.18; 18 Sqn ('O') 14.8.18; Engine failure on return from raid, FL, ran into shell hole 2.9.18 (Lt R Thurburn & 2/Lt AE Stock OK); Rep Pk 1 ASD 5.9.18; SOC 8.9.18

A7899 (RAF 3a) 1 ASD to 18 Sqn 18.9.18; Left 06.10 for high level raid on Wasnes-au-Bac, in combat with several EA Sancourt, last seen going NW after combat 27.9.18 (Lt RC Bennett DFC PoW & Lt NW Helwig DFC PoW)

A7900 (RAF 3a) At 2 AAP Hendon 7.6.18, allotted to EF; Rec Pk to 1 AI 5.7.18; 18 Sqn 12.7.18; Radiator shot through, engine seized, FL, overturned after running on to light railway Ligny 10.20 14.7.18 (2/Lt A Duncan & 2/Lt JH Dunbar OK); Rep Pk 1 ASD 17.7.18; SOC 19.7.18

A7901 (Eagle VII) Presentation Aircraft 'Jamnagar No.1'. At 2 AAP Hendon 27.12.17, allotted to EF; England to Rec Pk 4.1.18; 1 AI 6.1.18; 57 Sqn 7.1.18; Albatros D OOC Roulers 14.45 19.1.18 (Sgt ER Clayton & 2/Lt LLT Sloot); Albatros D OOC E of Ledeghem 12.30 13.3.18 (Capt A Roulstone & Lt DFV Page); After bombing Linselles attacked by six Albatros Ds one of which was sent down smoking 11.30 17.3.18 (Capt A Roulstone MC and 2/Lt WC Venmore both wounded); Scout OOC nr Irles 11.45 1.4.18 (Capt F McDC Turner OK & 2/Lt A Leach wounded); Landed at Fienvillers to deliver exposed plates to Photo Section, while on ground run into by 11 Sqn Bristol Fighter C4847, m/c cut in half between pilot's and observer's seats 11.4.18 (2/Lt FAW Mann & 2/Lt JT White both injured); 2 Adv Salvage Dump 19.4.18; Rep Pk 2 ASD 20.4.18; SOC 21.4.18

A7902 Once coded 'A'; also 'H'

A7903 (RAF 3a) At 2 AAP Hendon 3.6.18, allotted to EF; Rec Pk to 1 AI 30.6.18; 18 Sqn 24.7.18; Left on photo reconnaissance 09.05, went down E of lines 14.8.18 (Capt HR Gould MC & 2/Lt EF Jinman both killed)

A7904 (Eagle V) At 2 AAP Hendon 27.12.17, allotted to EF; England to Rec Pk 1.1.18; 1 AI and on to 57 Sqn 4.1.18; Albatros D OOC Lichtervelde 12.00 6.1.18 (2/Lt WE Green & 2/Lt EH Wilson); Albatros D OOC N of Thourout 13.15 25.1.18 (2/Lt JM Allen & 2/Lt FRS Wakeford); Pfalz OOC Bapaume 11.15 31.3.18 (2/Lt WE Green & 2/Lt HS Gros); Crashed into hangars on landing 6.6.18 (Lt WE Green & 2/Lt RH Shepherd OK); SOC Rep Pk 2 ASD 16.6.18

A7905 (Eagle VIII) 2 (N)ARD Greenhill/Coal Aston (coded 'D16' from previous unit); Arr Rec Pk ex UK 10.11.18; 6 AI, ferrying to 57 Sqn, EF on TO, FL, CW 2.1.19 (2/Lt HE Harden injured); SOC to Salvage

A7906 (RAF 3a) At 2 AAP Hendon 30.5.18, allotted to EF; Rec Pk to 1 AI 18.6.18; 18 Sqn 24.6.18; Overshot on landing, crashed in potato patch 10.8.18 (Capt HR Gould MC & 2/Lt RD Smith OK); Bboc 2 ASD 10.8.18; Rep Pk 2 ASD to 2 AI 23.10.18; To England 18.12.18

A7907 (RAF 3a) At 2 AAP Hendon 3.6.18, allotted to EF; Rec Pk to 1 AI 30.6.18; 18 Sqn 1.7.18; Albatros C OOC Esquerchin 07.30 and scout OOC 07.35 28.7.18 (Lt J Gillanders & 2/Lt E Walker); Left on raid 09.00, seen going SW in combat with 15 EA nr Albert 13.8.18 (Lt

A Puma-engined D.H.4 of No.27 Squadron. (via Mike O'Connor)

A D.H.4 of No.5 (Naval) Wing with a clear-view panel in the centre-section. (via J.J.Halley)

Unidentified D.H.4, probably at Waddington, coded '7' and the nicknamed 'WOUF-WOUF'. (via Terry Treadwell)

This unidentified D.H.4 has a white skull and crossbones motif painted on the nose. (J.M.Bruce/G.S.Leslie collection)

CF Drabble & 2/Lt RW Rawley both killed)

A7908 (Eagle V) At Makers 8.12.17, allotted to EF; Rep Pk 2 ASD 5.1.18 from Makers in case; 2 AI 28.2.18; 5N Sqn 12.3.18; In combat with EAs in raid on Busigny Dump, shot down nr Benin 16.3.18 (F/Cdr LW Ormerod DSC & FSL WLH Pattison DSC both killed)

A7909 No information

A7910 (RAF 3a) At 2 AAP Hendon 15.6.18, allotted to EF; Rec Pk to 1 AI 13.7.18; 18 Sqn 15.7.18; Engine cut out, crashed 19.7.18 (Capt JR Stewart slightly injured & 2/Lt H Buckner OK); SOC Rep Pk 1 ASD 22.7.18

A7911 (RAF 3a) At 2 AAP Hendon 3.6.18, Reallotted from Air Ministry for HQ Communications Flight to EF; Rec Pk to 1 AI 16.7.18; 18 Sqn 21.7.18; Badly shot up, attempted to land in cornfield but crashed Estrée-Couchy 05.30 28.7.18 (2/Lt A Pickin slightly injured & Sgt Mech WA Dyke DCM DFM DoW 14.8.18); Rep 1 ASD 30.7.18; SOC

A7912 (Eagle V) At 2 AAP Hendon 27.12.17, allotted to EF; Rec Pk to 1 AI 29.12.17; 57 Sqn 12.1.18; Left 11.50 on raid on Harlebeke, FTR 24.1.18 (Lt JO Beattie & 1/AM WJ Bellchamber both killed)

A7913 (Eagle VI) At Makers 8.12.17, allotted to EF; Rep Pk 2 ASD 12.1.18 from Makers in case; 2 AI 9.2.18; 25 Sqn 10.3.18; Pfalz DIII OOC & another down in flames Thourout 08.20 8.5.18 (Lt JE Pugh MC & 2/Lt WL Dixon); FTR photographic mission Bruges 16.40 29.6.18 (Lt BL Lindley MC killed & 2/Lt D Boe PoW)

A7914 No information

A7915 (Eagle VII) 1 (S)ARD Farnborough by 2.5.18, allotted to EF; England to Rec Pk and on to 2 AI 27.5.18; 205 Sqn 31.5.18; Bumped on landing, wings damaged 16.6.18 (Lt HG Kirkland & 2/Lt JC Walker both unhurt); Rep Pk 2 ASD 18.6.18; SOC 22.6.18

A7916 (Eagle VI) At 1 (S)ARD 2.5.18 allotted to EF; England to Rec Pk 20.5.18; 2 AI; 25 Sqn 25.5.18; Overshot aerodrome, landed heavily 16.6.18 (Lt J Webster & Sgt E Edwards); To Rep Pk 1 ASD; SOC 17.7.18; Rebuilt as F5833 17.7.18

A7917 217 Sqn by 20.9.18 (FM); FL Maxenzeal, nr Alost 17.12.18 (2/Lt RW Woodhead & 2/Lt GC Paish); Retd Sqn 19.12.18; 233 Sqn Dover 27.2.19

A7918 (RAF 3a) At 2 AAP Hendon 4.5.18 allotted to EF; RAF North Russia by 5.19

A7919 (RAF 3a) At 2 AAP Hendon 4.5.18 allotted to EF; To RAF North Russia?

A7920 (Eagle VIII) France to 8 AAP Lympne (via Dover) 13.9.18; 4 ASD Wissant to 217 Sqn 24.9.18; Tail skid post bent on TO, ran into ditch 27.9.18 (Lt TW Whittaker & Sgt E Farley); 233 Sqn Dover 27.2.19; At Joyce Green by 26.4.19, allocated 2 Comm Sqn Buc for special duty with HM The King of the Belgians; To 2 Comm Sqn Buc 4.19; FL successfully Evère 22.4.19

A7921 (RAF 3a) At 2 AAP Hendon 9.5.18 allotted to EF

A7922 (RAF 3a) At 2 AAP Hendon 9.5.18 allotted to EF

A7923 No information

A7924 (Eagle VIII) 4 ASD Wissant to 217 Sqn 24.9.18; Attacked by 16 EA, shot down in flames 4m E of Thourout 28.9.18 (1/Lt JE Gregory USAS & 2/Lt EM Bell both killed)

A7925 (Eagle VIII) 4 ASD Wissant to 217 Sqn 4.11.18; 233 Sqn Dover 1.3.19; At Guston Road Dover 24.4.19 reallotted from 5 Group to 2 Comm Sqn Buc for the use of the Air Attache Paris

A7926 England to Rec Pk 5.10.18; 5 AI 8.10.18; 3 AD 9.10.18; 2 AI to 57 Sqn 7.12.18, FL en route at Tubise (2/Lt JH Lorimer), arrived at Sqn 9.12.18; On landing flattened out too soon, pancaked 11.2.19 (2/Lt JH Lorimer & 2/Lt GB Allen OK)

A7927 Marske

A7928 No information

A7929 4 ASD by 11.18; 202 Sqn 4.11.18; SAD Farnborough for HMS *Argus* 6.1.19; 6 SD Ascot (for HMS *Argus*) W/E 16.1.19 - 30.1.19; Imperial Gift to New Zealand; NZPAF Sockburn ('J') by 1921

A7930 (Eagle VIII) At 1 (S)ARD Farnborough 3.4.18, allotted to E 1c for Dover-Dunkirk; Dover 4.4.18; 202 Sqn 8.5.18; 2 D-types OOC, rudder shot away in combat, crash landed on beach, wings and u/c damaged, nr Fort Mardyck 20.00 4.6.18 (FSL LH Pearson & G/L SE

Allatson); to 4 ASD; 2 SS Richborough 15.9.18

A7931 (RAF 3a) At 2 AAP Hendon 27.5.18, allotted to EF; Rec Pk to 1 AI 2.7.18; 18 Sqn 7.7.18; On photo recce attacked by seven Pfalz DIIIs one of which sent OOC Douai 08.00 20.7.18 (Lt RT Minors & Sgt Mech WA Dyke DCM); Pfalz DIII OOC Vitry-en-Artois 11.15 30.7.18 (Lt RT Minors & Lt WH Lyall); Engine seized, FL 2.9.18 (Lt RT Minors & 2/Lt H Buckner OK); Rep Pk 1 ASD 5.9.18; SOC 8.9.18 NWR

A7932 26 TS Narborough by 4.18

A7933 (Eagle VI, later Eagle V) At 2 AAP Hendon 24.1.18, allotted to EF; England to Rec Pk 27.1.18; 2 AI 17.2.18; 5N Sqn 24.3.18; Became 205 Sqn 1.4.18; Badly shot up while bombing Chaulnes Rly Stn, FL Bellevue 23.4.18 (Lt LF Cocks wounded & Lt HF Taylor unhurt); 2 ASD 27.4.18; Rebuilt as F6059 2.7.18

A7934 (Eagle VIII) 1(S)ARD Farnborough by 3.4.18; allotted to E 1c for Dover-Dunkirk; Dover by 27.4.18; 217 Sqn 9.5.18; With A8067 dropped 2x230-lb bombs each on U-boat escorted by 4 destroyers 15m NNW Ostende 19.10 19.5.18; 2-str biplane seaplane shot down in steep dive 08.30 1.6.18 (Lt AE Bingham & G/L H Tallboys); Damaged in hangar by A8082 taking off, Crochte 18.7.18; 4 ASD 19.7.18 - 25.10.18

A7935 (Eagle VIII) 1 (S)ARD Farnborough by 3.4.18, allotted to E 1c for Dover-Dunkirk; Dover 4.18; 217 Sqn ('E':'2') by 27.4.18; With A7772 dropped 2x230-lb bombs each on U-boat 25m NNE of Dunkirk 30.5.18; Attacked by 4 Pfalz DIII over Zeebrugge, shot down 1 in flames 31.5.18 (2/Lt GB Coward & 1/AM G/L GF Briggs observer wounded); Damaged in enemy air raid 5/6.6.18; After raid on Zeebrugge, patrol chased by 4 Pfalz, aircraft then fired on by Dutch troops on landing, overturned, Soesterburg airfield, Vlissingen, Zeeland 17.6.18 (2/Lt GB Coward & Lt JF Read interned); Retained by Dutch as *deH432*; Retd to RAF 12.3.20

A7936 (Eagle VIII) Recd Rec Pk ex UK 1.9.18; 2 AI 5.9.18; 3 ASD 5.9.18 (arr 6.9.18); 55 Sqn 14.9.18; Fokker DVII OOC Saarbrucken 14.30 6.11.18 (Lt RFH Norman & Capt JFD Tanqueray); Nose dived into wood, total wreck 7.1.19 (2/Lt DG Beaudry & 2/Lt WHS Kingsland OK); 2 ASD 17.1.19

A7937 (RAF 3a) At 8 AAP Lympne 10.4.18, allotted to EF; Rep Pk 1 ASD to Rec Pk 23.4.18; Rec Pk to 1 AI 16.5.18; 18 Sqn 31.5.18; Landed cross wind, u/c collapsed 30.6.18 (Lt J Gillanders & 2/Lt E Walker); Rep Pk 1 ASD 4.7.18; Rebuilt as F5835 7.8.18

A7938 10 TDS Harling Road by 6.18 - 8.18; 12 Sqn Germany 1920

A7939 (RAF 3a) At 2 AAP Hendon 3.6.18, Reallotted from Air Ministry for HQ Communications Flight to EF; 1 ASD to 18 Sqn 18.6.18; Left on raid 07.25, shot down by AA 09.40 14.7.18 (2/Lt D Mallett & 2/Lt JS Burn both PoW)

A7940 Recd Rec Pk ex UK for IF 9.11.18; 3 AD 9.11.18; 2 ASD, crashed 1.12.18; 6 AI to 57 Sqn 14.12.18; On mail flight crashed into trees in mist 6.3.19 (Lt FO Thornton & Lt PS Burnay both killed)

A7941 (Eagle VIII) 1 (S)ARD Farnborough by 3.4.18, allotted to E 1c for Dover-Dunkirk; Dunkirk Naval Wing 4.4.18; 217 Sqn W/E 25.4.18; Damaged in enemy air raid 5/6.6.18; Anti-submarine patrol, combat with 8 enemy seaplanes nr Zeebrugge, Brandenburg W.29 seaplane crashed in sea, shared A7683 19.40 29.7.18 (Lt RG Shaw & Lt UGA Tonge); still 217 Sqn 31.7.18; 4 ASD by 9.18; 2 SS Richborough 15.9.18; 217 Sqn by 28.9.18; Recd Rec Pk ex UK by 11.11.18

A7942 (Eagle VIII) 1 (S)ARD Farnborough by 3.4.18, allotted to E.1c for Dover-Dunkirk; Dunkirk Naval Wing 4.4.18; England to Rep Pk 1 ASD 11.4.18; 2 AI to 55 Sqn 17.5.18; On recce attacked by three Fokker DVII one of which sent OOC Sarrebourg, own a/c badly damaged 14.20 7.9.18 (2/Lt DJ Waterous DFC & 2/Lt CL Rayment DFC); 3 ASD 7.9.18

A7943 (RAF 3a) At 8 AAP Lympne 10.4.18, allotted to EF

A7944 UK to 31 Wing AP Mesopotamia 7.10.18; WO there 28.8.19

A7945 (Eagle VIII) 1 (S)ARD Farnborough by 3.4.18, allotted to E 1c for Dover-Dunkirk; Dunkirk Naval Wing 4.4.18; Dover by 27.4.18; 217 Sqn by 15.5.18; With A7996 dropped 2x230-lb bombs each on U-boat escorted by 4 destroyers 15m NNW of Ostende 19.05 19.5.18; Monoplane seaplane apparently OOC 08.30 1.6.18 (Lt FE Bridges & G/L HG Groves); Bounced landing after raid, u/c collapsed, went on nose 23.6.18 (Lt AM Phillips & 2/AM G/L H Tourlamain); 4 ASD 25.6.18 - 25.10.18

A7946 No information

A7947 No information

A7948 31 TDS Fowlmere; 121 Sqn Narborough by 5.18

A7949 UK to 31 Wing AP Mesopotamia 28.9.18; WO there 28.8.19

A7950 (RAF 3a) Presentation Aircraft 'Ontario'. At 2 AAP Hendon 30.3.18, allotted to EF; England to Rec Pk 21.4.18; Rep Pk 1 ASD 24.4.18; SOC 25.4.18

A7951 Arr Rec Pk ex UK 10.11.18; 2 AI to 57 Sqn 1.12.18 to at least 1.19

A7952 125 Sqn Fowlmere, lost speed on turn, sideslipped, dive in 28.6.18 (2/Lt HA Heritage killed)

A7953 to A7956 No information

A7957 (RAF 3a) At Makers 11.12.17, allotted to EF; Rep Pk 2 ASD 14.1.18 from Makers in case; 2 AI 24.2.18; 49 Sqn 8.3.18; 4 ASD and on to Rec Pk 2.4.18 (exchanged for D.H.9);1 AI 4.6.18; 18 Sqn 29.6.18; Scout OOC Vitry-Quierry La Motte 07.35 28.7.18 (Lt E Peskett & 2/Lt W Clark); Shot up in combat, FL nr Albert 25.8.18 (Lt WB Hogg OK & 2/Lt WE Baldwin DoW); Rep Pk 1 ASD 29.8.18; SOC 31.8.18 NWR

A7958 No information

A7959 (RAF 3a) At Makers 11.12.17, allotted to EF: Rep Pk 2 ASD 14.1.18 from Makers in case; Rep Pk 2 ASD to 2 AI 10.5.18; 1 AI 17.5.18; 18 Sqn 1.6.18; Landed in heavy storm with bad visibility, hit ridge, overturned 10.7.18 (2/Lt FC Edwardes & Sgt Mech LG Vredenburg OK); Rep Pk 1 ASD 11.7.18; Rebuilt as F5834 7.8.18

A7960 No information

A7961 No information

A7962 (Eagle VIII) 11 TDS Old Sarum by 29.5.18; To Eastbourne 26.6.18

A7963 Arr Rec Pk ex UK by 11.11.18; 6AI to 57 Sqn 12.3.19

A7964 (Eagle VI) 1 (S)ARD Farnborough by 2.5.18, allotted to EF; Rec Pk to 2 AI 9.6.18; 205 Sqn 12.6.18; Hit on ground by D9234 landing 11.8.18; Fokker DVII OOC W of St.Quentin 18.40 7.9.18 (2/Lt HF Taylor & 2/Lt J Golding); Fokker DVII OOC St.Quentin 17.50 15.9.18 (2/Lt HF Taylor & 2/Lt HS Mullen); Hit in raid on Busigny (pilot OK & 2/Lt HS Mullen wounded); 2 ASD 23.9.18; Rebuilt as H6858 3.10.18

A7965 44 TS Waddington by 2.18; 110 Sqn Sedgeford by 2.18

A7966 No information

A7967 (Eagle VII) At 1 (S)ARD 17.6.18; Allotted to EF; 2 AI to 25 Sqn 2.7.18; Turned over after heavy landing 20.7.18 (Lt AE Hulme & Sgt WB Gray OK); Rep Pk 2 ASD SOC 27.7.18 NWR

A7968 (Eagle VI) At Makers 11.1.18, allotted to EF; Rep Pk 2 ASD 2.2.18 from Makers in case; 2 AI to 25 Sqn 31.3.18; Damaged in heavy landing 28.5.18 (Lt AE Hulme & Cpl T Ramsden); Rebuilt as F5829 25.6.18

A7969 (Eagle VIII) 1 (S)ARD Farnborough by 25.5.18 for Dunkirk; Dover W/E 1.6.18; 4 ASD by 6.18; 217 Sqn 18.6.18; Badly shot about 22.7.18 (Capt DW Davies & Sgt GI White); Crashed on TO, badly damaged 22.8.18 (2/Lt LH Nesbitt & 2/Lt WA Spranklin both unhurt); 4 ASD 23.8.18; 2 SS Richborough 15.9.18; Rebuilt as H6858 3.10.18

A7970 (Eagle VIII) 44 TS Waddington 11.17 - 12.17; England to Rec Pk 3.10.18; 5 AI 7.10.18; 55 Sqn 24.12.18; Still at 55 Sqn 25.1.19, its only a/c then and unserviceable; 57 Sqn, on mail flight to Spa lost way and FL in Holland 1.3.19 (2/Lt HC Pendle)

A7971 (Eagle VIII) 1 Comm Sqn Kenley from/by 18.5.19 - @23.5.19

A7972 44 TS by Waddington 11.17; Rec Pk to 2 AI 6.8.18; 3 ASD 7.8.18; 55 Sqn 8.8.18; Shot down in combat with EAs in raid on Thionville Sidings 30.8.18 (2/Lt TH Laing & 2/Lt TFL Myring both killed)

A7973 (Eagle VII) Arr Rec Pk ex UK 23.8.18; 2 AI and on to 3 ASD 27.8.18; 55 Sqn 30.8.18; CW 21.10.18; 6 AP to 3 ASD 29.10.18

A7974 10 TDS Harling Road by 7.18

A7975 (RAF 3a) At 2 AAP Hendon 28.2.18, allotted to EF; England to Rec Pk 16.3.18; 1 AI 17.3.18; 18 Sqn

20.3.18; Pfalz in flames Estaires 20.15 20.5.18 (2/Lt G Leitch & Capt D Gale); Left 19.05 for bombing raid in 1st Army area, shot up in combat, landed OK 20.45 25.5.18 (2/Lt G Leitch & Capt D Gale OK); Rep Pk 1 ASD 26.5.18; Rebuilt as F5837 25.6.18

A7976 (Eagle V) At Makers 11.1.18, allotted to EF; Rep Pk 1 ASD to 1 AI 16.2.18; 2 AI 20.3.18; 5N Sqn 24.3.18; Left 09.35 for raid on Foucaucourt, FTR 28.3.18 (FSL JG Carroll & AGL GE Daffey both killed)

A7977 & A7978 No information

A7979 (Eagle VIII) At 8 AAP Lympne by 10.8.18; Arr Rec Pk ex UK 15.8.18; 3 ASD 17.8.18; 55 Sqn 17.8.18; 3 ASD 7.9.18; 55 Sqn 27.9.18; 3 ASD 27.9.18

A7980 (RAF 3a) 104 Sqn Andover, spun in off flat turn at 150ft 28.2.18 (2/Lt AA Gerow killed)

A7981 (RAF 3a) At 2 AAP Hendon 23.2.18, allotted to EF; England to Rec Pk 15.3.18; 1 AI 21.3.18; 18 Sqn 26.3.18; Casualty Report 31.7.18 says m/c badly strained and in poor condition, unfit for further service in the field; To Rec Pk and on to 8 AAP Lympne 8.8.18

A7982 (Eagle VIII) Arr Rec Pk ex UK for IF 21.8.18; to 2 AI and on to 3 ASD 23.8.18; 55 Sqn 5.10.18; TOC 6 AP 2.11.18; 3 ASD 11.11.18

A7983 46 TS Catterick by 15.1.18

A7984 (RAF 3a) At 2 AAP Hendon 23.2.18, allotted to EF; England to Rec Pk 15.3.18; 1 AI 21.3.18; 18 Sqn 26.3.18; EA OOC smoking Quiery La Motte-Vitry, shared A8049 20.50 1.6.18 (Lt RC Bennett & Lt PW Anderson); On engine test, crashed when RH wheel of u/c collapsed 7.6.18 (Lt RC Bennett & Lt PW Anderson OK); Rep Pk 1 ASD 8.6.18; Rebuilt as F6000 12.7.18

A7985 (Eagle VII) 44 TS Waddington by 11.17 - @28.2.18; 1 (S)ARD Farnborough by 1.5.18, allotted to EF "rebuilt m/c"; Rec Pk by 1.6.18; 2 AI to 205 Sqn 6.6.18; EF, FL nr aerodrome 4.7.18 (Lt RLMcK Barbour & 2/Lt JH Preston); Pfalz DIII in flames between Marcelcave and the lines 20.00 31.7.18 (Lt RLMcK Barbour & 2/Lt JH Preston); COL, u/c collapsed 29.8.18 (2/Lt FF Anslow & AM WJ Cleverley); COL 17.9.18 (2/Lt AN Hyde & 2/Lt WW Harrison unhurt); to 2 ASD; SOC 20.9.18

A7986 52 TS Catterick, lost control and spun in 25.1.18 (2/Lt JF Cheesman killed)

A7987 Rec Pk to 2 AI 19.8.18; 57 Sqn 21.8.18; Shot down in flames in combat with EAs 1m E of Marcoing about 12.00 16.9.18 (2/Lt JP Ferreira & 2/Lt LB Simmonds both killed)

A7988 Became *G-EAXH*

A7989 (RAF 3a) At 2 AAP Hendon 23.2.18, allotted to EF; England to Rec Pk 15.3.18; 1 AI 18.3.18; 18 Sqn 20.3.18; Albatros D crashed Bihucourt 17.30 26.3.18 (2/Lt HR Gould & Lt JM Brisbane); Scout crashed in flames Fresnes 09.15 30.3.18 (2/Lt LJ Balderson & Capt FTR Kempster); Left 12 noon for 2nd Army area, damaged by ground mg fire, FL, crashed 12.45 10.4.18 (2/Lt L Balderson & Lt G Bullen OK); Rep Pk 1 ASD 12.4.18; Rec Pk 15.4.18; England 20.4.18

A7990 (RAF 3a) At 2 AAP Hendon 23.2.18, allotted to EF; England to Rec Pk 16.3.18; 2 AI and on to 18 Sqn 17.3.18; Scout in flames and another OOC Estaires, shared A7859, A7998 & A8000 10.25 12.4.18 (Lt FJ Morgan & Sgt MV Kilroy); In action 30.5.18 (Lt J Mellish OK & Sgt G Braithwaite wounded); Whilst bombing Erquinghem at 12.00, attacked by 14 EA, observer 2/Lt E Walker sent an EA on tail OOC then the pilot stalled the m/c and fired into another EA above which went vertically down OOC, on returning flattened out too soon and "pancaked" from 10-15 feet 31.5.18 (2/Lt J Waugh & 2/Lt E Walker OK); Rep Pk 1 ASD 4.6.18 SOC 6.6.18 NWR

A7991 (RAF 3a)) At 2 AAP Hendon 11.3.18, allotted to EF; England to Rec Pk 19.3.18; 1 AI 3.4.18; 18 Sqn 10.4.18; FL due to engine seizing 11.4.18 (2/Lt LJ Balderson & Lt G Bullen OK); Rep Pk 1 ASD 13.4.18 (unfit); SOC 23.4.18

A7992 Dover by 10.18; Pool of Pilots 5.10.18

A7993 (375hp Eagle) 2 AAP Hendon to Medical Flt Hendon 2.4.18; AES Martlesham Heath 24.4.18 (experimental 250hp Rolls-Royce engine, sparking plug tests); Airco Hendon W/E 7.12.18 (convtd to D.H.4A with ungeared Eagle); AES Martlesham Heath by 31.12.18 (performance and climb, also KLG plugs); Left W/E 11.8.19

A7994 11 TDS Old Sarum by 3.7.18

A7995 (Eagle) photo at Hendon

A7996 (Eagle VIII) 1 (S)ARD Farnborough by 23.2.18; AAP Dover W/E 9.3.18 (erected in Repair Shop 13.3.18); 17N Sqn 20.3.18; Became 217 Sqn 1.4.18; With A7945 dropped 4x230-lb bombs on U-boat escorted by 4 destroyers 15m NNW of Ostende 19.05 19.5.18; 1 Pfalz sent down vertically OOC smoking between Zeebrugge & Ostende 20.15 17.6.18 (Lt AM Phillips & Sgt GI White); EF on TO, damaged 30.7.18 (2/Lt HA Pank & 2/Lt EM Ball both unhurt); to 4 ASD, to at least 25.10.18

A7997 Presentation Aircraft 'Gold Coast No.1'.

A7998 (RAF 3a) At 2 AAP Hendon 11.3.18, allotted to EF: England to Rec Pk 20.3.18; 1 AI 29.3.18; 18 Sqn 31.3.18; Scout in flames and another OOC Estaires, shared A7859, A7990 & A8000 10.25 12.4.18 (2/Lt AC Atkey MC & Sgt H Hammond); Photographic mission, hit by AA, crashed, wrecked Nieppe Forest 18.00-19.00 14.5.18 (Lt FJ Morgan DoW 16.5.18 & 2/Lt STJ Helmore killed), m/c total wreck and unsalvable

A7999 2 AAP Hendon 12.3.18, allotted to EF; Rec Pk 20.3.18; 1 AI 23.3.18; 18 Sqn 26.3.18; COL, wrecked and burnt 9.4.18 (2/Lt D Gordon OK & Cpl Lewis injured); Rep Pk 1 ASD 13.4.18; SOC 20.4.18

A8000 (RAF 3a) At 2 AAP Hendon 12.3.18, allotted to EF; England to Rec Pk 19.3.18; 1 AI 29.3.18; 18 Sqn 30.3.18; Scout in flames and another OOC Estaires, shared A7859, A7990 & A7998 10.25 12.4.18 (Capt AG Waller & 2/Lt J Waugh); White, red & yellow Pfalz OOC Phalempin 11.50 9.5.18 (2/Lt HR Gould & Capt MSE Archibald); Badly shot up in combat, FL in ploughed field nr Houdain 12.00 25.5.18 (2/Lt J Waugh & 2/Lt F Walker OK); Rep Pk 1 ASD 28.5.18; Rebuilt as F5839 25.6.18

A8001 (RAF 3a) At 2 AAP Hendon 12.3.18, allotted to EF; England to Rec Pk 17.3.18; 1 AI 21.3.18; 18 Sqn 22.3.18; Engine seized, crashed 25.3.18 (Lt FJ Morgan & Capt GG Roberts MC OK); Rep Pk 1 ASD 27.3.18; SOC 14.4.18

A8002 (Eagle) Presentation Aircraft 'Presented by The Colony of Mauritius No.2'. 1 SoN&BD Stonehenge, crashed nr Bristol 19.2.18 (2/Lt ET Evans killed)

A8003 UK to 31 Wing AP Mesopotamia 7.2.19

A8004 UK to 31 Wing AP Mesopotamia 2.8.18; WO at 63 Sqn 4.4.19

A8005 UK to 31 Wing AP Mesopotamia 2.8.18; WO at 63 Sqn 23.7.19

A8006 (Eagle VIII) 1 (S)ARD Farnborough by 23.2.18; AAP Dover W/E 9.3.18 (erected in Repair Shop); 217 Sqn 25.4.18; Damaged in enemy air raid 5/6.6.18; Crashed on TO, badly damaged 15.7.18 (Lt SJ Saunders & 2/Lt WA Spranklin both slightly injured); 4 ASD 16.7.18; 217 Sqn by 9.18; Crashed 9.18; 4 ASD 14.9.18 - 25.10.18

A8007 UK to 31 Wing AP Mesopotamia 2.18; WO there 10.6.19

A8008 UK to 31 Wing AP Mesopotamia 7.2.19; WO at 63 Sqn 3.12.19

A8009 UK to 31 Wing AP Mesopotamia 7.2.19; WO there 7.11.19

A8010 (RAF 3a) Presentation Aircraft 'North Queensland Grazier'. At 2 AAP Hendon 10.4.18, allotted to EF; England to Rec Pk 22.4.18; 1 AI 1.5.18;18 Sqn 15.5.18; Returning from raid on Valenciennes, Albatros D OOC Douai, shared A7833 & A8021 12.00 19.5.18 (2/Lt GWF Darvill & Lt EA Collis); Hit by shrapnel in 11.00 raid on Laventie 15.6.18 (Lt RT Minors OK & Lt LE Lyell wounded); On reconnaissance with A7799, attacked by six Pfalz DIIIs at Hulluch, one of which broke up 20.45 17.6.18 (Capt DA Stewart & Capt LI Collins); On photographic flight over Lille attacked by a Pfalz DIII which was sent down OOC 20.20 19.6.18 (Lt A Pickin & Sgt WA Dyke DCM); Landed heavily, u/c collapsed 7.7.18 (Lt RT Minors & Sgt Mech WA Dyke DCM OK); Rep Pk 1 ASD 9.7.18; Rebuilt as F6004 7.8.18

A8011 1 SoN&BD Stonehenge by 3.18

A8012 (Eagle VIII) 1 (S)ARD Farnborough by 5.18; 491 Flt

D.H.4 A8044 on floats for trials at Felixstowe 18.10.18. (via Jim Oughton)

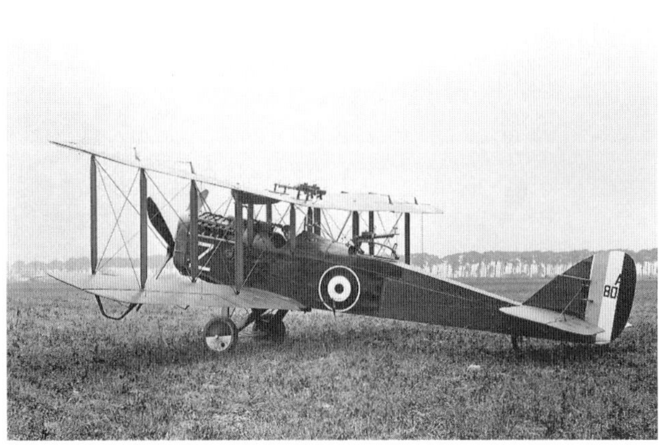

D.H.4 A8025 'Z' of No.202 Squadron. (J.M.Bruce/G.S.Leslie collection)

D.H.4 A8032 of No.1 Communications Squadron, Kenley. (via Terry Treadwell)

D.H.4 A8042 at No.4 School of Military Aeronautics, University of Toronto in 1918. (J.M.Bruce/G.S.Leslie collection)

55 Sqn D.H.4 A8073 brought down 26.6.18 at Hagenau by Ltn W.Rosenstein of Kest 1b. (J.M.Bruce/G.S.Leslie collection)

D.H.4 'B' of No.27 Squadron being bombed up at Serny on 17.2.18. In the background is a Nieuport 27 of No.32 Squadron.

Dover by 25.5.18 (W/E 1.6.18); 217 Sqn 1.6.18; Damaged in enemy air raid 5/6.6.18; 4 ASD by 9.6.18; 202 Sqn by 3.10.18; Pilot's gun muzzle attachment hit propeller, FL beach La Panne 5.10.18 (Lt NH Witter & 2/Lt AEE Lee); 4 ASD 5.10.18 - 25.10.18

A8013 (Eagle VIII) 1 (S)ARD Farnborough by 5.18; 491 Flt Dover by 25.5.18 (W/E 1.6.18); 217 Sqn 7.6.18; With A7773 dropped 2x230-lb bombs on U-boat nr CI Buoy, East Dyke 29.6.18 (Lt RM Berthe); Left 17.00 for bombing raid on Zeebrugge, shot down OOC by EA, BU in air 5m N of Ostende 19.45 30.6.18 (Lt CJ Moir & Sgt Mech G/L EE Hunnisett killed)

A8014 (RAF 3a) At 8 AAP Lympne 10.4.18, allotted to EF

A8015 No information

A8016 (Eagle VII) 8 AAP Lympne for EF by 3.4.18; Rec Pk 12.4.18; 2 AI 17.4.18; 25 Sqn 21.4.18; Overshot landing, crashed 22.7.18 (Lt HC Bryant & 2/Lt EF Boyce both unhurt); SOC 27.7.18; Rebuilt as F6222 31.7.18

A8017 (Eagle VII) 44 TS Waddington by 2.18; At 1 (S)ARD 17.6.18, allotted to EF; 2 AI to 57 Sqn 14.7.18; Fokker DVII dest Bourlon Wood 09.55 4.9.18 (Sgt Mech DE Edgley & Sgt JH Bowler); Fokker DVII OOC W of Bourlon 18.45 21.9.18 (Lt FO Thornton & 2/Lt HT Barnett); Fokker DVII OOC Cambrai 18.00 27.9.18 shared F2635 (Lt FO Thornton & 2/Lt FG Craig); 2 AI 30.11.18

A8018 (RAF 3a) At 8 AAP Lympne 10.4.18, allotted to EF; Rec Pk to 1 AI 17.5.18; 18 Sqn 26.5.18; Scout in flames and scout in vertical dive Bac St Maur 20.30-20.50 30.5.18 (Capt AG Waller & Lt BJ Blackett); Petrol pipe broke, FL in thick mist on heavy ground 29.6.18 (Capt HR Gould MC & Sgt LG Vredenburg OK); Rep Pk 1 ASD 30.6.18

A8019 (RAF 3a) At 2 AAP Hendon 8.4.18, allotted to EF; England to Rec Pk 25.4.18; Rec Pk to 1 AI 8.5.18; Left 1 AI for 18 Sqn, lost flying speed, crashed 25.5.18 (2/Lt G Leitch & Capt D Gale); Rep Pk 1 ASD 28.5.18; Rebuilt as F5840 25.6.18

A8020 (Eagle VII) At 1 (S)ARD 27.6.18, allotted to EF; Rec Pk to 2 AI 28.7.18; 3 ASD 29.7.18; 55 Sqn 31.7.18; 3 ASD 4.9.18; 55 Sqn 5.10.18; 2 ASD 16.1.19

A8021 (RAF 3a) At 2 AAP Hendon 10.4.18, allotted to EF; England to Rec Pk 8.5.18; 1 AI 11.5.18; 18 Sqn 16.5.18; Returning from raid on Valenciennes, Albatros D OOC Douai, shared A7833 & A8010 12.00 19.5.18 (Capt AG Waller & 1/Lt LK Ayres USAS); Landed in thick mist and crashed into sunken road 29.6.18 (Lt FM Macfarland & Capt D Gale OK); Rep Pk 2 ASD 30.6.18; SOC 9.7.18; Rebuilt as F6002 25.7.18

A8022 (Eagle VIII) 1 (S)ARD Farnborough by 5.18; 491 Flt Dover by 25.5.18 (W/E 1.6.18); 4 ASD Audembert 7.6.18; 217 Sqn 8.6.18; Broke wing landing 15.6.18 (Capt DW Davies & Sgt GJ Wilson); Pfalz DIII shot down OOC 17.6.18 (Capt DW Davies & Sgt G/L GI White); With A7867 dropped 2x230-lb bombs on U-boat 2m off Ostende Piers 27.6.18; COL 28.6.18 (Lt TW Whittaker & G/L GI White OK); 4 ASD 29.6.18; retd 217 Sqn; COL after A/S patrol, wings and u/c damaged 9.18 (Lt TW Whittaker & Sgt G/L GI White unhurt); 4 ASD 16.9.18 - @25.10.18

A8023 (Eagle VIII) 1 (S)ARD Farnborough by 5.18; 491 Flt Dover by 25.5.18 (W/E 1.6.18); 4 ASD Audembert to 217 Sqn 13.6.18; Shot down by EA, last seen in water 5m off Ostende 06.00 28.6.18 (Lt AE Bingham & Lt LJ Smith both PoW)

A8024 (RAF 3a) At 2 AAP Hendon 10.4.18, allotted to EF

A8025 (Eagle VIII) 1 (S)ARD Farnborough by 5.18; 491 Flt Dover by 25.5.18; 4 ASD 6.18; 202 Sqn ('Z') 6.6.18; Attacked by 5 EA off Middelkerke, damaged, landed safely 27.6.18 (Lt LH Pearson & 2/Lt E Darby DSM unhurt); Repaired on Sqn; Left 06.35, lost in storm over enemy lines, last seen nr Engel Dump 28.9.18 (Capt AV Bowater & Lt DL Melvin both PoW)

A8026 (RAF 3a) At 8 AAP Lympne 15.3.18, allotted to EF; England to Rec Pk 1.4.18; 1 AI 1.5.18; 18 Sqn 6.5.18;

bearings owing to darkness (21.20), tried to land in field, struck ridge and overturned 22.5.18 (2/Lt A Green & Lt F Loly OK): Rep Pk 1 ASD 25.5.18; SOC 26.5.18

A8027 (RAF 3a) At 8 AAP Lympne 15.3.18, allotted to EF; Rec Pk 31.3.18; 1 AI 15.5.18; 18 Sqn 26.5.18; FL at 13 Sqn 31.7.18 (2/Lt H Cardwell OK & Capt D Gale wounded); A/c returned to sqn 3.8.18; FL due to engine over heating, hit corn stack and overturned 22.8.18 (2/Lt H Cardwell OK & Lt G Thompson MC injured; Rep Pk 1ASD 25.8.18; SOC 28.8.18

A8028 (Eagle V) At Makers 30.1.18, allotted to EF; Rep Pk 2 ASD 23.2.18 from Makers in case; 2 AI to 25 Sqn 31.3.18; COL 30.6.18 (Lt CEH Allen & 2/Lt HG Wepener OK); Rep Pk 2 ASD SOC wrecked 20.7.18; Rebuilt as F6207

A8029 (Eagle VI) Deld 2 AAP Hendon by 9.5.18, allotted to EF; Rec Pk to 2 AI 13.6.18; 205 Sqn 18.6.18; Pfalz DIII shot down Bray 19.57 5.7.18; Pfalz DIII OOC La Flaguye 10.15 30.7.18 (both Lt EH Johnson & 2/Lt AR Crosthwaite); Pfalz DIII OOC Péronne, also attacked by D8387 c.08.00 11.8.18 (Lt EH Johnson & Lt HF Taylor); Casualty Report 17.8.18 says unfit for further service in the field, longerons strained; Rep Pk 2 ASD 21.8.18; To Rep Pk 1ASD; SOC 17.9.18, new number H7125 allotted for reconstruction

A8030 (Eagle V) Deld 2 AAP Hendon by 9.5.18, allotted to EF; England to Rec Pk 21.5.18; 2 AI 22.5.18; 205 Sqn 28.5.18; Casualty Report 27.6.18 says unfit; 2 AI to Rep Pk 2 ASD 2.7.18 (poor performance); Rebuilt as F6187 12.7.18

A8031 (Eagle VIII) Rec Pk to 2 AI and on to 57 Sqn 17.7.18 but returned to 2 AI the same day; 25 Sqn 26.7.18; Left 09.35 on photo recce, FTR, retd later 17.9.18 (Lt JH Latchford & 2/Lt J Pullar OK); Left 07.45 for recce Mons, FTR 27.9.18 (Lt DH Hazell & 2/Lt DB Robertson both killed)

A8032 (Eagle VIII, later RAF 3a) 1 (S)ARD Farnborough by 25.5.18 for Dunkirk; Yarmouth by 29.6.18 - 10.8.18; AZP, shot down *L70* in flames off Wells-next-the-Sea, nr the Blakeney Overfalls buoy and damaged *L65*, a/c then landed Sedgeford 5.8.18 (Mjr E Cadbury & Capt R Leckie); 534 Flt 273 Sqn Covehithe by 8.18 - 5.11.18; 'B' Flt 1 Comm Sqn Kenley 6.19; 24 Sqn? ('C') 1920 (visited Hawkinge)

A8033 (Eagle VIII) 1 (S)ARD Farnborough by 25.5.18 - 31.5.18 for Dunkirk (NTU?); Covehithe by 1.7.18 - 18.8.18; Became 534 Flt 273 Sqn Covehithe by 8.18 - 10.18; 534 Flt 273 Sqn Burgh Castle, 2 HACPs 9.11.18; 534 Flt 273 Sqn Covehithe, HACP 10.11.18; still Covehithe 27.11.18

A8034 At 2 AAP Hendon 21.1.18, allotted to EF; England to Rec Pk 28.2.18; 2 AI 11.3.18; 49 Sqn 12.3.18; 4 ASD and on to Rec Pk 2.4.18; 1 AI 2.5.18; 18 Sqn 7.5.18; Albatros D crashed nr Douai 11.40 21.5.18 (2/Lt GWF Darvill & 2/AM LG Vredenburg); On landing swerved sharply to avoid a Bristol Fighter, u/c collapsed, crashed 1.6.18 (Lt GWF Darvill & Sgt Mech H Hammond OK); Rep Pk 1 ASD 3.6.18; SOC, rebuilt as F6001 29.7.18

A8035 (RAF 3a) At 8 AAP Lympne 15.3.18, allotted to EF; Rec Pk 29.3.18; 18 Sqn 30.3.18; Ran over shell hole on take off, swerved and struck plough 8.4.18 (2/Lt GWF Darvill injured & Sgt H Wilkes OK); Rep Pk 1 ASD 13.4.18; SOC 23.4.18

A8036 UK to 31 Wing AP Mesopotamia 7.2.19

A8037 (RAF 3a) At 2 AAP Hendon 21.1.18, allotted to EF; England to Rec Pk 15.2.18; 1 AI 11.3.18; Rep Pk 1 ASD 18.3.18; SOC 19.3.18

A8038 (RAF 3a) At Makers 23.1.18, allotted to EF; England to Rep Pk 1 ASD 16.2.18; 1 AI 6.3.18; 18 Sqn 8.3.18; Pfalz crashed 12.55 15.3.18 (2/Lt DA Stewart & Sgt AOA Pollard); Aviatik C crashed Loupart Wood S of Bapaume 17.15 25.3.18 (2/Lt DA Stewart MC & Capt LI Collins); Albatros D crashed W of Douai 11.40 28.5.18 (Capt DA Stewart MC & Capt LI Collins MC); Scout DD smoking, Pfalz BU, Scout OOC Neuve Chapelle-Richebourg St Vaast 13.00 30.5.18 (Capt DA Stewart MC & Lt W Miller); Misjudged landing, landed in corn and turned on nose 6.7.18 (2/Lt D Mallett & 2/Lt S Burn OK); Rep Pk 1 ASD 7.7.18; SOC 10.7.18 NWR

A8039 (Eagle VIII) 1 (S)ARD Farnborough by 25.5.18 - 31.5.18 for Dunkirk (NTU?); Yarmouth by 29.6.18; AZP 5.8.18 (Lt RE Keys & AM AT Harman); AZP from Burgh Castle, FL nr Louth 6.8.18 (2 crew unhurt)

A8040 (Eagle VIII) 1 (S)ARD Farnborough by 25.5.18 - 31.5.18 for Dunkirk (NTU?); Yarmouth by 25.6.18 - 17.9.18; 'B' Flt 1 Comm Sqn Kenley 6.19

A8041 (RAF 3a) At Makers 23.1.18, allotted to EF; Makers to Rep Pk 2 ASD 12.2.18; 2 AI to 1 AI 3.4.18; 18 Sqn 11.4.18; Hit by shell at 14,000 feet during raid on Sainghin 12.5.18, FL at 5 Sqn 12.5.18 (Lt HR Gould OK & Capt MSE Archibald DoW); A/c back at sqn 13.5.18; Fokker Dr1 OOC Neuf Berquin 13.30 16.5.18 (Capt AG Waller & Capt FTR Kempster); Casualty Report 1.6.18 says three ply in bad condition and a heavy landing had caused it to split badly; 1 ASD 2.6.18 (Rec Pk?); Flown to England 4.6.18

A8042 Free issue to Canada; 4 School of Military Aeronautics, University of Ottawa 1918

A8043 (RAF 3a) At Makers 30.1.18, allotted to EF but this cancelled 8.2.18; At 2 AAP Hendon 15.2.18, Reallotted to EF; England to Rec Pk 27.2.18; 1 AI 5.3.18; 18 Sqn 6.3.18; Left 14.10, attacked by EAs, crashed Wavrin 16.3.18 (2/Lt RA Mayne wounded POW & Lt VW Scott MC killed) (claimed by Oblt Auffarth, Jasta 29, his 12th victory)

A8044 (Eagle VIII) 1 (S)ARD Farnborough by 25.5.18 - 31.5.18 for Dunkirk (NTU?); Covehithe ('B') by 9.7.18; AZP 5.8.18 (Lt WR Plaskitt & Sgt Keeling); Trials at Felixstowe fitted with floats 18.10.18; Became 534 Flt 273 Sqn Covehithe 8.18 - 10.18

A8045 (RAF 3a) At Makers 30.1.18, allotted to EF but this cancelled 8.2.18; At 8 AAP Lympne 15.3.18, Reallotted to EF; Rec Pk 31.3.18; Rec Pk to 1 AI 7.4.18; 18 Sqn 12.4.18; FL due to pressure trouble, ran into camouflaged ditch 20.4.18 (2/Lt J Waugh & Lt PW Anderson OK); Adv Salvage to Rep Pk 1 ASD 23.4.18; SOC 27.4.18

A8046 (Eagle VIII) 1 (S)ARD Farnborough by 25.5.18; AAP Dover 14.6.18; 4 ASD by 7.18; 217 Sqn 2.7.18; Crashed on TO 8.8.18 (Lt SW Whittaker & 2/Lt PJ Holmes); Crashed on TO, badly damaged 9.10.18 (Lt SW Whittaker & 2/Lt PJ Holmes both unhurt); 4 ASD by 25.10.18; Deleted 31.10.18 DBR

A8047 (RAF 3a) At 8 AAP Lympne 10.4.18, allotted to EF; Rec Pk 17.5.18; 1 AI 30.5.18; 18 Sqn 31.5.18; Crashed landing in thick mist on rough ground 29.6.18 (Lt E Peskett & 2/Lt W Clark OK); Rep Pk 1 ASD 30.6.18; Rebuilt as F6003 25.7.18

A8048 (RAF 3a) At Makers 30.1.18, allotted to EF; England to Rep Pk 4.3.18; 1 AI 21.3.18; 18 Sqn 2.4.18; Hit by ground fire 10.4.18 (Capt A Brooke and Capt E Powell both wounded); Scout OOC S of Laventie 11.45 5.6.18; Pfalz OOC Lens 20.00 10.6.18 (both Lt RC Bennett & Lt PW Anderson); In action 27.6.18 (Lt R Anderson OK & Lt PW Anderson wounded); In raid on Cantin Dump 8.8.18 (1/Lt TE Kearney USAS OK & Sgt Mech E Homer wounded); Casualty Report 13.8.18 says in poor condition and badly strained; Rep Pk 1 ASD 16.8.18 (unfit); SOC 18.8.18 NWR

A8049 (RAF 3a) At Makers 30.1.18, allotted to EF; 2 AI to 1 AI 16.4.18; 18 Sqn 21.4.18; EA OOC smoking Quiery La Motte-Vitry, shared A7984 20.50 1.6.18 (Lt J Smith & Sgt C Lines); Casualty Report 24.7.18 says unfit for further service in the field; 1 AI 28.7.18; Rec Pk 30.7.18; 8 AAP Lympne 2.8.18

A8050 (Eagle VIII) 4 ASD by 7.18; 217 Sqn 30.7.18; With A7772 dropped 4 bombs each on U-boat 3m NNE of Middelkerke 12.8.18; Test flight, COL, badly damaged 17.8.18 (Lt CW Bragg & 2/Lt GC Paish unhurt); to 4 ASD; 2 SS Richborough 15.9.18

A8051 (Eagle VIII) Rec Pk to 2 AI 4.8.18; 25 Sqn 30.8.18; Photo recce, observer wounded in combat, pilot landed to assist observer to hospital, he left the engine ticking over, two orderlies were asked to fill the observer's cockpit with ballast, whilst doing so the throttle accidentally opened, the m/c ran for 50 yards then turned over 25.9.18 (Capt S Jones OK & 2/Lt J Pullar wounded)

A8052 (Eagle VIII) Rec Pk to 2 AI 22.7.18; 25 Sqn 25.8.18; Left on recce to Maubeuge 15.15, FTR 3.10.18 (Sgt FP Clarke & Lt EWAG Middlecote both killed)

A8053 (RAF 3a) At Makers 23.1.18, allotted to EF; Makers to Rep Pk 2 ASD 18.2.18; 2 AI to England, crashed 3.4.18 (Lt CC Wood); Dismantled Dover and sent Farnborough, arr 11.4.18 for WOC

A8054 (Eagle VI) At Makers 23.1.18, allotted to EF; England to Rep Pk 1 ASD 9.3.18; 2 ASD 25.3.18; 25 Sqn 31.3.18; Left 06.35 for photographic mission in Bruges area, FTR 1.7.18 (Lt GE Dobeson & 2/Lt JE Pilling both killed)

A8055 (Eagle VIII) Rec Pk to 2 AI 22.7.18; 25 Sqn 31.7.18; 6 AI 13.5.19

A8056 (Eagle VIII) 217 Sqn by 9.8.18; Landed in cornfield nr aerodrome and smashed 16.8.18 (Capt DW Davies & Sgt GJ Wilson); Badly shot about in raid on Thourout, FL Morshoek, nr Abincourt 28.9.18 (Capt DW Davies & Sgt GJ Wilson); Flying again 4.10.18; Hit by ground fire 7.10.18 (Pilot unhurt & Sgt G/L GI White wounded); 98 Sqn 15.3.19 (arr 17.3.19); 1 ASD 25.3.19

A8057 (Eagle VIII) England to Rec Pk 8.8.18; 2 AI 11.8.18; 25 Sqn 5.9.18; Left on recce to Maubeuge 06.35, FTR 4.10.18 (Lt L Young killed & Sgt HE Whitehead died same day - as PoW?)

A8058 (Eagle VI) At Makers 30.1.18, allotted to EF; England to Rep Pk 14.3.18; 2 AI 25.3.18; 25 Sqn 27.3.18; FL due to bad weather, ran into bomb hole 20.4.18 (2/Lt FF Keen slightly injured & 2/Lt W Rudman MC OK); Adv Salvage to Rep Pk 1 ASD 22.4.18; SOC 27.4.18

A8059 (Eagle VIII) Deld 2 AAP Hendon 2.18; AAP Dover 23.2.18; 17N Sqn 5.3.18; Became 217 Sqn 1.4.18; With A7773 dropped 2x230-lb bombs each on U-boat 12m N of Zeebrugge 23.4.18; COL 5.5.18 (Lt JN Rutter & G/L HG Groves both unhurt); 4 ASD Guines 5.5.18 - 31.5.18; 4 ASD Audembert to 202 Sqn 17.7.18; Attacked by 5 EA, 1 sent down OOC Lissweghe 17.05 16.9.18 (Lt NH Witter & 2/Lt AEE Lee); 2-str (probably Rumpler) Zele-Termonde 13.05 30.10.18 (Lt NH Witter & 2/Lt AEE Lee); Crashed Zerkegen 10.12.18 (repaired locally); 98 Sqn 16.3.19; 1 ASD 18.3.19 (for 11 AP)

A8060 Arr Rec Pk ex UK for IF 19.8.18; to 2 AI and on to 3AD 23.8.18; 55 Sqn 23.8.18; WO 26.9.18 SOC

A8061 (Eagle VIII) 4 ASD by 8.18; 217 Sqn 25.8.18; FL in water just off beach nr La Panne 16.9.18 (2/Lt SJ Saunders & 2/Obs AM Turnbull USA both unhurt); 4 ASD 18.9.18 - 25.10.18

A8062 (RAF 3a) At Makers 30.1.18, allotted to EF; Rep Pk 2 ASD 25.2.18 from Makers in case; On ferry flight from 2 AI to 1 AI, engine cut out just after take off, attempted to turn, stalled and nosedived in, caught fire 3.4.18 (Lt W Russell killed & Capt HF Jenyns injured)

A8063 (Eagle VIII) Deld 2 AAP Hendon by 2.18; AAP Dover 24.2.18; 17N Sqn 13.3.18; Became 217 Sqn 1.4.18; While attempting to bomb enemy trawler spun in sea and wrecked 2½m N of Zeebrugge Mole 22.4.18 (Lt CF Parsons & AC1 G/L GS Gladwin captured by enemy trawler, PoW); Deleted 13.5.18

A8064 (RAF 3a) At Makers 30.1.18, allotted to EF; England to Rep Pk 1 ASD 11.3.18; 1 AI 12.4.18; 18 Sqn 13.4.18; Taking photographs over Aubers 14.00, attacked by five Pfalz one of which was sent down OOC 21.4.18 (2/Lt AC Atkey & Lt PW Anderson); Damaged when hit on the ground by 22 Sqn Bristol Fighter A7243 7.5.18; Rep Pk 1 ASD 9.5.18; SOC 11.5.18

A8065 (Eagle VIII) Deld 2 AAP Hendon by 2.18; AAP Dover 26.2.18; 17N Sqn 8.3.18; Became 217 Sqn 1.4.18; With A7846 dropped 2x230-lb bombs each on 4 destroyers 15m NNW Ostende 19.40 19.5.18; Attacked destroyer 21.5.18 (Lt GB Coward & PteI A/G SF Briggs); Left 02.35 for raid on Zeebrugge lock gates 28.5.18 (L/Col PFM Fellowes PoW wounded & Sgt FH Pritchard PoW) [credited Flgm Bieber of Seefrontstaffel]

A8066 (Eagle VIII) Deld 2 AAP Hendon by 2.18; AAP Dover 11.3.18; 17N Sqn 16.3.18; Became 217 Sqn 1.4.18; COL 22.4.18 (LM); 4 ASD Dunkirk by 25.5.18; 202 Sqn 15.9.18; FTR, last seen in storm over Nieuport 07.25 28.9.18 (Lt CR Moore & 2/Lt E Darby both PoW)

A8067 (Eagle VIII) Deld 2 AAP Hendon 2.18; AAP Dover 23.2.18; 17N Sqn 8.3.18; Became 217 Sqn 1.4.18; With A7934 dropped 2x230-lb bombs each on U-boat escorted by 4 destroyers 15m NNW Ostende 19.10 19.5.18; EF on TO, crashed into 2 aircraft 29.7.18 (Lt HS Matthews & Sgt E Farley); Repaired on Sqn; 98 Sqn 16.3.19; Rec Pk 18.3.19

A8068 (Eagle VI) At Makers 9.2.18, allotted to EF; England to Rep Pk 1 ASD 9.3.18; 2 AI 25.3.18; 57 Sqn 1.4.18; Photographic mission, in combat with 15 EA, shot up by Albatros W of Bapaume, damaged, COL 9.5.18 (Lt CM Powell & Sgt EEAG Bridger OK); Rep Pk 2 ASD 10.5.18; 2 AI 29.6.18; 57 Sqn 4.7.18; Crashed into stationary A7536 30.7.18 (Lt PWJ Timson & Lt AE Smith); Returning from raid engine cut out, FL in cornfield and wrecked 22.8.18 (Lt J Caldwell & Lt AM Barron OK); Rep Pk 2 ASD 23.8.18

An officer and a dog take an interest in the proceedings as a Scot handles the gun of a D.H.4 of No.18 Squadron in September 1917. (via Terry Treadwell)

A8069 (Eagle VI) At Makers 9.2.18, allotted to EF; England to Rep Pk 1 ASD 14.3.18; 2 ASD 25.3.18; 55 Sqn 29.3.18; Thionville raid 29.5.18 (Lt W Wild wounded & Lt CD Palmer OK); Tested after crash 9.6.18; 3 ASD 30.6.18; 55 Sqn ('E') 15.8.18; Shot up by EAs in raid on Thionville Sidings 30.8.18 (pilot OK & 2/Lt HTC Gompertz wounded); 3 ASD 30.8.18; 55 Sqn 30.10.18; 6 AP 19.11.18

A8070 (Eagle VII) At Makers 9.2.18, allotted to EF; At Rep Pk 2 ASD 1.4.18; 2 AI and on 57 Sqn 12.4.18; COL 15.5.18 (Lt TG Rhodes & Lt ED Spencer OK); Landed on one wheel, u/c collapsed, m/c wrecked 1.7.18 (Lt JMcC Lee & 2/Lt HS Musgrove OK); Rep Pk 2 ASD 3.7.18; SOC 11.7.18

A8071 (Eagle VII) At Makers 9.2.18, allotted to EF; England to Rep Pk 1 ASD 1.3.18; 2 ASD 23.3.18; 5N Sqn by 25.3.18; Became 205 Sqn 1.4.18; Triplane OOC Chaulnes Rly Stn 19.30 23.4.18 (Lt GE Siedle & Sgt CV Middleton); Shot about by AA, landed Bertangles 31.5.18 (Lt GE Siedle & Sgt CV Middleton unhurt); Rep Pk 2 ASD 1.6.18; Rebuilt as F6114 3.7.18

A8072 (Eagle VIII) 4 ASD by 8.18; 217 Sqn 19.8.18; 98 Sqn 6.3.19; 1 ASD 19.3.19

A8073 (Eagle VII) At Makers 9.2.18, allotted to EF; 2 ASD to 55 Sqn ('A') 25.3.18; Bombing raid on Karlsruhe, last seen in control S of Strasbourg landing in field N of Saverne 26.6.18 (2/Lt FFH Bryan & Sgt A Boocock both PoW) [Brought down at Hagenau by Ltn W Rosenstein, Kest 1b]

A8074 (Eagle VIII) Flown Lympne to 4 ASD Audembert 4.8.18; 217 Sqn by 14.8.18; TW by explosion while stationary on aerodrome 22.8.18; Wreckage to 4 ASD 23.8.18; 2 SS Richborough 15.9.18

A8075 (Eagle VII) At Makers 9.2.18, allotted to EF; 2 AI to 25 Sqn 27.3.18; Damaged in heavy landing 7.6.18 (Lt J Loupinsky & Sgt JR Wright); SOC Rep Pk 2 ASD 19.6.18

A8076 (RAF 3a) Presentation Aircraft 'Zanzibar No.6'. At Makers 30.1.18, allotted to EF but this cancelled 8.2.18; At 2 AAP Hendon 18.2.18, Reallotted to EF; England to Rec Pk 27.2.18; 1 AI 6.3.18; 18 Sqn 11.3.18; Scout OOC Avelin 12.00-13.00 15.3.18 (Capt AG Waller & Lt JM Brisbane); FL in heavy storm, overran and hit fence 30.3.18 (2/Lt P Harris & Cpl G Browne OK); Rep Pk 1 ASD 1.4.18; SOC 14.4.18

A8077 (Eagle VI) Presentation Aircraft 'Punjab No.4. Jind'. At 2 AAP Hendon 18.2.18, allotted to EF; England to Rec Pk 25.2.18; 1 AI 4.3.18; 25 Sqn 5.3.18; Hit shell hole making FL at disused aerodrome 11.3.18 (2/Lt AWP Cumming & 2/Lt VG Stanton OK); Rep Pk 2 ASD to Rep Pk 1 ASD by rail 2.4.18; SOC 14.4.18 NWR

A8078 (Eagle V) Presentation Aircraft 'Bombay No.1'; At 2 AAP Hendon 21.2.18, allotted to EF; England to Rec Pk 27.2.18; 2 AI 6.3.18; 25 Sqn 25.3.18; Left on bombing raid 12.15, shot up in combat with 10 EA, wounded observer managed to land a/c at Serny 21.4.18 (2/Lt JD Dingwall killed & Lt CM Sinclair wounded); SOC Rep Pk 1 ASD 25.4.18

A8079 (Eagle VIII) Deld 2 AAP Hendon by 3.18; AAP Dover 9.3.18; NAD Dunkirk 20.3.18; 4 ASD Guines 28.3.18; 202 Sqn by 7.4.18; Attacked by 5 Pfalz DIII over Donkerklok Battery, slightly damaged 27.6.18 (Capt J Robinson DFC uninjured & Lt FS Russell DSC slightly wounded); to 4 ASD; 202 Sqn 28.9.18; FL in mist on beach at low tide, crashed, DBR, salvaging 27.1.19 (2/Lt GC Cole & 2/Lt GP Muffey); WOC 6.2.19

A8080 (Eagle VI) At 2 AAP Hendon 26.2.18, allotted to EF; England to Rec PK 28.2.18; Rep Pk 1 ASD 6.3.18 "wrecked"; 205 Sqn 10.4.18; Crashed into D8405 on TO, CW 18.4.18 (Lt WE MacPherson unhurt); 2 ASD 18.4.18; SOC Adv Salvage Dump 19.4.18

A8081 (Eagle VIII) 4 ASD by 8.18; 217 Sqn 19.8.18; Hit ridge landing after A/S patrol and broke off u/c 5.9.18 (Capt DW Davies & Sgt GJ Wilson both unhurt); 4 ASD 9.9.18 - @25.10.18

A8082 (Eagle VIII) 1 (S)ARD Farnborough by 25.5.18; AAP Dover by 12.6.18; 4 ASD Audembert 13.6.18; 217 Sqn 2.7.18; Crashed into hangar on TO, wrecking A7934 & D8353, badly damaged 18.7.18 (Lt RM Berthe & Lt AC Lester unhurt); to 4 ASD, to at least 25.10.18

A8083 Fitted experimentally with 400hp Sunbeam Matabele; Allocated from RFC 16.2.18 for experiments; Deld 14 AAP Castle Bromwich to Hendon 5.5.18; RAE Farnborough 27.6.18 (performance and general tests); CFS Upavon 16.12.18 - 31.12.18 (performance tests for AES Martlesham Heath)

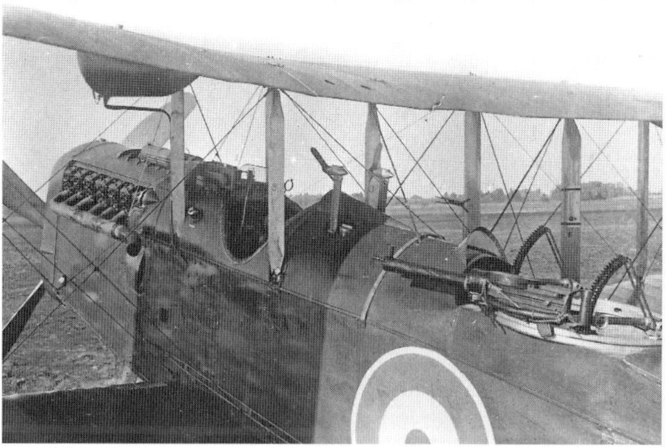

D.H.4 armament experiments at Martlesham Heath. (via Frank Cheesman)

A8084 (Eagle V) At 2 AAP Hendon 18.2.18, allotted to EF; Rec Pk 22.2.18; 2 AI 20.3.18; 5N Sqn 24.3.18; Became 205 Sqn 1.4.18; EF on TO, badly damaged 9.4.18 (Lt HD Evans & Sgt PL Richards unhurt); 2 Adv Salvage Dump 11.4.18; Rep Pk 2 ASD 20.4.18; SOC 22.4.18

A8085 Rec Pk to 2 AI 21.8.18; 57 Sqn 22.8.18; Engine damaged by EA fire on photographic reconnaissance, FL nr Mayenneville 6.9.18 (Lt JL Standish & Lt J Carrey OK); Controls shot away in combat on bombing raid 18.30, FL at 13 Sqn, wrecked 27.9.18 (2/Lt GJ Dickins wounded & 2/Lt AH Aitken unhurt)

A8086 (Eagle) At 8 AAP Lympne by 30.8.18; Rec Pk 1.9.18; 2 AI 3.9.18; 57 Sqn 4.9.18; Fokker DVII OOC 08.10 24.9.18; Left 16.30 on bombing raid, Fokker DVII OOC Cambrai 18.00, own a/c shot up in combat 27.9.18 (both 2/Lt FdeM Hyde OK & 2/Lt LH Eyres wounded)

A8087 (Eagle VI) Rec Pk to 2 AI 13.9.18; 25 Sqn 18.9.18

A8088 At 8 AAP Lympne by 24.8.18; Rec Pk to 2 AI 29.8.18; 57 Sqn 30.8.18; Fokker DVII OOC between Bantouzelle and Havrincourt Wood 17.25 19.9.18; Damaged in combat, FL at 15 Sqn, returned to sqn 20.9.18; Left 06.45, Fokker DVII in flames just after attack on Beauvais aerodrome, own a/c damaged in combat 08.10 24.9.18 (both Lt FG Pym & Sgt WCE Mason); Rep Pk 2 ASD 25.9.18; Rebuilt as H6882 25.10.18

A8089 (Eagle VI) At 8 AAP Lympne by 10.9.18; 2 AI to 205 Sqn 18.9.18; Left 17.35 to bomb Villers Outréaux, dived steeply with 2 Fokker DVII on tail, BU over Le Catelat 18.45 21.9.18 (Lt AN Hyde & 2/Lt WW Harrison both killed)

A8090 Skeleton a/c deld Farnborough, but either completed or replaced because (Eagle) at 8 AAP Lympne by 8.9.18; Rec Pk to 2 AI 13.9.18; 205 Sqn 18.9.18; 2 AI 24.9.18 (exchanged for D.H.9A); 57 Sqn 26.9.18; Bombing raid to Sanztoi, SE of Cambrai, Fokker DVII smoking E of Garmes, shared F7597 08.30, then shot down in flames 2.10.18 (2/Lt FHA Weale & 2/Lt E Preece both killed)

1 D.H.4 prototype to have been transferred from RNAS and renumbered B394. (275hp Eagle V)

B394 (Ex 3697) At 2 AAP Hendon 13.3.17 allotted to EF but this cancelled 16.3.17 "to be retained by Admiralty", keeping serial number 3697

5 D.H.4 rebuilds by 1(S)ARD Farnborough in the range B701 to B900

B774 (RAF 3a) At 1 (S)ARD 18.5.18, allotted to EF; Issued for EF W/E 1.7.18; Rec Pk to 1 AI 1.7.18; 18 Sqdn 1.7.18; Casualty Report 20.8.18 says due to faulty tail plane a/c will not climb and is unfit for further service in the field; Rec Pk 25.8.18; To England 26.8.18

B775 (RAF 3a) At 1(S)ARD 20.4.18, allotted to EF; England to Rec Pk 28.5.18; 1 AI 29.5.18; 18 Sqdn 8.6.18; Landed on one wheel 1.7.18 (Lt JK Smith & Sgt C Lines OK); Rep Pk 1 ASD 3.7.18

B776 (RAF 3a) At 1 (S)ARD 29.3.18, allotted to EF; Rec Pk to 1 AI 2.7.18; 18 Sqdn 2.7.18; Casualty Report 2.10.18 says a/c in poor condition, return to 1 ASD for complete overhaul recommended; 1 ASD 14.10.18

B882 (RAF 3a) At 1 (S)ARD 5.2.18, allotted to EF; but this was cancelled 18.3.18, a/c damaged; Issued for training W/E 13.5.18; The allotment to EF was reinstated 29.3.18; England to Rec Pk 10.5.18; 1 AI 18.5.18; 18 Sqdn 29.6.18; Fokker DrI OOC W of Douai 07.40 29.8.18 (Lt FM Macfarland & 2/Lt A Petersen); On practice flight COL 24.9.18 (2/Lt J Whitehead & 2/Lt H Cranfield OK); To Rep Pk 1 ASD 26.9.18

B884 (Eagle VI) En route to EF from 1 (S)ARD 27.12.17, allotted to EF; Rec Pk to 1 AI 6.1.18; 57 Sqn 26.1.18; Unable to keep up with formation, attacked by three Albatros D over Bousbecque one of which sent down OOC 08.00, then FL Bailleul 6.3.18 (Lt BE Sharwood-Smith OK & Sgt JC Lowe wounded); Casualty Report 22.4.18 says a/c had been damaged in several bad landings and return to depot recommended; Rep Pk 2 ASD; Rebuilt as F6070 2.7.18

1 D.H.4 ordered 11.7.16 under running Cont No 87/1/496 from the parent company and numbered B1482

B1482 26 TS Harlaxton by 11.6.18

100 D.H.4 ordered 3.4.17 under Cont No 87/A/1185 from F.W.Berwick & Co Ltd, London and numbered B2051 to B2150. (Mainly 200hp BHP, but some of the earlier a/c had RAF 3a)

B2051 (BHP) Deld 2 AAP Hendon; 2 TDS Lake Down/Stonehenge 6.9.17 - @22.11.17; 99 Sqn Old Sarum by 22.12.17; 98 Sqn Old Sarum 27.12.17; Half ARS 9.1.18

B2052 WEE Biggin Hill by 27.7.18

B2053 (BHP) At 2 AAP Hendon 29.9.17, allotted to EF; 1 ASD to 27 Sqn 8.11.17; Rep Pk 1 ASD 13.11.17; Casualty Report 14.11.17 says a/c damaged due to various bad landings; 27 Sqn 1.12.17; Lost in thick mist, FL and crashed 31.1.18 (2/Lt T Noad & 2/AM J Ferguson both OK); Rep Pk 1 ASD 4.2.18; SOC 26.4.18

B2054 7 Wing to 19 TS Hounslow 5.11.17; 18 Wing ARS Hounslow 6.11.17; 9 TS Norwich, diving in landing in snowstorm 26.12.17 (2/Lt CCA Norris killed)

B2055 (RAF 3a) 33 Wing ARS Lake Down to 29 Wing ARS Shawbury 22.11.17; 2 TDS Lake Down 28.11.17; 109 Sqn Lake Down by 11.3.18

B2056 Deld 2 AAP Hendon; 2 TDS Stonehenge 28.9.17

B2057 (RAF 3a) 103 Sqn Old Sarum by 19.12.17 - @22.1.18; 109 Sqn Lake Down by 9.3.18

B2058 No information

B2059 (RAF 3a) From Dover to France with 49 Sqn 8.11.17; 2 AI 15.2.18 (exchanged for Fiat-engined m/c); Rep Pk 1 ASD 7.4.18; SOC 8.4.18

B2060 (RAF 3a) From Dover to France with 49 Sqn 8.11.17; 2 AI 13.3.18 (exchanged for Fiat-engined m/c); Rep Pk 2 ASD by 1.4.18; SOC 25.4.18

B2061 2 TDS Lake Down, stalled on TO 11.11.17 (2/Lt CF Drabble & 1/AM Walkden both injured); SOC 16.11.17

B2062 (RAF 3a) From Dover to France with 49 Sqn 8.11.17; 2 AI 13.3.18 exchanged for Fiat-engined m/c; 18 Sqn 15.3.18; Casualty Report 19.3.18 says m/c overturned on landing, return to Depot for examination and overhaul recommended; Rep Pk 1 ASD 22.3.18; SOC 14.4.18

B2063 (RAF 3a) From Dover to France with 49 Sqn 8.11.17; 2 AI 11.2.18 (exchanged for Fiat-engined m/c); Rep Pk 1 ASD 2.4.18; SOC 8.4.18

B2064 (RAF 3a) At No 8 AAP Lympne 15.11.17, allotted to EF; 1 ASD to 18 Sqn 2.12.17; Caught by wind landing, qturned sharply onto ploughed land and turned over 18.1.18 (Lt HR Gould & Capt MSE Archibald); Rep Pk 1 ASD 26.1.18; SOC 4.2.18

B2065 (RAF 3a) At 2 AAP Hendon 3.6.18, Reallotted from Air Ministry for HQ Communications Flight to EF: Rec Pk to 1 AI 3.7.18 but back at Rec Pk 4.7.18; 1 AI 16.7.18; 18 Sqn 22.7.18; Left 06.00, returning from raid on Douai in combat Vitry, seen to go down smoking 07.35, FL E of lines 28.7.18 (Lt RV Irwin PoW DoW 2.10.18 & Sgt Mech GH Tench MM PoW DoW)

B2066 (RAF 3a) At No 8 AAP Lympne 15.11.17, allotted to EF; 1 AI to 18 Sqn 5.12.17; Scout OOC smoking nr Lens 14.00-14.30 25.1.18 (2/Lt D Richardson & Capt C L'Estrange); Photographic mission, met AA, combat with 2-str over Carvin, damaged, FL at 4 Sqn and crashed 12.30 28.1.18 (Lt JW Ritch & Capt R Roberts both OK); Rep Pk 1 ASD 31.1.18; 1 AI 15.4.18; 18 Sqn 21.4.18; Casualty Report 8.8.18 says unfit for further service in the field; Rec Pk 8.8.18; To England 12.8.18

B2067 (RAF 3a) At No 8 AAP Lympne 15.11.17, allotted to EF; Rec Pk to 2 AI 4.12.17; 49 Sqn 5.12.17; 2 AI 11.2.18 (exchanged for Fiat-engined m/c); SOC Rep Pk 1 ASD 8.4.18 NWR

B2068 (RAF 3a) At No 8 AAP Lympne 15.11.17, allotted to EF; 2 ASD to 18 Sqn 30.11.17; Wrecked 1.1.18; 2 AI to Rep Pk 2 ASD 3.1.18; 2 AI 7.5.18; 27 Sqn 11.5.18; On test flight COL 19.5.18 (Lt CE Hutcheson & 2/AM W Hilton); Rep Pk 2 ASD 21.5.18; SOC 7.6.18 NWR

B2069 (RAF 3a) At 2 AAP Hendon 3.6.18, Reallotted from Air Ministry for HQ Communications Flight to EF; Rec Pk to 1 AI 30.6.18; 18 Sqn 2.7.18; Misjudged landing struck ridge and crashed 4.8.18 (2/Lt B Champion & 2/Lt L McCall OK); Rep Pk 1 ASD 5.8.18; SOC 8.8.18 NWR

B2070 No information

B2071 (BHP) At 2 AAP Hendon 30.10.17, allotted to EF; England to Rec Pk 11.11.17; 27 Sqn 15.11.17; Casualty Report 16.11.17 reports faults not noticed when taken over from 1 ASD; Rep Pk 1 ASD 17.11.17; 27 Sqn 1.12.17; FL due to leaky radiator 3.12.17 (2/Lt S Hewett & Lt JJ Coleman both OK); Rep Pk 1 ASD 5.12.17; 2 AI 27.3.18; 27 Sqn ('R') 27.3.18; Red Albatros D OOC Fampoux-Arras 10.15 18.5.18 (not allowed); Pfalz DIII crashed Valenciennes-Anzin 10.50 20.5.18 (both Capt S Anderson & Lt WI Crawford); After bombing Flaby, badly shot up in combat, FL Beauvais 6.6.18 (Mjr GD Hill OK & 2/Lt CHF Nesbitt wounded); 9 AP 6.6.18; SOC Rep Pk 2 ASD 22.7.18 NWR

B2072 (BHP) At 2 AAP Hendon 7.11.17, allotted to EF; Rec Pk to Rep Pk 1 ASD 18.12.17 - @27.12.18; 1 AI to 27 Sqn 4.1.18; Rep Pk 1 ASD 9.4.18; SOC 10.4.18

B2073 (BHP) At 2 AAP Hendon 10.11.17, allotted to EF; England to Rec Pk 19.11.17; 1 AI and on to 27 Sqn 23.11.17; Bombing raid on "E.T." [??], FL Bully-Grenay, just our side of line 30.11.17 (2/Lt F Carr & 2/Lt PW Plant); Retd next day; Turned over taking off in cross wind 15.12.17 (2/Lt GR Norman OK & 2/AM A Hughesden cuts); Rep Pk 1 ASD 15.12.17; 2 AI 27.3.18; 27 Sqn 6.4.18; Bombing raid, badly shot up in combat with 7 Fokker DrI 22.4.18 (2/Lt EJ Smith OK & 2/Lt ECW Deacon killed); to Rep Pk 1 ASD; SOC 25.4.18

B2074 (BHP) AT 2 AAP Hendon 12.11.17, allotted to EF; England to Rec Pk 22.11.17; 27 Sqn 26.11.17; Split longeron 6.12.17; Rep Pk 1 ASD 7.12.17; 1 AI 28.12.17; 27 Sqn 29.12.17; FTR from raid on Denain, left at 09.50, last seen gliding down from 13,000 feet apparently with engine, trouble 4.1.18 (2/Lt KP Ewart & Lt AN Westlake MC both killed)

B2075 (BHP) At 2 AAP Hendon 12.11.17, allotted to EF;

England to Rec Pk 23.11.17; 27 Sqn 26.11.17; On raid FL due to engine trouble nr Béthune 28.11.17 (Lt AF Ingram & Lt AN Westlake); Rep Pk 1 ASD 29.11.17; Rep Pk 13.12.18; 1 AI 23.2.18; 2 AI 8.3.18; 27 Sqn ('P') 20.3.18; COL trying to avoid a collision, total wreck 28.3.18 (2/Lt DMcQ Smith & 2/Lt PW Plant); SOC 28.3.18

B2076 (BHP) At 2 AAP Hendon 19.11.17, allotted to EF; Rec Pk to Rep Pk 1 ASD 18.12.17; 1 AI 1.1.18; 27 Sqn 7.1.18; Left 10.30 on raid on Cambrai area, after dropping bombs attacked by 5 EA, controls shot up, COL nr Albert, m/c burnt as it was impossible to collect 26.3.18 (Capt MH Turner wounded & 2/Lt PS Driver killed); SOC wrecked

B2077 (BHP) At 2 AAP Hendon 13.11.17, allotted to EF; England to Rec Pk 21.11.17; 1 AI and on to 27 Sqn 23.11.17; Shot down in flames by Pfalz DIII over Marquion c.12.30 17.2.18 (2/Lt AW Greene & Sgt A Hughesden both killed)

B2078 (BHP) At 2 AAP Hendon 20.11.17, allotted to EF; England to Rec Pk 22.11.17; 1 AI and on to 27 Sqn 23.11.17; Returning from raid, caught by wind and turned over 2.12.17 (2/Lt WJ Henney & 2/Lt PS Driver OK); Rep Pk 1 ASD 3.12.17; 1 AI 27.1.18; 2 AI 12.3.18; 27 Sqn 12.4.18; Albatros D down OOC smoking Douai 16.00 8.5.18 (Lt SW Taylor & Sgt V Cummins); Left 05.05 for raid, in running fight SW of Péronne 19.15, FL Bertangles 13.5.18 (Lt SW Taylor unhurt & Lt WH Gibson severely wounded but continued to use his gun); To 2 Adv Salvage 13.5.18; SOC Rep Pk 2 ASD 6.6.18

B2079 (BHP) At makers 14.11.17, allotted to EF; 1 ASD by 12.12.17; 27 Sqn 16.12.17; Damaged in combat in bombing raid to Landrecies, overran aerodrome on return and crashed 24.3.18 (2/Lt GR Norman & 2/Lt RCD Oliver OK); Rep Pk 2 ASD 24.3.18; Rep Pk 1 ASD 7.4.18; SOC 8.4.18

B2080 (BHP) At Makers 14.11.17, allotted to EF; Rec Pk to 27 Sqn 11.12.17; Turned over on take off 28.12.17 (2/Lt CH Gannaway & 2/Lt FRD Wickham both OK); Rep Pk 1 ASD 1.1.18; 2 AI 25.3.18; Rep Pk 2 ASD by 1.4.18; 27 Sqn 15.5.18; Left 08.20, left formation E of lines, seen in control Chaulnes 6.6.18 (Lt MF Cunningham & 2/Lt WJ Stockins both killed)

B2081 (BHP) At Makers 14.11.17, allotted to EF; Rep Pk 1 ASD by 12.12.17; Height test, engine cut out, FL in barbed wire, overturned 21.12.17 (Lt SC Hollinghurst MC OK); Rep Pk 2 ASD by 31.12.17; 2 AI to 27 Sqn 31.3.18; Left 17.05 for raid on Bertangles, general engagement with 20-30 EA SW of Péronne, shot down in flames 10.5.18 (2/Lt LE Dunnett & 2/Lt DH Prosser both killed)

B2082 (BHP) At Makers 14.11.17, allotted to EF; Rep Pk 1 ASD to 1 AI 1.1.18; 27 Sqn 26.1.18; Crashed trying to land at 16 Sqn aerodrome after height test 2.3.18 (2/Lt HJT Wilkes killed & Sgt HR Eden injured), m/c total wreck.Rep Pk 1 ASD 4.3.18; SOC 5.3.18

B2083 (BHP) At Makers 14.11.17, allotted to EF; 1 ASD to 27 Sqn 10.12.17; Albatros D OOC Maria Aeltre 13.05 3.1.18 (2/Lt EA Coghlan & 2/AM HR Eden); Left on raid but had to return after 10 minutes with engine trouble, while standing on aerodrome hit by 25 Sqn's A7565 21.5.18 (Lt SW Taylor OK & 2/Lt D Moore lower right jaw fractured); SOC Rep Pk 2 ASD 23.5.18 NWR

B2084 (BHP) At 2 AAP Hendon 26.11.17, allotted to EF; Rec Pk to 27 Sqn 10.12.17; Engine trouble COL 11.3.18 (2/Lt DTC Rundle-Woolcock & Sgt A Everton OK); Rep Pk 2 ASD; Rep Pk 1 ASD by rail 1.4.18; SOC 8.4.18

B2085 (BHP) At 2 AAP Hendon 26.11.17, allotted to EF; Rec Pk to 27 Sqn 10.12.17; Raid on Roulers, as a result of AA and combat FL Houplines 2,000yds behind our front line trenches 25.1.18 (2/Lt DTC Rundle-Woolcock & 2/Lt JH Holland both OK); Rep Pk 1 ASD 29.1.18; SOC 26.4.18.

B2086 (BHP) At 2 AAP Hendon 27.11.17, allotted to EF; Rec Pk to 27 Sqn 13.12.17; 1 AI 3.2.18; Rep Pk 1 ASD 4.2.18; 2 AI 18.4.18; 27 Sqn 8.5.18; Attacked just after bombing Chaulnes, Albatros D OOC Roye 10.45 6.6.18 (Lt EA Coghlan & Lt JH Holland); Albatros D OOC W of Roye, shared A7597 7.6.18 (Lt EA Coghlan & Lt JH Holland); Albatros D in flames Roye 11.30, then attacked by a Fokker DrI 16.6.18 (Lt EA Coghlan wounded & Lt HM Stewart killed); Left 15.00 for bombing raid on Lille, hit by AA, shot up in combat with EA, retd 17.45 4.7.18 (2/Lt R Turner & Sgt V Cummins OK); To Rep Pk 2 ASD 4.7.18; SOC 27.7.18 NWR

B2087 (BHP) En route to EF 6.12.17, allotted to EF; Rep Pk 1 ASD to 1 AI and on to 27 Sqn 25.12.17; Albatros D OOC Maria Aeltre but badly damaged in combat 13.05 3.1.18 (2/Lt WJ Henney & 2/Lt PS Driver both OK); Rep Pk 1 ASD 6.1.18; 1 AI 24.2.18; 2 AI 8.3.18; 27 Sqn 26.3.18; Left 17.05 for raid on Bertangles, combat with 20-30 EA SW of Péronne, seen going down 10.5.18 (Lt AH Hill & Sgt Mech SR Richmond killed)

B2088 (BHP) At 2 AAP Hendon 1.12.17, allotted to EF; Rec Pk to 1 AI 28.12.17; 27 Sqn 4.1.18; Albatros D OOC Busigny 10.00 then engine seized, FL 8.3.18 (2/Lt J Gray & Lt JA McGinnis OK); Rep Pk 2 ASD 12.3.18; SOC 23.3.18

B2089 13 FS by 10.18 - @3.19

B2090 (BHP) At 2 AAP Hendon 3.12.17, allotted to EF; 1 ASD to 27 Sqn ('M') 24.12.17; COL 30.3.18 (2/Lt F Carr & 2/Lt JH Holland OK); Rep Pk 1 ASD 1.4.18; SOC 3.4.18

B2091 No information

B2092 (BHP) At 2 AAP Hendon 4.12.17, allotted to EF; Rec Pk to 1 AI 1.1.18; 27 Sqn 27.1.18; Albatros D down in spin Roubaix [not allowed] 09.00 3.5.18 (2/Lt GE Ffrench & Sgt V Cummins); Left on raid 06.30, fell behind formation due to engine trouble, FL N of Kemmel due to combat, crashed, impossible to salve due to proximity to lines 3.5.18 (2/Lt GE Ffrench & Sgt V Cummins OK)

B2093 (BHP) En route from Makers to EF 10.12.17, allotted to EF; Rep Pk 1 ASD to 1 AI 27.1.18; 27 Sqn ('G') 3.2.18; Flying to new aerodrome at Ruisseauville COL 29.3.18 (2/Lt MF Cunningham & 2/Lt GH Fozzard); Rep Pk 1 ASD 1.4.18; SOC 3.4.18

B2094 (BHP) At Makers 11.12.17, allotted to EF; Rep Pk 1 ASD to 1 AI 16.2.18; 27 Sqn 18.2.18; Albatros D apparently OOC Busigny then shot down in flames 10.00 8.3.18 (2/Lt JFRI Parkins & Lt RG Foley MC both killed)

B2095 126 Sqn Fowlmere by 7.18 until sqn disbanded 17.8.18; Midland Area FIS Lilbourne by 10.18

B2096 (BHP) 104 Sqn Andover to 98 Sqn Old Sarum 27.12.17; 99 Sqn Old Sarum by 13-23.1.18; 2 TDS Stonehenge 19.1.18; 98 Sqn Old Sarum by 28.1.18; 108 Sqn Lake Down 15.2.18; 109 Sqn Lake Down by 24.3.18

B2097 103 Sqn Old Sarum by 15.1.18 - @7.2.18

B2098 (BHP) Presentation a/c 'Jamnagar No.2'. At 2 AAP Hendon 21.12.17, allotted to EF; England to Rec Pk 13.1.18; 1 AI 24.1.18; 27 Sqn 26.1.18; FL at Honeghem having lost way in mist 31.1.18 (2/Lt CH Gannaway & 2/Lt RCD Oliver); Rep Pk 1 ASD 1.2.18; SOC 26.4.18

B2099 (BHP) Presentation a/c 'Jamnagar No.3'. At 2 AAP Hendon 21.12.17, allotted to EF; England to Rec Pk 21.1.18; 1 AI 27.1.18; 27 Sqn 31.1.18; Damaged in FL 12.4.18 (2/Lt GE Ffrench & 2/Lt W Spencer OK); 2 Adv Salvage Dump to Rep Pk 2 ASD 20.4.18

B2100 (BHP) At 1 (S)ARD 18.1.18 - 20.2.18, allotment to EF cancelled; 3 FS Bircham Newton by 8.18

B2101 (BHP) Presentation a/c 'Presented by The Colony of Mauritius No.9'. At 2 AAP Hendon 29.12.17, allotted to EF; England to Rec Pk 28.1.18; 1 AI 16.2.18; 27 Sqn 23.2.18; Left 13.20 on raid on Cambrai area, attacked by EA, FL Frevent 26.3.18 (Lt GE Wait & 2/Lt WG Hurrell OK); Rep Pk 1 ASD 31.3.18; SOC 3.4.18

B2102 (BHP) Presentation a/c 'Britons in Chile No.1'. At 2 AAP Hendon 29.12.17, allotted to EF; England to Rec Pk 24.1.18; 1 AI 27.1.18; 27 Sqn 3.2.18; Left 08.50 on bombing raid on Péronne, longeron hit by AA, crashed 11.10 1.4.18 (2/Lt F Carr & 2/Lt JH Holland OK); Adv Salvage to Rep Pk 1 ASD 9.4.18; SOC 10.4.18

B2103 (BHP) At Makers 20.12.17, allotted to EF; England to Rep Pk 1 ASD 9.1.18; 1 AI 16.2.18; 27 Sqn 18.2.18; Caught by gust of wind landing, turned on nose 26.2.18 (2/Lt AH Hill & Sgt V Cummins both OK); Rep Pk 1

ASD 27.2.18; SOC 7.3.18

B2104 (BHP) At Makers 20.12.17, allotted to EF; England to Rep Pk 14.1.18; 2 AI 6.3.18; 27 Sqn ('N') 13.3.18; Bombing raid on Busigny, taxied into 'R' on landing, broke prop 18.3.18 (2/Lt F Carr & 2/Lt JH Holland); Bird strike on prop 21.3.18 (same crew); Ground strafing troops from 1,000ft, m/c hit but retd OK 26.3.18 (same crew); Landed Villers-Bretonneux with burst radiator, owing to evacuation m/c left, RFA promised to burn it before leaving 26.3.18 (2/Lt HW Hewson & Sgt V Cummins)

B2105 (BHP) At 2 AAP Hendon 7.1.18, allotted to EF; England to Rec Pk 25.1.18; 1 AI 27.1.18; 27 Sqn 2.2.18; On returning from raid collided with a 25 Sqn D.H.4 17.2.18 (2/Lt T Noad & 2/Lt AD Wright both OK); Rep Pk 1 ASD 18.2.18; SOC 21.2.18

B2106 (BHP) At Makers 28.12.17, allotted to EF; England to Rep Pk 1 ASD 14.1.18; To England in case 26.4.18

B2107 (BHP) At Makers 9.1.18, allotted to EF; England to Rep Pk 1 ASD 21.1.18; 1 AI 23.2.18; 27 Sqn 27.2.18; COL at Candas 25.3.18 (2/Lt AH Hall & Sgt C Christian); Rep Pk 2 ASD 25.3.18; Rep Pk 1 ASD by rail 2.4.18; SOC 8.4.18

B2108 (BHP) At Makers 9.1.18, allotted to EF; England to Rep Pk 1 ASD 21.1.18; 1 AI 23.2.18; 2 AI 5.3.18; 27 Sqn 11.3.18; In combat in bombing raid to Landrecies, seen going down with EA on tail 24.3.18 (2/Lt BJ Johnstone & 2/Lt Lord CC Douglas both wounded); SOC wrecked

B2109 (BHP) At No 2 AAP Hendon 12.1.18, allotted to EF; England to Rec Pk 21.1.18; 1 AI 24.1.18; 27 Sqn 26.1.18; Wheel came off on landing, crashed 18.3.18 (Capt MH Turner & Lt JA McGinnis); Rep Pk 2 ASD; SOC 25.3.18

B2110 (BHP) Presentation a/c 'Malaya XXI The Tan Jiakkim'. At No 2 AAP Hendon 12.1.18, allotted to EF; England to Rec Pk 27.1.18; 1 AI 16.2.18; 2 ASD 12.3.18; 27 Sqn 17.4.18; Left 07.00 on raid, hit by AA before reaching objective, returned to aerodrome 22.4.18 (2/Lt CH Gannaway & 2/Lt WI Crawford OK); 2 AI and on to Rep Pk 2 ASD 23.4.18; 2 AI to 27 Sqn 29.6.18; Returning from raid on Tournai engine cut out, recrossed the lines with practically no engine, FL in trenches at Beaumetz 2.7.18 (Lt EJ Smith & Lt RH Norris OK); SOC Rep Pk 2 ASD 8.7.18 NWR

B2111 (BHP) At Makers 17.1.18, allotted to EF; England to Rep Pk 1 ASD 1.2.18; 2 AI 8.3.18; 27 Sqn 9.3.18; Shot down in bombing raid on Bapaume, left 07.45 26.3.18 (2/Lt GR Norman & 2/Lt RCD Oliver both PoW)

B2112 (BHP) At Makers 17.1.18, allotted to EF; England to Rep Pk 1 ASD 5.2.18; 1 AI 24.2.18; 27 Sqn 1.3.18; Bombing raid on Bavai, EF over target, fired green light but it picked up, crashed and overturned on landing 12.3.18 (2/Lt F Carr & 2/Lt W Spencer OK); Rep Pk 2 ASD 13.3.18; Rep Pk 1 ASD by rail 2.4.18; SOC 8.4.18

B2113 (BHP) At Makers 19.1.18, allotted to EF; England to Rep Pk 1 ASD 5.2.18; 1 AI 24.2.18; 27 Sqn ('S') 1.3.18; Albatros D down in spin just E of Valenciennes 10.50 20.5.18 (Lt HW Hewson & 2/Lt JD Parker); Scout down in spin Roye, own m/c badly damaged in combat 11.15 16.6.18 (Capt S Anderson DoW & Lt JH Holland badly wounded but continued to fire his gun until he collapsed); To Rep Pk 2 ASD 17.6.18; SOC 14.7.18 NWR

B2114 Midland Area FIS Lilbourne by 9.18

B2115 (BHP) Lympne by 6.18; Eastbourne W/E 25.6.18; 31 TDS Fowlmere, prop accident 10.10.18 (3/AM WH Haden seriously injured)

B2116 (BHP) At 2 AAP Hendon 22.1.18 - 7.2.18, allotted to EF (NTU?); 126 Sqn Fowlmere by 6.18 - 7.18

B2117 (BHP) At 2 AAP Hendon 22.1.18 - 7.2.18, allotted to EF

B2118 No information

B2119 (BHP) At 2 AAP Hendon 23.1.18 - 7.2.18, allotted to EF;

B2120 46 TS Catterick by 11.3.18

B2121 26 TS Narborough, stalled on right hand turn at 300ft, dived in 13.2.18 (2/Lt CA Law killed & 2/Lt JF Shaw DoI 19.2.18)

B2122 Deld CSD White City by 1.2.18; Shipped to Otranto 28.2.18; 224 Sqn Otranto by 11.5.18; Swung landing after raid on Cattaro seaplane base, hit hangar, damaged 2/Lt RB Picken's machine 23.8.18 (2/Lt SJ Chamberlain & Lt J Ellingham unhurt)

B2123 No information

B2124 No information

B2125 Deld CSD White City by 1.2.18; Cardiff Docks by 23.2.18; Shipped to 6 Wing Otranto 1.3.18; 224 Sqn Otranto by 28.4.18 - @1.5.18

B2126 (BHP) 52 TS Catterick by 4.18

B2127 8 AAP Lympne, HAPP 22.8.17 (2/Lt CH Drew); 49 TDS Catterick by 9.18

B2128 Deld CSD White City by 1.2.18; Cardiff Docks by 23.2.18; Shipped to 6 Wing Otranto 1.3.18; 224 Sqn Otranto by 7.4.18 - @1.5.18

B2129 (BHP) At Makers 12.2.18, allotted to EF; England to

D.H.4 B2131 being assembled at Chimino, near Taranto, Italy around April-May 1918. It later served with Nos.224 and 226 Squadrons. (via Frank Cheesman)

Rep Pk 1 ASD 26.2.18; 2 AI 31.3.18; 27 Sqn 3.4.18; bombing raid, engine cut over Valenciennes, FL E of lines nr Arras 19.5.18 (2/Lt FJ Bull & 2/Lt CB Law PoWs)

B2130 (BHP) At Makers 12.2.18, allotted to EF; England to Rep Pk 1 ASD 1.3.18; On test, collided with a hangar on landing, fuselage broke in three 9.3.18 (2/Lt JH Page & 2/AM JE Day); SOC 12.4.18

B2131 Deld CSD White City by 23.2.18; Shipped to 6 Wing Otranto 28.3.18; 224 Sqn Otranto by 11.5.18 - @6.18; 226 Sqn by 15.6.18; 224 Sqn by 1.7.18 - @17.8.18; AD Taranto to 'X' AD 28.6.19; WOC at ASD 25.8.19

B2132 (BHP) At Makers 13.2.18, allotted to EF; England to Rep Pk 1 ASD 4.3.18; 2 AI 26.3.18; 27 Sqn 27.3.18; Albatros or Pfalz D down in vertical dive smoking Valenciennes 11.15 20.5.18 (Lt GE Wait & 2/Lt FA Gledhill); Scout OOC Roye 10.45 6.6.18 (Lt SW Taylor & Lt WG Hurrell); 98 Sqn 1.3.19; FL Quelmes 2.3.19; 1 ASD 17.3.19; To England 18.3.19

B2133 (BHP) At Makers 13.2.18, allotted to EF; England to Rep Pk 1 ASD 9.3.18; 2 AI 13.4.18; 27 Sqn 27.4.18; Albatros D in flames 23.5.18; Fokker DrI OOC Flavy 19.00 8.6.18 (both Lt J Gray & Lt HE Gooding); Fokker DVII OOC W of Lille 1.7.18 (Lt EL Raworth & Lt GH Fozzard); Fokker DVII crashed nr Roye 18.30 8.8.18 (Lt BM Bowyer-Smythe & 2/Lt LJ Edwardes); 98 Sqn 1.3.19; 8 AAP Lympne 13.3.19

B2134 Deld CSD White City by 1.2.18; Shipped to 6 Wing Otranto 9.3.18; 224 Sqn Otranto by 7.4.18 - @1.5.18

B2135 (BHP) At Makers 13.2.18, allotted to EF; England to Rep Pk 1 ASD 26.2.18; 2 AI 11.3.18; 27 Sqn 25.3.18; Fokker DrI down in flames SW of Péronne & EA apparently OOC 19.15 10.5.18 (Lt FW Knight & Cpl FY McLauchlen); Fokker DrI OOC Flavy 19.00 8.6.18 (Lt FW Knight & Lt AR Sheppard); Fokker DVII apparently OOC smoking NW of Emerchicourt 09.45 27.9.18 (Lt FC Crummey & 2/Lt FT McKilligin); On landing ran into a shell hole and overturned 19.11.18 (Lt BM Bowyer-Smythe & 2/Lt WA Hall OK); 2 ASD 19.11.18

B2136 No information

B2137 Deld CSD White City 2.18; Shipped to Otranto 28.3.18; 224 Sqn Otranto by 11.5.18 - @17.8.18

B2138 No information

B2139 (BHP) At 2 AAP Hendon 26.2.18, allotted to EF; England to Rec Pk 29.3.18; 2 AI and on to 27 Sqn 31.3.18; Stationary on aerodrome having just landed, ran into by 25 Sqn's D9242 7.5.18 (Lt EA Coghlan & Lt VFS Dunton OK); To Rep Pk 2 ASD 10.5.18

B2140 No information

B2141 (BHP) At 2 AAP Hendon 26.2.18, allotted to EF; Reallotted from EF to Training 2.4.18;

B2142 Deld CSD White City 3.18; Shipped to Otranto 28.3.18; 224 Sqn Otranto by 11.5.18 - @15.6.18; Deleted by 13.7.18

B2143 (BHP) At Makers 4.3.18, allotted to EF but this cancelled 5.3.18; Deld CSD White City by 30.3.18; Shipped to Otranto 10.4.18; AR&ED Pizzone .18; AD Adriatic Group by 8.18; 224 Sqn Taranto by 27.9.18 - @31.1.19

B2144 (BHP) En route from Makers to France 5.3.18, allotted to EF; Arrived Rep Pk 1 ASD 15.3.18; 2 AI 12.4.18; 27 Sqn 22.4.18; Crashed just after taking off on raid 8.5.18 (Lt CH Gannaway & Sgt WEA Brookes OK); Rebuilt as F6078 3.7.18

B2145 (BHP) At Makers 4.3.18, allotted to EF; England to Rep Pk 1 ASD 16.3.18; 2 AI 13.4.18; 27 Sqn 23.4.18; Radiator burst, engine seized, FL nr Treizennes, ran into a ditch 9.5.18 (Lt CE Hutcheson & Lt HE Gooding); Rep Pk 2 ASD and SOC 16.5.18

B2146 Deld CSD White City by 7.3.18; Shipped to Otranto 25.3.18; AD Adriatic Group by 8.18; 224 Sqn Taranto by 25.9.18 - @4.10.18; Mudros by 12.18

B2147 Deld CSD White City by 7.3.18; Shipped to Otranto 25.3.18; AR&ED Pizzone .18; AD Taranto by 13.6.18; Deld Valona 5.9.18; 224 Sqn 5.9.18 - @31.1.19; AD Taranto to 'X' AD 28.6.19; WOC at ASD 25.8.19

B2148 Deld CSD White City by 7.3.18; Shipped to Otranto 21.4.18; AR&ED Pizzone .18; AD Adriatic Group by 8.18; 226 Sqn by 2.10.18; Mudros by 10.18 - @1.19

B2149 Deld CSD White City by 7.3.18; Shipped to Otranto 9.4.18; 224 Sqn Otranto by 11.5.18 - @15.6.18

B2150 (BHP) 44 TS Waddington by 20.4.18

14 D.H.4 built by Westland Aircraft Works, Yeovil under Cont No C.P.101977/17 and transferred from RNAS order, numbered B3955 to B3968. (275hp Eagle V/VI/VII)

B3955 (ex N5970 6.6.17) (Eagle VI) At Makers 6.6.17, allotted to EF; Yeovil to Lympne, crashed on arrival 8.6.17 (2/Lt RC Bryant); Repaired on site; ARS 1 AD 2.7.17; Collecting a/c for 55 Sqn made bad landing 7.7.17 (Lt AP Matheson & Lt GY Fullalove); ARS 1 AD 9.7.17; 55 Sqn ('3') 16.8.17; Practice flight COL 17.5.18 (2/Lt AC Hall OK); Rebuilt as F6166 3.7.18

B3956 (ex N5980 6.6.17) At Makers, allotted to EF 6.6.17; Reallotted to Training 7.6.17

B3957 (ex N5986) At Makers 12.6.17, allotted to EF England to ARS 1 AD 18.6.17; Tested 27.6.17; 55 Sqn ('6'), Albatros D OOC Mannheim 12.45 18.3.18 (2/Lt CA Bridgland & 2/Lt ER Stewart); In action 16.5.18 (Capt F Williams OK & 2/Lt JS Bradley wounded); Albatros D OOC Offenburg 07.25 30.7.18 (Capt F Williams MC & 2/Lt ER Stewart); Badly shot about 12.8.18 (2/Lt CA Bridgland OK & 2/Lt ER Stewart DFC killed); 3 ASD 12.8.18; 2 AI to 57 Sqn 8.12.18; Caught fire in the air just after take off due to carburettor trouble 26.1.19 (Lt FO Thornton OK)

B3958 (ex N5987) 44 TS Harlaxton by 8.17; Arr Rec Pk 1 ASD ex UK 25.8.18; 2 AI 26.8.18; 3 AD 27.8.18

B3959 (ex N5990) 44 TS Harlaxton by 8.17; Stalled on TO, insufficient flying speed 10.10.17 (2/Lt CR Bascombe killed & 2/Lt WF French injured)

B3960 (ex N5991) 51 TS Waddington by 7.17 - 8.17; 44 TS Waddington by 11.17 - @12.17; 51 Sqn ('6'); 51 TS Waddington, crashed in collision 21.1.18 (2/Lt A McGregor seriously injured)

The wreckage of D.H.4 B3960 of No.51 Training Squadron, Waddington after being involved in a mid-air collision on 21.1.18. (via Mike O'Connor)

B3961 (ex N5994) At Makers 13.6.17, allotted to EF England to ARS 1 AD 2.7.17; 55 Sqn 10.7.17; FTR 21.10.17 (Capt D Owen & 2/Lt B Harker)

B3962 (ex N5995) At Makers 13.6.17, allotted to EF England to ARS 1 AD 10.7.17; 55 Sqn 11.7.17; Left on raid 12.20 but returned soon after take off, tried to turn, m/c sideslipped then nose dived, crashing and bursting into flames 15.9.17 (2/Lt HNG Dann & 2/Lt FR Brotherhood both killed); ARS 1 AD 16.9.17; SOC 19.9.17

B3963 (ex N5998) At Makers 13.6.17, allotted to EF England to ARS 1 AD 10.7.17; 57 Sqn 12.7.17; Combat with Albatros DVs Houthulst 17.30 (Capt L Minot OK & Lt AF Britton wounded); Wrecked on landing 13.8.17 (2/Lt V Phillips & 2/Lt N Bell); ARS 1 AD 16.8.17; ARS 2 AD 31.8.17 for reconstruction; Rep Pk 2 ASD to 55 Sqn by rail 31.12.17; Stalled on take off, completely wrecked 17.2.18 (2/Lt W Legge & 2/Lt CL Rayment); WO 17.2.18 SOC

B3964 (ex N5999) At Makers 13.6.17, allotted to EF; England to ARS 1 AD 10.7.17; 57 Sqn 11.7.17; EA OOC Houthulst Forest 17.50 by pilot 27.7.17 (Lt DS Hall OK

& 2/Lt NM Pizey killed); Damaged landing on practice flight 6.9.17 (2/Lt CF Pritchard); ARS 1 AD 7.9.17; 25 Sqn 19.10.17; Returning from raid, bounced on landing and overturned 2.12.17 (2/Lt FV Bird & 2/AM LJW Bain); Rep Pk 1 ASD 3.12.17; SOC 7.2.18

B3965 (ex N6002) At Makers 13.6.17 allotted to EF England to ARS 1 AD 21.7.17; 55 Sqn 28.7.17; ARS 1 AD 26.9.17; SOC 29.9.17

B3966 (ex N6003) (Eagle VII) At Makers 13.6.17, allotted to EF England to ARS 1 AD 22.7.17; 55 Sqn 28.7.17; On 15.07 raid to Ingelmunster, attacked by 12 EA over Iseghem, controls damaged, FL and crashed nr aerodrome 12.8.17 (Capt GW Frost slightly injured & 2/Lt H Dunstan slightly wounded); ARS 1 AD; ARS 2 AD 31.8.17 for reconstruction; Became Rep Pk 2 ASD 1.11.17; To 55 Sqn by rail 25.2.18; FTR raid on Freiburg 13.3.18 (2/Lt C Gavaghan & Sgt A Brockbank both killed)

B3967 (ex N6006) At Makers 13.6.17, allotted to EF; England to ARS 1 AD 9.8.17; 55 Sqn ('4') 13.8.17; Albatros D OOC Neustadt 12.50 18.3.18 (Capt SB Collett & Lt G Bryer-Ash); Pfalz DIII crashed W of Oberndorf 07.30 20.7.18 (Lt PE Welchman & 2/Lt ER Beesley); Hit by mg fire while bombing Luxembourg, FL, wrecked 25.8.18 (Pilot OK & Sgt AS Allan MM killed); 3 ASD 4.9.18

B3968 At Makers 13.6.17, Taken over from RNAS, ex N6007 but allotment cancelled 25.7.17 being replaced by B3987 (ex N6380)

1 D.H.4 built by Westland Aircraft Works, Yeovil under Cont No C.P.101977/17 and transferred from RNAS order, numbered B3987. (200hp RAF 3a)

B3987 At Makers 25.7.17, allotted to EF; Taken over from RNAS, ex N6380 and in replacement for B3968; 8 AAP Lympne to ARS 1 AD 4.9.17; ARS 2 AD 12.9.17; 18 Sqn 19.10.17; Returning from FL engine cut out, landed heavily 24.3.18 (2/Lt WA Rochelle & 2/AM R Little); Rep Pk 1 ASD 28.3.18; SOC 31.5.18

100 D.H.4 ordered under Cont No 87/A/1413 from Vulcan Motor & Engineering Co (1906) Ltd, Southport and numbered B5451 to B5550. (230hp Puma)

B5451 Deld 2 TDS Boscombe Down 17.11.17; 98 Sqn Old Sarum by 23.1.18; 99 Sqn Old Sarum 16.2.18 - @1.3.18

B5452 9 TS Norwich (sic), on delivery from Farnborough to New Romney, hit post on aerodrome at dusk, CW, Hounslow 15.12.17 (2/Lt TC Moore injured)

B5453 Pool of Pilots Joyce Green by 7.18; 31 TDS Fowlmere

B5454 1 (O)SoAG New Romney, test flight, tailplane failed while manoeuvring, a/c broke up 20.6.18 (2/Lt DH Sessions MC & 1/AM H Munton both killed)

B5455 Deld Norwich to Narborough 24.12.17; Flown 28.12.17

B5456 3 (Aux)SoAG New Romney, caught fire at 30ft after descending from 1,000ft, crashed on landing, BO 28.1.18 (Lt CM White injured & Lt GJL Campbell unhurt)

B5457 At No.1 (S)ARD 4.1.18, allotted to EF; England to Rec Pk 16.2.18; 2 AI 27.3.18; Damaged landing, dismantled 5.4.18; Rep Pk 1 ASD 8.4.18; SOC 10.4.18

B5458 Deld 2 TDS Lake Down 27.11.17

B5459 At No.1 (S)ARD 4.1.18, allotted to EF; England to Rec Pk 15.2.18; 27 Sqn 29.3.18; Damaged in heavy landing 22.4.18 (2/Lt F Carr & 2/Lt JH Holland); 2 AI 22.4.18; Rep Pk 2 ASD 24.4.18; Rebuilt as F6164 3.7.18

B5460 105 Sqn Andover by 7.2.18; 6 TDS Boscombe Down by 1.5.18

B5461 No information

B5462 No information

B5463 26 TS Narborough, stalled on right hand turn at 300ft, dived in 23.2.18 (Lt HA Laws killed)

B5464 No information

B5465 69 TS Narborough by 7.18; 31 TDS Fowlmere 9.18 - 10.18

B5466 105 Sqn Andover by 14-16.2.18

B5467 11 TDS Old Sarum by 13.2.18

B5468 105 Sqn Andover by 6.2.18; Lost control while manoeuvring at low height, sideslipped in 13.2.18 (2/Lt WA Amor seriously injured)

B5469 26 TS Narborough by 3.18

B5470 No information

B5471 104 Sqn Andover by 13.2.18; 6 TDS Boscombe Down by 23.5.18 - @24.6.18

B5472 106 Sqn Andover, BU in air spinning out of loop 30.1.18 (2/Lt T Le Mesurier killed) [or B5492]

B5473 105 Sqn Andover by 20.2.18

B5474 No information

B5475 No information

B5476 26 TS Harlaxton by 12.6.18

B5477 105 Sqn Andover by 9-17.2.18

B5478 No information

B5479 No information

B5480 At 1 (S)ARD 18.3.18, allotted to EF; England to Rec Pk 29.3.18; 2 AI 1.4.18; 27 Sqn 2.4.18; COL 15.5.18 (Lt EL Raworth & Lt GH Fozzard OK); To 2 Adv Salvage 17.5.18; Rebuilt as F6165 3.7.18

B5481 Makers to Half ARS Old Sarum 11.1.18 by rail; 109 Sqn Lake Down by 12.5.18

B5482 1 SoN&BD Stonehenge by 14.3.18

B5483 1 SoN&BD Stonehenge by 22.7.18

B5484 1 SoN&BD Stonehenge, stalled on turn, spun in, caught fire 1.4.18 (Lt JW Richards (Can) & Lt CG Jacob both killed)

B5485 1 SoN&BD Stonehenge by 6.3.18 - 29.7.18

B5486 109 Sqn Lake Down, pulled out of dive too quickly, tail came off, crashed, BO 26.4.18 (2/Lt FG Edwards DoI 5.4.18)

B5487 105 Sqn Andover by 13.2.18; 6 TDS

B5488 No information

B5489 106 Sqn Andover, crashed 25.4.18 (Lt HM Whitcut, also British Army officers 2/Lt GJ Downey & 2/Lt FAR Richardson all killed)

B5490 105 Sqn Andover by 24.2.18

B5491 No information

B5492 106 Sqn Andover, crashed 30.1.18 (2/Lt T Le Mesurier killed) [or B5472]

B5493 No information

B5494 Old Sarum by 4.18

B5495 105 Sqn Andover, lost on cross-country flight, crashed Culham Bridge, Oxfordshire 13.3.18 (Lt LC Davies MC DoI 16.3.18)

B5496 No information

B5497 6 TDS Boscombe Down, stalled off flat turn at low altitude 3.5.18 (2/Lt EJ Whitehead killed)

B5498 No information

B5499 109 Sqn Lake Down by 27.6.18

B5500 CFS Netheravon 1918

B5501 At 2 (N)ARD 11.3.18, allotted to EF; At 1 (S)ARD 2.4.18, reallotted from EF to Training

B5502 52 TS Catterick by 3.18

B5503 At 2 (N)ARD 23.3.18, allotted to EF but reallotted to Training 2.4.18; 25 TS Thetford by 27.4.18

B5504 At 2 (N)ARD 23.3.18, allotted to EF but reallotted to Training 2.4.18; 25 TS Thetford by 22.4.18; 126 Sqn Fowlmere by 6.18 - 7.18

B5505 44 TS Waddington by 11.17 - @12.17; 46 TS Catterick by 8.18; 6 AI, mid-air collision 23.4.19 (Lt WG Jewitt injured & Lt JS Sherren injured) [serial uncertain, listed as "45505"]

B5506 At 2 (N)ARD 22.3.18, allotted to EF; England to Rec Pk 27.3.18; 27 Sqn ('J') 29.3.18; While leading formation of seven, running fight after bombing Peronne, 2 EA down in flames & 3 OOC 19.15 10.5.18 (Capt ML Doyle & Lt GS Chester); Fokker DVII OOC Mont Notre Dame 18.00 22.7.18 (Capt ML Doyle & Lt WG Hurrell); In raid on St Symphorien aerodrome Fokker DVII OOC 14.45 4.11.18 (Capt EJ Jacques & 2/Lt NP Wood); 98 Sqn 1.3.19; 8 AAP Lympne 14.3.19

B5507 No information

B5508 99 Sqn Old Sarum by 20.2.18; Lower wing broke off in flight 24.2.18 (2/Lt LL Brennan killed)

B5509 99 Sqn Old Sarum by 13-15.2.18

B5510 No information

B5511 No information

B5512 10 TDS Harling Road 11.18

B5513 No information

B5514 52 TS Catterick by 4.18; Turned with failing engine, crashed 1.5.18 (2/Lt JG McDonald DoI 2.5.18)

B5515 127 Sqn Catterick, prop accident 2.7.18 (2/AM F Ambler slightly injured); 46 TS Catterick 8.18

B5516 52 TS Catterick by 3.18
B5517 49 TDS Catterick by 10.18
B5518 No information
B5519 5 TS Wyton by 3.18; 1 TDS Wittering, stalled, sideslipped in on airfield 19.10.18 (F/Cdt AM Rennie killed)
B5520 126 Sqn Fowlmere by 6.18
B5521 6 TDS Boscombe Down by 25.5.18
B5522 4 (Aux) SoAG Marske by 20.3.18; 2 FS Marske ('16')
B5523 6 TDS Boscombe Down; 44 TS Waddington by 25.3.18
B5524 4 (Aux) SoAG Marske by 25.3.18; 2 FS 1918
B5525 6 TDS Boscombe Down
B5526 FF 12.4.18; 6 TDS Boscombe Down, tailplane failed, a/c broke up 9.5.18 (Lt RJ Griffiths & Pte JJ Leighton of 188th US Aero Sqn both killed)
B5527 6 TDS Boscombe Down, collided with lorry crossing aerodrome 3.7.18 (Lt L Hawkins seriously injured & 2/Lt SC Booth injured)
B5528 2 FS Marske 1918
B5529 44 TS Waddington, formation flight, stalled at 200ft, crashed 20.7.18 (2/Lt P Clifford USAS killed)
B5530 to B5532 No information
B5533 52 TS Catterick by 3.18
B5534 No information
B5535 52 TS Catterick by 3.18
B5536 Old Sarum 4.18
B5537 No information
B5538 FF 19.4.18; 31 TDS Fowlmere, aileron jammed, crashed 24.9.18 (2/Lt BC Fairchild & 2/Lt PS Griffith both OK)
B5539 35 TDS Duxford 4.18; 126 Sqn Fowlmere by 6.18 until sqn disbanded 17.8.18
B5540 No information
B5541 (BHP) 109 Sqn Lake Down, pilot lost control, stalled and dived in on attempting to land 19.5.18 (2/Lt JCA Barker killed & 2/AM J Stillman injured)
B5542 109 Sqn Lake Down by 11.5.18
B5543 109 Sqn Lake Down by 10.5.18
B5544 109 Sqn Lake Down by 13.6.18
B5545 109 Sqn Lake Down by 21.5.18
B5546 49 TDS Catterick by 8.18
B5547 No information
B5548 52 TS Catterick by 4.18
B5549 49 TDS Catterick by 8.18; WEE Biggin Hill by 26.9.18 [? - listed as DH9 .5549]
B5550 49 TDS Catterick by 8.18 - 10.18

D.H.4 rebuilds by No.1(S) ARD Farnborough numbered in the range B7731 to B8230

B7747 (RAF 3a) 8 AAP Lympne by 16.1.18; Rec Pk 18.1.18; 2 AI 5.2.18; 49 Sqn ('6') 6.2.18; On test flight, m/c was flying with left wing low, efforts to right this failed and it was difficult to get out of turn, FL, hit sunken road 16.2.18 (2/Lt AM Curtiss & 2/Lt V Gordon); Rep Pk 2 ASD 20.2.18; SOC 23.3.18
B7764 (Fiat A.12) At 1 (S)ARD 29.3.18, allotted to EF but reallotted to E.1c Home Anti Submarine for Cdr HA Williamson; At (S)ARD 27.6.18, allotted to EF, Eagle VI fitted; Rec Pk to 2 AI 1.8.18; 205 Sqn 14.8.18; Shot about by EA in raid on Busigny, FL nr Germaine 16.9.18 (Lt GC Matthews wounded & 2/Lt AG Robertson killed); 2 ASD 20.9.18; SOC 2 Salvage Dump 2 ASD 24.9.18
B7768 Dunkirk for delivery by 25.5.18
B7812 (Fiant A.12) Rec Pk to 2 AI 17.7.18; 3 ASD 18.7.18; 55 Sqn 18.7.18; 3 ASD 16.8.18; 55 Sqn 9.10.18; Crashed near aerodrome returning from raid 3.11.18 (2/Lt DC Fleischer killed & 2/Lt HB Mercier DoI); 6 AP 4.11.18; 3 ASD 5.11.18
B7818 (Fiat A.12) Issued for training W/E 27.5.18; 126 Sqn Fowlmere by 7.18 until sqn disbanded 17.8.18
B7819 (Fiat A.12) Issued for training W/E 27.5.18
B7826 (BHP) Issued for training W/E 17.6.18
B7854 (BHP) Issued for training W/E 1.7.18
B7857 (BHP) Issued for training W/E 13.5.18; 126 Sqn Fowlmere by 8.18 until sqn disbanded 17.8.18
B7865 (Eagle VI) At 1 (S)ARD 27.6.18, reallotted from 61 Wing to EF; 2 AI to 57 Sqn 30.6.18; Left 09.25 on photo recce Riencourt Dump, last seen over Bapaume 20.7.18 (Lt JT Kirkland killed & 2/Lt EI Riley PoW)
B7866 (Eagle VI) At 1 (S)ARD 28.5.18, allotted to EF; England to Rec Pk 29.5.18; 2 AI 30.5.18; 55 Sqdn 3.6.18; Bombing raid on Karlsruhe, driven down in combat over Saarbrucken 25.6.18 (Lt GA Sweet & 2/Lt CFR Goodyear both killed)
B7871 (BHP) Issued for training W/E 3.6.18
B7878 2 FS Marske 1918
B7885 (RAF 3a) At 1 (S)ARD 27.6.18, allotted to EF;
B7891 2 TDS Stonehenge by 22.1.18; 98 Sqn Old Sarum by 23.1.18 - 3.18; Martlesham Heath 4.9.18 - 31.1.19 (230hp Galloway Adriatic)
B7895 'B' Flt 1 Comm Sqn Kenley 6.19
B7910 (230hp Galloway Adriatic) To AES Martlesham Heath W/E 14.9.18 (Performance and general running); Norwich 22.1.19
B7911 (Eagle VIII) Arr Rec Pk 21.8.18; 2 AI 23.8.18; 2 AI to 25 Sqn 13.9.18; COL on test flight 18.10.18 (Lt JG Farquhar & 2/Lt I McEachran); At 1 ASD, u/s 10.18 (replaced by A7982); Rebuilt as H6887 31.10.18
B7925 Farnborough to Rec Pk but FL en route at Chappes 29.8.18; Rec Pk to 2 AI and on to 3 ASD 30.8.18; 55 Sqn 26.9.18; FTR, then located Port D'Atelier 10.11.18; Retd 14.11.18; Repaired in Sqn; 2 ASD 17.1.19
B7933 Left Farnborough 18.9.18; Arr Rec Pk 19.9.18; 2 AI and on to 3 ASD 20.9.18; 55 Sqn 28.9.18; In action 21.10.18 (Sgt EV Clare wounded); Fokker DVII OOC Saarbrucken 14.30 6.11.18 (Lt RFH Norman & Capt JFD Tanqueray): 2 ASD 17.1.19; 6 AI to 25 Sqn 15.3.19; 6 SS 13.5.19
B7937 4 ASD Wissant to 202 Sqn 14.11.18; 1(S)ARD Farnborough for HMS *Argus* 6.1.19; 6 SD Ascot (for HMS *Argus*) W/E 16.1.19 - @30.1.19
B7938 (Eagle VIII) 3 ASD to 55 Sqn 8.11.18; 2 ASD 17.1.19; 6 AI to 25 Sqn 21.3.19; 6 AI 13.5.19
B7939 Recd Rec Pk 1 ASD ex UK for IF 5.10.18; 5 AI 8.10.18; to 3 AD 9.10.18 but FL Fourneil, Paris 12.10.18, arr 3 AD 17.10.18; 57 Sqn, engine cut out on take off but before leaving the ground, wind lifted left wing up and turned m/c over 17.12.18 (2/Lt J Erskine seriously injured & Lt W Steele OK)
B7940 (Eagle VIII) Recd Rec Pk 1 ASD 30.8.18; 2 AI to 3 ASD 31.8.18; 55 Sqn 4.9.18; 6 AP 20.9.18; 3 ASD 21.9.18; On test at 2 AI engine failed struck trees and crashed 30.1.19 (2/Lt HS Sandiford & AC2 A Wardell both injured); SOC
B7941 (Eagle VIII) 4 ASD Wissant to 217 Sqn 16.10.18; 98 Sqn 6.3.19; 1 ASD 19.3.19; Retd UK
B7942 (Eagle VIII) 6IS to 57 Sqn 12.3.19; Casualty Report 16.3.19 says after two flights machine found to be defective
B7950 Recd Rec Pk ex UK for IF 9.11.18
B7951 (Eagle VIII) Imperial Gift to South Africa
B7962 (Eagle VIII) Imperial Gift to South Africa
B7964 (Eagle VIII) 4 ASD Wissant to 217 Sqn 22.10.18; 98 Sqn 6.3.19; 1 ASD 19.3.19; 6 AI to 57 Sqn 7.4.19
B7966 Recd Rec Pk ex UK for IF 8.11.18; 3 AD 9.11.18
B7967 Recd Rec Pk ex UK for IF 9.11.18; 3 AD 9.11.18
B7969 Used for communications in Rhineland post-war
B7976 (Eagle VIII) Imperial Gift to South Africa
B7977 6 TDS Boscombe Down, swung on TO, collided with hangar 13.9.18 (2/Lt BV Chinery slightly injured)
B7979 (Eagle VIII) Imperial Gift to South Africa; To South African Air Corps
B7982 Recd Rec Pk ex UK for IF 9.11.18; 3 AD 10.11.18; EF 13.11.18
B7985 495 Flt 246 Sqn Seaton Carew by 6.11.18
B7986 (Eagle VIII) 4 ASD to 202 Sqn 4.11.18; 233 Sqn Dover 6.3.19; At Joyce Green by 26.4.19, allocated 2 Comm Sqn Buc for special duty with HM the King of the Belgians
B7987 (Eagle) AES Martlesham Heath from 19.12.18 (general work & developing testing methods); Damaged W/E 1.2.19; Left W/E 8.7.19; AES Martlesham Heath by 7.10.19
B7991 (Eagle VIII) Imperial Gift to South Africa as *201*
B7992 (Eagle VIII) Imperial Gift to South Africa as *203*
B7993 (Eagle VIII) Imperial Gift to South Africa
B7976 (Eagle VIII) Imperial Gift to South Africa
B8005 (Eagle VIII) Imperial Gift to South Africa
B8013 (Eagle VIII) Imperial Gift to South Africa as *202*
B8016 (Eagle VIII) Imperial Gift to South Africa

D.H.4 B7941 of No.217 Squadron, seen postwar, appears to have a fuselage badge similar to that used by the U.S.Marines Northern Bombing Group, who sometimes flew No.217 Squadron's aircraft. (via Frank Cheesman)

D.H.4 B7964 of No.217 Squadron, seen postwar, probably at Bickendorf, also appears to have fuselage badge similar to that used by the U.S.Marines Northern Bombing Group. (via Frank Cheesman)

D.H.4 rebuild B7950 served post-war with the Independent Force

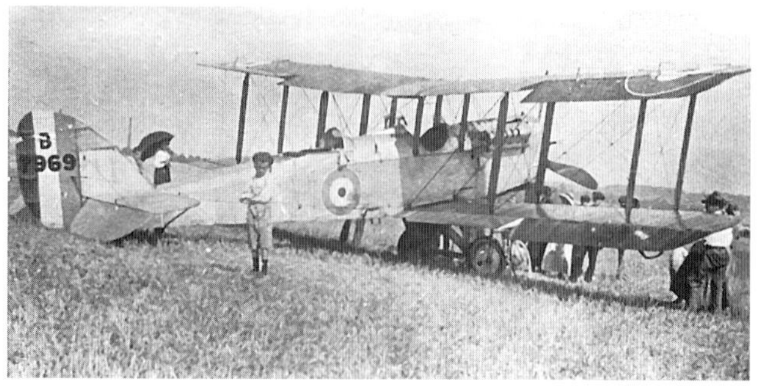

D.H.4 rebuild B7969 on post-war communications work in Rhineland. (J.M.Bruce/G.S.Leslie collection)

B8091 1 SoN&BD Stonehenge 2.18
B8125 1 SoN&BD Stonehenge 2.18

6 D.H.4 built by Westland Aircraft Works, Yeovil and numbered N6382 to N6387 for RNAS but renumbered B9434 to B9439 for RFC before delivery. (200hp RAF 3a)

B9434 At Makers 11.8.17, allotted to EF; England to ARS 1 AD 30.8.17; ARS 2 AD 4.9.17; 18 Sqn 8.9.17; Left 12.25, FTR 25.3.18 (Capt RP Fenn & Capt HW Barwell MC both killed)

B9435 At Makers 11.8.17, allotted to EF, England to ARS 1 AD 26.8.17; 18 Sqn 1.9.17; Albatros OOC Bourlon 14.20 16.9.17 (2/Lt JF Byron & 2/Lt EJ Detmold); Scout OOC during raid on Allenes 12.15 10.3.18 (2/Lt GWF Darvill & Sgt AOA Pollard); Struck ridge on landing, u/c torn away 18.3.18 (2/Lt R Smith & Sgt W Candy OK); Rep Pk 1 ASD 19.3.18; SOC 29.5.18

B9436 At Makers 11.8.17, allotted to EF; England to ARS 1 AD 31.8.17; ARS 2 AD 5.9.17; 18 Sqn 20.9.17; Albatros D OOC Gouy 11.15 24.9.17 (2/Lt CF Horsley & Lt AE Hahn); Engine shot through in combat, FL 2 Sqn aerodrome, hit ditch, crashed 11.40 6.3.18 (2/Lt WA Rochelle & Lt JM Brisbane both OK); Rep Pk 1 ASD 9.3.18; SOC 14.4.18

B9437 At Makers 11.8.17, allotted to EF; England to ARS 1 AD 14.9.17; ARS 2 AD 15.9.17; 18 Sqn 26.9.17; Engine choked and cut out just after take off 10.4.18 (2/Lt DB Richardson & 2/AM J Perigo both injured); Rep Pk 1 ASD 14.4.18; SOC 20.4.18

B9438 At Makers 11.8.17, allotted to EF; Allotment cancelled 24.8.17 but reinstated 29.8.17; England to ARS 1 AD 7.9.17 but FL on route, arrived 9.9.17 "Wrecked"; ARS 2 AD 5.10.17; 18 Sqn 31.10.17; Engine failure crashed 28.12.17 (Sgt W McCleary injured & Lt L Scott shaken); Rep Pk 1 ASD 1.1.18; SOC 23.7.18 NWR

B9439 At Makers 11.8.17, allotted to EF; En route Lympne to (S)ARD 6.9.17 allotment to EF cancelled, now on charge E.1 Repair Section

1 D.H.4 built by Westland Aircraft Works, Yeovil under Cont No C.P.103711/17 and transferred to RFC (Military Wing) on delivery, renumbered B9456. (200hp BHP)

B9456 (ex N6393) Westland Yeovil to 2 TDS Lake Down 15.9.17; 2 TDS Stonehenge 2.12.17 - @29.12.17; 98 Sqn Old Sarum to 107 Sqn Lake Down 15.2.18

1 D.H.4 built by Westland Aircraft Works, Yeovil under Cont No C.P.103711/17 and transferred to RFC (Military Wing) on delivery, renumbered B9458

B9458 (ex N6397) Fitted with high compression 230hp BHP engine No.S.D.5028 W.D.22702; Testing Sqn Martlesham Heath to replace A7462 22.9.17 (tests with Claudel Hobson carburettor and 4x112lb bombs; 2.18 tests with compass in lower plane, performance with new petrol, carburettor tests); Undercarriage under repair at Orfordness from week ending 6.7.18; Returned from Orfordness after repair during week ending 28.9.18; MAES Grain 31.10.18

2 D.H.4 built by Westland Aircraft Works, Yeovil and numbered N6401 & N6405 for RNAS but renumbered B9460 and B9461 for RFC before delivery. (200hp BHP)

B9460 At 2 AAP Hendon 26.9.17, allotted to EF; 1 AD to 27 Sqn 8.10.17; Casualty Report 11.4.18 says repairs needed would take more than 3 days, return to Depot recommended; 2 AI 15.4.18; Rep Pk 2 ASD 22.4.18; SOC 7.5.18

B9461 At 2 AAP Hendon 2.10.17, allotted to EF; 1 AD to 27 Sqn 18.10.17; COL 26.11.17 (2/Lt S Anderson & Lt W Ronald); Rep Pk 1 ASD 26.11.17; 1 AI 4.1.18; 27 Sqn 12.1.18; Forced to return from raid with engine trouble, engine cut out, FL just outside aerodrome 25.1.18 (2/Lt WS Mathew & Sgt A/G AJ Beavis); Rep Pk 1 ASD 27.1.18; SOC 26.4.18

1 D.H.4 built by Westland Aircraft Works, Yeovil and numbered N6409 for RNAS but renumbered B9470 for RFC before delivery. (200hp BHP)

B9470 At 2 AAP Hendon 25.10.17, allotted to EF; 1 AD to 27 Sqn 31.10.17; FL in field nr 5N Sqn aerodrome, crashed on take off 22.11.17 (Lt ECJ Elliott killed & 2/Lt H Townsend injured); Rep Pk 1 ASD 23.11.17; SOC 26.11.17

1 D.H.4 built up from spares by 7th Wing ARS Norwich and numbered B9471. (200hp BHP)

B9471 Deld 19 TS Hounslow 5.11.17

25 D.H.4 ordered 12.10.17 under Cont No A.S.29679/1/17 from Westland Aircraft Works, Yeovil and numbered B9476 to B9500. (200hp BHP unless otherwise stated)

B9476 Deld CSD White City 11.17; Shipped to 2 Wing Mudros 19.12.17 (no engine); Mudros by 3.18; Surveyed 2.3.18 (wrecked and burnt); Deleted 15.4.18

B9477 Deld CSD White City 11.17; Shipped to 2 Wing Mudros 2.1.18 (no engine); Mudros for erection by 4.3.18 - @24.3.18; Stavros by 6.18 & @4.8.18; Stavros by 10.18; Andrano by 10.18; Mudros by 10.18 (with Greeks); 220 Sqn Imbros by 20.10.18 - @2.11.18; To Greek Government

B9478 Deld Hendon W/E 17.11.17; RAE to Dover 24.11.17; RNASTE Cranwell W/E 1.12.17; Became 202 TDS Cranwell 1.4.18; To Redcar but FL nr Redcar 5.5.18; Became 57 TDS Cranwell 27.7.18 - @8.18

B9479 Deld RNASTE Cranwell W/E 7.12.17 - @30.3.18; Crashed 28.1.18 (pilot unhurt); Became 201/2 TDS Cranwell 1.4.18; 202 TDS Cranwell 17.6.18; Became 57 TDS Cranwell 27.7.18 - @11.18

B9480 Deld Observers School Flt Eastchurch W/E 24.11.17; HP Sqn Manston 28.11.17; DH4 School Manston 19.1.18; Became 203 TDS Manston 1.4.18; Became 55 TDS Manston (coded '6') 14.7.18; 55 TDS Narborough 9.18 - @10.18

D.H.4 B9480 of the Handley Page Squadron, Manston around December 1917. (RAF Museum P.735)

B9481 Deld HP Sqn Manston by 21.12.17; DH4 School Manston ('6') 19.1.18; Crashed 1.18; Deleted W/E 26.1.18

B9482 Deld HP Sqn Manston 28.11.17; DH4 School Manston ('7') 19.1.18; Became 203 TDS Manston ('7) 1.4.18 - @7.18; Crashed and overturned

B9483 Deld CSD White City 12.17; Hendon W/E 8.12.17; Collided with searchlight, badly damaged 11.12.17 (W/Cdr AM Longmore & PO Lee both injured); Surveyed 14.12.17; Deleted 19.12.18 DBR

B9484 Deld CSD White City 12.17; Hendon W/E 8.12.17; Dover 22.12.17; Paris 23.12.17; In transit by air to Otranto by 18.1.18; DH Flt 6 Wing Otranto by 21.3.18; Became 224 Sqn Otranto 1.4.18; Became 496/8 Flts 224 Sqn Otranto 9.18 - @10.18; Taranto by 10.18 - @1.19

B9485 Deld CSD White City 11.17; Shipped to 2 Wing Mudros 2.1.18; recd Mudros for erection by 24.3.18; 'G' Sqn 63 Wing 1.4.18; Engine trouble after TO, dived in from 200ft, BO 17.4.18 (2/Lt JH Taylor & Lt CC Betts both killed); Surveyed 20.4.18 wrecked; Deleted 11.5.18 wrecked

B9486 Deld HP Sqn Manston by road/rail W/E 26.11.17; DH4 School Manston (coded '8') 19.1.18; Became 203 TDS Manston 1.4.18 - @24.7.18

B9487 Deld HP Sqn Manston by road/rail by 26.11.17; DH4 School Manston (coded '9') 19.1.18; Became 203 TDS Manston ('9') 1.4.18; Became 55 TDS Manston (coded '9') 14.7.18; 55 TDS Narborough 9.18 - @11.18

B9488 (190hp Renault 8G) Deld RNASTE Cranwell for erection W/E 30.11.17; Became 202 TDS Cranwell 1.4.18; Became 57 TDS Cranwell 27.7.18 - @8.18

B9489 Deld RNASTE Cranwell for erection W/E 30.11.17 - @23.2.18; Became 202 TDS Cranwell 1.4.18; Became 57 TDS Cranwell 27.7.18 - @10.18

B9490 Deld HP Sqn Manston by road/rail W/E 27.11.17; DH4 School Manston (coded '10') 19.1.18; Became 203 TDS Manston 1.4.18 - @5.18; 4 ASD by 25.10.18

B9491 Deld HP Sqn Manston by road/rail W/E 30.11.17; DH4 School Manston (coded '9') 19.1.18; Became 203 TDS Manston 1.4.18; Landed on port wing and crashed 12.6.18

B9492 Deld CSD by 1.12.17; Shipped to 2 Wing Mudros 19.1.18 (no engine); arr Mudros by 3.18; 220 Sqn Imbros by 19.6.18 - @25.6.18; Mudros Repair Base by 10.18

B9493 Deld CSD White City 11.17; Shipped to 2 Wing Mudros 2.1.18 (no engine); Mudros (coded 'Z') by 3.18

B9494 (190hp Renault 8G) Deld RNASTE Cranwell for erection W/E 22.12.17; Became 201/2 TDS Cranwell 1.4.18

B9495 (190hp Renault 8G) Deld RNASTE Cranwell for erection W/E 7.12.17; Crashed, u/c damaged Cranwell North 5.4.18 (pilot unhurt); Flat spin, then spinning nose dive into ground 9.5.18 (2/Lt RJW Taylor killed); SOC 29.5.18

B9496 Deld RNASTE Cranwell W/E 7.12.17; Crashed landing, slightly damaged 28.3.18 (pilot unhurt); Became 202 TDS 1.4.18; Crashed near an Avro 504 13.6.18 (PFO HE Foster slightly injured)

B9497 Deld EAD Grain W/E 7.12.17 (fit Stokes gun); AP Dover 22.2.18; 11N Sqn 8.3.18; 12N Sqn 19.3.18; Crashed 30.3.18; To AD Dunkirk; Deleted 8.4.18

B9498 Deld EAD Grain W/E 15.12.17 (fit Stokes gun); AP Dover 27.2.18; 11N Sqn 20.3.18; Became 211 Sqn 1.4.18; Overshot landing 8.4.18 (Lt N Haigh & Lt CL Bray both unhurt); 4 ASD Guines 8.4.18; Deleted 8.4.18

B9499 Deld AP Dover (via Chingford) 11.12.17; 6N Sqn 19.1.18; 11N Sqn 11.3.18; Became 211 Sqn 1.4.18; 4 ASD Guines 9.4.18; 218 Sqn by 3.5.18; Dover W/E 24.5.18; 4 ASD Pilots Pool 26.6.18 - @10.7.18

B9500 Deld Hendon (via Brooklands) 14.12.17; Dover 22.12.17; Paris 23.12.17; Transit by air to 6 Wing by 18.1.18; DH4 Flt 6 Wing Otranto by 3.18; Became 224 Sqn 1.4.18 - @8.18; Damaged by seaplanes 13.6.18 (Lt EL Bragg & Lt PE Linder unhurt)

1 D.H.4 presumed rebuilt from spares and salvage, probably by 7th Wing ARS, Norwich, numbered B9951. (200hp BHP)

B9951 9 TS Norwich, undershot landing, hit belt of trees 23.11.17 (Sgt MJ Newall injured)

1 D.H.4 rebuild from spares and salvage by 6th Wing ARS Dover and numbered B9994. (200hp BHP)

B9994 By 6th Wing; 110 Sqn Sedgeford, caught fire in air, crashed 17.2.18 (2/Lt FB Evans killed)

100 D.H.4 to be ordered from Vulcan Motor & Engineering Co (1906) Ltd, Southport and numbered C1051 to C1150. Order not placed

50 D.H.4 ordered 4.9.17 under Cont No AS.24960 from The Aircraft Manufacturing Co Ltd, Hendon and numbered C4501 to C4550. (All 260hp Fiat A.12)

C4501 At 1 (S)ARD 19.10.17, allotted to EF; ARS 1 AD to ARS 2 AD 29.10.17; Rep Pk 2 ASD to 2 AI 11.1.18; Rep Pk 2 ASD 1.2.18; 2 AI 28.2.18; 49 Sqn 17.3.18; Left 10.30 to bomb Bray, FTR 28.3.18 (2/Lt GS Stewart killed & Lt DD Richardson PoW)

C4502 At 1 (S)ARD 19.10.17, allotted to EF; 8 AAP Lympne for France 31.10.17; Retd Farnborough 4.11.17; Rec Pk to 2 AI 3.2.18; 49 Sqn 11.2.18; FL nr Amiens due to ground mist and approaching darkness, Landed in ploughed field 27.2.18 (Lt JH Morris & 2/Lt AF Ferguson); To Rep Pk 2 ASD; SOC 18.3.18

C4503 At 1 (S)ARD 19.10.17, allotted to EF; FL Basingstoke Canadian Hospital, engine caught fire when backfired but put out 6.12.17; Allotment to EF cancelled 14.12.17, m/c to be W/O

C4504 At 1 (S)ARD 19.10.17, allotted to EF; Tested Farnborough 23.11.17; England to Rec Pk 3.2.18; 49 Sqn 14.3.18; Scout OOC Oisy-le-Verger 1010 23.3.18 (Pilot 2/Lt RA Curry wounded, observer Sgt W Kelsall OK); FL in ploughed field 24.3.18 (2/Lt C Bowman & 2/Lt PT Holligan); Rep Pk 2 ASD; By rail to Rep Pk 1 ASD 1.4.18

C4505 At 1 (S)ARD 19.10.17, allotted to EF; ARS 1 AD to ARS 2 AD 28.10.17; Rep Pk 2 ASD to 2 AI 14.1.18; 49 Sqn 11.2.18; Rep Pk 1 ASD and SOC 8.4.18

C4506 At 1 (S)ARD 19.10.17, allotted to EF; ARS 1 AD to ARS 2 AD 31.10.17; At Rep Pk 2 ASD 31.12.17; 49 Sqn 7.3.18; 1 AI 11.4.18; Rec Pk 17.4.18; England 20.4.18

C4507 At 1 (S)ARD 19.10.17, allotted to EF; ARS 1 AD to ARS 2 AD 28.10.17; Rep Pk 2 ASD to 2 AI 12.1.18; Rep Pk 2 ASD 18.1.18; 2 AI 15.2.18; 49 Sqn 16.2.18; Caught fire on landing 26.2.18 (2/Lt HL Rough & Lt V Dreschfeld both OK); To Rep Pk 2 ASD; SOC 23.3.18

C4508 At 1 (S)ARD 19.10.17, allotted to EF; En route to No.1 (S)ARD from Frimley 31.10.17, allotment to EF cancelled, now on charge E1 Repair Section

C4509 At 1 (S)ARD 19.10.17, allotted to EF; England to Rec Pk 16.3.18; 2 ASD 20.3.18; Rec Pk to England 1.4.18

C4510 At 1 (S)ARD 19.10.17, allotted to EF; ARS 1 AD to ARS 2 AD 28.10.17; Rep Pk 2 ASD to 2 AI 11.1.18; Rep Pk 2 ASD 1.2.18; 2 AI 19.2.18; 49 Sqn 7.3.18; 1 AI 6.4.18; Rec Pk 7.4.18; England 11.4.18;

C4511 At 1 (S)ARD 19.10.17, allotted to EF; England to Rec Pk 25.1.18; 2 AI 16.3.18; SOC 22.5.18 (NWR); sent to England in cases

C4512 At 1 (S)ARD 19.10.17, allotted to EF; Rec Pk to 2 AI 16.3.18; 49 Sqn 18.3.18; Adv Salvage to Rep Pk 1 ASD 9.4.18; SOC 12.4.18

C4513 At 1 (S)ARD 19.10.17, allotted to EF; En route from Hadlow to (S)ARD 4.2.18, to be W/O by (S)ARD)

C4514 At 1 (S)ARD 19.10.17, allotted to EF; England to Rec Pk 28.1.18; 2 AI 30.1.18; 2 AI to Rep Pk 2 ASD; SOC 25.5.18 (NWR); sent to England in cases

C4515 At 1 (S)ARD 19.10.17, allotted to EF; ARS 1 AD to ARS 2 AD 29.10.17; Rep Pk 2 ASD to 2 AI 12.1.18; Rep Pk 2 ASD 18.1.18; 2 AI 20.2.18; 49 Sqn 6.3.18; COL 17.3.18 (Lt RL Crofton & Sgt T Wills); Rep Pk 2 ASD 19.3.18; SOC 23.3.18

C4516 At 1 (S)ARD 19.10.17, allotted to EF; England to Rec Pk 28.1.18; 2 AI 30.1.18; Rep Pk 2 ASD 5.2.18; 2 AI 28.2.18; SOC Rep Pk 2 ASD 7.5.18

C4517 At 1 (S)ARD 19.10.17, allotted to EF; En route from Cove to (S)ARD 4.2.18, to be W/O by 1 (S)ARD

C4518 At 1 (S)ARD 19.10.17, allotted to EF; Tested Farnborough 26.11.17; En route Yarmouth (IoW) to 1 (S)ARD 14.12.17, allotment to EF cancelled, now on charge E.1a Repair Section

C4519 At 1 (S)ARD 19.10.17, allotted to EF; En route from North Weald to (S)ARD 6.2.18, to be W/O by 1 (S)ARD

C4520 At 1 (S)ARD 19.10.17, allotted to EF; England to Rec Pk 27.1.18; 2 AI 16.3.18; 49 Sqn 17.3.18; Bombing raid, petrol tank shot through in combat with EA Villers Bretonneaux, FL, crashed 10.00 25.3.18 (2/Lt C Bowman & Sgt W Kelsall OK); Adv Salvage to Rep Pk 1 ASD 10.4.18; SOC 14.4.18

C4521 At 1 (S)ARD 19.10.17, allotted to EF; 8 AAP Lympne by 16.2.18; Rec Pk 18.2.18; 2 AI 11.3.18; 49 Sqn 14.3.18; Rec Pk and on to England 12.4.18; At 57 Sqn by 22.3.19; Taking off from Cologne on mail service collided with an RE8 which was landing 4.4.19 (2/Lt HA Griffiths OK & 2/Lt ECW Bray injured)

C4522 At 1 (S)ARD 19.10.17, allotted to EF; Rec Pk to 2 AI 28.1.18; 49 Sqn 15.2.18; Adv Salvage to Rep Pk 1 ASD 11.4.18; SOC 14.4.18

C4523 At 1 (S)ARD 19.10.17, allotted to EF; Tested Farnborough 29.11.17; 8 AAP Lympne 27.1.18; Rec Pk 27.1.18; 2 AI 20.3.18; 49 Sqn 23.3.18; Rec Pk and on to England 12.4.18; 1(S)ARD Farnborough by 27.4.18 - @27.5.18 for Killingholme anti-submarine (use of W/Cdr HA Williamson); UK to Rec Pk 14.10.18; 3 AD 17.10.18 - @18.10.18; 6 AI to 57 Sqn 8.2.19

C4524 At 1 (S)ARD 19.10.17, allotted to EF; England to Rec Pk 15.3.18; 2 AI 18.3.18; 49 Sqn 24.3.18; Rec Pk 12.4.18; To England 14.5.18; 1(S) ARD Farnborough to Killingholme, but EF en route, FL Stallingborough, Lincs 31.5.18

C4525 At 1 (S)ARD 19.10.17, allotted to EF; Rec Pk to 2 AI 17.3.18; Rec Pk 4.4.18; Rep Pk 1 ASD 5.4.18; SOC 8.4.18

C4526 At 1 (S)ARD 19.10.17, allotted to EF; England to Rec Pk 24.1.18; 2 AI 2.2.18; 49 Sqn 11.2.18; COL 10.3.18 (2/Lt HL Rough & 2/Lt V Dreschfeld); Rep Pk 2 ASD; Railed to Rep Pk 1 ASD 1.4.18, arrived 4.4.18; SOC 8.4.18

C4527 At 1 (S)ARD 19.10.17, allotted to EF; ARS 1 AD to ARS 2 AD 29.10.17; SOC Rep Pk 2 ASD 16.11.17

C4528 At 1 (S)ARD 19.10.17, allotted to EF; England to Rec Pk 16.3.18; 2 AI 24.3.18; Rec Pk 1.4.18; To England 7.4.18

C4529 At 1 (S)ARD 19.10.17, allotted to EF; England to Rec Pk 4.2.18; 2 AI 24.2.18; Rec Pk 1.4.18; To England 25.7.18

C4530 At 1 (S)ARD 19.10.17, allotted to EF; England to Rec Pk 24.1.18; 2 AI 28.1.18; 49 Sqn 11.2.18; On practice flight engine cut out, m/c stalled and nose dived in bursting into flames 6.3.18 (Lt JH Morris killed & 1/AM WG Hasler injured); SOC Rep Pk 2 ASD 11.3.18

C4531 At 1 (S)ARD 19.10.17, allotted to EF; England to Rec Pk 16.3.18; 2 ASD 24.3.18; SOC 18.5.18 NWR; sent to England in cases

C4532 At 1 (S)ARD 19.10.17, allotted to EF; Rec Pk to 2 AI 29.1.18; At 2 ASD, overshot on landing and crashed 19.5.18 (2/Lt JA Dear); SOC 7.6.18 NWR

C4533 At 1 (S)ARD 19.10.17, allotted to EF; Farnborough to Lympne for France, but arr in dark so retd Farnborough 30.10.17; ARS 1 AD to ARS 2 AD 31.10.17; Became Rep Pk 2 ASD 1.11.17; 2 AI 12.1.18; Rep PK 2 ASD 12.2.18; SOC 18.5.18 NWR; sent to England in cases

C4534 At 1 (S)ARD 19.10.17, allotted to EF; Still at No.1 (S)ARD 21.11.17 when allotment cancelled, a/c to be W/O

C4535 At 1 (S)ARD 19.10.17, allotted to EF; England to Rec Pk 28.1.18; 2 AI 16.3.18; 49 Sqn 17.3.18; 1 AI 6.4.18; Rec Pk and on to England 7.4.18; Flown Hendon-Brough-Hendon 11.8.18

C4536 At 1 (S)ARD 19.10.17, allotted to EF; England to Rep Pk 2 ASD 6.1.18; FIAT special test 9.1.18; 2 AI and on to 49 Sqn 10.1.18; Rec Pk 12.4.18; To England 8.5.18

C4537 At 1 (S)ARD 19.10.17, allotted to EF; Rec Pk to 2 AI 15.3.18; Rep Pk 2 ASD; SOC 25.5.18 (NWR); sent to England in cases

C4538 At 1 (S)ARD 19.10.17, allotted to EF; England to Rec Pk 27.1.18; 2 AI 30.1.18; 49 Sqn 5.3.18; Propeller broke at 15,000 feet, fuselage twisted due to excessive vibration, FL nr aerodrome 23.3.18 (Capt WG Chambers & Lt WA Duncan); Rep Pk 2 ASD; Railed to Rep Pk 1 ASD 2.4.18; SOC 8.4.18 NWR

C4539 At 1 (S)ARD 19.10.17, allotted to EF; but still at (SARD) 19.12.17 when allotment cancelled, m/c to be W/O

C4540 At 1 (S)ARD 19.10.17, allotted to EF; England to Rec Pk 24.1.18; 2 AI 30.1.18; Rec Pk 1.4.18; England 20.4.18

C4541 to C4550 cancelled and reallocated
[Ten "Fiat airframes" were delivered to Rep Pk 1 ASD 11.17. Seven were dismantled for spares 15.3.18. The airframes were unserialled but presumably were the balance of the contract]

25 D.H.4 ordered 12.10.17 under Cont No A.S.29679 from Westland Aircraft Works, Yeovil and numbered D1751 to D1775. All to naval units. (200hp BHP)

D1751 Deld Dover 2.1.18; 6N Sqn 13.1.18; 11N Sqn 11.3.18; Hendon (via Dover) 15.3.18; Dunkirk 16.3.18; EF, FL

D.H.4 D1769 photographed on 13.5.18 with special fittings for ditching experiments at Grain. (J.M.Bruce/G.S.Leslie collection)

D.H.4 D1769 being ditched near a warship during ditching experiments around August 1918. (B.Robertson)

A close-up view of the paravane fitted to D.H.4 D1769 for ditching experiments at Grain. (W.J.Evans)

A close-up view of the containers built into the fuselage of D.H.4 D1769 for ditching experiments at Grain. (J.M.Bruce/G.S.Leslie)

AD Dunkirk 17.3.18; 11N Sqn 18.3.18; Became 211 Sqn 1.4.18; 4 ASD 8.4.18?; 218 Sqn 24.4.18; Crashed, damaged, Guston Road 8.5.18 (Lt BH Stata & Capt FET Hewlett); AP Dover repair 10.5.18; 491 Flt Dover by 25.5.18; 4 ASD 25.6.18; 2 SS Richborough 2.10.18

D1752 Deld Dover 22.12.17 - @12.1.18; AD Dunkirk by 17.1.18; 6N Sqn 19.1.18; 11N Sqn 11.3.18; Became 211 Sqn 1.4.18; 4 ASD 8.4.18; 218 Sqn 25.4.18; Dover W/E 24.5.18; Pilots Pool, crashed, to 4 ASD 25.10.18

D1753 Deld NAP Brooklands W/E 29.12.17; Dover 4.1.18; 6N Sqn 3.1.18; 11N Sqn 11.3.18; EF, FL, crashed 23.3.18 (FSL AG Storey & AGL HW Newsham); 4 ASD Guines 24.3.18; Deleted 8.4.18

D1754 Deld NAP Brooklands 1.18; Dover 13.1.18; 6N Sqn 27.1.18; 11N Sqn 11.3.18; Became 211 Sqn 1.4.18; 202 Sqn 16.4.18; Crashed on TO, BO 21.4.18 (Lt GH Whitmill killed); Surveyed 28.4.18; Deleted 15.5.18

D1755 Deld W/E 12.12.17 to Sunbeams Moorfield Works, Wolverhampton for experiments

D1756 Deld NAP Brooklands W/E 19.12.17; Dover 16.2.18; Deleted 15.5.18 DBR; Restored to commission; 491 Flt Dover by 25.5.18; Dunkirk 30.7.18; 4 ASD by 13.10.18

D1757 Deld NAP Brooklands W/E 19.12.17; AAP Dover 18.2.18; 11N Sqn 6.3.18; Became 211 Sqn 1.4.18; 202 Sqn 16.4.18; 218 Sqn 25.4.18 - @27.4.18; 202 Sqn (retd?) to Dover 28.4.18; COL Guston Rd, Dover 1.5.18 (Lt JH Eyres & 1/AM RH Peters uninjured); Broke propeller and crashed over edge of aerodrome Dover 9.5.18 (Lt JH Eyres injured); AP Dover repair 10.5.18; Surveyed 15.5.18; Deletion recommended 17.5.18; 491 Flt Dover by 24.5.18 (for deletion); 4 ASD 25.6.18; Deleted 5.7.18

D1758 Deld NAP Brooklands W/E 19.12.17; AAP Dover 21.2.18; 11N Sqn 12.3.18; 12N Sqn 16.3.18 - @30.3.18; Surveyed Dover 10.5.18; Deleted 15.5.18 DBR; Restored to commission; 491 Flt Dover by 25.5.18; Rec Pk 6.18; 2 ASD 18.6.18; 4 ASD Audembert 21.6.18; 4 ASD Pilots Pool by 3.7.18 - @13.7.18; 491 Flt Dover by 15.8.18; Pilots Pool to 4 ASD by road by 25.10.18

D1759 Deld CSD White City by 1.12.17; Shipped to 2 Wing Mudros 19.1.18; Mudros by 4.18; Repair Base Mudros by 25.7.18; F Sqn 62 Wing Mudros by 8.18 - @11.18; 220 Sqn Imbros by 28.10.18 - @1.19

D1760 Deld CSD White City by 1.12.17; Shipped to 2 Wing Mudros 19.1.18; 220 Sqn Imbros 7.6.18 - @1.19; To Greek Government

D1761 Deld CSD White City by 15.1.18; Shipped to Mudros 30.1.18; 224 Sqn by 21.4.18; Seen to spiral down to water apparently under control off Trieste Bay 22.8.18 (2/Lt JP Corkery & Lt EC Bragg both killed)

D1762 Deld CSD White City by 1.12.17; Shipped to 2 Wing Mudros 19.1.18; Stavros by 6.18 - @1.19

D1763 Deld CSD White City by 1.12.17; Shipped to 2 Wing

Westland-built D.H.4 D1773 at Yeovil. It was shipped to Mudros in early 1918 to serve with No.224 Squadron. (Westland Helicopters)

Mudros 30.1.18; Mudros by 3.18 - @4.18; Stavros by 6.18 - @2.8.18; Mudros Repair Base by 10.18 - @1.19

D1764 Deld Exptl Flt Gosport 11.1.18 - @10.18 (E/WT expts with RN Signal School, Portsmouth)

D1765 Deld CSD White City by 1.1.18; Shipped to Mudros 30.1.18; 224 Sqn by 7.4.18 - @11.5.18

D1766 Deld CSD White City by 1.1.18; Shipped to Mudros 30.1.18; Mudros by 3.18 - @4.18; Stavros by 6.18 & @10.9.18 - @1.19; 220 Sqn Imbros by 20.10.18

D1767 Deld AAP Hendon 1.18; RNASTE Cranwell 8.1.18; Crashed on nose Cranwell North 17.1.18; Became 202 TDS Cranwell 1.4.18; Became 57 TDS Cranwell 27.7.18 - @8.18

D1768 Deld AAP Hendon 1.18; RNASTE Cranwell W/E 18.1.18; O/t in wind and slightly damaged 26.2.18 (F/Cdr NR Cook DSC & PFO GC Bladon uninjured); Became 202 TDS Cranwell 1.4.18

D1769 (re-engined Puma) Deld NAP Brooklands by 19.1.18; ECD Grain 25.1.18 - @1.4.18 (hydrovane and fittings for flotation gear experiments); Grain Test Dept by 25.5.18; Tested with flotation gear 20.7.18; Ditching trials with double hydrovane 16.8.18; Ditching trials with wooden hydrovane 21.8.18; To Martlesham Heath c.31.10.18 (performance with 'Guardian Angel' parachute; Grain 2.11.18 (continue flotation trials)

D1770 Deld CSD White City by 15.1.18; Shipped to Mudros 30.1.18; G Sqn 2 Wing Mudros by 3.18; 66/67 Wings by 21.4.18; 226 Sqn by 25.5.18; F Sqn Mudros by 10.18

D1771 Deld CSD White City by 15.1.18; Shipped to Mudros 30.1.18; Mudros by 24.3.18 - @3.6.18; F Sqn Mudros by 6.18 - @1.19; To Greek Government; H.2 Flt RHNAS Stavros by 2.11.18

D1772 Deld CSD White City by 15.1.18; Shipped to Mudros 30.1.18; 224 Sqn by 7.4.18 - @13.6.18; AD Taranto by 7.18; 496/8 Flts 224 Sqn 2.9.18; FL 3,000 yds inside enemy lines NW of Fieri 21.9.18 (2/Lt AL Mawer & 2/Lt GE Hughes both PoW)

D1773 Deld CSD White City by 15.1.18; Shipped to Mudros 30.1.18; 224 Sqn by 7.4.18; Crashed on TO for raid on Otranto 9.6.18 (Lt WF Salton killed & 2/AM SW James seriously injured); Deleted 27.6.18

D1774 Deld CSD White City by 15.1.18; Shipped to Mudros 30.1.18; Mudros by 24.3.18 - @4.18; Mobile Sqn Mudros, wingtip hit flagstaff landing and caught fire 10.6.18 (Lt GM Scott & Boy W/T H Boyles both killed)

D1775 Deld CSD White City by 15.1.18; Shipped to Mudros 30.1.18; 224 Sqn Otranto by 7.4.18 - @30.4.18; Disposed of by 25.5.18 (not reported)

80 D.H.4 ordered 29.11.17 under Cont No AS.37726 (37762?) from The Aircraft Manufacturing Co Ltd, Hendon and numbered D8351 to D8430. (mainly fitted Eagle)

D8351 Deld 2 AAP Hendon .18; 1 Comm Sqn Hendon 30.7.18 - @11.8.18

D8352 Deld 2 AAP Hendon .18; 1 Comm Sqn Hendon 30.7.18 - @13.10.18

D8353 (Eagle VIII) 4 ASD to 217 Sqn 17.7.18; Damaged in hangar by A8082 taking off Crochte 18.7.18; 4 ASD 22.7.18; 4 ASD Wissant to 217 Sqn 1.10.18; Dropped 2x230-lb bombs, 1 failed to explode on U-boat 51°29'N 02°37'W 5.10.18; 233 Sqn Dover 1.3.19; At Joyce Green by 26.4.19, allocated 2 Comm Sqn Buc for special duty with HM The King of the Belgians

D8354 (Eagle IV) Deld 2 AAP Hendon W/E 11.7.18; Turnhouse W/E 15.8.18 - @1.19

D8355 (275hp Eagle) FF 29.7.18; Deld 2 AAP Hendon 30.7.18; 1 Comm Sqn Hendon/Kenley by 8.10.18; Taking off on flight to Paris, engine stopped at 20/30 feet, radiator empty of water, a/c stalled and crashed 3.5.19 (Capt EM Knott AFC killed, Sir Frederick H Sykes KCB, Controller General Civil Aviation injured)

D8356 3 ASD to 55 Sqn ('H') 4.9.18; FTR raid on Kaiserslautern 25.9.18 (2/Lt JB Dunn & 2/Lt HS Orange both killed)

D8357 (Eagle VII) 2 AAP Hendon for EF by 27.4.18, allotted to EF; Still at 2 AAP 10.5.18, allotment to EF cancelled crashed

D8358 (Eagle IV) Deld 2 AAP Hendon W/E 11.7.18; Turnhouse W/E 15.8.18 - @1.19

D8359 Deld 2 AAP Hendon .18; 1 Comm Sqn Hendon 30.7.18 - @18.11.18

D8360 (Eagle IV) Deld Islington W/E 15.8.18; Turnhouse by

8.18 - @1.19

D8361 (Eagle IV) Deld Islington W/E 15.8.18; Turnhouse by 8.18 - @1.19

D8362 (Eagle VI) CFS Upavon 7-21.12.18 (developing methods of testing for Martlesham Heath); Left by rail W/E 7.7.19

D8363 (Eagle VIII) 1 (S)ARD Farnborough to 8 AAP Lympne 8.7.18; 4 ASD Audembert 9.7.18; 217 Sqn 22.7.18; Burnt out when hit by A7863 while standing on aerodrome 22.8.18

D8364 Rec Pk to 2 AI 28.9.18; 57 Sqn 1.10.18 to at least 3.19; 49 Sqn Bickendorf ('5') c.6.19

D.H.4 D8364 '5' of No.49 Squadron at Bickendorf around June 1919. (RAF Museum P.9971)

D8365 (Eagle VI) 3 ASD to 55 Sqn 30.8.18; 3 ASD 4.9.18; 55 Sqn 16.9.18; Returning from raid on Kaiserlautern, COL 25.9.18 (2/Lt RV Gordon DoW & 2/Lt S Burbidge OK); 6 AP 27.9.18; 3 ASD 30.9.18

D8366 4 ASD to 217 Sqn but wings damaged and u/c wrecked on arrival 30.7.18 (Lt RF Johnson USN unhurt); retd 4 ASD; 4 ASD Wissant to 217 Sqn 16.10.18; 233 Sqn Dover 1.3.19

D8367 (Eagle VIII) 3 ASD to 55 Sqn and back to 3 ASD 4.9.18 wrecked

D8368 No information

D8369 (Eagle VIII) 3 ASD to 55 Sqn 22.8.18; 3 ASD 28.8.18; 55 Sqn 13.11.18; Delivering dispatches to Valenciennes 17.12.18 was left in the open there for six days, left 23.12.18 and FL at Abeele due to bad weather, was left in an unserviceable hangar for five days, m/c warped and distorted by incessant rain and has been dismantled being unsafe to fly (2/Lt CV Ronchi & 2/Lt S Burbidge OK); 2 ASD 14.1.19

D8370 (Eagle VIII) Allocated for transfer from RFC Hendon to Dover-Dunkirk Command by 30.3.18; 4 ASD Wissant to 217 Sqn 22.7.18; Seaplane shot down 17.9.18 (Lt AM Phillips & Lt NS Dougall); Reallotted from 5 Group to EF 11.4.19 for the use of Mjr RJ Bone DSO; To Mjr RJ Bone 1.3.19; At Joyce Green by 26.4.19, allocated 2 Comm Sqn Buc for special duty with HM the King of The Belgians; Joyce Green to Kenley 28.5.19; 'B' Flt 1 Comm Sqn Kenley 6.19

D8371 (Eagle VIII) Allocated for transfer from RFC Hendon to Dover-Dunkirk Command by 30.3.18; Yarmouth by 25.6.18 - @28.9.18 (at Covehithe 6.18)

D8372 (Eagle VI) At 2 AAP Hendon 7.3.18, allotted to EF; England to Rec Pk 11.3.18; 2 AI and on to 25 Sqn 12.3.18; Left at 06.50, tailplane damaged by AA, controls shot away, FL SE of Asq, overturned 07.50 27.3.18 (2/Lt FF Keen & Cpl T Ramsden OK)

D8373 (Eagle VI) At 2 AAP Hendon 12.3.18, allotted to EF; England to Rec Pk 16.3.18; 2 ASD 17.3.18; 55 Sqn ('G') 23.3.18; Wrecked on take-off 16.7.18 (Lt CR Whitelock killed & Lt G Bryer-Ash injured); 3 ASD 16.7.18; 55 Sqn 6.10.18; 2 ASD 17.1.19; SOC 13.6.19

D8374 (Eagle VIII) Allocated for transfer from RFC Hendon to Dover-Dunkirk Command by 30.3.18; 217 Sqn for erection by 10.9.18; Crashed, caught fire, nr Crochte aerodrome, BO 28.9.18 (2/Lt AF Tong killed & Sgt Mech G/L M Connolly injured)

D8375 (Eagle VI) At 2 AAP Hendon 11.3.18, allotted to EF; England to Rec Pk 23.3.18; 2 AI 23.3.18; 25 Sqn 27.3.18; Whilst stationary at aerodrome, crashed into by D9240 21.4.18; Adv Salvage to Rep Pk 1 ASD 23.4.18; SOC 27.4.18

D8376 (Eagle VIII) Presentation aircraft 'Zanzibar No.6'. Allocated for transfer from RFC Hendon to Dover-Dunkirk Command by 30.3.18; 4 ASD to 217 Sqn 17.7.18; COL, badly damaged 19.8.18 (Lt H Rudd and 2/Lt F Elliott both unhurt); 4 ASD by 9.18; 2 SS Richborough 15.9.18

D8377 (Eagle VI) At 2 AAP Hendon 14.3.18, allotted to EF; England to Rec Pk 20.3.18; 57 Sqn 23.3.18; Fokker DVII crashed at Roisel, the pilot baled out 10.35 14.8.18 (Lt EM Colet & Sgt Mech J Grant); On a test flight wheel collapsed on landing 4.9.18 (Mjr CAA Hiatt & 2/AM WJ Brinsden); SOC Rep Pk 1 ASD 25.9.18, new number H7147 allotted for reconstruction

D8378 (Eagle V) At 8 AAP Lympne 27.5.18, allotted to EF; 2 AI 4.7.18; 25 Sqn 6.7.18; Reconnaissance mission, in combat Mont St.Eloi, FL 08.30 16.9.18 (Lt C Brown OK & Lt EW Griffin killed); Rebuilt as H6885 25.10.18

D8379 (Eagle VI) At 2 AAP Hendon 11.3.18, allotted to EF; England to Rec Pk 15.3.18; 2 ASD 16.3.18; 5N Sqn by 25.3.18; Left 15.29 on bombing raid to Foucaucourt, FTR 27.3.18 (FSL EC Stocker & 1/AM CM Rendle both killed)

D8380 (Eagle VI) Presentation aircraft 'Women of Malaya. Malaya No.27'. At 2 AAP Hendon 14.3.18, allotted to EF; England to Rec Pk 20.3.18; 2 AI 23.3.18; 25 Sqn 27.3.18; Left on photo recce in the Tournai area 13.20, FTR 16.7.18 (Capt E Waterlow MC & Lt JM Mackie DCM MM both killed)

D8381 (Eagle VIII) Allocated for transfer from RFC Hendon to Dover-Dunkirk Command by 30.3.18; (now Eagle V) at 8 AAP Lympne 3.6.18, allotted to EF; Rec Pk to 2 AI 29.6.18; 25 Sqn 30.6.18; Rep Pk 2 ASD 15.9.18 "Unsuitable"

D8382 (Eagle V) At 8 AAP Lympne 27.5.18, allotted to EF; Rec Pk to 2 AI 18.6.18; 57 Sqn 23.6.18; Low bombing raid on Moislains aerodrome, Fokker DVII OOC 8.8.18 (Sgt Mech DE Edgley & 2/Lt FG Craig); Fokker DVII OOC nr Douai 11.00 16.8.18 (Lt LK Devitt & 2/Lt FG Craig); Left 14.55 for raid on Cambrai Annex Station, Fokker DVII OOC, own a/c damaged in combat 1.9.18 (Sgt Mech DE Edgley OK & Sgt Mech N Sandison wounded); SOC Rep Pk 1 ASD 25.9.18, new number allotted H7148 for reconstruction

D8383 (Eagle V) At 2 AAP Hendon 1.6.18, allotted to EF; Rec Pk to 2 AI 30.6.18; 25 Sqn 2.7.18; Reported as being unable to climb 15.8.18; SOC Rep Pk 1 ASD 17.9.18 ex Rec Pk, new number H7124 allotted for reconstruction

D8384 (Eagle VI later VIII) Allocated for transfer from RFC Hendon to Dover-Dunkirk Command by 30.3.18; 8 AAP Lympne by 31.5.18, allotted to EF; 2 AI 28.6.18; 3 ASD 1.7.18; 55 Sqn 8.7.18; 3 ASD 7.8.18; 55 Sqn 14.9.18; Fokker OOC S of Longuyan 29.10.18 (2/Lt GT Richardson & 2/Lt LJB Ward); Failed to return from a raid on the Burbach works, Saarbrücken 6.11.18 (pilot Lt GT Richardson PoW & 2/Lt LJB Ward killed); SOC 9.11.18

D8385 (Eagle VI) At 8 AAP Lympne 31.5.18, allotted to EF; Rec Pk to 2 AI 1.7.18; 57 Sqn 2.7.18; Photo mission, Fokker OOC Bancourt, own controls shot up nr Gommecourt 17.30, FL, hit trees, wrecked 30.8.18 (Lt LK Devitt OK & Sgt AC Lovesey wounded); SOC 2 Salvage Dump 3.9.18

D8386 (Eagle V) At 8 AAP Lympne 27.5.18, allotted to EF; Rec Pk to 2 AI 26.6.18; 55 Sqn 27.6.18; COL 17.7.18 (Lt C Young & Lt RA Butler); 3 ASD 17.7.18; 55 Sqn 23.8.18; Pfalz DIII broke up nr Kaiserslautern 25.9.18 (Lt WG Braid USAS OK & 2/Lt GS Barber killed); Crashed, CW 23.10.18 (Lt CE Reynolds DoI); 6 AP 27.10.18; 3 ASD 29.10.18

D8387 (Eagle VI) At 8 AAP Lympne 31.5.18, allotted to EF; Rec Pk to 2 AI and on to 205 Sqn 30.6.18; Damaged by AA 25.7.18 (observer 2/Lt PS Hartley wounded); flying again by 2.8.18; Engaged Pfalz DIII 08.00, afterwards OOC 11.8.18 (Lt WH Clarke & Lt CN Witham); FL after engaged by heavy AA 21.8.18 (Lt AN Hyde & 2/Lt WW Harrison unhurt); Retd 22.8.18; 2 AI exchanged for D.H.9A 1.9.18; Hounslow 21.9.18; Rep Pk 2 ASD 24.9.18

D8388 (Eagle VII) At 2 AAP Hendon 22.5.18, allotted to EF; 2 AI to 55 Sqn 6.6.18; Hit by AA in bombing raid on Metz 24.6.18 (2/Lt JR Bell & Sgt EV Clare OK); 2 ASD 24.6.18; 55 Sqn 25.6.18; Shot up in combat with EAs, fuel tank holed in Darmstadt raid, FL Luneville 16.8.18 (2/Lt TH Laing OK & 2/Lt N Wallace wounded); FTR raid on Kaiserslautern, believed hit by AA 25.9.18 (2/Lt RC Pretty & 2/Lt GR Bartlett both PoW)

D8389 (Eagle VI) At 2 AAP Hendon 22.5.18, allotted to EF; Rec Pk to 2 AI 5.6.18; 25 Sqn 10.6.18; Damaged in heavy landing 28.7.18 (2/Lt F Meehan unhurt; no passenger, ballast carried); Rep Pk 2 ASD 30.7.18; Rebuilt as F6232 6.8.18

D8390 (Eagle VIII) Dunkirk by 9.18; 4 ASD by rail 3.9.18; 202 Sqn 3.11.18; Rep Pk 4 ASD 11.18 (overhaul); 98 Sqn 15.3.19; Visited 217 Sqn, after TO on return, EF, FL in large wood WSW of Bruges, hit tree, crashed 16.3.19 (Capt RV James DFC injured); 1 ASD 19.3.19 WOC

D8391 (Eagle VIII) Arr Dunkirk (4 ASD?) 30.7.18; 4 ASD to 202 Sqn 13.10.18; 98 Sqn 16.3.19; 1 ASD 19.3.19

D8392 (Eagle V) At 2 AAP Hendon 27.4.18, allotted to EF; England to Rec Pk 4.5.218; 2 AI 8.5.18; 55 Sqn 16.5.18; EA OOC SW of Karlsruhe 31.5.18 (Lt CA Bridgland & 2/Lt ER Stewart); Hit by mg fire, COL, wrecked 16.7.18 (Lt E Blythe wounded & 2/Lt WH Currie killed); 3 ASD 16.7.18; 55 Sqn 13.9.18; On Kaiserslautern raid, Scout OOC 11.00, then crashed Vittremont 25.9.18 (2/Lt E Wood wounded in the leg & 2/Lt JD Evans OK); 6 AP 30.9.18; 3 ASD 4.10.18

D8393 (Eagle VIII) 217 Sqn by 18.10.18; 98 Sqn 17.3.19; 1 ASD 19.3.19; to England 23.3.19; Instrument Design Establishment, Biggin Hill by 9.20; Testing drift sight, crashed on turn at low altitude 31.3.21 (F/O NB Hemsley MBE killed & Mr E Fenton Terry DoI)

D8394 217 Sqn by 22.8.18; FL due to failing light Bergues 7.9.18; Crashed 23.10.18; 4 ASD 25.10.18; Deleted 31.10.18 DBR

D8395 (Eagle VII) At 2 AAP Hendon 27.4.18, allotted to EF; England to Rec Pk 8.5.18; On ferry flight, engine cut just after TO, FL, ran into dip in ground 12.5.18 (2/Lt VL Dowling); 2 AI 3.6.18; 25 Sqn 7.6.18; Overshot aerodrome crashed into rifle butts 6.7.18 (Lt CEH Allen & Lt JM Mackie DCM MM OK); SOC Rep Pk 2 ASD 11.7.18

D8396 (Eagle VII) At 2 AAP Hendon 27.4.18, allotted to EF; England to Rec Pk 7.5.18; 2 AI 12.5.18; 55 Sqn 16.5.18; Albatros OOC 12.8.18 (Lt CL Heater USA & Sgt A Allan); FTR raid on Thionville-Conflans 30.8.18 (2/Lt RIA Hickes & 2/Lt TA Jones both killed)

D8397 No information

D8398 (Eagle VII) England to Rec Pk 12.4.18; 2 AI 22.4.18; 57 Sqn 24.4.18; Pfalz OOC 19.6.18 (Capt CH Stokes & Sgt JH Bowler); Fokker OOC 31.7.18; Low bombing raid on Moislains aerodrome, Fokker DVII OOC 8.8.18 (both Lt A MacGregor & Lt JFD Tanqueray (Can)); Two EA OOC Havrincourt Wood 16.9.18; Two Fokker DVII OOC Marcoing and Havrincourt Wood 12.15 16.9.18; Fokker DVII OOC N of Fontaine Notre Dame 18.35 21.9.18 (all Capt CH Stokes & Lt RD Bovill); FTR from raid on Maubeuge Station, hit by AA, seen going down under control at 14.30 29.10.18 (Capt CH Stokes DoW 7.11.18 & 2/Lt LH Eyres PoW)

D8399 Deld 1(S)ARD Farnborough by 27.4.18 for Dunkirk; AAP Dover to 217 Sqn 18.5.18; EF, FL Nieuport Bains, abandoned, destroyed by enemy shellfire 30.5.18 (Capt HH Gonyou injured & Lt JF Reid unhurt); Deleted 15.6.18

D8400 (Eagle VII later VIII) Deld 1(S)ARD Farnborough by 27.4.18; Dover W/E 4.5.18; 491 Flt Dover by 25.5.18; 4 ASD Audembert 17.6.18; 217 Sqn by 29.6.18; COL Crochte 13.7.18 (Lt DW Davies & A/G H Tallboys unhurt); 4 ASD 18.7.18; 202 Sqn by 1.10.18; Flown from Varsennaere to 233 Sqn Dover, but crashed on FL in dark, Wanstone Court Farm, nr Swingate Downs aerodrome, damaged 6.3.19 (2/Lt LS Clarke); WOC 19.3.19 (for RTP)

D8401 (Eagle V) At 2 AAP Hendon 4.4.18, allotted to EF; England to Rec Pk 12.4.18; 2 AI 17.4.18; 205 Sqn 21.4.18; Left 09.55, FTR raid on Chaulnes Rly Stn, NW of Quesnel, last seen nr Aubercourt 18.5.18 (2/Lt HCR Conron & 2/Lt J Finnigan both killed); SOC 19.5.18

D8402 Deld 1(S)ARD Farnborough by 27.4.18; Dover to 4 ASD Guines W/E 24.5.18; 202 Sqn 26.5.18; Shot up, FL, slightly damaged 4.6.18 (Lt TA Warne-Browne unhurt & G/L Cpl Mech W Bowman slightly wounded); repaired on Sqn; U/c smashed on landing 22.7.18 (Lt FS Russell + another unhurt); While escorting A7632, both attacked Tervaette by 7 EA, shot up, but observer 2 EA OOC firing spare gun from shoulder, FL Rousbrugge railhead 29.7.18 (1/Lt W Chalaire USNR & AGL Pte1 AE Humphrey both badly wounded); 4 ASD repair 31.7.18; Dismantling from 24.10.18

D8403 (Eagle VIII) Deld 1(S)ARD Farnborough by 27.4.18; Hendon to Dover 22.5.18; 4 ASD Guines W/E 24.5.18; 217 Sqn 25.6.18; 2-str OOC 30.6.18 (Lt AM Phillips & AM2 G/L H Tourlamain); Wrecked landing nr Crochte 6.7.18 (Lt AM Phillips & Sgt Mech FW Shufflebotham unhurt); Repaired on Sqn; Damaged German destroyer 10.8.18; COL, badly damaged 16.8.18 (Lt SJ Saunders & 2/Lt C Fenteman-Coates both unhurt); to 4 ASD, still there 25.10.18

D8404 Deld 1(S)ARD Farnborough by 27.4.18 - @31.5.18 for Dunkirk

D8405 (Eagle V) At 2 AAP Hendon 25.3.18, allotted to EF; England to Rec PK and on to 2 AI 25.3.18; 5N Sqn 31.3.18, became 205 Sqn 1.4.18; Hit by A8080 on TO 18.4.18; Rep Pk 2 ASD 19.4.18; SOC 24.4.18

D8406 (Eagle V) Presentation a/c 'Presented by British Subjects of all Races in Siam'. At 2 AAP Hendon 25.3.18, allotted to EF; Rec Pk to 2 AI and on to 57 Sqn 1.4.18; Returning from raid on Bapaume, engine caught fire, crashed and completely burnt 23.4.18 (2/Lt WH Townsend US DoI & 2/Lt C Souchette killed); SOC Adv Salvage Dump 24.4.18

D8407 (Eagle VIII) Deld 1(S)ARD Farnborough 6.4.18 - @27.4.18; 491 Flt Dover by 25.5.18; 4 ASD Wissant by 8.18; 202 Sqn (coded 'S') 16.8.18; 98 Sqn 6.3.19; 1 ASD 18.3.19

D8408 Replaced by F1551

D8409 (Eagle VIII) Deld 1(S)ARD Farnborough 6.4.18 - @27.4.18; Dover by 31.5.18; 4 ASD Audembert by 6.18; 202 Sqn 23.6.18; FL Leffrinckhouke 16.11.18 (Lt WAE Pepler & 2/Lt JC Castle); FL Leffrinckhouke 24.12.18, flying again 30.12.18; SAD Farnborough for HMS *Argus* 6.1.19

D8410 (Eagle VII) At 2 AAP Hendon 4.4.18, allotted to EF; England to Rec Pk 12.4.18; 2 AI 19.4.18; Rep Pk 2 ASD 23.4.18; 2 AI 28.4.18; 25 Sqn 2.5.18; Stalled nr ground and pancaked 2.7.18 (Capt RL Whalley & 2/Lt HH Watson); SOC Rep Pk 2 ASD 8.7.18

D8411 (Eagle V) At 2 AAP Hendon 25.3.18, had been allotted to 1 SD to arrange store, reallotted to EF; England to Rec Pk and on to 1 AI 26.3.18; 57 Sqn 27.3.18; Left 10.05 on photographic mission, controls shot away, FL, spun in on landing at aerodrome 12.20 9.5.18 (Lt LdeV Weiner injured & Lt RW Rumsby DoI); To Rep Pk 2 ASD 10.5.18

D8412 (Eagle VII later Eagle VI) At 2 AAP Hendon 4.4.18, allotted to EF; England to Rec Pk and on to 205 Sqn 12.5.18; Pfalz DIII OOC Warfusée-Abancourt 11.15-11.30 7.7.18 (Lt RLMcK Barbour & 2/Lt JH Preston); Shot up by Pfalz DIII on its tail Chaulnes - Pont-les-Brie 15.40, which was later down OOC by A7587 10.8.18 (Lt JG Kerr unhurt; 2/Lt HW Hopton DoW 12.8.18); Rep Pk 2 ASD to Rep Pk 1 ASD 19.8.18; SOC 28.8.18, new number F6511 allotted in error for reconstruction, changed later to H7118

D8413 (Eagle VII later Eagle VIII) At 2 AAP Hendon 4.4.18, allotted to EF; England to Rec Pk and on to 2 AI 8.4.18; 25 Sqn 9.4.18 but damaged en route; 2 AI 11.4.18; Rep Pk 2 ASD 13.4.18; 2 AI 27.5.18; 55 Sqn 30.5.18; 3 ASD 8.7.18; 55 Sqn 6.9.18; FTR photo recce, believed shot down by AA 25.9.18 (2/Lt AJ Robinson & 2/Lt HR Burnett both killed)

D8414 (Eagle VI) At 2 AAP Hendon 4.4.18, allotted to EF; England to Rec Pk 11.4.18; 2 AI 12.4.18; Rep Pk 2 ASD 16.4.18; Rep Pk 2 ASD to 2 AI 6.6.18; 25 Sqn 10.6.18; Petrol pump seized, FL in shell hole 22.8.18 (Sgt FP Clarke & 2/Lt J Harrington OK); SOC Rep Pk 2 ASD 10.9.18 NWR

Vertical view of a No.57 Squadron D.H.4, photographed on 16.8.18. (J.M.Bruce/G.S.Leslie collection)

D8415 (Eagle VII) At 2 AAP Hendon 4.4.18, allotted to EF; England to Rec Pk and on to 57 Sqn ('A6') 12.4.18; 2 Fokker DVII OOC Roisel 10.30 14.8.18 (Lt JL Standish & Sgt Mech NM Belcher); Landed badly tail first then on one wheel which collapsed 22.8.18 (2/Lt FP Ferreira & 2/Lt LB Simmonds); SOC Rep Pk 1 ASD 6.9.18, new number H7121 allotted for reconstruction

D8416 At 2 AAP Hendon 26.6.18, allotted to EF; To Lympne for engine fitting and erection, Eagle V fitted; Hendon to Rec Pk and on to 2 AI 16.7.18; 57 Sqn 17.7.18; Left 08.15 for photo recce during raid on Péronne Bridge, went down E of lines 9.8.18 (Lt WJ Pitt-Pitts killed & 2/Lt HS Musgrove PoW DoW)

D8417 (Eagle VIII) Deld 1(S)ARD Farnborough 6.4.18 - @27.4.18; 491 Flt Dover by 25.5.18 - @31.5.18; 4 ASD Wissant by 25.10.18; 217 Sqn 4.11.18; 233 Sqn Dover 27.2.19; At Joyce Green by 26.4.19, allocated 2 Comm Sqn Buc for special duty with HM the King of the Belgians

D8418 (Eagle VIII later VII) Deld 1(S)ARD Farnborough 6.4.18 - @27.4.18; 4 ASD Guines by 25.5.18; Dover by 31.5.18; 4 ASD to 202 Sqn 28.6.18; 98 Sqn 15.3.19; 1 ASD Marquise 18.3.19

D8419 (Eagle VII) At 2 AAP Hendon 4.4.18, allotted to EF; England to Rec Pk 11.4.18; 57 Sqn 12.4.18; Aviatik forced to land 7.6.18 (Capt FMcDC Turner & Lt FL Walters); Low bombing raid on Moislains aerodrome, Fokker DVII dest (EA collided?) 8.8.18 (Capt FMcDC Turner & 2/Lt HS Musgrove); EA OOC smoking Bourlon Wood 09.55 4.9.18 (Capt A MacGregor & Sgt J Grant); Fokker DVII in flames W of Avèsnes-le-Sec 16.05 5.9.18 (Capt A MacGregor & Sgt J Grant); EA OOC 19.9.18 (Capt WE Green & Lt AM Barron MC); In combat with EA over Cambrai 18.20, last seen going down under control from 1,000ft 26.9.18 (Lt PWJ Timson & 2/Lt AN Eyre both killed)

D8420 (Eagle VIII) Deld 1(S)ARD Farnborough 6.4.18 - @27.4.18; 491 Flt Dover by 25.5.18 - @31.5.18; 4 ASD Wissant to 202 Sqn (coded 'F') 31.7.18; Attacked and badly shot up by Fokker DVII Blankenberghe-Zeebrugge 13.10 21.8.18 (Lt GR Hurst unhurt & Sgt LA Allen seriously wounded) [credited Ltn Osterkamp, Marine Jasta 2]; squadron repair; Hit by m/g fire 22.10.18; flying again by 28.10.18; 1(S)ARD Farnborough for HMS *Argus* 6.1.19; 6 SD Ascot by 1.19 for HMS *Argus*

D8421 (Eagle VI) At 2 AAP Hendon 26.6.18, allotted to EF; To Lympne for engine fitting and erection; Rec Pk to 2 AI 16.7.18; 205 Sqn 19.7.18; During raid on Péronne station, one of its 112-lb bombs knocked off the port wing of a Pfalz which was climbing 200 ft directly underneath it but did not explode 11.8.18 (Lt W Grossart & 2/Lt JB Leach); Badly shot about by EA in bombing raid on Busigny, then damaged by storm after landing 17.9.18 (Lt HF Taylor unhurt & 2/Lt HS Millen wounded); 2 ASD 20.9.18

D8422 (Eagle VIII) Deld 1(S)ARD Farnborough 6.4.18 - @27.4.18; Dover by 31.5.18; 4 ASD Wissant to 202 Sqn 13.8.18; COL on return from evening patrol 7.9.18 (1/Lt JF Moffett USNR & Cpl RK Hooper both unhurt); 4 ASD by lorry 7.9.18 - @25.10.18

D8423 (Eagle VIII) 4 ASD to 202 Sqn 1.9.18; 98 Sqn 6.3.19; 1 ASD 19.3.19

D8424 (Eagle VII) At 2 AAP Hendon 26.6.18, allotted to EF; To Lympne for engine fitting and erection; Rec Pk to 2 AI 16.7.18; 57 Sqn 17.7.18; Fokker OOC 10.8.18 (Lt A Newman & Sgt AT Wareing); EA crashed 24.9.18 (Lt A Newman & 2/Lt C Wilkinson); EA in flames, a/c damaged in combat, FL 26.9.18, (Capt A Newman OK & Lt EG Pernet wounded); Back at sqn 27.9.18 On practice flight stalled and landed on one wing and wheel 29.10.18 (Lt LS Harvey OK)

D8425 At 2 AAP Hendon 26.6.18, allotted to EF; To Lympne for engine fitting and erection; Rec Pk to 2 AI 17.7.18; 57 Sqn 20.7.18; Fokker DVII in flames & another OOC nr Ytres 08.00 29.8.18 (Lt FO Thornton OK & 2/Lt WH Thornton wounded); EA in flames 1.9.18 (Lt FO Thornton & 2/Lt FG Craig); EA OOC 5.9.18 (Lt FO Thornton & 2/Lt FG Craig); On practice flight COL 15.9.18 (Lt DJ Tarling); Rep Pk 1 ASD SOC 26.2.19

These D.H.4s of an unidentified unit carry assorted nose markings. (via Philip Jarrett)

D8426 At 2 AAP Hendon 26.6.18, allotted to EF; To Lympne for engine fitting and erection, Eagle VI fitted; Rec Pk to 2 AI 21.7.18; 25 Sqn 29.7.18; To England 18.1.19

D8427 At 2 AAP Hendon 26.6.18, allotted to EF; To Lympne for engine fitting and erection, Eagle VI fitted; Rec Pk to 2 AI 17.7.18; 25 Sqn 20.7.18; Crashed 18.9.18; Rebuilt as H6859 3.10.18

D8428 At 2 AAP Hendon 26.6.18, allotted to EF; To Lympne for engine fitting and erection; Rec Pk to 2 AI 6.7.18; 57 Sqn 1.8.18; On dual control instruction flight struck tree on landing, fuselage broke in three parts 9.8.18 Capt FMcDC Turner MC & Lt HEW Brying both injured); Rep Pk 2 ASD 10.8.18; SOC 19.8.18

D8429 (Eagle VI) At 2 AAP Hendon 26.6.18, allotted to EF; To Lympne for engine fitting and erection; Rec Pk to 2 AI 31.7.18; 205 Sqn 7.8.18; Pfalz DIII crashed W of Péronne during raid on Péronne station 07.58 11.8.18 (Lt GC Matthews & Sgt L Murphy); Damaged in combat with Fokker DVIIs during raid on Péronne station 11.00 13.8.18 (2/Lt FO McDonald wounded & Sgt FG Manning killed); General engagement, Fokker DVII leader (red nose, black fuselage with white diagonal stripe) crashed NW of Péronne 10.05 23.8.18 (2/Lt FO McDonald & Sgt L Murphy); Shot about by EA in raid on Busigny 16.9.18 (Lt EO Danger wounded & Lt AD Hollingsworth unhurt); 2 ASD 20.9.18

D8430 No information

50 D.H.4 built by Aircraft Manufacturing Co Ltd, Hendon and numbered D9231 to D9280. (mainly Eagle)

["A8059, A8063, A8065, A8066, A8067 & A8079 fitted Eagle VIII and replaced by D9231 to D9236"]

D9231 Replaced by F1552

D9232 (Eagle VII) Deld 2 AAP Hendon by 22.4.18, allotted to EF; England to Rec Pk 24.4.18; 205 Sqn 25.4.18; Pfalz DIII OOC in vertical dive Chaulnes-Rosières 17.42 3.5.18 (Capt E Dickson & AGL CV Robinson); COL, pilot fainted 15.5.18 (2/Lt WE MacPherson injured & 2/Lt JA Whalley unhurt); 2 ASD 17.5.18; Rebuilt as F6103 3.7.18

D9233 3 ASD to 55 Sqn 7.9.18; Wrecked 25.9.18; TOC 6 AP 30.9.18; 3 ASD 4.10.18

D9234 (Eagle V) At 2 AAP Hendon 10.5.18, allotted to EF; Rec Pk to 2 AI 2.6.18; 205 Sqn 6.6.18; Crashed into D.H.4 A7964 landing 11.8.18 (2/Lt FO MacDonald & 2/Lt JC Walker both unhurt); Rep Pk 2 ASD 14.8.18; SOC 19.8.18

D9235 (Eagle VI) England to Rec Pk 21.5.18; 2 AI 25.5.18; 25 Sqn 28.5.18; On landing overshot and crashed in sunken road 7.6.18 (Lt LA Hacklett & Sgt WC Elliott OK); 2 AI to 25 Sqn 16.8.18; On practice flight attacked by 5 EA Dixmude and FL at 108 Sqn 17.15 3.9.18 (Lt S Crosfield OK & 2/Lt EF Boyce killed)

D9236 (Eagle VI) At 2 AAP Hendon 13.5.18, allotted to EF; England to Rec Pk and on to 2 AI 29.5.18; 55 Sqn 3.6.18; On Koblenz raid, FL and crashed Chaumont 5.7.18 (2/Lt W Beer); 3 ASD 5.7.18; 55 Sqn 30.8.18; Wrecked, to 3 ASD 2.9.18

D9237 (Eagle VI) At 2 AAP Hendon 25.3.18, allotted to EF; Rec Pk to 2 AI 26.3.18; 25 Sqn 28.3.18; M/c turned on take off and left wing skid struck ground, crashed 31.3.18 (2/Lt CEH Allen & 2/Lt W Rudman MC OK); Rec Pk to Adv Salvage to Rep Pk 1 ASD 10.4.18; SOC 14.4.18

D9238 (Eagle VI) At 2 AAP Hendon 8.4.18, allotted to EF; England to Rec Pk and on to 2 AI 12.4.18; 205 Sqn ('P') 15.4.18; Albatros DV in flames 4-6m W of Chaulnes during raid on Chaulnes Rly Stn 11.25-11.30 18.5.18 (Capt E Dickson & AGL CV Robinson); Pfalz DIII in flames S of Bray 19.58 5.7.18 (Lt CJ Heywood unhurt & 2/Lt EA Dew wounded); Fokker DVII crashed E of Chaulnes 11.00-11.10 13.8.18 (Lt CJ Heywood & Sgt SF Langstone); 2 AI exchanged for DH 9A 1.9.18; Rec Pk 2.9.18; 8 AAP Lympne 4.9.18

D9239 (Eagle VI) At 2 AAP Hendon 8.4.18, allotted to EF; England to Rec Pk and on to 2 AI 12.4.18; 25 Sqn 15.4.18; Left 08.00 on bombing raid, hit by AA at 15,000ft, down in flames, crashed Aulnoye 20.5.18 (Lt AH Herring & 2/Lt RS Lasker both killed)

D9240 (Eagle VII) At 2 AAP Hendon 8.4.18, allotted to EF; England to Rec Pk 8.4.18; 2 AI and on to 25 Sqn 10.4.18; Returning from raid, crashed into D8375 on landing 21.4.18 (2/Lt S Jones & Cpl H Edwards OK); Adv Salvage to Rep Pk 1 ASD 23.4.18; SOC 27.4.18

D9241 (Eagle .VI) At 2 AAP Hendon 8.4.18, allotted to EF; England to Rec Pk 8.4.18; Rec Pk to 2 AI 10.4.18; 205 Sqn but crashed on arrival, new u/c fitted 11.4.18; Crashed 16.6.18 (Lt JC Wilson & Sgt SM MacKay); Crashed 30.6.18 (Lt JC Wilson & Sgt SF Langstone); 2 AI 24.9.18 (exchanged for D.H.9A); Rep Pk 2 ASD 28.9.18; 2 AI 27.9.18; Rep Pk 2 ASD 28.9.18; 57 Sqn, wrecked on landing 24.11.18 (2/Lt FH Thirkell & A/M2 TR Field OK)

D9242 (Eagle VI) At 2 AAP Hendon 8.4.18, allotted to EF; England to Rec Pk and on to 2 AI 12.4.18; 25 Sqn 22.4.18; Overshot on landing ran into 27 Sqn's B2139 7.5.18 (Lt J Loupinsky & Sgt JR Wright OK): To Rep

Pk 2 ASD; Rebuilt as F6136 3.7.18

D9243 (Eagle VI) At 2 AAP Hendon 8.4.18, allotted to EF; England to Rec Pk and on to 2 AI 12.4.18; 205 Sqn 13.4.18; Left 16.10, down in flat spin over Chaulnes Rly Stn 3.5.18 (Lt R Scott & 2/Lt TA Humphrey both killed); SOC in field 4.5.18

D9244 (Eagle) At 2 AAP Hendon 8.4.18, allotted to EF but this cancelled 10.4.18, a/c had crashed at Lympne

D9245 (Eagle VI) At 2 AAP Hendon 10.4.18, allotted to EF; Allotment to EF cancelled 4.5.18, a/c crashed at Joyce Green

D9246 (Eagle) At 2 AAP Hendon 8.4.18, allotted to EF; Allotment cancelled 16.4.18, damaged in transit

D9247 (Eagle) At 2 AAP Hendon 8.4.18, allotted to EF; England to Rec Pk 19.4.18; 2 AI 20.4.18; 25 Sqn 21.4.18; COL 20.5.18 (Lt AE Hulme & 2/Lt D Boe); To Rep Pk 2 ASD; Rebuilt as F6104 3.7.18

D9248 (Eagle VI) At 2 AAP Hendon 8.4.18, allotted to EF; England to Rec Pk and on to 2 AI 12.4.18; 57 Sqn 20.4.18; After raid on Bapaume Dump, Fokker Drl in flames and Fokker Drl OOC Ervillers to Vimy 20.10-20.25 then damaged by enemy fire FL 10.6.18 (Lt CW Peckham & Sgt J Grant OK); COL when u/c gave way, probably damaged by AA 16.6.18 (Lt CW Peckham & 2/Lt EI Riley); Rep Pk 2 ASD 18.6.18; SOC 22.6.18

D9249 (Eagle VI) At 2 AAP Hendon 10.4.18, allotted to EF; England to Rec Pk 12.4.18; 2 AI 21.4.18; 57 Sqn 22.4.18; Ran into a hole on landing and turned over 22.5.18 (Lt H Erskine & Sgt JS Macdonald OK); SOC Rep Pk 2 ASD 4.6.18; Rebuilt as F5827 25.6.18

D9250 (Eagle VI later VII) At 2 AAP Hendon 26.4.18, allotted to EF; England to Rec Pk 1.5.18; 1 AI 3.5.18; 2 AI 6.5.18; 205 Sqn 14.5.18; Left 07.30, FTR raid on Busigny, last seen with 2 EA on tail 16.9.18 (2/Lt FF Anslow PoW & Sgt L Murphy killed)

D9251 (Eagle VI) At 2 AAP Hendon 26.4.18, allotted to EF; England to Rec Pk and on to 2 AI 1.5.18; 25 Sqn 2.5.18; Recce, petrol tank punctured by shrapnel then attacked by EA, FL in shelled area just behind our lines, CW 10.45 21.5.18 (Lt LLK Straw & 2/Lt HH Watson OK); To Rep Pk 2 ASD; SOC 26.5.18

D9252 At 2 AAP Hendon 26.4.18, allotted to EF; 8 AAP Lympne to Rec Pk 3.5.18; 2 AI 8.5.18; 25 Sqn 16.5.18; Stalled nr ground 30.5.18 (Capt RL Whalley & Sgt CAF Johnson); To Rep Pk 2 ASD; Rebuilt as F6133 3.7.18

D9253 (Eagle VI) At 2 AAP Hendon 24.4.18, allotted to EF; England to Rec Pk and on to 2 AI 1.5.18; 205 Sqn 2.5.18; Test flight, EF, FL, crashed nr Bellancourt 9.5.18 (Lt HCR Conron unhurt & 2/Lt Deacon slightly injured); 2 ASD 10.5.18; Rebuilt as F6167 3.7.18

D9254 (Eagle VII) At 2 AAP Hendon 29.4.18, allotted to EF; England to Rec Pk 1.5.18; 2 AI 6.5.18; Rebuilt as F6168 3.7.18

D9255 (Eagle VI) At 2 AAP Hendon 29.4.18, allotted to EF; England to Rec Pk and on to 2 AI 1.5.18; 205 Sqn 4.5.18; Yellow and green Fokker DrI in flames W of Chaulnes 16.05 17.5.18; COL 15.7.18 (both Lt R Chalmers & 2/Lt SH Hamblin); Pfalz DIII in flames crashed Chaulnes 15.50 10.8.18 (Capt JM Mason & Sgt WJH Middleton); Raid on Busigny, Fokker DVII OOC 10m W of Bray 09.30 16.9.18 (2/Lt KG Nairn & 2/Lt NR McKinley); 2 AI exchanged for DH9A 28.9.18; 25 Sqn Casualty Report 18.10.18 says unsuitable, will not climb; To 2 ASD and on to Rec Pk 18.10.18; 8 AAP Lympne 22.10.18

D9256 (Eagle VII) At 2 AAP Hendon 30.4.18, allotted to EF; England to Rec Pk 1.5.18; 2 AI 5.5.18; 205 Sqn 11.5.18; Shot about by Fokker DrI, landed Cagny 11.05 5.6.18 (Lt WV Theron & Sgt HF Monday both unhurt); Rep Pk 2 ASD 7.6.18; Rebuilt as F6139 3.7.18

D9257 (Eagle VI) At 2 AAP Hendon 30.4.18, allotted to EF; England to Rec Pk 1.5.18; 2 AI 2.5.18; 57 Sqn 9.5.18; On practice flight attempting to land, misjudged distance engine did not pick up, m/c fell 30 feet and was wrecked 27.6.18 (Lt JB Cunningham & 2/Lt EI Riley OK); SOC Rep Pk 2 ASD 8.7.18 ex 2 Adv Salvage Dump

D9258 (Eagle VII) At 2 AAP Hendon 30.4.18.allotted to EF; 2 AI to 57 Sqn 16.5.18; On landing pancaked from about 3ft 15.7.18 (Lt G Anderson & 2/Lt HS Musgrove OK); Rep Pk 2 ASD 17.7.18; SOC 14.8.18 NWR

D9259 (Eagle VI) At 2 AAP Hendon 30.4.18, allotted to EF; England to Rec Pk 1.5.18; 2 AI 2.5.18; 25 Sqn 8.5.18; Casualty Report 11.6.18 says performance only good up to 7000 feet and "useless for our work"; Rebuilt as F5832 26.6.18

D9260 (Eagle VI) At 2 AAP Hendon 30.4.18, allotted to EF; England to Rec Pk 1.5.18; 2 AI to 205 Sqn 16.5.18; Pfalz DIII OOC by observer Rosières 08.25 20.5.18 (Lt R Chalmers & 2/Lt SH Hamblin); COL on or W/E 24.5.18 (repaired); Crashed into N6004 on aerodrome 11.6.18 (Lt WE MacPherson & Lt CF Ambler unhurt); Rep Pk 2 ASD 12.6.18; SOC 26.6.18 NWR

D9261 (Eagle VI) At 2 AAP Hendon 18.5.18, allotted to EF; England to Rec Pk 19.5.18; 2 AI 20.5.18; 57 Sqn 21.5.18; Engine cut out just after take off, crashed, CW 11.6.18 (Lt TG Rhodes and Lt ED Spencer both killed)

D9262 (Eagle VI) At 2 AAP Hendon 11.5.18, allotted to EF; Rec Pk to 2 AI 15.5.18; 57 Sqn 19.5.18; Two Fokker DVIIs OOC Bray to Péronne and back 18.10-18.50 10.8.18 (Capt WE Green & Lt CG Smith); Fokker DVII OOC Ytres 08.00 29.8.18 (Capt WE Green & Lt AM Barron MC); On sqn move to Vert Galant, engine cut out on landing hit telegraph wires 19.9.18 (Lt JW Hartley & Lt LH Eyres OK)

D9263 (Eagle VI) At 2 AAP Hendon 18.5.18, allotted to EF; England to Rec Pk and on to 2 AI 20.5.18; 57 Sqn 21.5.18; Scout probably Albatros OOC smoking SE of Arras 10.30 9.6.18 (Lt A Newman MC & Sgt NM Belcher); Wrecked on landing 18.6.18 (Lt A Newman & Sgt NM Belcher OK); Landing in strong wind left wing hit rudder of m/c already landed 10.7.18 (Lt JB Cunningham & Sgt AT Wareing); Rep Pk 2 ASD 12.7.18; Rebuilt as F6209 24.7.18

D9264 (Eagle VI) At 2 AAP Hendon 17.5.18, allotted to EF; Rec Pk to 2 AI 7.6.18; 57 Sqn 12.6.18; On practice flight landed in high wind one wing down, wrecked 23.6.18 (2/Lt HC Aylmer OK); Rebuilt as F6186 12.7.18

D9265 (Eagle VI) At 2 AAP Hendon 17.5.18, allotted to EF; England to Rec Pk and on to 2 AI 19.5.18; 55 Sqn 20.5.18; Damaged in bad landing 25.6.18 (2/Lt W Beer & 2/AM J McEwan OK); To Rep Pk 2 ASD 25.6.18; 3 ASD to 55 Sqn 21.9.18; Casualty Report 23.12.18 says due to the approach of bad weather, FL in open field nr Flers, m/c warped and distorted by incessant rain and now unfit to fly (2/Lt HC Pendle & Lt JA Shepherd MC OK);SOC by 28.12.18

D9266 (Eagle VI) England to Rec Pk and on to 2 AI 20.5.18; 25 Sqn 21.5.18; Left 08.30, hit by AA SW of Valenciennes, seen going down under control 7.6.18 (Lt LA Hacklett & Sgt WC Elliott both PoW)

D9267 (Eagle VI) At 2 AAP Hendon 27.5.18, allotted to EF; England to Rec Pk 30.5.18; 2 AI 3.6.18; 57 Sqn 7.6.18; Hit by EA fire, FL Doullens-Frévent road 10.8.18 (Sgt DE Edgley & Sgt N Sandison); Last seen at 14,000ft over Quesnoy at 11.10 gliding in a NE direction apparently under control going NE 16.8.18 (2/Lt WH Kilbourne PoW & 2/Lt DE Stephens PoW DoW 19.8.18)

D.H.4 D9269 'F' of No.205 Squadron in flight. It has a clear-view panel in the centre section. (RAF Museum P.21398)

D9268 (Eagle VI) England to Rec Pk and on to 2 AI 21.5.18; To 55 Sqn 22.5.18 but returned engine overheating; To 55 Sqn 27.5.18; Lost formation changing tanks, FL Martigny-les-Bains 3.6.18 (2/Lt JR Bell & Sgt EV Clare): SOC Rep Pk 2 ASD 10.7.18 (ex 6AP)

D9269 At 2 AAP Hendon 4.6.18, allotted to EF; Rec Pk to 2 AI 15.6.18; 205 Sqn ('F') 16.6.18; Pfalz DIII OOC 11.00-11.10 13.8.18 Péronne (Lt WH Clarke & 2/Lt CN Witham); Fokker DVII dest NE of Péronne 23.8.18 (2/Lt FO MacDonald & Sgt SM MacKay); Fokker DVII OOC 4.9.18 (Lt DJT Mellor & Sgt WJH Middleton); 2 AI exchanged for DH 9A; 57 Sqn 29.9.18; Left 07.00, in combat with EA NE of Beauvois, FTR 1.10.18 (2/Lt AH Mills-Adams & 2/Lt P Scherek both killed)

D9270 (Eagle VII) At 2 AAP Hendon 27.5.18, allotted to EF; 2 AI to 55 Sqn 15.6.18; Wrecked 1.8.18 (2/Lt CJ Kidder & Sgt V Foulsham); 3 ASD 2.8.18; 55 Sqn 6.10.18; Damage in combat 21.10.18 (2/Lt C Turner & 2/Lt CJ Knight); 2 ASD 17.1.19; 25 Sqn to 6 SS 13.5.19

D9271 (Eagle VI) At 2 AAP Hendon 1.6.18, allotted to EF; Rec Pk to 2 AI 15.6.18; 25 Sqn 17.6.18; Left 05.55 on recce, in combat with 30 EA, shot up Courtrai area 7.9.18 (2/Lt CH Saffery OK & 2/Lt J Harrington wounded)

D9272 (Eagle VI) At 2 AAP Hendon 28.5.18, allotted to EF; England to Rec Pk and on to 2 AI 30.5.18; 25 Sqn 3.6.18; Struck tree on landing 9.6.18 (Lt LFV Atkinson injured & 2/Lt HH Watson OK); To Rep Pk 2 ASD; SOC 23.6.18 NWR

D9273 At 2 AAP Hendon 4.6.18, allotted to EF; Rec Pk to 2 AI 15.6.18; 55 Sqn 16.6.18; Bombing raid on Darmstadt, shot down in combat with EAs 16.8.18 (2/Lt EA Brownhill & 2/Lt WT Madge both killed)

D9274 (Eagle VI) At 2 AAP Hendon 4.6.18, allotted to EF; Rec Pk to 2 AI 9.6.18; 25 Sqn 12.6.18; Overshot aerodrome, in trying to take off u/c caught in long corn 1.7.18 (Lt R de Bruyn OK & Lt MF St Clair-Fowles injured); SOC Rep Pk 2 ASD 11.7.18

D9275 (Eagle VI) At 2 AAP Hendon 4.6.18, allotted to EF; Rec Pk to 2 AI 9.6.18; 55 Sqn 13.6.18; FTR raid on Oberndorf, shot down in flames over target 20.7.18 (Lt C Young & Lt RA Butler both killed)

D9276 (Eagle VII) At Makers 5.6.18, allotted to EF; Rec Pk to 2 AI 16.6.18; 57 Sqn 17.6.18; Fokker DVII OOC Bapaume-St Leger 19.45 then FL at French aerodrome at Montagne 19.6.18 (Lt CW Peckham & 2/Lt EI Riley), back at Sqn 20.6.18; Left 03.40 for bombing raid, last seen Bapaume going south 23.6.18 (2/Lt ADR Jones & Sgt JT Ward both PoW)

D9277 (Eagle VI) Deld 3 AAP Norwich by 10.5.18; At 2 AAP Hendon 3.6.18, allotted to EF; 2 AI to 205 Sqn 12.6.18; Bombing raid, hit by flak 17.6.18 (Capt J Gamon wounded); Red Fokker DVII, spun in, crashed into trees 1m NE of Bethencourt 15.05 21.8.18 (Lt WH Clarke & 2/Lt CN Witham); Light green, white tailed Fokker DVII OOC & another DD St.Quentin-Brie 09.00-09.15 6.9.18 (Lt EH Johnson & 2/Lt AR Crosthwaite); Damaged by storm 17.9.18; 2 ASD 17.9.18

D9278 (Eagle V) At 2 AAP Hendon, allotted to EF; Rec Pk to 2 AI 28.6.18; 57 Sqn 29.6.18; Left on raid 17.00, damaged in combat, FL Frohen le Grand 20.00 10.8.18 (2/Lt DH Thomas OK & 2/Lt JK Mitchell killed); Rep Pk 2 ASD 12.8.18; To Rep Pk 1 ASD, SOC 11.9.18, allotted new number H7123 for reconstruction

D9279 (Eagle VII) At 2 AAP Hendon 10.6.18, allotted to EF; 8 AAP Lympne to Rec Pk 5.7.18; 2 AI to 25 Sqn 7.7.18; Left 07.55 on photographic mission Renaix area, FTR 10.7.18 (Lt J Loupinsky PoW wounded & Sgt JR Wright PoW)

D9280 (Eagle V) At 2 AAP Hendon 4.6.18, allotted to EF; Rec Pk to 2 AI 18.6.18; 57 Sqn 23.6.18; COL, misjudged wind which was gusty and drifted into sunken road just off aerodrome 1.8.18 (Lt JL Standish & 2/Lt AE Doncaster OK); SOC Rep Pk 2 ASD 14.8.18 NWR

5 D.H.4 ordered under Cont No 35a/216/C.127 from Aircraft Manufacturing Co Ltd, Hendon and numbered E4624 to E4628. (Eagle V)

E4624 At 2 AAP Hendon 25.3.18, allotted to EF; England to Rec Pk 25.3.18; 2 ASD 26.3.18; 5N Sqn 31.3.18; Became 205 Sqn 1.4.18; COL from raid aborted by bad visibility, caught fire, bomb exploded 24.4.18 (Lt RC Day injured & Sgt SM MacKay unhurt); SOC Adv Salvage Dump 2 ASD 26.4.18

E4625 At 2 AAP Hendon 25.3.18, allotted to EF; England to Rec Pk 25.3.18; 2 AI 26.3.18; 57 Sqn 31.3.18; Returned from raid due to engine vibrating, wrecked on landing 18.5.18 (Lt A Newman MC & Lt EG Pernet OK); Rebuilt as F6120 3.7.18

E4626 At 2 AAP Hendon 4.5.18, allotted to EF; England to Rec Pk 4.5.18; 2 AI 7.5.18; 57 Sqn 16.5.18; In action 23.6.18 (Lt E Erskine wounded & 2/Lt EI Riley OK); Left 08.45 of bombing recce Sancourt Dump, in combat on return, damaged, hit hangar landing 16.8.18 (2/Lt JP Ferreira OK & Sgt Mech NM Belcher wounded); Rep Pk 1 ASD 16.8.18; Rebuilt 31.8.18, numbered F6513 in error, changed to H7120

E4627 At 2 AAP Hendon 18.5.18, allotted to EF; England to Rec Pk 19.5.18; 2 AI and on to 25 Sqn 20.5.18; On practice flight throttle broke, crashed 24.9.18 (2/Lt JE Mann OK)

E4628 England to Rec Pk and on to 2 AI 21.5.18; 57 Sqn 22.5.18; Propeller hit ground on take off and broke m/c hit ridge and crashed 6.6.18 (Lt WH Kilbourne & Cpl J Simmons OK); Rep Pk 2 ASD; SOC 18.6.18 NWR

2 D.H.4 ordered under Cont Nos A.S.77726 & 87/A/496 from Aircraft Manufacturing Co Ltd, Hendon to replace D8408 and D9231, and numbered F1551 and F1552. (275hp Eagle V)

F1551 At 2 AAP Hendon 22.5.18, allotted to EF; England to Rec Pk and on to 2 AI 30.5.18; 205 Sqn 3.6.18; COL from bombing raid on Chaulnes Rly Stn 19.6.18 (Lt EO Danger & 2/Lt AD Hollingsworth unhurt); 2 ASD 19.6.18; Rebuilt as F6076 3.7.18

F1552 At 2 AAP Hendon 28.5.18, allotted to EF; Rec Pk to 2 AI 3.6.18; Rep Pk 2 ASD to 5 AI 10.10.18; 2 AI to 57 Sqn 16.10.18; 98 Sqn 21.2.19; To 1 ASD Marquise but COL, wrecked 24.2.19

100 D.H.4 ordered 13.4.18 under Cont No 35a/660/C.540 from The Glendower Aircraft Co Ltd, London and numbered F2633 to F2732. (The contract was for fuselages less wings)

F2633 (Eagle VII) Rec Pk to 2 AI 15.9.18; 205 Sqn 18.9.18; Fokker DVII dest 21.9.18 (Lt EH Johnson & Sgt Mech WJH Middleton); 2 AI exchanged for DH9A 25.9.18; 57 Sqn 27.9.18; FTR from raid on Maubeuge Station, left at 08.45, last seen over St Vaast-la-Vallée heading W having left formation 27.10.18 (2/Lt DU Thomas & 2/Lt AH Aitken both killed)

F2634 Rec Pk to 2 AI 30.8.18; 57 Sqn 31.8.18; Photo recce, attacked by EA, COL 16.9.18 (Lt G Anderson killed & Sgt Mech JS Macdonald injured); To 6SS; To England 1.19

F2635 (Eagle VI) Rec Pk to 2 AI 17.9.18; 57 Sqn 18.9.18; Fokker DVII OOC Cambrai shared A8017, 1800 27.9.18 (Lt FL Harding & 2/Lt IS Woodhouse); Ran into hedge landing at Spa 22.2.19 (Lt AD Stubbs & 2/Lt LE Morris)

F2636 Rec Pk to 2 AI 2.10.18; 57 Sqn 3.10.18; Flying from Spa to Paris, ran into dense fog nr Paris, hit telegraph wires then hedge, crashed 22.12.18 (2/Lt RR Gilpin killed & Mjr Gen CD Rhodes USAS injured)

F2637 No information

F2638 Shipped from 3AD to England via Port Depot Rouen 13.1.19

F2639 No information

F2640 (Eagle VIII) Rec Pk to 217 Sqn (via 202 Sqn) 25.10.18; 98 Sqn 16.3.19; 1 ASD 17.3.19; to England 18.3.19

F2641 Rec Pk to 5 AI 8.10.18; 6 AI to 25 Sqn 5.5.19; 6 SS 13.5.19

F2642 No information

F2643 (Eagle VIII) 202 Sqn to 217 Sqn 25.10.18; 202 Sqn to 98 Sqn 16.3.19; 1 ASD 18.3.19 (to OC 91 Wing)

F2644 Conv D.H.4A?; 1 Comm Sqn Hendon/Kenley by 17.10.18; Visit to Paris, after getting new prop from St.Omer, snow had thawed, tried to get out of field 170yds long, hit willow tree on canal bank, jumped canal and ditch, overturned, WO 28.1.19 (Lt CH Drew); Transferred from 1 Comm Sqn Hendon to EF 6.2.19 for

D.H.4 F2650 'S' of No.55 Squadron in a hangar towards the end of 1918. (J.M.Bruce/G.S.Leslie collection)

D.H.4A F2664 of No.2 Communications Squadron, Buc, has H.M.A.P. 'LADY IRIS' painted on the nose. (via Frank Cheesman)

D.H.4A F2665 of No.2 Communications Squadron at Buc in October 1918. (via Don Neate)

D.H.4A F2699, believed to be at Marske, later became G-EAHF. (J.M.Bruce/G.S.Leslie collection)

W/O by 11 AP 6.2.19
F2645 217 Sqn to 98 Sqn 16.3.19
F2646 No information
F2647 No information
F2648 2 AI to 57 Sqn 1.12.18; FL and crashed N of Namur 8.12.18 (Capt A Newman MC & Lt AM Barron OK).
F2649 No information
F2650 (Eagle VIII) 3 ASD to 55 Sqn ('S') 2.11.18; 2 ASD 16.1.19; 205 Sqn by 3.19
F2651 1 ASD to England 3.3.19
F2652 8 AAP Lympne by 21.10.18; Rec Pk 22.10.18; 2 AI 24.10.18; 57 Sqn by 1.19
F2653 (Eagle VII) Rec Pk to 2 AI 17.10.18; 57 Sqn 8.11.18; Mail flight, on return from Cologne, tried to land owing to snowstorm, stalled and crashed 20.3.19 (2/Lt AS Smith killed & Lt RM Dixon OK)
F2654 8 AAP Lympne, tested 8.11.18; Tested Hendon 4.2.19
F2655 1 ASD to England 4.1.19; Conv D.H.4A; 'A' Flt 1 Comm Sqn Kenley by 21.4.19 - 6.19
F2656 2 AAP Hendon to Rec Pk 8.10.18; 57 Sqn 9.10.18; Fokker DVII in flames Pont-sur-Sambre 10.15, elevator controls shot away, FL Izel 27.10.18 (2/Lt NH Leech OK & 2/Lt E Till DoW 6.11.18); FL Acheux due to bad weather, damaged landing 28.11.18 (Lt NH Leech OK); 2 AI 30.11.18; 91 Wing to 1 ASD 19.3.19
F2657 Rec Pk to 2 ASD 22.10.18; 1 ASD to 216 Sqn 3.1.19
F2658 (Eagle VI) At 8 AAP Lympne 24.12.18 allotted to SE Area for 1 Comm Sqn Hendon
F2659 Shipped from 3 AD to England via Port Depot Rouen 21.1.19
F2660 Shipped from 3 AD to England via Port Depot Rouen 12.1.19
F2661 No information
F2662 (Eagle VIII) 57 Sqn, FL having lost way, on take-off struck a mound knocking off u/c, overturned 21.1.19 (Lt FO Thornton & 2/Lt JF Blick OK)
F2663 Conv D.H.4A; 2 Comm Sqn Buc
F2664 Conv D.H.4A; 2 Comm Sqn Buc (named 'HMAP Lady Iris') (General Seely's aircraft, fitted with silencers); 1 Comm Sqn Kenley to RAE 3.5.19
F2665 Conv D.H.4A; 2 Comm Sqn Buc 10.18
F2666 Conv D.H.4A; 1 Comm Sqn Kenley 4.19 - 9.19
F2667 to F2669 No information
F2670 (c/n P.7) Became *G-EANK*
F2671 (c/n P.8) Became *G-EANL*
F2672 Became *G-CYBW*
F2673 Became *G-CYDB*
F2674 No information
F2675 Became *G-EAYE* (ferry marks to Belgian AF)
F2676 No information
F2677 Became *G-EAYJ* (ferry marks to Belgian AF)
F2678 Became *G-EAXN* (ferry marks to Belgian AF)
F2679 No information
F2680 Became *G-EAXO* (ferry marks to Belgian AF)
F2681 Conv D.H.4A; 2 Comm Sqn; 1 Comm Sqn
F2682 Became *G-AUBZ*, later *VH-UBZ*
F2683 No information
F2684 Became *G-EAYH* (ferry marks to Belgian AF)
F2685 No information
F2686 Became *G-EAXD* (ferry marks to Belgian AF)
F2687 No information
F2688 No information
F2689 Became *G-EAYR* (ferry marks to Belgian AF)
F2690 No information
F2691 Became *G-AUCM*, later *VH-UCM*
F2692 No information
F2693 Became *G-EAYI* (ferry marks to Belgian AF)
F2694 Conv D.H.4A; Became *G-EAHG*
F2695 No information
F2696 No information
F2697 Became *G-EAXE* (ferry marks to Belgian AF)
F2698 Became *G-EAXI* (ferry marks to Belgian AF)
F2699 Conv D.H.4A (believed to be at Marske); Became *G-EAHF*

F2700 No information
F2701 No information
F2702 Conv D.H.4A; Became *G-EAJC*
F2703 No information
F2704 Conv D.H.4A; Became *G-EAJD*
F2705 Imperial Gift to Canada; Became *G-CYBO*; TOC 26.10.20; SOC 30.11.28
F2706 Imperial Gift to Canada; Became *G-CYDM*; TOC 26.10.20; SOC 30.11.28
F2707 Imperial Gift to Canada; Became *G-CYEM*; TOC 26.10.20; SOC 30.11.28
F2708 Imperial Gift to Canada; Became *G-CYDN*; TOC 26.10.20; SOC 30.11.28
F2709 Imperial Gift to Canada; Became *G-CYBU*; TOC 26.10.20; SOC 30.11.28
F2710 Imperial Gift to Canada; Became *G-CYBV*; TOC 26.10.20; Crashed High River 1.8.21 WOC
F2711 Imperial Gift to Canada; Became *G-CYDK*; TOC 26.10.20; SOC 30.11.28
F2712 Imperial Gift to Canada; Became *G-CYDL*; TOC 26.10.20; SOC 30.11.28
F2713 Imperial Gift to Canada; Became *G-CYCW*; TOC 26.10.20; SOC 30.11.28
F2714 Imperial Gift to Canada; Became *G-CYEC*; TOC 26.10.20; SOC 30.11.28
F2715 to F2732 No information (storage only?)

100 D.H.4 ordered 12.4.18 under Cont No 35a/669/C.544 from Palladium Autocars Ltd, London and numbered F5699 to F5798. (Eagle VI/VI/VIII)

F5699 (Eagle) At Makers 10.6.18, allotted to EF; To be dispatched to 2 AAP Hendon for fitting and erection, Eagle VI fitted; Rec Pk to 2 AI and on to 25 Sqn 7.7.18; Lost bearings in mist, landed at dummy aerodrome and crashed in deep ridge 31.7.18 (Lt C Brown & 2/Lt H Roberts); Rebuilt as F6234 7.8.18
F5700 (Eagle VIII) At Makers 10.6.18, allotted to EF; To be dispatched to 2 AAP Hendon for fitting and erection; 8 AAP Lympne to Rec Pk 31.7.18; 2 AI 3.8.18; 3 ASD 4.8.18; 55 Sqn 7.8.18; Wrecked 13.8.18 (Lt EP Critchley wounded & Sgt SE Lewis killed); 3 ASD 13.8.18; 55 Sqn 26.9.18; 2 ASD 17.1.19
F5701 (Eagle VII) Arr Rec Pk 21.8.18; 2 AI 26.8.18; 3 ASD 27.8.18; 55 Sqn 30.8.18; Albatros DV in flames N of Offenburg 11.00 15.9.18 (Capt BJ Silly MC DFC & Lt J Parke DFC); Scout OOC nr Kaiserslautern 25.9.18 (Lt J Cunliffe & 2/Lt GE Little); 2 ASD 17.1.19; 6 AI to 25 Sqn 22.3.19; 6 SS 13.5.19
F5702 (Eagle V) At 2 AAP Hendon 25.7.18 allotted to EF; Rec Pk to 2 AI 16.8.18; 57 Sqn 16.8.18; On landing struck ridge and u/c collapsed 4.9.18 (2/Lt DJ Tarling OK); SOC Rep Pk 1 ASD 27.9.18
F5703 (Eagle VII) Rec Pk to 2 AI 25.7.18; 3 ASD and on to 55 Sqn 26.7.18; EA OOC 14.8.18 (Lt DJ Waterous & 2/Lt CL Rayment); Shot up in Darmstadt raid, wrecked on landing 16.8.18 (observer 2/Lt AC Roberts wounded); 3 ASD 23.8.18
F5704 (Eagle VIII) 217 Sqn by 19.9.18; Returning from bombing raid on Ostende, crashed, TW, W of Furnes 28.9.18 (Lt AR Padmore & Sgt Mech G/L FW Shufflebotham both killed); remains to 4 ASD; Deleted 31.10.18 DBR
F5705 Arr Rec Pk 17.8.18; 2 AI 21.8.18; 3 ASD 22.8.18; 55 Sqn 23.8.18; 3 ASD 7.9.18
F5706 (Eagle VIII) 202 Sqn ('T') by 30.9.18; 98 Sqn 15.3.19; 1 ASD 17.3.19
F5707 (Eagle VII) 4 ASD to 202 Sqn 9.10.18; 233 Sqn Dover 6.3.19; At Joyce Green by 26.4.19, allocated 2 Comm Sqn Buc for special duty with HM the King of the Belgians
F5708 217 Sqn by 20.9.18 (FM); Engine trouble, FL Wusburgh 28.9.18 (Lt HS Stidston & Sgt Mech MC Day); COL 20.11.18 (2/Lt RW Woodhead & Pte1 PG Bradley); 233 Sqn Dover 1.3.19
F5709 Dunkirk by rail to 4 ASD 29.8.18 - @25.10.18
F5710 (Eagle VII) 3 ASD to 55 Sqn 31.8.18; TOC 6 AP 19.9.18; 3 ASD 21.9.18
F5711 (Eagle VI) 3 ASD to 55 Sqn 19.8.18; Damaged in combat in Thionville-Conflans raid 30.8.18 (pilot OK & 2/Lt CE Thorpe DoW); 3 ASD 30.8.18
F5712 (Eagle VII) 3 ASD to 55 Sqn 29.8.18; Bombing raid on Mannheim, shot down nr Hagenau, seen going down under control 16.9.18 (2/Lt W.E.["Biggles"] Johns PoW wounded & 2/Lt AE Amey killed)
F5713 3 ASD to 55 Sqn 30.8.18; 3 ASD 7.9.18; 55 Sqn 17.9.18; Wrecked 29.9.18; 6 AP 2.10.18; 3 ASD 4.10.18
F5714 (Eagle VIII) 3 ASD to 55 Sqn 23.8.18; 3 ASD 4.9.18; 55 Sqn 15.9.18; FTR raid on Kaiserslautern Works, believed hit by AA 25.9.18 (2/Lt GB Dunlop & 2/Lt AC Heyes both PoW)
F5715 (Eagle VIII) 4 ASD Wissant to 217 Sqn 29.9.18; Sank into rut taxying for TO, damaged 29.9.18 (Lt LH Nesbitt & Sgt E Farley); flying again next day; 98 Sqn 16.3.19; 1 ASD 19.3.19
F5716 Rec Pk to 2 AI 25.9.18; 57 Sqn 27.9.18; Overshot on landing and ran into sunken road 30.9.18 (Lt AE Bourns & Lt MG Robson MC OK)
F5717 No information
F5718 Rec Pk to 57 Sqn 9.10.18; Crashed on take off 15.4.19 (2/Lt DG Beaudry & LAC D Harper OK)
F5719 (Eagle VI) Recd Rec Pk 17.10.18; 57 Sqn 13.10.18; Left 09.20 on recce, FTR 4.11.18 (2/Lt W Kinghorn DoW 5.11.18 & 2/Lt W Rushton killed)
F5720 Shipped from 3AD to England via Port Depot Rouen 13.1.19
F5721 (Eagle VIII) 202 Sqn (transit ex 4 ASD?) to 217 Sqn 25.10.18; Propeller accident 9.11.18 (1/AM H Joseph slightly injured); 233 Sqn Dover 1.3.19; At Joyce Green by 26.4.19, allocated 2 Comm Sqn Buc for special duty with HM The King of the Belgians
F5722 (Eagle VIII) Recd Rec Pk ex UK for IF 8.10.18; 5 AI 8.10.18; 3 AD 9.10.18; 55 Sqn ('Y') 5.11.18; 2 ASD 17.1.19; 6 AI to 57 Sqn 5.4.19
F5723 No information

D.H.4 F5706 'T' of No.202 Squadron in flight. (J.M.Bruce/G.S.Leslie collection)

D.H.4 'T' of No.202 Squadron, probably F5706, on the ground. (via Mike O'Connor)

D.H.4A F5764 of No.1 Communications Squadron banking whilst engaged in transporting delegates from London to Paris for the 1919 Peace Conference. (via Frank Cheesman)

F5724 1 ASD to England 4.1.19

F5725 (Eagle VIII) Rec Pk to 5 AI 4.10.18; Rec Pk to 2 AI 18.10.18; 3 ASD to 55 Sqn 22.10.18; On recce grey Fokker DVII OOC Metz-Montoy 12.15 3.11.18 (Capt DRG Mackay DFC & 2/Lt HTC Gompertz); Left on bombing raid, last seen going down under control Thionville-Metz, FTR 10.11.18 (Capt DRG Mackay DFC PoW DoW & 2/Lt HTC Gompertz PoW)

F5726 Rec Pk to 2 AI 22.10.18; 57 Sqn 9.11.18

F5727 (Eagle VII) 8 AAP Lympne by 10.10.18; Rec Pk 11.10.18; 2 AI 14.10.18; 57 Sqn, left 09.20 on practice flight, FTR 4.11.18 (Lt LdeV Wiener & 2/Lt HG Dixon both killed)

F5728 (Eagle VI) 2 AI to 57 Sqn 8.11.18; Casualty Report 22.1.19 says m/c has been exposed to the weather for a considerable time and a complete overhaul is required; To 2 ASD

F5729 (Eagle) 8 AAP Lympne by 8.10.18; Rec Pk 9.10.18; 2 AI 17.10.18; To England 13.1.19

F5730 2 AI to 55 Sqn 31.12.18; 2 ASD 17.1.19; 57 Sqn, engine cut out just after take off 31.3.19 (2/Lt DP Fulton injured)

F5731 (Eagle VIII) Took off from 2 AI on ferry flight, stalled on climbing turn and crashed on aerodrome 1.3.19 (2/Lt WJ Wickens seriously injured); M/c to be RTP

F5732 Shipped by 3 AD to England via Port Depot Rouen 21.1.19

F5733 8 AAP Lympne by 23.10.18; Rec Pk to Farnborough (via Lympne & Croydon) 4.1.19

F5734 Rec Pk to 2 AI 23.10.18; To England 8.1.19; 'A' Flt 1 Comm Sqn Kenley 6.19

F5735 8 AAP Lympne by 21.10.18; 1 ASD to England 3.1.19

F5736 8 AAP Lympne by 19.10.18; Rec Pk 21.10.18; 2 AI 24.10.18; To England 4.1.19; 'A' Flt 1 Comm Sqn Kenley by 6.19

F5737 (Eagle VIII) 55 Sqn 24.12.18; 2 ASD 17.1.19; On ferry flight from 2 ASD to 6 AI ran into stationary Snipe E8324 on landing 13.3.19 (Lt AH Moor)

F5738 Rep Pk 2 ASD to 2 AI 29.10.18; 25 Sqn 8.11.18

F5739 (Eagle VIII) Rep Pk 2 ASD to 2 AI 16.10.18; 25 Sqn, left 07.20 on recce to Maubeuge, shot up in combat, retd 10.05 30.10.18 (Lt DS Crumb & Lt TA Chilcott both unhurt); Rep Pk 2 ASD 30.10.18

F5740 Rep Pk 2 ASD to 2 AI 25.10.18; To England 4.1.19

F5741 Rep Pk 2 ASD to 2 AI 22.10.18; 57 Sqn 9.11.18; On landing due to hard ground and little head wind ran some considerable distance and fell into trench 17.11.18 (2/Lt SCH Biddle & 2/Lt WG Anderson)

F5742 1 ASD to England 8.1.19

F5743 (Eagle VIII) FF 25.10.18; Rep Pk 2 ASD to 2 AI 27.10.18; Deld 2 AAP Hendon to 1 Comm Sqn, lost way flying from Hendon to Paris on passenger service tried to land because of bad weather, banked near ground and nose dived into an English orchard 26.2.19 (Lt LA Hacklett killed & Lt S Graham RNVR Ministry of Shipping seriously injured [DoI?])

F5744 (Eagle VII) 8 AAP Lympne to Hendon 9.2.19; Reallotted 29.4.19 from SE Area for 1 Comm Sqn to EF

F5745 (Eagle) 8 AAP Lympne, tested 6-7.11.18; 'A' Flt 1 Comm Sqn Kenley 6.19

F5746 (Eagle VI) 8 AAP Lympne, tested 7-10.11.18; Allotted to SE Area for 1 Comm Sqn Hendon 23.12.18

F5747 8 AAP Lympne, tested 6.11.18; 37 Sqn 30.11.18; To store 17.12.18

F5748 8 AAP Lympne, tested 18.11.18; Hounslow to 1 Comm

Sqn Hendon 2.12.18
F5749 85 Sqn by 14-22.1.19
F5750 No information
F5751 To France by boat 22.10.18; TOC 7.11.18
F5752 To France by boat 22.10.18; TOC 7.11.18
F5753 To France by boat 3.11.18; TOC 13.11.18
F5754 To France by boat 23.10.18; TOC 7.11.18
F5755 To France by boat 3.11.18; TOC 13.11.18
F5756 To France by boat 30.10.18; TOC 13.11.18; At 57 Sqn 6.19
F5757 To France by boat 30.10.18; TOC 7.11.18
F5758 No information
F5759 'B' Flt 1 Comm Sqn Kenley 6.19
F5760 (Eagle VI) At 8 AAP Lympne 18.12.18 reallotted from EF to Store
F5761 (Eagle V) At 8 AAP Lympne 18.12.18 reallotted from EF to Store
F5762 (Eagle V) At 8 AAP Lympne 18.12.18 reallotted from EF to Store
F5763 (Eagle VI) At 8 AAP Lympne 18.12.18 reallotted from EF to Store
F5764 (Conv D.H.4A 3-seater) 'A' Flt 1 Comm Sqn Kenley 2.19 - 6.19; Became *G-EAWH*
F5765 to F5773 No information
F5774 Became *G-EAXP*
F5775 to F5778 No information
F5779 Became *G-EAYF*
F5780 No information
F5781 (Eagle VIII) At 8 AAP Lympne 10.1.19 allotted to EF; Reallotted to 86 Wing Hendon for London Lisbon flight; 7.2.19
F5782 (Eagle VIII) At 8 AAP Lympne 9.1.19 allotted to EF; Still at Lympne 10.3.19 allotment to EF cancelled;
F5783 (Eagle VIII) At 8 AAP Lympne 9.1.19 allotted to EF; Still at Lympne 10.3.19 allotment to EF cancelled; 1 Comm Sqn Kenley, carrying mail, flying low over Newcastle due to mist and low cloud, ran out of fuel before reaching aerodrome, FL in football field, crashed, Newcastle-on-Tyne 2.10.19 (F/O FHG Shepard seriously injured & F/O A Page unhurt)
F5784 (Eagle VIII) At 8 AAP Lympne 9.1.19 allotted to EF; Reallotted from EF to 86 Wing Hendon for London Lisbon flight 7.2.19; 2 Comm Sqn Buc, crashed on test flight 17.9.19 (F/Lt TA Cooch killed)
F5785 (Eagle VIII) At 8 AAP Lympne 9.1.19 allotted to EF; Reallotted to Midland Area for 27 Group Bircham Newton for England to Delhi and Australia flight 13.2.19
F5786 (Eagle VIII) At 8 AAP Lympne 9.1.19 allotted to EF; Reallotted to Midland Area for 27 Group Bircham Newton for England to Delhi and Australia flight 13.2.19
F5787 (Eagle VIII) At 8 AAP Lympne 10.1.19 allotted to EF; Reallotted to Midland Area for 27 Group Bircham Newton for England to Delhi and Australia flight 13.2.19
F5788 (Eagle VIII) At 8 AAP Lympne 9.1.19 allotted to EF; Reallotted to Midland Area for 27 Group Bircham Newton for England to Delhi and Australia flight
F5789 (Eagle VIII) At 8 AAP Lympne 10.1.19 allotted to EF; Still at Lympne 10.3.19 allotment to EF cancelled
F5790 (Eagle VIII) At 8 AAP Lympne 10.1.19 allotted to EF; Still at Lympne 10.3.19 allotment to EF cancelled
F5791 (Eagle VIII) At 8 AAP Lympne 10.1.19 allotted to EF; Still at Lympne 10.3.19 allotment to EF cancelled
F5792 No information
F5793 No information
F5794 Became *G-EAXJ*
F5795 No information
F5796 (Eagle VIII) 202 Sqn by 3.19; 98 Sqn 15.3.19
F5797 Became *G-EAYV*
F5798 No information

D.H.4 rebuilds at depots in France in range F5801 to F6300. Range continued to F6513 in error

F5825 (Eagle) Rebuilt ex A7838 25.6.18; Rec Pk to 2 AI 23.8.18; 57 Sqn 24.8.18; FTR, last seen at 8,000ft between Denain and Douai under control but being followed by 2 EA 07.45 29.8.18 (Lt J Caldwell & Sgt AT Wareing both killed)
F5826 (Eagle VI) Rebuilt ex A7716 25.6.18; Rep Pk 1 ASD to Rec Pk 24.7.18; 2 AI 29.7.18; 25 Sqn 1.8.18; Propeller struck ground and broke on take off, crashed 1.10.18 (2/Lt AL Wilcox OK); Rebuilt as H6873 17.10.18
F5827 (Eagle) Rebuilt ex D9249 25.6.18; Rep Pk 1 ASD to Rec Pk and on to 2 AI 1.9.18; 57 Sqn 2.9.18; Shot down in flames E of Bourlon 18.45 21.9.18 (2/Lt OMcL Turnball & 2/Lt DFV Page both killed)
F5828 (Eagle) Rebuilt ex A7790 25.6.18; Rep Pk 1 ASD to Rec Pk and on to 2 AI 1.9.18; 57 Sqn 3.9.18; Albatros D shot down 4.9.18 (Sgt DE Edgley & Sgt JH Bowler); Fokker DVII OOC Marcoing 11.25 5.9.18 (Sgt DE Edgley OK & Sgt JH Bowler wounded); Fokker DVII OOC Havrincourt Wood 12.30 16.9.18 (Sgt DE Edgley & Sgt AC Lovesey); FL due to storm, hit ridge on landing, u/c collapsed 29.9.18 (Lt Fde M Hyde & Sgt Mech R Taggart OK)
F5829 (Eagle) Rebuilt ex A7968 25.6.18; Rep Pk 1 ASD to Rec Pk 4.9.18; 2 AI 5.9.18; 57 Sqn 6.9.18; U/c and propeller wrecked in landing 20.9.18 (Lt GJ Dickins & Lt AH Aitken); Rep Pk 2 ASD 22.9.18
F5830 (Eagle VIII) Rebuilt ex A7442 25.6.18; 2 AI to Rep Pk 2 ASD 5.8.18; 1 ASD by 8.18 - @9.18; 25 Sqn, on reconnaissance flight, FL Hangard road 7.10.18 (2/Lt FW Seed OK & 2/Lt HC Shires injured)
F5831 (Eagle VI) Rebuilt ex A7417 25.6.18; Rec Pk to 2 AI 24.7.18; 57 Sqn 31.7.18; Attacked by 6 Fokker DVII over St Leger, damaged 11.45 1.8.18 (Lt FG Pym & Sgt WCE Mason); Casualty Report 21.8.18 says m/c is tail heavy, will not climb and a complete overhaul is required; Rep Pk 2 ASD 22.8.18 - @9.18
F5832 (Eagle) Rebuilt ex D9259 26.6.18; Rep Pk 1 ASD to Rec Pk 1.7.18; 2 AI 1.7.18; 25 Sqn 2.7.18; Combat damaged on photo recce to Landrecies, engine shot through, FL 19.10 22.7.18 (Lt S Jones & Lt MF St.Clair-Fowles both unhurt), to be repaired in the sqn; Landed short, u/c caught by corn at edge of aerodrome and swept off 4.8.18 (Lt S Jones & 2/Lt JE Hermon OK); SOC Rep Pk 2 ASD 11.8.18 NWR
F5833 Rebuilt ex A7916 17.7.18; 5Rep Pk 1 ASD to Rec Pk and on to 2 AI 5.9.18; 57 Sqn 6.9.18; Left 13.25 on practice flight, FTR 4.11.18 (2/Lt LS Harvey & 2/Lt F Heath MM); Later returned; Left behind 25.11.18 (overheating); 2 ASD 14.12.18
F5834 Rebuilt ex A7959 7.8.18
F5835 Rebuilt ex A7937 7.8.18; Rep Pk 1 ASD to 1 AI 3.10.18
F5836 Rebuilt ex A7684 7.8.18; Tested at Rep Pk 1ASD 14.10.18.
F5837 (RAF 3a) Rebuilt ex A7975 25.6.18; Rec Pk to 1 AI 16.7.18; 18 Sqn 29.7.18; Pfalz OOC just W of Somain 11.00 13.8.18 (Lt GWF Darvill & Lt J Fenwick); In raid on Wasnes -Au-Bac Fokker DVII OOC c.12.40 27.9.18 (Lt GF Lane & Lt G Thompson MC); COL 23.10.18; Rep Pk 1 ASD 17.10.18 (sic)
F5838 (RAF 3a) Rebuilt ex A7483 25.6.18; Rep Pk 1 ASD to Rec Pk 24.7.18; 18 Sqn 2.8.18; Badly shot up 31.8.18 (2/Lt C Mason & Lt EA Collis MM OK); Rep Pk 1 ASD 3.9.18; SOC 5.9.18 NWR
F5839 (RAF 3a) Rebuilt ex A8000 25.6.18; Rec Pk to 1 AI 4.8.18; 18 Sqn 10.8.18; Left 13.55 on photographic mission, shot down by AA W of Bourlon Wood 3.9.18 (Lt FM Macfarland & 2/Lt A Petersen both killed); SOC in field 3.9.18
F5840 (RAF 3a) Rebuilt ex A8019 25.6.18; Rep Pk 1 ASD to Rec Pk 2.8.18; 1 AI 4.8.18; 18 Sqn 11.8.18; Engine failure, lost flying speed and crashed nr aerodrome 1.9.18 (Lt L Hudson OK & 2/Lt L McCall minor facial injuries); SOC Rep Pk 1 ASD 6.9.18
F6000 Rebuilt.ex A7984 12.7.18
F6001 Rebuilt ex A8034 29.7.18; Rec Pk to 18 Sqn 31.8.18; In 07.45 raid on Aubigny 4.9.18 (Pilot OK & Sgt Mech CA Cribbes wounded); 1 ASD 30.10.18 exchanged for D.H.9A
F6002 (RAF 3a) Rebuilt ex A8021 25.7.18; Rep Pk 2 ASD to 1 AI 23.9.18; 18 Sqn 25.9.18; 2 AI 19.11.18 (exchanged for D.H.9A); To England 11.3.19
F6003 Rebuilt ex A8047 25.7.18
F6004 Rebuilt ex A8010 7.8.18; Rep Pk 1 ASD to 1AI 5.10.18
F6059 Rebuilt ex A7933 2.7.18; Rep Pk 2 ASD to 2 AI 5.7.18; 57 Sqn 6.7.18; Left 07.10 for photo recce Moislains aerodrome, last seen at 1,000 over target in combat

8.8.18 (2/Lt LL Brown DFC (Can) & 2/Lt AE Doncaster both PoW); SOC 8.8.18

F6070 (Eagle VIII) Rebuilt ex B884 2.7.18; Rep Pk 2 ASD to 2 AI 4.7.18; 205 Sqn 5.7.18; Pfalz DIII crashed and burnt Rosières-Chaulnes 19.15 8.8.18 (Lt AR McAfee & Sgt L Murphy); Photo recce, COL 25.8.18 (Lt W Grossart & 2/Lt JJ Rowe unhurt); SOS 26.8.18

F6075 (Eagle VI) Rebuilt ex A7776 3.7.18; Rep Pk 2 ASD to 2 AI 1.8.18; 57 Sqn 12.8.18; Returning from practice flight landed heavily on one wheel 21.8.18 (2/Lt DU Thomas & 2/Lt LB Simmonds OK); Rep Pk 2 ASD 23.8.18 - @9.18

F6076 (Eagle VIII) Rebuilt ex F1551 3.7.18; 25 Sqn, m/c sideslipped nr ground and crashed 21.12.18 (Lt C Addenbrooke & 2/Lt HJ Rayment OK)

F6077 Rebuilt ex A7619 3.7.18; Rep Pk 2 ASD to 2 AI 13.9.18; 205 Sqn 18.9.18; 2 AI exchanged for DH9A 24.9.18; 57 Sqn 25.9.18; Taking off on practice flight, stalled and hit telegraph wires 27.9.18, m/c destroyed by fire (2/Lt EA Smith killed & 2/Lt AL Symes injured); SOC Rep Pk 2 ASD 29.9.18

F6078 Rebuilt ex B2144 3.7.18; Rep Pk 2 ASD to 2 AI 1.10.18; 1 AI 3.10.18; 1 ASD to UK but crashed en route at Southgate, Middx 26.11.18 (Lt JH Whitham & Capt Prince Antoine of Orleans (Can Army) both killed)

F6096 Rebuilt ex A7452 3.7.18; Rep Pk 2 ASD to 2 AI 30.7.18; 57 Sqn 10.8.18; Fokker DVII BU and another OOC Roisel 10.30 14.8.18 (Lt G Anderson & 2/Lt DE Stephens); Fokker DVII OOC Cherisy 09.45 19.8.18 (Lt G Anderson & Lt TC Danby); FTR, last seen going down under control SE of Cambrai closely followed by 6 EA 14.00 1.9.18 (2/Lt JG Dugdale & 2/Lt FB Robinson both PoW)

F6099 (Eagle VIII) Rebuilt ex A7744 3.7.18; 2 AI to 25 Sqn 18.9.18

F6103 (Eagle V) Rebuilt ex D9232 3.7.18; 2 AI to 25 Sqn 15.8.18; FL and crashed due to bad weather 8.9.18 (Lt C Brown & Lt EW Griffin OK); SOC Rep Pk 2 ASD 30.9.18

F6104 Rebuilt ex D9247 3.7.18; Rep Pk 2 ASD to 2 AI 25.7.18; 205 Sqn 14.8.18; Fokker DVII OOC in raid on Rochy 19.05 30.8.18 (Lt GC Matthews & 2/Lt JB Leach); 2 AI exchanged for DH9A 1.9.18; 57 Sqn 2.9.18; Collided with A7774 on landing and destroyed by fire 8.12.18 (Lt AV Dearden OK).

D.H.4 F6104 of No.57 Squadron in late 1918. (via Mike O'Connor)

F6114 Rebuilt ex A8071 3.7.18; Rep Pk 2 ASD to 2 AI 16.9.18; 57 Sqn 17.9.18; Photographing bombing raid, in combat with EA, FL 62 Sqn airfield 18.30 27.9.18 (Lt EM Coles unhurt & 2/Lt C Wilkinson wounded)

F6119 (Eagle V) Rebuilt ex A7464 3.7.18; Rep Pk 2 ASD to 2 AI 13.9.18; 205 Sqn 18.9.18; COL when u/c struck top of RE hangar after returning from raid on Villers Outréaux with engine trouble, bomb exploded 20.9.18 (Lt WV Theron DoI & 2/Lt JJ Rowe injured); SOC 2 Salvage Dump, 2 ASD 23.9.18

F6120 (Eagle VIII) Rebuilt ex E4625 3.7.18; 2 AI to 25 Sqn 18.9.18; Left sqn 19.5.19

F6127 (Eagle VI) Rebuilt ex A7657 3.7.18; 2 AI to 25 Sqn 14.8.18; On practice flight engine failed, crashed 28.8.18 (2/Lt RL Henning injured); SOC Rep Pk 2 ASD 2.10.18

F6133 Rebuilt ex D9252 3.7.18; Rep Pk 2 ASD to 2 AI 7.9.18; 57 Sqn 16.9.18; Left on bombing raid on Marcoing 11.30, last seen nr Arras going SW 17.9.18 (2/Lt WA Wilson & 2/Lt HH Senior both PoW)

F6136 (Eagle V) Rebuilt ex D9242 3.7.18; Rep Pk 2 ASD to 2 AI 25.7.18; 205 Sqn 7.8.18; COL from bombing raid on Doingt station 20.8.18 (Lt GC Matthews & 2/Lt HS Mullen OK); Rep Pk 1 ASD 25.8.18; SOC 6.9.18, new number allotted H7122 for reconstruction

F6139 (Eagle VII) Rebuilt ex D9256 3.7.18; Rep Pk 2 ASD to 2AI 7.9.18; 57 Sqn 17.9.18; On practice flight, FL, wrecked 1.10.18 (2/Lt E Solomons injured); SOC Rep Pk 2 ASD 4.10.18

F6164 Rebuilt ex B5459 3.7.18; Rep Pk 2 ASD to 2 AI 30.7.18; Rec Pk 9.8.18; 1 AI 19.8.18; 18 Sqn 24.8.18; Two Albatros D OOC SW of Somain 07.30, then with petrol tank shot through FL Le Hamel 29.8.18 (2/Lt A Duncan & Sgt R Asher); COL 7.9.18 (2/Lt J Whitehead & 2/Lt H Cranfield OK); Rep Pk 1 ASD 10.9.18; SOC 13.9.18 (NWR)

F6165 Rebuilt ex B5480 3.7.18; Rep Pk 2 ASD to 2 AI 6.8.18; Rec Pk 9.8.18; 18 Sqn 15.8.18; Fokker DVII OOC Pailleul 13.45 4.9.18 (Lt RC Bennett DFC & 2/Lt A Lilley); Left 10.45 on photo recce, shot up in combat with EA, retd 13.35 24.9.18 (Lt RC Bennett DFC & 2/Lt A Lilley OK); Rep Pk 1 ASD 26.9.18

F6166 Rebuilt ex B3955 3.7.18; Rep Pk 2 ASD to 2 AI 3.8.18; Rec Pk 9.8.18; 18 Sqn 19.8.18; COL 23.8.18 (2/Lt R Johnston & 2/Lt H Buckner OK); Rep Pk 1 ASD 25.8.18; SOC 28.8.18 (NWR)

F6167 Rebuilt ex D9253 3.7.18; Rep Pk 2 ASD to 2 AI 25.7.18; 57 Sqn 9.8.18; Fokker DVII OOC Suzanne 19.05 10.8.18 (Lt JL Standish & Lt WH Thornton); In combat 16.8.18 (Lt WJ Barber OK & Sgt EEAG Bridger killed); FTR, last seen in combat with EAs at 8,000ft between Denain and Douai 07.45 29.8.18 (Sgt Mech THC Davies & 2/Lt WTS Lewis both PoW)

F6168 Rebuilt ex D9254 3.7.18; Rep Pk 2 ASD to 2 AI 28.7.18; 57 Sqn 9.8.18; Shot up in action 1.9.18 (Lt AL Platt OK & Lt J Howard-Brown wounded); Raid on Marcoing 5.9.18 (Lt AL Platt OK & Lt GAF Riley wounded); FTR, shot down in flames 18.35 5.9.18 (Lt AL Platt & Lt CE Kinton both killed)

F6169 (Eagle VI) Rebuilt ex A2144 3.7.18; Rep Pk 2 ASD to 2 AI 22.7.18; 205 Sqn 12.8.18; O/t landing from bombing raid, stalled, nosedived into ground, TW 1820 22.8.18 (2/Lt JB Cunningham killed & Sgt EB England injured); SOC 2 Salvage Dump 24.8.18

F6186 Rebuilt ex D9264 12.7.18; Rep Pk 2 ASD to 2 AI 28.10.18

F6187 Rebuilt ex A8030 12.7.18; 2 AI to 57 Sqn 30.8.18; Photographing bombing raid on Awoingt, in combat with EA, down in control from 10,000ft over Cambrai 18.20 26.9.18 (Lt FG Pym PoW wounded & Sgt WCE Mason PoW DoW)

F6207 Rebuilt ex A8028 20.7.18; Rep Pk 2 ASD to 5 AI 7.10.18; 57 Sqn, lost formation in mist, engine cut out, landed at 62 Sqn, m/c landed cross wind on one wheel 11.10.18 (2/Lt AV Dearden & 2/Lt F Brown)

F6209 Rebuilt ex D9263 24.7.18

F6212 Rebuilt ex A7713 25.7.18

F6214 Rebuilt ex A7507 25.7.18

F6215 Rebuilt ex A7626 15.7.18; To England 8.1.19

F6222 Rebuilt ex A8016 31.7.18; Rep Pk 2 ASD to 5 AI and on to 57 Sqn 9.10.18; 98 Sqn 21.2.19; 8 AAP Lympne 24.2.19

F6232 Rebuilt ex D8389 6.8.18; Rep Pk 2 ASD to 25 Sqn 6.10.18; 6 AI 13.5.19

F6234 Rebuilt ex F5699 7.8.18; Rep Pk 2 ASD to 2 AI 17.10.18; 57 Sqn 30.10.18; 98 Sqn 21.2.19; 8 AAP Lympne 24.2.19

F6236 Rebuilt ex A2174 10.8.18

F6511 Rebuilt Rep Pk 1 ASD ex D8412 28.8.18, incorrect serial given, renumbered H7118

F6512 Rebuilt Rep Pk 1 ASD ex A7561 28.8.18, incorrect serial given, renumbered H7119

F6513 Rebuilt Rep Pk 1 ASD ex E4626 28.8.18, incorrect serial given, renumbered H7120

D.H.4A H5894 of No.1 Communications Squadron in May 1919. (via Norman Franks)

D.H.4A H5895, possibly in South Russia. (via Jack Meaden)

2 D.H.4 ordered under Cont No 35a/1692/C.1795 from Aircraft Manufacturing Co Ltd, Hendon and numbered F7597 & F7598

F7597 Rec Pk to 57 Sqn 18.8.18; Fokker DVII OOC Le Transloy 15.15 23.8.18 (2/Lt DU Thomas & Lt JFD Tanqueray); Fokker DVII OOC N of Ytres 08.00 29.8.18 (2/Lt DU Thomas & 2/Lt CG Smith); Fokker DVII OOC Marcoing 11.20 5.9.18 (2/Lt DU Thomas & 2/Lt IS Woodhouse); Fokker DVII in flames Havrincourt Wood 12.15 16.9.18 (Lt PWJ Timson slightly wounded & 2/Lt IS Woodhouse OK); Bombing raid to Cambrai, Fokker DVII OOC smoking E of Garmes, shared A8090 08.30, then FTR 2.10.18 (Lt JWMcN Ramsay US & Sgt Mech JF Turner both killed)

F7598 (Eagle VII) Rec Pk to 2 AI 27.9.18; 25 Sqn 28.9.18; Stalled on take-off, fouled telegraph wires 21.1.19 (Lt C Addenbrooke & Sgt J Bourne OK)

1 D.H.4 rebuild by No.5(W) ARD, Yate numbered F9511

F9511 (RAF 3a) At (E)ARD 23.1.19 reallotted from EF to Store.

1 D.H.4 built by The Glendower Aircraft Co Ltd, London and numbered H5290

H5290 Rec Pk to 2 AI 3.10.18; 57 Sqn 4.10.18; Fokker DVII OOC Hargnies 10.15 27.10.18 (2/Lt SCH Biddle wounded & Sgt Mech A Curtiss OK) 2 AI 30.11.18

46 D.H.4 ordered 15.8.18 under Cont No 35a/2556/C.2849 from Waring & Gillow Ltd, London and numbered H5894 to H5939

H5894 Conv to D.H.4A; 1 Comm Sqn Kenley; The first aircraft on London-Paris route; FL in English Channel, missing 15.5.19
H5895 Conv to D.H.4A; Possibly in South Russia
H5896 Became *G-EAYX* (ferry marks to Belgian AF)
H5897 No information
H5898 Became *G-EAYS* (ferry marks to Belgian AF)
H5899 to H5901 No information
H5902 Became *G-EAYG* (ferry marks to Belgian AF)
H5903 No information
H5904 No information
H5905 Became *G-EAVL* (D.H.4A)
H5906 to H5914 No information
H5915 Became *O-BAIN*
H5916 To Belgian Air Force as 'B11' (11 Escadrille)
H5917 to H5924 No information
H5925 Became ADC No.0-2; To *O-BABI*
H5926 No information
H5927 No information
H5928 (covered cockpit). Became *O-BARI* (D.H.4A)
H5929 Became *O-BATO* (D.H.4A)
H5930 No information
H5931 Became *O-BALO* (or H5921?)
H5932 No information
H5933 No information
H5934 Became *G-EAXF* (ferry marks to Belgian AF)
H5935 No information
H5936 Became *O-BADO*
H5937 Became No.17, 10ème Belgian AF
H5938 No information
H5939 Became *G-EAMU* (D.H.4A)

H6843 to H7342 were allocated for the renumbering of aircraft rebuilt in France, a few of which went to naval units. Many such numbers were given to rebuilds which had originally been incorrectly renumbered in the range F6320 onwards. D.H.4s in this range as follows

H6858 Rebuilt ex A7964 3.10.18
H6859 Rebuilt ex D8427 3.10.18
H6873 Rebuilt ex F5826 17.10.18
H6881 Rebuilt ex A7820 23.10.18
H6882 Rebuilt ex A8088 25.10.18
H6885 Rebuilt ex D8378 25.10.18
H6887 Rebuilt ex B7911 31.10.18
H7118 (Eagle VIII) Renumbered ex F6511 28.8.18; Rep Pk 1 ASD to 2 AI 13.10.18; 57 Sqn 28.10.18; Damaged landing at Cologne on mail flight 17.1.19 (2/Lt WF Smith OK)
H7119 Renumbered ex F6512 28.8.18; Rep Pk 1 ASD to 2 AI 22.10.18
H7120 (Eagle VIII) Renumbered ex F6513 31.8.18; Rep Pk 1 ASD to 25 Sqn 7.10.18; Left sqn 19.5.19
H7121 Rebuilt ex D8415 6.9.18; Tested at Rep Pk 1 ASD 25.10.18; 2 AI to 25 Sqn 8.11.18; Stalled at 50ft on turn and dived in while landing 9.5.19 (2/Lt JG Barclay killed); 6 SS 13.5.19
H7122 Rebuilt ex F6136 6.9.18; To England 3.1.19
H7123 Rebuilt ex D9278 11.9.18; Rep Pk 1 ASD to 57 Sqn 8.10.18; 2 AI 30.11.18
H7124 Rebuilt ex D8383 17.9.18
H7125 Rebuilt ex A8029 17.9.18
H7147 Rebuilt ex D8377 25.9.18; 6 AI to 57 Sqn 14.12.18; On mail flight, FL, m/c badly damaged and looted by civilians 21.1.19 (2/Lt WE Hall & Lt W Steele)
H7148 (Eagle VIII) Rebuilt ex D8382 25.9.18; 2AI to 57 Sqn 1.12.18; 98 Sqn 21.2.19; 8 AAP Lympne 24.2.19

1 D.H.4 ordered 16.9.18 under Cont No 35a/2149/C.2512 from Palladium Autocars Ltd, London and numbered H8263

H8263 (Eagle VIII) Original sample conversion to D.H.4A; At 8 AAP Lympne 11.1.19 allotted to EF; Still at Lympne 10.3.19 allotment to EF cancelled

50 D.H.4 put forward 1.17 and ordered under Cont No C.P.101977/17 from Westland Aircraft Works, Yeovil for RNAS use and numbered N5960 to N6009 & built Yeovil. (275hp Eagle V/VI/VII) [N5995 onwards had higher u/c]

N5960 (Twin Vickers guns) Deld Hendon 20.3.17; Martlesham Heath 30.3.17; AD Dunkirk by 26.4.17; 2N Sqn 2.5.17; Crashed and wrecked 19.5.17 (FSL JF Chisholm & S/L CS Fox injured); AD Dunkirk by 24.5.17; Deleted 27.6.17

N5961 (Eagle V) Deld Dover 7.4.17; AD Dunkirk 7.4.17; 2N Sqn 16.4.17 - @21.10.17; AD Dunkirk by 24.10.17 - @24.1.18; 12N Sqn by 29.1.18 - @23.2.18; AD Dunkirk by 28.2.18; 5N Sqn 28.2.18; Albatros OOC in

Loading mail into a D.H.4 of No.1 Communications Squadron on the Kenley/Hendon mail run for British troops involved in the post-war Occupation Forces in Germany. (via Frank Cheesman)

raid on Busigny aerodrome 11.02 18.3.18 (F/Cdr CPO Bartlett & G/L W Naylor); Became 205 Sqn 1.4.18; Ran into hole on aerodrome landing, wrecked 7.4.18 (Lt L Jolly injured & G/L L James unhurt); Rep Pk 2 ASD 8.4.18; SOC 26.4.18

N5962 (275hp Eagle VII/V/VII) Deld AD Dunkirk 4.17; 5N Sqn 14.5.17 - @15.6.17; AD Dunkirk by 21.6.17; 5N Sqn 11.8.17 (Eagle V by 12.17]; Albatros D.V OOC Aertrycke aerodrome 11.40 8.12.17 (FSL E Dickson & AC1 AGL R Shaw); AD Dunkirk 12.1.18; 2N Sqn 12.3.18; Became 202 Sqn 1.4.18; Left 06.10 in storm, last seen nr Engel Dump 28.9.18 (Lt R Ringrose & 2/Lt H Hollings both killed); Deleted 15.10.18

N5963 Deld Dover 16.4.17; AD Dunkirk 20.4.17; 2N Sqn 29.4.17; Spotting for warship shoot on Zeebrugge, attacked by yellow biplane with dark green crosses, which was shot down into sea 12.5.17 (FSL LN Glaisby & OSL V Greenwood); Escort to 3696 on recce to Ostende, last seen over Oostduinkerke Bains 1m astern heading for shore 26.5.17 (FSL W Houston-Stewart & OSL CL Haines both killed)

N5964 (Eagle V) Deld AD Dunkirk 4.17; 2N Sqn 26.4.17; AD Dunkirk by 24.5.17; 2N Sqn 26.6.17; AD Dunkirk by 9.9.17; 2N Sqn 23.9.17; AD Dunkirk by road 7.12.17; 12N Sqn W/E 7.2.18; 2N Sqn 8.3.18; COL 12.3.18 (FSL AG Storey); Wrecked, 18.3.18; Still 2N Sqn 21.3.18; AD Dunkirk 25.3.18; 4 ASD Guines 28.3.18; Deleted 8.4.18

N5965 (Eagle V) Deld AD Dunkirk by 3.5.17; 2N Sqn 10.5.17; COL 22.8.17 (FSL ECR Stoneman); AD Dunkirk by 23.8.17; 2N Sqn 8.9.17; Fuel tank holed by flak, FL on beach, nosed-up, La Panne 24.1.18 (FSL FS Russell & Observer unhurt); Flying escort to N5997 contact lost at 16.45 and went in sea off La Panne 11.3.18 (FSL CG Macdonald & G/L AAM1 PJ Capp both drowned); Wreckage picked up 16.3.18; Deleted 18.3.18

N5966 (Eagle V) Deld AD Dunkirk (via Bournemouth and Dover) 29.4.17; 2N Sqn 19.5.17 - @2.6.17; AD Dunkirk by 7.6.17; 2N Sqn 24.7.17 - @3.9.17; AD Dunkirk by 6.9.17; 2N Sqn ('E') by 4.10.17; Became 202 Sqn ('E') 1.4.18; LM 6.4.18; NFT

N5967 (Eagle VI) Deld AD Dunkirk (via Dover) 29.4.17; 5N Sqn 30.4.17; COL 9.9.17 (FSL CH Pownall & AC2 CS Osborn); AD Dunkirk by 13.9.17; 5N Sqn ('A1') 23.9.17; Eagle V by 12.17; Swung on TO, hit bomb dump, wrecked 10.3.18 (FSL NA Taylerson & AGL GE Daffey unhurt); still 5N Sqn 21.3.18; 4 ASD Guines by 30.3.18; 2 ASD 4.18; Rep Pk 1 ASD 7.4.18; SOC 8.4.18

N5968 (Eagle VII) Deld AD Dunkirk 5.8.17; 5N Sqn 9.8.17; Crashed and destroyed by fire nr Houthulst Forest 13.1.18 (FSL H Willis DoI & AGL AM2 A Foster injured); Deleted 21.1.18

N5969 (Eagle V later VI) Deld AD Dunkirk by 10.5.17; 2N Sqn ('K') by 12.5.17; EA OOC 8.8.17 (F/L FE Sandford & F/L OGL Pickup); Very misty, hit tree on landing, u/c collapsed, broke prop 23.2.18 (FSL LHN Langworthy OK); Became 202 ('G') Sqn 1.4.18; EA OOC 2.5.18 (FSL LF Pendred & Lt NH Jenkins); Albatros DV in flames 17.45 9.5.18 (Lt RHV Fowler & Lt IH McClure) [but this aircraft also claimed by C66 of 213 Sqn]; Ferried to 98 Demobilisation Sqn but EF at 1,000 ft en route, FL Setques Pool Pilots' Range, u/c sank in hole 15.3.19 (2/Lt PR Spivey); Retd 1 AD salvage 17.3.19

N5970 Transferred to RFC as B3955

N5971 (Eagle VI) Deld AD Dunkirk by 5.17; 5N Sqn 10.5.17; Attacked by EA during raid on Aertrycke aerodrome 20.7.17 (FSL LN Glaisby & AM2 LV Saw both wounded); AD Dunkirk by 26.7.17; 5N Sqn ('G') by 2.8.17; AD Dunkirk W/E 30.8.17; 5N Sqn by 4.10.17; Damaged in collision with Capt Bailey 12.3.18; AD Dunkirk by 14.3.18; 4 ASD Guines 28.3.18; Deleted 8.4.18

N5972 (Fitted twin Vickers and Lewis gun) (Eagle VI) Deld AD Dunkirk by 5.17; 2N Sqn ('J') 23.5.17 - @27.5.17; AD Dunkirk by 31.5.17; 2N Sqn 5.7.17; Crashed on ridge landing Bergues 6.3.18 (FSL LH Pearson); Smashed in collision 21.3.18; AD Dunkirk 23.3.18; 4 ASD Guines 28.3.18; Deleted 8.4.18

N5973 Deld Eastbourne 16.5.17 (transit); Dover 17.5.17; AD Dunkirk 19.5.17; 2N Sqn 9.6.17; COL 27.6.17 (FSL

D.H.4 N5963 of No.202 Squadron on 24.1.18. It has a built-up gun ring and a local modification of a streamlined shield for a camera under its fuselage. (J.M.Bruce/G.S.Leslie collection)

Sgt Allen DFM leaning against D.H.4 N5966 'E' of No.202 Squadron. On the rear fuselage is some kind of winged motif. (J.M.Bruce/G.S.Leslie collection)

D.H.4 N5967 'A1' of No.5N Squadron. In the background is a Sopwith B1. (J.M.Bruce/G.S.Leslie collection)

D.H.4 N5969 'G' of No.202 Squadron. (via Frank Cheesman)

An experimental cover fitted to the cylinder block of D.H.4 N5977 of 5N Squadron. (via J.M.Bruce/G.S.Leslie collection)

F/Cdr C.P.O.Bartlett DSC and Col Dugdale in D.H.4 N5974, about to fly a "tourist" trip over the lines. (via Terry Treadwell)

D.H.4 N5978 'B3' of No.5N Squadron has a spinner fitted to its 4-bladed propeller, twin Vickers guns and a built-up rear cockpit.

D.H.4 N5988 'K' of 'B' Flight No.202 Squadron has two-colour wheel discs. (via Frank Cheesman)

AC Jones killed & OSL CB Orfeur DoI 1.7.17); Deleted AD Dunkirk 20.8.17

N5974 (Eagle VI to 12.17; To Eagle V 1.18) Deld AD Dunkirk by 5.17; 5N Sqn 23.5.17; Attacked by Albatros returning from raid on Ghistelles aerodrome 7.7.17 (Pilot unhurt & LM WJ Edwards wounded); Attacked by EA returning from raid on Aertrycke aerodrome 20.7.17 (FSL WF Cleghorn unhurt & AM1 G/L WR Burdett wounded); AD Dunkirk by 26.7.17; 5N Sqn 30.7.17; Crashed 27.1.18; AD Dunkirk by 31.1.18; Deleted 18.2.18 wrecked

N5975 Shipped to Aegean; 2 Wing Imbros by 1.12.17 - @1.1.18; Marsh by 13.3.18; Imbros by 24.3.18; Mudros by 3.18 - 4.18; C Sqn 2 Wing Imbros; Repair Base Mudros by 6.18; F Sqn 62 Wing, tested 22.7.18; Mudros 24.7.18; Mudros by 7.18 - @30.1.19

N5976 Shipped to Aegean; Imbros by 1.12.17; Marsh by 1.1.18 - @2.3.18 (250hp Eagle); Imbros by 24.3.18 - 4.18; Repair Base by 6.18; C Sqn 2 Wing Imbros; F Sqn 62 Wing Mudros by 8.18; 62 Wing Marsh by 10.18; Repair Base Mudros by 10.18; 222 Sqn Mudros by 14.11.18

N5977 (Twin Vickers guns) (Eagle VIII later V) Deld Dover 25.5.17; AD Dunkirk 26.5.17; 5N Sqn 28.5.17 - @6.7.17; AD Dunkirk by 12.7.17; 5N Sqn 30.7.17 - @11.8.17; AD Dunkirk by 16.8.17; 5N Sqn 11.9.17 - @4.12.17; Damaged and forced down at Frontier airfield 21.9.17 (FSL NP Playford slightly wounded); NAD Dunkirk by 13.12.17 - @31.12.17; 12N Sqn by 7.2.18; 17N Sqn 8.3.18; Became 217 Sqn 1.4.18; Crashed 4.5.18; 4 ASD Guines 5.5.18; 11 AP to 202 Sqn 15.3.19 (transit); 98 Sqn 16.3.19; 1 ASD 18.3.19; To England 18.3.19

N5978 (Twin Vickers guns) Deld AD Dunkirk (via Dover) 26.5.17; 5N Sqn ('B3') 28.5.17; Yellow Albatros shot down after bombing Aertrycke aerodrome 20.7.17 (F/Cdr INC Clarke DSC & O/L RS St.John); AD Dunkirk by 26.7.17 - @23.8.17; 5N Sqn by 30.8.17; Crashed 19.11.17; AD Dunkirk 20.11.17 - @22.11.17; Deleted by 29.11.17

N5979 Deld AD Dunkirk by 31.5.17; 2N Sqn 2.6.17; Crashed and wrecked on TO 8.6.17 (F/L GE Harvey & AAM1 G/L W Bowman); AD Dunkirk by 14.6.17; Deleted 27.6.17

N5980 Transferred to RFC as B3956

N5981 Deld AD Dunkirk by 31.5.17; 2N Sqn 5.6.17; Crashed on TO, landed on French Sopwith Triplane *F17*, both wrecked 27.6.17 (FSL LN Glaisby & OSL V Greenwood); AD Dunkirk 28.6.17; Deleted 20.8.17

N5982 (Eagle VI) Deld AD Dunkirk by 14.6.17; 5N Sqn 18.6.17; Shot away 2 propeller blades testing gun after raid on Sparappelhoek aerodrome 23.7.17 (F/Cdr RJ Slade and observer unhurt); Shot down during raid on Oostcamp 30.1.18 (FSL FTP Williams & AC1 G/L CA Leitch both killed); Deleted 4.2.18

N5983 Deld AD Dunkirk by 7.6.17; 2N Sqn 13.6.17; COL and wrecked 21.8.17 (F/L CJ Wyatt & OSL AI Hutt both killed); Deleted AD Dunkirk 3.9.17

N5984 Allocated Mudros 1.5.17; Shipped to Aegean; D Sqn 2 Wing Stavros by 29.11.17 - @1.1.18; Marsh by 13.3.18; Imbros by 20.3.18; G Sqn by 3.18 - 5.18; F Sqn by 6.18

N5985 (Eagle VI) Deld Hendon (via Eastbourne) 15.6.17; AD Dunkirk 17.6.17; 2N Sqn 20.6.17; AD Dunkirk 6.17; 2N Sqn 25.6.17; Fuel tank hit by shrapnel, FL La Panne 24.1.18 (retd 25.1.18); Became 202 Sqn 1.4.18; Attacked by 2 Albatros, FL Bray Dunes, o/t in water, badly damaged 18.20 4.5.18 (Lt JP Everitt seriously wounded & Lt WR Stennett killed); Salved, to 4 ASD, still there 31.5.18; Taken in hand at 4 ASD 15.10.18; Awaiting reconstruction 26.10.18; NFT

N5986 Transferred to RFC as B3957

N5987 Transferred to RFC as B3958

N5988 (Eagle VI later VIII) Deld AD Dunkirk by 7.17; 5N Sqn 2.7.17 - @28.2.18; AD Dunkirk by 3.18; 2N Sqn ('K') 12.3.18; FL on beach W of Nieuport 24.3.18; Became 202 Sqn ('K') 1.4.18; To 233 Sqn Dover but arrived in dark, FL, damaged Westcliffe Golf Links, St.Margarets Bay 6.3.19 (2/Lt E Tompkins unhurt); WOC 19.3.19

N5989 (Eagle VII) Deld Hendon 21.6.17; Dover 23.6.17; AD Dunkirk 24.6.17; 2N Sqn ('L') by 28.6.17; Became 202 Sqn ('L') 1.4.18; In action with EA nr Zeebrugge, petrol tank hit, badly damaged 4.5.18 (Capt GW Biles uninjured & Lt EE Gowing seriously wounded); For repair; Retd 202 Sqn, COL 18.7.18 (2/Lt AC Reeman unhurt); 4 ASD 20.7.18

N5990 Transferred to RFC as B3959

N5991 Transferred to RFC as B3960

N5992 (Eagle VI) Deld Dover 1.7.17; AD Dunkirk 2.7.17; 5N

A colourful D.H.4, N5997 'M' of No.202 Squadron, showing an excellent view of the near-standard Lewis-Scarff gun mounting arrangement. (via Terry Treadwell)

Sqn 14.7.17; AD Dunkirk by 26.7.17; 5N Sqn ('B5') 20.8.17; Crashed W/E 15.11.17; EF en route bombing raid on Aertrycke aerodrome, FL on beach, crashed 1,000yds W of Nieuport 27.1.18 (FSL FTP Williams); Shot up bombing troops and transport E of Villers Bretonneux, crashed 30.3.18 (FSL CJ Heywood uninjured & AGL TW Jones wounded); SOC Repair Pk 2 ASD 4.4.18

N5993 (Eagle V) Deld Dover 1.7.17; AD Dunkirk 2.7.17; 5N Sqn 20.7.17; Eagle VI by 12.17; AD Dunkirk 27.2.18; 2N Sqn 13.3.18; Became 202 Sqn 1.4.18; Scout OOC smoking 19.15 4.6.18 (Lt HS Round & Ptel AE Humphrey); Dived into sea 2km E of Loon Plage, nr Calais road 10.8.18 (2/Lt AC Reeman & Ptel WG Shepherd both killed); Wreckage to 4 ASD 11.8.18; Deleted 15.8.18

N5994 Transferred to RFC as B3961

N5995 Transferred to RFC as B3962

N5996 (Eagle V) Deld AD Dunkirk by 12.7.17; 5N Sqn 13.7.17; Crashed W/E 5.11.17; Crashed W/E 15.11.17; NAD Dunkirk W/E 6.12.17; 5N Sqn 22.2.18; AD Dunkirk W/E 7.3.18; 4 ASD Guines 28.3.18; 202 Sqn ('E') 18.5.18; 1 black scout shot down into sea 1m off Zeebrugge Mole 19.15 4.6.18 (Lt AL Godfrey & 2/Lt E Darby DSM); Combat with 5 Pfalz at Middelkerke 27.6.18 (Lt JF Moffett USNR unhurt & Lt WD Jeans wounded); FL beach 500 yds E of Zuydcoote Semaphore 28.6.18; Retd 4 ASD 28.6.18 (now Eagle VII)

N5997 (Eagle VI) Deld AD Dunkirk 7.17; 2N Sqn ('M') (zig-zag on fuselage and nose-thumbing devil on fin) 12.7.17; Became 202 Sqn ('M') 1.4.18; Albatros D.V OOC 6m WNW of Ostende 06.55 2.4.18 (Capt CR Vaughan & Lt IH McClure); Seaplane in sea 10m off Ostende 10.10 3.6.18 (Lt AL Godfrey & 2/Lt C Taylor); In combat off Zeebrugge 4.6.18 (Lt JP Everitt unhurt & Lt IH McClure seriously wounded); Repaired on squadron; 1-str into sea off Ostende, then EF, FL ½m E of La Panne 17.6.18 (Lt HS Round & 2/Lt W Taylor OK); Shot down into sea from 300ft by m/g fire over Zeebrugge Mole during bombing raid on Zeebrugge 07.05 18.10.18 (F/L R Coulthard & 2/Lt L Timmins)

N5998 Transferred to RFC as B3963

N5999 Transferred to RFC as B3964

D.H.4 N6000 'B1', the usual aircraft of Capt C.P.O.Bartlett of No.206 Squadron. (via Frank Cheesman)

N6000 (Eagle VI) Deld AD Dunkirk (via Dover) 10.7.17; 5N Sqn ('B1') 13.7.17; Albatros DV OOC Ostende-Blankenberghe 12.10 17.2.18; Albatros DV OOC St.Pierre Capelle c.13.00 18.2.18 (both F/L E Dickson & AGL W Naylor); Tested after crash 9.3.18; EA OOC Honnecourt 21.3.18; Albatros DV crashed 10.45 27.3.18 (both F/Cdr CPO Bartlett DSC & AGL W Naylor); Became 205 Sqn ('B1') 1.4.18; Pfalz OOC 10.15 1.4.18 (Capt CPO Bartlett DSC & AGL W Naylor); Attacked by 2 scouts, 1 red/black/white Pfalz with stripes over wings sent down in steep dive smoking 13.50 7.4.18 (Capt CR Lupton DFC & AGL 1/AM AG Wood); Crashed 12.4.18 (Capt CPO Bartlett & G/L AM1 FS Jackson); Left 12.37 for raid on La Motte, rudder controls shot away, FL, hit telegraph wires nr Corbie 17.4.18 (Capt CR Lupton DFC & AGL AG Wood both unhurt); For 2 ASD

N6001 (Eagle VI) Deld AD Dunkirk 23.7.17; 5N Sqn 24.7.17; Albatros DV crashed & another OOC Busigny aerodrome and dump c.11.00 16.3.18 (F/L SR Watkins & S/Cdr SJ Goble DSO DSC); Attacked by 5 Pfalz, 1 shot down by rear gun, then 2 Fokker DrIs manoeuvring on to its tail collided and fell locked together, catching fire on crashing Rainecourt 10.00 28.3.18 (F/Cdr CPO Bartlett & AGL W Naylor); Became 205 Sqn 1.4.18; Retd early with engine trouble, COL 16.15 12.4.18 (Lt R Chalmers & Lt JEH Chadwick unhurt); To 2 Salvage Dump 15.4.18; SOC Rep Pk 2 ASD 26.4.18

N6002 Transferred to RFC as B3965

N6003 Transferred to RFC as B3966

N6004 (Twin Vickers guns) (Eagle VI) Deld AD Dunkirk (via Dover) 24.7.17; 5N Sqn ('B35') 24.7.17; Fokker DrI destroyed 09.12 30.3.18 (F/Lt J Gamon & OSL FH Stringer); Became 205 Sqn 1.4.18; Fokker Dr.I in flames, then Pfalz OOC Chaulnes Rly Stn 19.50 23.4.18 (Capt J Gamon & Lt R Scott); Pfalz DIII crashed nr Mericourt, brought down by concerted fire from rear gunners of 8 machines in tight formation 08.30 20.5.18 (Capt J Gamon & Sgt J Jones); Crashed into by D9260 on aerodrome 11.6.18 (Capt J Gamon & Sgt PL Richards unhurt); 2 ASD 12.6.18; SOC 26.6.18 NWR

N6005 (Eagle VI) Deld AD Dunkirk (via Eastchurch & Dover) 29.7.17; 5N Sqn 30.7.17 - @4.12.17; NAD Dunkirk by 6.12.17; 5N Sqn 17.2.18; 1 NAP Dunkirk 21.2.18; 5N Sqn, 27.2.18; Albatros DV OOC Mont D'Origny aerodrome 10.30-10.45 9.3.18 (FSL GE Siedle & Sgt AGL WJH Middleton); Combat damage, FL nr Doullens after raid on Busigny Dump 16.3.18 (FSL GM Cartmel & AGL AM1 RB Wilcox both injured); For survey by 21.3.18; SOC 8.4.18 NWR

N6006 Transferred to RFC as B3967

N6007 Transferred to RFC as B3968 (NTU); Deld AD Dunkirk by 8.17; 5N Sqn 9.8.17; Crashed 16.8.17 (FSL AH Garland & G/L EG Symonds injured); AD Dunkirk by 23.8.17; Destroyed by fire on night of 1.10.17; Surveyed 17.10.17; Deleted 23.10.17 burnt

N6008 Deld AD Dunkirk (via Dover) 9.8.17; 5N Sqn 9.8.17; Crashed in sea on bombing raid on Blankenberghe 19.12.17 (FSL SS Richardson & AC1 G/L RA Furby both killed); Surveyed 24.12.17; Deleted 28.12.17 lost

N6009 (Eagle VII by 12.17 - 2.18, later Eagle VIII) Deld AD Dunkirk by 2.8.17; 5N Sqn by 13.8.17; Crashed by 10.1.18; 2 EA shot down in raid on Busigny aerodrome & dump, shared A7644 09.44-11.48 16.3.18 (F/Cdr CR Lupton DSC & 1/AM AGL G Smith); EA claimed shot down (endorsed indecisive) 18.3.18 (FSL GE Siedle & Sgt AGL WJH Middleton); Albatros DV OOC SW of Vendhuile 15.20 22.3.18 (F/Cdr CR Lupton DSC & 1AM AGL AG Wood); Became 205 Sqn 1.4.18; BU over Amiens returning from raid on Chaulnes Rly Stn 9.5.18 (Capt CR Lupton DSC & G/L 1/AM AG Wood both killed)

50 D.H.4 put forward 1.17 and ordered under Cont Nos C.P.102623 & C.P.103711/17 from Westland Aircraft Works, Yeovil for RNAS use and numbered N6380 to N6429. (200hp BHP)

N6380 Transferred to RFC as B3987 (RAF 3a)

N6381 Deld Eastbourne 19.8.17 (transit); 2N Sqn 20.8.17 (via Dover); AD Dunkirk 23.8.17; 2N Sqn by 25.8.17; AD Dunkirk by 30.8.17; 2N Sqn by 3.9.17; AD Dunkirk 9.9.17; 2N Sqn 23.9.17; 12N Sqn 12.1.18 - @2.2.18; NAD Dunkirk by 7.2.18; 12N Sqn W/E 14.3.18; Crashed, wrecked 28.3.18; 4 ASD Guines 28.3.18; Deleted 8.4.18

N6382 Transferred to RFC as B9434 (RAF 3a)

N6383 Transferred to RFC as B9435 (RAF 3a)

N6384 Transferred to RFC as B9436 (RAF 3a)

N6385 Transferred to RFC as B9437 (RAF 3a)

N6386 Transferred to RFC as B9438 (RAF 3a)

N6387 Transferred to RFC as B9439

N6388 Deld AD Dunkirk (via Dover) 26.8.17 - @6.9.17; 2N Sqn by 9.9.17 - @14.9.17; AD Dunkirk by 20.9.17; Dest by fire on night of 1.10.17; Surveyed 17.10.17; Deleted 22.10.17 burnt

N6389 Deld Dunkirk (via Eastbourne) 3.9.17 - @6.9.17; 2N

Westland-built D.H.4 N6383 was renumbered B9435 on being issued instead to the Royal Flying Corps (via Mike O'Connor)

Sqn by 11.9.17; In action 21.10.17 (S/Cdr PFM Fellowes & FSL WR Stennett wounded); Crashed into searchlight in mist on landing and badly damaged St.Pol 27.1.18 (FSL LH Pearson); AD Dunkirk 21.2.18; Dover W/E 28.3.18; Became 491 Flt Dover by 25.5.18 - @31.5.18; 4 ASD by 6.18; 5 Group (Dunkirk?); 2 SS Richborough 9.18

N6390 Deld AD Dunkirk by 6.9.17; 2N Sqn 15.9.17; FL Clacton after special operation 5.12.17; Hendon 6.12.17; AAP Dover 11.3.18 (repair); 6N Sqn 20.3.18; Became 206 Sqn 1.4.18 [left by 6.4.18]; 218 Sqn by 3.5.18; Dover W/E 24.5.18; 4 ASD by 6.18; Pilots Pool; 4 ASD; WOC 30.9.18 general fatigue

N6391 Deld Hendon 12.9.17; AD Dunkirk 13.9.17; 2N Sqn 19.9.17 - @30.9.17; AD Dunkirk by 4.10.17 - @23.2.18; 12N Sqn by 28.2.18; Crashed in field nr aerodrome, BO 15.3.18 (FSL CW Emmett killed); Remains AD Dunkirk 18.3.18; 4 ASD Guines 28.3.18; For deletion by 31.3.18

N6392 Deld Hendon 12.9.17; AD Dunkirk 13.9.17; 2N Sqn 2.10.17; EF, FL Yarmouth after special operation 5.12.17; Dover 6.12.17; Dunkirk 8.12.17; 2N Sqn by 29.12.17; 12N Sqn 6.3.18; Became 212 Sqn 1.4.18; 218 Sqn by 3.5.18; Slightly damaged landing Dover 20.5.18 (Lt JB Palmer & Sgt G/L G Barlow unhurt); AAP Dover W/E 24.5.18; 4 ASD Audembert 17.6.18; 4 ASD Pilots Pool by 28.9.18; 2 SS Richborough 9.18

N6393 Transferred to RFC as B9456

N6394 Deld AD Dunkirk by 27.9.17; 2N Sqn 2.10.17; AD Dunkirk by 11.17; 2N Sqn 21.11.17 (comparison of 2 and 4 blade propellers); Dover 11.12.17 (overhaul); to 12N Sqn but thick weather, sideslipped to ground trying to ascertain whereabouts, badly damaged nr Hardingham (nr Cap Gris Nez) 28.2.18 (FSL J Hardman slightly injured); 12N Sqn W/E 7.3.18 - @28.3.18; 4 ASD Guines by 30.3.18; Deleted 8.4.18

A camouflaged D.H.4 of another squadron visiting the No.150 Squadron aerodrome at either Kirec or Salonika around May 1918. (via Frank Cheesman)

N6395 Deld Hendon W/E 21.9.17; Burgh Castle 19.9.17; Yarmouth 23.9.17; HACP 12.12.17 (F/L GWR Fane DSC); Became 490 Flt Yarmouth 25.5.18; Covehithe by 6.18; With F.2As N4549 & N4550 & D.H.9 D5209 engaged 5 EA 12m E of Shipwash LV 16.9.18

N6396 Deld Hendon 21.9.17; Yarmouth 24.9.17; Became 490 Flt Yarmouth by 25.5.18 - @6.18; Burgh Castle by 12.6.18

N6397 Transferred to RFC as B9458

N6398 Deld CSD White City 19.9.17; To 2 Wing Otranto (less engine) 24.9.17; Shipped 4.10.17; Mudros Repair Base without engine by 1.12.17 - @1.1.18; Mudros by 3.18; Possibly the Mudros machine on reconnaissance which EF, FL, sideslipped to ground, burnt out ½m from aerodrome 26.2.18 (T/F/L J Moore & Lt CE Palmer both killed)

N6399 Deld CSD White City for 2 Wing 3.10.17; Shipped to Aegean 31.10.17; arr Mudros by 1.12.17 - @1.1.18; 2 Wing by 3.18; Became 62 Wing 1.4.18 - @6.18; 62 Wing Stavros by 10.18 - @30.1.19; Transferred to Greek Government

N6400 Deld CSD White City for 2 Wing 3.10.17; Shipped to Aegean 31.10.17; arr Mudros by 1.12.17 - @1.1.18; 2 Wing Stavros by 3.18; Became 62 Wing Stavros 1.4.18 - 6.18; Repair Base Mudros by 5.18; F Sqn 62 Wing Mudros by 7.18; Repair Base Mudros by 10.18; 220 Sqn Imbros by 28.10.18; F Sqn 62 Wing Mudros by 11.18 - @30.1.19

N6401 Transferred to RFC as B9460

N6402 Deld AD Dunkirk by 27.9.17; 2N Sqn 2.10.17; Crashed nr Fort Mardyck, BO 7.1.18 (FSL CR Barber & S/L HR Easby killed); Deleted 4 ASD 21.1.18

N6403 Deld Dover W/E 6.10.17; 2N Sqn 26.11.17; Landed Little Bentley, Essex, after special operation 5.12.17; Hendon by 6.12.17; Dover W/E 9.2.18; 17N Sqn 16.2.18; Crashed, wrecked 27.2.18; NAD Dunkirk 27.2.18; 4 ASD Guines 28.3.18; Deleted 8.4.18

N6404 Deld Hendon W/E 27.10.17 (ex Gosport Works); Grain W/E 3.11.17; Dover 10.12.17; 2N Sqn 12.12.17; Hendon (via Dover) 3.1.18; 6N Sqn Dover by 17.1.18; 11N Sqn 7.3.18; 12N Sqn W/E 14.3.18 - @30.3.18; Petite Synthe to 218 Sqn 21.4.18; Overshot, went round again hit flagstaff, CW Guston Road 1.5.18 (Lt EA Lawson & Lt LH Herridge both shaken); Deletion recommended 3.5.18

N6405 Felixstowe to Hendon W/E 15.12.17; Transferred to RFC as B9461

N6406 Shipped to Aegean 27.10.17; arr Mudros for erection by 1.12.17 - @1.1.18; Marsh by 18.1.18; Imbros by 3.18 - @5.18

N6407 Deld Hendon W/E 13.10.17; RNASTE Cranwell W/E 9.11.17; Freiston by 11.17; RNASTE Cranwell by 1.18; Crashed, badly damaged Spittlegate 4.3.18 (pilot unhurt); Became 201/2 TDS Cranwell 1.4.18 - @5.18

N6408 Deld Dover W/E 13.10.17; 2N Sqn 23.11.17; Became 202 Sqn 1.4.18; 218 Sqn 3.5.18; Dover W/E 24.5.18; 491 Flt Dover by 25.5.18 - @31.5.18; 4 ASD by 25.10.18 for Pool; 217 Sqn by 3.19; HQ RAF with 11 AP 20.3.19

N6409 Transferred to RFC as B9470

N6410 Shipped to Aegean 27.10.17; arr 2 Wing Mudros for erection by 1.12.17 - @1.1.18; Marsh by 18.1.18; Mudros, shot down on reconnaissance of battlecruiser *Goeben* 22.3.18 (F/Cdr TR Hackman & O/L TH Piper PoWs)

N6411 Shipped to Aegean 10.11.17; C Sqn 2 Wing Mudros by 3.18; Marsh by 13.3.18; Mudros by 3.18; Became 62 Wing Mudros 1.4.18 - @5.18; Repair Base Mudros by 6.18; 226 Sqn Pizzone; Transferred to Greek Government by 10.18 - @11.18

N6412 Deld W/E Hendon 3.11.17; Observers School Flt Eastchurch W/E 10.11.17; HP Sqn Manston 28.11.17; DH4 School Manston ('1') 19.1.18; Became 203 TDS Manston 1.4.18; Became 55 TDS Manston 14.7.18 - @11.18

N6413 Deld Hendon W/E 10.10.17; Observers School Eastchurch W/E 10.11.17; HP Sqn Manston 28.11.17; Collided with Pup landing Manston 5.1.18 (FSL LH Pearson); DH4 School Manston 19.1.18

N6414 Deld War School Manston W/E 20.10.17; HP Sqn Manston 2.1.18; DH4 School Manston 19.1.18; Became 203 TDS Manston 1.4.18 - @7.18

N6415 Deld War Flt Manston W/E 27.10.17; HP Sqn Manston 28.10.17; DH4 School Manston 19.1.18 - @30.3.18; DH4 Sqn Manston by 5.4.18; Controls failed, dived in 16.6.18 (F/Cdt PK Mason injured)

N6416 Deld War School Manston W/E 27.10.17; HP Sqn Manston on/by 27.10.17; AGP 31.10.17/1.11.17; Shipped to Aegean 10.11.17; arr 2 Wing Mudros for erection by 1.1.18; Marsh by 3.3.18; Mudros by 3.18;

D.H.4s of No.5N Squadron lined up at Petite Synthe. (via Frank Cheesman)

Became 62 Wing Mudros 1.4.18 - @5.18; F Sqn 62 Wing Imbros by 6.18 - @7.18 (large sunburst on fuselage with 'SULTAN SELIM II' written on sun; also with 'MOORQ' written on sun)

N6417 Deld CSD White City 29.10.17; Shipped to Aegean 14.11.17; in transit to 6 Wing by 28.12.17; 6 Wing Otranto by 1.2.18; 224 Sqn (named 'BOUNCING BERTIE') 1.4.18 - @16.12.18; AD Taranto to 'X' AD Abu Qir 28.6.19; WOC at ASD 25.8.19

N6418 Deld CSD White City 10.17; Shipped to Aegean 14.11.17; In transit to 6 Wing by 28.12.17; 6 Wing Otranto by 1.2.18; 224 Sqn ('8') 1.4.18; Shot down in flames returning from bombing attack in Gulf of Cattaro 6.9.18 (Lt RB Picken & Lt AF Hodgskin both killed)

N6419 Deld CSD White City 10.17; Shipped to Aegean 20.11.17; In transit to 6 Wing Otranto by 28.12.17; Marsh by 19.3.18; Imbros by 3.18 - @6.18; C Sqn 62 Wing Imbros by 5.18 - @28.6.18; Taranto by 1.19

N6420 Deld CSD White City 10.17; Shipped to Aegean 14.11.17; In transit to 6 Wing by 28.12.17; 2 Wing Mudros by 29.1.18 - @29.1.18 (F/Cdr LA Hervey & S/L S Chryssids); G Sqn 2 Wing Mudros by 3.18; Became G Sqn 62 Wing Mudros 1.4.18 - @5.18; Repair Base Mudros by 6.18; 226 Sqn Pizzone; Repair Base Mudros by 10.18 - @30.1.19

N6421 Deld CSD White City 10.17; Shipped to Otranto 12.12.17 - @18.1.18; 224 Sqn ('1') by 21.4.18 - @7.18; 496/8 Flts 224 Sqn Andrano by 2.10.18 - @11.10.18; Taranto by 1.19; AD Taranto to 'X' AD Abu Qir 28.6.19; WOC at ASD 25.8.19

N6422 Deld CSD White City 10.17; Shipped to Aegean 12.12.17; In transit to Taranto by 18.1.18; 6 Wing Otranto by 24.3.18; Became 66/67 Wing Otranto 1.4.18 - @21.4.18; 224 Sqn by 28.4.18 - @13.6.18; AD Taranto by 8.18; 496/8 Flts 224 Sqn 23.10.18 - @23.12.18; Taranto by 1.19; AD Taranto to 'X' AD Abu Qir 28.6.19; WOC at ASD 25.8.19

N6423 Deld CSD White City 10.17; Shipped to Aegean 12.12.17; arr Mudros for erection by 1.1.18; G Sqn 2 Wing Mudros by 24.3.18; Became G Sqn 62 Wing Mudros 1.4.18; Mudros Base by 4.18 - @5.18; Stavros by 6.18; Repair Base Mudros by 10.18 - @30.1.19

N6424 Deld CSD White City 10.17; Shipped to Aegean 12.12.17; arr Mudros for erection by 1.1.18; 2 Wing Mudros by 2.18; Became 62 Wing Mudros 1.4.18 - 5.18; Imbros by 6.18

N6425 Deld AAP Brooklands to Eastchurch 10.11.17; HP Sqn Manston 28.11.17; DH4 School Manston ('4') 17.1.18; Became 203 TDS Manston 1.4.18

N6426 Deld Observers School Flt Eastchurch W/E 10.11.17; Manston W/E 1.12.17; Gunnery School Flt Eastchurch by 29.12.17; Became 204 TDS Eastchurch 1.4.18 - @28.7.18

N6427 Deld RNASTE Cranwell W/E 23.11.17; Freiston by 11.17; RNASTE Cranwell by 1.12.17; Crashed, propeller and u/c damaged Cranwell North 16.1.18 (pilot unhurt); Became 201/2 TDS Cranwell 1.4.18 - @5.18

N6428 Deld RNASTE Cranwell 19.11.17 (W/T trials); Detd Wireless Experimental Establishment Biggin Hill 6.3.18; Retd Cranwell; Became 201/2 TDS Cranwell 1.4.18; WT Establishment Biggin Hill 29.5.18

N6429 Deld RNASTE Cranwell W/E 7.12.17 [Oxford to Cranwell 28.1.18]; Became 201/2 TDS Cranwell 1.4.18

Unidentified incidents

23.4.17 55 Sqn, attacked by EA in raid on Boue (pilot unhurt; 2/Lt FL Oliver wounded)

29.4.17 55 Sqn, in action (Lt GG Sturt wounded)

4.5.17 55 Sqn, hit by shrapnel (Capt FS Moller wounded & observer OK)

6.6.17 55 Sqn, raid on Reckem (pilot OK & 2/Lt WH Bolam wounded)

20.7.17 55 Sqn, bombing raid (pilot OK & 2/AM A Tibbles wounded)

28.7.17 18 Sqn, hit by trench fire (Pilot OK & 2/Lt GR Willis wounded)

12.8.17 55 Sqn, in action (Pilot unhurt & 2/Lt HKR Bent wounded)

18.8.17 55 Sqn, shot up by AA (2/Lt GF Mackay wounded)

25.9.17 18 Sqn, combat during photographic mission (pilot OK & Lt GC Langford wounded)

23.11.17 18 Sqn, hit by AA (Capt ER Cottier & Capt JA Mansfield both wounded)

4.12.17 55 Sqn, hit by AA (pilot OK & Lt A Sattin slightly wounded)

30.1.18 25 Sqn, in action (pilot OK & AG 2/AM CN Harvey killed)

5.2.18 25 Sqn, in action (pilot unhurt & AG Sgt Hupper wounded)

12.2.18 "A7418" 55 Sqn, returned from raid on Offenburg, COL Besancon (Lt WB Andrew & 2/Lt FG Todd both killed)

7.3.18 "5256" (BHP) 1 SoN&BD Stonehenge, crashed, no details (Sgt L Mears & 2/Lt WH Collins both killed)

14.3.18 18 Sqn, crashed nr St.Omer on delivery (Lt NK Adams killed)

17.3.18 27(?) Sqn, in action (pilot OK & Sgt AJ Perkins wounded)

25.3.18 30 Sqn, recce Baghdad, engine hit, FL, a/c burnt (Lt Col JE Tennant & Mjr PCS Hobart both PoW, rescued 28.3.18)

26.3.18 25 Sqn, in action (pilot OK & 2/Lt J Mitchell DoW 3.4.18)

28.3.18 18 Sqn, in action (2/Lt DO Robinson wounded & observer OK)

28.3.18 25 Sqn, in action (pilot unhurt but Sgt AH Muff wounded)

16.5.18 55 Sqn, shot up in bombing raid on Saarbrucken (Lt JS Bradley unhurt & 2/Lt WI Parke wounded)

16.5.18 55 Sqn, shot up in bombing raid on Saarbrucken (pilot OK & 2/Lt FW Roak wounded)

24.5.18 226 Sqn Italy, crashed (Lt PBS Wood & 1/AM F Johnson both killed)

8.6.18 25 Sqn, reconnaissance (pilot OK & 2/Lt WH Dixon DoW 23.6.18)

16.6.18 25 Sqn, photographic mission (pilot OK & Sgt CAF Johnson wounded)

16.6.18 "5263" 26 TS Narborough, EF, fuel starvation, started to turn back, sideslipped into field, crashed (2/Lt TDH Alderton killed & 2/Lt J Oakes injured)

1.7.18 226 Sqn, crashed on TO to bomb Cattaro (Lt CRW Pascoe & 1/AM AF Bugden both killed)

21.7.18 224 Sqn, shot down by fighter into sea nr Platamona Point, south of Cattaro (Lt EL Bragg & Lt PE Lindner both killed)

2.8.18 [D.H. Type?] 67 Wing, in raid on Cattaro, damaged by gunfire, FL on shore SE side of Malaluka Bay, 20m SE of Cattaro (Capt EP Hardman & Gnr JF Hartney both PoW)

2.8.18 57 Sqn, in combat (pilot OK & Sgt CG Sowden wounded)

12.8.18 25 Sqn, in combat (pilot unhurt & Sgt T Lumley wounded)

12.8.18 25 Sqn, in combat (pilot unhurt & Sgt WB Gray wounded)

14.8.18 27 Sqn (one coded 'O'), two a/c collided during raid on Cambrai (2/Lt AFMillar & 2/Lt JB Lee; 2/Lt J Dickson & Sgt Mech SP Percival; all killed))

26.8.18 67 Wing, force landed in sea 30m NE of Brindisi during raid on Tirana aerodrome (not found, crew unknown)

3.5.19 (D.H.4A) 9th Wing France, EF at 250ft, turned back, stalled, dived in (2/Lt AHB Steel & Mjr HH Robinson both killed)

D.H.4A G-EAMU 'City of York', piloted by F.L.Barnard, winner of the King's Cup Air Race held on 8-9.9.22. (via Terry Treadwell)

D.H.4 - CIVIL AND OVERSEAS USE

UNITED KINGDOM

A number of D.H.4 variants received British civil registrations, as follows:

F2699 D.H.4A ex *F2699* Regd [adopting interim ex military serial] 18.7.19 to Aircraft Transport & Travel Ltd, Hendon. Regd *G-EAHF* [CofR 188] 31.7.19 to same owner. C of A [122] issued 7.8.19. Flew Hounslow to Le Bourget in 2hrs 30min carrying grouse, newspapers, leather goods and Devon Cream 25.8.19. Flew first civil air mail to France at 2s 6d per ounce 10.11.19. Crashed Caterham, Surrey 11.12.19. Regn cld 1.20.

K-141 D.H.4R c/n "G7/67" Modified by Airco to D.H.4R Racer sesquiplane with Napier Lion. Regd 16.6.19 to Aircraft Transport & Travel Ltd, Hendon. FF Hendon 21.6.19 and winner of Aerial Derby at Hendon same day. Regd *G-EAEW* [CofR 127] 31.7.19 to same owner. No C of A issued. Scrapped 1920. Regn cld 6.20.

K-142 D.H.4 c/n "G7/63" Regd 16.6.19 to Aircraft Transport & Travel Ltd, Hendon. Ff 21.6.19 and came third in Aerial Derby at Hendon same day. Regd *G-EAEX* [CofR 128] 31.7.19 to same owner. No CofA issued. Scrapped 1920. Regn cld 4.20.

G-EAEW see K-141

G-EAEX see K-142

G-EAHF see F2699

G-EAHG D.H.4A ex *F2694* Regd [CofR 189] 5.8.19 to Aircraft Transport & Travel Ltd, Hendon. C of A [123] issued 7.8.19. Demonstrated at First Air Traffic Exhibition in Amsterdam 25.8.19. En route Paris to London, forced to ditch in English Channel due to bad weather 29.10.19. Regn cld 1.20.

G-EAJC D.H.4A ex *F2702* Regd [CofR 237] 7.8.19 to Aircraft Transport & Travel Ltd, Hendon. C of A [170] issued 19.8.19. Flew first commercial passenger service from Hounslow to Le Bourget at a fare of 20 guineas 25.8.19. C of A lapsed 18.8.20. Regn cld 11.20.

D.H.4A G-EAVL operated by Handley Page Transport in 1920.

The sole D.H.4R K-141/G-EAEX.

[Aircraft Transport and Travel ceased operations on 17.2.20, unable to compete with subsidised foreign airlines]

G-EAJD D.H.4A ex *F2704* Regd [CofR 238] 7.8.19 to Aircraft Transport & Travel Ltd, Hendon. C of A [174] issued 22.8.19. C of A lapsed 21.8.20. Regn cld 11.20.

G-EAMU D.H.4 ex *H5939* Regd [CofR 335] 9.19 to S Instone & Co Ltd, t/a Instone Air Line, Hendon; named "City of Cardiff". CofA [234] issued 7.10.19. Used by the company for the carriage of ship's documents plus two passengers. Converted to D.H.4A and new C of A [300] issued 11.2.20. Renamed "City of York" in 1922. Won King's Cup Air Race 8-9.9.22. CofA lapsed 11.3.24. Transferred to Imperial Airways Ltd, Croydon 31.3.24; regd [CofR 1074] to them 10.6.24. Regn cld [undated].

G-EANK D.H.4 c/n P.7 ex *F2670* Regd [CofR 351] 20.9.19 to Aircraft Transport & Travel Ltd, Hendon. C of A [225] issued 2.10.19. Temporary use only, regn cld as sold abroad 4.20.

G-EANL D.H.4 c/n P.8 ex *F2671* Regd [CofR 352] 20.9.19 to Aircraft Transport & Travel Ltd, Hendon. C of A [216] issued 24.9.19. Temporary use only, regn cld as sold 4.20.

G-EAVL D.H.4A Limousine ex *H5905*Regd [CofR 596] 13.9.20 to Handley Page Ltd, Cricklewood [and operated by Handley Page Transport]. C of A [434] issued 12.11.20. Made record flight to Paris flying in half a gale with two passengers in 1hr 48min 4.1.21. Regn cld as crashed 4.21; prior to CofA expiry on 11.11.21.

G-EAWH D.H.4A ex *F5764* Regd [CofR 631] 17.2.21 to Handley Page Ltd, Cricklewood [and operated by Handley Page Transport]. C of A [466] issued 16.4.21. Regn cld 5.1.23, prior to CofA expiry on 15.4.23.

G-EAXD D.H.4 ex *F2686* Regd [CofR 666] 3.6.21 to Aircraft Disposal Co Ltd, Croydon. No CofA issued. Ferried to Belgian Air Force 6.21. Regn cld as sold abroad 13.10.21.

G-EAXE D.H.4 ex *F2697* Regd [CofR 667] 3.6.21 to Aircraft Disposal Co Ltd, Croydon. No CofA issued. Ferried to Belgian Air Force 6.21. Regn cld as sold abroad 13.10.21.

G-EAXF D.H.4 ex *H5934* Regd [CofR 668] 3.6.21 to Aircraft Disposal Co Ltd, Croydon. No CofA issued. Ferried to Belgian Air Force 6.21. Regn cld as sold abroad 13.10.21.

G-EAXH D.H.4 ex *A7988* Regd [CofR 671] 15.6.21 to Aircraft Disposal Co Ltd, Croydon. No CofA issued. Ferried to Belgian Air Force 6.21. Regn cld as sold abroad 13.10.21.

G-EAXI D.H.4 ex *H5934* Regd [CofR 672] 15.6.21 to Aircraft Disposal Co Ltd, Croydon. No CofA issued. Ferried to Belgian Air Force 6.21. Regn cld as sold abroad 13.10.21.

G-EAXJ D.H.4 ex *F5794* Regd [CofR 673] 15.6.21 to Aircraft Disposal Co Ltd, Croydon. No CofA issued. Ferried to Belgian Air Force 6.21. Regn cld as sold abroad 13.10.21.

G-EAXN D.H.4 ex *F2678* Regd [CofR 677] 27.6.21 to Aircraft Disposal Co Ltd, Croydon. No CofA issued. Ferried to Belgian Air Force 7.21. Regn cld as sold abroad 13.10.21.

G-EAXO D.H.4 ex *F2680* Regd [CofR 678] 27.6.21 to Aircraft Disposal Co Ltd, Croydon. No CofA issued. Ferried to Belgian Air Force 7.21. Regn cld as sold abroad 13.10.21.

G-EAXP D.H.4 ex *F5774* Regd [CofR 679] 27.6.21 to Aircraft Disposal Co Ltd, Croydon. No CofA issued. Ferried to Belgian Air Force 7.21. Regn cld as sold abroad 13.10.21

G-EAYE D.H.4 ex *F2675* Regd [CofR 698] 30.7.21 to Aircraft Disposal Co Ltd, Croydon. No CofA issued. Ferried to Belgian Air Force 8.21. Regn cld as sold abroad 13.10.21.

G-EAYF D.H.4 ex *F5779* Regd [CofR 699] 30.7.21 to Aircraft Disposal Co Ltd, Croydon. No CofA issued. Ferried to Belgian Air Force 8.21. Regn cld as sold abroad 13.10.21.

G-EAYG D.H.4 ex *H5902* Regd [CofR 700] 30.7.21 to Aircraft Disposal Co Ltd, Croydon. No CofA issued. Ferried to Belgian Air Force 8.21. Regn cld as sold abroad 13.10.21.

G-EAYH D.H.4 ex *F2684* Regd [CofR 701] 30.7.21 to Aircraft Disposal Co Ltd, Croydon. No CofA issued. Ferried to Belgian Air Force 8.21. Regn cld as sold abroad 13.10.21.

G-EAYI D.H.4 ex *F2693* Regd [CofR 703] 25.8.21 to Aircraft Disposal Co Ltd, Croydon. No CofA issued. Ferried to Belgian Air Force 9.21. Regn cld as sold abroad 13.10.21.

G-EAYJ D.H.4 ex *F2677* Regd [CofR 704] 25.8.21 to Aircraft Disposal Co Ltd, Croydon. No CofA issued. Ferried to Belgian Air Force 9.21. Regn cld as sold abroad 13.10.21.

G-EAYR D.H.4 ex *F2689* Regd [CofR 714] 4.10.21 to Aircraft Disposal Co Ltd, Croydon. No CofA issued. Ferried to Belgian Air Force 10.21. Regn cld as sold abroad 13.10.21.

G-EAYS D.H.4 ex *H5898* Regd [CofR 715] 4.10.21 to Aircraft Disposal Co Ltd, Croydon. No CofA issued. Ferried to Belgian Air Force 10.21. Regn cld as sold abroad 13.10.21.

G-EAYV D.H.4 ex *F5797* Regd [CofR 720] 13.10.21 to Aircraft Disposal Co Ltd, Croydon. No CofA issued. Ferried to Belgian Air Force 10.21. Regn cld as sold abroad 28.11.21.

G-EAYX D.H.4 ex *H5896* Regd [CofR 722] 21.10.21 to Aircraft Disposal Co Ltd, Croydon. No CofA issued. Ferried to Belgian Air Force 11.21. Regn cld as sold abroad 28.11.21.

ARGENTINA

In 1920 an unidentified D.H.4A was shipped to Major Shirley G Kingsley, Buenos Aires and until c.1924-25 it was operated by the Rio Platte Aviation Co. This was an Argentine company, known locally as both the Sociedad Rioplatense de Aviacion and Cia. Rioplatense de Aviacion. Major Kingsley made a pioneer business flight from Buenos Aires to Port Alegre in August 1920, this being on charter to an Argentine bank.

A German diplomatic report listed the Argentine Escuela de Aviacion Militar (EAM) with one DH-4 around 26 May 1920. US reports never mentioned it, so presumably either it was short-lived, or related to Major Kingsleys machine.

AUSTRALIA

Two D.H.4s came on to the Australian civil register, these being:

G-AUBZ ex *F2682* To CJ de Garis, Australia 1920. To RJP Parer, Melbourne 12.20. Won Australian Aerial Derby 28.12.20; regd to Parer's Commercial Aviation Service Ltd [CofR 30] 28.6.21. Sold 7.3.22, regd [CofR 70] 9.10.22 to Q.A.N.T.A.S. Ltd, Longreach; shipped by rail, arriving 12.8.22. Used on Charleville to Cloncurry mail route, flew 50,000 miles in two months. Hit telephone wires landing Gilford Park Station, SW of Longreach 6.6.23 (FG Huxley). Rebuilt with roof to passenger cabin, reflown 5.24. Regd 17.12.27 to Matthews Aviation Pty Ltd, Essendon for joy flights and named "Cock Bird"; later renamed "The Lachlan" with 4 open cockpits for passengers. Regd *VH-UBZ* 1929. Reconverted to taxi work as D.H.4A in 1930; renamed "Spirit of Melbourne". From 24.12.31 made several experimental flights from Launceston to Flinders Island. CofA lapsed 28.10.33. Regd 13.9.34 to Pioneer Air Services Pty Ltd, Essendon. Sold 3.7.35 [but not regd] to Mrs A McKeown, Brunswick, Vic. Sold 2.3.36 [but not regd] to Aerat Passenger Flying Pty Ltd, Essendon. Regn cld 10.11.40.

G-AUCM (ex *F2691*) Shipped by sea to CJ de Garis, Australia 1920. Test flown Glenroy 27.11.20. Flown to Perth, arr 2.12.20. Flew Brisbane to Melbourne in one day 16.1.21. Regd [CofR 31/CofA 26] 28.6.21 to CJ de Garis, Melbourne. Intended flight Hobart to New Zealand 7.21 by FS Briggs prohibited by CAB. Flew Melbourne to Alice Springs, becoming first aircraft to land 9.9.21. Regd [CofR 67] 13.9.22 to Larkin Aircraft Supply Co Ltd and sold 8.24 [but not regd] to Australian Aerial Services Ltd; named "Scrub Bird". Sold 18.1.27 to Bululo Goldfields Aeroplane Service Ltd, Lae, NG. Sold 6.29 to The Morlae Airline, Lae, NG; regd to them 8.29. WFU in New Guinea 30.6.30. Regn cld 15.7.30.

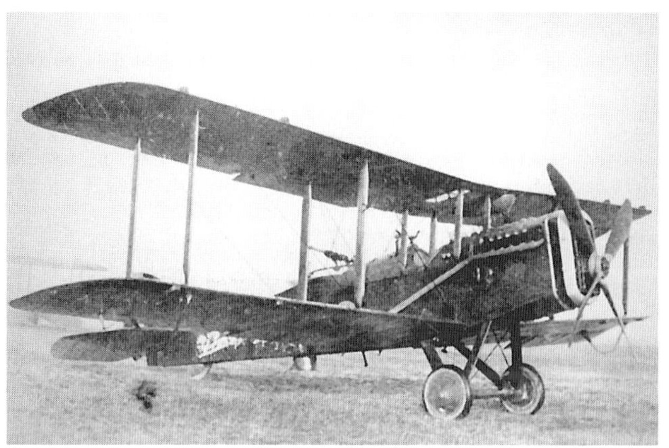

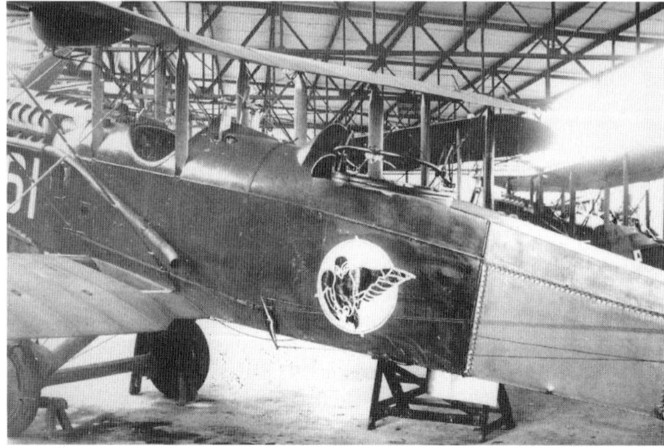

A miscellany of Belgian military D.H.4s

BELGIUM

Numbers of D.H.4s and D.H.4As were supplied to Belgium, for both civil and military use. [See also under D.H.9]

Civil use

SNETA (Société Nationale pour l'Etude des Transports Aériens) was formed on 1 March 1919 by Lt Avi Georges Nélis with the help of King Albert. Its aims were aeronautical research and its industrial, commercial or colonial applications; the development of national, international and colonial airlines for the transportation of people, goods and mail; and the construction and maintenance of aeronautical equipment for both civil and military purposes (this last point gave birth to SABCA).

Initially, several war surplus D.H.9s were bought from the Aircraft Disposal Company. By 19 March 1920, SNETA had 9 D.H.4, 6 D.H.9, 3 Breguet XIV, 10 Rumpler, 4 LVG C.VI, 6 Farman F.60 Goliath, 1 Avro 504, 5 SPAD 33 and 1 Ansaldo A.300.

The D.H.9s were used on the Brussels-Croydon-Cricklewood route, the first journey from Brussels to London being achieved on 25 May 1920 with one of the D.H.9s. Collaboration with the Dutch KLM and French CMA companies allowed the opening on 2 May 1921 of an Amsterdam-Brussels-Paris route.

1921 was a disastrous year for SNETA, with 11 aircraft being lost, amongst them D.H.4s and a Farman Goliath. The worst event was on 27 September of that year; a hangar fire at Evère destroyed the 7 aircraft inside, these being 3 D.H.4, 2 Goliath, 1 Rumpler C IV and 1 SPAD 33.

In June 1922, SNETA, considering that its development and research work was finished, suspended its activities in order to form an air transport society. The status of the (Societé Anonyme Belge pour l'Exploitation de la Navigation Aérienne (SABENA) was approved in March 1923 and it was officially constituted on 23 May 1923, when it inherited 1 D.H.4, 4 D.H.9, 1 Farman F.60, 3 Bleriot-SPAD, 3 Rumpler and 1 Ansaldo from SNETA.
[See under D.H.9 for SABCA]

Civil registered aircraft:

O-BABI D.H.4 (ex *H5925*) Deld ex Cricklewood 10.8.20 as *O-2*. Regd [CofR 27] 20.8.20 to SNETA, Brussels. Transferred to SABENA. Crashed Addington, nr Croydon 25.2.21.

O-BADO D.H.4 (ex *H5936*) Regd [CofR 28] 20.8.20 to SNETA. Dbf in hangar fire Brussels/Evère 27.9.21.

O-BAIN D.H.4 (ex *H5915*) Regd [CofR 30] 21.8.20 to SNETA. Crashed Hawkinge, Kent 25.1.21.

Note: The above two were probably dd ex Cricklewood 11.8.20 as *O-3* and *O-4*, order unknown.

O-BALO D.H.4 (ex *H5931*) Regd [CofR 35] 8.9.20 to SNETA. Crashed Strasbourg, France 5.5.24.

O-BARI D.H.4A (ex *H5928*) Regd [CofR 34] 8.9.20 to SNETA. Dbf in hangar fire Brussels/Evère 27.9.21.

O-BATL Reserved for unidentified D.H.4, deld by ADC 21.3.21. Transferred to Belgian Air Force instead.

O-BATO D.H.4A (ex *H5929*) Regd [CofR 31] 21.8.20 to SNETA. Dbf in hangar fire Brussels/Evère 27.9.21. Note: This may have been the D.H.4 deld ex Cricklewood 12.8.20 as *O-5*.

O-BATU Reserved for unidentified D.H.4, deld by ADC 23.3.21. Transferred to Belgian Air Force instead.

Military use

In March 1919, a Belgian detachment of No.1 (Communication) Squadron RAF, Kenley, based at Buc, became a separate unit as No.2 (Communications) Squadron RAF. Its strength included a number of D.H.4s and D.H.4As earmarked for special duty with His Majesty the King of the Belgians. These included A7920, B7986, D8353, D8370, D8417, F5707 and F5721. The squadron disbanded on 14 October 1919.

The D.H.4 was the first aircraft type to go into service with the Belgian Air Force (Aviation Militaire Belge) after the First World War. A major reorganisation took place in 1924, followed by another in 1926. The service was renamed Aéronautique Militaire in 1930.

A total of 68 D.H.4s was eventually received, these being serialled *E1* to *E68* under the wings. H5937 is known to have become marked '17' with the 10ème Escadrille, but no Belgian records survive of previous RAF identities due to many documents being lost during the Second World War. In total, 53 surplus RAF machines were bought from 1919 onwards, and 15 more were built in 1926 by SABCA.

British records indicate that in March 1921 two D.H.4s were received from the Aircraft Disposal Company, these having initially been intended to receive civil registrations O-BATL and O-BATU. These were followed by a further 19 between June and November 1921, initially bearing British registrations G-EAXD/XE/XF/XH/XI/XJ/XN/XO/XP/YE/YF/YG/YH/YI/YJ/YR/YS/YV/YX (q.v.) for ferry purposes. Fortunately, previous RAF identities for these do survive in British records

The original intention was to equip 1ère, 11ème, 6ème and 10ème Escadrilles, but in the event initial deliveries went to 10ème, 11ème and 12ème Escadrilles of Vème Groupe. The further deliveries in 1921 went to 1ère, 6ème and 11ème Escadrilles, followed by 10ème Escadrille in 1922. All were based at Bierset from 1923.

Belgian D.H.4 units:

1ère Escadrille d'Observation (Mephisto Escadrille)
- formed in 1919 at Evère as part of II/1Aé, and had D.H.4s until these were replaced by D.H.9s.

2ème Escadrille d'Observation (Gull Escadrille)
- based at Evère, moving to Goetsenhoven in 1922 as part of II/1Aé, and was equipped with D.H.4s and Bréguet XIVs.

3ème Escadrille d'Observation (Holly Leaf Escadrille)
- at Goetsenhoven with Bréguet XIVs and Ansaldo from 1922. There is no evidence that either the D.H.4 or the D.H.9 was ever flown, but the possibility cannot be ruled out.

6ème Escadrille d'Observation (Bee Escadrille)
- based at Evère post-war as part of II/1Aé, and had some ex-RAF D.H.4s on strength up until 1925.

9ème Escadrille
- joined 11ème and 12 ème in Vème Groupe to complete its complement.

10ème Escadrille
- in Vème Groupe

11ème Escadrille de Combat et de Bombardment (White Paper Hen Escadrille)
- Disbanded in August 1919, it reformed at Berchem Ste Agathe in March 1920 in Vème Groupe equipped initially with Hanriot HD-1s, Fokker D VIIs and Sopwith Camels, but later totally re-equipped with RAF surplus D.H.4s. It moved temporarily to Wilrijk on 9 July 1920, returning to Berchem Ste Agathe on 1 August 1920. Later that year it joined the occupation forces in Germany, to be based at Bochum, and shortly after moving the first D.H.4 arrived. During 1921 it became completely equipped with the type. Sergent pilote Lermusiau was killed in a D.H.4 accident on 22 October 1920. On 5 January 1922 the unit returned to Belgium, to be based at Bierset, where D.H.4 *E52* crashed on 1 May 1922, killing both the pilot, Sergent G. Stenhout, and Sergent Albert Godts. Moved to Schaffen early in 1923, disbanding there on 19 February 1923.

12ème Escadrille
- formed in Germany at Bochum during 1920/1. In Vème Groupe.

NOTE:
The suffixes *ère* and *ème* refer to an ordinal unit number: 1ère is première (first), 2ème deuxième (second), etc. It could also be written with only the *e*: 1e, 2e, etc.
In shortened form, 9/II/3Aè means ninth Escadrille of the second Groupe of the third Groupement (later Regiment) d'Aéronautique. Each escadrille was given a name and a badge. Unfortunately an insignia was not attached permanently to the same number, but could be given to various escadrilles following renumbering or re-organisations, which can sometimes make unit identification difficult when studying photographs. Escadrilles could also move within Groupes and Regiments. Two different Groupes (one of fighter and another of reconnaissance, for instance) might have a 1ère Escadrille with a different insignia. So it can be important to indicate the Groupe and Groupement (or Regiment) or the insignia to know the exact Escadrille at any given time.

Imperial Gift D.H.4 F2714 prior to becoming G-CYEC.

CANADA

Twelve D.H.4s were allocated 10.20 as Imperial Gift Aircraft for the Canadian Air Board, Civil Operations Branch, for use on forestry patrols etc. Of these, G-CYDB, G-CYDL, G-CYDN and G-CYEC were issued to No.2 (Operations) Squadron, CAF, which formed 1.4.25 at High River, and were in use until it disbanded there 1.7.27. Several were converted in service to the equivalent of D.H.4Bs. The survivors were all officially struck off charge in November 1928.

G-CYBO ex *F2705* TOC 30.11.20; Converted to DH-4B; SOC 30.11.28
G-CYBU ex *F2709* TOC 26.10.20; Flown at High River and Borden; SOC 30.11.28
G-CYBV ex *F2710* TOC 29.11.20; Crashed High River, Cat A 1.8.21; SOC
G-CYBW ex *F2672* TOC 1.2.21; Crashed High River, Cat A 31.5.21; SOC 7.7.21
G-CYCW ex *F2713* TOC 1.2.21; Flown as single-seater at High River; SOC 30.11.28
G-CYDB ex *F2673* TOC 1.2.21; Flown by 2 Sqn at High River; SOC 4.12.24
G-CYDK ex *F2711* TOC 19.4.21; Crashed Waldemar, Cat A 23.4.22; SOC
G-CYDL ex *F2712* TOC 19.4.21; Converted to DH-4B; Flown by 2 Sqn at High River; SOC 30.11.28
G-CYDM ex *F2706* TOC 19.4.21; Converted to DH-4B; Airworthy in 1927. SOC 30.11.28
G-CYDN ex *F2708* TOC 16.3.21; Converted to DH-4B; Flown by 2 Sqn at High River; SOC 2.2.25
G-CYEC ex *F2714* TOC 2.8.21; Converted to DH-4B; Flown by 2 Sqn at High River; SOC 2.11.28
G-CYEM ex *F2707* TOC 7.6.22; Crashed High River, Cat A 28.7.24; SOC 1.8.24

CHILE

In 1919, twelve D.H.4s were to have been supplied to Chile, but there is no evidence that these were ever sent.

CUBA

Six Boeing-built DH-4M-1s were supplied, numbered *11 to 16*, for use by the Cuerpo de Aviacion. All six were damaged in a hurricane in 1926, being subsequently repaired. One was written off, and parts used for repair of the remaining five were ordered c.20 December 1928. Another was written off, and then in 1929 the remaining four were grounded, being deemed fire traps.

GREECE

A number of D.H.4s were transferred to the Greek Government for use by the Royal Hellenic Naval Air Service. They included B9477, D1760, D1761, N6399 and N6411.

Imperial Gift D.H.4 G-CYDM.

A Mexican Air Force DH-4B numbered '10'. (via Dan Hagedorn)

Mexican Air Force DH-4Bs numbered 2 and 19 in front of the hangars at Balbuena airfield. (via Dan Hagedorn)

A group standing in front of an American-built Mexican Air Force DH-4B in 1924. In the centre is W/Col Ralph O'Neill. (Manuel Ruiz Ramero via Dan Hagedorn)

A Mexican D.H.4B at Isapuato in 1924. (via Dan Hagedorn)

MEXICO

At least 13, and possibly as many as 20 ex-US DH-4Bs were supplied to the Fuerza Aérea Mexicana (Mexican Air Force), as part of the aid given by the American government to president General Alvaro Obregon in 1924, when his old friend Lic.Adolfo de la Huerta led an unsuccessful rebellion. The latter had taken exception to General Plutarco E.Calles being selected as the next president, and not himself.

The DH-4B was chosen on the recommendation of Col.Asm.Rafael (Ralph) O'Neill, a World War I fighter pilot who been born in Mexico of an Irish father and a Mexican mother. He had flown Nieuport 28C.1s and later Spad XIIIs with the 147th Aero Squadron, 1st Pursuit Group and had claimed 11 enemy aircraft of which 6 were confirmed. He had been promoted to 1st Lieutenant on 16 October 1918, and after returning to the United States post-war was discharged from the USAS on 9 February 1919. He was later hired to modernise the Mexican Air Service, and after making his report he was appointed chief of the Service, later becoming a technical adviser and chief training instructor at the aviation school at Balbuena airfield.

Known Mexican serials are 1 to 13 and also 19. Only two ex-USAS serials are known, these being A.S.22-1154 and A.S.22-1187. At least seven are known to have been lost in accidents and by rebel action, and by 17 February 1928 only two remained in the Order of Battle.

NETHERLANDS

D.H.4 A7935 of 217 Sqn forced landed on Soesterberg airfield on 17.6.18, being the only interned aircraft to land on a Dutch airfield. It was fired on by Dutch troops as it came into land, and overturned on touching down. 2/Lt GB Coward & Lt JF Read were interned, and their aircraft was repaired and taken on charge by the Dutch as *deH432*, being listed as operational on 1.11.18. It was returned to the RAF on 12.3.20.

NEW ZEALAND

Two D.H.4s were supplied to New Zealand as Imperial Gift machines:

A7929 Arrived New Zealand 19.3.19. Erected and ff 11.19. To NZPAF, Sockburn 14.6.23. Wfu Wigram 1930 and burnt.

A7893 Arrived New Zealand 19.3.19. Erected and ff 11.19. To NZPAF, Sockburn 14.6.23; coded "J". Wfu Wigram 1930 and burnt.

NICARAGUA

Two American-built DH-4Bs were supplied to Nicaragua in late 1921, but these were never uncrated, being subsequently returned to the USA to avoid payment.

PERSIA

In January 1924 four D.H.4s were purchased by Persia from Russia. Nothing further is known.

RUSSIA

A Russian order was placed in 1917 for 50 D.H.4s fitted with the 260hp Fiat A.12, but with the onset of winter these could not be delivered. Russia agreed to relinquish the order against a promise of 75 in the spring of 1918. The order was then taken over by the RFC as C4501-C4550.

In 1917 an incomplete set of drawings was provided to the Duks factory in Moscow for the production of the D.H.4 under licence, this factory being later restyled GAZ No.1 (Gosudarstvenny aviatzionny Zavod 1 or State Aircraft Factory No.1) . Following the Revolution, production commenced with the availability of FIAT A.12 engines. The first (c/n 2262) was test flown on 2 June 1920, followed by c/n 2293 on 15 June. C/n's

A Russian D.H.4 on wheels. (Alexandrov/Woodman)

A Russian D.H.4 on skis. (Alexandrov/Woodman)

A Russian D.H.4 on floats. (Alexandrov/Woodman)

2301 to 2321 were flown in 1921, and probably 2294 to 2321, then 2397 to 2436 in 1922/23. Production was to have continued with 35 Maybach-engined aircraft and a further 39 with FIATS. For winter operation the wheels could be replaced by skis.

In June 1918 the RAF had a flight of eight D.H.4s to support the Allied landings at Murmansk. Later, FIAT-powered D.H.4s were used both in North Russia and at Baku. At least five American-built DH-4Bs were captured by the RKKVF, including 63893, 63934 and 63954.

By 1921 about 10-15 Russian-built D.H.4s were in service, being mostly transferred from the Ukraine to Tambov. Units known to have flown the type in varying numbers are:
Aviaskadra No.2.
2nd Otryad of the DVK.
Military School of Observers at Leningrad.
School of Military Pilots in Moscow.
3rd Otdel'nyi razvedivatel'nyi aviatryad, Gomel'.
13th Otdel'nyi razvedivatel'nyi aviatryad, Luga.
16th (later 8th) Otdel'nyi razvedivatel'nyi aviatryad, Irkutsk.
1st, 3rd and 5th Otdel'nyi razvedivatel'nye aviatsionnye eskadrilii .
1st, 5th, 12th, 15th and 17th Otdel'nyi razvedivatel'nye aviatryady.
VVS HQ of the Leningrad Military District.
1st High School of Military Pilots, Moscow
Strel'bom School, Serpukhov (later Orenburg)
Training Eskadri'ya (later Akademiya VVS)

The Russian-built D.H.4s did not live up to expectations, and production was stopped, attention then turning to the D.H.9.

SOUTH AFRICA

Ten D.H.4s fitted with Eagle engines were presented to the Union of South Africa in 1920 by the Overseas Club of London. They had serial numbers B7951, B7962, B7976, B7979, B7991, B7992, B7993, B8005, B8013 and B8016. The aircraft flew initially with these serials until 1924 when they were renumbered in the SAAF serial system introduced that year, being given serial numbers from 201 to 210, though not necessarily in that order.

The first D.H.4 was assembled in October 1921 and the last one in February 1926. They were allotted to Swartkop aerodrome, firstly with No.1 Squadron and later to the Flying Training Squadron.

During the Industrial Strike of 1922, D7991 flew several reconnaissance sorties over the areas concerned. In one of these, on 13 March, the observer, Air/Cpl WH Jones, was hit by a stray bullet and killed.

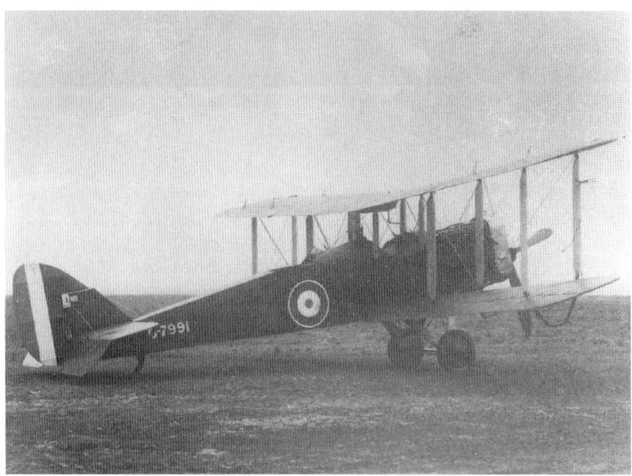

D.H.4 B7991 was reserialled 201 in South African service. (via Ken Smy)

Swartkop aerodrome lies at an altitude of 1,490m (4,770ft) which over the years has caused problems with engine power for service performance. An aircraft with more engine power was obviously needed, but financial constraints at the time prohibited the purchase of additional aircraft. The answer was to re-engine the existing types. Two Armstrong Siddeley Jaguar Mk.VI engines were purchased and installed in D.H.4s 204 and 208, the first of which flew in April 1927. These two aircraft were known in SAAF service as D.H.9J and were re-serialled as SAAF 151 and 152. Later that year, four Bristol Jupiter VI engines were bought for same purpose and were fitted into D.H.4s 201 and 203, and in D.H.9s 138 and ,147. These aircraft were reserialled 153 to 156, the first one flying in January 1928. They were known in service as the M'pala.

A further development took place the following year. Ten Jupiter VIII engines had been bought for the Westland Wapiti that had now been ordered to replace the D.H.4 and D.H.9. It was decided to temporarily install these engines in the D.H.4 and D.H.9 pending delivery of the Wapitis, the majority of which were to be locally built. The first such conversions involved D.H.9 airframes but three D.H.4s were allotted for conversion, numbers 202, 205 and 206. These further modified aircraft were known in SAAF service as the Mantis. In 1930 the conversion project was halted and the partly converted aircraft struck off charge.

Individual histories

201 (ex B7991) No.1 Sqn 10.21- 3.26; Converted to Mpala *153*
202 (ex B8013) No.1 Sqn 2.23 - 6.26; Force landed 24.4.28; Converted to Mantis
203 (ex B7992) No.1 Sqn 1923 - 6.25; Converted to Mpala *154*
204 No.1 Sqn 9.25 - 3.26; Converted to D.H.9J *151*
205 No.1 Sqn 9.25 - 9.26; FTS 1.27; Crashed 27.11.27; Conversion to Mantis cancelled
206 No.1 Sqn 6.26 - 12.26; FTS 1.27; Crashed 3.9.28; Conversion to Mantis cancelled
207 No.1 Sqn 6.26 - 12.26; FTS 1.27; Cr Swartkop; BER. SOC 1929
208 No.1 Sqn 9.26 - 12.26; FTS 1.27; Converted to D.H.9J *152*
209 FTS 3.27 - 6.29; Force landed at Swartkop 1929; SOC 1930
210 FTS 12.27 - 9.28; Crashed Swartkop 6.11.28; SOC 1929

SPAIN

A number of D.H.4s were ferried to Spain in 1921 for use by the Spanish Air Force, being later used in Morocco. 37 were issued with "registrations" *M-MHAC, M-MHDE to M-MHEN.*
[For further information see the D.H.9 section of this book]

Spanish Air Force D.H.4 M-MHDO at Croydon awaiting delivery 1921. (via Frank Cheesman).

TURKEY

At the end of the First World War, the Ottoman Air Force had on its inventory two captured D.H.4s. These were damaged ex-RAF machines which had been shot down over Turkish territory, one being practically demolished.

U.S.A.

Military use

In 1917, U.S. military flying activities were the responsibility of the Aviation Section of the Signal Corps, with four squadrons in the United States, two in Panama and one in the Phillipines. With the entry of America into World War I on 6 April 1917, there came a rapid expansion in both squadrons and equipment, much of the latter being of foreign origin or basic design.

On 18 October 1917, the DH-4 was ordered into production in the United States, fitted with a 420hp Liberty engine and referred to as the "Liberty Plane". Deliveries began in February 1918, the monthly totals being quoted as: February - 9; March - 4; April - 15; May - 153; June - 336; July - 484; August - 224; September - 757; October - 1,097; November - 1,072, December - 436. Then January to April 1919 - 254 (Total 4,841). Three manufacturers shared this production, being the Dayton-Wright Company of Dayton, Ohio (3,106), the Fisher Body Division of General Motors of Cleveland, Ohio (1,600) and the Standard Aircraft Corporation of Patterson, New Jersey (140) [the total of 4,846 for these does not quite tally with the total monthly production figures]. After the Armistice, orders were cancelled for an intended further 7,502 from these and other manufacturers.

The first American-built machines arrived in France on 11 May 1918 . Within two months they were arriving in quantity, and on 2 August a formation of 18 Liberty-engined aircraft of the 135th Aero Squadron flew across the front-line trenches. Subsequent flights went as much as 160 miles into enemy territory.

The DH-4 was the mainstay of the bombardment and observation units of the Air Service, American Expeditionary Force in France. 499 aircraft had actually reached the squadrons before the Armistice, of which 417 had been actually utilised on the Front. Of these 33 were lost due to enemy action, 4 lost over the lines not due to enemy action and 249 crashed at the front. References to it as a "flaming coffin" were unjustified, only 8 of those aircraft lost being sent down in flames, despite the universal use of incendiary bullets. Personnel losses were 38 killed in action (16 down in flames), 8 wounded, 10 missing and 20 prisoners-of war.

Self-sealing fuel tanks, which were in use on French Salmons and Breguets, had been offered to the front-line Air Service as early as August 1917, but refused. In September 1918 they were requested, and the first order for experimental self-sealing tanks was placed on 18 October, but when the first pair were delivered three days later they were too large and had to be redesigned. The first corrected ones arrived on 28 October, but were not installed in a DH-4 until 12 November, the day after the Armistice

Operational DH-4 unit strength on 11 November 1918 was 196, comprising:

FIRST ARMY
1st Pursuit Group HQ - 1; 1st Day-Bombing Group HQ - 2; 11th Sqn - 18; 20th Sqn - 19; 166th Sqn - 21; 24th Sqn - 1; 91st Sqn - 2; 50th Sqn - 16.

SECOND ARMY
85th Sqn - 11; 100th Sqn - 17, 163rd Sqn - 18; 135th Sqn - 21; 168th Sqn - 15; 8th Sqn - 17; 354th Sqn - 17.

By the time of the Armistice 1,213 had arrived in France, of which 155 had been passed on to the US Navy. A further 227 were delivered to France up to 12 February 1919. These can be broken down as follows:

Zone of Advance Air Depots to 12.2.19 (figures to 11.11.18 in brackets) -
1st Air Depot, Colombey-les-Belles 440 (410); 4th Air Depot 83 (83); 5th Air Depot, Vinets 134 (135); Clamecy-Gievres 11 (nil). TOTAL 668 (628)
Schools to 12.2.19 (to 11.11.18 in brackets) -
Orly sections Fabrications Aéronautics 2 (2); Orly for shipment to England 37 (36); 1st AIC, Paris 9 (9); 2nd AIC, Tours 28 (18); 3rd AIC, Issoudun 178 (158); 7th AIC, Clermont-Ferrand 57 (46); Aerial Gunnery School, St.Jean-des-Monts 75 (61); 2nd Aer School, Chatillon 43 (22); 2nd AOS, Souge 10 (3); Instruction, ASPC No.2 1 (1); Chaumont 1 (nil); Coetquidan 1 (nil). TOTAL 442 (356).
Deliveries to 12.2.19 (to 11.11.18 in brackets) -
Total delivered 1,110 (984); Crashed during test flight and en route to delivery points 75 (59); Disassembled for spare parts 43 (44); Ready for delivery 32 (67); In process of assembly nil (55); In cases as received from USA 180 (4). TOTAL 1,440 (1,113)

Many overseas DH-4s were piled up and burned after the Armistice, rather than being returned to the USA.

Smaller numbers were built post-war, and numerous American-built DH-4 variants existed, having official designations as follows:

DH-4	Basic WW1 Americanised "Liberty Plane".
DH-4Amb-1	One-seater ambulance conversion.
DH-4Amb-2	Two-seater ambulance conversion.
DH-4Ard	Cross-country dual-control version as modified by Air Repair Depot, Ardmont, ALbama; 165-gallon main tank; 7hrs fuel supply
DH-4B	Major redesign of DH-4 with pilot and main fuel tank interchanged so that the pilot was in the same location as in the D.H.9; Standard Liberty 12 installation; 88-gallon, plain, main tank [not leak-proof?]; 8-gallon reserve.
DH-4B-1	Standard Liberty 12 installation; 110 gallon main tank; 8 gallon reserve.
DH-4B-2	Standard Liberty 12 installation; 76 gallon, leak-proof main tank; 7 gallon reserve.
DH-4B-3	Standard Liberty 12 installation; 135 gallon main tank; 8 gallon reserve.

DH-4 P-31 (A.S.32083) fitted with Grain-type flotation gear. (J.M.Bruce/G.S.Leslie collection)

XDH-4B-5 Honeymoon Express P-76 (A.S.23432), fitted with an Austin D-5 engine, participated in the New York - Toronto air race in August 1919. (via Gordon Swanborough).

XDH-4L P-123 (S.C.62948) was a cleaned up racer with a narrow rear fuselage and a Liberty engine. (via Philip Jarrett)

DH-4B P-139 (A.S.63639) was a high altitude aircraft with a supercharged geared Liberty engine and long undercarriage. (J.M.Bruce/G.S.Leslie Collection)

DH-4B (P-188) A.S.63757 fitted with Siddeley Jaguar in 1924. (via Gordon Swanborough)

DH-4B P-226 (A.S.64356) had a revised cockpit position and oversize wheels. (via Gordon Swanborough)

D.H.4B P-277 (A.S.64587) was a Curtiss D-12 testbed. (via Bruce Robertson)

DH-4B-5 P-288 (A.S.23-1200) "Honeymoon Express". (via Gordon Swanborough)

DH-4B-4 Airways aircraft with Liberty 12 installation prepared in accordance with drawing No. 0104000; 110 gallon main tank; 8 gallon reserve.
XDH-4B-5 "Honeymoon Express"; Experimental airways aircraft built in accordance with Engineering Division's drawings for carrying passengers or freight.
DH-4BD Duster aircraft; Standard DH-4B equipped with duster apparatus.
DH-4BG Gas Barrage aircraft; Standard DH-4B equipped with chemical smoke screen apparatus.
DH-4BK Standard DH-4B equipped for night flying.
DH-4BM Standard DH-4B modified with rear seat and rear baggage compartment only.
DH-4BM-1 Transport version of DH-4BM, built in accordance with specifications from Office, Chief of Air Service; Dual control, including instruments; 110 gallon main tank; 8 gallon reserve.
DH-4BM-2 Transport version of DH-4BM, built in accordance with specifications from Office, Chief of Air Service; 135 gallon main tank; 8 gallon reserve.
XDH-4BP Experimental single-seat photographic aircraft; Liberty 12 installation; cameras mounted in front cockpit.
DH-4BP-1 Peacetime photographic aircraft; Liberty 12 installation, adapted to vertical mapping, oblique and motion picture photography in accordance with drawing No. X-39241.
XDH-4BP-2 Experimental photographic aircraft; Liberty 12 installation; 135 gallon main tank; 8 gallon reserve; USD-9A wings.
DH-4BP-3 Photographic aircraft similar to DH-4BP-1; Liberty 12 installation; Adapted to vertical mapping, oblique and motion picture photography in accordance with drawing No. X-47746; 110 gallon main tank; 8 gallon reserve.
XDH-4BS Experimental aircraft; Liberty 12 engine equipped with supercharger in accordance with drawing No. X-38250; 88 gallon main tank; 8 gallon reserve.
DH-4BT Training aircraft; standard DH-4B with modified dual control including instruments and rear seat.
DH-4BW Test bed for 300hp Wright-Hispano "H" engine.
DH-4C DH-4B test bed for 350hp Packard 1A-1237 engine; Modified fuselage.
XDH-4L Experimental aircraft; Cleaned-up cross-country racer; Liberty 12 installation, 185 gallon, 9 hour fuel supply.
DH-4M Liberty 12 installation; "Modernised" DH-4/DH-4B with new steel tube fuselage; 53 built by Boeing
DH-4M-1 Liberty 12 installation; Arc-welded metal fuselage in accordance with A.S. Specification 1560 or A.S. Specification 1561-B; 76 gallon main tank; 8 gallon reserve; 97 built by Boeing.
DH-4M-1K DH-4M-1 equipped as target tug.
DH-4M-1T DH-4M-1 conversions to dual-control trainer; 22 converted.
DH-4M-2 Liberty 12 installation; Metal fuselage in accordance with A.S. Specification 1567; 110 gallon main tank; 8 gallon reserve; 135 built by Atlantic (Fokker).
DH-4M-2A DH-4M-2 equipped for operation on airways.
DH-4M-2K DH-4M-2 equipped as target tug.
DH-4M-2P Photographic aircraft; Liberty 12 installation; Metal fuselage in accordance with A.S. Specification 1569; 110 gallon main tank; 8 gallon reserve.
DH-4M-2S Supercharged aircraft; Liberty 12 installation; Metal fuselage in accordance with A.S. Specification 1568; 88 gallon main tank; 8 gallon reserve.
DH-4M-2T DH-4M-2 equipped as dual control trainer.

Orders were placed with the Dutch Fokker company to provide gas-welded steel tube fuselages for American-built DH-4s, in place of the wooden fuselages. In all, 135 metal frame fuselages were built from 1924 at Teterboro, in the former buildings of the liquidated Witteman-Lewis company. Designated the DH-4-M2, and fitted with a 110-gallon main tank, these comprised 100 rebuilt aircraft and 35 complete aircraft, use being also made of the nearby Hasbrouck Heights airfield. The Fokker establishment at Hasbrouck Heights was designated the Atlantic Aircraft Corporation.

Many wartime DH-4s built by Dayton-Wright, Fisher and Standard were rebuilt post-war. Some retained their original serial numbers, but others were given new serials when they were rebuilt.

A Transcontinental Aeroplane race was held between 8 October and 4 November 1919. The winner of the round trip was a DH-4 flown by 2/Lt A.Pearson and Sgt R.Atkinson with a flying time of 48 hours 14 minutes 8 seconds. A DH-4 crewed by 1/Lt B.W.Maynard and Sgt W.E.Klein had the best overall time, this being 9 days 4 hours 26 minutes 8 seconds.

Plane numbers of aircraft assigned to McCook Field

Numerous DH-4 variants were evaluated at McCook Field with various experimental installations, these having local plane numbers painted on the fin. The following are known:

P-16 DH-4 (serial unknown). Converted to DH-4 Bluebird trainer, surveyed 25.11.19
P-21 DH-4 A.S.32071. Wrecked at Erie, Pa., 20.1.19
P-31 DH-4 A.S.32083. Fitted with flotation gear. Wrecked Selfridge Field, MI, 10.9.19
P-34 DH-4 A.S.32341. Salvaged 1.4.21
P-35 DH-4 A.S.32321. Condemned 20.10.20
P-49 DH-4 A.S.32344. Modified to DH-4B, wrecked Wilbur Wright Field, OH, 4.4.21
P-56 DH-4 Bluebird trainer A.S.31108. Wrecked Detroit, MI, 24.4.20
P-76 XDH-4B-5 Honeymoon Express A.S.23432. Participated in New York - Toronto race.
P-77 DH-4L A.S.62945. Transferred to Hazelhurst Field, NY 13.6.19
P-78 DH-4 A.S.30130. Assigned to General Kenly
P-79 DH-4L A.S.62946. Wrecked Fort Wayne, IN 4.7.20
P-81 DH-4 A.S.30894. Transferred to Langley Field, VA, 22.8.19
P-82 DH-4 A.S.30723. Transferred to Kelly Field, TX, 4.6.20
P-85 DH-4 Honeymoon Express A.S.40128. Wrecked Centerville, IN, 19.1.23
P-91 DH-4 A.S.30727. Wrecked 20.8.19 near Dayton, OH
P-92 DH-4 A.S.30590. Transferred to Kelly Field, TX, 4.6.20
P-93 DH-4 A.S.30855. 300-hp Wright-Martin H engine. Wrecked 20.12.21
P-94 DH-4 A.S.30913. Transferred to Langley Field, VA, 23.10.19
P-102 DH-4 A.S.30632. Transferred to Langley Field, VA, 1.11.19
P-105 DH-4 A.S.30846. Transferred to Kelly Field, TX., 4.6.20
P-107 DH-4L A.S.62947. Wrecked McCook Field 25.6.20
P-109 DH-4 A.S.23075. Wrecked Leesburg, VA. Salvaged at Bolling Field, DC 25.2.21
P-122 DH-4 A.S.30855. 300-hp Wright-Martin H engine. Transferred to Wilbur Wright Field, OH, 1.8.21
P-123 DH-4L S.C.62948. Narrow rear fuselage. Wrecked near Keyser, W. VA, 3.10.21
P-125 DH-4 A.S.22856. Transferred to Langley Field, VA, 28.11.19
P-126 DH-4 A.S.23369. Transferred to Wilbur Wright Field, OH, 12.7.21
P-130 DH-4Amb A.S.63278. Transferred to Bolling Field, DC, 8.9.20
P-131 DH-4B A.S.63413.
P-133 DH-4B A.S.63697. 300-hp Wright-Martin H engine. Surveyed 25.4.21
P-134 DH-4C A.S.63279. Wrecked Moundsville, W. VA, 13.8.21. Also listed as wrecked in White Mountains, N.H.
P-136 DH-4C A.S.63280. Wrecked Wilbur Wright Field, OH, 19.6.20 and repaired.
P-137 DH-4B A.S.63600. Salvaged 6.6.23
P-139 DH-4B A.S.63639. High altitude with supercharged geared Liberty engine and long undercarriage. Still active 1.5.25
P-157 DH-4B A.S.63747. Transferred Fairborne Air Intermediate Depot, OH, 8.7.21
P-158 DH-4B A.S.63719. Transferred Fairborne Air Intermediate Depot, OH, 8.7.21
P-160 DH-4 A.S.22909. Transferred to Fairborne Air Intermediate Depot, OH
P-173 DH-4B A.S.64009. Fitted with Liberty 6-cylinder engine. Transferred to Langley Field, VA, 26.9.22

DH-4B P-292 (A.S.22-1128) was fitted experimentally with skis. (via Gordon Swanborough)

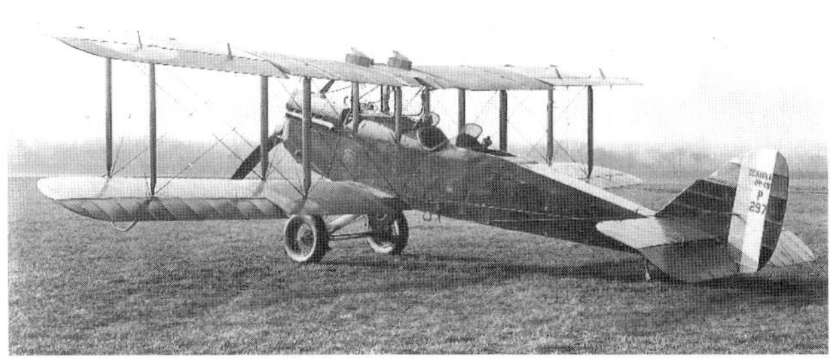

DH-4B P-297 (A.S.22-1117) fitted with experimental Curtiss wing radiators

DH-4B P-297 (A.S.22-1117) fitted with an underslung radiator

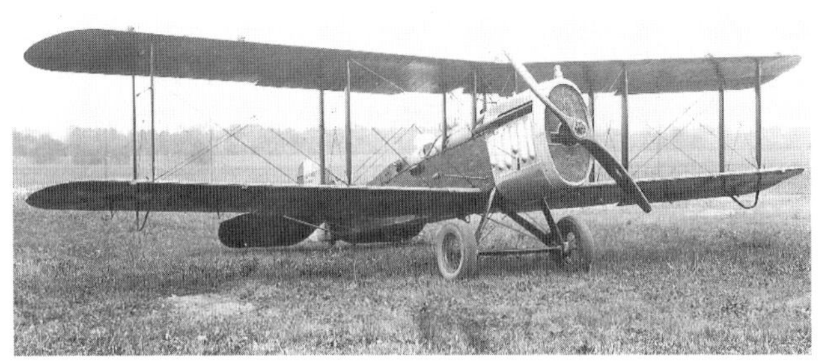

DH-4B P-297 (A.S.22-1117) fitted with dual radiators

P-174 DH-4B A.S.64008. Surveyed 2.10.24

P-175 DH-4B A.S.64007. Wrecked Wilbur Wright Field, OH

P-188 DH-4B A.S.63757. 300-hp Wright-Martin H engine, fitted with Wright radial 1.1.24, fitted with Siddeley Jaguar 23.5.24, fitted with Wright radial 1.5.25

P-190 DH-4B A.S.63181. Turbo supercharged Liberty; Wrecked about 22.6.22

P-191 DH-4B A.S.64535. Surveyed 3.9.22

P-192 DH-4B A.S.64539. Transferred to Bolling Field, DC, 10.7.23

P-193 DH-4L A.S.64593. Transferred to Montgomery, AL, 6.12.26

P-194 DH-4B A.S.63896. Wrecked, surveyed 7.12.22

P-211 DH-4B A.S.68209. Surveyed 2.1.23

P-218 DH-4B A.S.63698. Wrecked 16.10.22

P-219 DH-4B A.S.63710. Surveyed 28.4.25

P-220 DH-4B A.S.68214. Transferred to Fairborne Air Intermediate Depot 11.5.22

P-226 DH-4B A.S.64356. Revised cockpit position and oversize wheels; Surveyed 4.10.26

P-237 DH-4B A.S.64468. Rejected and returned to Wilbur Wright Field, OH, 6.4.22

P-247 DH-4B A.S.22-517. Wrecked, surveyed 1.10.22

P-251 DH-4BP-1 A.S.22-511. Transferred to Wilbur Wright Field, OH, 24.7.23

P-252 DH-4B A.S.64354. Transferred to Fairborne Air Intermediate Depot 5.7.23

P-256 DH-4B A.S.22-528. Inverted Liberty engine. Surveyed 18.8.26

P-257 DH-4B A.S.22-523. Transferred to Fairborne Air Intermediate Depot 7.7.25

P-258 DH-4B A.S.22-520. Transferred to Fairborne Air Intermediate Depot 7.12.22

P-261 DH-4B A.S.64281. Surveyed 2.1.23

P-271 DH-4B A.S.22-586. Surveyed 2.7.23

P-275 DH-4B A.S.22-596. Surveyed 2.6.25

P-277 DH-4B A.S.64587. Curtiss D-12 testbed. Surveyed 8.3.27

P-287 DH-4B A.S.22-587. Surveyed 24.7.25

P-288 DH-4B-5 A.S.23-1200. Surveyed 11.2.25

P-289 DH-4B A.S.22-1110. Surveyed 10.7.25

P-292 DH-4B A.S.22-1128. Fitted skis; Transferred to Fairborne Air Intermediate Depot 27.1.27

P-296 DH-4B A.S.22-1124. Surveyed 6.8.23

P-297 DH-4B A.S.22-1117. Wing skin radiator experiments. Surveyed 30.1.25

P-298 DH-4B-3 A.S.22-1107. Surveyed 21.11.25

P-299 DH-4B A.S.22-1123. Surveyed 8.3.27

P-300 DH-4B-P2 A.S.22-1121. Surveyed 2.2.27

P-301 DH-4B-3 A.S.22-1122. Surveyed 24.7.23 (23.7.24?)

P-302 DH-4B-3 A.S.22-1125. Transferred to Fairborne Air Intermediate Depot 27.1.27

P-312 DH-4BP-1 A.S.23-553. Surveyed 8.2.26

P-315 DH-4BP-1 A.S.23-552. Transferred to Fairborne Air Intermediate Depot 3.12.23

P-329 DH-4B A.S.23-669. Fitted with complete wing cellule from a Loening COA-1 amphibian by the Gallaudet Aircraft Corp. in 1922. Surveyed 21.2.25

P-332 XC0-7 A.S.23-109. Surveyed 23.5.24

P-334 DH-4B-3 A.S.23-420. Surveyed 29.9.24

P-336 DH-4B-4 A.S.24-111. Transferred to Phillips 9.3.26

P-337 XDH-4M-1 A.S.68592. Transferred to Boston airport 27.2.25

P-359 DH-4B-4 A.S.24-247. Rebuild by Fairfield Air Intermediate Depot.

P-363 DH-4M-1 A.S.32319. Transferred to Fairborne Air Intermediate Depot 3.1.27

P-366 DH-4M-1 A.S.31412. Transferred to Fairborne Air Intermediate Depot 10.11.24

P-368 XCO-7B A.S.31216. Out of commission by 16.3.26

P-369 XC0-8 A.S.23163. Atlantic rebuild from DH-4, fitted with N-struts and outsize wheels. Surveyed 8/30

P-371 DH-4M-1 A.S.24-301.

P-382 DH-4B-4 A.S.24-253. Possibly converted from DH-4 63416 by Curtiss; Transferred to Fairborne Air Intermediate Depot 27.1.27

P-388 X-DH-4B-5 A.S.23-691. Surveyed 1.12.25

P-389 DH-4B A.S.23-697. Surveyed 18.8.26

DH-4B P-329 (A.S.23-669) had Gallaudet-built Loening wings from a COA-1 amphibian. (via Gordon Swanborough)

P-390 DH-4B A.S.32894.
P-391 DH-4M-1 A.S.32752. Transferred to Maxwell Field, AL, 22.3.27
P-392 DH-4M-1 A.S.32476.
P-393 DH-4M-1 A.S.31386. Transferred to Fairborne Air Intermediate Depot 24.3.27
P-397 DH-4BS A.S.26-21.Surveyed 18.1.27
P-398 DH-4BK A.S.26-30. Transferred to Fairborne Air Intermediate Depot 27.1.27
P-423 DH-4BK A.S.26-29.
P-425 DH-4BP-2 A.S.30805. Transferred to Scott Field 11.25
P-426 DH-4M-2 A.S.32858.
P-427 DH-4M-2 A.S.31871. Transferred to Fairborne Air Intermediate Depot 25.2.27
P-428 DH-4M-2P A.S.31839.
P-429 DH-4B A.S.23-672.
P-433 DH-4M-2P A.S.30479.
P-435 DH-4M-2S A.S.63945. Transferred to Fairborne Air Intermediate Depot 27.1.27
P-436 DH-4M-2S A.S.31955.

U.S.ARMY SQUADRONS

By 1918, the U.S. Air Service had adopted a designation of numbering units in which blocks of numbers were allocated according to the task involved. Nos.1 to 399 were reserved for Service squadrons, 400 to 599 to Construction squadrons, 600 to 799 to Supply squadrons, 800 to 999 to Repair squadrons and 1000 onwards to Replacement squadrons. Thus aircraft squadrons were generally numbered in the 1 to 399 series, an exception being No.800 squadron. They were initially all known as Aero squadrons, but the word 'Aero' was dropped on 14 March 1921. Then from 25 January 1923 the word squadron was prefixed by the task, such as Observation, Pursuit, Attack etc.

Regarding DH-4 squadrons intended for service on the Western Front, the practice was that the enlisted personnel, on arrival in the UK, were posted as separate flights to various RFC training bases in order to gain experience of servicing the aircraft they were eventually to operate. This did not always prove possible in practice, as the training units they were attached to were sometimes flying types other than the D.H.4. In the meantime, the pilots and observers underwent continuation training in their respective function at the appropriate RFC schools/aerodromes or, exceptionally, through attachment to a British squadron operating in France. When a US squadron was required in France, the whole personnel was formed up and it then moved to its base in France to where its aircraft were delivered from their designated supply depot either by ferry pilots or by the squadron pilots.

The following squadrons are known to have flown DH-4 variants as either full or partial equipment.

2nd Aero/Observation Squadron
Formed 5.6.19 as 2nd Aero Squadron with DH-4 as partial equipment at Rockwell Field, CA; Fort Mills, Corregidor 24.12.19; Kindley Field, Corregidor 15.10.20; Redesignated 2nd Squadron 14.3.21; Redesignated 2nd Observation Squadron 25.1.23; Nichols Field, Luzon 6.29; Re-equipped 1931.

3rd Aero/Pursuit Squadron
Formed 13.5.19 as 3rd Aero Squadron with DH-4 as main (later partial) equipment at Mitchel Field, NY; Hazelhurst Field, NY 29.5.19 to 28.6.19; Manila, Luzon 2.12.19; Clark Field, Luzon 15.10.20 Redesignated 3rd Squadron 14.3.21; Redesignated 3rd Pursuit Squadron 25.1.23; Re-equipped 1931.

4th Aero/Observation Squadron
Formed 23.6.19 as 4th Aero Squadron with DH-4 as main equipment at Hazelhurst Field, NY; Mitchel Field, NY 11.19 to 8.1.20; Luke Field, HA 24.1.20; Schofield Barracks, HA 6.2.20; Redesignated 4th Squadron 14.3.21; Redesignated 4th Observation Squadron 25.1.23; Luke Field, HA 11.1.27; Squadron re-equipped in 1929.

5th Aero/Observation Squadron
Formed 24.10.19 as 5th Aero Squadron with DH-4 as major equipment at Hazelhurst Field, NY; Mitchel Field, NY 11.19 (operated from Langley Field, VA 6.5.21 - 26.10.21); Redesignated 5th Squadron 14.3.21; Redesignated 5th Observation Squadron 25.1.23; Re-equipped 1928.

6th Aero/Pursuit Squadron
Formed 23.6.19 as 6th Aero Squadron with DH-4 as partial equipment at Ford Island (later Luke Field), HA; Mitchel Field, NY 11.19 to 8.1.20; Luke Field, HA 24.1.20; Redesignated 6th Squadron on 14.3.21; Redesignated 6th Pursuit Squadron on 25.1.23; Wheeler Field, HA 11.1.27; Squadron re-equipped during 1930.

7th Aero/Observation Squadron
Based as 7th Aero Squadron by 1919 at Coco Walk (later France Field), CZ with DH-4 as main equipment; Redesignated 7th Squadron 14.3.21; Redesignated 7th Observation Squadron 25.1.25; DH-4s withdrawn 1931.

8th Aero/Attack Squadron
Based Winchester as 8th Aero Squadron and later equipped with DH-4 for Corps Observation from 8.12.17; Dartford c.24.12.17 (detts at Thetford, Wyton & Northolt); Thetford 1.5.18; Amanty, France 11.7.18 (assigned to 4th Corps for the Lorraine, St.Mihiel areas); Ourches, France 31.8.18; Toulon, France 29.9.18; Saizerais 23.10.18; Colombey-les-Belles, France 11.2.19; Fargues-St.Hilaire, France 22.2.19; In transit 18.4.19; Mitchel Field, NY 3.5.19; Kelly Field, TX 25.5.19 (flt detd McAllen, TX 25.7.19; McAllen, TX 13.8.19 (flt detd Laredo, TX 15.8.19-3.8.20 & Pope Field, NC from 13.8.20); Redesignated 8th Squadron 14.3.21; Kelly Field, TX 2.7.21 (flight detd Pope Field. NC to 26.11.21); Redesignated 8th Attack Squadron 25.1.23; Fort Crockett, TX 30.6.26 and re-equipped.

Commanding Officers: Lt JG Hinant (7.18), 2/Lt JD Halsteid (8.18).

9th Aero Squadron
Based Winchester as 9th Aero Squadron equipped partially with DH-4 from c.8.12.17; Grantham (Spittlegate?) c.26.12.17; To France 7.8.18 (for Night Observation in the Lorraine, St.Mihiel, Meuse-Argonne areas); Colombey-les-Belles, France 23.8.18; Amanty, France 28.8.18; Vavincourt, France 21.9.18; Preutin, France 21.11.18; Trier, Germany 5.12.18; Colombey-les-Belles, France 18.5.19; Marseilles, France 25.5.19; In transit 7.6.19; Mitchel Field, NY 23.6.19; Park Field, Tenn 12.7.19; March Field, CA 22.7.19; Rockwell Field, CA 2.8.19 (flt detd Calexico, CA 4.20); March Field, CA 15.11.19; Rockwell Field, CA 11.12.19; Mather Field, CA 27.4.20; Redesignated 9th Squadron 14.3.21; Disbanded 29.6.22.

11th Aero/Bombardment Squadron
Based Stamford as 11th Aero Squadron equipped with DH-4 for Bombardment from c.7.1.18; Waddington 24.6.18; To France 7.8.18 (for Day Bombing in the Lorraine, St.Mihiel, Meuse-Argonne areas); Delouze, France 26.8.18; Amanty, France 6.9.18; Maulan, France 24.9.18; Colombey-les-Belles, France 17.1.19; Guitres, France 1.2.19; St.Denis de Pile, France 19.2.19; Sablons, France 9.3.19; Libourne, France 13.4.19; In transit 16.4.19; Mitchel Field, NY 2.5.19 with DH-4 as partial equipment; Hazelhurst Field, NY 5.5.19; Ellington Field, TX 26.5.19; Fort Bliss, TX c.22.6.19; Kelly Field, TX 8.11.19; Redesignated 11th Squadron 14.3.21; Langley Field, VA 30.6.22; Redesignated 11th Bombardment Squadron 25.1.23; Disbanded 19.5.27.

Pilot and observer teams in France collecting American-built DH-4s at Romarintin, south of Orleans, in the summer of 1918. (via Terry Treadwell)

12th Aero/Observation Squadron
Based Mitchel Field, NY from 17.6.19 as 12th Aero Squadron with DH-4 as partial equipment; Scott Field, IL 6.7.19; Kelly Field, TX 13.10.19; Fort Bliss, TX 9.1.20 (flt detd Douglas, AZ from 10.1.20); Nogales, AZ 12.4.29 (flt still detd Douglas); To Douglas, AZ c.2.21 (flt detd Nogales, AZ); Fort Bliss, TX 28.9.21 (detd at Fort Sam Houston, TX after 26.6.24); Redesignated 12th Observation Squadron 25.1.23; Fort Sam Houston, TX 22.6.26 and DH-4s withdrawn.

13th Attack Squadron
Formed 14.3.21 as 13th Squadron ex 104th Aero Squadron at Fort Bliss, TX (Flt detd Marfa, TX) with DH-4 a main equipment; Kelly Field, TX 2.7.21; Redesignated 13th Attack Squadron 25.1.23; Disbanded 27.6.24

15th Aero/Observation Squadron
Formed 22.8.17 as 15th Aero Squadron at Mineola, NY with DH-4 as partial equipment; Disbanded 18.9.19.

Reformed 21.9.21 as 15th Squadron at Chanute Field, IL with DH-4 as partial equipment; Kelly Field, TX 1.6.21; Redesignated 15th Observation Squadron 25.1.23; Disbanded 1.8.27

16th Observation Squadron
Formed 7.12.21 as 16th Squadron at Fort Riley, KS with DH-4 as main equipment; Redesignated 16th Observation Squadron 25.1.23; Re-equipped 1926.

17th Pursuit Squadron
Formed 14.3.21 as 17th Squadron at Kelly Field, TX with DH-4s as partial equipment; Ellington Field, TX 1.7.21; Selfridge Field, MI 1.7.22; Redesignated 17th Pursuit Squadron 25.1.23; DH-4s withdrawn 1925.

18th Observation Squadron
Formed 11.7.22 as 18th Squadron at Bolling Field, DC with DH-4s as partial equipment; Redesignated 18th Observation Squadron 25.1.23; Disbanded 18.2.25.

19th Pursuit Squadron
Formed 1.5.23 as 19th Pursuit Squadron at Wheeler Field, HA with DH-4 as partial equipment; Luke Field, HA 15.1.24; DH-4s withdrawn 1926.

20th Aero/Bombardment Squadron
Based Stamford from 7.1.18 as 20th Aero Squadron later with DH-4 for Bombardment as main equipment; In transit to France 7.8.18 (for Day Bombing in the Lorraine, St.Mihiel, Meuse-Argonne areas); Delouze 26.8.18; Amanty 7.9.18; Maulan 23.9.18; Colombey-les-Belles 16.1.19; Guitres 1.2.19; St.Denis de Pile 5.2.19; Libourne 27.2.19; Retd to USA 4.19; Mitchel Field, NY 2.5.19 now with DH-4 as partial equipment; To Kelly Field, TX c.25.9.19; Redesignated 20th Squadron 14.3.21; Langley Field, VA 30.6.22; Redesignated 20th Bombardment Squadron 25.1.23; DH-4s withdrawn 1929.

22nd Aero/Observation Squadron
Based from 6.5.18 as 22nd Aero Squadron with HQ and 'A' Flt at Petite Synthe (attd 211 Sqn & 4 ASD Guines), 'B' Flt at Bois de Roche (attd 205 Sqn) and 'C' Flt at Conteville (attd 49 Sqn) with DH-4 as main equipment; From 11.6.18 HQ and 'A' Flt at Petite Synthe (attd 211 Sqn), 'B' Flt at Bois de Roche (attd 205 Sqn) and 'C' Flt at Fourneuil (attd 49 Sqn which had moved 2.6.18); Sqn reassembled at Guines 24.6.18; Issoudun 26.6.18; Orly 7.7.18; Toul 16.8.18; Belrain 22.9.18; To Grand c.29.1.19; Colombey-les-Belles 18.4.19; Le Mans 6.5.19; Retd to USA; Mitchel Field, NY until disbanded 16.6.19.
Commanding Officer: Lt JC Kennedy (8.18)

Reformed 14.3.21 as 22nd Squadron ex 135th Aero Squadron at Post Field, OK (dett to Montgomery, AL 4.11.21); Montgomery, AL 30.11.21 (dett to Pope Field, NC 26.11.21); Redesignated 22nd Observation Squadron 25.1.23; DH-4s withdrawn c.1927.

23rd Bombardment Squadron
Formed 1.10.21 as 23rd Squadron at March Field, CA with DH-4 as partial equipment; Luke Field, HA 29.3.22; Redesignated 23rd Bombardment Squadron 25.1.23; DH-4s withdrawn 1929.

24th Aero/Pursuit Squadron
Based as 24th Aero Squadron at Wye from 31.1.18 with DH-4 later as partial equipment (detts Sedgeford, Wyton, London Colney (to 7.3.18 & Croydon (from 7.3.18)); Narborough 1.5.18; To France 19.7.18; St.Maxent 22.7.18; Ourches 6.8.18 (assigned to 4th Corps for army observation work in the Lorraine & St.Mihiel areas); Gondreville-sur-Moselle 22.8.18; Vavincourt 22.9.18 (dett at Souilly 9-18.10.81 & 27.10.18 - 6.11.18); Weissenthurm, Germany 7.5.19; Retd USA 14.7.19 and discarded DH-4s.
Commanding Officer: Lt HA Miller (7.18 - 8.18), 2/Lt WJ Johnston (8.18).

As 24th Squadron received further DH-4s as partial equipment in 1922 at Mitchel Field, NY; France Field, CZ 30.4.22; Redesignated 24th Pursuit Squadron 25.1.23; DH-4s withdrawn by 1930.

26th Attack Squadron
Formed 15.9.21 as 26th Squadron at Kelly Field, TX with DH-4s; Redesignated 26th Attack Squadron 25.1.32; Disbanded 27.6.24

27th Aero/Pursuit Squadron
Returned from France as 27th Aero Squadron and based from Garden City, NY from 19.3.19, now with DH-4 as partial equipment; Selfridge Field, MI 28.4.19; Kelly Field, TX 31.8.19; Redesignated 27th Squadron 14.3.21; Ellington Field, TX 1.7.21; Selfridge Field, MI 1.7.22; Redesignated 27th Pursuit Squadron 25.1.23; DH-4s withdrawn 1925.

28th Aero/Bombardment Squadron
Based as 28th Aero Squadron from 6.5.18 with HQ Flt at Alquines, France (attd 206 Sqn), 'A' Flt at Alquines (attd 98 Sqn - which moved to Coudekerque 25.5.18 and Ruisseauville 6.6.18), 'B' Flt at Serny (attd 18 Sqn) and 'C' Flt at Ruisseauville (attd 25 Sqn); From 1.6.18 HQ Flt ("18 Misc") at Alquines with D.H.9 (attd 206 Sqn), 'A' Flt at Ruisseauville with D.H.9 (attd 98 Sqn), 'B' Flt at Serny with D.H.4 (attd 18 Sqn) and 'C' Flt at Ruisseauville with D.H.4 (attd 25 Sqn)
[This per RAF records, though US records suggest equipped with Spads but trained on DH-4].

Commanding Officer: Lt JC Mille (7.18 - 8.18)

Reformed 20.9.21 as 28th Squadron at Mather Field, CA with DH-4 as main equipment initially; Disbanded 28.6.22.

Reformed 1.9.22 as 28th Squadron at Clark Field, Luzon; Kindley Field, Corregidor 9.22;Camp Nichols, Luzon 11.22; Clark Field, Luzon 12.22; Redesignated 28th Bombardment Squadron 25.1.23; Camp Nichols, Luzon 4.6.23; DH-4s withdrawn 1928.

37th Aero Squadron
By 1918 as 37th Aero Squadron at Issoudon, France with DH-4 as partial equipment; Bordeaux c.6.1.19; Retd USA c.18.3.19.

41st School Squadron
Formed 7.7.22 as 41st Squadron at Kelly Field, TX with DH-4 as main equipment; Redesignated 41st School Squadron 25.1.23; DH-4s withdrawn 1928.

Men of the U.S.Army Signal Corps surrounding the wreckage of what appears to be DH-4 A.S.29662. (via Frank Cheesman)

42nd Aero/School Squadron
Based by 1918 as 42nd Aero Squadron at Wilbur Wright Field, OH, possibly with some DH-4 as partial equipment; Disbanded 21.2.19.

Reformed 5.7.22 as 42nd Squadron at Kelly Field, TX; Redesignated 42nd School Squadron 25.1.23; DH-4s withdrawn by 1931.

43rd School Squadron
Formed 7.7.22 as 43rd Squadron at Kelly Field, TX with DH-4 as partial equipment; Redesignated 43rd School Squadron 25.1.23; DH-4s withdrawn by 1929.

44th Aero/Observation Squadron
Formed 30.6.17 as 44th Aero Squadron at Wilbur Wright Field, OH possibly with DH-4 as partial equipment; Redesignated Squadron K 10.18.

Reformed 10.6.22 as 44th Squadron at Post Field, OK with DH-4 as main equipment; Redesignated 44th Observation Squadron 25.1.23; March Field, CA 25.6.27; Disbanded 31.7.27.

49th Aero Squadron
Formed 14.3.21 as 49th Squadron ex 166th Aero Squadron at Kelly Field, TX with DH-4 as partial equipment; Langley Field, VA 20.5.21; Kelly Field, TX 26.10.21; Langley Field, VA 30.6.22; Aberdeen Proving Ground, MD 17.8.22; Langley Field, VA 18.1.28; Redesignated 49th Bombardment Squadron 25.1.23; DH-4s withdrawn 1929.

50th Aero/Observation Squadron
Based Romsey as 50th Aero Squadron from 24.1.18 with DH-4s later for Army Observation as main equipment; Grantham 4.2.18; Winchester [Flower Down?] 3.7.18; To France 13.7.18 (for the Lorraine, St.Mihiel, Meuse-Argonne areas); Amanty 27.7.18; Behonne 4.9.18; Bicqueley 8.9.18; Remicourt 24.9.18; Clermont-en-Argonne 28.10.18; Langres 6.12.18 (operated from Longeau; 'B' Flt at Clermont-en-Argonne to 18.12.18 and then Clamency; 'C' Flt at Clermont-en-Argonne to 12.12.18 and then La Valbonne); Clamency 19.1.19; Retd USA 19.4.19; Mitchel Field, NY 9.5.19; Scott Field, IL 27.5.19; Langley Field, VA 8.19; Redesignated 50th Squadron 14.3.21; Redesignated 50th Observation Squadron 25.1.23; Brooks Field, TX 25.6.27; Disbanded 1.8.27.

54th School Squadron
Formed 31.7.27 in 13th School Group as 54th School Squadron at March Field, CA with DH-4 as partial equipment; Disbanded 30.4.31.

55th Pursuit Squadron
Formed 15.11.30 at Mather Field, CA as 55th Pursuit Squadron with DH-4 as partial equipment in 1931.

72nd Bombardment Squadron
Formed 1.5.23 as 72nd Bombardment Squadron at Luke Field, HA with DH-4 as main equipment; DH-4s withdrawn 1929.

74th Aero Squadron
Formed 22.2.18 as 74th Aero Squadron at Waco, TX believed with DH-4; Call Field, TX 1.3.18; Hazelhurst Field, NY 29.7.18; Roosevelt Field, NY 9.18; Garden City, NY by 28.1.19; Langley Field, VA 17.6.19; Disbanded 25.9.19.

77th Pursuit Squadron
Formed 15.11.30 as 77th Pursuit Squadron at Mather Field, CA with some DH-4 on strength in 1931.

85th Aero Squadron
In France in 1918 as 85th Aero Squadron, assigned to the Front 25.10.18, for Army Observation in the Lorraine area with DH-4s; Still in France 1.4.19, but not by 1.5.19; No further details available.

88th Aero/Observation Squadron
Retd 27.6.19 ex France as 88th Aero Squadron to Mitchel Field with DH-4 as main equipment; Scott Field, IL 11.7.19; Langley Field, VA 5.9.19; Redesignated 88th Squadron 14.3.21 (operated from Charleston, VA 3-8.9.21; dett Charleston to 10.21); Wilbur Wright Field, OH 11.10.22; Redesignated 88th Observation Squadron 25.1.23; Brooks Field, TX 7.5.27; Disbanded 1.8.27.

90th Aero Squadron
Retd 5.5.19 ex France as 90th Aero Squadron to Hazelhurst Field, NY with DH-4 as main equipment (flight detd Eagle Pass, TX 2.9.19 until 11.6.20); Sanderson, TX 29.11.19 (Flight detd Del Rio, TX 12.6.20 - 30.6.21); Redesignated 90th Squadron 14.3.21; Kelly Field, TX 2.7.21; Redesignated 90th Attack Squadron 25.1.23; Fort Crockett, TX 1.7.26 (dett Fort Huachuca. AZ 7.4.29 - 2.5.29); DH-4 withdrawn by 1932.

91st Aero/Observation Squadron
From 14.12.17 as 91st Aero Squadron at Amanty, France with DH-4s as partial equipment (assigned 1st Army for observation work in the Lorraine, St.Mihiel, Meuse-Argonne areas); Gondreville-sur-Moselle 24.5.18; Vavincourt 21.9.18 (dett at Souilly from 16.10.18); Preutin 21.11.18; Trier, Germany 4.12.18; Coblenz 3.1.19; Colombey-les-Belles 17.4.19; Le Mans 6.5.19; Brest 19.5.19; Retd USA 3.6.19; Mitchel Field, NY 17.6.19; Park Field, Tenn 4.7.19; Rockwell Field, CA 29.9.19; Mather Field, CA 3.11.19; Ream Field, CA 24.1.30 (detts El Centro & Calexico, CA 17.3.20 - 30.7.20); Rockwell Field, CA 30.4.20 (flt detd Eugene, OR with dett at Medford, OR 6.20 - c.9.20); Mather Field, CA 3.11.20 (dett at Rockwell Field, CA to 1.21); Redesignated 91st Squadron 14.3.21; Eugene, OR 5.21 (dett at Medford, OR & flt at Camp Lewis, WA to c.9.21); Crissy Field, CA 12.10.21 (dett at Eugene, OR 8.22 - 9.22); Redesignated 91st Observation Squadron 25.1.23; DH-4s withdrawn c.1928.
Commanding Officer: Mjr RN Reynolds (7.18 - 8.18).

94th Aero/Pursuit Squadron
Retd from France as 94th Aero Squadron, based Mitchel Field, NY from 1.6.19 with DH-4s as partial equipment; Selfridge Field, MI 27.6.19; Kelly Field, TX c.31.8.19; Redesignated 94th Squadron 14.3.21; Ellington Field, TX 1.7.21; Selfridge Field, MI 1.7.22; Redesignated 94th Pursuit Squadron 25.1.23; DH-4s withdrawn when consolidated with 103rd Squadron 8.4.24.

95th Aero/Pursuit Squadron
Formed 12.8.19 as 95th Aero Squadron at Selfridge Field, MI with DH-4s as partial equipment; Kelly Field, TX 31.8.19; Redesignated 95th Squadron 14.3.21; Ellington Field, TX 1.7.21; Selfridge Field, MI 1.7.22; Redesignated 95th Pursuit Squadron 25.1.23; DH-4s withdrawn 1925.

96th Aero/Bombardment Squadron
Based by 1918 as 96th Aero Squadron at Clermont-Ferrand, France with DH-4s as partial equipment for day bombardment; Amanty 18.5.18 (assigned to 1st Army for the St.Mihiel, Lorraine, Meuse-Argonne areas); Maulan 23.9.18; Colombey-les-Belles 10.1.19; St.Denis-de-Pile 13.2.19; Libourne 12.4.19; Retd to USA 16.4.19; Arr Mitchel Field, NY 2.5.19; Ellington Field, TX 26.5.19; Camp Furlong, NM c.28.6.19; Fort Bliss, TX 3.7.19 (flight detd Douglas, AZ c.10.8.19 - 10.1.20); Kelly Field, TX 12.1.20; Langley Field, VA 20.5.20; Redesignated 96th Squadron 14.3.21; Kelly Field, TX 26.10.21; Langley Field, VA 30.6.22; Redesignated 96th Bombardment Squadron 25.1.23; DH-4s withdrawn 1928.
Commanding Officer: Mjr HM Brown (7.18 - 8.18).

99th Aero/Observation Squadron
Returned from France as 99th Aero Squadron and based from 24.5.19 at Mitchel Field, NY with DH-4s as partial equipment; Hazelhurst Field, NY 25.5.19; Camp Alfred Vail, NJ 7.19; Bolling Field, DC 17.8.19; Redesignated 94th Squadron 14.3.21; Redesignated 99th Observation Squadron 25.1.23; Kelly Field, TX 23.6.27; Disbanded 31.7.27.

100th Aero Squadron
Formed 27.8.17 at Kelly Field, TX as 100th Aero Squadron with DH-4 for Bombardment; St.Maxient, France 2.1.18; Redesignated 800th Aero Squadron 1.2.18.

104th Aero Squadron
At Upavon as 104th Aero Squadron from 24.12.17 (detts Salisbury to 6.6.18, Andover to 6.6.18, Yatesbury to 6.6.18); Netheravon 24.3.18; Salisbury 6.6.18; Winchester 10.7.18; in transit 19.7.18; St.Maxient with DH-4 as main equipment 22.7.18 (for Corps Observation work in the Lorraine, St.Mihiel, Meuse-Argonne areas); Epiez 4.8.18; Luxeuil-les-Bains 8.8.18; Soilly 8.9.18; Foucaucourt 20.9.18; Parois 4.11.18 (flt detd Barricourt 10.11.18); Belrain 30.11.18; Colombey-le-Belles 14.1.19; St-Denis-de-Pile 29.1.19; Libourne 3.2.19; Bordeaux 10.4.19; Retd to USA 18.4.19; At Roosevelt Field, NY from c.28.4.19 with DH-4 as main equipment; To Mitchell Field, NY c.1.5.19; To Fort Bliss, TX c.15.5.19; To Kelly Field, TX 6.19; Fort Bliss, TX 6.11.19 flt detd Marfa, TX 5.11.19 - 3.9.20, also Post Field 10.9.20 - 4.11.20 & Marfa, TX 4.11.20 - 14.3.21); Redesignated 13th Attack Squadron 14.3.21.
Commanding Officer: Lt CH Reynolds (7.18).

106th Observation Squadron
Formed 16.1.24 as 106th Observation Squadron ex 114th Observation Squadron at Birmingham, AL with DH-4s as partial equipment; DH-4s withdrawn 1933.

114th Observation Squadron
Formed 1.5.23 as 114th Squadron ex 135th Observation Squadron at Birmingham, AL with DH-4s as partial equipment; Redesignated 106th Observation Squadron 16.1.24.

115th Observation Squadron
Formed 16.6.24 as 115th Observation Squadron at Los Angeles, CA with DH-4s as partial equipment until these were withdrawn in 1932.

118th Observation Squadron
Formed 1.11.23 as 118th Observation Squadron at Hartford, CTn with DH-4s as partial equipment until these were withdrawn in 1932.

135th Aero/Observation Squadron
Based from 8.1.18 as 135th Aero Squadron at Waddington with DH-4 as main equipment for Corps Observation (detts at Scampton and South Carlton to 27.2.18); in transit to France 24.6.18 (for the Lorraine & St.Mihiel areas); Issoudun 2.7.18; Amanty 19.7.18; Ourches 30.7.18; Toul 30.9.18; Colombey-les-Belles 10.2.19; Tresses 23.2.19; Bordeaux 18.4.19; Retd to USA 25.4.19; Arr Hazelhurst Field, NY c.7.5.19; (Flt detd Fort Leavenworth, KS 30.4.20 - 30.6.20 & 6.9.20 - 3.11.20); Redesignated 22nd Squadron 14.3.21.

Reformed 21.1.22 as 135th Squadron at Birmingham, AL with DH-4s as partial equipment; Redesignated 135th Observation Squadron 25.1.23; Redesignated 114th Observation Squadron 1.5.23.
Commanding Officer 7.18 - 8.18: 1/Lt AB Thaw.

147th Aero Squadron
At Garden City, NY as 147th Aero Squadron from 19.3.19 with DH-4 as partial equipment; Selfridge Field, MI 27.4.19; Kelly Field, TX 31.8.19; Redesignated 17th Aero Squadron 14.3.21.

154th Observation Squadron
Formed 24.10.25 as 154th Observation Squadron at Little Rock, AK with DH-4s as partial equipment until these were withdrawn by 1934.

163rd Aero Squadron
In France in 1918 as 163rd Aero Squadron, assigned to the Front 27.10.18, with DH-4 for Day Bombardment; Ordered to be demobilised 8.4.19; Still in France 1.4.19, but not by 1.5.19; No details.

166th Aero Squadron
Based from 25.3.18 as 166th Aero Squadron at Catterick equipped with DH-4 for Bombardment; In transit to France 7.8.18 (for Day Bombing in the Meuse-Argonne area); Delouze 26.8.18; Vinets-sur-Aube 1.9.18; Delouze 7.9.18; Amanty 21.9.18; Maulan 25.9.18; Joppecourt 22.11.18; Trier, Germany 5.1.19; Colombey-les-Belles, France 17.4.19; Le Mans 3.5.19; Brest 19.5.19; Retd to USA 3.6.19; Mitchel Field, NY 17.6.19, now with DH-4 as partial equipment; Ellington Field, TX 7.19; Kelly Field, TX 26.9.19; Redesignated 49th Squadron 14.3.21.

168th Aero Squadron
In France as 168th Aero Squadron, assigned to the Front 30.9.18, with DH-4 for Corps Observation in the Lorraine area; Still in France 1.4.19, but not by 1.5.19; No details.

278th Aero Squadron
In France in 1918 as 278th Aero Squadron, assigned to the Front 29.10.18, with DH-4 for Army Observation in the Lorraine area; Still in France 1.4.19, but not by 1.5.19; No further details.

DH-4 A.S.32143 was shot down south of Metz by Oblt Wenig, CO of Jasta 80b, on 7 September 1918. (via Frank Cheesman)

354th Aero Squadron
In France in 1918 as 354th Aero Squadron, assigned to the Front 21.10.18, with DH-4 for Corps Observation in the Lorraine area; Still in France 1.4.19, but not by 1.5.19; No further details.

800th Aero Squadron
Formed 1.2.18 as 800th Aero Squadron by redesignating 100th Aero Squadron at St.Maxient, France; Champ de Tir de Souge 28.2.18 (HQ & 'A' Flt) (by 8.18, 'B' Flt at Coetquidan under 1/Lt H Wilder; 'C' Flt at Valdahon under 1/Lt M Chapman); Retd to USA 4.19 and based Mitchel Field, NY; Disbanded 2.7.19.
Commanding Officer 8.18: 1/Lt RE Bowers.

US ARMY SERIAL NUMBERS

Up until 1921 US Army aircraft were allocated airframe serial numbers in a straight sequence commencing at No.1 for the Wright Brothers Model A of 1909 and progressing to almost 70,000 by mid-1921. From the beginning of the 1922 fiscal year, which actually began on 1 July 1921, aircraft were serialled with the fiscal year number followed by an individual number beginning at 1 each fiscal year. Under both systems the full serial number included the prefix A.S. to indicate Air Service. Until May 1918 the prefix S.C. had been used, but this was dropped when the Air Service was removed from its jurisdiction. When the Air Service became the U.S. Army Air Corps on 2 July 1926 the prefix was changed to A.C.. Such prefixes were not always painted on the aircraft. A number of aircraft were rebuilt and then received random serial numbers. Surviving information on the serial number allocations of U.S. Army DH-4 variants is incomplete, but known batches and examples are as follows [the A.S. prefix is used in all cases, rather than attempt to distinguish the earlier S.C. prefixes]:

Known U.S. production and rebuilds

Aeromarine
DH-4B rebuilds (US Air Corps Contract No.35522):
A.S.22-1100 to 1142

Atlantic Aircraft Corporation
This was the name given to the American branch of the Fokker company. DH-4B and DH-4M-2 rebuilds.

DH-4B:
A.S.62995 to 63000
A.S.63063 to 63209
A.S.23-425 to 427

DH-4B (US Air Corps Contract No.35622):
A.S.23-406

DH-4M (US Air Corps Contract No.201524):
A.S.22864 to A.S.22884
A.S.23163 to A.S.23330
A.S.23381 to A.S.23410
A.S.23609 to A.S.23629
A.S.23683
A.S.23942 to A.S.23947
A.S.28808
A.S.29129
A.S.30063 to A.S.30099
A.S.30355 to A.S.30360
A.S.30452
A.S.30459 to A.S.30479
A.S.30640
A.S.30731 to A.S.30917
A.S.30184 to A.S.31167
A.S.31231
A.S.31258
A.S.31366
A.S.31377
A.S.31556
A.S.31575
A.S.31624 to A.S.31690
A.S.31756 to A.S.31807
A.S.31820 (bought by France)
A.S.31827
A.S.31829 (bought by France)
A.S.31844
A.S.31850
A.S.31856
A.S.31858 (bought by France)
A.S.31871 to 31886
A.S.31929 to 31936 (bought by France)
A.S.31940 to 31949
A.S.31955 (bought by Phillipines)
A.S.31958
A.S.62945
A.S.62969
A.S.63545
A.S.63680
A.S.64611 to 64627

DH-4M (US Air Corps Contract No.26186):
A.S.62969
A.S.63005 to 63053
A.S.63220 to 63369
A.S.22-257
A.S.22-356 to 359
A.S.23-685 to 688
A.S.23-702
A.S.23-716 to 725
A.S.23-732
A.S.23-740 to 743
A.S.23-751 to 757
A.S.23-766 to 774
A.S.24-034 to 037

DH-4M (US Air Corps Contract No unknown):
A.S.64562

Boeing
Converted 111 Liberty-engined DH-4s to DH-4Bs, these being delivered between 6 March and 1 July 1920 with new serial numbers. 50 of these were returned to Boeing in 1923 for reworking, when they were given further new serial numbers.
Built a considerable number of DH-4s in the twenties as the Model 16. Most were supplied to the US military, but c/n 652 was built for civil use and c/n's 653-658 were DH-4Bs for Cuba.

The CO-7 was a Boeing-built variant fitted with a new thick-section tapered wing of which only two were built (A.S.31216 and A.S.23-109). A single CO-8 variant (A.S.23163) was also built by Atlantic, this being fitted with Loening wings and used by Captain A.W.Stevens for high altitude and long-range photography experiments.

DH-4B:
A.S.63461 to 63507
A.S.63761 to 63823
A.S.63936
[NOTE - A.S.63398 to 63475, A.S.63639 to 63672, A.S.63764 to 63800 and A.S.68140 to 68220 have been quoted for the batches Boeing DH-4B rebuilds, put probably mistakenly]

DH-4B (US Air Corps Contract No.34022):
A.S.22-1002 to 1038

Lts Lowell Smith and Paul Richter demonstrating flight refuelling on 27.6.23. (via Terry Treadwell)

DH-4M (US Air Corps Contract No.117323):
A.S.23570 to 23579
A.S.24171 to 24304
A.S.24319 to 24330
A.S.29133 to 29136
A.S.29183
A.S.30131 to 30284
A.S.30422 to 30446
A.S.30456
A.S.30517 to 30520
A.S.30708
A.S.32205
A.S.32377
A.S.32703

DH-4M (US Air Corps Contract No.140324):
A.S.22886 to 23109
A.S.23340
A.S.23447
A.S.24318
A.S.29125
A.S.29138 to 29154
A.S.30954 to 31082
A.S.31184 to 31220
A.S.31242 to 31246
A.S.31260 to 31345
A.S.31368
A.S.31382 to 31498
A.S.31561
A.S.31578
A.S.31715 (bought by France)
A.S.31835
A.S.31909
A.S.31956
A.S.32087 to 32188
A.S.32247 to 32319
A.S.32461 to 32578
A.S.32733 to 33049
A.S.24-451 to 454

DH-4M (US Air Corps Contract No.625):
A.S.68591 to 68592

Cox-Klemin
DH-4B rebuilds (US Air Corps Contract No.83023):
A.S.23-699
A.S.23-709 to 715

Dayton-Wright
Received wartime contracts for 4,000 DH-4s, to be numbered A.S.29059 to A.S.33058. Of these, 3,101 were completed, A.S.29160 to A.S.30058 being cancelled after the Armistice. A later order for 1,000 was also cancelled at the Armistice. In addition, 2 DH-4 Honeymoon Express (A.S.23432 and A.S.40128) and four DH-4L (A.S.62945 to A.S.62948) were ordered and completed, as well as two DH-4P-1 (A.S.42126 and A.S.42127).

Douglas
At least one DH-4B rebuild.

DH-4: M-328 to M-427 [Post Office mail numbers]
DH-4: M-605 to M-647 [Post Office mail numbers]
DH-4B (JN-2C) A.S.26-003

Fisher Body
4,000 DH-4 were ordered on wartime contracts, to be numbered A.S.22804 to A.S.25803 and A.S.36232 to A.S.37231, but only the first 1,600 of these (A.S.22804 to A.S.24403) were completed, the remainder being cancelled after the Armistice.

Post-war rebuilds were numbered as follows:

A.S.64279. DH-4B
A.S.64464. DH-4M
A.S.22-1053 to 1058. DH-4B (US Air Corps Contract No.34522)
A.S.23-423. DH-4B
A.S.24-247 to 253. DH-4B
A.S.24-457. DH-4B
A.S.25-161 to 163. DH-4B

Gallaudet
DH-4B and DH-4M rebuilds.

DH-4B (US Air Corps Contract No.82923):
A.S.23-660 to 674
A.S.24-115 to 131
A.S.25-078 to 083

L.W.F. Corporation
DH-4B rebuilds:
A.S.64496 to 64559
A.S.64587

Naval Aircraft Factory
DH-4B rebuilds. Included A6113 to A6192, also A6514, for the US Marine Corps.

Standard
500 DH-4 were ordered on a wartime contract, to be numbered A.S.39368 to A.S.39867. Only 140 were completed, A.S.39508 being cancelled after the Armistice.

Thomas-Morse
DH-4B rebuilds (US Air Corps Contract No.35622):
A.S.22-1155 to 1188

Witteman-Lewis
DH-4B and DH-4M rebuilds.

DH-4B (US Air Corps Contract No.34522):
A.S.22-1060 to 1094

DH-4B (US Air Corps Contract No.83123):
A.S.23-726
A.S.23-730
A.S.23-738
A.S.23-744
A.S.23-758
A.S.25-085 to 089

Unknown companies
DH-4B rebuilds:
A.S.68656
A.S.23-459 to 463
A.S.23-467 to 471
A.S.23-515 to 524
A.S.23-552
A.S.24-051 to 054
A.S.24-064 to 085
A.S.24-095
A.S.25-046 to 048
A.S.25-052
A.S.25-054
A.S.25-107
A.S.25-131
A.S.25-445

Known individual details

"1755" DH-4. 7th Aviation Instruction Center, France, 1918
A.S.1378x DH-4. Rich Field, TX, spun nr a/f 19.11.18 (Cdt RD Burdin minor injuries & passenger killed)
A.S.22349 DH-4. Brooks Field, taxying accident, Hillsboro, TX 13.4.23 (1/Lt RG Breene unhurt); Repaired
A.S.22505 DH-4B. Crissy Field, FL in bad weather, Eugene, OR 6.2.23 (1/Lt RL Maughan unhurt)
A.S.22509 DH-4. Scott Field, FL N of a/f in fog 8.12.23 (1/Lt C Elleman & passenger both unhurt)
A.S.22804 to A.S.25803. Ordered from Fisher. Cancelled from 24404
A.S.22811 DH-4
A.S.22846 DH-4. Wright Field, hit trees nr a/f 2.12.18 (2/Lt JU Brumbach killed)
A.S.22856 DH-4 McCook Field P-125
A.S.22864 DH-4M-2S. Langley Field 1927
A.S.23873 DH-4B-1. To US Navy as *A6379*
A.S.22884 XCO-7 (ex DH-4M-1). Boeing-built as Type 42 (c/n 520)
A.S.22886 DH-4M-1. Boeing rebuild (c/n 529). Kelly Field 1927
A.S.22894 DH-4B-1. To US Navy as *A6376*
A.S.22896 DH-4B-1. To US Navy as *A6382*
A.S.22899 DH-4B-1. To US Navy as *A6383*
A.S.22909 DH-4. McCook Field P-160
A.S.22911 DH-4B-1. To US Navy as *A6384*
A.S.22912 DH-4M-1. Boeing rebuild (c/n 539). Kelly Field, spun in 6m N of a/f 16.4.26 (2/Lt PB Fuoua)
A.S.22951 DH-4M. EF, FL nr Big Foot, TX 20.1.26 (EB Storiting)
A.S.22974 DH-4M-1. Boeing rebuild (c/n 559). Kelly Field, FL, crashed 2m S of a/f, 12.12.25 (2/Lt RW Gibson)
A.S.22979 DH-4M-1. Boeing rebuild (c/n 569). Kelly Field 1927; Crashed nr Yturri Field, TX 24.6.29 (2/Lt LC Wilson)
A.S.22981 DH-4M-1. Boeing rebuild (c/n 579). Kelly Field 1927; Crashed nr Brooks Field 6.2.30 (Cdt Thomas)
A.S.23000 DH-4M-1. Boeing rebuild (c/n 588); to DH-4M-1T. San Antonio Air Intermediate Depot 1927
A.S.23006 DH-4M-1. Boeing rebuild (c/n 597)
A.S.23007 DH-4M-1. Boeing rebuild (c/n 606). Luke Field 1927; Crashed nr Kaneohe, HI 10.3.30 (1/Lt LBF Griffin & Sgt Thermenos)
A.S.23042 DH-4B-1. To US Navy as *A6387*
A.S.23049 DH-4B-1. To US Navy as *A6385*
A.S.23060 DH-4B. To US Navy as *A6373*
A.S.23075 DH-4. McCook Field P-109
A.S.23102 DH-4B-1. To US Navy as *A6377*
A.S.23109 XCO-7A (ex DH-4M-1). Boeing-built as Type 42 (c/n 519)
A.S.23130 DH-4. Langley Field, turned at low speed, sideslipped in 9.11.18 (2/Lt EF Eagan killed)
A.S.23131 DH-4B-1. To US Navy as *A6388*
A.S.23163 XC0-8. McCook Field P-369
A.S.23177 DH-4M-2. San Antonio Air Intermediate Depot 1927
A.S.23196 DH-4M-2K. Fairfield Air Intermediate Depot 1927; Hit pole nr Augusta, GA 1.6.27 (1/Lt ME Gross)
A.S.23198 DH-4B-1. To US Navy as *A6386*
A.S.23201 DH-4M-2K. Langley Field 1927; Crashed 3m N of Casterville, TX 14.9.28 (Cdt SO Yoder)
A.S.23207 DH-4M-2. Langley Field 1927; Hit tree landing nr Berne, IN 16.10.27 (2/Lt JG Hopkins)
A.S.23256 DH-4M-2. Bolling Field, DC 1927
A.S.23262 DH-4M-2. Fairfield Station Supply 1927; Ground looped, Yturri Field, TX 18.12.29 (Cdt CE Smith)
A.S.23287? DH-4. Camp Stotsenberg, Pampanga, Phillipines. engine failure, forced landed, hit flagpole, crashed 12.8.20 (2/Lt WC Maxwell killed)
A.S.23306 DH-4M-2. Chanute Field 1927
A.S.23330 DH-4M-2. FL nr Charleston, SC 22.9.25 (Sgt D Johnson); Marshall Field 1927
A.S.23331 DH-4B-1. To US Navy as *A6378*
A.S.23340 DH-4M-1. Boeing rebuild (c/n 530). FL nr Langley Field 11.9.25 (Cpl LC Lee)
A.S.23352 DH-4B-1. To US Navy as *A6381*
A.S.23369 DH-4. McCook Field P-126
A.S.23376 DH-4B-1. To US Navy as *A6380*
A.S.23381 DH-4M-2. Marshall Field 1927
A.S.23405 DH-4. Camp Benning, Ca, overturned landing in electric storm, high wind and rain, Deepstop, CA 10.7.20 (Capt HA Dogan slightly injured & passenger killed)
A.S.23410 DH-4M-2. Fairfield Air Intermediate Depot 1927; Crashed, DBR, nr La Jolla, CA 6.2.30 (Cdt AS Mansfield)
A.S.23420 DH-4B. McCook Field, EF, FL 2m S of Dayton, OH 18.6.24 (1/Lt JA McCready)
A.S.23432 XDH-4B5. McCook Field P-76
A.S.23447 DH-4M-1. Boeing rebuild (c/n 540). FL nr Williamsburg 5.10.25 (S/Sgt F Tyler); Post Field 1927; EF, FL 15m E of March Field, CA 10.8.28 (Cdt HJ Zimmerman)
A.S.23458 DH-4B. McCook Field, hit tree on TO, Knoxville, TN 11.12.23 (2/Lt CL Williams minor injuries & passenger unhurt)
A.S.23466 DH-4B. Crissy Field, EF on T/O 11.3.24 (Sgt RH Fatt unhurt)
A.S.23570 DH-4M-1. Boeing rebuild (c/n 490). San Antonio Air Intermediate Depot 1927; Kelly Field, collided with A.S.24330 landing 1.4.27 (2/Lt JW Bowman)
A.S.23574 DH-4M-1. Boeing rebuild (c/n 476)
A.S.23578 DH-4M-1. Boeing rebuild (c/n 475). San Antonio Air Intermediate Depot 1927
A.S.23579 DH-4M-1. Boeing rebuild (c/n 472). France Field, CZ 1927
A.S.23609 DH-4M-2. Marshall Field 1927
A.S.23614 DH-4M-2. Air Corps dett Fort Levenham 1927
A.S.23683 DH-4M-2. Bolling Field, DC 1927; Crashed Fort Crockett, TX 29.1.31 (2/Lt MM Beach)
A.S.23698 Rebuilt as A.S.22-257
A.S.23707 Renumbered A.S.25-078
A.S.23715 DH-4B-1. Edgewood Arsenal 1927
A.S.23763 DH-4. Detroit, MI, struck flagpole, crashed 11.11.18 (2/Lt EC Morrow killed)
A.S.23783 DH-4. Hit flagpole nr Detroit, MI 11.11.18 (2/Lt KC Norrow killed)
A.S.23792 DH-4B-1 (later DH-4B-2). To US Navy as *A6372* [or 23792?]
A.S.23797 DH-4B-1. To US Navy as *A6374*
A.S.23798 DH-4B-1. To US Navy as *A6375*
A.S.23805 DH-4B. Post Field, hit fence landing in fog 22.2.24 (Cpl LD Frederick unhurt)
A.S.23816 DH-4B-1. To US Navy as *A6368*
A.S.23822 DH-4B-1. To US Navy as *A6369*
A.S.23824 DH-4B-1. To US Navy as *A6370*
A.S.23825 & 23826. DH-4B-1. To US Navy as *A6356* & *A6357*
A.S.23828 DH-4B-1. To US Navy as *A6371*
A.S.23829 & 23830. DH-4B-1. To US Navy as *A6358* & *A6359*
A.S.23842 DH-4B-1 (later DH-4B-2). To US Navy as *A6352*
A.S.23886 Renumbered A.S.25-083
A.S.23920 Renumbered A.S.25-085, later A.S.23-753
A.S.23921 DH-4B-1. To US Navy as *A6364*
A.S.23926 DH-4B-1. To US Navy as *A6365* or *A6366*
A.S.23939 DH-4B-1. To US Navy as *A6367*
A.S.23947 DH-4M-2. Selfridge Field 1927; Crashed nr Yturri, TX 11.6.29 (2/Lt GF Smith)
A.S.23962 DH-4. Post Field, turning to land, wing struck ground, a/c overturned, burst into flames 27.10.19 (Mjr WH Sanders killed)
A.S.23980 DH-4B-1. To US Navy as *A6360*
A.S.23986 DH-4B-1. To US Navy as *A6361*
A.S.23989 DH-4B-1. To US Navy as *A6362*
A.S.23991 DH-4B-1. To US Navy as *A6363*
A.S.23994 DH-4B-1. To US Navy as *A6353*
A.S.24000 DH-4B-1. To US Navy as *A6354*
A.S.24006 DH-4. Transcontinental Reliability Flight, landed in poor field, hit tree, Bustleton, PA 5.10.19 (Lt Col TF Dodd killed & passenger unhurt)
A.S.24016 DH-4B-1. To US Navy as *A6355*
A.S.24158 DH-4A. Kelly Field, hit flagpole, crashed nr a/f 21.5.20 (2/Lt AM St.John & passenger both killed)
A.S.24171 DH-4M-1. Boeing rebuild (c/n 468). Kelly Field 1927
A.S.24174 DH-4. Luke Field, NY, spun in from formation, burnt out 24.10.41 (1/Lt UL Sergant & Sgt VE Vickers both killed)
A.S.24180 DH-4M-1. Boeing rebuild (c/n 462); Kelly Field, landing accident 6.10.25 (2/Lt WT Meyer); to DH-4M-1T; Brooks Field 1927; Crashed nr March Field 3.4.29 (Cdt Sullivan)
A.S.24185 DH-4M-1. Boeing rebuild (c/n 466); to DH-4M-1T. Kelly Field 1927; Hit tree nr Red Rock, TX 8.7.27 (Sgt B Wallace)

DH-4 A.S.22811.

Boeing XCO-7A 23109. (via Gordon Swanborough)

Atlantic XCO-8 23163 (P-369). (via Gordon Swanborough)

A DH-4 variant with outsize wheels and modified exhaust pipes. (Frank Yeoman via Frank Cheesman)

A DH-4 squadron poses for the camera with its mounts.

A DH-4 variant with the code '10 on the nose'. (D.M.Hannah)

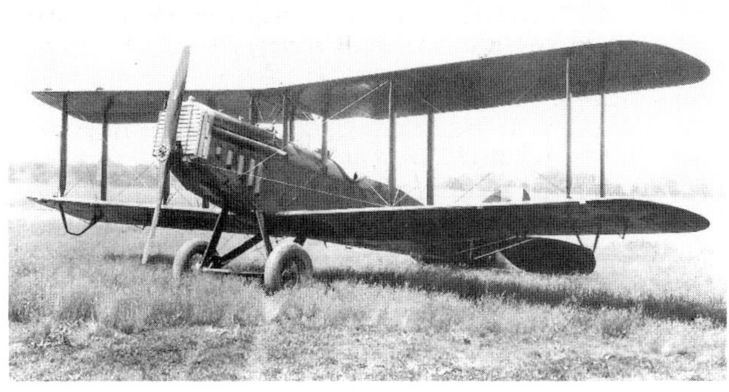

A D.H.4B with a modified radiator.

A DH-4B with a modified exhaust pipe.

A.S.24189 DH-4M-1. Boeing rebuild (c/n 477). Kelly Field 1927
A.S.24190 DH-4. Turned to avoid mountain with failing motor, spun in, Sanderson, TX 24.4.20 (2/Lt DM Hansoll & Sgt JW Welch both killed)
A.S.24224 DH-4. To US Postal Service
A.S.24227 DH-4. To US Postal Service
A.S.24232 DH-4B. Chanute Field, IL, EF, FL nr a/f 19.6.24 (1/Lt DM Reeves unhurt)
A.S.24239 DH-4. To US Postal Service
A.S.24259 DH-4. 11th Aero Sqn, Marfa, TX 6.19
A.S.24297 DH-4M-1. Boeing rebuild (c/n 470). Kelly Field 1927
A.S.24298 DH-4M-1. Boeing rebuild (c/n 479). San Antonio Air Intermediate Depot 1927; Crashed nr Brooks Field 20.8.30 (Cdt LR Sandell)
A.S.24300 DH-4M-1. Boeing rebuild (c/n 485). Rockwell Air Intermediate Depot 1927; Crashed nr March Field 4.6.29 (Cdt Church)
A.S.24301 DH-4M-1. Boeing rebuild (c/n 463). Wright Field 1927
A.S.24302 DH-4M-1. Boeing rebuild (c/n 484). Kelly Field 1927
A.S.24303 DH-4M-1. Boeing rebuild (c/n 488). Luke Field 1927; Crashed nr Kawaihawai, HI 18.8.30 (2/Lt WJ Scott)
A.S.24304 DH-4M-1. Boeing rebuild (c/n 496). Inst. Arkansas National Guard, Little Rock 1927
A.S.24305 DH-4M-1. Boeing rebuild (c/n 469); to DH-4M-1T. Kelly Field 1927
A.S.24307 DH-4M-1. Boeing rebuild (c/n 473). Stalled Fort Sam Houston N, TX 4.2.27 (Cdt RH Ranney)
A.S.24314 DH-4M-1. Boeing rebuild (c/n 494). San Antonio Air Intermediate Depot 1927
A.S.24318 DH-4M-1. Boeing rebuild (c/n 495); to DH-4M-1T. Kelly Field 1927
A.S.24319 DH-4M-1. Boeing rebuild (c/n 492). Kelly Field 1927
A.S.24324 DH-4M-1. Boeing rebuild (c/n 486). Kelly Field 1927
A.S.24325 DH-4M-1. Boeing rebuild (c/n 482). Kelly Field 1927
A.S.24328 DH-4M-1. Boeing rebuild (c/n 489). Luke Field 1927; Crashed Mokapu Peninsular, HI 3.6.30 (2/Lt JH Davis)
A.S.24330 DH-4M-1. Boeing rebuild (c/n 481). Kelly Field, collided with A.S.23570 landing 1.4.27; Crashed nr March Field 7.5.28 (Cdt HE Hall); Crashed nr Caniss, CA 3.10.29 (Cdt Johnson)
A.S.24558 DH-4M. Boston Airport, EF on T/O, FL 29.6.24 (1/Lt FB Valentine)
A.S.25037 DH-4. Kelly Field, engine failure, forced landed, hit building, crashed, caught fire 12.10.20 (Sgt CB Allen killed)
A.S.25381 DH-4M. T/O accident nr Lisbon, OH 13.6.27
A.S.25455 DH-4B. Fort Bliss, EF on T/O, Denver, CO 16.6.24 (1/Lt RH Clark & passenger unhurt)
A.S.27107 DH-4B. Kelly Field, EF, FL on a/f 7.3.24 (2/Lt CN O'Conner)
A.S.28808 DH-4M-2. Fairfield Air Intermediate Depot 1927
A.S.28494 DH-4B. Kelly Field 8.20
A.S.29059 to A.S.33058. Ordered from Dayton-Wright. Cancelled from A.S.29160
A.S.29061 DH-4. Sideslipped in off bank, Ellington Field 23.2.19 (2/Lt CS Price killed)
A.S.29125 DH-4M-1. Boeing rebuild (c/n 550). Luke Field 1927
A.S.29129 DH-4M-2. Fairfield Air Intermediate Depot 1927; Crashed nr March Field 14.11.29 (Cdt CC Beyer killed)
A.S.29133 DH-4M-1. Boeing rebuild (c/n 499). San Antonio Air Intermediate Depot 1927; Accident, Brooks Field, TX 24.11.30 (Cdt L Williams)
A.S.29136 DH-4M-1. Boeing rebuild (c/n 510). Kelly Field 1927; Crashed in mountains, San Juan Capistran, CA 16.6.28 (Cdt WR Shepherd)
A.S.29138 DH-4M-1. Boeing rebuild (c/n 560). France Field, CZ 1927
A.S.29154 DH-4M-1. Boeing rebuild (c/n 570). Kelly Field 1927; Crashed 3m S of Brooks Field 2.5.28 (Cdt I Best killed)
A.S.29183 DH-4M-1. Boeing rebuild (c/n 509). Mid-air collision with A.S.32975 nr San Antonio, TX 7.1.27 (Cdt CS Shields killed)
A.S.29662 DH-4. Wrecked
A.S.30065 DH-4B-1. To US Navy as *A6392*
A.S.30066 DH-4M-2P. Langley Field 1927; Crashed nr Kelly Field, TX 7.2.30 (Cdt EM Rouse)
A.S.30067 DH-4B-1. To US Navy as *A6397*
A.S.30099 DH-4M-2P. Richards Field 1927; Crashed nr Brooks Field 5.11.29 (Sgt JL Waught)
A.S.30130 DH-4. McCook Field P-78
A.S.30131 DH-4M-1. Boeing rebuild (c/n 491). Kelly Field 1927
A.S.30135 DH-4M-1. Boeing rebuild (c/n 502). France Field, CZ 1927
A.S.30138 DH-4B-1. To US Navy as *A6391*
A.S.30142 DH-4B-1. To US Navy as *A6398*
A.S.30152 DH-4B-1. To US Navy as *A6393*
A.S.30155 DH-4B-1. To US Navy as *A6390*
A.S.30174 DH-4B-1. To US Navy as *A6396*
A.S.30186 DH-4B-1. To US Navy as *A6394*
A.S.30210 DH-4M-1. Boeing rebuild (c/n 493). Kelly Field 1927
A.S.30248 DH-4M-1. Boeing rebuild (c/n 471). Langley Field 1927
A.S.30251 DH-4M-1. Boeing rebuild (c/n 480). Kelly Field 1927; Spun in nr Brooks Field 5.12.28 (Cdt PH Atkinson killed)
A.S.30280 DH-4M-1. Boeing rebuild (c/n 504). Luke Field 1927
A.S.30284 DH-4M-1. Boeing rebuild (c/n 467). Luke Field 1927; Crashed nr Waimanalo, HI 1.10.30 (2/Lt HW Darr)
A.S.30346 Renumbered A.S.24-437
A.S.30355 DH-4M-2. Langley Field 1927; Crashed nr Kelly Field, TX 7.4.31 (2/Lt HA Hughes killed)
A.S.30422 DH-4M-1. Boeing rebuild (c/n 464). Kelly Field 1927; Circuits & bumps, crashed 2m E of March Field 20.2.28 (Cdt BI Boradman [Boardman?] killed)
A.S.30433 DH-4M-1. Boeing rebuild (c/n 503). Kelly Field 1927; Accident 9m S of Victorville, CA 21.2.29 (Cdt JM Elivca)
A.S.30443 DH-4M-1. Boeing rebuild (c/n 465). San Antonio Air Intermediate Depot 1927
A.S.30446 DH-4M-1. Boeing rebuild (c/n 487). Kelly Field 1927; Crashed nr Loruse, TX 1.3.28 (Cdt JM Peyton)
A.S.30452 DH-4M-2K. Aberdeen Proving Ground 1927
A.S.30456 DH-4M-1. Boeing rebuild (c/n 474). San Antonio Air Intermediate Depot 1927; Crashed nr Brooks Field

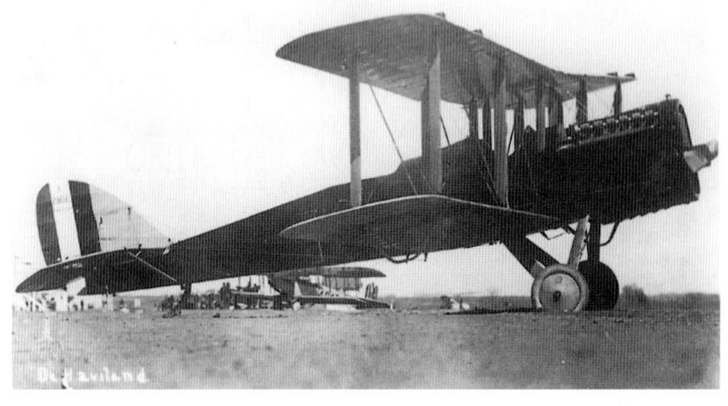

DH-4 A29152. (via D.M.Hannah)

A DH-4 fitted with a Lamblin radiator.

A formation of DH-4Ms, led by A.S.31219. (via D.M.Hannah)

9.4.30 (2/Lt BC Muse)
A.S.30459 DH-4M-2P. Fairfield Air Intermediate Depot 1927
A.S.30466 DH-4M-2. Bolling Field, DC 1927
A.S.30469 DH-4M-2. Middletown Air Intermediate Depot 1927; Accident, Bayside, TX 9.9.30 (1/Lt FD Lynch)
A.S.30479 DH-4M-2P. McCook Field P-433; Wright Field 1927
A.S.30517 DH-4M-1. Boeing rebuild (c/n 501). Rockwell Air Intermediate Depot 1927
A.S.30520 DH-4M-1. Boeing rebuild (c/n 483). San Antonio Air Intermediate Depot 1927; Crashed nr Elmendorf Field, TX 4.4.29 (Lt Murttia)
A.S.30590 DH-4. McCook Field P-92
A.S.30607 DH-4M-2P. Bolling Field, DC 1927
A.S.30632 DH-4. McCook Field P-102
A.S.30640 DH-4M-2K. Langley Field 1927; Crashed nr Langley Field 28.8.28 (Lt CW Carnish)
A.S.30708 DH-4M-1. Boeing rebuild (c/n 506); to DH-4M-1T; Crashed nr Eagle Pass, TX while landing 20.12.26 (2/Lt DF Fritch)
A.S.30723 DH-4. McCook Field P-82
A.S.30727 DH-4. McCook Field P-91
A.S.30731 DH-4M-2P. San Antonio Air Intermediate Depot 1927
A.S.30752 DH-4M-2P. Mitchel Field 1927; Crashed nr Benaides, TX 9.3.29 (Lt Lowe)
A.S.30753 DH-4M. Circuits & bumps, crashed nr Hempstead, NY 22.6.26 (Mjr WL Moose & passenger both killed)
A.S.30800 DH-4M-2P. Chanute Field 1927; Crashed nr Kelly Field, TX 19.8.31 (2/Lt FH Robinson)
A.S.30805 DH-4BP-2. McCook Field P-425; Scott Field Station Supply 1927; Crashed nr Gulf, TX 5.10.29 (1/Lt WK Moran)
A.S.30807 DH-4M. Crashed nr Kelly Field, TX 7.4.31 (Mr C Hu)
A.S.30812 DH-4M-2. San Antonio Air Intermediate Depot 1927
A.S.30813 DH-4M-2P. France Field, CZ 1927
A.S.30814 DH-4M-2. Inst. Colorado National Guard, Denver 1927
A.S.30817 DH-4M-2. Ditched off Hampton Roads 25.3.26 (Cdt EJ Rogers); Recovered and rebuilt; Woodward Field 1927
A.S.30845 DH-4B. Spun in nr Del Rio, TX 20.6.19 (2/Lt OE Grazier & passenger both killed)
A.S.30846 DH-4. McCook Field P-105
A.S.30855 DH-4. McCook Field P-93 and P-122
A.S.30859 DH-4M. Mid-air collision nr Chenute Field, IL 22.12.26 (2/Lt RH Lawter & passenger both killed)
A.S.30875 DH-4M. Ditched off Barnegat Inlet, NJ 17.2.27 (2/Lt WL Harris & passenger both killed)
A.S.30880 DH-4M-2. Marshall Field 1927; Crashed nr Los Angeles, CA 23.4.29 (2/Lt HF Brown)
A.S.30885 DH-4M-2. San Antonio Air Intermediate Depot 1927; Marked '116' at one time
A.S.30886 DH-4M-2. San Antonio Air Intermediate Depot 1927
A.S.30892 DH-4M-2P. Mitchel Field 1927
A.S.30894 DH-4. McCook Field P-81
A.S.30895 DH-4. Spun in nr Fulshier, TX 23.5.19 (2/Lt FP Manaker killed)
A.S.30897 DH-4. Attempted to land in darkness, hit roof of building, nr Austin, TX 6.9.19 (1/Lt MA Bateman killed)
A.S.30913 DH-4. McCook Field P-94
A.S.30954 DH-4M-1. Boeing rebuild (c/n 497). Kelly Field 1927
A.S.30980 DH-4M-1. Boeing rebuild (c/n 511). Kelly Field 1927
A.S.30995 DH-4. Low flying, spun in off steep bank, tank exploded, a/c caught fire, Polester(?), TX 30.5.19 (2/Lt ES Sladen killed)
A.S.31062 DH-4. 20th Aero Sqn, bombing raid on troops at Buzancy-Bois de Barricourt, in combat with Fokker DVII nr Buzancy, shot down OOC in flames nr Bayonville, pm 23.10.18 (2/Lt JH Weimer & 1/Lt HE Turner both killed)
A.S.31079 DH-4. Partial engine failure, turned and crashed, Montgomery, AL 29.12.19 (2/Lt CW Schumacher killed)
A.S.31082 DH-4M-1. Boeing rebuild (c/n 580). Hit fence nr Consales, TX, while landing 8.6.26 (Cdt EL McMillan)
A.S.31084 DH-4M-2P. Post Field 1927
A.S.31095 DH-4M-2P. Phillipines 1927
A.S.31108 DH-4. McCook Field P-56
A.S.31135 DH-4M-2. Kelly Field 1927
A.S.31159 DH-4M-2P. Kelly Field 1927
A.S.31164 DH-4M-2. Mitchel Field 1927
A.S.31167 DH-4M-1. Boeing rebuild (c/n 580)

Ground crew swinging the propeller of a DH-4 in the snow in late 1918. (via Terry Treadwell)

A.S.31184 DH-4M-1. Boeing rebuild (c/n 589). France Field, CZ 1927

A.S.31200 DH-4M-1. Boeing rebuild (c/n 598). Rockwell Air Intermediate Depot 1927

A.S.31202 DH-4M-1. Boeing rebuild (c/n 607). Kelly Field 1927; Crashed nr Oceanside, CA 20.10.28 (Cdt LI Harmon); '24' on nose at one time

A.S.31205 DH-4M-1. Boeing rebuild (c/n 541). Dallas 1927; Crashed nr March Field 7.11.29 (Cdt JM Poicomb)

A.S.31216 XCO-7B (ex DH-4M-1). Boeing-built as Type 42 (c/n 521). McCook Field P-368

A.S.31219 DH-4M-1. Boeing rebuild (c/n 531). EF, FL, crashed Scott AFB, IL 28.11.26 (1/Lt WF Robinson)

A.S.31220 DH-4M-1. Boeing rebuild (c/n 551); Crashed nr Shines, TX 23.4.25 (S/Sgt BR Erstwine)

A.S.31231 DH-4M. Ditched in California Bay, CA 26.3.28 (2/Lt TJ Munchof killed & passenger seriously injured)

A.S.31242 DH-4M-1. Boeing rebuild (c/n 561). Kelly Field, crashed nr a/f 16.2.27 (Cdt JW Green killed)

A.S.31246 DH-4M-1. Boeing rebuild (c/n 571); to DH-4M-1T. San Antonio Air Intermediate Depot 1927; Crashed Crissy Field 19.6.31 (2/Lt AR Kingham)

A.S.31260 DH-4M-1. Boeing rebuild (c/n 581). Luke Field 1927

A.S.31262 DH-4M-1. Boeing rebuild (c/n 590). Rockwell Air Intermediate Depot 1927

A.S.31265 DH-4M-1. Boeing rebuild (c/n 599). Rockwell Air Intermediate Depot 1927

A.S.31271 DH-4M-1. Boeing rebuild (c/n 608). March Field 1927; Crashed nr Santa Barbara 22.6.29 (Cdt Museholder)

A.S.31274 DH-4M-1. Boeing rebuild (c/n 522). Sand Point 1927; Ditched in San Francisco Bay 14.6.31 (Lt RB Hurst)

A.S.31287 DH-4M-1. Boeing rebuild (c/n 532). Scott Field Station Supply 1927; Crashed nr Brooks Field 9.2.28 (AF Hallinger)

A.S.31298 DH-4M-1. Boeing rebuild (c/n 542); EF, FL nr Ealstead, TX 22.8.25 (Cdt JF Buckman)

A.S.31301 DH-4M-1. Boeing rebuild (c/n 552). Luke Field 1927; 4th Sqn Luke Field, crashed Waimanalo Beach, HI 19.11.28 (Lt D Goodrich unhurt)

A.S.31306 DH-4M-1. Boeing rebuild (c/n 562); to DH-4M-1T. Brooks Field 1927

A.S.31307 DH-4M-1. Boeing rebuild (c/n 572). Kelly Field 1927; Crashed nr March Field 7.11.29 (Cdt JA Anderson)

A.S.31318 DH-4M-1. Boeing rebuild (c/n 582). Luke Field 1927

A.S.31335 DH-4B-1. To US Navy as *A6399*

A.S.31345 DH-4M-1. Boeing rebuild (c/n 591). FL, nosed over nr Kahuku Point, HI 2.9.26 (Capt H Pascale)

A.S.31366 DH-4B-2K. Mitchel Field 1927; Crashed nr Coast Guard Stn, NY 16..27 (2/Lt JW Boman)

A.S.31368 DH-4M-1. Boeing rebuild (c/n 600). Luke Field 1927; Crashed nr Waimanalo, HI 14.3.29 (Lt JT Hutchinson)

A.S.31382 DH-4M-1. Boeing rebuild (c/n 609)

A.S.31377 DH-4M-2P. Fort Sam Houston 1927

A.S.31386 DH-4M-1. Boeing rebuild (c/n 523). McCook Field P-393; Bowman Field 1927

A.S.31391 DH-4M-1. Boeing rebuild (c/n 533). Kelly Field 1927

A.S.31412 DH-4M-1. Boeing rebuild (c/n 543). McCook Field P-366, landing accident 17.10.24 (1/Lt EV Pettis & passenger unhurt); Fairfield Air Intermediate Depot 1927

A.S.31425 DH-4M-1. Boeing rebuild (c/n 553). Kelly Field 1927; Crashed nr Brooks Field 1.5.29 (2/Lt JC Banta)

A.S.31450 DH-4M-1. Boeing rebuild (c/n 563). Kelly Field 1927

DH-4 '40' of the 2nd Aviation Instruction Center, Tours in October 1918.

A.S.31483 DH-4M-1. Boeing rebuild (c/n 573). Luke Field 1927; FL nr Wahiawa, HI 21.8.30 (2/Lt JB Stanley)
A.S.31497 DH-4M-1. Boeing rebuild (c/n 583). San Antonio Air Intermediate Depot 1927; Crashed nr Yturri Field, TX 14.1.28 (Cdt EWF Pierce)
A.S.31498 DH-4M-1. Boeing rebuild (c/n 592). Rockwell Air Intermediate Depot 1927; Crashed 10m SE of March Field, CA 13.8.28 (Cdt RM Winn)
A.S.31512 DH-4B-1. To US Navy as *A6401*
A.S.31556 DH-4M-2A. Brooks Field 1927
A.S.31561 DH-4M-1. Boeing rebuild (c/n 601). Kelly Field 1927
A.S.31575 DH-4M-2. Langley Field, FL nr a/f 13.6.27 (1/Lt FB McConnell & passenger both killed)
A.S.31578 DH-4M-1. Boeing rebuild (c/n 610). Luke Field 1927
A.S.31624 DH-4M-2P. Scott Field Station Supply 1927; Crashed nr Kelly Field 7.8.29 (2/Lt AR Meashawn)
A.S.31627 DH-4M-2P. Luke Field 1927
A.S.31629 DH-4M-2A. San Antonio Air Intermediate Depot 1927
A.S.31632 DH-4M-2. San Antonio Air Intermediate Depot 1927; Crashed nr Capital City, TX 1.4.29 (Cdt Catron)
A.S.31638 DH-4M-2P. France Field, CZ 1927
A.S.31639 DH-4M-2P. Wright Field 1927
A.S.31656 DH-4M-2A. San Antonio Air Intermediate Depot 1927
A.S.31666 DH-4M-2A. Kelly Field 1927
A.S.31668 DH-4B-1. To US Navy as *A6389*
A.S.31690 DH-4M-2. Air Corps dett Fort Levenham 1927
A.S.31715 DH-4M-1. Boeing rebuild (c/n 524). Langley Field 1927
A.S.31756 DH-4M. Crashed nr Nixon, TX 6.3.26 (Cdt JC Soper)
A.S.31792 DH-4M-2. Scott Field Station Supply 1927
A.S.31803 DH-4M-2. Crashed Logan Field 12.11.25 (Lt JH Howard); Repaired; Still Logan Field 1927
A.S.31807 DH-4M-2. Mitchel Field 1927; Crashed nr Southton, TX 16.4.30 (2/Lt SH Ayre killed)
A.S.31818 To A.S.68165, later A.S.25-089
A.S.31827 DH-4M-2. Kelly Field 1927; Crashed nr Brooks Field 5.7.30 (Cdt MM Stephenson)
A.S.31829 DH-4M-2. Chanute Field 1927; Crashed nr Kelly Field 23.10.28 (2/Lt J Burwell minor injuries)
A.S.31835 DH-4M-1. Boeing rebuild (c/n 534). Fairfield Air Intermediate Depot 1927; Crashed nr March Field, CA 20.2.30 (Cdt JA Anderson)
A.S.31839 DH-4M-2P. McCook Field P-428. Langley Field 1927
A.S.31844 DH-4M-2. 95th Division 1927
A.S.31850 DH-4M-2. Middletown Station Supply 1927
A.S.31856 DH-4M-2. Fairfield Air Intermediate Depot 1927; Crashed nr Edsons, AL 17.2.27 (1/Lt Niergarth & passenger both killed)
A.S.31858 DH-4M-2. Boston Airport 1927; Crashed nr Aquila, TX 2.12.28 (Capt AB McDaniel)
A.S.31871 DH-4M-2. McCook Field P-427; Wright Field 1927
A.S.31873 DH-4M-2. San Antonio Air Intermediate Depot 1927
A.S.31886 DH-4M-2. Kelly Field 1927; Crashed nr El Dorado, AR 7.7.27 (1/Lt RF Stearly)
A.S.31909 DH-4M-1. Boeing rebuild (c/n 544). San Antonio Air Intermediate Depot 1927
A.S.31912 DH-4M-2. Langley Field 1927
A.S.31916 DH-4M-2. Boston Airport 1927
A.S.31919 DH-4M-1. Boeing rebuild (c/n 478). Kelly Field 1927; Crashed nr Torbert, TX 23.7.27 (2/Lt OF Carlson)
A.S.31929 DH-4M-2A. Brooks Field 1927; Crashed nr Palestine, TX 26.4.27 (CB Oldfield)
A.S.31936 DH-4M-2. Fairfield Air Intermediate Depot 1927; Crashed nr Brooks Field 27.12.30 (2/Lt JW Atchinson)
A.S.31940 DH-4M-2. Bolling Field, DC 1927
A.S.31943 DH-4B-1. To US Navy as *A6395*
A.S.31949 DH-4M-2. Marshall Field 1927
A.S.31955 DH-4M-2S. McCook Field P-436. Wright Field 1927; Crashed nr Fort Crockett, TX 18.2.29 (2/Lt JH Williamson)
A.S.31956 DH-4M-1. Boeing rebuild (c/n 554); to DH-4M-1T. San Antonio Air Intermediate Depot 1927
A.S.31958 DH-4M-2S. Fairfield Air Intermediate Depot 1927
A.S.32071 DH-4. McCook Field P-21
A.S.32077 DH-4. Dayton-Wright built (400hp Liberty). Attd 55 Sqn 7.18
A.S.32083 DH-4. McCook Field P-31
A.S.32084 DH-4. Dayton Field, test flight, spun in nr Moraine City, OH 2.5.18 (Lt Col HJ Damon killed)
A.S.32087 DH-4M-1. Boeing rebuild (c/n 564). Kelly Field 1927; Crashed nr March Field 7.12.28 (Cdt MT Williams)
A.S.32093 DH-4M-1. Boeing rebuild (c/n 574). Phillipines 1927
A.S.32098 DH-4. Testing Dept, Wilbur Wright Field, Fairford, OH, BU in firing dive from 15,000ft 19.6.18 (1/Lt FS Patterson & 2/Lt LA Swan both killed)
A.S.32104 DH-4M-1. Boeing rebuild (c/n 584). Inst. Missouri National Guard, St.Louis 1927
A.S.32143 DH-4. Shot down by Oblt Wenig, CO of Jasta 80b, south of Metz 7.9.18
A.S.32151 DH-4B. To US Navy as *A3277*
A.S.32155 DH-4B. To US Navy as *A3271*
A.S.32158 DH-4B. To US Navy as *A3254*
A.S.32160 DH-4B. To US Navy as *A3250*
A.S.32163 DH-4B. To US Navy as *A3274*
A.S.32172 DH-4M-1. Boeing rebuild (c/n 593). Luke Field 1927; Crashed at Luke Field, HI 24.12.30 (1/Lt RR Brown)
A.S.32178 DH-4B. To US Navy as *A3319*
A.S.32188 DH-4M-1. Boeing rebuild (c/n 602); to DH-4M-1T. Brooks Field 1927; Crashed nr Camp Jones, CA 30.5.28 (Capt B Benson killed & passenger seriously injured)
A.S.32198 DH-4B. To US Navy as *A3260*
A.S.32199 DH-4. To US Navy as *A3263*; US base Ardres by 24.10.18; To USMC as *D10*
A.S.32200 DH-4. Hit tree landing nr Stockton, CA 12.11.19 (2/Lt CM Rudd killed)
BUT DH-4B. To US Navy as *A3251*
A.S.32201 DH-4B. To US Navy as *A3268*
A.S.32202 DH-4B. To US Navy as *A3267*
A.S.32203 DH-4B. To US Navy as *A3258*?
A.S.32205 DH-4M-1. Boeing rebuild (c/n 507). Little Rock 1927
A.S.32206 DH-4B. To US Navy as *A3248*
A.S.32207 DH-4B. To US Navy as *A3280*
A.S.32209 DH-4B. To US Navy as *A3265*
A.S.32210 DH-4B. To US Navy as *A3249*
A.S.32212 DH-4B. To US Navy as *A3255*
A.S.32216 DH-4B. To US Navy as *A3252*
A.S.32224 DH-4B. Coded '5' and running housewife with stick motif
A.S.32226 DH-4B. To US Navy as *A3247*
A.S.32229 DH-4B. To US Navy as *A3256*
A.S.32232 DH-4B. To US Navy as *A3283*
A.S.32240 DH-4B. To US Navy as *A3272*
A.S.32244 DH-4B. To US Navy as *A3296*
A.S.32247 DH-4M-1. Boeing rebuild (c/n 611). Luke Field 1927; Crashed Hawaii 5.10.29 (M/Sgt BR Ertwins); A/c repaired
A.S.32255 DH-4. To US Navy as *A3262*. To USMC as D-6
A.S.32256 DH-4B. To US Navy as *A3285*
A.S.32261 DH-4B. To US Navy as *A3257*
A.S.32265 DH-4B. To US Navy as *A3253*
A.S.32268 DH-4. To US Navy as *A3246*
A.S.32272 DH-4B. To US Navy as *A3259*
A.S.32273 DH-4B. To US Navy as *A3298*?
A.S.32274 DH-4. To US Navy as *A3261*. US base Ardres by 24.10.18; To USMC Naval Northern Bombing Group as *D11*
A.S.32280 DH-4B. To US Navy as *A3317*
A.S.32281 DH-4B. To US Navy as *A3321*
A.S.32286 DH-4. 20th Aero Sqn, bombing raid on Dun-sur-Meuse, in combat for 35min with 12 Fokker DVII, shared victory, then brought down by Ltn A Greven, Jasta 12 10.55 26.9.18 (2/Lt GB Wiser & 1/Lt GR Richardson both PoW)
A.S.32289 DH-4. Forestry patrol, engine failure, went into tail spin 7.10.19 (2/Lt HW Webb killed)
A.S.32291 DH-4. Transcontinental Reliability Flight (air race), crashed attempting to land, pilot thrown out, Saratoga, WY 10.10.19 (2/Lt EV Wales killed)
A.S.32292 DH-4. To US Navy as *A3245*
A.S.32293 DH-4B. To US Navy as *A3297*
A.S.32296 DH-4B. To US Navy as *A3320*
A.S.32299 DH-4. To US Navy as *A3276*
A.S.32300 DH-4B. To US Navy as *A3324*

XCO-7B A.S.31216 (P-368). (via Gordon Swanborough)

DH-4 A.S.32098 in silver finish. (via Gordon Swanborough)

DH-4B A.S.32224, coded '5' and running housewife with stick motif

Unserialled DH-4Amb-2 with the side door open to show the stretcher.

DH-4 32286 of 20th Aero Squadron in which 2/Lt G.B.Wise and 1/Lt G.Richardson were brought down at 10.55 on 26.9.18 by Ltn A.Greven of Jasta 12. (J.M.Bruce/G.S.Leslie collection)

DH-4 A.S.32344. (MAP)

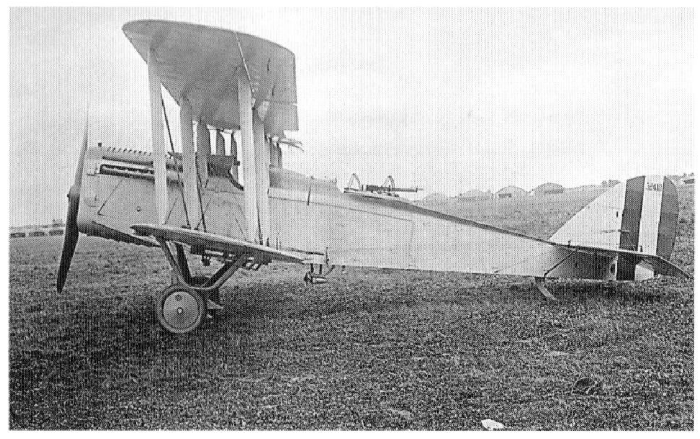

D.H.4 A.S.32410 with silver finish. (J.M.Bruce/G.S.Leslie collection)

A.S.32899 DH-4M A.S.32899, coded 7 aft of horned skull motif in a circle, and named 'MARY ALICE'.

A.S.32308 DH-4B. To US Navy as *A3281*
A.S.32309 DH-4B. To US Navy as *A3266*
A.S.32314 DH-4B. To US Navy as *A3302*
A.S.32318 DH-4. To US Navy as *A3299*
A.S.32319 DH-4M-1. Boeing rebuild (c/n 525). sMcCook Field P-363; Schoen Field 1927; Crashed nr Brooks Field 28.2.29 (2/Lt GD Henderson)
A.S.32321 DH-4. McCook Field P-35
A.S.32329 DH-4B. To US Navy as *A3279*
A.S.32333 DH-4. Engine failed on take-off, sideslipped in off turn at 60ft, nr Rockwell Field, CA, 20.10.19 (1/Lt GW Puryear killed)
BUT To US Navy as *A3312*
A.S.32335 DH-4. To US Navy as *A3275*
A.S.32337 DH-4. To US Navy as *A3273* or *A3311*
A.S.32338 DH-4B. To US Navy as *A3286*
A.S.32341 DH-4. McCook Field P-34
A.S.32344 DH-4. McCook Field P-49
A.S.32347 DH-4B. To US Navy as *A3322*
A.S.32349 DH-4B. To US Navy as *A3315*
A.S.32351 DH-4B. To US Navy as *A3308*
A.S.32354 DH-4. To US Navy as *A3278*
A.S.32357 DH-4B. To US Navy as *A3305* or *A3310*
A.S.32360 DH-4. To US Navy as *A3264*; To USMC as D-9
A.S.32363 DH-4B. To US Navy as *A3314*
A.S.32369 DH-4B. To US Navy as *A3292*
A.S.32370 DH-4B. To US Navy as *A3304* [or 32310?]
A.S.32371 DH-4B. To US Navy as *A3291*
A.S.32372 DH-4B. To US Navy as *A3294*
A.S.32377 DH-4M-1. To US Navy as *A3316*. Boeing rebuild (c/n 505). Crashed nr Kelly Field 31.3.26
A.S.32378 DH-4B. To US Navy as *A3306*
A.S.32380 DH-4. To US Navy as *A3270*
A.S.32381 DH-4B. To US Navy as *A3307*
A.S.32384 DH-4B. To US Navy as *A3290*
A.S.32387 DH-4. To US Navy as *A3269*
A.S.32389 DH-4B. To US Navy as *A3313*
A.S.32390 DH-4B. To US Navy as *A3309*
A.S.32395 DH-4B. To US Navy as *A3288*
A.S.32398 DH-4. Transcontinental Reliability Flight (air race), attempted to glide into small field, went into tail spin at 150ft, crashed in pond nr Salt Lake City, UT 8.10.19 (Mjr DA Crissey & Sgt V Thomas both killed)
A.S.32403 DH-4B. To US Navy as *A3289*
A.S.32404 DH-4B. To US Navy as *A3282*
A.S.32405 DH-4. To US Navy as *A3300*
A.S.32407 DH-4B. To US Navy as *A3323*
A.S.32411 DH-4B-1. To US Navy as *A3287*
A.S.32413 DH-4B. To US Navy as *A3295*
A.S.32414 DH-4B. To US Navy as *A3284*
A.S.32416 DH-4B. To US Navy as *A3303*
A.S.32417 DH-4B. To US Navy as *A3301*
A.S.32420 DH-4B. To US Navy as *A3293*
A.S.32438 DH-4B. To US Navy as *A3318*
A.S.32457 DH-4. 20th Aero Sqn, France ('19') 1918
A.S.32460 DH-4. (Dayton-Wright built) McCook Field, crashed on test, nr Dayton, OH 27.6.18 (Mr A Freeman & Mr R Ahlers both killed)
A.S.32461 DH-4M-1. Boeing rebuild (c/n 535); to DH-4M-1T. Brooks Field 1927; Accident nr Kelly Field, TX 3.12.29 (Cdt AW Mason)
A.S.32476 DH-4M-1. Boeing rebuild (c/n 545). McCook Field P-392; Wright Field 1927
A.S.32488 Renumbered A.S.25-46
A.S.32492 DH-4. 20th Aero Sqn, bombing raid on Dun-sur-Meuse, in combat with 12 Fokker DVII, patrol took sharp turn after dropping bombs causing break up of formation, engine hit, a/c OOC in flames but recovered, pilot about to jump but saw observer alive 10.55 26.9.18 (Capt MC Cooper wounded/burnt PoW & 1/Lt EC Leonard wounded PoW)
A.S.32502 DH-4. 55 Sqn RAF to 6 AP 22.9.18; 3 ASD 30.9.18
A.S.32503 DH-4. 20th Aero Sqn, bombing raid on railway yards Milly-Devant-Dun, in combat with 12 Fokker DVIIs, US Spads came to assistance, shared victory, own a/c shot up 12.26 10.10.18 (1/Lt LB Edwards OK & 2/Lt EB Christian wounded)
A.S.32512 DH-4M-1. Boeing rebuild (c/n 555); to DH-4M-1T. Kelly Field 1927; Accident, March Field, CA 19.7.29 (Cdt Rimball)
A.S.32530 DH-4M-1. Boeing rebuild (c/n 565). Kelly Field 1927; Crashed nr March Field 28.7.30 (1/Lt JR Glascock)
A.S.32538 DH-4M-1. Boeing rebuild (c/n 575); to DH-4M-1T. Kelly Field 1927
A.S.32578 DH-4M-1. Boeing rebuild (c/n 585). Rockwell Air Intermediate Depot 1927
A.S.32584 DH-4. 20th Aero Sqn, bombing raid on Dun-sur-Meuse, in combat with 12 Fokker DVII, shared victory, own a/c shot up, FL 10.55 26.9.18 (1/Lt SC Howard OK & 1/Lt EA Parrott killed)
A.S.32670 DH-4. To US Navy as *A3434*
A.S.32699 DH-4. 168th Aero Sqn, France ('7', named 'Mary Alice') 11.18
A.S.32700 DH-4. Engine failure, forced landed, hit trees, Stockton, CA 10.11.19 (pilot killed)
A.S.32703 DH-4M-1. Boeing rebuild (c/n 500); to DH-4M-1T. San Antonio Air Intermediate Depot 1927
A.S.32772 DH-4M-1. Inst. Minnesota National Guard, St.Paul 1927
A.S.32733 DH-4M-1. Boeing rebuild (c/n 594); to DH-4M-1T. Kelly Field 1927
A.S.32734 DH-4M-1. Boeing rebuild (c/n 603). Phillipines 1927
A.S.32739 DH-4M-1. Boeing rebuild (c/n 612). Luke Field 1927; DH-4M. 7nd BS, 5th BG, circuits & bumps, hit HT wire and crashed nr Wahiawa Angle N, HI 2.9.27 (Capt JW Signer killed)
A.S.32748 DH-4. 20th Aero Sqn, bombing raid on railway yards at Dun-sur-Meuse, in combat with 12 Fokker DVII, US Spads came to assistance, shared victory, own a/c shot up 12.25 10.10.18 (1/Lt SC Howard OK & 2/Lt SC Hicks wounded)
A.S.32752 DH-4M-1. Boeing rebuild (c/n 526). McCook Field P-391; Maxwell Field 1927
A.S.32772 DH-4M-1. Boeing rebuild (c/n 536)
A.S.32792 DH-4. 20th Aero Sqn, bombing raid on Dun-sur-Meuse, in combat with 12 Fokker DVII, shared victory, own a/c shot up 10.55 26.9.18 (2/Lt DB Harris & 2/Lt E Forbes both killed)
A.S.32807 DH-4M-1. Boeing rebuild (c/n 508)
A.S.32814 DH-4M-1. Boeing rebuild (c/n 546). Fairfield Air Intermediate Depot 1927
A.S.32815 DH-4M-1. Boeing rebuild (c/n 556); to DH-4M-1T. Brooks Field 1927; Crashed nr Hensley Field, TX 21.6.30 (Cdt WC Kent)
A.S.32819 DH-4. 20th Aero Sqn, bombing raid on Dun-sur-Meuse, in combat with 12 Fokker DVII nr Clery-la-Grand, shared victory, own a/c shot up 10.55 26.9.18 (1/Lt RP Matthews & 2/Lt EA Taylor both killed)
A.S.32833 DH-4M-1. Boeing rebuild (c/n 566). San Antonio Air Intermediate Depot 1927
A.S.32847 DH-4M-1. Boeing rebuild (c/n 576). Luke Field 1927; Accident nr Wheeler Field, HI 1.2.29 (1/Lt RJ Minty)
A.S.32855 DH-4M-1. Boeing rebuild (c/n 586). Luke Field 1927; 72nd BS, crashed at night, Luke Field, HI 9.7.29 (1/Lt CA Kuntz killed)
A.S.32857 DH-4M-1. Boeing rebuild (c/n 595); to DH-4M-1T. Kelly Field 1927
A.S.32858 DH-4M-2. McCook Field P-426
A.S.32862 DH-4M-1. Boeing rebuild (c/n 498); to DH-4M-1T. Kelly Field 1927
A.S.32879 DH-4M-1. Boeing rebuild (c/n 604); to DH-4M-1T. Fort Crockett 1927; Accident nr Brooks Field, TX 10.2.28 (Cdt JD Nedwed)
A.S.32888 DH-4M-1. Boeing rebuild (c/n 613). Luke Field 1927
A.S.32890 DH-4M-1. Boeing rebuild (c/n 527). Bolling Field, DC 1927
A.S.32894 DH-4B/DH-4M-1. Boeing rebuild (c/n 537). McCook Field P-390; Wright Field 1927
A.S.32899 DH-4M. Coded 7 aft of horned skull motif in circle, and named 'MARY ALICE'.
A.S.32901 DH-4M-1. Boeing rebuild (c/n 547); to DH-4M-1T. Brooks Field 1927
A.S.32903 DH-4M-1. Boeing rebuild (c/n 557); to DH-4M-1T. Kelly Field 1927
A.S.32915 DH-4. 20th Aero Sqn, bombing raid on Dun-sur-Meuse, in combat with 12 Fokker DVII, own a/c shot up 10.55 26.9.18 (1/Lt PN Rhinelander & 1/Lt HC Preston both killed
A.S.32920 DH-4M-1. Boeing rebuild (c/n 567). Kelly Field 1927

A newly completed D.H.4 in the Standard Aircraft Corporation factory at Patterson, New Jersey in 1917. (via Philip Jarrett)

A.S.32932 DH-4M-1. Boeing rebuild (c/n 577). EF, FL, Wheeler Field, HI 21.6.26 (MJ Smith); Rockwell Air Intermediate Depot 1927; Accident 20m N of Victorville, CA 21.2.29 (Cdt H Brummuel)

A.S.32951 DH-4M-1. Boeing rebuild (c/n 549)

A.S.32956 DH-4M-1. Boeing rebuild (c/n 587). Phillipines 1927

A.S.32957 DH-4M-1. Boeing rebuild (c/n 596). Rockwell Air Intermediate Depot 1927; EF, FL nr Oceanside, CA 13.6.28 (Cdt E Martin)

A.S.32962 DH-4. 20th Aero Sqn, bombing raid on troops at Buzancy-Bois de Barricourt, shot up in combat with Fokker DVIIs nr Buzancy 15.25 23.10.18 (1/Lt KG West OK & 1/Lt WF Frank slightly wounded)

A.S.32975 DH-4M-1. Boeing rebuild (c/n 605). Mid-air collision with A.S.29183 nr San Antonio, TX 7.1.27 (Cdt RE Terrell killed)

A.S.32984 DH-4M-1. Boeing rebuild (c/n 614). Luke Field 1927; Crashed on landing, nr Waimanalo, HI 2.5.27 (1/Lt JL Davidson); A/c repaired

A.S.32994 DH-4M-1. Boeing rebuild (c/n 528). Aberdeen Proving Ground 1927

A.S.32996 DH-4M-1. Boeing rebuild (c/n 538). Crashed nr Bennetts Creek, VA 1925 (Capt JG Colgan); Fort Sam Houston 1927

A.S.32998 DH-4M-1. Boeing rebuild (c/n 548); Crashed 15m E of March Field, CA 24.8.28 (GH Plufher)

A.S.33006 DH-4M-1. Boeing rebuild (c/n 558); to DH-4M-1T. San Antonio Air Intermediate Depot 1927

A.S.33027 DH-4M-1. Boeing rebuild (c/n 568). Crashed nr Kelly Field, TX 15.11.26 (Cdt FS Wilbur)

A.S.33049 DH-4M-1. Boeing rebuild (c/n 578). Phillipines 1927

A.S.33172 DH-4M. Crashed at Luke Field, HI 25.7.27 (Capt HC Drayton)

A.S.34105(?) DH-4B. Kelly Field, hit flagpole in poor visibility, flew into ground 21.5.20 (2/Lt AM St.John & Pte CL Buehler both killed)

A.S.36232 to A.S.37231. Cancelled order from Fisher

A.S.39368 to A.S.39867. Ordered from Standard. Cancelled from 39508

A.S.39403 DH-4. Roosevelt Field, crashed into crowd nr Scranton, PA (Lt GP Ziesmer & another killed; 3 seriously injured)

A.S.39406 DH-4. Circuits & bumps, overshot into another field while landing, overturned, Roosevelt Field 20.11.19 (2/Lt EF Gaskell killed)

A.S.40060 DH-4B. McCook Field P-43

A.S.40128 DH-4. McCook Field P-85

A.S.4029x DH-4. 6th Aero Sqn Luke Field, accident Fort Kamehameha, HI 18.11.18 (2/Lt WG Crowdus minor injuries)

A.S.42041 DH-4B. Langley Field, EF, FL nr a/f 13.8.24 (1/Lt JR Wilkinson unhurt)

A.S.42126 & A.S.42127. DH-4P-1 ordered from Dayton-Wright

A.S.45087 DH-4. 147th Sqn 1st Pursuit Gp, Kelly Field, EF, FL, hit building nr New Braumfels, TX 12.10.20 (Sgt CB Allen killed)

A.S.62945 DH-4L. McCook Field P-77, later DH-4M-2S Langley Field 1927

A.S.62946 DH-4L. McCook Field P-79

A.S.62947 DH-4L. McCook Field P-107

A.S.62948 DH-4L. McCook Field P-123

A.S.62969 DH-4B. Kelly Field, T/O accident 20.12.21 (Capt FA Place seriously injured); Later DH-4M-2T at Kelly Field 1927

A.S.62973 DH-4B. Kelly Field, circuits & bumps, tail spin from 1,000ft, crashed nr a/f, burst into flames 8.6.20 (Cdt H Brawley & Cdt RW Ellington both killed)

A.S.62990 DH-4B. Hit tree nr Lufkin, TX 22.4.22 (PFC RL Mitchell minor injuries)

A.S.62994 DH-4B. Pope Field, stalled landing, wing dipped, crashed, totally wrecked 29.4.21 (1/Lt JE Virgin & 1/Lt HA Bartram both killed)

A.S.62995 DH-4B. Phillipines 1927

A.S.62999 DH-4B. Caught by gust of wind while landing, crashed, Watkins Station, TX 3.3.20 (2/Lt JE Greer killed)

A.S.63000 DH-4B. Groundlooped Kelly Field, TX 2.8.23 (Cdt Lamont)

Boeing-built DH-4M-1 A.S.31202 in 1927.
(via Gordon Swanborough)

Atlantic-built DH-4M-2 A.S.30885. (via Gordon Swanborough)

A Hollywood-based DH-4 painted up for a film.

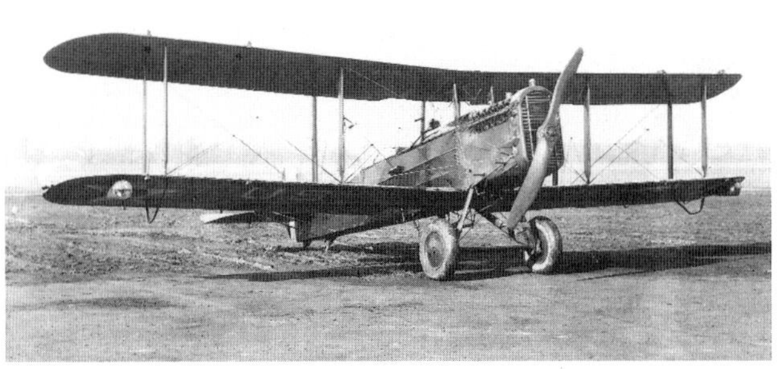

D.H.4M-2T A.S.31....

DH-4 A.S.696.. marked '8'.

Boeing-built XDH-4M-1 prototype P-337 (A.S.68592).
(via Gordon Swanborough)

A DH-4 variant fitted with special skis.

An experimental fitment of machine guns on both port and starboard mainplanes of an American DH-4. (via Frank Cheesman)

A.S.63005 DH-4M-2T. San Antonio Air Intermediate Depot 1927
A.S.63016 DH-4B. Landing accident, Fort Collins, CO 26.5.22 (Capt R Derby unhurt)
A.S.63023 DH-4B. Post Field, EF, FL on a/f 5.11.23 (Cdt JA Collins unhurt)
A.S.63033 Post Field, collided with A.S.63604 during manoeuvre, crashed with engine full on, burnt out (1/Lt HJT Lanfall & Pte GE Hubbard both killed)
A.S.63039 DH-4B. Air Service Observation School, Post Field, Fort Sill, OK, failed to pick up speed on TO from soft ground, badly damaged 29.7.21 (Mjr JW Jones & 1/Lt JE Parker OK)
A.S.63049 DH-4M. Crashed on TO, Corning, CA 4.7.21 (Cdt CG Stanton & passenger unhurt)
A.S.63053 DH-4M-2T. San Antonio Air Intermediate Depot 1927
A.S.63058 DH-4B. Post Field, bad weather, FL 8m W of Waller, TX 8.3.22 (Lt Col PW Beck unhurt)
A.S.63081 DH-4B. Phillips Field, EF, crashed New Castle, MD 2.11.23 (1/Lt WH Bleakley & passenger both minor injuries)
A.S.63080 DH-4B-1. Bolling Field, DC 1927
A.S.63082 DH-4B. Langley Field, VA, EF at 100ft on TO, pancaked, lost u/c 11.8.21 (Cdt VD Lovell OK)
A.S.63128 DH-4B. Post Field, Fort Sill, OK, cross-country, fog and rain, poor visibility, rolled into a buffalo hollow landing 25.12.20 (Cdt CW Knetchel & Cdt JH Livingston OK); EF on T/O, Leadville, CO 25.5.25 (1/Lt EG Shrader)
A.S.63129 DH-4B. Post Field, Fort Sill, OK, on take-off had to zoom to avoid 2 crashed a/c [see A.S.63582], insufficient speed, fell from 10ft on to one wing 10.8.21 (1/Lt SP Walker & mechanic OK)
A.S.63131 DH-4B. Langley Field, VA, throttle rod became disconnected in flight, FL, pulled up to avoid man walking on beach, CW, Buckroe Beach 29.7.21 (Cdt RP Bodeen & Cdt WC Breedlone both OK)
A.S.63146 DH-4B. Langley Field, VA, EF at 2,000ft, FL in water nr Sandy Beach Point, VA 17.6.21 (Cdt GG Willard & Cdt C Iraine OK); A/c salved
A.S.63168 DH-4B. Landing accident, Roseburg, OR 18.7.22 (1/Lt JP Morgan & passenger both unhurt)
A.S.63170 DH-4B. Phillipines 1927
A.S.63181 DH-4B. McCook Field P-190
A.S.63220 DH-4M-2T. Kelly Field 1927
A.S.63223 DH-4B. Kelly Field, stalled on step turn, spun in, burst into flames 22.10.20 (Cdr JH Turney & Cdt S Szymanski both killed)
A.S.63229 DH-4B. EF, FL nr Vista, TX 15.3.22 (1/Lt RW Gamblin)
A.S.63240 DH-4B. Post Field, FL on a/f 23.6.22 (Cdt AL Caperton)
A.S.63242 DH-4Ard. Flying School, flew into severe storm during cross-country, FL, crashed 15.5.21 (1/Lt CA Cover & Lt CE Miller OK)
A.S.63244 DH-4B. 20th Aero Sqn, Kelly Field, TX, returning in formation from Camp Stanley, EF, FL in small field, sideslipped in, crashed, caught fire, 9m N of Kelly Field/10m from San Antonio on Blanco road 20.8.20 (Lt IC Stenson & F/Cdt EH Burson both killed)
A.S.63249 DH-4B. FL nr Stockdale, TX 21.12.21 (1/Lt AR McConnell)
A.S.63278 DH-4Amb. McCook Field P-130
A.S.63279 DH-4C. McCook Field P-134
A.S.63280 DH-4C. McCook Field P-136
A.S.63337 DH-4B. Post Field, ran out of fuel, FL Lancaster, TX 22.12.23 (1/Lt SB Ebert unhurt)
A.S.63366 DH-4B. Post Field, bad weather, FL 3m W of a/f 14.2.22 (Cdt HJ Wright killed & passenger minor injuries)
A.S.63369 DH-4M-2T. Kelly Field 192
A.S.63370 DH-4B. Oklahoma City, steep turn near ground, crashed, burst into flames 18.7.20 (2/Lt R Browne & Sgt CR Burleson)
A.S.63376 DH-4B. Post Field, landing accident 17.1.22 (1/Lt JE Parker unhurt); Repaired; Post Field, landing accident nr Chicasha, OK 4.5.22 (1/Lt P Evert)
A.S.63383 DH-4M. Ferrying, crashed on landing, caught fire, Fort Worth, TX 28.11.21 (Lt AL Thornton unhurt)
A.S.63385 DH-4B. Post Field, hit fence nr Monohans, TX on T/O 22.5.22 (1/Lt HW Prosser unhurt)
A.S.63387 DH-4B. Kelly Field, EF on T/O, FL Fort Clark, TX 13.12.21 (Lt HF Sessions unhurt)
A.S.63390 DH-4B. T/O accident, Denver, CO 24.5.22 (Capt JW Signer unhurt)
A.S.63395 DH-4B. Post Field, T/O accident, Dallas, TX 8.5.22 (1/Lt CH Howard unhurt)
A.S.63397 DH-4B. Schoen Field, IN, landing accident 15.7.24 (2/Lt RW Douglas & passenger both unhurt)
A.S.63399 DH-4B. Sand Point Field, FL in fog 10m from Brinnon, WA 16.9.24 (1/Lt TJ Koenig minor injuries)
A.S.63403 DH-4B. Post Field, landing accident Fort Sill, OK 22.5.22 (Capt WH Crom unhurt); Post Field, landing accident, Oklahoma City 11.4.23 (2/Lt AH Rich)
A.S.63406 DH-4B. Kelly Field, spun in landing 15.2.24 (2/Lt WS Smith killed)
A.S.63408 DH-4B. Selfridge Field, EF, FL nr Huntsberg, OH 30.11.22 (pilot unhurt)
A.S.63409 DH-4B. Post Field, bad weather, EF, FL nr Hazelton, KS 21.5.21 (1/Lt P Evert unhurt); Unit?, Corning, Tehama County, CA, EF on T/O, FL on bumpy ground, lost u/c, completely wrecked 4.7.21
A.S.63413 DH-4B. McCook Field P-131
A.S.63415 DH-4B. Langley Field, EF, FL among bomb holes, hit edge of creek, nosed over 14.7.21 (JG O'Neal minor injuries)
A.S.63416 DH-4B. Langley Field, VA, hit ridge landing, nosed over, completely wrecked 27.7.21 (Cdt LE McLaughlin & Cdt J Johnson OK)
A.S.63417 DH-4B. Fisher-built body with Dayton-Wright tail, modelled by L.W.F. Co, assembled Aberdeen proving ground; Air Service Flying School, Langley Field, VA, photographic flight, control stick installed in reverse on assembly, a/c stalled, completely wrecked, 4.2.21 (2/Lt EB Bobzien of 7th Photographic Section minor injuries & 2/Lt HJ Martin of 1st AOS unhurt)
A.S.63422 DH-4B. Langley Field, EF, FL 4m W of Danville, VA 25.8.24 (1/Lt HB Smith & passenger both unhurt)
A.S.63448 DH-4B. USN Group at Mitchel Field, EF, FL 19.10.20 (pilot unhurt)
A.S.63451 DH-4B. USN Group at Mitchel Field, stalled landing 19.10.20 (pilot unhurt)
A.S.63454 DH-4B. Northfield, MA, hit tree landing, crashed 15.9.20 (2/Lt HH Spencer killed & passenger minor injuries)
A.S.63456 DH-4B, Spun in 1m S of Austin, TX 23.2.21 (Cdt EE Allen & passenger both killed)
A.S.63458 DH-4B. Post Field, spun into ground on a/f 17.11.21 (Lt RB Wriston unhurt)
A.S.63461 to A.S.63507 DH-4B. Boeing rebuilds as Type 16 (c/n's 88-134)
A.S.63461 DH-4B. Crissy Field, landing accident, Sand Point Field, WA 27.9.24 (Lt Col EP Lahur unhurt)
A.S.63465 DH-4B. 91st Sqn (Observation), dett 'A' Flt, Medford, OR, forest patrol, struck air pocket at 7ft while landing, badly damaged 29.6.21 (Sgt MB Rouse & Mr CM Parsons OK)
A.S.63466 DH-4B. 91st Sqn (Observation), Camp Lewis, WA, EF at 300ft during circuits and bumps, ditched in lake 15.6.21 (Cdt CW Hillman & Pte RH Wilkerson OK)
A.S.63475 DH-4B. Phillipines 1927
A.S.63480 DH-4B. 6th Pursuit Sqn Luke Field, mid-air collision, crashed into Pearl Harbor, HI 30.10.22 (1/Lt TV Hynes killed)
A.S.63482 DH-4B. Crissy Field, landing accident, San Jose, CA 6.9.23 (Sgt LL Heffing & passenger both unhurt)
A.S.63487 DH-4B. 91st Sqn (Observation), Camp Lewis, WA (coded '10'), heavy landing on port wheel, overturned, nr Meadow Park, WA 15.7.21 (1/Lt RS Worthington & Mjr CAC Lyons of the Artillery Corps both OK)
A.S.63488 DH-4B. 91st Sqn (Observation (coded '11') 1921
A.S.63501 DH-4B. Unit unknown, recd 29.5.20; EF, spun in from 1,000ft, crashed, exploded on impact, nr Alturas, CA 10.7.20 (Sgt W Haney, Cpl AA Salcido & Civ BH Roble all killed)
A.S.63503 DH-4B. 1st Sqn (Observation (coded '9') 1921
A.S.63506 DH-4B. Luke Field, NY, took off cross-wind, stalled, crashed, burnt out 16.9.21 (1/Lt JF Armstrong, Sgt

DH-4B, probably A.S.63413 (P-131), with supercharged Liberty and controllable pitch propeller. (J.M.Bruce/G.S.Leslie collection)

DH-4B A.S.63819.

A DH-4, possibly DH-4BW A.S.63697 (P-133), with a Wright-Hispano engine.

DH-4 A.S.6392., seen here at Cranwell, was allocated for use by the U.S. Air Attachés. (via Peter Green)

PJ White & [Civ?] BA Gipson all killed)

A.S.63525 DH-4B (L.W.F.) 4th Sqn (Observation), EF at 200ft on TO, FL Ford Island, Pearl Harbor, BO 13.7.21 (Mjr SH Wheeler & Sgt TA Kelly both killed) [but see A.S.63626]

A.S.63529 DH-4B. 4th Sqn (Observation), tactical mission attack on Kekepa Island, windward Oahu, Hawaii, lost power at 2,000ft, FL 100yds offshore 12.7.21 (1/Lt UC Boquet minor injuries & Sgt ML Drew OK)

A.S.63536 DH-4B. Langin Field, WV, ground collision 2.10.23 (1/Lt CB Deshields & passenger both unhurt)

A.S.63544 DH-4B. Post Field, unable to pull out of dive from 3,500ft, completely wrecked 12.5.21 (Sgt AL Bloomquist & Civ CK McCullough both killed)

A.S.63545 DH-4M-2S. Fairfield Air Intermediate Depot 1927

A.S.63561 DH-4B. Langley Field, dived in from 300ft 27.4.21 (1/Lt EH Wood & Sgt RO Bryson both killed)

A.S.63565 DH-4B. Post Field, Fort Sill, OK, struck road landing 1.8.21 (1/Lt JE Parker & 2 Range Guards OK)

A.S.63567 DH-4B. Post Field, hit pole landing 22.9.21 (1/Lt RB Walker)

A.S.63570 DH-4B. Post Field, EF, FL 1m W of a/f 1.5.22 (1/Lt WR Peck)

A.S.63582 DH-4B. 22nd Sqn, Post Field, Fort Sill, OK, formation take-off, tail cut off by following a/c 10.8.21 (1/Lt E Davis & Sgt RL Fair OK)

A.S.63594 DH-4B. Post Field, Fort Sill, OK, tailspin from c.500ft, totally wrecked 1.8.21 (Capt J McRae & 1/Lt FW Nunemacher both killed)

A.S.63596 DH-4B. Post Field, Fort Sill, OK, struck obstacle landing 1.8.21 (1/Lt FB Valentine & 1/Lt FW Nunemacher OK)

A.S.63600 DH-4B. McCook Field P-137

A.S.63601 DH-4B. EF, FL nr Cement, OK 7.5.22 (1/Lt RHV Stackhouse)

A.S.63603 DH-4B. Post Field, landing accident nr Duncan, OK 22.10.21 (pilot unhurt)

A.S.63604 DH-4B. Post Field, collided with A.S.63033 during manoeuvre, crashed with engine full on, burnt out (Capt F Loomie & Pte PN Smith both killed)

A.S.63613 DH-4B. Hit by civil a/c while landing, Beeville, TX 2.12.21 (1/Lt L Andrews minor injuries)

A.S.63616 DH-4B. Post Field, landing accident 28.10.21 (1/Lt CP Prime unhurt)

A.S.63620 DH-4B. Luke Field, hit HT wire Kipapa Gulch, HI 14.10.22 (1/Lt WH Manzelman killed)

A.S.63626 DH-4B. Luke Field, NY, EF at 300ft on take-of, turned back, dived in from 120ft, burst into flames 12.7.21 (Mjr SH Wheeler & Sgt TA Kelly both killed) [but see A.S.63525]

A.S.63627 DH-4B. Post Field, landing accident 16.11.21 (Lt SB Ebert)

A.S.63628 DH-4B. To US Navy as *A5884*

A.S.63629 DH-4B. USMC, nosed over landing Parris Island 30.8.20 (pilot unhurt)

A.S.63639 DH-4B. McCook Field P-139

A.S.63651 DH-4B. 50th Aero Sqn, Langley Field, VA (coded '11'), lost bearings in fog and low cloud, dived in from 200ft avoiding towers, completely wrecked 27.4.21 (Master Sgt NC Bryant killed & 1/Lt TH Ward DoI)

A.S.63653 DH-4B. Unit unknown, prop damaged, ran out of fuel, FL on beach, u/c struck water on TO, overturned, CW, 3m S of Munden, VA 21.7.21 (1/Lt WL Boyd & passenger unhurt)

A.S.63656 DH-4B. Langley Field, VA, pancaked landing in small field, u/c collapsed, Virginia Beach, VA 24.6.21 (1/Lt CB Austin & passenger unhurt

A.S.63657 DH-4B. Luke Field, EF on T/O, ditched in Pearl Harbor 4.5.22 (Capt RK Kirkpatrick unhurt)

A.S.63666 DH-4B. Langley Field, VA, ground looped landing, hit fence attempting to take-off again, skidded for 100ft 15.8.21 (Cdt HR Angell shaken & Pte Smith minor injuries)

A.S.63670 DH-4B. Landing accident nr Macon GA 20.1.21 (Lt JK McDuffle)

A.S.63672 DH-4M. EF on T/O, FL, Alturas, CA 30.9.21 (Cdt CS Stanton)

A.S.63676 DH-4B. 50th Aero Sqn?, Langley Field, VA, took off with three 100lb bombs for live bombing exercise,

wingtip clipped tree, rolled over and dived in, bombs exploded 7.6.21 (Cdt NR Thompson & Cdt CA Bevan both killed)
A.S.63680 DH-4M-2S. Wright Field 1927
A.S.63690 DH-4B. T/O accident off New Point Comf, VA 11.7.21 (1/Lt DV Gaffney unhurt)
A.S.63696 DH-4B Boeing built as Type 16 (c/n 135)
A.S.63697 DH-4BW. McCook Field P-133
A.S.63698 DH-4B. McCook Field P-218
A.S.63709 DH-4B. Recd Godman Field, Camp Knox 28.11.20; Cross-country to Martinsville, IN, nosed over in soft ground on arrival 4.2.21 (Lt RR Brown & Lt OW Broberg both slightly injured)
A.S.63710 DH-4B. McCook Field P-219
A.S.63719 DH-4B. McCook Field P-158
A.S.63747 DH-4B. McCook Field P-157
A.S.63757 DH-4B. McCook Field P-188
A.S.63761 to A.S.63823 DH-4B (Boeing rebuilds as Type 16, c/n's 136 to 198)
A.S.63763 DH-4B. Mather Field, Sacramento, CA, engine failure on cross-country, FL, crashed 1m N of Roseville, CA 12.2.21 (Cdt LH Scott OK)
A.S.63764 DH-4B. Phillipines 1927
A.S.63768 DH-4B. Crissy Field, landing accident, crashed nr Reno, NV 2.6.24 (Cpl RH Fatt unhurt)
A.S.63772 DH-4B. Phillipines 1927
A.S.63778 DH-4B. Crissy Field, landing accident 18.3.24 (Capt JW Signer & passenger unhurt)
A.S.63779 DH-4B. Crissy Field, FL in bad weather, crashed nr Elk Grove 17.1.24 (1/Lt OC Wilson & passenger both minor injuries)
A.S.63780 DH-4B. Rockwell Field, FL in bad weather, 49m from San Diego, CA 7.12.22 (1/Lt CL Webber & passenger both killed
A.S.63790 DH-4B. 91st Sqn (Observation), coded '9'
A.S.63791 DH-4B. 91st Sqn (Observation), Municipal Field, Eugene, OR, while at local landing field, Medford Field, OR, hit tree top on TO, crashed, BO 9.7.21 (1/Lt S Carter minor injuries & Obs J Burman OK) BUT DH-4B. Mather Field, hit hill nr Placeville, CA 13.12.21 (Cdt SD Dubose & passenger both minor injuries)
A.S.63801 DH-4B. Crissy Field, CA, landing accident 8.2.22 (1/Lt BS Catlin & passenger unhurt)
A.S.63800 DH-4B. Phillipines 1927
A.S.63813 DH-4B. Brooks Field, FL in bad weather, nr Fauke, AR 24.4.24 (1/Lt CF Woolsey & passenger unhurt)
A.S.63819 DH-4
A.S.63827 DH-4B. Mitchel Field 1927
A.S.63832 DH-4B. Post Field, T/O accident nr Medicine Park, 7m S of Fort Sill 10.2.22 (1/Lt P Evert minor injuries)
A.S.63844 4th Observation Sqn, Wheeler Field, HI, spun in ½m from a/f 29.1.23 (1/Lt R Julian killed)
A.S.63860 DH-4B1. Selfridge Field, heavy rain, unable to climb through cloud, EF over Detroit River, FL on bank. overturned, BO 20.8.21 (1/Lt JT Hutchison OK)
A.S.63873 DH-4B. Luke Field, EF on T/O, ditched in Pearl Harbor 28.10.23 (1/Lt AB Ballard unhurt)
A.S.63887 DH-4B. 96th Sqn, Langley Field, VA, Flew low over bathers at Ocean View Beach, VA, zoomed low over life lines to avoid bathers, pancaked into sea 13.6.21 (Cdt GD Roberts & Pte RR Darien OK); A/c salved
A.S.63891 DH-4. Langley Field, engine backfired and caught fire, FL in swamp, Poquosen, VA, 4m S of airfield 25.7.21 (Cdt HE Elliott slightly injured)
A.S.63893 DH-4B. Captured and flown in Russia by RKKVF
A.S.63896 DH-4B. McCook Field P-194
A.S.63910 DH-4B. Selfridge Field, EF at 500ft, FL nr York River, VA 29.8.21 (Cdt LP Hudson slightly injured)
A.S.63915 DH-4B. Langley Field, hit tree on take-off, crashed, burst into flames 31.8.21 (Cdt AJ Ferenchak & Cdt SC Chapkowitz both killed)
A.S.63916 DH-4B (Gallaudet-built). Langley Field, EF, FL in field, overshot, hit tree, completely wrecked, 6m from Coastguard Stn, Virginia Beach, VA 17.6.21 (Cdt TG McLaughlin minor injuries & Cdt RD Carr unhurt)
A.S.6392. DH-4B. Allocated to U.S.Air Attache in the United Kingdom
A.S.63925 DH-4B. To US Navy as *A5984*
A.S.63927 DH-4B. To US Navy as *A5985*
A.S.63934 DH-4B. Captured and flown in Russia by RKKVF
A.S.63936 DH-4B. To US Navy as *A5986*. (Boeing rebuild as Type 16 - c/n 135)
A.S.63937 DH-4B. To US Navy as *A5987*
A.S.63938 DH-4B. To US Navy as *A5988*
A.S.63943 DH-4B. To US Navy as *A5989*
A.S.63945 DH-4M-2S. McCook Field P-435
ALSO reported as DH-4B captured and flown in Russia by RKKVF [error for A.S.63954?]
A.S.63946 DH-4B. To US Navy as *A5990*
A.S.63947 DH-4B. To US Navy as *A5991*
A.S.63951 DH-4B. To US Navy as *A5992*
A.S.63954 DH-4B. Captured and flown in Russia by RKKVF; Used by VVS HQ of the Leningrad Military District; WO 1929
A.S.63956 to 63958. DH-4B. To US Navy as *A5993* to *A5995*
A.S.63963 DH-4B. To US Navy as *A5996*
A.S.63968 & 63969. DH-4B. To US Navy as *A5997* & *A5998*
A.S.63975 & 63976. DH-4B. To US Navy as *A5999* & *A6000*
A.S.63979 DH-4B. To US Navy as *A6001*
A.S.63981 DH-4B. 4th Group (Observation), Manila, PI, cross-country Manila to Clark Field, EF, FL in rough water Manila Bay 27.6.21 (Capt IC Baker & Mjr CO Staples OK)
A.S.63983 DH-4B. 50th Sqn Langley Field, VA, u/c damaged landing in formation 14.6.21 (Cdt HH Gallup & Cdt Holden OK)
A.S.63987 DH-4B. 50th Aero Sqn, Langley Field, VA, EF on TO, crashed, Fair Grounds, Richmond, VA, badly damaged 18.8.21 (Cdt VD Lovell OK)
A.S.64007 DH-4B. McCook Field P-175, EF, FL on a/f 10.6.22 (1/Lt BR Lewis unhurt)
A.S.64008 DH-4B. McCook Field P-174
A.S.64009 DH-4B. McCook Field P-173
A.S.64256 DH-4B. Langley Field, EF, FL nr a/f 2.9.22 (1/Lt GC McDonald unhurt)
A.S.64257 DH-4B. Langley Field, T/O accident 20m from Fayetteville, NC 13.10.23 (S/Sgt DF Kearns & passenger both unhurt)
A.S.64279 DH-4B. Luke Field 1927
A.S.64281 DH-4B. McCook Field P-261
A.S.64351 DH-4B. Chaute Field, landing accident, Carlinville, IL 15.9.23 (Cpl LG Wilson unhurt)
A.S.64354 DH-4B. McCook Field P-252
A.S.64356 DH-4B. McCook Field P-226; Chanute Field, EF, FL nr Tipton, MO 2.12.23 (1/Lt WG Smith & passenger both unhurt)
A.S.64467 DH-4B. 4th Sqn Wheeler Field (coded '55'), EF, FL (1/Lt FA Lundell OK)
A.S.64464 DH-4M-2S. Chanute Field 1927
A.S.64466 DH-4B. 4th Observation Sqn, Wheeler Field, HI, EF, FL on airfield 27.2.24 (Mjr REM Goolrick unhurt)
A.S.64468 DH-4B. McCook Field P-237
A.S.64496 DH-4B. 19th Pursuit Sqn, Luke Field, EF, FL Cook Ranch House, HI 2.6.24 (1/Lt E Eubanks)
A.S.64497 DH-4B. 4th Observation Sqn, Wheeler Field, HI, landing accident 16.10.23 (Lt FC Wheeler unhurt)
A.S.64503 DH-4B. Luke Field 1927
A.S.64509 DH-4B. Mitchel Field, landing accident 2.4.23 (1/Lt E Hyndshaw unhurt); Mitchel Field, FL in bad weather, Crosswick, NJ 23.9.23 (Capt FM Brady & passenger unhurt)
A.S.64510 DH-4B. Mitchel Field, landing accident 12.9.24 (1/Lt HB Chandler & passenger unhurt)
A.S.64518 DH-4B. Langley Field, FL Westernpoint, MD 27.9.23 (1/Lt RH Finty unhurt)
A.S.64535 DH-4B. McCook Field P-191
A.S.64536 DH-4B. Langley Field, EF on T/O, FL 20.2.22 (1/Lt WB Souza unhurt & passenger minor injuries)
A.S.64539 DH-4B. McCook Field P-192
A.S.64544 DH-4B. McCook Field, ran into bad rain storm and thick cloud, short of fuel, FL in bad country, damaged 8.7.21 (1/Lt GW Hoskins OK & Mech CF Schory minor injuries)
A.S.64545 DH-4B. Landing accident, Carmichaels, PA 11.4.23 (1/Lt FP Booker unhurt)
A.S.64547 DH-4B. Mitchel Field, FL in bad weather, nr Stamford, CT 23.11.23 (Sgt SH Turner)
A.S.64553 DH-4B. 9th Observation Sqn, Mitchel Field, NY, FL in small rolling field, u/c leg torn off, overturned, nr

A Boeing-built DH-4M at Seattle in 1924. (via Gordon Swanborough)

Norwich, CT 10.10.23 (1/Lt DE Rowland unhurt & Sgt J Murin minor injuries)

A.S.64558 DH-4B. Boston Airport (MA), EF on TO, rolled into mud 28.6.24 (1/Lt FB Valentine & 1/Lt RA Nagle unhurt); McCook Field, landing accident 1.10.24 (1/Lt HR Wells & passenger both unhurt)

A.S.64559 DH-4B. Mitchel Field 1927

A.S.64562 DH-4M-2S. Langley Field 1927

A.S.64572 DH-4B. Landing accident, Columbus, OH 16.3.23 (Lt MN Stewart minor injuries)

A.S.64585 DH-4B. Norton Field, landing accident Columbus, OH 17.1.25 (M/Sgt P Biesoit & passenger unhurt)

A.S.64586 DH-4B. EF, FL nr Richmond, IN 12.4.23 (Mjr HJ Knerr minor injuries)

A.S.64587 DH-4B. McCook Field *XP277*, Curtiss D-12 testbed

A.S.64593 DH-4L. McCook Field P-193; EF, FL on South MT, nr Marion, IN (pilot unhurt); Crashed 15m W of Gettysburg, PA 8.11.26 (2/Lt HW Downing)

A.S.64607 DH-4B. 4th Sqn Wheeler Field, stalled on TO, crashed 2m W of Hilo, HI 21.2.24 (1/Lt WO Goldsborough)

A.S.64611 DH-4M-2S. Langley Field 1927

A.S.64620 DH-4B. Mitchel Field, EF on T/O, FL, Lakehurst NAS, 31.5.24 (Capt RA Kinloch & passenger both unhurt)

A.S.64627 DH-4M-2S. Fairfield Air Intermediate Depot 1927; Circuits & bumps, crashed nr Southville, VA 5.10.29 (Lt HJ Osterman & passenger both killed)

A.S.64629 DH-4B. Ditched in Hudson River, nr Mitchel Field 20.12.24 (Sgt SH Turner minor injuries)

A.S.64832 DH-4B. Langley Field, landing accident 13.3.22 (M/Sgt P Biesiot)

A.S.64633 DH-4B. McCook Field, EF on T/O, FL on a/f 10.1.24 (1/Lt Hutchinson & passenger unhurt)

A.S.65348 DH-4. FL due to fog and low cloud, overturned, John Skinner Farm Hayfi, Veazie, ME 2.9.22 (Lt FB Valentine & Lt C Lintens unhurt)

A.S.65690 DH-4. While ferrying, EF, FL on beach, high wave caught undercarriage, nr Comfort Point 11.7.21

A.S.68002 DH-4B. FL in bad weather, N of Prince Frederick, MD 15.15.21 (1/Lt CA Cover unhurt)

A.S.68008 DH-4Ard. Carlstrom Field, Arcadia, FL, returning from cross-country to Dayton, FL, landed after dark, crashed, caught fire 22.2.21 (2/Lt RC McDonald & Capt FN Shumaker OK)

A.S.68036 DH-4B. Carlstrom Field, FL, landing accident, caught fire (1/Lt L Claude & 5 others minor injuries)

A.S.68042 DH-4B. Roberts Field, EF in fog, FL nr Birmingham, AL 20.11.23 (Capt AN Duncan & passenger both unhurt)

A.S.68050 DH-4B. Landing accident, Selma, AL 11.4.23 (Mjr R Brown unhurt)

A.S.68057 DH-4B. Carlstrom Field, FL, landing accident 14.2.22 (Cdt GC McGinley minor injuries)

A.S.68113 DH-4B. Kelly Field, mid-air collision with another D.H.4B nr airfield 8.5.24 (2/Lt SL Thompson & a civilian both killed)

A.S.68114 DH-4B. 44th Observation Sqn, Post Field, spun, caught fire, nr Leon, OK 12.4.24 (1/Lt SB Ebert killed)

A.S.68120 DH-4B. Mitchel Field, EF, FL Smithtown Branch Line, NY 15.2.25 (Cpl HR Angell & passenger unhurt)

A.S.68134 DH-4B. Flew into ground nr Sweeney, TX 30.4.22 (1/Lt Ellis minor injuries)

A.S.68144 DH-4B. Kelly Field, TX, ran out of fuel at 700ft in storm, FL, nosed over, Laringen, TX 27.5.21 (1/Lt MG Estabrook Jnr OK)

A.S.68148 DH-4B. Post Field, landing accident 27.10.21 (1/Lt SC Skamp unhurt)

A.S.68160 DH-4B. Air Service Observation School, Post Field, Fort Sill, OK, stalled landing, wing hit ground, DBR 2.12.20 (Cdt CR Covell & Cdt JC Richardson OK)

A.S.68161 DH-4B. Post Field, Fort Sill, OK, flat tyre, stbd wing hit ground landing 7.8.21 (1/Lt FC Nelson & Staff Sgt EC Chambers of 22nd Sqn OK)

A.S.68162 DH-4B. EF, FL nr Ellington Field, TX 23.9.21 (1/Lt EE Glenn unhurt); Landing accident, Laurie Field, WV 11.12.22 (1/Lt RR Yeager & passenger unhurt)

A.S.68165 Rebuild ex A.S.31818; To A.S.25-089

A.S.68166 DH-4Amb-1.

A.S.68167 DH-4B, stalled and crashed nr a/f 10.2.23 (Lt HJ Martin & passenger both killed)

A.S.68171 DH-4B. Landing accident, Kelly Field, TX 22.12.21

A.S.68178 DH-4B. Kelly Field, spun in 2m N of a/f 2.9.24 (Lt TM Conroy & passenger both killed)

A.S.68180 DH-4B. Landing accident, Colorado Springs, CO 26.5.22 (1/Lt RHV Stackhouse unhurt)

A.S.68184 DH-4B. Kelly Field No.2, TX, undercarriage collapsed on landing 25.5.21 (1/Lt HA Craig OK)

A.S.68188 DH-4Amb-2

A.S.68203 DH-4B. Post Field, EF, FL 4m E of Fort Sill, OK 18.4.22 (1/Lt WR Peck unhurt)

A.S.68204 DH-4B. Post Field, landing accident 11.12.21 (Capt JW Kelly minor injuries)

A.S.68208 DH-4B-1. Inst. California National Guard, Los

Angeles 1927
A.S.68209 DH-4B. McCook Field P-211
A.S.68214 DH-4B. McCook Field P-220
A.S.68219 DH-4BP-1. Mitchel Field 1927
A.S.68220 DH-4BP-1 Chanute Field 1927
A.S.68226 DH-4B. Phillips Field, MD, landing accident 14.9.24 (S/Sgt LP Hudson unhurt)
A.S.68236 DH-4B. Post Field, landing accident 11.12.21 (Capt C Giffin unhurt)
A.S.68564 Renumbered A.S.25-054
A.S.68590 to A.S.68592. XDH-4M-1. Boeing-built prototypes (c/n's 515 - 517)
A.S.68591 DH-4M-1. Luke Field 1927
A.S.68592 XDH-4M-1. McCook Field P-337. Langley Field 1927
A.S.68645 DH-4B. Crissy Field, landing accident, Reno, NV 4.6.24 (1/Lt WR Swenley & passenger both unhurt)
A.S.68647 DH-4B. Crissy Field, landing accident 17.7.22 (1/Lt RE Selff & passenger unhurt); Landing accident nr Blairsden, CA 17.8.22 (1/Lt RE Selff unhurt)
A.S.68656 D.H.4B. Crissy Field, landing accident 15.11.23 (Mjr GH Brett); DH-4B-1 at Bolling Field, DC 1927
A.S.68661 DH-4B. Kelly Field, EF, FL Jourdanton, TX 5.1.25 (Cdt JH Collins unhurt)
A.S.68669 DH-4B. Crissy Field, EF, FL on a/f, hit MT 4.8.22 (Sgt F Kelly unhurt)
A.S.68673 DH-4B. Crissy Field, fog, FL on beach nr a/f 26.10.22 (1/Lt JB Patrick unhurt)
A.S.68676 DH-4B. Kelly Field, EF, FL N of a/f 19.8.24 (1/Lt SM Hopkins)
A.S.68677 DH-4B. Kelly Field, caught fire in air, FL 3m S of Coutoule, TX 19.3.23 (Capt TS Voss & passenger both unhurt)
A.S.68678 DH-4B. Camp Hancock, EF on T/O, FL, crashed Augusta, GA 11.6.22 (1/Lt R Aldsworth & passenger seriously injured)
A.S.68853 DH-4B. Post Field, landing accident 14.12.21 (1/Lt WN Brookley minor injuries & passenger unhurt)
A.S.22-238 DH-4B. Landing accident, San Mateo, CA 28.2.23 (1/Lt JB Patrick & passenger unhurt)
A.S.22-257 DH-4 Atlantic rebuild ex A.S.23698. To DH-4M-2T in 1925; Fairfield Service Section 1927; Brooks Field, hit tree ne airfield 25.1.28 (2/Lt JR Harhum)
A.S.22-268 DH-4B. Fort Bliss, landing accident 23.11.23 (Capt TW Hastey & passenger unhurt)
A.S.22-349 Kelly Field, structural failure 200yds N of airfield 5.5.24 (2/Lt BW Chidlaw)
A.S.22-351 DH-4B. Brooks Field, damaged in hangar fire, Hat Box Field, OK 19.11.24
A.S.22-356 to 22-359 DH-4M. Atlantic rebuilds; To DH-4M-2T in 1925
A.S.22-356 DH-4M-2T. Kelly Field 1927
A.S.22-358 DH-4B. Kelly Field, hit tree landing, 10m N of airfield 13.6.24 (2/Lt JH Hicks)
A.S.22-359 DH-4M-2T. Kelly Field 1927; Crashed nr Windmill Field, TX 26.4.29 (Lt Hudson)
A.S.22-362 DH-4B. Brooks Field, EF, FL 26m N of Comstock, TX 3.2.24 (S/Sgt RL Mitchell); Ground fire, Fort Scott, KS 24.12.24 (2/Lt LO Craigis)
A.S.22-365 DH-4B. Brooks Field, FL nr airfield in fog 4.12.22 (1/Lt LR Hewitt & passenger unhurt)
A.S.22-394 DH-4B. Mitchel Field, EF, FL 4m from Woonsocket, RI 8.9.24 (1/Lt KS Hoag minor injuries)
A.S.22-411 DH-4B. Brooks Field, EF on TO, FL, Seagoville, TX 22.12.23 (2/Lt RC Ashley minor injuries)
A.S.22-506 DH-4B. Crissy Field, landing accident 3.78.22 (1/Lt RE Selff)
A.S.22-510 DH-4B. Chanute Field, EF, FL nr Rantoul, IL 12.5.24 (1/Lt HH Carr)
A.S.22-511 DH-4B. McCook Field P-251
A.S.22-513 DH-4BP-1. 8th Photo Sqn, Boston Airport, MA, fast landing, overshot, stalled in 10.10.23 (1/Lt HB Chandler & Sgt HJ Hendricks both unhurt)
A.S.22-514 DH-4B. McCook Field, landing accident 31.10.22 (M/Sgt P Biesott)
A.S.22-517 DH-4B. McCook Field P-247
A.S.22-520 DH-4B. McCook Field P-258; Weather closed in, FL nr New London, CT 8.11.22 (1/Lt SP Mills unhurt)
A.S.22-521 DH-4B. FL in fog, hit tree 6m W of Dayton, OK 21.3.42 (S/Sgt JG O'Neal)
A.S.22-523 DH-4B. McCook Field P-257
A.S.22-528 DH-4B. McCook Field P-256
A.S.22-586 DH-4B. McCook Field P-271. Builder unknown
A.S.22-587 DH-4B. McCook Field P-287. Builder unknown
A.S.22-591 DH-4B. Crissy Field, hit HT wire landing nr Del Monte, CA 24.11.22 (1/Lt LF Post)
A.S.22-594 DH-4B. Mitchell Field, EF, fuel blockage, FL, hit stone wall, M.Aldege Farm, Cumberland, RI 8.9.24 (1/Lt ES Hoag & P1C LH Jankowski both minor injuries)
A.S.22-595 DH-4B. Crashed on TO Port Jervis 14.3.23 (1/Lt P Melville); Phillips Field, EF, FL 2m E of Elizaville, NY 10.7.24 (1/Lt CF Bond & passenger both unhurt)
A.S.22-596 DH-4B. McCook Field P-275. Builder unknown
A.S.22-599 DH-4B. Builder unknown
A.S.22-693 DH-4B. Chanute Field, landing accident nr Rantoul 7.6.24 (1/Lt CH Mills)
A.S.22-1000 to 22-1049 DH-4B. Boeing rebuilds as Type 16 (c/n's 412-461)
A.S.22-1002 DH-4B. Phillipines 1927
A.S.22-1004 DH-4B. Phillipines 1927
A.S.22-1005 DH-4B. Phillipines 1927
A.S.22-1006 DH-4B. Phillipines 1927
A.S.22-1007 DH-4B. Phillipines 1927
A.S.22-1008 DH-4B. Phillipines 1927
A.S.22-1011 to A.S.22-1019 DH-4B. Phillipines 1927
A.S.22-1018 DH-4B. To DH-4B-K
A.S.22-1022 DH-4B. To DH-4BP-1
A.S.22-1038 DH-4B. Luke Field 1927
A.S.22-1045 DH-4B. 4th Observation Sqn, hit HT wire, Waipahu Plantation, HI 23.7.25 (Lt JF McBlain seriously injured)
A.S.22-1049 DH-4B. 4th Observation Sqn, hit HT wire, Waipahu Plantation, HI 23.7.25 (2/Lt JA Wyatt killed)
A.S.22-1053 to 22-1058 DH-4B. Fisher rebuilds
A.S.22-1055 DH-4B. Phillipines 1927
A.S.22-1060 to 22-1094 DH-4B. Wittman rebuilds
A.S.22-1060 to A.S.22-1062. DH-4B. Phillipines 1927
A.S.22-1067 DH-4B. Phillipines 1927
A.S.22-1068 DH-4B. Phillipines 1927
A.S.22-1070 DH-4B. Phillipines 1927
A.S.22-1072 DH-4B. Phillipines 1927
A.S.22-1076 DH-4B. Phillipines 1927
A.S.22-1077 DH-4B. Phillipines 1927
A.S.22-1079 DH-4B. Phillipines 1927
A.S.22-1082 DH-4B. Phillipines 1927
A.S.22-1091 DH-4B. Phillipines 1927
A.S.22-1092 DH-4B. Phillipines 1927
A.S.22-1094 DH-4B. Phillipines 1927
A.S.22-1093 DH-4B. France Field, CZ 1927
A.S.22-1100 to 22-1142 DH-4B. Aeromarine rebuilds
A.S.22-1100 DH-4B. Inst. New York National Guard, Staten Island 1927
A.S.22-1104 DH-4M. 11th Bombardment Sqn, landing accident, Langley Field 4.7.24 (Sgt HD Herron)
A.S.22-1107 DH-4B-3. McCook Field P-298
A.S.22-1110 DH-4B. McCook Field P-289
A.S.22-1113 DH-4B. Phillips Field, EF, FL 2m from Aberdeen, MD 19.2.25 (Capt A Nilsen & passenger both unhurt)
A.S.22-1115 DH-4B. Boston Airport, ferrying to Mitchel Field, FL in fog, hit trees, burnt out, nr Sakonnet Pt, Little Compton, RI 13.6.24 (Capt LH Knight minor injuries)
A.S.22-1116 DH-4B. Marshall Field, spun in on airfield 25.11.24 (Capt D Bedinger & passenger both killed)
A.S.22-1117 DH-4B. McCook Field P-297
A.S.22-1120 DH-4M-2T. Kelly Field 1927
A.S.22-1121 DH-4B-P2. McCook Field P-300
A.S.22-1122 DH-4B-3. McCook Field P-301
A.S.22-1123 DH-4B. McCook Field P-299
A.S.22-1124 DH-4B. McCook Field P-296
A.S.22-1125 DH-4B-3. McCook Field P-302
A.S.22-1126 DH-4M-2T. Langley Field 1927
A.S.22-1128 DH-4B. McCook Field P-292
A.S.22-1131 DH-4B. Chanute Field, EF, FL, crashed on airfield 12.8.24 (1/Lt FP Albrook & passenger both seriously injured)
A.S.22-1139 DH-4M-2T. Langley Field 1927
A.S.22-1142 DH-4M-2T. Kelly Field 1927; Crashed Matagorda, TX 17.1.31 (2/Lt RE Cobb)
A.S.22-1149 DH-4B. Grisard Field, landing accident 11.8.24 (1/Lt DM Outcalt & passenger unhurt)

A Boeing-built DH-4M-1T dual control trainer. (via Gordon Swanborough)

A.S.22-1152 DH-4B. Langin Field, spun in nr Moundsville, WV 23.4.24 (1/Lt A Elbro & passenger both minor injuries)
A.S.22-1154 DH-4B. To Mexican Air Force
A.S.22-1155 to 22-1188 DH-4B. Thomas-Morse rebuilds
A.S.22-1168 DH-4B. Langley Field, EF, FL, N of airfield 20.10.24 (1/Lt HF Sessions & passenger both minor injuries)
A.S.22-1170 DH-4BG. Edgewood Arsenal 1927
A.S.22-1180 DH-4B. Accident, Minneapolis Field 1.7.27
A.S.22-1182 DH-4B. Langley Field, crashed on landing Bristol, VA 23.8.24 (2/Lt JA Collins & passenger unhurt)
A.S.22-1187 DH-4B. Chanute Field, landing accident 25.4.24 (2/Lt CH Howard); To Mexican Air Force
A.S.22-1188 DH-4B. Inst. Arkansas National Guard, Little Rock 1927
A.S.23-109 XC0-7A Boeing-built (c/n 519). Marked A.S.23102 in error. McCook Field P-332
A.S.23-406 DH-4B. Atlantic rebuild. To DH-4M-2T 1925. Kelly Field 1927
A.S.23-408 DH-4B. Kelly Field, spun in, caught fire 17.4.24 (1/Lt WA Frederick & passenger both killed)
A.S.23-415 DH-4. Bolling Field, DC, FL in bad weather, Brandywine, MD 19.1.25 (Capt CB Oldfield)
A.S.23-418 DH-4B. Chanute Field, TO accident, Fort Crook, NW 15.9.24 (1/Lt JJ Devery)
A.S.23-420 DH-4B-3. McCook Field P-334
A.S.23-421 DH-4B. Langley Field, FL in bad weather, crashed 16m E of Moundsville (1/Lt T Brooks killed)
A.S.23-423 DH-4B. Fisher rebuild. Kelly Field 1927 as DH-4M-2T
A.S.23-425 DH-4B. Atlantic rebuild; To DH-4M-2T 1925; San Antonio Air Intermediate Depot 1927
A.S.23-426 DH-4B. Atlantic rebuild; To DH-4M-2T 1925
A.S.23-427 DH-4B. Atlantic rebuild; To DH-4M-2T 1925; Kelly Field 1927
A.S.23-444 DH-4B. Kelly Field, mid-air collision 18,11,23 (1/Lt PT Wagner killed)
A.S.23-451 DH-4B. Kelly Field, mid-air collision 18.11.23 (1/Lt WR Peck minor injuries)
A.S.23-459 to 23-463 DH-4B. rebuilds
A.S.23-460 Chanute Field 1927 as DH-4BP-1
A.S.23-463 Chanute Field 1927 as DH-4BP-1
A.S.23-465 DH-4B. Chanute Field, EF on T/O, FL 1m NW of Schoen Field, IN 22.5.24 (1/Lt DM Reeves & passenger unhurt)
A.S.23-467 to 23-471 DH-4B. rebuilds
A.S.23-467 DH-4BP-1. Kelly Field 1927
A.S.23-471 DH-4B. France Field, CZ 1927
A.S.23-503 DH-4B. Selfridge Field, EF, FL on ice, Maumee Bay, OH 14.3.24 (Cpl L Manning) unhurt); A/c salved
A.S.23-507 DH-4B, Maxwell Field, EF, FL 7m E of Montgomery, AL 8.11.24 1/Lt EM Morris & passenger unhurt)
A.S.23-511 DH-4BM-1 rebuild ex A.S.25-52
A.S.23-515 DH-4B-4 rebuild
A.S.23-516 to 23-522 DH-4B rebuilds
A.S.23-516 DH-4B. Chanute Field, FL in fog, hit HT wires, 1m NW of Paxton, IL 28.3.24 (Capt AE Easterbrook)
A.S.23-523 DH-4B rebuild
A.S.23-527 DH-4B. Post Field, EF, FL 10m E of Ponca City, OK 8.10.23 (2/Lt JF McBlain & passenger both unhurt)
A.S.23-524 DH-4B rebuild
A.S.23-552 DH-4B. McCook Field P-315; Rebuilt as DH-4BP-1
A.S.23-553 DH-4B. McCook Field P-312; Rebuilt as DH-4BP-1
A.S.23-557 DH-4M rebuild
A.S.23-574 DH-4M. Kelly Field, crashed 3m S of airfield, BO 19.4.27 (1/Lt ED Raney killed)
A.S.23-660 to 23-674 DH-4M. Gallaudet rebuilds
A.S.23-669 DH-4B. McCook Field P-329; Hit tree trunk nr Wright Field 7.1.25 (1/Lt EH Barksdale & passenger unhurt)
A.S.23-672 DH-4B. McCook Field P-429; Fairfield Air Intermediate Depot 1927
A.S.23-674 DH-4B-2. Inst. Massachusetts National Guard, Boston 1927
A.S.23-680 DH-4B. Selfridge Field, EF, FL Oscada Field, MI 25.5.24 (1/Lt TW Blackburn & passenger unhurt)

A.S.23-682 DH-4B. Brooks Field, EF, FL nr Chicotah, OK 23.4.23 (1/Lt C McMullen)
A.S.23-685 to 23-688 DH-4B. Atlantic rebuilds; To DH-4MT in 1925
A.S.23-685 DH-4M-2T. San Antonio Air Intermediate Depot 1927; Brooks Field, crashed nr airfield 20.2.30 (2/Lt DT Skuvey)
A.S.23-688 DH-4M-2Y. Kelly Field 1927 as DH-4M-2T
A.S.23-691 DH-4B-5. "Honeymoon Express". Engineering Division rebuild with 2-seat rear cabin. McCook Field P-388
A.S.23-697 DH-4B. McCook Field P-389; Rebuilt as DH-4N
A.S.23-699 DH-4B. Cox-Klemin rebuild. Fairfield Air Intermediate Depot 1927
A.S.23-702 DH-4M. Atlantic rebuild; To DH-4M-T in 1925; Kelly Field 1927
A.S.23-703 DH-4M. Atlantic rebuild; To DH-4M-T in 1925; Kelly Field 1927
A.S.23-707 DH-4B. Logan Field 1927
A.S.23-708 DH-4B; To DH-4M-2T. Kelly Field 1927
A.S.23-709 to 23-715 DH-4B. Cox-Klemin rebuilds
A.S.23-711 DH-4B. Pope Field 1927
A.S.23-716 DH-4B. Crashed nr Mitchell Field 5.1.28 (J Tactail)
A.S.23-716 to 23-725 DH-4M. Atlantic rebuilds. To DH-4M-2T
A.S.23-716 DH-4M-2T. Kelly Field 1927
A.S.23-717 DH-4M-2T. Kelly Field 1927
A.S.23-722 DH-4M-2T. Kelly Field 1927; Crashed nr Eagle Pass, TX 27.9.30 (2/Lt GR Atkinson)
A.S.23-723 DH-4M-2T. San Antonio Air Intermediate Depot 1927; March Field, CA, crashed nr airfield 29.7.29
A.S.23-725 DH-4M-2T. Kelly Field 1927
A.S.23-726 DH-4M. Witteman-Lewis rebuild
A.S.23-730 DH-4M. Witteman-Lewis rebuild
A.S.23-732 DH-4M. Atlantic rebuild. Kelly Field 1927 as DH-4M-2T; Crashed nr March Field 22.5.30 (2/Lt HH Dekaye killed)
A.S.23-738 DH-4B-2. Witteman-Lewis rebuild
A.S.23-740 to 23-743 DH-4M. Atlantic rebuilds; To DH-4M-2T
A.S.23-743 DH-4M-2T. Kelly Field 1927
A.S.23-744 DH-4B. Witteman-Lewis rebuild
A.S.23-751 to 23-757 DH-4M. Atlantic rebuilds; To DH-4M-2
A.S.23-751 DH-4M-2T. Kelly Field 1927
A.S.23-753 DH-4B ex A.S.23920; To DH-4BM; To DH-4M-2; Became A.S.25-085
A.S.23-757 DH-4M-2T. Kelly Field 1927
A.S.23-758 DH-4B. Witteman-Lewis rebuild. Air Corps dett Fort Levenham 1927
A.S.23-766 to 23-774 DH-4B. Atlantic rebuilds; To DH-4M-2
A.S.23-766 DH-4M-2T. Kelly Field 1927
A.S.23-774 DH-4M-2T. Kelly Field 1927
A.S.23-1107 to 23-1125 DH-4B rebuilds
A.S.23-1200 DH-4B-5. McCook Field P-288
A.S.23-1249 DH-4B-5. Engineering Division rebuild
A.S.23-1328 DH-4B rebuild
A.S.23-1329 DH-4B. Kelly Field, spun in 14.12.23 (1/Lt EV Willis & passenger both killed)
A.S.24-22 DH-4B. Kelly Field, crashed on landing 27.7.24 (2/Lt TM Conroy & passenger unhurt)
A.S.24-29 DH-4B. Fort Bliss, crashed on landing (2/Lt CE O'Conner & passenger both unhurt)
A.S.24-30 DH-4B. 47th School Sqn, Brooks Field, hit tree, caught fire, 1m NE of Pendleton 18.12.23 (Capt HE Sturchen & passenger both killed)
A.S.24-34 to 24-37 DH-4M. Atlantic rebuilds; Became DH-4M-2 in 1925
A.S.24-34 DH-4M-2T. Kelly Field 1927
A.S.24-37 DH-4M-2T. San Antonio Air Intermediate Depot 1927
A.S.24-38 DH-4B. Brooks Field, landing accident, Hondo, TX 17.6.24 (2/Lt T Griffiss & passenger unhurt)
A.S.24-51 to 24-54 DH-4B rebuilds; To DH-4BP-1
A.S.24-51 DH-4BP-1. Pope Field 1927
A.S.24-53 DH-4BP-1. Chanute Field, crashed nr airfield 7.7.27 (2/Lt JM Fitsmaurice)
A.S.24-54 DH-4BP-1. Chanute Field 1927
A.S.24-64 to 24-85 DH-4B. rebuilds
A.S.24-64 DH-4B. France Field, CZ 1927
A.S.24-66 DH-4B. France Field, CZ 1927
A.S.24-70 DH-4B. France Field, CZ 1927
A.S.24-73 DH-4B. France Field, CZ 1927
A.S.24-77 DH-4B. France Field, CZ 1927
A.S.24-85 DH-4B. France Field, CZ 1927
A.S.24-95 DH-4B rebuild. Phillipines 1927
A.S.24-111 DH-4B-4 McCook Field P-336
A.S.24-115 to 24-131 DH-4B. Gallaudet rebuilds
A.S.24-117 Conv DH-4S. Aberdeen Proving Ground 1927
A.S.24-131 DH-4B-1. Sand Point 1927
A.S.24-247 to 24-253 DH-4B. Fisher rebuilds; To DH-4B-4 at Fairfield Air Intermediate Depot
A.S.24-247 DH-4B-4. McCook Field P-359; Wright Field 1927
A.S.24-249 DH-4B. Chanute Field, FL in bad weather, nr Zionsville, IN 17.1.25 (2/Lt HG Peterson)
A.S.24-250 DH-4B-4. Fairfield Station Supply 1927
A.S.24-251 DH-4B. Langley Field, landing accident, nr Evansville, WV 13.2.25 (Cpl HR Angell)
A.S.24-253 DH-4B-4. McCook Field P-382; Fairfield Station Supply 1927
A.S.24-301 DH-4M-1. McCook Field P-371; Boeing rebuild given further new serial number
A.S.24-302 to 24-436 Not used, possibly intended for 135 Atlantic DH-4M-2 rebuilds which in the event retained their original numbers
A.S.24-430 DH-4B. Brooks Field, landing accident 20.8.24 (Cdt BA Bridget)
A.S.24-437 DH-4B. Fisher rebuild ex A.S.30346
A.S.24-451 to 24-454 DH-4M. Boeing rebuilds as Type 16 (c/n's 451-454)
A.S.24-451 DH-4M-1. Luke Field 1927
A.S.24-452 DH-4M-1. Luke Field 1927
A.S.24-453 DH-4M-1. FL nr Turkey Point, MD 9.9.26 (1/Lt HL George)
A.S.24-454 DH-4M-1. France Field, CZ 1927
A.S.25-45 DH-4B. Clover Field, landing accident Ventura Field 18.2.25 (1/Lt HS Kenyon & passenger unhurt)
A.S.25-46 DH-4B-1 rebuild ex A.S.32488. Inst. Washington National Guard, Spokane 1927
A.S.25-48 DH-4BM-1 rebuilds
A.S.25-52 DH-4BM-1 rebuild ex A.S.23-511. Pope Field 1927 as DH-4BM Special
A.S.25-54 DH-4B rebuild ex A.S.68564. To DH-4BP-1. Luke Field 1927
A.S.25-69 DH-4BM-1 Clover Field 1927
A.S.25-78 to 25-83 DH-4B. Gallaudet rebuilds
A.S.25-78 DH-4BK rebuild ex A.S.23707; Aberdeen Proving Ground 1927; Circuits & bumps, EF on TO, crashed nr Middletown, PA 25.5.27 (Mjr H Geiger killed)
A.S.25-83 DH-4BM-1 rebuild ex A.S.23886; Pearson Field 1927
A.S.25-85 to 25-89 DH-4B. Witteman rebuilds
A.S.25-85 DH-4BM rebuild ex A.S.23-753, ex A.S.23920
A.S.25-89 DH-4BM-1 rebuild ex A.S.68165, ex A.S.31818; Clover Field, CA, crashed nr airfield 26.7.26 (1/Lt GP Eien)
A.S.25-107 DH-4B rebuild. Chanute Field 1928 as DH-4B-4
A.S.25-121 XDH-4B5 rebuild by Engineering Division; Became a.S.26-021
A.S.25-131 DH-4B rebuild. Clover Field 1927 as DH-4BM-1
A.S.25-161 to 25-163 DH-4BK. Fisher rebuilds
A.S.25-163 DH-4B. Crashed nr Crissy Field, CA 12.7.27
A.S.25-445 DH-4B rebuild. Bolling Field 1927 as DH-4BM
A.S.25-447 DH-4M. Curtiss-Wright rebuild
A.S.26-003 DH-4B. Douglas rebuild. Inst. Tennessee National Guard, Nashville 1927 as DH-4BM
A.S.26-021 XDHB-5 rebuild by Engineering Division, ex A.S.25-121; ALSO DH-4BS McCook Field P-397
A.S.26-029 & 26-030 DH-4B rebuilds
A.S.26-029 DH-4BK. McCook Field P-423
A.S.26-030 DH-4BK. McCook Field P-398; DH-4K at Wright Field 1927

Unidentified:
27.7.18 DH-4 "A.S.3834". Rich Field, spun in 6m W of Waco, TX 27.7.18 (2/Lt HC Winter & passenger both killed)
25.8.18 DH-4. 135th Aero Sqn, photo mission Lahayville-Bouillonville, in combat with 4 EA, rudder shot up, spun down, FL in trenches, crashed (2/Lt WC Suiter OK & 1/Lt LA Smith wounded)
4.9.18 DH-4. Crashed State Fairground, Indianapolis, IN
12.9.18 DH-4. 8th Aero Sqn, FTR combat with EA, pm? (1/Lt HW Mitchell PoW & 2/Lt JW Artz PoW wounded)
12.9.18 DH-4. 20th Aero Sqn, contact patrol St. Mihiel, lost in rain clouds at 300ft, FL east of lines (1/Lt GM Crawford

An Atlantic-built DH-4M-2K fitted with target towing gear. (via Gordon Swanborough)

PoW & 2/Lt JG O'Toole (attd from 96th Sqn) wounded PoW)

12.9.18 DH-4. 50th Aero Sqn, left 10.30?, contact patrol in support of 82nd Division, believed hit by ground fire, crashed Thionville (1/Lt HleN Stevens & 2/Lt EH Gardiner both killed)

12.9.18 DH-4. 135th Aero Sqn, artillery recce, became lost in low clouds & wind, FL Switzerland (1/Lt TJD Fuller & 1/Lt V Brookhart both interned)

12.9.18 DH-4. 135th Aero Sqn, contact patrol, left 0530, forced low by clouds, hit by US shell & blew up, crashed, caught fire (2/Lt JE Bowyer & 1/Lt AT Johnson both killed)

12.9.18 DH-4. 135th Aero Sqn, contact patrol?, in combat with 6 Fokker DVII, shot up but returned (1/Lt GM Chritzman & 1/Lt MJ Reed OK)

12.9.18 DH-4. 135th Aero Sqn, line recce in bad weather, combat with 6 Fokker DVII shot down in flames nr Vilcey-sur-Trey (1/Lt WC Suiter DSC & 2/Lt GE Morse DSC both killed)

13.9.18 DH-4. 8th Aero Sqn, no details (1/Lt EG West wounded)

13.9.18 DH-4. 8th Aero Sqn, FTR running combat with Fokker DVII (1/Lt HB Rex & 2/Lt WF Gallagher both killed)

13.9.18 DH-4. 50th Aero Sqn, contact patrol, shot up by rifle fire, FL near lines to help observer but found dead (1/Lt DC Beebe OK & 2/Lt FK Bellows killed)

14.9.18 DH-4. 11th Aero Sqn, bombing raid on Conflans, in combat with Fokker DVIIs, shot down in spiral from 8,000ft (1/Lt FT Shoemaker wounded PoW & 2/Lt RH Groner injured PoW)

14.9.18 DH-4. 11th Aero Sqn, bombing raid on Conflans, shared victory, then shot down in combat with Fokker DVIIs (2/Lt H Shidler PoW & 2/Lt HH Sayre killed)

16.9.18 DH-4. 20th Aero Sqn, bombing raid on Conflans, through drop-outs had reached target alone, then also chased back by EAs, hit by AA nr Etain, down OOC but recovered, then engine failed, FL, crashed just west of lines (1/Lt AF Seaver DSC & 1/Lt JY Stokes DSC both OK)

18.9.18 DH-4. 11th Aero Sqn, bombing raid on La Chaussée, difficult cloud conditions, in combat with 10 Fokker DVII, controls shot up, caught fire, FL nr Olley, crashed east of lines (1/Lt TD Hooper (Sqn CO) wounded PoW & 1/Lt RR Root wounded PoW)

18.9.18 DH-4. 11th Aero Sqn, bombing raid on La Chaussée, difficult cloud conditions, in combat with Fokker DVIIs, shot down in flames (1/Lt JC Tyler & 1/Lt HH Strauch both killed)

18.9.18 DH-4. 11th Aero Sqn, bombing raid on La Chaussée, difficult cloud conditions, in combat with Fokker DVIIs, shot down in flames MIA (1/Lt LS Harter & 1/Lt McR Stephenson both killed)

18.9.18 DH-4. 11th Aero Sqn, led bombing raid on La Chaussée, difficult cloud conditions, in combat with Fokker DVIIs, fuel tank hit, then hit by AA, FL (1/Lt RF Chapin & 2/Lt CB Laird both PoW)

18.9.18 DH-4. 11th Aero Sqn, bombing raid on La Chaussée, difficult cloud conditions, combat with Fokker DVIIs, 1 possible EA, fought back to lines then FL nr Damloup (1/Lt VP Oatis & 2/Lt RJ Guthrie both OK, the only crew to survive this combat)

18.9.18 DH-4. 11th Aero Sqn, bombing raid on La Chaussée, difficult cloud conditions, combat with Fokker DVIIs shot down in flames by Ltn H Besserof Jasta 12 (1/Lt ET Comegys & 2/Lt AR Carter both killed)

5.10.18 DH-4. 50th Aero Sqn, search for "Lost Battalion" of 308th Regt trapped in ravine by enemy fire, shot down, crashed Binarville (1/Lt GR Phillips & 2/Lt MH Brown both OK)

5.10.18 DH-4. 50th Aero Sqn, search for "Lost Battalion" of 308th Regt trapped in ravine by enemy fire, shot down, crashed Vienne-le-Chateau (1/Lt SC Bird & 1/Lt WA Bolt both OK)

6.10.18 DH-4. 50th Aero Sqn, search for "Lost Battalion" of 308th Regt trapped in ravine by enemy fire, shot up by ground fire (1/Lt M Graham OK & 2/Lt JE McCurdy severely wounded)

6.10.18 DH-4. 50th Aero Sqn, search for "Lost Battalion" of 308th Regt trapped in ravine by enemy fire, shot up by ground fire down nr Binarville (2/Lt HE Goettler killed & 2/Lt ER Bleckley DoW - both awarded Medal of Honor for this action)

7.10.18 DH-4. 50th Aero Sqn, located the "Lost Battalion" of 308th Regt trapped in ravine by enemy fire, shot up (1/Lt RM Anderson & 1/Lt WJ Rogers OK)

8.10.18 DH-4. 50th Aero Sqn, shot up on food drop (1/Lt FC Slater wounded)

10.10.18 DH-4. 8th Aero Sqn, patrol attacked by 12 Fokker DVII shot down in flames, infantry reported seeing pilot on wing holding strut and attempting to control a/c until he fell off at 50ft (1/Lt CS Garrett & 1/Lt RJ Cochran both killed)

10.10.18 DH-4. 20th Aero Sqn, bombing raid on rail yards at Dun-sur-Meuse, in combat with 12 Fokker DVII shot clown (1/Lt WC Potter DSC & 1/Lt HW Wilmer both killed)

23.10.18 DH-4. 20th Aero Sqn, bombing raid, in combat with Fokker DVIIs nr Buzancy, radiator shot up (Capt CG Sellers DSC OK & 1/Lt PH Buckley wounded)

23.10.18 DH-4. 166th Aero Sqn, no details (Pilot OK & 2/Lt RW Steele wounded/injured)

23.10.18 DH-4. 166th Aero Sqn, bombing raid, shot up (Pilot OK & 1/Lt G Todd wounded)

27.10.18 DH-4. 11th Aero Sqn, after bombing raid on Briquenay, shot up in combat with Fokker DVIIs, FL, crashed (1/Lt DC Malcolm OK & 1/Lt LW Springer wounded)

29.10.18 DH-4. 135th Aero Sqn, photo recce Mars-la-Tour, shot up in combat with 7 Fokker DVII, FL (1/Lt EC Landon OK & 1/Lt PH Aldrich DSC killed)

31.10.18 DH-4. 166th Aero Sqn, bombing raid on Tailly-Barricourt, EAs seen using Barricourt-Bayonville road as airstrip, shot up in combat with 13 Fokker DVII (1/Lt S Pickard wounded & 2/Lt SL Cockrane killed)

1.11.18 DH-4. 168th Aero Sqn, no details (1/Lt RM Armstrong wounded & observer OK) [or 5.11.18?]

3.11.18 DH-4. 8th Aero Sqn, FTR low recce (2/Lt WW Royce & 2/Lt JJ McIlvaine both PoW)

3.11.18 DH-4. 168th Aero Sqn, low recce (Pilot OK & 1/Lt EA Hassett wounded)

3.11.18 DH-4. 168th Aero Sqn, low recce, shared KB down in flames 0930 (1/Lt ER Clark & 1/Lt BF Giles)

3.11.18 DH-4. 168th Aero Sqn, low recce, shared KB down in flames 0930 (2/Lt RG Conant & Lt Col JF Curry)

4.11.18 DH-4. 11th Aero Sqn, left late, shot down by AA in bombing raid on Cheveney-le-Chateau (1/Lt CJ Gatton & 1/Lt GE Bures both killed)

4.11.18 DH-4. 11th Aero Sqn, bombing raid on Cheveney-le-Chateau, shot up in combat with 18 Fokker DVII (1/Lt Newby wounded & 1/Lt JR Pearson severely wounded)

4.11.18 DH-4. 11th Aero Sqn, bombing raid on Cheveney-le-Chateau, in combat with Fokker DVIIs, heavily shot up, fuel tank on fire, down in flames, crashed nr Stenay (1/Lt DE Coates & 2/Lt LR Thrall both killed)

4.11.18 DH-4. 50th Aero Sqn, FTR (2/Lt DC Beebe & 2/Lt MK Lockwood both PoW)

4.11.18 DH-4. 168th Aero Sqn, no details (Pilot OK & /1/Lt E Pendell wounded) [or 5.11.18?]

5.11.18 DH-4. 20th Aero Sqn, after bombing raid on Mouzon, engine hit in combat with Fokker DVIIs at 12,000ft, went down partly under control, then sideslipped in Martincourt (1/Lt SP Mandell DoW & 2/Lt RW/RB Fulton PoW)

5.11.18 DH-4. 20th Aero Sqn, bombing raid on Mouzon, in combat with Fokker DVIIs at 13,000ft after drop, chased down by EA, went down in flames (1/Lt KG West & 1/Lt WF Frank both killed)

5.11.18 DH-4. 20th Aero Sqn, bombing raid on Mouzon, in combat with Fokker DVIIs Mouzon-Stenay, fuel tank & engine shot up, FL east of lines (1/Lt LB Edwards & 1/Lt KC Payne both PoW)

5.11.18 DH-4. No.14? 20th Aero Sqn, bombing raid on Mouzon, in combat with Fokker DVIIs Dun-sur-Meuse, shared victory 0925 - 0945 (2/Lt LP Kotpfgen OK & Cpl RC Alexander slightly wounded)

8.11.18 DH-4. 8th Aero Sqn, FTR (2/Lt CB Robinson & 2/Lt DD Watson both PoW)

28.6.19 DH-4. FL 25m E of New Bern, NC (Lt R Johnson unhurt)

19.7.19 DH-4 "82". Lost in fog, FL, crashed 12m W of Bellefonte, PA (Lt C Lamborn killed)

20.8.19 DH-4. Missing en route Yuma - San Diego (2/Lt FD Waterhouse & another both missing)

23.8.19 DH-4. Kelly Field, spun in nr airfield (2/Lt RH Haslam & passenger both killed)

4.10.19 DH-4 Bluebird trainer. Transcontinental Reliability Flight (air race), flew into trees in heavy mist, Prospect Mt, Port Jarvis, nr Middletown, NY (Mjr P Frissell killed & passenger seriously injured))

8.10.19 DH-4 Bluebird trainer. Transcontinental Reliability Flight (air race), engine failure, forced landed, sideslipped in nr Deposit, NY (Col GC Brant unhurt & observer 2/Lt WP Nevitt killed)

8.10.19 DH-4. Transcontinental Reliability Flight (air race), FL nr Candice, NY (1/Lt DB Gish & passenger unhurt)

9.10.19 DH-4. FL in Lake Erie (Lt AM Roberts & passenger both minor injuries)

9.10.19 DH-4. Transcontinental Reliability Flight (air race), EF, FL nr Plymouth, PA (2/Lt GC McDonald)

15.10.19 DH-4. Spun in nr Evanston, WY (2/Lt F Kirby & passenger both killed)

11.1.20 DH-4. Crashed nr Silver Creek, AZ (pilot unhurt & passenger killed)

6.3.20 DH-4 "512". Engine failure, stalled, dived in vertically, Post Field 6.3.20 (2/Lt FH Utley killed)

21.7.20 DH-4. FL, crashed off Long Island, NY (1/Lt CL Mitcap unhurt & passenger minor injuries)

19.8.20 DH-4. Missing en route Yuma-San Diego, AZ (2/Lt FD Waterhouse & passenger missing)

28.8.20 DH-4A. 2nd Observation Sqn, Luke Field, missing en route Oahu-Molokai Field (Lt RP Fox missing)

9.10.20 DH-4. Mitchel Field, LI, engine problem at 900ft, crashed ½m from Brood Street (Capt HM Smith)

12.2.21 DH-4B. Landing accident, Marfa Field, TX (1/Lt CB Deshields & passenger unhurt)

16.2.21 DH-4B. El Paso, TX, hit bump on airfield landing after dusk (1/Lt LL Harvey & Sgt WP Rhodes OK)

19.2.21 DH-4. Rolled over landing nr Long Branch, NJ (Lt W Fitzpatrick & passenger unhurt)

10.3.21 DH-4B. Nogales, AZ, wheel broke and tyre burst on take-off in high wind, totally wrecked (2/Lt HW Prosser & Pte H Williamson OK)

14.3.21 DH-4B. Fort Bliss, TX, cross-country flight, overshot landing, caught by wind, swung, wing hit parked a/c, both totally wrecked (1/Lt BE Lewis & Master Sgt RE Wiseman)

15.4.21 DH-4B. 'A' Flt, 12th Squadron, Douglas, AZ, u/c collapsed taxying out (1/Lt CE Shankle & Pte G Johnson OK)

22.4.21 DH-4B. 'B' Flt. 8th Squadron, Laredo, TX, test flight, crashed on landing, (1/Lt HG Crocker & Pte ED Seaman OK)

24.5.21 DH-4B. Port Bliss, TX, sideslipped landing cross-wind in small field at Roswell, NM (1/Lt CB Deshields & Staff Sgt T Shakespeare OK)

1.6.21 DH-4B, Douglas, AZ, FL 40m N of airfield (1/Lt FM Paul & passenger both unhurt)

4.6.21 DH-4B. Aberdeen, Idaho, bomb dropped off and exploded nr airfield (1/Lt C Eliason killed)

7.6.21 DH-4B. Mather Field, turned at low speed after take-off, crashed, burnt out (Cdt HE Page & Cdt JW Weatherby both killed)

7.6.21 DH-4B. Douglas, AZ, engine failure, FL, hit small ditch, u/c broke, went on nose,3m NE of airfield (1/Lt F Paul injured & Staff Sgt E Nendell slightly injured)

16.6.21 DH-4B. Douglas, AZ, engine overheating, climbed to cool it down but engine stopped, forced landing on rough ground, broke u/c, overturned, 15m WSW of Fort Huachaoa (Capt TW Hasty & Sgt RF Mants OK)

27.6.21 DH-4B. Mather Field, spun in nr Visalia, CA (Cdt HE Page & passenger both killed)

1.7.21 DH-4B. Douglas, AZ, engine failure, forced landed 40m N of airfield (1/Lt F Paul & Pte M Johnson OK)

6.7.21 DH-4B. EF, FL 30m S of Medford, OR (S/Sgt ML Helpman & passenger both minor injuries)

23.7.21 DH-4B. Edenton, NC, tried to land to avid rainstorm, axle broke landing, overturned (Cdt JJ Fretz OK)

27.7.21 DH-4B. EF at 200ft, turned back, spun in, caught fire, Weissenthurm, [Germany] (1/Lt KD Guenther & Cpl OL Rogers both killed)

3.9.21 DH-4B. Crashed nr Johnstown (Lt Goodrich & passenger)

3.9.21 DH-4B. Crashed nr Harper, WV (Lt Liebhauser)

4.9.21 DH-4B. Montague, CA, steep bank at 200ft, caught by gust, crashed, overturned, caught fire (Cdt RJ Hooly & Sgt TJ Thieziel both killed)

4.9.21 DH-4B. Spun in, caught fire, nr Montague, CA (Cdt RG Noelp & another both killed)

21.10.21 DH-4B-1. Port Matherson, Ga, overshot landing, crashed, completely wrecked (Capt LE Appleby killed)
26.10.21 6th Sqn Luke Field, spun in from 2,000ft, Waipio Peninsula, HI (Lt UC Boquet killed)
21.12.21 DH-4B. Fog, FL nr Bremond, TX (Capt CB Oldfield)
30.12.21 DH-4B. Kelly Field, stalled at low altitude, crashed (Capt F Place killed)
5.22 DH-4A. Ditched 500yds off Haleiwa, HI (Lt WJ White seriously injured)
19.5.22 DH-4B. Carlstrom Field, hit wires, spun in 1m from airfield (Pte MG McLauglin killed)
22.6.22 DH-4A. Ditched in Honolulu harbour, HI (Lt WD Clark unhurt)
8.22 DH-4A. 4th Sqn, hit parked DH-4, HT wire, Wheeler Field, HI (Capt AE King) [before 9.8.22]
6.8.22 DH-4. Crashed on TO, nr Pablo Beach, FL (Lt JS Doolittle unhurt)
8.10.22 DH-4. Landing accident, Kerville, TX (1/Lt P Holland minor injuries)
3.11.22 DH-4B. Ran out of fuel, FL 2.5m S of Prattville, AL 3.11.22 (Lt EC Harper)
12.11.22 DH-4. 5th Observation Sqn, circuits and bumps, crashed nr Brainard Field, Hartford, CT, WO (Lt J Blaney killed)
14.11.22 DH-4B. Logan Field, crashed nr airfield while landing (1/Lt EG Shrader killed & passenger seriously injured)
6.12.22 DH-4. Crashed nr Barton, MD (Sgt Loupious unhurt & passenger minor injuries)
29.2.23 DH-4B. Kelly Field, circuits & bumps, crashed 7m E of Laredo, TX (Lt FT Honsinger & passenger both killed)
18.3.23 DH-4. Fort Bliss, crashed on circuits and bumps (2/Lt KP Brown & passenger both killed)
23.4.23 DH-4. 57th School Sqn, pilot assigned to 27th Sqn (T/Sgt MN Rowland killed)
25.5.23 DH-4B. Bolling Field, DC, circuits & bumps, crashed nr airfield (Mjr T Duncan & passenger both killed)
21.7.23 DH-4. FL in bad weather, Edenton, NC (Cdt JB Frotz & passenger OK)
8.8.23 DH-4. 4th Observation Sqn, taxying accident, Wheeler Field, OH (Lt WB Clarke)
23.8.23 DH-4. 4th Observation Sqn, FL Luke Field, HI (Lt FC Wheeler)
8.5.24 DH-4B. Kelly Field, mid-air collision with A.S.68113 nr airfield (Lt White)
29.5.24 DH-4B. Kelly Field, spun in (2/Lt NP Beasley killed)
5.6.24 Kelly Field, mid-air collision with another A.S.22-364, 2m N of airfield 5.6.24 (Lt SL Stewart & passenger both killed)
11.10.24 DH-4B. Scott Field, IL, T/O accident 11.10.24 (1/Lt WT Atkinson unhurt & passenger minor injuries)
26.1.25 DH-4B. EF, FL Vineland, NJ (1/Lt DG Lingle & passenger both unhurt)
6.25 DH-4. Crissy Field, en route to Rockwell Field, EF, engine caught fire, FL on beach, Newport Beach, CA, a/c o/t in surf (Sgt C Guile OK)
16.7.25 DH-4. Accident Bolling Field, DC
8.10.25 DH-4B. Crashed nr Chanute Field, IL (Lt WL Wheeler killed & passenger minor injuries)
c.1926 DH-4. 16th Observation Sqn, Fort Crook, Omaha, en route to Fairfield, OH - EF, FL 40m from Iowa City, hit fence, one wing torn loose (Sgt OW Haynes); Repaired and arr Fairfield two days later
19.7.28 DH-4. Tyre burst landing, overturned, Portland Airport, Scarborough, MI (Lt G Lusk & Mech W Russell unhurt)

U.S.Navy

During the First World War, the US Navy received 155 DH-4s on transfer from the War Department, these being numbered A3245 to A3324 and A3384 to A3458. Many served with the Marine Corps in France.

The 1st Marine Aviation Force was organised in Florida, four squadrons being sent to France as the Day Wing, Northern Bombing Group. Disembarking at Brest on 30 July 1918, a headquarters was established at Bois-en-Ardres, having landing grounds in the Calais area with Squadrons A and B at Oye and Squadron C at La-Fresne. 72 American-built DH-4s were earmarked for transfer from the US Army for their use, to be shipped from the USA to the US Navy supply base at Pauillac, 30 miles from Bordeaux. However, the first deliveries took some time to assemble, and the first of these did not reach the squadrons until 7 September, most having been inadvertently sent to England; some Liberty-engined D.H.9As were sent from England in partial substitution. Pending further DH-4 deliveries, Marine pilots were attached to Nos.217 and 218 RAF squadrons, to help overcome a shortage of RAF pilots, these pilots serving in rotation so that each went on at least three raids.

On 5 October, Squadron D arrived at La-Fresne, and the four squadron were then redesignated Nos.7 to 10 Squadrons to conform with the Northern Bombing Group identification system. Seven days later the Marine squadrons began flying missions independently of the RAF, and on 14th Captain Robert S.Lytle of Squadron 9 led five DH-4s and three D.H.9As to drop 2,218lbs of bombs on Thielt railway yards in Belgium.

The DH-4s received new local numbers D-1 onwards, but by the time of the Armistice only 16 had actually reached the Marines in France; 20 Liberty-engined D.H.9As had also been received by then. A total of 14 raids was carried out between 14 October and 11 November, dropping 18,972lbs of bombs, in addition to 15,140lbs dropped by USMC crews whilst attached to RAF squadrons.

The insignia of this organisation was the American style roundel in place of the globe in the normal Marine Corps insignia. This was applied to all Marine Corps aircraft in France. A few aircraft in the United States were incorrectly painted with this insignia after the squadrons returned home.

The Marine Corps insignia on the fuselages of most aircraft of the Day Wing of the Northern Bombing Group were painted incorrectly on the starboard side. Rules of heraldry require the emblem to face the enemy, so in this case it should be looking forward. It is most noticeable in the position of wrongly-painted "dragging anchors"; the Marine Corps emblem has a right and a left as worn on the collar of the coat or shirt.

Known details of individual aircraft in France:

D-1 (A3295) Squadron C (later Squadron D); Attd 218 Sqdn 29.9.18; Bombing raid on Lichtervelde Railway Yards 1.10.18 (Capt RS Lytle USMC & Sgt A Wiman USMC) [the first US Marine Aviation operation with its own a/c, attd 218 Sqn]; Fokker OOC Coudekerque 08.15 8.10.18 (Lt R Talbot & Cpl RG Robinson); Bombing raid on Thielt, in combat with 12 EA on return of which 1 shot down and another unconfirmed, own a/c shot up, FL Hondschoote 14.10.18 (2/Lt R Talbot OK & Cpl RG Robinson wounded); Retd Northern Bombing Group 11.10.18 [sic]
D-2 (A3260) Squadron A, Forced landed Petit Fort Philipe, Gravelines 10.12.18
D-3 (A3269) Squadron A (later Squadron B, then Squadron C); Bombing raid on Thielt, in combat with 12 EA on return, EF, FL, hit by ground fire and AA while landing 14.10.18 (Capt RS Lytle & Cpl A Wiman both OK); A/c dismantled and salvaged after dark by Marine ground crews and returned to base [number D-3 uncertain]
D-4 (A3300) Squadron A; Later Squadron C; Redesignated Squadron 9 5.10.18; Bombing raid on Melle in dense fog, attacked by 3 EA in in combat over Ghent, shot up, crashed 22.10.18 (1/Lt HC Norman & 1/Lt CW Taylor both killed)
D-5 (A3280) Squadron B, later Squadron C; Bore US Marine Corps Globe and Anchor insignia imposed on Allied fuselage roundel
D-6 (A3262) Squadron C
D-7 (A3299) Squadron B
D-8 (A3278) Squadron C; Retd USA post-war; At Miami coded '7'
D-9 (A3264) Squadron C
D-10 (A3263) Squadron C
D-11 (A3261) Squadron C; Ardres by 24.10.18; Squadron 10 (coded 'D'), Bombing raid on Lokeren Railway Yard, lost way, engine trouble, FL, nose bent and radiator damaged, Steenheve, Schoondijke, Holland 12.00 27.10.18 (2/Lt F Nelms Jnr & 2/Lt JF Gibbs interned but soon retd Squadron 10); Dutch proposal to buy a/c for study purposes 3.12.18; Proposal rfused by War Ministry 28.2.19; Proposal repeated 14.6.19; US Naval attaché asked Chef Marine Staff (CMS) for whereabouts of a/c in connection with transport to USA 1.7.19 (nothing further known)
D-12 (A3270) Squadron C
D-13 (A3279) Squadron C

U.S.Marine Corps DH-4 A3280 'D-5' in France with the Northern Bombing Group in 1918. (via Gordon Swanborough)

D-14 (A3433) Squadron C, later Squadron D
D-15 (A3432) Squadron C, later Squadron D
D-16 (A3435) Squadron C, later Squadron D
D-17 (A3434) Squadron C, later Squadron D

Post-World War I, the US Navy obtained a total of 177 ex-Army DH-4Bs from the War Department. Initial deliveries in 1920 and 1921 comprised the following:

A5809-5814 (6)
A5834-5839 (6)
A5870-5884 (15)
A5982-6001 (20)

These 47 aircraft were followed by two further batches which were reworked by the Naval Aircraft Factory at Philadelphia before entering service between 1921 and 1923:

A6113-6192 (80)
A6352-6401 (50)

The above airframes included 73 DH-4B-1s, modified with a fuel capacity increase from 96 to 118 gallons, and other minor improvements. Serial numbers of the DH-4B-1s were A5877, A6155, A6164, A6173-6192 and A6352-6401

A further development of the basic DH-4B airframe resulted in the DH-4B-2. While the exact nature of the changes in this model are unclear, indications from the aircraft history cards suggest that it was an unarmed personnel transport. Known conversions, the majority from DH-4B-1s, were A6134, A6159, A6160, A6166, A6167, A6170, A6172, A6177, A6352, A6377 and A6380. One final DH-4B-2, A6514, was built from spares by the Naval Aircraft Factory in 1924, making a total of 12 for the type.

Perhaps the most unusual of the Navy DH-4Bs were the ambulance conversions, in which the upper rear fuselage was modified with a "turtledeck" housing to accommodate a stretcher. According to the history cards, only two of these were produced, A6113 and A6386, but photographic evidence exists for a third, A6125, while the ambulance compartment of A6386 was transferred at a later date to A6180. Although not the most modern of aircraft when serving in the early and mid-twenties, the DH-4B proved to be a useful general-purpose workhorse for the Navy and Marines at a time when money for new equipment was severely limited. The major problems with the design lay with the fuselage longerons, which were prone to twisting and splitting, and the undercarriage, which was considered to be of insufficient strength for regular operations from rough fields.

Quite clearly, these faults had also been recognised by the Army which, in 1923, contracted with Boeing for the DH-4M-1 model. Styled O2B-1 observation aircraft under the Navy aircraft designation system, these were rebuilt DH-4s utilising the original flying surfaces on new welded tubular steel fuselages, being the result of studies of the Fokker DVIIs brought to the USA after the war, and fitted with a strengthened landing gear.

Thirty such aircraft were delivered to the Navy in 1925 under conract numbes Aero-61 and Bu-25 carrying the serial numbers A6898-A6927. Five of these, A6919 and A6924-A6927, were converted to O2B-2s with extra equipment for cross-country flights, again, as with the DH-4B-2s, probably for use as transports for senior officers. Most of the surviving DH-4s and O2Bs had been retired by the end of 1928, with only two O2Bs continuing into early 1929.

Navy Service

On the United States east coast most of the Navy DH-4Bs served either at Anacostia as utility transports or at Pensacola as trainers. Small numbers were used for testing at the Naval Aircraft Factory, Naval Proving Ground, Dahlgren, and the Naval Air Station Hampton Roads (Norfolk). One of the latter participated in arresting gear trials on a platform specially constructed at the air station, while a few others were assigned to the Navy's first aircraft carrier, USS *Langley*, but it is not known whether they ever landed aboard. A single DH-4B-1 served briefly at NAS Lakehurst, the Navy's centre for lighter-than-air aviation.

Deliveries to the west coast went mainly to the Pacific Fleet Air Squadrons at San Diego, beginning with Spotting Squadrons 3 and 4 in 1922. On 1 July of that year these units became Observation Squadrons 2 and 1 respectively, assigned to the Battle Fleet (VO-1B and VO-2B). Their DH-4Bs were operated until 1925 and participated in Fleet Exercises at such locations as Puerto Rico, Panama and Hawaii. The only other Navy DH-4Bs to be based on the west coast were a few assigned to the reserve unit at Sand Point, Seattle in 1926/7. Further west, the Naval Air Station at Pearl Harbor also operated a few between 1926 and 1928.

The small number of Navy O2Bs served at Anacostia and Philadelphia from 1925 to 1928.

Marine Corps Service

Post-war, the Marine Corps was the larger user of the DH-4B and its aircraft were the only ones to see combat. At the time initial

This DH-4 was cleaned up for personal use by 'Billy' Mitchell.

deliveries were being made in 1920, all Marine aviation was in the process of being moved from Marine Flying Field, Miami, Florida. Squadron D arrived at Santo Domingo (Dominican Republic) on 26 February 1919, Squadron E at Port au Prince (Haiti) on 31 March, Squadron B at Parris Island (South Carolina) on 12 June, Squadron C at Quantico (Virginia) on 13 June and squadron A also at Quantico on 20 September 1919. Quantico was considered the headquarters, and was to remain the centre of Marine Aviation for many years. Both overseas squadrons operated in support of Marine ground units which were present on the island of Hispaniola to protect US interests during a period of political instability.

In 1921, DH-4Bs of the Group at Quantico participated in the experimental bombing of captured German battleships by which Brigadier General "Billy" Mitchell demonstrated the ability of aircraft to sink a capital ship, albeit stationary in the water and undefended. In April of that year, Lt Col Thomas C.Turner led a flight of two DH-4Bs from Washington, DC, to Santo Domingo to establish a record for the longest unguarded flight over land and water made up to that time by US Navy or Marine personnel.

New organisational structures emerged in 1922 with the formation, at Quantico, of the 1st Marine Aviation Group, and the redesignation of the overseas units as Marine Observation Squadrons 1 (Santo Domingo) and 2 (Haiti). These latter titles were usually abbreviated to VO-1M and VO-2M, although it may have been the late twenties before the 'M' for Marine suffix obtained official sanction. Aircraft of VO- squadrons carried identification markings consisting of the squadron number, a circular letter with a diagonal slash across it to denote that it was an observation squadron, and an individual number. The slash was used to distinguish the letter "O" from the numeral "0".

In September 1923, two Marine DH-4Bs made another impressive long distance flight, from Haiti to Saint Louis, Missouri, to attend that year's National Aircraft Races. Through 1923 deliveries of DH-4Bs continued to the same three operating locations, the next change coming the following year when the Marines were withdrawn from the Dominican Republic.

VO-1M transferred to San Diego in July 1924, where it became part of the newly formed 2nd Marine Aviation Group. Thus, by the end of that year Marine DH-4Bs were to be found at Quantico, San Diego and with VO-2M at Port au Prince.

By January 1925 the 1st Marine Aviation Group had a mixed bag of 25 operational aircraft, these including nine DH-4B-1s all based at Quantico. Welcome new equipment, in the form of Boeing O2B-1s, reached Quantico and Port au Prince in the spring of that year, although there were only enough to supplement rather than replace the older DH-4Bs. On 1 September 1925 VF-3 formed with DH-4Bs at San Diego in a new 2nd Marine Aviation Group.

At the beginning of 1926 the assignments were:

1st Marine Aviation Group, Quantico	DH-4B, O2B-1
2nd Marine Aviation Group, San Diego	DH-4B
VO-2M, Haiti	DH-4B, O2B-1

Further organisational change in July 1926 saw the 1st and 2nd Marine Aviation Groups become respectively the Aircraft Squadrons, East Coast Expeditionary Force and the West Coast Expeditionary Force, these being components of the "Mud Marines" Expeditionary Force on each coast. Their DH-4Bs/O2Bs we assigned to newly formed squadrons, VO-1M at San Diego and VO-3M and VO-4M at Quantico.

With the new year of 1927 came a new challenge for Marine aviators when attacks on American property and citizens in Nicaragua led to the commitment of the 5th Marine regiment in

DH-4s at the Aberdeen, MD, naval base from which 'Billy' Mitchell's demonstration were carried out. Possibly some of these aircraft took part in the bombing of surrendered German warships. (via Frank Cheesman)

A preserved DH-4 in U.S.Marine Corps markings photographed in 1966. (via Frank Cheesman)

January. On 18 February 1927, VO-1M, as it was now known, embarked at San Diego with six DH-4Bs and two DH-4B-1s for Nicaragua, where it set up base in a sports field at the edge of the city of Managua, to cooperate with the Nicaraguan air force in combating guerrilla rebel forces. Three months later it was joined by the six O2B-1s of VO-4M from Quantico. At the end of June most of the personnel from the VO-1M detachment were withdrawn, although the aircraft remained behind with VO-4M. Fighting continued spasmodically in Nicaragua for several years.

VO-5M formed at San Diego and was then shipped to China in May 1927 as support for ground Marines who had been landed at Shanghai to protect the International Settlement there from the effects of a Civil War. 1927 was certainly a busy year for Marine aviation, bringing not only greatly expanded overseas commitments, but also new equipment for the observation squadrons.

Squadron renumbering became effective from 1 July 1927, Marine DH-4B/O2B squadrons changes being as follows:

VO-3M	Quantico	(to VO-6M)
VO-1M	San Diego	(to VO-8M)
VO-4M	Nicaragua	(to VO-7M)
VO-2M	Haiti	(to VO-9M)
VO-5M	China	(to VO-10M)

To build up the aviation component of the Second Marine Brigade, VO-6M was formed on 1 July 1927 by redesignating Division 1 VO Squadron 3 at Quantico; with six O2B-1s, it departed on 26 January 1928 for duty with the Second Marine Brigade in Nicaragua.

In the meantime, however, the DH-4 and its variants was becoming obsolete, being mainly replaced in the Marine squadrons by Vought O2U Corsairs. The old wooden-longeroned DH-4Bs could now be retired, though a few survived into 1928 with VOs-7M,-8M and -9M. The newer O2Bs served throughout that year with VOs-7M,-9M and -10M, but by early 1929 they too had gone.

Naval DH-4 Individual Histories

80 DH-4M "Chasse type" (sic) under Contracts 30-Z-2, SC Order 20047, CR-386, SE-653 & Bu-18. All ex Army, renumbered A3245 to A3324. [A3247 was a DH-4B]

[N.B. As deliveries began before the Armistice, it seems likely that these were originally DH-4s, some of which may later have been brought up to DH-4M standard]

A3245 (ex A.S.32292) To England via Brooklyn 24.9.18 for Northern Bombing Group; Returned USA; NAF 5.9.19; Shipped to Pacific Fleet 16.11.21, arrived there 14.12.21; VO-1, overshot whilst landing, uundercarriage collapsed on rough ground, San Diego 7.11.22 (Lt FB Connell); San Diego 2.1.23; Reported in poor condition 26.2.23; SOC 24.3.23

A3246 (ex A.S.32268) To England via Brooklyn 24.9.18 for Northern Bombing Group; Retd USA; NAF 5.9.19; Great Lakes 27.2.20; SOC 11.4.21

A3247 (ex A.S,32226) (to DH-4B) To England via Brooklyn 24.9.18 for Northern Bombing Group; Retd USA; NAF 5.9.19; Shipped to Pacific Fleet 16.11.21, arr 14.12.21; VO-1B, EF, ditched San Francisco Bay 28.10.22 (L/Cdr MB McComb); SOC 3.2.23

A3248 (ex A.S.32206) VS-3, heavy landing San Diego, 10.7.22 (Ens GS Hasselman)

A3249 (ex A.S.32210) VO-2B, landing accident, San Diego 12.12.22 (Lt JH Stevens)

A3250 (ex A.S.32160)

A3251 (ex A.S.32200)

A3252 (ex A.S.32216)

A3253 (ex A.S.32265)

A3254 (ex A.S.32158)
A3255 (ex A.S.32212)
A3256 (ex A.S.32229)
A3257 (ex A.S.32261)
A3258 (ex A.S.32203?)
A3259 (ex A.S.32272)
A3260 (ex A.S.32198) To Northern Bombing Group as D-2
A3261 (ex A.S.32274) To Northern Bombing Group as D-11
A3262 (ex A.S.32255) To Northern Bombing Group as D-6
A3263 (ex A.S.32199) To Northern Bombing Group as D-10
A3264 (ex A.S.32360) To Northern Bombing Group as D-9
A3265 (ex A.S.32209)
A3266 (ex A.S.32309)
A3267 (ex A.S.32202)
A3268 (ex A.S.32201)
A3269 (ex A.S.32387) To Northern Bombing Group as D-3
A3270 (ex A.S.32380) To Northern Bombing Group as D-12
A3271 (ex A.S.32155)
A3272 (ex A.S.32240)
A3273 (ex A.S.32337) USN, FL nr Miami 1.1.19
A3274 (ex A.S.32163) USMC, EF, spun in, Parris Island 25.6.20
A3275 (ex A.S.32335) USN, FL nr Miami 12.4.19
A3276 (ex A.S.32299) Miami (coded 'C') 1919; SOC Parris Island 4.6.20 (deterioration)
A3277 (ex A.S.32151)
A3278 (ex A.S.32354) To Northern Bombing Group as D-8
A3279 (ex A.S.32329) To Northern Bombing Group as D-13
A3280 (ex A.S.32207) To Northern Bombing Group as D-5
A3281 (ex A.S.32308)
A3282 (ex A.S.32404)
A3283 (ex A.S.32232)
A3284 (ex A.S.32414) VO-1B, tailskid hit railroad tie, Rosamond Field 12.10.22 (Lt BR Holcombe); Axle failed landing Rockwell Field, CA 23.10.22 (Lt JD Barner); Ground collision with truck, San Diego 18.1.23 (AMMIC JM Larson)
A3285 (ex A.S.32256)
A3286 (ex A.S.32338) VS-4, EF, FL nr San Diego 26.4.22 (Ens RR Auerswald unhurt); VO-1B, hit HT wires near Rogers Field, Los Angeles 28.11.22 (CEM FM Linder)
A3287 (ex A.S.32411) (DH-4B-1)
A3288 (ex A.S.32395)
A3289 (ex A.S.32403)
A3290 (ex A.S.32384)
A3291 (ex A.S.32371)
A3292 (ex A.S.32369)
A3293 (ex A.S.32420)
A3294 (ex A.S.32372)
A3295 (ex A.S.32413) To Northern Bombing Group as D-1
A3296 (ex A.S.32244)
A3297 (ex A.S.32930) To Northern Bombing Group (attd 217 Sqdn by 3.10.18)
A3298 (ex A.S.32273?) Anacostia, EF, FL, Hampton Roads 30.8.24 (L/Cdr EF Stone)
A3299 (ex A.S.32318) To Northern Bombing Group as D-7
A3300 (ex A.S.32405) To Northern Bombing Group as D-4
A3301 (ex A.S.32417)
A3302 (ex A.S.32314)
A3303 (ex A.S.32416)
A3304 (ex A.S.32310 or 32370)
A3305 (ex A.S.32357)
A3306 (ex A.S.32378)
A3307 (ex A.S.32381)
A3308 (ex A.S.32351)
A3309 (ex A.S.32390)
A3310 (ex A.S.32357)
A3311 (ex A.S.32337)
A3312 (ex A.S.32333)
A3313 (ex A.S.32389)
A3314 (ex A.S.32363) VO-2B, spun in from heavy cloud, nr San Diego 31.10.22 (Lt OW Erickson unhurt)
A3315 (ex A.S.32349)
A3316 (ex A.S.32377)
A3317 (ex A.S.32280)
A3318 (ex A.S.32438)
A3319 (ex A.S.32178)
A3320 (ex A.S.32296)
A3321 (ex A.S.32281)
A3322 (ex A.S.32347)
A3323 (ex A.S.32407)
A3324 (ex A.S.32300)

75 DH-4B under Contracts 30-Z-2, CR-564, SE-9623 & Bu-18. All ex Army, renumbered A3384 to A3458. A3384 = DH-4B-2, A3385-A3392 = DH-4, A3393 = DH-4B-2, A3394 = DH-4B-2, A3395-3397 = DH-4, A3398 = DH-4B-1, A3399-A3401 = DH-4, A3402 = DH-4B-1, A3401-3444 = DH-4, A3445 = DH-4B-1 and A3446-A3458 = DH-4. Previous Army numbers unknown. Information available for the following:

A3384 NAS Anacostia, EF, FL, nr Baltimore, MD 2.4.26 (Lt HC Rodd)
A3388 NAS Anacostia, crashed nr airfield 12.4.22
A3393 NAS Anacostia, EF, FL, crashed, nr Hill's Grove Field, Warwick, RI 26.5.24 (Lt AW Gorton minor injuries & Lt CAF Sprage unhurt)
A3394 NAS Anacostia, hit tree landing Sweet Briar Field 22.5.26 (Lt LW Curtin); Repaired; FL in bad weather, hit fence, nr Chilston, VA 9.12.26 (L/Cdr FW Pennoyer)
A3397 MCAS Quantico, crashed nr Haverford, PA, in bad weather 12.6.22 (Capt JE Davis)
A3398 Anacostia, Axle broke landing nr Patterson, NJ 25.9.24 (Lt R Bota); FL in bad weather, hit ditch, DBR, Bowie Field, MD 29.5.25 (Lt PE Gillespie minor injuries)
A3401 USMC Quantico, EF, FL nr airfield 22.9.21; Repaired; 1st Marine Aviation Group, ran out of fuel, FL nr Quantico 21.3.23 DBR (1/Lt AR Holderby III)
A3403 To Philadelphia for overseas 26.6.18; To England via Brooklyn 1.10.18; Retd USA; NAF 5.9.19; To Hampton for Marine Force 6.12.19 (arr 29.12.19); To Gallaudet Corpn 8.20
A3404 To Philadelphia for overseas 27.6.18; To England via Brooklyn 2.10.18; Retd USA; NAF 5.9.19; To Hampton for Marine Force 6.12.19 (arr 29.12.19); To Gallaudet Corpn 8.20
A3405 To Philadelphia for overseas 27.6.18; To England via Brooklyn 2.10.18; Retd USA; NAF 5.9.19; Transferred to US Army 29.5.20
A3410 USN, EF, FL in Potomac River 9.6.21
A3411 EF, FL, hit telegraph pole landing, Parris Island 21.9.21 (pilot minor injuries); DBR
A3414 1st Marine Aviation Group, ground looped into hangar while landing, Quantico 26.9.23 (2/Lt GH Towner Jnr)
A3417 USN, crashed nr Dunn, NC 5.2.21
A3420 To Philadelphia for overseas 2.7.18; Nothing further known
A3432 To Northern Bombing Group as D-15
A3433 To Northern Bombing Group as D-14
A3434 To Northern Bombing Group as D-17
A3435 To Northern Bombing Group as D-16
A3436 To Philadelphia for overseas 10.7.18; Brooklyn 8.11.18; US Marine Corps Miami 14.12.18; Paris Island, SC 16.6.19; Dayton 1.9.20 (to be conv DH-4B); No further details until SOC 4.5.29; From NAF to N E High School, Philadelphia 9.5.29; SOC
A3437 USN Quantico, EF on TO, crashed, 1.4.21 DBR
A3441 USN Quantico, crashed nr airfield 20.8.21
A3442 USN Quantico, FL nr airfield 6.8.21
A3443 MCAS Quantico, ran out of fuel, FL 6m E of Moundsville, WV 6.10.22 DBR (2/Lt F Christian)
A3446 1st Marine Aviation Group, Quantico, ground looped landing Remington, VA 27.8.23 DBR (Capt LE Woods)
A3447 To Philadelphia for overseas 13.7.18; Brooklyn 8.11.18; US Marine Corps Miami 14.12.18; Quantico 23.5.19; Dayton 4.9.20 (to be conv DH-4B by Army)
A3449 USN, hit trees on approach, Parris Island 30.7.20 DBR

6 DH-4B under Contract 2-Z-21. All ex Army, renumbered A5809 to A5814. Previous Army numbers unknown

A5809 Haiti 3.20; Squadron E; EF, FL in trees, Port au Prince 27.4.21
A5810 Haiti 3.20; Squadron E; EF, FL Port au Prince 9.8.20 (2/Lt JG Bowen killed);
A5811 Haiti 3.20; Squadron E; VO-2M; SOC 30.11.25 (deteriorated)
A5812 Haiti 3.20; Squadron E; Axle broke, Port au Prince 25.1.21 (pilot minor injuries); VO-2M; Damaged landing Port au Prince 25.9.21, used for parts; SOC 18.4.22
A5813 Haiti 3.20; Squadron E; Axle broke, Hinch Field 23.2.21; VO-2M; SOC 23.4.24 (worn out)
A5814 Haiti 3.20; Squadron E; EF, FL, crashed Sarte Dau, Haiti 5.10.21

A U.S.Navy DH-4 variant flying from Pensacola. (via Gordon Swanborough)

6 DH-4B under Contract 2-Z-21. All ex Army, renumbered A5834 to A5839. Previous Army numbers unknown

A5834 Santo Domingo 12.20; VO-1M; San Diego 5.27; SOC 27.8.27 (obsolete)
A5835 Santo Domingo 12.20 (flown at Santo Domingo by Major Alfred A Cunningham, USMC in 1922); VO-1M; Crashed on TO, San Pedro de Macoris 7.12.22 (1/Lt WJ Wallace unhurt)
A5836 Santo Domingo 12.20; VO-1M; SOC 16.6.22 (deteriorated)
A5837 Santo Domingo 12.20; Port au Price, Haiti 12.21; VO-2M; Rudder locked in flight, crashed, Port au Prince 13.9.22 (2/Lt JF Plachta unhurt)
A5838 Santo Domingo 12.20; VO-1M; Stalled on TO, Monte Cristo, Santo Domingo City 27.3.24 (WO M Wodarczyk unhurt)
A5839 Santo Domingo 12.20; SOC 16.5.21 (deteriorated)

15 DH-4B under Contract 2-Z-21. All ex Army, renumbered A5870 to A5884. Previous Army numbers mostly unknown

A5870 USMC Parris Island 8.20; Hit cables and crashed on approach 20.8.20 (Lt JH Weaver killed)
A5871 USMC Parris Island 8.20; EF, ditched at sea 23.8.20
A5872 USMC Parris Island 8.20; EF, crashed nr airfield 1.11.20
A5873 USMC Parris Island 8.20; U/c collapsed landing Greenville 10.9.20; Quantico 4.21; SOC 15.2.22 (deteriorated)
A5874 Parris Island 8.20; Quantico 10.21; SOC 15.2.22 (deteriorated)
A5875 Parris Island 8.20; Quantico 10.21; NAS Pensacola, EF, FL, nosed over nr airfield 1.12.21; SOC 15.2.22 (deteriorated)
A5876 Parris Island 8.20; Quantico 10.21; SOC 20.4.23 (deteriorated)
A5877 (DH-4B-1) VO-1M Santo Domingo 7.24; Port au Prince, SOC 8.9.25 (worn out)
A5878 Santo Domingo; Port au Prince 1.22; Destroyed by fire following oil leak 20.2.22
A5879 Santo Domingo; Port au Prince 7.21; VO-2M; Hit pig on take-off Aux Cayes Field, forced to ditch offshore 24.2.24 (Capt JT Moore unhurt)
A5880 Santo Domingo; Port au Prince 7.21; SOC 23.4.24 (deteriorate)
A5881 Santo Domingo; Wrecked 8.8.21
A5882 Santo Domingo; 1st Air Sqdn [VO-1M]; EF, crashed Santo Domingo City 29.4.22 (Capt HH Shepherd unhurt)
A5883 Santo Domingo; SOC 13.7.23 (worn out)
A5884 Santo Domingo; EF, crashed Port au Prince 15.4.21 (pilot minor injuries)

20 DH-4B under Contracts 2-Z-21 & C&R 51-21. All ex Army, renumbered A5982 to A6001. Previous Army not identified

A5982 10.21 Hampton Roads; SOC 18.10.21 (damaged beyond repair)
A5983 10.21 Hampton Roads; SOC 19.9.22 (overstressed during arresting gear trials)
A5984 San Diego (VO-2B); U/c collapsed landing, DBR 31.7.22
A5985 VO-2B, u/c collapsed landing, San Diego 8.8.22 (Lt OW Erickson)
A5986 VO-1B 7.22; San Diego; VO-1B 3.23; San Diego 4.24; VO-2B; Crashed on TO, Glendale, CA 15.10.24
A5987 Spotting Sqdn No.4 4.22; VO-1B; USN San Diego, heavy landing 24.4.22 (Lt OW Erickson minor injuries); Damaged at San Diego 23.1.23; SOC 24.3.23
A5988 San Diego; SOC 18.10.21
A5989 VO-1B 9.22; Engine caught fire, FL, crashed nr San Diego 6.11.23 (ACMM JE Rawlings)
A5990 VO-1B 9.22; San Diego; SOC San Diego 20.4.23 (deteriorated)
A5991 VO-1B 9.22; SOC San Diego 24.3.23 (deteriorated)
A5992 USN San Diego; Stalled on approach turn when engine failed, spun in 8.9.21 (pilot seriously injured)
A5993 VO-2B 9.22; SOC 24.3.23 (deteriorated)
A5994 VO-2B 9.22; SOC 19.10.22 (deteriorated)
A5995 VO-2B 9.22; San Diego, DBR 23.2.23
A5996 Pacific Fleet Air Squadrons; EF, ditched off San Diego 25.4.22 (Lt DA Musk unhurt)
A5997 VO-2B 7.22; Crashed on landing, San Diego 27.7.22 (Lt DA Musk)
A5998 VO-2B; EF, ditched off San Diego 8.9.22 (Lt GT Owen unhurt)
A5999 Pacific Fleet Air Squadrons; SOC 18.4.22 (dismantled for spares)

A6000 VO-1B 9.22; SOC San Diego 20.4.23 (deteriorated)
A6001 VO-2B 9.22; VO-2B, heavy landing, structural failure, nr NAS San Diego 19.3.25 (L/Cdr MB McComb); SOC San Diego 11.8.25 (deteriorated)

80 DH-4B-1 & DH-4B-2 under Contract 2-Z-46. All ex Army, converted at Naval Aircraft Factory and renumbered A6113 to A6192. Previous Army numbers unidentified

A6113 NAF 12.21 (conv DH-4Amb-1); SOC 16.6.22
A6114 San Diego 11.21; VO-1B; VO-2B 11.23; EF, ditched off Point Fermin, CA 10.6.24 (L/Cdr MB McComb); Salvaged and repaired; Hit ditch landing, Rosedale Field, CA 20.1.25 (Lt FB Stump); Crashed nr San Diego 24.6.25; SOC San Diego 15.8.25 (not repaired)
A6115 San Diego 11.21; VO-2B; Accident with VO-2B 1.25; U/c collapsed landing, Glendale Field, CA 15.8.24 (Lt H Schmidt); Crashed nr San Diego 24.6.25; SOC San Diego 11.8.25 (not repaired)
A6116 San Diego 11.21; VO-2B; SOC San Diego 30.11.25 (worn out)
A6117 San Diego 11.21; VO-2B; SOC San Diego 30.11.25 (obsolete)
A6118 San Diego 11.21; VO-1B; Ground looped landing, San Diego 10.4.23 (Lt HS Kendall); Ground looped landing, DBR, San Emicion, CA 6.9.23 (Lt HS Kendall)
A6119 San Diego 11.21; VS-4, landing accident 22.5.22 (Lt MF Schoeffel); SOC 2.8.22 (lack of spare parts for repair)
A6120 San Diego 11.21; VO-1B 6.24; SOC San Diego 11.8.25 (deteriorated)
A6121 San Diego 11.21; VO-2B; Hit haystack on TO, crashed nr San Diego 2.7.23 (ACMM SR Shore minor injuries)
A6122 San Diego 11.21; VO-1B; Controls jammed, crashed nr San Diego 13.2.23
A6123 San Diego 11.21; VO-1B; San Diego 6.23; VO-1B; SOC 13.12.23
A6124 San Diego 11.21; VO-2B; Accident VO-2B 4.23; SOC 13.7.23
A6125 San Diego 11.21; Landed in bunker on golf course, San Diego 22.5.22 (Lt EP McKellar); VO-2B; San Diego 3.25; SOC 26.11.26 (deteriorated)
[NB. Became DH-4Amb-1 conversion]

U.S.Navy DH-4Amb-1 in flight. (via Gordon Swanborough)

A6126 San Diego 11.21; VO-2B; SOC 21.2.23
A6127 San Diego 11.21
A6128 San Diego 11.21; VO-1B; San Diego 4.24; 2nd Aviation Group 11.25. Quantico 12.26; SOC 30.7.27 (worn out)
A6129 San Diego 11.21; VO-1B; VO-2B 4.24; San Diego 3.25; SOC 11.8.25
A6130 San Diego 11.21; VO-2B; VO-1B 3.23; EF, FL Spanish Bight 29.3.23 (ACMM RB Lawrence); San Diego 5.23; SOC 9.11.23
A6131 San Diego 11.21; Pacific Fleet Air Squadrons; EF, ditched in San Diego Bay, nosed over 8.6.22 (Lt BH Wyatt)
A6132 San Diego 11.21; VO-2B; Landed on one wheel, San Diego 27.11.22 (L/Cdr PM Bates); San Diego 7.23; SOC 9.11.23
A6133 San Diego 11.21; VO-2B, EF, FL, undershot, San Diego 22.5.24 (Lt LW Curtin); USMC San Diego 3.25; Pensacola 8.25; SOC 30.7.27 (obsolete)
A6134 (conv DH-4B-2) San Diego 11.21; VO-2B; Marines, San Diego 3.25; Quantico 3.28; SOC 27.8.28 (obsolete)
A6135 Quantico 1.22; 1st Aviation Group; EF, FL, crashed 19.10.23 (Capt AR Presley); EF, ditched, 26.1.25 (2/Lt TL Cagle); SOC 30.11.25 (structural failure)
A6136 Quantico 1.22; 1st Aviation Group; Crashed on landing, nr Badham, SC 12.5.24 (Lt JM Shoemaker)
A6137 Quantico 1.22; 1st Aviation Group; Quantico, EF, FL nr Widewater 23.2.24 (1/Lt LN Medaris)
A6138 Quantico 1.22; 1st Aviation Group; SOC 29.3.26 (deteriorated)
A6139 Quantico 1.22; 1st Aviation Group; Quantico, hit mountain in fog, nr Uniontown, PA 25.6.23 (Capt FP Mulcahy minor injuries)
A6140 Quantico 1.22; 1st Aviation Group; FL after dark, DBR, Quantico 18.9.23 (Capt JF Moriarty)
A6141 San Diego 12.21; Spotting Sqdn No.3; Became VO-2B 1.7.22; Stalled on approach, crashed nr Encinitas, CA, BO 7.7.22 (Ens RR Auerswald seriously injured)
A6142 San Diego 12.21; VO-2B; Landing accident, San Diego 26.2.24 (ACMM FW Moy); San Diego 4.24; Crashed nr San Diego, DBR 24.6.25
A6143 San Diego; VO-1B; EF, ditched off San Diego 19.9.22 (Lt BH Wyatt unhurt)
A6144 San Diego 12.21; VO-1B; SOC 19.2.23 (worn out)
A6145 Pensacola 3.22; SOC 26.11.26 (worn out)
A6146 Anacostia 1.22; Hit ditch landing Dahlgren Field 11.5.22 (Lt HJ Brow); National Aircraft Factory 9.23; SOC at NAF 30.6.27 (deteriorated)
A6147 Port au Prince 1.22; SOC Port au Prince 23.4.24 (worn out)
A6148 Port au Prince 1.22; VO-2M; EF, FL in trees, Port au Prince 15.7.24 (1/Lt WL McKittrick unhurt)
A6149 Port au Prince 1.22; SOC Port au Prince 23.12.25 (deteriorated)
A6150 Port au Prince 1.22; VO-2M; EF, stalled and crashed, nr Cape Haitien Field 24.1.25 (1/Sgt PP Tolusciak killed)
A6151 Port au Prince 1.22; VO-2M; Caught fire in flight, FL nr Cape Haitien 3.2.24 (Sgt PP Tolusciak unhurt)
A6152 Port au Prince 1.22; VO-2M; EF, FL, stalled, ditched in shallow water off L'Arcahaec 19.8.25 (1/Lt AR Holderby III unhurt)
A6153 Quantico 1.22; 1st Aviation Group; Taxying out, hit by A6917 landing, DBR, Quantico, 22.3.26 (Mt Sgt A Paschal)
A6154 Quantico 1.22; SOC 11.8.25 (deteriorated)
A6155 (DH-4B-1) Quantico 1.22; 1st Aviation Group; Hit tree landing Quantico 23.9.23 (Mjr RS Geiger); Hit stump landing 26.8.24 (Gy Sgt A Paschel); EF, FL in trees, Quantico 23.4.25 (1/Lt NW Abbott)
A6156 Quantico 1.22; 1st Aviation Group; Groundlooped landing, DBR 19.5.23 (2/Lt GF Cowie)
A6157 Quantico 1.22; Failed to recover from spin, nr Gettysburg, PA 26.6.22 (Capt GW Hamilton killed)
A6158 Quantico 1.22; Quantico, EF on TO, hit fence, DBR, Bellefonte, PA 9.7.27 (1/Lt VM Guymon)
A6159 (conv DH-4B-2) Pensacola 3.22; Anacostia 7.22; NAF 7.24; Anacostia 3.26; AP HB Hubert hit by prop starting); NAF 2.28; SOC 2.6.28 (obsolete)
A6160 (conv DH-4B-2) Pensacola 4.22; Anacostia 7.22; NAF 7.24; Anacostia 3.26; U/c collapsed landing Moristown Field, TN 26.7.28 (Lt GT Owen); SOC 2.6.28 (uneconomical to repair)
A6161 Santo Domingo 5.22; VO-1M; Hit trees 11.10.22 (2/Lt GW Kirkman unhurt); Repaired; Landed in swamp, overturned, Sameni Ba..... 2.1.24 (2/Lt JN Smith unhurt)
A6162 Santo Domingo 5.22; VO-1M; EF, crashed Azua 12.3.24 (1/Sgt BF Belcher unhurt)
A6163 Santo Domingo 5.22; Oil leak, FL, DBR 18.10.22
A6164 (DH-4B-1) Santo Domingo 5.22; VO-1M; West Coast Expeditionary Force, San Diego; EF, FL, DBR, nr Tucson, AZ 14.12.26 (Gunner M Wodarczyk)
A6165 NAF for USS *Langley* 11.22; EF, FL, hit ditch nr Vandalia, IL 4.10.23 DBR
A6166 (conv DH-4B-2) Anacostia 3.22; SOC 1.8.23 (deterioration)
A6167 (conv DH-4B-2) Anacostia 3.22; SOC 30.6.27 (obsolete)
A6168 USS *Langley* 11.22; Hampton Roads 12.23; EF on TO, FL, Hampton Roads 25.2.24 (Ens WB Gwin minor injuries); Hampton Roads 5.27; SOC 30.6.27 (deterioration)
A6169 USS *Langley* 11.22; Hampton Roads 12.23; Struck tree on TO, crashed, BO, Hampton Roads 6.12.24 (L/Cdr CY Johnston)

A6170 (conv DH-4B-2) USS *Langley* 11.22; Anacostia 8.23; EF on TO, crashed, BO, Hampton Roads 11.8.27 (Lt SH Arthur)
A6171 USS *Langley* 11.22; Dahlgren Roads 10.23; SOC 31.10.26 (worn out)
A6172 (conv DH-4B-2) Anacostia 6.22; Dahlgren 3.26; SOC 30.11.28 (obsolete)
A6173 Quantico 5.23; 1st Marine Aviation Group; Fog, FL in peach orchard, hit fence on landing, DBR, Cataba Island, MI 13.11.24 (Capt RJ Archibald)
A6174 Quantico 5.23; Port au Prince 10.24; VO-1M; EF, FL, crashed into tree, nr Milot, Haiti 9.6.25 (1/Lt WL McKittrick unhurt)
A6175 Quantico 5.23; 1st Marine Aviation Group; SOC 25.4.27 (deterioration)
A6176 Quantico 5.23; 1st Marine Aviation Group; While parked, hit by A6179, Quantico 16.2.25; SOC 25.4.27 (deterioration)
A6177 (conv DH-4B-2) Quantico 6.23; VO-1M 8.24; San Diego 3.25; Sand Point (Seattle) 5.26; Accident 11.4.27; SOC 28.5.27
A6178 Quantico 6.23; U/c collapsed on landing, BO, nr Bryan, OH 26.10.23 (Capt AR Presley)
A6179 Quantico 6.23; 1st Marine Aviation Group; Hit parked A6176 landing, Quantico 16.2.25 (2/Lt WO Brice); SOC 25.4.27 (deterioration)
A6180 (DH-4B-1Amb) USMC Quantico 6.23; Axle broke landing Niamo-Black Airport, IL, 5.12.23 (Capt LE Woods); Port au Prince 10.24; SOC 28.10.27 (deterioration)
A6181 Quantico 6.23; 1st Marine Aviation Group; Quantico, EF, FL, crashed, DBR, nr Moundsville, WV 11.4.24 (Lt FM Maile);
A6182 Quantico 8.23; VO-1M; VO-2M, stalled, spun in from 200ft, BO, Port au Prince 28.5.24 (1/Lt WS Hallenberg killed)
A6183 VO-1M 11.23; San Diego 6.25; Pearl Harbor 6.26; SOC 2.6.28 (obsolete)
A6184 VO-1M Santo Domingo 11.23; EF, FL, hit ditch, nr Irvine, CA 23.9.24 (Capt JF Moriarty); San Diego 11.26; SOC 30.6.27 (obsolete)
A6185 VO-1M Santo Domingo 11.23 & 8.24; Aircraft Squadron, Battle Force 10.25; VO-2B, collided in fog with TS-1 of VF1B, ditched off Oceanside, CA 24.10.25 (Lt LC Stevens minor injuries)
A6186 Anacostia 5.24; FL in bad weather, DBR, nr Millerville, MD 3.10.25 (Lt FO Rogers)
A6187 Anacostia 5.24; Heavy landing, Anacostia 16.7.24 (Lt WM Dillon); Overshot landing, hit ditch, DBR, Dahlgren, VA 27.8.25 (L/Cdr AC Davis)
A6188 NAF 4.24; SOC 25.4.27 (worn out)
A6189 Quantico 8.23; 1st Marine Aviation Group; Quantico, crashed on TO, wrecked, nr Cumnor, VA 14.4.26 (Capt JT Moore)
A6190 Port au Prince 7.23; VO-1M; VO-1M San Diego 8.24; San Diego 2.26; VO-8M, mid-air collision with A6376, nr San Diego 15.3.28 (2/Lt LH Dewine killed)
A6191 Port au Prince 9.23; VO-2M; Hit tree on TO 8.3.24 (Sgt PP Tolusciak unhurt); Crashed Port au Prince 31.1.25 DBR
A6192 Quantico 8.23; 1st Marine Aviation Group; Quantico, EF, FL nr Langley Field 27.2.24 (Capt AR Presley); EF, FL, crashed, DBR, Cutter Point, MD 25.8.25 (1/Lt CF Schilt)

50 DH-4B-1 & DH-4B-2 under Contract 2-Z-46. All ex Army, renumbered A6352 to A6401. Previous Army numbers mostly identified

A6352 (ex A.S.23842) (conv DH-4B-2) Pensacola 11.22; Ground collision, Pensacola 30.1.23 (2/Lt AR Holderby III); EF, FL, hit fence, nr Summerdale, AL 9.2.24 (Lt CG McGauly); Stalled on TO, Pensacola 27.3.24 (Acr NH Craven); SOC 26.11.26 (deterioration)
A6353 (ex A.S.23994) Hampton Roads 11.22; VO-2B 1.23; Crashed on landing Kailua Field, Pearl Harbor 22.8.23 DBR (ACMM JM Frosio)
A6354 (ex A.S.24000) Hampton Roads 11.22; VO-2B 2.23; San Diego 4.24; SOC 30.6.27 (deterioration)
A6355 (ex A.S.24016) VO-2B 1.23; VO-1,. axle failed landing Eugene, OR 11.9.23 (Lt HS Kendall); San Diego 3.25; SOC 11.8.25 (deterioration)
A6356 (ex A.S.23825) VO-2B 1.23; Undershot landing San Diego 20.9.23 (Lt JH Campman); SOC 11.8.25 (deterioration)
A6357 (ex A.S.23826) Pensacola; Damaged in mid-air collision with A6378 nr NAS Corry Field, landed safely 17.3.24 (Lt HM Mullinnix); SOC 26.11.26 (deterioration)
A6358 (ex A.S.23829) Hampton Roads 11.22; VO-2B 1.23; Night landing, flew into ground, San Diego 24.11.23 (Lt LW Curtin minor injuries)
A6359 (ex A.S.23830) Hampton Roads 11.22; VO-2B 1.23; Overshot landing San Diego 30.8.23 DBR (Lt OW Erickson)
A6360 (ex A.S.23980) Hampton Roads 11.22; VO-2B 1.23; Marines, San Diego 3.25; Pensacola 8.25; SOC 30.6.27 (worn out)
A6361 (ex A.S.23986) VO-2B 1.23; VO-1B 12.23; VO-2B 4.24; San Diego 3.25; 2nd Marine Aviation Group, San Diego 10.25; VO-1M 1927; SOC Nicaragua 30.7.27 (deterioration)
A6362 (ex A.S.23989) Pensacola 11.22; Collided with A6365 landing Pensacola 4.3.23; Fog, settled in turn at low altitude, crashed in Pensacola Bay 18.2.24 (Lt HM Mullinnix unhurt)
A6363 (ex A.S.23991) VO-2B 1.23; VO-1B 8.23; VO-2B, EF, FL nr San Diego 26.10.23 (Lt SE Haddon); SOC 28.5.27 (worn out)
A6364 (ex A.S.23921) Hampton Roads 11.22; VO-1B 1.23; EF, ditched off San Diego 7.5.23 (ACMM Scheltz unhurt)
A6365 (ex A.S.23926) Pensacola 11.22; Collided with A6362 landing Pensacola 4.3.23 (Lt JR Kyle); Axle broke, nosed over, Pensacola 4.2.24 (Lt MA Sciur); SOC 30.7.27 (obsolete)
A6366 (ex A.S.23926) Hampton Roads 11.22; VO-1B 2.23; Overturned landing San Diego 2.8.23 DBR (Lt JD Barner)
A6367 (ex A.S.23939) Hampton Roads 11.22; VO-1B 2.23; Axle broke landing nr Bakersfield, CA 6.9.23 (Lt JF Maloney); San Diego 11.23; Ferrying San Diego to Anacostia, crashed on TO, hit fence, BO, Cheyenne, WY 22.12.23 (Lt JD Price unhurt)
A6368 (ex A.S.23816) Pensacola 11.22; Hit fence on TO Chopers Field 6.3.22 (Lt JF Maloney); EF on approach, crashed, Pensacola 28.8.23 (Lt HI Booker)
A6369 (ex A.S.23822) VO-2B 12.22; Marines, San Diego 3.25; SOC Nicaragua 30.7.27 (deterioration)
A6370 (ex A.S.23824) Hampton Roads 11.22; VO-1B 1.23; VO-2B 4.24; Stalled and spun in nr San Diego, BO 18.2.25 (Lt WS Garrett killed)
A6371 (ex A.S.23828) Hampton Roads 11.22; VO-1B 1.23; Pearl Harbor 5.26; SOC 2.6.28 (obsolete)
A6372 (ex A.S.23772 or 23792) Pensacola 11.22; SOC 26.11.26 (deteriorated)
A6373 (ex A.S.23060) Hampton Roads 11.22; VO-2B 1.23; Ground looped landing San Diego 19.3.23 (ACMM JM Frosio); San Diego 8.24; 2nd Marine Aviation Group 2.26; VO-1M, stalled on landing, Managua, Nicaragua 14.3.27 (2/Lt FH Scribner unhurt)
A6374 (ex A.S.23797) Hampton Roads 11.22; VO-1B 1.23; VO-2B 8.24; EF on TO, FL, crashed, DBR, nr Wilmington Field, CA 5.3.25 (AP FW Moy)
A6375 (ex A.S.23198 or 12798) Pensacola 11.22; Lost control on TO, ditched Pensacola Bay 6.3.23 (Lt D Kiefer unhurt)
A6376 (ex A.S.22894) VO-2B 1.23; San Diego 7.24; Marines, San Diego 7.24; VO-8M, mid-air collision with A6190, nr San Diego 15.3.28 (1/Lt JD Swartwout killed)
A6377 (ex A.S.23102) (conv DH-4B-2) VO-2B 1.23; Anacostia 6.24; NAF 8.24; Hampton Roads 4.26; Dahlgren 7.26; SOC 30.11.28 (obsolete)
A6378 (ex A.S.23331) VO-1B 1.23; San Diego, flew into beach in fog, nr Half Moon Bay, CA 23.10.23 (L/Cdr RA Burg minor injuries)
A6379 (ex A.S.22873) Pensacola 2.23; Mid-air collision with A6357 nr NAS Corry Field 17.3.24 (Lt CD Porter killed)
A6380 (ex A.S.23376) (conv DH-4B-2) VO-2B 1.23; VO-1B 10.23; VO-2B 4.24; Landing accident, Wilmington Field, CA 21.5.24 (Acmm FW Moy); San Diego 3.25; 2nd Marine Aviation Group 10.25; SOC Nicaragua 27.8.27 (deterioration)
A6381 (ex A.S.23352) VO-2B 1.23; VO-1B 10.23; San Diego 4.24; 2nd Marine Aviation Group 10.25; SOC Nicaragua 30.7.27 (deterioration)
A6382 (ex A.S.22896) Pensacola 2.23; Hit stake on TO 8.8.23 (Lt L Charles); EF, FL, undershot, Pensacola 9.6.24 (Lt LA Pope); SOC 25.4.27 (deterioration)

A6383 (ex A.S.22899) VO-2B 1.23; San Diego 6.24; SOC 30.11.25 (worn out)
A6384 (ex A.S.22911) Quantico 1.23; 1st Marine Aviation Group; EF, FL, BO, nr Universal, PA 29.7.25 (2/Lt TL Cagel killed)
A6385 (ex A.S.23049) Pensacola 2.23; SOC 26.11.26 (deterioration)
A6386 (ex A.S.23198) (DH-4B-1Amb) Quantico 8.24; Port au Prince 10.24; SOC VO-9M 1.10.28 (obsolete)
A6387 (ex A.S.23042) VO-2B 1.23; Prop failed, San Diego 27.11.23 (Lt HS Woodman); San Diego 3.25; SOC 11.8.25 (worn out?)
A6388 (ex A.S.23131) USS *Langley*; Anacostia; NAS Lakehurst, crashed on TO, 27.11.23 (Lt JH Hykes minor injuries); Hit by strong gust of wind on TO, crashed, NJ 26.11.27
A6389 (ex A.S.31668) VO-2B 1.23. Ground looped landing San Diego, DBR 11.3.24 (Lt CW Smith)
A6390 (ex A.S.30145) Pensacola 2.23; Crashed nr Pensacola, DBR 2.4.25
A6391 (ex A.S.30138) VO-1B 5.23; VO-2B 11.24; San Diego 3.25; Strut failed taxying San Diego 14.9.26 (AP WL Elmore); SOC 30.6.27 (worn out)
A6392 (ex A.S.30065) VO-2B 1.23; VO-1B 12.23; VO-2B 4.24; San Diego 3.25; Pearl Harbor 6.26; SOC 2.6.28 (obsolete)
A6393 (ex A.S.30152) VO-1B 1.23; San Diego 4.24; West Coast Expeditionary Force 11.26; VO-7M, EF on TO, hit tree nr Ocotal, Nicaragua 16.9.27 (2/Lt JC Harmon minor injuries)
A6394 (ex A.S.30186) VO-2B 1.23; Hit cactus plant on TO, Homestead Field, Molokai, Hawaii 2.8.23 DBR (Lt MT Seligman)
A6395 (ex A.S.31943) San Diego 12.22; SOC 30.6.27 (deterioration)
A6396 (ex A.S.30174) Quantico 1.23; 1st Marine Aviation Group; FL in foggy weather, DBR, nr Camp Meade, MD 14.10.25 (Capt JE Davis)
A6397 (ex A.S.30067) Quantico 10.24; Port au Prince; Nicaragua 4.27; VO-7M, EF, FL, nr Managua, Nicaragua 10.1.28 (Sgt LH Pabst unhurt); DBR
A6398 (ex A.S.30142) San Diego 12.22; VO-1B 6.23; Axle failed landing San Diego 7.6.23 (Lt JD Lowry); Ground looped landing, u/c collapsed, Fort Clayton, Panama Canal Zone 18.1.24 (Lt DN Logan unhurt)
A6399 (ex A.S.31335) Quantico 1.23; Dahlgren 1.26; 1st Marine Aviation Group, Quantico 3.26; Became lost in bad weather, crew baled out nr Quantico 14.4.26 (1/Lt NW Abbott killed)
A6400 San Diego 1.23; VO-1B; VO-2B 4.24; Heavy landing, Sierra service field, CA 18.2.25 (Lt FB Stump)
A6401 (ex A.S.31512) Quantico 1.23; 1st Marine Aviation Group; Overran and crashed on attempted take-off through slush and snow, Quantico 11.3.24 (Mjr RE Rowell)

1 DH-4B-2 built from spares at Naval Aircraft Factory in 1924 and numbered A6514

A6514 Anacostia 7.24; EF, FL, Logan Field, MD 22.9.24 (Lt RA Ofstie); Conv to racing plane by 6.26; To Pensacola for (ground?) instructional purposes 4.27; SOC 28.5.27

O2B-1 Individual Histories

A6898 Deld NAF 10.3.25 (arr 31.3.25); Hampton Roads for Port au Prince 20.7.25 (arr 21.7.25); VO-2M 28.9.25; Became VO-9M 1.7.27; SOC after tropical service 1.10.28
A6899 Deld NAF 10.3.25 (arr 31.3.25); Hampton Roads for Port au Prince 20.7.25 (arr 21.7.25); VO-3M Quantico 8.12.25; U/c damaged landing 2.3.26 (ROS); To San Diego for West Coast Expeditionary Force, China (3rd Brigade) 29.3.27 (arr 27.4.27); VO-5M; Became VO-10M 1.7.27; SOC 8.8.28 (deterioration, China)
A6900 Deld NAF 12.3.25 (arr 31.3.25); Hampton Roads for Port au Prince 20.7.25 (arr 21.7.25); Port au Prince 30.7.25; VO-2M Port au Prince, ('2Ø3') 28.9.25; Badly damaged landing 29.5.26; Became VO-9M Port au Prince 1.7.27; Assessed as beyond economical repair 18.4.28; SOC 2.6.28

U.S.Marine Corps Boeing O2B-1s A6900 and A6903 of VO-2M Port au Prince around 1925/6. (via Gordon Swanborough)

A6901 Deld NAF 10.3.25 (arr 31.3.25); Hampton Roads for Port au Prince 20.7.25 (arr 21.7.25); VO-2M Port au Prince 8.8.25; Became VO-9M Port au Prince 1.7.27; SOC after tropical service 1.10.28 (obsolete)
A6902 Deld NAF 10.3.25 (arr 31.3.25); Hampton Roads for Port au Prince 20.7.25 (arr 21.7.25); Port au Prince 30.7.25; To VO-2M Port au Prince; Became VO-9M Port au Prince 1.7.27; SOC 29.12.28 (obsolete)
A6903 Deld NAF 10.3.25 (arr 31.3.25); Hampton Roads for Port au Prince 20.7.25 (arr 21.7.25); Port au Prince 30.7.25; To VO-2M Port au Prince ('2Ø6'); Became VO-9M Port au Prince 1.7.27; Control stick sheared, forced landed, DBR, Port au Prince 31.1.28; SOC 27.2.28
A6904 Deld VO-3M ('3Ø3') Quantico 3.25 (arr 6.4.25); U/c damaged landing 4.6.26 (ROS); Badly damaged landing 7.2.27; To San Diego for West Coast Expeditionary Force, China (3rd Brigade), arr 27.4.27; VO-5M; Became VO-10M ('10Ø3') 1.7.27; Reported wings and tail surfaces warped etc 18.6.28; SOC 8.8.28 (deterioration, China)
A6905 Deld VO-3M Quantico 3.25 (arr 6.4.25); VO-2M Port au Prince 2.3.26; Became VO-9M Port au Prince 1.7.27; Hit trees and crashed, fuselage broke in two at rear cockpit, Port de Paix, Haiti 21.2.28; SOC 26.4.28
A6906 Deld VO-3M Quantico 3.25 (arr 6.4.25); Port au Prince 2.3.26 (storage); Deteriorated in storage, SOC 29.3.29 (obsolete)
A6907 Deld VO-3M Quantico 3.25 (arr 6.4.25); VO-2M Port au Prince 2.3.26; Became VO-9M Port au Prince 1.7.27; U/c damaged landing 19.4.28; SOC after tropical service 1.10.28 (obsolete)
A6908 Deld VO-3M Quantico 3.25 (arr 6.4.25); Became VO-6M 1.7.27; SOC 31.1.29 (u/s after long and continuous service); "To be held until 1.5.29 for School"
A6909 Deld VO-3M Quantico 3.25 (arr 6.4.25); Std wings and wheel damaged landing 4.1.27; VO-4M Nicaragua 11.5.27; Became VO-7M 1.7.27; EF, FL, crashed, burnt out Quilali, Nicaragua 14.2.28; SOC 31.3.28
A6910 Deld VO-3M Quantico 3.25 (arr 6.4.25) [flown by Major Charles A.Lutz, a successful Marine air racer]; To San Diego for West Coast Expeditionary Force, China (3rd Brigade) 29.3.27 (arr 27.4.27); VO-5M; Became VO-10M 1.7.27; Reported wings and tail surfaces warped etc 18.6.28; SOC 8.8.28 (deterioration, China)
A6911 Deld VO-3M Quantico 3.25 (arr 6.4.25); VO-2B 11.3.26; To San Diego for West Coast Expeditionary Force, arr 27.12.26; Badly damaged landing ...abens, TX 14.1.27; Rebuilt, then retd WCEF San Diego 19.8.27; To Nicaragua for VO-7M 24.10.27 (arr 10.11.27); Reported wings warped etc 16.2.28; SOC 31.3.28 (deterioration)
A6912 Deld VO-3M Quantico 24.3.25 (arr 22.4.25); Badly damaged landing Camp Meade 9.9.26; To VO-4M Nicaragua 11.5.27; EF, FL, San Francisco, Nicaragua 3.12.27; VO-8M San Diego, crashed, DBR 13.1.28; SOC 27.2.28
A6913 Deld VO-3M Quantico 21.3.25 (arr 22.4.25); To VO-4M Nicaragua 11.5.27; Became VO-7M 1.7.27; Crashed Nicaragua, DBR 21.10.27; SOC 27.12.27
A6914 Deld VO-3M Quantico 21.3.25 (arr 22.4.25); Badly damaged landing 28.1.27; To San Diego for West Coast Expeditionary Force, China (3rd Brigade) 29.3.27 (arr 27.4.27); VO-5M; Became VO-10M 1.7.27; Reported wings warped etc 18.6.28; SOC 8.8.28 (deteriorated, China)
A6915 Deld VO-3M Quantico 21.3.25 (arr 22.4.25); To VO-4M Nicaragua 11.5.27; Became VO-7M 1.7.27; Crashed into mountain, burnt out, Qhilali, Nicaragua 8.10.27; SOC 27.12.27
A6916 Deld VO-3M Quantico 20.3.25 (arr 22.4.25); To San Diego for West Coast Expeditionary Force, China (3rd Brigade) 29.3.27 (arr 27.4.27); VO-5M; Became VO-10M 1.7.27; Reported wings warped etc 18.6.28; SOC 8.8.28 (deterioration, China)
A6917 Deld VO-3M Quantico 20.3.25 (arr 22.4.25); Hit DH-4B A6153 while landing, badly damaged landing 22.3.26; To San Diego for West Coast Expeditionary Force, China (3rd Brigade) 29.3.27 (arr 27.4.27); VO-5M; Became VO-10M 1.7.27; Reported wings warped etc 30.4.28; SOC 2.6.28 (deterioration, China)
A6918 [Converted to O2B-2?] Deld Quantico 3.25; Anacostia 22.4.25 (less engine); Ferrying Cdr Rogers from NAF to Mitchell Field, crashed in bad weather at Charlestown, Mil 4.12.25; NAF 23.12.25 (arr 28.12.25); Anacostia 16.4.26; EF, FL, DBR, Charleston, MD 19.1.27; NAF 28.2.27 (arr 11.3.27); SOC 25.4.27
A6919 [Converted to O2B-2] Deld Quantico 3.25; Anacostia 22.4.25 (less engine); Badly damaged in tornado, Anacostia 18.11.27; SOC 30.11.27
A6920 Deld VO-3M Quantico 3.25 (arr 22.4.25); To VO-4M Nicaragua 11.5.27; Lower wings and u/c demolished landing 20.6.27; Became VO-7M 1.7.27; Reported in poor condition 16.2.28; SOC 31.3.28 (deterioration)
A6921 Deld VO-3M Quantico 3.25 (arr 22.4.25); Engine written off, a/c undamaged 20.8.26; Loss of control, crashed, DBR, Occoquan, VA 16.2.27; SOC 28.3.27
A6922 Deld VO-3M Quantico 3.25 (arr 22.4.25); EF, ditched, Potomac River, DBR 1.2.26; SOC 29.3.26
A6923 Deld VO-3M Quantico 3.25 (arr 22.4.25); To VO-4M Nicaragua 11.5.27; Became VO-7M 1.7.27; Reported in poor condition 16.2.28; SOC 31.3.28 (deterioration)
A6924 [Converted to O2B-2] Deld Quantico 3.25 (arr 29.4.25); To NAF 29.4.25 (arr 4.5.25); Anacostia 24.11.25 (arr 26.11.25); Forced landed York River, to Hampton Roads for repair 2.1.26; Anacostia 8.2.26; FL, a/c OK, Moundsville, VA 18.8.26; EF, ditched, Potomac River 23.5.27; SOC 9.6.27
A6925 [Converted to O2B-2] Deld Quantico 3.25 (arr 29.4.25); To NAF 29.4.25 (arr 7.5.25); Anacostia 18.11.25; U/c collapsed on landing, Rochester, NY 19.9.27; NAF 24.9.27; SOC 2.6.28 (obsolete)
A6926 [Converted to O2B-2] Deld Quantico 3.25 (arr 29.4.25); To NAF 29.4.25 (arr 7.5.25); Anacostia 30.11.25; Crashed 8.10.26; To NAF; Anacostia, struck hump on landing, Baltimore, MD, DBR 30.5.27; SOC 9.6.27
A6927 [Converted to O2B-2] Deld Quantico 3.25 (arr 29.4.25); To NAF 29.4.25 (arr 7.5.25); Anacostia 19.11.25; EF on take-off, ditched in Potomac River 15.9.27; SOC 28.10.27

[NB. SOC = "stricken" in US naval terminology]

Boeing O2B-1 A6925 is the nearest aircraft in this line-up at Anacostia.

The L.W.F.-built J.2, a DH-4 fitted with two wing-mounted Liberty engines for use by the U.S. Mail Services. (via Gordon Swanborough)

Civil use

De Havilland records show that c/n's 138 and 139 were allocated to two DH-4Bs, fitted with Liberty engines and supplied to a Major Davidson in the USA.

A DH-4B was operated by the US Air Attachés, London, and based at Kenley. On 26.9.26 it crashed near Whyteleafe, Surrey and caught fire following engine failure, the pilot, Mjr C.L.Tinker. Assistant Military Attaché (Aviation), being injured and passenger Cdr Robert A.Burg, Assistant Naval Attaché (Aviation), dying in hospital of his injuries. *[see photograph on page 109]*

A considerable number of DH-4s were operated on civilian services in the USA in the twenties, before any formal scheme of registration was introduced. Many were operated by the US Air Mail Service, the fuselages being marked 'U.S.MAIL' with an individual number, these including *60 to 110, 183, 186, 245, 250, 255, 253, 3212, 24224, 24227 & 24239*, the last three of these presumably still bearing their former military serial numbers. Also the Bellanca Mailplane conversion of a D.H.4, *509*.

In 1927, a more formal registration system was brought in. Few details are available, but the following are believed to be registrations of DH-4s then listed:-

NS-1	to NS-13. Batch regd to Dept of Commerce, Washington. *[Some doubts about this being a complete block of DH-4s]*
NS-11	DH-4B c/n 422
NS-12	DH-4B By 1929, shown in register as "sold - owner unknown"
NS-13	c/n 379
NS-89	DH-4M1
C114	DH4-B c/n 4. Built Maywood, IL 1925. Regd 4.27. Regd [1928] to Robertson Air Co, Anglum, MO. *[Note. The whole batch NC93 to NC118 has been reported, but this is thought to be erroneous.]*
C125	DH4-B c/n 110. Built Maywood, IL 1925. Regd 4.27. Regd [1928] to Robertson Air Co, Anglum, MO.
C126	DH4-B c/n unknown. Built Maywood, IL 1925. Regd 4.27. Regd [1928] to Robertson Air Co,

A DH-4 modified as the Dayton-Wright Cruiser for civil use, fitted with a car-type radiator. (J.M.Bruce/G.S.Leslie collection)

A DH-4 much modified fitted with an Ashmussen radial engine, for civil use.

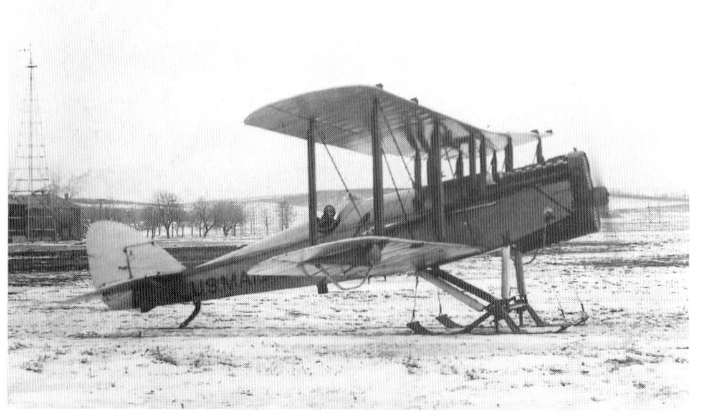

A miscellany of U.S.Air Mail Service D.H.4s

DH-4 modified as the Bellanca Mailpane '509'

	Anglum, MO.
C127	DH4-B c/n 114. Built Maywood, IL 1925. Regd 4.27. Regd [1928] to Robertson Air Co, Anglum, MO.
C128	DH4-B c/n 113. Built Maywood, IL 1925. Regd 4.27. Regd [1928] to Robertson Air Co, Anglum, MO.
C299	DH4-B c/n 299 [sic - build date 1926] Regd 6.27. Regd 1928 to McDaneld & Shelton, Arcadia, CA.
332	DH-4 Special
M-430	DH-4. Crashed nr Eugene, OR (WJ Chamberlain)
447	DH-4B c/n 347
449	No information
NC489	DH4-M1 c/n 652 [Boeing-built as DH-4 Mail] Regd *NS489* 1928 to US Dept of Agriculture, Tallulah, LA [and regd with c/n ÐA-4, which may be simply fleet number] Regd *489* 1.36 to DW Lenahan, Middletown, NY. Later *N489* and post-war to Crawford Auto-Aviation Museum, Cleveland, OH; painted as *A.S.63786*. On loan to US Air Force Museum, Dayton, OH. Also painted in US Mail c/s as "67".
640	DH-4B Western Air Express (WAE)
812	DH-4B c/n 100
915	DH-4B c/n 372
1487	DH-4B c/n A.98
1488	DH-4B c/n A.99
1498	DH-4M c/n 361
1827	DH-4B c/n 381
1828	DH-4B c/n 57
1934	DH-4 with Clark Y Wing c/n 428
3211	DH-4B
3212	Flown by US Postal Service [but also reported as Standard J-1]
3258	DH-4M-1. Ex *A2169*. Regd *3258* [1.36] as Vance De Havilland DH-4 [c/n DHV-3] to G.Lincoln Air Service, Hollywood, CA. Later to *NX3258* and to Wings & Wheels Collection, Florida [quoted c/n ET-4 relates to post-war rebuild by Edgar Tobin]; To Georgia 1981. To Airventure Museum, OR and on loan to Boeing Museum of Flight, WA; painted as US Mail "166".
3360	c/n DA.2 [Department of Agriculture?]
3361	No information
3494	c/n 383
5629	DH-4 Mail
7588	DH-4B c/n 400
9350	DH-4M1 c/n ET.3 [rebuild by Edgar Tobin]
NC57E	DH-4B c/n 395 [or C57E]
NC65E	Boeing DH-4M-1 c/n ET-2 [rebuild by Edgar Tobin]
NC278E	DH-4B c/n 412
NC97M	DH-4B ex *23-707* [c/n quoted as "707"]
NC299V	No information
N249B	In 1961/68, a wreck recovered from a 1922 Utah crash site was rebuilt and regd *N249B* [c/n quoted as "249"] . This is now on display in the National Postal Museum, Washington, DC.
N981RM	Restored and extant

Known Survivors

Kermit Weeks has an unidentified DH-4 on rebuild for his Fantasy of Flight Museum, Polk City, FL.

A DH-4 Replica built by the Museum staff is on display in Marine Corps Air-Ground Museum, Quantico, VA.

The National Air & Space Museum, Washington, DC displays "21959", c/n A.15101.

N249B Rebuild on display in the National Postal Museum, Washington, DC.

NC489 On loan to US Air Force Museum, Dayton, OH. Variously painted as *A.S.63786* and U.S. Mail "67".

N981RM Restored and extant

Survivor N489 *painted up as U.S.Air Mail Service No.67. (via Gordon Swanborough)*

D.H.4 - INDEX OF U.S.MILITARY NAMES

Note. Where only a date is given, this relates to the list of unidentified incidents.

Prototype D.H.9 A7559 in May 1918 during trials of a 230-lb underwater bomb at Orfordness. On the top outer port wing is a static head indicator. (J.M.Bruce/G.S.Leslie collection)

D.H.9 & D.H.9A - SERIAL LISTING

1 D.H.9 prototype conversion from D.H.4 ordered 28.9.17 and numbered A7559

A7559 Production D.H.4 convtd to prototype D.H.9 under Cont No A.S.17569 & A.S.21273/1/17 dated 23.1.17 (Galloway-built BHP); Orfordness by 16.2.18; Trials of 230-lb underwater bomb 5.18

100 D.H.9 ordered 29.6.17 under Cont Nos A.S.17570 & A.S.22860 (BR.113) from Westland Aircraft Works, Yeovil and numbered B7581 to B7680. All originally intended for use by naval units. Initially ordered as D.H.4. (B7581 to B7590 250hp FIAT A.12 at first but refitted 230hp BHP for overseas, remainder 230hp BHP)

B7581 Deld 10 AAP Brooklands 1.18 (refitted B.H.P.); AP Dover 24.1.18; 4 ASD Guines 1.4.18; 211 Sqn 12.4.18; Shot up 17.7.18 (Lt JF Drake OK & 2/Lt NG Breeze wounded); EA OOC in flames 11.00 1.11.18 (Lt JF Drake & 2/Lt GJ Moore); 2 ASD 2.2.19 (unfit to fly Channel)

B7582 Deld 10 AAP Brooklands by 13.1.18 (refitted B.H.P.); Cranwell to AAP Hendon 28.1.18 (comms work); B.H.P. by 2.18; 1 Comm Sqn Hendon 23.7.18; Martlesham 10.8.18

B7583 Deld AP Dover 21.1.18; 6N Sqn 16.2.18; Became 206 Sqn 1.4.18; Went on nose landing 21.4.18 (Lt LN Warren & 1/Pte JT O'Brien unhurt); to 1 ASD; 206 Sqn 27.4.18; Casualty Report 26.5.18 says unfit; Rep Pk 1 ASD 29.5.18 (overhaul); 2 ASD 25.6.18; 98 Sqn 28.6.18; Left 04.50 for bombing raid, combat with 30 EA, shot up, FL nr Château Thierry 25.7.18 (Lt JH Nicholas unhurt & 2/Lt GK Carruthers killed); 9 AP 28.7.18; SOC Rep Pk 1 ASD 3.9.18

B7584 Deld 10 AAP Brooklands 2.18 (refitted B.H.P.); AP Dover W/E 9.2.18; 202 Sqn 4.5.18; 4 ASD 24.7.18

B7585 Deld 10 AAP Brooklands 2.18 (refitted B.H.P.); AP Dover 19.2.18; 217 Sqn 16.5.18; Damaged in enemy air raid 5/6.6.18; 4 ASD Guines 27.7.18 - @3.10.18

B7586 Deld 10 AAP Brooklands 2.18 (refitted B.H.P.); AP Dover W/E 9.2.18; 6N Sqn 23.2.18; Became 206 Sqn 1.4.18; FL nr Busnes after fight with six Fokker DrI over Estaires during bombing raid, BO 23.4.18 (2/Lt LM Whittington injured & A/G 1/Pte S Jones wounded); SOC in field 27.4.18

B7587 Deld 10 AAP Brooklands (refitted B.H.P.); AP Dover W/E 9.2.18; 6N Sqn 19.2.18; Became 206 Sqn 1.4.18; Left 17.07 for bombing raid on Armentières railway station, attacked by 2 Fokker DrI, shot up, EF, FL nr Winnezeele 18.15 11.5.18 (Lt GA Pitt unhurt & 2/Lt CE Anketell MM killed); Rep Pk 1 ASD 14.5.18; SOC 15.5.18

B7588 Deld 10 AAP Brooklands 2.18 (refitted B.H.P.); AP Dover 2.18; 6N Sqn 21.2.18 - @28.3.18; 211 Sqn by 6.4.18; Hit rut landing, nose up 25.4.18 (2/Lt ETM Routledge & 2/Lt IAB McTavish); Rep Pk 1 ASD 25.4.18; SOC 5.5.18 but Bboc 11.5.18; Rebuilt; 2 AI 26.6.18; 104 Sqn 28.6.18; 3 ASD 18.8.18

B7589 Deld 10 AAP Brooklands 2.18 (refitted B.H.P.); AP Dover W/E 9.2.18; 6N Sqn 18.2.18; EF, FL Bray Dunes 10.3.18; Became 206 Sqn 1.4.18; COL from raid 20.4.18 (Lt EJ Stedman & A/G CG Smith); Rep Pk 1 ASD 25.4.18; SOC 5.5.18

B7590 Deld 10 AAP Brooklands 2.18 (refitted B.H.P.); AP Dover 28.2.18; 11N Sqn 16.3.18; 6N Sqn 29.3.18; Crashed 1.4.18; Deleted AD Dunkirk 3.4.18

B7591 Deld 10 AAP Brooklands to AP Dover 15.2.18; 6N Sqn 27.2.18; Shot down 1 of 6 Albatros DV, spiral nosedive, crashed & burnt in floods between St.Pierre Capelle & the lines 14.40 9.3.18 (F/Cdr TF Le Mesurier DSC & PO AGL JJ Ryan); Became 206 Sqn 1.4.18; FL Sally, then Bruigny 25.4.18; EF, FL in ploughed field, o/t Beutin, nr Etaples 29.4.18 (Lt JV Turner & 2/Lt EW Tatnall); Rep Pk 1 ASD 3.5.18; SOC 4.5.18

B7592 Deld 10 AAP Brooklands to AP Dover 15.2.18; AD Dunkirk by 23.2.18; 6N Sqn 26.2.18; FL on beach Oost Dunkirk-Coxyde 9.3.18 (FSL AM Bannatyne & AC1 AGL RA Hollingsbee both wounded); Became 206 Sqn 1.4.18; 4 ASD Guines by 6.4.18 (Pilots Pool by 18.6.18); 2 SS Richborough 2.10.18

B7593 Deld 10 AAP Brooklands to AP Dover 21.2.18; Damaged 17.3.18; 202 Sqn 4.5.18; Bounced on ridge on

TO, on nose 14.9.18 (Lt LF Pendred & 2/Lt HS Saunders unhurt); 4 ASD 15.9.18 - @25.10.18

B7594 Deld 10 AAP Brooklands to AP Dover 26.2.18; 11N Sqn 20.3.18; 6N Sqn 29.3.18; Became 206 Sqn 1.4.18; Left 18.15, last seen in combat with EA over Menin 19.40 19.5.18 (2/Lt FG Reddie & 2/Lt AC Howell-Jones both killed); SOC in field 20.5.18

B7595 Deld 10 AAP Brooklands to AP Dover 16.2.18; 6N Sqn 26.2.18; AP Dover by 18.3.18; 11N Sqn 20.3.18; 6N Sqn 29.3.18; Became 206 Sqn 1.4.18; Badly damaged by AA nr Merville 9.5.18 (Lt EA Burn & 2/Lt AH Mitchener both unhurt); Rep Pk 1 ASD 13.5.18; SOC 14.5.18

B7596 Deld 10 AAP Brooklands to AP Dover W/E 23.2.18; AD Dunkirk to 6N Sqn 23.2.18 (but retd bad weather, arr 26.2.18); Became 206 Sqn 1.4.18; EA in flames 3.5.18 (Lt LN Warren & 1/Pte JT O'Brien); EA OOC thick smoke Halvin 1.7.18; EA OOC & EA DD Roulers 29.7.18; Pfalz DIII Scout crashed 2m N of Menin & Pfalz DIII in flames 19.20-19.35 29.7.18; Pfalz DIII OOC & Pfalz DIII BU in air Menin-Wervicq 08.30 1.8.18 (all Lt LN Warren & Lt LA Christian); Wrecked by 30.9.18, to be retd; 206 Sqn by 12.18; EF, FL Lissendorf on ferry flight 19.12.18 (2/Lt NE Latham & Cpl Lloyd both unhurt); 8 SS repair

B7597 Deld 10 AAP Brooklands 11.2.18; AP Dover W/E 23.2.18; 6N Sqn 28.2.18; Became 206 Sqn 1.4.18; EF on TO, FL 4.7.18 (2/Lt RH Stainbank & 2/Lt CO Shelswell both unhurt); Rep Pk 1 ASD 7.7.18, SOC 10.7.18, NWR

B7598 Deld 10 AAP Brooklands to AP Dover 19.2.18; Left Dover for 6N Sqn but landed Manston, then returned to Dover but COL 27.2.18 (FSL VCM Tiarks); 4 ASD 5.4.18; 211 Sqn 15.4.18; Damaged by AA fire Bruges-Ostende 9.7.18 (Lt H Axford & Cpl F Wilkinson both unhurt); Rep Pk 1 ASD 10.7.18; SOC 13.7.18 NWR

B7599 Deld 10 AAP Brooklands to AP Dover W/E 23.2.18; 6N Sqn by 21.2.18; Became 206 Sqn 1.4.18; Ferried Boisdinghem-Alquines but COL 17.4.18 (Lt VCM Tiarks & AGL 1/Pte HW Williams both unhurt); Adv Salvage to Rep Pk 1 ASD 22.4.18

B7600 Deld 10 AAP Brooklands to AP Dover 21.2.18; 6N Sqn 27.2.18; Crashed 18.3.18 (FSL LE Oakeshott & AGL Dray); Flying by 22.3.18; Became 206 Sqn 1.4.18; 211 Sqn 6.4.18; EF nr aerodrome, tried to turn, spun in, BO 15.5.18 (2/Lt CK Flower & 2/Lt IAB McTavish both killed); Salvage to Rep Pk 1 ASD 17.5.18; SOC 18.5.18 NWR

B7601 Deld 10 AAP Brooklands to AP Dover 26.2.18; 218 Sqn Dover 24.4.18; EF, damaged 30.5.18 (Lt BH Stata); 4 ASD 31.5.18 (Pilots Pool by 1.7.18)

B7602 Deld 10 AAP Brooklands to AP Dover 23.2.18; 6N Sqn 8.3.18; Became 206 Sqn 1.4.18; Crashed nr Wylder due to mist 11.5.18 (Lt CM Hyslop & 2/Lt FS Ganter both unhurt); Rep Pk 1 ASD 16.5.18; SOC 17.5.18 NWR

B7603 Deld 10 AAP Brooklands to AP Dover 21.2.18; 6N Sqn 6.3.18; Became 206 Sqn 1.4.18; 211 Sqn 6.4.18; In combat, FL Zuydcoote 16.9.18 (Capt WD Gairdner OK & 2/Lt HM Moodie DoW just after landing); EA OOC 11.00 4.11.18 (Capt WD Gairdner & Lt BJ Paget); 98 Sqn 26.2.19

B7604 Deld 10 AAP Brooklands to AP Dover 23.2.18; 6N Sqn 8.3.18; AD Dunkirk 12.3.18 (engine test); 6N Sqn by 14.3.18 - @21.3.18; AD Dunkirk by 26.3.18; 4 ASD Guines 1.4.18; 211 Sqn 6.4.18; Left 10.20 for bombing raid on Varssenaere aerodrome, in combat with 5 EA Boetschouck, then caught by heavy AA, crashed west of lines 21.5.18 (Lt RFC Metcalfe & 2/Lt DR Bradley unhurt); Rep Pk 1 ASD 25.5.18; Rebuilt as F5847 25.6.18

B7605 Deld 10 AAP Brooklands to AP Dover 23.2.18; 6N Sqn 8.3.18; Became 206 Sqn 1.4.18; COL after bombing raid 25.4.18 (Lt WL Coleridge & 2/Lt RW Brigstock both unhurt); Rep Pk 1 ASD 28.4.18; SOC in field 28.4.18

B7606 Deld 10 AAP Brooklands to DH4 School Manston 23.2.18; Became 203 TDS Manston 1.4.18; Crashed 12.4.18 (2/Lt JH Evierson & 2/Lt JH Holland both injured)

B7607 Deld 10 AAP Brooklands to DH4 School Manston 23.2.18; Became 203 TDS Manston 1.4.18 - @5.18

B7608 Deld 10 AAP Brooklands to DH4 School Manston 23.2.18; Became 203 TDS Manston ('3A') 1.4.18; Became 55 TDS Manston 14.7.18: Firing practice, left wing folded back as a/c dived vertically into sea with engine full on 24.7.18 (F/Cdt TT Whitley & 1/AM A Capes both killed)

B7609 Deld 10 AAP Brooklands by 23.2.18; DH4 Sqn Manston W/E 8.3.18; Became 203 TDS Manston ('4A') 1.4.18; Became 55 TDS 14.7.18; Crashed on test 20.11.18 (2/Lt FP Adams OK)

D.H.9 B7609 '4A' of No.203 TDS Manston in 1918. (RAF Museum P.16195)

B7610 Deld 10 AAP Brooklands 1.3.18; DH4 Sqn Manston W/E 8.3.18; Pancaked landing 11.3.18 (FSL KHG Tilley & FSL EE Ward unhurt); Became 203 TDS Manston 1.4.18; EF at 150ft on TO, turned back, sideslipped, crashed, BO 2.5.18 (2/Lt SP Inman injured)

B7611 Deld Mullion (via Prawle Point) 23.3.18; Padstow by 12.4.18; Mullion, tested 17.4.18; Padstow 19.5.18; Became 494 Flt 250 Sqn Padstow 30.5.18; Hit by DH.6 B2965 landing 18.9.18 (2 crew unhurt) BUT England to Rec Pk 1.5.18

B7612 Deld 10 AAP Brooklands to Mullion by rail 26.3.18; Prawle Point 27.4.18; COL 26.5.18; Became 492 Flt Prawle Point 30.5.18; 236 Sqn Mullion by 8.18

B7613 Deld 10 AAP Brooklands to Mullion 18.3.18; Prawle Point W/E 2.5.18; 493 Flt Mullion 5.18; Padstow 17.5.18; Dropped 100-lb bomb on U-boat, but no results seen 50°36'N 05°11'W 17.20 18.9.18 (Lt HW Whale & Lt T Terrell); Became 494 Flt 250 Sqn Padstow 30.5.18 - @11.10.18

B7614 Deld 10 AAP Brooklands to AP Dover 6.3.18; Calais 16.3.18; 11N Sqn 17.3.18; Became 211 Sqn 1.4.18; Left 14.35, attacked by 6 EA on PR mission, badly shot up, FL and crashed, CW nr Oudecappelle 13.8.18 (Lt CH Miller wounded & Cpl SJ Bence killed); Rep Pk 1 ASD 14.8.18; SOC 17.8.18 NWR

B7615 Deld 10 AAP Brooklands to AP Dover 8.3.18; 11N Sqn 20.3.18; 6N Sqn 31.3.18; Became 206 Sqn 1.4.18; Bombing raid, FL, o/t 1m SE of aerodrome 12.4.18 (Lt H Mitchell & AM CF Costen unhurt); Rep Pk 1 ASD 15.4.18; SOC 19.4.18

B7616 Deld 10 AAP Brooklands to AP Dover 11.3.18; 11N Sqn 20.3.18; 4 ASD Guines (crashed) 28.3.18 - @25.10.18

B7617 Deld 10 AAP Brooklands to AP Dover 8.3.18; 11N Sqn 20.3.18; 6N Sqn 29.3.18; Became 206 Sqn 1.4.18; Crashed nr aerodrome on landing, caught fire, bombs exploded 12.4.18 (Lt R Robinson killed & Sgt G Woodgate unhurt); Wreckage to Rep Pk 1 ASD 15.4.18; SOC 19.4.18

B7618 Deld 10 AAP Brooklands to AP Dover 15.3.18; 11N Sqn 24.3.18; 6N Sqn 29.3.18; Became 206 Sqn 1.4.18; COL from bombing raid 17.4.18 (Lt LM Whittington & 1/Pte S Jones both unhurt); Adv Salvage to Rep Pk 1 ASD 22.4.18; SOC 25.4.18

B7619 Deld 10 AAP Brooklands to AP Dover 15.3.18; 11N Sqn 23.3.18; 6N Sqn 29.3.18; Became 206 Sqn 1.4.18; COL 12.4.18 (Lt EHP Bailey & 2/Lt CE Anketell both unhurt); Rep Pk 1 ASD 15.4.18; SOC 19.4.18

D.H.9 B7623 'L' of No.211 Squadron after being forced down in Holland and interned on 16.8.18. (via Frank Cheesman)

D.H.9 B7632 of No.211 Squadron around September 1918 (J.M.Bruce/G.S.Leslie collection)

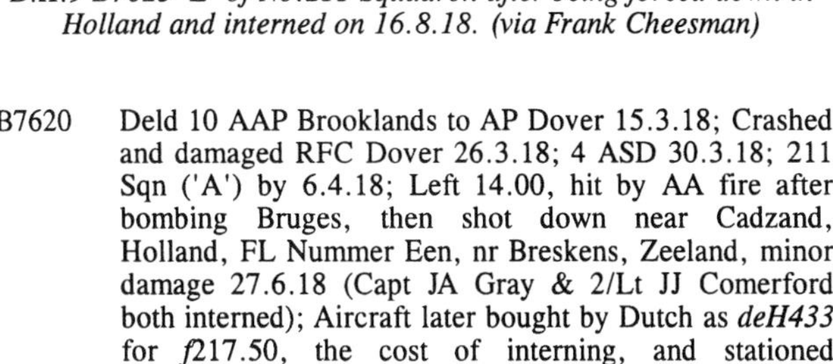

B7620 Deld 10 AAP Brooklands to AP Dover 15.3.18; Crashed and damaged RFC Dover 26.3.18; 4 ASD 30.3.18; 211 Sqn ('A') by 6.4.18; Left 14.00, hit by AA fire after bombing Bruges, then shot down near Cadzand, Holland, FL Nummer Een, nr Breskens, Zeeland, minor damage 27.6.18 (Capt JA Gray & 2/Lt JJ Comerford both interned); Aircraft later bought by Dutch as *deH433* for *f*217.50, the cost of interning, and stationed Soesterberg for training KNIL (Dutch East Indies Army) pilots

B7621 Deld 10 AAP Brooklands to AP Dover 16.3.18; 4 ASD Guines 3.4.18; 211 Sqn 12.4.18, crashed 29.4.18 (Lt JF Drake & 2/Lt NG Breeze); COL 13.6.18 (Lt JF Drake & 2/Lt NG Breeze both unhurt); Rep Pk 1 ASD 13.6.18; SOC 5.7.18 NWR

B7622 Deld 10 AAP Brooklands to AP Dover 15.3.18; 11N Sqn 23.3.18; 6N Sqn 29.3.18; Flat turn into wind in hailstorm, dived in, CW St.Marie Cappell 31.3.18 (FSL LE Oakeshott DoI same day & FSL HW Dray DoI 4.4.18); 4 ASD 2.4.18; Deleted 8.4.18

B7623 Deld 10 AAP Brooklands to AP Dover 16.3.18; 4 ASD Guines to 211 Sqn ('B':'L') 7.4.18; COL 10.7.18 (1/Lt DR Harris USAS & 2/Lt WL Bing); Left 10.30, badly hit by AA fire NE of Bruges, seen gliding down OK, gave emergency signals and FL with dead engine, having been damaged by rifle fire, Zoudekerque, Zeeland, landed intact 12.30 16.8.18 (1/Lt DR Harris USAS & 2/Lt J Munro both interned) [a camera thrown overboard by the crew was found next day]; SOC in field 16.8.18; Became Dutch *deH438*; Retd RAF 12.3.20

B7624 Deld 10 AAP Brooklands to AP Dover 16.3.18; 4 ASD Guines 1.4.18; 211 Sqn ('P') 7.4.18; In action 13.7.18 (Capt HM Ireland OK & 2/Lt CWT Coleman wounded); Engine damaged in combat, FL on beach La Panne 20.7.18 (Capt HM Ireland unhurt & Mjr R Loraine wounded in leg); Raid on Bruges Docks, fired on by German and Dutch coastal guards, engine hit, FL and burnt by crew, Sas van Gent (Hoofdplaat), Zeeland 09.30 8.8.18 (2/Lt LK Davidson & 2/Lt WL Bing both interned); SOC in field 8.8.18

B7625 Deld 10 AAP Brooklands to AP Dover 15.3.18; 211 Sqn 20.4.18; Struck bump landing, wiped off u/c 6.5.18 (Lt GH Baker & 2/Lt TB Dodwell both unhurt); Rep Pk 1 ASD 9.5.18; SOC 11.5.18

B7626 Deld 10 AAP Brooklands to AP Dover 16.3.18; 4 ASD Guines 3.4.18; 211 Sqn ('O') 12.4.18; In action 3.10.18 (2/Lt CC Brouncker OK & 2/Lt DJ Avery wounded); EA BU in air, shared D551 & E8962 11.00 4.11.18 (2/Lt CH Dickins & 2/Lt AM Adams); 2 ASD 22.2.19 unfit for further service in field

B7627 Deld 5 AAP Bristol by 30.3.18; AP Dover by 3.4.18; 202 Sqn 4.5.18; 4 ASD Pilots Pool 24.7.18; EF, FL, stalled, wrecked 21.10.18 (2/Lt RC Treen slightly injured); 4 ASD by 25.10.18; Deleted 31.10.18 DBR

B7628 Deld 5 AAP Bristol to AP Dover but landed RFC Dover and crashed 26.3.18 (Lt HF Game), then to Dover; 491 Flt Dover 25.5.18; 4 ASD Audembert 7.6.18; 218 Sqn by 1.8.18; Pfalz DIII OOC 07.55 13.8.18 (Lt AWE Reeves & 2/Lt GM Worthington); Fokker DVII OOC Stalhille aerodrome 09.43 20.9.18 (Lt AM Anderson & Sgt J Harris); 4 ASD by air 11.10.18 (time expired)

B7629 Deld 5 AAP Bristol 20.3.18; AP Dover 29.3.18; 4 ASD Guines 1.4.18; 211 Sqn ('K') 7.4.18; Hit railway signal post on TO 2.6.18 (Lt GT Scott & 2/Lt PR Thornton both unhurt); Rep Pk 1 ASD 3.6.18; SOC 6.6.18 NWR

B7630 Deld 5 AAP Bristol by 30.3.18; AAP Dover 2.4.18; 202 Sqn 4.5.18; 4 ASD 25.6.18 (later Pilots Pool); EF, FL, starboard wing hit tree, nosed in 3.10.18 (Sgt J Stewart slightly injured); 4 ASD by 25.10.18

B7631 Deld 1 SD late 3.18; Armament School Uxbridge by 10.8.18; WO 11.18

B7632 Deld 5 AAP Bristol by 30.3.18; AAP Dover 2.4.18; 211 Sqn 7.4.18; COL 12.4.18 (Lt NA Taylersen & A/G LC Norman); 4 ASD Guines 13.4.18 - @27.4.18; Rep Pk 1 ASD by 5.18; 1 AI 7.5.18; 4 ASD by 25.5.18 - @31.5.18; 211 Sqn by 9.18, crashed; 4 ASD 29.9.18; To England 2.4.19 [BUT not mentioned in Sqn record, and 211 did not send its aircraft to 4 ASD]

B7633 Deld 1 SD by 3.18; In transit to Mudros 8.18; Recd 'X' AD 2.9.18; 144 Sqn 24.10.18; 'X' AD 26.11.18; 'A' Flt 142 Sqn 28.2.19; WO at 142 Sqn 12.6.19
BUT RAF South Russia to Russian Aviation Corps 8.19

B7634 Deld 5 AAP Bristol 27.3.18; AAP Dover 2.4.18, allotted to EF; England to Rec Pk 21.4.18; 98 Sqn 27.4.18; At aerodrome crashed into by C6073 18.5.18 (Lt AM Phillips & Lt NC McDonald OK); Rep Pk 1 ASD 22.5.18; SOC 23.5.18 BWR

B7635 Deld 5 AAP Bristol by 30.3.18; AAP Dover 2.4.18 - 5.18; 217 Sqn by 16.5.18; 218 Sqn 24.9.18; FL on Sqn transfer to Vert Galant 16.11.18 (Lt JA Eyres & AM M Dawson); Marquise 30.12.18; SOC 1 ASD 21.1.19

B7636 Deld 5 AAP Bristol, tested 5.4.18; En route to Dover from E.1c (Dover-Dunkirk) 6.4.18, reallotted to EF; England to Rec Pk 20.4.18; 49 Sqn 30.4.18; Engine cut out at 14,000ft the other side of the lines, glided back to aerodrome, struck ridge on landing, pancaked 19.5.18 (Lt JA Yates & Lt FC Aulagnier OK); Rep Pk 2 ASD 23.5.18; Rebuilt as F6171 3.7.18

B7637 Deld 5 AAP Bristol by 30.3.18; AAP Dover 2.4.18; 4 ASD Guines 7.4.18; 211 Sqn ('I') 7.4.18; Badly shot up in bombing raid between Ostende & Nieuport 9.5.18 (Lt FJ Islip unhurt & 2/Lt E Cooke wounded); Rep Pk 1 ASD 13.5.18; SOC 14.5.18

B7638 Deld 5 AAP Bristol by 30.3.18 - @5.4.18, reallotted from E1c (Dover-Dunkirk) to EF; Dover to 8 AAP Lympne W/E 4.5.18; Rec Pk 3.5.18; 1 AI 7.5.18; 211 Sqn 11.5.18; FL in field 12.6.18 (Lt JF Drake & 2/Lt NG Breeze both unhurt); Rep Pk 1 ASD 13.6.18; SOC 5.7.18 NWR

B7639 Deld Mullion (via Helston) 4.18; Tested 23.4.18; Prawle Point 28.4.18; Became 492 Flt 254 Sqn Prawle Point by 25.5.18; COL 26.5.18

B7640 Deld Mullion (via Helston) W/E 27.3.18; Prawle Point 28.4.18; Surveyed 10.5.18 wrecked; Deleted 18.5.18

B7641 Deld 5 AAP Bristol W/E 27.3.18; At AAP Dover 5.4.18 allotted to EF; England to Rec Pk 20.4.18; 1 AI 25.4.18; 98 Sqn 28.4.18; Attempting to land when wind caught one wing tip causing other wing to hit ground 30.4.18 (Capt RW Bell & Lt AA Malcolm); Rep Pk 1 ASD 3.5.18; SOC 4.5.18

B7642 Deld 5 AAP Bristol W/E 27.3.18; 10 AAP Brooklands by 4.18; Yarmouth 6.4.18 (anti-sub); Dropped 2x100-lb bombs on U-boat 8m NE of Shipwash LV 9.5.18; 490 Flt Yarmouth by 25.5.18 - @18.6.18; HACP 10.6.18; Covehithe by 6.18

B7643 Deld 5 AAP Bristol W/E 27.3.18; AAP Dover 2.4.18; 211 Sqn 7.4.18; COL 13.4.18 (2/Lt GH Baker & Pte2 HW Newsham) both unhurt; 4 ASD Guines 14.4.18; 2 SS Richborough 15.9.18

B7644 Deld 1 SD 27.3.18; In transit to Mudros 8.18; Recd 'X' AD ex UK 2.9.18; 144 Sqn 25.10.18; 'X' AD 26.11.18; 28 TS Aboukir .19

B7645 Deld 1 SD 27.3.18; In transit to Mudros 8.18; Recd 'X' AD ex UK 10.8.18; 144 Sqn .18; 'X' AD 26.11.18; 'A' Flt 142 Sqn 28.2.19; 31 Wing AP 24.3.19

B7646 Deld 1 SD 27.3.18; In transit to Mudros 8.18; Recd 'X' AD 17.8.18; 144 Sqn 24.10.18; 'X' AD 26.11.18

B7647 Deld 10 AAP Brooklands 28.3.18; Yarmouth 6.4.18 (anti-sub); 490 Flt Yarmouth 25.5.18 - @6.7.18

B7648 Deld 10 AAP Brooklands 28.3.18 for RNAS (NTU); reallotted to EF 9.4.18; Allotment to EF cancelled 15.6.18, returned to Makers

B7649 Deld 10 AAP Brooklands 28.3.18 for RNAS (NTU); reallotted from E.1c Home Anti-Submarine to EF 9.4.19; England to Rec Pk 12.4.18; 1 AI 17.4.18; 49 Sqn ('V') 22.4.18; Fokker Drl OOC E of Bray 12.10 9.5.18 (Lt N Braithwaite & 2/Lt FP Bellingan); Scout OOC S of Bray 11.00, combat damaged and FL and crashed Bertangles 19.5.18 (Lt N Braithwaite & Lt FP Bellingan both wounded); Rep Pk 2 ASD 20.5.18; Rebuilt as F6066 2.7.18

Overshot landing, damaged u/c and wings 8.6.18 (Capt MG Baskerville & Chief Mech SH Newton), repaired on Sqn; Crashed, CW on local flight Capelle 24.6.18 (Lt HVM Hoskins seriously injured); to 4 ASD

B7657 Deld 10 AAP Brooklands by 20.4.18, allotted to EF; England to Rec Pk 28.4.18; 98 Sqn 30.4.18; Left 12.15 for bombing raid on Bruges, hit by AA, down in spin 31.5.18 (Capt GD Horton & Lt HJ McConnell both killed)

B7658 At 10 AAP Brooklands 22.4.18, allotted to EF; England to Rec Pk 1.5.18; 1 AI 7.5.18; 206 Sqn 15.5.18; Sqn move, EF, COL Alquines 5.6.18 (Lt CM Hyslop & Sgt JW Pacey unhurt); Rep Pk 1 ASD 8.6.18; SOC 11.6.18 NWR

B7659 At 5 AAP Bristol 25.4.18 allotted to EF;Reallotted to E.1C for Mediterranean 1.5.18; AAP Dover W/E 15.5.18; Shipped to Italy?; 226 Sqn Pizzone by 28.5.18; Became 472/4 Flts 226 Sqn Pizzone 9.18

B7660 Deld 5 AAP Bristol by 3.5.18; AAP Dover W/E 15.5.18; 218 Sqn W/E 24.5.18; Damaged by AA fire Ostende 12.6.18 (Capt JF Chisholm & 2/AM LA Locke unhurt); to 4 ASD; 218 Sqn 27.9.18; Fokker Drl OOC Thourout 09.35-09.40 29.9.18 (Capt CS Iron & 2/Lt C Ford); 98 Sqn 21.1.19; 8 AAP Lympne (via Rec Pk) 9.2.19

B7661 At 10 AAP Brooklands 22.4.18, allotted to EF; England to Rec Pk 1.5.18; 1 AI 4.5.18; 211 Sqn 8.5.18; Albatros D crashed into wood & caught fire nr Blankenberghe 12.20 19.5.18 (Lt JS Forgie & 2/Lt JS Muir); Left 10.15, last seen behind formation over target Varssenaere aerodrome 21.5.18 (2/Lt HE Tansley &

D.H.9 B7651 '1' of the Wireless Experimental Establishment, Biggin Hill in 1918. (RAF Museum P.21495)

D.H.9A prototype B7664 fitted with an Eagle VIII engine. (J.M.Bruce/G.S.Leslie collection)

B7650 Deld 10 AAP Brooklands 28.3.18 for RNAS (NTU); Re allotted to EF 9.4.18; England to Rec Pk 1.5.18; 98 Sqn 2.5.18; Left 05.30 for bombing raid on Menin, hit by AA shrapnel E of lines 10.5.18 (Lt FA Laughlin & 1/AM RJ Weston OK); Rep Pk 1 ASD 13.5.18; SOC 14.5.18 NWR

B7651 Deld 10 AAP Brooklands 28.3.18 for RNAS (NTU); WEE Biggin Hill ('1') by 4.18 - @28.5.18

B7652 WEE Biggin Hill ('2') by 29.5.18

B7653 Deld 10 AAP Brooklands by 13.4.18; England to Rec Pk 28.4.18; 99 Sqn 1.5.18; Landed too fast, turned on nose 25.6.18 (Lt J Whattam & 2/Lt TH Wiggins OK); 3 ASD to 104 Sqn 22.8.18; Raid on Mannheim, formation attacked by EA, FTR 7.9.18 (2/Lt JE Kemp PoW & 2/Lt EB Smailes PoW DoW 13.9.18)

B7654 At 10 AAP Brooklands 15.4.18, allotted to EF; England to Rec Pk 1.5.18; 1 AI 4.5.18; 206 Sqn 8.5.18; COL 19.5.18 (Lt S Gillott & 2/Lt FS Ganter both unhurt); Rep Pk 1 ASD 20.5.18; SOC 21.5.18 NWR

B7655 At 10 AAP Brooklands 22.4.18, allotted to EF; Rec Pk to 2 AI 2.7.18; 3 ASD 4.7.18; 104 Sqn 7.7.18; EF over wood SSW of airfield, crashed in wood, wrecked 12.7.18 (2/Lt GH Patman & 2/Lt AB Rattray both injured); SOC 12.7.18

B7656 Deld 5 AAP Bristol by 25.4.18, allotted to EF; Tested 29.4.18; AAP Dover for Dover-Dunkirk Cd by 11.5.18, reallotted from EF to E.1C for Dover-Dunkirk Command; 218 Sqn by 29.5.18; Damaged landing 29.5.18 (Lt WF Purvis unhurt), repaired on Sqn;

2/Lt NB Harris PoWs); SOC in field 21.5.18

B7662 Deld Mullion W/E 11.5.18; 493 Flt 236 Sqn Mullion by 25.5.18; Prawle Point 12.6.18; On return from patrol crashed Gaspell, BO 19.6.18 (Lt FStP Harran DoI 20.6.18 & AC2 F Fairbrother killed)

B7663 Deld Mullion W/E 11.5.18; 493 Flt 236 Sqn Mullion by 25.5.18 - @3.6.18; Padstow by 17.7.18

B7664 Trial combination of D.H.9A airframe and 375hp Eagle VIII engine; Deld Martlesham Heath 17.8.18 (comparison tests with Liberty-engined D.H.9A); AES Orfordness 10.9.18

B7665 Deld Mullion W/E 11.5.18; 494 Flt 250 Sqn Padstow 24.5.18, FL in sea, towed in by trawler 14.6.18 (crew saved)

B7666 Deld Mullion W/E 11.5.18; 493 Flt 236 Sqn Mullion by 25.5.18; 492 Flt Prawle Point 254 Sqn 12.6.18 - @23.10.18; 493 Flt 236 Sqn Mullion by 29.10.18 - @30.10.18

B7667 Deld 5 AAP Bristol by 27.4.18; At Dover 11.5.18, reallotted from EF to E.1c for Dover-Dunkirk Command; 218 Sqn by 31.5.18; Crashed in sea, last seen above clouds at 12/14,000ft off Nieuport 10.6.18 (2/Lt RW Robinson & G/L 1/Pte HA Claydon both drowned)

B7668 Deld 5 AAP Bristol by 26.4.18 - 20.5.18, allotted to EF; Rec Pk by 23.5.18; 206 Sqn 25.5.18; Left 17.35, seen over Courtrai 19.20 29.7.18 (Lt G Cheston USAS & Sgt JW Pacey both killed); SOC in field 31.7.18

B7669 Deld 5 AAP Bristol by 27.4.18, allotted to EF; Tested

A D.H.9 cockpit in 1918. The mounting for the Vickers gun (not installed) is above the switch panel for the instrument lights. There are six small lights, three of which are set round the compass. Top centre is the fuel system tank selector. The hole in the windscreen is for an Aldis sight. (via Philip Jarrett)

30.4.18; At Dover 11.5.18, reallotted from EF to E.1C for Dover-Dunkirk Command; 217 Sqn 18.5.18; Damaged in enemy air raid 5/6.6.18; 4 ASD Pilots Pool 13.6.18; 2 SS Richborough 15.9.18

B7670 Deld 5 AAP Bristol 26.4.18, allotted to EF; reallotted from EF to E.1c for the Mediterranean 1.5.18; Shipped to Italy; 226 Sqn Pizzone by 28.4.18; Became 472/4 Flts 226 Sqn Pizzone 9.18 - @1.19; AD Taranto to 'X' AD 28.6.19; AP Baghdad by 20.7.20 - @24.7.20; 55 Sqn by 7.20 - @25.9.20

B7671 Deld 5 AAP Bristol by 5.5.18; 491 Flt Dover W/E 24.5.18; 218 Sqn 1.6.18; Hit by AA Bruges Docks 16.9.18 (Lt HD McLaren & Sgt G Barlow OK); 4 ASD 16.9.18 - @25.10.18

B7672 Presentation Aircraft 'Presented by Patrick Burns Esq of Calgary, Alberta'. AAP Dover W/E 15.5.18; 218 Sqn W/E 24.5.18; Fokker DVII crashed in sea 07.30 14.7.18; Pfalz DIII OOC S of Ostende 07.55 13.8.18 (Lt AC Lloyd & Sgt J Harris); Pfalz DIII in flames Ghistelles aerodrome 13.25 15.8.18 (both Lt AWE Reeves & 2/Lt GM Worthington); 8 AAP Lympne 14.1.19

B7673 Deld 5 AAP Bristol by 27.4.18; AAP Dover to 218 Sqn W/E 24.5.18; Hit by AA Zeebrugge 07.30 14.7.18 (Lt AM Anderson unhurt & 2/Lt CJ Swatridge slightly wounded); Raid on Zeebrugge, left formation, lost Blankenberghe-Zeebrugge 16.7.18 (Lt JA Pugh PoW & 2/Lt J Ankers killed) [credited Ltn Poss of Seefrontstaffel]; Deleted 31.7.18

B7674 Deld 5 AAP Bristol by 1-4.5.18, allotted to EF; England to Rec Pk 20.5.18; 1 AI 21.5.18; 98 Sqn 23.5.18; Left 04.00 for bombing raid on Bruges, in combat with at least 2 EA, last seen in flames in steep spiral E of Ostende 28.5.18 (Lt FH Reilly DoW & Lt RMcK Hall killed)

B7675 Deld 5 AAP Bristol by 29.4.18, allotted to EF; reallotted from EF to E.1c for Dover-Dunkirk Command 11.5.18; 211 Sqn to Rep Pk 1 ASD 17.5.18; SOC 18.5.18 NWR

B7676 Deld AAP Dover W/E 15.5.18; 218 Sqn W/E 24.5.18; Overshot landing from raid, hit lorry 23.6.18 (Lt H Fawdry & 2/Lt JS Cryan); To 4 ASD; 2 SS Richborough 2.10.18

B7677 Deld 5 AAP Bristol by 4.5.18; AAP Dover W/E 15.5.18; 218 Sqn W/E 1.6.18; Badly damaged in raid on Ostende 5.7.18 (Lt BH Stata & 2/Lt CVR Browne OK); 4 ASD Guines 8.7.18; 4 ASD Audembert by 9.18; 218 Sqn 29.9.18; Fokker DVII down in flames Cortemarcke 09.40 29.9.18 (Lt FP Mulcahy USMCR & Cpl TL McCullough USMCR); 98 Sqn 21.1.19; 8 AAP Lympne 12.2.19

B7678 Deld 5 AAP Bristol by 6.5.18, allotted to EF; England to Rec Pk 20.5.18; 1 AI 22.5.18; 206 Sqn 27.5.18; Pfalz DIII crashed nr Ledeghem 19.40 29.7.18 (Lt HA Schlotzhauer USAS OK & Cpl HW Williams wounded); Left 07.40 on bombing raid, FTR 5.10.18 (2/Lt LH Prime PoW DoW 6.10.18 & 2/Lt C Hancock PoW)

B7679 Deld 5 AAP Bristol by 20.5.18-7.6.18, allotted to EF; Rec Pk to 1 AI 11.6.18; 211 Sqn 14.6.18; Bombing raid on Bruges 16.8.18 (Lt GH Baker wounded); 2 ASD 22.2.19 (unfit to fly Channel)

B7680 Deld 5 AAP Bristol by 20.5.18, allotted to EF; Rec Pk to 1 AI 12.6.18; 206 Sqn 13.6.18; Fokker DVII OOC, own a/c shot up Roulers 16.05 29.8.18 (2/Lt AJ Garside & Sgt WS Blyth both wounded); Burst radiator, FL, crashed Elseghem 22.11.18 (Lt GA Pitt & Lt HOFB Blew both unhurt); 8 SS for repair

D.H.9 rebuilds from salvage by No.1 (Southern) ARD Farnborough in range B7731 to B8230

B7749 No information

B7886 Deld SoTT Halton 9.7.18 - @1.1.19

B7912 11 TDS Old Sarum, EF, FL, crashed 25.10.18 (Lt PG Hutton slightly injured)

B7945 (Puma) Rep Pk 1 ASD to Rep Pk 2 ASD 10.10.18; 2 AI 15.10.18; Martlesham Heath (via 1 (S)ARD Farnborough) 22.12.18 (general work and developing testing methods); AES Orfordness 23.1.19

D.H.9 Rebuild from spares and salvage by No.3 (Western) ARD Yate in range B8841 to B9030

B8854 (D.H.9/Puma) 29 TS Croydon, climbed too steeply on turn, stalled at low height, crashed 20.5.19 (Lt AL Russell & F/Sgt JGS Watts both injured)

100 D.H.9 ordered 29.6.17 under Cont Nos 87/A/1413, A.S.17570 & A.S.19175 (BR.113) from Vulcan Motor & Engineering Co (1906) Ltd, Southport and numbered B9331 to B9430. Probably ordered as D.H.4 initially. (230hp Puma)

B9331 To France with 107 Sqn 5.6.18; Crashed 29.6.18 (Lt BE Gammell & 2/Lt W Middleton OK); Rep Pk 1 ASD 1.7.18; SOC 5.7.18 NWR

B9332 At 2 AAP Hendon 23.5.18, reallotted from 218 Sqn (Mob) Dover to EF; Rec Pk to 2 AI 3.6.18; 98 Sqn 8.6.18; Left 07.15 for bombing raid on Cambrai Rlwy Stn, in combat with 20 EA, shot down, FL in control E of lines 17.6.18 (Lt WJT Atkins & Sgt Mech JH Reed both PoW)

B9333 England to Rec Pk 30.5.18; 2 AI 31.5.18; 103 Sqn 6.6.18; Aileron came off, cause unknown, crashed Enquinegatte 12.7.18 (2/Lt CA Posey & 2/Lt CC Dance both injured); SOC Rep Pk 1 ASD 15.7.18

B9334 England to Rec Pk 31.5.18; 2 AI 6.6.18; 49 Sqn 9.6.18; Bombing raid, hit by AA 10.50, down OOC over Seclin 27.6.18 (Lt JC Robinson & 2/Lt LG Cocking both PoW)

B9335 At 2 AAP Hendon 29.5.18, allotted to EF; England to Rec Pk 4.6.18; 2 AI 14.6.18; 49 Sqn 15.6.18; Left 15.50, FTR bombing raid on Marne Bridges 16.7.18 (2/Lt J Aitken & Sgt SW Melbourne both killed)

B9336 AES Orfordness by 11.9.18

B9337 No information

B9338 At 2 AAP Hendon 31.5.18, reallotted from Training Division to EF; Rec Pk to 2 AI 18.6.18; 27 Sqn 19.6.18; Taking off on raid, m/c stalled, flat turned and crashed from about 80ft, m/c in flames, bombs exploded 7.7.18 (2/Lt ES Morrison & Lt PFH Webb both killed)

B9339 At 2 AAP Hendon 30.5.18, reallotted from Training Division to EF; England to Rec Pk 31.5.18; 2 AI 1.6.18; 104 Sqn 5.6.18; 3 ASD 25.8.18

B9340 At 2 AAP Hendon by 3.6.18, 108 Sqn (Mob) Kenley 7.6.18; reallotted to EF 29.6.18; 2 AI to 49 Sqn 1.7.18; FL due to bad weather, crashed 3.8.18 (2/Lt H Hartley & 2/AM WA Rayer), m/c dismantled and collected by Rep Pk 1 ASD; SOC 3.9.18 NWR

B9341 2 FS Marske, stalled and spun in, BO 17.8.18 (F/Cdt HWW Williams killed & Sgt TS Robinson DoI 18.8.18)

B9342 No information

B9343 At 4 AAP Lincoln 21.6.18, reallotted from Midland Area to EF; Rec Pk to 1 AI 22.6.18; 103 Sqn 6.18 - @14.3.19

B9344 At 4 AAP Lincoln 7.6.18, allotted to EF; Rec Pk to 2AI 18.6.18; 49 Sqn 21.6.18; Fokker DVII crashed nr Chery-Charteuve 19.00 25.7.18 (Capt LR Charron & Lt WA Owens); Fokker DVII in flames Bethencourt 18.30 8.8.18; Fokker DVII OOC S of Bethencourt 06.20 9.8.18 (both Lt H Ford & 2/Lt J Whitehead); Left 09.15, last seen over Péronne 10.8.18 (2/Lt H Hartley & Sgt Mech OD Beetham both PoW)

B9345 At 4 AAP Lincoln 7.6.18, allotted to EF; 2 AI 18.6.18; 98 Sqn 19.6.18; Albatros Scout crashed and burnt Fôret de Ris 17.20 16.7.18; Fokker DVII BU and another OOC Douai 08.40-09.00 29.8.18 (all Lt WG Davis & Sgt Mech JK Ison); Casualty Report 9.10.18 says unfit for war flying; 2 ASD 13.10.18; 49 Sqn 10.18; Fokker DVII crashed Elougies 11.25 28.10.18; Fokker DVII in flames Hautmont 13.20 1.11.18 (both 2/Lt JW Birkenshaw & 2/Lt EVG Bramble); Still 49 Sqn 29.5.19

B9346 At 4 AAP Lincoln 7.6.18, allotted to EF; Rec Pk to 1 AI 24.6.18; to 211 Sqn but COL 26.6.18 (Lt CM Ducking); Flying again 28.6.18; Left 15.20 for raid on Ostende, hit by AA nr Zeebrugge, FL in sea 4m N of Nieuport 17.35 13.7.18 (2/Lt W Gilman & AC1 WJ Atkinson both drowned) [BUT credited by Germans to Flgm Blaas, Marine Jasta 3]; SOC in field 13.7.18

B9347 At 4 AAP Lincoln 21.6.18, reallotted from 61 Wing to EF; Rec Pk to 2 AI 23.6.18 104 Sqn 26.6.18; 3 ASD 7.7.18; 99 Sqn ('T') 29.8.18; EA dest 30.8.18 (Lt MJ Poulton & Lt S Lane); Bombing raid on Arnaville junction, in combat with EA 13.9.18 (2/Lt JL Hunter (Can) wounded in leg & 2/Lt TH Swann OK); Bombing raid on Metz-Sablon railway, last seen in combat with 30-40 EA 26.9.18 (Capt PE Welchman MC DFC PoW DoW & 2/Lt TH Swann PoW wounded)

B9348 At 4 AAP Lincoln 7.6.18, allotted to EF; Rec Pk to 1 AI 23.6.18; 211 Sqn ('F') 24.6.18; 2 ASD 22.2.19

D.H.9 B9348 'F' of No.211 Squadron at Clery in November 1918. The pilot is Lt C.H.Miller and the observer 2/Lt A.B.Belford. (via Stuart Taylor)

B9349 At 4 AAP Lincoln 7.6.18, allotted to EF; 1 AI to 49 Sqn 28.6.18; Pfalz DIII OOC E of Douai 09.05 1.7.18 (Sgt SJ Oliver & Sgt A Davies); COL 9.7.18 (Sgt SJ Oliver & Sgt RA Wootton); To Rep Pk 2 ASD; Rebuilt as F6231 6.8.18

B9350 At 4 AAP Lincoln 7.6.18, allotted to EF; Rec Pk to 1 AI 29.6.18; 107 Sqn 1.7.18; COL 14.8.18 (Lt LE Gosden & Lt WA Smith OK); SOC Rep Pk 2 ASD 13.9.18 (ex 9 AP) NWR

B9351 Tested 1 AAP Coventry 5.7.18; 9 TDS Shawbury by 10.18 - @3.19

B9352 No information

B9353 Tested 1 AAP Coventry 25-27.6.18

B9354 Tested 1 AAP Coventry 18-28.6.18

B9355 Tested 1 AAP Coventry 5-6.7.18; Rec Pk to 2 AI 16.7.18; 3 ASD 4.8.18; 104 Sqn 23.8.18; Damaged by AA in raid on Morhange aerodrome 4.9.18 (Lt J Wrighton OK & Sgt FHJ Denney wounded); To 3 ASD

B9356 Tested 1 AAP Coventry 21.6.18; 131 Sqn Shawbury

B9357 & B9358 No information

B9358 Tested 1 AAP Coventry 26.6.18;

B9359 Tested 1 AAP Coventry 1.7.18; 9 TS Sedgeford by 10.7.18; Midland Area FIS Lilbourne by 10.18

B9360 Tested 1 AAP Coventry 29.6.18; 7th (T) Wing by 6.18; 9 TS Sedgeford by 6.7.18

B9361 Tested 1 AAP Coventry 6.7.18; 7 TDS Feltwell by 9.18

B9362 Tested 1 AAP Coventry 1.7.18; 10 TDS Harling Road by 7.18

B9363 Tested 1 AAP Coventry 28-29.6.18; 10 TDS Harling Road, prop accident 3.7.18 (1/AM J McKendrick injured); 55 TS Narborough by 9.19

B9364 Tested 1 AAP Coventry 27.6.18-16.7.18

B9365 No information

B9366 Rec Pk to 2 AI 21.7.18; 3 ASD 22.7.18; 99 Sqn ('Y') 22.7.18; Bombing raid on Metz-Sablon railway, in combat with 30-40 EA, heavily shot up, crashed Pont-à-Mousson, wrecked 26.9.18 (2/Lt S McKeever wounded & 2/Lt N Boniface OK)

B9367 11 TDS Old Sarum by 21.7.18

B9368 Tested 1 AAP Coventry 5-6.7.18; Prop accident 6.7.18 (Lt GW Hemsworth OK & 1/AM R Maxwell injured)

B9369 Deld 1 AAP Coventry 7.18; Tested 6.7.18; 491 Flt 233 Sqn Dover 9.7.18; EF, FL in sea and sank, attempted salve Dover Harbour 8.8.18 (Lt HG Sullivan & 2/Lt CD Churchill unhurt); WOC 1.9.18

B9370 Deld 1 AAP Coventry 7.18; 491 Flt Dover 26.7.18; Stalled landing, port wing hit ground, u/c collapsed, badly damaged 29.8.18 (Lt DL Melvin); ARS Dover by 30.8.18; Retd 491 Flt 233 Sqn Dover by 12.18
B9371 Deld 1 AAP Coventry by 7.18; 491 Flt 233 Sqn Dover 20.7.18; 10 TDS Harling Road by 10.18
B9372 to B9377 No information
B9378 1 TDS Wittering 1918
B9379 & B9380 No information
B9381 1 TDS Wittering, spun in off turn 29.9.18 (F/Cdt JH McLaurin killed & Pte W Christopherson of 172nd US Aero Sqn DoI)
B9382 10 TDS Harling Road 10.18
B9383 1 TDS Wittering, stalled on turn at 300ft, sideslipped in 3.1.19 (F/Cdt C Thompson & F/Cdt FC Vincent both DoI)
B9384 No information
B9385 10 TDS Harling Road 11.18
B9386 Deld 6 SD Ascot W/E 18.7.18; Shipped to Adriatic Group 10.8.18; Mudros by 10.18 - @1.19; 226 Sqn Otranto
B9387 Deld 6 SD Ascot W/E 18.7.18; Shipped to Adriatic Group 10.8.18; 226 Sqn Otranto; Taranto by 10.18 - @1.19; AD Taranto to 'X' AD 28.6.19; ASD to 'H' Unit, Sudan 7.12.19
B9388 Deld 6 SD Ascot W/E 18.7.18; Shipped to Adriatic Group 15.8.18; AD Taranto by 17.8.18; 226 Sqn Otranto; Mudros by 10.18 - @1.19; Sold to Anti-Bolshevik Government
B9389 Deld 6 SD Ascot W/E 25.7.18; Shipped to Adriatic Group 15.8.18; 226 Sqn Otranto; Mudros by 10.18 - @1.19
B9390 Deld 6 SD Ascot W/E 25.7.18; Shipped to Adriatic Group 15.8.18; 226 Sqn by 2.10.18; Mudros by 10.18 - @1.19
B9391 Deld 6 SD Ascot W/E 25.7.18; Shipped to Adriatic Group 15.8.18; AD Taranto by 17.8.18; 226 Sqn by 2.10.18; Taranto by 10.18; Mudros by 10.18 - @1.19
B9392 Deld 6 SD Ascot W/E 1.8.18; Shipped to Aegean Group 15.8.18; 226 Sqn Pizzone; Taranto by 10.18 - @1.19; AD Taranto to 'X' AD 28.6.19; ASD to 'H' Unit, Sudan 7.12.19 - @2.20
B9393 Deld 6 SD Ascot W/E 1.8.18; To Docks W/E 12.9.18; Shipped to Mudros 13.9.18; Mudros by 10.18 - @1.19; Sold to Anti-Bolshevik Government
B9394 Tested 1 AAP Coventry 17.8.18; Rec Pk to 2 AI 21.8.18; 3 ASD 24.8.18; 99 Sqn 28.9.18; In action 23.10.18 (2/Lt AR Collis wounded); EA OOC 30.10.18 (Capt H Sanders & Lt GH Power); In raid on Buhl aerodrome, Pfalz DIII crashed S of Arzchviller 14.00 6.11.18 (2/Lt WA Warwick & Lt LH Burrows); 3 ASD 13.11.18
B9395 Presentation a/c 'Australia No.28, Queensland No.3, The Mackenzie Tooloombah'. Tested 1 AAP Coventry 25.7.18; Rec Pk to 2 AI 30.7.18; 49 Sqn ('O') 4.8.18 - @29.5.19
B9396 to B9401 No information
B9402 Norwich to 10 TDS Harling Road 14.10.18
B9403 Tested 1 AAP Coventry 13.8.18; Norwich to 10 TDS Harling Road 14.10.18; Crashed landing on rough ground, totally wrecked 6.11.18 (Sgt W Grant seriously injured)
B9404 Tested 1 AAP Coventry 14.8.18; 10 TDS Harling Road 10.18; 3 (T) Group Navigation School, Norwich by 9.19
B9405 to B9416 No information
B9417 Rec Pk to 108 Sqn 3.10.18; Left 08.05 for bombing raid on Mousron, hit by AA E of Zillebeke, FL crashed in shell hole nr Ypres 9.10.18 (Lt JG Kershaw & 2/Lt WL Walker unhurt), unsalvable
B9418 1 Observers School Eastchurch by 10.18; Became 2 MOS Eastchurch 28.12.18 - @1.19
B9419 2 MOS Eastchurch by 3.19 - @7.19
B9420 120 Sqn Bracebridge Heath by 9.18; 15 TDS Hucknall by 10.18
B9421 Rec Pk to 2 AI 20.9.18; 98 Sqn 3.10.18; Attack on Mons railway station 30.10.18 (pilot 2/Lt WG Davies wounded in hand & Lt RHS Grundy OK); Shot up in combat with 20 EA in attack on Mons railway station 1.11.18 (Capt RV James OK & Capt AWB Becher wounded in leg); Damaged by EA fire 9.11.18 (Lt WH Whitlock & Lt HS Boocock OK); Rep Pk 1 ASD 12.11.18
B9422 to B9424 No information
B9425 2 SoN&BD Andover, EF, stalled attempting to sideslip into field 22.10.18 (Lt LS Davis & Sgt F Clews both slightly injured)
B9426 to B9430 No information

300 D.H.9 ordered 29.6.17 under Cont No A.S.17570 (BR.113) from G & J Weir Ltd, Glasgow and numbered C1151 to C1450. Originally ordered as D.H.4. (230hp Puma)

C1151 Arr AES Martlesham Heath 28.2.18 (Remy ignition tests & photographic trials); AES Orfordness 13.3.18 - 10.18
C1152 44 TS Waddington by 1.18 - @3.18
C1153 Tested 1 AAP Coventry 8.5.18 [prefix?]; 44 TS Waddington by 19.6.18
C1154 Tested 1 AAP Coventry 8-22.5.18 [prefix?]; 31 TDS Fowlmere, FF 13.10.18; Crashed due to breaking of aileron control cable 19.10.18 (Lt TWA Radcliffe & F/Cdt Baner both OK); Midland Area FIS Lilbourne by 11.18
C1155 Tested 1 AAP Coventry 8.4.18 - 5.6.18 [prefix?]; 7 TDS Feltwell, prop accident 12.9.18 (3/AM A Brown seriously injured)
C1156 No information
C1157 25 TS Thetford; 6 TDS Boscombe Down by 6-31.7.18
C1158 Presentation a/c 'Jamnagar No.3'. At 4 AAP Lincoln 28.6.18, reallotted from SW Area to EF; 1 AI to 108 Sqn 29.9.18; Engine cut out sideslipped and crashed 1.11.18 (Lt GS Daniel & Lt E Holder OK); SOC 3.11.18 NWR; Bboc 19.12.18; 98 Sqn 23.1.19
C1159 Deld Stamford to 25 TS Thetford 7.4.18
C1160 1 AAP Coventry to [46 TS?] Catterick 13.3.18 [prefix?]; 44 TS Waddington, spun in off flat turn 21.6.18 (Lt JGH De Roeper seriously injured) [prefix?]
C1161 2 FS Marske ('61'); 44 TS Waddington, on seeing another a/c in front while landing, started to go round

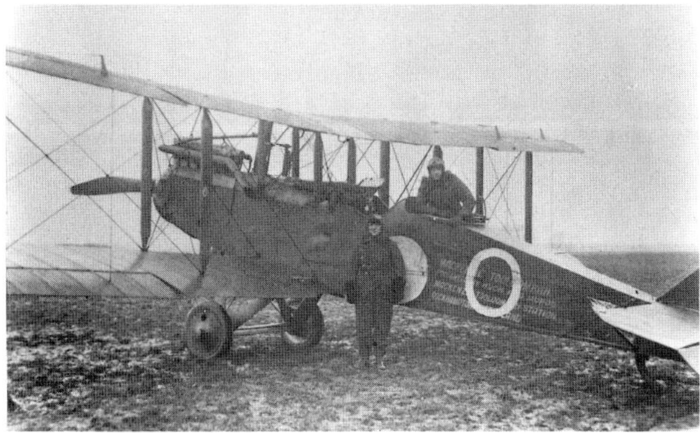

D.H.9 B9395 'O' of No.49 Squadron 'Australia No.28, Queensland No.3, The Mackenzie Tooloombah' was one of a large number of Australian presentation aircraft. (G.S.Leslie/J.M.Bruce collection)

D.H.9 C1151 was used by Aeroplane Experimental Station at Martlesham Heath for Remy ignition tests & photographic trials, later moving to Orfordness. (MAP)

D.H.9 C1161 of No.2 Fighting School, Marske. (via Terry Treadwell)

D.H.9 C1169 of an unidentified unit has 'Uncle Sam' on the nose in Gothic script. (RAF Museum)

again but went into flat spin on turn near ground, crashed 1.5.18 (Lt WA Stahl seriously injured & Pte B Wright slightly injured)

C1162 110 Sqn Sedgeford by 27.5.18; 4 SoN&BD Thetford by 11.18 [prefix?]

C1163 Tested 1 AAP Coventry 9.5.18 [prefix?]; 44 TS Waddington by 7.18

C1164 46 TS Catterick 1918; 52 TS Catterick by 6.18; Became 49 TDS Catterick 15.7.18 - @9.18

C1165 Presentation a/c 'Baroda No.16'.

C1166 At 4 AAP Lincoln 30.5.18, reallotted from Training Division to EF; England to Rec Pk 31.5.18; 2 AI 3.6.18; 98 Sqn 8.6.18; In combat over Lille 11.15 9.7.18 (Lt AE Simpson wounded & 2/Lt HTG Robey OK); Left 06.15 for raid on Bazoches Rlwy Junction, in combat with EA, damaged by enemy fire 20.7.18 (Lt F Carpenter & Lt FE Donkin OK); 9 AP 22.7.18; SOC Rep Pk 1 ASD 3.9.18 NWR

C1167 No information

C1168 Rec Pk to 1 AI 12.6.18; 211 Sqn 14.6.18; In action 17.6.18 (2/Lt J Steel Muir wounded); Lost way, landed Yarmouth, then landed Manston due to storm 7.9.18; Retd Sqn 9.9.18; Damaged by AA, FL Möeres 7.10.18 (Lt JL McAdam & Sgt Mech H Lindsay both wounded); 2 ASD 22.2.19 (unfit to fly Channel)

C1169 Tested 1 AAP Coventry 9.5.18 [prefix?]; 44 TS Waddington by 6.18 - @7.18; Named "Uncle Sam"

C1170 No information

C1171 25 TS Thetford by 20.5.18

C1172 At 1 AAP Coventry 21.3.18, allotted to EF; England to Rec Pk 11.4.18; 49 Sqn ('O') 12.4.18; FL during heavy rain storm and crashed due to bad visibility 3.8.18 (2/Lt AL Murray & Sgt Mech CG Mock); SOC Rep Pk 2 ASD 23.8.18 (ex 2 Salvage Dump)

C1173 At 4 AAP Lincoln 21.3.18, allotted to EF; England to Rec Pk 22.4.18; 2 AI 6.5.18; 49 Sqn 10.5.18; Scout crashed and burnt Harbonnières 19.1519.5.18 (Lt RC Stokes & Lt RAV Scherk); On landing a sudden gust of wind caught the RH plane causing the LH plane to strike the ground, the m/c turned on its nose 25.5.18 (Lt RC Stokes & 1/Pte LC Norman); Rep Pk 2 ASD 28.5.18; Rebuilt as F6072 3.7.18

C1174 At 4 AAP Lincoln 21.3.18, allotted to EF; England to Rec Pk 12.4.18; 1 AI 17.4.18; 98 Sqn 21.4.18; On take off at a height of 10ft engine cut out, stalled, crashed 19.5.18 (Lt GD Horton & Lt HJ McConnell OK); Rep Pk 1 ASD 28.5.18; SOC 29.5.18 NWR

C1175 At 4 AAP Lincoln 23.3.18, allotted to EF; England to Rec Pk 25.4.18; 206 Sqn 1.5.18; Crashed into telephone wires Boisdinghem 15.5.18 (Lt EA Burn & 2/Lt AH Mitchener unhurt); Rep Pk 1 ASD 19.5.18; SOC 20.5.18

C1176 At 4 AAP Lincoln 25.3.18, allotted to EF; England to Rec Pk 25.4.18; Rec Pk to 2 AI 2.5.18; 49 Sqn 6.5.18; Fokker DrI OOC E of Bray 12.10 9.5.18 (Lt FW Lowen & 2/Lt J Sharp); Scout OOC Harbonnières 19.15 19.5.18 (Lt FW Lowen & Lt FB Dennison); Fokker DrI OOC Flavy-Le-Martel 10.45 7.6.18 (Lt FW Lowen & 2/Lt J Sharp); On practice flight engine cut out, FL, 6.7.18 (Lt GS Ramsay & 3/AM H Knowles OK); To Rep Pk 2 ASD; SOC 28.7.18 NWR

C1177 At 4 AAP Lincoln 27.3.18, allotted to EF; England to Rec Pk 25.4.18; 98 Sqn 30.4.18; Pfalz DIII OOC 5m SE of Ypres 14.45, then engine cut out, FL, crashed 2.5.18 (Capt RW Bell & Lt AA Malcolm both OK); Rep Pk 1 ASD 6.5.18; 1 AI 24.6.18; 206 Sqn 28.6.18; Left 14.15 on long reconnaissance, hit by mg fire, FTR 29.6.18 (Lt C Eaton & 2/Lt EW Tatnall both PoW); SOC in field 1.7.18

C1178 At 4 AAP Lincoln 27.3.18, allotted to EF; England to Rec Pk 15.5.18; 2 AI 20.5.18; 49 Sqn 21.5.18; On landing the wind caught the RH wing when 3ft off the ground causing the a/c to turn to left and crash on nose 25.5.18 (Sgt SJ Oliver & Sgt W Lee); Rep Pk 2 ASD 26.5.18; Rebuilt as F6073 3.7.18

C1179 Rec Pk to 2 AI 7.7.18; 107 Sqn 9.7.18; In action 30.10.18 (2/Lt RC Creamer wounded & Sgt JP Hazell OK); On delivery flight from 107 Sqn to 98 Sqn Demobilisation Unit engine failed on take off, nose dropped, a/c hit F6073 which was stationary 1.3.19 (2/Lt CF Robinson OK); 1 ASD 3.3.19

C1180 England to Rec Pk 14.5.18; 1 AI 19.5.18; 98 Sqn 22.5.18; Crashed into a cart in a field adjoining the aerodrome 28.5.18 (Lt RL Tilly & Lt CP Harrison); Rep Pk 1 ASD 30.5.18; SOC 5.7.18 NWR

C1181 England to Rec Pk 16.5.18; 1 AI 19.5.18; 206 Sqn 21.5.18; Fokker DrI crashed and burnt Bac St.Maur, shared C6240 12.00 7.6.18 (Lt LA Christian & 2/Lt EW Tatnall); Hit by Camel B7413 on TO, CW 17.6.18 (Lt FA Brock & Cpl LH Hartford USAS); Rep Pk 1 ASD 19.6.18; SOC 22.6.18 NWR

C1182 4 (Aux) SoG Marske ('6'), wrecked; Tested Harling Road 8.11.18

C1183 2 FS Marske ('35' or ''39')

C1184 2 FS Marske by 8.18

C1185 FF 27.4.18; 4 (Aux) SoAG Marske 27.4.18; Pulled up sharply from dive, wings and tail fell off 1.5.18 (Lt RG Tunbridge killed).

C1186 117 Sqn Fermoy ('1')

C1187 & C1188 No information

C1189 1 FS Turnberry ('107') by 4.9.18; 14 TDS Boscombe Down by 8.18 - @9.18

C1190 1 FS Turnberry ('108')

C1191 No information

C1192 1 FS Turnberry by 6.9.18; 57 TDS Cranwell by 18.9.18

C1193 FF 15.5.18; 44 TS Waddington, stalled and spun landing (Lt EG Jones seriously injured); Repaired?; Left leading edge of tailplane fractured 20.5.18 (Lt EF Matthew & Pte FD Booth both OK)

C1194 51 TS Waddington by 15.6.18; 44 TS Waddington by 3.7.18; EF, FL, crashed 29.7.18 (2/Lt CF Kearns OK)

C1195 No information

C1196 44 TS Waddington 5.18 - 7.18; Crashed 15.5.18

C1197 44 TS Waddington, practice formation flight, mid-air collision at 3,000ft with Camel B6384 9.7.18 (2/Lt CV Felhauer killed)

C1198 44 TS Waddington by 6.18

C1199 44 TS Waddington by 18.6.18

C1200 44 TS Waddington by 2.7.18; Spun in 4.12.18 (F/Cdt AL Taylor (Can) seriously injured)

C1201 44 TS Waddington, mid-air collision with DH6 C7251 of 47 TS during aerial fighting practice 7.6.18 (2/Lt RE

D.H.9 C1223 '2' of No.52 Training Depot Station, Cramlington in 1918. (RAF Museum P.21565)

Heater killed)
C1202 No information
C1203 Deld 75 TS Cramlington 5.18; Aerial firing at Newbiggin range, stbd side of tailplane collapsed, a/c spun in 14.5.18 (Lt CW Brown seriously injured)
C1204 Deld 4 AAP Lincoln by 24.4.18, allotted to EF; allotment to EF cancelled 14.5.18, crashed on test
C1205 At 4 AAP Lincoln 26.4.18, allotted to EF; England to Rec Pk 14.5.18; 1 AI and on to 98 Sqn 18.5.18; Returning from raid on landing swerved to avoid a Handley Page and turned over 30.5.18 (Lt LW Strugnell & Sgt C Lomax); Rep Pk 1 ASD 31.5.18; SOC 5.7.18 NWR
C1206 Deld 4 AAP Lincoln by 5.18; 491 Flt Dover 15.5.18 - @14.6.18; Despatched 2.6.18 (sic); 218 Sqn by 6.18; Damaged 18.6.18 (Lt BH Stata & 2/Lt CVR Browne); Yellow 2-str in flames shared by formation Ostende 18.25 5.7.18 (Capt WF Cleghorn & 2/Lt GJL Potts); Shot up in combat with EAs 28.9.18 (2/Lt F Nelms USMCR wounded & 2/Lt CC Barr USMC DoW 6.10.18); 4 ASD 6.10.18 repair; Deleted 15.10.18 general fatigue
C1207 Deld Dover by 15.5.18; 218 Sqn W/E 1.6.18; Hit by AA, down in flames off Zeebrugge 11.8.18 (Lt H Fawdry & 2/Lt JS Cryan both killed); Deleted 31.8.18
C1208 Deld 491 Flt Dover by 25.5.18; Despatched 2.6.18; 98 Sqn by 9.6.18; Left 10.00 on bombing raid, believed in combat with EA, seen going down east of lines S of Bois de Biez 12.6.18 (Lt FC Wilton & Sgt Mech JH Reed safe)
C1209 75 TS Cramlington by 9.7.18
C1210 Deld 491 Flt Dover W/E 24.5.18; AAP Dover to 218 Sqn 7.6.18; COL 15.6.18 (Lt CF Smith & Sgt G/L RS Joysey); To 4 ASD; 2 SS Richborough 2.10.18
C1211 Deld 491 Flt Dover W/E 24.5.18; 218 Sqn (Code 'VI') by 6.18; During raid on Zeebrugge Mole, hit by AA over Belgian coast, glided with stopped engine into Holland, red/white flares were fired over Breskens, FL still carrying 8 bombs of ca. 10kg, damaged u/c and lower wing, Breskens, Zeeland 29.6.18 (Lt WF Purvis & 2/AM LA Locke both interned) [credited Flgm Zenses, Marine Jasta 2]; Deleted 31.7.18; Transported to Soesterberg, became Dutch *deH434*; Retd RAF 20.3.20
C1212 At 4 AAP Lincoln 11.5.18, allotted to EF; England to Rec Pk 19.5.18; 2 AI 21.5.18; 27 Sqn 22.5.18; Albatros D OOC Roye 10.45 6.6.18 (Lt DB Robertson wounded & Sgt SB Percival unhurt); Fokker DVII crashed Bethencourt 17.00 9.8.18 (2/Lt IL Dutton & 2/Lt T Brown); Fokker DVII crashed nr Bohain and Ponchaux 18.25 25.9.18 and another FL (2/Lt CM Allan & Sgt WE Smith); Fokker DVII in flames Emerchicourt 09.45 27.9.18 (2/Lt CM Allan & 2/Lt CE Robinson): Fokker DVII in flames Mons, pilot baled out 28.10.18 (2/Lt IL Dutton & Sgt SF Briggs); Left 06.45 on bombing raid, shot up by AA St.Remy, FL 10.11.18 (2/Lt IL Dutton & 2/Lt GH Wilson both unhurt); 2 ASD 10.11.18;
C1213 At 4 AAP Lincoln 7.6.18, allotted to EF; Rec Pk to 1 AI 19.6.18; 103 Sqn by 17.7.18; Left 06.00 on bombing raid, in combat with EA, seen going down E of lines, crashed nr Houplines 22.7.18 (2/Lt CT Houston & 2/Lt JK Clarke both killed)
C1214 Presentation a/c 'Elizabeth Campbell of Inverell Station'. At 4 AAP Lincoln 13.6.18, allotted to EF; Prop accident

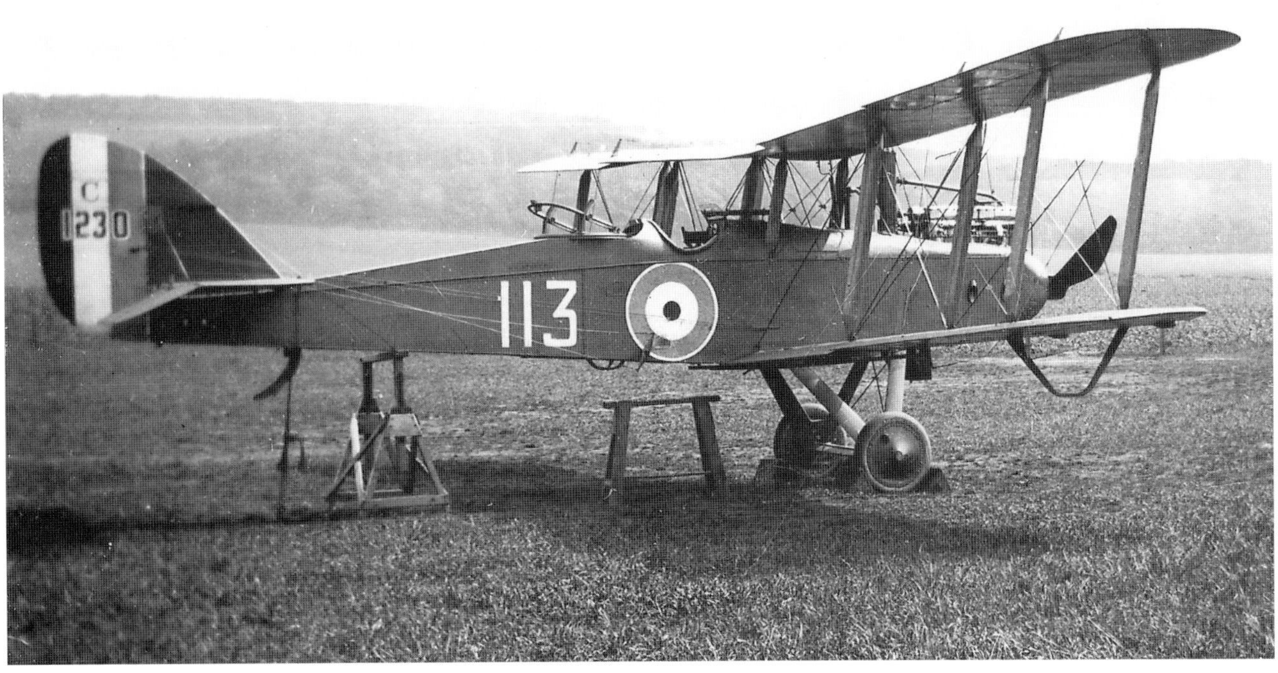

D.H.9 C1230 '113' of No.1 Fighting School, Turnberry in 1918. (Jimmy McCudden via Frank Cheesman)

24.8.18 (2/AM G Syrett injured); Rec Pk to 1 AI 7.9.18
C1215 1 SoAG Turnberry by 5.18
C1216 1 FS Turnberry by 4.9.18
C1217 & C1218 No information
C1219 109 Sqn Lake Down by 30.7.18; 1 FS Turnberry by 1.11.18 [prefix?]
C1220 1 FS Turnberry by 10.18 - 1.11.18
C1221 & C1222 No information
C1223 52 TDS Cramlington ('2'), spun in from low height on turn 31.10.18 (2/Lt GG Scott seriously injured & Sgt CJ Martin unhurt)
C1224 120 Sqn by 6.18; 52 TDS Cramlington, photographing, spun in off gliding turn at low height 30.7.18 (2/Lt FA Bird seriously injured & Sgt WG Daiber USAS slightly injured)
C1225 75 TS Cramlington by 17.6.18
C1226 No information
C1227 49 TDS Catterick by 11.18
C1228 & C1229 No information
C1230 1 FS Turnberry ('113') by 5.18 - @6.18; 120 Sqn by 9.18
C1231 1 FS Turnberry, BU in air, dived into sea which was 20ft deep at low tide 5.6.18 (Lt HW Elliott & Lt RB Reed both killed; Reed was of Aviation Section, US Service Signals Corps)
C1232 to C1235 No information
C1236 49 TDS Catterick by 11.18 - 2.19
C1237 49 TDS Catterick, dived in off flat turn 13.8.18 (F/Cdt NS Ton slightly injured)
C1238 120 Sqn by 6.18
C1239 52 TDS Cramlington, flat turn at 100ft on TO, stalled, dived in, BO 5.11.18 (2/Lt GH Woodland & 3/AM FG Ryder both killed)
C1240 57 TDS Cranwell by 29.9.18
C1241 44 TS Waddington, fainted at 14,000ft, crashed 17.9.18 (F/Cdt LCJ Jennings seriously injured)
C1242 & C1243 No information
C1244 57 TDS Cranwell, propeller accident 6.8.18 (Cpl Mech VG Davis seriously injured)
C1245 57 TDS Cranwell by 27.8.18 - @9.18
C1246 to C1248 No information
C1249 51 TS Waddington by 8.18
C1250 Deld ECD Grain by 1.4.18 - @25.5.18; 57 TDS Cranwell by 8.18; Nosed up in rough ground 9.18
C1251 to C1255 No information
C1256 44 TS Waddington, tailplane collapsed while practising air firing 29.7.18 (F/Cdt CF Fesser killed)
C1257 to C1259 No information
C1260 44 TS Waddington by 7.18; Hendon by 27.7.18 - @10.8.18
C1261 Deld Turnhouse W/E 13.6.18; Crashed 19.9.18 (Lt JC Ambler injured & 2/Lt W Smith slightly injured); Deleted W/E 10.10.18
C1262 No information
C1263 75 TS Cramlington by 20.6.18
C1264 Deld 1 FS Turnhouse W/E 13.6.18 - @30.1.19
C1265 109 Sqn Lake Down by 2.8.18; 1 FS Turnberry by 4.8.18 - @5.9.18; 14 TDS Lake Down by 10.18
C1266 to C1267 No information
C1268 1 FS Turnberry by 3.8.18
C1269 No information
C1270 57 TDS Cranwell by 18.9.18; 1 FS Turnberry ('DII 107'), crashed on shore
C1271 & C1272 No information
C1273 2 FS Marske ('22') by 8.18
C1274 6 AAP Renfrew, propeller accident 6.6.18 (2/AM L Markham killed); 2 FS Marske 1918; 120 Sqn Hawkinge by 3.19 - 8.19
C1275 & C1276 No information
C1277 120 Sqn Bracebridge Heath by 9.18
C1278 120 Sqn Bracebridge Heath by 9.18
C1279 Allocated RN (no details)
C1280 Allocated RN (no details)
C1281 Was to be RN; 120 Sqn by 9.18
C1282 Allocated RN (no details)
C1283 Allocated RN (no details)
C1284 Allocated RN (no details)
C1285 Allocated RN (no details)
C1286 Deld Dover 5.18; 219 Sqn W/E 1.6.18
C1287 Allocated RN (no details)
C1288 Allocated RN (no details)
C1289 Allocated RN (no details); Unidentified unit, prop accident 29.9.18 (Sgt Haslett injured)
C1290 57 TDS Cranwell by 9.18
C1291 Allocated RN (no details)
C1292 Was to be RN; 120 Sqn by 9.18; 15 TDS Hucknall by 11.18, EF on TO, spun in 7.2.19 (Lt JE Schingh killed) [or D1292]
C1293 57 TDS Cranwell by 29.8.18
C1294 6 AAP Renfrew to AAP Dover 26.6.18; 4 ASD Audembert 28.6.18; 218 Sqn 29.6.18; Fokker DrI OOC off Zeebrugge 07.20 14.7.18 (Lt CLW Brading & G/L Sgt F Smith); Heavily damaged in attack by EA on Belgian coast, EF, FL, overturned, prop broke, Vrouwenpolder beach, Zeeland 5.9.18 (Lt JG Munro (S African) & 2/Lt TW Brodie both interned unhurt); Deleted 15.9.18; Became Dutch *deH441*; Retd RAF
C1295 218 Sqn to 4 ASD 25.7.18; 4 ASD Pilots Pool, crashed; 4 ASD by 25.10.18
C1296 1 AI to Alquines 18.6.18 (by Rec Pk); 492 Flt 254 Sqn Prawle Point by 18.8.18 - @27.10.18; Imperial Gift to Australia; Became *A6-9*
C1297 Deld 492 Flt 254 Sqn Prawle Point by 6.10.18 - @19.10.18; COL 8.10.18 (2/Lt RJ Thompson seriously injured & 3/AM AHW Busby injured)
C1298 Deld 492 Flt 254 Sqn Prawle Point by 8.18 - @7.11.18
C1299 Deld 492 Flt 254 Sqn Prawle Point by 8.18 - @31.10.18
C1300 Padstow by 4.10.18; EF, FL, damaged Harlyn Bay 21.10.18 (pilot unhurt)
C1301 Deld Padstow by 12.4.18; Became 494 Flt 250 Sqn Padstow by 25.5.18; COL 17.9.18 (2 crew unhurt)
C1302 Deld 493 Flt 236 Sqn Mullion by 11.18; East Fortune by 20.11.18
C1303 494 Flt 250 Sqn Padstow by 28.10.18 - @31.10.18
C1304 494 Flt 236 Sqn Mullion, EF, stalled and spun in on TO 18.1.19 (2/Lt RJ Cotterell killed)
C1305 Mullion by 11.18; To Prawle Point but missing en route 7.11.18 (Lt D Lamb & AM Lownes) [presumably returned later]
C1306 493 Flt 236 Sqn Mullion by 25.9.18 - @28.10.18
C1307 East Fortune by 12.18; Lake Down 15.12.18 (arr 18.12.18)
C1308 52 TS Catterick by 6.18; Became 49 TDS Catterick 15.7.18 - @9.18; NE Area FIS Redcar by 9.18
C1309 to C1312 No information
C1313 Imperial Gift to India
C1314 & C1315 No information
C1316 Presentation a/c 'Georgetown. Presented by Scottish Munition Workers'. At Makers 27.6.18, allotted to EF; To 6 AAP Renfrew; Rec Pk to 2 AI 17.7.18; 5 AI to 27 Sqn 20.7.18; Left 16.15 for raid, shot up by mg fire, FL 9.8.18 (Lt CB Sanderson OK & Sgt A Dobell wounded); 2 AI 15.8.18; SOC Rep Pk 2 ASD 5.9.18 NWR
C1317 & C1318 No information
C1319 49 TDS Catterick, stalled on gliding turn at 500ft, spun in 21.8.18 (2/Lt FC Barlow seriously injured)
C1320 1 SoAN&BD Stonehenge by 7.18; 8 TDS Netheravon by 4.19 - @19.8.19
C1321 FF 13.7.18; 9 TDS Shawbury, leading edge of tailplane failed pulling out of dive while on test 23.7.18 (Lt RB Slade & F/Sgt F Alsopp both killed)
C1322 2 (N)ARD Greenhill/Coal Aston 1918
C1323 1 FS Turnberry by 5.8.18
C1324 1 FS Turnberry by 3.11.18
C1325 52 TS Catterick by 6.18; Became 49 TDS Catterick 15.7.18 - @9.18
C1326 Deld Yarmouth by 1.8.18; 555/6 Flts 219 Sqn Manston 13.8.18; Crashed 23.9.18 (Lt SW Orr & 2/Lt JW Davies); 218 Sqn (via Dover) 29.9.18; Returning from raid on Melle Siding, FL, crashed Wulveringhem 14.10.18 (Lt SW Orr slightly injured & 2/Lt JW Davies seriously injured); 4 ASD 17.10.18; Deleted 31.10.18 DBR
C1327 Deld Yarmouth by 8.18; 555/6 Flts 219 Sqn Manston 10.8.18; 218 Sqn (via Dover) 29.9.18; Returning from bombing raid, FL on beach and crashed nr Dunkirk 18.10.18 (2/Lt J Jackson & Sgt J Mathers); 4 ASD 19.10.18 - @25.10.18
C1328 Deld Yarmouth by 8.18; 555/6 Flts 219 Sqn Manston 12.8.18; 218 Sqn (via Dover) 29.9.18; Engine burnt out over Bruges during raid, FL 200 yds inside British lines, crashed, shelled 18.10.18 (2/Lt CM Arias unhurt & 2/Lt

Wg Cdr Keevor running up the engine of D.H.9 C1357 'A' of No.117 Squadron at Fermoy in 1919. (J.M.Bruce/G.S.Leslie collection)

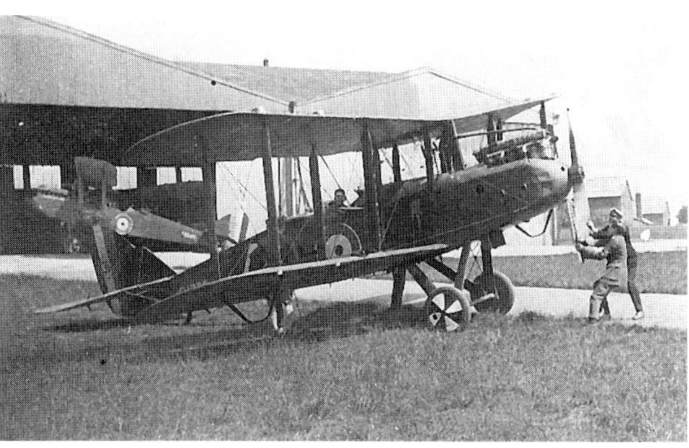

D.H.9 C1385 'A' of No.2 Marine Observers School, Eastchurch in 1919. In the background is D5646. (RAF Museum P.15587)

MJ Clark injured); Deleted 31.10.18
C1329 Deld Yarmouth by 11.8.18; 555/6 Flts 219 Sqn Manston 13.8.18 - @9.18
C1330 Deld 555/6 Flts 219 Sqn Manston by 10.8.18 - @9.18
C1331 Deld 219 Sqn Manston by 12.4.18; 555/6 Flts 219 Sqn Manston 26.6.18 - @9.18
C1332 Deld 219 Sqn Manston by 12.4.18; 555/6 Flts 219 Sqn Manston 26.6.18; 218 Sqn (via Dover) 29.9.18; Returning from raid, COL St.Pol 16.10.18 (2/Lt J Jackson & Sgt J Mathers); 4 ASD 16.10.18 - @25.10.18
C1333 1 FS Turnberry by 4.8.18; Took off cross-wind, turned downwind, stalled, spun in from 30ft, BO 5.9.18 (F/Cdt A McLean & 2/Lt WA Rymal both killed)
C1334 1 FS Turnberry, mid-air collision, crashed Minnybae Farm, nr Turnberry 23.8.18 (2/Lt A McFarlan & F/Cdt AA Hepburn both killed; Hepburn's body found about 1m away at Ballochneil Wood)
C1335 No information
C1336 57 TDS Cranwell by 28.9.18; 14 TDS Lake Down by 10.18
C1337 22 TDS Gormanston by 16.9.18
C1338 No information
C1339 22 TDS Gormanston by 8.9.18
C1340 22 TDS Gormanston by 4.10.18
C1341 At Makers 27.6.18, allotted to EF; To 6 AAP Renfrew; Rec Pk to 1 AI 22.8.18; 206 Sqn 24.8.18; Returning from raid crashed due to high wind and heavy rain 29.9.18 (Lt H McLean & 2/Lt HP Hobbs OK); To Rep Pk 1 ASD 30.9.18
C1342 At Makers 27.6.18, allotted to EF; To 6 AAP Renfrew; Rec Pk to 2 AI 18.10.18; 108 Sqn 9.11.18; 8 AAP Lympne 18.1.19
C1343 to C1354 No information
C1355 22 TDS Gormanston by 30.8.18
C1356 No information
C1357 117 Sqn Fermoy ('A') 1919
C1358 to C1363 No information
C1364 49 TDS Catterick by 11.18 - 2.19
C1365 52 TS Catterick by 6.18; Became 49 TDS Catterick 15.7.18 - @9.18
C1366 to C1369 No information
C1370 Collinstown 1919
C1371 No information
C1372 57 TDS Cranwell by 26.9.18; 1 FS Turnberry, stalled on climbing turn, fell into sea 20.10.18 (Lt JS Brown & 2/Lt CA Fletcher both killed)
C1373 57 TDS Cranwell by 18.9.18
C1374 57 TDS Cranwell by 29.9.18; 1 FS Turnberry, severe engine vibration, FL, crashed 25.11.18 (Lt KF Piper seriously injured & F/Cdt J Hughes DoI when petrol-soaked clothing caught alight from a match in hospital) [prefix?]
C1375 No information
C1376 Crashed on nose c.1920
C1377 & C1378 No information
C1379 44 TS Waddington, FL, wrecked turning in mist 5.9.18 (Sgt JH Peace seriously injured)
C1380 MOS Aldeburgh by 11.18
C1381 MOS Aldeburgh by 9.18 - @10.18; 120 Sqn Hawkinge by 3.19 - 8.19
C1382 to C1384 No information
C1385 2 MOS Eastchurch ('A') by 3.19 - @7.19
C1386 No information
C1387 Deld 493 Flt Mullion by 6.18; Damaged in storm 8.6.18; 493 Flt 236 Sqn Mullion 20.8.18; COL, slightly damaged 1.9.18 (pilot unhurt)
C1388 & C1389 No information
C1390 57 TDS Cranwell by 9.18
C1391 Imperial Gift to India
C1392 Imperial Gift to India
C1393 RAE from/by 2.9.20 (FIAT engine radiator tests; General test 28.3.23; Landing load test 17.4.25); Last flown 28.9.27
C1394 to C1446 No information
C1447 22 TDS Gormanston by 10.18
C1448 to C1450 No information

80 D.H.9 ordered 16.12.17 under Cont No 87/A/1185 (BR.113) from F.W.Berwick & Co Ltd, London and numbered C2151 to C2230. (200hp BHP)

C2151 At 7 AAP Kenley 23.3.18, allotted to EF; To Penhurst, caught fire, FL in field 26.4.18 (Lt H Shaw OK); England to Rec Pk 9.5.18; 1 AI 12.5.18; 98 Sqn 17.5.18; Scout in nose dive W of Comines 13.50 18.5.18 (Capt EA Fawcus & Lt GD Dardis); Ran into ditch on landing 26.5.18 (Lt WS Eason OK); Rep Pk 1 ASD 29.5.18; SOC 5.7.18 NWR
C2152 At 7 AAP Kenley 26.3.18, allotted to EF; England to Rec Pk 2.5.18; 2 AI 6.5.18; 27 Sqn 16.5.18; COL 29.5.18 (Lt H Wild & Sgt J Little); Rep Pk 2 ASD to 2 AI 25.7.18; 5 AI 28.7.18; 49 Sqn 31.7.18; Left 14.00, last seen going down Dreslincourt in control and landing 8.8.18 (Lt JA Yates & 2/Lt GR Schooling both PoW)
C2153 At 7 AAP Kenley 9.4.18, reallotted from EF to DPD for special ferry work; Martlesham to Hendon 1.8.18 - @10.8.18; 99 Sqn [photo]
C2154 England to Rec Pk and on to 1 AI 2.5.18; 206 Sqn 8.5.18; EF on TO, FL nr aerodrome, wrecked 10.5.18 (Lt L Childs slightly injured & 2/Lt FW Chester unhurt); Rep Pk 1 ASD 14.5.18; SOC 17.5.18 NWR
C2155 At 7 AAP Kenley 2.4.18, allotted to EF; England to Rec Pk 27.4.18; 99 Sqn 30.4.18; Rep Pk 2 ASD 6.5.18; Rebuilt as F6065 2.7.18
C2156 At 7 AAP Kenley 2.4.18 allotted to EF; England to Rec Pk 20.4.18; 206 Sqn 25.4.18; COL after raid 14.5.18 (Lt EA Burn & 1/Pte WS Blyth both unhurt); Rep Pk 1 ASD 19.5.18; Rebuilt as F5849 25.6.18
C2157 At 7 AAP Kenley 2.4.18, allotted to EF; England to Rec Pk 12.4.18; 206 Sqn 21.4.18; Left 17.41, shot down in flames Bailleul-Kemmel between 18.00 & 19.00 3.5.18 (Lt AE Steele & 2/Lt A Slinger both killed); SOC in field 3.5.18
C2158 At 7 AAP Kenley 2.4.18, allotted to EF; England to Rec Pk 14.5.18; 1 AI 17.5.18; 98 Sqn 18.5.18; Damaged in enemy night raid Coudekerque 5/6.6.18; 4 ASD by 20.6.18; 218 Sqn 6.9.18; Attacked by 2 EA Zeebrugge-Ostende, FL, completely wrecked, Deutsche Bank Channel, mouth of River Schelde off Walcheren (Deurloo) 15.9.18 (Lt WS Mars & 2/Lt HE Power

rescued by Dutch Navy and interned, both slightly injured); Deleted 31.10.18; The fishing boats *ARN11* and *VL136* (the captains were awarded *f* 25 each) found the wreck which was later salvaged by the *Coertzen* and transported to Vlissingen

C2159 Hendon by 14.6.18 - @25.7.18

C2160 Shipped to Otranto 20.4.18; 226 Sqn by 25.5.18

C2161 Shipped to Otranto 20.4.18; 224 Sqn by 9.6.18; Missing en route Taranto 20.10.18 (2/Lt JTR Profitt killed)

C2162 Shipped to Otranto 20.4.18; 226 Sqn by 25.5.18 - @6.18; Disposed of by 25.7.18

C2163 103 Sqn Old Sarum by 25.4.18; 1 SoN&BD Stonehenge, cross-country tests, stalled and dived in [believed nr Dorchester] 16.8.18 (2/Lt WF Maker killed & Sgt S Chapman seriously injured)

C2164 119 Sqn Duxford by 5.18; Spun in 15.8.18 (2/Lt JTF Neary seriously injured)

C2165 5 TS Wyton by 5.18; 31 TS Wyton, prop accident 10.6.18 (Pte D Caudill injured)

C2166 31 TS Wyton, spun in from 1,500ft 9.5.18 (2/Lt RSC Hall seriously injured)

C2167 & C2168 No information

C2169 49 TDS Catterick by 7.18; 75 TS Cramlington by 14.7.18; 52 TDS Cramlington 15.7.18

C2170 To France with 104 Sqn 19.5.18; Left 09.35 for bombing raid on Karlsruhe, on return met 5 EA, engine probably hit, went down E of Vosges east of lines 25.6.18 (Lt SCM Pontin & 2/Lt J Arnold both PoW)

BUT 104 Sqn, bombing raid on Karlsruhe, formation in combat over Saverne, red & white Albatros OOC just before reaching target & blue & white Pfalz DIII SS in spin over target 09.10 11.8.18

m/c regarded as badly strained and should be returned to ASD for repair (Lt V Mercer-Smith & 2/Lt AE Durling OK); SOC Rep Pk 1 ASD 17.7.18 ex 9 AP NWR

C2178 At 2 AAP Hendon 1.5.18, allotted to EF; England to Rec Pk 9.5.18, 98 Sqn 11.5.18; Left on low reconnaissance, lost way tried to land at Marquise, flat turn without flying speed, side slipped and nose dived in 24.5.18 (Lt HW Whale & Sgt ER McDonald both seriously injured): Rep Pk 1 ASD 26.5.18; SOC 27.5.18

C2179 At 2 AAP Hendon 8.5.18, allotted to EF; England to Rec Pk 17.5.18; 2 AI 23.5.18; 104 Sqn 27.5.18; Raid on Mannheim, in combat with 15 EA from approach to target, FTR 22.8.18 (Lt GHB Smith & Sgt W Harrop MM both PoW)

C2180 At 2 AAP Hendon 8.5.18, allotted to EF; England to Rec Pk 18.5.18; 1 AI 20.5.18; 211 Sqn 22.5.18; Pancaked landing, crashed 1.6.18 (2/Lt HH Palmer & 2/Lt JS Muir); Rep Pk 1 ASD 2.6.18; SOC 5.7.18 NWR

C2181 AAP Hendon for EF by 1.5.18; To France with 107 Sqn 5.6.18; Crashed on aerodrome 12.6.18 (Lt AM Rosenbleet & 2/Lt WJ Palmer); To Rep Pk 2 ASD; Rebuilt as F6213 25.7.17

C2182 To France with 107 Sqn 5.6.18; Left on raid 06.25, FTR, last seen over Tournai, believed hit by AA 11.7.18 (Lt JD Cook & 2/Lt HH Ankrett both killed)

C2183 To France with 107 Sqn 5.6.18; Left on raid 06.25, FTR, last seen over Tournai 11.7.18 (Lt RA Arnott & Lt HR Whitehead both wounded PoW)

C2184 At 2 AAP Hendon 23.5.18, reallotted from 218 Sqn (Mob) Dover to EF; England to Rec Pk and on to 2 AI 28.5.18; 1 ASD to 98 Sqn 8.6.18; On test flight ran into hollow on landing which spun m/c round, crashed

A D.H.9 fitted with a FIAT engine. (French Air Museum)

A D.H.9 of No.25 Training Depot Station, Thetford with an ornate swastike-like device on the nose. (J.M.Bruce/G.S.Leslie collection)

C2171 (Puma) FF 6.5.18; 1 SoN&BD Stonehenge by 7.18; Engine fell out in air, FL, struck telephone post, crashed 21.11.18 (Sgt WW Parker injured & Sgt RT Haspinall DoI)

C2172 [108 Sqn?] Lake Down by 14.5.18

C2173 At 2 AAP Hendon 29.4.18, allotted to EF; England to Rec Pk 3.5.18; 2 AI 4.5.18; 99 Sqn 9.5.18; Designated as an "emergency" a/c on raid, crashed on TO 16.7.18 (Lt FT Cockburn & Sgt A Foulsham)

C2174 At 2 AAP Hendon 29.4.18, allotted to EF; England to Rec Pk 7.5.18; 1 AI 21.5.18; 98 Sqn 22.5.18; Albatros D OOC Ghistelles 19.40 29.5.18 (Lt AM Phillips & Lt NC MacDonald); Damaged in enemy night raid on aerodrome 5/6.6.18; To 4 ASD 6.18; 491 Flt 233 Sqn Dover 25.10.18 - @12.18

C2175 At 2 AAP Hendon 1.5.18, allotted to EF; England to Rec Pk 17.5.18; 206 Sqn 25.5.18; Defective 11.6.18, for Rep Pk 1 ASD; Recommended to be retd, not suitable 21.6.18; to 1 ASD, flown to England 26.6.18

C2176 At 2 AAP Hendon 1.5.18, allotted to EF; England to Rec Pk 14.5.18; 1 AI 18.5.18; 206 Sqn 19.5.18; Missing last seen at 5,000ft in heavy AA 2m E of Ostende 25.6.18 (2/Lt F Daltrey PoW wounded & 1/Pte R Shephard killed)

C2177 At 2 AAP Hendon 1.5.18, allotted to EF; England to Rec Pk 14.5.18; 1 AI 17.5.18; 103 Sqn 18.5.18; FL due to failure in water circulation 6.6.18, returned 7.6.18 but

13.6.18 (2/Lt WV Thomas); Rep Pk 1 ASD 16.6.18; SOC 17.6.18 NWR

C2185 At 2 AAP Hendon 23.5.18, reallotted from 218 Sqn (Mob) Dover to EF; England to Rec Pk 22.5.18; 49 Sqn 25.5.18; Bombing raid on Fourneuil, Albatros DV DD Roye 10.00 5.6.18 (Sgt SJ Oliver OK & Sgt EG Jones); Two Pfalz DIII down smoking between Tricot and Courcelles 15.00, main petrol tank shot through, FL Fouquerolles 15.30 11.6.18 (Lt RC Stokes & 2/Lt CE Pullen); To 9 AP; SOC Rep Pk 1 ASD 17.7.18 NWR

C2186 Deld Hendon to Dover W/E 24.5.18; 218 Sqn by 20.5.18; COL 12.6.18 (Lt JRA Barnes & G/L Sgt RJ Williams unhurt); repaired on Sqn; COL after raid on Bruges 9.7.18 (Capt EF Chamberlain USMC & 2/Lt FH Bugge); to 4 ASD; 2 SS Richborough 15.9.18

C2187 At 2 AAP Hendon 23.5.18, reallotted from 218 Sqn (Mob) Dover to EF; England to Rec Pk 27.5.18; 1 AI 28.5.18; 206 Sqn 30.5.18; FL due to engine trouble and crashed 6.6.18 (Lt F Daltrey slightly injured & 2/Lt MG Penny OK); CW, SOC in field 8.6.18

C2188 At 2 AAP Hendon 23.5.18, reallotted from 218 Sqn (Mob) Dover to EF; England to Rec Pk 31.5.18; Rec Pk to 1 AI 1.6.18; 2 AI 12.6.18; 49 Sqn 13.6.18; On practice flight engine trouble, crashed 30.6.18 (Lt MD Allen & 2/Lt J Ross); Rep Pk 2 ASD 5.7.18; SOC 28.7.18 NWR

C2189 No information

C2190 109 Sqn Lake Down by 21.6.18

C2191 At 2 AAP Hendon 1.6.18 for 109 Sqn (Mob) Lake Down as a training m/c; To sqn 5.6.18 - @7.6.18

C2192 Rec Pk to 2 AI 29.7.18; 3 ASD 1.8.18; 99 Sqn 3.8.18; Hit in engine by AA, FL nr Bar-le-Duc 25.8.18 (Sgt HH Wilson & Sgt FL Lee); 3 ASD 25.8.18

C2193 Rec Pk to 2 AI 31.7.18; 206 Sqn 1.8.18; Fokker DVII in flames, crashed E of Messines 18.50 13.8.18 (Lt RH Stainbank & 2/Lt EW Richardson); Bombing raid, radiator hit by AA, crashed 09.35 5.10.18 (Sgt Mech G Packman slightly injured & 2/Lt JW Kennedy unhurt); to Rep Park 1 ASD

C2194 Rec Pk to 2 AI 5.8.18; 27 Sqn 9.8.18; Bombing raid, left 05.30, in combat with EA Duisans, engine shot up, FL 23.8.18 (Lt PV Holder & 2/Lt H Pitkin OK); 9 AP 24.8.18; SOC Rep Pk 2 ASD 16.9.18

C2195 8 AAP Lympne to Rec Pk 1.8.18; 1 AI 4.8.18; 103 Sqn 7.8.18; Collided with a cow on landing 13.8.18 (Lt DM Darroch OK & 2/Lt HG Stirrup broken nose); Rep Pk 1 ASD 14.8.18; SOC 23.8.18; To be rebuilt as F6451 but cancelled 17.9.18 & WOC 29.9.18

C2196 Arr Rec Pk 7.18 (u/s replaced by C2917); 2 AI 28.7.18; 49 Sqn 7.8.18; Left 14.05 in raid on Bethencourt bridge, damaged by AA, FL nr Amiens 8.8.18 (Lt MD Allen wounded & 2/Lt J Ross killed); SOC Rep Pk 2 ASD 13.9.18 (ex 9 AP)

C2197 Arr Rec Pk 1.8.18; 2 AI 6.8.18; 3 ASD 12.8.18; 99 Sqn 12.9.18; Aileron controls shot away by EA fire, crashed in field nr aerodrome on return 25.9.18 (2/Lt MJ Poulton slightly injured & Sgt FL Lee DFM OK); 6 AP 25.9.18; 3 ASD 30.9.18

C2198 Rec Pk to 2 AI 3.8.18; 3 ASD 4.8.18; 99 Sqn 13.9.18; 3 ASD 25.9.18; 166 Sqn Bircham Newton 1.19

C2199 8 AAP Lympne by 29-30.7.18; Rec Pk to 1 AI 4.8.18; 206 Sqn 9.8.18; Left 05.05 for low recce, FTR 11.8.18 (Lt EHP Bailey & Lt R Milne both killed); SOC in field 11.8.18

C2200 At 2 AAP Hendon 29.5.18, allotted to EF; Rec Pk to 2 AI 7.6.18; 103 Sqn 8.6.18; Left 10.00 for bombing raid on Roye, last seen between Roye and lines 16.6.18 (2/Lt V Mercer-Smith & Sgt J Hamilton both wounded PoW)

C2201 At Makers in case 29.5.18, allotted to EF; Rec Pk to 2 AI 20.6.18; 104 Sqn 25.6.18; 3 ASD 11.7.18 (wrecked); 104 Sqn 8.9.18; 6 AP 12.9.18; 3 ASD 19.9.18

C2202 At 2 AAP Hendon 30.5.18, allotted to EF; Rec Pk to 2 AI 7.6.18; 49 Sqn 8.6.18; Fokker DVII OOC Sergy 18.20 22.7.18 (Lt JA Keating USA & 2/Lt EA Simpson); Badly shot up in raid on Bethencourt bridge, COL 9.8.18 (Lt JA Keating USAS & 2/Lt EA Simpson OK); SOC Rep Pk 2 ASD 10.9.18 (ex 9 AP)

C2203 At Makers in case 29.5.18, allotted to EF; Rep Pk 2 ASD to 2 AI 5.7.18; 5 AI 17.7.18; 98 Sqn 20.7.18; Left 05.00 for raid on Péronne Rlwy, last seen rising above clouds nr Amiens 8.8.18 (2/Lt W Goffe PoW & Sgt JL May PoW wounded)

C2204 Rec Pk to 1 AI 12.8.18; 103 Sqn 13.8.18; On photographic mission attacked by 7 Fokker DrIs nr Laventie observer injured but continued firing, 1 EA BU and another OOC 17.50 30.8.18 (Lt GB Hett OK & 2/Lt CE Eddy shot through thigh); Bombing raid to Hirson Rlwy Stn, Fokker DVII OOC and another in flames E of Tournai 16.50 23.10.18 (2/Lt LW Marchant & 2/Lt EA Slater); Fokker DVII "fell like a stone" and crashed S of Moustier 09.55 30.10.18 (Sgt A Shepherd & Sgt WJ Westcott); Engine trouble FL in ploughed field 6.2.19 (Sgt CR Haigh OK)

C2205 Rec Pk to 1 AI 19.8.18; 108 Sqn 21.8.18; Fokker DVII crashed in the sea Ostende shared C6314 & D3107 11.20 7.9.18 (2/Lt CR Knott OK & 2/Lt FD McClinton wounded); After bombing Ingelmunster station at 17.35, formation attacked by 33 EA between target and Roulers 3 EA in flames, 1 BU and 2 OOC shared D499, D5835, D5845, D7342, E605, E5435, E8871 & F5847 1.10.18 (Capt CG Haynes & 2/Lt G Brown); Left on bombing raid, hit by British AA, engine seized 15.40, FL, crashed Baerle 4.11.18 (2/Lt EB Thomson & 2/Lt CM Donald unhurt); 8 SS 10.11.18

C2206 Rec Pk to 2 AI 6.8.18; 98 Sqn 9.8.18; Left 06.30 for raid on Clery, attacked by EA and FL Faloise on very rough ground, u/c torn off 11.8.18 (Lt HJ Fox & Lt WR Sellar OK); Rep Pk 2 ASD 14.8.18; SOC 2.10.18

C2207 Deld Martlesham Heath without engine 18.7.18 - @31.5.19 (fitted high compression, high speed BHP); Left by 9.6.19

C2208 Imperial Gift to India

C2209 No information

C2210 At Makers 29.5.18, allotted to EF; Rec Pk to 1 AI 27.6.18; 211 Sqn 28.6.18; Travelling flight, hit ridge landing, u/c collapsed 6.12.18 (2/Lt HC Thomas & 3/AM EW Morgan both unhurt); 7 SS 7.12.18

C2211 At Makers in case 29.5.18, allotted to EF; Rep Pk 2 ASD to 5 AI 25.7.18; 98 Sqn 28.7.18; On test flight FL due to ignition trouble, taking off m/c caught in corn and crashed 7.8.18 (Lt EW Langford & Lt NC McDonald); Rep Pk 2 ASD 9.8.18; SOC 23.8.18 NWR

C2212 At Makers 3.6.18, allotted to EF; Rec Pk to 2 AI 16.6.18; 27 Sqn 17.6.18; On practice flight crashed on take off 18.7.18 (2/Lt RC Rogers OK); 9 AP 20.7.18;

C2213 At Makers 3.6.18, allotted to EF; 2 AI to 103 Sqn 18.6.18; DFW down smoking Steenwerck 3.7.18 (Capt KT Dowding & 2/Lt CE Eddy); On practice flight lost propeller in the air, crashed 28.8.18 (Lt LW Marchant OK); Rep Pk 1 ASD 30.8.18; SOC 2.9.18 NWR

C2214 & C2215 No information

C2216 8 AAP Lympne by 19.8.18; Rec Pk 21.8.18; 1 AI 16.10.18; 108 Sqn 19.10.18; Fokker DVII crashed and burnt S of Ghent 14.10 28.10.18 (2/Lt HG Daulton & Sgt W Greenwood); EA OOC Sotteghem, shared D613, E676, E8959, E8980, E9026 & F1118 09.40-10.10 4.11.18 (2/Lt HG Daulton & Sgt J Crowther): In Denderleeuw raid EA OOC E of Sotteghem shared D613, D5845, D7357, E8980, E9028 09.05 9.11.18 (2/Lt HN Tiplady OK & 2/Lt FLP Smith DoW); 98 Sqn 23.1.19; 8 AAP Lympne 12.2.19

C2217 8 AAP Lympne by 4.8.18; Rec Pk to 2 AI 8.8.18; 107 Sqn 10.8.18; Water tank burst, engine seized, FL 1.10.18 (2/Lt C Houlgrave & 2/Lt WM Thomson OK), faulty soldering was blamed

C2218 Imperial Gift to India

C2219 Imperial Gift to India

C2220 At Makers 10.6.18, reallotted from Store to EF; Rep Pk 1 ASD to Rec Pk 4.7.18; 2 AI 5.7.18; 3 ASD 7.7.18; 104 Sqn 8.7.18; 3 ASD 31.7.18 (wrecked); 99 Sqn 29.9.18; 6 AP 7.10.18; 3 ASD 8.10.18

C2221 At Makers 10.6.18, reallotted from Store to EF; 2 AI to 98 Sqn 13.7.18; Scout in flames then scout crashed 17.20 16.7.18; Pfalz DIII crashed Forêt de Fère 08.00 18.7.18 (all Lt FC Wilton & Lt CP Harrison MC); Fokker DrI in flames Barleux 18.15 8.8.18; Fokker DVII OOC Somain 18.15 30.8.18 (both Lt FC Wilton & Capt GH Gillis); In raid on Valenciennes Rlwy Stn Pfalz DIII OOC Denain 10.35, own a/c shot up 16.9.18 (2/Lt WV Thomas & Sgt CHO Allwork OK); Rep Pk 2 ASD 19.9.18; SOC 23.9.18

C2222 At Makers 10.6.18, reallotted from Store to EF; Rep Pk 2 ASD to 2 AI 4.7.18; 49 Sqn 5.7.18; EF, crashed 26.7.18 (2/Lt JG Andrews slightly injured & 2/Lt J Churchill unhurt)

C2223 At Makers 10.6.18, reallotted from Store to EF; Rep Pk 2 ASD to 2 AI 9.7.18; To 5 AI but returned due to misty weather, on landing collided with D2955 15.7.18 (2/Lt JH Stringfellow DoI 22.7.18); SOC Rep Pk 2 ASD 16.7.18 (ex 2 AI) NWR

C2224 At Makers 10.6.18, reallotted from Store to EF; Rep Pk 1 ASD to Rec Pk 10.7.18; 1 AI 13.7.18; 103 Sqn 25.7.18; Fokker DVII OOC E of Tournai 16.50 23.10.18 (Sgt WJ McNeill & 2/Lt J Davison); Left 12.00 on bombing raid, brought down Louvain 4.11.18 (Lt JG Carey & 2/Lt DC McDonald both PoW)

C2225 No information

C2226 35 TDS Duxford by 11.11.18

C2227 35 TDS Duxford by 9.18 - @19.10.18

C2228 31 TDS Fowlmere 9.18

C2229 31 TDS Fowlmere 1918

C2230 & C2231 No information

C2232 16 Group, despatched 9 AAP Newcastle 19.10.18 - @24.10.18 (outside block)

300 D.H.9 ordered 28.9.17 to Cont No A.S.17569 (BR.112 & 162) from Aircraft Manufacturing Co Ltd, Hendon and numbered C6051 to C6350. (230hp BHP unless otherwise stated)

D.H.9 C6051, the first machine from the Airco production line. (via Mike O'Connor)

C6051 (Puma) Deld AES Martlesham Heath 6.11.17; AES Orfordness 9.11.17; Testing Sqn Martlesham Heath 28.11.17; Rec Pk 18.12.17; 27 Sqn 22.12.17 "for evaluation and report"; Rep Pk 2 ASD 28.2.18; Standing on aerodrome crashed into by a 25 Sqn m/c 25.3.18; SOC Rep Pk 1 ASD 2.4.18 NWR

C6052 (Fiat A.12) Deld AES Martlesham Heath 8.1.18 (performance with 230-lb bombs); AES Orfordness 18.1.18; AES Martlesham Heath 25.1.18 (bomb load tests); AES Orfordness 12.2.18; AES Martlesham Heath 17.2.18; AES Orfordness by 3.18 - @6.18; AES Martlesham Heath by 11.18

C6053 Deld AES Martlesham Heath 22.12.17 (performance tests with and without gap in lower plane; with bombs, prop and radiator tests); Record endurance flight 18.2.18 (Capt HJT Saint DSC & Thompson); AES Orfordness 20.4.18 - 6.18; Martlesham to AES Orfordness 16.9.18

C6054 Became *G-EAAA*

C6055 2 AAP Hendon, took off for Martlesham Heath, but stalled on turn, spun in, totally wrecked at Hendon 13.1.18 (Lt FHV Wise & 2/Lt A Payne both killed) [believed to be the first D.H.9 fatalities]

C6056 No information

C6057 4 (Aux) SoAG Marske by 30.4.18; 1 SoN&BD Stonehenge by 20.6.18 - @12.18

C6058 (Liberty 12) Sold to American Government; Shipped USA for evaluation; To McCook Field as plane *P-17*

C6059 2 AAP Hendon to 98 Sqn Old Sarum 9.2.18; 99 Sqn Old Sarum 8.3.18 - @11.3.18; 11 TDS Boscombe Down by 11.18

C6060 Deld Martlesham to replace crashed C6055 29.1.18 (first production a/c - performance and radiator tests); 2 AAP Hendon to 98 Sqn Old Sarum 12.2.18; 2 AAP Hendon 23.2.18; RAE Farnborough 2.3.18 - last mentioned 27.3.18

C6061 2 AAP Hendon to 98 Sqn Old Sarum 13.2.18; 99 Sqn Old Sarum 8.3.18 - @10.3.18; [108 Sqn?] Lake Down by 12.5.18; 6 TDS Boscombe Down

C6062 2 AAP Hendon to 98 Sqn Old Sarum 6.2.18; 99 Sqn Old Sarum 8.3.18

C6063 110 Sqn Sedgeford/Kenley 3.18 - 6.18

C6064 2 AAP Hendon to 98 Sqn Old Sarum 13.2.18; (Not at 98 Sqn by 14.3.18); 99 Sqn Old Sarum by 15.4.18; 14 TDS Lake Down by 10.8.18

D.H.9 C6053 setting out from Martlesham Heath on 18.2.18 for a record endurance flight, piloted by Capt HJT Saint DSC with observer Thompson. (via Frank Cheesman)

D.H.9 C6078, fitted with a 430hp prototype Napier Lion engine, was tested at both Martlesham Heath and Farnborough. (via Frank Cheesman)

C6065 1 SoN&BD Stonehenge by 20.3.18

C6066 2 AAP Hendon to 98 Sqn Old Sarum 11.2.18; 99 Sqn Old Sarum 8.3.18; 103 Sqn Old Sarum ('F') by 13.3.18 - @19.4.18

C6067 2 AAP Hendon to 98 Sqn Old Sarum 11.2.18; 99 Sqn Old Sarum 8.3.18; 98 Sqn Old Sarum by 9.3.18; 103 Sqn Old Sarum by 27.2.18 - 22.3.18; Southern Trg Bde School of Instruction by 3.18 - @6.18

C6068 2 AAP Hendon to 98 Sqn Old Sarum 13.2.18; 99 Sqn Old Sarum by 19.2.18-17.3.18; 11 TDS Old Sarum by 3.6.18 - @10.18

C6069 103 Sqn Old Sarum by 17.2.18

C6070 Sold to French Government 1.18

C6071 110 Sqn Sedgeford 3.19; Stalled and spun in 23.4.18 (Lt HV Brisbin seriously injured & Lt T Phillips injured)

C6072 110 Sqn Sedgeford 3.18; 11 TDS Old Sarum, turning near ground on bad weather, stalled and dived in from 150ft 20.4.18 (2/Lt RG Young seriously injured & 2/Lt AF Tong injured)

C6073 98 Sqn Old Sarum by 14.3.18; In France with Sqn 1.4.18; Took off on raid but engine cut out, in landing collided with B7634 18.5.18 (Lt GD Horton & Lt CP Harrison OK); Rep Pk 1 ASD 22.5.18; SOC 11.8.18 NWR

C6074 1 SoN&BD Stonehenge by 10.3.18

C6075 105 Sqn Andover by 21.2.18; Stalled landing 19.3.18 (2/Lt H Nelson DoI)

C6076 110 Sqn Sedgeford 3.18

C6077 44 TS Waddington by 30.6.18 - @1.7.18

C6078 FF RAF Farnborough 15.2.18 (fitted with a prototype 430hp Lion engine); AES Martlesham Heath 27.3.18; RAF/RAE Farnborough 29.3.18; FL Littlehampton 29.8.18 (Capt J Palethorpe & Mr Fender); Retd RAE Farnborough 12.9.18; AES Martlesham Heath 12.10.18 (performance with recce and bomb loads); Established a new world's altitude record of 30,500ft 2.1.19 (Capt A Lang & Lt EW Blower); Airco Hendon W/E 8.2.19; Believed to Spain in 1919

C6079 2 AAP Hendon to 98 Sqn Old Sarum 23.2.18; In France with Sqn 1.4.18; KB attacked 06.45-07.15, observer jumped but parachute did not open, KB did not catch fire 21.4.18 (Lt CJ Gillan & Lt W Duce); Left 11.30, EF in raid on Gheluvelt, seen to glide down west over target 25.4.18 (Lt CJ Gillan & Lt W Duce both PoW)

C6080 2 AAP Hendon to 98 Sqn Old Sarum 23.2.18 (not to France); 11 TDS Old Sarum by 6.18

C6081 At 98 Sqn Old Sarum by 14.3.18; In France with Sqn 1.4.18; Crashed on take off when got into slipstream of another m/c 11.4.18 (2/Lt CG Tysoe & 2/Lt NC MacDonald); Adv Salv to Rep Pk 1 ASD; SOC 25.4.18

C6082 26 TS Harlaxton by 2.18; 1 SoN&BD Stonehenge by 7.3.18; 4 (Aux) SoAG Marske by 24.4.18; 1 SoN&BD Stonehenge, stalled on turn, spun in 21.6.18 (2/Lt LS Morck DoI 26.6.18 & Sgt HC Minty killed)

C6083 At 98 Sqn Old Sarum by 14.3.18; In France with Sqn 1.4.18; Albatros DV OOC Armentières, shared C6105 07.00 21.4.18 (Capt RW Bell & Lt AA Malcolm); Returning from raid tried to land in fog, left wing hit tree, crashed 25.4.18 (Capt RW Bell & Lt AA Malcolm); SOC Rep Pk 1 ASD 28.4.18

C6084 2 AAP Hendon to 98 Sqn Old Sarum 28.2.18; Not to France with sqn

C6085 2 AAP Hendon to 98 Sqn Old Sarum 23.2.18; In France with Sqn 1.4.18; Returning from raid, shot down in combat with EA Westuleteren 3.5.18 (Lt FA Loughlin OK & 2/Lt TRG Cooke wounded); Rep Pk 1 ASD 6.5.18; Rebuilt as F5845 25.6.18

C6086 105 Sqn Andover by 24.3.18; 6 TDS Boscombe Down by 30.6.18

C6087 2 AAP Hendon to 98 Sqn Old Sarum 6.3.18; In France with sqn 1.4.18; Controls shot away, crashed nr Lyndy 18.4.18 (Lt SB Walsh & Lt CT de Guise OK); Rep Pk 1 ASD 23.4.18; SOC 25.4.18

C6088 Hendon by 2.18; Martlesham 24.2.18; 10 TDS Harling Road by 6.18 - 7.18

C6089 (Puma) FF 27.2.18; 6 TDS Boscombe Down; 110 Sqn Sedgeford, leading edge of tailplane failed 21.5.18 (Capt GJ MacLean & 1/AM EAE Hart both slightly injured)

C6090 2 AAP Hendon to 98 Sqn Old Sarum 12.3.18; In France with Sqn 1.4.18; Returning from a raid lost speed on turn, went into a flat spin nr aerodrome 12.4.18 (2/Lt HW Brown & Lt DGJ Odlam both injured); Adv Salvage to Rep Pk 1 ASD SOC 27.4.18

C6091 2 AAP Hendon to 98 Sqn Old Sarum 6.3.18; Not to France with Sqn

C6092 At 2 AAP Hendon 28.2.18, allotted to EF: reallotted to 99 Sqn (Mob) Old Sarum 5.3.18; Reallotted to 98 Sqn Old Sarum 9.3.18 (NTU); 8 AAP Lympne by 12.4.18; Rec Pk 19.4.18; 2 AI 21.4.18; 99 Sqn 27.4.18; FL Colombey-Les-Belles 25.8.18 (2/Lt DF Brooks & 2/Lt R Buckby); 3 ASD 25.8.18

C6093 At 2 AAP Hendon 27.2.18, allotted to EF; reallotted to 99 Sqn (Mob) Old Sarum 5.3.18; Reallotted to EF 2.4.18; Rep Pk 1 ASD to 1 AI 2.4.18; 49 Sqn 11.4.18; Scout OOC Harbonnières 19.15 19.5.18 (Lt HL Rough & Lt V Dreschfeld); COL in severe hail storm which obstructed visibility 22.5.18 (Lt H Mallet & 2/Lt CB Edwards OK); Rep Pk 2 ASD 25.5.18; Rebuilt as F6172 3.7.18

C6094 At 2 AAP Hendon 28.2.18, allotted to EF; England to Rec Pk 11.3.18; 2 AI 31.3.18; 1 AI 3.4.18; 49 Sqn 6.4.18; Albatros DV OOC smoking Keyem 18.15 20.4.18 (Lt GA Leckie & Lt GR Cuttle); Left 09.40, in combat with EA, seen gliding down under control E of Bray 12.10 9.5.18 (Lt GA Leckie & Lt GR Cuttle MC both killed)

C6095 2 AAP Hendon to 98 Sqn Old Sarum 6.3.18; In France with Sqn 1.4.18; Raid on Neuf Berquin 12.4.18 (Capt RNG Atkinson OK & Lt V Brent wounded); Wrecked 2.5.18; SOC Rep Pk 1 ASD 4.5.18

C6096 121 Sqn Narborough by 23.7.18

C6097 (Puma) 99 Sqn Old Sarum by 17.3.18; 11 TDS Old Sarum, stalled on turn near ground, spun in, BO 14.5.18 (2/Lt HD Preston & Pte EL Messenger USAS both killed)

C6098 At 2 AAP Hendon 27.2.18, allotted to EF: reallotted to 99 Sqn (Mob) Old Sarum 5.3.18 - @22.3.18

C6099 No information

C6100 2 AAP Hendon to 98 Sqn Old Sarum 6.3.18; In France with Sqn 1.4.18; Returning from raid, lost way, landed at Icques, in trying to avoid ridge, took off again but lacked sufficient flying speed and caught ridge knocking off u/c 30.4.18 (Lt CJ Stanfield injured & 2/Lt NC MacDonald OK); Left on raid 11.50 but had to return due to engine trouble, on landing m/c bounced but in taking off engine failed to pick up, crashed 16.5.18 (Lt AG Baker & 1/AM D Wentworth OK); Rep Pk 1 ASD and SOC 21.5.18 NWR

C6101 2 AAP Hendon to 98 Sqn Old Sarum 28.2.18; In France with Sqn 1.4.18; Left 12 noon, bombing raid on Menin, in combat with 18 EA, OOC, BU going down vertically in flames over Gheluvelt 3.5.18 (Lt RA Holiday & 2/Lt CB Whyte killed)

C6102 2 AAP Hendon to 98 Sqn Old Sarum 28.2.18 (not to France with sqn)

C6103 2 AAP Hendon to 98 Sqn Old Sarum 6.3.18; In France with Sqn 1.4.18; Fokker DrI OOC Menin 12.45 3.5.18 (2/Lt W Lamont & Lt HBB Wilson); Left on raid 17.30, last seen 4m W of Courtrai below the formation with the centre section on fire 15.5.18 (2/Lt W Lamont PoW & Lt HBB Wilson PoW DoW 18.7.18)

C6104 2 AAP Hendon to 98 Sqn Old Sarum 15.3.18; In France with sqn 1.4.18; EA OOC Menin-Wervicq 19.20 8.5.18 (Lt CD Taylor & Lt JR Jackman); Longeron shot through 1.6.18 (Lt CD Taylor & Lt JR Jackman OK); Casualty Report 5.6.18 says repairs not satisfactory and recommends return to depot; To 4 ASD; Transferred from EF to 5 Group 6.18; 2 SS Richborough 15.9.18

C6105 2 AAP Hendon to 98 Sqn Old Sarum 6.3.18; In France with Sqn 1.4.18; Albatros DV OOC Armentières, shared C6083 07.00 21.4.18; Returning from Courtrai raid Pfalz DIII in flames and another OOC Becelaere 15.00 2.5.18 (all Capt DVD Marshall & 2/Lt HA Lamb); Left on raid but had to return due to engine trouble, trying to land lost flying speed banked and spun in 16.5.18 (Lt JH Bryer & 1/AM RJ Weston both injured); Rep Pk 1 ASD 21.5.18; SOC 22.5.18

C6106 2 AAP Hendon to 98 Sqn Old Sarum 8.3.18; In France with Sqn 1.4.18; EA in flames Menin-Wervicq 19.20 8.5.18 (Lt RE Dubber & Sgt ER McDonald); Crossing the Lines engine trouble developed, pilot decided to land at St Omer, in doing so hit ridge knocking off u/c

D.H.9 'A' of No.211 Squadron in 1918 had the individual letter incorporated in the nickname 'ACME'. (via Frank Cheesman)

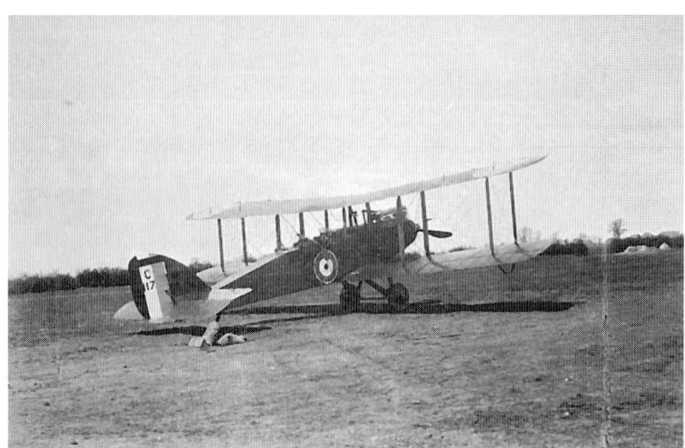

D.H.9 C6117 was named 'Umpikoff' when serving with No.31 Training Squadron at Wyton. (W.J.Evans)

D.H.9A C6122 was the prototype conversion from a D.H.9, being fitted with a 400hp Liberty engine. (via Frank Cheesman)

D.H.9 C6109 'P' of No.207 Squadron at Ruisseauville in 1918. (W.J.Evans)

21.5.18 (Lt HW Whale & Lt CP Harrison OK); Rep Pk 1 ASD 22.5.18; Rebuilt as F5846 25.6.18

C6107 2 AAP Hendon to 98 Sqn Old Sarum 6.3.18 (not to France with sqn); 103 Sqn Old Sarum, EF at 200ft on TO from Hillsea Drill Ground, turned back, stalled, dived in 26.3.18 (2/Lt RC Bark DoI 28.3.18 & Cpl LN Witley killed)

C6108 2 AAP Hendon to 98 Sqn Old Sarum 6.3.18; In France with sqn 1.4.18; Fokker DrI OOC Bailleul-Armentières 07.00 21.4.18 (Lt AM Phillips & Lt CP Harrison); Fokker DVII in flames Menin-Wervicq 19.20 8.5.18 (Lt CC MacDonald wounded & Lt CP Harrison OK) - landed at Calais, retd sqn 10.5.18; Just after take off right wing dropped, crashed 27.5.18 (Lt RL Tilly & Lt CP Harrison); Rep Pk 1 ASD 30.5.18; SOC 5.7.18 NWR

C6109 (BHP) At 2 AAP Hendon 27.2.18, allotted to EF; England to Rec Pk 15.3.18; 2 AI 20.3.18; 27 Sqn ('P') 31.3.18; Left 08.55 for bombing raid, EA on tail 2m W of Roye, spun in 16.6.18 (Lt H Wild & Sgt Mech E Scott both killed)

C6110 (BHP) At 2 AAP Hendon 27.2.18, allotted to EF; England to Rec Pk 11.3.18; 2 ASD 20.3.18; Rep Pk 2 ASD to 2 AI 27.5.18; 49 Sqn 31.5.18; Fokker DVII OOC smoking S of Lille 17.15 4.7.18 (Lt HP Mallett & 2/Lt CB Edwards); Left 14.05 for raid on Bethencourt Bridge, FTR 8.8.18 (Lt HP Mallett & 2/Lt R Kelly both PoW slightly wounded)

C6111 31 TS Wyton (named 'Impikoff') by 5.18; Prop accident on start-up 1.5.18 (Sgt Mech NC Piggott OK); Stalled left wing correcting bad bump, spun in 7.8.18 (Lt LA Knight & 2/Lt EB Jones both slightly injured)

C6112 103 Sqn Old Sarum by 14.3.18 - @19.4.18

C6113 At 2 AAP Hendon 1.3.18, allotted to EF but reallotted to 99 Sqn (Mob) Old Sarum 5.3.18; In France with Sqn by 17.5.18; FTR from Offenburg raid, last seen gliding down NE of St Die 22.7.18 (2/Lt F Smith & Sgt F Coulson wounded); SOC 23.7.18

C6114 (BHP) At 2 AAP Hendon 27.2.18, allotted to EF; England to Rec Pk 20.3.18; 2 AI 31.3.18; 1 AI 2.4.18; 49 Sqn ('M') 7.4.18; Left 09.30, Scout OOC Flavy-le-Martel 11.00, then hit by AA Fresnoy-Le Roye, FL 11.45 7.6.18 (Lt AH Curtis & Sgt A Davis OK); To 9 AP; SOC Rep Pk 1 ASD 15.7.18 NWR

C6115 Allotment to 98 Sqn Old Sarum cancelled 9.3.18

C6116 At 2 AAP Hendon 28.2.18, allotted to EF but reallotted to 99 Sqn (Mob) Old Sarum 5.3.18; Reallotted to EF 30.3.18; England to Rec Pk 29.3.18; 49 Sqn 11.4.18; Casualty Report 6.7.18 says complete overhaul desirable; 2 AI 8.7.18; Rec Pk 15.7.18; England 22.7.18

C6117 5 TDS Easton-on-the-Hill by 3.18; 31 TS Wyton (named 'Umpikoff')

C6118 At 2 AAP Hendon 28.2.18, allotted to EF; England to Rec Pk 10.3.18; Rep Pk 1 ASD 17.3.18; Rec Pk 20.4.18; 1 AI 22.4.18; Rep Pk 23.4.18; Rec Pk and on to 98 Sqn 1.5.18; Damaged in enemy air raid on the night of 5-6.6.18; Rep Pk 1 ASD 14.6.18; SOC 5.7.18 NWR

C6119 & C6120 No information

C6121 At 2 AAP Hendon 28.2.18, allotted to EF; England to Rec Pk 10.3.18; 2 AI 31.3.18; 1 AI 2.4.18; 49 Sqn 7.4.18; Taxied into ditch 25.4.18 (Lt DS Cramb & Lt RC Stokes OK): Rep Pk 1 ASD 28.4.18; 1 AI to 206 Sqn 20.6.18; Left 18.29, last 20.15 seen 2m N of Gheluve 25.7.18 (2/Lt FT Heron & 2/Lt CJ Byrne both killed); SOC in field 26.7.18

C6122 Prototype conversion to D.H.9A (400hp Liberty). FF 19.4.18; Fairlop to Hendon 12.5.18; Martlesham Heath 15.5.18 (performance & fuel consumption); Crashed 15.8.18

C6123 1 SoN&BD Stonehenge by 23.8.18 - @1.2.19

C6124 4 (Aux) SoAG Marske by 24.4.18; 1 SoN&BD Stonehenge by 14.6.18 - @3.9.18 BUT 110 Sqn Kenley 7.18

C6125 4 (Aux) SoAG Marske by 2.5.18; 110 Sqn Kenley 7.18; SoN&BD, EF, FL downwind in cornfield, overturned 21.7.18 (Lt GA Le Moine unhurt & 2/Lt GE Hunt killed)

C6126 110 Sqn Kenley 7.18

C6127 No information

C6128 1 SoN&BD Stonehenge by 7.18; Imperial Gift to India

C6129 4 (Aux) SoAG Marske by 4.5.18; 110 Sqn Kenley 7.18; 1 SoN&BD Stonehenge 7.18 - @28.8.18

C6130 4 (Aux) SoAG Marske by 24.4.18; 1 SoN&BD Stonehenge by 22.6.18 - @24.8.18

C6131 No information

C6132 Desp UK to AD Aboukir 12.3.20 [? - listed as D6132]

C6133 At 2 AAP Hendon 28.2.18, allotted to EF but this cancelled 1.3.18; 99 Sqn 3.4.18; Bringing m/c from England engine cut out, FL in soft ground 16.5.18 (2/Lt RF Freeland & 1/AM CW Mills); To Rep Pk 2 ASD; Rebuilt as F6196 17.7.18

C6134 In France with 98 Sqn 1.4.18; Pfalz DIII BU Ghistelles 19.40 29.5.18 (Lt DA Macartney & Lt GD Dardis); Damaged in enemy night raid Coudekerque 5/6.6.18; To 4 ASD, transferred to 5 Group 6.18; 4 ASD to 2 SS Richborough 2.10.18

C6135 En route 98 Sqn Old Sarum 1.4.18, reallotted from 99 Sqn (Mob) Old Sarum to EF; England to Rec Pk 29.3.18; 49 Sqn ('U':'S') 3.4.18; Left 15.00 for bombing raid on Fives Rlwy Junction, shot through in combat, COL 17.30 4.7.18 (Lt CAB Beattie & Sgt FL Roberts); Rep Pk 2 ASD 6.7.18; Rebuilt as F6183 11.7.18

C6136 At 2 AAP Hendon 14.3.18, allotted to EF; England to Rec Pk 4.4.18; 206 Sqn 26.4.18; Left 18.15, badly shot about by EA, FL Teteghem 20.5.18 (Lt PW Birkbeck uninjured & 2/Lt W Susman wounded); Rep Pk 1 ASD 24.5.18; Rebuilt as F5850 25.6.18

C6137 At 2 AAP Hendon 1.4.18, reallotted from 104 Sqn (Mob) Andover to EF; England to Rec Pk 2.5.18; 2 AI 7.5.18; 99 Sqn 16.5.18; Left 09.55 for bombing raid on Bensdorf, in combat with EAs N of Dieuze, chased down in spin from 2,000ft 27.5.18 (Lt DA MacDonald & 2/Lt FH Blaxill both PoW)

C6138 At 2 AAP Hendon 1.4.18, reallotted from 104 Sqn (Mob) Andover to EF; England to Rec Pk 8.4.18; 49 Sqn 12.4.18; On raid tested Vickers gun at 10,000ft, shot propeller, excessive vibration caused engine to fall out 22.4.18 (Sgt SJ Oliver slight internal injuries and shock & Sgt W Kelsall broken leg); 4 ASD 24.4.18 - @31.5.18

C6139 At 2 AAP Hendon 14.3.18, allotted to EF; England to Rec Pk 7.4.18; Rep Pk 1 ASD 8.4.18; Rebuilt as F5841 25.6.18

C6140 99 Sqn to Rep Pk 2 ASD 29.4.18; 49 Sqn 25.5.18; 2 Albatros DV OOC Assinvilles 05.00 10.6.18; Fokker DVII apparently OOC Mont Notre Dame (not claimed) 19.00 25.7.18 (both 2/Lt ED Astbury & 2/Lt WN Hartley); Fokker DVII OOC Bois de Bourlon 19.00 25.8.18 (Lt ED Asbury & Lt RAV Scherk); Casualty Report 28.8.18 says unfit for further service in the field; Rec Pk to 8 AAP Lympne 15.9.18

C6141 No information

C6142 At 2 AAP Hendon 1.4.18, reallotted from 104 Sqn (Mob) Andover to EF; England to Rec Pk 11.5.18; 1 AI 14.5.18; 98 Sqn 15.5.18; Left 04.35, shot up in bombing raid on Armentières 17.5.18 (Lt RE Dubber & Sgt ER McDonald OK); Rep Pk 1 ASD SOC 21.5.18 NWR

C6143 103 Sqn Old Sarum by 20-24.3.18; Not to France with sqn 5.18

C6144 Eastbourne by 6.4.18

C6145 99 Sqn Old Sarum by 1.4.18; To France with Sqn 3.5.18; Albatros D OOC Saarbrücken-Homburg 07.15 5.7.18 (Lt KD Marshall & 2/Lt O Bell); Practice flight COL 27.7.18 (Lt FT Cockburn & 2/Lt AT Bowen); FTR from Saarbrücken raid, last seen at 6,000ft over St.Avold 31.7.18 (Lt EL Doidge (Can) & Lt HT Melville both killed)

C6146 99 Sqn Old Sarum by 21-30.3.18; reallotted from 99 Sqn (Mob) Old Sarum to EF 30.3.18; England to Rec Pk 29.3.18; 49 Sqn 2.4.18; On landing approach propeller stopped, lost flying speed and pancaked 3.4.18 (Lt C Bowman & Lt PT Holligan); 4 ASD 4.4.18; 2 SS Richborough 15.9.18; 6 TDS Boscombe Down

C6147 At 2 AAP Hendon 1.4.18, reallotted from 104 Sqn (Mob) Andover to EF; This cancelled 8.4.18, crashed on test

C6148 A Flt 104 Sqn Andover Spring 1918; 6 TDS Boscombe Down

C6149 To France with 99 Sqn 3.5.18; Hit by AA in Offenburg raid 25.6.18 (Lt H Sanders OK & Lt WWL Jenkin killed); In action 20.7.18 (Lt G Martin OK & 2/Lt TK Ludgate wounded); Missing after combat N of Dieuze 31.7.18 (2/Lt TM Richie PoW & Lt LWG Stagg killed)

C6150 To France with 103 Sqn 9.5.18; In action 13.6.18 (2/Lt CJ Bayly wounded in leg & 2/Lt JB Russell OK); Observer fell out of m/c over the Lines 2.7.18 (Lt RH Dunn OK & 2/Lt TH Soute killed); On reconnaissance attacked by Pfalz which was sent OOC La Bassée-Estaires 20.20 4.7.18 (Capt JS Stubbs & 2/Lt CC Dance); Misjudged landing due to failing light, 21/20 6.7.18 (Lt RH Dunn & Lt HC Hinchcliffe OK); Rep Pk 1 ASD 7.7.18; SOC 10.7.18, NWR

C6151 103 Sqn Old Sarum by 13.3.18; To France with Sqn 9.5.18; On take off engine cut out at 20ft, crashed 4.6.18 (Capt H Turner & Lt RE Dodds OK); 9 AP 7.6.18; SOC Rep Pk 1 ASD 17.7.18 NWR

C6152 Presentation Aircraft 'Shanghai Britons'. reallotted from 99 Sqn (Mob) Old Sarum to EF 30.3.18; England to Rec Pk 29.3.18; 1 AI 1.4.18; 206 Sqn 1.4.18; COL 21.5.18 (Lt RH Stainbank & 2/Lt FC Taylor); Rep Pk 1 ASD 23.5.18; SOC 24.5.18 NWR

C6153 99 Sqn by 21.3.18; To France with Sqn 3.5.18; Returned from Kaiserslautern with engine trouble, crashed 6.7.18 (Capt AD Taylor & Lt HS Notley); 3 ASD to 104 Sqn 30.10.18; Ran out of fuel FL in Holland wrecked 4.1.19 (Lt F Wallis & 2/Lt CB Parker OK); SOC 10.1.19

C6154 At Rep Pk 1 ASD 1.4.18 (accommodated for 99 Sqn); Reallotted 2.4.18 from 99 Sqn (Mob) to EF; 98 Sqn, on landing turned to avoid another a/c, wheels caught in rut, u/c knocked off 9.5.18 (Lt LT Hockley & Lt HBB Wilson OK); Rep Pk 1 ASD 13.5.18; SOC 14.5.18

C6155 Being brought to France by 99 Sqn, overshot aerodrome, wheels caught in trench and ripped off 4.5.18 (Lt NS Harper & Cpl Harding); 2 ASD 17.5.18; 103 Sqn 5.18; Left on bombing raid 18.25, shot up, retd 19.45 9.6.18 (Lt JGH Chrispin & Lt EA Wadsworth OK); 9 AP 9.6.18; SOC Rep Pk 1 ASD 13.7.18

C6156 14 TDS Lake Down by 31.7.18 - 5.9.18

C6157 To France with 103 Sqn 9.5.18; Crashed nr Chateau de la Versine 10.6.18 (Lt FH Sillem & Sgt HW Cornell OK); To 9 AP; SOC Rep Pk 1 ASD 20.7.18 NWR

C6158 At Rep Pk 1 ASD 1.4.18 "accommodated for 99 Sqn"; reallotted to EF 2.4.18; Rep Pk 1 ASD to 1 AI 2.4.18; 206 Sqn 18.4.18; Overshot landing, crashed into trailer 12.6.18 (Sgt R Jackson & 1/Pte WS Blyth); Rep Pk 1 ASD 14.6.18; 4 ASD 17.6.18; SOC Rep Pk 1 ASD 5.7.18 NWR

C6159 At 7 AAP Kenley 2.4.18, allotted to EF; England to Rec Pk 10.5.18; 206 Sqn 16.5.18; FTR bombing raid, last seen in combat NW of Roulers 07.10 19.5.18 (2/Lt BF Dunford & 2/Lt FF Collins both killed); SOC 20.5.18

C6160 At 7 AAP Kenley 22.4.18, allotted to EF; England to Rec Pk 3.5.18; 2 AI 6.5.18; 49 Sqn 16.5.18; Engine cut out just after take off, crashed 19.5.18 (Capt W Mitton injured & Lt TF Harvey OK); SOC Rep Pk 2 ASD 24.5.18

C6161 At 7 AAP Kenley 2.4.18, allotted to EF; England to Rec Pk 11.5.18; 1 AI 15.5.18; 206 Sqn 17.5.18; Left 18.15, last seen in combat nr Menin, left formation west of lines and turned back 19.5.18 (2/Lt H Mitchell & AM CF Costen both PoW); SOC 20.5.18

C6162 At 7 AAP Kenley 2.4.18, allotted to EF; England to Rec Pk 18.5.18; 49 Sqn 20.5.18; Tail down landing, wheels held by rut, m/c turned on wing 30.7.18 (Lt JA Yates & 1/AM JW Deal both unhurt); SOC Rep Pk 1 ASD 3.9.18 (ex 9 AP)

C6163 At 7 AAP Kenley 2.4.18, allotted to EF; At AAP Brooklands by 9.5.18; Rec Pk 10.5.18; 1 AI 19.5.18; 206 Sqn 20.5.18; Left 12.05, damaged by AA shrapnel in bombing raid, FL Acquin 23.5.18 (Capt GLE Stevens & Lt LA Christian unhurt); Rep Pk 1 ASD 23.5.18; SOC 27.5.18 NWR

C6164 At 7 AAP Kenley 2.4.18, allotted to EF;

C6165 At 7 AAP Kenley 2.4.18, allotted to EF; Rec Pk to 2 AI 13.7.18; 5 AI 17.7.18; 107 Sqn 19.7.18; On take-off trying to avoid a 205 Sqn m/c got into the backwash of another m/c and crashed 4.11.18 (2/Lt O Lane & 2/Lt WJ Mabb OK)

C6166 At 7 AAP Kenley 2.4.18, allotted to EF; England to Rec

Lt O'Day standing by the embellished nose of a D.H.9 at Harling Road. (J.M.Bruce/G.S.Leslie collection)

A D.H.9 fitted with a camera gun. (J.M.Bruce/G.S.Leslie collection)

A D.H.9 fitted with static turn indicator equipment. (Gordon Kinsey)

Flt Lt H.G.Crowe seated in the cockpit of a D.H.9 fitted with a special cartridge collector at Fermoy in 1920 (J.M.Bruce/G.S.Leslie collection)

Close-up of a D.H.9 cockpit whilst being used for parachute experiments. (J.M.Bruce/G.S.Leslie collection)

An airman climbing into a D.H.9 before participating in parachute experiments. (J.M.Bruce/G.S.Leslie collection)

Pk 10.5.18; 1 AI and on to 98 Sqn 18.5.18; Lost cowling in bombing raid on Roulers Railway Stn, possibly hit by AA, glided down, crashed 21.5.18 (Lt AM Phillips & Lt NC MacDonald OK); Rep Pk 1 ASD 26.5.18; SOC 29.5.18

C6167 At 7 AAP Kenley 2.4.18, allotted to EF; England to Rec Pk and on to 1 AI 28.5.18; 211 Sqn 30.5.18; Hit by AA, EF on bombing raid, FL beach 3.6.18 (Lt GH Baker & 2/Lt TB Dodwell); COL 16.6.18 (2/Lt ETM Routledge & 2/Lt JFJ Peters unhurt); Rep Pk 1 ASD 16.6.18; SOC 20.6.18 NWR

C6168 No information

C6169 At 7 AAP Kenley 2.4.18, allotted to EF; England to Rec Pk 19.5.18; 2 AI 21.5.18; 27 Sqn 22.5.18; Albatros D OOC Roye 10.45 6.6.18 (Lt FG Powell & Sgt V Cummins); Left 16.20, low strafing, longeron shot through, retd 19.00 10.6.18 (Lt FG Powell & Sgt Mech J Little OK); Rep Pk 2 ASD 12.6.18; 2 AI and on to 107 Sqn 10.8.18; Left 07.35 on bombing raid, FTR 4.9.18 (Lt BE Gammell DoW 7.9.18 & 2/Lt F Player killed)

C6170 At 7 AAP Kenley 2.4.18, allotted to EF; England to Rec Pk 9.5.18; 1 AI 11.5.18; 98 Sqn 18.5.18; Left 16.10 for bombing raid on Courtrai Rlwy Stn, shot up in combat with EA 25.6.18 (Lt G Richmond & Sgt F Sefton OK); Rep Pk 1 ASD 27.6.18; SOC 29.6.18, NWR

C6171 104 Sqn Andover by 20.4.18; To France with Sqn 19.5.18; 3 ASD 6.7.18; 104 Sqn 30.10.18; SOC 21.1.19

C6172 To France with 103 Sqn 9.5.18; Left 14.30 on bombing raid, found nr Montdidier 12.6.18 (2/Lt WR McGee & 2/Lt H Thompson both killed)

C6173 104 Sqn Andover by 13.4.18

C6174 At 2 AAP Hendon 1.4.18, reallotted from 104 Sqn (Mob) Andover to EF; England to Rec Pk 11.4.18; 1 AI 15.4.18; 98 Sqn 22.4.18; Approaching aerodrome, engine cut out when a/c at about 50ft, stalled, crashed 3.5.18 (Lt SB Welch & Lt CT de Guise both slightly injured); Rep Pk 1 ASD 7.5.18

C6175 England to Rec Pk 3.4.18; 1 AI 22.4.18; 49 Sqn 23.4.18; Engine began to overheat, landed to make examination but landed in soft sand and overturned 22.5.18 (Lt ED Asbury & Lt FP Dennison OK); 2 ASD 26.5.18; Rebuilt as F6095 3.7.18

C6176 98 Sqn Old Sarum; In France with Sqn 1.4.18; EA OOC Menin-Wervicq 19.20 8.5.18 (Lt F Smethurst & Lt EGT Chubb); Landing from a practice flight wing caught tree, crashed 11.5.18 (Lt A Sevastopulo & Lt F Smethurst OK); SOC Rep Pk 1 ASD 15.5.18

C6177 At 2 AAP Hendon 1.4.18, reallotted from 104 Sqn (Mob) Andover to EF; England to Rec Pk 7.4.18; 49 Sqn 11.4.18; FTR from photo reconnaissance, last seen at 08.25 over Bertangles 15.5.18 (Capt WG Chambers & Lt RC Burky USAS both killed)

C6178 No information

C6179 To France with 103 Sqn 9.5.18; KB dest, own a/c damaged Seclin 11.00 20.5.18 (Capt JS Stubbs & 2/Lt CC Dance OK); Scout in flames & scout OOC Fretoy, 7m SW of Hour, shared C6192, D5569 & D1007 16.20 6.6.18 (Capt JS Stubbs & 2/Lt CC Dance); Combat damaged, retd 08.30 22.7.18 (Lt CA Hallawell & Sgt EJW Watkinson unhurt); Rep Pk 1 ASD 25.7.18; SOC 28.7.18 NWR

C6180 At 2 AAP Hendon 1.4.18, reallotted from 104 Sqn (Mob) Andover to EF; England to Rec Pk 7.4.18; 1 AI 23.4.18; 206 Sqn 25.4.18; EF, FL Clairmarais 6.6.18 (Capt JW Mathews & Lt C Knight unhurt); Rep Pk 1 ASD 10.6.18; SOC 5.7.18 NWR

C6181 At 2 AAP Hendon 1.4.18, reallotted from 104 Sqn (Mob) Andover to EF; England to Rec Pk 4.4.18; 49 Sqn 11.4.18; Scout OOC Maricourt 0605 17.5.18 (Lt CG Capel & 1/Pte J Knight); Two scouts OOC Harbonnières 19.15, damaged in combat, EF, FL Raineville 19.5.18 (Lt CG Capel & 1/Pte J Knight both wounded); Rep Pk 2 ASD 22.5.18; Rebuilt as F6141 3.7.18

C6182 At 2 AAP Hendon 1.4.18, reallotted from 104 Sqn (Mob) Andover to EF; England to Rec Pk 2.4.18; 49 Sqn 11.4.18; Stalled on take-off, crashed 25.4.18 (Lt FD Nevin & Sgt C Fathers both OK); Rep Pk 1 ASD 28.4.18; SOC 5.5.18

C6183 At 2 AAP Hendon 2.4.18, allotted to EF; England to Rec Pk 7.4.18; 49 Sqn 11.4.18; FL, crashed in wheatfield 2.6.18 (Lt H Ford & 1/AM SE Carr both injured; Rep Pk 2 ASD 2.6.18; SOC 16.6.18 NWR

C6184 At 2 AAP Hendon 1.4.18, reallotted from 104 Sqn (Mob) Andover to EF; England to Rec Pk 3.4.18; 49 Sqn 11.4.18; Photographic mission, in combat with EA, seen going down 10.45 7.6.18 (Lt GC McEwan & Lt TF Harvey killed); SOC 16.6.18

C6185 To France with 103 Sqn 9.5.18; Hit by shrapnel in raid on Estaires 17.00 20.5.18, (2/Lt CT Houston OK & 2/Lt JK Clarke wounded); Crashed just after take off, the cause said to be bomb dropping off and upsetting trim of a/c 12.6.18 (Lt FH Sillem & Sgt HW Cornell OK); 9 AP to Rep Pk 1 ASD SOC 20.7.18 NWR

C6186 To France with 103 Sqn 9.5.18; Damaged by AA in raid on Seclin 20.5.18 (Lt J Austin-Sparks OK & 2/Lt TOW Wrightson wounded); Rep Pk 1 ASD 24.5.18; Rebuilt as F5848 25.6.18

C6187 25 TS Thetford by 4.18 - @7.6.18

C6188 No information

C6189 99 Sqn Old Sarum, turned too near ground, spun in 10.4.18 (2/Lt QW Bannister killed & 2/Lt EJC Kidd DoI)

C6190 No information

C6191 In France with 99 Sqn by 17.5.18; COL 19.7.18 (1/Lt P Dietz USAS & 2/Lt EJ Munson); 3 ASD 19.7.18; 104 Sqn 27.9.18; 6 AP 30.10.18; 3 ASD 3.11.18

C6192 103 Sqn Old Sarum by 5.18; To France with Sqn 9.5.18; Scout in flames & scout OOC Fretoy, 7m SW of Hour, shared C6179, D5569 & D1007 16.20 6.6.18 (Capt KT Dowding & 2/Lt CE Eddy); Left 10.00 for bombing raid on Roye, last seen over Crapeau Mesnil, possible direct hit by AA 16.6.18 (2/Lt S Hirst & Lt JM Hughes both killed)

C6193 No information

C6194 England to 103 Sqn 17.5.18; Overshot on landing 7.6.18 (Lt DM Darroch & 1/AM WJ Westcott OK); To 9 AP; Rep Pk 1 ASD, SOC 9.7.18 NWR

C6195 99 Sqn Old Sarum by 5.4.18; Bringing m/c from England lost way, landed on soft ground in trench and crashed 16.5.18 (2/Lt HD West & 1/AM L Speed); Rep Pk 2 ASD 16.5.18; Rebuilt as F6125 3.7.18

C6196 Hendon to 99 Sqn 18.4.18; To France with Sqn 3.5.18; Scout crashed W of Molsheim, shared D1032 16.00 22.7.18; Albatros D shot down, pilot fell out Lahr 07.15 30.7.18 (both Sgt HH Wilson & Sgt FL Lee); Shot down St.Avold in raid on Saarbrücken 31.7.18 (Lt WJ Garrity (Can) & Lt GH Stephenson both PoW)

C6197 No information

C6198 At 2 AAP Hendon 2.4.18, allotted to EF; England to Rec Pk 29.5.18; 1 AI 30.5.18; 98 Sqn, damaged in enemy night raid Coudekerque 5/6.6.18; To 4 ASD, transferred to 5 Group 6.18; 2 SS Richborough 15.9.18

C6199 At 2 AAP Hendon 3.4.18, allotted to EF; England to Rec Pk 7.4.18; 1 AI 12.4.18; 98 Sqn 18.4.18; Fokker DrI OOC Bailleul-Armentières, m/c combat damaged 07.00 21.4.18 (Lt CJ Stanfield OK & Lt FH Wrigley wounded in foot); Rep Pk 1 ASD 25.4.18; SOC 5.5.18; Bboc 11.5.18; Rebuilt as F5842 25.6.18

C6200 From Old Sarum to France with 103 Sqn 12.5.18; Left on raid 08.00, last seen over Armentières spinning down slowly OOC 20.7.18 (2/Lt SE Carson & 2/Lt T Hawkins both killed)

C6201 Shipped to Mudros 20.4.18 BUT 44 TS Waddington by 6.18 - 7.18

C6202 99 Sqn Old Sarum by 20.4.18; In France with 99 Sqn by 17.5.18; Fitted large carburettor intakes; In combat on Saarbrücken raid around 07.15 5.7.18 (Capt WD Thom OK & Lt CG Claye killed); 3 ASD 6.7.18; 104 Sqn 12.8.18; Raid on Mannheim, in combat with EAs on return, FTR 22.8.18 (2/Lt J Valentine & 2/Lt CG Hitchcock both PoW)

C6203 To France with 103 Sqn 9.5.18; Left 18.55 for bombing raid, in combat with 4 EA, seen gliding down over wood Warsy-Liglières 5.6.18 (Capt H Turner & 2/Lt G Webb both killed)

C6204 2 AAP Hendon for EF 6.4.18; England to Rec Pk 1.5.18; 1 AI 4.5.18; 98 Sqn 9.5.18; Attempting to land lost flying speed, swung and knocked u/c off 15.5.18 (Lt LT Hockley & Sgt C Lomax OK); Rep Pk 1 ASD 18.5.18; SOC 20.5.18 NWR

C6205 Shipped to Mudros 20.4.18; Imbros by 25.5.18; 220 Sqn

by 10.18; 222 Sqn Imbros by 14-16.11.18; Repair Base Mudros by 10.18 - @1.19

C6206 31 TS Wyton by 9.5.18; Crashed off sharp turn near ground 23.6.18 (Lt JF Byron injured & Mr L Cass civilian killed)

C6207 To France with 103 Sqn 9.5.18; "Bounced and twisted" on landing 23.5.18 (2/Lt IW Leiper & 1/AM J Buffery OK); Rep Pk 1 ASD 26.5.18; Rebuilt as F5844 25.6.18

C6208 Shipped to Mudros 20.4.18; 226 Sqn by 25.5.18 - @7.18; AD Taranto by 29.8.18

C6209 At 2 AAP Hendon 3.4.18, allotted to EF; England to Rec Pk 17.5.18; 49 Sqn 20.5.18; Attacking ground targets a direct hit on a two-str and two EA on fire 9.6.18 (Capt HL Rough wounded & Lt V Dreschfeld OK): Pfalz DIII OOC Orvillers 14.45 11.6.18 (Capt FW Lowen & Lt V Dreschfeld); Fokker DVII in flames and another crashed Fresnes 20.50 9.8.18 (Lt SB Welch & 2/Lt DC Roy); Left 16.05 to bomb Evreux aerodrome, in combat with EA, tailplanes shot away, last seen going down with right hand side of tail plane crumpled up in slow spin over Moeuvres 25.8.18 (Lt SB Welch & 2/Lt DC Roy both killed)

C6210 8 AAP Lympne 27.4.18, reallotted from EF to 99 Sqn (Mob) Old Sarum; To France with sqn 3.5.18; Scout OOC NE of Saarebourg 09.15 2.7.18 (Capt WD Thom & Lt CG Claye); Bombing raid, radiator hit on return, FL, crashed Jaenmanie, wrecked 30.7.18 (2/Lt G Martin wounded & 2/Lt SGHE Burton killed); 3 ASD to 99 Sqn 5.10.18; 3 ASD 13.11.18; 2 AI 1.12.18

C6211 Hendon for EF 6.4.18

C6212 At 2 AAP Hendon 3.4.18, allotted to EF; England to Rec Pk 8.5.18; 1 AI 14.5.18; 98 Sqn 17.5.18; Albatros D OOC Snollighem 14.30 1.6.18 (Capt FA Laughlin & 2/Lt H Tasker); Damaged in enemy night raid 5/6.6.18; To 4 ASD, transferred from EF to 5 Group 6.18; 218 Sqn 9.8.18; In combat 11.8.18 (Lt KR Campbell unhurt & Sgt AE Powell slightly wounded); COL, damaged 29.8.18 (Lt GF Smith & 2/Lt B Archer); 4 ASD 1.9.18; 2 SS Richborough 2.10.18

C6213 Shipped to Mudros 20.4.18

C6214 Arr Salonika AP ex UK 1.7.18; 47 Sqn from 2.8.18 (squadron's first a/c); Crashed on special duty Hajdarli to Sofia 11.10.18 (Lt EC White & Sgt Mech E Aston); SOC at Salonika AP 24.10.18

Lt L.F.Mead seated in the cockpit of D.H.9 C6215 of No.47 Squadron at Tbilisi in 1918. (via Don Neate)

C6215 Arr Salonika AP ex UK 17.7.18; Salonika AP to 47 Sqn 12.8.18; Crashed nr Amberkoj 31.12.18 (Mjr FA Bates); 17 Sqn by 25.2.19; Salonika AP 27.6.19; WO 3.10.19

C6216 Arr Salonika AP ex UK 29.7.18; 47 Sqn 26.8.18; Salonika AP to 17 Sqn 26.7.19

C6217 Arr Salonika AP ex UK 29.7.18; 47 Sqn by 10.8.18 - 9.18; Salonika AP to 17 Sqn 26.7.19

C6218 Arr Salonika AP 29.7.18 ex UK; 47 Sqn; Mail flight to Sofia 5.11.18 and to Bucarest 14.12.18; WO 30.1.19.

C6219 Arr Salonika AP ex UK 29.7.18; 17 Sqn by 26.9.18; Salonika AP for dismantling 7.12.18; "A" Flight 17 Sqn by 13.3.19; WO at 17 Sqn 27.6.19

C6220 Deld 2 AAP Hendon by 8.5.18; Allotted to 109 Sqn (Mob) 20.6.18; Reallotted to 108 Sqn (Mob) Kenley 24.6.18 and then to EF 29.6.18; Rec Pk to 1 AI 1.7.18; 206 Sqn 2.7.18; Pfalz DIII down smoking, crashed Neuve Eglise 07.25 7.8.18 (Lt H Stier USAS & Sgt J Chapman DSM); EF, COL 23.8.18 (Lt JD Russell & 2/Lt B Knee unhurt); Rep Pk 1 ASD 24.8.18; SOC 12.9.18 NWR

C6221 Shipped to Mudros 20.4.18; 226 Sqn by 25.5.18 - @8.18

C6222 Shipped to Mudros 20.4.18; Repair Base Mudros by 25.5.18; 220 Sqn by 3-4.7.18; Stavros by 10.18 - @1.19

C6223 Deld 2 AAP Henson 27.4.18, allotted to EF; England to Rec Pk 1.5.18; 1 AI 4.5.18, 98 Sqn 6.5.18; EA BU Menin Wervicq 19.20 8.5.18 (Capt EA Fawcus & Lt GD Dardis); FL at St Omer 19.5.18; Engine having been repaired was ready to fly off when damaged by collision with a Camel taking off 22.5.18 (Lt GD Horton & Lt HJ McConnell); Rep Pk 1 ASD 24.5.18; SOC 5.7.18 NWR

C6224 Shipped to Mudros 20.4.18; 226 Sqn by 25.5.18 - @2.10.18; Taranto by 10.18 - @1.19; AD Taranto to 'X' AD 28.6.19; ASD to 206 Sqn 20.11.19

C6225 No information

C6226 Duxford by 18.6.18; 35 TDS Duxford by 10.18?

C6227 Arr 'X' AD ex UK 25.6.18; 144 Sqn 7.7.18; 'C' Flt 29.7.18; Trg Bde to 144 Sqn 14.8.18; Salonika AP 16.11.18; 17 Sqn Amberkoj by 8.12.18; to Salonika AP 13.2.18

C6228 Arr 'X' AD ex UK 17.6.18; 144 Sqn 8.8.18; 'X' AP 6.9.18; 144 Sqn to 'X' AD 26.11.18

C6229 Arr 'X' AD ex UK 27.6.18; 144 Sqn by 4.8.18; Mudros by 10.18; 17 Sqn Amberkoj to Salonika AP 13.12.18; 17 Sqn to 47 Sqn 16.12.18; Salonika AP to 17 Sqn 21.5.19; WO 18.7.19

C6230 Arr 'X' AD ex UK 27.6.18; 'B' Flt 144 Sqn by 7.8.18; Stalled on turn at low height dived in 11.8.18 (Capt AL Fleming MC DoI & Lt GK Cathles of 27KBS attd killed); WO 14.8.18

C6231 Arr 'X' AD ex UK 25.6.18; 'X' AP 11.8.18; 144 Sqn 16.8.18; Rescued the crew of C6298 17.9.18 (2/Lt JS Wesson & Lt W Steele); Landed behind enemy lines on bombing raid 28.9.18 (2/Lt JS Wesson & Lt W Steele both PoW); WOC 6.10.18

C6232 Arr 'X' AD ex UK 25.6.18; 144 Sqn 24.8.18; 'X' AP to 'X' AD 16.10.18

C6233 Arr Salonika AP ex UK 6.8.18; 'B' Flt 17 Sqn Amberkoj 20.12.18; Prop broke landing in soft ground en route San Stefano 16.2.19 (Lt RR Macnaughton & AC2 NA Hicken); WO at Salonika AP 29.9.19

C6234 Arr Salonika AP ex UK 6.8.18; 47 Sqn 17.9.18; Salonika AP 27.4.19; Salonika AP to ASD 26.9.19

C6235 Arr Salonika AP ex UK 17.7.18; 47 Sqn by 24.8.18; WO at 17 Sqn 10.4.19

C6236 Arr Salonika AP ex UK 6.8.18; 47 Sqn 1.9.18; Salonika AP to 47 Sqn for service in Russia 21.4.19; At 47 Sqn Ekaterinodar 27.5.19; Erected 12.6.18; COL 20.6.19 (Lt GH Clavey & AM FJ Smith); Sqn records dated 11.8.19 say lost through enemy action on special mission with the Caucasian Army
BUT 206 Sqn Helwan by 12.19; Became 4 Sqn 1.2.20

C6237 No information

C6238 At 2 AAP Hendon 23.5.18, reallotted from 218 Sqn (Mob) Dover to EF; England to Rec Pk 27.5.18; 1 AI and on to 98 Sqn 28.5.18; Albatros D OOC 19.40 29.5.18 (Lt CD Taylor & Lt JR Jackman); Returning from practice flight wheel caught in rut causing crash 30.5.18 (Lt WS Eason OK); Rep Pk 1 ASD 31.5.18; SOC 5.7.18 NWR

C6239 No information

C6240 At 2 AAP Hendon 30.4.18, allotted to EF; England to Rec Pk 10.5.18; 1 AI 11.5.18; 206 Sqn 14.5.18; Fokker DrI crashed and burnt, shared C1181 Bac St.Maur 12.00 7.6.18 (Capt GLE Stevens & Lt C Eaton); Pfalz DIII crashed Zonnebeke 12.32 12.6.18 (Capt GLE Stevens & Lt LA Christian); Hit in radiator by AA approaching target, unable to keep up with formation on return flight, running fight (15.25-15.40) Nazareth, nr Ghent with 3 Fokker DVII, one of which BU in air, then crashed Aeltre-Pucques 30.10.18 (Sgt Mech G Packman & 2/Lt JW Kennedy unhurt); to Rep Pk 1 ASD

C6241 Imperial Gift to Australia; Became *A6-26*

C6242 to C6244 No information

C6245 6 Wing Otranto by 18.3.18 (or C6255?); Imperial Gift to India

C6246 Imperial Gift to Australia; Became *A6-27*

C6247 At 2 AAP Hendon 30.5.18, allotted to EF; Rec Pk to 2 AI 6.6.18; 27 Sqn 7.6.18; Fokker DVII left wing crumpled W of Lille 08.10 1.7.18 (Lt BM Bowyer-Smythe & Sgt WB Harold); 98 Sqn 1.3.19; 1 ASD 8.3.19; 8 AAP Lympne 8.3.19;

C6248 At 2 AAP Hendon 30.4.18, allotted to EF; England to Rec Pk 12.5.18; 1 AI 16.5.18; 98 Sqn 17.5.18; Damaged in enemy night raid Coudekerque 5/6.6.18; To 4 ASD, transferred to 5 Group 6.18; 2 SS Richborough 2.10.18

C6249 25 TS Thetford by 30.6.18; 35 TDS Duxford by 1.10.18

C6250 Deld Hendon to Dover W/E 24.5.18; 218 Sqn by 20.5.18; Slightly damaged after raid 12.6.18 (Lt JW Kennedy & G/L 1/Pte EWS Curtis unhurt); COL 18.6.18 (Lt JW Kennedy & 1/Pte EWS G/L Curtis unhurt); Yellow Pfalz DIII DD 18.15 5.7.18; Albatros DV down in sea shared by formation Zeebrugge 07.10 14.7.18 (both Capt JF Chisholm & G/L Sgt RJ Williams); Engine cut, landed crosswind, badly damaged 18.8.18 (Bos CJ O'Connor USN & QM C Van Galder unhurt); 4 ASD 20.8.18; 2 SS Richborough 15.9.18

C6251 At 2 AAP Hendon 9.5.18, allotted to EF; England to Rec Pk and on to 1 AI 25.5.18; 103 Sqn 27.5.18; Engine seized up at 500ft, FL, crashed 5.6.18 (Lt EA Windridge & 2/Lt VW Allen OK); To 9 AP; SOC Rep Pk 1 ASD 7.6.18

C6252 At 2 AAP Hendon by 1.6.18; 107 Sqn (Mob) Lake Down 4.6.18; To France with sqn 5.6.18; Left at 06.33 for raid on Courmont-Fère-en-Tardenois, FTR 18.7.18 (Lt FN Mollet & 2/Lt B Rawlings both killed)

C6253 At 2 AAP Hendon 30.5.18, allotted to EF; Rec Pk to 2 AI 2.6.18; 103 Sqn 7.6.18; Pfalz DIII OOC nr Roye 11.35 16.6.18; Scout OOC Estaires 1500 25.6.18 (both 2/Lt DM Darroch & Lt BA Tussaud); COL 5.8.18 (2/Lt DC McDonald & Lt HG Stirrup OK); Rep Pk 1 ASD 7.8.18; SOC 9.8.18 NWR

C6254 No information

C6255 9 TDS Shawbury by 10.18 - @3.19

C6256 From Andover to France with 104 Sqn 19.5.18; Bombing raid on Karlsruhe, went down E of lines 26.6.18 (2/Lt CG Jenyns PoW wounded & 2/Lt HC Davis killed)

C6257 No information

C6258 9 TDS Shawbury by 10.18 - @3.19

C6259 120 Sqn Cramlington by 5.18; 75 TS Cramlington by 21.6.18

C6260 From Andover to France with 104 Sqn 19.5.18; Bombing raid on Karlsruhe, shot up in combat with 5 EA, believed nr Maroncourt, FL, crashed 25.6.18 (Lt FW Mundy wounded & 2/Lt HAB Jackson DoW); Repaired; 3 ASD to 99 Sqn ('3') 3.8.18; In raid on Arnaville junction Fokker DVII crashed 17.25 13.9.18 (2/Lt WT Jones & 2/Lt EC Black); 3 ASD 25.9.18; Re-TOC EF 25.11.18; 2 AI 1.12.18

C6261 (Puma) FF 1.5.18; 75 TS Cramlington, believed prop burst and struck wings, tailplane failed, a/c broke up, fuselage and engine fell in street in Newcastle-upon-Tyne 9.5.18 (2/Lt RC Forster killed)

C6262 104 Sqn Andover by 5.5.18; To France with Sqn 19.5.18; On Metz-Sablon raid driven down under control Ars 07.05 1.7.18 (Lt GC Body & Lt WG Norden both PoW)

C6263 From Andover to France with 104 Sqn 19.5.18; Flying from Paris to Azelot, engine failed, FL on rough ground struck ditch 29.5.18 (2/Lt WJ Rivett-Carnac & 2/AM WH Escott); Rep Pk 2 ASD 29.5.18; Rebuilt as F6064 26.6.18

C6264 From Andover to France with 104 Sqn 19.5.18; Scout crashed Metz 07.00 1.7.18 (2/lt RJ Gammon & 2/Lt PE Appleby); Bombing raid on Karlsruhe, Albatros OOC down in vertical dive over Saverne on return 09.10 11.8.18 (Lt E Cartwright & Sgt AL Windridge); On Mannheim raid EA broke up Saverne, then later two OOC 12.50 7.9.18; Pfalz DIII crashed nr Metz 11.05, then with radiator shot through FL at French aerodrome nr Nancy, wrecked 15.9.18 (all Capt RJ Gammon & Lt PE Appleby); 6 AP 24.9.18; 3 ASD 30.9.18

C6265 At 2 AAP Hendon 26.4.18, allotted to EF; England to Rec Pk 1.5.18; 206 Sqn 4.5.18; COL, CW 19.6.18 (Lt FT Heron & 2/Lt CO Shelswell unhurt); Rep Pk 1 ASD 21.6.18; SOC 23.6.18 NWR

C6266 "Reporting from England" for 104 Sqn 25.5.18, landed with engine trouble at Sézanne, took off, FTR, it is believed that having lost way, FL in German lines at Pont-à-Mousson c.11.30 (Lt W Bruce & Sgt DG Smith both killed)

C6267 From Andover to France with 104 Sqn 19.5.18; Bombing raid on Hagendingen, in combat with EA, shot up, FL nr Toul 13.6.18 (2/Lt WJ Rivett-Carnac wounded & 2/AM WE Flexman DoW); SOC Rep Pk 2 ASD 8.7.18 (ex 6 AP)

C6268 104 Sqn, "Reporting from Paris", landed in the dark 21.50 20.5.18 (Lt E Cartwright & 2/AM J Lornie); To 3 ASD 5.18; 3 ASD to 104 Sqn 8.9.18; 6 AP 17.9.18; 3 ASD 19.9.18; To England 1.10.18

C6269 At 2 AAP Hendon by 1.6.18; 107 Sqn (Mob) Lake Down 4.6.18; To France with 107 Sqn 5.6.18; Collided on ground with D5669 1.7.18 (Lt RA Arnott & 2/Lt HR Whitehead OK); Rep Pk 1 ASD 2.7.18; SOC 5.7.18 NWR

C6270 At 2 AAP Hendon 8.5.18, allotted to EF; Rec Pk to 1 AI 13.7.18; 211 Sqn 15.7.18; Stalled landing from bombing raid, CW 17.10.18 (2/Lt J Hart & 2/Lt TE Drake both slightly injured); Remains to Rep Pk 1 ASD 17.10.18

C6271 At 2 AAP Hendon 9.5.18, allotted to EF; England to Rec Pk 26.5.18; 1 AI 29.5.18; 98 Sqn 31.5.18; Left 11.45 on bombing raid on Bruges, FTR 1.6.18 (2/Lt IA Peers US & 1/AM D Wentworth DFM both PoW)

C6272 At 2 AAP Hendon 9.5.18, allotted to EF; England to Rec Pk 26.5.18; 2 AI to 104 Sqn 9.6.18; Wrecked on take off 1.7.18 (Lt A Moore & Lt FP Cobden); Rep Pk 2 ASD 1.7.18; 3 ASD to 99 Sqn 7.8.18; Bombing raid on

D.H.9 C6260 '3' in which Lt H.Sanders returned safely from a raid on Mannheim on 7.9.18 (via Frank Cheesman)

This C-serialled D.H.9 has 'SOLO MACHINE' painted under the cockpit, believed to be at Waddington. (via Terry Treadwell)

Metz-Sablon railway, last seen in combat with 30-40 EA 26.9.18 (2/Lt CRG Abrahams & 2/Lt CH Sharp both killed)

C6273 At 2 AAP Hendon 8.5.18, allotted to EF; England to Rec Pk 26.5.18; 1 AI 28.5.18; 98 Sqn by 2.6.18; Damaged in enemy air raid on the night of 5/6.6.18; To 4 ASD, transferred from EF to 5 Group 6.18; 2 SS Richborough 15.9.18

C6274 At 2 AAP Hendon 22.5.18, reallotted from 218 Sqn (Mob) Dover to EF; England to Rec Pk 25.5.18; 1 AI 26.5.18; 98 Sqn 27.5.18; Left 13.45 for bombing raid, seen in spin over Bruges, reported shot down around 16.30 3.6.18 (Lt BA Bird & Lt AR Cowan both PoW)

C6275 At 2 AAP Hendon 8.5.18, allotted to EF; Rec Pk to 206 Sqn 25.5.18; COL 16.6.18 (Lt AJ Garside & 2/Lt MG Perry unhurt); Rep Pk 1 ASD 18.6.18; SOC 25.6.18 NWR

C6276 At 2 AAP Hendon 8.5.18, allotted to EF; England to Rec Pk 25.5.18; 1 AI 26.5.18; 98 Sqn 30.5.18; Damaged in enemy night raid Coudekerque 5/6.6.18; To 4 ASD, transferred from EF to 5 Group 6.18; 211 Sqn by 17.6.18; 4 ASD to 2 SS Richborough 15.9.18

C6277 WEE Biggin Hill ('3') by 12.5.18 - @9.7.18 (fixed aerial); 24 Sqn to Croydon 1.7.19 (for Directorate of Research); Air Council Inspection Sqn 22.8.19; At Manston, allocated Poland 3.20, but not sent

C6278 At 2 AAP Hendon 8.5.18, allotted to EF; England to Rec Pk 25.5.18; 2 AI 26.5.18; 99 Sqn 30.5.18; Hit by AA in Metz-Sablon raid 1.6.18 (Lt V Beecroft OK & Lt HT Melville slightly wounded); Damaged in Karlhaus raid 1.7.18 (Capt V Beecroft OK & Lt RP Connell slightly wounded); Scout broke up Sarreguemines 07.30 5.7.18 shared D7232 (Capt V Beecroft & 2/Lt BSW Taylor); FTR from Saarbrücken raid, missing after combat at St Avold/N of Dieuze 31.7.18 (Lt SMcB Black (Can) & 2/Lt E Singleton both PoW)

C6279 At 2 AAP Hendon 23.5.18, reallotted from 218 Sqn (Mob) Dover to EF; Rec Pk to 1 AI 4.6.18; 2 AI to 27 Sqn 12.6.18; FL at French aerodrome 25.7.18 (Lt RC Rogers wounded & Lt JV Lee OK); Shot through by AA Izel le Hameau, FL 11.00 7.8.18 (2/Lt HM Brown & Sgt HW Cornell both OK); 9 AP 9.8.18; SOC Rep Pk 2 ASD 18.9.18

C6280 204 TDS Eastchurch by 13.7.18 - @11.18; 2 MOS Eastchurch by 2.19

C6281 Arr 'X' AD ex UK 17.8.18; 144 Sqn 28.8.18; 'X' AP to 144 Sqn 6.9.18; Salonika AP 2.12.18; 'B' Flt 17 Sqn by 17.12.18 - @7.1.19; At Salonika AP 29.5.19

C6282 At 2 AAP Hendon 8.5.18, allotted to EF; Rec Pk to 1 AI 25.5.18; 211 Sqn 27.5.18; Hit in raid on Bruges docks (2/Lt JS Forgie wounded 18.6.18 & 2/Lt R Simpson OK); Sideslipped on landing 29.6.18 (2/Lt CO Carson & Cpl H Lindsay unhurt); 1 ASD 30.6.18; SOC 3.7.18 NWR

C6283 Deld 6 SD Ascot W/E 15.8.18; At docks W/E 19.9.18; Shipped to Mudros in SS *Hazlemere* W/E 17.10.18, but damaged en route

C6284 10 TDS Harling Road, caught fire at 2,000ft, crashed, WO 29.10.18

C6285 No information

C6286 2 MOS Eastchurch by 3.19 - @7.19

C6287 At 2 AAP Hendon 23.5.18, allotted to EF; England to Rec Pk 31.5.18; 211 Sqn 1.6.18; EF, FL on beach Gravelines 24.6.18 (2/Lt ETM Routledge & 2/Lt JFJ Peters unhurt); Rep Pk 1 ASD 24.6.18; SOC 27.6.18 NWR

C6288 No information

C6289 At 2 AAP Hendon 23.5.18, reallotted from 218 Sqn (Mob) Dover to EF; Rec Pk by 6.18; 1 AI 1.7.18; 206 Sqn 8.7.18; Pfalz DIII OOC 20.00-20.15 25.7.18 (2/Lt FA Brock & Sgt Mech LH Rowe); In combat 27.9.18 (2/Lt FA Brock OK & Sgt Mech LH Rowe wounded); Left on bombing raid 05.30, last seen Neuve Eglise 7.8.18 (2/Lt FA Brock MM & Cpl CH Cullimore both killed)

C6290 Arr 'X' AD ex UK 17.8.18; 'X' AD to 17 TDS El Firdan 14.11.18; 'Z' Sqn to 142 Sqn 14.6.19; ASD 9.10.19; SOC 13.11.19

C6291 10 TDS Harling Road by 6.18

C6292 1 Observers School Eastchurch by 10.18 - @11.18

C6293 Arr 'X' AD ex UK 11.7.18; 144 Sqn 19.8.18; 16 Wing Salonika 16.11.18; 'C' Flt 17 Sqn Amberkoj to Salonika AP 7.12.18; 'A' Flt 17 Sqn by 18.5.19; WO 3.10.19

The serial number of this D.H.9, surrounded by Australian troops is unclear, but could be C6293. (via Terry Treadwell)

C6294 Arr 'X' AD ex UK 11.7.18; 144 Sqn 16.8.18; Salonika AP 2.12.18; 'C' Flt 17 Sqn Amberkoj ('3') 7.12.18; Test flight, damaged landing 17.12.18 (2/Lt R Walker & AM NA Hicken); Salonika AP 19.12.18; 17 Sqn 1.4.19; Recd South Russia Instructional Mission 3.11.19; To GOC Russian Aviation 10.11.19; Later Soviet Russian Air Fleet (RKKVF?)

D.H.9 C6294 '3' of No.17 Squadron crashed on landing 17.12.18. (Stewart Taylor)

C6295 Arr 'X' AD ex UK 11.7.18; Palestine Brigade 4.10.18; 'X' AP to 144 Sqn 10.10.18; 'X' AF 26.11.18; 'C' Flt 142 sqn Suez 28.2.19; 31 Wing AP 24.3.19

C6296 Arr 'X' AD ex UK 16.7.18; 144 Sqn 17.8.18; 'X' AD 26.11.18

C6297 Arr 'X' AD ex UK 16.7.18; 144 Sqn Junction Station ('3') 27.8.18; FL in enemy territory after raid on Deraa, crew uninjured 16.9.18 (2/Lt TL Gitsham rejoined unit 5.10.18; 2/Lt CGH Thomas also survived); M/c bombed and burnt by 1 Sqn AFC, SOC by 144 Sqn 22.9.18

C6298 Arr 'X' AD ex UK 16.7.18; 144 Sqn 2.8.18; Bombing mission, FL in enemy territory, destroyed 17.9.18 (Lt B Heath & 2/Lt FE Horley rescued by C6231, both OK); SOC 22.9.18

C6299 Arr 'X' AD ex UK 3.8.18; 144 Sqn Junction Station 17.9.18; Salonika AP 16.11.18; 17 Sqn by 25.11.18; 47 Sqn to 17 Sqn 16.12.18; 'B' Flt 17 Sqn Amberkoj by 3.1.19; 47 Sqn to 17 Sqn 16.12.18

C6300 Arr 'X' AD ex UK 3.8.18; 'X' AP 15.9.18; 144 Sqn Junction Station 19.9.18; Salonika AP 2.12.18; 47 Sqn 29.12.18; Salonika AP 16.4.19; 'B' Flt 17 Sqn by 7.6.19 (described as a Salonika AP m/c); COL at Salonika AP 16.6.19 (Lt SM Sharpe & Lt FL Goodacre); WOC 17.6.19

C6301 Arr 'X' AD ex UK 3.8.18; 144 Sqn 3.9.18; 'X' AP 28.9.18; 'X' AD 16.10.18; SOC at ASD 13.11.19

C6302 Arr 'X' AD ex UK 3.8.18; 144 Sqn 15.9.18; In action 19.9.18 (Pilot unhurt & 2/Lt FE Horley wounded); 'X'

D.H.9 C6297 '3' of No.144 Squadron after force landing in Turkish territory following a raid on Deraa on 16.9.18. The cloth circle indicates that the ground is too rough to permit a rescue attempt by the photographing aircraft. Both crew members later returned safely. (via Frank Cheesman)

AP 28.9.18; 'X' AD 16.10.18; AW&SP to 'C' Flt 142 Sqn Suez 3.4.19; FL en route Ismailia 19.8.19 (Lt JH Code & AC Hinton)

C6303 Arr "X" AD ex UK 25.7.18; 144 Sqn 1.8.18; Salonika AP 16.11.18; 17 Sqn by 25.2.19; Salonika AP 28.5.19; ASD 26.9.19

C6304 Arr 'X' AD ex UK 3.8.18; 'X' AP 11.9.18; 144 Sqn 12.9.18; Salonika AP 2.12.18; 'A' Flt 17 Sqn by 1.2.19; WO at 17 Sqn 17.6.19

C6305 Arr 'X' AD ex UK 3.8.18; 144 Sqn 29.8.18; Attacking retreating Turkish troops on Ferweh-Buseiliyeh road 21.9.18, FL in enemy territory 21.9.18 (2/Lt KMH Marriott & L/Cpl WJ Westley both killed); WOC 28.9.18

C6306 No information

C6307 From Andover to France with 104 Sqn ('B') 19.5.18; FTR bombing raid on Metz, last seen gliding E of lines 1.7.18 (Lt TL McConchie & 2/Lt KCB Woodman both PoW)

C6308 108 Sqn Lake Down, spun in off turn at low height 9.6.18 (Lt AM Bain injured)

C6309 Arr 'X' AD ex UK 3.8.18; 'X' AP 15.9.18; 144 Sqn 16.9.18; Salonika AP 16.11.18; 'C' Flt 17 Sqn by 2.12.18; Salonika AP 13.12.18; 47 Sqn 31.12.18; Crashed on test 4.1.19 (2/Lt T Dowsett); SOC at 47 Sqn 11.1.19

C6310 Arr 'X' AD ex UK 3.8.18; 144 Sqn 15.9.18; 'X' AP to 'X' AD 16.10.18; WO at ASD 13.11.19
BUT 6 Wing Otranto by 18.3.18

C6311 Arr 'X' AD ex UK 3.8.18; 144 Sqn 24.10.18; 'X' AD 26.11.18; 'B' Flt 142 Sqn Suez 11.3.19

C6312 Arr 'X' AD ex UK 25.7.18; 144 Sqn 1.8.18 (to 'C' Flt 5.8.18); Salonika AP 2.12.18; 'A' Flt 17 Sqn by 2.4.19; Crashed on demonstration flight 13.4.19 (Mjr SG Hodges & Lt HA Fourte); at 17 Sqn SOC 2.5.19

C6313 Arr 'X' AD ex UK 3.8.18; 144 Sqn 19.9.18; 'X' AP to 'X' AD 16.10.18; WO at ASD 13.11.19

C6314 At 8 AAP Lympne 19.7.18 for 109 Sqn (Mob) Lake Down; Reallotted to EF 29.7.18; 1 AI to 108 Sqn 24.8.18; Fokker DVII crashed in the sea Ostende, shared C2205 & D3107 11.20 7.9.18 (2/Lt R Russell & 2/Lt GB Pike); In Lichtervelde raid Fokker DrI OOC at Gits and Fokker DVII OOC Staden shared C6345, D1080, D3092, D5622, D5759, D7208, E669, E5435 & F5847 11.45 21.9.18 (Lt R Russell & Lt WL Walker); Left on solo recce 10.35, FTR 23.10.18 (Capt CG Haynes & Lt G Brown both killed)

C6315 At 8 AAP Lympne 19.7.18 for 109 Sqn (Mob) Lake Down; Reallotted to EF 29.7.18; Rec Pk to 2 AI 10.8.18; 49 Sqn 12.8.18; Left 19.30 on bombing raid, badly shot up, FL Osterville 23.8.18 (2/Lt ST Franks & 2/Lt SP Scott OK); SOC Rep Pk 2 ASD 24.9.18 ex 9 AP.

C6316 [108 Sqn?] Lake Down by 12.5.18; 109 Sqn Lake Down by 19.6.18

C6317 Lake Down, burst tyres landing Eastbourne 20.5.18 (stayed overnight); 136 Sqn by 6.18 - 7.18; 14 TDS Lake Down by 12-13.8.18

C6318 No information

C6319 To France with 107 Sqn 5.6.18; Oil pipe broke in air, covered screen & blurred goggles when landing, crashed 30.7.18 (2/Lt AT Reid & 2/Lt WJ Bradshaw); SOC Rep Pk 1 ASD 3.9.18 (ex 9 AP)

C6320 [108 Sqn?] Lake Down by 15.5.18; To France with 107 Sqn 5.6.18; Left 05.40 for raid on Brie Bridge, seen going down E of lines 9.8.18 (2/Lt SJ Hill PoW & 2/AM FA Ellery DoW)

C6321 218 Sqn by 20.5.18; Damaged in combat nr Ostend 12.6.18 (Lt CLW Brading & G/L Sgt RS Joysey OK); EF on overshoot, CW 7.7.18 (Lt CLW Brading & G/L

Sgt F Smith unhurt); to 4 ASD for repair; 2 SS Richborough 15.9.18

C6322 218 Sqn by 20.5.18; 4 ASD Pilot Pool by 2.6.18; Crashed; WOC 30.9.18 DBR

C6323 Imperial Gift to Australia; Became *A6-28*

C6324 To France with 107 Sqn 5.6.18; Bad landing 15.6.18 (Lt G Beveridge & Lt WH Newman OK); Rep Pk 2 ASD 19.6.18; Rebuilt as F6205 18.7.18

C6325 14 TDS Lake Down/Boscombe Down by 11.8.18 - @9.18

C6326 4 ASD Guines, tested 1.6.18; 4 ASD to 491 Flt 233 Sqn Dover 23.10.18 - @16.12.18

C6327 Deld 6 SD Ascot W/E 15.8.18; At docks W/E 19.9.18; Shipped to Mudros in SS *Hazlemere* W/E 17.10.18, but damaged en route

C6328 Deld 6 SD Ascot W/E 15.8.18; At docks W/E 19.9.18; Shipped to Mudros in SS *Hazlemere* W/E 17.10.18, but damaged en route

C6329 Deld 6 SD Ascot W/E 15.8.18; At docks W/E 19.9.18; Shipped to Mudros in SS *Hazlemere* W/E 17.10.18, but damaged en route

C6330 Deld 6 SD Ascot W/E 15.9.18; Shipped 12.9.18; AP Taranto by 10.18; 'X' AD 1.4.19

C6331 Deld 6 SD Ascot W/E 15.9.18; Shipped 12.9.18; AP Taranto by 10.18; 'X' AD 1.7.19

C6332 Deld 6 SD Ascot W/E 15.9.18; Shipped 12.9.18; AD Taranto by 10.18; 'X' AD 28.6.19

C6333 SOC Rep Pk 1 ASD 26.8.18 ex Rec Pk.

C6334 Deld 6 SD Ascot W/E 15.9.18; Shipped to Taranto 21.9.18; AP Taranto by 10.18; 'X' AD 1.4.19

C6335 Recd Rec Pk ex UK for IF 8.18; Rec Pk to 2 AI 10.8.18; 3 ASD 20.8.18; 104 Sqn 5.10.18; 3 ASD 29.10.18

C6336 Arr Salonika AP 25.8.18 ex UK; 'C' Flt 17 Sqn 10.11.18; Salonika AP for dismantling 5.12.18; 'A' Flight 17 Sqn by 18.2.19; COL 16.3.19 (2/Lt LF Mead & 2/Lt HA Fourte); SOC 7.4.19.

C6337 Arr Salonika AP 25.8.18 ex UK; 47 Sqn 21.4.19 for service in South Russia; At 47 Sqn Ekaterinodar by 27.5.19; Erected 12.6.19; Sold to Anti-Bolshevik Government

C6338 Arr Salonika AP 29.8.18; 'B' Flight 17 Sqn 21.10.18; WO 17 Sqn 3.10.19

C6339 Arr Salonika AP ex UK 25.8.18; 'B' Flight 17 Sqn 29.9.18; Salonika AP for dismantling 5.12.18; Tested 'A' Flt 17 Sqn 18.5.19; Recd South Russia Instructional Mission 3.11.19; To Russian Aviation Corps 24.11.19

C6340 At 7 AAP Kenley 29.5.18, allotted to EF; Rec Pk to 2 AI and on to 27 Sqn 12.6.18; Fokker DVII smoking probably crashed in wood nr Coiney 19.20 21.7.18 (Lt CE Hutchinson & Sgt HW Cornell); Practice flight, stalled at 600ft, dived in, BO 24.7.18 (2/Lt CE Robinson & 2/Lt WH Telfer both killed)

C6341 At 7 AAP Kenley by 19.6.18 for 108 Sqn (Mob); To Sqn by 6.7.18;

C6342 At 7 AAP Kenley by 19.6.18 for 108 Sqn (Mob); 108 Sqn by 6.18; Rec Pk to 2 AI 26.6.18; 3 ASD 30.7.18; 99 Sqn 31.7.18; FTR from raid on Buhl aerodrome, seen going down under control, FL nr Baccarat 27.8.18 (Lt G Broadbent & Lt TH Swann OK); 3 ASD 30.8.18; To England 1.10.18

C6343 At 7 AAP Kenley 11.6.18 for 109 Sqn (Mob); reallotted to EF 14.6.18; 2 AI to 104 Sqn 27.6.18; 5 AI to 107 Sqn 17.7.18; Left 05.40 for raid on Brie Bridge, in combat with 25 Fokker DVII nr Péronne, Fokker DVII dest & 2 others OOC Fresnes 06.55 - 07.15, own a/c shot up, pilot fainted, observer landed a/c, crashed Villers Bretonneux 9.8.18 (Lt G Beveridge wounded & 2/Lt C Dunlop unhurt); SOC Rep Pk 2 ASD 27.8.18 (ex 2 Salvage Dump)

C6344 At 7 AAP Kenley 29.5.18, allotted to EF; Rec Pk to 2 AI 10.6.18; 103 Sqn 12.6.18; COL 21.6.18; SOC Rep Pk 1 ASD 26.6.18 NWR

C6345 At 7 AAP Kenley by 20.6.18 for 108 Sqn (Mob); At Sqn by 6.7.18; To France with Sqn 22.7.18; In Lichtervelde raid Fokker DrI OOC Gits and Fokker DVII OOC Staden, shared C6314, D1080, D3092, D5622, D5759, D7208, E669, E5435 & F5847 11.45 21.9.18 (Lt AAS Milne & Sgt W Greenwood); On formation practice collided with D3113 at 5,000ft 8.10.18 (2/Lt RS Herbert & Sgt GR Hext both killed); Rep Pk 1 ASD 10.10.18 SOC

C6346 At 7 AAP Kenley 29.5.18, allotted to EF; Rec Pk to 2 AI and on to 27 Sqn 9.6.18; Left 08.55 on bombing raid, seen in combat with EA W of Roye, went down in flames 16.6.18 (2/Lt WH Vick PoW wounded & Lt FRG Spurgin killed)

C6347 At 7 AAP Kenley 11.6.18 for 109 Sqn (Mob); reallotted EF 14.6.18; Rec Pk to 2 AI 30.6.18; 27 Sqn 1.7.18; FL due to bad weather, overturned in soft ploughed ground 2.8.18 (Lt HP Schoeman & 2/Lt FF McKilligin); Rep Pk 1 ASD 8.8.18; SOC 3.9.18

C6348 At 7 AAP Kenley 11.6.18 for 109 Sqn (Mob); reallotted EF 14.6.18; Rec Pk to 1 AI 24.6.18; 211 Sqn ('C') 26.6.18; EF on TO, FL, crashed in corn, o/t 7.8.18 (Capt RM Wynne-Eyton & 2/Lt TB Dodwell unhurt); Badly damaged by AA over Bruges, FL in the Wielingen, 2m from coast, sank off Breskens 12.30 16.8.18 (Capt RM Wynne-Eyton & 2/Lt TB Dodwell both badly wounded, both rescued by a Dutch guard boat, later 2 torpedo boats & HMS *Hydra* arrived, interned); SOC 16.8.18

C6349 At 7 AAP Kenley 11.6.18 for 109 Sqn (Mob); reallotted EF 14.6.18; Rec Pk to 1 AI 27.6.18; 98 Sqn 29.6.18; In combat over Lille 11.35 9.7.18 (Capt OCW Johnsen OK & Lt HA Lamb killed); Albatros D crashed nr Ville-en-Tardenois 08.05 18.7.18; Fokker DrI crashed 19.50 20.7.18 (both Capt OCW Johnsen & Capt GHP Whitfield); Left 04.50, combat with 30 EA east of lines, shot up 25.7.18 (Capt OCW Johnsen & Capt GHP Whitfield unhurt); 9 AP 28.7.18; SOC Rep Pk 1 ASD 3.9.18

C6350 Completed as a D.H.9A prototype (Eagle VIII) [the other was B7664]; Replaced by E5435; 2 AAP Hendon to AES Martlesham Heath 23.2.18; BU in the air 16.3.18 (Lt KK Muspratt MC & F/Sgt S Ashby both killed)

D.H.9 C6311 of No.142 Squadron at Heliopolis in 1919.
RAF Museum P.2220

D.H.9A prototype C6350 was test flown at Martlesham Heath.
(via Frank Cheesman)

500 D.H.9 ordered 30.10.17 under Cont No A.S.26928 (BR.162 & 238) from Cubitt Ltd/National Aircraft Factory No.1, Waddon and numbered D451 to D950. (200hp BHP)

D451 9 TDS Shawbury by 10.18 - 3.19; Base Depot RAF Novorossisk to 7 Sqn Russian Aviation Corps 14.2.20
D452 No information
D453 31 TDS Fowlmere by 10.18; Midland Area FIS Lilbourne by 11.18
D454 207 TDS Chingford by 5.18
D455 9 TDS Shawbury by 10.18 - 3.19
D456 11 TDS Old Sarum by 30.5.18
D457 At 2 AAP Hendon 8.5.18 allotted to EF; England to Rec Pk 18.5.18; 49 Sqn 21.5.18; Pfalz DIII OOC confirmed crashed NE of Douai 10.20 27.6.18 (Lt AJP Estlin & Lt EH Tredcroft); In action 16.7.18 (Lt GS Ramsay OK & Lt JT Peacock killed); Left 14.00 for low bombing raid on Bethencourt Bridge, shot up, retd 16.15 8.8.18 (Lt GS Ramsay & 2/Lt BT Gillman both OK); SOC Rep Pk 2 ASD 18.9.18
D458 103 Sqn Old Sarum; 11 TDS Old Sarum by 22.5.18
D459 At 2 AAP Hendon 8.5.18 allotted to EF; England to Rec Pk 18.5.18; 1 AI 20.5.18; 206 Sqn 21.5.18; COL 10.6.18 (Lt EHP Bailey & 2/Lt WD McKinnon unhurt); Wrecked, to Rep Pk 1 ASD 11.6.18; SOC 5.7.18 NWR
D460 At 2 AAP Hendon 23.5.18, reallotted from 108 Sqn (Mob) Lake Down to EF; Rec Pk to 2 AI 4.6.18; 98 Sqn 8.6.18; Tested 29.6.18 (tail heavy); On test flight caught in rut on landing and crashed 11.7.18 (2/Lt JH Davies & Lt HTG Robey OK); SOC Rep Pk 1 ASD 15.7.18
D461 At 2 AAP Hendon 30.5.18, allotted to EF; Rec Pk to 2 AI 10.6.18; 49 Sqn 11.6.18; Left 13.45 for bombing raid, hit by AA, retd 16.05 17.6.18 (Lt AJP Estlin & Lt RHV Scherk both unhurt); SOC Rep Pk 1 ASD 15.7.18
D462 At 2 AAP Hendon 23.5.18, reallotted from 218 Sqn (Mob) Dover to EF; England to Rec Pk 25.5.18; 49 Sqn 26.5.18; Returning from bombing raid, broke up at 12,000ft 30.5.18 (Lt RHB Stevens & Ptel LC Norman both killed)
D463 At 2 AAP Hendon 30.5.18, allotted to EF; Rec Pk to 2 AI 8.6.18; 49 Sqn 13.6.18; COL 18.6.18 (Lt RC Stokes & Lt FC Aulagnier OK); To 9 AP 19.6.18; Rep Pk 1 ASD, SOC 11.7.18 NWR
D464 At 2 AAP Hendon 3.6.18, allotted to EF; Rec Pk to 2 AI 11.6.18; 103 Sqn 12.6.18; Misjudged landing and crashed 29.6.18 (Lt AET Tyrell & 2/Lt IB Corey OK); Rep Pk 1 ASD 30.6.18; SOC 1.7.18 NWR
D465 & D466 No information
D467 At 2 AAP Hendon 6.6.18, allotted to EF; Rec Pk to 1 AI 11.6.18; 2 AI and on to 98 Sqn 12.6.18; Preparing to land got into "air bump" at only 200ft, unable to get out and crashed 13.6.18 (Lt IV Lawrence & Lt JR Jackman); To Rep Pk 1 ASD 16.6.18; SOC 19.6.18 NWR
D468 At 2 AAP Hendon by 3.6.18; 108 Sqn (Mob) 7.6.18; At 108 Sqn Kenley 29.6.18, reallotted from SE Area for 108 Sqn (Mob) to EF; Rec Pk to 1 AI 29.6.18; 98 Sqn 3.7.18; Fokker DrI OOC Lille by observer 11.35 9.7.18 (2/Lt F Carpenter & 2/Lt FE Donkin); Left at 05.25, shot up by EA, engine failed, crashed at St Venant 11.7.18 (2/Lt F Carpenter & 2/Lt FE Donkin both OK); SOC 12.7.18 wrecked
D469 At 2 AAP Hendon 23.5.18, reallotted from 218 Sqn (Mob) Dover to EF; England to Rec Pk 22.5.18; 27 Sqn 25.5.18; Left 16.15 on low strafing mission, FTR, last seen SE of Dormans 15.7.18 (Lt HGS Phipson & 2/Lt NCL Auster both killed)
D470 At 2 AAP Hendon 6.6.18, allotted to EF; Via 8 AAP Lympne to Rec Pk 7.7.18; 1 AI 8.7.18; Collecting m/c from 1 AI for 103 Sqn, spun in from 200ft 9.7.18 (2/Lt JH Smith killed); Rep Pk 1 ASD 9.7.18; SOC 13.7.18
D471 1 SoN&BD Stonehenge by 12.18; Spun in after flat turn at 200ft 7.1.19 (2/Lt PE Kearney DoI & Sgt RR Harper killed)
D472 203 TDS Manston by 6.18; Became 55 TDS Manston 14.7.18; 55 TDS Narborough 12.9.18 - @11.18
D473 55 TDS Manston by 9.18; 1 Observers School, Eastchurch by 10.18 - @11.18
D474 At 2 AAP Hendon 1.6.18 for 108 Sqn (Mob) Kenley as a training machine; To sqn 8.6.18; Reallotted to D of T for Manston Scout Pool 28.6.18; Pool of Pilots Manston/Joyce Green by 3.19-8.19
D475 At 2 AAP Hendon by 17.6.18 for 108 Sqn (Mob); At Sqn by 21.6.18; reallotted to EF 29.6.18; Rec Pk to 2 AI 3.7.18; 27 Sqn 3.7.18; Overshot landing ground and crashed 15.7.18 (2/Lt SM Feurer OK); 9 AP 17.7.18; Rep Pk 1 ASD SOC 3.9.18
D476 At 2 AAP Hendon for 108 Sqn (Mob) Kenley 13.6.18; To sqn 27.6.18; Reallotted to D of T for Manston Scout Pool 28.6.18; Observers School 1918; Hit mast of barge 19.10.18 (Lt JA Radcliffe slightly injured)
D477 At 2 AAP Hendon by 21.6.18 for 108 Sqn (Mob) Kenley; At Sqn 29.6.18, reallotted to EF; Rec Pk to 1 AI 30.6.18; 107 Sqn 1.7.18; Struck ridge on landing 8.7.18 (Lt RA Arnott & Lt HR Whitehead OK); Rep Pk 1 ASD SOC 12.7.18 NWR
D478 At 2 AAP Hendon 6.6.18, allotted to EF; Rec Pk to 2 AI 13.6.18; 107 Sqn 14.6.18; Struck sunken road on landing Metringhem 7.7.18 (Lt JR Brown & AM JC Hazell OK); Rep Pk 1 ASD SOC 12.7.18 NWR
D479 At 2 AAP Hendon for 108 Sqn (Mob) Kenley 17.6.18; To sqn 26.6.18; Reallotted to D of T for Manston Scout Pool 28.6.18; Pool of Pilots Manston by 7.18; EF, FL and crashed Sandwich, Kent 3.9.18 (Capt SA Hamilton-Bowyer); Air Observers School 1918
D480 At 2 AAP Hendon for 108 Sqn (Mob) Kenley 11.6.18; Reallotted to EF 15.6.18; Rec Pk to 2AI 16.6.18; 103 Sqn 18.6.18; COL 21.6.18 (Lt JL Roberts & 2/Lt JY Round); Rebuilt as F6057 28.6.18
D481 At Makers 3.6.18, allotted to EF; 2 AI to 3 ASD 2.7.18; 104 Sqn 6.7.18; 3 ASD 13.7.18; 104 Sqn 8.11.18; Crashed Essey, nr Nancy 9.11.18; Engine failed, landed badly 4.1.19 (2/Lt RF Lynch & AM Linion OK); SOC 10.1.19
D482 At Makers 3.6.18, allotted to EF; Rec Pk to 1 AI and on to 211 Sqn 30.6.18; Left 07.00, direct hit by AA between Ypres & Roulers, FL, crashed west of lines, TW 29.9.18 (2/Lt JL McAdam unhurt & 2/Lt TW Kelly killed); Salvage to 1 ASD 1.10.18
D483 At Makers 3.6.18, allotted to EF; Rec Pk to 2 AI and on to 99 Sqn 28.6.18; Rep Pk 2 ASD, SOC 10.7.18
D484 At Makers 3.6.18, allotted to EF; 8 AAP Lympne to Rec Pk 6.7.18; 1 AI 7.7.18; 103 Sqn 9.7.18; Left 06.10 for recce, in combat with EA, FTR 1.11.18 (2/Lt PS Tennant & 2/Lt GLP Drummond both PoW wounded)
D485 Presentation Aircraft 'Faridkot No.1'. At Makers 3.6.18, allotted to EF; Rec Pk to 1 AI 3.8.18; 103 Sqn 5.8.18; Crashed 28.10.18 (Lt R Jackson & Sgt EG Stevens OK); 1 ASD 30.10.18
D486 At Makers 3.6.18, allotted to EF; Rec Pk to 2AI 29.6.18; Standing outside a hangar at 2AI ran into by AW D5023 1.7.18; To Rep Pk 2 ASD and SOC 8.7.18 NWR
D487 At Makers 3.6.18, allotted to EF; Rec Pk to 2 AI 10.9.18; 3 ASD 15.9.18; 104 Sqn 23.10.18; Pfalz DIII OOC Buhl 14.00 6.11.18 (2/Lt P Hopkinson & Lt CC Blizard); SOC 1 ASD 21.1.19
D488 At Makers 3.6.18, allotted to EF; Rec Pk to 2 AI 7.7.18; 107 Sqn 9.7.18; Damaged in bad landing 17.7.18 (Lt JV Turner & Lt RO Baird OK); SOC Rep Pk 1 ASD 3.9.18 (ex 9 AP) NWR
D489 At Makers 3.6.18, allotted to EF; Rec Pk to 1 AI 2.7.18; 103 Sqn 5.7.18; Slight AA hit while bombing Erquinghem, u/c collapsed on landing 9.8.18 (Lt G Butters & Lt CN Wilson unhurt); Left 08.00 for raid on Fives, met formation of 50 Fokker DVII & DrI at 10-16,000 over Lille on return, seen going down in spin around 09.45 after being attacked by 2 EA, but flattened out at 2,000ft 16.9.18 (2/Lt WH Cole & Sgt S Hookway both killed)
D490 At Makers 3.6.18, allotted to EF; Rec Pk to 2 AI 17.7.18; 5 AI 7.18; 27 Sqn 20.7.18; Left on raid 15.55, FTR, last seen in combat going down over Mont Notre Dame 22.7.18 (2/Lt SM Feurer & 2/Lt HB Steckley both killed)
D491 6 TDS Boscombe Down, spun in from 500ft during cross-country practice 19.8.18 (2/Lt ME Rowe killed)
D492 Presentation Aircraft 'Faridkot No.2'. 2 SoN&BD Andover, stalled taking off in cross wind over row of houses, crashed 26.9.18 (2/Lt NK Johnson & F/Cdt GJ Wheeler both injured)
D493 2 FS Marske by 7.18 - 8.18
D494 No information

D.H.9 D506 'H' of No.27 Squadron.
(via Mike O'Connor)

D495 203 TDS Manston by 7.18; Became 55 TDS 14.7.18 - @11.18

D496 At Makers 3.6.18, allotted to EF; To 7 AAP Kenley; Rec Pk to 1 AI 15.7.18; 103 Sqn 22.7.18; Bombing raid on Péronne, oil pipe broken, overnight at 207 Sqn airfield 16.8.18 (2/Lt G Butters & Lt MS Lewin); Fokker DVII crashed nr Chappelles-à-Wattines 14.40 30.10.18 (Lt CA Hallawell & Sgt EJW Watkinson); FL, crashed 17.1.19 (Lt WN Wilson & 2/Lt G Butters): RTP 25.1.19

D497 Arr Rec Pk 8.8.18; 2 AI to 3 ASD 12.8.18; 104 Sqn 22.8.18; 6 AP 25.10.18; 3 ASD 31.10.18

D498 No information

D499 At Makers 27.6.18, allotted to EF; To 7 AAP Kenley; For 108 Sqn (Mob) by 18.7.18; To France with Sqn 22.7.18; Hit by AA on Ostende raid 27.8.18 (Lt JEH Dakin OK & 2/Lt JW Ritchie wounded); After bombing Ingelmunster station at 17.35 attacked by 33 EA between target and Roulers 3 EA in flames, 1 EA BU and 2 OOC shared C2205, D5835, D5845, D7342, E605, E5435, E8871 & F5847 1.10.18 (2/Lt CR Knott & Lt G Windle); FL Mardyke 14.10.18 (2/Lt CR Knott & Lt G Windle), repaired in sqn; In action 26.10.18 (2/Lt CR Knott wounded & Lt G Windle OK); On landing hit small store with u/c, nose dived in 23.11.18 (2/Lt JSG Holmes and 2/Lt JB Fletcher both injured); 11 SS 6.12.18

D500 No information

D501 Arr Rec Pk 31.7.18; 2 AI 31.7.18; 3 ASD 31.7.18; 104 Sqn 2.8.18; FTR 11.8.18 (2/Lt JE Parke & 2/Lt WW Bradford)

D502 At Makers 27.6.18, allotted to EF; At 7 AAP Kenley 24.7.18 for 109 Sqn (Mob) Lake Down; To Sqn 26.7.18; Reallotted IF 29.7.18; Arr Rec Pk 31.7.18; 2 AI 3.8.18; 49 Sqn 5.8.18; Left 07.25 on bombing raid, shot down in flames in combat SW of Mons 30.10.18 (2/Lt BW Cotterell & Sgt WH Gumbley both killed)

D503 To US Government

D504 At Makers 27.6.18, allotted to EF; To 7 AAP Kenley; Rec Pk to 2 AI 6.8.18; 98 Sqn 9.8.18; Left 06.40, in combat with Fokker DVII W of lines, down in flames over lines, crashed Roiselle 19.8.18 (Lt CH Roberts & 2/Lt JH Davies both killed)

D505 No information

D506 At Makers 27.6.18, allotted to EF; To 7 AAP Kenley; Rec Pk to 2 AI 3.8.18; 27 Sqn ('H') 7.8.18; 98 Sqn 1.3.19; 1 ASD 8.3.19; 8 AAP Lympne 8.3.19;

D507 & D508 No information

D509 Rec Pk to 2 AI 30.7.18; 3 ASD 31.7.18; 99 Sqn 31.7.18; Crashed on aerodrome 7.8.18 (Lt JL Hunter & 2/Lt W Shaw); 3 ASD 7.8.18

D510 No information

D511 At Makers 27.6.18, allotted to EF; To 7 AAP Kenley; To France with 108 Sqn 22.7.18; Left 10.16 for raid on Ostende Docks, believed hit by AA, seen going down at 9,000ft towards SE Ostende 3.9.18 (2/Lt A Preston & Sgt H Stewart both PoW)

D512 & D513No information

D514 Imperial Gift to India

D515 AAP Kenley by 10.18

D516 Became *G-EAXG* (D.H.9C c/n 16)

D517 Deld 7 AAP Kenley by 9.18; Rec Pk to 1 AI 26.9.18; 1 AI to 211 Sqn 30.9.18; Left 11.00 for photo recce, attacked by 4 EA at 14,000ft over Maubeuge, damaged 1.11.18 (2/Lt PM Keary unhurt & 2/Lt AK Robinson slightly wounded); 7 SS 2.11.18 for 2 ASD

D518 Hucknall to RAE 16.7.19

D519 to D523 No information

D524 Imperial Gift to India

D525 3 (T) Group Navigation School, Norwich to 4 SoN&BD Thetford 4.9.19

D526 3 ASD to 104 Sqn 21.10.18; Damaged in raid on Buhl aerodrome 6.11.18 (Lt JW Richards & 2/Lt EG Stevens both wounded); Engine over heated, FL cross wind and crashed 17.12.18 (2/Lt W McCullagh & Sgt WH Ball OK); SOC 27.12.18

D527 5 TDS Easton-on-the-Hill by 7.18; 3 ASD by 9.18; 99 Sqn 26.9.18; Hit by AA 10.10.18 (Pilot unhurt & 2/Lt WHR Jarvis wounded); FL Neufchateau 11.11.18; 3 ASD 13.11.18

D528 No information

D529 55 TDS Narborough by 1.19

D530 3 ASD to 104 Sqn 20.9.18; Bombing raid 18.10.18 (Lt JW Richards OK & 2/Lt AM Mitchell wounded); 6 AP 23.10.18

D531 No information

D532 Left 7 AAP Kenley 3.9.18; Rec Pk 4.9.18; 2 AI 6.9.18; 3 ASD 7.9.18; 104 Sqn 14.9.18; In combat with many EAs in raid on Metz-Sablon Railway, FL Sivry, crashed, wrecked 15.9.18 (2/Lt AA Baker & Sgt HE Tonge both wounded); 3 ASD 15.9.18

D533 No information

D534 ARS to 1 SoN&BD 15.12.18 - @17.1.19

D535 Rec Pk to 2 AI 16.9.18; 27 Sqn 1.10.18; Left 09.40 for bombing raid to Mons, radiator hit in combat with EA over target, FTR 28.10.18 (2/Lt CM Allan & 2/Lt JP Coleman both PoW)

D536 to D538 No information

D539 Rep Pk 2 ASD to 2 AI 1.10.18; 103 Sqn 9.10.18; Left 15.10 on bombing raid, damaged 23.10.18 (Capt DM Darroch & Lt FM Loly both wounded); 1 ASD 27.10.18

D540 2 SoN&BD Andover by 10.18

D541 Rec Pk to 2 AI 14.9.18; 27 Sqn 26.9.18; 98 Sqn 5.3.19

D542 No information

D543 At Burton-on-Trent W/E 10.10.18; 6 SD Ascot W/E 31.10.18 for Mudros; Shipped W/E 21.11.18; Unloaded from SS *Diyatalana* on/by 25.1.20; TOC Base Depot RAF Novorossisk 14.2.20; Sold to Anti-Bolshevik Government

D544 England to Rec Pk 1.9.18; 2 AI 3.9.18; 3 ASD 4.9.18; 99 Sqn 14.9.18; Bombing raid on Metz-Sablon railway, in combat with 30-40 EA, Scout OOC nr Metz by observer who was then killed 26.9.18 (Lt HD West (Can) unhurt & 2/Lt JW Howard killed); Pfalz DIII crashed SW of Buhl 14.00 6.11.18 (Lt F Crosbie-Choppin & 2/Lt AT Bower); 3 ASD 13.11.18; 2 AI 1.12.18

D545 & D546 No information

D547 6 AI to 211 Sqn 1.12.18; 98 Sqn 24.2.19

D548 & D549 No information

D550 7 AAP Kenley by 9.18; Rec Pk to 1 AI 16.10.18; 103 Sqn 25.10.18; Fokker DVII crashed nr Montroeuil-au-Bois, N of Leuze 14.30 30.10.18 (Capt JS Stubbs DFC & Lt CG Bannerman); 98 Sqn 10.3.19; 8 AAP Lympne 14.3.19

D551 Rec Pk to 1 AI 7.9.18; 211 Sqn ('X') 30.9.18; EA BU in air, shared B7626 & E8962 11.00 4.11.18 (2/Lt WG Watson & Sgt Obs C Lamont); Delivering 211 Sqn m/c to 98 Sqn demobilisation unit, FL due to weather conditions 28.2.19 (Lt A Adams of 98 Sqn shock and abrasions); 1 ASD 3.3.19

D552 At 7 AAP Kenley 16.9.18 for 117 Sqn (Mob) Norwich as a training m/c; To Sqn 23.9.18 - 10.18

D553 At Burton-on-Trent W/E 10.10.18; 6 SD Ascot W/E 31.10.18 for Mudros; Shipped W/E 21.11.18

D554 Arr 'X' AD ex UK 24.11.18; Salonika AP 3.4.19; 17 Sqn 26.7.19

D555 Deld 7 AAP Kenley by 10.18; 4 ASD to 218 Sqn 16.10.18; 98 Sqn 21.1.19; 8 AAP Lympne 12.2.19

D556 3 ASD to 104 Sqn 27.10.18; Rec Pk 21.1.19; To

England 2.4.19

D557 Rep Pk 2 ASD to 2 AI 14.10.18; 98 Sqn 28.10.18; Bombing raid to Mons Rlwy Stn, combat with 30 EA, Fokker DVII crashed nr Mons 11.30 30.10.18 (2/Lt JM Brown & Sgt Mech T Tedder unhurt); 8 AAP Lympne 12.2.19; Crashed San Stefano 1923 (207 Sqn?)

D558 Rec Pk to 1 AI 4.10.18; 98 Sqn but on landing at sqn one wheel caught the wing of another m/c 29.10.18 (2/Lt JW Brown OK); Rep Pk 1 ASD 1.11.18; 103 Sqn by 3.19; 8 AAP Lympne 14.3.19

D559 Rec Pk to 1 AI 4.10.18; 206 Sqn by 11.18; 104 Sqn ('E'); 49 Sqn handed in to 1 ASD 15.7.19

D560 Deld 7 AAP Kenley by 9.18; Rec Pk to 1 AI 1.10.18; 206 Sqn by 10.18; Left 07.45, shot down 08.30 nr Aelbecke by Oblt H Auffahrt (his 23rd) 5.10.18 (Lt CT Knight USAS & 2/Lt JH Perring both PoW)

D561 At Burton-on-Trent W/E 10.10.18; 6 SD Ascot W/E 31.10.18 for Mudros; Shipped W/E 21.11.18; TOC Base Depot RAF Novorossisk 14.2.20; Sold to Anti-Bolshevik Government

D562 Arr 'X' AD ex UK 18.11.18; 269 Sqn Port Said 23.11.18; 'B' Flt 142 Sqn Suez 18.3.19; ASD Egypt 12.8.19

D563 No information

D564 3 ASD to 104 Sqn 18.9.18 TOC 6 AP 24.10.18; 3 ASD 31.10.18

D565 Rep Pk 1 ASD to 1 AI 23.9.18; 211 Sqn 26.9.18; Left 11.30 for bombing raid on Courtrai, shot down in flames in running fight Cambrai - Ypres 11.30 29.9.18 (1/Lt W Henley-Mooney USAS PoW wounded & 2/Lt VA Fair MC killed)

D566 7 AAP Kenley by 9.18; 2 AI to 107 Sqn 2.10.18; 98 Sqn 5.3.19; To England 13.3.19

D567 No information

D568 Rec Pk to 1 AI 26.9.18; 211 Sqn 30.9.18; Bombing raid, hit by AA over Menin, badly damaged, COL 2.10.18 (2/Lt PM Keary & 2/Lt RM Alston unhurt); to Rep Pk 1 ASD; Used in Burma postwar for a survey of the Irrawaddy River

D569 Rec Pk to 1 AI 2.10.18; 206 Sqn ('A') 10.18; Fokker DVII in flames nr Lendelede, shared D5782 14.40 14.10.18 (Capt RNG Atkinson MC & 2/Lt JS Blanford); Badly smashed Jahlay-Saart 19.4.19; to 1 ASD

D570 Rep Pk 2 ASD to 5 AI 4.10.18; 27 Sqn 10.18; Pilot wounded in raid on Mons, FL at Serny, 28.10.18 (Lt E Bryant wounded & Lt WG Lacey OK); Back at sqn 29.10.18; 98 Sqn 6.3.19; Waddon 13.3.19 (for Salvage Depot, Croydon Factory)

D571 No information

D572 Rep Pk 2 ASD to 2 AI 13.10.18; 27 Sqn 26.10.18; Left 12.25 on bombing raid on Valenciennes, shot up, FL 4.11.18 (2/Lt HD Williams & 2/Lt HB Smith both unhurt); 2 ASD 4.11.18

D573 Arr 'X' AD ex UK 18.11.18; 269 Sqn Port Said 23.11.18; 'A' Flt 142 Sqn Suez 18.3.19; Crashed 27.4.19 (Lt HM Fletcher & AC Johnson)
BUT 1 Observers School Eastchurch by 10.18 - @12.18

D574 & D575 No information

D576 Deld 7 AAP Kenley by 10.18; SMOP Dover by 11.18

D577 No information

D578 Aerial Co-operation School, Cowes to RAE 8.7.19; Retd Aerial Co-operation School, Cowes 22.7.19

D579 Deld 7 AAP Kenley by 10.18; 4 SoN&BD Thetford to 10 TDS Harling Road 5.11.18

D580 Deld 7 AAP Kenley by 10.18; Naval Flt 219 Sqn Manston 30.10.18 - @16.12.18

D581 No information

D582 7 AAP Kenley by 10.18; Rec Pk to 98 Sqn 23.11.18; Ran into ditch on landing 26.12.18 (Lt JHW Haswell & AM3 AS Jay OK); 1 ASD 7.1.19

D583 7 AAP Kenley by 10.18

D584 Rep Pk 2 ASD to 2 AI 25.10.18; 104 Sqn, crashed & WO 21.1.19; Rec Pk 21.1.19

D585 At Burton-on-Trent W/E 10.10.18; 6 SD Ascot W/E 31.10.18 for Mudros; Shipped W/E 21.11.18
BUT Imperial Gift to India

D586 No information

D587 491 Flt 233 Sqn Dover

D588 At 7 AAP Kenley 21.12.18 reallotted from EF to SE Area for Wireless Telephony School, Bournemouth

D589 7 AAP Kenley by 10.18

D590 2 ASD to 218 Sqn 14.12.18; 98 Sqn 21.1.19; Retd UK 15.2.19

D591 No information

D592 1 ASD to 108 Sqn 23.11.18; 103 Sqn 24.1.19

D593 Aerial Co-operation School, Cowes to RAE 8.7.19; Retd Aerial Co-operation School, Cowes 22.7.19

D594 No information

D595 48 TDS Waddington by 1.19

D596 No information

D597 At Burton-on-Trent W/E 10.10.18; 6 SD Ascot W/E 31.10.18 for Mudros; Shipped W/E 21.11.18; Presumably not shipped; 491 Flt 233 Sqn Dover by 16.12.18; Bad weather, FL Dungeness, slightly damaged 20.12.18 (2/Lt HH Lewis & 2/Lt RA Darby OK); 212 Sqn by 2.19

D598 At 7 AAP Kenley 9.10.18 for 119 Sqn (Mob) Wyton; To sqn there 13.10.18; Reallotted by 18.11.18; 73 Wing Yarmouth, stalled and crashed 5.12.18 (2/Lt L Leeming DoI & 2/Lt ED Warren killed)

D599 & D600 No information

D601 7 AAP Kenley by 10.18; 108 Sqn? ('D'); Imperial Gift to India

D602 206 Sqn Helwan ex France 29.7.19; 47 Sqn ('T', named 'NIOBE') by 6.20 - @7.20

D603 No information

D604 At 7 AAP Kenley 15.10.18 for 117 Sqn (Mob) Norwich; To sqn 23.11.18; With 117 Sqn to Tallaght 23.3.19; Midland Area FIS Lilbourne by 1.19(?) - 9.19

D605 4 ASD to 218 Sqn 16.10.18; Left at Fréthun 27.10.18

D606 Last wartime delivery. 206 Sqn Helwan ex France 10.8.19; ASD Aboukir 14.8.19

D607 ASD to 107 Sqn 15.11.18; 98 Sqn 5.3.19; 8 AAP Lympne 14.3.19

D608 No information

D609 Rep Pk 2 ASD to 2 AI 30.10.18; 107 Sqn 4.11.18; 98 Sqn 1.3.19; 8 AAP Lympne 6.3.19

D610 At 7 AAP Kenley 15.10.18 for 117 Sqn (Mob) Norwich; At sqn by 31.10.18

D611 Imperial Gift to India

D612 534 Flt 273 Sqn Covehithe by 5.11.18 - @22.11.18; HACPs 5.11.18 & 7.11.18; Imperial Gift to India

Believed to be Flight Commanders visiting Martlesham Heath for instruction, D.H.9 D601 'D' nearest. (H.S.Clark)

D.H.9 D602 'D', named 'NIOBE', of No.47 Squadron in the Middle East around June-July 1920. (via Philip Jarrett)

D613 Rec Pk to 1 AI 22.10.18; 108 Sqn 24.10.18; EA OOC 4.11.18; EA OOC Sotteghem 09.40-10.10 4.11.18 shared C2216, E676, E8959, E8980, E9026, F1118; EA OOC E of Sotteghem shared C2216, D5845, D7357, E8980 & E9028 09.05 9.11.18 (both Capt R Russell & Lt JE Hermon); 98 Sqn 23.1.19; 8 AAP Lympne 13.2.19
D614 6 AI to 107 Sqn 14.1.19; 98 Sqn 5.3.19; 8 AAP Lympne 14.3.19
D615 No information
D616 At 7 AAP Kenley 18.10.18 for 117 Sqn (Mob) Norwich; To sqn 29.10.18 - 11.18
D617 No information
D618 Deld at NAF Waddon W/E 10.10.18; 6 SD Ascot W/E 24.10.18 for Mudros; Shipped W/E 21.11.18; Sold to Anti-Bolshevik Government; Later Soviet Russian Air Fleet (RKKVF)
D619 At 7 AAP Kenley 29.10.18 for 120 Sqn (Mob) Bracebridge; To sqn 31.10.18 - @15.11.18
D620 Deld at NAF Waddon W/E 10.10.18; 6 SD Ascot W/E 24.10.18 for Mudros; Shipped W/E 21.11.18; Sold to Anti-Bolshevik Government; In service with Soviet Russian Air Force (RKKVF) by 11.20
D621 No information
D622 Deld at NAF Waddon W/E 10.10.18; 6 SD Ascot W/E 24.10.18 for Mudros; Shipped W/E 21.11.18; Sold to Anti-Bolshevik Government
D623 7 AAP Kenley by 10.18
D624 & D626 No information
D627 7 AAP Kenley by 10.18
D628 At 7 AAP Kenley 29.10.18 for 120 Sqn (Mob) Bracebridge; To sqn ('A4') 30.10.18, took woollen goods and food to Belgium to relieve scarcity there 1.19; Used on Cologne-Folkestone air mail service 3.19; still with 120 Sqn at Hawkinge 3.19 - 8.19
D629 To Greek Government
D630 RAE (supercharger experiments)
D631 to D634 No information
D635 At 7 AAP Kenley 29.10.18 for 120 Sqn (Mob) Bracebridge; At sqn by 9.12.18; 1 ASD Marquise 4.3.19; 98 Sqn to Rec Pk 16.3.19
D636 1 ASD to 103 Sqn 26.11.18; 98 Sqn 16.3.19; 1 ASD 17.3.19; 206 Sqn Helwan ex France 29.7.19; ASD Aboukir 16.10.19; WO 13.11.19
D637 No information
D638 At 7 AAP Kenley 30.1.19 reallotted from EF to Store; Imperial Gift to South Africa as *117*
D639 No information
D640 To Greek Government
D641 & D643 No information
D644 Deld at NAF Waddon W/E 10.10.18; 6 SD Ascot W/E 24.10.18 for Mudros; Shipped W/E 21.11.18; ASD Aboukir ex UK 6.1.20
D645 Deld at NAF Waddon W/E 10.10.18 for Mudros; Imperial Gift to India
D646 To Greek Government
D647 No information
D648 49 Sqn, handed in to 1 ASD 14.7.19
D649 'Z' Unit .19; Crashed Berbera, British Somaliland 15.2.20
D650 IAAD; Imperial Gift to India, shipped SS *Hatimura* 8.20
D651 (240hp Puma) Sold to Estonian Government; To Estonian AF as *No.28*
D652 ASD Mesopotamia, WO 13.11.19
D653 No information
D654 To Greek Government
D655 & D656 No information
D657 Imperial Gift to South Africa as *111*
D658 At 7 AAP Kenley 30.1.19 reallotted from EF to Store; To Greek Government
D659 At 7 AAP Kenley 30.1.19 reallotted from EF to Store; Imperial Gift to South Africa
D660 (240hp Puma) Sold to Estonian Government; To Estonian AF as *No.30*; Crashed Tallinn 1.20
D661 Ferrying, FL Lopcombe Corner 12.9.19
D662 No information
D663 Imperial Gift to South Africa
D664 CFS Upavon by 15.5.18; To Greek Government
D665 Imperial Gift to South Africa as *118*
D666 To Greek Government
D667 To Greek Government
D668 Rec Pk to 1 AI 3.9.18; Imperial Gift to South Africa as *104*
D669 'Z' Unit; Crashed El Afwena, British Somaliland 31.1.20
D670 Imperial Gift to South Africa
D671 To Greek Government
D672 & D673 No information
D674 England to Rec Pk 7.10.18; 2 AI 10.10.18; 3 ASD 13.10.18; To Greek Government
D675 Imperial Gift to South Africa as *106*
D676 No information
D677 England to Rec Pk 7.10.18; 2 AI 13.10.18; 3 ASD 15.10.18; Imperial Gift to South Africa as *105*
D678 To Greek Government
D679 'Z' Unit by 1.20 - @3.20
D680 Imperial Gift to South Africa
D681 Imperial Gift to South Africa as *108*
D682 No information
D683 Imperial Gift to South Africa as *101*
D684 To Greek Government
D685 No information
D686 To Greek Government
D687 Imperial Gift to South Africa
D688 Imperial Gift to South Africa
D689 No information
D690 Imperial Gift to South Africa as *107*
D691 & D692 No information
D693 (230hp Puma) Sold to Estonian Government; To Estonian AF as *No.29*
D694 At Rep Pk 2 ASD 19.10.18; 27 Sqn; 98 Sqn 5.3.19
D695 Imperial Gift to South Africa as *109*
D696 120 Sqn Bracebridge Heath by 10.18
D697 to D950 cancelled 11.18 (factory closes 31.12.18) - but some further deliveries evidently made from supposedly cancelled range, as follows:
D697 To Greek Government
D698 Imperial Gift to South Africa as *110*
D699 No information
D700 'Z' Unit by 1.20 - @3.20
D703 Imperial Gift to South Africa as *114*
D704 To Greek Government
D705 Imperial Gift to South Africa
D725 Fowlmere ('18') by 10.18
D812 IAAD; Imperial Gift to India, shipped SS *Hatimura* 8.20

500 D.H.9 ordered 15.10.17 under Cont No A.S.32754/17 (BR.162 & 638) from Crossley Motors/ National Aircraft Factory No.2, Heaton Chapel and numbered D1001 to D1500. (230hp Puma)

D1001 117 Sqn Beaulieu from 6.18; EF, attempted to turn back, spun in, BO, Hucknall 3.7.18 (2/Lt HL Prior killed)
D1002 At 4 AAP Lincoln 2.4.18, allotted to EF; England to Rec Pk 25.4.18; 49 Sqn 30.4.18; Fokker Drl OOC Suzanne 16.15 17.5.18 (Lt FD Nevin OK & Lt HP Roberts wounded); Left 05.05 for raid on Bray, last seen Harbonnières 19.5.18 (2/Lt FD Nevin & Sgt H Barfoot both killed)
D1003 4 AAP Lincoln for EF by 6.4.18; England to Rec Pk 19.5.18; 103 Sqn 21.5.18; Pfalz DIII OOC smoking W of Armentières 17.30 13.7.18 (Lt J Austin-Sparks & Lt FM Loly); Raid on Armentières 31.7.18 (Lt MS Lewin OK & 2/Lt K Nixon wounded); Pfalz DIII crashed Lomme 08.30hrs 10.8.18; Fokker DVII crashed S of Armentières 11.15 25.8.18 (both Capt J Austin-Sparks & Lt FM Loly); Crashed on practice flight 4.11.18 (Lt SW Taylor & Lt WBH Eaton OK); Rep Pk 2 ASD 9.11.18
D1004 44 TS Waddington, starting accident 1.6.18 (Boy PH Bowers injured)
D1005 44 TS Waddington by 6.18 - 7.18
D1006 Deld 491 Flt Dover W/E 24.5.18; Bercq 7.6.18; 218 Sqn, COL from raid 21.6.18 (Lt W Bentley & 2/Lt AJ Cunningham both unhurt); To 4 ASD; 2 SS Richborough 2.10.18
D1007 At 4 AAP Lincoln 11.5.18, allotted to EF; England to Rec Pk 22.5.18; 103 Sqn 25.5.18; Scout in flames & another OOC Fretoy, 7m SW of Hour, shared C6179, C6192 & D5569 16.20 6.6.18; "Pfalz-type" OOC Lagny 18.30 9.6.18 (both 2/Lt IW Leiper & 1/Pte J Buffery); Left 19.45, last seen E of lines going east 9.6.18 (Lt EA Windridge & 2/Lt VW Allen both killed); SOC 11.6.18

D.H.9 D1001 bears the inscription the rear fuselage: 'BUILT BY CROSSLEY MOTORS LTD AEROPLANE WORKS MANCHESTER'. It was the first aircraft from National Aircraft Factory No.2'. (J.M.Bruce/G.S.Leslie collection)

D1008 At 4 AAP Lincoln 14.5.18, allotted to EF; England to Rec Pk 26.5.18; 2 AI 27.5.18; 99 Sqn 30.5.18; 104 Sqn 31.5.18; Left 05.00 for bombing raid on Landau Stn, formation attacked both on way and return, shot up by EA 30.6.18 (2/Lt FH Beaufort (US) & 2/Lt CGV Pickard); 3 ASD 30.6.18; 99 Sqn 15.8.18; 3 ASD 25.9.18; 99 Sqn 27.10.18; Hit by shrapnel 6.11.18 (pilot 2/Lt LV Russell wounded); 6 AP 9.11.18; 3 ASD 12.11.18

D1009 Presentation Aircraft 'River Plate'.

D1010 At 4 AAP Lincoln 24.5.18, reallotted from Training Division to EF; Then reallotted to E.1C for 61 Wing for 218 Sqn (Mob) Dover; 491 Flt Dover by 25.5.18 (W/E 1.6.18); 98 Sqn 4.6.18; Left 07.30 on raid, signal to return was given due to bad weather, seen gliding down into cloud and apparently got into spin 16.6.18 (Lt LW Strugnell & Sgt C Lomax both killed); Rep Pk 1 ASD 17.6.18; SOC 21.6.18

D1011 5 TS Wyton, prop accident 15.8.18 (Pte TR Keefore USAS of 151st US Sqn injured)

D1012 At 4 AAP Lincoln 27.5.18, allotted to EF; England to Rec Pk 30.5.18; 1 AI 1.6.18; 206 Sqn 7.6.18; Left 03.30 on long reconnaissance, went down east of lines 24.6.18 (Lt WC Cutmore & 2/Lt WG Duncan both killed); SOC in field 25.6.18

D1013 At 4 AAP Lincoln 20.5.18, allotted to EF; England to Rec Pk 27.5.18; 1 AI 28.5.18; 98 Sqn 29.5.18; Left 12.15 for raid on Bruges Docks, shot up by AA, retd 15.00 31.5.18 (Lt IA Peers USA & 1/AM D Wentworth who was awarded DFM for act of gallantry on this operation); SOC 1 ASD 5.7.18 NWR

D1014 9 TDS Shawbury by 10.18 - 3.19

D1015 At 4 AAP Lincoln 8.6.18, allotted to EF; Rec Pk to 1 AI 23.6.18; 206 Sqn 25.6.18; Pfalz DIII shot down 1½m E of Ypres 19.20-19.35 29.7.18 (2/Lt JFS Percival & 2/Lt FJ Paget); Pfalz crashed 2m SW of Menin 08.30 1.8.18 (2/Lt JFS Percival OK & 2/Lt FJ Paget wounded); COL 9.8.18 (Lt AJ Garside & 2/Lt C Hancock unhurt); Rep Pk 1 ASD 10.8.18; SOC 13.8.18 NWR; Rebuilt as F6453 23.8.18

D1016 Presentation Aircraft 'Jamnagar No.2'; At 4 AAP Lincoln 22.5.18, allotted to EF; Rec Pk to 2 AI 1.9.18; 107 Sqn 5.9.18; Bombing raid on St.Quentin, EA OOC but damaged by enemy action, FL, crashed 27.9.18 (2/Lt HW Gill & 2/Lt JR Thompson unhurt); SOC Rep Pk 2 ASD 3.10.18

D1017 218 Sqn, COL after raid on Ostende 5.7.18 (Lt W Bentley & 2/Lt AJ Cunningham); 4 ASD 5.7.18; 2 SS Richborough 15.9.18

D1018 FF 4 AAP Lincoln 3.6.18; 1 FS Turnberry ('A-09'), crashed probably due to a temporary loss of control during a climbing turn while testing Lewis gun 21.6.18 (Lt HB Redler & Capt IHD Henderson both killed); That the crew changed places in flight was not held to have been a contributory factor

D1019 At 4 AAP Lincoln 8.6.18, allotted to EF; Rec Pk to 2 AI 27.6.18; 99 Sqn ('C') 28.6.18; Practice flight, wrecked 14.8.18 (2/Lt DF Brooks & 2/Lt R Buckby); 3 ASD 14.8.18

D1020 No information

D1021 At 4 AAP Lincoln 30.5.18, reallotted from Training Division to EF; England to Rec Pk 30.5.18; 1 AI 31.5.18; 211 Sqn ('K') 2.6.18; Sideslipped, COL 25.6.18 (2/Lt HH Palmer & Pte1 WJ Atkinson); Rep Pk 1 ASD 26.6.18; SOC 29.6.18 NWR

D1022 At 4 AAP Lincoln 1.6.18, allotted to EF; 1 AI to 98 Sqn 14.6.18; On landing swerved to avoid another m/c and crashed 9.7.18 (2/Lt WV Thomas & 2/Lt GK Carruthers OK); To Rep Pk 1 ASD 10.7.18; SOC 13.7.18 NWR

D1023 At 4 AAP Lincoln 21.6.18, reallotted from 61 Wing to EF; Rec Pk to 1 AI 1.7.18; 103 Sqn 6.7.18; Left on reconnaissance 03.40, last seen W of lines going north 9.7.18 (2/Lt RH Dunn & 2/Lt HC Hinchcliffe both PoW)

D1024 At 4 AAP Lincoln 1.6.18, allotted to EF; 1 AI to 206 Sqn 18.6.18; Fokker DVII in flames W of Sotteghem 15.25-15.40 30.10.18 (Lt AJ Garside & Sgt J Chapman DFM); Left in open when sqn arrived Nivelles, wings and fuselage became warped, for 8 SS overhaul 14.4.19

D1025 AES Orfordness by 6.18; AES Martlesham Heath by 10.18

D1026 At 4 AAP Lincoln 7.6.18, allotted to EF; Rec Pk to 2 AI 23.6.18; 99 Sqn 25.6.18; Albatros D OOC 10m SW of Strasbourg 07.00 20.7.18 (Lt G Broadbent & Sgt J Jones); Engine hit, FL nr Baccarat 22.7.18 (Lt G Broadbent & Sgt J Jones); 3 ASD 22.7.18; 104 Sqn 15.9.18; 3 ASD 17.9.18

D1027 7th (T) Wing by 6.18

D1028 Rec Pk to 4 ASD 9.7.18; 218 Sqn 31.7.18; Hit by AA, FL on beach 2m E of Zeebrugge, wrecked, shelled and destroyed, submerged by tide 11.8.18 (Lt WS Mars & 2/Lt HE Power both unhurt); 4 ASD 12.8.18; 2 SS Richborough 15.9.18

D1029 Rec Pk to 2 AI 22.7.18; 3 ASD and on to 99 Sqn

24.7.18; FTR from Saarbrücken raid 31.7.18, missing after combat over St.Avold (Lt F Smith & 2/Lt KH Ashton both PoW)

D1030 3 FS Sedgeford by 10.18

D1031 No information

D1032 Rec Pk to 2 AI 16.7.18; 3 ASD 17.7.18; 99 Sqn 17.7.18; Scout crashed W of Molsheim, shared C6196 16.00 22.7.18 (2/Lt LV Dennis & 2/Lt FW Woolley); FTR from Saarbrücken raid, in combat with 40 EA over St Avold/N of Dieutze 31.7.18 (2/Lt LV Dennis & 2/Lt FW Woolley both killed)

D1033 3 FS Sedgeford, stalled and spun in 4.11.18 (2/Lt TT Williams injured & Lt FL Mitchell slightly injured)

D1035 Midland Area FIS Lilbourne by 9.18

D1036 No information

D1037 Midland Area FIS Lilbourne by 9.18

D1038 At 4 AAP Lincoln 28.6.18, reallotted from SE Area to EF; Rec Pk to 1 AI 3.7.18; 107 Sqn 9.7.18; Crashed in sunken road landing at new aerodrome 15.7.18 (2/Lt G Beveridge injured & 2/Lt WH Newman seriously injured)

D1039 3 FS Bircham Newton by 9.18; 35 TDS Duxford by 9.18?

D1040 No information

D1041 9 TDS Shawbury by 10.18 - 1.19

D1042 Tested 1 AAP Coventry 30.6.18; 3 FS Bircham Newton by 7.18 - 8.18

D1043 Presentation Aircraft 'Newfoundland No.1'; In Ireland by 1.19

D1044 At Makers 19.6.18 for 109 Sqn (Mob) Lake Down; 1 AAP Coventry 3.7.18; To Sqn 20.7.18; Reallotted to IF 29.7.18; Rec Pk to 2 AI and on to 3 ASD 31.7.18; 99 Sqn 4.8.18; Crashed outside aerodrome on practice flight 19.8.18 (Lt JL Hunter & Lt TH Swann); 3 ASD 19.8.18

D1045 No information

D1046 Presentation Aircraft 'Zanzibar No.8'; At Makers 26.6.18, allotted to EF; To 4 AAP Lincoln; Rec Pk to 2 AI 28.7.18; 5 AI 30.7.18; Lost while ferrying to 9th Brigade area and captured 31.7.18 (Lt DC Townley PoW)

D1047 At Makers 19.6.18 for 109 Sqn (Mob) Lake Down; 1 AAP Coventry 9.7.18; Reallotted SE Area 29.7.18; 491 Flt 233 Sqn Dover 31.7.18 - @12.18; 120 Sqn Hawkinge by 7.19

D1048 Tested 1 AAP Coventry 17.7.18 [prefix?]; Rec Pk to 2 AI 3.8.18; 3 ASD 4.8.18; 104 Sqn 12.8.18; Raid on Mannheim, in combat with EAs, FTR 22.8.18 (2/Lt RJ Searle PoW & 2/Lt CGV Pickard killed)

D1049 At 4 AAP Lincoln 28.6.18, reallotted from SE Area to EF; 8 AAP Lympne to Rec Pk 6.7.18; 1 AI 7.7.18; 107 Sqn 15.7.18; Left 05.40 for raid on Brie Bridge, in combat with 7 Fokker DVII, 1 shot down SW of Villers Carbonnel 9.8.18 (2/Lt FT Stott & AM WJ Palmer); Fokker DVII shot down 4.9.18; FL in shelled area due to engine failure 28.10.18 (2/Lt O Lane & Sgt SG Walker OK)

D1050 Presentation Aircraft 'Jamnagar No.1'. At Makers 26.6.18, allotted to EF; To 4 AAP Lincoln; England to Rec Pk 8.8.18; 2 AI 10.8.18; 3 ASD 12.8.18; 104 Sqn 13.8.18; Hit in raid on Metz-Sablon Railway 13.9.18 (2/Lt RH Rose OK & 2/Lt TJ Bond wounded); FTR raid on Buhl aerodrome 6.11.18 (2/Lt HL Wren & 2/Lt WH Tresham both PoW)

D1051 Presentation a/c 'Zanzibar No.12'; At Makers 26.6.18, allotted to EF; To 4 AAP Lincoln; Rec Pk to 206 Sqn 28.7.18; Pfalz DIII BU in air Neuve-Eglise 07.25 7.8.18 (Lt EA Burn & Capt WA Carrothers); Throttle came off in air, FL nr aerodrome 1.10.18 (Lt HW Campbell & 2/Lt CO Thompson)

D1052 At 4 AAP Lincoln 25.7.18 for 109 Sqn (Mob) Lake Down; Reallotted SE Area 29.7.18; 491 Flt 233 Sqn Dover by 15.8.18; 218 Sqn 29.9.18; Returning from raid on railway junction nr Bruges, EF, FL on beach, crashed, badly damaged, W of Mardyck 17.10.18 (Sgt GM Rowley & Sgt HG Pearce both unhurt); 4 ASD 19.10.18 - @25.10.18

D1053 At 4 AAP Lincoln 25.7.18 for 109 Sqn (Mob) Lake Down; Reallotted SE Area 29.7.18; 534 Flt 273 Sqn Covehithe by 30.8.18 - @28.10.18; IAAD; Imperial Gift to India, shipped SS *Hatimura* 8.20

D1054 Presentation Aircraft 'Punjan No.6, Nabha'; At Makers 26.6.18, allotted to EF; To 4 AAP Lincoln; Rec Pk to 2 AI 25.7.18; 5 AI 26.7.18; 98 Sqn 28.7.18; Left 05.30 for raid on Feuillères Bridge, last seen gliding down west, east of lines with steam coming from radiator 9.8.18 (Lt F Carpenter & Sgt ER McDonald both PoW); SOC 10.8.18

D1055 Rep Pk 2 ASD to 2 AI 9.8.18; 107 Sqn 10.8.18; Photographic mission, in combat with EA 17.55, oil tank shot up, engine seized, FL, crashed 1.10.18 (2/Lt LE Gooden & 2/Lt WA Smith both unhurt)

D1056 No information

D1057 55 TS Narborough by 9.19; 3 (T) Group Navigation School, Norwich 27.9.19

D1058 203 TDS Manston by 7.18

D1059 55 TDS Manston by 26.7.18

D1060 At Makers 19.6.18 for 109 Sqn (Mob) Lake Down; 1 AAP Coventry 3.7.18; To Sqn 22.7.18; Reallotted to IF 29.7.18; Rec Pk to 2 AI and on to 3 ASD 30.7.18; SOC Rep Pk 2 ASD 24.8.18 NWR

D1061 At Makers 20.6.18 for 109 Sqn (Mob) Lake Down; 1 AAP Coventry 9.7.18; To Sqn 22.7.18; Reallotted to IF 28.7.18; Rec Pk to 2 AI 3.8.18; 3 ASD 4.8.18; 104 Sqn 13.8.18; 3 ASD 23.8.18

D1062 No information

D1063 2 AI to 107 Sqn 14.8.18; Crashed due to broken throttle control 1.10.18 (2/Lt CS Howley & 2/Lt M Witham)

D1064 Rep Pk 1 ASD to Rec Pk and on to 2 AI 10.8.18; 107 Sqn 15.8.18; On practice flight throttle broke, struck telegraph wires on landing 23.9.18 (Lt H Cunningham & Lt AC Garwood OK)

D1065 14 TDS Lake Down by 8.18

D1066 At Makers 19.6.18 for 109 Sqn (Mob) Lake Down; 1 AAP Coventry 3.7.18; To Sqn 20.7.18; Reallotted to IF 29.7.18; England to 2 AI 31.7.18; 3 ASD 4.8.18; 104 Sqn 12.8.18; 3 ASD 21.8.18

D1067 No information

D1068 14 TDS Lake Down by 13.8.18 - @9.18

D.H.9 D1068 was flown by No.14 Training Depot Station at Lake Down in 1918. (W.J.Evans)

D1069 to D1073 No information

D1074 Rep Pk 1 ASD, ferrying to 2 ASD, EF on take-off, badly damaged 8.8.18 (Lt EW Everiss OK); For repair by Rep Pk 1 ASD; Rebuilt as F6450 19.8.18

D1075 Rec Pk to 2 AI 7.8.18; 49 Sqn 9.8.18; Left 16.05, FTR raid on Etreux, hit by AA over Cambrai, last seen gliding down over Mazinghem 25.8.18 (Lt CH Stephens & 2/Lt AB Henderson both PoW)

D1076 & D1077 No information

D1078 557/8 Flts 212 Sqn Yarmouth by 21.8.18 - @10.18

D1079 534 Flt 273 Sqn Covehithe by 5.8.18 - @12.18; AZP 5.8.18 (Lt FR Bicknell & Sgt Bull)

D1080 Rec Pk to 108 Sqn 12.8.18; Fokker DVII crashed and burnt in fight from Oudenburgh to Schoore 17.35-17.55, shared E605 21.8.18 (2/Lt ATW Boswell & 2/Lt W Bolt); In Lichtervelde raid Fokker DrI OOC Gits and Fokker DVII OOC Staden, shared C6314, C6345, D3092, D5622, D5759, E669, E5435 & F5847 11.45 21.9.18 (2/Lt ATW Boswell & 2/Lt W Bolt); Left 12.07 for bombing raid, last seen W of Menin flying W above clouds at 3,000ft 3.10.18 (2/Lt ATW Boswell & 2/Lt RP

Capt D.R.MacLaren DSO MC & Bar DFC of No.46 (Camel) Squadron at Busigny in late October 1918. The D.H.9 is believed to be D1109 of No.98 Squadron which was based about 20 miles away at Abscon. (via Mike O'Connor)

Gundill both killed)

D1081 557/8 Flts 212 Sqn Yarmouth by 14.8.18 - @10.18; Manston to Handley Page, Cricklewood for Polish Military Purchase Mission on free issue 23.3.20

D1082 4 ASD to 218 Sqn 31.8.18; COL from raid, CW 7.9.18 (Lt HP Brumell & Sgt RS Joysey both unhurt); 4 ASD 8.9.18; 2 SS Richborough 15.9.18

D1083 4 ASD to 218 Sqn 16.8.18; COL from raid 31.8.18 (Lt WS Mars & 2/Lt HE Power both unhurt); 4 ASD 1.9.18; 2 SS Richborough 2.10.18

D1084 No information

D1085 4 ASD to 218 Sqn 27.8.18; Fokker DVII OOC NW of Bruges 16.35 15.9.18 (Lt BH Stata & 2/Lt CVR Brown); Met storm returning from raid, BU, spun in, CW, Wulveringhem 28.9.18 (Lt BH Stata & 2/Lt CVR Brown both killed)

D1086 109 Sqn by 6.18; 211 Sqn by 1.11.18; 6 AI by 2.19; 211 Sqn 12.2.19; 98 Sqn 23.2.19; 98 Sqn to 8 AAP Lympne 6.3.19; 206 Sqn Helwan ex France 10.8.19; ASD Aboukir 14.8.19

D1087 No information

D1088 218 Sqn by 29.9.18; FL 1.10.18 (Lt KR Campbell & 2/Lt LA Churchill), retd later; Left at Fréthun when squadron moved 23.10.18, still there 31.10.18

D1089 4 ASD to 218 Sqn 16.8.18; COL from raid on Bruges, badly damaged 22.8.18 (Lt FJ Burslem & 2/Lt B Hutchinson); 4 ASD 23.8.18; 218 Sqn 9.10.18; 98 Sqn 21.1.19; 8 AAP Lympne 12.2.19

D1090 Tested 1 AAP Coventry 18.8.18 [prefix?]

D1091 SOC Rec Pk 23.9.18 destroyed by enemy action

D1092 Tested 1 AAP Coventry 17.8.18 [prefix?]; Rec Pk to 2 AI 6.9.18; 27 Sqn 7.9.18; Fokker DVII OOC W of Bohain 18.15 25.9.18 (Capt JR Webb & 2/Lt WA Hall); Fokker DVII in flames then broke up Busigny, shared D2873 09.45 29.9.18 (Capt JR Webb & 2/Lt WA Hall): Left 09.35 for bombing raid to Mons, damaged by AA, retd 12.30 28.10.18 (Capt JR Webb & 2/Lt LJ Edwardes both OK)

D1093 Tested 1 AAP Coventry 24-25.8.18 [prefix?]

D1094 6 TDS Boscombe Down, stalled on turn at 500ft, spun in 27.10.18 (2/Lt ELR Delteil killed)

D1095 No information

D1096 Marine Observers School Aldeburgh by 10.18; Became 1 MOS Aldeburgh 1.1.19 - @3.19; 120 Sqn Hawkinge by 3.19 - 8.19

D1097 Tested 1 AAP Coventry 18.8.18 [prefix?]; ; Rec Pk to 2 AI 23.8.18; 49 Sqn 2.9.18; In action 24.9.18 (2/Lt EC Moore USAS & 2/Lt L Eteson both wounded); Crashed into shell dump on take off, m/c destroyed by fire 24.11.18 (Lt GW Waddington injured & Sgt Mech B Riley killed)

D1098 Marine Observers School Aldeburgh by 10.18; Became 1 MOS Aldeburgh 1.1.19

D1099 & D1100 No information

D1101 1 SoN&BD Stonehenge by 17.7.19

D1102 Wrecked 26.10.18 SOC

D1103 & D1105 No information

D1106 Rep Pk 1 ASD to Rec Pk 8.9.18; 2 AI 13.9.18; 98 Sqn 17.9.18; Left 07.30 for bombing raid on Bertry aerodrome, in combat with 8 EA, damaged, crashed 27.9.18 (Lt G Richmond & 2/Lt P Fish unhurt); Rep Pk 2 ASD 30.9.18; SOC 3.10.18

D1107 Rep Pk 2 ASD to 2 AI 24.9.18; 107 Sqn by 10.18; Left 10.58 for bombing raid on Mons Station, FTR 9.10.18 (2/Lt DE Webb & 2/Lt JH Thompson both killed)

D1108 Rep Pk 1 ASD to Rec Pk 12.9.18; 2 AI 13.9.18; 49 Sqn 25.9.18; Left 05.55 for bombing raid on Aulnoye Junction, shot up, retd 08.55 9.10.18 (2/Lt WA Crich & Sgt Mech HL Dodson both unhurt)

D1109 2 AI to 5 AI 8.10.18; 98 Sqn ('N/D'?) by 23.10.18; Left 11.30 on bombing raid, radiator shot up in combat with EA Bouvignies, engine seized, FL 1.11.18 (2/Lt HW Whitlock & Mjr E Crewdson unhurt); Rep Pk 1 ASD 5.11.18

D1110 Rep Pk 1 ASD to 1 AI 18.9.18; 108 Sqn 28.9.18; Left 06.23 on solo recce to Ghent, FTR 22.10.18 (2/Lt CF Cave killed & 2/Lt H McNish believed killed)

D1111 Rep Pk 2 ASD to 5 AI 8.10.18; 107 Sqn 10.10.18; Lost bearings, FL, hit sunken road on take off 21.12.18 (2/Lt CW Daggett & Sgt R Reed both slightly injured)

D1112 1 ASD to 98 Sqn 29.10.18; 8 AAP Lympne 7.2.19

D1113 & D1114 No information

D1115 Imperial Gift to Australia; Became *A6-1*

D1116 No information

D1117 35 TDS Duxford by 11.11.18; Turned to port at 400ft after TO, stalled and spun in, BO 24.1.19 (Lt E Nichols

killed)
D1118 117 Sqn by 4.11.18
D1119 Imperial Gift to Australia; Became *A6-2*
D1120 No information
D1121 1 AAP Coventry to Dover 23.9.18
D1122 491 Flt 233 Sqn Dover to 4 ASD Audembert 26.9.18; 218 Sqn 29.9.18; Fokker DVII OOC Lichtervelde 0935 29.9.18 (Lt JH Sprott & 2/Lt SJ Lewin); 98 Sqn 21.1.19; 8 AAP Lympne 12.2.19;
D1123 202 Sqn for evaluation by 10.18, crashed; AP 4 ASD 24.10.18 (then taken in hand 4 ASD)
D1124 No information
D1125 1 TDS Wittering by 12.11.18
D1126 1 TDS Wittering by 13.11.18
D1127 Imperial Gift to Australia; Became *A6-3*
D1128 No information
D1129 NE Area FIS Redcar by 10.18 - @11.19; Imperial Gift to Australia; Became *A6-4*
D1130 3 FS Bircham Newton by 10.18; 52 TDS Cramlington by 10.18
D1131 52 TDS Cramlington by 10.18
D1132 5 TDS Easton-on-the-Hill .18; 117 Sqn by 11.18
D1133 & D1134 No information
D1135 3 FS Bircham Newton by 10.18
D1136 No information
D1137 4 ASD Audembert to 218 Sqn 29.9.18 - @LM 18.10.18
D1138 to D1140 No information
D1141 Recd 'X' AD ex UK 24.11.18; 206 Sqn Helwan 16.7.19
D1142 Recd 'X' AD ex UK 24.11.18; Salonika AP 19.2.19; 47 Sqn for service in South Russia 21.4.19; At Ekaterindodar with 47 Sqn by 3.6.19; Crashed at aerodrome 18.7.19 (Lt AH Day & Lt ST Fripp); W/O 19.8.19.
D1143 Recd 'X' AD ex UK 24.11.18; 'A' Flt 142 Sqn Suez 22.1.19; RAF North Russia by 8.19; ; In service with Soviet Russian Air Force (RKKVF) by 12.20

The wreckage of D.H.9 D1149 'Z' of No.206 Squadron, Helwan, after crashing into a building and demolishing the top storey on 22.11.19. (via Philip Jarrett)

D1144 Recd 'X' AD ex UK 24.11.18; Salonika AP 3.4.19; 17 Sqn 26.7.19
D1145 Recd 'X' AD ex UK 24.11.18; Salonika AP 3.4.19; 17 Sqn 26.7.19
D1146 Recd 'X' AD ex UK 24.11.18; Salonika AP 3.4.19; 17 Sqn 26.7.19
D1147 Recd 'X' AD ex UK 24.11.18; Salonika AP 3.4.19; 17 Sqn 26.7.19
D1148 Recd 'X' AD ex UK 24.11.18; Salonika AP 3.4.19
D1149 Recd 'X' AD ex UK 24.11.18; 206 Sqn ('Z') 16.7.19; Crashed into building and demolished top storey, WO 22.11.19
D1150 Recd 'X' AD ex UK 24.11.18; Salonika AP 21.2.19; WO 7.3.19
D1151 Sold to Anti-Bolshevik Government; TOC Base Depot RAF Novorossisk 14.2.20
D1152 To Greek Government
D1153 Sold to Anti-Bolshevik Government; TOC Base Depot RAF Novorossisk 14.2.20; To 7 Sqn Russian Aviation Corps 14.2.20; In service with Soviet Russian Air Force (RKKVF) as "84/1153" by 10.23
D1154 5 TDS Easton-on-the-Hill 1918; Midland Area FIS Lilbourne by 1.19 - 2.19
D1155 Recd 'X' AD ex UK 24.11.18
D1156 Recd 'X' AD ex UK 24.11.18
D1157 Recd 'X' AD ex UK 24.11.18; 6 TDS Boscombe Down
D1158 & D1159 No information
D1160 7 TDS Feltwell, prop accident 29.10.18 (1/AM EC Humphrey seriously injured) [prefix?]
D1161 Rep Pk 2 ASD to 2 AI 26.10.18; 49 Sqn 2.11.18; 2 AI 8.12.18, exchanged for D.H.9A
D1162 No information
D1163 Rep Pk 2 ASD by 22.10.18; 2 AI 24.10.18; 49 Sqn ('Z') 1.11.18; 1 ASD 14.7.19

D.H.9 D1163 'Z' of No.49 Squadron, flown by Lt J.F.Higgins, seen at Bavai on 1.4.19. (via Cross & Cockade)

D1164 46 TS Catterick by 9.18 - 10.18
D1165 Rep Pk 2 ASD to 2 AI 24.10.18; 218 Sqn 2.11.18; Pfalz DIII in flames NW of Hautmont 11.35 4.11.18 (Lt JRA Barnes & Sgt F Smith); 8 AAP Lympne 14.1.19
D1166 Rec Pk to 1 AI 14.10.18; 108 Sqn 16.10.18; Returning from raid overshot, took off to avoid running into hangar but u/c hit roof 19.10.18 (Lt JD Sloss & Sgt W Greenwood OK); SOC 20.10.18
D1167 206 Sqn, ferry flight, crashed Sitault 1.12.18 (Sgt Mech JW Duffield Harding & Sgt G Woodgate both injured)
D1168 RAF North Russia by 7.19
D1169 At 15 AAP Manchester 8.10.18 for 119 Sqn (Mob) Wyton; With sqn by 22.10.18; Reallotted by 18.11.18
D1170 At 15 AAP Manchester 8.10.18 for 119 Sqn (Mob) Wyton; With sqn by 22.10.18; Reallotted by 18.11.18
D1171 At 15 AAP Manchester 8.10.18 for 119 Sqn (Mob) Wyton; With sqn by 22.10.18; Reallotted by 18.11.18; 25 TS Thetford by 12.18; 6 AI by 1.19; 211 Sqn 2.1.19; 98 Sqn 23.2.19; 8 AAP Lympne 8.3.19
D1172 At 15 AAP Manchester 8.10.18 for 119 Sqn (Mob) Wyton; FL at Madby en route to sqn 29.10.18; At sqn by 4.11.18; Reallotted by 18.11.18; At Wyton 21.12.18 reallotted from EF to Midland Area; 35 TDS Duxford by 6.1.19
D1173 At 15 AAP Manchester 8.10.18 for 119 Sqn (Mob) Wyton; With sqn by 29.10.18; Reallotted by 18.11.18;

At Wyton 21.12.18 reallotted from EF to Midland Area

D1174 At 15 AAP Manchester 8.10.18 for 119 Sqn (Mob) Wyton; With sqn by 29.10.18; Reallotted by 18.11.18; At Wyton 21.12.18 reallotted from EF to Midland Area

D1175 At 15 AAP Manchester 8.10.18 for 119 Sqn (Mob) Wyton; With sqn by 29.10.18; Reallotted by 18.11.18

D1176 At 15 AAP Manchester 11.10.18 for 120 Sqn (Mob) Bracebridge as a training m/c; To sqn 30.10.18; Midland Area FIS Lilbourne by 23.9.19 [prefix?]

D1177 Presentation Aircraft 'Britons in Chile No.1'; At 15 AAP Manchester 11.10.18 for 120 Sqn (Mob) Bracebridge as a training m/c; Still at 15 AAP 2.1.19; 120 Sqn Hawkinge by 3.19 - 8.19

D1178 At 15 AAP Manchester 12.10.18 for 120 Sqn (Mob) Bracebridge as a training m/c; To sqn 26.10.18; Wyton 1.19

D1179 Midland Area FIS Lilbourne by 1.19

D1180 4 SoN&BD Thetford 11.18; Sideslipped in 6.1.19 (2/Lt C Marks killed)

D1181 At 15 AAP Manchester 18.10.18 for 117 Sqn (Mob) Norwich; To sqn 29.10.18; EF, crashed in sea flying from Gormanston 25.7.19

D1182 At 15 AAP Manchester 16.10.18 for 117 Sqn (Mob) Norwich; To sqn 29.10.18; 4 SoN&BD Thetford by 11.18

D1183 At 15 AAP Manchester 16.10.18 for 117 Sqn (Mob) Norwich; At sqn by 2.11.18

D1184 No information

D1185 At 15 AAP Manchester 16.10.18 for 117 Sqn (Mob) Norwich; To sqn 2.11.18

D1186 No information

D1187 Imperial Gift to Australia; Became *A6-5*

D1188 At 15 AAP Manchester 16.10.18 for 117 Sqn (Mob) Norwich; To sqn 2.11.18

D1189 No information

D1190 At 15 AAP Manchester 16.10.18 for 117 Sqn (Mob) Norwich; To sqn 7.11.18; Hit telegraph wires on turn 13.12.18 (Capt CC Brill slightly injured & 2/AM TW Moore unhurt)

D1191 35 TDS Duxford by 5.12.18

D1192 At 15 AAP Manchester 22.10.18 for 120 Sqn (Mob) Bracebridge; To sqn 7.11.18; still with 120 Sqn at Hawkinge 3.19 - 8.19

D1193 120 Sqn Hawkinge by 3.19 - 8.19

D1194 No information

D1195 AAP Shotwick by 1.19

D1196 At 15 AAP Manchester 29.10.18 for 120 Sqn (Mob) Bracebridge; AAP Shotwick by 1.19

D1197 At 15 AAP Manchester 1.11.18 for 120 Sqn (Mob) Bracebridge; To sqn ('B') 8.11.18, took woollen goods and food to Belgium to relieve scarcity there 1.19, and with sqn until at least 8.19; To Aircraft Transport & Travel Ltd (used on Belgian service)

D1198 to D1201 No information

D1202 9 TDS Shawbury by 9.12.18

D1203 No information

D1204 At 15 AAP Manchester 29.10.18 for 120 Sqn (Mob) Bracebridge; To sqn 7.11.18; still with 120 Sqn at Hawkinge 3.19 - 8.19; Coded 'C.15' (Turnberry?)

D1205 No information

D1206 At 15 AAP Manchester 29.10.18 for 120 Sqn (Mob) Bracebridge; At sqn by 9.12.18 - @1.19; still with 120 Sqn at Hawkinge 3.19 - 8.19

D1207 At 15 AAP Manchester 29.10.18 for 120 Sqn (Mob) Bracebridge; To sqn 5.11.18

D1208 At 15 AAP Manchester 29.10.18 for 120 Sqn (Mob) Bracebridge; To sqn by 7.11.18 - @1.19

D1209 At 15 AAP Manchester 29.10.18 for 120 Sqn (Mob) Bracebridge; To sqn 8.11.18 - @1.19

D1210 At 15 AAP Manchester 29.10.18 for 120 Sqn (Mob) Bracebridge; On test before delivery, stalled landing 8.11.18 (Lt GR Whittaker seriously injured & Lt E Birch injured)

D1211 Presentation Aircraft 'Faridkot No.2'; At 15 AAP Manchester 29.10.18 for 120 Sqn (Mob) Bracebridge; Still at 15 AAP 27.12.18; OSR&AP Shrewsbury 28.12.18; 47 Sqn by 2.20 - @3.20

D1212 At 15 AAP Manchester 4.11.18 for 120 Sqn (Mob) Bracebridge; To sqn 3.12.18 - @1.19

D1213 At 15 AAP Manchester 29.10.18 for 120 Sqn (Mob) Bracebridge; To sqn 12.11.18 - @1.19; still with 120 Sqn at Hawkinge 3.19 - 8.19

D1214 At 15 AAP Manchester 29.10.18 for 120 Sqn (Mob) Bracebridge; At sqn by 9.12.18 - @1.19; still with 120 Sqn at Hawkinge 3.19 - 8.19

D1215 35 TDS Duxford ('G') 1918

D1216 At 15 AAP Manchester 29.10.18 for 120 Sqn (Mob) Bracebridge; At sqn ('A5') by 9.12.18; still with 120 Sqn at Hawkinge 3.19 - 8.19

D1217 At 15 AAP Manchester 4.11.18 for 120 Sqn (Mob) Bracebridge; To sqn 3.12.18; still with 120 Sqn at Hawkinge 3.19 - 8.19

D1218 54 TDS Fairlop by 11.18; 49 TDS Catterick, crashed in fog 24.11.18 (Lt MWH Mackay & Lt WH Halfpenny both killed)

D1219 At 15 AAP Manchester 4.11.18 for 120 Sqn (mob) Bracebridge; To sqn 13.11.18; In France 21.3.19 reallotted from 120 Sqn to EF

D1220 At 15 AAP Manchester, engine backfired 13.11.18 (2/AM FRN Prosser seriously injured)

D1221 to D1229. Sold to Belgian Government

D1230 to D1237 No information

D1238 Imperial Gift to Australia

D1239 No information

D1240 No information

D1241 No information

D1242 5 TDS Easton-on-the-Hill .18

D1243 491 Flt 233 Sqn Dover

D1244 44 TS Waddington, spun in off flat turn at 100ft 13.8.18 (2/Lt AN Metcalf seriously injured) [prefix?]

D1245 Last wartime delivery

D1246 At 6 SD Ascot 5.12.18 reallotted from EF to Store; Sold to Estonian Government; To Estonian AF as *No.27* (240hp Puma)

D1247 At 6 SD Ascot 5.12.18 reallotted from EF to Store; Imperial Gift to India

D1248 At 6 SD Ascot 5.12.18 reallotted from EF to Store; Imperial Gift to India

D.H.9 D1204 'C.15', believed at Turnberry post-war. (RAF Museum P.17102)

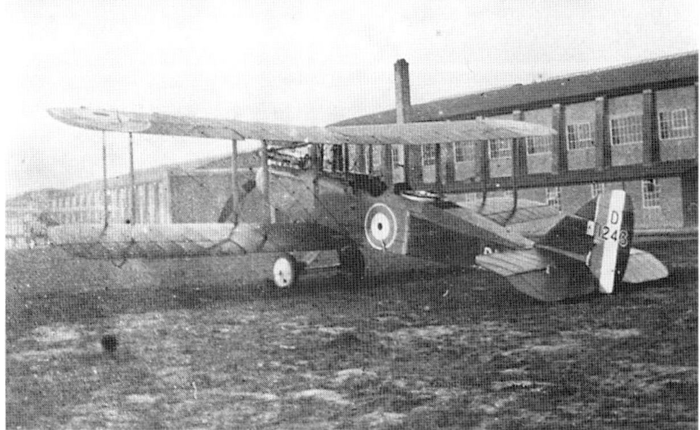

D.H.9 D1243 was flown by No.491 Flt, No.233 Squadron at Dover. (via Mike O'Connor)

D1249 Presentation Aircraft 'Jamnagar No.2'; New aircraft 28.12.18; 15 AAP Manchester by 1.19
D1250 No information
D1251 Presentation Aircraft 'Malaya XXI, The Tanjiak K.M.'; Midland Area AP by 8.19
D1252 Presentation Aircraft 'Presented by British subjects of all Races in Siam'; New aircraft 28.12.18
D1253 Presentation Aircraft 'Zanzibar No.12'; New aircraft 28.12.18.
D1254 Presentation Aircraft 'Presented by the Colony of Mauritius No.2'; New aircraft 28.12.18; 15 AAP Mmanchester by 1.19
D1255 Presentation Aircraft 'Baroda No.16'; New aircraft 28.12.18; 15 AAP Manchester by 1.19; 120 Sqn Hawkinge by 5.19
D1256 No information
D1257 Presentation Aircraft 'Malaya No.27 Bejina'; New aircraft 28.12.18; Imperial Gift to Australia; 15 AAP Disbury by 1.19; Became *A6-7*
D1258 Presentation Aircraft 'Gold Coast No.11'; New aircraft 28.12.18; 15 AAP Manchester by 1.19; 24 Sqn to Croydon for D of R 1.7.19; ACIS 22.8.19; Left 11.19; Manston to Handley Page, Cricklewood for Polish Military Purchase Mission on free issue 23.3.20
D1259 Presentation Aircraft 'Presented by the Colony of Mauritius No.9'; New aircraft 28.12.18
D1260 Presentation Aircraft 'North Queensland Grazier'; New aircraft 28.12.18; 15 AAP Manchester by 1.19
D1261 2 FS Marske by 3.19
D1262 Presentation Aircraft 'Georgetown. Presented by Scottish Munitions Workers'; New aircraft 28.12.18
D1263 Presentation Aircraft 'Gold Coast No.1'; New aircraft 28.12.18; 15 AAP Manchester by 1.19
D1264 to D1272 No information
D1273 6 SD Ascot, allotted Anti-Bolshevik Government for General Denikin; Re-allotted Polish Military Purchase Mission on free issue 22.4.20; Despatched port for shipment in SS *Neptune* 27.4.20
D1274 No information
D1275 6 SD Ascot, allotted Anti-Bolshevik Government for General Denikin; Re-allotted Polish Military Purchase Mission on free issue 22.4.20; Despatched port for shipment in SS *Neptune* 28.4.20
D1276 131 Sqn Shawbury
D1277 131 Sqn Shawbury
D1278 6 SD Ascot, allotted Anti-Bolshevik Government for General Denikin; Re-allotted Polish Military Purchase Mission on free issue 22.4.20; Despatched port for shipment in SS *Neptune* 30.4.20
D1279 to D1281 No information
D1282 Imperial Gift to India
D1283 to D1291 No information
D1292 15 TDS Hucknall by 11.18, EF on TO, spun in 7.2.19 [or C1292]
D1293 & D1294 No information
D1295 Free issue to Chile Government
D1296 Free issue to Chile Government
D1297 To Chile [but not on official list]
D1298 to D1304 No information
D1305 SOC Egypt d/d 22.8.18
D1306 No information
D1307 To Chile [Not on official list]
D1308 Free issue to Chile Government
D1309 & D1314 No information
D1315 6 TDS Boscombe Down by 21.10.18
D1316 109 Sqn by 12.18
D1317 to D1324 No information
D1325 6 SD Ascot, allotted Anti-Bolshevik Government for General Denikin; Re-allotted Polish Military Purchase Mission on free issue 22.4.20; Despatched port for shipment in SS *Neptune* 28.4.20
D1326 Free issue to Chile Government
D1327 Free issue to Chile Government
D1328 49 Sqn, handed in to 1 ASD 15.7.19
D1329 to D1339 No information
D1340 Irish FIS Curragh by 14.12.18
D1341 to D1346 No information
D1347 Became *G-EBEG* (ferry markings)
D1348 No information
D1349 47 Sqn by 9.19
D1350 No information

D.H.9 D1651 of No.44 Training Squadron, Waddington. (RAF Waddington collection)

D1351 47 Sqn by 9.19 - @3.20
D1352 & D1353 No information
D1354 Covehithe; 47 Sqn by 9.19 - @10.19
D1355 Covehithe
D1356 to D1359 No information
D1360 22 TDS Gormanston by 11.18
D1361 to D1374 No information
D1375 47 Sqn by 9.19
D1376 to D1408 No information
D1409 RAF North Russia (Southern Area) by 8.19
D1410 & D1411 No information
D1412 RAF North Russia (Southern Area) by 8.19
D1413 to D1444 No information
D1445 22 TDS Gormanston by 11.18
D1446 22 TDS Gormanston by 23.11.18
D1447 to D1450 No information
D1451 to D1500 cancelled 26.3.19

100 D.H.9 ordered 28.6.17 under Cont No A.S.17994 (BR.113) from Mann, Egerton & Co Ltd, Norwich and numbered D1651 to D1750

D1651 44 TS Waddington
D1652 44 TS Waddington
D1653 Deld 3 AAP Norwich 3.18; Yarmouth W/E 23.3.18; Became 490 Flt Yarmouth by 25.5.18; EF, FL in sea, sank 14.8.18 (crew rescued by F.2A N4542)
D1654 Deld 3 AAP Norwich 3.18; Yarmouth W/E 23.3.18; Became 490 Flt Yarmouth by 25.5.18; 534 Flt 273 Sqn Covehithe by 25.6.18 - @9.18
D1655 Deld 3 AAP Norwich 3.18; Yarmouth W/E 30.3.18; AZP 13.4.18 (F/Cdr E Cadbury & OSL FL Wills); Became 490 Flt Yarmouth by 25.5.18 - @15.6.18; HSMP 10.6.18; Covehithe by 6.18; Manston Naval Flt by 7.18; 534 Flt 273 Sqn Covehithe by 1.8.18 - @15.11.18; 2x100-lb bombs dropped on British submarine *C.25*, missed 8.8.18; 534 Flt 273 Sqn Burgh Castle, HACP 9.11.18
D1656 Deld 3 AAP Norwich 3.18; Yarmouth W/E 30.3.18; AZP 13.4.18 (Capt GWR Fane & OSL S Plowman); Became 490 Flt Yarmouth 25.5.18 (212 Sqn 20.8.18) - @15.10.18
D1657 Shipped from West India Docks to Otranto 27.4.18; AD Taranto by 7.18; 472/4 Flts 226 Sqn Pizzone by 8.18
D1658 Shipped from West India Docks to Otranto 27.4.18; AD Taranto by 7.18; 472/4 Flts 226 Sqn Pizzone by 8.18
D1659 Shipped from West India Docks to Otranto 27.4.18; AD Taranto by 7.18; 472/4 Flts 226 Sqn Pizzone by 8.18; In sea 30m NE of Brindisi during raid on Durazzo 08.05 26.8.18 (Lt JF George & Ptel W Copley)
D1660 Shipped from West India Docks to Otranto 27.4.18; AD Taranto by 7.18; 224 Sqn by 8.18; 66/67 Wing, EF, FL in sea after raid on Durazzo, sank 17.9.18 (2 crew picked up unhurt by Italian destroyer)
D1661 Shipped from West India Docks to Otranto 27.4.18; AD Taranto by 7.18 - @8.18; 224 Sqn by 2.10.18 - @23.10.18; Pizzone by 10.18; 472/4 Flts 226 Sqn

Pizzone
D1662 Shipped from West India Docks to Otranto 27.4.18; 226 Sqn Pizzone by 7.18; Became 472/4 Flts 226 Sqn Pizzone 9.18 - @2.10.18; Mudros by 10.18 - @1.19
D1663 At 3 AAP Norwich 5.4.18, reallotted from E 1C (Dover-Dunkirk) to EF; England to Rec Pk 12.4.18; 206 Sqn 19.4.18; Badly damaged by AA 3.5.18 (Lt T Roberts & Sgt J Chapman DFM unhurt); Rep Pk 1 ASD 7.5.18; Rebuilt as F5843 25.6.18
D1664 At 3 AAP Norwich 5.4.18, reallotted from E 1c (Dover-Dunkirk) to EF but this cancelled 13.4.18, crashed at Lympne
D1665 At 3 AAP Norwich 5.4.18, reallotted from E 1c (Dover-Dunkirk) to EF; England to Rec Pk 1.5.18; 1 AI 18.5.18; 98 Sqn 21.5.18; Pilot began to feel unwell, shut off engine but only had partial control, glided straight down into ploughed field crashed 19.6.18 (2/Lt AL Perry-Keene & Sgt Mech RT Wallace OK); Rep Pk 1 ASD 20.6.18; SOC 24.6.18 NWR
D1666 At 3 AAP Norwich 5.4.18, reallotted from E 1c (Dover-Dunkirk) to EF; England to Rec Pk 1.5.18; 2 AI 7.5.18; 99 Sqn 16.5.18; Albatros D in flames, Lahr 07.20 30.7.18; EA OOC on Saarbrücken raid 31.7.18 (both Capt AD Taylor & Lt HS Notley); Crashed & WO 24.8.18 (Capt AD Taylor & Lt O Bell both killed)
D1667 At 3 AAP Norwich 5.4.18, reallotted from E 1c (Dover-Dunkirk) to EF; England to Rec Pk 1.5.18; 1 AI 3.5.18; 98 Sqn 5.5.18; Shot up E of lines by AA in bombing raid on Armentières 17.5.18 (Lt FH Reilly & Lt RMcK Hall OK); SOC Rep Pk 1 ASD 21.5.18 NWR
D1668 At 3 AAP Norwich 10.4.18, allotted to EF; England to Rec Pk 27.4.18; 99 Sqn ('6') 30.4.18 [16.5.18?]; Raid on Hagendingen 24.5.18 (2/Lt WJ Garrity OK & 2/Lt MR Skinner wounded); EA OOC in raid on Thionville 27.6.18 (Lt CA Vick & 2/Lt E Beale); EA OOC 30.7.18 (2/Lt WJ Garrity & 2/Lt HT Melville); Hit by AA in raid on rail targets 13.9.18 (Capt V Beecroft OK & Lt HS Notley wounded); 6 AP 30.9.18; 3 ASD 4.10.18
D1669 At 3 AAP Norwich 8.4.18, allotted to EF; England to Rec Pk 27.4.18; 99 Sqn 1.5.18; OP, in combat with EA E of Thionville, shot down in flames, BU near Alsdorf 27.6.18 (Lt EA Chapin (US) & 2/Lt TH Wiggins both killed)
D1670 At 3 AAP Norwich 8.4.18, allotted to EF; England to Rec Pk 1.5.18; 2 AI 2.5.18; 99 Sqn 9.5.18; Raid on Thionville, EA shot down in flames 27.6.18 (Lt H Sanders wounded & 2/Lt W Walker OK); FTR from raid on Arnaville junction, shot down NW of Pont-a-Mousson, m/c broke up over American lines 13.9.18 (2/Lt EE Crosby & 2/Lt CP Wogan-Brown both killed); Wreckage to 6 AP 16.9.18; 3 ASD 20.9.18
D1671 Deld 3 AAP Norwich 28.3.18; 25 TS Thetford; by 26.4.18
D1672 Deld 3 AAP Norwich 28.3.18; 31 TDS Fowlmere, detd to 10 TDS Harling Road 29.10.18
D1673 Deld 3 AAP Norwich 28.3.18
D1674 104 Sqn Andover by 9.5.18; To France with Sqn 19.5.18; FL nr Azelot on raid on Metz-Sablon 22.6.18 (2/Lt MJ Du Cray injured & 2/Lt RL Philip OK): To 2 ASD 24.6.18; 3 ASD 23.7.18; 99 Sqn 30.7.18; 3 ASD 15.8.18 (wrecked)
D1675 From Andover to France with 104 Sqn 19.5.18; Damaged in combat in bombing raid on Karlsruhe 25.6.18 (2/Lt AW Robertson wounded & Lt MH Cole OK); 3 ASD 25.6.18; 99 Sqn 14.8.18; Wrecked 30.8.18; 3 ASD 1.9.18
D1676 (BHP) At 2 AAP Hendon 26.4.18, allotted to EF; Propeller accident 8.5.18 (Pte G Fowlds injured); England to Rec Pk 8.5.18; 2 AI 10.5.18; 27 Sqn by 27.5.18; Taking off for raid, taxied into a depression and wiped off u/c 1.7.18 (Lt HP Schoeman & 2/Lt J Gray OK); Rep Pk 2 ASD 1.7.18; Rebuilt as F6239 12.8.18
D1677 1 SofN&BD Stonehenge by 7.18
D1678 At 2 AAP Hendon 29.4.18, allotted to EF; England to Rec Pk 8.5.18; 2 AI 10.5.18; 27 Sqn; On landing to avoid another m/c stalled and sideslipped in 30.6.18 (Lt WJ Dalziel OK & Lt RH Shepherd slightly injured); SOC Rep Pk 2 ASD 5.7.18
D1679 At 2 AAP Hendon 29.4.18, allotted to EF; England to Rec Pk 7.5.18; 2 AI 10.5.18; 99 Sqn 19.5.18; FTR from Offenburg Railway raid, formation attacked by EA nr target, last seen going down under control over Molsheim with steam coming from radiator 20.7.18 (Lt FE Thompson & 2/Lt SC Thornley both PoW)
D1680 At 2 AAP Hendon 29.4.18, allotted to EF; England to Rec Pk 17.5.18; 49 Sqn 20.5.18; Bombing raid on Roye, indecisive combat Ham 08.40 6.6.18 (Sgt SJ Oliver OK; Sgt EG Jones badly wounded in leg); On practice flight landed in cornfield and ran into ditch 27.6.18 (2/Lt HP Bell OK); Rebuilt as F6074 3.7.18
D1681 Deld 492 Flt 254 Sqn Prawle Point 24.5.18; Landed and CW Paignton, Devon 9.6.18
D1682 Deld 492 Flt 254 Sqn Prawle Point 22.5.18 - @27.10.18; Longside by 15.11.18
D1683 Deld 492 Flt 254 Sqn Prawle Point by 25.5.18; 494 Flt 250 Sqn Padstow W/E 30.5.18
D1684 Deld 492 Flt 254 Sqn Prawle Point 24.5.18 - @6.18; Tested 27.5.18
D1685 Deld 492 Flt 254 Sqn Prawle Point 24.5.18; Tested 27.5.18; Dropped 2x230-lb bombs on U-boat 50°17'N 03°05'W 9.6.18 (Capt RR Thornely DSC & AM Ford)
D1686 Deld 492 Flt 254 Sqn Prawle Point 24.5.18; Tested 27.5.18; FL, slightly damaged Hallsands 6.6.18; still there 25.6.18
D1687 At 3 AAP Norwich 30.4.18, allotted to EF; England to Rec Pk 8.5.18; 1 AI 10.5.18; 98 Sqn 12.5.18; Pfalz DIII OOC just W of Bruges 14.10 31.5.18 (Lt DA Macartney & Lt GD Dardis); Pfalz DIII crashed Inchy-Moevres 09.40 17.6.18 (Lt CH Roberts & Sgt Mech GW Slater); Left 16.30, damaged by AA, FL 1.7.18 (Lt CH Roberts & Sgt GW Slater OK); Rep Pk 1 ASD 2.7.18; SOC 5.7.18 NWR
D1688 Deld 3 AAP Norwich 27.4.18 for Dunkirk; 8 AAP Lympne by 27.5.18; Rec Pk 29.5.18; reallotted from E.1c Dover-Dunkirk Command to EF 30.5.18; 1 AI 31.5.18; 206 Sqn 13.6.18; Hit rut landing 23.11.18 (Lt GW Welch & 2/Lt TH Lowe unhurt); retd 8 SS for repair
D1689 At 3 AAP Norwich 3.5.18, allotted to EF; England to Rec Pk 8.5.18; 1 AI 9.5.18; 206 Sqn 12.5.18; EA shot down OOC when squadron attacked by 8 Pfalz DIII E of Ypres 28.7.18 (Lt GA Pitt & G/L Sgt G Betteridge); Returning from bombing Courtrai Rly Stn, attacked by 20 Pfalz DIII, 1 in flames crashed W of Courtrai & 1 in spin 19.20-19.35, then thick fog nr aerodrome, EF, FL in wood, lost wings in treetops, W of Quercamp 28.7.18 (Lt GA Pitt & G/L Sgt G Betteridge unhurt); Rep Pk 1 ASD 15.8.18; SOC 19.8.18
D1690 En route 3 AAP Norwich to 103 Sqn Salisbury, FL in mist and low cloud, spun in on landing, CW, Guston Road 6.5.18 (Lt GF Townsend slightly injured); Surveyed 7.5.18; For deletion by 24.5.18; WOC Dover 21.7.18
D1691 Deld Dover W/E 15.5.18; 218 Sqn by 20.5.18; After raid on Ostende, EF, FL on sands on French/Belgian border 25.6.18 (Lt EH Dixon & 2/Lt PK Wilson unhurt); repaired on sqn; Overshot, hit D7241 1.8.18; Badly shot up by EA 12.8.18; 4 ASD 12.8.18; 233 Sqn Dover by 16.10.18; 4 ASD 18.10.18; 218 Sqn 24.10.18; 98 Sqn 21.1.19; 8 AAP Lympne 12.2.19
D1692 No information
D1693 At 3 AAP Norwich 8.5.18, allotted to EF; England to Rec Pk 10.5.18; 1 AI 14.5.18; 211 Sqn 16.5.18; Left 10.10 on test with extra driftwires, port wing folded up crossing over trenches at 20ft Pervyse, CW 26.5.18 (Capt TF Le Mesurier DoI & 2/Lt R Lardner killed); Salvaged to 8 AP 27.5.18; SOC in field
D1694 Deld 491 Flt Dover W/E 24.5.18; Bergues 7.6.18; 98 Sqn by 3.6.18; Left 07.15 for bombing raid on Cambrai Rlwy Stn, in combat with 20 EA, shot down in flames 17.6.18 (Lt DA Macartney & Lt JR Jackman both killed)
D1695 At 3 AAP Norwich 9.5.18, allotted to EF; England to Rec Pk 10.5.18; 1 AI 16.5.18; 206 Sqn 21.5.18; Stalled on turn after TO and spun in, BO 22.5.18 (2/Lt EP Morgan DoI & 2/Lt FC Taylor killed); Rep Pk 1 ASD 23.5.18; SOC 27.5.18
D1696 121 Sqn Narborough by 5.18; 10 TDS Harling Road by 6.18; 26 Wing ARS Thetford 5.7.18; Overturned at one time
D1697 121 Sqn Narborough by 5.18
D1698 No information
D1699 At 3 AAP Norwich 13.5.18, allotted to EF; England to

D.H.9 D1710, believed at the Central Flying School, Upavon, has a horizontal semi-circular marking on the rudder. (W.J.Evans)

Rec Pk 16.5.18; 1 AI 18.5.18; 206 Sqn 21.5.18; EF, FL Droglandt 23.6.18 (Lt T Roberts & 2/Lt RW Brigstock unhurt); Rep Pk 1 ASD 25.6.18; SOC 27.6.18 NWR

D1700 At 3 AAP Norwich 13.5.18, allotted to EF; England to Rec Pk 27.5.18; 98 Sqn 28.5.18; Damaged in enemy night raid Coudekerque 5/6.6.18; 4 ASD, transferred to 5 Group 6.18; Crashed 28.9.18; Rep Pk 4 ASD 28.9.18 - 11.18

D1701 At 3 AAP Norwich 13.5.18, allotted to EF; England to Rec Pk 19.5.18; 211 Sqn ('V') 25.5.18; Left 14.35, attacked by 6 Fokker DVII on PR mission, FL and crashed between Forthem & Loo, SE of Furnes 13.8.18 (1/Lt AF Bonnalie USAS & 2/Lt TB Dodwell both unhurt); Rec Pk 1 ASD 14.8.18; SOC 27.8.18 NWR

D1702 At 3 AAP Norwich 16.5.18, allotted to EF; Rec Pk to 1 AI 2.6.18; England to Rec Pk 29.5.18; 2 AI 11.6.18; 27 Sqn 12.6.18; Albatros D OOC 2m W of Roye 11.20 16.6.18 (Lt BM Bowyer-Smythe & Sgt WB Harold); Returning from raid collided in the air with E634 14.8.18 (2/Lt JH Dickson & Sgt SB Percival both killed)

D1703 25 TS Thetford by 5.18; 31 TDS Fowlmere; 5 TDS Easton-on-the-Hill 1918

D1704 Duxford by 6.18

D1705 No information

D1706 17 TS Yatesbury by 4.18 - 5.18; 69 TS Narborough by 6.18

D1707 No information

D1708 Deld 3 AAP Norwich by 25.5.18; Dover (via Eastbourne) 29.6.18; 4 ASD Audembert 30.6.18; 218 Sqn 2.7.18; Yellow Albatros in flames Ostende, shared formation 18.25 5.7.18 (Capt MG Baskerville & Sgt J Harris); EF, FL, folded up and wrecked, Groede, Zeeland 07.15 16.8.18 (Lt AC Lloyd & 2/Lt MG Wilson both interned) [credited Oblt Theo Osterkamp, Marine Jasta 1]; Aircraft interned

D1709 24 Sqn by 8.19 (for General Game)

D1710 Possibly CFS

D1711 Allocated 250 Sqn HQ Padstow by 25.5.18; 492 Flt 254 Sqn Prawle Point by 23.7.18; 493 Flt 236 Sqn Mullion 15.8.18 - @18.10.18

D1712 Allocated 250 Sqn HQ Padstow by 25.5.18; 492 Flt 254 Sqn Prawle Point by 23.7.18; 493 Flt 236 Sqn Mullion by 8.18; Crashed owing to broken drift wire Poldhu Creek 15.10.18 (pilot unhurt)

D1713 494 Flt 250 Sqn Padstow by 25.5.18; Retd with engine trouble, COL 18.10.18

D1714 494 Flt 250 Sqn Padstow by 25.5.18; COL 16.6.18 (2/Lt AEN Ashford & 2/Lt JD Davidson both injured)

D1715 At 3 AAP Norwich 28.5.18, allotted to EF; England to Rec Pk 29.5.18; 2 AI 30.5.18; 49 Sqn 2.6.18; Albatros DV in flames Assinvilliers 04.40 10.6.18 (Capt G Fox-Rule & Lt EH Tredcroft); Hit by ground fire 17.7.18 (Capt G Fox-Rule OK & Lt EH Tredcroft wounded); Fokker DVII OOC Bois de D Ole 19.00 25.7.18 (Capt G Fox-Rule & Lt RAV Scherk); Fokker DVII OOC

The Mann, Egerton work force looking at D.H.9 D1716, an early production machine from their factory, at the Aylsham Road, Norwich test aerodrome. (via Terry Treadwell)

smoking Marchalpot 17.00 9.8.18 (Capt G Fox-Rule & Lt SP Scott); Hit by AA Erincourt, FL 100 yards from enemy lines, set on fire and abandoned 08.10 19.8.18 (Lt ER Wallington & 2/Lt JD Hall OK)

D1716 At 3 AAP Norwich 28.5.18, allotted to EF; England to Rec Pk 29.5.18; 2 AI 30.5.18; 104 Sqn 3.6.18; Overshot on landing on return from Saarbrücken raid 24.6.18 (2/Lt RJ Searle & 2/Lt J Arnold OK); 3 ASD 24.6.18; 99 Sqn 3.8.18; Crashed on aerodrome 28.8.18 (2/Lt JL Hunter & 2/Lt TH Swann); 3 ASD 28.8.18; To England 1.10.18

D1717 At 3 AAP Norwich 30.5.18, allotted to EF; Rec Pk to 2 AI 3.6.18; 98 Sqn 8.6.18; Left 16.40, in combat with 12 EA S of Soilly, spiralled down OOC 16.7.18 (Capt EBG Morton & Lt FA Shaw both killed)

D1718 At 3 AAP Norwich 4.6.18, allotted to EF; 1 AI to 206 Sqn 6.6.18; Fokker DVII crashed NW of Nieppe 11.15 30.8.18; KB shot down Frelinghem-Deulemont 4.9.18 (both Capt RNG Atkinson MC & 2/Lt FS Ganter); Bombing raid, hit by AA, all controls shot away, crashed in shell holes nr Ypres 09.00 5.10.18 (Capt RNG Atkinson MC & 2/Lt JS Blanford); to Rep Pk 1 ASD

D1719 At Makers 29.5.18, allotted to EF; Rec Pk to 2 AI 24.7.18; 5 AI 24.7.18; 27 Sqn 26.7.18; Left 17.20 on low strafing raid on Voyennes, shot down by Oblt Auffarth, Jasta 29, 8.8.18 (2/Lt LH Forrest & 2/Lt SWP Foster-Sutton both PoW); SOC 8.8.18

D1720 At Makers 29.5.18, allotted to EF; Rep Pk 2 ASD to 2 AI 11.7.18; 5 AI 15.7.18; 98 Sqn 18.7.18; EF, FL 30.7.18 (2/Lt WV Thomas & Mjr ET Newton-Clare DSO unhurt); New engine taken out to m/c but due to bad weather decided to tow it in, then stbd wheel collapsed, overturned; 9 AP 5.8.18

D1721 At Makers 29.5.18, allotted to EF; Rep Pk 1 ASD to Rec Pk and on to 2 AI 2.7.18; 98 Sqn 3.7.18; left 06.30 for raid on Clery, FTR 11.8.18 (Lt SD Connolly PoW & 2/Lt EH Clayton PoW DoW 24.8.18); SOC 11.8.18

D1722 At Makers 29.5.18, allotted to EF; Rep Pk 2 ASD to 2 AI 28.7.18; 5 AI 29.7.18; 107 Sqn 31.7.18; Left 05.40 for raid on Brie Bridge, FTR 9.8.18 (2/Lt H Butterworth & 2/Lt RO Baird both killed); SOC 9.8.18

D1723 At 3 AAP Norwich 8.6.18, allotted to EF; Rec Pk to 2 AI and on to 49 Sqn 11.6.18; Left 10.55 for raid on Ricquesbourg, last seen going down under control nr Orvilliers 13.6.18 (1/Lt HH Giles & 2/Lt EM Nicholas both PoW)

D1724 At 3 AAP Norwich 8.6.18, allotted to EF; Rec Pk to AI 12.6.18; 98 Sqn 14.6.18; At 07.30 as part of a formation of four a/c was attacked by 14 EA, observer shot down a Pfalz DIII which "crumpled up", the EA then withdrew and Austin was badly wounded by AA, the attack was renewed and Austin shot down a Pfalz DIII in flames, with engine shot through FL just behind our lines, a/c shelled, on landing observer was found to have DoW 11.7.18 (2/Lt FC Wilton OK & 2/Lt EV Austin DoW); SOC Rep Pk 1 ASD 17.7.18 NWR

D1725 At 3 AAP Norwich 8.6.18, allotted to EF; Rec Pk to 2 AI 14.6.18; 107 Sqn 16.6.18; Bombing raid on Lille, shot up in combat with Fokker DVIIs, observer killed and fell on controls, crashed 79 Sqn aerodrome 10.7.18 (Lt SR Coward OK & Lt PA Hand killed); To Rep Pk 1 ASD, SOC 13.7.18 NWR

D1726 At 3 AAP Norwich 8.6.18, allotted to EF; Rec Pk to 2 AI 18.6.18; 27 Sqn 19.6.18; On practice flight COL 1.7.18 (2/Lt IL Dutton & Sgt Mech W Maggs); Rep Pk 2 ASD 3.7.18; Rebuilt as F6237 10.8.18

D1727 Deld 3 AAP Norwich 6.18; 8 AAP Lympne (via Dover) 18.6.18; In France 21.6.18, reallotted from 61 Wing to EF; Rec Pk to 2 AI and on to 49 Sqn 19.6.18; Left 19.10 in attack on Marne bridges, damaged in combat, COL Petit Becurre 16.7.18 (2/Lt CAB Beattie & Sgt Mech FL Roberts both wounded); SOC 16.7.18 NWR

D1728 Deld 3 AAP Norwich 6.18; 8 AAP Lympne (via Dover) 18.6.18; Rec Pk to 1 AI 19.6.18; 206 Sqn 20.6.18; In France 21.6.18, reallotted from 61 Wing to EF; COL 16.8.18 (Lt TC Story unhurt); Rep Pk 1 ASD 17.8.18; SOC 21.8.18 NWR

D1729 At 3 AAP Norwich 21.6.18, reallotted from 61 Wing to EF; Rec Pk to 2 AI 21.6.18; 104 Sqn 25.6.18; FL, crashed, St.Dizier 30.6.18 (Lt OJ Lange & Sgt EG McCabe both wounded); 3 ASD 30.6.18; 104 Sqn 13.8.18; Raid on Mannheim, in combat with EAs on return, radiator hit, patrol followed it down to 6,000ft but became separated, spun down but landed OK 22.8.18 (Capt JB Home-Hay MC DFC & Sgt WT Smith DCM MM both PoW)

D1730 In France 22.6.18, reallotted from 61 Wing to EF; Rec Pk to 1 AI 23.6.18; 206 Sqn 25.6.18; Left 16.40 on long recce, FTR 7.7.18 (Lt JR Harrington & 2/Lt CL Bray both killed); SOC in field 8.7.18

D1731 At Makers 8.6.18, allotted to EF; 1 AI to 98 Sqn 28.6.18; Pfalz DIII OOC near Douai 07.30 11.7.18 (Capt OCW Johnsen & Capt GHP Whitfield); On landing u/c caught in ridge, crashed 16.7.18 (Lt RT Ingram & 2/Lt JL Stevenson OK); 9 AP 19.7.18; SOC Rep Pk 1 ASD 3.9.18 NWR

D1732 At Makers 8.6.18, allotted to EF; Rec Pk to 5 AI 21.7.18; 49 Sqn 20.7.18; On practice flight, crashed 9.11.18 (2/Lt SF Morrissey & Capt RW Course OK)

D1733 At Makers 8.6.18, allotted to EF; Rec Pk to 1 AI 28.7.18; 108 Sqn ('G') 29.7.18; To Stonehenge 4.8.18 for special bombing course, back at sqn 4.9.18; Left 14.15 for bombing raid on Bruges, hit by AA over target, FL, overturned, badly damaged, Cadzand, Holland 15.9.18 (Capt WRE Harrison & 2/Lt C Thomas interned); SOC 15.9.18; Became Dutch *deH443* [not confirmed by Dutch reports]

D1734 At Makers 8.6.18, allotted to EF; Rec Pk to 1 AI 29.6.18; 107 Sqn 30.6.18; Fokker DVII dest 9.7.18 (2/Lt JR Brown & AM JP Hazell); Damaged in combat with EA Le Breuil 16.7.18 (2/Lt BE Gammell OK & 2/Lt W Middleton DoW); SOC Rep Pk 1 ASD 3.9.18 NWR

D1735 131 Sqn Shawbury 1918; 3 FS Bircham Newton by 7.18 - 8.18; 10 TDS Harling Road 1918

D1736 35 TDS Duxford by 20.9.18

D1737 35 TDS Duxford by 9.9.18

D1738 10 TDS Harling Road 1918; 3 FS Sedgeford by 4.19

D1739 At Makers 17.6.18 for 108 Sqn (Mob); reallotted to Store 19.6.18

D1740 At Makers 17.6.18 for 108 Sqn (Mob); reallotted to Store 19.6.18; 10 TDS Harling Road 1918

D1741 At Makers 17.6.18 for 108 Sqn (Mob); reallotted to Store 19.6.18; 46 TS Catterick

D1742 At Makers 17.6.18 for 108 Sqn (Mob); reallotted to Store 19.6.18; 46 TS Catterick; Became 49 TDS Catterick 15.7.18 - @9.18

D1743 52 TS Catterick by 6.18; Became 49 TDS Catterick 15.7.18 - @10.18

D1744 49 TDS Catterick by 9.18 - @12.18

D1745 49 TDS Catterick, FL in failing light, hit tree and crashed nr Stockton 13.9.18 (F/Cdt HG Paines slightly injured)

D1746 52 TS Cramlington 9.18

D1747 MOS Aldeburgh by 8.18; Became ASIPOP Aldeburgh 28.12.18; Became 1 MOS Aldeburgh 1.1.19 - 2.19

D1748 No information

D1749 MOS Aldeburgh by 8.18 - @12.18

D1750 4 ASD to 218 Sqn 3.8.18; Fokker DVII OOC Cortemarcke, shared U.S. D.H.4 A3205 (Lt R Talbot USMC & Cpl RG Robinson USMC) 08.15 8.10.18 (Lt HW Matthews & 2/Lt HW Murray); 98 Sqn 21.1.19; 8 AAP Lympne 12.2.19

100 D.H.9 ordered 19.11.17 under Cont No A.S.34886 (B.R.228) from Short Bros, Rochester and numbered D2776 to D2875. (Ordered with 260hp FIAT A.12, but changed to 230hp Puma)

D2776 99 Sqn Old Sarum by 10-17.3.18; 14 TDS Lake Down by 8.18; Imperial Gift to India

D2777 14 TDS Lake Down by 6.7.18

D2778 At 8 AAP Lympne 28.2.18, allotted to EF but reallotted to Training 1.3.18

D2779 8 AAP Lympne to 5 TDS Easton-on-the-Hill 15.3.18; 110 Sqn Sedgeford by 4.18; U/c broken landing 14.5.18 (2/Lt CBE Lloyd OK)

D2780 Hounslow 1918; 31 TS Wyton, went out of control on sharp turn near ground, crashed 3.5.18 (2/Lt C Knight seriously injured)

D2781 Deld 2 AAP Hendon 3.18; AAP Dover 18.3.18; 11N Sqn 23.3.18; Became 211 Sqn ('M') 1.4.18; EA claimed

OOC 13.7.18 (Lt ES Morgan & 2/Lt R Simpson); Left 11.35, hit by AA over Zeebrugge, FL Groede, Zeeland 25.7.18 (Sgt RS Gude interned & Sgt HM Partridge interned DoW) [pilot flew as fast as possible to Holland to get help for observer who was hurried to hospital but died of his wounds]; SOC 25.7.18

D2782 Deld 2 AAP Hendon 3.18; Chingford 18.3.18 (transit); AAP Dover 20.3.18; 11N Sqn 23.3.18; Became 211 Sqn 1.4.18; Damaged by AA 14.7.18 (2/Lt HH Palmer wounded & 2/Lt WC Snowden unhurt); 2 ASD 22.2.19 (unfit to fly Channel)

D2783 Deld 2 AAP Hendon 3.18; AAP Dover 21.3.18; 6N Sqn 24.3.18; Became 206 Sqn 1.4.18; Casualty Report 13.5.18 says unfit for further service in the field; Rep Pk 1 ASD 31.5.18 (overhaul); Rec Pk to 1 AI 14.6.18; 206 Sqn 16.6.18; Left 18.08, hit by EA fire, FL Estrée Blanche 26.6.18 (Lt C Eaton & Lt EW Tatnall unhurt); Rep Pk 1 ASD 26.6.18; SOC 2.7.18 NWR

D2784 Deld 2 AAP Hendon 3.18; AAP Dover 23.3.18; 4 ASD Guines 1.4.18; 211 Sqn 7.4.18; Fokker Drl destroyed Zeebrugge Mole 9.5.18 (Lt W Gilman & 2/Lt R Lardner): Left 11.00, last seen Ostende-Nieuport in formation believed crashed nr Uytkerke 12.00 19.5.18 (Lt NA Taylerson & Lt CL Bray both killed)

D2785 Deld 2 AAP Hendon 3.18; Cranwell 24.3.18; Became 202 TDS Cranwell 1.4.18; SOC 29.5.18

D2786 Deld EAD Grain 12.3.18; ECD Grain by 1.4.18 - @23.6.18 (flotation gear experiments); 2 ASD, SOC 24.8.18 NWR

D2787 Deld 2 AAP Hendon 3.18; Cranwell ('111') 24.3.18; Became 202 TDS Cranwell 1.4.18; Spun in from 500ft 12.7.18 (2/Lt WL Lanigan killed)

D2788 Deld 2 AAP Hendon 3.18; Cranwell 24.3.18; Became 201/2 TDS Cranwell 1.4.18

D2789 Deld 7 AAP Kenley 12.3.18 (for D of T); Cranwell (via Lympne) 31.3.18 - @4.18

D2790 Deld 7 AAP Kenley 12.3.18 (for D of T); Cranwell (via Lewes) 29.3.18 - @17.7.18

D2791 Deld 7 AAP Kenley 12.3.18 (for D of T); Cranwell (via Lewes) 29.3.18; Chingford 14.4.18; Cranwell 24.4.18

D2792 Deld 7 AAP Kenley 12.3.18 (for D of T); Cranwell (via Lewes) 29.3.18; Engine trouble, FL, stalled in 24.4.18 (Lt CM Bates killed)

D2793 Shipped to Otranto 10.4.18; AD Taranto by 7.18; 226 Sqn by 8.18; Left Pizzone 05.30, FTR raid on Cattaro 30.8.18 (2/Lt GW Cooper & Cpl WA Easman both killed)

D2794 Shipped to Otranto 10.4.18; AD Taranto by 7.18; 224 Sqn by 29.7.18; Stalled and o/t on landing Valona 29.8.18 (FSL SJ Chamberlain & Lt MI Brockbank both unhurt)

D2795 Deld 12.3.18; Shipped to Otranto 10.4.18; 224 Sqn by 7.18 - @11.18; Raid on Cattaro 6.9.18 (2/Lt RT Gray, observer, slightly wounded); AP Taranto to 'X' AD 28.6.19

D2796 Deld 12.3.18; Shipped to Otranto 10.4.18; AD Taranto by 7.18; 224 Sqn by 7.18; Accident c.23.10.18 (2/Lt N Holroyde slightly injured)

D2797 Deld 12.3.18; Shipped to Mudros 22.4.18; 220 Sqn Imbros by 30.6.18 - @4.11.18; Stavros by 11.18 - @1.19

D2798 Deld 12.3.18; Shipped to Otranto 10.4.18; AD Taranto by 7.18; 226 Sqn by 8.18; Taranto by 1.19; AP Taranto to 'X' AD 28.6.19; 'Z' Unit British Somaliland by 1.20 - 5.4.20

D2799 8 AAP Lympne by 30.3.18; Cranwell 6.4.18; En route 12 TS Thetford, crashed Sproughton, Suffolk 20.4.18; Cranwell by 1.19

D2800 Shipped from West India Docks to Otranto 27.4.18; 268 Sqn Calafrana by 6.18 - @1.19

D2801 Shipped from West India Docks to Otranto 27.4.18; 268 Sqn Calafrana by 6.18 - @1.19

D2802 Shipped from West India Docks to Otranto 27.4.18; 226 Sqn by 7.18; FTR raid on Cattaro 30.8.18 (Lt J McDonald DFC PoW & Cpl E Sutcliffe killed)

D2803 Shipped from Cardiff to Mudros 7.5.18; Shipped to Mudros 18.7.18; Stavros by 10.18 - @1.19; 553 Flt 221 Sqn ('I', possibly named 'DAPHNE'), crashed 3.2.19 (Capt JWP Grigson & Lt OR Gayford DFC)

D2804 Shipped from Cardiff to Mudros 7.5.18; Shipped to Mudros 18.7.18; Stavros by 7.8.18 - @15.5.18; 226 Sqn, lost 5.9.18 (Lt HTB Williams & Lt EC Finzi both killed)

D2805 At 2 AAP Hendon 16.4.18, allotted to EF; Rec Pk to 1 AI 17.5.18; 98 Sqn 18.5.18; Albatros D fell "in cartwheels" smoking nr Gheluwe 06.55 19.5.18 (Lt AG Baker & Lt AR Cowan); Pfalz DIII OOC just W of Bruges 14.10 31.5.18; After raiding Bruges docks, Pfalz DIII OOC nr Ostende 16.20 3.6.18 (both Lt F Smethurst & Lt EGT Chubb); Damaged in enemy air raid on the night of 5/6.6.18; To 4 ASD, transferred from EF to 5 Group 6.18; Pilots Pool, crashed, to 4 ASD by road by 25.10.18

D2806 119 Sqn Duxford, EF, turned back, crashed 14.5.18 (2/Lt S Walker killed)

D2807 (BHP) 123 Sqn Duxford, EF, stalled, dived in, BO 29.5.18 (2/Lt JE Machin killed)

D2808 52 TDS Cramlington by 8.18

D2809 31 TS Wyton, crashed on delivery, overturned 30.4.18 (2/Lt HC Dakin slightly injured)

D2810 (Puma) 131 Sqn Shawbury, test flown 24.3.18; 129 Sqn Duxford, broke up in dive, tailplane failed 27.4.18 (Lt GW Whalley & F/Sgt GL Evans both killed)

D2811 131 Sqn Shawbury

D2812 To France with 104 Sqn 19.5.18; Pfalz DIII OOC Saarebourg, shared D5729 16.25 7.7.18 (Capt EA McKay & 2/Lt RAC Brie); Raid on Mannheim, in combat with 8 EAs 5m E of lines on way out, radiator hit, last seen going down under control Vosges 22.8.18 (Capt EA McKay MC DFC & Lt RAC Brie both PoW)

D2813 52 TDS Cramlington by 9.18; 49 TDS Catterick by 1.19 - 2.19

D2814 No information

D2815 9 TDS Shawbury by 10.18 - 3.19

D2816 No information

D2817 9 TDS Shawbury by 10.18 - 3.19

D2818 9 TDS Shawbury by 27.11.18

D2819 & D2820 No information

D2821 25 TS Thetford by 17-18.5.18; 221 Sqn Petrovsk .18; Became *G-EALJ*

D2822 No information

D2823 Duxford by 6.18; 35 TDS Duxford by 10.18?; Midland Area FIS Feltwell, prop accident 1.7.19 (Mjr A Gray seriously injured)

D2824 No information

D2825 (F.I.A.T.) RAE Farnborough by 16.7.18 (engine & altitude tests, gliding tests, control column tests, short wave radio coils); Radiator test, damaged in mid-air collision 23.1.19 (Lt Muir & Lt HM Garner); Gosport 4.8.20; Deck landing trials HMS *Eagle* on/from 9.8.20; RAE Farnborough 13.8.20 (general testing); Flight refuelling contact trials as tanker with Virginia J8236 as receiver 7.8.30

D2826 At 2 AAP Hendon by 19.6.18 for 108 Sqn (Mob); Damaged landing at Kenley 25.6.18.

D2827 No information

D2828 9 TDS Shawbury by 10.18 - 3.19

D2829 No information

D2830 203 TDS Manston by 6.18; Became 55 TDS Manston 14.7.18; Spun in from 500ft 22.8.18 (F/Cdt H Marshall injured)

D2831 202 TDS Cranwell by 5.18; Became 57 TDS Cranwell 27.7.18 - @16.8.18

D2832 57 TDS Cranwell by 24.7.18 - @9.18

D2833 57 TDS Cranwell by 19.7.18 - @9.18

D2834 57 TDS Cranwell by 25.7.18 - @23.8.18

D2835 Deld 6 SD Ascot W/E 1.7.18; Shipped 25.8.18; Mudros by 10.18 - @1.19

D2836 Deld 6 SD Ascot W/E 1.7.18; Shipped 25.8.18; Mudros by 10.18 - @1.19

D2837 No information

D2838 Deld 6 SD Ascot W/E 1.7.18; Shipped 25.8.18; Mudros by 10.18 - @1.19; Tested AD Hinaidi 27.5.22, then to 8 Sqn 27.5.22 (arr 29.5.22)

D2839 Salonika AP ex UK 25.8.18; 'B' Flight 17 Sqn Amberkoj 10.10.18; FL Amarynthos on Athens-Salonika flight 4.4.19, arrived Salonika 11.4.19 (Capt SG Frogley & Lt A Mercer); WO Salonika AP 1.5.19

D2840 Salonika AP ex UK 25.8.18; Mail flights to Sofia 21.10.18 and to Sofia and Bucharest 23.11.18; 47 Sqn for service in south Russia 21.4.19; At Ekaterinodar with 47 Sqn by 27.5.19; With E8994 in indecisive combat

D.H.9 D2781 from Short Bros at Rochester, still in factory finish. (J.M.Bruce/G.S.Leslie collection)

D.H.9 D2781, now with No.211 Squadron and coded 'M', after coming down in Holland on 25.7.18 (J.M.Bruce/G.S.Leslie collection)

D.H.9 D2786 was involved in flotation gear experiments at Grain during 1918. (J.M.Bruce/G.S.Leslie collection)

Short-built D.H.9 D2789 being refuelled. (via Philip Jarrett)

A mechanic working on the engine of D.H.9 D2780 at Hounslow in 1918. (via Norman Franks)

D.H.9 D2803 '1' of No.221 Squadron, Petrovsk, after being crashed on 3.2.19. (J.M.Bruce/G.S.Leslie collection)

A D.H.9 of No.221 Squadron, believed to be D2803 which was flown by Capt JWP Grigson & Lt OR Gayford. (J.M.Bruce/G.S.Leslie collection)

D.H.9 D2825 during deck landing trials on 9.8.20. HMS Eagle has early fore-and-aft type arrester wires to prevent aircraft going over the side. (J.M.Bruce/G.S.Leslie collection)

with Russian Nieuport, Dubovka 11.00 16.9.19 (Lt AH Day & Lt H Buckley); From 'A' Dett to Store for repair fuselage only 3.11.19; Sold to Anti-Bolshevik Government

D2841 Shipped to Mudros 18.5.18; Repair Base Mudros by 6.18; G Sqn 2 Wing Mudros by 6.18; F Sqn 62 Wing Mudros by 11.18; Imbros by 10.18 - @1.19; Salonika AP by 4.19; 47 Sqn 21.4.19; Sold to Anti-Bolshevik Government 'A' dett to repair South Russia with Mission 3.11.19

D2842 Shipped to Mudros 18.5.18; Repair Base Mudros by 6.18; F Sqn 62 Wing Mudros by 7.18; 220 Sqn Imbros by 27.10.18; 221 Sqn Imbros 23.12.18 - @1.19; Sold to Anti-Bolshevik Government; RAF South Russia to Russian Aviation Corps 8.19; Later Soviet Russian Air Fleet (RKKVF)

D2843 Shipped to Mudros 18.5.18; Repair Base Mudros by 6.18; F Sqn 62 Wing Mudros by 9.18 - @11.18; Taranto by 10.18; 220 Sqn Imbros by 27.10.18 - @16.11.18; Salonika AP by 4.19; 47 Sqn 21.4.19; RAF South Russia to Russian Aviation Corps 8.19

D2844 Shipped to Mudros 18.5.18; Repair Base Mudros by 6.18; Stavros by 29.8.18; Imbros 14.10.18; 222 Sqn Mudros by 1.11.18; 222 Sqn San Stefano 14.11.18 - @1.19; Salonika AP by 4.19; 47 Sqn 21.4.19; Sold to Anti-Bolshevik Government 1919

D2845 16 Wing Salonika ex UK 25.8.18; Salonika AP to 'B' Flt 17 Sqn 4.10.18; On move to San Stefano, spun in from 600ft 16.2.19 (Lt GM Metcalfe injured & AC1 H Plumb OK); WO 28.2.19

D2846 Salonika AP ex UK 13.10.18; 47 Sqn for service in south Russia 21.4.19; 47 Sqn Ekaterinodar by 3.6.19; Erected 17.7.19; FL in hostile territory, m/c burnt 30.7.19 (Capt H Elliot DFC & Lt HS Laidlaw rescued by D2942)

D2847 Deld 6 SD Ascot W/E 13.6.18; Salford Docks W/E 25.7.18; Shipped to Mudros 1.8.18; Repair Base Mudros by 10.18 - @1.19; Sold to Anti-Bolshevik Government 1919; AP Simferopol to A Flt Crimean Group RAF South Russia 15.2.20 - @3.20; Bolshevik 1½ Strutter with snow skids DD 2m SW of Novo-Aleksyeeka 15.20, two men ran out 18.2.20 (Capt JWP Grigson DFC & Capt CF Gordon OBE MC); EF, FL 3m N of Djaukoi 22.2.20 (Mjr R Collishaw DSO DSC DFC & Capt CF Gordon OBE MC)

D2848 Deld 6 SD Ascot W/E 13.6.18; To West India Docks W/E 11.7.18; Shipped to Mudros 18.7.18; Mudros by 9.18; Repair Base Mudros by 10.18 - @1.19; 222 Sqn Mudros by 2.11.18; 222 Sqn San Stefano 14.11.18

D2849 Deld 6 SD Ascot W/E 13.6.18; Salford Docks W/E 25.7.18; Shipped to Mudros 1.8.18; Deleted Mudros 10.18

D2850 Deld 6 SD Ascot W/E 13.6.18; Salford Docks W/E 25.7.18; Shipped to Mudros 1.8.18; Deleted Mudros 10.18

D2851 Deld 6 SD Ascot W/E 13.6.18; Salford Docks W/E 25.7.18; Shipped to Mudros 1.8.18; 222 Sqn Mudros by 28.10.18; Repair Base Mudros by 10.18 - @1.19

D2852 Deld 6 SD Ascot W/E 13.6.18; Salford Docks W/e 25.7.18; Shipped to Mudros 1.8.18; Repair Base Mudros by 10.18

D.H.9 D2854 of No.221 Squadron, Petrovsk, in 1919 (via J.J.Halley)

D2853 Deld 6 SD Ascot W/E 13.6.18; Shipped West India Docks to Mudros 18.7.18; Mudros by 9.18; 478/480 Flts 222 Sqn Mudros by 28.10.18; Repair Base Mudros by 10.18 - @1.19; Sold to Anti-Bolshevik Government; 1 Volunteer Arm Sqn (Russian), South Russia 1919

D2854 Deld 6 SD Ascot W/E 13.6.18; Shipped West India Docks to Mudros 18.7.18; Mudros by 9.18; Repair Base Mudros by 10.18 - @1.19; 478/480 Flts 222 Sqn Mudros by 28.10.18; 222 Sqn San Stefano 14.11.18; 221 Sqn Petrovsk 1919

D2855 At 8 AAP Lympne 23.5.18, allotted to EF; Rec Pk to 1 AI 1.6.18; 206 Sqn 11.6.18; Last seen over Menin 08.40 1.8.18 (Capt JW Mathews & Lt WA John both killed); SOC 1.8.18

D2856 Deld 8 AAP Lympne by 25.5.18, allotted to EF; Rec Pk to 107 Sqn 9.6.18; EA OOC 25.7.18; Raid on Brie Bridge, in combat with Fokker DVII, 1 shot down with front gun & BO 2m W of Haplincourt 05.50 9.8.18; EA crashed 9.8.18; EA OOC 29.10.18 (all Capt FM Carter & Lt AWH Arundell); 98 Sqn 6.3.19; Rec Pk 16.3.19

D2857 At 8 AAP Lympne 30.5.18, allotted to EF; Rec Pk to 2 AI 10.6.18; 103 Sqn 11.6.18; Hit telegraph pole in mist 29.6.18 (Capt AH Curtis & Lt IB Corey OK); SOC Rep Pk 1 ASD 2.7.18 NWR

D2858 Rec Pk to 2 AI 6.8.18; 98 Sqn 9.8.18; Left 06.10 for bombing raid on Somain, damaged in combat with 30-40 Fokker DVII, FL Daunville 29.8.18 (2/Lt TW Sleigh OK & Lt AA Douglas wounded); SOC Rep Pk 2 ASD 13.9.18 NWR

D2859 8 AAP Lympne to Rec Pk 2.8.18; 2 AI to 98 Sqn 7.8.18; Taking off had to throttle down to avoid m/c in front preventing m/c from climbing, u/c hit corn, crashed, m/c completely burnt 8.8.18 (Lt WV Thomas OK & Lt HTG Robey injured)

D2860 8 AAP Lympne by 8.7.18; Rec Pk 1.8.18; To 2 AI and on to 3AD 1.8.18; 99 Sqn 4.8.18 ('1'); Returning from aborted raid, wrecked 12.9.18 (Lt MJ Poulton & Sgt FL Lee); 6 AP 15.9.18; 3 ASD 20.9.18; SOC 5.10.18

D2861 Rec Pk to 2 AI 6.8.18; 49 Sqn 10.8.18; Left 08.30, Fokker DVII crashed Bois d'Havrincourt wood then shot down in flames 14.8.18 (2/Lt JG Andrews & 2/Lt J Churchill both killed)

D2862 England to Rec Pk 4.8.18; 2 AI 10.8.18; 3 ASD 1.9.18 104 Sqn 30.10.18; Taking a pilot to 2 AI to collect a new m/c, COL when u/c collapsed 31.12.18 (Lt EC Stringer & 2/Lt JN Ogilvy); To Rep Pk 2 ASD

D2863 Rec Pk to 2AI 3.8.18; 98 Sqn 7.8.18; In combat in raid on Clery 11.8.18 (Sgt Mech HW Bush OK & Sgt Mech EA Swayne wounded); Fokker DVII OOC 5m SW of Cambrai 18.15, then engine seized, glided back and FL nr Cappy 3.9.18 (Lt CG Gowing OK & 2/Lt JGW Halliday killed); Rep Pk 2 ASD 7.9.18; SOC 15.9.18 NWR

D2864 52 TS Catterick by 6.18; Became 49 TDS Catterick 15.7.18 - @10.18

D2865 No information

D2866 At Makers 25.5.18, allotted to EF; Rec Pk to 1 AI 28.6.18; 103 Sqn 29.6.18; COL 31.7.18 (Lt TM Phillips & 1/AM E Halliwell both unhurt); Rep Pk 1 ASD 2.8.18; SOC 4.8.18 NWR

D2867 At Makers 25.5.18, allotted to EF; Rep Pk 2 ASD to 2 AI 5.7.18; 27 Sqn 8.7.18; COL, said to be bad landing on unfamiliar aerodrome 15.7.18 (2/Lt RC Walters & Lt FW Chester OK); 9 AP 19.7.18; SOC Rep Pk 1 ASD 1.8.18 NWR

D2868 At Makers 25.5.18, allotted to EF; Rec Pk to 2 AI 28.6.18; 104 Sqn 29.6.18; Bombing raid on Kaiserslautern, formation attacked on outward and return journeys, in combat with EA, last seen going down under control Homburg-Dieuze, reported shot down by a Halberstadt C 7.7.18 (Lt A Moore PoW & Lt FP Cobden killed)

D2869 At Makers 25.5.18, allotted to EF; Rep Pk 2 ASD to 2 AI 6.7.18; 98 Sqn 13.7.18; Returning from raid, u/c caught in rut on landing, crashed 16.7.18 (2/Lt FJ Fogarty & Sgt Mech RT Wallace OK); To 9 AP 19.7.18; SOC Rep Pk 1 ASD 3.9.18 NWR

D2870 46 TS Catterick by 10.18

D2871 No information

D2872 At Makers 10.6.18, allotted to EF; Rep Pk 2 ASD to 49 Sqn 28.6.18; Damaged by AA crashed Montmort 19.20

15.7.18 (2/Lt CC Conover OK & Sgt RS Dobbie wounded); SOC Rep Pk 1 ASD 3.9.18

D2873 At Makers 10.6.18, allotted to EF; Rec Pk to 2 AI 1.7.18; 27 Sqn 2.7.18; Hit on raid 17.7.18 (Lt R Turner & Sgt WB Harold both wounded); Fokker DVII crashed 2m W of Péronne 10.45 13.8.18 (Lt CE Hutcheson & Sgt WE Smith); Fokker DVII in flames then broke up Busigny, shared with D1092 09.45 27.9.18 (2/Lt TA Dickinson & 2/Lt WJ Diment); Returning from raid, burst into flames nr aerodrome, crew both jumped, m/c destroyed 1.11.18 (Lt CE Hutcheson & 2/Lt EA Hooper both killed)

D2874 At Makers 10.6.18, allotted to EF; 8 AAP Lympne by 3.7.18; Rec Pk and on to 2 AI 4.7.18; 27 Sqn 7.7.18; Low strafing mission 8.8.18 (pilot 2/Lt TA Dickinson OK & 2/Lt NF Frome wounded); Failed to come out of a dive, landed in a pond, totally submerged, WO 19.11.18 (2/Lt TA Dickinson & Capt IH Stockwood bruised and shaken)

D2875 At Makers 10.6.18, allotted to EF but this cancelled 20.6.18 and retained for conversion for ship's aeroplane; 8 AAP Lympne by 6.8.18; Experimental Station Butley by 17.1.19

400 D.H.9 ordered 19.11.17 under Cont No A.S.17569 (BR.228) from Aircraft Manufacturing Co Ltd, Hendon and numbered D2876 to D3275. (230hp Puma)

D2876 At 2 AAP Hendon 20.6.18 for 109 Sqn (Mob); Reallotted to 108 Sqn (Mob) 28.6.18; Not to France with sqn 22.7.18.

D2877 At 2 AAP Hendon 25.5.18, allotted to EF; Rec Pk to 2 AI and on to 103 Sqn 13.6.18; Scout OOC La Bassée 2030 4.7.18 (Lt RE Dodds & 2/Lt JB Russell); Pfalz DIII OOC and another in spin N of Estaires 16.30-17.00 11.8.18; 2 Fokker DVII OOC Lomme area 11.05 (all Lt RE Dodds & 2/Lt IB Corey); Left 09.30, seen in combat, FTR 24.9.18 (2/Lt CH Heebner & 2/Lt D Davenport both killed)

D2878 At 2 AAP Hendon 25.5.18, allotted to EF; Rec Pk to 2 AI 29.6.18; 2 AI to 99 Sqn 30.6.18; 3 ASD by 7.18; 104 Sqn 4.7.18; Bombing raid on Kaiserslautern, formation attacked on outward and return journeys, last seen going down under control Homburg-Dieuze 7.7.18 (2/Lt MJ DuCray PoW & 2/Lt NH Wildig killed)

D2879 At 2 AAP Hendon 21.6.18 for 109 Sqn (Mob); Reallotted to 108 Sqn (Mob) 28.6.18; At sqn by 17.7.18, but not to France with sqn 22.7.18

D2880 At 2 AAP Hendon 20.6.18 for 109 Sqn (Mob) Lake Down; Reallotted to 108 Sqn (Mob) 28.6.18; At sqn by 4.7.18; To France with sqn 22.7.18; Swerved on take off on practice flight, swung in circle and crashed into huts 10.8.18 (2/Lt AAS Milne & Sgt W Greenwood); Rep Pk 1 ASD 12.8.18; SOC 15.8.18 NWR

D2881 At 2 AAP Hendon 21.6.18 for 109 Sqn (Mob) Lake Down; Reallotted to 108 Sqn (Mob) 28.6.18; At 7 AAP Kenley 23.7.18 reallotted to EF; Rec Pk to 2 AI 25.7.18; 3 ASD 28.7.18; 104 Sqn 29.7.18; Raid on Ehrang Rlwy Junction, direct hit by AA, folded up, fell on D7229 13.8.18 (Lt FH Beaufort US & 2/Lt HO Bryant both killed)

D2882 At 2 AAP Hendon 20.6.18 for 109 Sqn (Mob) Lake Down; Reallotted to 108 Sqn (Mob) 28.6.18; To France with Sqn 22.7.18; Radiator hit by AA in raid on Ostende Docks, FL on beach 11.8.18 (Mjr SS Halse & Lt HD Buchanan); Returning from FL at Coudekerque, u/c was found to have been damaged on take off 3.10.18 (2/Lt CR Knott & Cpl Mech RG Pelling); Rep Pk 1 ASD 6.10.18

D2883 Deld 6 SD Ascot W/E 13.6.18; Salford Docks W/E 25.7.18; Shipped to Mudros 1.8.18; Repair Base Mudros by 10.18 - @1.19; Sold to Anti-Bolshevik Government; RAF South Russia to Russian Aviation Corps 8.19

D2884 Deld 6 SD Ascot W/E 13.6.18; Salford Docks W/E 25.7.18; Shipped to Mudros 1.8.18; Repair Base Mudros by 10.18; To Greek Government by 1.19; Allocated *G-EALJ* (NTU)

D2885 Deld 6 SD Ascot W/E 13.6.18; Salford Docks W/E 25.7.18; Shipped to Mudros 1.8.18; 222 Sqn Mudros by 29.10.18; Repair Base Mudros by 10.18 - @1.19

D2886 Deld 6 SD Ascot W/E 13.6.18; Salford Docks W/E 25.7.18; Shipped to Mudros 1.8.18; Mudros by 10.18 - @1.19; Sold to Anti-Bolshevik Government 1919

D2887 Deld 6 SD Ascot W/E 27.6.18; Salford Docks W/E 25.7.18; Shipped to Mudros 1.8.18; Mudros by 10.18 - @1.19; 222 Sqn Mudros by 11.18; 222 Sqn San Stefano 14.11.18

D2888 Deld 6 SD Ascot W/E 13.6.18; Salford Docks W/E 25.7.18; Shipped to Mudros 1.8.18; Repair Base Mudros by 10.18 - @1.19; Sold to Anti-Bolshevik Government 1919

D2889 Islington by 13.6.18; 6 SD Ascot W/E 20.6.18; West India Docks 11.7.18; Shipped to Mudros 18.7.18; ? Sqn 62 Wing Mudros, FTR bombing attack, crashed Anatolia 20.9.18 (Lt EPO Haughton & Gnr A Weller both PoW)

D2890 Islington by 13.6.18; 6 SD Ascot W/E 20.6.18; West India Docks 11.7.18; Shipped to Mudros 18.7.18; Mudros by 9.18; Mudros, deleted 10.18 BUT flew Bristol-Hendon-Martlesham 25.6.18

D2891 Deld 6 SD Ascot W/E 15.8.18; Shipped 21.9.18; Taranto by 11.18 - @1.19; AP Taranto to 'X' AD 28.6.19; ASD Aboukir to 142 Sqn 7.10.19; 5 Sqn by 8.20

D2892 Deld 6 SD Ascot W/E 15.8.18; Shipped 21.9.18; Taranto by 1.19; 'X' AD 1.4.19; RAF South Russia to Russian Aviation Corps 24.11.19

D2893 Deld 6 SD Ascot W/E 15.8.18; Shipped 21.9.18; Taranto by 11.18; 'X' AD 1.4.19; Sold to Anti-Bolshevik Government; RAF South Russia to Russian Aviation Corps 8.19

D2894 Deld 6 SD Ascot W/E 15.8.18; Shipped 21.9.18; Taranto by 11.18; 'X' AD 1.4.19; Sold to Anti-Bolshevik Government; RAF South Russia to Russian Aviation Corps 8.19

D2895 Deld 6 SD Ascot W/E 15.8.18; Shipped to Taranto 21.9.18; 'X' AD 1.4.19; Sold to Anti-Bolshevik Government 1919

D2896 Deld 6 SD Ascot W/E 15.8.18; Shipped to Taranto 21.9.18; Taranto by 11.18; 'X' AD 1.4.19; Sold to Anti-Bolshevik Government; RAF South Russia to Russian Aviation Corps 8.19

D2897 (200hp BHP) Tested Martlesham Heath 1.6.18 - 12.8.18 [flown Lympne-Gosport en route Bristol 24.6.18]

D2898 Arr Martlesham Heath W/E 1.6.18 (prop tests); Lympne to Gosport (en route Bristol) 24.6.18; AES Orfordness by 8.18; Waddon 12.8.19

D2899 11 TDS Old Sarum, crashed on rooftop in fog nr London 19.1.19 (Capt SB Collett & Lt MV Stewart both slightly injured)

D2900 No information

D2901 11 TDS Old Sarum by 10.18

D2902 11 TDS Old Sarum by 10.18; Spun in on turn, caught fire, bombs exploded 5.11.18 (Sgt CG Angeloff killed)

D2903 6 TDS Boscombe Down by 21.10.18

D2904 49 TDS Catterick (known as "The Coffin", possibly black with white trim) by 2.19

D2905 49 TDS Catterick by 10.18 - @11.18

D2906 Shipped to Aegean; 226 Sqn by 2.10.18

D2907 Shipped to Aegean; 226 Sqn .18

D2908 49 TDS Catterick by 9.18 - 10.18

D2909 49 TDS Catterick by 11.18 - 2.19

D.H.9 D2904 of No.49 Training Depot Station, Catterick was known as "The Coffin", and was probably painted black with white trim. (J.M.Bruce/G.S.Leslie collection)

D29.., another individually-painted D.H.9 of No.49 Training Depot Station, Catterick. (via Frank Cheesman)

D.H.9 D2933 of No.3 School of Navigation & Bomb Dropping, Helwan. (via Mike O'Connor)

D2910 Shipped to Otranto 24.5.18; AR&ED Pizzone .18; AD Taranto by 7.18; 224 Sqn Andrano 17.8.18 - @2.10.18; Taranto by 11.18 - @1.19; AP Taranto to 'X' AD 1.7.19

D2911 Shipped to Otranto 24.5.18; AR&ED Pizzone .18; AD Taranto by 7.18 - @8.18; 226 Sqn by 2.10.18; Mudros by 10.18 - @1.19

D2912 Shipped to Otranto 24.5.18; AR&ED Pizzone .18; AD Taranto by 8.18; 224 Sqn by 2.10.18; Mudros by 10.18 - @1.19; 47 Sqn by 11.18; Sold to Anti-Bolshevik Government 1919

D2913 Shipped to Otranto 24.5.18; AR&ED Pizzone .18; AD Taranto by 7.18 - @8.18; Mudros by 10.18 - @1.19

D2914 Deld Barry Docks 24.5.18; Shipped to Otranto 14.6.18; Repair Base Mudros by 10.18

D2915 Deld Barry Docks 24.5.18; Shipped to Mudros 14.6.18; Mudros by 9.18

D2916 On charge IF 23.7.18 reallotted from EF to IF; Rec Pk to 2 AI 24.7.18; 3 ASD 25.7.18; 99 Sqn 26.7.18; FTR from Ludwigshaven raid, attacked from behind by 6 EA, seen going down under control E of Saarebourg 7.9.18 (Lt G Broadbent & 2/Lt MA Dunn both PoW)

D2917 Rec Pk to 2 AI 29.7.18; 3 ASD 29.7.18 (at Paris 31.7.18); 104 Sqn 1.8.18; Raid on Mannheim, in combat with EAs, FTR 22.8.18 (1/Lt HP Wells USAS PoW & 2/Lt JJ Redfield USAS PoW wounded)

D2918 Rec Pk to 211 Sqn ('D') 28.7.18; Left 09.50, shot down on bombing raid, wreckage in sea 7/9m N of Gravelines 7.9.18 (Lt ES Morgan DFC & 2/Lt R Simpson both killed, picked up in sea by French); SOC in field 7.9.18

D2919 On ferry flight from 2 AAP Hendon to 8 AAP Lympne went OOC and crashed 8.8.18 (Lt CR Perring of Central Dispatch Pool DoI 9.8.18)

D2920 On delivery flight from 2 AI to 98 Sqn right wheel burst on landing, m/c swerved and crashed 5.8.18 (Lt CH Roberts OK); Rep Pk 2 ASD 7.8.18; SOC 18.9.18.

D2921 Deld Yarmouth by 7.18; 555/6 Flts 219 Sqn Manston 28.7.18; EF, FL, starboard wing & u/c smashed 15.8.18 (Lt EWT Fussell & Sgt Mech DA Alderton); 218 Sqn (via Dover) 29.9.18; Landed St.Pol after hit by AA fire in raid on Melle 13/14.10.18 (Lt W Bentley pilot wounded); Spun after TO, CW 20.10.18 (Lt CS Oegger & Sgt Paschal USA both unhurt); 4 ASD 21.10.18 - @25.10.18

D2922 Deld Yarmouth by 7.18; 555/6 Flts 219 Sqn Manston 30.7.18; FL nr Minster 10.8.18; 218 Sqn (via Dover) 29.9.18; Shot up 2.10.18 (Lt FG Burden wounded); U/s, burnt on squadron, SOC 22.1.19

D2923 555/6 Flts 219 Sqn Manston by 3.8.18 - @9.18

D2924 Deld Yarmouth by 7.18; 555/6 Flts 219 Sqn Manston 30.7.18; Overshot landing, sideslipped into field and caught fire 12.8.18 (Lt JW Ratcliffe & Sgt Mech DA Alderton both slightly injured)

D2925 Deld Yarmouth by 7.18; 555/6 Flts Manston 30.7.18 - @9.8.18

D2926 Recd 'X' AD ex UK 19.10.18; 18 TDS Ismailia 30.12.18; 16 TDS Heliopolis to ASD Aboukir 2.10.19; WO 13.11.19

D2927 Recd 'X' AD ex UK 19.10.18; to TDS 1.1.19; 5 FS Heliopolis by 3.19 (flown by 'Z' Sqn); 'X' AP 4.6.19;

D.H.9 D2931 'S' of No.104 Squadron at Buhl, after being forced down there on 12.8.18 by Ltn Monnington. (via Frank Cheesman).

206 Sqn Helwan 9.8.19 - @10.19

D2928 Recd 'X' AD ex UK 19.10.18; 3 SoN&BD Helwan 4.1.19; 5 FS Heliopolis to 'X' AP 4.6.19; 206 Sqn 26.7.19; ASD Aboukir and WO 18.12.19

D2929 Recd 'X' AD ex UK 19.10.18; 3 SoN&BD Helwan 6.1.19; 5 FS Heliopolis .19; Crashed with 'Z' Sqn 31.5.19 (unit attd 5 FS); 'X' AP 4.6.19

D2930 Recd 'X' AD ex UK 19.10.18; 'B' Flt 142 Sqn Suez 1.3.19; 'X' AP to ASD Aboukir 8.8.19; WO 10.9.19

D2931 At Makers 27.5.18, allotted to EF: Rec Pk to 2 AI 5.7.18; 3 ASD 7.7.18; 104 Sqn ('S') 8.7.18; Combat with 23 EA, shot down at Buhl by Ltn K Monnington, Jasta 18 and captured 12.8.18 (2/Lt OF Meyer & Sgt AC Wallace both PoW)

D2932 At Makers 27.5.18, Allotted to EF; 2 AI to 104 Sqn 28.6.18; 3 ASD 12.7.18; 104 Sqn 22.9.18; Shot down OOC over Metz 23.10.18 (2/Lt BS Case PoW DoW 10.11.18 & 2/Lt H Bridger PoW wounded)

D2933 Recd 'X' AD ex UK 19.10.18; 3 SoN&BD Helwan 7.1.19; Arabian Desert Party to 31 Wing AP 18.8.19; SOC 7.11.19

D2934 Recd 'X' AD ex UK 18.10.18

D2935 Recd 'X' AD ex UK 18.10.18; AW & SP (sic) to 142 Sqn 3.4.19; EF, crashed 20.4.19 (Lt CB Cockman & Lt LET Burley); WO at 142 Sqn 15.12.19

D2936 No information

D2937 Recd 'X' AD ex UK 19.10.18; 'C' Flt 142 Sqn Suez 22.1.19; WO at 142 Sqn 17.9.19

D2938 Recd 'X' AD ex UK 18.10.18; 'B' Flt 142 Sqn Suez 22.1.19; WO at 142 Sqn 11.9.19

D2939 No information

D2940 Deld 6 SD Ascot W/E 15.8.18; Shipped to Mudros 11.10.18; 47 Sqn by 14.9.19; 'A' dett RAF Instructional Mission South Russia by 17.10.19 (repairing); Sold to Anti-Bolshevik Government

D2941 Deld 6 SD Ascot W/E 15.8.18; Shipped 27.9.18; Taranto by 11.18 - @1.19; AP Taranto by 3.19; 'X' AD 1.4.19

D2942 Recd 'X' AD ex UK 24.11.18; TOC Salonika AP 19.2.19; 47 Sqn for service in south Russia 21.4.19; 47 Sqn Ekaterinodar by 3.6.19; Although gravity tank holed, landed and rescued crew of D2846 which had FL in hostile territory 30.7.19 (Capt WF Anderson & 2/Lt JDB Mitchell) - on the return flight Lt Mitchell stood on the lower plane blocking the hole in the tank with his thumb; Damaged in raid on Tsaritsyn 6.8.19 (Capt WF Anderson OK & 2/Lt JDB Mitchell wounded in foot); Still 47 Sqn 16.9.19; 'A' dett RAF Instructional Mission South Russia by 17.10.19 (crashed or awaiting write-off); Sold to Anti-Bolshevik Government; AP Simferopol to A Flt Crimean Group RAF South Russia 18.2.20 - @3.20

D2943 Recd 'X' AD ex UK 24.11.18; Salonika AP 19.2.19; 47 Sqn for service in south Russia 21.4.19; 47 Sqn Ekaterinodar by 2.6.19; Erected 11.8.19; To White Russian Forces

D2944 Recd 'X' AD ex UK 24.11.18; Salonika AP 19.2.19; 47 Sqn for service in south Russia 21.4.19; At 47 Sqn Ekaterinodar by 2.6.19; 'A' dett RAF Instructional Mission South Russia by 17.10.19 (repairing); Sold to Anti-Bolshevik Government; Later Soviet Russian Air Fleet (RKKVF)

D2945 3 ASD by 9.18; 104 Sqn 12.9.18; Crashed 24.9.18 (Lt AV Goble & 2/Lt GA Faulkner both seriously injured); 6 AP 2.10.18; 3 ASD 4.10.18

D2946 & D2947 No information

D2948 Deld 6 SD Ascot W/E 15.8.18; To docks W/E 19.9.18; Shipped to Mudros 11.10.18; Repair Base Mudros by 1.19; Sold to Anti-Bolshevik Government 1919

D2949 & D2950 No information

D2951 Recd 'X' AD ex UK 24.11.18; 222 Sqn Mudros ('5'), crashed 18.12.18 (Lt BH Church seriously injured & Lt RB Poole DoI 19.12.18); 'X' AD to 206 Sqn Helwan 16.7.19' 'Z' Force, Somaliland ('W') by 10.19

D2952 No information

D2953 Recd 'X' AD ex UK 24.11.18; Salonika AP 19.2.19; 47 Sqn for service in south Russia 21.4.19; At 47 Sqn Ekaterinodar 27.5.19; Erected for 'C' Flt 47 Sqn 25.6.19; Sqn records dated 11.8.19 say lost through enemy action on special mission with the Caucasian Army

D2954 Recd 'X' AD ex UK 24.11.18; 206 Sqn Helwan 16.7.19; WOC at 206 Sqn 11.12.19

D2955 At Makers 27.5.18, reallotted from Store to EF; Rep Pk 2 ASD to 2 AI 11.7.18; Left on ferry flight from 2 AI to 5 AI, returned due to misty weather, on landing collided with C2223, caught fire 15.7.18 (Lt AS Rayner badly burned, DoI); SOC Rep Pk 2 ASD 16.7.18 NWR

D2956 At Makers 27.5.18, reallotted from Store to EF; Rep Pk 2 ASD to 2 AI 15.7.18; 5 AI to 107 Sqn 21.7.18; Engine cut due to water in carburettor 3.8.18 (Lt JV Turner & Lt SL Dunlop); SOC Rep Pk 1 ASD 13.8.18 NWR

D2957 No information

D2958 Deld 6 SD Ascot W/E 15.8.18; To docks W/E 19.9.18; Shipped to Mudros 11.10.18; Repair Base Mudros by 1.19; Sold to Anti-Bolshevik Government 1919

D2959 No information

D2960 At 2 AAP Hendon for 108 Sqn (Mob) Kenley by 5.6.18; At Sqn by 10.6.18; reallotted to EF 29.6.18; Rec Pk to 2 AI 1.7.18; 3 ASD 2.7.18; 104 Sqn 4.7.18; Raid on Trier, formation met 24 EA, petrol tank hit over Metz, last seen diving for lines 1.8.18 (Lt WH Goodale & 2/Lt LC Prentice USAS both killed)

D2961 At 2 AAP Hendon by 5.6.18 for 108 Sqn (Mob); At Sqn by 8.6.18; Wrecked 29.6.18

D2962 Deld 6 SD Ascot W/E 15.8.18; To docks W/E 19.9.18; Shipped on SS *Hazlemere* W/E 17.10.18 but damaged en route Mudros

D2963 Deld 494 Flt 250 Sqn Padstow by 29.6.18; EF, FL in sea, 1 bomb exploded on hitting water 24.7.18 (Capt N Wadham & 2/Lt AGV Reeves both slightly injured)

D2964 Deld 494 Flt 250 Sqn Padstow 6.18; Landed with broken wing 13.7.18; Bombed U-boat 50°28'N 05°15'W 28.7.18; still Padstow 23.10.18

D2965 Deld 494 Flt 250 Sqn Padstow by 25.5.18 - @31.9.18

D2966 Deld 494 Flt 250 Sqn Padstow 6.18 - @8.7.18

D2967 Deld 6 SD Ascot W/E 15.8.18; To docks W/E 19.9.18; Shipped on SS *Hazlemere* W/E 17.10.18 but damaged en route Mudros

D2968 Deld 494 Flt 250 Sqn Padstow by 25.5.18; 492 Flt Prawle Point by 8.18; Dropped 230-lb bomb on U-boat 50°11'N 03°43'W 20.35 10.8.18 (2/Lt RJ Thompson & 3/AM AHW Busby); COL Gara Rock owing to thick mist 29.10.18 (2 crew unhurt)

D2969 Allocated 250 Sqn HQ Padstow by 25.5.18; 492 Flt 254 Sqn Prawle Point by 9.18

D2970 to D2972 No information

D2973 Allocated Mudros 19.3.18 (was to have been Taranto); To 'X' AD ex UK; 16 Wing 21.2.19

D2974 Allocated Mudros 19.3.18 (was to have been Taranto)

D2975 Allocated Mudros 19.3.18 (was to have been Taranto)

D2976 Allocated Mudros 19.3.18 (was to have been Taranto)

D2977 Allocated Mudros 19.3.18 (was to have been Taranto)

D2978 Allocated Mudros 19.3.18 (was to have been Taranto): 3 TDS Lopcombe Corner; Imperial Gift to India

D2979 Allocated Mudros 19.3.18 (was to have been Taranto)

D2980 & D2981 No information

D2982 6 TDS Boscombe Down by 13.11.18

D2983 Imperial Gift to India

D2984 to D2986 No information

D2987 5 TDS Easton-on-the-Hill 1918; 31 TDS Fowlmere; Midland Area FIS Lilbourne by 11.18

D2988 No information

D2989 49 TDS Catterick by 2.19

D2990 to D2996 No information

D2997 6 TDS Boscombe Down by 21.10.18 - @8.11.18; Imperial Gift to India

D2998 & D2999 No information

D3000 Imperial Gift to Australia; Became *A6-10*

D3001 6 TDS Boscombe Down by 21.10.18

D3002 Deld 6 SD Ascot W/E 20.6.18; Shipped to Taranto 4.7.18; AD Taranto by 8.18; AR&ED Pizzone by .18; 224 Sqn Taranto by 11.18 - @1.19; AP Taranto to 'X' AD 28.6.19; 'Z' Unit British Somaliland by 1.20 - @4.20 (used as spares)

D3003 Deld 6 SD Ascot W/E 20.6.18; West India Docks W/E 11.7.18; Shipped to Mudros 18.7.18; Mudros by 9.18; Stavros, tested 11.10.18; 222 Sqn Mudros by 31.10.18; Repair Base Mudros by 10.18 - @1.19

D3004 Deld 6 SD Ascot W/E 20.6.18; West India Docks W/E 11.7.18; Shipped to Mudros 18.7.18; Mudros by 9.18;

A downward-firing Lewis gun fitment on a D.H.9. (J.M.Bruce/G.S.Leslie collection)

The wreckage of two D.H.9s after a German attack on RNAS Dunkerque. (J.M.Bruce/G.S.Leslie collection)

The D.H.9s of No.67 Wing which took part in a raid on Cattaro on 1.7.18. (J.M.Bruce/G.S.Leslie collection)

A D.H.9 of 'A' Flight No.17 Squadron with an elephant insignia on the nose. The pilot may be Capt F.W.Hudson. (Stewart Taylor)

Loading mail into a No.120 Squadron D.H.9 at Hawkinge post-war. (via Frank Cheesman)

A flame-damper on a D.H.9 at Thetford or Netheravon, possibly for night attacks on Zeppelins. Note Vickers gun. (via David Birch)

Two captured D.H.9s in a War Booty Exhibition at Munich. They were possibly both of No.104 Squadron, forced down on the same raid. (via Frank Cheesman)

A D.H.9 of 'A' Flight No.104 Squadron at Azelot with the individual letter 'P' repeated under the nose. The pilot is believed to be Captain Ewart Garland. (via Frank Cheesman)

D.H.9 D3039 'Z' of No.99 Squadron after going down out of control at Puttelange on 31.7.18. (via Frank Cheesman)

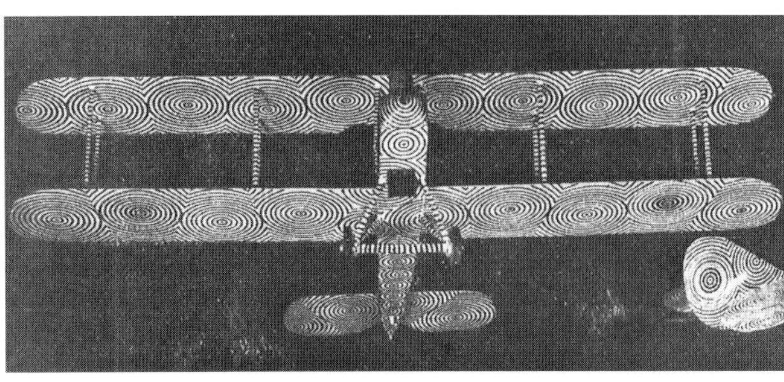

A proposal by Snowden Gamble for an optical illusion painting scheme for D.H.9s. (via Bruce Robertson)

Repair Base Mudros by 10.18 - @1.19; Sold to Anti-Bolshevik Government

D3005 Deld 6 SD Ascot W/E 20.6.18; Shipped to Taranto 4.7.18; AD Taranto by 8.18; 226 Sqn by 2.10.18; Taranto by 10.18; 224 Sqn by 4.12.18; AD Taranto to 'X' AD 28.6.19 - 1920 (then at Ismailia)

D3006 Deld 6 SD Ascot W/E 20.6.18; Shipped to Taranto 4.7.18; AD Taranto by 8.18; AR&ED Pizzone by .18; Taranto by 10.18; Mudros by 10.18 - @1.19

D3007 Deld 6 SD Ascot W/E 20.6.18; Shipped to Taranto 4.7.18; AD Taranto by 8.18; AR&ED Pizzone by .18; 226 Sqn by 2.10.18; 223 Sqn Mudros ('11') by 10.18 - @1.19

D3008 Deld 6 SD Ascot W/E 20.6.18; Shipped to Taranto 4.7.18; AD Taranto by 8.18; 224 Sqn by 2.10.18; Mudros by 10.18 - @1.19

D3009 Deld 6 SD Ascot W/E 20.6.18; Shipped to Taranto 4.7.18; AD Taranto by 8.18

D3010 Deld 6 SD Ascot W/E 20.6.18; Shipped to Taranto 17.7.18; AD Taranto by 8.18; 226 Sqn by 2.10.18; Mudros by 10.18 - @1.19; 186 Devt Sqn Gosport 1919

D3011 Deld 6 SD Ascot W/E 20.6.18; Shipped to Taranto 17.7.18; Mudros by 10.18 - @1.19

D3012 Deld 6 SD Ascot W/E 20.6.18; Shipped to Taranto 4.7.18; AD Taranto by 8.18; AR&ED Pizzone by .18

D3013 & D3014 No information

D3015 'F' Flt 186 Devt Sqn Gosport 1919

D3016 No information

D3017 Imperial Gift to Australia; Arrived Australia 5.11.20; Became *A6-11*; Became *G-AUMB*, later *VH-UMB*

D3018 Imperial Gift to India

D3019 55 TS Narborough, crashed landing Hucknall 2.5.19 (Sgt ED Chaundy)

D3020 55 TDS Narborough by 11.18

D3021 to D3027 No information

D3028 At Makers 6.6.18 for 108 Sqn (Mob); 2 AAP Hendon 17.6.18; At 108 Sqn 21.6.18; Reallotted to D of T for Manston Scout Pool 28.6.18; Pool of Pilots Manston/Joyce Green by 6.18 - @10.18; No 2 Observer School, Manston

D3029 At Makers 6.6.18 for 108 Sqn (Mob); 2 AAP Hendon 20.6.18; With sqn by 29.6.18; To France with 108 Sqn 22.7.18; Ran into ditch on landing from practice flight 28.7.18 (2/Lt WF Long & Sgt W Greenwood both unhurt); Rep Pk 1 ASD 30.7.18; SOC 3.8.18 NWR

D3030 11 TDS Old Sarum by 11.18

D3031 31 TDS Fowlmere by 11.18 - 1.19

D3032 5 TDS Easton-on-the-Hill by 1918; 31 TDS Fowlmere by 12.18; Propeller accident 25.1.19 (Sgt A Frost seriously injured); EF, FL, caught telegraph wires, stalled and spun in 9.8.19 (Sgt A Stockton injured & Sgt SC Pomfret slightly injured)

D3033 3 ASD by 9.18; 99 Sqn 14.9.18; 3 ASD 25.9.18; 99 Sqn 27.10.18; 3 ASD 13.11.18; 49 Sqn; Handed in to 1 ASD 15.7.19

D3034 31 TDS Fowlmere

D3035 3 ASD by 9.18; 104 Sqn 13.9.18; Pfalz DIII crashed S of Metz 08.40 14.9.18 (Capt EJ Garland & Lt WC Bottrill); 1 ASD 21.1.19

D3036 At Makers 19.6.18, reallotted from Store to EF; To 8 AAP Lympne by 8.7.18 for engine fitting and erection; Rec Pk to 1 AI 9.7.18; 107 Sqn 15.7.18; Practice flight, crashed in French lines 9.11.18 (2/Lt WA Oates USAS & 2/Lt WJB Penman both injured)

D3037 2 SoN&BD Andover by 10.18

D3038 No information

D3039 At Makers 19.6.18, reallotted from Store to EF; To 8 AAP Lympne for engine fitting and erection; 2 AI 16.7.18; 3 ASD to 99 Sqn ('Z') 17.7.18; Crashed taking off on raid 20.7.18 (1/Lt P Dietz USAS & Sgt HS Bynon): Petrol tank shot through on Saarbrücken raid, last seen going down under control at Puttelange 31.7.18 (Lt MTS Papenfus DFC wounded PoW & Lt AL Benjamin PoW)

D3040 3 ASD by 9.18; 99 Sqn 28.9.18; Shot down 6.11.18 (2/Lt CEW Thresher PoW & 2/Lt W Glew PoW DoW 7.11.18)

D3041 3 ASD to 99 Sqn 27.8.18; Pfalz DIII OOC just S of Metz 09.00 14.9.18 (Capt WG Stevenson & Sgt J Jones); 6 AP 12.10.18; 3 ASD 15.10.18

D3042 3 ASD by 9.18; 99 Sqn 28.9.18; 3 ASD 13.11.18

D3043 55 TDS Narborough by 10.18; Became 55 TS Narborough 14.3.19; To Castle Bromwich 8.8.19

D3044 No information

D3045 At Makers 19.6.18, reallotted from Store to EF; To 8 AAP Lympne by 9.7.18 for engine fitting and erection; Rec Pk to 1 AI 15.7.18; 2 AI 20.7.18; 5 AI 22.7.18; 98 Sqn 24.7.18; Left 06.30 for raid on Roisel Stn, shot up in combat with EA, damaged, crashed 19.8.18 (2/Lt JM Brown & 2/Lt H Lawrence OK); 9 AP 20.8.18; SOC Rep Pk 2 ASD 18.9.18.

D3046 At Makers 19.6.18, reallotted from Store to EF; To 8 AAP Lympne for engine fitting and erection; Rec Pk 13.7.18; 1 AI 15.7.18; 2 AI 20.7.18; 5 AI 21.7.18; 49 Sqn 22.7.18; Wheel came off in flight, COL 31.7.18 (2/Lt JG Renshaw & 3/AM C Ferris both unhurt); SOC Rep Pk 1 ASD 3.9.18 NWR (ex 9 AP)

D3047 At Makers 19.6.18, reallotted from Store to EF; To 8 AAP Lympne by 7.7.18 for engine fitting and erection; Rec Pk to 1 AI 15.7.18; 103 Sqdn 22.7.18; Propellor burst in the air, crashed 12.8.18 (Lt CH Heebner & 2/Lt CS Harding OK); Rep Pk 1 ASD 14.8.18; SOC 17.8.18 NWR

D3048 At Makers 19.6.18, reallotted from Store to EF; To 8 AAP Lympne by 13.7.18 for engine fitting and erection; Rec Pk to 2 AI 16.7.18; 3 ASD 17.7.18; 99 Sqn 19.7.18; Crashed on return from bombing raid 15.8.18 (2/Lt EL McCowen & 2/Lt W Shaw both injured); SOC 15.8.18

D3049 2 SoN&BD Andover by 10.18

D3050 At Makers 8.6.18, allotted to EF; Rep Pk 1 ASD to Rec Pk 5.7.18; 2 AI 7.7.18; 98 Sqn 11.7.18; KB burned near Treloup then crashed 17.45 16.7.18 (2/Lt WV Thomas & 2/Lt HTG Robey); 9 AP 18.7.18; SOC Rep Pk 1 ASD 3.9.18 NWR

D3051 At Makers 8.6.18, allotted to EF; Rep Pk 2 ASD to 2 AI 28.7.18; 5 AI 30.7.18; 98 Sqn ('S') 31.7.18; 8 AAP Lympne 16.1.19

D3052 At Makers 8.6.18, allotted to EF; Rec Pk to 2 AI 5.7.18; 49 Sqn 8.7.18; Fokker DVII OOC Bethencourt 18.20 8.8.18; Fokker DVII OOC Falvy 06.30 9.8.18; Fokker DVII OOC smoking Marchelepot 17.00 9.8.18 (all Capt C Bowman & Lt PT Holligan); Fokker DVII OOC Bavai 17.05 24.9.18 (Capt C Bowman DFC & 2/Lt CB Edwards); Crashed 24.11.18 (Lt CF Cogswell & Lt JD Hall OK)

D3053 At Makers 8.6.18, allotted to EF; Rep Pk 2 ASD to 2 AI 9.8.18; 98 Sqn ('E') 9.8.18; On landing from practice flight tyre burst causing m/c to swing on wing tip and crash 28.8.18 (2/Lt FJ Keble & 2/Lt CH Senecal OK); 9 AP 30.8.18; SOC Rep Pk 2 ASD 13.9.18 NWR

D3054 At Makers 8.6.18, allotted to EF; Rep Pk 1 ASD to Rec Pk 14.7.18; 1 AI 15.7.18; 5 AI 21.7.18; To 49 Sqn but returned, damaged on landing 20.7.18 (Lt HL Arnott); Dismantled after salvage 24.7.18; 1 AI by rail 25.7.18; SOC 1 ASD 3.9.18 NWR

D3055 At Makers 10.6.18 for 108 Sqn (Mob); At Sqn by 3.7.18; To France with Sqn 22.7.18; Left 07.30 on photo reconnaissance of Ardoye Dump, weakened by AA damage and not under full control, crashed on landing 22.8.18 (2/Lt R Russell & 2/Lt GB Pike OK); Rep Pk 1 ASD 24.8.18; SOC 12.9.18 NWR

D3056 At Makers 19.6.18, reallotted from Store to EF; To 8 AAP Lympne for engine fitting and erection; Rec Pk to 5 AI 19.7.18; 49 Sqn 20.7.18; Red-nosed Fokker DVII OOC Mont Notre Dame 19.00 25.7.18 (2/Lt AR Spurling & Sgt Mech FW Bell); Left 16.35 on bombing raid, at 18.55 cut off from formation by cloud, flew west for 20 minutes, thinking they were over own lines and seeing an aerodrome were going to land to find position when attacked by a Fokker DVII, a formation of about 30 Fokkers was seen below, dived into centre of formation firing "continuously" leaving three in flames and one crashed, time 19.15, a/c damaged, FL at 1 ASD 24.8.18 (Lt AR Spurling & Sgt Mech FW Bell OK); Rebuilt & renumbered F6452 in error Rep Pk 2 ASD 26.8.18; Renumbered H7075

D3057 At Makers 19.6.18, reallotted from Store to EF; To 8 AAP Lympne for engine fitting and erection; Rec Pk to 5 AI 19.7.18; 107 Sqn 20.7.18; COL 31.7.18 (2/Lt AT Reid & 2/Lt WJ Bradshaw both unhurt)

D3058 At Makers 19.6.18, reallotted from Store to EF; To 8 AAP Lympne for engine fitting and erection; Rec Pk to 2 AI 21.7.18; 5 AI 21.7.18; 49 Sqn 22.7.18; In trying to avoid another m/c on aerodrome swerved and crashed in cornfield 8.8.18 (Lt SB Welch & 2/Lt DC Roy); Rep Pk 2 ASD SOC 13.9.18 (ex 9 AP) NWR

D3059 At Makers 19.6.18, reallotted from Store to EF; To 8 AAP Lympne by 8.7.18 for engine fitting and erection; Rec Pk to 2 AI 13.7.18; 5 AI 17.7.18; 107 Sqn 19.7.18; Struck ridge on landing, u/c broke 28.7.18 (Lt JE Emtage & 2/Lt P Willis both unhurt); SOC Rep Pk 1 ASD 3.9.18 NWR (ex 9 AP)

D3060 At Makers 28.6.18, reallotted from Store to EF; To 8 AAP Lympne by 8-22.7.18 for engine fitting and erection; Rec Pk to 2 AI 25.7.18; 5 AI 28.7.18; 98 Sqn ('R') 28.7.18; Raid on Péronne Rlwy Bridge, Pfalz DIII crashed Bequincourt, SW of Péronne 15.20 8.8.18 (Sgt ER McDonald & Sgt Mech RT Wallace); Attempting to land at Beugnatre, crashed and caught fire causing bombs to explode, a/c destroyed 1.10.18 (Lt FK Heywood killed & Sgt Mech RT Wallace badly burnt)

D3061 Deld 6 SD Ascot W/E 20.6.18; Shipped to Taranto 17.7.18; AD Taranto by 8.18

D3062 Deld 6 SD Ascot W/E 20.6.18; Shipped to Taranto 17.7.18; AD Taranto by 8.18; Repair Base Mudros by 10.18; 224 Sqn 17.10.18 - @1.19

D3063 Deld 6 SD Ascot W/E 20.6.18; Shipped to Taranto 17.7.18; AD Taranto by 8.18

D3064 5 TDS Easton-on-the-Hill .18; Midland Area FIS Lilbourne by 1.19

D3065 At Makers 28.6.18, reallotted from Store to EF; To 8 AAP Lympne for engine fitting and erection; Rec Pk to 5 AI 19.7.18; 27 Sqn 20.7.18; Returning from raid overshot on landing and crashed into medical tent 11.8.18 (Lt RS Walter & Lt H Pitkin OK); 9 AP 13.8.18; SOC Rep Pk 2 ASD 10.9.18 NWR

D3066 No information

D3067 98 Sqn 1919; 49 TDS Catterick by 2.19

D3068 & D3069 No information

D3070 117 Sqn Tallaght 1919

D3071 No information

D3072 5 TDS Easton-on-the-Hill 1918; Midland Area FIS Lilbourne by 1.19

D3073 to D3076 No information

D3077 6 TDS Boscombe Down by 28.9.18

D3078 At Makers 28.6.18, reallotted from Store to EF; To 8 AAP Lympne for engine fitting and erection; Rec Pk to 2 AI 25.7.18; 5 AI 26.7.18; 98 Sqn 28.7.18; FTR on Péronne Rlwy Bridge, left 12.50, 8.8.18 (Capt FG Powell & Capt GHP Whitfield both PoW wounded)

D3079 98 Sqn by 10.18; Rec Pk 21.3.19

D3080 No information

D3081 At 6 Sqn in France 11.3.19 reallotted from SW Area to EF; 'M' Flt from 14.7.19

D3082 At Makers 28.6.18, reallotted from Store to EF; To 8 AAP Lympne for engine fitting and erection; Rec Pk to 5 AI 19.7.18; 98 Sqn 20.7.18; Pfalz DIII OOC Douai 08.50 29.8.18 (Lt FJ Fogarty & Sgt Mech RT Wallace); Landing at new aerodrome ran into E8875 27.10.18 (Lt WV Thomas & 2/Lt WS Woodall OK); Rep Pk 1 ASD 5.11.18

D3083 No information

D3084 At Makers 28.6.18, reallotted from Store to EF; To 8 AAP Lympne by 20.7.18 for engine fitting and erection; On charge IF 23.7.18 reallotted from EF to IF; Rec Pk to 2 AI and on to 3 ASD 24.7.18; 104 Sqn 26.7.18; Combat with 23 EA, 5m E of lines, fuel tank hit 12.8.18 (Lt GH Patman & 2/Lt JMS Macpherson both killed)

D3085 At Makers 28.6.18, reallotted from Store to EF; To 8 AAP Lympne for engine fitting and erection; 2 AI to 5 AI 24.7.18; 49 Sqn 27.7.18; COL 7.8.18 (Lt RC Stokes & 2/Lt CE Pullen OK); SOC Rep Pk 2 ASD 16.9.18 (ex 9 AP)

D3086 & D3087 No information

D3088 At Makers 28.6.18, reallotted from Store to EF; To 8 AAP Lympne by 22.7.18 for engine fitting and erection; In France 24.7.18 reallotted to IF; Rec Pk to 2 AI 26.7.18; 3 ASD 28.7.18; 104 Sqn 29.7.18; Shot down in raid on Metz-Sablon 13.8.18 (2/Lt EC Clarke killed & Lt JLC Sutherland MC PoW died)

D3089 No information

D3090 14 TDS Lake Down by 13.7.18 - @7.8.18

D3091 At 2 AAP Hendon by 1.7.18 for 108 Sqn (Mob); 108 Sqn Kenley, EF landing, hit house, TW 8.7.18 (2/Lt F Shaw injured & 2/Lt CG Mobbs seriously injured)

D3092 At 2 AAP Hendon by 1.7.18 for 108 Sqn (Mob); To France with Sqn 22.7.18; In Lichtervelde raid Fokker DrI OOC Gits and Fokker DVII OOC Staden shared C6314, C6345, D1080, D5622, D5759; D7208, E669, E5435 & F5847 11.45, then chased down in spiral by 2 EA from 10,000ft 21.9.18 (Lt DA Shanks & Sgt RJ Sear both killed)

D3093 8 AAP Lympne to Rec Pk 5.7.18; 1 AI 7.7.18; 211 Sqn 10.7.18; Left 11.30 for bombing raid on Courtrai, shot down smoking but in control c.12.00 in running fight when formation attacked by 40/50 EA Ypres-Cambrai 29.9.18 (Lt AG White & 2/Lt JB Blundell both killed)

D3094 4 ASD to 218 Sqn 13.7.18; EF, FL on beach Hooglade 6.10.18 (Lt HW Matthews & 2/Lt B Archer); 4 ASD 6.10.18 (repair)

D3095 218 Sqn by 28.7.18; After raid on Ostende harbour crashed nr Beaumaris 4.8.18 (2/Lt EH Attwood & 2/Lt FK Wilson both injured); 4 ASD 4.8.18; 2 SS Richborough 2.10.18

D3096 Rec Pk to 2 AI 10.7.18; 5 AI 22.7.18; 98 Sqn 24.7.18; Whilst photographing Frise bridge attacked by two Pfalz DIII one of which was sent down OOC 10.30 9.8.18 (Lt JH Nicholas & 2/Lt APC Bruce); Left 06.15, in combat Albert, driven down E of lines 29.8.18 (2/Lt HJ Fox wounded & 2/Lt WR Sellar killed)

D3097 8 AAP Lympne to Rec Pk 7.7.18; 1 AI 8.7.18; 98 Sqn 13.7.18; left 06.30 for raid on Clery, FTR 11.8.18 (2/Lt BC Geary & 2/Lt EH Edgell both killed)

D3098 Rec Pk to 1 AI 10.7.18; 107 Sqn 15.7.18; Damaged in bad landing 17.7.18 (Lt FT Stott & AM WJ Palmer OK); Rep Pk 1 ASD SOC 3.9.18 (ex 9 AP)

D3099 218 Sqn by 1.8.18; U/c collapsed landing, badly damaged 11.8.18 (Lt HW Matthews & 2/Lt B Archer both unhurt); 4 ASD 12.8.18; 2 SS Richborough 15.9.18

D3100 Rec Pk to 2 AI 10.7.18; 3 ASD 14.7.18; 104 Sqn 15.7.18; 3 ASD 24.7.18; 3 ASD to 104 Sqn 5.10.18; 3 ASD 29.10.18; 104 Sqn 8.11.18; En route from Azelot to Blangey, COL 21.11.18 (2/Lt W McCullagh & AM Potter OK); SOC 29.11.18

D3101 Rec Pk to 2 AI 9.7.18; 3 ASD 18.7.18; 104 Sqn 18.7.18; 3 ASD 31.7.18 wrecked; 104 Sqn 30.10.18; FTR from raid on Buhl aerodrome 6.11.18 (2/Lt A Hemingway & Sgt GA Smith both killed)

D3102 14 TDS Lake Down, u/c caught top plane of another a/c

D.H.9 ambulance D3117 '6' of 'Z' Force, Somaliland in 1919-20. (via Peter Green)

Capt J.F.Goodman (Somali Camel Corps) being removed from D.H.9 ambulance D3117 '6' of 'Z' Force at Eil dur Elan 1.2.20. (via Frank Cheesman)

on TO 29.7.18 (Lt E Cropper slightly injured)

D3103 No information

D3104 11 TDS Old Sarum by 10.18

D3105 14 TDS Lake Down by 2.19; Stalled after EF on TO and dived in 1.2.19 (Capt SH Bell injured & Lt HW Heyward slightly injured)

D3106 At Makers 28.6.18, reallotted from Store to EF; To 8 AAP Lympne by 24.7.18 for engine fitting and erection; Rec Pk to 2 AI 7.8.18; 107 Sqn 9.8.18; Left on bombing raid 07.35, FTR 4.9.18 (2/Lt JC Boyle PoW & 2/Lt FCB Eaton killed); SOC 5.9.18

D3107 At Makers 28.6.18, reallotted from Store to EF; To 8 AAP Lympne for engine fitting and erection; Rec Pk to 1 AI 28.7.18; 108 Sqn ('P') 29.7.18; Hit by AA 13.8.18 (2/Lt HL McLellan OK & Sgt EF Kimpton wounded); Fokker DVII crashed in sea Ostende, shared C2205 & C6314 11.20 7.9.18 (2/Lt HL McLellan & 2/Lt FX Jackson); Left 14.15 for bombing raid on Bruges, FL, ran into canal, Souburg, Holland c.17.45 15.9.18 (2/Lt FB Cox wounded & Lt JJ Lister unhurt both interned); A/c fell on its side and killed a soldier while being salvaged; Scrapped

D3108 No information

D3109 6 TDS Boscombe Down by 2.10.18; 14 TDS Lake Down, dived in, believed fainted 19.10.18 (Lt EL Capreal & Lt CB Smith both seriously injured)

D3110 & D3112 No information

D3113 At Makers 25.6.18 for 109 Sqn (Mob) Lake Down; At 2 AAP Hendon by 1.7.18, reallotted to 108 Sqn (Mob); At sqn by 9.7.18; Tested 8 AAP Lympne 19.7.18; To France with sqn 22.7.18; To Stonehenge 4.8.18 for special bombing course, back at sqn by 6.9.18; On formation practice collided with C6345 at 5,000ft 8.10.18 (2/Lt HG Daulton & Sgt FGL King OK)

D3114 At Makers 25.6.18 for 109 Sqn (Mob) Lake Down; 2 AAP Hendon 6.7.18; To Sqn 9.7.18 but crashed landing at Lake Down; WOC

D3115 At Makers 25.6.18 for 109 Sqn (Mob) Lake Down; 2 AAP Hendon 3.7.18, reallotted to 108 Sqn (Mob); Not to France with sqn 22.7.18

D3116 At Makers 25.6.18 for 109 Sqn (Mob) Lake Down; 2 AAP Hendon 6.7.18; Reallotted to 108 Sqn (Mob) 11.7.18; At sqn by 13.7.18; To France with sqn 22.7.18; A wheel gave way on landing, overturned 1.8.18 (2/Lt WF Long & Sgt W Greenwood); Rep Pk 1 ASD 1.8.18; SOC 5.8.18 NWR

D3117 At Makers 24.6.18 for 110 Sqn (Mob) Kenley as a training machine; 2 AAP Hendon 3.7.18; To 110 Sqn 9.7.18; Reallotted to SE Area 10.8.18; Pilots and Observers AF&AGS Leysdown by 8.18 - @2.19; Propeller accident 26.11.18 (1/AM FW Parsons injured); 'Z' Unit British Somaliland ('6') by 12.19 - @5.4.20 (Used as ambulance)

D3118 55 TDS Manston by 7.18; Stalled on turn, spun in from 500ft 29.7.18 (F/Cdt RJ Wickham seriously injured & 2/AM GF Frost killed)

D3119 203 TDS Manston by 7.18

D3120 Sold to Anti-Bolshevik Government; Base Depot RAF Novorossisk to Russian Aviation Corps 14.2.20

D3121 Sold to Anti-Bolshevik Government

D3122 At Makers 28.6.18, reallotted from Store to EF; To 8 AAP Lympne for engine fitting and erection; On charge IF 23.7.18 reallotted to IF; Arr Rec Pk 20.7.18; 2 AI 21.7.18; 3 ASD 22.7.18; 104 Sqn 22.7.18; Wrecked 14.9.18; 6 AP 17.9.18; 3 ASD 19.9.18; To England 1.10.18; To Anti-Bolsheviks

D3123 Sold to Anti-Bolshevik Government; TOC Base Depot RAF Novorossisk 14.2.20; SOC 5.3.20

D3124 Sold to Anti-Bolshevik Government; TOC Base Depot RAF Novorossisk 14.2.20; To Russian Aviation Corps 14.2.20

D3125 No information

D3126 Sold to Anti-Bolshevik Government

D3127 Sold to Anti-Bolshevik Government; TOC Base Depot RAF Novorossisk 14.2.20; To Russian Aviation Corps 14.2.20

D3128 Sold to Anti-Bolshevik Government

D3129 Sold to Anti-Bolshevik Government; Later Soviet Russian Air Fleet (RKKVF)

D3130 Sold to Anti-Bolshevik Government; TOC Base Depot RAF Novorossisk 14.2.20

D3131 Sold to Anti-Bolshevik Government

D3132 Sold to Anti-Bolshevik Government; TOC Base Depot RAF Novorossisk 14.2.20; SOC 5.3.20

D3133 Sold to Anti-Bolshevik Government

D3134 Sold to Anti-Bolshevik Government; TOC Base Depot RAF Novorossisk 14.2.20; To Russian Aviation Corps 14.2.20

D3135 No information

D3136 Imperial Gift to New Zealand; Became *G-NZAH*

D3137 Sold to Anti-Bolshevik Government; TOC Base Depot RAF Novorossisk 14.2.20; To Russian Aviation Corps 14.2.20; Later Soviet Russian Air Fleet (RKKVF)

D3138 No information

D3139 Imperial Gift to New Zealand; New Zealand Air Transport Co 1921; Became *G-NZAM*

D3140 No information

D3141 47 Sqn by 8.19

D3142 Unit? [211 or 218 Sqn?], FL, irreparably damaged Breskens, Zeeland 16.8.18 DBR (crew presumably interned) [Fitted Puma No.6526]

D3143 Recd 'X' AD ex UK 18.8.18; 'X' AP to 144 Sqn 28.8.18; FL in enemy territory on raid on Afule 19.9.18 (Capt IM Matheson & Lt CD Walinck rescued by an F.2b of 1 Sqn AFC); M/c destroyed; SOC 22.9.18

D3144 Recd 'X' AD ex UK 3.10.18; 17 TDS El Firdan 12.11.18; 5 FS Heliopolis by 3.19; 'X' AP 4.6.19; 206 Sqn Helwan 9.7.19; SOC at 206 Sqn 13.12.19
BUT 'Z' Force, Somaliland ('V') 1919

D3145 No information

D3146 Recd 'X' AD ex UK 17.9.18; 144 Sqn 25.10.18; 'X' AD 26.11.18

D3147 Recd 16 Wing ex UK 13.10.18; Arr Salonika AP 13.10.18 ex UK; 47 Sqn for service in south Russia 21.4.19; At 47 Sqn Ekaterinodar by 3.6.19; Erected 12.7.19; U/c smashed landing 18.7.19 (Lt JR Hatchett & Lt EJ Cronin); Crashed just after take off 20.8.19 (Lt JR Hatchett & Lt HE Simmons); Sold to Anti-Bolshevik

Government
D3148 No information
D3149 Arr Salonika AP ex UK 13.10.18; 47 Sqn for service in south Russia 21.4.19; At 47 Sqn Ekaterinodar by 3.6.19; Erected 17.7.19; 'A' dett RAF Instructional Mission South Russia by 17.10.19; Sold to Anti-Bolshevik Government
D3150 Arr Salonika AP ex UK 13.10.18; 47 Sqn 30.12.18; Salonika AP to 47 Sqn for service in south Russia 21.4.19; At 47 Sqn Ekaterinodar by 3.6.19; Erected 4.7.19; Sqn records dated 11.8.19 say lost through enemy action on special mission with the Caucasian Army
D3151 Arr Salonika ex UK 25.9.18; 'B' Flt 17 Sqn, damaged on landing Mudros 7.11.18 (Lt A Dickson & Col Heywood); 17 Sqn Amberkoj to Salonika AP 13.12.18; 17 Sqn 1.5.19
D3152 Deld 6 SD Ascot W/E 25.7.18; To docks W/E 29.8.18; Shipped to Mudros 6.9.18 - @10.18; Repair Base Mudros by 1.19; Sold to Anti-Bolshevik Government; RAF South Russia to Russian Aviation Corps 8.19
D3153 Deld 6 SD Ascot W/E 25.7.18; To docks W/E 29.8.18; Shipped to Mudros 6.9.18 - @10.18; Repair Base Mudros by 1.19; Sold to Anti-Bolshevik Government 1919
D3154 Deld 6 SD Ascot W/E 25.7.18; To docks W/E 29.8.18; Shipped to Mudros 6.9.18 - @10.18; Repair Base Mudros by 1.19; Sold to Anti-Bolshevik Government 1919
D3155 Deld 6 SD Ascot W/E 25.7.18; To docks W/E 29.8.18; Shipped to Mudros 6.9.18 - @10.18; Repair Base Mudros by 1.19
D3156 & D3158 No information
D3159 5 TDS Easton-on-the-Hill .18
D3160 At Makers 24.7.18 allotted to EF; Rep Pk 1 ASD to 2 AI 9.8.18; 107 Sqn 10.9.18; Engine trouble, landed at Rep Pk 2 ASD and retained there 14.8.18 (Lt DH Tyler & Lt WJ Bradstreet OK); 2 AI 14.8.18; 107 Sqn 5.9.18; 98 Sqn 1.3.19; 8 AAP Lympne 6.3.19
D3161 At Makers 24.7.18 allotted to EF; Rep Pk 2 ASD to 2 AI 9.8.18; 27 Sqn 10.8.18; Fokker DVII with two red stripes on each wingtip OOC between Prement and Brancourt 18.20 25.9.18 (Lt BM Bowyer-Smythe & Sgt HW Cornell); Left 06.05 on bombing raid, damaged in combat with EA over Aulnoye 10.10.18 (Lt BM Bowyer-Smythe & Lt WG Lacey both OK); Rep Pk 2 ASD 10.10.18;
D3162 At Makers 24.7.18 allotted to EF; Rep Pk 1 ASD to Rec Pk 10.8.18; 1 AI to 103 Sqn 27.8.18; In raid on Fives Stn Fokker DVII crashed N of St André 11.30 6.9.18; Fokker DVII OOC Wasnes-au-Bac 09.15 27.9.18 (both Capt JS Stubbs DFC & 2/Lt CC Dance); 98 Sqn 16.3.19
D3163 At Makers 24.7.18 allotted to EF; Rep Pk 2 ASD to 2 AI 10.8.18; 27 Sqn 12.8.18; Left 03.50 for bombing raid on Bohain, last seen in control Le Catelat 25.9.18 (2/Lt CB Sanderson PoW DoW 17.10.18 & Sgt J Wilding PoW wounded)
D3164 At Makers 24.7.18 allotted to EF; Rep Pk 1 ASD to Rec Pk 7.8.18; 2 AI and on to 49 Sqn 10.8.18; Left 16.05, hit by AA returning from raid on Etreux, crashed Izel le Hameau, damaged 19.35 25.8.18 (Lt CC Conover & 2/Lt SP Scott OK); SOC Rep Pk 2 ASD 2.10.18 (ex 9 AP)
D3165 At Makers 24.7.18 allotted to EF; Rep Pk 2 ASD to 2 AI 6.8.18; 49 Sqn 8.8.18; Fokker DVII OOC NW of Marquion 17.15 27.9.18 (2/Lt LC Ellis & Sgt Mech F Davies); COL 17.1.19 (Lt LW Boland & 2/Lt JB Tinn)
D3166 At Makers 24.7.18 allotted to EF; Rec Pk to 2 AI 10.8.18; SOC Rep Pk 2 ASD 2.10.18 (ex 2 AI)
D3167 At Makers 24.7.18 allotted to EF; Rep Pk 2 ASD to 2 AI 10.8.18;
D3168 At Makers 24.7.18 allotted to EF; Rec Pk to 2 AI 13.8.18; 3 ASD 19.8.18; 104 Sqn 24.8.18; Wrecked 29.10.18; 6 AP 2.11.18; 3 ASD 12.11.18
D3169 At Makers 24.7.18 allotted to EF; Rep Pk 2 ASD by 12-13.8.18; 2 AI to 98 Sqn 21.8.18; Fokker DVII OOC Somain 18.15 30.8.18; On landing wheel caught in rut spinning m/c on to wingtip 4.9.18 (Lt WV Thomas & Capt AWB Becher OK); Rep Pk 2 ASD 6.9.18; SOC 15.9.18 NWR
BUT 98 Sqn, returning from raid on Valenciennes Rlwy Stn Fokker DVII OOC Oisy 10.45 16.9.18 (Capt OCW Johnsen & 2/Lt CH Thompson) (combat report and sqn daily records have D3169; however weekly returns of a/c at 98 Sqn show this a/c not at the sqn 16.9.18)
D3170 At Makers 24.7.18 allotted to EF; Rec Pk to 2 AI 16.8.18; 49 Sqn 24.8.18; Left 15.55 for bombing raid on Busigny, hit by gunfire, retd safely 17.30 30.8.18 (2/Lt ST Franks & 2/Lt A Dewhirst); SOC Rep Pk 2 ASD 30.9.18 (ex 9 AP)
D3171 At Makers 24.7.18 allotted to EF; Rep Pk 2 ASD to 2 AI 9.8.18; 98 Sqn 10.8.18; Wheel caught in rut on landing, crashed 27.9.18 (Lt EW Langford & Lt J Andrews OK); Rep Pk 2 ASD 29.9.18
D3172 At Makers 24.7.18 allotted to EF; Rec Pk to 2 AI 9.8.18; 27 Sqn 10.8.18; Left 06.30 for bombing raid on Busigny, seen going down OOC over target 29.9.18 (2/Lt HS Thomas & 2/Lt T Brown both killed)
D3173 At Makers 24.7.18 allotted to EF; 2 AI to 27 Sqn 24.8.18; On test flight crashed due to carburettor trouble 4.9.18 (2/Lt J Cocksedge & 1/AM A Simpson OK); 9 AP 5.9.18; SOC Rep Pk 2 ASD 23.9.18
D3174 to D3178 No information
D3179 Special Instruction Flight Almaza 7.20 - 12.20 (prefix unconfirmed)
D3180 Imperial Gift to India; Became *G-IAAB*
D3181 1 TDS Wittering by 8.18; 31 TDS Fowlmere by 9.18 - 11.18
D3182 Imperial Gift to Australia; Became *A6-12*; Arrived Australia 5.11.20;
D3183 & D3184 No information
D3185 Imperial Gift to India
D3186 Imperial Gift to Australia; Became *A6-13*
D3187 Imperial Gift to Australia; Shipped on SS *Australmad*; allotted CFS (Australia), Point Cook 24.9.20; 1 FTS AAF, Point Cook 31.3.21; Became *A6-14* 3.10.21
D3188 Imperial Gift to India
D3189 Imperial Gift to Australia; Became *A6-15*
D3190 Imperial Gift to India
D3191 Imperial Gift to Australia; Shipped on SS *Australmad*; allotted CFS (Australia), Point Cook 24.9.20; 1 FTS AAF, Point Cook 31.3.21; Became *A6-16* 3.10.21
D3192 Imperial Gift to India
D3193 Imperial Gift to India
D3194 To Greek Government
D3195 Imperial Gift to Australia; Became *A6-17*
D3196 Imperial Gift to Australia; Became *A6-18*
D3197 Imperial Gift to India
D3198 Rec Pk to 2 AI 23.8.18; 49 Sqn 26.8.18; On practice formation flight, engine cut on TO, crashed 5.9.18 (Lt WH Stone killed & 2/Lt VA Fair injured); SOC 2 Salvage Dump 14.9.18
D3199 To Greek Government
D3200 Imperial Gift to India
D3201 Imperial Gift to India
D3202 Imperial Gift to Australia; Arrived Australia 6.10.20; Became *A6-19*
D3203 Desp UK to AD Aboukir 12.3.20; SF Almaza by 7.20; Imperial Gift to Australia
D3204 Imperial Gift to India
D3205 To Greek Government
D3206 To Greek Government
D3207 Imperial Gift to Australia; Shipped on SS *Australmad*; allotted CFS (Australia), Point Cook 24.9.20; 1 FTS AAF, Point Cook 31.3.21; Became *A6-20* 3.10.21
D3208 Imperial Gift to India
D3209 Arr Rec Pk, but COL, CW 15.8.18
D3210 Rec Pk to 1 AI 31.8.18; 211 Sqn 12.9.18; Hit by AA returning from raid on Bruges, EF, FL by railway N of aerodrome, crashed into hedge 15.9.18 (2/Lt JM Payne unhurt & Lt CT Linford slightly wounded); Rep Pk 1 ASD 17.9.18; SOC 20.9.18
D3211 Arr Rec Pk 16.8.18; 2 AI and on to 3 ASD 30.8.18; 104 Sqn 5.9.18; Shot up in raid on Metz-Sablon railway 15.9.18 (Lt J Wrighton OK & 2/Lt WE Jackson DoW); 3 ASD 21.9.18
D3212 No information
D3213 Arr Rec Pk 8.8.18; 2 AI 10.8.18; 3 ASD 12.8.18; 99 Sqn 15.8.18; On practice flight crashed nr aerodrome 26.8.18 (Lt WHG Gillett & 2/Lt JLMcI Oliphant OK); Bombing raid on Metz-Sablon railway, in combat with 30-40 EA, FTR 26.9.18 (2/Lt WHG Gillett & 2/Lt H

Crossley both wounded PoW)

D3214 Rec Pk to 2AI 13.8.18; 27 Sqn 15.8.18; On take off bomb released and exploded causing crash 7.9.18 (Capt JR Webb & 2/Lt H Pitkin); 2 Adv Salvage Dump 7.9.18; SOC Rep Pk 2 ASD 14.9.18 NWR

D3215 Arr Rec Pk 8.8.18; 2 AI 9.8.18; 3 ASD 12.8.18; 99 Sqn 19.8.18; Hit by EA fire in raid on Conflans and Doncourt aerodromes 30.8.18 (2/Lt WA Warwick OK & 2/Lt CG Russell killed); Shot up in raid on Metz-Sablon Rlwy 14.9.18 (2/Lt JG Dennis DFC & 2/Lt HG Ramsay both wounded); 3 ASD 25.9.18

D3216 No information

D3217 3 FS (Bircham Newton?) by 8.18

D3218 Arr Rec Pk 15.8.18; 2 AI 18.8.18; 3 ASD 18.8.18; 99 Sqn 25.8.18; Shot down after bombing Metz-Sablon Rlwy 13.9.18 (2/Lt FA Wood USAS & 2/Lt C Bridgett both killed)

D3219 Arr Rec Pk 16.8.18; 2 AI 18.8.18; 3 ASD 19.8.18; 104 Sqn 25.8.18; 6 AP 25.10.18; 3 ASD 31.10.18

D3220 Imperial Gift to Australia; Shipped on SS *Australmad*; allotted CFS (Australia), Point Cook 24.9.20; 1 FTS AAF, Point Cook 31.3.21; Became *A6-21* 3.10.21

D3221 203 TDS Manston by 7.18

D3222 11 TDS Old Sarum, steep turn on windy day, dived in, BO 6.10.18 (2/Lt CH Edgecombe killed & 2/Lt D Forster DoI 7.10.18)

D3223 At Makers 24.7.18 allotted to EF; Rep Pk 2 ASD to 2 AI 10.8.18; 49 Sqn 14.8.18; Returning from raid on Etreux aerodrome sent a red tailed Fokker DVII down in flames Moeuvres 19.00hrs 25.8.18 (Lt WK Jenne & 2/Lt L Eteson); Left 09.35 for bombing raid to St.Ghislain, shot up, retd 12.15 26.10.18 (2/Lt WE McDermott & 2/Lt RH St.Amory both OK)
BUT WO with 'S' Sqn attd 5 FS Heliopolis 27.5.19

D3224 At Makers 24.7.18 allotted to EF; Rec Pk to 1 AI 13.8.18; 206 Sqn 14.8.18 - @30.9.18

D3225 2 AI to 98 Sqn 21.8.18; On landing m/c caught a bump and bounced high, engine would not respond and having lost flying speed crashed 23.8.18 (Lt TW Sleigh & Lt J Andrews); 9 AP 24.8.18; SOC Rep Pk 2 ASD 18.9.18

D3226 Rec Pk to 1 AI 12.8.18; 206 Sqn 13.8.18; Left 07.20 for recce, last seen nr Dunkirk 2.9.18 (2/Lt HA Scrivener PoW wounded & Sgt CH Davidson PoW DoW same day); SOC in field 3.9.18

D3227 2 AI to 49 Sqn 27.8.18; Left 15.55 for bombing raid on Busigny, hit by gunfire, retd safely 17.10 30.8.18 (Lt CC Conover & 2/Lt SP Scott OK); SOC Rep Pk 2 ASD 2.10.18 (ex 9 AP)

D3228 Rec Pk to 2 AI 23.8.18; 3 ASD 30.8.18; 99 Sqn 2.9.18; Practice flight,COL 25.9.18 (2/Lt FL Brown & 2/Lt FO Cook); 6 AP to 3 ASD 30.9.18

D3229 2 AI to 27 Sqn 13.8.18; Casualty Report 17.2.19 says m/c waterlogged, fuselage badly twisted and main and tail planes warped; To 6 SS 25.2.19

D3230 Arr Rec Pk ex UK 16.8.18; 3 ASD 24.8.18; 104 Sqn 25.9.18; Wrecked St.Clermont 29.10.18; 6 AP 4.11.18; 3 ASD 5.11.18

D3231 No information

D3232 73 Wing Yarmouth by 11.8.18; Swung, stalled and crashed on TO, CW 21.8.18 (Lt JW Ritch & Lt TFP Llewellyn both injured)

D3233 Rec Pk to 211 Sqn 12.8.18; While stationary, hit by 20 Sqn Bristol Fighter E2603 23.11.18; 2 ASD 24.11.18

D3234 4 ASD by 8.18; 218 Sqn 18.8.18; Pfalz DIII OOC Blankenberge 16.20 24.8.18 (Lt W Bentley & 2/Lt AJ Cunningham); FL 21.12.18 (local repair); 98 Sqn 21.1.19; 8 AAP Lympne (via Rec Pk) 4.2.19

D3235 14 TDS Lake Down by 14.8.18; Prop accident 31.8.18 (F/Sgt J Watson unhurt & 1/AM E Sharples injured)

D3236 Rec Pk to 2 AI 9.8.18; 107 Sqn 10.8.18; 98 Sqn 6.3.19; 8 AAP Lympne 14.3.19

D3237 Arr Rec Pk 8.8.18; 27 Sqn 10.8.18; Fokker DVII OOC Etreux 18.30 25.8.18 (2/Lt J Cocksedge & 2/Lt JE Hermon); Fokker DVII OOC Ponchaux 1825hrs 25.9.18 (2/Lt J Cocksedge & Sgt HWJ Roach); Left 06.30 for bombing raid on Busigny, had to bank to miss another a/c landing, crashed 09.30 29.9.18 (2/Lt J Cocksedge OK & 2/Lt CP Robinson wounded); SOC Rep Pk 2 ASD 3.10.18

D3238 Arr Rec Pk 6.8.18; 2 AI 8.8.18; To 3 ASD but crashed Le Bourget 12.8.18; SOC Rep Pk 2 ASD 13.9.18 NWR

D3239 Rec Pk to 2 AI 10.8.18; 98 Sqn 12.8.18; After attacking Bertry aerodrome Pfalz DIII OOC Le Catelat 09.40 27.9.18 (2/Lt WV Thomas & 2/Lt P Fish); Returning from raid on Mons railway station, in combat with 30 EA, Fokker DVII BU and crashed in flames, own a/c damaged in combat 11.30 30.10.18 (Lt WV Thomas OK & Lt WS Woodall wounded in wrist)

D3240 219 Sqn Manston by 9.8.18

D3241 Rec Pk to 1 AI 15.8.18; 211 Sqn 17.8.18; Left 11.00 for photo mission, last seen going down S of Maubeuge with 10 EA attacking 1.11.18 (2/Lt JM Payne & 2/Lt WG Gadd both PoW)

D3242 Naval Flt 219 Sqn Manston by 3.8.18 - @21.11.18; Manston to Handley Page, Cricklewood for Polish Military Purchase Mission on free issue 25.3.20

D3243 Rec Pk to 2 AI 11.8.18; 3 ASD 13.8.18; 99 Sqn 1.9.18; On practice flight COL 19.9.18 (Lt CEW Thresher & 2/Lt JW Howard); 3 ASD 25.9.18; 99 Sqn 27.10.18; COL, radiator, undercarriage etc smashed 4.11.18; 6 AP 9.11.18

D3244 Arr Rec Pk 11.8.18; 2 AI 12.8.18; 98 Sqn 14.8.18; Pfalz DIII OOC Douai-Valenciennes 17.55 30.8.18 (2/Lt CG Gowing & 2/Lt JGW Halliday); Pfalz DIII OOC Oisy 10.40 16.9.18 (2/Lt CG Gowing & 2/Lt WV Philpott); 8 AAP Lympne 7.2.19

D3245 Arr Rec Pk 10.8.18; 2 AI 14.8.18; 3 ASD 15.8.18; 104 Sqn 23.8.18; In combat with many EAs in raid on Metz-Sablon Rlwy, FTR 15.9.18 (2/Lt LG Hall USAS PoW DoW & 2/Lt WD Evans PoW)

D3246 1 SoN&BD Stonehenge by 2.9.18

D3247 SOC Rec Pk 14.8.18, destroyed by fire.

D3248 Arr Rec Pk 4.8.18; 2 AI 6.8.18; 3 ASD 13.8.18; 104 Sqn 8.9.18; Fokker DVII broke up Ecouvier 12.40 29.10.18 (Capt IW Leiper wounded & 2/Lt LG Best OK); En route Azelot to Blangey wrecked on take off 21.11.18 (2/Lt LC Pitts & 3/AM SH Wilcox); 6 AP 23.11.18; SOC 29.11.18

D3249 Rec Pk to 206 Sqn 10.8.18; Thick ground mist, crashed, CW 6.9.18 (2/Lt SM Desmond & 1/AM A Helliwell both DoI); SOC Rep Pk 1 ASD 11.9.18

D3250 Rec Pk to 1 AI 11.8.18; SOC Rep Pk 1 ASD 12.9.18 NWR (ex 1 AI)

D3251 1 AI to 211 Sqn ('E') 17.8.18; Left 13.30, dropped 2 bombs on Bruges docks, radiator hit by AA, EF at 8,000ft, glided to Holland, FL Breskens, Zeeland, no further damage 15.55 24.9.18 (2/Lt J Olorenshaw & 2/Lt RL Kingham both interned unhurt); Became Dutch *deH444* [not confirmed by Dutch reports]; Retd to RAF 12.3.20

D3252 Rec Pk to 1 AI 14.8.18; 211 Sqn 14.8.18; Landed fast, overshot, o/t 26.9.18 (2/Lt GC Hope & 2/Lt AB Bedford unhurt); Rep Pk 1 ASD 26.9.18

D3253 4 ASD to 218 Sqn 18.8.18; 98 Sqn 21.1.19; 8 AAP Lympne 12.2.19

D3254 Rec Pk to 1 AI 22.8.18; 103 Sqn 29.8.18; Left 08.00 for raid on Fives, presumed hit by AA on return, seen to go down OOC smoking over Lomme but flattened out at 1,000ft c.09.45 16.9.18 (Capt FA Ayrton PoW & 2/Lt BP Jenkins PoW DoW 20.10.18)

D3255 No information

D3256 Rec Pk to 1 AI 15.8.18; 206 Sqn 17.8.18; COL from bombing raid, into tree in thick mist 29.9.18 (Lt AL Seddon & 1/Pte AF Bailey unhurt), to be retd

D3257 Rec Pk to 1 AI 14.8.18; 206 Sqn 15.8.18; EF, FL 11.10.18 (Lt CH Denny & Pte1 S Jones unhurt); to Rep Pk 1 ASD

D3258 Rec Pk to 2 AI 13.8.18; 3 ASD 19.8.18; 104 Sqn 15.9.18; 2 ASD 17.1.19; SOC 21.1.19

D3259 Presentation Aircraft 'Biggar Parish No.4'. Rec Pk to 1 AI 23.8.18; 211 Sqn 25.8.18; Returning ferry pilot to Marquise, FL Teteghem aerodrome in strong wind, hit bump, o/t 7.10.18 (2/Lt EJ Stevenson & Lt Wretham both unhurt); Rep Pk 1 ASD 8.10.18

D3260 Rec Pk to 2 AI 9.8.18; 49 Sqn 10.8.18; Left 07.25 on bombing raid to St.Denis, shot up in combat, retd 08.45 30.10.18 (Capt H Ford & 2/Lt J Whitehead both unhurt)

D3261 Presentation Aircraft 'Presented by His Highness the Maharajah of Bikanir No.12'. At 8 AAP Lympne 23.1.19 allotted to SE Area for Store

D3262 Rec Pk to 2 AI 10.8.18; 98 Sqn 12.8.18; Left 08.00 for raid on Valenciennes Rlwy Stn, in combat with 20 EA,

D.H.9 D3271 of No.218 after force landing at Vlissingen on 26.9.18. (via Frank Cheesman)

Pfalz DIII crashed and burnt 4m W of Valenciennes 10.35 16.9.18 (2/Lt JH Nicholas & 2/Lt APC Bruce); Left 14.05 for raid on Hirson Rlwy Stn, probably shot down between the target and Guise homeward bound 23.10.18 (2/Lt HH Rofe & 2/Lt APC Bruce both PoW)

D3263 Arr Rec Pk 11.8.18; 3 ASD 13.8.18; 104 Sqn 13.8.18; Pfalz DIII OOC just S of Metz 13.00 13.9.18 (2/Lt A MacKenzie & 2/Lt CE Bellord); Shot down OOC on Metz-Sablon raid 15.9.18 (2/Lt A MacKenzie & 2/Lt CE Bellord both killed)

D3264 Arr Rec Pk 15.8.18; 2 AI and on to 3 ASD 17.8.18; 99 Sqn ('F') 26.8.18; FTR from raid on Metz-Sablon, left 07.25, last seen going down under control Metz 14.9.18 (2/Lt WF Ogilvy & 2/Lt GH Shipton both PoW)

D3265 Rec Pk to 2 AI 29.8.18; 49 Sqn 31.8.18; In action 24.9.18 (2/Lt JF Higgins OK & 2/Lt LC Belcher wounded); Left 07.25 on bombing raid to St.Denis, shot up in combat, retd 09.45 30.10.18 (2/Lt JF Higgins & 2/Lt EN Andrews both unhurt)

D3266 Rec Pk to 2 AI 13.8.18; 27 Sqn 15.8.18; 98 Sqn 5.3.19; 1 ASD 17.3.19

D3267 Rec Pk to 2 AI 24.8.18; 98 Sqn 29.8.18; Left 08.00 for raid on Valenciennes Rlwy Stn, in combat with 20 EA, last seen in combat S of Douai 16.9.18 (2/Lt FJ Keble & 2/Lt CH Senecal both PoW)

D3268 Arr Rec Pk 14.8.18; 2 AI 17.8.18; 3 ASD 18.8.18; 104 Sqn 22.8.8; Raid on Mannheim, in combat with EAs, FTR 7.9.18 (Sgt E Mellor killed & Sgt J Bryden PoW)

D3269 Rec Pk to 2 AI 22.8.18; 49 Sqn 25.8.18; Left 14.25 for raid on Douai Station, hit by AA, crashed on return 17.10 3.9.18 (2/Lt BG Pool & Sgt Mech RA Campbell unhurt); SOC Rep Pk 2 ASD 30.9.18 (ex 9 AP)

D3270 3 ASD by 8.18; 99 Sqn 1.9.18; Raid on Buhl aerodrome 25.9.18 (2/Lt HE King OK & 2/Lt JLMcI Oliphant wounded); Pfalz DIII OOC smoking Buhl 14.00 6.11.18 (2/Lt HE King & Lt T Llewellyn); 3 ASD 13.11.18; 2 AI 1.12.18

D3271 4 ASD to 218 Sqn 21.8.18; Fokker DVII OOC Bruges 09.20 20.9.18 (Capt JF Chisholm DSC DFC & Sgt RJ Williams); Radiator hit by AA after bombing Bruges Docks, EF, broke propeller landing on beach in front of Grand Hotel, Vlissingen, Zeeland, steered into sea to avoid breakwater, went on nose, 26.9.18 (Capt JF Chisholm DSC DFC & Sgt RJ Williams both interned); Deleted 15.10.18; Repaired and became Dutch *deH446* [not confirmed by Dutch records]; Retd to RAF less engine 12.3.20

D3272 4 ASD to 218 Sqn 21.8.18; Raid on Bruges, attacked by 4 Fokker DVII and a 2-str, Fokker D.VII OOC smoking W of Bruges 09.30 20.9.18 (Lt EH Attwood & 2/Lt AE Smith); Last seen in steep dive with 5 EA on tail, Lichtervelde 09.45 29.9.18 (2/Lt JL Pritchard & 2/Lt AE Smith both killed); Deleted 15.10.18

D3273 Arr Rec Pk 9.8.18; 2 AI 16.8.18; 3 ASD 17.8.18; 104 Sqn 23.8.18; 3 ASD 23.8.18

D3274 (240 hp BHP) Rec Pk to 1 AI 12.8.18; 103 Sqn ('M') 13.8.18; Fokker DVII OOC and another crashed S of Armentières 11.15 25.8.18 (Capt JS Stubbs DFC & 2/Lt JB Russell DFC); Rep Pk 1 ASD 28.8.18; SOC 31.8.18

D3275 (Eagle VIII) 1 Comm Sqn Hendon by 2.4.19; FL due to mist, collided with hill 10.4.19 (2/Lt G Gorrill & Rowland Kenny Esq both injured)

200 D.H.9 ordered from G & J Weir Ltd, Cathcart, Glasgow and numbered D4011 to D4210. Order cancelled and serials re-allocated

300 D.H.9 ordered 10.7.17 under Cont No A.S.20391 (BR.162) from Alliance Aeroplane Co/Waring & Gillow Ltd, Hammersmith and numbered D5551 to D5850 (50 sub-contracted to Wells Aviation Co Ltd, Chelsea). (230hp Puma)

D5551 2 AAP Hendon to 98 Sqn Old Sarum 21.2.18; 99 Sqn Old Sarum 5.3.18; 108 Sqn Lake Down, prop accident 19.4.18 (2/AM H Barker seriously injured); 14 TDS Lake Down by 16.7.18 - @9.8.18

D5552 At 2 AAP Hendon 14.3.18, allotted to EF; England to Rec Pk 24.3.18; 2 AI 31.3.18; By road to Salvage Section 6.4.18; SOC Rep Pk 1 ASD 5.5.18

D5553 104 Sqn by 3.18, but not to France with Sqn 5.18.

D5554 At 2 AAP Hendon 26.2.18, allotted to EF but reallotted to 99 Sqn (Mob) Old Sarum 5.3.18; Reallotted to EF 30.3.18; England to Rec Pk 29.3.18; 49 Sqn 2.4.18; About to land, stalled coming out of a turn and nose dived in 1.5.18 (Lt DS Cramb slightly injured & Sgt FA Bardsley cuts and shock); SOC Rep Pk 1 ASD 4.5.18

D5555 48 TS Waddington, ran into airman on ground 26.4.18 (Lt W Chalaire unhurt & 3/AM H Watson DoI); 44 TS Waddington by 7.18

D5556 26 TS Narborough by 10.3.18 - @25.4.18; 9 TS Sedgeford by 10.6.18; 69 TS Narborough by 7.18

D5557 103 Sqn

D5558 99 Sqn Old Sarum 15.3.18; To France with Sqn 3.5.18; Landed too slowly in strong wind, fell on one wing 27.5.18 (2/Lt V Beecroft & 2/Lt HT Melville); Rep Pk 2 ASD 28.5.18; Rebuilt as F6055 26.6.18

D5559 At 2 AAP Hendon 26.2.18, allotted to EF but reallotted to 99 Sqn (Mob) Old Sarum 5.3.18; Stalled on turn at 200ft, sideslipped, dived in 15.3.18 (2/Lt WE Sinclair killed)

D5560 107 Sqn Lake Down, wings broke away at 2,000ft in dive 22.3.18 (Capt LV Thorowgood & 2/Lt AHC Evans both killed)

D5561 No information

D5562 5 TS Wyton by 5.18; 31 TS Wyton, stalled landing, sideslipped in, goggles blurred by rain 11.8.18 (F/Cdt E Grimshaw slightly injured)

D5563 At 2 AAP Hendon 12.4.18, allotted to EF; England to Rec Pk 1.5.18; 49 Sqn 2.5.18; Attempting to land, saw another a/c directly in its path, turned but having lost flying speed was unable to level out before one wing hit the ground 4.5.18 (Lt FW Lowen & 1/AM E Martin OK): Rep Pk 2 ASD 6.5.18; Rebuilt as F6170 3.7.18

D5564 & D5565 No information

D5566 99 Sqn to Rep Pk 1 ASD 30.4.18; SOC 5.5.18; bboc week ending 31.5.18; Rec Pk to 2 AI 29.6.18; 27 Sqn 30.6.18; Fokker DVII dived into houses on the outskirts of Valenciennes 18.15 3.9.18 (Lt EJ Jacques & 2/Lt NP Wood); Practice flight COL at unfamiliar aerodrome in bad light 24.10.18 (2/Lt E Sidey & 2/Lt EA Hooper OK); 2 ASD 24.10.18

D5567 105 Sqn Andover by 22.3.18 - @9.4.18; 11 TDS Old Sarum by 20.6.18

D5568 To France with 99 Sqn 3.5.18; Albatros OOC 24.5.18 (2/Lt EL Doidge & Lt W Walker); 3 ASD 7.7.18; 104 Sqn 26.8.18; 6 AP 17.9.18; 3 ASD 19.9.18

D5569 103 Sqn Old Sarum by 20.4.18; To France with Sqn 9.5.18; Scout in flames and scout OOC Fretoy, shared C6179, C6192, D1007 16.20 6.6.18 (2/Lt CH Heebner & 2/Lt WR Henderson); Left 07.50 for bombing raid on Tournai, seen in combat over Barcy going W at 14,000ft, Fokker DVII OOC Mainvault 09.55 then FTR, but OK 30.10.18 (Sgt Mech WJ McNeill & Sgt Mech EG Stevens)

D5570 99 Sqn Old Sarum by 16.3.18; To France with 99 Sqn 3.5.18; Bombing on Hagendingen 24.5.18 (2/Lt O Jones wounded & 2/Lt E Beale unhurt); Left 04.45, attacked by several EA in bombing raid on Offenburg, chased down in control emitting steam S of Strasbourg 25.6.18

(Lt NS Harper & 2/Lt DG Benson (Can) both killed)

D5571 allotted to 103 Sqn (Mob) Old Sarum but reallotted to EF 2.4.18; Rec Pk to 1 AI 2.4.18; 98 Sqn 12.4.18; Left 07.50 for Menin, last seen going down Gheluwe-Wervicq 29.4.18 (Lt CG Tysoe PoW & 2/Lt CV Carr PoW wounded)

D5572 To France with 103 Sqn 9.5.18; In combat Fromelles-Wavrin 8.7.18 (2/Lt HD Humphreys OK & 2/Lt WS Marshall slightly wounded); Left 09.50 on raid on Haubourdin, seen to spin down and crash, presumed to have been hit by AA 18.9.18 (Lt TM Phillips & 2/Lt RE Owen both killed)

D5573 To France with 99 Sqn 3.5.18; Damaged by AA in raid on Metz 18.15 23.6.18 (Lt HD West (Can) & 2/Lt J Levy OK); 2 ASD 24.6.18; 3 ASD to 99 Sqn 3.8.18; Bombing raid on Metz-Sablon railway, in combat with 30-40 EA, shot down nr Pullingen 26.9.18 (Lt LG Stern & Lt FO Cook killed)

D5574 104 Sqn Andover by 12.4.18; 11 TDS Old Sarum by 22.7.18

D5575 No information

D5576 At 2 AAP Hendon 14.3.18, allotted to EF; England to Rec Pk 23.3.18; 1 AI 1.4.18; 49 Sqn 7.4.18; Scout OOC smoking Flavy-Le Martel 10.45 7.6.18 (Capt G Fox-Rule & Lt EH Tredcroft); Pfalz DIII in flames Fignières 18.40 10.6.18; Pfalz DIII in vertical dive Honvillers 14.45 11.6.18 (both Lt H Ford & Lt HH Jones); Casualty Report 6.7.18 says complete overhaul desirable; Rep Pk 2 ASD 8.7.18; 2 AI 20.9.18; 8 AAP Lympne 29.9.18; 1 (S)ARD to Islington 5.11.18

D5577 103 Sqn Old Sarum, tested 23.4.18; To France with Sqn 9.5.18; Pfalz DIII dest Haubourdin-Bac St.Maur 09.50 8.7.18 (2/Lt JGH Chrispin & 2/Lt EA Wadsworth); COL 4.8.18 (Lt DM Darroch & Lt BA Tussaud); Rep Pk 1 ASD 9.8.18; SOC 11.8.18 NWR

D5578 At 2 AAP Hendon 1.4.18, reallotted from 104 Sqn (Mob) Andover to EF; England to Rec Pk 7.4.18; 49 Sqn 11.4.18; Crashed after combat c.18.15 over Keyem 20.4.18 (Lt BW Robinson & Sgt TJ Willis both PoW)

D5579 To France with 104 Sqn 19.5.18; Engine failure, bad landing in cross wind 6.6.18 (Lt WJ Rivett-Carnac & 2/AM JC Wilderspin OK); Rep Pk 2 ASD 6.6.18; Rebuilt as F6113 3.7.18

D5580 SOC 1 ASD 5.7.18 NWR

D5581 104 Sqn Andover by 3.18; To France with 104 Sqn 19.5.18; On test flight hit ridge on landing, u/c collapsed, turned on nose 7.6.18 (Lt OJ Lange & 1/AM GA Smith OK); 3 ASD 7.6.18; 104 Sqn 8.9.18; Hit by AA in raid on Metz-Sablon 14.9.18 (2/Lt GH Knight wounded in thigh & 2/Lt FF Bates OK); Raiding the same target, controls shot away, COL 15.9.18 (2/Lt F Barker & 2/Lt FF Bates both injured); 6 AP 17.9.18; 3 ASD 19.9.18

D5582 At 2 AAP Hendon 1.4.18, reallotted from 104 Sqn (Mob) Andover to EF; England to Rec Pk 3.4.18; 1 AI 12.4.18; To 206 Sqn but crashed on arrival, bad ground Drionville 15.4.18 (Lt AE Steele & 1/Pte A/G FC Bevis both injured); Adv Salvage to Rep Pk 1 ASD 22.4.18; SOC 25.4.18

D5583 131 Sqn Shawbury (flown by 2/Lt HG Lowe); 9 TDS Shawbury by 10.18 - 1.19

D5584 No information

D5585 At 2 AAP Hendon 1.4.18, reallotted from 104 Sqn (Mob) Andover to EF; England to Rec Pk 7.4.18; 49 Sqn 12.4.18; Fokker DrI OOC E of Bray 12.00 9.5.18 (Lt G Ezard & Sgt H Barfoot); Fokker DrI OOC Chaulnes 19.15 9.5.18 (Lt FD Nevin & Lt FC Aulagnier); In combat with Pfalz, gun jambed, control wires except rudder controls shot away, succeeded in bringing m/c back to aerodrome 10.6.18 (Lt LR Charron OK & Lt FE Dennison wounded); To 9 AP 10.6.18; Rep Pk 1 ASD, SOC 9.7.18, NWR

D5586 123 Sqn Duxford, stalled landing from height test at night, crashed 15.8.18 (F/Cdt F McClive seriously injured)

D5587 131 Sqn Shawbury; 9 TDS Shawbury, stalled and crashed while turning at low speed near ground Prees Heath, Shropshire 25.8.18 (2/Lt A Dunn DoI 26.8.18 & Pte F Baskerville killed)

D5588 & D5589 No information

D5590 At 2 AAP Hendon 15.4.18, allotted to EF; England to Rec PK 8.5.18; 1 AI 10.5.18; 206 Sqn 15.5.18; Pfalz DIII OOC 1½m E of Ypres 19.20-19.35 29.7.18 (Lt EA Burn & Capt WA Carrothers); Pfalz DIII OOC Menin-Wervicq 08.30 1.8.18 (Lt CS Johnston & 2/Lt AB Sangster); Left on raid 05.11, FTR 13.8.18 (Lt CS Johnson & 2/Lt AB Sangster both killed)

D5591 & D5593 No information

D5594 To France with 103 Sqn 9.5.18; COL 17.5.18 (Lt HR Herbert & 2/Lt HTG Robey both injured); Rep Pk 1 ASD 20.5.18; SOC 21.5.18.

D5595 No information

D5596 At 2 AAP Hendon 1.4.18, reallotted from 104 Sqn (Mob) Andover to EF; Rec Pk to 49 Sqn 11.4.18; On travelling flight landed at 57 Sqn to enquire location, EF on take off, crashed into a wood 9.6.18 (Lt G Ezard injured & Lt CAB Beattie OK); To 9AP

D5597 No information

D5598 To France with 104 Sqn 19.5.18; Overshot on landing and ran onto ditch 16.6.18 (1/Lt WL Deetjen USA & Cpl HV Jurgens OK); 2 ASD 16.6.18; 3 ASD .18; 104 Sqn 30.7.18; 3 ASD 31.7.18; 104 Sqn 27.10.18; Wrecked 5.11.18; 6 AP 8.11.18; 3 ASD 9.11.18

D5599 131 Sqn Shawbury; 41 TDS London Colney, ran into fog, FL 10.7.18 (Lt CL Cumming unhurt & Lt GO Slade slightly injured); 9 TDS Shawbury by 10.18 - 1.19

D5600 At 2 AAP Hendon 16.4.18, allotted to EF; England to Rec Pk 3.5.18; 2 AI 6.5.18; 27 Sqn 17.5.18; Engine trouble, COL 22.5.18 (Lt CE Hutcheson & Sgt WB Harold OK); Rep Pk 2 ASD 29.5.18; Rebuilt as F6112 3.7.18

D5601 137th US Aero Sqn, prop accident 10.5.18 (Cpl C Jenkins seriously injured) [he was probably attached to an RAF unit]

D5602 & D5603 No information

D5604 2 AAP Hendon to 1 SoN&BD Stonehenge 3.5.18 - @3.9.18 BUT 110 Sqn Kenley 6.18

D5605 To France with 103 Sqn 9.5.18; Albatros DV OOC Douai 11.00 22.5.18 (Lt EA Windridge & 2/Lt VW Allen); Landed cross wind, pulled up to avoid another m/c, pancaked 26.5.18 (Lt DM Darroch & 1/AM WJ Westcott); Rep Pk 1 ASD 27.5.18; SOC 30.5.18 NWR

D5606 At 2 AAP Hendon 2.4.18, allotted to EF; England to Rec Pk 8.4.18; 1 AI 12.4.18; 206 Sqn 18.4.18; COL 26.5.18 (Lt TH Wood); Rep Pk 1 ASD 30.5.18; SOC 5.7.18, NWR

D5607 & D5608 No information

D5609 At 2 AAP Hendon 9.4.18, allotted to EF; England to Rec Pk 1.5.18; 206 Sqn 4.5.18; Left 14.14 for long reconnaissance, engagement with EA, FL in shell hole No Man's Land, unable to salve 30.6.18 (Lt EA Burn injured & 2/Lt CO Shelswell unhurt); SOC in field

D5610 7 TDS Feltwell, stalled on turn at 20ft, dived in 29.5.18 (2/Lt RC Townsend killed & Lt ER Watts seriously injured)

D5611 (Puma) FF 12.4.18; Deld 119 Sqn Duxford 4.18; EF, spun in from 700ft, burnt 29.7.18 (2/Lt JS Ross of 119 Sqn & 2/Lt DR Evans of 123 sqn both killed)

D5612 No information

D5613 131 Sqn Shawbury, stalled on turn, spun in, BO 25.5.18 (2/Lt G Roper killed)

D5614 131 Sqn Shawbury, spun in off turn 10.6.18 (2/Lt A Williams slightly injured)

D5615 At 2 AAP Hendon by 19.6.18 for 108 Sqn (Mob); At Sqn by 3.7.18; To France with Sqn 22.7.18; Pancaked on landing and hit dugout 8.8.18 (Lt A Preston & Lt WR Jackson OK); Rep Pk 1 ASD 9.8.18; SOC 11.8.18 NWR

D5616 At 2 AAP Hendon 15.4.18, allotted to EF; England to Rec Pk 2.5.18; 2 AI 7.5.18; 27 Sqn 12.5.18; Left 06.10, bombing raid on Maria Aeltre, engine fell off, crashed Sains-lès-Pernes, wrecked 23.5.18 (Lt GE Ffrench & Cpl FY MacLauchlan both killed); SOC 23.5.18

D5617 No information

D5618 44 TS Waddington by 6.18 - 7.18; 15 TDS Hucknall by 10.18

D5619 35 TDS Thetford, prop accident 19.10.18 (2/AM T Clayton seriously injured)

D5620 131 Sqn Shawbury; 9 TDS Shawbury by 10.18 - 3.19

D5621 52 TS Catterick by 6.18; Became 49 TDS Catterick 15.7.18; Stalled on turn at 500ft with failing engine, spun in 13.8.18 (2/Lt RS Murray DoI 14.8.18)

D.H.9 D5645, seen here with underwing serials, served briefly with No.108 Squadron. (J.M.G.Gradidge)

D.H.9 D5656 bears the presentation inscription 'ROYAL MARINES PLYMOUTH'. (D.M.Hannah)

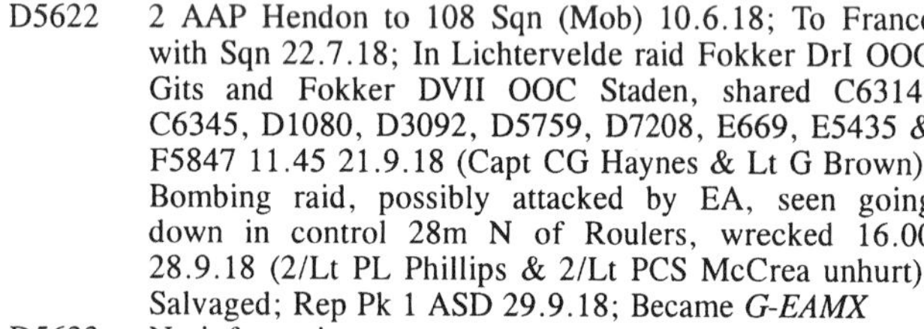

D5622 2 AAP Hendon to 108 Sqn (Mob) 10.6.18; To France with Sqn 22.7.18; In Lichtervelde raid Fokker DrI OOC Gits and Fokker DVII OOC Staden, shared C6314, C6345, D1080, D3092, D5759, D7208, E669, E5435 & F5847 11.45 21.9.18 (Capt CG Haynes & Lt G Brown); Bombing raid, possibly attacked by EA, seen going down in control 28m N of Roulers, wrecked 16.00 28.9.18 (2/Lt PL Phillips & 2/Lt PCS McCrea unhurt); Salvaged; Rep Pk 1 ASD 29.9.18; Became *G-EAMX*

D5623 No information

D5624 At 2 AAP Hendon 16.4.18, allotted to EF; England to Rec Pk 25.4.18; 211 Sqn 1.5.18; Forced to land crosswind as 2 other aircraft in way on ground, starboard wing hit ground, on nose 29.5.18 (Lt ETM Routledge & Cpl H Lindsay unhurt); Rep Pk 1 ASD 30.5.18; SOC 5.7.18 NWR

D5625 (High compression Puma) To Martlesham Heath 5.5.18 (carburettor tests); Hendon 5.6.18; Villacoublay 6.6.18; Hendon 7.6.18; AEE/AES Martlesham Heath by 31.12.18; Left by air W/E 7.7.19

D5626 & D5627 No information

D5628 206 Sqn by 10.19- @2.20; 47 Sqn by 6.20 ('X')

D5629 To France with 107 Sqn 5.6.18; COL 25.6.18 (2/Lt SS George & AM FG Machir); Struck furrow on take off for target practice damaging u/c, COL 8.7.18 (2/Lt A Donaldson & 2/Lt DMcN Livingstone OK); SOC Rep Pk 1 ASD 14.7.18

D5630 At 2 AAP Hendon 16.4.18, allotted to EF; England to Rec Pk 1.5.18; 1 AI 3.5.18; 98 Sqn 5.5.18; Victory 8.5.18 (Capt RW Bell & 2/Lt AA Malcolm); Left 04.30 for high reconnaissance Hazebrouck, shot down S of Thiepval 17.5.18 (Capt RW Bell & Lt AA Malcolm both killed); SOC 17.5.18

D5631 121 Sqn Narborough by 5.18 - @30.6.18; 49 TDS Catterick by 7.18

D5632 120 Sqn Cramlington by 5.18 - @10.18

D5633 104 Sqn Andover, rudder bar jammed, lost speed, stalled and dived in [Thruxton?] 19.5.18 (Sgt W Gunn, also 1/AM TT House of 215 Sqn, both killed)

D5634 & D5635 No information

D5636 At 2 AAP Hendon by 7.6.18 for 108 Sqn (Mob) Kenley; reallotted to EF 15.6.18; Rec Pk to 2 AI 25.6.18; Rep Pk 2 ASD to 2 AI 24.10.18; 49 Sqn 1.11.18; 2 AI 8.12.18, exchanged for D.H.9A

D5637 No information

D5638 MOS Leysdown by 8.18 - @2.19

D5639 & D5643 No information

D5644 52 TS Cramlington by 10.198

D5645 At 2 AAP Hendon 21.6.18 for 108 Sqn (Mob); Listed as crashed 28.6.18

D5646 233 Sqn; 1 Observers School Eastchurch by 10.18; Became 2 MOS Eastchurch 28.12.18 - @7.19

D5647 To France with 107 Sqn 5.6.18; Left on raid at 06.20, FTR, last seen over Tournai, in combat with EA? 11.7.18 (2/Lt AT Simons & 2/Lt TF Blight both PoW wounded)

D5648 No information

D5649 At Makers 14.6.18 for 110 Sqn (Mob) Kenley as a training m/c; Reallotted to Store 17.6.18; Imperial Gift to India

D5650 2 AI to 104 Sqn 29.5.18; Crashed 7.7.18; 3 ASD to 99 Sqn 27.9.18; Pfalz OOC 23.10.18 (Lt W Hodder & Lt L Burrows); Pfalz DIII OOC smoking Buhl 6.11.18 (Lt WC Jeffries & Sgt EVG Chalmers); 3 ASD 13.11.18

D5651 107 Sqn, return 14.6.18 says still in England; Joined 107 Sqn from England 5.7.18; Fokker DVII OOC Blendain, SW of Tournai 08.45 11.7.18 (Lt A Holden & 2/Lt H Bradbury); Aerial firing practice propeller shot through and broken crashed in the sea nr Wimereux 5.9.18 (Lt WF Long & 2/Lt FC King OK); Salved from sea; SOC Rep Pk 1 ASD 7.9.18 NWR

D5652 & D5653 No information

D5654 At 2 AAP Hendon 21.5.18, allotted to EF; England to Rec Pk 28.5.18; 1 AI 29.5.18; 98 Sqn 31.5.18; Damaged in enemy air raid on night of 5/6.6.18; To 4 ASD, transferred to 5 Group 6.18; 218 Sqn 13.9.18; FTR from raid on Thourout, last seen over target 12.00 28.9.18 (2/Lt TM Steele & 2/Lt G Gedge both PoW)

D5655 No information

D5656 Presentation Aircraft 'Royal Marines Plymouth'; At 2 AAP Hendon 15.6.18, reallotted from SE Area for 108 Sqn (Mob) Kenley to EF; Rec Pk to 2 AI 17.6.18; To 49 Sqn 19.6.18 but COL (Lt J Aitken); To 9 AP; SOC Rep Pk 1 ASD 13.7.18 NWR

D5657 107 Sqn Lake Down, engine trouble, stalled and dived in landing 1.6.18 (Lt OJ Marchbank DoI 2.6.18 & Lt K Kennedy seriously injured)

D5658 At 2 AAP Hendon 24.5.18, reallotted from Training Division to EF; England to Rec Pk 25.5.18; 2 AI 26.5.18; 104 Sqn 29.5.18; Wrecked 7.7.18 (Lt HD West & Lt E Beale); SOC 7.7.18

D5659 No information

D5660 99 Sqn by 4.9.18

D5661 Deld 2 AAP Hendon 5.18; AAP Dover W/E 24.5.18; 218 Sqn by 31.5.18; Ran into ditch landing after raid 15.6.18 (Lt WF Purvis & 2/AM G/L TR Barber unhurt); To 4 ASD; 218 Sqn 19.10.18; FL Oye 22.10.18 (Lt JRA Barnes & 2/Lt FE Green unhurt)

D5662 & D5663 No information

D5664 To France with 107 Sqn 9.6.18 but crashed on arrival at Rec Pk; SOC Rep Pk 1 ASD 5.7.18 NWR

D5665 To France with 107 Sqn 5.6.18; Overshot landing, hit raised road 20.7.18 (2/Lt JV Sillars & AM SG Walker OK); SOC Rep Pk 1 ASD 3.9.18 NWR (ex 9 AP)

D5666 To France with 107 Sqn 5.6.18; Albatros DV OOC Tournai 08.20 11.7.18; EA OOC 18.7.18 (both Capt WH Dore & 2/Lt JE Wallace); Left 05.40 for raid on Brie Bridge, in combat, last seen going down in flames east of lines 06.30 9.8.18 (Capt WH Dore & 2/Lt JE Wallace both killed); SOC 9.8.18

D5667 AAP Dover to Chingford 13.3.18; 4 ASD to 218 Sqn 1.8.18; Returning from raid, spun in from 800ft on aerodrome, BO 19.8.18 (Lt JE Wase & 2/Lt JC Cavanagh both killed); WOC 31.8.18

D5668 To France with 107 Sqn 5.6.18; Left 12.40 for raid on Brie Bridge, nr Péronne in terrible rain, combat with Fokker DVIIs, FTR 8.8.18 (2/Lt JK Gaukroger & 2/Lt EL Doncaster both killed)

D5669 To France with 107 Sqn 5.6.18; Collided on ground with C6269 1.7.18 (2/Lt JK Gaukroger OK & 2/Lt DMcN Livingstone injured); Rep Pk 1 ASD 2.7.18; SOC 7.7.18 NWR

D5670 52 TS Cramlington by 10.18
D5671 No information
D5672 At 2 AAP Hendon by 5.6.18 for 108 Sqn (Mob); At Sqn by 8.6.18; Reallotted to D of T for Manston Scout Pool 28.6.18; Pool of Pilots Manston/Joyce Green 8.18 - @11.18; Became *G-EAMX*
D5673 52 TS Cramlington by 10.18
D5674 121 Sqn Narborough by 26.7.18; Stalled and dived in from 50ft 30.7.18 (2/Lt LF Callaway slightly injured) BUT 51 Sqn Marham, prop accident 30.7.18 (Cpl Lochaffee of 92nd US Aero Sqn slightly injured)
D5675 to D5680 No information
D5681 1 SoN&BD Stonehenge by 7.18
D5682 107 Sqn Lake Down, stalled at low height, dived in 1.6.18 (2/Lt RR Bourner killed & Boy J Durran injured)
D5683 Deld 2 AAP Hendon 5.18; AAP Dover W/E 24.5.18; 218 Sqn W/E 1.6.18; Fokker DVII OOC Zeebrugge 10.20 27.6.18 (Capt MG Baskerville & 2/Lt AJ Cunningham); Pfalz DIII OOC Bruges-Ostende 16.50-17.20 5.9.18; Fokker DVII BU Bruges 16.30 15.9.18 (both Lt GH Howarth & 2/Lt FJ Gallant); u/s, burnt on site, SOC 22.1.19
D5684 To France with 107 Sqn 5.6.18; Left on raid at 06.33, FTR 18.7.18 (Capt RE Dubber & Lt CB Dickie both killed)
D5685 No information
D5686 At Makers 14.6.18 for 110 Sqn (Mob) Kenley as a training m/c; 2 AAP Hendon 2.7.18; At Sqn 9.7.18; Reallotted to SE Area 10.8.18; Marine Observers School Leysdown by 8.18 - 2.19; IAAD; Imperial Gift to India, shipped SS *Hatimura* 8.20; Became *G-IAAS*, later *VT-AAS*
D5687 Deld 2 AAP Hendon 5.18; AAP Dover W/E 24.5.18; 218 Sqn by 20.5.18; COL 10.6.18 (Lt EH Dixon & G/L Sgt RJ Williams unhurt); Repaired on Sqn; Dived in combat with Fokker DVII, BU in air over Blankenberge, Fokker then shot down by Camel C65 27.6.18 (Lt C Briggs & 2/Lt WH Warner both killed)
D5688 (Puma) At 2 AAP Hendon 23.5.18, reallotted from 218 Sqn (Mob) Dover to EF; Approaching Lympne, tailplane failed 25.5.18 (Chief Mech AH Reffell of Central Dispatch Pool, London OK); Rec Pk to 1 AI 4.6.18; 98 Sqn 8.6.18; Hit by AA Forêt de Nesle 22.7.18 (Lt EW Langford OK & 2/Lt H Ridley wounded); Practice flight, into flat turn, then spinning nose dive, BO 31.7.18 (2/Lt EW Gordon & 2/Lt LFC Sayers both killed); SOC 1.8.18
D5689 At Makers 14.6.18 for 110 Sqn (Mob) Kenley; as a training m/c; 2 AAP Hendon 25.6.18; To Sqn 2.7.18; Reallotted to SE Area 10.8.18; Marine Observers School Leysdown 8.18 - 2.19; IAAD; Imperial Gift to India, shipped SS *Hatimura* 8.20
D5690 At 2 AAP Hendon 23.5.18, reallotted from 218 Sqn (Mob) Dover to EF; England to Rec Pk 31.5.18; 2 AI 2.6.18; 103 Sqn 7.6.18; Left 16.15 on bombing raid, fuel tank and rudder shot up, FL, crashed 5.7.18 (2/Lt CT Houston & 2/Lt JK Clarke OK); Rep Pk 1 ASD, SOC 9.7.18, NWR
D5691 to D5695 No information
D5696 At 2 AAP Hendon 23.5.18, reallotted from 108 Sqn (Mob) Lake Down to EF; England to Rec Pk 29.5.18; 1AI 30.5.18; 206 Sqn 7.6.18; EF, FL, crashed on sunken road running through aerodrome 12.6.18 (Lt H Stier USAS & 2/Lt WG Duncan); Rep Pk 1 ASD 15.6.18; SOC 5.7.18 NWR
D5697 At 2 AAP Hendon 6.6.18, allotted to EF; Rec Pk to 2 AI 8.7.18; 5 AI 18.7.18; 107 Sqn 20.7.18; Engine cut out on take off, crashed 8.1.19 (2/Lt JV Sillars & AC1 A Adams OK)
D5698 to D5700 No information
D5701 At 2 AAP Hendon 24.5.18, reallotted from Training Division to EF; England to Rec Pk and on to 27 Sqn 25.5.18; On raid on Chaulnes, FL before crossing the lines due to oil pipe bursting and engine failure, crashed into hedge 6.6.18 (Lt CE Hutchinson & Lt FRG Spurgin); 9 AP 6.6.18; Rebuilt as F6098 3.7.18
D5702 & D5703 No information
D5704 At 2 AAP Hendon 23.5.18, reallotted from 218 Sqn (Mob) Dover to EF; Rec Pk to 27 Sqn 25.5.18; Standing on aerodrome when crashed into by 32 Sqn SE5a D6858 28.6.18; SOC Rep Pk 2 ASD 29.7.18 NWR
D5705 to D5708 No information
D5709 At 2 AAP Hendon 25.7.18 for 109 Sqn (Mob) Lake Down; Reallotted to "Naval Developments" 29.7.18; 557 Flt 212 Sqn Yarmouth by 1.8.18 - @27.9.18; AZP 5.8.18 (Lt WK Prendergast & 2/Lt E Gray); With F.2A N4549, N4550 & D.H.4 N6395 engaged 5 EA 12m off Shipwash LV 16.9.18; IAAD; Imperial Gift to India, shipped SS *Hatimura* 8.20
D5710 At 2 AAP Hendon by 7.6.18 for 108 Sqn (Mob) Kenley; reallotted to EF 14.6.18; Rec Pk to 2 AI 16.6.18; 27 Sqn 17.6.18; On landing tried to clear another m/c on the ground, could not pick up sufficient flying speed and crashed in corn at the edge of the aerodrome 4.8.18 (Lt JR Webb & Lt AF Millar OK); SOC Rep Pk 2 ASD 8.8.18 NWR
D5711 No information
D5712 4 ASD to 218 Sqn 9.8.18; In combat with EA over Cortemarck, Fokker DVII OOC 17.50, but own a/c badly shot up 28.9.18 (Lt ER Brewer USMC & Sgt HB Wershiner USMC both wounded); 4 ASD 6.10.18 - @25.10.18
D5713 1 Observers School Eastchurch by 12.18; Became 2 MOS Eastchurch 28.12.18 - @2.19
D5714 Rec Pk to 1 AI 14.8.18; 211 Sqn 16.8.18; Damaged by AA returning from bombing raid, FL, COL Ypres-Courtrai 29.9.18 (2/Lt VGH Phillips & 2/Lt AF Taylor both unhurt); Rep Pk 1 ASD 30.9.18
D5715 No information
D5716 Rec Pk to 2 AI 23.8.18; 49 Sqn 26.8.18; COL 30.8.18 (2/Lt AJ Girardot & Sgt Mech R Reid); SOC Rep Pk 2 ASD 23.9.18 (ex 9 AP)
D5717 218 Sqn, engine hit by AA fire during raid on Zeebrugge Mole, EF, FL Biggekerke, Zeeland 31.7.18 (Lt LWC Pearce & 2/Lt FH Bugge interned unhurt); Deleted 15.8.18; Became *H437* with Dutch forces [serial allocation not confirmed by reports]; Retd to RAF 12.3.20
D5718 & D5719 No information
D5720 At 2 AAP Hendon 31.5.18, allotted to EF; Rec Pk to 2 AI 7.6.18; 104 Sqn 9.6.18; Left 05.00 for bombing raid on Landau Stn, formation attacked both on way and return, shot down in flames in combat with 20 EA on return 30.6.18 (1/Lt WL Deetjen (US) & 2/Lt MH Cole both killed); SOC 30.6.18
D5721 At 2 AAP Hendon for 108 Sqn (Mob) by 5.6.18; At Sqn by 10.6.18; Pool of Pilots Manston/Joyce Green by 7.18 - @8.19
D5722 At 2 AAP Hendon 29.5.18, allotted to EF; Rec Pk to 1 AI 16.6.18; 98 Sqn 17.6.18; On test flight engine cut out immediately after take off, nose dived in 27.6.18 (Mjr ET Newton Clare slightly hurt & Sgt Mjr H Grainger injured); Rep Pk 1 ASD & SOC 28.6.18
D5723 At 2 AAP Hendon 6.6.18, allotted to EF; Rec Pk to 2 AI 14.6.18; 98 Sqn 16.6.18; Had to return from raid due to engine giving insufficient revs, attempting to land crashed in a ploughed field adjoining the aerodrome 17.6.18 (Lt IV Lawrence & Sgt PJ Sprange both OK); Rep Pk 1 ASD 18.6.18; SOC 21.6.18 NWR
D5724 No information
D5725 Lincoln to Midland Area FIS Lilbourne 15.10.18; 31 TDS Fowlmere 10.18; U/c fouled top of stationary 504 C707 on TO, TW 1.11.18 (2/Lt C Warboys injured & Lt LR Harvey slightly injured)
D5726 No information
D5727 204 TDS Eastchurch by 6.18
D5728 1 Observers School Eastchurch by 10.18; Became 2 Marine Observers School Eastchurch 28.12.18 - @7.19
D5729 At 2 AAP Hendon 6.6.18, allotted to EF; Rec Pk to 2 AI 21.6.18; 104 Sqn 25.6.18; Pfalz DIII OOC Metz area 07.05 1.7.18; Pfalz DIII OOC Saarebourg 16.25 7.7.18 shared D2812 (both 2/Lt E Cartwright & 2/Lt AGL Mullen); Raid on Mannheim, in combat with EAs, FTR 22.8.18 (Lt E Cartwright & Lt AGL Mullen both killed)
D5730 10 TDS Harling Road by 7.18; 31 TDS Fowlmere; 120 Sqn Bracebridge Heath by 9.18
D5731 1 Observers School Eastchurch by 11.18 - @12.18
D5732 No information
D5733 6 SD Ascot, allotted Anti-Bolshevik Government for General Denikin; Re-allotted Polish Military Purchase Mission on free issue 22.4.20; Despatched port for shipment in SS *Neptune* 27.4.20

D5734 No information
D5735 35 TDS Duxford by 22.10.18
D5736 & D5737 No information
D5738 1 SoN&BD Stonehenge by 9.8.18
D5739 & D5740 No information
D5741 Rec Pk to 1 AI 8.7.18; 103 Sqn 9.7.18; 98 Sqn 11.3.19; 1 ASD 20.3.19
D5742 Erected by Wells Aviation Co; 491 Flt 233 Sqn Dover by 20.7.18 - @15.8.18; Eastbourne repair 8.18; 491 Flt 233 Sqn Dover 13.9.18; 218 Sqn 24.9.18; FTR from raid 26.9.18 (2/Lt JT Aitken PoW DoW 28.9.18 & 2/Lt OR Hibbert PoW)
D5743 & D5747 No information
D5748 RAE Farnborough from/by 4.11.18 (various engines inc 260hp Fiat A.12; fitted with duplicated bracing wires; fitted special tailplane; magneto coupling tests; oil tests; altitude tests); To Hendon 22.11.18; Retd Farnborough 31.12.18 (experimental water system test 8.12.19); FL Godalming, Surrey 15.5.20
D5749 1 AI to 103 Sqn 16.9.18; In combat 27.9.18 (2/Lt WS Marchant OK & 2/Lt HS Crees wounded); Left 07.50 for bombing raid on Tournai, seen S of target going west, FTR 30.10.18 (Sgt Mech CS Silvester & 2/Lt H Langdale both PoW)
D5750 Rec Pk to 1 AI 31.8.18; 206 Sqn 3.9.18; Took off crosswind, stalled, crashed 20.9.18 (2/Lt C Knight USAS & 2/Lt JH Perring both unhurt); Rep Pk 1 ASD 21.9.18; SOC 23.9.18
D5751 Desp UK to AD Aboukir 12.3.20 [? - listed as D5251]
D5752 No information
D5753 Rec Pk to 1 AI 31.8.18; 206 Sqn 7.9.18 - @30.9.18
D5754 493 Flt 236 Sqn Mullion by 9.18; Tested 28.9.18; East Fortune 5.11.18 (arr 11.11.18)
D5755 RAE from/by 3.1.19 (used for comparative landing trials with H1940 (High Lift) version fitted with Handley Page section wing); FL Gosport 12.11.19 (F/O JFT Barrett & Mr Jenner); Retd 13.11.19; EF, FL Tolworth, near Kingston-on-Thames, Surrey 14.5.23; still at RAE 10.24
D5756 Marine Observers School Leysdown by 8.18 - 2.19; IAAD; Imperial Gift to India, shipped SS *Hatimura* 8.20
D5757 & D5758 No information
D5759 At Makers 19.6.18 for 109 Sqn (Mob) Lake Down; Reallotted to 108 Sqn (Mob) 28.6.18; At 2 AAP Hendon by 29.6.18; To France with 108 Sqn 22.7.18; To Stonehenge 4.8.18 for special bombing course, back at sqn by 10.9.18; In Lichtervelde raid Fokker DrI OOC Gits and Fokker DVII OOC Staden, shared C6314, C6345, D1080, D5622, D7208, E669, E5435 & F5847, hit by AA at 11,000ft and BU 11.45 21.9.18 (2/Lt HL McLellan & 2/Lt FX Jackson both killed)
D5760 49 TDS Catterick by 1-6.11.18
D5761 to D5764 No information
D5765 Imperial Gift to India
D5766 Arr Rec Pk 8.8.18; 2 AI 10.8.18; 3 ASD 12.8.18; 104 Sqn 22.8.18; Fokker DVII broke up Ecouvier 12.40 then wrecked Clermont 29.10.18 (Lt JR Tansey & 2/Lt JM Scott); 6 AP 5.11.18; 3 ASD 9.11.18
D5767 to D5772 No information
D5773 At Makers 28.6.18, allotted to EF; To 2 AAP Hendon; Rec Pk to 2 AI 29.8.18; 3 ASD 31.8.18; Deld 104 Sqn but COL 14.9.18; 104 Sqn by 31.10.18; Fokker DVII on fire Buhl aerodrome 14.00 6.11.18 (2/Lt J Wrighton & Sgt WH Bell); Engine cut out landed in ploughed field, m/c turned over 4.1.19 (Lt PC Saxby & Lt ED Aldridge OK); SOC 10.1.19
D5774 Imperial Gift to India
D5775 & D5776 No information
D5777 Became *G-EBEH*
D5778 No information
D5779 At Makers 28.6.18, allotted to EF; To 2 AAP Hendon; Rec Pk to 2 AI 31.8.18; 98 Sqn 4.9.18; Pfalz DIII OOC just N of Honnecourt 09.45 27.9.18; Pfalz DIII crashed Mons-Valenciennes 13.50 1.11.18 (both 2/Lt HW Bush & Sgt Mech CHO Allwork); 8 AAP Lympne 12.2.19
D5780 & D5781 No information
D5782 Rec Pk to 1 AI 7.8.18; 206 Sqn 9.8.18; Fokker DVII OOC E of Messines 18.50 13.8.18 (Capt T Roberts & 2/Lt CO Shelswell); Fokker DVII in flames crashed nr Lendelede, shared D569 14.40 14.10.18 (Lt H McLean & 2/Lt HP Hobbs); Collided with taxying 43 Sqn Snipe E8013 while landing 9.2.19 (Capt T Roberts & Sgt Pugh unhurt); to 9 SS for repair
D5783 & D5784 No information
D5785 Arr Rec Pk 1.9.18; 2 AI 5.9.18; 3 ASD 5.9.18 (arr 6.9.18); 104 Sqn 12.9.18; 6 AP 25.10.18; 3 ASD 31.10.18
D5786 Rec Pk to 2 AI 7.8.18; To 3ASD 12.8.18; 104 Sqn 17.8.18; 1 ASD 21.1.19
D5787 & D5788 No information
D5789 1 ASD Marquise, accident 27.9.18 (Lt CW Arkle killed)
D5790 At Makers 19.6.18 for 109 Sqn (Mob) Lake Down; Reallotted to 108 Sqn (Mob) 28.6.18; At 2 AAP Hendon by 29.6.18; At sqn by 8.7.18; To France with 108 Sqn 22.7.18; COL due to gust of wind 27.7.18 (2/Lt HL McLellan & Lt HD Buchanan both unhurt); Rep Pk 1 ASD 30.7.18; SOC 3.8.18 NWR
D5791 2 SoN&BD Andover, EF after TO, turned back, stalled on turn, crashed 17.10.18 (2/Lt P Richardson & 2/Lt IH Gilbert both injured)
D5792 Acoustic Test Flt, Butley to Martlesham Heath 11.11.18 (performance tests with/without Connor silencer); Acoustic Test Flt, Butley 23.11.18; Martlesham Heath W/E 14.12.18 (performance with exhaust manifold silencer); Acoustic Test Flt, Butley 31.12.18
D5793 At Makers 19.6.18 for 109 Sqn (Mob) Lake Down; 2 AAP Hendon 23.7.18; Reallotted "Naval Developments" 29.7.18; 557/8 Flts 212 Sqn Yarmouth by 5.8.18 - @7.9.18; AZP, attacked *L70* which was later brought down by A8032, COL Sedgeford 5.8.18 (Capt CS Iron & Lt HG Owen unhurt); IAAD; Imperial Gift to India, shipped SS *Hatimura* 8.20
D5794 No information
D5795 To Greek Government
D5796 & D5797 No information
D5798 Rec Pk to 108 Sqn 3.10.18; Left 09.41 for bombing raid on Sotteghem, oil tank hit by AA Denterghem 10.26, FL west of lines, damaged 1.11.18 (Lt JG Kershaw & Lt WL Walker both unhurt); 8 SS 5.11.18
D5799 Became *G-EBEP*
D5800 To Greek Government
D5801 No information
D5802 At Makers 19.6.18 for 109 Sqn (Mob) Lake Down; 2 AAP Hendon 24.7.18; Reallotted "Naval Developments" 29.7.18; Yarmouth, AZP, FTR 5.8.18 (Capt DGB Jardine & Lt ER Munday both killed; Jardine's body washed up Verduse, W coast of Jutland 26.9.18)
D5803 No information
D5804 1 SoN&BD Stonehenge, sideslipped off sharp turn near ground 23.10.18 (2/Lt JH Clark MM & Bar DoI 4.11.18 & 2/Lt OM Huby killed)
D5805 No information
D5806 'D' Flt Devt Sqn Gosport by 6.19; Netheravon
D5807 557/8 Flts 212 Sqn Yarmouth by 19.9.18 - @15.10.18
D5808 No information
D5809 At Makers 19.6.18 for 109 Sqn (Mob) Lake Down; 2 AAP Hendon 25.7.18; Reallotted "Naval Developments" 29.7.18; Yarmouth, AZP 5.8.18 (Capt CB Sproatt & Capt J Hodson); COL, wrecked 10.8.18 (2 crew unhurt)
D5810 & D5813 No information
D5814 Imperial Gift to India
D5815 No information
D5816 Presentation a/c 'Faridkot No.3', fitted modified engine cowling. At Makers 28.6.18, allotted to EF; To 2 AAP Hendon; Rec Pk to 1 AI 1.8.18; 206 Sqn 4.8.18; Left 05.30, combat with EA, forced down, crashed nr Grasse-Payelle, CW 7.8.18 (Lt JFS Percival & 2/Lt J Lowthian both injured); Rep Pk 1 ASD 9.8.18; SOC 11.8.18 BUT 1 SoN&BD Stonehenge by 12.18
D5817 1 SoN&BD by 12.18 - @16.1.19
D5818 Imperial Gift to India
D5819 to D5828 No information
D5829 At Makers 28.6.18, allotted to EF; To 2 AAP Hendon; Rec Pk to 2 AI 22.8.18; 98 Sqn 24.8.18; Left 06.10, after attacking Somain Rlwy Stn forced to fly below the formation due to slight engine trouble, attacked, combat 08.40-09.00, elevator controls shot away and observer badly wounded but shot down a Fokker DVII in flames and another sent down OOC, a/c badly damaged, elevators shot up, FL between Mory and Vraucourt some 30 yards from the front line and under enemy fire, m/c unsalvable 29.8.18 (2/Lt JM Brown OK & 2/Lt H Lawrence badly wounded); BUT scout OOC

Valenciennes 10.30 16.9.18 (2/Lt TW Sleigh & 2/Lt AH Fuller) [Note combat report and sqn daily records have D5829, but sqn weekly returns of a/c do not have this a/c at 98 Sqn 16.9.18; see also D3169]

D5830 to D5834 No information

D5835 At Makers 28.6.18, allotted to EF; To 2 AAP Hendon; Rec Pk to 1 AI 17.8.18; 108 Sqn 20.8.18; After bombing Ingelmunster station at 17.25 formation attacked by 33 EA between the target and Roulers, 3 EA in flames, 1 BU and 2 OOC shared C2205, D499, D5845, D7342, E605, E5435, E8871 & F5847 but FTR 1.10.18 (Lt F Hopkins & 2/Lt JW Firth both killed).

D5836 & D5837 No information

D5838 Presentation Aircraft 'Presented by H.H. The Maharaja of Bikanir No.9'. 8 AAP Lympne to Rec Pk 17.9.18; 1 AI 4.10.18; 206 Sqn 6.10.18; Hit rut landing 12.11.18 (Lt AL Seddon & 2/Lt EW Richardson both unhurt)

D5839 to D5841 No information

D5842 Rec Pk to 1 AI 29.6.18; 103 Sqn 30.6.18; Shot down in fight over the target Santes 10.25 24.9.18 (2/Lt HC Noel DoW & Sgt LC Owens PoW)

D5843 Arr Rec Pk and on to 2 AI 3.9.18; 3 ASD 4.9.18; 104 Sqn 12.9.18; Bombing raid, FL St.Mihiel 29.10.18 (pilot 2/Lt PJ Waller wounded); 99 Sqn 5.11.18; 3 ASD 14.11.18 (rebuild)

D5844 No information

D5845 'Presented by H.H. The Maharaja of Bikanir No.10'. At Makers 28.6.18, allotted to EF; To 2 AAP Hendon; Rec Pk to 1 AI 17.9.18; 108 Sqn 29.9.18; After bombing Ingelmunster station at 17.25 formation attacked by 33 EA between the target and Roulers, 3 EA in flames, 1 BU and 2 OOC shared C2205, D499, D5835, D7342, E605, E5435, E8871 & F5847, then crashed 1.10.18 (2/Lt JG Kershaw & 2/Lt WL Walker OK); On Denderleeuwe raid EA OOC E of Sotteghem, shared C2216, D613, D7357, E8980 & E9028 09.05 9.11.18 (Lt JG Kershaw OK & Lt HS Gargett wounded); Reconnaissance 10.11.18 (Lt W Marsden wounded & Lt W McGowen OK); 98 Sqn 23.1.19; 8 AAP Lympne 13.2.19

D5846 Imperial Gift to India

D5847 & D5848 No information

D5849 Deld 6 SD Ascot for Mudros W/E 17.10.18; RAF North Russia (Southern Area) by 7.19 - @8.19

D5850 At 2 AAP Hendon 18.10.18 for 119 Sqn (Mob) Wyton; Crashed at Dunstable en route to sqn 24.10.18

100 D.H.9 ordered 5.1.18 under Cont No A.S.42381 (BR.228) from Westland Aircraft Works, Yeovil and numbered D7201 to D7300. (230hp Puma)

D7201 Deld 5 AAP Filton by 20.5.18-1.6.18, allotted to EF; Rec Pk to 2 AI 7.6.18; 49 Sqn 10.6.18; Low bombing, Albatros DV OOC Cuveilly 15.00, own a/c controls shot up Mointierz 15.30, engine trouble, FL 11.6.18 (Lt C Bowman OK & Lt V Gordon wounded); To 9 AP; Rep Pk 1 ASD SOC 22.7.18 NWR

D7202 Deld 5 AAP Filton by 20.5.18, allotted to EF; Rec Pk to 1 AI 2.6.18; 2 AI and on to 98 Sqn 12.6.18; Pfalz DIII OOC Inchy-Moevres 09.40 17.6.18 (Sgt Mech HW Bush & Sgt Mech J Reay); Left 15.30 for raid on Cambrai-Ville Rlwy Junction, in combat with 6 EA 17.55, but shot down OOC in spin by AA, crashed W of Cambrai 3.9.18 (2/Lt RT Ingram & 2/Lt KJW Dennitts both killed)

D.H.9 D7204 'J' of No.211 Squadron after being forced down at Zuidzande on 24.8.18. (via Frank Cheesman)

D7203 Deld 5 AAP Filton by 17.5.18-8.6.18, allotted to EF; Rec Pk to 2 AI and on to 103 Sqn 12.6.18; 98 Sqn 10.3.19; 8 AAP Lympne 14.3.19

D7204 Deld 5 AAP Filton by 17.5.18-8.6.18, allotted to EF; Rec Pk to 1 AI 12.6.18; 211 Sqn ('J') 16.6.18; Badly shot up 26.6.18 (Lt HN Lett & Pte2 HW Newsham); Left 13.10, hit by AA over Bruges Docks, FL, went on nose, Zuidzande, Zeeland c.16.30 24.8.18 (Lt JA Dear & 2/Lt JFJ Peters both interned); SOC 24.8.18

D7205 Deld 5 AAP Filton by 4-28.6.18, allotted to EF; Rec Pk to 2 AI 28.7.18; 3 ASD 1.8.18; 104 Sqn 1.8.18; In combat with many EAs in raid on Metz-Sablon Rlwy, FTR 15.9.18 (2/Lt RH Rose & 2/Lt EL Baddeley both PoW)

D7206 Deld 5 AAP Filton by 17.5.18-17.6.18, allotted to EF; Rec Pk to 98 Sqn 19.6.18; Out of fuel, crashed into tree landing St.Forgeau 24.7.18 (Lt W Goffe unhurt & Sgt JL May slightly injured); to be sent to 9 AP when salved; SOC Rep Pk 1 ASD 3.9.18 (ex 9 AP)

D7207 Deld 5 AAP Filton by 4.6.18, allotted to EF; SOC Rec Pk 14.8.18, destroyed by fire

D7208 Deld 5 AAP Filton by 4.6.18, allotted to EF; Rec Pk to 2 AI 30.7.18; 108 Sqn 3.8.18; In Lichtervelde raid Fokker DrI OOC Gits and Fokker DVII OOC Staden, shared C6314, C6345, D1080, D3092, D6522, D5759, E669, E5435 & F5847 11.45 21.9.18 (2/Lt PL Phillips & 2/Lt PCS McCrea); Left 14.47 for raid on Courtemarck Dump, FTR, last seen descending under control nr Roulers followed by two EA 24.9.18 (2/Lt JM Dandy & Sgt CP Crites both PoW)

D7209 Dismantled, parts used for spares

D7210 Deld 5 AAP Filton by 4.6.18, allotted to EF; On charge IF 23.7.18 reallotted to IF; Rec Pk to 2 AI and on to 3 ASD 24.7.18, 104 Sqn 24.7.18; Raid on Mannheim, in combat with EAs, FTR 7.9.18 (2/Lt WEL Courtney PoW & 2/Lt AR Sabey PoW DoW 11.9.18)

D7211 Shipped to Mudros 18.5.18; Repair Base Mudros by 6.18 & 10.18 - @1.19; To Greek Government; H.2 Flt RHNAS Thasos/Stavros by 10.10.18 - @2.11.18

D7212 Shipped to Mudros 18.5.18; Repair Base Mudros by 6.18; 220 Sqn Imbros, crashed 22.7.18 (Lt LG Steel & Lt FC Smith both killed)

D7213 Deld 6 SD Ascot W/E 25.5.18; Shipped to Mudros 15.6.18; Aegean Group, FL and captured 17.10.18 (Lt W Bamber & Lt KG Withers both PoW)

D7214 Deld 6 SD Ascot W/E 25.5.18; Shipped to Mudros 15.6.18; Stavros by 19.8.18 - @1.19; Crashed 5.11.18 (2/Lt RC Morrison slightly injured & 2/Lt JR Barrett seriously injured)

D7215 and D7216 cancelled

D7217 to D7220 No information

D7221 Deld 5 AAP Filton by 20.5.18, allotted to EF; England to Rec Pk 25.5.18; 2 AI 26.5.18; 49 Sqn 27.5.18; Shot up, ran into tree on landing 5.6.18 (Lt CAB Beattie OK & Sgt AI Boyack killed); Rep Pk 2 ASD 5.6.18; SOC Rep Pk 1 ASD 17.7.18 ex 9 AP, NWR

D7222 Deld 5 AAP Filton by 22-24.5.18, allotted to EF; England to Rec Pk 26.5.18; 2 AI and on to 27 Sqn 30.5.18; Left 13.50 for low strafing Montdidier, shot through, retd 16.15 11.6.18 (Lt F Carr & Lt JH Holland OK); 9 AP 12.6.18; Rep Pk 2 ASD to 2 AI 6.7.18; 49 Sqn 8.7.18; COL 27.7.18 (2/Lt ST Franks & Sgt RA Campbell both unhurt); SOC Rep Pk 1 ASD 3.9.18 NWR (ex 9 AP)

D7223 Deld 5 AAP Filton by 24-25.5.18, allotted to EF; England to Rec Pk 28.5.18; 2 AI 29.5.18; 99 Sqn 1.6.18; Bombing raid on Lahr, combat with 5 EA NW of Schlettstadt, BU in air 30.7.18 (1/Lt P Dietz USAS & 2/Lt HW Batty both killed)

D7224 Presentation a/c 'Presented by Patrick Burns Esq of Calgary, Alberta'. Deld 5 AAP Filton by 28.5.18, allotted to EF; England to Rec Pk 31.5.18; 1 AI 1.6.18; 98 Sqn ('H') 8.6.18; Fokker Dr1 in flames by observer 20.7.18 (Lt CH Roberts & Sgt Mech GW Slater); Left 16.30, shot up in combat with 30 EA east of lines 25.7.18 (Lt CH Roberts OK & Sgt Mech GW Slater

DoW 1.8.18); 9 AP 28.7.18; SOC Rep Pk 1 ASD 3.9.18 NWR

D7225 Deld 5 AAP Filton by 28.5.18, allotted to EF; England to Rec Pk 30.5.18; 2 AI 31.5.18; 104 Sqn 3.6.18; Bombing raid on Karlsruhe, Pfalz DIII down in vertical dive over Saverne on return 09.10 11.8.18 (Capt JB Home-Hay & Sgt WT Smith DCM MM); WO 15.8.18 SOC

D7226 Deld 5 AAP Filton by 28.5.18, allotted to EF; England to Rec Pk 31.5.18; 2 AI 1.6.18; 103 Sqn 6.6.18; Left 13.15 on bombing raid, shot up by EA, retd 16.00 16.6.18 (Capt KT Dowding & Lt CE Eddy OK); SOC Rep Pk 1 ASD 13.7.18 (ex 9 AP) NWR

D7227 Deld 5 AAP Filton by 28.5.18, allotted to EF; England to Rec Pk 30.5.18; 1 AI 2.6.18; 98 Sqn 8.6.18; After bombing Cambrai Rly station Pfalz DIII crashed Inchy-Moeuvres 09.40 17.6.18 (Capt FA Laughlin & Lt H Tasker); Pfalz DIII OOC Don 19.30 11.7.18 (Lt G Richmond & Sgt Mech F Sefton); Landed too near edge of aerodrome, swerved to avoid parked machines, hit building 24.7.18 (2/Lt BC Geary & 2/Lt EH Edgell both unhurt); 9 AP 25.7.18; SOC Rep Pk 1 ASD 3.9.18 NWR

D7228 Deld 5 AAP Filton by 30.5.18-2.6.18, allotted to EF; Rec Pk to 2 AI 5.6.18; 1 AI to 98 Sqn 8.6.18; Engine failed shortly after take off, pilot tried to turn back but had lost flying speed and dived in 25.6.18 (Lt HEA Reynolds slightly injured & Lt HA Lamb OK); SOC wrecked 27.6.18

D7229 Deld 5 AAP Filton by 30.5.18, allotted to EF; Rec Pk to 2 AI 3.6.18; 104 Sqn 5.6.18; Bombing raid on Saarbrücken railways and factories, shot up in combat with EA, but landed OK nr aerodrome Azelot 24.6.18 (Lt OJ Lange slightly wounded & Sgt GT Smith wounded); 3 ASD 25.6.18; 104 Sqn 11.8.18; Raid on Ehrang Rlwy Junction, fallen on by D2881 which was hit by AA fire and folded up 13.8.18 (2/Lt HPG Leyden & Sgt AL Windridge both killed)

D7230 Deld 5 AAP Filton by 31.5.18-1.6.18, allotted to EF; England to Rec Pk 2.6.18; 1 AI 5.6.18; 98 Sqn 8.6.18; Got into spin just after take off and crashed on aerodrome 30.6.18 (Lt HG Goddard & Sgt Mech CW Moulden both injured); Rep Pk 1 ASD 1.7.18; SOC 4.7.18 NWR

D7231 At Makers 25.5.18, allotted to EF; Rec Pk to 2 AI 26.6.18; 49 Sqn 6.7.18; Left 17.55 for raid on Bethencourt Bridge, seen going down in flames nr target 8.8.18 (Lt GS Ramsey & 2/Lt WN Hartley both killed)

D7232 At Makers 25.5.18, allotted to EF; 2 AI to 99 Sqn 28.6.18; Scout broke up Sarreguemines 07.30 5.7.18 shared C6278 (Sgt HH Wilson & Sgt FL Lee); Engine hit in Metz-Sablon raid FL 6.7.18 (Sgt HH Wilson & Sgt FL Lee OK); 3 ASD 7.7.18; 104 Sqn 22.8.18; Bombing raid on Metz-Sablon railway, in combat with many EA, last seen over Verny 26.9.18 (Lt OL Malcolm & 2/Lt GV Harper both killed)

D7233 At Makers 25.5.18, allotted to EF; Rec Pk to 2 AI and on to 3 ASD, then 99 Sqn 30.6.18; Albatros D OOC just W of the target Lahr 07.10 30.7.18 (Capt V Beecroft & Lt BSW Taylor); On Conflans raid FL Amanty a French airfield nr Toul with fuel problems 30.8.18, returning 31.8.18 stalled and crashed on take off (Sgt HH Wilson & 2/Lt HE Alsford both killed)

D7234 At Makers 25.5.18, allotted to EF; Rep Pk 2 ASD to 2 AI 5.7.18; 49 Sqn 9.7.18; Left 17.20 for raid on Sapeney, in combat with EA at 2,000ft over Grand Rozoy, seen going down under control, FTR 20.7.18 (Sgt SJ Oliver & Sgt A Davis both PoW)

D7235 1 SoN&BD by 12.18 - @1.19

D7236 No information

D7237 1 SoN&BD Stonehenge by 2.19

D7238 1 SoN&BD Stonehenge by 12.18; 8 TDS Netheravon by 4.19

D7239 Deld 5 AAP Filton by 3.6.18; AAP Dover 7.6.18; 4 ASD Audembert 7.6.18; 218 Sqn 6.18; COL from raid 26.6.18 (Lt JA Pugh & 2/Lt MG Wilson unhurt); 4 ASD by 10.18; 2 SS Richborough 2.10.18

D7240 Deld 5 AAP Filton 6.18; AAP Dover 7.6.18; 218 Sqn by 30.6.18; Returning from raid, crashed nr Calais, engine damaged 19.7.18 (Lt HP Brumell & Sgt RS Joysey); Crashed on beach nr Calais after raid, badly damaged 29.8.18 (Lt HP Brumell & 2/Lt G Gedge); To 4 ASD; 2 SS Richborough 2.10.18

D7241 Deld 5 AAP Filton 6.18; AAP Dover 7.6.18; 218 Sqn by 5.7.18; EA in flames, shared formation 18.25 5.7.18 (Lt GWE Hanmer & Sgt AE Powell); Hit by D1691 overshooting, badly damaged 1.8.18; 4 ASD 3.8.18; 491 Flt 233 Sqn Dover by 8.10.18; 4 ASD 13.10.18; 218 Sqn 21.10.18; Returning from bombing raid, FL, crashed Bisseghem 9.11.18 (2/Lt CM Arias & Sgt RG Pearce unhurt); to 2 ASD

D7242 Deld 5 AAP Filton by 11.6.18; AAP Dover 12.6.18; 4 ASD Audembert 13.6.18; 218 Sqn by 2.7.18; Probably accounted for the Pfalz DIII OOC 2.7.18 (Lt H Fawdry & 2/Lt JS Cryan); Albatros crashed 2/3m N of Nieuport 18.35 5.7.18 (Lt H Fawdry & 2/Lt JS Cryan); Pfalz DIII OOC Ghistelles aerodrome 13.25 15.8.18 (Lt HP Brumell & Sgt RS Joysey); 4 ASD 20.10.18 - @25.10.18 (overhaul, time expired)

D7243 Deld 5 AAP Filton by 11.6.18; AAP Dover 12.6.18; 491 Flt Dover 16.6.18; EF, FL Maidstone 31.7.18; Became 491 Flt 233 Sqn Dover 31.8.18 - @16.12.18; 120 Sqn Hawkinge by 3.19 - 8.19

D7244 No information

D7245 Deld 5 AAP Filton by 12.6.18; AAP Dover 13.6.18; 491 Flt Dover 16.6.18; Landed on rough ground at edge of aerodrome, u/c wrecked, wings damaged 18.8.18 (Lt LG Sullivan unhurt); To ARS Guston Road; 491 Flt 233 Sqn Dover by 9.18; 218 Sqn loan 24.9.18; Tested 491 Flt 26.9.18; Retd 218 Sqn by 1.19; 98 Sqn 21.1.19; 8 AAP Lympne 12.2.19

D7246 Deld 5 AAP Filton by 12.6.18; AAP Dover 13.6.18; 491 Flt Dover 16.6.18; On convoy escort patrol FL in sea due to engine failure 9m SW of Beachy Head, only engine salved 25.8.18 (Lt DL Melvin & Lt GL Coombes picked up by British destroyer HMS *Orion*)

D7247 Deld 5 AAP Filton by 13-15.6.18, reallotted from 61 Wing to EF; Rec Pk to 2 AI 16.6.18; 98 Sqn 17.6.18; Two Albatros Ds OOC one of which was smoking S of Roulers 19.30 30.6.18; Pfalz DIII wing fell off nr Fère-en-Tardenois 19.00 25.7.18 (all Sgt Mech HW Bush & Sgt ER McDonald); Travelling to new aerodrome misjudged height on landing due to failing light and landed heavily 3.8.18 (Sgt Mech HW Bush & 1/AM C Wood); 9 AP 5.8.18

D7248 Deld 5 AAP Filton by 12.6.18; AAP Dover 13.6.18; 491 Flt Dover 16.6.18 (233 Sqn 31.8.18); 218 Sqn 29.9.18; Returning from raid, EF, FL in sea off Ostende, sank 18.10.18 (2/Lt MJ Carroll & Sgt AJ Oliver both unhurt); Deleted 31.10.18

D7249 Deld 5 AAP Filton by 14-15.6.18, reallotted from 61 Wing to EF; Rec Pk to 2 AI 17.6.18; 103 Sqn 19.6.18; Fokker DVII OOC Haubourdin-Santes 10.27 24.9.18 (Lt JGH Chrispin & 2/Lt CG Bannerman); Fokker DVII OOC Wasnes au Bac 09.15 27.9.18 (Capt DM Darroch & 2/Lt EA Wadsworth); Returning from low level raid on Roubaix aerodrome two Fokker DVIIs crashed NW of Leuze 14.40 30.10.18, own a/c shot up 30.10.18 (Lt GB Hett unhurt & 2/Lt JJ Nicholls DoW); FL Le Bourget 17.11.18; Repaired at RAF Paris, back at sqn by 9.12.18; Incorrect timing on gears caused propeller to break and engine to race 21.1.19 (Lt JGH Chrispin DFC & Lt CG Bannerman); RTP 25.1.19

D7250 8 AAP Lympne (via AAP Dover) 18.6.18; Rec Pk to 2 AI and on to 98 Sqn 19.6.18; Reallotted from 61 Wing to EF 21.6.18, A/c then in France; On landing m/c caught in rut, swung round and crashed 2.7.18 (Lt F Carpenter & Lt FE Donkin OK); Rep Pk 1 ASD 4.7.18; SOC 6.7.18 NWR

D7251 to D7300 cancelled 15.6.18

100 D.H.9 ordered 29.11.17 under Cont No A.S.37725 (BR.228) from F.W.Berwick & Co Ltd, London and numbered D7301 to D7400. Some delivered as spares to 3 SD Milton. Cancelled from D7331. (230hp BHP)

D7301 No information

D7302 At Makers 15.6.18 for 108 Sqn (Mob); 2 AAP Hendon by 25.6.18; 108 Sqn ('N') by 4.7.18; To France with Sqn 22.7.18; Left 1553 18.8.18, FTR, last seen making rapid descent over Ostende after hit by AA 18.8.18 (Capt RSS Ingram & 2/Lt AW Wyncoll both POWs)

D.H.9 D8302 'N' of No.108 Squadron after being shot down by AA near Ostende on 18.8.18. (via Frank Cheesman)

D7303 to D7307 No information
D7308 Prawle Point by 30.11.18; 14 TDS Lake Down 18.12.18
D7309 3 FS Bircham Newton by 7.18 - 8.18
D7310 3 FS Bircham Newton by 9.18; Crashed 8.10.18 WO
D7311 3 FS Bircham Newton by 8.18
D7312 At Makers 29.6.18 allotted to EF; Rec Pk to 2 AI 26.7.18; 3 ASD and on to 104 Sqn 1.8.18; 3 ASD 11.8.18 wrecked
D7313 At Makers 29.6.18 allotted to EF; Rec Pk to 2 AI 28.7.18; Took off on ferry flight to 3 ASD, engine failed, crashed and burst into flames 28.7.18 (2/Lt CN Barker badly burnt); Rep Pk 2 ASD SOC 1.8.18 NWR
D7314 At Makers 29.6.18 allotted to EF; At Rec Pk crashed into by 12 Sqn's RE8 B6573 28.7.18; SOC Rep Pk 1 ASD 8.8.18 NWR
D7315 At Makers 29.6.18 allotted to EF; Rec Pk to 1 AI 28.7.18; 206 Sqn 30.7.18; Left 08.55, seen just W of lines, but crashed E of lines 12.8.18 (Lt JC Ivens & 2/Lt CA Atkins both PoW); SOC in field 14.8.18; Salvaged in No Man's Land by 103 Sqn 7.9.18; SOC 7.9.18
D7316 2 AI to 107 Sqn 10.8.18; On practice flight COL 1.11.18 (Lt WA Oates USAS OK)
D7317 Rep Pk 2 ASD to 2 AI 4.8.18; 27 Sqn 4.8.18; Left 17.20 on low strafing mission, last seen in combat with 2 EA over Voyennes 8.8.18 (2/Lt HM Brown & 2/Lt DE Chase both PoW)
D7318 Rep Pk 1 ASD to Rec Pk and on to 2 AI 10.8.18; 3 ASD 12.8.18; 104 Sqn 18.8.18; On Mannheim raid 7.9.18 engine not running well had to fly 2,000ft below the formation, in combat EA destroyed, m/c damaged 7.9.18 (Lt JW Richards OK & Sgt WE Reast wounded in head, DoW 9.9.18); 6 AP 18.9.18; 3 ASD 19.9.18
D7319 Rec Pk to 2 AI 13.8.18; 49 Sqn 19.8.18; Engine trouble, COL just after take off 25.8.18 (Lt ER Wallington & 2/Lt JD Hall)
D7320 Rec Pk to Rep Pk 1 ASD, on to 108 Sqn 9.8.18; Raid on Zeebrugge, engine hit by AA Ostende, seen diving nr Ostende beach 11.30, FL 100yds W of Ostende Pier 30.8.18 (2/Lt KAW Leighton & 2/Lt WR Jackson PoW)
D7321 2 AI to 49 Sqn 11.8.18; Got into slipstream of another a/c on take off, lost control and crashed 23.8.18 (Lt ER Wallington & 2/Lt JD Hall); SOC Rep Pk 2 ASD 10.9.18 (ex 9 AP)
D7322 Rec Pk to 1 AI 11.8.18; 206 Sqn 11.8.18; Badly shot up by AA fire Armentières 17.15 29.8.18 (Lt CL Cumming unhurt & 2/Lt B Knee slightly wounded); Rep Pk 1 ASD 31.8.18; SOC 2.9.18 NWR
D7323 2 AI to 98 Sqn ('Z') 12.8.18; Pfalz DIII in flames Valenciennes 13.15 9.10.18 (2/Lt EAR Lee & 2/Lt AA Douglas); Left 09.30 for bombing raid to Mons Rlwy Stn, combat with EAs W of Mons on return, FTR 30.10.18 (2/Lt EAR Lee & 2/Lt AA Douglas both killed)
D7324 At Makers 23.7.18 allotted to EF; Rec Pk to 1 AI 30.8.18; 103 Sqn 16.9.18; Left 06.00 on recce, hit by AA, FL and crashed La Motte 29.9.18 (Capt J Austin-Sparks & Lt JB Russell DFC both wounded); Rep Pk 1 ASD 1.10.18
D7325 At Makers 23.7.18 allotted to EF; Rep Pk 2 ASD to 2 AI 7.9.18; 98 Sqn 17.9.18; Returning from raid on Mons Rlwy Stn, combat with 30 EA W of Mons, shot down 1130 30.10.18 (Lt DW Holmes & 2/Lt JE Prosser both killed)
D7326 No information
D7327 98 Sqn ('Z') by 10.18
D7328 to D7330 No information
D7331 to D7400 cancelled 3.5.18

50 D.H.9 ordered 20.8.18 under Cont No 35a/1548/C.1649 (BR.509) from F.W.Berwick & Co Ltd, London and numbered D7331 to D7380

D7331 No information
D7332 3 FS Bircham Newton ('6') by 8.18; Crashed 11.18
D7333 SOC Rep Pk 1 ASD 7.9.18 (ex Rec Pk) NWR
D7334 Rec Pk to 2 AI 24.8.18; 98 Sqn ('Q') 30.8.18; Returning from Cambrai, Pfalz DIII in flames Demicourt 18.00 3.9.18 (2/Lt EAR Lee & 2/Lt EG Banham); Left 07.15 for bombing raid on Grévillers, in combat, FL, crashed in shell hole 27.9.18 (2/Lt EAR Lee & 2/Lt EG Banham both injured); SOC Rep Pk 2 ASD 3.10.18
D7335 Rec Pk to 2 AI and on to 98 Sqn 30.8.18; Pfalz DIII BU SW of Cambrai 18.15 3.9.18; Pfalz DIII OOC 5m E of Valenciennes 12.40 and a Pfalz DIII OOC Mons 13.15 9.10.18 (all 2/Lt TW Sleigh & 2/Lt AH Fuller); Raid to Mons Rlwy Stn, combat with 30 EA, FL Odamez 30.10.18 (Lt EW Langford & Lt J Andrews both unhurt); A/c shelled, unsalvable
D7336 Rec Pk to 1 AI 23.8.18; 108 Sqn ('G') 31.8.18; Left 14.15 for bombing raid on Bruges, hit by AA, crashed inverted Zierikzee c.17.00 15.9.18 (Lt JJ McDonald & Lt GE McManus both interned); Used by Dutch as *deH442* [not confirmed by Dutch reports]
D7337 Rep Pk 1 ASD to Rec Pk 11.9.18; 1 AI 17.9.18; 103 Sqn 20.9.18; Fokker DVII in flames and another OOC Leuze 16.50 23.10.18 (Sgt TW Haines & 2/Lt DC McDonald); Fokker DVII OOC Leuze 16.10 26.10.18 (Lt PS Tennant & 2/Lt GLP Drummond); Fokker DVII crashed Chapelle-à-Wattines 14.35 30.10.18 (Sgt TW Haines & 2/Lt DC McDonald)

D7338 1 AI to 211 Sqn 16.9.18; Bombing raid on Roulers, port aileron shot away by EA, FL outside aerodrome, hit bump, o/t 07.00 29.9.18 (2/Lt JM Payne & 2/Lt WG Gadd both unhurt); 1 ASD 29.9.18
D7339 Rep Pk 1 ASD to Rec Pk 12.9.18; 2 AI 13.9.18; 107 Sqn 28.9.18; On aerial firing practice lost flying speed and dived in, m/c destroyed by fire 22.10.18 (2/Lt CP Lee killed & 2/Lt AH Butler injured)
D7340 1 AI to 108 Sqn 23.9.18; Left on raid but when at 200ft appeared to sideslip, crashed 28.9.18 (2/Lt PA Haynes DoI & 2/Lt C Donald killed)
D7341 Rec Pk to 2 AI 14.9.18; 107 Sqn 25.9.18; 98 Sqn 1.3.19; 8 AAP Lympne 8.3.19
D7342 Rec Pk to 1 AI 16.9.18; 108 Sqn 23.9.18; After bombing Ingelmunster station at 17.25, formation attacked by 33 EA between the target and Roulers 3 EA in flames, 1 BU and 2 OOC shared C2205, D499, D5835, D5845, E605, E5435, E8871 & F5847, FTR last seen in control nr Roulers 1.10.18 (Lt GA Featherstone & 2/Lt F Owen both killed).
D7343 Rec Pk to 2 AI 10.9.18; 3 ASD 13.9.18; 99 Sqn 14.9.18; 3 ASD 13.11.18
D7344 No information
D7345 Left Hendon 1.9.18; Arr Rec Pk 3.9.18; 2 AI and on to 3 ASD 5.9.18; 104 Sqn 14.9.18; 3 ASD 16.9.18, wrecked
D7346 Arr Rec Pk 9.9.18; 2 AI 14.9.18; 98 Sqn 28.9.18; Left 14.05 for bombing raid on Hirson Rlwy Stn, shot up in combat with enemy formation 23.10.18 (2/Lt FC Wilton & Capt GH Gillis OK); 2 AI 26.10.18; To Rep Pk 2 ASD but overshot landing, overturned in ploughed field 27.10.18 (2/Lt CFE Arthur & Lt GE Gillett OK)
D7347 Rec Pk to 2 AI 14.9.18; 27 Sqn 26.9.18; Left 06.45 for raid on Aulnoye, hit by AA before reaching objective, engine seized, recrossed the lines and FL at Moeuvres 30.9.18 (Lt E Bryant & 2/Lt WJ Diment OK); Rep Pk 1 ASD 4.10.18
D7348 to D7350 No information
D7351 Rec Pk to 2 AI 16.9.18; 98 Sqn 28.9.18; Returning from raid on Hirson railway station, formation had to land at 62 Sqn airfield due to bad visibility, D7351 dived to avoid another m/c but the controls had jammed, unable to pull out, crashed 23.10.18 (Lt TW Sleigh & Lt AH Fuller OK)
D7352 Presentation a/c 'Presented by H.H. The Maharaja of Bikanir No.11'. Rec Pk to 2 AI 16.9.18
D7353 2 AI to 5 AI 10.10.18; 98 Sqn 28.10.18; On reconnaissance 4.11.18 (Lt EW Longford & Lt J Andrews both wounded); 8 AAP Lympne 12.2.19
D7354 Rep Pk 2 ASD by 24.9.18; 2 AI 25.9.18
D7355 Rep Pk 2 ASD to 2 AI 18.10.18; 27 Sqn 30.10.18; Left 12.25 on bombing raid, shot down over St.Symphorien aerodrome 4.11.18 (2/Lt JG Symonds & Lt WG Lacey MC both killed)
D7356 Rep Pk 2 ASD to 5 AI 16.10.18; 27 Sqn, left 12.25 on bombing raid, shot down over St.Symphorien aerodrome 4.11.18 (2/Lt WJ Potts & Sgt CW Metcalfe both PoW)
D7357 2 AI to 108 Sqn 7.11.18; EA OOC E of Sotteghem, shared C2216, D613, D5845, E8980, E9028 09.05 9.11.18 (2/Lt C Campbell & 2/Lt JTR Wynne); 98 Sqn 23.1.19; 8 AAP Lympne 13.2.19
D7358 6 AI to 211 Sqn 9.12.18; to 98 Sqn 26.2.19; 1 ASD 5.3.19
D7359 Arr 206 Sqn Helwan ex France 25.7.19; 47 Sqn by 6.20
D7360 Rep Pk 2 ASD to 2 AI 22.10.18; 27 Sqn by 12.18; 98 Sqn 5.3.19; 47 Sqn by 5.20
D7361 Rep Pk 2 ASD to 2 AI 23.10.18; 98 Sqn 4.11.18; 8 AAP Lympne 12.2.19
D7362 Rec Pk to 1 AI 29.9.18; 211 Sqn 30.9.18; Left 09.45 on photo mission, hit by AA, seen to land in enemy territory SW of Charleroi 10.11.18 (2/Lt CH Thomas PoW & 2/Lt JHR Smith killed)
D7363 No information
D7364 Flown Thetford to Harling Road 17.10.18; 4 SoN&BD Thetford by 11.18
D7365 & D7366 No information
D7367 4 SoN&BD Thetford by 11.18
D7368 557/8 Flts 212 Sqn Yarmouth by 15.10.18 - @31.10.18; IAAD, Imperial Gift to India, shipped SS *Hatimura* 8.20
D7369 Rec Pk to 1 AI by 10.18; 211 Sqn ('V') 7.10.18 but FL Petite Synthe en route; Thick mist, landed Boussières, crashed 30.11.18 (Lt DF Taber USA & 2/Lt JM McLellan both unhurt) (for 1 ASD); 7 SS Bohain 1.12.18
D7370 At 8 AAP Lympne 28.1.19 reallotted from EF to SE Area for Store
D7371 1 ASD to 103 Sqn 1.11.18; Crashed 22.1.19 (Sgt CR Haigh OK); Being returned to 1 ASD 8.3.19
D7372 3 FS Sedgeford by 3.19; 206 Sqn by 5.19; 1 ASD to 49 Sqn 19.6.19; Handed in to 1 ASD 14.7.19
D7373 Rep Pk 2 ASD to 2 AI 25.10.18; 218 Sqn 14.11.18; Stalled on landing 9.12.18 (2/Lt MJ Carroll & 2/Lt T James both unhurt); to 2 ASD; SOC 16.12.18
D7374 & D7375 No information
D7376 Arr 206 Sqn Helwan ex France 27.7.19
D7377 Arr 206 Sqn Helwan ex France 10.8.19; ASD Aboukir 14.8.18
D7378 On test flight at Rep Pk 1 ASD engine, failed to pick up, a/c turned over on soft ground 17.1.19 (2/Lt T Rennie)
D7379 Rep Pk 2 ASD to 2 AI 25.10.18;
D7380 206 Sqn, flying accident 14.5.19 (2/Lt SH Gibbs DoI & Sgt A Page killed)
"D7386" Rep Pk 2 ASD to 2 AI 16.10.18

100 D.H.9 ordered 24.1.18 under Cont No A.S.41634 (BR.228) from G & J Weir, Cathcart, Glasgow and numbered D9800 to D9899. (200hp BHP)

D9800 to D9802 No information
D9803 49 TDS Catterick by 10.18
D9804 to D9806 No information
D9807 Presentation Aircraft 'City of Glasgow, Canada'
D9808 119 Sqn Wyton by 11.18; 117 Sqn Tallaght by 7.4.19; Midland Area FIS Lilbourne by 7.10.19
D9809 No information
D9810 49 TDS Catterick by 10.18
D9811 49 TDS Catterick by 10.18
D9812 No information
D9813 49 TDS Catterick by 10.18
D9814 1 FTS Netheravon by 11.24 (prefix?)
D9815 No information
D9816 49 TDS Catterick by 10.18; 1 FTS Netheravon by 11.24 - @12.24 (prefix?)
D9817 to D9819 No information
D9820 49 TDS Catterick, stalled on turn at 500ft, spun in 16.11.18 (Lt CA Songhurst seriously injured)
D9821 No information
D9822 25 TDS Tallaght by 12.18
D9823 No information
D9824 Arr 206 Sqn Helwan ex UK 29.7.19; 'X' AD 8.8.19; 206 Sqn to ASD Aboukir 14.8.19; 206 Sqn 26.12.19; 47 Sqn by 5.20; Lost speed on climbing turn on TO, stalled and spun in Almaza 3.9.20 (O/O BCS Bright killed)
D9825 No information
D9826 1 FS Turnberry by 6.11.18; 1 FTS Netheravon by 11.24 (prefix?)
D9827 to D9834 No information
D9835 Arr 206 Sqn Helwan ex UK 29.7.19; ASD Aboukir 16.9.19
D9836 49 Sqn, en route to 1 ASD, FL nr Morschenich, destroyed by fire 8.7.19 (2/Lt J Turner)
D9837 At 6 SD Ascot 5.12.18 reallotted from EF to Store; Sold to Estonian Government; To Estonian AF as *No.32* (230hp Puma)
D9838 At 6 SD Ascot 5.12.18 reallotted from EF to Store; To Greek Government
D9839 to D9842 No information
D9843 83 Sqn by 1.19
D9844 22 TDS Gormanston by 10.18
D9845 to D9855 No information
D9856 22 TDS Gormanston by 5.19
D9857 to D9860 No information
D9861 49 TDS Catterick by 1.19
D9862 to D9866 No information
D9867 22 TDS Gormanston by 10.18
D9868 23 TDS Baldonnel, stalled after EF on TO and spun in 3.2.19 (F/Cdt J Littley burnt to death)
D9869 to D9881 No information
D9882 22 TDS Gormanston by 10.18
D9883 22 TDS Gormanston by 10.18
D9884 No information
D9885 to D9899 cancelled 12.18 (factory closed 31.12.18)

D.H.9 D9883 of No.22 Training Depot Station, Gormanstown in late 1918. (H.S.Clarke)

100 D.H.9 ordered 26.1.18 under Cont No A.S.2341 (BR.113, 228 & 332) from Whitehead Aircraft Co Ltd, Richmond, Surrey and numbered E601 to E700. (230hp Puma)

E601 Deld 10 AAP Brooklands, tested 27/28.6.18; Manston Naval Flight by 6.18; Covehithe 29.7.18; Became 534 Flt 273 Sqn Covehithe by 1.9.18 - @31.10.18

E602 At 7 AAP Kenley for 108 Sqn (Mob); To France with sqn 22.7.18; Left 17.15 on raid on Jabbeke dump, hit by AA nr Bruges, unable to reach Holland, went down in sea nr Ostende 19.8.18 (2/Lt JM Dunlop & 2/Lt FF Schorn both PoW)

E603 110 Sqn Kenley 7.18; Manston to 557/8 Flts 212 Sqn Yarmouth 22.7.18 - @31.10.18

E604 Manston to 557/8 Flts 212 Sqn Yarmouth 13.8.18; FL Alberswick, nr Southwold, wrecked 19.8.18 (2 crew unhurt)

E605 7 AAP Kenley to 108 Sqn (Mob) by 12.7.18; To France with Sqn 22.7.18; Shot down Fokker DVII 2.8.18 (2/Lt AAS Milne & 2/Lt GE McManus); Fokker DVII crashed and burnt in fight from Oudenberg to Schoore, shared D1080 17.35-17.55 21.8.18 (2/Lt AAS Milne & 2/Lt GE McManus); After bombing Ingelmunster station at 17.25 formation attacked by 33 EA between the target and Roulers, 3 EA in flames, 1 BU and 2 OOC shared C2205, D499, D5835, D5845, D7342, E5435, E8871 & F5847 1.10.18 (2/Lt AAS Milne & Sgt W Greenwood); Left 06.22 on bombing raid to Audenarde, combat with EA, shot down in flames E of Courtrai 14.10.18 (Lt HW Bingham & 2/Lt FW Woolley both killed)

E606 Eastchurch to Manston 6.7.18 - @8.18

E607 55 TS Narborough to Castle Bromwich 6.8.19

E608 Artillery & Infantry Co-op School Worthy Down by 6.18 - 7.18; Wireless School Worthy Down by 11.7.18 - @24.9.18

E609 Artillery & Infantry Co-op School Worthy Down by 7.18; Wireless School Worthy Down by 2.7.18 - @9.7.18

E610 2 FS Marske, flat turn at 300ft, stalled, spun in 28.8.18 (2/Lt AJ Goring seriously injured & F/Cdt H Hill killed)

E611 Imperial Gift to India; Became *G-IAAQ* later *VT-AAQ*

E612 Covehithe by 11.18; Imperial Gift to India

E613 11 TDS Boscombe Down by 11.18

E614 15 TDS Hucknall by 10.18 - @11.18

E615 to E617 No information

E618 49 TDS Catterick by 11.18; TOC Base Depot RAF Novorossisk 27.2.20; SOC 5.3.20

E619 49 TDS Catterick by 10.18 - 11.18

E620 In transit to Mudros 10.18; Recd 'X' AD ex UK 2.9.18; 144 Sqn 25.10.18; 'X' AD 26.11.18

E621 At Makers 28.6.18, Allotted to EF; To 7 AAP Kenley; Rec Pk to 2 AI 26.7.18; 5 AI 28.7.18; 107 Sqn 29.7.18; Left 05.40 for raid on Brie Bridge, FTR 9.8.18 (2/Lt JE Emtage & 2/Lt P Willis MM (Can) both killed

E622 At Makers 28.6.18, Allotted to EF; To 7 AAP Kenley; 8 AAP Lympne to Rec Pk 24.7.18; 2 AI 26.7.18; 5 AI 28.7.18; 98 Sqn 29.7.18; In raid on Péronne Rlwy bridge, came out of cloud and saw a Halberstadt C directly below, this was attacked, it glided down and COL Foy 15.05 8.8.18 (Lt F Carpenter & 2/Lt NC MacDonald); Landing after practice flight, undershot, flat turned into the wind, stalled hit a ridge and crashed 23.8.18 (Lt FJ Keble & Sgt Mech RT Wallace OK); 9 AP 25.8.18; SOC Rep Pk 2 ASD 24.9.18

E623 At Makers 28.6.18, Allotted to EF; To 7 AAP Kenley; Rec Pk to 2 AI 25.7.18; 5 AI 28.7.18; 49 Sqn 31.7.18; Returning from raid on Aulnoye Junction, formation attacked by 40 EA, Pfalz red tail yellow planes crashed W of Forêt de Mormal 17.30 24.8.18 (Lt MD Allen & 2/Lt WA Owens); In combat over Moeuvres at 19.00 25.8.18 (Lt MD Allen OK & Lt F Maudesley wounded); Fokker DVII OOC smoking W of Aulnoye 08.10 9.10.18; Fokker DVII in flames St.Denis 09.15 30.10.18; Fokker DVII in flames Blangy 08.45 4.11.18 (all Capt MD Allen & 2/Lt WA Owens); COL 21.4.19 (Lt JN Bitton & Lt H Taylor MC OK)

E624 Rec Pk to 2 AI 28.7.18; Sent to IF to replace D7313 which had crashed and burnt; Le Bourget 29.7.18; 3 ASD 30.7.18 ; 104 Sqn 31.7.18; 3 ASD 1.8.18; Pool of Pilots by 5.19 (prefix?)

E625 to E629 No information

E630 RAE from/by 3.3.19 - 6.3.20 (supercharger experiments)

E631 Rep Pk 1 ASD to Rec Pk and on to 2 AI 31.7.18; 1 AI to 103 Sqn 1.8.18; Bombing Péronne in mist, lost formation, landed 207 Sqn airfield 15.8.18 (Lt G Butters & Lt MW Lewin retd next morning); Crashed 25.10.18 (Sgt WH White & Cpl Mech OH Armitage both killed); 1 ASD 27.10.18

E632 England to France 8.18; Rep Pk 2 ASD to 2 AI 4.8.18; 3 ASD 7.8.18; 99 Sqn 8.9.18; Bombing raid on Metz-Sablon railway, in combat with many EAs, 26.9.18 (Lt SC Gilbert & 2/Lt R Buckby both killed)

E633 Rep Pk to Rec Pk 30.7.18; 2 AI 31.7.18; 107 Sqn 5.8.18; Left 05.40 for raid on Brie Bridge, believed FL Villers Bretonneux and laid out wounded 9.8.18 (2/Lt SR Coward PoW wounded & 2/Lt LG Cooper PoW DoW)

E634 Rep Pk 2 ASD to 2 AI 3.8.18; 27 Sqn 6.8.18; Returning from raid, aerial collision with D1702 and wrecked 14.8.18 (2/Lt AF Millar & 2/Lt JV Lee both killed)

E635 Rec Pk to 2 AI 6.8.18; 49 Sqn 9.8.18; FL nr Mont St Eloi 25.8.18 (2/Lt AL Murray OK & Sgt RW Buchan wounded); 2 AI by 1.19; 211 Sqn 13.2.19; 98 Sqn 23.2.19; Rec Pk 4.3.19; To England 6.3.19

E636 Rec Pk to 2 AI 6.8.18; 49 Sqn 8.8.18; In combat over Fresnes 9.8.18 (Lt RC Stokes & Lt CE Pullen both wounded); Left 11.45 for bombing raid on Valenciennes, hit by AA, retd 14.50 3.10.18 (2/Lt LWD Peacock & Sgt R Reid unhurt)

E637 to E648 No information

E649 Sold to Anti-Bolshevik Government; TOC Base Depot RAF Novorossisk 14.2.20; To Russian Aviation Corps 14.2.20

E650 Sold to Anti-Bolshevik Government; Unloaded from SS *Diyatalana* on/by 25.1.20; TOC Base Depot RAF Novorossisk 14.2.20

E651 Sold to Anti-Bolshevik Government; TOC Base Depot RAF Novorossisk, to 7 Sqn Russian Aviation Corps 14.2.20

E652 Sold to Anti-Bolshevik Government; Unloaded from SS *Diyatalana* on/by 25.1.20; TOC Base Depot RAF Novorossisk 14.2.20; To Russian Aviation Corps 14.2.20

E653 to E656 No information

E657 SOC Rep Pk 1 ASD 6.9.18 ex England; Rebuilt as H7076

E658 Rep Pk 1 ASD to Rec Pk 5.9.18; 2 AI 7.9.18; 49 Sqn 17.9.18; Left 14.50 on raid on Aulnoye Junction, FTR 24.9.18 (Lt HJ Bennett PoW DoW 25.9.18 & 2/Lt RH Armstrong PoW)

E659 Rep Pk 1 ASD to Rec Pk 8.9.18; 2 AI 10.9.18; 3 ASD 15.9.18; 104 Sqn 21.10.18; En route from Azelot to Blangy, FL at Paris Depot with unserviceable engine 21.11.18 (Lt ST Crowe & 3/AM T Lee); SOC 29.11.18

E660 Rep Pk 1 ASD to Rec Pk and on to 1 AI 7.9.18; 103 Sqn 25.9.18; On dusk recce attacked by two Fokker DVIIs one of which down OOC 1630 28.10.18 (Sgt H Driver & Sgt H Huckle); COL, fuselage broke in half 6.1.19 (Capt R Jackson & Lt EA Slater OK); Rep Pk 1 ASD 14.1.19

E661 Rep Pk 1 ASD to Rec Pk 4.9.18; 2 AI 5.9.18; 107 Sqn 7.9.18; Pilot seized with cramp necessitating FL 23.10.18 (Lt CEF Searle & 2/Lt ET Shone)
E662 Rep Pk 2 ASD to 2 AI 17.9.18; 98 Sqn 1.10.18; On test flight landed at 19 Sqn airfield, crashed into hangar and destroyed by fire 11.10.18 (2/Lt DH Grigg killed & 2/Lt SStC Stone injured)
E663 No information
E664 Rep Pk 2 ASD to 2 AI 26.9.18; 5 AI 9.10.18; 107 Sqn 23.10.18; 98 Sqn 6.3.19; 8 AAP Lympne 14.3.19
E665 Rep Pk 2 ASD to 2 AI 13.9.18; 27 Sqn 1.10.18; FL on raid on Tournai 14.10.18 (Lt J Cocksedge OK & Lt HG Biltcliffe wounded); Back at sqn 15.10.18 98 Sqn 5.3.19
E666 Rep Pk 2 ASD to 2 AI 23.9.18; 107 Sqn 22.10.18; 98 Sqn 1.3.19; Lympne 6.3.19
E667 Rec Pk to 2 AI 4.9.18; 49 Sqn 5.9.18; Crashed 17.9.18 (Lt ER Wallington & Sgt T Potter); To Rep Pk 2 ASD; 2 AI 18.10.18; 107 Sqn 30.10.18; 98 Sqn 6.3.19; 8 AAP Lympne 14.3.19
E668 Rec Pk to 1 AI 3.9.18; 108 Sqn 16.9.18; 8 AAP Lympne 18.1.19
E669 Rec Pk to 1 AI 6.9.18; 108 Sqn 16.9.18; In Lichtervelde raid Fokker DrI OOC Gits and Fokker DVII OOC Staden, shared C6314, C6345, D1080, D3092, D5622, D5759, D7208, E5435 & F5847 11.45 21.9.18 (2/Lt AS Jones & Sgt R Richardson); Left 10.35 in raid on Cortemarck dump, hit by AA nr target, last seen going down in spin but appeared to be under partial control 27.9.18 (2/Lt AS Jones & Sgt R Richardson both killed)
E670 No information
E671 11 TDS Old Sarum, stalled at 50ft gliding in to land, dived in 10.2.19 (Lt AO Greeves injured)
E672 Rec Pk to 2 AI 23.9.18; 98 Sqn ('R') 2.10.18; Crashed on landing 26.10.18 (Lt WH Whitlock & Sgt H Brigham); Returning from raid on Mons Rlwy Stn Fokker DVII crashed in flames W of Mons 11.30 30.10.18 (Lt WH Whitlock & Sgt Mech F Sefton); 1 ASD 16.11.18
E673 No information
E674 Arr Rec Pk 7.9.18; 2 AI 10.9.18; 3 ASD 13.9.18; 104 Sqn 15.9.18; SOC 21.1.19
E675 Rec Pk to 2 AI 13.9.18; 49 Sqn 25.9.18
E676 Rec Pk to 108 Sqn 7.10.18; EA OOC Sotteghem, shared C2216, D613, E8959, E8980, E9026 & F1118 09.40-10.10 4.11.18 (2/Lt EB Thomson & 2/Lt EL Chafe who was slightly wounded); Oil pipe burst FL on rough ground crashed 12.11.18 (2/Lt AH Gooch & Sgt W Jackson OK); SOC in field 14.11.18
E677 Rec Pk to 2AI 13.9.18; Rep Pk 2 ASD 14.9.18; 2AI 18.10.18; 107 Sqn by 2.19; 8 AAP Lympne 14.3.19
E678 No information
E679 1 TS Turnberry, flat turn after TO, spun in 31.12.18 (2/Lt CA Hillock DoI & pupil 2/Lt J Millikin killed)
E680 to E683 No information
E684 55 TS Narborough by 8.19 - 9.19
E685 No information
E686 Deld 6 SD Ascot for Mudros W/E 17.10.18; Shipped/left W/E 7.11.18; TOC Base Depot RAF Novorossisk 14.2.20; To Russian Aviation Corps 14.2.20; Sold to Anti-Bolshevik Government
E687 Deld 6 SD Ascot for Mudros W/E 17.10.18; Shipped/left W/E 7.11.18; Base Depot RAF Novorossisk to Russian Aviation Corps 14.2.20;
E688 Deld 6 SD Ascot for Mudros W/E 17.10.18; Shipped/left W/E 7.11.18; TOC Base Depot RAF Novorossisk 14.2.20; SOC 5.3.20; Sold to Anti-Bolshevik Government
E689 Deld 6 SD Ascot for Mudros W/E 31.10.18; Shipped/left W/E 7.11.18; TOC Base Depot RAF Novorossisk 14.2.20; SOC 5.3.20; Sold to Anti-Bolshevik Government; To Soviet Russian Air Corps (RKKVF)
E690 Deld 6 SD Ascot for Mudros W/E 17.10.18; Shipped/left W/E 21.11.18; TOC Base Depot RAF Novorossisk 14.2.20; SOC 5.3.20; Sold to Anti-Bolshevik Government; To Soviet Russian Air Corps (RKKVF)
E691 Rec Pk to 1 AI 16.10.18; 211 Sqn 18.10.18; Hit on ground by another m/c 27.10.18; to 7 SS 28.10.18; SOC in field
E692 Rec Pk to 2 AI 14.10.18; 98 Sqn 28.10.18; Returning from raid on Mons two Fokker DVIIs in flames 11.30 30.10.18 (2/Lt FC Wilton & Capt GH Gillis); 8 AAP Lympne 7.2.19
E693 No information
E694 2 AI to 27 Sqn 7.11.18; 98 Sqn 5.3.19
E695 2 AI to 49 Sqn 22.11.18; FL at Maubeuge on sqn move to Bickendorf 29.5.19 (2/Lt LWD Peacock & AC2 RJ Ashton)
E696 At 7 AAP Kenley 13.9.18 for 117 Sqn (Mob) Norwich as a training m/c; To Sqn 23.9.18
E697 At 7 AAP Kenley 14.9.18 for 117 Sqn (Mob) Norwich as a training m/c; To Sqn 26.9.18 - 10.18
E698 At 7 AAP Kenley 16.9.18 for 117 Sqn (Mob) Norwich as a training m/c; To Sqn 23.9.18 but FL Tydd St Mary; TOC 3 AAP Norwich
E699 At 7 AAP Kenley 16.9.18 for 117 Sqn (Mob) Norwich as a training m/c; At Sqn by 5.10.18; Crashed on landing 28.10.18 (2/Lt F Latimer unhurt & 2/Lt HDH Williams injured)
E700 Rec Pk to 1 AI 1.10.18; 108 Sqn 3.10.18; Attempting to take off from FL in ploughed field struck post and crashed 1.11.18 (Lt GS Daniel & Lt E Holder OK); Rep Pk 1 ASD 4.11.18

400 D.H.9A ordered 26.1.18 under Cont No A.S.4291 (also A.S.2341/18) from Whitehead Aircraft Co Ltd, Richmond, Surrey and numbered E701 to E1100. (400hp Liberty 12A)

E701 2 SoN&BD Andover by 10.18
E702 3 ASD to 110 Sqn 22.10.18; Wrecked 23.10.18; 6 AP 26.10.18; 3 ASD 29.10.18; SOC W/E 30.11.18
E703 3 ASD to 110 Sqn 21.10.18; COL 16.1.19 (2/Lt WA Peters & 2/Lt LR Robins); SOC 21.1.19
E704 3 ASD to 110 Sqn 22.10.18; Badly wrecked in FL in snow on mail flight to Cologne 29.3.19 (Lt MJ Lewin OK)
E705 3 ASD to 110 Sqn 23.10.18; Wrecked 23.10.18; 6 AP 26.10.18; 3 ASD 29.10.18
E706 2 AI to 25 Sqn 11.11.18; 99 Sqn to 6 AI on landing pilot over estimated aerodrome, engine would not pick up in time to take off again, caught corner of a hangar 23.4.19 (2/Lt DC Bain OK); To be RTP
E707 2 AI to 18 Sqn 12.11.18; Test flight at Bickendorf struck wreckage of a German m/c on landing which tore u/c off 26.2.19 (Lt JKS Smith & 2/Lt RH Walker OK)
E708 1 AI to 18 Sqn 30.10.18; Engine cut out at 7,000ft, crashed into a hut on landing 9.11.18 (2/Lt K Holmes & 2/Lt E Lay OK); Rep Pk 2 ASD 9.11.18;
E709 1 AI to 18 Sqn 30.10.18; Throttle control broke, FL, struck shell hole and crashed 10.11.18 (2/Lt AR Hunt & 2/Lt J Collins OK); 2 ASD 10.11.18
E710 At 7 AAP Kenley 16.11.18 for 155 Sqn (Mob) Chingford; Reallotted to 123 Sqn Upper Heyford by 14.12.18 on disbandment of 155 Sqn 12.12.18; 123 Sqn by 12.18 - 1.19
E711 Arr Rec Pk 28.10.18; 3 ASD 30.10.18; 99 Sqn 14.11.18; On landing engine cut out, m/c hit tree 14.3.19 (2/Lt JHW Wilcox & 2/Lt PE Bullock OK)
E712 No information
E713 7 AAP Kenley by 10.18 - 1.19; 110 Sqn by 4.1.19
E714 No information

D.H.9A E716 'F' of No.205 Squadron. (via Philip Jarrett)

A wartime photograph of D.H.9A E726. (via Frank Cheesman)

A post-war photograph of D.H.9A E726 coded 'B3' with No.207 Squadron in 1926. (via Frank Cheesman)

E715 47 Sqn Ekaterinodar by 15.8.19; 'A' Flt, 'A' Dett, RAF Trg Mission South Russia 12.19; Sold to Anti-Bolshevik Government; Later Soviet Russian Air Fleet (RKKVF)

E716 Arr Rec Pk 9.11.18 - @11.11.18; 205 Sqn ('F') post-war; 'A' dett RAF Instructional Mission South Russia by 17.10.19

E717 Arr Rec Pk 9.11.18 - @11.11.18; 2 AI to 18 Sqn 19.11.18; Engine lost all water and seized, crashed 9.3.19 (Lt B Champion & 2/Lt E Lay OK)

E718 TOC EF 21.11.18; 99 Sqn by 17.1.19; COL due to bad ground 7.4.19 (2/Lt HW Atherton & Lt JSF Watson)

E719 TOC EF 22.11.18; 110 Sqn 11.1.19; Crashed on mail flight to Cologne 31.3.19 (2/Lt HG Bennett OK)

E720 3 ASD to 99 Sqn 14.11.18; On mail flight crashed Gerpinnes 25.2.19 (2/Lt DC Bain & 2/Lt FS Smith)

E721 3 ASD to 99 Sqn 13.11.18 - @17.1.19

E722 No information

E723 110 Sqn from 11.18; 2 AI 28.11.18

E724 PD Ascot; AD Drigh Rd; 27 Sqn 4.24

E725 On ferry flight from 2 AI overshot and ran into railway 20.11.18 (Lt AG Bathurst-Norman)

E726 At 8 AAP Lympne 28.1.19 allotted to EF; Reallotted to Store 6.2.19; 1 FTS Netheravon 6.22 - 8.22; 207 Sqn (B3) 1926; PD Ascot; AD Aboukir; 4 FTS 10.28; Engine disintegrated at 1,500ft on cross-country, a/c started to spin, crashed Tel el Kebir, Egypt, Cat W 23.1.30 (F/L VJ Somerset-Thomas & passenger parachuted safely) [but see S871]

E727 At 8 AAP Lympne 19.11.18 for 155 Sqn (Mob) Chingford; Reallotted to 123 Sqn Upper Heyford 21.11.18 - @1.19

E728 At 8 AAP Lympne 28.1.19 reallotted from Midland Area for D of T for No 4 SoN&BD Thetford to EF but reallotted to Store 6.2.19; Reallotted to EF 8.2.19; PD Ascot; AD Drigh Rd; 27 Sqn (A) 2.23 - 1.24; 60 Sqn 4.25 (dual control?); Swung on TO and collided with E8646 14.9.25 (F/O CJ Pooley OK)

E729 At 8 AAP Lympne allotted to EF 28.1.19 but reallotted to Store 6.2.19; Reallotted to EF 8.2.19; 57 Sqn, crashed on flight to Cologne 15.6.19 (Lt WS Eason)

E730 At 8 AAP Lympne 19.11.18 for 155 Sqn (Mob) Chingford; Reallotted to 123 Sqn Upper Heyford 21.11.18 - @12.18

E731 At 8 AAP Lympne 19.11.18 for 155 Sqn (mob) Chingford; Reallotted to 123 Sqn Upper Heyford 21.11.18; To sqn 3.1.19; Tested IAAD 5.5.23; Crashed Sealand Road, Chester 19.6.23 (P/O HCECP Dalrymple slightly injured); PD Ascot; AD Aboukir; 4 FTS 11.24 - 9.25; AD Aboukir rebuilt as ER731 and conv DC; 4 FTS 8.27 - 3.28; Bounced landing and stalled, crashed Abu Sueir WOC 26.3.28 WOC

E732 At 8 AAP Lympne 19.11.18 for 155 Sqn (mob) Chingford; Reallotted to 123 Sqn Upper Heyford 21.11.18 - @1.19; Left UK for AD Aboukir 12.3.20

E733 At 8 AAP Lympne 28.1.19 reallotted from Midland Area for D of T for No 4 SoN&BD Thetford to EF but reallotted to Store 6.2.19; Reallotted to EF 8.2.19; Still at Lympne 19.4.19 allotted to EF

E734 At 8 AAP Lympne 27.11.18 for 123 Sqn Upper Heyford - @1.19

E735 At 8 AAP Lympne 19.11.18 for 155 Sqn (Mob) Chingford; Reallotted to 123 Sqn Upper Heyford 21.11.18 - @1.19

E736 Sold to American Government; Transferred to USMC Northern Bombing Group, France

E737 Sold to American Government; Transferred to USMC Northern Bombing Group, France

E738 Sold to American Government; Transferred to USMC Northern Bombing Group, France

E739 Transferred to USMC Northern Bombing Group, France NOTE - Not on official list of sales to American Government

E740 Sold to American Government; Transferred to USMC Northern Bombing Group, France

E741 Sold to American Government; Transferred to USMC Northern Bombing Group, France

E742 to E744 No information

E745 APS 23.12.19 - 2.20

E746 DH record and fitted Lion II; Andover; RAE 11.11.19 - 13.8.30 (engine, u/c, performance, ceiling, gyro rudder control, auto control tests)

E747 No information

E748 DH record, fitted Lion II and wide undercarriage; RAE 7.19; Went on nose landing *Argus* at Spithead 26.8.21 (F/O JH Bryer); U/c smashed landing Farnborough 18.7.19 (Capt E Gribben & Mr Mitchell); DH 25.10.26; RAE 30.10.26 - 8.27

E749 (Lion) RAE from/by 21.8.19 - @23.4.20 (engine & radiator tests); Delny to Leuchars 19.10.20; Cranwell to RAE Farnborough 22.12.20 (210 Sqn crew)

E750 DH record and fitted Lion II; Regd *G-EAOF* 9.10.19 to Aircraft Transport & Travel Ltd for Government mail service; Hounslow to RAE Farnborough 10.4.20; Retd RAF 6.20; 24 Sqn by 4.21 - @5.21 (for Chief of Air Staff)

E751 No information

E752 DH record and fitted Lion II; Regd *G-EAOG* 9.10.19 to Aircraft Transport & Travel Ltd for Government mail service; Retd RAF 6.20; HMS *Eagle* Trials Flight 6.20 (deck landing trials); Cranwell to RAE Farnborough 22.12.20 (210 Sqn crew)

E753 DH record and fitted Lion II; Regd *G-EAOH* 9.10.19 to Aircraft Transport & Travel Ltd for Government mail service; Retd RAF 4.20; Hendon; AEE 7.4.20 (performance tests); Gosport 7.20 (HMS *Eagle* landing trials - on 6.7.20?); AEE W/E 3.7.20 - @8.20 (performance & consumption), then to Donibristle

E754 DH record and fitted Lion II; Regd *G-EAOI* 9.10.19 to Aircraft Transport & Travel Ltd for Government mail service; Retd RAF 6.20; 210 Sqn Gosport to RAE Farnborough 25.6.20 (engine tests); Retd 210 Sqn Gosport to at least 6.9.20; PD Ascot; AD Hinaidi; 8 Sqn

E755 RAE from 8.6.20 (various tests including development of supercharged Lion); Last flown 31.1.27

E756 DH record and fitted Lion II; Regd *G-EAOJ* 9.10.19 to Aircraft Transport & Travel Ltd for Government mail service; Retd RAF 6.20; 210 Sqn Gosport by 19.7.20 - 10.20

E757 DH record and fitted Lion II; Regd *G-EAOK* 9.10.19 to Aircraft Transport & Travel Ltd for Government mail

Lion-engined D.H.9A E748, piloted by F/O J.H.Bryer after going on its nose while landing on HMS Argus at Spithead on 26.8.21. (via Philip Jarrett)

service; Retd RAF 6.20

E758 PD Ascot; AP Baghdad; 30 Sqn 6.20; AP Baghdad to 30 Sqn 11.3.22; Lost, FL, u/c collapsed in rough ground , Cat W 3.7.22 (F/O CGF Arthur OK); AD Hinaidi, RTP

E759 & E760 No information

E761 At 7 AAP Kenley 28.1.19 reallotted from Midland Area to EF but reallotted 30.1.19 to SE Area for Store; 47 Sqn Ekaterinodar by 15.8.19; Sold to Anti-Bolshevik Government 1919

E762 & E763 No information

E764 At 7 AAP Kenley 19.11.18 for 155 Sqn (Mob) Chingford; 155 Sqn by 12.18; 221 Sqn 1919; Sold to Anti-Bolshevik Government 1919

E765 At 7 AAP Kenley 19.11.18 for 155 Sqn (mob) Chingford; 155 Sqn by 12.18; Sold to Anti-Bolshevik Government 1919

E766 221 Sqn by 7.19; Sold to Anti-Bolshevik Government 1919

E767 47 Sqn Ekaterinodar by 15.8.19 - 10.19; 'A' dett RAF Instructional Mission South Russia by 17.10.19; Sold to Anti-Bolshevik Government

D.H.9A of HMS Eagle Trials Flight landing on the carrier in June 1920. (J.M.Bruce/G.S.Leslie collection)

E768 RAF North Russia (Southern Area) by 5.19

E769 RAF North Russia (Southern Area) (Beresnik) by 6.19; Overturned c.8.19 (Capt JIT Jones)

E770 To Russia 1919; RAF North Russia (Southern Area) by 6.19; Bombing raid on Ignatofokai, u/c collapsed landing 26.6.19 (Lt CF Kearns); Deliberately burnt on landing 16.9.19 (Obs KJ Hook) BUT DH recond (c/n 167)

E771 RAF North Russia

E772 RAF North Russia, uc/ collapsed landing BUT 3 FS Sedgeford by 3.19

E773 PD Ascot; AP Hinaidi; 30 Sqn; FL in desert, crashed Iraq 14.6.22 WOC (F/O FJH Ayscough)

E774 PD Ascot; AD Drigh Rd; 99 Sqn by 2.20; 60 Sqn 4.20; 27 Sqn

E775 RAE from/by 17.4.19 (engine and climb tests); DH recond and fitted prototype Lion II installation; RAE 1.5.20 (high speed propeller etc); Westlands 9.3.22 (fit oleo u/c); RAE 29.3.22; FL Black Down, Hants 24.10.23 (repaired); RAF Base Gosport 29.3.24 (deck trials landed HMS *Eagle* 8.4.24); RAE 24.4.24; recond and refitted Liberty; PD Ascot; AD Hinaidi; 30 Sqn 26.7.28 - 12.28; AD Hinaidi Trg Flt 1.7.30 - 1.31

E776 PD Ascot; Arr AD Aboukir ex UK 11.3.20; AP Baghdad; 30 Sqn ('A') by 5.20 - 1.22; EF, FL Kirkuk 28.8.20 ROS

E777 PD Ascot; Left UK for AD Aboukir 12.3.20; From Egypt to Mesopotamia with 8 Sqn (ordered 10.1.21); AD Hinaidi by 6.22 - @7.22; AP Hinaidi to 55 Sqn 5.3.23; AD Hinaidi 4.23; 30 Sqn 1.24; Retd UK; DH recond (c/n 166)

E778 PD Ascot; AP Baghdad; 47 Sqn 3.22; 30 Sqn 2.22 - 6.22; AD Hinaidi to 8 Sqn 12.5.23

E779 PD Ascot; AP Baghdad; 84 Sqn; Destroyed when bomb accidentally exploded 1.11.20 WOC

E780 30 Sqn, bombing raid, FL 15m from Rustamabad in NW Persia 8.12.20 (P/O W Sidebottom shot by Bolsheviks trying to escape; AC2 L Wilkon retd unhurt); Possibly "780" in service with Soviet Russian Air Force (RKKVF) by 2.23

E781 to E784 No information

D.H.9A E802 of No.30 Squadron around 1929. (via Philip Jarrett)

D.H.9A E873 of No.84 Squadron c.1926 with a Club design on the fin and all four suit designs on the nose. (via Philip Jarrett)

E785 PD Ascot; AP Baghdad; Rebuilt AD Hinaidi 3.23 - 11.23; 8 Sqn 11.23; FL Alepo, Iraq 4.7.24; Recond and conv DC; 8 Sqn; 60 Sqn ('Q') 5.26 - 1.30; 27 Sqn ('G')
E786 PD Ascot; AP Baghdad; 30 Sqn 1.22; 84 Sqn, stalled and spun in on TO Shaibah 8.6.22 (F/O FJW Mellersh & F/O CE Kelly both slightly injured)
E787 84 Sqn by 11.21
E788 PD Ascot; 8 Sqn by 4.21; AP Hinaidi 4.1.22; To 8 Sqn 1.23 - 6.23; 55 Sqn 1.25 - 6.25; Retd UK; DH recond on Cont No 579165/25 (c/n 257)
E789 PD Ascot; AD Aboukir; 47 Sqn ('X') 2.23; 4 FTS 8.24 - 3.25; Retd UK; DH recond on Cont No 579165/25 (c.n 230); RAF (Cadet) College; 84 Sqn 12.27 - 4.28; 55 Sqn 4.28
E790 PD Ascot; AP Hinaidi; 55 Sqn; Overturned on landing with flat tyre 21.3.21 WOC
E791 PD Ascot; AP Baghdad; 84 Sqn by 7.21
E792 PD Ascot; AD Aboukir; AP Iraq by 6.21; AD Aboukir rebuilt as ER792; 47 Sqn 11.2.24 - 5.24
E793 Allocated 5(E) ARD Henlow for Australia by 2-9.1.20; Imperial Gift to Australia, became *A1-2*
E794 Imperial Gift to Australia, became *A1-3*
E795 Imperial Gift to Australia, became *A1-4*
E796 Left UK for 55 Sqn 16.2.20; Arr ASD Aboukir 25.2.20; A&GS 12.29 - 1.30
E797 (conv DC); Harling Road; 1 FTS Netheravon 9.21 - 10.21; AEE 11.24; HAD 23.7.26
E798 1 FTS Netheravon 3.22 - 6.22
E799 PD Ascot; AD Drigh Rd 8.22; AW/CN 7.9.22
E800 PD Ascot; AP Baghdad; 30 Sqn 9.21 - 10.22; SOC AP Hinaidi 1.23
E801 No information
E802 5 FTS by 11.24 - @1.25; PD Ascot; AD Hinaidi; 84 Sqn 1.28 - 3.28 (red triangle design); 30 Sqn ('A') 1928 - 1930
E803 1 FTS Netheravon 9.21; PD Ascot; AD Hinaidi; HQ RAF Trans-Jordan, mail machine, undercarriage collapsed on landing 15.10.22 (F/O AdeCMcG Denny unhurt & AC1 P Rutley injured); 55 Sqn 7.25; 84 Sqn (Club marking) 12.27 - 5.28; While stationary run into by Wapiti J9091 (Cat M), Cat M 29.1.30 (Sgt ER White OK)
E804 No information
E805 PD Ascot; AP Baghdad; 30 Sqn 5.23 - 10.23; Retd UK; DH recond on Cont No 579165/25 (c/n 171)
E806 & E807 No information
E808 Sold to Anti-Bolshevik Government
E809 & E810 No information
E811 PD Ascot; AD Hinaidi tested 11-15.12.22; 30 Sqn
E812 39 Sqn ('9'); PD Ascot; AD Drigh Rd; 60 Sqn ('V') 4.28; Crashed, 1928 SOC
E813 No information
E814 39 Sqn ('9') 12.23 - 6.25
E815 No information
E816 PD Ascot; AP Baghdad; 30 Sqn 19.9.20
E817 Sold to Anti-Bolshevik Government
E818 Sold to Anti-Bolshevik Government
E819 & E820 No information
E821 PD Ascot; AP Baghdad; 30 Sqn 5.20; Crashed, Shergat, Mesopotamia, salvaged 19.8.20; AP Baghdad; 30 Sqn; Crashed landing in deep snow, Kasvin, 9.2.21 WOC
E822 PD Ascot; AP Baghdad; 30 Sqn by 5.20; FL after shot through petrol tanks, shot down on take-off, Diwaniyah, 10.7.20; Repaired; Shot down on TO Diwaniyah, 28.7.20; Abandoned on evacuation
E823 to E826 No information
E827 100 Sqn 11.22; 5 FTS 11.24 - 12.24; PD Ascot; AD Aboukir; 14 Sqn 7.26 - 7.27
E828 PD Ascot; AD Hinaidi 6.23 - 8.23; 30 Sqn 8.23; DH recond (c/n 153); PD Ascot; AD Drigh Rd; 27 Sqn ('A') 5.27; Dived to ground from 100ft after going round again, Miramshah, 14.2.28 WOC (F/Lt S Graham)
E829 to E834 No information
E835 Left UK for ASD Aboukir 20.2.20
E836 to E841 No information
E842 PD Ascot; AD Drigh Rd; AP Lahore; tested as "PATRIA" for Portuguese Airmens Flight 5.24
E843 PD Ascot; AD Drigh Rd; 30 Sqn 11.24; 8 Sqn 12.25 - 1.26; 55 Sqn 2.26 - 8.26
E844 PD Ascot; AD Drigh Rd; 27 Sqn ('F'); AP Lahore 6.24
E845 PD Ascot; AD Drigh Rd; AP Lahore 4.3.24 - 7.24; 27 Sqn; Caught fire in air, FL, crashed, Thall, 27.11.24 (Sgt GE Campbell & LAC CT Cave both injured)
E846 PD Ascot; AD Drigh Rd; AP Lahore 5.4.24 - 6.24; 27 Sqn, height test with full war load, hit bungalow on landing, Risalpur, 28.6.24 (Sgt CD Strickland & AC CE Upton both slightly injured)
E847 PD Ascot; AD Hinaidi; 30 Sqn 1.25
E848 S of AG&B Eastchurch by 9.21 - 12.22; PD Ascot; AD Hinaidi; 55 Sqn ('B2') 5.25 - 3.26; Retd UK; PD Ascot; AD Drigh Rd; 30 Sqn 6.27; 30 Sqn ('X') 30; 27 Sqn ('F')
E849 PD Ascot; AD Hinaidi; 30 Sqn by 7.22 - @12.22; 84 Sqn (Club marking) 1.23; 30 Sqn by 5.23; AD Hinaidi 9.23 - 3.24 (rebuild)
E850 PD Ascot; AD Hinaidi; 30 Sqn 2.22 - 10.22; AD Hinaidi 1.23; 55 Sqn 18.7.23; 47 Sqn ('D') (named "PERSEUS") 4.26; Heavy landing, Helwan 1926; AD Hinaidi rebuilt as ER850; 14 Sqn 12.27 - 4.28
E851 84 Sqn by 6.22
E852 To 6 ASD Ascot (via Farnborough) for packing 20.9.20; Arr 207 Sqn 10.20; Tested 20.10.20; EF, FL in sea 1.8.22; Presume salved; 207 Sqn 12.22 - 6.23; PD Ascot; AD Hinaidi; 30 Sqn 11.27 - 2.28
E853 to E855 No information
E856 207 Sqn 8.22
E857 DH rebuilt and renumbered J7012 (c/n 92)
E858 No information
E859 DH rebuilt and renumbered J7016 (c/n 96)
E860 No information
E861 DH rebuilt and renumbered J7009 (c/n 89)
E862 1 FTS Netheravon 7.22
E863 1 FTS Netheravon 10.20 - 7.22; DH recond as DC (c/n 71); PE Ascot; Tested AD Hinaidi 28.12.22; AD Hinaidi 9.24
E864 No information
E865 RAE Farnborough by/from 7.6.21 (glider experiments) (detd MAES Grain for aerial target experiments 13-16.6.21, 30.6.21, 8.8.21 & 10-11.8.21); MAES Grain 23.11.21; RAE 1.2.22 - 9.23 (VP metal airscrew); 55 Sqn 10.23; AP Lahore 8.24; Reid UK; DH recond; RAE 1.25 - 4.25 (test Fairey-Reed duralumin airscrews); PD Ascot; AD Aboukir; 14 Sqn (comms) 5.28 - 10.28
E866 1 FTS Netheravon 1923; Tested IAAD 11.12.23 - 4.2.24; Crashed, Theydon Bois, Essex, 15.12.23 (F/O TWS Brown OK); Repaired on site
E867 RAE (supercharged Liberty) by/from 15.3.21; Last flown RAE 22.11.29
E868 12 Sqn 11.23 - 2.24; PD Ascot; AD Hinaidi; 84 Sqn (Swastika marking), crashed in duststorm, l0m from Shaibah, 12.26
E869 39 Sqn (9) 1923; A&AEE 11.24; HAD; Northolt 19.7.26 HAD 10.28 - 1.29; RAF College 6.29 - 10.29
E870 RAE Farnborough by/from 20.5.21 (glider experiments) (detd MAES Grain for aerial target experiments 13-16.6.21, 30.6.21, 8.8.21 & 10.8.21); MAES Grain by 24.11.21; RAE by 1.2.22 - @30.3.22 (general testing); DH recond; Westlands; RAE 17.1.23 - 14.2.25 (test on steel airscrews); PD Ascot; AD Aboukir; 14 Sqn 5.28; Overturned Burka 5.28 (pilot G/Capt LWB Rees VC)
E871 6 SD Ascot to pack 9.20; AD Aboukir to 207 Sqn 1.11.20; 207 Sqn 11.22 - 3.24; 1 FTS Netheravon 10.25; HAD 3.29; PD Ascot; AD Aboukir; 4 FTS; Out of control, Abu Sueir, 21.1.30 (F/Lt VJ Somerset-Thomas made first successful parachute jump outside UK) [but see E726]
E872 39 Sqn ('1') 1927
E873 39 Sqn; PD Ascot; AD Hinaidi 7.24 - 8.24; 30 Sqn 11.24; 84 Sqn 9.25 - 9.27 (club design)
E874 39 Sqn ('4')
E875 PD Ascot; AD Hinaidi 7.23; 55 Sqn 15.10.23; Retd UK; DH recond on Cont No 579165/25 (c/n 176); PD Ascot; AD Drigh Rd; 60 Sqn ('Q') [or E785 'Q'?]
E876 IAAD 4.23; 39 Sqn ('4') 6.23 - 7.23; Heliopolis by 10.4.23; 55 Sqn ('B5') 12.23 [doubtful]; PD Ascot; AD Drigh Rd; 60 Sqn 5.26; AD Drigh Rd 12.29
E877 PD Ascot; AD Hinaidi; 14 Sqn; Retd UK?; PD Ascot; AD Drigh Rd; 27 Sqn ('B') 4.26 - 12.26; 60 Sqn 1928 - 1929
E878 PD Ascot; AD Drigh Rd; AP Lahore 2.5.24; 60 Sqn ('8') 6.24 - 12.24; AP Lahore 12.24; AD Drigh Rd 7.25; 60 Sqn 7.25 - 5.26; 60 Sqn ('7') landed on back,

Peshawar; Crashed 11.27 (F/Lt CW Busk MC); AD Drigh Rd; 60 Sqn ('T') 6.28; 60 Sqn ('O') 8.28; AD Drigh Road 31.12.28; 60 Sqn ('Z') 29.1.29; Crashed in night landing, Risalpur, 15.11.29 (Sgt WC Henley)

E879 PD Ascot; AD Drigh Rd; HQ RAF India ('9') 1.25

E880 D Ascot; AD Drigh Rd; AP Lahore 2.24; 60 Sqn 7.24 - 12.24; HQ RAF India; 60 Sqn 11.9.25; EF due to storm damage, FL, Dera Ismail Khan, Waziristan, 3.5.26 (Sgt D Munro); Repaired; Damaged by whirlwind, 5.5.26; AD Drigh Rd; 27 Sqn (J) 7.27; Crashed Pubbi 25.10.27; 60 Sqn 8.28; 27 Sqn 7.29 - 5.30

E881 & E882 No information

E883 1 FTS Netheravon 4.21 - 7.22; 24 Sqn, struck tree on take-off, Kenley, 14.8.22 (F/O WJ Cooke slightly injured)

E884 PD Ascot; AD Drigh Rd; 27 Sqn ('H') 10.24 - 12.24

E885 No information

E886 PD Ascot; AD Hinaidi; 8 Sqn ('O'); 55 Sqn 1.25 - 4.25

E887 PD Ascot; AD Hinaidi 31.8.23 - 9.23; 55 Sqn ('CII') 10.23 - 2.24; Retd UK; DH recond (c/n 175); PD Ascot; AD Drigh Rd; 27 Sqn 6.26 - 4.27; AD Drigh Road; AP Lahore 7.4.28; 27 Sqn 9.28; 60 Sqn 6.29; To AD Drigh Rd 3.30; (DC?)

E888 No information

E889 PD Ascot; AD Hinaidi; 30 Sqn 12.24 - 1.25; Retd UK; 1 FTS Netheravon 7.28

E890 DH recond and conv DC; PD Ascot; AD Aboukir; 4 FTS 1922 - 10.23; Overturned, Abu Sueir 1923;

E891 to E898 No information

E899 From Egypt to Mesopotamia with 8 Sqn (ordered 10.1.21); 8 Sqn by 1.21; 84 Sqn, crashed in night landing Shaibah, Cat W 16.9.22 (F/O JL Airey injured & AC1 B Hayes killed)

E900 Completed 16.4.19; Arr 5(E) ARD Henlow 3.12.19 - @9.1.20 for Australia; Imperial Gift to Australia, became *A1-5*

E901 Arr 5(E) ARD Henlow 5.12.19 - @9.1.20 for Australia; Imperial Gift to Australia, became *A1-6*

E902 1 FTS Netheravon, undershot, struck ridge landing, TW 1.12.23 (P/O F Boston slightly injured)
BUT 1 FTS, accident 1.12.23 (Sgt JS Sheppard & F/L JW Woodhouse DSO MC both slightly injured)

E903 Allocated 5(E) ARD Henlow for Australia by 2-9.1.20; Imperial Gift to Australia, became *A1-7*

E904 Arr 5(E) ARD Henlow 3.12.19 - @9.1.20 for Australia; Imperial Gift to Australia, became *A1-8*

E905 Allocated 5(E) ARD Henlow for Australia by 2-9.1.20; Imperial Gift to Australia, became *A1-9*

E906 Arr 5(E) ARD Henlow 3.12.19 - @9.1.20 for Australia; Imperial Gift to Australia, became *A1-10*

E907 Arr 5(E) ARD Henlow 5.12.19 - @9.1.20 for Australia; Imperial Gift to Australia, became *A1-11*

E908 Arr 5(E) ARD Henlow 3.12.19 - @9.1.20 for Australia; Imperial Gift to Australia, became *A1-12*

E909 Allocated 5(E) ARD Henlow for Australia by 2-9.1.20; Imperial Gift to Australia, became *A1-13*

E910 Allocated 5(E) ARD Henlow for Australia by 2-9.1.20; Imperial Gift to Australia, became *A1-14*

E911 PD Ascot; 30 Sqn 12.20; AD Hinaidi 6.22 - 7.22; AD Hinaidi 2.23 - 11.23; 8 Sqn 11.23 - 6.24; Retd UK; DH recond on Cont No 579165/25 (c/n 172); PD Ascot; AD Drigh Rd; 60 Sqn ('V') 5.26 - 10.26; AD Drigh Rd; 27 Sqn 29.2.28 - 2.29

E912 30 Sqn 2.21 - 4.21

E913 84 Sqn 12.20; 5 FTS, FL in fog en route Hendon to Shotwick, overturned and wrecked, Shenstone, Staffs 22.2.23 (F/O DL Evans unhurt)

E914 PD Ascot; AD Hinaidi; 30 Sqn 14.12.22 - 9.23; 8 Sqn ('P') 3.24; AD Hinaidi 7.24; 8 Sqn 10.24 - 12.24; Retd UK?; AD Aboukir; 4 FTS ('4'); Rebuilt as ER914; While stationary, hit by J8202, Abu Sueir, Cat W 17.1.30 (LAC CP Clement slightly injured)

E915 Left UK for 55 Sqn 16.2.20; Arr ASD Aboukir 25.2.21; PD Ascot; AP Baghdad; 47 Sqn 12.20 - 2.22; 30 Sqn 3.22; COL Baghdad 15.9.22

E916 Allocated 5(E) ARD Henlow for Australia by 2-9.1.20; Imperial Gift to Australia, became *A1-15*

E917 84 Sqn by 2.20 (?); RAE by/from 5.10.20 (engine & radiator tests; tropical radiator); HAD 23.3.24; RAE 5.1.26 - 9.7.26; PD Ascot; AD Hinaidi rebuilt as ER917; 45 Sqn ('6') 8.29 - 9.29

E918 PD Ascot; AP Hinaidi; 55 Sqn; Shot down in hostile territory, nr Dasht-i-Harir, Iraq 5.5.21 WOC (F/L RS Maxwell & observer rescued by F2775)

E919 PD Ascot; AD Aboukir; 8 Sqn Suez by 1.21 - 2.21; 4 FTS 1.22 - 4.22

E920 PD Ascot; AD Hinaidi; 30 Sqn 9.22; Arr AD Aboukir ex UK 10.3.20

E921 to E923 No information

E924 5 FTS; EF on starting to go round again, FL cross wind in standing corn in high wind, 21.9.22 WOC (F/O FF Inglis & P/O OB Swain both unhurt)

E925 DH recond (c/n 79)

E926 1 FTS Netheravon 6.22 - 7.22; PD Ascot; AD Hinaidi; 55 Sqn 5.28

E927 PD Ascot; AD Hinaidi; 55 Sqn 12.24 - 2.25

E928 PD Ascot; AD Aboukir; 47 Sqn 5.23; AD Aboukir rebuilt as ER928; 4 FTS 4.24 - 1.25; Crashed and overturned, c.24; 47 Sqn, crashed, caught fire on impact, BO, Cat W 10.8.26 (F/O HG Slater & AC1 TR Harvey both killed)

E929 No information

E930 AD Hinaidi 6.2; 30 Sqn 7.22 - 11.22; AD Hinaidi 3.23

E931 PD Ascot; AD Hinaidi test 11.11.22; To 55 Sqn 11.22

E932 PD Ascot; AD Hinaidi 5.22; 84 Sqn 4.23

E933 & E934 No information

E935 PD Ascot; AD Drigh Rd; 27 Sqn 2.24

E936 No information

E937 PD Ascot; AD Drigh Rd 3.22 - 4.23; AP Lahore AW/CN 29.3.24; 27 Sqn; EF, crashed, Risalpur, 25.4.24; 60 Sqn ('2') 2.26 - 4.26 [but squadron had letter codes by then!]

E938 41 Sqn 10.23 - 11.23; A&GS 12.25

E939 & E940 No information

E941 PD Ascot; AD Aboukir; 14 Sqn 9.23

E942 PD Ascot; AD Drigh Rd; 27 Sqn 1.24

E943 PD Ascot; AD Hinaidi 9.25; 55 Sqn 9.25

E944 PD Ascot; AD Hinaidi; 30 Sqn 10.24; Hit bump landing, overturned Kirkuk 6.12.24 (Sgt E Smith-Marriott unhurt & AC1 TH Walton slightly injured); 8 Sqn 7.25; 55 Sqn 7.25 - 1.26; 30 Sqn ('X') 9.26 - 1.28

E945 PD Ascot; AD Hinaidi to 30 Sqn 7.7.23

E946 No information

E947 PD Ascot; AD Hinaidi; 55 Sqn 31.7.23

E948 39 Sqn ('1') 6.23 - 7.23; PD Ascot; AD Aboukir; 4 FTS 9.24

E949 & E950 No information

E951 PD Ascot; AD Drigh Rd; AP Lahore 24.4.24; AP Lahore 10.24; 27 Sqn ('F') 1924 - 1925; 60 Sqn ('S') 1925 - 4.26; AD Drigh Road conv DC 1926; 60 Sqn 1.27; AD Drigh Rd 1.30

E952 PD Ascot; AD Hinaidi 2.23; 84 Sqn 27.3.23 - 11.23; Rebuilt AD Hinaidi 12.23 - 1.24; 55 Sqn, wheel hit mound of earth landing, Hagena, Iraq, 27.3.24 (F/O BMFS Leete & AC1 F Atkinson both slightly injured); 8 Sqn 9.25

E953 PD Ascot; AD Drigh Rd; AP Lahore 18.1.24 - 2.24; 27 Sqn 2.24; Throttled back too soon after take-off from Risalpur for Nowshera, crashed on FL in bad ground, 15.7.24 (F/O CA Mason & LAC WH Fearn both OK)

E954 Tested IAAD 20.4.23; PD Ascot; AD Hinaidi; 30 Sqn

Dual control conversion D.H.9A E951 at Drigh Road, Karachi in 1926. (via Ray Vann)

D.H.9A E954, the No.8 Squadron CO's aircraft, with E843 just visible beneath the fuselage. (MoD Photo Library)

Whitehead production, including E964, E962 and E960. (B.Robertson)

2.25 - 3.25; 8 Sqn 10.25 (CO's a/c); 55 Sqn 7.26; 84 Sqn 12.27 - 2.28 (swastika design)

E955 1 FTS Netheravon 7.25 11.25; HAD; Hendon 5.4.27

E956 PD Ascot; AD Aboukir; 4 FTS by 8.24; Landing downwind, choked engine, crashed and overturned, Abu Sueir, BO, Cat W 5.9.24 (F/O J Masser-Bennetts slightly injured)

E957 24 Sqn 4.23; Propeller accident, Kenley, 10.10.24; ARS HAD (overhaul); A&AEE 20.2.26

E958 AD Hinaidi to 30 Sqn 26.7.23

E959 39 Sqn 8.22; DH recond on Cont No 579165/25 (c/n 223); PD Ascot; AD Aboukir; 47 Sqn ('BII' in 1926, also 'Bl' & 'B2') 6.7.26 - @3.27; AD Aboukir rebuilt as ER959; 14 Sqn 7.28 - 5.29

E960 2 FTS Duxford 2.21 - 2.22; 39 Sqn ('7') 1923 - 1924; DH rebuilt and renumbered J7017 (c/n 97); PD Ascot; AD Hinaidi; 84 Sqn 11.24 - 12.24; Iraq CF 3.26 - 4.26; 84 Sqn 4.26

E961 PD Ascot; AD Hinaidi 7.23; 8 Sqn 13.10.23; 30 Sqn 6.24; PD Ascot; AD Aboukir; 4 FTS

E962 98 Sqn; PD Ascot; AD Aboukir; 47 Sqn 11.22 - 12.22; 4 FTS 10.23 - 12.23

E963 PD Ascot; AD Aboukir; 4 FTS 1.22; Retd UK?; AD Aboukir 10.23; 84 Sqn 11.23; AD Hinaidi 12.23; 55 Sqn 2.25 - 12.25; 84 Sqn 1.28; Fouled wingtip of J7872 on take-off, Shaibah, Cat W 3.8.28 (Sgt HP Murray OK)

E964 No information

E965 PD Ascot; AD Aboukir; 4 FTS 9.21 - 2.22

E966 100 Sqn 11.22 - 1.23; PD Ascot; AD Hinaidi; 55 Sqn ('B3') 10.1.27 - 7.27

E967 39 Sqn, spun in from 300ft steep climbing turn downwind on take-off, Spittlegate, BO 28.3.22 (F/O CW Bragg & LAC W Warne both killed); once coded "B"

E968 PD Ascot; AD Aboukir; 47 Sqn; AD Aboukir rebuilt as ER968

E969 DH recond on Cont No 579165/25 (c/n 229); 1 SoTT 5.27 - 9.27

E970 RAF (Cadet) College 8.23 - 10.23; RAF (Cadet) College 10.27 - 5.29

E971 24 Sqn 3.22

E972 No information

E973 PD Ascot; AD Drigh Rd; AP Lahore 12.23; 27 Sqn 22.3.24; Crashed on landing, Tank, 25.6.24; 60 Sqn

E974 Arr Rec Pk 13.10.18; 3 ASD 17.10.18; 39 Sqn Spittlegate, landed downwind in rough weather, swept down and hit cottage, Digby, 21.12.21 (F/O CG Halliday slightly injured & AC2 HR Warry unhurt)

E975 1 SoN&BD Stonehenge by 11.2.19; Tested IAAD 11-13.6.23

E976 PD Ascot; AP Baghdad; 8 Sqn ('A') 1920

E977 99 Sqn 12.19 - 4.20; Redes 27 Sqn 1.4.20; 60 Sqn 6.23 - 7.23; AD Drigh Rd to 60 Sqn ('1') 1.4.24; Struck pylon on take-off, Risalpur 14.6.24 (F/O ELW Aitken)

E978 No information

E979 DH recond (c/n 18); TOC Waddon 6.12.21; PD Ascot; AD Drigh Rd; 60 Sqn ('Y') 1925; EF, FL, Tank, 4.3.26 (Sgt D Munro); 60 Sqn 1.8.26 - 9.26; AD Drigh Rd; 27 Sqn 17.3.27; 60 Sqn to 9.29 (DC?)

E980 No information

E981 PD Ascot; AD Hinaidi; 55 Sqn ('BI') 10.22

E982 to E988 No information

E989 DH recond (c/n 22); TOC Waddon 22.12.21

E990 No information

E991 Imperial Gift to Canada; Not registered

E992 Imperial Gift to Canada; Became *G-CYBI*; TOC 17.9.20; Used Camp Borden; SOC 18.5.26

E993 Imperial Gift to Canada; Became *G-CYBN*; TOC 11.10.20; Cat B Camp Borden 22.11.20; SOC 18.2.29

E994 Imperial Gift to Canada; Became *G-CYAK*; TOC 19.7.20; SOC 18.2.29

E995 Imperial Gift to Canada; Became *G-CYBF*; TOC 18.9.20; Used Camp Borden; SOC 18.2.29

E996 Imperial Gift to Canada; Became *G-CYAN*; TOC 19.7.20; SOC 23.9.27

E997 Imperial Gift to Canada; Became *G-CYAZ*; TOC 10.9.20; Cat A Winnipeg 30.9.20; SOC 1.2.22

E998 110 Sqn Kenley 8.18; Imperial Gift to Canada; Became *G-CYAJ*; TOC 19.7.20; SOC 23.9-27

E999 Imperial Gift to Canada; Became *G-CYDO*; TOC 18.6.20; SOC 23.9.27

E1000 Imperial Gift to Canada; Became *G-CYAD*; TOC 18.6.20; Crashed Morley, Alta, 23.8.20; SOC 18.2.29

E1001 Imperial Gift to Canada; Became *G-CYCG*; TOC 16.12.20; Cat C Camp Borden 20.12.20; SOC 23.9.27

E1002 Imperial Gift to Canada; Became *G-CYAO*; TOC 18.6.20; Used at Morley, Alta; SOC 12.2.22

E1003 to E1010 No information

E1011 20 TDS Shallufa by 24.12.18

E1012 & E1013 No information

E1014 155 Sqn Chingford by 11.18 [prefix?]

E1015 to E1039 No information

E1040 Deld 10.19

E1041 to E1100 cancelled 11.18

The wreckage of D.H.9A E977 '1' of No.60 Squadron after F/O E.L.W.Aitken struck a pylon while taking off at Risalpur on 14.6.24. (via Philip Jarrett)

D.H.9A (400hp Liberty). Basic instrumentation plus extra stop-watch & added piping with turncock to left side. (via Philip Jarrett)

D.H.9A fitted with an experimental sprung undercarriage. (J.M.Bruce/G.S.Leslie collection)

D.H.9 engine fitted with an Ad Astra Silencer . during 1918. (J.M.Bruce/G.S.Leslie collection)

D.H.9A fitted with jettisonable undercarriage. (via J.M.Bruce/G.S.Leslie collection)

D.H.9A being launched in the Solent at 4,000lb weight from an S.1.L catapult on HMS Ark Royal 12.11.30. (via Bruce/Leslie)

A D.H.9, believed after landing in Turkey post-war. (via Gordon Swanborough)

D.H.9A 193M, an early example of an RAF ground instructional serial, mis-painted as M193 on the rudder. (J.M.Bruce/G.S.Leslie collection)

Capt D.Carruthers, OC 'A' Flight, flying a D.H.9A of No.123 (Canadian) Squadron, Upper Heyford in the Spring of 1919. (via Stewart Taylor)

D.H.9A E8407, the first of its type to emerge from the Airco production line. (via Philip Jarrett)

2 D.H.9 ordered 25.3.18 & 2.4.18 respectively under Cont No A.S.17569 from The Aircraft Manufacturing Co Ltd, Hendon to replace D.H.9A conversions C6350 & C6122, and numbered E5436 & E5437. (230hp Puma)

E5435 At 7 AAP Kenley for 108 Sqn (Mob) 19.6.18; At sqn by 3.7.18; To France with sqn 22.7.18; Propeller and U/C smashed 28.7.18 (Mjr SS Halse & 2/Lt GS Spencer), repaired in sqn; In Lichtervelde raid Fokker DrI OOC Gits and Fokker DVII OOC Staden shared C6314, C6345, D1080, D3092, D5622, D5759, D7208, E669 & F5847 11.45 21.9.18 (2/Lt PA Haynes & Lt G Windle); After bombing Ingelmunster station at 17.25 formation attacked by 33 EA between the target and Roulers, 3 EA in flames, 1 BU and 2 OOC shared C2205, D499, D5835, D5845, D7342, E605, E8871 & F5847 1.10.18 (2/Lt GC Page & Sgt P Hoolihan); 8 AAP Lympne 18.1.19

E5436 10 TDS Harling Road, propeller accident 4.2.19 (Lt R Brett injured)

400 D.H.9A ordered 21.3.18 under Cont No 35a/412/C.291 from Aircraft Manufacturing Co.Ltd, Hendon and numbered E8407 to E8806. (400hp Liberty 12A)

E8407 1 FTS Netheravon 7.22 - 8.22

E8408 & E8409 No information

E8410 Presentation Aircraft 'Nizam of Hyderabad No.10'. At 7 AAP Kenley 2.8.18 for 110 Sqn (Mob) Kenley; To Sqn by 23.8.18; To France with Sqn 31.8.18; Went down with tail off nr Mannheim 16.9.18 (Sgt A Haigh & Sgt J West both killed)

E8411 2 AI to 205 Sqn 27.9.18; EF after raid on Wassigny, FL, crashed Bois de Buire 9.10.18 (2/Lt HF Taylor & 2/Lt MLV Hill unhurt); to 2 ASD

E8412 At 7 AAP Kenley 9.8.18 for 110 Sqn (Mob) Kenley; Reallotted to EF 22.8.18; Rec Pk to 5 AI 8.10.18; Delivering m/c to 25 Sqn COL 20.10.18 (Lt R de Bruyn & 2/Lt WLA Wilkinson)

E8413 At 7 AAP Kenley 9.8.18 for 110 Sqn (Mob) Kenley; Reallotted to EF 22.8.18; Rec Pk to 5 AI 4.10.18; 205 Sqn from 9.10.18; COL from raid on Charleroi 4.11.18 (Lt RJV Pulvertoft & 2/Lt WM Newton unhurt); U/c crashed on landing new aerodrome Maubeuge 27.11.18 (2/Lt PJ Baker unhurt); to 2 ASD

E8414 Deld AES Martlesham Heath but crashed on arrival 11.9.18 (for engine tests); Repaired on site; Acoustic Testing Flt, Butley W/E 26.10.18; AES/AEE Martlesham Heath 26.10.18; Left by air W/E 23.6.19

E8415 Rec Pk to 18 Sqn 29.9.18; Photo bombing mission, combat with EA over Mons 11.00, damaged, FL 207 Sqn airfield 27.10.18 (Lt R Johnson unhurt & 2/Lt A Toes killed); Rep Pk 2 ASD 27.10.18

E8416 At 7 AAP Kenley 21.12.18 reallotted from EF to SW Area for D of T for Wireless Telephony School Bournemouth; 1 SoN&BD Stonehenge by 4.19 - @7.19

E8417 No information

E8418 Rec Pk to 205 Sqn 18.9.18; COL after raid on Wassigny 8.10.18 (2/Lt RJV Pulvertoft unhurt & 2/Lt W Haviland injured); to 2 ASD

E8419 Rec Pk to 205 Sqn 23.9.18; Recce 29.9.18 (Lt HG Kirkland wounded & 2/Lt CO'N Daunt killed); Flying again 8.10.18; COL from bombing raid on Wassigny 9.10.18 (Lt AL Monger & 2/Lt WM Newton unhurt); to 2 ASD

E8420 8 AAP Lympne to Rec Pk 13.9.18; 2 AI 13.9.18; to 3 ASD 14.9.18 (arr 18.9.18); 110 Sqn 21.9.18; Shot up in raid on Frankfurt 25.9.18 (2/Lt NN Wardlaw OK & Sgt WH Neighbour killed); 3 ASD 25.9.18; 57 Sqn by 5.19 (sic)

E8421 Arr Rec Pk 9.9.18; 2 AI 13.9.18; 3 ASD 13.9.18 (arr 14.9.18); 110 Sqn 21.9.18; Bombing raid to Kaiserslautern-Pirmasens in poor weather, heavy combat, FTR 5.10.18 (Lt RCP Ripley & 2/Lt FS Towler both killed)

E8422 8 AAP Lympne to Rec Pk 13.9.18; 2 AI 13.9.18; 3 ASD 15.9.18 (arr 16.9.18); 110 Sqn 16.9.18; FTR raid on Frankfurt 25.9.18 (Sgt HW Tozer & Sgt W Platt both

killed)
E8423 Left Kenley 18.9.18; Arr Rec Pk 20.9.18; 2 AI 20.9.18; 3 ASD 22.9.18 (arr 23.9.18); 99 Sqn 25.9.18; 6 AP 21.10.18; 3 ASD 11.11.18
E8424 1 AI to 18 Sqn 16.12.18
E8425 No information
E8426 1 AI to 18 Sqn 30.10.18; Landing at 20 Sqn, hit ridge and crashed 9.3.19 (Capt RT Minors & Lt W Ballentine OK)
E8427 Left 2 AAP Hendon for IF 15.9.18; Rec Pk 6.10.18; 2 AI 13.10.18; 3 ASD 14.10.18; TOC EF 15.11.18; 2 AI to 49 Sqn ('A') 8.12.18 - @29.5.19; Went on nose landing Bavai 20.2.19
E8428 Rec Pk to 2 AI 18.9.18; Rep Pk 2 ASD to 2 AI 27.10.18; 25 Sqn 3.11.18; Ran into obstruction on landing 23.11.18 (2/Lt F Ollenbittle & 2/Lt FHH White OK); Rep Pk 2 ASD 23.11.18; 18 Sqn, on ferry flight to 1 ASD engine failed crashed 20.1.19 (Mjr WH Ewen); M/c collected by 2 ASD
E8429 At 8 AAP Lympne 27.1.19 reallotted from EF to SW Area for No 2 School of N & BD Andover; Sold to Anti-Bolshevik Government
E8430 At 2 AAP Hendon 24.1.19 reallotted from EF to Store
E8431 No information
E8432 No information
"D8432" Recd Rec Pk ex UK for IF 28.10.18; 3 ASD 28.10.18
E8433 Arr Rec Pk 20.9.18; 2 AI 21.9.18; 3 ASD 21.9.18; 99 Sqn 25.9.18; SOS 99 Sqn 19.10.18 CW; 6 AP 22.10.18;
E8434 Arr Rec Pk 9.9.18; 2 AI 13.9.18; 3 ASD 13.9.18; 110 Sqn 15.9.18; In combat over Mannheim 15.20 16.9.18 (Lt JB Wilkinson unhurt & 2/Lt HM Kettener wounded); 6 AP 16.10.18; 3 ASD 3.11.18
E8435 No information
E8436 Supposedly Presentation Aircraft 'Infantry Records Office No.7 District Warwick', but actually F952 with false temporary inscription and serial
E8437 Rec Pk to 2 AI 24.9.18; 205 Sqn 25.9.18; EF, COL on aerodrome 7.1.19 (Lt KK Gould unhurt); to 2 ASD
E8438 Rec Pk to 5 AI 5.10.18; 205 Sqn 13.10.18; EF, FL nr Tournai 5.2.19 (2/Lt SJ Furze); Salved by 10th Bde for 2 ASD
E8439 Arr Rec Pk 20.9.18; 2 AI 21.9.18; 3 ASD 22.9.18 (arr 23.9.18); 110 Sqn 29.9.18; Bombing raid to Kaiserslauten-Pirmasens in poor weather, heavy combats with EAs, FTR 5.10.18 (2/Lt DP Davies & 2/Lt HMD Speagell both PoW)
E8440 Recd Rec Pk ex UK for IF 25.9.18, crashed, dismantling by 30.9.18
E8441 & E8443 No information
E8444 MAEE Grain, flotation tests off Nore LV from HMS *Slinger*, CW, beached 27.11.20; DH recond; MAEE (immersion tests)
E8445 COL on delivery flight from 2 ASD to 6 AI 27.3.19 (Lt GE Gillett OK)
E8446 No information
E8447 18 Sqn by 6.19 - @7.19
E8448 57 Sqn by 18.4.19
E8449 Sold to American Government post-war, to USA, apparently for performance comparison with the USD-9A
E8450 India, u/c collapsed landing
E8451 Sold to American Government; To USMC Northern Bombing Group
E8452 Sold to American Government; To USMC Northern Bombing Group
E8453 Sold to American Government; To USMC Northern Bombing Group
E8454 Sold to American Government; To USMC Northern Bombing Group
E8455 Sold to American Government; To USMC Northern Bombing Group
E8456 No information
E8457 (First with new type tailplane) ECD Grain, fitted detachable wings, flotation gear & detachable wheels, air tested, then to Fleet 4.19; 1 FTS Netheravon 1923; Tested IAAD 23-27.4.23
E8458 Twickenham from W/E 12.9.18; Turnhouse W/E 24.10.18; Disposed 1.19
E8459 Twickenham from W/E 12.9.18; Turnhouse W/E 24.10.18; Disposed 1.19
E8460 No information
E8461 PD Ascot; AD Drigh Rd; 27 Sqn
E8462 No information
E8463 Sold to American Government; To USMC Northern Bombing Group
BUT 1 FTS Netheravon, caught fire on ground, Cat W 2.5.27 (F/O MJ Du Cray & Cpl J Harriman OK)
E8464 AES Orfordness by 10.18
E8465 Sold to American Government; To USMC Northern Bombing Group as *E-1* (attd 217 Sqn 3-13.10.18); Dropping rations Stadenberg 2/3.10.18 (Capt RS Lytle USMC & Sgt A Wiman); Bombing raid to Thourout, EA dest 3.10.18 (1/Lt R Talbot USMC & Cpl RG Robinson); US base Ardres by 24.10.18
E8466 Sold to American Government; To USMC Northern Bombing Group as *E-3* (attd 217 Sqn 3-13.10.18); US Base Ardres by 24.10.18; WO 15.11.18
E8467 Sold to American Government; To USMC Northern Bombing Group as *E-9* (attd 217 Sqn 3-13.10.18)
E8468 PD Ascot; AD Drigh Rd; 27 Sqn; During attack on village, port plane hit by bomb from another aircraft, dived in, Palose, Waziristan, 28.12.22 (F/O EE Turner DFC & AC1 Sly both killed); WOC
E8469 Sold to American Government; To USMC Northern Bombing Group as *E-8* ; US base Ardres by 24.10.18
E8470 Sold to American Government; To USMC Northern Bombing Group
E8471 1 FTS Netheravon 9.24; PD Ascot; AD Aboukir; Issued out 16.12.25
E8472 Sold to American Government; To USMC Northern Bombing Group as *E-4*; WO 29.9.18
E8473 PD Ascot; AD Drigh Rd; 60 Sqn ('5') 10.23; Stalled after take-off, port wing touched ground, Risalpur, Cat W 29.4.24 (F/L JW Baker)
E8474 PD Ascot; AP Hinaidi; 8 Sqn; Collided in practice formation flight with H102 and crashed nr Hinaidi, Cat W 13.1.22 (F/L AG Peace AFC & AC2 WS Browne both killed)
E8475 Sold to American Government; To USMC Northern Bombing Group as *E-5*
E8476 Sold to American Government; To USMC Northern Bombing Group as *E-7*; US Base Ardres by 24.10.18; Evidently retd RAF; PD Ascot; AD Hinaidi Trg Flt 5.30 - 1.31
E8477 Sold to American Government; To USMC Northern Bombing Group *E-2* by 11.18
E8478 Sold to American Government; To USMC Northern Bombing Group as *E-18*
E8479 18 Sqn, crashed on take off, LH wheel sank into soft ground and collapsed 28.3.19 (Lt B Champion OK)
E8480 Sold to American Government; To USMC Northern Bombing Group as *E-6*
E8481 3 ASD to 110 Sqn 23.10.18; 2 AI 28.11.18; 49 Sqn 8.12.18; Crashed on arrival at Bickendorf during sqn move 29.5.19 (Capt SH Gaskell & Sgt FW Thomson)
E8482 3 ASD to 110 Sqn 22.10.18; On mail duty crashed nr Sittingbourne in fog 5.3.19 (Lt AR McDonald & Lt HC Hinchcliffe)
E8483 3 ASD to 99 Sqn ('1F') 21.10.18 - @27.1.19

D.H.9A E8483 '1F' of No.99 Squadron.
(J.M.Bruce/G.S.Leslie collection)

E8484 3 ASD to 110 Sqn 17.10.18; FTR bombing raid on Frankfurt 21.10.18 (2/Lt AWR Evans & Lt RWL Thompson both PoW)
E8485 3 ASD to 99 Sqn 22.10.18; Lost bearings and crashed on landing 16.11.18 (2/Lt HE King & 2/AM S Winter OK); 4 FTS? ('3')
E8486 10 AP to 49 Sqn 18.4.19; Engine trouble just after take off, crashed on aerodrome 28.4.19 (2/Lt J Turner & Lt JN Bitton OK)
E8487 At 2 AAP Hendon 12.2.19 reallotted from SE Area for d on landing to EF; At Grain 26.2.19 reallotted to SE Area for Grain for war wastage on squadrons mobilising; 2 FTS Duxford 7.22 - 9.22; 5 FTS, EF, FL, Willaston, Cheshire, WOC 17.12.23 (P/O BL Young slightly injured)
E8488 No information
E8489 Deld Turnhouse W/E 24.10.18; Disposed 1.19; 39 Sqn, spun in from 100ft on take-off, Spittlegate, DBF 24.4.23 (F/O MC Trench & P/O FS Harris both killed)
E8490 Deld Turnhouse W/E 24.10.18; Disposed 1.19
E8491 Deld Turnhouse W/E 24.10.18; Disposed 1.19; Grand Fleet SoAF&G by 9.19; 39 Sqn ('1' & '11') by 6.23 - @7.23; CFS by 2.31
E8492 Deld Turnhouse W/E 24.10.18 - @30.1.19
E8493 At 8 AAP Lympne 19.11.18 for 155 Sqn (Mob) Chingford; Reallotted to 123 Sqn Upper Heyford 21.11.18 - @1.19; DH recond; 1 FTS Netheravon 8.24; Crashed and u/c ripped off 1.12.24; Recond; PD Ascot; AD Hinaidi; 84 Sqn 10.26 - 2.27; 55 Sqn 1928
E8494 At 8 AAP Lympne 27.11.18 for 123 Sqn (Mob) Upper Heyford; 123 Sqn by 12.18 - @1.19
E8495 At 8 AAP Lympne 27.11.18 for 123 Sqn (Mob) Upper Heyford; 123 Sqn by 12.18 - @1.19
E8496 PD Ascot; AD Hinaidi; 8 Sqn; allowed insufficient time for a/c ahead to get clear on take-off, collided with H3529, caught fire on impact, BO, Cat W 19.4.26 (Sgt J Gaillie OK); SOC 26.4.26
E8497 PD Ascot; AP Baghdad; 30 Sqn 2.22; 47 Sqn 6.22
E8498 PD Ascot; AP Baghdad; Trg Flt, Central Air Comm Sqn, Shaibaih; Unit disbanded 31.3.21; AP Baghdad; 30 Sqn 14.7.21 - 1.22
E8499 PD Ascot; AP Baghdad; 8 Sqn 1920
E8500 PD Ascot; AD Drigh Rd 11.22; AP Lahore 5.12.22; 27 Sqn 5.1.23
E8501 Sold to American Government; USMC Northern Bombing Group as *E-19*
E8502 Sold to American Government; To USMC Northern Bombing Group as *E-11*
E8503 Sold to American Government; To USMC Northern Bombing Group
E8504 Sold to American Government; To USMC Northern Bombing Group as *E-12*
E8505 Sold to American Government; To USMC Northern Bombing Group
E8506 Sold to American Government; To USMC Northern Bombing Group as *E-13*; Retd RAF; PD Ascot; AD Hinaidi test 22.12.22
E8507 Sold to American Government; To USMC Northern Bombing Group as *E-10*
E8508 Rec Pk to 1 AI 16.10.18; 205 Sqn by 27.11.18 - @3.1.19; 18 Sqn; Engine lost water, seized, FL in ploughed field and crashed 27.4.19 (2/Lt JA Watton & 2/Lt WP Perry OK)
E8509 2 AI to 25 Sqn 7.11.18; 99 Sqn, crashed 15.4.19 (Capt WD Thom OK)
E8510 Deld Turnhouse W/E 24.10.18 - @30.1.19; 24 Sqn, stalled on turn at 150ft after TO and dived in Kenley 4.1.23 (F/O I Glyn-Roberts OK)
E8511 No information
E8512 Deld Turnhouse W/E 24.10.18 - @30.1.19; served post-war; PD Ascot; AD Hinaidi; 55 Sqn ('B4') 3.25 - 10.26; 30 Sqn 1.28 - 2.28
E8513 Deld Turnhouse W/E 24.10.18 - @30.1.19; 2 FTS Duxford 11.22 - 7.23; A&GS 10.23 - 10.24; PD Ascot; AD Hinaidi; 30 Sqn 11.27; Ground collision with F.2b J7622, Cat R 19.12.27 (F/O KC Garvie); AD Hinaidi (repairs) 12.4.28
E8514 Deld Turnhouse W/E 24.10.18 - @30.1.19; 2 FTS Duxford 12.22; PD Ascot; AD Hinaidi 12.23; 8 Sqn 1.24; AOC Iraq 6.24; 30 Sqn 7.25; 84 Sqn 5.28 - 6.28
E8515 Deld Turnhouse W/E 24.10.18 (fitted hydrovanes and wingtip floats); Disposed 1.19
E8516 Turnhouse from 10.18 - @12.18; Disposed by 1.19
E8517 to E8520 No information
E8521 Recd Rec Pk ex UK for IF 24.10.18; 3 ASD 9.11.18; TOC EF 13.11.18; 2 AI to 18 Sqn 23.11.18
E8522 Rebuilt by Armstrong-Whitworth at RAE as Tadpole and renumbered J6585
E8523 Recd Rec Pk ex UK for IF 13.10.18; 3 ASD 13.10.18 (arr 17.10.18); 110 Sqn 17.10.18; FL, engine failure 21.10.18 (Lt Leigh & Sgt F Quilter); 6 AP 24.10.18; 3 ASD 26.10.18; Shipped to England via Port Depot Rouen 12.1.19
E8524 At 2 AAP Hendon 4.10.18 for 155 Sqn (Mob) Chingford; At Sqn by 21.10.18
E8525 At 2 AAP Hendon 10.10.18 for 155 Sqn (Mob) Chingford; At Sqn by 21.10.18; 57 Sqn, COL 3.3.19 (Lt WJ Barber OK)
E8526 At 2 AAP Hendon 10.10.18 for 155 Sqn (Mob) Chingford; FL en route to sqn 24.10.18, To 7 AAP Kenley; Still there 12.12.18 when sqn disbanded and at 28.1.19 when reallotted from SW Area to EF
E8527 No information
E8528 8 AAP Lympne by 23.10.18; Rec Pk for IF 23.10.18; 3 ASD 30.10.18; 49 Sqn 8.12.18; 18 Sqn 8.6.19
E8529 Recd Rec Pk ex UK for IF 24.10.18; 3 ASD 28.10.18
E8530 At 2 AAP Hendon 12.10.18 for 155 Sqn (Mob) Chingford; At Sqn by 18.10.18
E8531 At 2 AAP Hendon 10.10.18 for 155 Sqn (Mob) Chingford; At Sqn by 18.10.18 - 11.18
E8532 Arr Rec Pk 23.10.18 for IF; For EF by 11.11.18
E8533 1 AI to 18 Sqn 1.11.18; Landed slightly cross wind spun round on nose and tore u/c off 4.11.18 (Lt RW Thurburn & 2/Lt HPA O'Mant); Rep Pk 2 ASD 4.11.18
E8534 At 2 AAP Hendon 12.10.18 for 155 Sqn (Mob) Chingford; Cranwell Workshops ('C') 1918
E8535 At 2 AAP Hendon 28.12.18reallotted from EF to CTD for Instrument Section of D Air Arm
E8536 At 2 AAP Hendon 17.10.18 for 155 Sqn (Mob) Chingford; 155 Sqn by 10.18
E8537 205 Sqn to Sart 26.2.19; 57 Sqn ('A') by 21.3.19 - @5.19
E8538 Sold to American Government; To USMC Northern Bombing Group as *E-15*
E8539 Sold to American Government; To USMC Northern Bombing Group as *E-14*; WO 21.11.18
E8540 Sold to American Government; To USMC Northern Bombing Group as *E-16 or E-22*
E8541 Sold to American Government; To USMC Northern Bombing Group as *E-21*; WO 16.11.18
E8542 Sold to American Government; To USMC Northern Bombing Group as *E-20*
E8543 Sold to American Government; To USMC Northern Bombing Group
E8544 Sold to American Government; To USMC Northern Bombing Group
E8545 Sold to American Government; To USMC Northern Bombing Group
E8546 No information
E8547 At 2 AAP Hendon 17.10.18 for 155 Sqn (Mob) Chingford; 155 Sqn by 12.18

D.H.9A E8553 'N' of No.155 Squadron just after landing at Fowlmere after flying from Chingford. (RAF Museum P.3669)

A Birger 'Ad Astra' silencer fitted to an RAE Puma-engined D.H.9 in 1921. (via J.M.Bruce)

E8548 At 2 AAP Hendon 18.10.18 for 155 Sqn (mob) Chingford; At Sqn by 25.10.18 - 11.18
E8549 PD Ascot; AD Hinaidi 1.23
E8550 & E8551 No information
E8552 2 AI to 18 Sqn 21.11.18
E8553 155 Sqn Fowlmere ('N') 1918
E8554 1 SoN&BD by 31.3.19 - @7.19; Tipped on nose [no date]
E8555 At 7 AAP Kenley 30.1.19 reallotted from EF to SE Area for Store; 47 Sqn Ekaterinodar by 15.8.19; Sold to Anti-Bolshevik Government; Later Soviet Russian Air Fleet (RKKVF)
E8556 No information
E8557 Recd Rec Pk ex UK for IF 5.11.18; 3 ASD 9.11.18; 2 AI to 25 Sqn 27.11.18
E8558 No information
E8559 2 AI to 49 Sqn 8.12.18 - @29.5.19
E8560 3 ASD to 99 Sqn 14.11.18; On mail flight FL nr Namur 17.12.18 (2/Lt G Jones & Lt LH Burrows OK)
E8561 3 ASD to 99 Sqn 13.11.18; FL 20.12.18 (Lt LB Duggan & Lt WJ Tremellen OK)
E8562 3 ASD to 99 Sqn 14.11.18; COL 17.3.19 (2/Lt RR Martin & Mjr Cameron OK)
E8563 3 ASD to 99 Sqn 13.11.18; COL, hit trees 20.1.19 (Lt LB Duggan & 2/Lt EE Bricknell both killed)
E8564 2 AI to 49 Sqn ('C') 8.12.18 - @29.5.19
E8565 Sold to American Government; To USMC Northern Bombing Group
E8566 Sold to American Government; To USMC Northern Bombing Group
E8567 Sold to American Government; To USMC Northern Bombing Group
E8568 Sold to American Government; To USMC Northern Bombing Group
E8569 At 2 AAP Hendon 4.11.18 for 156 Sqn (Mob) Wyton; On disbandment of 156 Sqn 21.11.18 allotted to 123 Sqn Upper Heyford; To sqn 17.12.18 - @1.19
E8570 Sold to American Government; To USMC Northern Bombing Group
E8571 Sold to American Government; To USMC Northern Bombing Group
E8572 TOC EF 26.11.18; 6 AI to 57 Sqn 18.3.19; Crashed at Sorennes 3.4.19 (Lt EG Gaff & Lt AS White)
E8573 3 ASD to 99 Sqn 14.11.18; Overshot aerodrome when attempting to land then nose dived and crashed 16.11.18 (2/Lt GRA Dick & 1/AM L Speed OK); PD Ascot; AD Drigh Rd; 27 Sqn 12.23 - 3.24
E8574 & E8575 No information
E8576 At 2 AAP Hendon 12.4.19 reallotted from SE area to EF;
E8577 1 ASD to 6 AI 28.1.19; 18 Sqn ('D'), on sqn move to Bickendorf, hit sunken road on landing and bumped heavily on hard ground 8.2.19 (Lt DF Brooks & LAC F Beaumont OK)
E8578 1 ASD to 18 Sqn 13.3.19
E8579 On ferry flight from 2 AI misjudged take off struck bank 7.12.18 (2/Lt SF Morrissey OK)
E8580 At 2 AAP Hendon 12.4.19 reallotted from SE Area to EF; PD Ascot; AD Hinaidi; 55 Sqn 1926; 30 Sqn ('A') 7.27 - 1.28
E8581 At 2 AAP Hendon 30.12.18 reallotted from EF to SE Area for 123 Sqn (Mob) Upper Heyford; Tested 2 AAP Hendon 18.1.19, then to 123 Sqn; Propeller broke in dive 13.2.19
E8582 No information
E8583 USMC Northern Bombing Group
E8584 At 2 AAP Hendon 12.4.19, allotted to EF; PD Ascot; AD Drigh Rd; 27 Sqn; EF, FL, Nakband, NWF, 19.12.23 (F/O CA Mason & LAC D Croft both unhurt); AP Lahore 12.23; 27 Sqn 1.24 - 6.24; 27 Sqn ('5') 6.25 - 7.25; 60 Sqn ('N') 3.26; AD Drigh Road 1927; 60 Sqn ('Y') 4.8-27; U/c collapsed landing, Miranshah 7.28 (F/Sgt EA Steers); Repaired; 60 Sqn 10.28
E8585 At 2 AAP Hendon 4.11.18 for 156 Sqn (Mob) Wyton; On disbandment of 156 Sqn 21.11.18 allotted to 123 Sqn; Allotment changed to Midland Area 14.12.18
E8586 At 2 AAP Hendon 4.11.18 for 156 Sqn (Mob) Wyton; On disbandment of 156 Sqn 21.11.18 allotted to 155 Sqn Chingford
E8587 At 2 AAP Hendon 2.12.18 reallotted from IF to EF; 2 FTS Duxford 7.23; 5 FTS; Collided with 504K landing, Shotwick, 2.8.23 (P/O AE Steward unhurt)
E8588 At 2 AAP Hendon 7.11.18 for 156 Sqn (mob) Wyton; On disbandment of 156 Sqn 21.11.18 allotted to 123 Sqn; Allotment changed 14.12.18 to Midland Area; Still at Hendon 12.4.19, allotted to EF; PD Ascot; AD Hinaidi; 84 Sqn 7.25 - 8.25
E8589 At 2 AAP Hendon 12,4,19, allotted to EF; PD Ascot; AD Hinaidi by 7.23; 84 Sqn 14.8.23 - 7.24; Retd UK; DH recond on Cont No 579165/25 (c/n 174); PD Ascot; AD Drigh Rd; 27 Sqn ('F') 8.26 - 5.27
E8590 Completed 9.11.18; At 2 AAP Hendon 12.4.19, allotted to EF; Arr 5(E) ARD Henlow 3.12.19 - @9.1.20 for Australia; Imperial Gift to Australia, arr 16.6.20; Exhibited by Australian War Museum in Exhibition Building, Nicholson Street, Melbourne 19.6.20 - 3.7.20; CFS (AAC), Point Cook by 1920; 1 FTS Point Cook 31.3.21; Became *A1-26* 3.10.21
E8591 At 2 AAP Hendon 12.4.19, allotted to EF; 5 FTS Shotwick, wind dropped while landing towards hangars, left wing hit hut while avoiding two civilian a/c, o/t 11.8.22 (P/O BJ Hanstock unhurt)
E8592 4 FTS 9.24; Retd UK; DH recond (c/n 78); PD Ascot; AD Drigh Rd; 60 Sqn 11.25
E8593 PD Ascot; AD Hinaidi; 84 Sqn; Crashed on landing, 8.11.20; WOC
E8594 No information
E8595 PD Ascot; AD Drigh Rd 8.22; 27 Sqn, returning from bombing raid, stalled landing, overturned 14.3.23 (F/L PG Scott injured & Sgt AB Lewis unhurt)
E8596 DH recond on Cont No 726079/26 (c/n 309); A&AEE (15 Sqn) 6.26; HAD 6.27; 14 Sqn by 7.28
E8597 Allocated 5(E) ARD Henlow for Australia by 2-9.1.20; Imperial Gift to Australia, became *A1-27*
E8598 Left UK for 25 Sqn 16.2.20; Arr AD Aboukir 25.2.20; 47 Sqn, smoke bomb ignited in flight, FL, BO, Orbendofa 15.4.21 (F/L EB Grenfell slightly burned & F/O CA Horn unhurt)
E8599 PD Ascot; AD Aboukir; AD Aboukir rebuilt as ER8599; 47 Sqn 4.25; Overturned landing [no date]
E8600 No information
E8601 PD Ascot; AP Baghdad; 84 Sqn; FL, nr.Hillah, 3.8.20

WOC

E8602 At 2 AAP Hendon 1.11.18 for 156 Sqn (Mob) Wyton; 156 Sqn disbanded 21.11.18, allotment changed to 155 Sqn (Mob) Chingford 23.11.18; At sqn by 26.11.18; PD Ascot; AD Hinaidi; 30 Sqn 2.29

E8603 57 Sqn by 1.3.19; FL Clavier 13.3.19 (2/Lt AS Smith & Lt RM Dixon)

E8604 No information

E8605 601 Sqn 8.28

E8606 At 2 AAP Hendon 4.11.18 for 156 Sqn (Mob) Wyton; On disbandment of 156 Sqn 21.11.18 reallotted to 123 Sqn Upper Heyford; Still at 2 AAP 12.4.19 reallotted from SE Area to EF; PD Ascot; AD Drigh Rd; AP Lahore 12.23

E8607 At 2 AAP Hendon 1.11.18 for 156 Sqn (Mob) Wyton; To sqn 19.11.18; On disbandment of 156 Sqn 21.11.18 reallotted to 123 Sqn Upper Heyford; At sqn by 5.12.18; At 1 ASD 30.1.19 reallotted from SE Area for 123 Sqn (Mob) to EF

E8608 At 2 AAP Hendon 12.4.19 allotted to EF

E8609 No information

E8610 DH record (c/n 49); 24 Sqn 1924

E8611 At 2 AAP Hendon 12.4.19 reallotted from SE Area to EF; Gosport 1919/20; Recond; PD Ascot; AD Drigh Rd; 27 Sqn 1925; 60 Sqn, ground collision with two F.2Bs on take-off for cross-country, Miranshah, 17.12.25 (F/O NWF Mason OK); To AD Drigh Rd; 60 Sqn 8.27

E8612 No information

E8613 At 2 AAP Hendon 7.11.18 for 156 Sqn (Mob) Wyton; On disbandment of 156 Sqn 21.11.18 allotted to 155 Sqn Chingford

E8614 57 Sqn by 5.19

E8615 DH record (c/n 47); PD Ascot; AD Aboukir; 47 Sqn 10.23; AD Aboukir rebuilt as ER8615 12.24 - 1.25; 4 FTS 1.25 - 3.25; 47 Sqn 4.25; AD Aboukir 5.25 - 7.25; 4 FTS 5.26 - 2.28

E8616 Arr 5(E) ARD Henlow 3.12.19 - @9.1.20 for Australia; Imperial Gift to Australia; CFS (AAC), Point Cook by 1920; Used for experimental work with petrol tanks; Crashed in Bass Strait 23.9.20 (Capt WJ Strutt & Sgt AG Dalzell both killed); SOC 31.12.20

E8617 No information

E8618 At 2 AAP Hendon 7.11.18 for 156 Sqn (Mob) Wyton; On disbandment of 156 Sqn 21.11.18 allotted to 155 Sqn Chingford;155 Sqn by 12.18

E8619 PD Ascot; AD Drigh Rd 12.22; AP Lahore 12.22; 27 Sqn 11.1.23

E8620 At 2 AAP Hendon 12.4.19 allotted to EF

E8621 No information

E8622 DH record (c/n 48); 39 Sqn ('5') 12.23 - 2.24; PD Ascot; AD Hinaidi 4.26; 55 Sqn 5.26; 8 Sqn ('N') 1926; 84 Sqn 8.27 - 2.28

E8623 At 2 AAP Hendon 7.11.18 for 156 Sqn (Mob) Wyton); On disbandment of 156 Sqn 21.11.18 allotted to 123 Sqn Upper Heyford; 123 Sqn by 12.18 - @1.19; Tested 2 AAP Hendon 15.1.19; 60 Sqn ('3') by 1.25 - @2.25

E8624 At 2 AAP Hendon 7.11.18 for 156 Sqn (Mob) Wyton; On disbandment of 156 Sqn 21.11.18 allotted to 123 Sqn Upper Heyford; Still at 2 AAP 12.4.19 reallotted from SE Area to EF; PD Ascot; AD Drigh Rd; AP Lahore 3.23

E8625 At 2 AAP Hendon 12.4.19 allotted to EF; PD Ascot; AD Hinaidi by 7.22; 55 Sqn 3.25 - 5.25; 84 Sqn (spade marking) 10.25 - 1.26

E8626 No information

E8627 At 2 AAP Hendon, allotted to EF; IAAD 4.23; A&AEE 3.24; A&AEE 7.27; DH record (c/n 177); 601 Sqn 8.28

E8628 5 FTS; Structural failure, broke up in loop, crashed in sea, Heswall, Cheshire, 26.3.23 (P/O RE Brooke-Hunt killed)

E8629 PD Ascot; AD Drigh Rd; AP Lahore; Port wing damaged, 2.9.22; AD Drigh Rd; AP Lahore 18.3.23; Dardoni 1.4.23; AP Lahore 10.23; 27 Sqn 10.23; Flew into tree on TO, caught fire, BO, Cat W 29.1.24 (F/O DJ Hugh-Jones killed & Cpl Hall DoI 11.2.24)

E8630 At 2 AAP Hendon 14.2.19 reallotted from SE Area for Store to EF

E8631 At 2 AAP Hendon 12.4.19 allotted to EF; PD Ascot; AD Hinaidi 8.24; 55 Sqn ('A3') 8.24 - 10.24; Retd UK; 39 Sqn ('3') (Named 'CELICIA') 12.26 - 7.27

E8632 Sold to American Government; To USMC Northern Bombing Group; Retd RAF; PD Ascot; AD Drigh Rd; AP Lahore 31.1.24; 27 Sqn 5.24; 60 Sqn ('6') 1924; Crashed, Risalpur 1925

E8633 Sold to American Government; To USMC Northern Bombing Group

E8634 Sold to American Government; To USMC Northern Bombing Group

E8635 Sold to American Government; To USMC Northern Bombing Group

E8636 PD Ascot; AD Drigh Rd; AP Lahore 31.1.24; 27 Sqn 5.24; 60 Sqn ('6') 1924; Crashed Risalpur 1925 (F/O LW Aiken)

E8637 PD Ascot; AD Aboukir; 47 Sqn 4.24; 4 FTS; Crashed and overturned, Abu Sueir, early 20's; AD Aboukir rebuilt as DC ER8637; 4 FTS, lost wheel on landing Abu Sueir; Retd UK; DH Recond on Cont No 579165/25 (c/n 177); 60 Sqn 4.26 - 5.26; 27 Sqn 2.27; Crashed on delivery to AD from Kohat when port wing and nose dropped landing, Drigh Rd, 24.4.30; 27 Sqn; AD Drigh Rd 24.4.31

E8638 No information

E8639 PD Sealand; AD Drigh Rd; 8 Sqn 8.22; 70 Sqn 3.23

E8640 55 Sqn ('B3') 10.22; FL in soft ground in desert and overturned, Cat W 23.4.23 (F/O HW Westaway)

E8641 PD Ascot; AD Drigh Rd; 27 Sqn ('I') 8.23; 60 Sqn 9.23; Crashed Lahore, 2.10.23; AD Drigh Rd; 60 Sqn, struck calf landing, Lahore 24.4.24 (F/O CFH Grace & Cpl AG Woods both unhurt); AP Lahore 12.24; 27 Sqn 2.25 - 3.25; 27 Sqn 10.26 - 2.27; EF, FL 27.10.26 (repaired)

E8642 206 Sqn by 12.19; PD Ascot; AD Hinaidi; 8 Sqn by 12.22 - 5.23; 39 Sqn ('V') by 4.25 - @8.26; 4 FTS; AD Aboukir rebuilt as DC ER8642; 4 FTS 8.27 - 12.28; 45 Sqn, flew into ground in fog after take-off, Helwan, 20.11.29 WOC

E8643 PD Ascot; AD Hinaidi by 6.22; 30 Sqn; EF while landing, 3.9.22 (F/O TA Langford-Sainsbury OK); 55 Sqn 10.23; 8 Sqn

E8644 PD Ascot; AD Hinaidi; 55 Sqn ('B3') 3.23

E8645 PD Ascot; AD Hinaidi 5.23 (fit special tanks); 55 Sqn 10.23

E8646 PD Ascot; AD Aboukir; 47 Sqn 4.9.23 - 1.24; PD Ascot; AD Drigh Rd; 27 Sqn 8.25 - 9.25; 60 Sqn; Damaged in take-off collision with E728, 14.9.25; AD Drigh Rd; 27 Sqn ('I') 1.27 - 3.27; AD Drigh Rd to 60 Sqn ('R'?) 26.9.28; AD Drigh Rd 1.5.30

E8647 PD Ascot; AD Drigh Rd; 27 Sqn; AP Lahore 14.4.24

E8648 PD Ascot; AD Drigh Rd; AP Lahore 4.23; AP Lahore 2.24 - 5.24; 60 Sqn 11.24; FL, Sorarogha, NWF 15.4.25; 60 Sqn, crashed Arawali, 4.4.26 (F/O DJ Lloyd & Lt WJ Vezey RE both killed)

E8649 PD Ascot; AD Aboukir rebuilt as ER8649; 4 FTS 5.25; Crashed 1926 WOC

E8650 Longmore's personal aircraft (name 'JAN' on nose) 1923; 84 Sqn 1923 (Red heart marking, named 'TRELAWNY'); 8 Sqn 4.23 - 7.23; AD Hinaidi 7.23; 8 Sqn 11.9.23; 84 Sqn 2.25; AD Hinaidi (DC) 11.25

E8651 PD Ascot; RAF Amman, test flight, overturned landing 22.2.23 (F/O G Horsfield unhurt & AC2 EJ Hogan slightly injured); AD Hinaidi 5.23; 55 Sqn ('B3') 12.25 - 1.26; 30 Sqn; Stalled on turn after take-off, Kirkuk, 24.4.28 WOC

E8652 DH recond (c/n 46); PD Ascot; AD Hinaidi to 30 Sqn 7.5.23; 55 Sqn 3.26

E8653 205 Sqn to Hesdin (via Valenciennes) 21.2.19

E8654 39 Sqn, mid-air collision with J7087, crashed, BO, Spittlegate, 5.6.24 (F/O RH Daly & Sgt WH Brewer both killed)

E8655 DH recond (c/n 154); PD Ascot; AD Hinaidi test 16.12.22; 84 Sqn 17.2.23 - 11.23; AD Drigh Rd; 27 Sqn 4.26; 60 Sqn ('Y') 1.27 - 7.28; 84 Sqn 10.28 (DC); 60 Sqn ('Z') 10.28 - 3.30

E8656 PD Ascot; AD Drigh Rd; 27 Sqn 10.24 - 3.25; Retd UK; DH recond; 605 Sqn 25.10.26 - 16.8.27

E8657 PD Ascot; AD Hinaidi to 8 Sqn 26.7.23; 55 Sqn 10.26 - 1.27

E8658 PD Ascot; AD Hinaidi; 55 Sqn 4.25 - 5.25; 30 Sqn; While parked, hit by F.2b F4341 whose pilot had left it unattended with the engine running, Cat R 4.4.27; 84 Sqn 4.30 - 5.30

E8659 PD Ascot; AD Drigh Rd; AP Lahore 7.2.24 - 6.24; 60 Sqn, photo survey of Wazai area, EF, FL in river bed in mountainous country, Khaisora River, Waziristan, 28.6.24 (F/O HE Greenberry unhurt)
E8660 PD Ascot; AD Drigh Rd; AP Lahore 25.2.24; 60 Sqn 7.24 - 1.25; 27 Sqn ('M') 6.25 - 1.28; AP Lahore; 60 Sqn ('I'); AP Lahore; 60 Sqn ('V') 29.10.28; Crashed NWF, Cat W 26.12.28 (S/Ldr RHG Neville OK)
E8661 PD Ascot; AD Aboukir; 4 FTS; Stalled at low height, spun in, BO, Cat W 2.4.24 (Sgt AC Murray killed)
E8662 PD Ascot; AD Aboukir; 47 Sqn, hit tree on TO Ahurabbad, Egypt 2.9.24 (F/O GH Huxham slightly injured & LAC DE Edwards unhurt); AD Hinaidi 4.26
E8663 98 Sqn by 10.18; PD Ascot; AD Hinaidi 7.23; 84 Sqn 24.8.23
E8664 No information
E8665 PD Ascot; AD Drigh Rd 3.23 - 4.23; AP Lahore 21.4.23; 60 Sqn 7.23; AP Lahore 4.24 - 5.24; 60 Sqn ('10') 5.24 - 7.25; HQ RAF India 9.25; 27 Sqn 19.9.25; AD Drigh Rd 1.26; 60 Sqn 5.27; 27 Sqn ('L') 1929; 60 Sqn ('R'?) 9.29; To AD Drigh Rd 3.30 - 4.30
E8666 PD Ascot; AD Hinaidi 6.23; 8 Sqn 13.7.23; AD Hinaidi 4.24; 84 Sqn 5.24 - 11.24; Retd UK; 500 Sqn
E8667 No information
E8668 PD Ascot; AD Hinaidi to 55 Sqn 24.9.23; 30 Sqn 6.27 - 12.27
E8669 DH recond; PD Ascot; AD Hinaidi 5.23; 8 Sqn ('O'); 84 Sqn, in desert, lost power on take-off in limited space, crashed, BO, Cat W 14.4.25
E8670 PD Ascot
E8671 PD Ascot; AD Drigh Rd; AP Lahore 3.23; 60 Sqn ('4') 2.24; Crashed on landing, 12.2.24 (Sgt D Munro); Repaired; AP Lahore 8.24; 60 Sqn 8.24; AP Lahore 10.24; 60 Sqn; FL, Risalpur, 29.3.25; AD Drigh Road 1927; Convtd DC; 60 Sqn ('V'?) 6.28 - 3.30
E8672 IAAD, tested 18-23.4.23; 39 Sqn (3) 4.25 - 7.25; PD Ascot; AD Drigh Rd; 60 Sqn 8.28 - 3.30
E8673 39 Sqn 1923; PD Ascot; AD Drigh Rd; Convtd DC; 27 Sqn ('E') 1923; AP Lahore 1.24; 27 Sqn ('B') 1.24 - 12.24; AD Drigh Rd; 60 Sqn 6.25 - 10.25; 27 Sqn 2.27; 60 Sqn 10.29 - 4.30

D.H.9A E8673 'E' of No.27 Squadron in 1923. (RAF Museum P.7557)

E8674 PD Ascot; AD Drigh Rd; AP Lahore 3.23; 60 Sqn; Struck bump landing 2.6.24 (F/O AJ Carlielle & AC1 S Gould both OK); AP Lahore 11.24; 27 Sqn ('G') 12.24 - 3.25; 60 Sqn ('8') 11.25 - 3.26
E8675 Tested IAAD 5-7.11.23; Inland Area CF 4.24; PD Ascot; AD Aboukir; 4 FTS 1.26; 14 Sqn 1.28 - 10.28
E8676 PD Ascot; AD Drigh Rd; 60 Sqn 8.23
E8677 Tested IAAD 27.4.23 - 1.5.23; 5 FTS Shotwick, dived in on turn, nr.Chester, 19.6.23 (P/O HCECP Dalrymple slightly injured)
E8678 PD Ascot; AD Drigh Rd; 31 Sqn, spun in Dardoni 11.10.23 (F/O M Tallentire DoI 14.10.23 & AC1 AL Young DoI 12.10.23)
E8679 2 FTS Duxford 11.22 - 6.23
E8680 Tested IAAD 3.5.23 & 8.6.23; PD Ascot; AD Hinaidi; 8 Sqn ('A') 12.25; FL, nosed up, Aleppo, Syria 1926; 55 Sqn 5.26
E8681 2 FTS Duxford 2.21; 207 Sqn ('A') 6.7.22 - 6.24; U/c collapsed 17.4.24; PD Ascot; AD Aboukir; 14 Sqn 11.25 - 8.26
E8682 & E8683 No information
E8684 PD Ascot; AD Hinaidi 6.23 - 7.24 (fit LR tanks); 8 Sqn 7.23 - 6.24; Retd UK; PD Ascot; AD Drigh Rd; 30 Sqn 10.24 - 12.24
E8685 39 Sqn 5.23; 5 FTS 9.23; PD Ascot; AD Drigh Rd; 27 Sqn ('I') 4.26 - 3.27; AD Drigh Road 8.27; 60 Sqn ('X') 8.27; EF, FL, Thal, NWF 19.3.29 (Sgt WC Henley); Repaired; 60 Sqn ('V') 4.29 - 4.30, AD Drigh Rd 4.30
E8686 1 FTS Netheravon 10.25 - 11.25; HAD; 605 Sqn 25.10.26; HAD; 60 Sqn 16.8.27 - 1.28
E8687 PD Ascot; AD Drigh Rd; 60 Sqn; 27 Sqn 1929 - 1930
E8688 PD Ascot; AD Hinaidi 4.23; 8 Sqn 5.23 - 6.23; Retd UK; HAD 10.26; PD Ascot; AD Hinaidi; 14 Sqn 10.29
E8689 PD Ascot; AD Hinaidi 3.23; To Latvian Air Force as *3K*
E8690 No information
E8691 2 FTS Duxford by 11.20 - 10.22
E8692 2 FTS Duxford 2.21; S of AG&B 9.21; Renamed A&GS 1.4.22 - 1.24; PD Ascot; AD Hinaidi; 55 Sqn 5.25; 8 Sqn ('C') 1925
E8693 PD Ascot; AD Hinaidi 28.6.23
E8694 2 FTS Duxford 6.23 - 7.23; DH recond (c/n 140); 1 FTS Netheravon 6.25 - 11.25; PD Ascot; AD Hinaidi; 84 Sqn 4.28; After night landing, taxied into J7876 which had burst wheel landing and had taxied out of flare path to await assistance, Cat M 27.8.28 (F/O FB Tomkins OK)
E8695 39 Sqn ('9'), lost flying speed and dived into ground after take-off, Spittlegate, BO, Cat W 29.9.23 (P/O EB Coventry & Cpl W Wardle both killed)
E8696 A&AEE (15 Sqn) 6.26
E8697 & E8698 No information
E8699 DH rebuilt and renumbered J7308 (c/n 125)
E8700 DH rebuilt and renumbered J7307 (c/n 124)
E8701 No information
E8702 DH rebuilt and renumbered J7309 (c/n 126)
E8703 to E8709 No information
E8710 DH rebuilt and renumbered J7306 (c/n 123)
E8711 PD Ascot; AD Hinaidi to 30 Sqn 21.3.23; AD Hinaidi 6.23 - 11.23; 84 Sqn 11.23; Retd UK; HAD 4.27; 605 Sqn 23.5.27; Crashed on take-off, Manston, 4.8.29 BO
E8712 No information
E8713 PD Ascot; AD Hinaidi; 14 Sqn 9.23; 30 Sqn 10.28 - 1.29
E8714 to E8716 No information
E8717 PD Ascot; AD Drigh Rd; AP Lahore 31.12.23 - 6.24; 60 Sqn ('12') 11.24; Crashed in FL, Renala Khurd, nr Lahore, Cat W 22.1.25 (Sgt D Munro)
E8718 & E8719 No information
E8720 PD Ascot; AD Hinaidi to 55 Sqn 29.3.23
E8721 39 Sqn 12.23; PD Ascot; AD Drigh Rd; 60 Sqn 3.26 - 1.27
E8722 22 Sqn; DH recond and conv DC; 27 Sqn 6.24 - 1.25; AP Lahore; 60 Sqn 20.5.27; Crashed on take-off 28.9.27 (F/L JW Baker MC DFC); Repaired; 60 Sqn 10.27 - 3.30
E8723 PD Ascot; AD Drigh Rd; 27 Sqn ('Aa'), test flight after fitting new radiator, u/c collapsed on rough ground landing, Risalpur, 21.3.24 (F/O HW Westaway & AC1

D.H.9A E8680 'A' of No.8 Squadron after force landing at Aleppo in 1926. (via Philip Jarrett)

F Callicott both unhurt); AD Drigh Rd; 27 Sqn ('A') 12.24 - 3.25
E8724 2 FTS Duxford 7.23 - 9.23; 1 FTS Netheravon, stalled on flat turn after taking off towards rising ground, petrol tanks burst, Farnborough, BO, Cat W 14.3.24 (Cpl IB Shelley killed)
E8725 39 Sqn 8.22 - 12.23, DH record (c/n 149); PD Ascot; AD Drigh Rd; 27 Sqn ('A') 12.25 - 6.26; AD Drigh; 27 Sqn 28.5.38 but crashed en route, Rohri, NWF
E8726 PD Ascot; AD Drigh Rd; 60 Sqn, collided with F2782 on starting Risalpur, 23.1.24 (F/O CFH Grace & F/O CW Rugg both unhurt); AD Drigh Rd; 60 Sqn ('3'); Crashed landing, Risalpur, Cat W 14.10.24 (F/L JW Baker MC DFC)
E8727 PD Ascot; AD Aboukir; 47 Sqn 9.22; Retd UK; PD Ascot; AD Drigh Rd; 60 Sqn
E8728 PD Ascot; AD Aboukir; 47 Sqn 1.22 - 2.22; Retd UK; DH record on Cont No 579165/25 (c/n 225); PD Ascot; AD Hinaidi; 84 Sqn 3.28 - 9.28
E8729 PD Ascot; AD Drigh Rd 4.23; 60 Sqn; EF on take-off, Risalpur, 30.7.23; EF on TO Risalpur 24.9.23 (F/O WN Cumming slightly injured & F/O M Tallentire unhurt); AD Drigh Rd; AP Lahore 20.2.24; 60 Sqn 5.24 - 6.24; 27 Sqn ('G') 10.24; 60 Sqn 11.24; EF, FL crashed, Bastan, Baluchistan, Cat W 20.7.25 (P/O NWF Mason)
E8730 PD Ascot; Arr AD Hinaidi 1.23; 84 Sqn 10.2.23
E8731 PD Ascot; AD Drigh Rd; 60 Sqn 3.24 - 5.24
E8732 PD Ascot; AD Drigh Rd; AP Lahore 4.23; 60 Sqn 7.23 - 9.23 [doubtful - E8752 intended?]
E8733 PD Ascot; AD Aboukir; 47 Sqn 3.24 - 5.24; AD Aboukir rebuilt as ER8733; 4 FTS 4.25 - 11.27
E8734 PD Ascot; AD Hinaidi to 8 Sqn 2.5.23 - 6.23; AD Hinaidi 10.23 - 11.23 (rebuild); 84 Sqn 8.24
E8735 PD Ascot; AD Hinaidi 11.23
E8736 PD Ascot; AD Aboukir; 4 FTS 6.24; AD Aboukir rebuilt as ER8736; U/c collapsed (F/O JMJCJI Rock de Besombes)
E8737 to E8739 No information
E8740 PD Ascot; AD Drigh Rd 4.23
E8741 207 Sqn ('A2') 3.24 - 8.24; 1 FTS Netheravon 7.25 - 10.25; 84 Sqn 1928
E8742 DH recond and convtd DC; PD Ascot; AD Drigh Rd; AP Lahore 6.2.23; 27 Sqn ('H'); Port tyre burst taxying, u/c collapsed Risalpur, 28.1.24 (F/L S Graham MC unhurt & Sgt GE Campbell slightly injured); 27 Sqn ('H') 1.25; AD Drigh Rd 2.26; 27 Sqn 4.27 - 7.27
E8743 PD Ascot; AD Hinaidi to 55 Sqn ('B3') 27.2.23 - 4.23
E8744 PD Ascot; AD Hinaidi 1.23; 70 Sqn 3.23; Retd UK; DH recond (c/n 155); PD Ascot; AD Aboukir; 47 Sqn; 14 Sqn ('A') 2.26; Crashed on nose; AD Aboukir 4.2.27; Rebuilt as ER8744
E8745 PD Ascot; AD Drigh Rd; 60 Sqn; To Latvian Air Force as *6K*
E8746 PD Ascot; AD Drigh Rd; 60 Sqn
E8747 No information
E8748 AD Hinaidi 1.23
E8749 No information
E8750 1 FTS Netheravon 11.24; PD Ascot; AD Drigh Rd; 60 Sqn
E8751 PD Ascot; AD Aboukir; 4 FTS 10.23; Flying low, struck boat mast on Suez Canal, crashed on nose, nr Nefisna, Egypt, BO, Cat W 23.12.25 (P/O CW Woodbyrne DoI & AC1 AT Grom seriously injured)
E8752 PD Ascot; AD Drigh Rd; 60 Sqn ('11') 9.23; AP Lahore 7.24 - 8.24; 60.Sqn; Hit by H3534 taxying, Risalpur 14.11.24 (F/L JW Baker MC DFC); Repaired; 60 Sqn; EF, FL Latchi, NWF 25.11.24 (Sgt D Munro); 60 Sqn ('Z') 12.24 - 5.25; 60 Sqn ('P') 1.26
E8753 PD Ascot; AD Hinaidi to 8 Sqn 28.7.23; Std wheel collapsed landing and overturned, 1.7.24 WOC BUT 60 Sqn by 12.15
E8754 PD Ascot; AD Hinaidi; 8 Sqn ('O') 6.8.23 - 1.24 (personal a/c of Salmond, AOC); AD Hinaidi; Recd UK; 207 Sqn ('A4'); DH recond on Cont No 579165/25 (c/n 178); 60 Sqn 3.27; EF, FL 4.12.28 (Sgt C Howells); Repaired; 60 Sqn 12.28 - 1.29; 27 Sqn 6.29 - 5.30
E8755 PD Ascot; AD Hinaidi; 30 Sqn 3.24; Swung landing, tyre burst and overturned, Hinaidi 29.5.24; Swung landing, port tyre burst and overturned, Hinaidi 5.8.24 (F/O RL Edward unhurt & F/O PR Cawdell slightly injured); AD Hinaidi; Recd UK; 1 FTS Netheravon by 10.24 - @11.24; DH recond on Cont No.579165/25 (c/n 173); AP Lahore 3.27; 60 Sqn ('X') 3.27; To AD Drigh Rd 4.30
E8756 PD Ascot; AD Hinaidi; 55 Sqn 7.25
E8757 PD Ascot; AD Hinaidi; 55 Sqn 1925; 30 Sqn 9.27
E8758 PD Ascot; AD Hinaidi; 30 Sqn 12.5.23; Recd UK; 207 Sqn ('A4') 6.25; DH recond (c/n.157); 60 Sqn ('R') 12.27 - 8.29; 27 Sqn ('E')
E8759 1 FTS Netheravon 11.24 - 8.25; DH recond on Cont No 579165/25 (c/n 254); RAF (Cadet) College 4.28 - 6.28
E8760 PD Ascot; AD Aboukir; 47 Sqn; EF, FL, 28.12.23; 4 FTS 27.10 25; 47 Sqn, hit by H3519 landing in formation, Cat W 26.3.26 (F/O CJK Caggle OK)
E8761 PD Ascot; AD Hinaidi 5.24; Recd UK; DH recond (c/n 161); PD Ascot; AD Drigh Rd; 27 Sqn ('G') 1924 - 1925; 60 Sqn ('Y'); Crashed on landing, 1925; Recd UK; RAF (Cadet) College 2.28 - 4.28
E8762 At 2 AAP Hendon 21.2.19 allotted to EF; Irish FIS Curragh by 14.12.18 [unlikely?]
E8763 At 2 AAP Hendon 12.2.19 allotted to EF; Still at 2 AAP Hendon 12.4.19 allotted to EF; PD Ascot; AD Hinaidi 1.24; 84 Sqn 1.24; AD Hinaidi 2.24
E8764 At 2 AAP Hendon 12.2.19 allotted to EF; PD Ascot; AD Hinaidi 1.23; 55 Sqn 3.2.23; 8 Sqn 1.25 - 7.25; 55 Sqn 10.25; 8 Sqn 10.26
E8765 At 2 AAP Hendon 1.2.19 reallotted from SE Area for Store to EF; At Richborough 5.3.19 allotted to Elope; RAF North Russia (Southern Area) by 7.19 - @9.19; 3 Sqn 1921 - 1922

D.H.9A E8765 in North Russia in 1919.
(via Frank Cheesman)

E8766 At 2 AAP Hendon 5.2.19 allotted to EF; Still at 2 AAP Hendon 12.4.19 allotted to EF; 24 Sqn 4.21; Crashed 5.21; 24 Sqn 11.22
E8767 At 2 AAP Hendon 26.2.19 allotted to EF; RAE from/by 30.6.19 - 21.8.25 (engine, u/c and balance tests)
E8768 At 2 AAP Hendon 5.2.19 allotted to EF; Still at 2 AAP Hendon 12.4.19 allotted to EF; 25 Sqn, wrecked 27.5.19; 6 SS 6.6.19
E8769 At 2 AAP Hendon 12.4.19 allotted to EF; PD Ascot; AD Drigh Rd; 27 Sqn ('A')
E8770 At 2 AAP Hendon 21.2.19 allotted to EF
E8771 At 2 AAP Hendon 21.2.19 allotted to EF; 1 ASD to 25 Sqn 21.5.19; AD Hinaidi 10.23
E8772 PD Acton; AD Drigh; AP Lahore 8.24
E8773 At 2 AAP Hendon 21.2.19 allotted to EF
E8774 At 2 AAP Hendon 24.2.19 allotted to EF; PD Ascot; AD Drigh Rd; AP Lahore 4.23
E8775 At 2 AAP Hendon 19.4.19 allotted to EF; Still at 2 AAP Hendon 12.4.19 allotted to EF
E8776 At 2 AAP Hendon 12.4.19 allotted to EF;
E8777 At 2 AAP Hendon 21.2.19 allotted to EF
E8778 No information
E8779 To Latvian Air Force as PY1PY
E8780 DH recond (c/n 19); TOC Waddon 14.12.21
E8781 Became *G-EBLC*
E8782 DH recond (c/n 21); TOC Waddon 19.12.21
E8783 No information
E8784 To Latvian Air Force as *10*
E8785 To Latvian Air Force as *4K*
E8786 1 FTS Netheravon 10.24
E8787 To Latvian Air Force as *5K*
E8788 DH recond (c/n 17); TOC Waddon.3.12.21; Became *G-EBAC*; Regd 5.12.21; Sold overseas 12.1.22

E8789 To Latvian Air Force
E8790 No information
E8791 Became *G-EAXC*
E8792 PD Ascot; AD Drigh Rd 2.23; AP Lahore 10.3.23; 60 Sqn 3.23; 27 Sqn 1.24 - 3.25; U/c collapsed landing, Rawalpindi, 2.6.24 (F/O HW Westaway & F/L CP Barber both unhurt); Repaired; 27 Sqn, dived low to drop bombs, shot down and crashed with bombs, caught fire on impact, BO, Torra Tukka, Cat W 21.3.25 (F/O EJ Dashwood & F/O NC Hayter-Hames both killed)
E8793 PD Ascot; AD Aboukir; 47 Sqn 24.9.23 - 2.24; 47 Sqn 10.24 - 3.25
E8794 PD Ascot; AD Hinaidi; 8 Sqn 9.24 - 5.23; PD Ascot; AD Aboukir; 47 Sqn; 4 FTS, after practice formation, E9887 broke away at 1,200ft and collided with E8794, both pilots being dazzled by sun, Cat M 1.11.27 (Cpl LJ Dixon) [2 crew members to hospital, not clear which a/c]; WOC 25.11.27
E8795 No information
E8796 PD Ascot; AD Hinaidi 1.24; 55 Sqn ('CI') 3.24; 60 Sqn to AP Lahore 28.3.24; AD Hinaidi; 55 Sqn ('CI') 18.2.27; Crashed, Hillah, 19.8.27 WOC
E8797 AD Hinaidi 8.23
E8798 PD Ascot; AD Hinaidi 6.23; 55 Sqn 12.9.23 - 11.23; Recd UK; PD Ascot; AD Aboukir; 4 FTS 5.28
E8799 PD Ascot; AD Drigh Rd; 27 Sqn 8.23; 60 Sqn ('O') 3.24; FL Rawalpindi 4.3.24 (P/O AF Hutton); AP Lahore 12.24; 60 Sqn; EF, FL 20.7.25 (P/O NWF Mason); AP Lahore; 60 Sqn ('2 ') 24.10.25; Crashed on landing 29.11.25 (P/O NWF Mason); To AD Drigh Rd, repaired by 21.12.25; 60 Sqn ('Z') 5.26 - 1.27; 27 Sqn 10.28; 60 Sqn 10.28
E8800 No information
E8801 PD Ascot; 84 Sqn 1921; AD Hinaidi 7.23
E8802 Sold to Soviet Russian Air Force (RKKVF)
E8803 PD Ascot; AD Drigh Rd; 60 Sqn; Undershot landing Risalpur 20.4.23 (F/O DS Allen & F/Lt APV Daly both slightly injured); Undershot and hit telephone wires, Risalpur, 1.7.23; AP Lahore 12.23; AP Lahore 4.24
E8804 From Egypt to Mesopotamia with 8 Sqn (ordered 10.1.21); 84 Sqn ('X') 1.21 - 1.23
E8805 PD Ascot; AD Hinaidi; 30 Sqn 10.22 - 1.23; AD Hinaidi 1.23; 55 Sqn ('B2') 24.4.23 - 5.23; Recd UK; DH recond on Cont No 726079/26 (c/n 156); 207 Sqn ('C4) 6.25; DH recond on Cont No 726079/26 (c/n 310); HAD 7.28
E8806 Deld 1.3.19; PD Ascot; AD Hinaidi; 8 Sqn 8.22 - 11.22; 55 Sqn ('CII') 6.24 - 1.26; AD Hinaidi 1926; 84 Sqn 8.26

200 D.H.9 ordered 23.3.18 under Cont No 351/418/C.296 (BR.394) from Aircraft Manufacturing Co Ltd, Hendon and numbered E8857 to E9056. (230hp Puma)

E8857 Rec Pk to 2 AI 31.8.18; 27 Sqn 4.9.18; Left 16.00 for bombing raid on Bohain, shot down in flames W of target 25.9.18 (2/Lt AV Cosgrove & 2/Lt SC Read both killed)
E8858 14 TDS Lake Down by 12.8.18; Practising forced landing, stalled on turn at 1,000ft, dived in 27.8.18 (2/Lt LR Marsh injured)
E8859 3 ASD to 104 Sqn 27.10.18; Pfalz DIII OOC Jametz 12.45, but combat damaged crashed and wrecked St Mihiel 29.10.18 (2/Lt L Hart wounded & 2/Lt T Bailey OK); 6 AP 4.11.18; 3 ASD 5.11.18
E8860 3 ASD to 99 Sqn 10.11.18; 3 ASD 13.11.18
E8861 8 AAP Lympne by 13.9.18; Rec Pk to 2 AI 20.9.18; 5 AI 7.10.18; 107 Sqn 10.10.18; 98 Sqn 5.3.19; 8 AAP Lympne 14.3.19
E8862 8 AAP Lympne by 30.8.18; Rec Pk to 2 AI 1.9.18; 107 Sqn 5.9.18; Struck ridge on landing 19.10.18 (Lt HRT Hughes & 2/Lt AH Baker)
E8863 Rec Pk to 2 AI 30.8.18; 98 Sqn 4.9.18; Fokker DVII BU Le Cateau 12.45 2.10.18 (Lt HF Mulhall & Lt SStC Stone); Left 09.30 for bombing raid on Mons Rlwy Stn, combat with EAs over Mons on return, FTR 30.10.18 (Lt HF Mulhall PoW & Lt JC Pritchard killed)
E8864 8 AAP Lympne to Rec Pk 19.9.18; 2 AI 21.9.18; 49 Sqn 25.9.18; In raid on Aulnoye junction 9.10.18 (2/Lt SC Lambert OK & 2/Lt J Warren wounded); COL 12.11.18 (Lt LW Boland & 2/Lt NJ Spence OK)
E8865 Rec Pk to 2 AI 3.9.18; 98 Sqn 5.9.18 - @19.1.19
E8866 Rec Pk to 2 AI 29.8.18; 49 Sqn 31.8.18; 2 AI 8.12.18, exchanged for D.H.9A
E8867 Rec Pk to 2 AI 18.10.18; 98 Sqn 1.11.18; 8 AAP Lympne 7.2.19
E8868 2 AI to 107 Sqn 3.10.18; In combat 29.10.18 (pilot OK & 2/Lt RB Williamson killed); 98 Sqn 5.3.19; 8 AAP Lympne 14.3.19
E8869 8 AAP Lympne by 21.8.18; Rec Pk 22.8.18; 2 AI 23.8.18; 49 Sqn 29.8.18; Left 14.50 for bombing raid on Aulnoye Junction, in combat with EAs W of Forêt de Mormal on return, FTR 24.9.18 (Capt ED Asbury & 2/Lt BT Gillman both killed)
E8870 No information
E8871 Rec Pk to 1 AI 3.9.18; 108 Sqn 16.9.18; After bombing Ingelmunster station at 17.25 formation attacked by 33 EA between the target and Roulers, 3 EA in flames, 1 BU and 2 OOC shared C2205, D499, D5835, D5845, D7342, E605, E5435 & F5847 1.10.18 (Lt ATW Boswell & 2/Lt RP Gundill); Left 06.22 on bombing raid to Audenaarde, combat with EA, last seen going down OOC in spiral E of Courtrai with EA on tail 14.10.18 (2/Lt PL Phillips & 2/Lt PCS McCrea both PoW)
E8872 Rec Pk to 1 AI 17.9.18; 211 Sqn 29.9.18; Bombing raid, pilot wounded by EA fire just before reaching target but carried on, observer wounded by EA fire on the way back and aileron controls shot away, FL just behind British lines just W of Roulers at 10.00, attempts to collect m/c were frustrated by shell fire 5.10.18 (2/Lt VGH Phillips & 2/Lt AF Taylor both wounded); Remains to 1 ASD, only engine and gun salved; 8 AP 8.10.18 & WOC
E8873 Rec Pk to 206 Sqn ('D') 13.10.18 - @30.1.19
E8874 Rec Pk, tested 16.9.18; St.Omer 24.9.18; 1 AI 2.10.18; 206 Sqn by 18.10.18; Fokker DVII in flames Sotteghem, nr Ghent 10.00-10.15 4.11.18 (2/Lt H McLean & 2/Lt HP Hobbs)
E8875 Rec Pk to 2 AI 27.8.18; 98 Sqn 30.8.18; On landing at new aerodrome ran into by D3082 27.10.18 (Lt JM Brown & Sgt Mech F Sefton OK); Rep Pk 1 ASD 5.11.18
E8876 No information
E8877 Rec Pk to 1 AI 23.8.18; 206 Sqn 30.8.18; Caught fire in air Buschbell 31.1.19 (Lt CL Cumming & 2/Lt AJ Waters both killed); SOC in field
E8878 8 AAP Lympne by 11.9.18; Rec Pk to 1 AI 16.9.18; 206 Sqn 21.9.18
E8879 No information
E8880 Rec Pk to 1 AI 27.9.18; 211 Sqn 30.9.18; Fokker DVII destroyed S of Charleroi 15.15 9.11.18 (Lt WF Blanchfield & 2/Lt TR Lole); 98 Sqn 23.2.19; 8 AAP Lympne 8.3.19
E8881 Rec Pk to 4 ASD 15.9.18; 218 Sqn 25.9.18; Bombing raid to Lichtervelde, attacked by 8 Fokker DrI over Cortemarck, Fokker DrI in flames & another OOC 17.50, m/c badly shot up 28.9.18 (Lt HD McLaren DFC unhurt & Sgt G Barlow wounded); 4 ASD 4.10.18
E8882 Imperial Gift to India
E8883 Rec Pk by 13.9.18; 4 ASD Audembert 18.9.18; 218 Sqn 25.9.18; Left on bombing raid to Thourout, last seen crossing lines 12.00 28.9.18 (Lt HP Brumell & Sgt RS Joysey both PoW); Deleted 15.10.18
E8884 8 AAP Lympne to Rec Pk 7.9.18; 1 AI 12.9.18; 103 Sqn 25.9.18; Grey Fokker DVII with red tail OOC Mainvault 09.35 30.10.18 (Capt RE Dodds & 2/Lt IB Corey); Two EA destroyed on ground Roubaix aerodrome 14.20 30.10.18 (Mjr MHB Nethersole & 2/Lt IB Corey); Damaged landing on bad ground 8.3.19 (2/Lt MS Lewin & 2/Lt G Butters OK); W/O by 11.3.19
E8885 3 ASD to 99 Sqn 28.9.18; 3 ASD 13.11.18
E8886 99 Sqn by 3.11.18; 3 ASD 13.11.18
E8887 No information
E8888 'F' Flt 186 Development Sqn Gosport by 6.19
E8889 No information
E8890 11 TDS Old Sarum, hit hangar on cross-wind TO 6.10.18 (Lt SE Pitt seriously injured & Pte JC Bowman USA injured)
E8891 No information
E8892 & E8893 No information
E8894 Imperial Gift to India
E8895 No information

E8896 Deld Brockworth W/E 10.10.18 for Taranto; Left/shipped W/E 14.11.18
E8897 Deld Brockworth W/E 10.10.18 for Taranto; Left/shipped W/E 14.11.18
E8898 Deld Brockworth W/E 10.10.18 for Taranto; Left/shipped W/E 14.11.18
E8899 Deld Brockworth W/E 10.10.18 for Taranto; Left/shipped W/E 14.11.18
E8900 Deld Brockworth W/E 10.10.18 for Taranto; Left/shipped W/E 14.11.18
E8901 Deld Brockworth W/E 10.10.18 for Taranto; Left/shipped W/E 14.11.18
E8902 Deld Brockworth W/E 10.10.18 for Taranto; Left/shipped W/E 14.11.18
E8903 At 1 AAP Coventry 4.1.19 reallotted from EF to Belgian Government; Allotment presumably cancelled; Coventry to RAE Farnborough 25.4.19 (undercarriage test 21.8.19); AEE Martlesham Heath 31.10.19 (new type release valve and altitude control); RAE 20.5.20
E8904 No information
E8905 At 1 AAP Coventry 4.1.19 reallotted from EF to Belgian Government
E8906 to E8908 No information
E8909 IAAD; Imperial Gift to India, shipped SS *Hatimura* 8.20
E8910 At 1 AAP Coventry 4.1.19 reallotted from EF to Belgian Government; Sold to Belgian Government
E8911 No information
E8912 At 1 AAP Coventry 4.1.19 reallotted from EF to Belgian Government
E8913 Deld Brockworth W/E 10.10.18 for Taranto; Left/shipped W/E 14.11.18
E8914 Deld Brockworth W/E 17.10.18; 6 SD Ascot W/E 24.10.18 for Mudros; Left/shipped W/E 21.11.18
E8915 Deld Brockworth W/E 17.10.18; 6 SD Ascot W/E 24.10.18 for Mudros; Left/shipped W/E 28.11.18; Imperial Gift to India
E8916 Deld Brockworth W/E 17.10.18; 6 SD Ascot W/E 24.10.18 for Mudros; Left/shipped W/E 28.11.18; To Greek Government
E8917 Deld Brockworth W/E 17.10.18; 6 SD Ascot W/E 24.10.18 for Mudros; Left/shipped W/E 28.11.18; To Greek Government
E8918 1 ASD to 103 Sqn 3.11.18; COL at 4 ASD 23.11.18 (Sgt H Driver & Sgt HS Garnett); To Rep Pk 1 ASD
E8919 8 AAP Lympne by 23-24.10.18; 103 Sqn by 2.19
E8920 2 AI to 49 Sqn 14.11.18; 2 AI 8.12.18, exchanged for D.H.9A
E8921 2 AI to 49 Sqn 10.11.18
E8922 No information
E8923 8 AAP Lympne by 23.10.18; 1 AI to 108 Sqn 4.11.18; 98 Sqn 23.1.19; 8 AAP Lympne 13.2.19; 'Z' Unit British Somaliland 7.19 - @1.20
E8924 Deld 6 SD Ascot W/E 12.9.18; Shipped to Taranto 14.11.18; 'A' dett RAF South Russia Instructional Mission to storage 3.11.19; Sold to Anti-Bolshevik Government
E8925 Deld 6 SD Ascot W/E 12.9.18; Shipped to Taranto 14.11.18; Sold to Anti-Bolshevik Government; RAF Instructional Mission South Russia to Russian Aviation Corps 8.19
E8926 Deld 6 SD Ascot W/E 12.9.18; Shipped to Taranto 14.11.18; Sold to Anti-Bolshevik Government
E8927 Deld 6 SD Ascot W/E 12.9.18; Shipped to Taranto 14.11.18; 'A' dett RAF Instructional Mission South Russia by 17.10.19; To Store 3.11.19; Sold to Anti-Bolshevik Government
E8928 Deld 6 SD Ascot W/E 12.9.18; Shipped to Taranto 14.11.18; Sold to Anti-Bolshevik Government
E8929 Deld 6 SD Ascot W/E 12.9.18 for Taranto; Left/shipped W/E 21.11.18; Arr ASD Aboukir ex UK 30.9.19
E8930 1 ASD to 98 Sqn 4.11.18 - @19.1.19; 15 TS Hucknall, EF, engine overheated, FL, crashed on bumpy ground 8.5.19 (F/L GF Sharman & 2/Lt VB Leach both slightly injured)
E8931 Rep Pk 2 ASD to 2 AI 18.10.18; 98 Sqn ('Z') 1.11.18; Temp to 40 Sqn 17.1.19; Retd 98 Sqn; Oil failure due to excessive cold caused damage to engine, m/c further damaged in FL 29.1.19 (Lt JM Brown OK); 1 ASD 3.2.19
E8932 Tested at Rep Pk 1 ASD 18.9.18; SOC Rep Pk 1 ASD 27.9.18 damaged by enemy action, allotted new number H7201 for reconstruction
E8933 Rep Pk 2 ASD to 5 AI 7.10.18; 2 AI to 27 Sqn 8.11.18; Casualty Report 17.2.19 says m/c waterlogged, fuselage twisted, main and tail planes warped; To 6 SS 25.2.19
E8934 Rep Pk 1 ASD to 1 AI 21.9.18; 108 Sqn 26.9.18; In action on Ingelmunster raid 1.10.18 (Lt S Whellock and 2/Lt JW White both wounded); Left 15.30 for solo reconnaissance, FTR 6.10.18 (2/Lt W Freer & 2/Lt JW Neil both killed)
E8935 Rep Pk 2 ASD to 2 AI 27.10.18; 107 Sqn; 27 Sqn by 12.18; 98 Sqn 1.3.19; 1 ASD 8.3.19; 8 AAP Lympne 8.3.19; 206 Sqn by 12.19
E8936 Rep Pk 1 ASD to 1 AI 21.9.18; 211 Sqn 25.9.18; Left 11.30 to bomb Staden, last seen W of target in control after raid 28.9.18 (2/Lt WJ Johnson PoW DoW 13.10.8 & Sgt Mech WE Jones MM PoW)
E8937 Rep Pk 2 ASD to 2 AI 23.10.18; 211 Sqn 4.11.18; 98 Sqn 26.2.19; 8 AAP Lympne 13.3.19
E8938 SOC Rep Pk 1 ASD 27.9.18 damaged by enemy action, allotted new number H7202 for reconstruction
E8939 Arr Rec Pk 3.9.18; 2 AI and on to 3 ASD 6.9.18 (arr 7.9.18); 99 Sqn 9.10.18; Crashed through hangar 5.11.18; 3 ASD 5.11.18; SOC 7.11.18
E8940 Deld 6 SD Ascot W/E 12.9.18; Shipped to Taranto W/E 21.11.18; Arr ASD Aboukir ex UK 30.9.19
E8941 Arr 'X' AD ex UK 1.12.18; 206 Sqn Helwan 16.7.19 - @12.19; 'Z' Unit ('U') British Somaliland by 10.19 - @1.20
ALSO 501 Sqn, crashed Hawkinge 7.11.30 (prefix?)
E8942 Deld 6 SD Ascot W/E 15.10.18; To Docks W/E 31.10.18; Shipped to Taranto 14.11.18; 'A' dett RAF Instructional Mission South Russia by 17.10.19; Sold to Anti-Bolshevik Government; To Russian Aviation Corps 24.11.19
E8943 Arr 'X' AD ex UK 1.12.18; 206 Sqn Helwan 16.7.19
E8944 Deld 6 SD Ascot W/E 17.10.18; Shipped to Taranto 14.11.18; 'A' dett RAF Instructional Mission South Russia by 17.10.19; Sold to Anti-Bolshevik Government
E8945 Sold to Anti-Bolshevik Government; Deld 6 SD Ascot W/E 12.9.18; Left Shipped to Mudros W/E 21.11.18; Unloaded from SS *Diyatalana* on/by 25.1.20; TOC Base Depot RAF Novorossisk 14.2.20; To White Russian Forces; Later Soviet Russian Air Fleet (RKKVF)
E8946 Deld 6 SD Ascot W/E 17.10.18; To docks W/E 31.10.18; Shipped to Taranto 14.11.18
E8947 Deld 6 SD Ascot W/E 12.9.18; To docks W/E 31.10.18; Shipped to Taranto 14.11.18; Sold to Anti-Bolshevik Government; RAF Instructional Mission South Russia to Russian Aviation Corps 8.19
E8948 Deld 6 SD Ascot W/E 12.9.18; To docks W/E 31.10.18; Shipped to Mudros 14.11.18; Sold to Anti-Bolshevik Government
E8949 Deld 6 SD Ascot W/E 12.9.18; To docks W/E 31.10.18; Shipped to Mudros 14.11.18; Sold to Anti-Bolshevik Government; RAF Instructional Mission South Russia to Russian Aviation Corps 8.19
E8950 Deld 6 SD Ascot W/E 12.9.18; To docks W/E 31.10.18; Shipped to Mudros 14.11.18; Sold to Anti-Bolshevik Government; RAF Instructional Mission South Russia to Russian Aviation Corps 24.11.19; Later Soviet Russian Air Fleet (RKKVF)
E8951 Deld 6 SD Ascot W/E 12.9.18; To docks W/E 31.10.18; Shipped to Mudros 14.11.18; 'A' dett RAF South Russian Instructional Mission by 17.10.19; To Store 3.11.19; Sold to Anti-Bolshevik Government; To Russian Aviation Corps 24.11.19; Later Soviet Russian Air Fleet (RKKVF)
E8952 Deld 6 SD Ascot W/E 12.9.18; To docks W/E 31.10.18; Shipped to Mudros 14.11.18; Sold to Anti-Bolshevik Government; RAF Instructional Mission South Russia to Russian Aviation Corps 24.11.19; Later Soviet Russian Air Fleet (RKKVF)
E8953 Deld 6 SD Ascot W/E 12.9.18; At docks 10.18; Shipped to Mudros 14.11.18; AP Simferopol to A Flt Crimean Group RAF South Russia 13.2.20; Crashed landing on bad ground at height 12.3.20
E8954 Rec Pk to 1 AI 1.10.18; 211 Sqn 3.10.18; EA OOC 1.11.18 (2/Lt CC Brouncker & Sgt Mech PC Siverton); Overshot landing, failed to clear sunken road, crashed 14.12.18 (Lt MF Mousley & 2/Lt W Norrie unhurt); 7 SS Bohain 16.12.18

E8955 Rec Pk to 1 AI and on to 103 Sqn 1.10.18; Left on bombing raid 11.42, hit by AA, FL, COL, caught fire 8.10.18 (Sgt J McKie killed & 2/Lt ALAM Pitot DoI)
E8956 8 AAP Lympne to Rec Pk 21.9.18; 1 AI 29.9.18
E8957 8 AAP Lympne by 25.9.18; 4 ASD to 218 Sqn 19.10.18; COL 14.1.19 (2/Lt RA Whitehead & AM Barnes unhurt); to 2 ASD
E8958 4 ASD Audembert to 218 Sqn 29.9.18; Left am, lost over enemy lines when dropping rations at Stadenburg 2.10.18 (Capt WF Cleghorn DFC killed & Lt FH Stringer DSC PoW); Deleted 15.10.18
E8959 8 AAP Lympne by 25.9.18; Rec Pk to 1 AI 4.10.18; 108 Sqn 4.10.18; EA OOC Sotteghem, shared C2216, D613, E676, E8980, E9026 & F1118 09.40-10.10 4.11.18 (2/Lt HN Tiplady & 2/Lt FLP Smith); 98 Sqn 23.1.19; 8 AAP Lympne 13.2.19
E8960 4 ASD to 218 Sqn 9.10.18; COL after bombing raid, badly damaged 18.10.18 (Lt JRA Barnes & 2/Lt FE Green both unhurt); 4 ASD 20.10.18 - @25.10.18
E8961 At Rec Pk, tested 29.9.18
E8962 8 AAP Lympne by 26.9.18; Rec Pk to 1 AI 5.10.18; 211 Sqn 8.10.18; EA BU in air, shared B7626 & E8962 11.00 4.11.18 (both Lt EG Gaff & 2/Lt WJ Large); EF on TO, swung avoiding rut 30.11.18 (2/Lt EJ Stevenson & Sgt J Smith unhurt); 7 SS Bohain 1.12.18; for 2 ASD
E8963 to E8969 No information
E8970 18 Sqn, on take-off wing skid buried itself in soft earth causing m/c to swing and turn on nose, u/c torn off 31.12.18 (2/Lt DLH Moore & 2/Lt HS Cranfield OK)
E8971 49 Sqn, handed in to 1 ASD 14.7.19
E8972 3 ASD to 104 Sqn 30.10.18; Fokker DVII OOC Lorquin 14.10 6.11.18 (2/Lt BH Stretton & 2/Lt H Grieve); SOC 21.1.19
E8973 No information
E8974 3 ASD to 104 Sqn 6.11.18; En route Azelot to Blangy, FL Doullens and wrecked 21.11.18 (2/Lt AW Hardwick & 3/AM White); To Rep Pk 2 ASD; SOC 29.11.18
E8975 to E8977 No information
E8978 3 ASD to 104 Sqn 28.10.18; FTR bombing raid 29.10.18 (2/Lt HD Arnott & Lt B Johnson both killed)
E8979 No information
E8980 Rep Pk 2 ASD to 2 AI 7.10.18; 108 Sqn 18.10.18; EA OOC Sotteghem, shared C2216, D613, E676, E8959, E9026 & F1118 09.40-10.10 4.11.18; EA OOC E of Sotteghem, shared C2216, D613, D5845, D7357 & E9028 09.05 9.11.18 (both 2/Lt JD Sloss & 2/Lt JD Todd); Then left at 13.05 on raid to Denderleeuwe, combat with 12 Fokker DVII, shot up by EA and AA, FL Audenarde 9.11.18 (2/Lt JD Sloss DoW 23.11.18 & 2/Lt JD Todd wounded); To Rep Pk 1 ASD 15.11.18
E8981 49 Sqn by 20.6.19; Handed in to 1 ASD 15.7.19
E8982 Rep Pk 2 ASD to 2 AI 18.10.18; 98 Sqn 1.11.18; On landing pilot mistook wind direction, a gust of wind swung m/c round, crashed 7.11.18 (2/Lt W Geary & Sgt Mech T Tedder OK); Rep Pk 1 ASD 11.11.18
E8983 SOC Rep Pk 1 ASD 27.9.18 damaged by enemy action, allotted new number H7203 for reconstruction
E8984 Rep Pk 2 ASD to 2 AI 31.10.18; 108 Sqn 8.11.18; 98 Sqn 23.1.19; 8 AAP Lympne 15.2.19
E8985 No Information
E8986 Deld docks W/E 19.9.18; Shipped to Mudros W/E 3.10.18 - @30.1.19; Sold to Anti-Bolshevik Government
E8987 Deld 6 SD Ascot W/E 12.9.18; To docks W/E 31.10.18; Shipped to Mudros 14.11.18; 'A' dett RAF Instructional Mission South Russia by 17.10.19; Sold to Anti-Bolshevik Government
E8988 Deld docks W/E 19.9.18; Shipped to Mudros W/E 3.10.18 - @30.1.19; Sold to Anti-Bolshevik Government
E8989 No information
E8990 To docks W/E 19.9.18; Shipped to Mudros W/E 3.10.18 - @30.1.19; 222 Sqn Mudros/San Stefano by 14.11.18; Sold to Anti-Bolshevik Government
E8991 Deld docks W/E 19.9.18; Shipped to Mudros W/E 3.10.18 - @30.1.19; To Greek Government
E8992 Deld docks W/E 19.9.18; Shipped to Mudros W/E 3.10.18 - @30.1.19; Sold to Anti-Bolshevik Government
E8993 Arr 'X' AD ex UK 28.11.18; Salonika AP 19.2.19; 47 Sqn for service in south Russia 21.4.19; At 47 Sqn Ekaterinodar by 27.5.19; COL returning from raid on Tsaritsyn 22.6.19 (2/Lt CC Reynolds & 2/Lt CP Primrose DFC); 'A' dett South Russian Instructional Mission for repair 3.11.19; Sold to Anti-Bolshevik Government
E8994 Arr 'X' AD ex UK 28.11.18; TOC Salonika AP 19.2.19; 47 Sqn for service in south Russia 21.4.19; At 47 Sqn Ekaterinodar by 3.6.19; Erected 12.8.19; Attacked a boat towing a balloon setting the balloon alight 28.8.19 (Capt WF Anderson OK & Capt JL McLennan MC DoW); KB moored on beach set on fire Shirokoe 15.30 15.9.19; With D2840 in indecisive combat with Russian Nieuport, Dubovka 11.00 16.9.19 (Lt EJ Cronin & Lt A Mercer); Bombed barge carrying 8 FBA flying boats on deck, several FBAs wrecked 17.9.19 (both Capt WF Anderson & Lt R Addison); 'A' dett RAF Instructional Mission South Russia by 17.10.19; Sold to Anti-Bolshevik Government (NTU?); 47 Sqn by 3.20
E8995 3 ASD to 104 Sqn 30.10.18; SOS 21.1.19; En route to 12 AAP Hawkinge 14.3.19 reallotted from EF to SE Area; 120 Sqn Hawkinge by 3.19 - 8.19
E8996 Arr 'X' AD ex UK 18.11.18; 269 Sqn Port Said 25.11.18; 'X' AP Kantara 14.3.19; 'Z' Sqn for Arabian Desert Expedition 6.7.19; 16 TDS Heliopolis to AD Aboukir 12.2.20
E8997 Arr 'X' AD ex UK 18.11.18; 269 Sqn Port Said 25.11.18; 'X' AP Kantara 14.3.19; 'B' Flt 142 Sqn Suez 7.5.19; ASD Aboukir 7.8.19; SOC 14.8.19
E8998 Arr 'X' AD ex UK 18.11.18; 269 Sqn Port Said 25.11.18; 'C' Flt 142 Sqn Suez 14.3.19; AP Baghdad (repair) to 55 Sqn 21.8.20
E8999 Arr 'X' AD ex UK 18.11.18; 269 Sqn Port Said 25.11.18; 'B' Flt 142 Sqn Suez 14.3.19; AP Baghdad by 7.20 (rebuild); To 55 Sqn hy 8.20
E9000 No information
E9001 206 Sqn, lost in fog, FL in Holland 3.3.19 (Lt C Workman & AM E Rogan both injured)
E9002 No information
E9003 2 AI to 27 Sqn 16.11.18; 98 Sqn 1.3.19; To England 16.3.19; 120 Sqn Hawkinge by 3.19 - 8.19
E9004 No information
E9005 No.1 Aerial Ranges by 18.12.18; Meteorological Flight 91 Wing, Berck-sur-Mer, crashed 25.4.19 (Capt CKM Douglas & Sgt Williams)
E9006 No information
E9007 2 AI to 27 Sqn 22.11.18; 98 Sqn 1.3.19; FL Quelmes 2.3.19; 8 AAP Lympne 8.3.19; Arr 206 Sqn Helwan ex France 27.7.19 (with 'Z' Unit Somaliland ('Y') 9.19); ASD Aboukir 29.12.19
E9008 No information
E9009 3 ASD to 99 Sqn 6.11.18; 3 ASD 14.11.18; 2 AI 1.12.18
E9010 & E9011 No information
E9012 3 ASD to 99 Sqn 8.11.18; 3 ASD 13.11.18; On ferry flight from 3 ASD to 2 AI flew into the side of a hill at Moreuil in thick fog 20.11.18 (Lt AG Bathurst-Norman killed)
E9013 No information
E9014 Rep Pk 2 ASD to 2 AI 18.10.18; 98 Sqn 4.11.18; Landed too near edge of aerodrome, in swerving to avoid hangars u/c was wrenched off 31.12.18 (Lt RL Lawson & Lt RU Hoddinott OK): 1 ASD 7.1.19
E9015 1 ASD to 108 Sqn 7.12.18; 98 Sqn 23.1.19; 8 AAP Lympne 13.2.19
E9016 Rep Pk 2 ASD to 2 AI 31.10.18; 98 Sqn 9.11.18; 8 AAP Lympne 7.2.19
E9017 No information
E9018 Arr 206 Sqn Helwan ex France 25.7.19; ASD Aboukir 1.12.19
E9019 4 SoN&BD Thetford by 11.18
E9020 No information
E9021 SMOP Dover by 10.18 - @11.18; 212 Sqn by 2.19 - @3.19 (A/S training); 120 Sqn Hawkinge by 3.19 - 8.19
E9022 Deld 555/6 Flts 219 Sqn Manston 13.10.18; HACP 5.11.18; Manston to Handley Page, Cricklewood for Polish Military Purchase Mission on free issue 19.3.20
E9023 No information
E9024 4 SoN&BD Thetford by 10.18 - 11.18
E9025 Deld 555/6 Flts 219 Sqn Manston 8.10.18 - @11.18
E9026 Rec Pk to 1 AI 22.10.18; 108 Sqn 23.10.18; EA OOC Sotteghem 09.40-10.10 shared C2216, D613, E676, E8959, E8980 & F1118, then FL with radiator and oil tank shot through 10.11.18 (Lt W Marsden wounded &

Lt W McGowan OK); 98 Sqn 23.1.19; 8 AAP Lympne 13.2.19; En route to 12 AAP Hawkinge 14.3.19 reallotted from EF to SE Area; 120 Sqn Hawkinge by 3.19 - 8.19

E9027 120 Sqn Hawkinge by 3.19 - 8.19

E9028 Rec Pk to 1 AI 9.10.18; 108 Sqn 10.10.18; On photo recce over Ledeberg attacked by five Fokker DVIIs one of which was sent down OOC smoking 12.00-12.20 30.10.18 (2/Lt RTO Hawthorne & Sgt P Hoolihan); EA OOC E of Sotteghem, shared C2216, D613, D5845, D7357, E8980 09.05 9.11.18 (2/Lt RTO Hawthorne & 2/Lt WM Elvery); 103 Sqn 24.1.19; 98 Sqn 10.3.19; 1 ASD 23.3.19

E9029 Rec Pk to 1 AI 5.10.18; 206 Sqn ('J') 6.10.18 - @4.19, crashed on nose in hedge in snow [no date]; 49 Sqn by 20.6.19; Handed in to 1 ASD 14.7.19

E9030 Rec Pk to 1 AI 9.10.18; 108 Sqn 13.10.18; 98 Sqn 23.1.19; 8 AAP Lympne 13.2.19; En route to 12 AAP Hawkinge 14.3.19 reallotted from EF to SE Area

E9031 Deld 555/6 Flts 219 Sqn Manston 8.10.18; HACP 4.11.18; Manston to Handley Page, Cricklewood for Polish Military Purchase Mission on free issue 23.3.20

E9032 Deld 557/8 Flts 212 Sqn Yarmouth by 15.10.18 - @28.10.18

E9033 No information

E9034 Rec Pk to 1 AI 7.10.18; 108 Sqn 7.10.18; Left 09.36 for bombing raid on Melle, hit by AA Ghent, seen going down NW with water streaming from radiator 24.10.18 (Capt R Russell & 2/Lt GB Pike unhurt); Salved & Bboc 108 Sqn 29.10.18; At 108 Sqn write-off applied for 25.1.19

E9035 No information

E9036 SMOP Dover by 10.18; Landed in dark, ran into bank, damaged propeller, tailskid and lower wings, 8 AAP Lympne 13.11.18 (Lt GW Stallard)

E9037 SMOP Dover by 10.18 - @11.18; 212 Sqn by 3.19 (A/S training)

E9038 1 ASD to 103 Sqn 27.10.18; 98 Sqn 11.3.19

E9039 At 2 AAP Hendon 18.10.18 for 119 Sqn (Mob) Wyton; Reallotted to EF 26.10.18

E9040 to E9042 No information

E9043 15 TDS Hucknall by 10.18

E9044 15 TDS Hucknall by 10.18 - @11.18

E9045 15 TDS Hucknall by 10.18 - @11.18

E9046 Presentation a/c 'The J.M.Dixon No.1'. 1 ASD to 98 Sqn 9.11.18; 8 AAP Lympne 12.2.19

E9047 No information

E9048 At 2 AAP Hendon 17.10.18 for 117 Sqn (Mob) Norwich; FL Thurmaston en route to sqn 29.10.18; At sqn by 12.11.18

E9049 4 ASD by 10.18; 218 Sqn 23.10.18; FL on delivery at French aerodrome Calais 24.10.18 (Lt KR Campbell & Lt LA Churchill both unhurt); to 4 ASD 24.10.18

E9050 At 2 AAP Hendon 17.10.18 for 117 Sqn (Mob) Norwich; At sqn by 2.11.18

E9051 & E9052 No information

E9053 15 TDS Hucknall by 10.18; Spun in off flat turn 9.11.18 (2/Lt CJS Tainton seriously injured)

E9054 At 2 AAP Hendon 10.10.18 for 119 Sqn (Mob) Wyton; At sqn 17.10.18; Reallotted by 18.11.18

E9055 Arr ASD Aboukir ex UK 30.9.19

E9056 Arr ASD Aboukir ex UK 30.9.19

100 D.H.9A ordered 20.3.18 under Cont No 35a/413/C292 from Mann, Egerton & Co Ltd, Norwich and numbered E9657 to E9756 (400hp Liberty 12A)

E9657 Grain by 2.19 - @8.19 (fit flotation gear); DH recond

E9658 & E9659 No information

E9660 Presentation a/c 'Hyderabad No.9'. At 3 AAP Norwich 3.8.18 for 110 Sqn (Mob) Kenley; To France with 110 Sqn 31.8.18; Attacked by 3 EA on return from raid on Frankfurt, shot 1 down but aileron controls shot away, ran out of petrol, crashed in the Vosges, crew set fire to a/c 25.9.18 (Lt CBE Lloyd slightly injured & 2/Lt HJC Elwig both PoW)

E9661 At 3 AAP Norwich 3.8.18 for 110 Sqn (Mob) Kenley; To Sqn 10.8.18;

E9662 Rec Pk to 205 Sqn 12.8.18 (its first D.H.9A); COL 1.10.18 (2/Lt G Bannerman unhurt); to 2 ASD

E9663 No information

D.H.9A E9665 '7' of the Wireless Experimental Establishment, Biggin Hill. (via J.M.Bruce/G.S.Leslie)

E9664 31 TDS(?) Fowlmere

E9665 Deld 3 AAP Norwich, tested 21.8.18; WEE Biggin Hill ('7') by 17.9.18; At Biggin Hill 15.2.19 reallotted from Store to EF

E9666 No information

E9667 3 FS Bircham Newton by 8.18 - @4.19

E9668 No information

E9669 Deld 3 AAP Norwich, tested 27.8.18; 1 SoN&BD Stonehenge, climbing turn on windy and bumpy day, stalled on turn, spun in 22.9.18 (Lt HK Dudley-Scott & F/Cdt J Wilcock both killed)

E9670 Deld 3 AAP Norwich, tested 24.8.18

E9671 Deld 3 AAP Norwich, tested 24.8.18; 1 SoN&BD Stonehenge by 18.2.19

E9672 Deld 3 AAP Norwich, tested 22.8.18

E9673 212 Sqn Yarmouth, swung on TO and crashed into fence *28.8.18 (Lt GW Stallard); 2 MOS Eastchurch by 3.19 - @7.19; PD Ascot; AD Hinaidi 3.24

E9674 to E9680 No information

E9681 1 SoN&BD Stonehenge by 10.18; APS 10.21

E9682 No information

E9683 PD Ascot; AD Drigh Rd 10.22; AP Lahore 17.1,1.22; 27 Sqn 3.23; AP Lahore 10.23; 27 Sqn 17.11.23 - 1924; 60 Sqn 9.24; Crashed on edge of aerodrome while landing, Risalpur, 22.10.24 (P/O NWF Mason OK); 27 Sqn 10.27 - 7.28; 60 Sqn 8.28 - 3.30

E9684 AD Hinaidi 5.22

E9685 PD Ascot; AD Aboukir; 84 Sqn 10.21; 4 FTS 7.25; Crashed and caught fire, Cat W 19.8.26

E9686 No information

E9687 PD Ascot; AD Drigh Rd 7.25; AP Lahore 4.24 (conv DC); 27 Sqn 9.24; AP Lahore; 60 Sqn ('N'?) 11.25 - 1.27; 27 Sqn ('A') 10.28; U/c collapsed in heavy landing

E9688 PD Ascot; AD Hinaidi; 84 Sqn 5.24; 55 Sqn 1.25; Recd UK?; 4 FTS 4.26 - 2.28

E9689 Fitted experimental flotation gear by JS White at Cowes; Grain 26.3.20; Repairs 19.4.20; Ready for trials 3.5.20; Hauled ashore after flotation tests 9.7.20; Declared surplus 3.8.20

E9690 DH recond (c/n 72); 30 Sqn 12.24 - 8.25; 55 Sqn 8.26

E9691 PD Ascot; AP Baghdad; 30 Sqn; EF, FL in river, Karradesh, nr.Baghdad 20.2.21 WOC

E9692 Arr 5(E) ARD Henlow 3.12.19 - @9.1.20 as free gift for Australia; Imperial Gift to Australia, became *A1-28*

E9693 PD Ascot; Arr ASD Aboukir 25.2.20; 47 Sqn ('U') 11.20

E9694 Allocated 5(E) ARD Henlow as free gift for Australia by 2-9.1.20; Imperial Gift to Australia, became *A1-29*

E9695 & E9696 No information

E9697 AES Grain by 3.19; AEE Martlesham W/E 22.5.19; Gosport for trials in HMS *Eagle* W/E 5.6.19; AES/AEE Grain by 8.19 (fitted Gratze hydrovane wing floats & air bags; AEE Martlesham Heath W/E 22.5.20; Gosport W/E 5.6.20 (for trials in *Eagle*); 2 FTS Duxford 10.22 - 12.22

E9698 8 AAP Lympne, tested 6-10.11.18; 6 AI to 18 Sqn 13.2.19

E9699 18 Sqn by 6.19

D.H.9A E9709 'S' of No.10 Training Depot Station, Harling Road. (J.M.Bruce/G.S.Leslie collection)

D.H.9A E9711 'A' of No.110 Squadron during the winter of 1918/19. (via Norman Franks)

D.H.9A E9735 'H' of No.18 Squadron after coming to grief at Bickendorf on 8.2.19. (J.M.Bruce/G.S.Leslie collection)

D.H.9A E9746 of No.156 Squadron. (J.M.Bruce/G.S.Leslie collection)

E9700 No information
E9701 No information
E9702 2 FS Marske 1918
E9703 PD Ascot; AD Aboukir; 4 FTS
E9704 Deld 3 AAP Norwich, tested 18.9.18
E9705 Rec Pk to 2 AI 3.10.18; 25 Sqn. left 08.15 for photo recce to Maubeuge, FTR 4.11.18 (Lt LLK Straw & 2/Lt P Cartwright both killed)
E9706 Rec Pk to 2 AI 28.9.18; to Paris 5.10.18; 3 ASD to 110 Sqn 9.10.18; 6 AP 17.10.18; 3 ASD 20.10.18
E9707 Rec Pk to 2 AI 18.10.18; 205 Sqn 29.10.18; COL new aerodrome Maubeuge 27.11.18 (Lt WH Clarke & 2/Lt CN Witham); flying again 8.12.18; Still 205 Sqn 2.19; 10 TDS Harling Road; Once coded 'A' (crashed)
E9708 Deld 3 AAP Norwich, tested 24.9.18
E9709 10 TDS Harling Road ('S'); 57 Sqn by 18.4.19
E9710 110 Sqn by 30.11.18 - @1.19
E9711 3 ASD to 110 Sqn ('A') 27.10.18; COL at Valenciennes on mail flight 11.2.19 (Lt TG Griffiths & 2/Lt WW Pritchard OK)
E9712 No information
E9713 Rec Pk to 5 AI 5.10.18; 205 Sqn 14.10.18 - @3.1.19; 57 Sqn by 5.19
E9714 Rec Pk to 5 AI 8.10.18
E9715 Rep Pk 2 ASD to 5 AI and on to 107 Sqn 17.10.18; At 2 AI 18.10.18 returned from FL (Lt LA West); 18 Sqn 30.10.18; On mail flight crashed in snow storm at Profondeville 27.3.19 (Capt RT Minors DoI)
E9716 Deld 3 AAP Norwich, tested 29.9.18; Rec Pk to 5 AI 5.10.18; 205 Sqn 14.10.18 - @3.1.19
E9717 Arr Rec Pk 16.10.18; To 3 ASD but wrecked en route 17.10.18 (2/Lt CM Thomson); Back at 2 ASD 21.10.18
E9718 No information
E9719 Deld 3 AAP Norwich, tested 14.10.18; Rec Pk to Paris 24.10.18
E9720 Arr Rec Pk 16.10.18; 2 AI 24.10.18; to 3 ASD 24.10.18, FL Auxi-le-Chateau; 2 AI to 49 Sqn 8.12.18 - @29.5.19
E9721 Rec Pk to Paris 17.10.18; 205 Sqn from 8.12.18; COL 7.2.19 (Capt PJ Barnett unhurt); to Repair Park 2 ASD
E9722 Arr Rec Pk 17.10.18; To Paris 24.10.18; 3 ASD to 110 Sqn 27.10.18 - @1.19
E9723 No information
E9724 Deld 3 AAP Norwich, tested 9.10.18; Rec Pk 24.10.18; 3 ASD 1.11.18
E9725 At 3 AAP Norwich 19.10.18 for 155 Sqn (Mob) Chingford; At sqn by 1.11.18
E9726 Deld 3 AAP Norwich 17.10.18 for 155 Sqn (Mob) Chingford; At Sqn by 25.10.18
E9727 Arr Rec Pk 24.10.18; 2 AI to 18 Sqn 21.11.18
E9728 No information
E9729 Deld 3 AAP Norwich, tested 16.10.18
E9730 Rec Pk to 2 AI 24.10.18; 18 Sqn 9.11.18; 6 SS 4.1.19
E9731 2 AI to 205 Sqn, COL with D.H.9 F6074 of 107 Sqn, WO 10.11.18 (2/Lt SJ Furze); SOC in field
E9732 At 3 AAP Norwich 19.10.18 for 155 Sqn (Mob) Chingford; At Sqn by 4.11.18
E9733 At 3 AAP Norwich by 18.10.18 for 155 Sqn (Mob) Chingford; At Sqn by 25.10.18; On ferry flight from Rec Pk to 6 AI, landed downwind, ran into soft ground and turned on nose 24.12.18 (Lt FF Woodyer OK)
E9734 No information
E9735 2 AI to 18 Sqn ('H') 21.11.18; On sqn move to Bickendorf ran into hole on landing, turned on nose 8.2.19 (Lt W Henderson & Cpl C Bradley OK)
E9736 At 3 AAP Norwich 22.10.18 for 156 Sqn (Mob) Wyton as a training m/c; To Sqn 25.10.18; Allotted to 123 Sqn Upper Heyford 21.11.18 on disbandment of 156 Sqn
E9737 At 3 AAP Norwich 23.10.18 for 156 Sqn (Mob) Wyton as a training m/c; EF, crashed en route delivery to sqn 27.10.18 (Capt AC McKelvie slightly injured); W/O
E9738 At 3 AAP Norwich 25.10.18 for 156 Sqn (Mob) Wyton; To sqn 7.11.18; Allotted to 123 Sqn Upper Heyford 21.11.18 on disbandment of 156 Sqn
E9739 At 3 AAP Norwich 25.10.18 for 156 Sqn (Mob) Wyton; To sqn 31.10.18; Allotted to 123 Sqn Upper Heyford 21.11.18 on disbandment 156 Sqn
E9740 At 3 AAP Norwich 25.10.18 for 156 Sqn (Mob) Wyton; To sqn 31.10.18; Allotted to 123 Sqn Upper Heyford 21.11.18 on disbandment 156 Sqn; At 123 Sqn by

5.12.18; U/s at Buc 12.5.19 (reallotted EF for write-off wef 6.5.19)
E9741 At 3 AAP Norwich for 155 Sqn (Mob) Chingford; To Sqn 1.11.18
E9742 2 AI to 18 Sqn 21.11.18; On sqn move to Bickendorf, misjudged landing and overran aerodrome, attempted to avoid hangar turned sharply and wrenched u/c off 8.2.19 (Lt L Hudson & Cpl A Henson OK)
E9743 99 Sqn, COL 6.1.19 (2/Lt WT Jones & Sgt AJ Renfree)
E9744 At 3 AAP Norwich 22.10.18 for 156 Sqn (Mob) Wyton; To sqn 7.11.18; Allotted to 123 Sqn Upper Heyford 21.11.18 on disbandment of 156 Sqn
E9745 Deld 3 AAP Norwich, tested 29.10.18
E9746 At 2 AAP Hendon 2.11.18 for 156 Sqn (Mob) Wyton; To sqn 7.11.18; Allotted to 123 Sqn Upper Heyford 21.11.18 on disbandment of 156 Sqn; Still 123 Sqn 5.12.18
E9747 Sold to Anti-Bolshevik Government
E9748 No information
E9749 47 Sqn Ekaterinodar by 15.8.19; Sold to Anti-Bolshevik Government; A Flt Crimean Group RAF South Russia by 4.3.20
E9750 Sold to Anti-Bolshevik Government
E9751 47 Sqn Ekaterinodar by 15.8.19; Sold to Anti-Bolshevik Government; 'A' dett RAF Instructional Mission South Russia by 17.10.19
E9752 47 Sqn Ekaterinodar by 15.8.19; Sold to Anti-Bolshevik Government
E9753 No information
E9754 Deld 3 AAP Norwich to AES Martlesham Heath 24.11.18 (special petrol tests); Left W/E 15.2.19
E9755 No information
E9756 Grain by 7.19

100 D.H.9A ordered 21.3.18 under Cont No 35a/414/C.293 from The Vulcan Motor & Engineering Co (1906) Ltd, Southport and numbered E9857 to E9956. (400hp Liberty 12A)

E9857 Grain by 2.19 - @8.19 (fitted flotation gear); MAES Grain to RAE Farnborough 20.6.21; PD Ascot; AD Hinaidi to 84 Sqn 4.8.23
E9858 2 AI to 49 Sqn 8.12.18 - @29.5.19; RAF Base Gosport 6.25 - 7.25
E9859 At 15 AAP Manchester 2.1.19 reallotted from EF to SW Area for D of T for No 1 SoN&BD Stonehenge; Still at Manchester 19.4.19 when reallotted to EF
E9860 At (E) ARD 15.2.19 allotment to EF Cancelled, a/c WOC
E9861 At 15 AAP Manchester 19.2.19 allotted to EF
E9862 At 15 AAP Manchester 19.2.19 allotted to EF; 57 Sqn by 6.19
E9863 At 15 AAP Manchester 24.4.19 allotted to EF
E9864 57 Sqn by 6.19
E9865 At 15 AAP Manchester 20.3.19 allotted to EF
E9866 No information
E9867 At 15 AAP Manchester 27.3.19 allotted to EF
E9868 Sold to American Government; To USMC Northern Bombing Group
E9869 Sold to American Government; To USMC Northern Bombing Group
E9870 Sold to American Government; To USMC Northern Bombing Group
E9871 Sold to American Government; To USMC Northern Bombing Group
E9872 Sold to American Government; To USMC Northern Bombing Group
E9873 Sold to American Government; To USMC Northern Bombing Group
E9874 Sold to American Government; To USMC Northern Bombing Group as *E-17* late 1918
E9875 Sold to American Government; To USMC Northern Bombing Group
E9876 To USMC Northern Bombing Group
NOTE - Not on official list of aircraft sold to American Government
E9877 to E9883 No information
E9884 No information
E9885 PD Ascot; AD Hinaidi; 55 Sqn; FL after hit by bullet in petrol tank and overturned in soft ground, Aqra, Iraq, Cat W 5.2.23 (F/O PW Lingwood OK)
E9886 No information
E9887 PD Ascot; AD Hinaidi 6.23; AD Aboukir; 4 FTS 7.27; After practice formation, broke away at 1,200ft and collided with E8794, both pilots being dazzled by sun Cat W 1.11.27 (F/O JH Hutchinson) [2 crew members to hospital, not clear which a/c]; AD Aboukir; Rebuilt as ER9887; 4 FTS
E9888 PD Ascot; AD Drigh Rd; 60 Sqn ('11') 1.24; Crashed on landing, 23.4.24 (Sgt D Munro); Repaired; 60 Sqn; EF,FL Shamshattu, NWF, 25.7.24 (Sgt D Munro); AD Drigh Rd 28.7.24; 60 Sqn 17.10.24 - 4.25
E9889 & E9890 No information
E9891 1 SoTT Halton 6.24 - 9.25; DH recond on Cont No 579165/25 (c/n 256); PD Ascot; AD Hinaidi; 84 Sqn 1.28 - 5.28; Ground collision, Cat M 13.1.28 (S/Ldr AH Peck OK)
E9892 & E9893 No information
E9894 PD Ascot; AD Hinaidi to 30 Sqn 19.2.23; AD Hinaidi 6.23 (fitted 550-lb bomb rack); 30 Sqn 27.6.23; 47 Sqn 7.26 - 8.26
E9895 PD Ascot; AD Aboukir; 4 FTS 8.24 - 9.24; Recd UK; DH recond; A&AEE 4.28 (test Wapiti slots); Vickers Brooklands 1933 (long-stroke oleo u/c)
E9896 At 15 AAP Manchester 19.2.19, allotted to EF
E9897 At 15 AAP Manchester 19.2.19, allotted to EF
E9898 110 Sqn, flying accident 8.6.19 (Lt WN Wilson & Lt GG Bannerman both killed)
E9899 At 15 AAP Manchester 19.2.19 allotted to EF
E9900 PD Ascot; AD Drigh Rd; 47 Sqn ('Y') 7.20; Flying from Helwan to Heliopolis to form escort to Baghdad, lost speed, spun in Heliopolis, Cat W 14.8.21 (F/O SH Potter killed)
E9901 & No information
E9902 At 15 AAP Manchester 19.2.19 allotted to EF
E9903 No information
E9904 At 15 AAP Manchester 19.2.19 allotted to EF
E9905 & E9906 No information
E9907 At 15 AAP Manchester 19.2.19 allotted to EF
E9908 PD Ascot; From Egypt to Mesopotamia with 8 Sqn (ordered 10.1.21); 8 Sqn 1.21; 30 Sqn 12.21; Engine cut on take-off, Cat W 1.9.22 (F/O GA Atkinson OK)
E9909 PD Ascot; AP Baghdad; 55 Sqn 1920 - 1921; 84 Sqn 6.22; FL in sandstorm en route Samarra, Iraq 22.6.22; Retd base; Bounced landing, Cat W 13.9.22 (F/O JS Harrison OK)
E9910 PD Ascot; AD Aboukir; 4 FTS 4.22; Spun in from 500ft, Abu Sueir, Cat W 23.8.22 (F/O HF Potter killed & F/O FWG Bedford DoI)
E9911 PD Ascot; AP Baghdad; 30 Sqn 1.21 - 3.21; 55 Sqn ('B3') 1921 - 6.22; AD Hinaidi 1.23; 55 Sqn; 9.1.24; Air mail delivery, turned too quickly, stalled, crashed, BO, Cat W 22.7.24
E9912 PD Ascot; AP Hinaidi to 55 Sqn ('B4') 11.6.21; Crashed on landing, Zakho LG, 11.1.22 (F/O PW Lingwood OK); 55 Sqn ('BIII') 6.22
E9913 PD Ascot; AP Hinaidi 6.22; 8 Sqn; Test flight, stalled and dived into ground from 1,000ft, Hinaidi, BO 23.8.22 (F/O RL Hartley AFC & AC1 A Glasby both killed)
E9914 AD Hinaidi 6.22
E9915 PD Ascot; AP Baghdad; Trg Flt, Central Air Comm Sqn, Shaibah; Unit disbanded 31.3.21
E9916 & E9917 No information
E9918 DH recond (c/n 163); PD Ascot; AD Hinaidi; 30 Sqn 6.22 - 8.22; AD Hinaidi; 30 Sqn 6.11.22; AD Hinaidi 3.23 (rebuild); 84 Sqn ('V') 16.6.23; Tipped on nose Shaibah 24.12.23; 55 Sqn 1929 - 1930
E9919 PD Ascot; AP Hinaidi; 84 Sqn, DBR when Cooper bomb dropped off H66 and exploded on take-off Nasiriyah, Cat W 30.9.21, (F/O BE Hobart DCM severely injured & LAC AW Graham slightly injured)
E9920 No information
E9921 PD Ascot; AP Hinaidi; 8 Sqn; Hit ridge and stalled on take-off Amadia LG, Cat W 31.10.22 (F/O HR Sayes OK)
E9922 PD Ascot; AP Baghdad; 30 Sqn 6.21 - 1.22; Retd UK; PD Ascot; AD Aboukir; 14 Sqn 5.28 - 4.30
E9923 No information
E9924 PD Ascot; AD Drigh Rd; AP Lahore; 27 Sqn (E') 10.24
E9925 PD Ascot; AD Drigh Rd; 27 Sqn; EF, FL 7m N of Fort Sandeman, 18.12.24; 60 Sqn ('X') 3.25; AD Drigh Rd to 60 Sqn 20.11.25; AD Drigh Rd 28.1.26; AP Lahore

3.27; 60 Sqn 3.27 - 10.28; 27 Sqn 3.29

E9926 No information

E9927 Recd Rec Pk ex UK for IF 9.8.18; 3 AD 17.8.18 [? - listed as D.H.9 D9927]

E9928 No information

E9929 At 15 AAP Manchester 14.4.19, allotted to EF; 18 Sqn by 7.19; 1 FTS Netheravon 9.27

E9930 At 15 AAP Manchester 14.4.19, allotted to EF: 6 AI to 25 Sqn 10.6.19; PD Ascot; AD Hinaidi; 30 Sqn 3.4.23

E9931 AD Hinaidi 5.22

E9932 to E9936 No information

E9937 PD Ascot; AD Aboukir; ('E') in Egypt; 47 Sqn 1.25 - 2.25; 14 Sqn

E9938 PD Ascot; AD Hinaidi to 30 Sqn 22.3.23 - 4.23

E9939 PD Ascot; AD Hinaidi 2.24 - 3.24; 55 Sqn 3.25; 8 Sqn; 39 Sqn by 1928

E9940 to E9946 No information

E9947 PD Ascot; AD Drigh Rd; 60 Sqn 5.23

E9948 PD Ascot; AD Drigh Rd; 27 Sqn ('C') 10.24 - 3.25; 27 Sqn 11.26; Crashed Jhelum, 20.9.27 (F/O EG Olson); Retd UK; PD Ascot; AD Drigh Rd 1928; AP Lahore 7.4.28; 60 Sqn 8.28; AP Lahore; 60 Sqn 6.29; 27 Sqn 7.29; 60 Sqn to AD Drigh Rd 16.2.30

E9949 PD Ascot; AD Drigh Rd; 60 Sqn ('9') 8.23 - 1.25; Returning from Dardoni after recce over Waziristan, EF, FL, Jand Junction, NWF 23.7.24 (Sgt WW Smalley unhurt); 60 Sqn 10.24 - 1.25

E9950 Tested IAAD 4.23 - 18.6.23; A&GS 7.23- 1.24

E9951 2 FTS Duxford 11.22 - 5.23; DH recond (c/n 141); 1 FTS Netheravon 9.25; While landing collided with stationary J7023, Cat R 13.10.25 (Lt (F/O RAF) E Chase RN OK); DH repair and recond on Cont No 579165/25 (c/n 231)

E9952 to E9955 No information

E9956 Deld 25.1.19; PD Ascot; AD Aboukir rebuilt as ER9956; 4 FTS 1926

300 D.H.9A ordered 26.3.18 under Cont No 35a/409/C297 from Cubitt Ltd/ National Aircraft Factory No.1, Waddon and numbered F1 to F300. Cancelled 14.9.18

[Reported that 142 completed, but no evidence of this has come to light, and none appear to have either entered service or been sold]

150 D.H.9A ordered 21.3.18 under Cont No 35a/414/C293 from Westland Aircraft Works, Yeovil and numbered F951 to F1100. (400hp Liberty 12A)

F951 Deld 5 AAP Bristol by 27.6.18; 99 Sqn post-war 9.18 [but not up to 31.12.18]

F952 Deld 5 AAP Bristol by 25.6.18; For photographic purposes given false temporary presentation name 'Infantry Records Office No.7 District Warwick' and serial "E8436"; 2 FS Marske ('17') 1918

F953 Deld 5 AAP Bristol by 30.6.18-1.7.18

F954 Coded '8'

F955 Deld 5 AAP Bristol by 28.6.18; 557/8 Flts Yarmouth by 7.18

F956 Deld 5 AAP Bristol by 1.7.18; 555/6 Flts Manston to 557/8 Flts 212 Sqn Yarmouth 22.7.18; Attacked U-boat which rose to surface and attacked aircraft W of Smith's Knoll Pillar Buoy, engine disabled, FL in sea, taken in

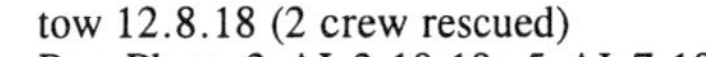

tow 12.8.18 (2 crew rescued)

F957 Rec Pk to 2 AI 3.10.18; 5 AI 7.10.18; 25 Sqn 10.18; Photo mission, Albatros C dest W of Maubeuge, then FL due to engine failure 4.11.18 (Lt JH Latchford & Lt HLH Tate OK); Rep Pk 2 ASD 4.11.18

F958 Deld 5 AAP Bristol by 30.6.18-4.7.18; 555/6 Flts 219 Sqn Manston 1918

F959 Deld 5 AAP Bristol by 30.6.18; 557/8 Flts 212 Sqn Yarmouth by 21.8.18

F960 No information

F961 Deld 5 AAP Bristol by 18.7.18

F962 No information

F963 Deld 5 AAP Bristol by 7.7.18; Became F9515

F964 Deld 5 AAP Bristol by 3.7.18; Photograph with US mechanics

F965 No information

F966 Deld 5 AAP Bristol by 24.7.18; AES Martlesham Heath 1.8.18 (bomb load tests); AES Orfordness 30.8.18 - 10.18; AES Orfordness by 8.8.19 [still there then?]

F967 Rec Pk to 2 AI 29.7.18; 3 ASD 30.7.18; 99 Sqn 28.8.18; Damaged during raid on Aricourt 2.11.18 (Lt H Sanders OK & Lt GH Power injured); 2 ASD 27.11.18; 2 AI to 49 Sqn but COL 14.12.18 (Lt BA Whitmore & 3/AM J Dorrance OK)

F968 No information

F969 PD Ascot; AD Aboukir; 4 FTS Abu Sueir Abu Sueir 5.24 - 6.25; 47 Sqn

F970 Tested IAAD 18-20.12.23; PD Ascot; AD Hinaidi; 84 Sqn 1.25; Crashed, Shaibah, 3.26 (Sgt G....)

F971 No information

F972 Deld 5 AAP Bristol by 27.7.18

F973 1 SoN&BD Stonehenge ('2')

F974 No information

F975 1 SoN&BD Stonehenge by 6.18

F976 No information

F977 Presentation Aircraft 'Hyderabad No.18'. At 7 AAP Kenley 5.8.18 for 110 Sqn (Mob) Kenley; To Sqn 21.8.18; To France with Sqn 31.8.18; Wrecked 25.9.18; 6 AP 29.9.18; 3 ASD 30.9.18; 99 Sqn 13.11.18; COL 19.3.19 (Lt JG Kershaw OK)

F978 Presentation Aircraft 'Hyderabad No.14'. At 7 AAP Kenley 2.8.18 for 110 Sqn (Mob) Kenley; At sqn by 26.8.18 ('C'); To France with sqn 31.8.18; 2 AI 28.11.18; 99 Sqn; COL 15.2.19 (Lt TCS Tuffield & Lt WJ Tremellen)

F979 7 AAP Kenley to AES Martlesham Heath 21.9.18 (prop tests, also performance and consumption tests with Zenith carburettor) - @3.5.19; Gosport for trials in HMS *Eagle* W/E 5.6.19; To AEE Martlesham Heath W/E 15.5.20; Gosport for trials in HMS *Eagle* W/E 22.5.20; 2 FTS Duxford 12.22 - 2.23; DH recond (c/n 147); PD Ascot; AD Drigh Rd; AP Lahore; 27 Sqn 1926; 60 Sqn 1927; AD Drigh Rd to 60 Sqn ('S') 22.2.28; EF, FL, Guyranwala, NWF, 27.11.28 (Sgt WC Henley); 27 Sqn c.30; 60 Sqn, also coded 'Y' and 'T'

F980 Presentation Aircraft 'Hyderabad No.2'. At 7 AAP Kenley 2.8.18 for 110 Sqn (Mob) Kenley; At Sqn by 24.8.18; To France with Sqn 31.8.18; Pfalz OOC Saverne 11.15 25.9.18 (2/Lt A Brandrick & Sgt TW Harman); Bombing raid to Kaiserslautern-Pirmasnes in poor weather, heavy combats with EAs, FTR 5.10.18

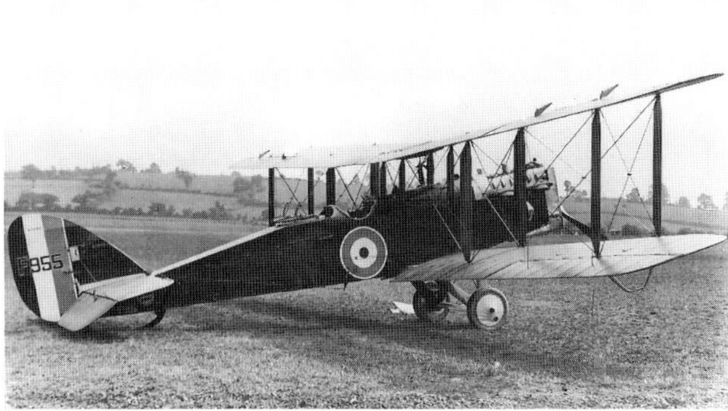

D.H.9A F955 of Nos.557/558 Flights, Yarmouth in August 1918. (J.M.Bruce/G.S.Leslie collection)

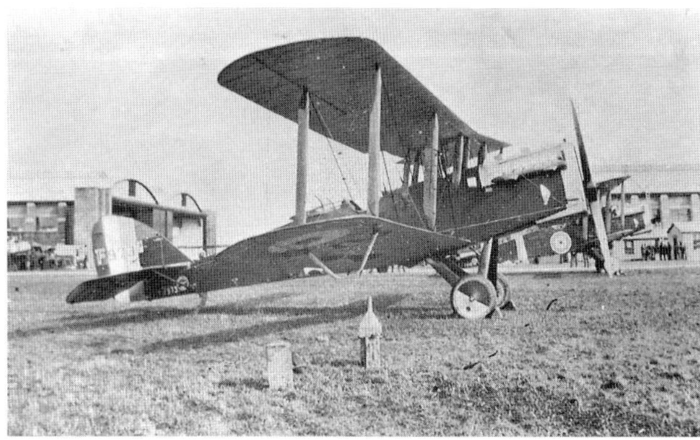

D.H.9A F973 '2' of No.2 School of Navigation & Bomb Dropping, Stonehenge. (J.M.Bruce/G.S.Leslie collection)

(2/Lt A Brandrick PoW & 2/Lt HC Eyre killed)

F981 Presentation Aircraft 'Hyderabad No.17'. At 7 AAP Kenley 2.8.18 for 110 Sqn (Mob) Kenley; To Sqn 21.8.18; To France with Sqn 31.8.18; On test flight from 3AD, landed 2 AD USAS Latrecy for directions, engine did not pick up taking off from muddy ground, wing struck bush, crashed, BO 18.10.18 (Lt HE Futcher & Lt JG Moore both badly burned, Futcher DoI 21.10.18)

F982 3 FS Sedgeford by 12.18

F983 Presentation Aircraft 'Hyderabad No.1'. Deld 5 AAP Bristol by 27.7.18 for 110 Sqn (Mob) Kenley; To Sqn 31.7.18 (but not with sqn to France 31.8.18); Left 7 AAP Kenley 10.9.18; Arr Rec Pk 11.9.18; 3 ASD to 110 Sqn 13.9.18; 6 AP 8.10.18; 3 ASD 9.10.18; 99 Sqn; COL 13.2.19 (Lt EH Buxton OK)

F984 Deld 5 AAP Bristol by 24.7.18 for 110 Sqn (Mob) Kenley; To Sqn 31.7.18 (but not with sqn to France 31.8.18); Rec Pk to 2 AI 1.10.18; 3 ASD 8.10.18 (arr 11.10.18); 110 Sqn 17.10.18; FTR bombing raid on Frankfurt 21.10.18 (Lt SL Mucklow & 2/Lt R Riffkin both PoW)

F985 Presentation Aircraft 'Hyderabad No.4'. At 5 AAP Bristol 24.7.18 for 110 Sqn (Mob) Kenley; To Sqn 31.7.18; To France with Sqn 31.8.18; FTR from Frankfurt raid, separated from formation, lost, ran out of oxygen and nearly out of fuel, FL nr Buchenbeuren in Hunsruck 21.10.18 (Mjr LGS Reynolds & 2/Lt MW Dunn PoWs)

F986 Presentation Aircraft 'Hyderabad No.5'. Deld 5 AAP Bristol by 24.7.18; for 110 Sqn (Mob) Kenley; To Sqn 31.7.18; To France with Sqn 31.8.18; 3 ASD to 110 Sqn 17.10.18; FTR from bombing raid on Frankfurt 21.10.18 (2/Lt JORS Saunders & 2/Lt WJ Brain both killed)

F987 At 5 AAP Bristol 25.7.18 for 119 Sqn (Mob) Kenley; Left 7 AAP Kenley 17.9.18; Arr Rec Pk 18.9.18; 2 AI 19.9.18; To 3 ASD 19.9.18 but FL 20km N of Le Bourget; 110 Sqn by 30.11.18; Crashed on mail flight to Cologne 26.3.19 (Lt R Burgess OK & Lt WDC Hutton DoI 28.3.19)

F988 At 5 AAP Bristol 25.7.18 for 110 Sqn (Mob) Kenley: To Sqn 2.8.18; Collided with F991 at Stonehenge, believed by pilots "showing off" on delivery to 1 SoN&BD [DATE?]

F989 Deld 5 AAP Bristol by 27.7.18 for 110 Sqn (Mob) Kenley; To Sqn but COL, CW 1.8.18

F990 Rec Pk to 205 Sqn 1.9.18; Fokker DVII OOC Busigny 15.20 15.9.18 (Lt CJ Heywood & Sgt SF Langstone); EF, FL struck fence Dinant 20.1.19 (Lt RE Morton unhurt); to 2 ASD

F991 At 5 AAP Bristol 27.7.18 for 110 Sqn (Mob) Kenley; To Sqn 1.8.18; Collided with F988 at Stonehenge, believed by pilots "showing off" on delivery to 1 SoN&BD [DATE?]

F992 Presentation Aircraft 'Hyderabad No.8'. At 7 AAP Kenley 2.8.18 for 110 Sqn (Mob) Kenley; To Sqn 8.8.18; To France with Sqn 31.8.18; Shot down in raid on Frankfurt 25.9.18 (Lt LS Brooke & 2/Lt A Provan both killed)

F993 Presentation Aircraft 'Hyderabad No.6'. At 7 AAP Kenley 2.8.18 for 110 Sqn (Mob) Kenley; To Sqn 8.8.18; To France with Sqn 31.8.18; Shot down 2 EA in raid on Frankfurt, then FL Epinal 25.9.18 (Lt RP Brailli OK & Lt RF Casey wounded); 6 AP 9.10.18; 3 ASD 11.10.18; 6 AI to 25 Sqn 13.2.19; PD Ascot; AD Drigh Rd; 27 Sqn 11.21 - 1.23; AP Lahore to 60 Sqn; EF, FL on arrival Risalpur 5.5.24 (Sgt D Munro); Repaired; 60 Sqn 8.24 - 11.24

F994 No information

F995 Presentation Aircraft 'Hyderabad No.15'. At 7 AAP Kenley 12.8.18 for 110 Sqn (Mob) Kenley; To Sqn ('E') 19.8.18; To France with Sqn 31.8.18; On Frankfurt raid FL nr Toul 21.10.18 (Lt SB Bradley & Sgt AH Banks); 6 AP 29.10.18

F996 Presentation Aircraft 'Hyderabad No.11'. At 7 AAP Kenley 2.8.18 for 110 Sqn (Mob) Kenley; To Sqn 8.8.18; To France with Sqn 31.8.18; Wrecked 16.9.18; 6 AP 21.9.18; 3 ASD 22.9.18; 110 Sqn 23.10.18; 2 AI 28.11.18; 205 Sqn 8.12.18; COL 19.1.19 (Lt RLMcK Barbour unhurt); to 2 ASD; To England 11.3.19

F997 Presentation Aircraft 'Hyderabad No.3'. At 7 AAP Kenley 2.8.18 for 110 Sqn (Mob) Kenley; To Sqn 8.8.18; To France with Sqn 31.8.18; Down smoking nr Mannheim 16.9.18 (Lt HV Brisbin & 2/Lt RS Lipsett both PoW)

F998 No information

F999 No information

F1000 Presentation Aircraft 'Hyderabad No.7'. At 7 AAP Kenley 7.8.18 for 110 Sqn (Mob) Kenley; To Sqn ('B') 2.8.18; To France with Sqn 31.8.18; Damaged in Frankfurt raid, FL, wrecked 25.9.18 (Lt HJ Cockman DFC wounded & 2/Lt CHB Stevenson OK); 6 AP 29.9.18; 3 ASD 30.9.18; 99 Sqn 13.11.18; COL on mail flight 20.12.18 (2/Lt G Jones & 2/Lt MJ Poulton OK)

F1001 205 Sqn Verviers ('L')

F1002 & F1003 No information

F1004 Presentation Aircraft 'Hyderabad No.12'. At 7 AAP Kenley 7.8.18 for 110 Sqn (Mob) Kenley; To Sqn 13.8.18; To France with Sqn 31.8.18; Wrecked 13.9.18; 6 AP 19.9.18; 3 ASD 21.9.18

F1005 Presentation Aircraft 'Hyderabad No.16'. At 7 AAP Kenley 8.8.18 for 110 Sqn (Mob) Kenley; To Sqn 19.8.18; To France with Sqn 31.8.18; Fokker DVII OOC Neustadt 14.30 25.9.18 (Capt ACH Groom & Capt GE Lange): Forced down over Koblenz with fractured petrol tank in bombing raid on Frankfurt 21.10.18 (Capt WE Windover & 2/Lt JA Simson both PoW)

F1006 557/8 Flts 212 Sqn Yarmouth, from Burgh Castle to Holt 3.9.18

F1007 Rec Pk to 2 AI 3.9.18; 205 Sqn 7.9.18; Photo recce, red-nosed Fokker DVII in flames Le Cateau 15.30 9.10.18 (Lt JG Kerr & 2/Lt G Gardner); COL from raid, u/c collapsed 4.11.18 (Capt W Grossart & 2/Lt CN Witham both unhurt); COL Halluin West 24.11.18 (Lt RK Rose unhurt); to 2 ASD

F1008 Rec Pk to 205 Sqn ('G') 1.9.18; 2 ASD 1.2.19 (poor condition)

F1009 Rec Pk to 205 Sqn 1.9.18; 2-str in flames W of Roisel 17.00 15.9.18 (2/Lt FO McDonald & 2/Lt JB Leach); Damaged by storm 17.9.18; 2 ASD 26.9.18

F1010 Presentation Aircraft 'Hyderabad No.12A'. At 7 AAP Kenley 8.8.18 for 110 Sqn (Mob) Kenley; To Sqn 21.8.18; To France with Sqn 31.8.18; Fokker DVII OOC nr Saverne 12.30 25.9.18 (Capt AG Inglis & 2/Lt WGL Bodley); Bombing raid to Kaiserslautern-Pirmanses in poor weather, heavy combats with EAs, 5.10.18 (Capt AG Inglis & 2/Lt WGL Bodley both PoW); Became one of the exhibits at the Deutsche Luftfahrt Sammlung in Berlin; It survived an RAF raid 22-23.11.43 and was found in Poland post-war; In Krakow Museum 1968; The fuselage only exchanged for Spitfire LF.XVI SM411 on 15.6.77; Rebuilt at Cardington and went to RAF Museum Hendon 1983; Extant

F1011 Arr Rec Pk 7.9.18; 2 AI 13.9.18; 3 ASD 17.9.18; 110 Sqn 18.9.18; Fokker DVII OOC W of Kaiserslautern 14.00 5.10.18 (Lt W Armstrong & Sgt WGH Ambler); On ferry flight Bettoncourt to Auxi-le-Chateau, FL and wrecked 17.11.18 (2/Lt RD Gardner & Cpl Mech E Reed OK)

F1012 No information

F1013 Rec Pk to 2 AI 16.9.18; 205 Sqn 18.9.18; COL 23.10.18 (2/Lt FO McDonald & 2/Lt RM Allen); Crashed in fog Bertangles 7.12.18 (2/Lt FO McDonald & Capt W Grossart unhurt)

F1014 Rec Pk to 205 Sqn 10.9.18; White-tailed Fokker DVII crashed nr Neuvillette-Mont d'Origny 16.40 3.10.18 (Lt RLMcK Barbour & Capt MEM Wright); Fokker DVII destroyed Busigny 08.30 9.10.18 (Lt RLMcK Barbour & Capt MEM Wright); COL 10.10.18 (2/Lt WB Esplin & 2/Lt W Wilson unhurt); flying again by 23.10.18; Fokker DVII OOC nr Charleroi 10.35 9.11.18 (2/Lt WB Esplin & 2/Lt CHL Needham); still 205 Sqn 2.1.19; Travelling flight to Louveterie, COL Ans 7.1.19 (Lt WB Esplin & 2/Lt CHL Needham unhurt); To England 11.3.19

F1015 Rec Pk to 2 AI 16.9.18; 205 Sqn 17.9.18; In action 21.9.18 (Lt WH Clarke OK & 2/Lt W Tunstall wounded); Crashed on TO 27.10.18 (2/Lt AM Duggan & 2/Lt LA Drain unhurt); No further trace

F1016 Rec Pk to 205 Sqn 1.9.18; Hannover C in flames 2m N

of St.Quentin, then Fokker DVII BU in air S of St.Quentin c.08.45 16.9.18 (Lt WE Macpherson & 2/Lt CF Ambler); Damaged by storm 19.9.18; 2 ASD 24.9.18

F1017 Rec Pk to 205 Sqn 1.9.18; EF, crashed nr aerodrome, TW 6.9.18 (Lt WE Macpherson unhurt & 2/Lt CF Ambler cut); SOS 6.9.18

F1018 7 AAP Kenley to Arr Rec Pk 13.9.18; 2 AI 15.9.18; to 3 ASD 16.9.18 but FL Louvres; 99 Sqn 14.11.18; On mail flight engine cut out crashed nr Cologne 14.2.19 (Lt LB Duggan & Capt TEH Birley OK)

F1019 Rec Pk to 2 AI 18.9.18; 205 Sqn ('C') 21.9.18; Silver grey Fokker DVII crashed into small wood Vaux-le-Prêtre, N of Brancourt-le-Grand 13.40 29.9.18 (Lt RLMcK Barbour & Capt MEM Wright); COL Valenciennes 18.1.19 (Lt HF Taylor unhurt); to 2 ASD

F1020 Arr Rec Pk 20.9.18; 2 AI 21.9.18; 3 ASD 22.9.18; 110 Sqn 6.10.18; 6 AP 23.10.18; 3 ASD 19.10.18

F1021 Arr Rec Pk 21.9.18; 2 AI 23.9.18; 3 ASD 24.9.18; 110 Sqn ('W') 26.9.18; Fokker DVII OOC between 13.00-14.00 5.10.18 (2/Lt P King & 2/Lt RG Vernon); Bombing raid on Frankfurt, shot down by EA nr target 21.10.18 (2/Lt P King PoW & 2/Lt RG Vernon PoW DoW same day)

F1022 Rec Pk to 205 Sqn 23.9.18; Left 08.35 for bombing raid, last seen in combat with EA going E nr Florennes 9.11.18 (Lt EH Johnson & Sgt Mech GE Grundy both killed)

F1023 Arr Rec Pk 20.9.18; 2 AI 23.9.18; 3 ASD 24.9.18; 110 Sqn ('J') 26.9.18; Wrecked on aerodrome 4.1.19; 2 ASD 10.1.19; 24 Sqn by 10.22 - 4.23; DH recond on Cont No 579165/25 (c/n 255); 1 FTS 8.24 - 7.25

F1024 Rec Pk to 2 AI 23.9.18; 205 Sqn 23.9.18; Shot up in combat 3.10.18 (Pilot unhurt & Sgt Mech WJH Middleton DoW 4.10.18); 1 ASD 10.18; 205 Sqn 13.10.18; White-tailed green fuselage Fokker DVII in flames N of Namur 10.11 9.11.18 (2/Lt FO McDonald & Sgt AP Pearce); 1 ASD by 11.18; 205 Sqn 12.11.18; 57 Sqn by 12.3.19; Casualty Report 24.3.19 says a/c transferred to 57 Sqn when 205 Sqn disbanded, it had not been in a hangar since 10.18, a/c waterlogged and soggy, return to depot for a complete overhaul recommended

F1025 Rec Pk to 2 AI 27.9.18; 205 Sqn 2.10.18; Fokker DVII OOC Maubeuge 15.35 4.11.18 (Mjr EG Joy & 2/Lt LA Drain); COL Germund 7.1.19 (Lt WH Clarke & Lt WR McKinlay unhurt); SOC

F1026 First in batch with new type tailplane

F1027 Left 7 AAP Kenley 17.9.18; Arr Rec Pk 18.9.18; 2 AI 18.9.18; to 3 ASD 18.9.18 (arr 20.9.18); 110 Sqn 26.9.18; Two EA OOC Treves and Kaiserslautern 5.10.18 (2/Lt ARS Proctor & Sgt F Quilter); 6 AP 21.10.18; 3 ASD 3.11.18

F1028 Arr Rec Pk 23.9.18; 2 AI 23.9.18; 3 ASD 24.9.18; 110 Sqn 26.9.18; On ferry flight Bettoncourt to Auxi-le-Chateau, FL and crashed 17.11.18 (Lt AR MacDonald & Sgt FW Hawkes OK); 3 ASD 17.11.18

F1029 Arr Rec Pk 26.9.18; 2 AI 27.9.18; 3 ASD 27.9.18 (arr 28.9.18 via Paris); 110 Sqn 28.9.18; FTR bombing raid on Frankfurt 21.10.18 (Lt J McLaren-Pearson & Sgt TW Harman both PoW)

F1030 Arr Rec Pk 16.9.18; 2 AI 17.9.18; 3 ASD 17.9.18; 110 Sqn 18.9.18; shot down in raid on Frankfurt 25.9.18 (Capt A Lindley & Lt CR Gross both PoW)

F1031 Left 7 AAP Kenley 18.9.18; Arr Rec Pk 20.9.18; 2 AI 21.9.18; 3 ASD 22.9.18 (arr 23.9.18); 99 Sqn 25.9.18; Stalled and nose dived in 4.3.19 (Lt TCS Tuffield & 2/Lt WJ Tremellen both seriously injured)

F1032 Arr Rec Pk 27.9.18; 2 AI 30.9.18; 3 ASD 1.10.18; 110 Sqn 5.10.18; Engine seized up, FL on bad ground nr Béthune 4.1.19 (Lt RP Brailli & 2/Lt CHB Stevenson OK); SOC 4.1.19

F1033 Arr Rec Pk 21.9.18; 2 AI 21.9.18; 3 ASD 22.9.18 (arr 23.9.18); 99 Sqn 25.9.18; 2 AI 27.11.18; 49 Sqn 8.12.18 - @29.5.19

F1034 Arr Rec Pk 24.9.18; 2 AI 24.9.18; to 3 ASD 28.9.18 (arr 29.9.18); 110 Sqn ('H') 5.10.18; 6 AP 17.10.18; 3 ASD 20.10.18

F1035 Arr Rec Pk 20.9.18; 2 AI 21.9.18; to 3 ASD 22.9.18 (arr 23.9.18); 99 Sqn 25.9.18; 6 AP 5.10.18; 3 ASD 11.10.18; 2 AI to 49 Sqn 8.12.18 - @29.5.19

F1036 Arr Rec Pk 26.9.18; 2 AI 27.9.18; Paris 27.9.18; 3 ASD 28.9.18; 110 Sqn 29.9.18; In combat on Kaiserslautern raid 5.10.18 (2/Lt NN Wardlaw OK & 2/Lt CJ May wounded); 6 AP 15.10.18; 3 ASD 20.10.18; 18 Sqn; COL, pilot claimed m/c was flying right wing low and he had difficulty in flying straight, on landing m/c struck ground with RH wheel and crashed 5.4.19 (Lt E Peskett & AC1 G Tunks)

F1037 No information

F1038 Arr Rec Pk 26.9.18; 2 AI 26.9.18; Propeller struck ground on take off, crashed total wreck 27.9.18 (Lt RI Drake slight facial injuries); Dismantling by 30.9.18

F1039 Arr Rec Pk 26.9.18; 2 AI 26.9.18; Paris 26.9.18; 3 ASD 29.9.18; 99 Sqn 2.10.18; 2 AI 27.11.18; 49 Sqn 8.12.18 - @29.5.19

F1040 UK to Rec Pk 25.9.18; 2 AI 25.9.18; 205 Sqn 27.9.18; COL 1.10.18 (2/Lt RE Morton & 2/Lt LA Drain); 110 Sqn 5.10.18; 6 AP 12.10.18; 3 ASD 15.10.18

F1041 Arr Rec Pk 26.9.18; 2 AI 28.9.18; Paris 2.10.18; 3 ASD 3.10.18; 110 Sqn 5.10.18; 3 ASD 6.10.18

F1042 Arr Rec Pk 28.9.18; 18 Sqn 1.10.18; On landing did a flat turn to avoid a hangar and struck ground heavily with RH wheel 22.10.18 (2/Lt G Carter & 2/Lt R Walker)

F1043 UK to Rec Pk 25.9.18; 2 AI 25.9.18; 205 Sqn 27.9.18; Green Fokker DVII in flames Grougis 16.08 11.10.18 (Capt AR McAfee & Sgt W Jones); LM 27.11.18

F1044 UK to Rec Pk 25.9.18; 2 AI 26.9.18; 205 Sqn 27.9.18; Crashed into F.2B E2255 of 20 Sqn 13.10.18 (Lt KG Nairn & 2/Lt G Bannerman unhurt); to 2 ASD

F1045 Rec Pk to 2 AI but forced landed 27.9.18, arr 3.10.18; 5 AI 8.10.18; 25 Sqn, crashed into by a French m/c at Maubeuge aerodrome 9.2.19; 6 AI 9.2.19

F1046 Rec Pk to 18 Sqn 1.10.18; On mail flight lost bearings, landed to ascertain whereabouts, ran into concealed dyke and crashed 5.4.19 (Lt HR Leach OK)

F1047 1 ASD to 18 Sqn 28.9.18; Struck ridge landing at 110 Sqn Maisoncelle 6.4.19 (Lt LR Haskell OK)

F1048 UK to Rec Pk 25.9.18; 2 AI 25.9.18; 205 Sqn ('T') 27.9.18; On low reconnaissance 22.10.18 (2/Lt EB Fielden OK & 2/Lt A Hesketh wounded); Crashed u/c landing new aerodrome Maubeuge 27.11.18 (2/Lt EB Fielden & Sgt Pawley); To England 23.2.19; 57 Sqn 9.3.19; Landing after test turned over due to bad ground 5.4.19 (Capt A MacGregor DFC & Capt JFD Tanqueray)

D.H.9A F1048 'T' of No.205 Squadron in Rhineland during the winter of 1918/19. (J.M.Bruce/G.S.Leslie collection)

F1049 Rec Pk to 2 AI 27.9.18; 205 Sqn 1.10.18; Fokker DVII OOC Charleroi 9.11.18 (Lt RJV Pulvertoft & 2/Lt WM Newton) [presumed F1049, but last digit of serial indistinct]; U/c crashed new aerodrome Maubeuge 27.11.18 (2/Lt G Gardner & Lt PN Melitus); Engine cut, crashed on aerodrome 17.1.19 (Lt WE Dipple); to 2 ASD To England 11.3.19

F1050 2 SoN&BD Andover 10.18 [? - listed as E1050]

F1051 Rec Pk to 2 AI 27.9.18; 18 Sqn 28.9.18; Casualty Report lists defects 17.3.19; To 8 SS for repair

F1052 No information

F1053 Arr Rec Pk 25.9.18; 2 AI 27.9.18; Paris 27.9.18; 3 ASD 4.10.18; 110 Sqn 6.10.18; 6 AP 15.10.18; 3 ASD 20.10.18; Shipped to England via Port Depot Rouen

F1054 Arr Rec Pk 27.9.18; 2 AI 27.9.18; Paris 28.9.18; 3 ASD 29.9.18; 110 Sqn 5.10.18; Crashed on mail flight to Cologne 9.3.19 (Lt RR Spencer OK); To 8 SS
F1055 2 SoN&BD Andover 10.18 [? - listed as E1055]
F1056 No information
F1057 No information
F1058 Rec Pk to 2 AI 27.9.18; 18 Sqn 28.9.18; Ran into hidden ditch on landing 6.12.18 (2/Lt E Carter & Lt Sparcrop OK); 6 SS 11.12.18
F1059 No information
F1060 3 ASD to 110 Sqn 22.10.18; Overran landing in bad weather, wrecked 20.1.19 (Lt SB Bradley & Sgt AH Banks OK); M/c transferred to 57 Sqn for return to the nearest repair depot; 1 ASD 26.2.19
F1061 3 ASD to 110 Sqn 17.10.18; 6 AP 23.10.18; 3 ASD 18.10.18; Shipped to England via Port Depot Rouen
F1062 2 AI to 99 Sqn 30.12.18; COL at Spa on mail flight 6.3.19 (Lt HAL Pattison & 2/Lt WE Lowrie)
F1063 3 ASD to 110 Sqn 17.10.18; 6 AP 23.10.18; 3 ASD 26.10.18; SOC W/E 30.11.18
F1064 49 TDS Catterick 9.18; 3 ASD to 110 Sqn 21.10.18; 6 AP 27.10.18; 3 ASD 29.10.18
F1065 3 ASD to 110 Sqn 22.10.18; Wrecked on landing 1.1.19 (Lt GT Griffith & 2/Lt RW Jones)
F1066 No information
F1067 Rec Pk to 1 AI 22.10.18; 18 Sqn 16.11.18
F1068 Rec Pk to 2 AI 3.10.18; 25 Sqn, left 12.35 on photo recce, Avesnes, FTR 3.11.18 (2/Lt RG Dobeson & 2/Lt FG Mills both PoW)
F1069 Rec Pk to 1 AI 16.10.18
F1070 Rec Pk to 2 AI 22.10.18; 18 Sqn 6.11.18
F1071 Arr Rec Pk 6.10.18; To 5 AI but FL Louvres 8.10.18, WO
F1072 Rec Pk to 2 AI 18.10.18; 18 Sqn 5.11.18
F1073 Test flown at Yeovil 2.10.18
F1074 At 7 AAP Kenley 15.10.18 for 155 Sqn (Mob) Chingford; At sqn by 1.11.18; 205 Sqn, FL nr Spa 7.2.19 (Capt AR McAfee unhurt); to 2 ASD
F1075 1 SoN&BD Stonehenge by 13.5.19; 207 Sqn 5.22 - 7.22
F1076 At 7 AAP Kenley 9.10.18 for 155 Sqn (Mob) Chingford; To Sqn 17.10.18;
F1077 At 7 AAP Kenley 9.10.18 for 155 Sqn (Mob) Chingford
F1078 At 7 AAP Kenley 14.10.18 for 155 Sqn (Mob) Chingford; Crashed en route to sqn 11.11.18
F1079 At 7 AAP Kenley 14.10.18 for 155 Sqn (Mob) Chingford
F1080 6 AI to 18 Sqn ('R') 14.1.19; Misjudged landing, struck ploughed land short of the aerodrome and turned over 1.3.19 (Lt RW Thurburn & Sgt T Carr OK); 8 SS 2.3.19
F1081 Arr Rec Pk 5.11.18; 3 ASD 9.11.18
F1082 At 7 AAP Kenley 28.4.19, reallotted from Store to EF
F1083 At 7 AAP Kenley 17.10.18 for 155 Sqn (Mob) Chingford; Unidentified landing ('R'), lost undercarriage landing [no date]
F1084 At 7 AAP Kenley 23.10.18 for 156 Sqn (Mob) Wyton as a training m/c; To sqn 5.11.18; Allotted to 123 Sqn Upper Heyford 21.11.18 on disbandment of 156 Sqn; At 123 Sqn by 11.12.18; 47 Sqn Ekaterinodar by 15.8.19
F1085 At 7 AAP Kenley 28.4.19, reallotted from Store to EF; At 8 AAP Lympne 27.1.19 reallotted from EF to SW Area for No 2 School of N & BD Andover
F1086 At 8 AAP Lympne 27.1.19 reallotted from EF to SW Area for No 2 School of N & BD Andover; Sold to Anti-Bolshevik Government; 47 Sqn Ekaterinodar by 15.8.19; 'A' Dett RAF Instructional Mission South Russia by 10.19; Bomb dropped from rack just after TO, crashed, other bomb exploded, BO, Beketovka 24.10.19 (F/Lt BGH Keymer DFC & Lt DB Thompson both killed)
F1087 47 Sqn Ekaterinodar by 15.8.19 - @10.19; Sold to Anti-Bolshevik Government; In service with Soviet Russian Air Force (RKKVF) by 12.21 - 1922
F1088 At 7 AAP Kenley 31.10.18 for 156 Sqn (Mob) Wyton; On disbandment of 156 Sqn 21.11.18 allotted to 123 Sqn Upper Heyford; Changed to Midland area 14.12.18; 47 Sqn Ekaterinodar by 15.8.19; Sold to Anti-Bolshevik Government
F1089 At 7 AAP Kenley 5.11.18 for 156 Sqn (Mob) Wyton; On disbandment of 156 Sqn 21.11.18 allotted to 123 Sqn Upper Heyford; 123 Sqn by 12.18 - @1.19; 47 Sqn Ekaterinodar by 15.8.19; Sold to Anti-Bolshevik Government; 'A' dett RAF Instructional Mission South Russia

D.H.9A F1098 'Q' and others of No.60 Squadron at Kohat on 18.1.27. (RAF Museum P.1087)

F1090 At 8 AAP Lympne 27.1.19 reallotted from EF to SW Area for 2 SoN&BD Andover; Sold to Anti-Bolshevik Government
F1091 At 8 AAP Lympne 27.1.19 reallotted from EF to SW Area for 2 SoN&BD Andover; 47 Sqn Ekaterinodar by 15.8.19; Sold to Anti-Bolshevik Government
F1092 At 8 AAP Lympne 27.1.19 reallotted from EF to SW Area for 2 SN&BD Andover; Sold to Anti-Bolshevik Government
F1093 At 7 AAP Kenley 21.12.18 reallotted from EF to SE Area for D of T for Pilots' Pool Joyce Green; PD Ascot; AP Baghdad; 84 Sqn 1.21; AD Hinaidi 26.6.23; 84 Sqn 12.23; 84 Sqn 2.25 - 3.25; 55 Sqn; Crashed on take-off, Nasiriyah, 16.10.27
F1094 552 Flt 221 Sqn ('G') .19; 47 Sqn Ekaterinodar by 15.8.19; Sold to Anti-Bolshevik Government; 'A' dett RAF Instructional Mission South Russia by 17.10.19 - @12.19
F1095 At 8 AAP Lympne 21.1.19 reallotted from EF to SW Area for No 2 School of N & BD Andover; 552 Flt 221 Sqn ('G') 1919; Sold to Anti-Bolshevik Government
F1096 Arr Rec Pk 10.11.18; 3 ASD 10.11.18; TOC EF 18.11.18
F1097 No information
F1098 WEE Biggin Hill ('8') by 4.11.18 - 3.20; PD Ascot; AD Drigh Rd; 60 Sqn ('8') 5.24; AD Drigh Rd; AP Lahore; 60 Sqn ('Q') 3.26 - 1.27 (India height record 1.27); 27 Sqn 1928; 27 Sqn 2.30; AD Drigh Rd 23.5.30
F1099 At 2 AAP Hendon 7.11.18 for 156 Sqn (Mob) Wyton; On disbandment of 156 Sqn 21.11.18 allotted to 123 Sqn Upper Heyford; 123 Sqn by 12.18 - @1.19
F1100 At 7 AAP Kenley 16.11.18 for 155 Sqn (Mob) Chingford; 57 Sqn 9.3.19; On landing turned over due to bad ground 8.4.19 (2/Lt FdeM Hyde & Capt Todd OK)

200 D.H.9 ordered 23.3.18 under Cont No 35a/416/C.295 (BR.396) from Waring & Gillow Ltd, Hammersmith, London and numbered F1101 to F1300. (230hp Puma)

F1101 to F1103 No information
F1104 Imperial Gift to India
F1105 No information
F1106 557/8 Flts 212 Sqn Yarmouth by 17.10.18
F1107 No information
F1108 No information
F1109 557/8 Flts 212 Sqn Yarmouth by 10.18
F1110 No information
F1111 Sold to Anti-Bolshevik Government; Deld 6 SD Ascot W/E 24.10.18; Shipped to Mudros W/E 21.11.18; Unloaded from SS *Diyatalana* on/by 25.1.20; TOC Base Depot RAF Novorossisk 14.2.20
F1112 to F1114No information
F1115 Deld 6 SD Ascot W/E 24.10.18; Shipped to Mudros W/E 21.11.18
F1116 No information
F1117 Manston, HACP 4.11.18; still Manston 3.19; Air Council Inspection Sqn by 8.19 (1 Group Ex Officers)
F1118 Rec Pk to 1 AI 16.10.18; 108 Sqn 20.10.18; EA OOC

Sotteghem, shared C2216, D613, E676, E8959, E8980 E9026 09.40-10.10 then FTR 4.11.18 (2/Lt W Shackleton & Lt JE Radley both PoW)
F1119 to F1124 No information
F1125 IAAD; Imperial Gift to India, shipped SS *Hatimura* 8.20
F1126 RAF North Russia by 9.8.19 - @10.8.19
F1127 Arr Rec Pk 7.11.18, wrecked on arrival; 6 AI to 211 Sqn 8.12.18; 98 Sqn 23.2.19; 8 AAP Lympne 6.3.19
F1129 No information
F1130 No information
F1131 At 2 AAP Hendon 11.9.18 for 117 Sqn (Mob) Norwich as a training m/c; At Sqn by 25.9.18 - @10.18
F1132 No information
F1133 Deld 6 SD Ascot W/E 24.10.18; Shipped to Mudros W/E 21.11.18; RAF North Russia by 21.7.19 - @8.19
F1134 to F1136 No information
F1137 218 Sqn by 2.10.18 - @8.10.18
F1138 Sold to Anti-Bolshevik Government; TOC Base Depot RAF Novorossisk 14.2.20; SOC 5.3.20; Later Russian Air Fleet (RKKVF)
F1139 At 2 AAP Hendon 28.12.18, reallotted from EF to 120 Sqn (Mob) Bracebridge; To sqn 31.12.18 until at least 8.19
F1140 Sold to Belgian Government
F1141 Sold to Belgian Government
F1142 Deld 6 SD Ascot W/E 24.10.18; Shipped to Mudros W/E 21.11.18
F1143 Deld 6 SD Ascot W/E 24.10.18; Shipped to Mudros W/E 21.11.18; RAF North Russia (Southern Area) by 24.8.19 - @26.8.19
F1144 Rep Pk 2 ASD to 5 AI 8.10.18; 49 Sqn 13.10.18; Ran into shell hole on take off crashed 4.11.18 (2/Lt JW McKinty & Sgt Mech RA Campbell)
F1145 No information
F1146 No information
F1147 'X' AD to Salonika AP 21.2.19; 47 Sqn for service in Russia 21.4.19; 47 Sqn Ekaterinodar by 3.6.19; Sqn records dated 11.8.19 say lost through enemy action on special mission with the Caucasian Army; Later to Soviet Russian Air Fleet (RKKVF)
F1148 Sold to Belgian Government; Became *O-BEAU*
F1149 Rep Pk 2 ASD to 2 AI 17.10.18; 211 Sqn 10.11.18; 98 Sqn 23.2.19; 8 AAP Lympne 6.3.19.
F1150 No information
F1151 At 8 AAP Lympne 24.1.19 reallotted from EF to SE Area for Store; To Russian Aviation Corps
F1152 No information
F1153 Lopcombe Corner to Stonehenge 12.9.19; Imperial Gift to India

Presentation D.H.9A F1154, seen here at Hendon, was inscribed '3rd Batt. The Durham Light Infantry'. (via Peter Green)

F1154 Presentation aircraft '3rd Batt. The Durham Light Infantry'
F1155 & F1156 No information
F1157 Rep Pk 2 ASD to 2 AI 14.10.18; 211 Sqn 29.10.18; Left 11.30 on tactical recce, FTR 4.11.18 (2/Lt CC Brouncker & 2/Lt CD Macdonald both killed)
F1158 No information
F1159 Rec Pk to 206 Sqn 1.10.18; Left 15.42, last seen British side of lines nr Deulemont 16.15 3.10.18 (Sgt Mech R Walker PoW wounded & 1/Pte AF Bailey missing believed killed)
F1160 Tested 2 AAP Hendon 10.1.19
F1161 1 SoN&BD Stonehenge by 2.19
F1162 & F1163 No information
F1164 Arr 'X' AD ex UK 24.11.18; Salonika AP 21.2.19; 47 Sqn for South Russia 21.4.19; 47 Sqn Ekaterinodar by 3.6.19; Erected 11.8.19; 'A' dett RAF Instructional Mission South Russia by 17.10.19; Sold to Anti-Bolshevik Government
F1165 120 Sqn Hawkinge by 3.19 - 8.19
F1166 Tested 2 AAP Hendon 9.1.19
F1167 Rec Pk to 1 AI 22.10.18; 108 Sqn 27.10.18; 98 Sqn 23.1.19; 8 AAP Lympne 13.2.19
F1168 RAF North Russia (Southern Area) by 6.18 - @22.8.19; Later Soviet Russian Air Fleet (RKKVF)
F1169 to F1171 No information
F1172 1 Comm Sqn Hendon/Kenley by 5.19; Became 24 Sqn 1.2.20 (C of C)
F1173 At 2 AAP Hendon by 28.12.18, reallotted from EF to 120 Sqn (Mob) Bracebridge; 120 Sqn by 1.19; Tested 2 AAP Hendon 17.3.19; Air Council Inspection Sqn by 8.19 (for Gen Seeley); Manston to Handley Page, Cricklewood for Polish Military Purchase Mission on free issue 19.3.20
F1174 Deld Hendon to Manston Naval Flt 3.10.18; Manston, prop starting accident 4.10.19 (Pilot F/O IS Bell unhurt; AC2 C Culley injured); Manston to Handley Page, Cricklewood for Polish Military Purchase Mission on free issue 24.3.20
F1175 No information
F1176 At 2 AAP Hendon 17.10.18 for 117 Sqn (Mob) Norwich; To sqn 30.12.18 - @9.19
F1177 & F1178 No information
F1179 Observers School of Recce & Aerial Photography Shrewsbury, EF, dived in off turn at 400ft, BO 18.2.19 (Lt CE Preece & AC1 H Welsh both killed)
F1180 Arr 'X' AD ex UK 24.11.18; 20.6 Sqn Helwan 16.7.19; Special Instruction Flight Almaza by 7.20 - @11.20
F1181 Presented to Canada 2.19 to help form nucleus of RCAF
F1182 At 2 AAP Hendon 4.10.18 for 119 Sqn (Mob) Wyton; At Sqn by 29.10.18; Reallotted by 18.11.18
F1183 No information
F1184 Imperial Gift to India
F1185 104 Sqn by 8.12.18; Rec Pk 21.1.19; En route to 12 AAP Hawkinge 14.3.19 reallotted from EF to SE Area; 120 Sqn Hawkinge by 3.19 - 8.19
F1186 No information
F1187 47 Sqn Ekaterinodar, on landing crashed into F1196 17.10.19 (Lt JJ Clow & Lt W Bourne)
F1188 At 2 AAP Hendon 4.10.18 for 119 Sqn (Mob) Wyton; At Sqn by 29.10.18; Reallotted by 18.11.18
F1189 Tested 2 AAP Hendon 3.1.19
F1190 At 2 AAP Hendon 9.10.18 for 119 Sqn (Mob) Wyton; At sqn by 29.10.18; Reallotted to EF; TOC EF 13.11.18; 1 ASD to 108 Sqn 8.12.18; 98 Sqn 23.1.19; 8 AAP Lympne 13.2.19
F1191 Manston, HACP 10.11.18 (prefix?)
F1192 No information
F1193 Arr 'X' AD ex UK 24.11.18; TOC Salonika AP 19.2.19; 47 Sqn for service in south Russia 21.4.19; 47 Sqn Ekaterinodar by 3.6.19; Engine failure, crashed Dimskaya 10.6.19 (Lt EC White & Lt JW Webb OK); Flying again 19.6.19; 'A' Dett Instructional Mission south Russia to store w/e 3.11.19 for repair, fuselage only; Sold to Anti-Bolshevik Government
F1194 & F1195No information
F1196 47 Sqn Ekaterinodar, damaged when crashed into by F1187 which was landing 17.10.19
F1197 No information
F1198 At 2 AAP Hendon 16.10.18 for 117 Sqn (Mob) Norwich; To sqn 19.12.18 - @1.19
F1199 No information
F1200 2 AI to 27 Sqn 22.11.18; 98 Sqn 1.3.19; 8 AAP Lympne 8.3.19;
F1201 Presentation Aircraft 'City of Glasgow, Canada'. Tested 2 AAP Hendon 12.1.19; Sold to Belgian Government; Became *No.8*, 8th Belgian Sqn [sic]
F1202 Arr 'X' AD ex UK 24.11.18; TOC Salonika AP 19.2.19; 47 Sqn for service in South Russia 21.4.19; At 47 Sqn Ekaterinodar by 3.6.19; Erected 4.7.19; 'A' Dett Instructional Mission south Russia to store w/e 3.11.19,

D.H.9A F1210 at Beresnik, North Russia, around August 1919. (via Frank Cheesman)

fuselage only; Sold to Anti-Bolshevik Government
F1203 Presentation Aircraft 'Australia No.26'. Tested 2 AAP Hendon 1.3.19
F1204 Sold to Belgian Government
F1205 No information
F1206 Deld Hendon to Manston Naval Flight 26.11.18 - @1.19
F1207 & F1208 No information
F1209 In service with Soviet Russian Air Force (RKKVF) 7.20
F1210 RAF Contingent, Bereznik, North Russia 1919
F1211 to F1212 No information
F1213 Arr 'X' AD ex UK 24.11.18; 206 Sqn Helwan 16.7.19
F1214 & F1215 No information
F1216 Became *G-EBEJ*
F1217 6 SD Ascot, allotted Anti-Bolshevik Govt for General Denikin; Re-allotted Polish Military Purchase Mission on free issue 22.4.20; Despatched port for shipment in SS *Neptune* 28.4.20
F1218 No information
F1219 4 SoN&BD Thetford by 11.18 [prefix?]
F1220 No information
F1221 Became *O-BLAC*
F1222 Presentation Aircraft 'Australia No.26, Queensland No.2, The Banchory' (presented by E.Landerdale Ramsey of Banchory.); Tested 2 AAP Hendon 2.4.19
F1223 (to D.H.9C) Became *O-BELG*, later *G-EBUN*, later *VT-AAL*
F1224 1 ASD to 103 Sqn 27.11.18; 98 Sqn 10.3.19; 1 ASD 17.3.19
F1225 Arr Rec Pk 4.11.18; 3 ASD 9.11.18; Meteor Flight by 7-21.7.19
F1226 1 FS Turnberry by 3.11.18 [prefix?]
F1227 Presentation Aircraft 'Australia No.27, Victoria No.2, The Murroa'.
F1228 to F1230 No information
F1231 At 2 AAP Hendon 10.10.18 for 119 Sqn (Mob) Wyton; Reallotted to 117 Sqn (Mob) Norwich 18.10.18; At sqn by 2.11.18; Arr Rec Pk 7.11.18; 3 ASD 9.11.18
F1232 Sold to Anti-Bolshevik Government; Deld 6 SD Ascot W/E 24.10.18; Shipped to Mudros W/E 21.11.18; TOC Base Depot RAF Novorossisk 14.2.20; To Russian Aviation Corps 14.2.20
F1233 Deld 6 SD Ascot W/E 24.10.18; Shipped to Mudros W/E 21.11.18; Arr ASD Aboukir ex UK 10.1.20; To Russian Aviation Corps
F1234 At 2 AAP Hendon 14.10.18 for 119 Sqn (Mob) Wyton; Reallotted to 117 Sqn (Mob) Norwich 18.10.18; To sqn 29.10.18 - @4.19.
F1235 to F1237 No information
F1238 Imperial Gift to Australia; Shipped on SS *Australmad*; allotted CFS (Australia), Point Cook 24.9.20; 1 FTS AAF, Point Cook 31.3.21; Became *A6-6* 3.10.21
F1239 & F1240No information
F1241 55 TS Narborough by 8.19 - 9.19 [prefix?]
F1242 At 2 AAP Hendon 16.10.18 for 117 Sqn (Mob) Norwich; At sqn by 7.11.18 - @12.18
F1243 Sold to Russia
F1244 & F1245 No information
F1246 Imperial Gift to India
F1247 Deld 6 SD Ascot W/E 24.10.18; Shipped to Mudros W/E 21.11.18; To RAF in North Russia
F1248 Deld 6 SD Ascot W/E 24.10.18; Shipped to Mudros W/E 21.11.18
F1249 No information
F1250 Deld 6 SD Ascot W/E 24.10.18; Shipped to Mudros W/E 21.11.18

D.H.9 F1255 was probably with No.15 Training Depot Station at Hucknall. (via J.M.Bruce/G.S.Leslie collection)

F1251 Arr AES Martlesham Heath W/E 12.4.19 (Zenith carburettor tests); Left by air W/E 7.7.19
F1252 Imperial Gift to New Zealand; New Zealand Flying School, Auckland
F1253 & F1254No information
F1255 15 TDS Hucknall by 10.18 (prefix?); Presented to Canada 2.19 to help form nucleus of RCAF
F1256 & F1257 No information
F1258 Tested 2 AAP Hendon 24.3.19; Sold to French Government; In Musée de l'Air, Chalais-Meudon, near Paris by 1957, fuselage marked 'A' Battery, 2nd Siege Artillery, Reserve Brigade
F1259 to F1262No information
F1263 120 Sqn Hawkinge by 3.19 - 4.19; 6 AI to 49 Sqn 8.6.19; 1 ASD 14.7.19
F1264 to F1268 No information
F1269 'A' dett for repair South Russia Instructional Mission 3.11.19
F1270 & F1271 No information
F1272 At 7 AAP Kenley 3.12.18 reallotted from EF to Midland Area
F1273 & F1274 No information
F1275 Sold to Belgian Government
F1276 No information
F1277 3 (T) Group Navigation School, Norwich, crashed on TO Feltwell 2.9.19 (Sgt DS Chaundy) [prefix?]
F1278 Became *G-EAQM*
F1279 6 AI to 211 Sqn 11.2.19; 98 Sqn 23.2.19; 8 AAP Lympne 6.3.19
F1280 No information
F1281 At Fairlop 6.2.19, allotment to EF cancelled, WOC
F1282 Imperial Gift to India
F1283 49 Sqn, handed in to 1 ASD 14.7.19
F1284 No information
F1285 Sold to Russia
F1286 Became *G-EBEI* (ferry markings)
F1287 No information
F1288 4 SoN&BD Thetford
F1289 & F1290 No information
F1291 At 2 AAP Hendon 29.10.18 for 120 Sqn (Mob) Bracebridge; Still at AAP 27.12.18; 120 Sqn by 1.19
F1292 15 TDS Hucknall by 11.18 (prefix?)
F1293 Sold to Belgian Government; Became *O-BIEN*, later *OO-IEN*
F1294 Tested 2 AAP Hendon 30.1.19; 49 Sqn, handed in to 1 ASD 14.7.19
F1295 Imperial Gift to Australia; Shipped on SS *Australmad*; allotted CFS (Australia), Point Cook 24.9.20; To 1 AD; Retd CFS 21.2.21; 1 FTS AAF, Point Cook 31.3.21; Became *A6-8* 3.10.21
F1296 to F1299 No information
F1300 Deld 15.3.19; To Greek Government

50 D.H.9A ordered 28.3.18 on BR.437 under Cont No 35a/573/C.472 from Westland Aircraft Works, Yeovil and numbered F1603 to F1652. (400hp Liberty 12A)

F1603 to F1608 No information
F1609 Deld RAE Farnborough 18.12.18; AD Taranto to 'X' AD 28.6.19; SOC at ASD Aboukir 28.8.19
F1610 No information
F1611 At 7 AAP Kenley 31.10.18 for 156 Sqn (Mob) Wyton; To sqn by 12.11.18; Allotted to 123 Sqn on disbandment of 156 Sqn 21.11.18; 1 Sqn CAF; 1 FTS 4.21; 24 Sqn 3.22 - 7.22; Irish Flt 8.22 - 7.22; Tested IAAD 4.5.23; 39 Sqn 6.23; 39 Sqn ('6') 1924; 39 Sqn ('4'); A&AEE 3.26 - 6.26; A&AEE (15 Sqn) 6.11.26
F1612 The same unit as F.K.8 H4467
F1613 No information
F1614 PD Ascot; AD Hinaidi; 30 Sqn 2.24; AD Hinaidi 7.24
F1615 PD Ascot; AD Hinaidi 5.23 - 6.23 (fit special tank); 30 Sqn 8.23
F1616 Westland 25.10.18; Feltham 19.11.18; Shrewsbury 5.7.19; Spittlegate 26.3.20 (storage); First flew there 21.6.22 (20hrs 15min); 'A' Flt 207 Sqn ('A') 28.9.22 - @2.24; Hit wireless mast 6.7.23; 1 FTS Netheravon, practice landing, wheel buckled, went on nose 20.5.25 (Lt (F/O RAF) JE Vallance RN & passenger OK)
BUT 6 SD Ascot for packing 9.20; 207 Sqn, tested 31.10.20
F1617 No information

D.H.9A F1612, with the tail of F.K.8 H4467 visible behind, appears to have a camera protruding under the observer's cockpit. (via Philip Jarrett)

F1618 At 7 AAP Kenley 16.11.18 for 155 Sqn (Mob) Chingford; 6 AI to 205 Sqn, COL Verviers 13.2.19 (Lt YH Sox); to 2 ASD
F1619 Arr Rec Pk 9.11.18; 3 ASD 9.11.18
F1620 No information
F1621 24 Sqn Kenley by 10.20
F1622 31 TDS Fowlmere by 10.18
F1623 AP Lahore; 60 Sqn ('7') 22.7.23 - 10.23; 60 Sqn ('11') 2.24 - 5.24; AP Lahore; 27 Sqn 22.3.25 - 9.25
F1624 & F1625 No information
F1626 552 Flt 221 Sqn ('F') 1919; Sold to Anti-Bolshevik Government
F1627 to F1630 No information
F1631 PD Ascot; AD Hinaidi; 8 Sqn 17.5.23; AD Hinaidi 8.23; 5 Sqn 1.24
F1632 Rebuilt 1921 as H.P. X.4B and renumbered J6914 (was to have been J6906)
F1633 No information
F1634 At Bristol AAP 27.11.18 for 123 Sqn (Mob) Upper Heyford; To sqn by 31.12.18 - @1.19
F1635 1 SoN&BD Stonehenge by 12.2.19 - @7.19; Old Sarum
F1636 At Cranwell 16.4.19 allotted to EF; RAF (Cadet) College, Cranwell
F1637 to F1639 No information
F1640 PD Ascot; AD Hinaidi 6.22; 8 Sqn; Crash on landing Halebja, Iraq 6.9.22 (S/Ldr GH Bowman); burnt by enemy
F1641 PD Ascot; AD Aboukir; 47 Sqn 9.23 - 11.23; Retd UK; DH recond on Cont No 726079/26 (c/n 316); HAD 9.27; 39 Sqn 11.27 - 8.28; HAD 7.29
F1642 PD Ascot; AD Hinaidi 5.22 - 9.22; AD Hinaidi by 2.23; 55 Sqn 20.9.23; Spun in from 1,500ft, Mosul, Cat W 14.12.23
F1643 PD Ascot; AD Drigh Rd; 27 Sqn, formation practice, overturned landing, shock absorber broke, Risalpur, 9.3.22 (F/O SB Harris unhurt & F/O RB Luard slightly injured)
F1644 PD Ascot; AP Baghdad; 84 Sqn 2.21 - 4.22; Propeller accident, Sargassh Urynka, 2.2.21 (F/O JB Stockbridge slightly injured); Crashed on landing, Cat W 12.4.22 (P/O CE Kelly)
F1645 4 FTS Abu Sueir 11.24 - 10.25
F1646 FF 17.6.20; 24 Sqn, test flight, flat spin off low climbing turn, BO, Kenley 12.7.20 (F/O VO Reynolds & AC2 Mech P Braithwaite both killed)
F1647 to F1651 No information
F1652 Deld 23.11.18

100 D.H.9 ordered 15.4.18 under Cont No A.S.19174 from Westland Aircraft Works, Yeovil and numbered F1767 to F1866. (230hp Puma)
[NOTE. Delivery doubtful as batch not in Ministry of Munitions statistics of Output of Aeroplanes 1914 to 1919]

F1767 to F1792 No information
F1793 25 TS Thetford 1918 [doubtful?]
F1794 to F1844 No information
F1845 6 TDS Boscombe Down by 21.10.18

F1846 to F1855 No information
F1856 6 TDS Boscombe Down by 13.11.18
F1857 to F1866 No information

170 D.H.9A ordered 25.4.18 on BR.398 under Cont No 35a/781/C.669 from F.W.Berwick & Co, London and numbered F2733 to F2902. (400hp Liberty 12A)

F2733 Arr Rec Pk 17.10.18; 3 ASD 2.11.18
F2734 1 AI to 18 Sqn ('W') 1.11.18; Misjudged landing in bad weather, ran into ploughed land, overturned 22.3.19 (Lt RW Thurburn OK)
F2735 At 2 AAP Hendon 4.10.18 for 155 Sqn (Mob) Chingford as a training m/c; With sqn by 22.10.18 - 11.18
F2736 At 2 AAP Hendon 4.10.18 for 155 Sqn (Mob) Chingford as a training m/c; At Sqn by 21.10.18;
F2737 Arr Rec Pk 16.10.18; To Paris 24.10.18; 3 ASD to 99 Sqn 14.11.18; Lost bearings in fog, COL at French aerodrome 16.11.18 (Sgt CFR Hemphill & 2/AM AT Hancock OK); 3 ASD 18.11.18
F2738 Arr Rec Pk 22.10.18; To 2 AI but FL weather Auxi-le-Chateau 24.10.18; 3 ASD 27.10.18; 2 AI to 49 Sqn 15.12.18; 6 AI 8.6.19
F2739 (Liberty) Arr Rec Pk 23.10.18; FL due to engine failure 30.10.18 (Lt A Russell); 99 Sqn 1919
F2740 At 2 AAP Hendon 12.10.18 for 155 Sqn (Mob) Chingford; FF 17.10.18; to Sqn by 22.10.18; Engine failed, pilot lost control, FL, stalled, crashed West Essex Golf Links 3.12.18 (2/Lt T Richardson & Sgt CHC Noyes both killed)
F2741 At 2 AAP Hendon 15.10.18 for 155 Sqn (Mob) Chingford; To sqn by 22.10.18
F2742 First in batch with new type tailplane
F2743 PD Ascot; AD Aboukir; 4 FTS Abu Sueir
F2744 18 Sqn by 7.19 - @8.19
F2745 No information
F2746 1 SoN&BD Stonehenge by 29.4.19
F2747 Rebuilt as H7204 17.12.18
F2748 No information
F2749 At 2 AAP Hendon 30.12.18 reallotted from EF to SE Area for 123 Sqn (Mob) Upper Heyford; 123 Sqn by 12.18 - 1.19
F2750 No information
F2751 On ferry flight from 6 AI to 205 Sqn engine gave out, FL crashed, a/c "mysteriously" caught fire 20.1.19 (Lt ASM Meyrick-Jones)
F2752 & F2753No information
F2754 At 2 AAP Hendon 4.11.18 for 156 Sqn (Mob) Wyton; On disbandment of 156 Sqn 21.11.18 allotted to 155 Sqn Chingford; At sqn by 3-11.12.18

D.H.9A F2755 of No.2 Squadron, CAF at Shoreham. In the background is captured Rumpler CVII 9949. (J.M.Bruce/G.S.Leslie collection)

F2755 At 2 AAP Hendon 4.11.18 for 156 Sqn (Mob) Wyton; On disbandment of 156 Sqn 21.11.18 allotted to 123 Sqn Upper Heyford; At sqn by 10.12.18; 2 Sqn CAF Shoreham; PD Ascot; AD Drigh Rd
F2756 57 Sqn by 6.19 - 7.19
F2757 PD Ascot; AD Aboukir; 4 FTS Abu Sueir 12.27 - 3.28
F2758 No information
F2759 2 AAP Hendon, prop accident 2.12.18 (2/AM C Ford injured)
F2760 & F2761 No information
F2762 PD Ascot; AD Aboukir; 47 Sqn 2.23; En route to AD Aboukir, stalled on gliding turn at 20ft, Helwan, 21.7.24 (F/O MB Mackay & Cpl HJ Bath both injured)
F2763 27 Sqn 1920; PD Ascot; AD Aboukir 4.25 - 6.25; Rebuilt as FR2763; 4 FTS Abu Sueir ('6') 10.25 - 5.27; Remains on Abu Sueir dump 1929
F2764 At 2 AAP Hendon 28.2.19 reallotted from Midland Area to EF; Still at 2 AAP Hendon 12.4.19 allotted to EF; PD Ascot; AD Hinaidi; 84 Sqn 2.25 - 3.25
F2765 At 2 AAP Hendon 12.4.19, allotted to EF
F2766 At 2 AAP Hendon 28.1.19 allotted to EF
F2767 At 2 AAP Hendon 28.1.19 allotted to EF; Still at 2 AAP Hendon 20.3.19 allotted to EF
F2768 At 2 AAP Hendon 28.1.19 allotted to EF; Still at 2 AAP Hendon 18.3.19 allotted to EF
F2769 At 2 AAP Hendon 28.1.19 allotted to EF; Still at 2 AAP Hendon 27.3.19 allotted to EF
F2770 PD Ascot; AP Hinaidi; 55 Sqn 2.22 - 3.22
F2771 PD Ascot; AD Hinaidi; 30 Sqn 5.24; 8 Sqn 6.24; 30 Sqn 10.24 - 3.25; Retd UK; 39 Sqn 8.27 - 3.28
F2772 PD Ascot; AD Drigh Rd; 27 Sqn ('E') 12.24 - 9.25; 27 Sqn ('C')
F2773 No information
F2774 PD Ascot; AD Drigh Rd; AP Lahore 28.1.23; 27 Sqn ('L') 7.23; 60 Sqn, crashed on take-off 10.9.24 (P/O CH Ratcliffe & AC WJT Gomm both slightly injured); 27 Sqn, crashed, Arawali, 11.24
F2775 PD Ascot; AP Baghdad; 55 Sqn 5.8.20; Port tyre burst on landing, Cat W 4.6.21 (F/O HW Westaway)
F2776 2 AAP Hendon 12.4.19 allotted to EF; Arr 5(E) ARD Henlow 5.12.19 - @9.1.20 for Australia; Imperial Gift to Australia; CFS (AAC), Point Cook, Ff 14.5.20 (Capt AT Cole); Forced landed Point Cook 29.6.20 (Capt AT Cole); To 1 FTS Laverton 31.3.21; Became *A1-16* 3.10.21
F2777 At 2 AAP Hendon 28.1.19 allotted to EF; Tested 26.2.19; Still at 2 AAP Hendon 27.3.19 allotted to EF;
F2778 DH recond; 55 Sqn ('CIII') 1926
F2779 At 2 AAP Hendon 12.4.19 allotted to EF; Arr 5(E) ARD Henlow 5.12.19 - @9.1.20 for Australia; Imperial Gift to Australia; CFS (AAC), Point Cook by 1920 (used for experimental work with petrol tanks); Set Australian altitude record of 27,000ft 17.6.20 (Capt A Cole & Capt H De La Rue); To 1 FTS Laverton 31.3.21; Became *A1-17* 3.10.21
F2780 At 2 AAP Hendon 12.4.19 allotted to EF;
F2781 At 2 AAP Hendon 12.4.19 allotted to EF; 39 Sqn 9.22; RAF (Cadet) College, Cranwell 2.24 - 1.30
F2782 PD Ascot; AD Drigh Rd; 27 Sqn ('J') 9.10.22; Hit by E8726 of 60 Sqn, Risalpur, 23.1.24; AP Lahore 10.24 - 12.24
F2783 PD Ascot; AD Drigh Rd; 30 Sqn 1920; 27 Sqn
F2784 PD Ascot; Arr AD Aboukir 10.3.20; 47 Sqn 4.22
F2785 PD Ascot; AP Baghdad; 30 Sqn; Shot through longerons, 15.7.20; Repaired; FL on rough ground in desert, Cat W 14.5.21
F2786 No information
F2787 PD Ascot; Left UK for 55 Sqn 16.2.20; Arr ASD Aboukir 25.2.20; Retd UK?; RAF (Cadet) College, Cranwell 9.24 - 10.24; AD Drigh Rd; 27 Sqn ('K') 12.28 - 1.30
F2788 IAAD; RAF (Cadet) College, Cranwell 21.11.24; PD Ascot; AD Drigh Rd; 27 Sqn
F2789 to F2792 No information
F2794 At 2 AAP Hendon 14.2.19 reallotted from SE Area for Store to EF; Still at 2 AAP Hendon for EF 12.4.19; PD Ascot; AD Aboukir; 47 Sqn 3.22 - 9.22
F2795 At 2 AAP Hendon 14.2.19 reallotted from SE Area for Store to EF
F2796 At 2 AAP Hendon 14.2.19 reallotted from SE Area for Store to EF; Still at 2 AAP Hendon for EF 12.4.19; PD Ascot; AD Aboukir 4.24; 4 FTS Abu Sueir; Crashed; Retd UK; Repaired; A&AEE 7.26 - 8.26; RAE 19.8.26; A&GS Eastchurch 11.27 - 5.30
F2797 At 2 AAP Hendon 1.2.19 reallotted from SE Area for Store to EF
F2798 At 2 AAP Hendon 1.2.19 reallotted from SE Area for Store to EF; At Richborough 5.3.19 reallotted to

"Elopeforce" (the Allied EF to Archangel); RAF North Russia (Southern Area) by 6.19

F2799 At 2 AAP Hendon 1.2.19 reallotted from SE Area for Store to EF; At Richborough 5.3.19 reallotted to "Elope"; RAF North Russia (Southern Area) by 6.19

F2800 At 2 AAP Hendon 1.2.19 reallotted from SE Area for Store to EF

F2801 At 2 AAP Hendon 1.2.19 reallotted from SE Area for Store to EF; 18 Sqn, crashed Merheim, Cologne 30.6.19; To Canada; Crashed Camp Borden

F2802 At 2 AAP Hendon 1.2.19 reallotted from SE Area for Store to EF

F2803 At 2 AAP Hendon 1.2.19 reallotted from SE Area for Store to EF; At Richborough 5.3.19 allotted to Elope; RAF North Russia (Southern Area) by 6.19

F2804 At 2 AAP Hendon 1.2.19 reallotted from SE Area for Store to EF; At Richborough 5.3.19 allotted to Elope; RAF North Russia (Southern Area) by 6.19

F2805 At 2 AAP Hendon 1.2.19 reallotted from SE Area for Store to EF; At Richborough 5.3.19 allotted to Elope; RAF North Russia (Southern Area) by 29.6.19 - @7.19

F2806 At 2 AAP Hendon 14.2.19 reallotted from SE Area for Store to EF; Still at 2 AAP Hendon 12.4.19 allotted to EF; PD Ascot; AD Aboukir; Rebuilt a FR2806; 4 FTS Abu Sueir 'A' Flt, u/c collapsed landing [no date] (LAC Thom); AD Hinaidi by 1.23

F2807 At 2 AAP Hendon 21.2.19 allotted to EF; PD Ascot; AD Aboukir; 4 FTS Abu Sueir 10.23; Spun in from 800ft, 2m NW of Abu Sueir, BO, Cat W 17.10.24 (F/O RG Peckover killed)

F2808 At 2 AAP Hendon 7.2.19 allotted to EF

F2809 From Egypt to Mesopotamia with 8 Sqn (ordered 10.1.21); 8 Sqn 1.21; 30 Sqn 9.21

F2810 PD Ascot; AP Baghdad; 30 Sqn 9.21 - 2.22

F2811 No information

F2812 PD Ascot; AD Drigh Rd 8.22; AP Lahore 4.9.22; 27 Sqn 9.22; AP Lahore 2.24; 60 Sqn ('12') 2.24; Crashed on landing, Risalpur, 14.5.24 (Sgt WW Smalley & AC2 AE White unhurt); 60 Sqn 2.25

F2813 PD Ascot; AD Aboukir; 4 FTS Abu Sueir 10.23 - 12.23; AD Hinaidi; 55 Sqn ('B4') 12.26 - 6.27

F2814 No information

F2815 PD Ascot; AD Hinaidi from 10.23; 30 Sqn 1927

F2816 PD Ascot; AD Aboukir; 4 FTS crashed and broke back, Abu Sueir, c.22/3; AD Aboukir 8.24

F2817 PD Ascot; AD Hinaidi by 1.23; 30 Sqn 1.23 - 3.23

F2818 6 SD Ascot for packing 9.20; 'A' Flt 207 Sqn ('A'), tested 3.11.20 - 8.24; DH recond (c/n 142); RAF (Cadet) College, Cranwell 4.28 - 7.28

F2819 207 Sqn 5.23 - 8.24; PD Ascot; AD Hinaidi; 55 Sqn 1927

F2820 6 SD Ascot for packing 9.20; 207 Sqn, tested 26.10.20 - 1923

F2821 to F2827 No information

F2828 DH rebuilt and renumbered J7304 (c/n 121)

F2829 to F2832 No information

F2833 PD Ascot; AP Baghdad; 30 Sqn 3.20; FL Shora, Mesopotamia, 17?.8.20; Repaired and overhauled on Sqn; AP Baghdad 18.9.20; 55 Sqn; Crashed on landing, Cat W 15.6.21 (F/O F Carpenter OK)

F2834 No information

F2835 PD Ascot; AP Baghdad; 30 Sqn 4.20 - 6.20; EF, FL, went on nose returning from bombing raid, 25.4.20; Repaired on Sqn

F2836 PD Ascot; AP Baghdad; 8 Sqn; FL and crashed nr. Baghdad West, Cat W 26.10.21 (F/O RE Keys DFC & another both OK)

F2837 Desp UK to AD Aboukir 12.3.20

F2838 30 Sqn by 4.20 - 6.20; EF, FL, overturned 24.4.20 (repaired on Sqn); Shot through petrol tanks and lower plane, 17.7.20; 84 Sqn, shot down while dropping food to a stranded F.2b crew, FL in river, Dangatora, 20m SW of Samarra, Iraq, crew seen to wade ashore, 22.9.20 (F/O HCE Bockett-Pugh DFC & F/O IDR McDonald MC DFC taken prisoner and killed)

F2839 PD Ascot; AD Hinaidi to 84 Sqn (Spade motif on fin) 19.6.23 - @12.23; 84 Sqn 6.24 - 10.24 & 4.25; 84 Sqn 5.26 - 4.27

F2840 PD Ascot; AD Hinaidi; 30 Sqn

F2841 No information

F2842 PD Ascot; AD Hinaidi; 8 Sqn by 12.22; AD Hinaidi 28.10.23; DH recond on Cont No 579165/25 (c/n 176); PD Ascot; AD Hinaidi; 55 Sqn ('CIII') 1926

F2843 PD Ascot; AD Hinaidi; 8 Sqn 1.23; AD Hinaidi by 2.23

F2844 PD Ascot; AD Hinaidi by 6.22 - @7.22; 8 Sqn; Hit buried object landing into sun, Kirkuk LG, Cat W 10.8.22 (F/O GL Carter OK)

F2845 PD Ascot; AP Baghdad to 55 Sqn 28.6.21 - @3.22

F2846 PD Ascot; AD Hinaidi to 84 Sqn 18.6.23 - @9.23; Rebuilt; 30 Sqn 10.24; AD Hinaidi 14.10.24

F2847 PD Ascot; AD Aboukir; 4 FTS Abu Sueir ('5') 10.23 - 11.23; Crashed; Retd UK; DH recond on Cont No 726079/26 (c/n 311); 39 Sqn by 2.26; Hendon to HAD 16.6.27

F2848 PD Ascot; AD Hinaidi to 84 Sqn 27.3.23; AD Hinaidi to 84 Sqn ('Z') 3.8.23; Crashed on landing 1924

F2849 No information

F2850 PD Ascot; AD Hinaidi; 55 Sqn 12.25; 55 Sqn ('A2') 1927; FL in sandstorm, hit ditch and overturned, Guchan, Iraq, 3.2.28

F2851 Northolt 11.25; RAE 11.25, A&AEE 30 11.25 - 1.26; 39 Sqn 8.28; HAD 7.29; 601 Sqn 3.30

F2852 No information

F2853 PD Ascot, AD Hinaidi 8.24; Retd UK; 39 Sqn 8.27; 30 Sqn

F2854 207 Sqn by 12.24; 5 FTS Sealand by 1.26

F2855 PD Ascot; AD Hinaidi; 30 Sqn 5.23; AD Hinaidi 5.23; 30 Sqn 28.8.23

F2856 PD Ascot; AD Hinaidi; 8 Sqn 1.24; 84 Sqn; FL in dust storm and overturned, Jalibah, Iraq 25.2.24; AD Hinaidi 10.24; 8 Sqn 3.25

F2857 PD Ascot; AD Aboukir; 47 Sqn 11.24; AD Aboukir rebuilt as FR2857; 4 FTS Abu Sueir 1927

F2858 PD Ascot; AD Hinaidi; 8 Sqn ('M') 12.23 - 12.24; Retd UK; 39 Sqn 9.27 - 3.28

F2859 RAF (Cadet) College, Cranwell 4.28

F2860 to F2865 No information

F2866 Sold to Soviet Russian Air Force (RKKVF)

D.H.9A F2818 and others of 'A' Flight, No.207 Squadron. (via Dave Birch)

D.H.9A F2851 and another of No.601 Squadron, with two of their Wapiti replacements in the hangar at Hendon in 1930. (RAF Museum P.7505)

F2867 (Eagle VIII) Became *G-EBAN*
F2868 (Eagle VIII) Became *G-EBCG*
F2869 DH recond (c/n 23); Waddon 27.12.21
F2870 Sold to Soviet Russian Air Force (RKKVF)
F2871 No information
F2872 Deld 28.6.19; Became *G-EBGX* (Lion)
F2873 to F2902 cancelled 12.18
BUT
F2878 Ferried Croydon to Hendon 8.7.19 (sic)

D.H.9 rebuilds at Depots in France numbered in range F5801 onwards

F5841 Rebuilt ex C6139 25.6.18; 1 AI to 206 Sqn 30.6.18; Collided with telegraph wires ferrying to Linselles 24.10.18 (Lt RH Stainbank & 2/Lt EW Richardson unhurt); to Rep Pk 1 ASD

F5842 Rebuilt ex C6199 25.6.18; Rec Pk to 2AI 29.6.18; 103 Sqn, left 09.20, attacked by 4 EA at 4,000ft, seen with damaged tail, FTR 24.9.18 (Lt HC Noely killed & Sgt LC Ovens PoW)

F5843 Rebuilt ex D1663 25.6.18; Rec Pk to 1 AI 30.6.18; 98 Sqn 1.7.18; Left 06.15 for raid on Saponay, badly damaged by AA, crashed 20.7.18 (Lt HVR Roberts-Taylor & 2/Lt SG Bates OK); 9 AP 22.7.18; Rep Pk 1 ASD 1.8.18; SOC 3.9.18

F5844 Rebuilt ex C6207 25.6.18; Rec Pk to 2 AI 30.6.18; 3 ASD 1.7.18; 104 Sqn 6.7.18; Hit by mg fire in raid on Thionville, FL, wrecked 13.8.18 (2/Lt JC Uhlman & 1/Lt P Sutherland USAS both wounded); 3 ASD 15.8.18

F5845 Rebuilt ex C6085 25.6.18; Rep Pk 1 ASD to Rec Pk and on to 2AI 1.7.18 but COL (Lt HA Airey); To Rep Pk 2 ASD; 5 AI 10.10.18; 2 AI to 49 Sqn 30.10.18 - @30.6.19

F5846 Rebuilt ex C6106 25.6.18; Rep Pk 1 ASD to Rec Pk 25.7.18; 2 AI 9.8.18; 107 Sqn 10.8.18; Left 10.58 for bombing raid on Mons Station, FTR 9.10.18 (2/Lt C Hargrave PoW & Lt WM Thompson PoW DoW 20.10.18)

F5847 Rebuilt ex B7604 25.6.18; 1 AI to 108 Sqn 4.9.18; In Lichtervelde raid Fokker DrI OOC Gits and Fokker DVII OOC Staden, shared C6314, C6345, D1080, D3092, D5622, D5759, D7208, E669, E5435 11.45 21.9.18 (Lt AM Matheson & Lt HS Gargett); After bombing Ingelmunster station at 17.25 formation attacked by 33 EA between the target and Roulers, 3 EA in flames, 1 BU and 2 OOC shared C2205, D499, D5835, D5845, D7342, E605, E5435 & E8871, then FTR 1.10.18 (Lt AM Matheson & 2/Lt FR Eveleigh both PoW)

F5848 Rebuilt ex C6186 25.6.18; Rec Pk to 1 AI 30.6.18; 206 Sqn 6.7.18; Left 17.35, crashed due to enemy activity in vicinity of Rousbrugge-Haringhe 29.7.18 (Lt RH Stainbank & 2/Lt EW Richardson both injured); Rep Pk 1 ASD 3.8.18; SOC 7.8.18

F5849 Rebuilt ex C2156 25.6.18; Rep Pk 1 ASD to Rec Pk 7.7.18; 2 AI 8.7.18; 107 Sqn 9.7.18; FTR, left at 06.33 18.7.18 (2/Lt SS George & AM FG Machir)

F5850 Rebuilt ex C6136 25.6.18; Rep Pk 1 ASD to Rec Pk and then on to 2 AI 4.7.18; 27 Sqn 5.7.18; COL 7.7.18 (2/Lt RS Walter OK); Rep Pk 2 ASD 8.7.18; SOC 29.7.18 NWR

F6054 Rebuilt ex C6263 26.6.18

F6055 (B.H.P.) Rebuilt ex D5558 26.6.18; 2 AI to 5 AI 15.7.18; Rep Pk 2 ASD to 2 AI 13.10.18; 98 Sqn by 27.10.18; Left 09.30 for bombing raid on Mons Rlwy Stn, combat with EAs over Mons on return, FTR 30.10.18 (2/Lt TW Sleigh PoW & 2/Lt EPW Dyke killed)

F6057 Rebuilt ex D480 28.6.18; 2 AI to 98 Sqn 24.8.18; Returning from raid on Valenciennes Rlwy Stn Pfalz DIII OOC Oisy 10.30 16.9.18 (Lt RL Lawson & Lt RHS Grundy); Had to return from raid on Hirson railway station due to bad visibility, aerodrome missed, landed in adjacent rough ground and turned on nose 23.10.18 (Lt RL Lawson & Lt RHS Grundy OK)

F6065 Rebuilt ex C2155 2.7.18; Rep Pk 2 ASD to 2 AI 11.7.18; 5 AI 15.7.18; 27 Sqn 17.7.18; COL trying to avoid another m/c 11.8.18 (2/Lt FC Wiltshaw & 2/Lt FF McKilligin); 9 AP 12.8.18; SOC Rep Pk 2 ASD 18.9.18

F6066 Rebuilt ex B7649 2.7.18; Rep Pk 2 ASD to 2 AI 15.7.18; 5 AI 19.7.18; 107 Sqn 20.7.18; Two Fokker DVII destroyed SW of Péronne 07.30 9.8.18 (Capt AJ Mayo & 2/Lt JW Jones); Left on raid 16.15 9.8.18, FTR (Capt AJ Mayo & 2/Lt JW Jones both killed)

F6072 Rebuilt ex C1173 3.7.18; Rep Pk 2 ASD to 2 AI 13.7.18; 107 Sqn 22.8.18; 98 Sqn 1.3.19; 8 AAP Lympne 8.3.19; Arr 206 Sqn Helwan ex France 29.7.19; 'X' AD 8.8.19

F6073 Rebuilt ex C1178 3.7.18; ASD to 107 Sqn ('6') 15.11.18; Stationary on ground about to be delivered to 98 Sqn demobilisation unit when hit by C1179 1.3.19 (2/Lt WF Long); 1 ASD 3.3.19.

F6074 Rebuilt ex D1680 3.7.18; Rep Pk 2 ASD 9.18; 2 AI 14.10.18; 107 Sqn 25.10.18; Collided with 205 Sqn a/c E9731 10.11.18 (Lt A Holden & AM C Chirgwin)

F6095 Rebuilt ex C6175 3.7.18; Rep Pk to 2 AI 28.10.18; 211 Sqn 4.11.18; 98 Sqn 24.2.19

F6098 Rebuilt ex D5701 3.7.18; 2 AI to 49 Sqn 31.8.18; Left 14.50 for bombing raid on Aulnoye Junction, in combat with EAs W of Forêt de Mormal on return, 24.9.18 (Lt CC Conover PoW & 2/Lt HJ Pretty PoW wounded)

F6112 Rebuilt ex D5600 3.7.18; Rep Pk 2 ASD to 2 AI 8.8.18; 107 Sqn 10.8.18; Left 14.25 for raid on Roisel-Clery-Vitry stations, attacked by 8 Fokker DVII 21.8.18 (2/Lt HC Curtis & 2/Lt FG Davies both killed)

F6113 Rebuilt ex D5579 3.7.18; 2 AI to 98 Sqn 8.11.18; 8 AAP Lympne 12.2.19

F6125 Rebuilt ex C6195 3.7.18; 2 AI to 49 Sqn 4.9.18; Raid on Aulnoye junction 2.10.18 (2/Lt BG Pool wounded & 2/Lt WA Greig OK); 2 AI 8.12.18, exchanged for D.H.9A

F6141 Rebuilt ex C6181 3.7.18; Rep Pk 2 ASD to 2 AI 14.8.18; 49 Sqn 23.8.18; Returning from practice flight got into flat spin nr the ground 1.9.18 (2/Lt EC Moore & 2/Lt A Mauvy OK)

F6170 Rebuilt ex D5563 3.7.18; On test flight at 2 AI wheel collapsed on landing, a/c turned on nose 31.7.18 (Lt H Dear); SOC Rep Pk 2 ASD 3.8.18 NWR (total flying time 26 minutes)

F6171 Rebuilt ex B7636 3.7.18; Rep Pk 2 ASD to 2 AI 19.7.18; 5 AI 24.7.18; 27 Sqn 25.7.18; Ran into cornfield on landing, overturned on TO 31.7.18 (2/Lt J Cocksedge & Sgt JR Dimberline both unhurt); To 9 AP; Rep Pk 1 ASD SOC 3.9.18 NWR

F6172 Rebuilt ex C6093 3.7.18; Rep Pk 2 ASD to 2 AI and on to 5 AI 19.7.18; 107 Sqn ('F') 20.7.18; Left 07.35 for raid on Valenciennes-Marguette, FTR 4.9.18 (Lt ERL Sproule & 2/Lt GT Coles both PoW)

F6183 Rebuilt ex C6135 11.7.18; Rep Pk 2 ASD by 20.8.18; 2 AI to 49 Sqn 25.8.18; Fokker DVII broke up N of Cambrai 09.10, then damaged by AA, FL 1.10.18 (2/Lt JB Gunn & 2/Lt EVG Bramble); 2 AI 8.12.18, exchanged for D.H.9A

F6196 Rebuilt ex C6133 17.7.18; Rep Pk 2 ASD to 2 AI 28.10.18; 218 Sqn 2.11.18; 98 Sqn 21.1.19; 8 AAP Lympne 12.2.19

F6205 Rebuilt ex C6324 18.7.18

F6213 Rebuilt ex C2181 25.7.18; Rec Pk to 2 AI 19.10.18; 107 Sqn 8.11.18; 98 Sqn 1.3.19; 1 ASD 17.3.19

F6231 Rebuilt ex B9349 5.8.18

F6237 Rebuilt ex D1726 10.8.18

F6239 Rebuilt ex D1676 12.8.18

F6450 Rebuilt ex D1074 20.8.18

F6451 Rebuilt ex C2195 17.9.18, but cancelled and reverted to C2195 29.9.18

F6452 Rebuilt ex D3056 23.8.18, renumbered H7075

F6453 Rebuilt ex D1015 23.8.18

1 rebuild by 5(Eastern) ARD Henlow in range F9496 to F9545

F9515 Rebuilt ex F963; At 5 (E)ARD 23.1.19 allotted to Store

200 D.H.9A ordered 4.7.18 under Cont No.35a/1918/C.2105 from Aircraft Manufacturing Co Ltd, Hendon and numbered H1 to H200. (400hp Liberty 12A)

H1 Deld 15.2.19; PD Ascot; AP Hinaidi; 30 Sqn by 4.22; Axle bent on landing, Sulaimania, 5.9.22 (F/O D Maclaren OK); Burned on evacuation

H2 PD Ascot; AD Baghdad 8.22 - 10.22

H3 S of TT Manston 9.21; 39 Sqn 5.23 - 12.23; 5 Sqn; 55

Sqn
H4 PD Ascot; AD Drigh Rd; 60 Sqn 7.23
H5 Allocated 5(E) ARD Henlow by 2-9.1.20 for Australia; Imperial Gift to Australia, became *A1-1*
H6 to H9 No information
H10 PD Ascot; AP Baghdad to 55 Sqn 24.7.20; Crashed 17.8.20; AD Hinaidi by 7.23
H11 to H15 No information
H16 A&GS Eastchurch 11.22 - 6.23
H17 SoTT (Home), Manston, propeller accident, 8.3.20 (F/Sgt CL Parsön slightly injured); S of AG&B 1.21; S of TT Home 8.21 - 9.21
H18 No information
H19 207 Sqn; Lost control when W/T operator caught foot between dual control and camera fitting, a/c spun in, San Stefano, 4.6.23 (F/O ES Edwardes seriously injured & AC1 A Smith unhurt)
H20 & H21 No information
H22 PD Ascot; AD Hinaidi to 207 Sqn ('A4') 16.4.24 - @12.24; 84 Sqn 1928
H23 3 Sqn 3.22; PD Ascot; AD Drigh Rd; AP Lahore 1.3.24; 27 Sqn ('Aa') 4.24; Recd UK?; 55 Sqn; U/c torn off
H24 PD Ascot; AD Hinaidi; 30 Sqn, COL Shaibah 19.5.21; 8 Sqn ('E) 10.24 - 1.25; Coded ('L) once
H25 No information
H26 PD Ascot; Arr AD Aboukir ex UK 10.3.20; 55 Sqn 21.7.20; Crashed 17.8.20; 30 Sqn by 5.21 - @8.21; 47 Sqn 9.21 - 2.22; AD Aboukir; 4 FTS Abu Sueir 10.23 - 10.24
H27 No information
H28 PD Ascot; AD Drigh Rd; 27 Sqn ('A) 12.20; EF at 7,000ft, FL, crashed on a nullah, Walla LG 11.4.22 (F/L RTB Houghton & F/O RJM de St.Leger both slightly injured); A/c burnt to prevent it falling into hands of raiders
H29 PD Ascot; AD Drigh Rd; 27 Sqn ('C)
H30 & H31 No information
H32 RAF North Russia (Southern Area) by 17.6.19 - @6.9.19
H33 to H39 No information
H40 PD Ascot; AD Baghdad; 30 Sqn by 7.20; FL in snow, Hamad, NW Persia, Cat W 18.2.21
H41 PD Ascot; AD Drigh Rd; 27 Sqn 2.22 - 1.23; AP Lahore 2.23
H42 8 Sqn by 12.21 - 1.22; AD Hinaidi by 5.22 - 6.22
H43 PD Ascot; From Egypt to Mesopotamia with 8 Sqn (ordered 10.1.21); 8 Sqn by 1.21 - @2.21; AD Hinaidi; 30 Sqn 10.22 - 1.23
H44 PD Ascot; AP Hinaidi; 30 Sqn 2.22; 14 Sqn ('B)
H45 PD Ascot; AP Hinaidi; 30 Sqn; EF, FL 24.3.22
H46 PD Ascot; AP Baghdad; 55 Sqn, crashed on landing, Mosul, Cat W 5.5.21
H47 PD Ascot; AP Baghdad; 8 Sqn, damaged in storm, 22.11.21; Retd AP Baghdad for rebuilding
H48 PD Ascot; AD Drigh Rd; 27 Sqn; U/c broke in fast landing on rough ground, Risalpur, 25.4.21 (F/L JL Vachell MC & Army Mjr Humphreys both unhurt); 47 Sqn ('M'); Overturned landing
H49 From Egypt to Mesopotamia with 8 Sqn (ordered 10.1.21); 30 Sqn by 5.22
H50 No information
H51 PD Ascot; AD Drigh Rd; 27, Sqn; Drifted while landing and u/c collapsed, Risalpur, 30.8.21
H52 PD Ascot; AD Drigh Rd; 27 Sqn; Photographic flight, crashed on landing, Risalpur 7.6.20 (F/L JL Vachell MC unhurt & AC2 CE Upton slightly injured); Inability to land with Vickers gun fitted, Risalpur, 14.12.20 (F/L JL Vachell MC & Army Lt Heaton both unhurt); AD Drigh Rd 7.22; AW/CN 6.9.22; 27 Sqn 9.22 - 2.23; 60 Sqn ('7') 1923; AP Lahore 5.24; 60 Sqn 2.25; Crashed on landing, Sorarogha, NWF, Cat W 4.4.25 (S/Ldr TF Hazell OK)
H53 PD Ascot; From Egypt to Mesopotamia with 8 Sqn (ordered 10.1.21); 8 Sqn by 1.21 - @2.21; AD Hinaidi to 30 Sqn 2.10.22 - 5.24; 55 Sqn ('CIV') 10.24; To UK 1.25; PD Ascot; AD Hinaidi; 55 Sqn ('A2') 10.26 - 1.27; U/c collapsed landing
H54 PD Ascot; AD Hinaidi; 8 Sqn; Crashed landing, Sulaimania, Cat W 2.6.22 (F/L J Leacroft MC OK)
H55 55 Sqn 3.27; Unidentified Sqn ('V), forced landed
H56 PD Ascot; Left Uk for AD Aboukir 26.3.20; AD Hinaidi; 84 Sqn by 11.20 - @10.21; To AD Hinaidi 11.21 (rebuild); 84 Sqn by 2.22 - @10.22; Recd AD Hinaidi by 6.23; SOC 7.23
H57 PD Ascot; AP Baghdad; 55 Sqn; FL in hostile country and looted by Arabs, Cat W 22.4.21
H58 PD Ascot; AP Baghdad; 84 Sqn; Shot down, nr.Khidr, Iraq, Cat W 22.9.20
H59 PD Ascot; AP Baghdad; 84 Sqn; Destroyed when bomb accidentally exploded, Cat W 1.11.20
H60 PD Ascot; AP Baghdad; 30 Sqn mid-1920; 84 Sqn
H61 AD Hinaidi by 6.22
H62 PD Ascot; AP Baghdad; 55 Sqn 1.8.20; EF, FL in hostile territory, 1.11.20; destroyed by insurgents
H63 Left UK for Mesopotamia 23.2.20
H64 PD Ascot; AD Drigh Rd; 45 Sqn mid-1922 [too early?]; 27 Sqn
H65 & H66 No information
H66 PD Ascot; AP Baghdad; 30 Sqn mid-1920; 84 Sqn, 112-lb bomb dropped at low altitude and exploded on take-off, a/c crashed and set on fire, Nasiriyeh, Cat W 30.9.21 (F/O M Hyslop & AC2 E Plummer both killed) (E9919 also DBR in explosion)
H67 PD Ascot; AP Baghdad; Baghdad; 55 Sqn 31.8.21 - 3. 22
H68 PD Ascot; AP Baghdad; 30 Sqn by 3.20; FL due to rifle fire 14.6.20; Salved but DBR
H69 No information
H70 PD Ascot; AD Drigh Rd; 27 Sqn 11.21; EF on tests, FL east of Risalpur Cantonment 11.2.21 (F/O JWF Merer & LAC GF Cockell both unhurt); Leaving on bombing raid, stalled on turn and crashed, BO, Dardoni, 17.8.22 (F/O DC Duncan & F/O RB Luard both killed)
H71 1 SoN&BD Stonehenge by 4.2.19; PD Ascot; AD Baghdad; 30 Sqn 19.9.20; Shot down by rifle fire, nr.Kifl, Iraq 12.10.20; Burnt by Arabs
H72 PD Ascot; AD Drigh Rd; 27 Sqn ('D) 1920 - 1921, u/c collapsed landing [no date]; 27 Sqn ('C') 11.22; AP Lahore 20.2.23; AD Drigh Rd 2.23; 60 Sqn ('8) 2.24; EF, crashed in FL, 15.4.24 (Sgt D Munro); AD Drigh Rd; 60 Sqn ('10) 7.25 - 9.25; HQ RAF India 9.25 (flown Quetta-Peshawar 20.9.25; 27 Sqn ('C) 9.26 - 10.27; Crashed 1926 (repaired); 60 Sqn 1928; 60 Sqn 18.12.29 - 3.30
H73 No information
H74 PD Ascot; AD Drigh Rd; 60 Sqn
H75 & H76 No information
H77 PD Ascot; AP Baghdad; 55 Sqn 7.21; Crash landed, Mosul, Cat W 31.8.21 (F/O CD Spiers)
H78 PD Ascot; AP Baghdad; 30 Sqn 20.1.22; FL in desert and hit sand ridge, Cat W 23.4.22 (F/O GA Atkinson OK)
H79 PD Ascot; AP Baghdad; 55 Sqn; FL and abandoned when petrol tank burst on recce, Nisibin, Iraq, Cat W 9.8.21 (F/O J Silvester & another OK)
H80 PD Ascot; AP Baghdad; 30 Sqn mid-1920; Crashed 13.1.21
H81 PD Ascot; AP Baghdad; 55 Sqn 7.20 - 8.20; 30 Sqn; FL in sandstorm, overturned in irrigation ditch, Khidire, Iraq, 8.4.21
H82 PD Ascot; AD Aboukir; Rebuilt as HR82; 47 Sqn 1.23 - 5.23; AD Aboukir 7.24; 4 FTS Abu Sueir 8.24; Hit by J7304 on overshoot, Abu Sueir, Cat W 22.5.25
H83 PD Ascot; AD Aboukir; 47 Sqn 3.22 - 5.22
H84 PD Ascot; AD Aboukir; 4 FTS Abu Sueir 4.23 - 10.23
H85 PD Ascot; AD Aboukir; 47 Sqn 9.21 - 2.22; AD Aboukir test 27.6.24; Rebuilt as HR85; 14 Sqn Amman, undershot, struck railway and overturned, Ramleh, 30.12.24 (F/O FCT Rowe slightly injured & LAC G Harding unhurt)
H86 PD Ascot; AP Baghdad; 30 Sqn by 5.20 - @6.20; AP Baghdad to 55 Sqn 23.7.20 - @8.20; 30 Sqn 1921; Crashed Quizil Robat 14.4.22
H87 No information
H88 PD Ascot; AD Aboukir; 47 Sqn 10.1.23 - 5.23; Recd UK; DH recond (c/n 160); PD Ascot; AD Hinaidi; 55 Sqn 1926; Std outer front strut fouled tailplane of another a/c while in formation, Cat M 8.7.29 (F/Sgt KR Boulton OK)
H89 PD Ascot; AD Drigh Rd; AP Lahore 26.2.23; 27 Sqn ('A') 3.23 - 9.23; AP Lahore 10.23 - 11.23; 27 Sqn

('C); 60 Sqn ('9) 1924; Flames from exhaust, presumed faulty throttle barrel, landed safely 17.3.25; AD Drigh Rd; 60 Sqn 6.25; 27 Sqn 6.25; Crashed 1926; AD Drigh Rd; 27 Sqn, minor crash 17.3.27; 27 Sqn 11.27; FL and u/c torn off landing, Drigh Rd, 22.3.29; AD Drigh Rd; 60 Sqn 11.29 - 4.30; Ran into Wapiti J9402 of 11 Sqn while taxying for take-off, Kohat, Cat M 30.11.29 (F/L DJ McBain OK)

H90 PD Ascot; AP Baghdad; 30 Sqn; Crashed in bad landing in sandstorm, Cat W 9.6.21 (F/O HGW Lock)

H91 PD Ascot; AP Baghdad; 55 Sqn 8.20 - 8.21; 6 Sqn, spontaneous combustion of Very light in locker during raid on Mosul 17.8.21 (F/O HSP Walmsley OK & F/O ET Carpenter injured); 84 Sqn by 10.21 - 9.22

H92 PD Ascot; AP Baghdad to 55 Sqn 7.8.20; 8 Sqn Suez by 1.21

H93 AD Aboukir rebuilt as DC HR93; 208 Sqn 1923

H94 No information

H95 PD Ascot; AD Drigh Rd; 27 Sqn ('H) 1922; 27 Sqn ('M)

H96 PD Ascot; AD Baghdad by 6.20; 55 Sqn 21.8.20 - @6.21; AP Baghdad (recond) 27.8.21; 84 Sqn 7.22

H97 PD Ascot; AP Baghdad to 55 Sqn 5.8.20; Crashed 9.8.20

H98 & H99 No information

H100 AP Baghdad by 6.21

H101 PD Ascot; AP Baghdad; 30 Sqn 1920 - 1921

H102 PD Ascot; AP Baghdad; 55 Sqn 4.8.20; 8 Sqn; Collided in practice flight formation with E8474, crashed nr Hinaidi, Cat W 13.1.22 (F/O FH Barton killed & AC2 G Pattinson slightly injured)

H103 No information

H104 PD Ascot; From Egypt to Mesopotamia with 8 Sqn (ordered 10.1.21); 8 Sqn by 1.21 - @2.21; 30 Sqn, COL Baghdad West, Cat W 20.6.22 (F/L S Kinkead DSO DSC DFC OK)

H105 PD Ascot; AP Baghdad; Trg Flt, Central Air Comm Sqn, Shaibah; Unit disbanded 31.3.21; 30 Sqn by 5.21 - @6.21; 30 Sqn 1.22

H106 PD Ascot; AD Baghdad; 55 Sqn 31.8.21 - 9.21

H107 PD Ascot; AP Baghdad; 47 Sqn 1.7.21; 30 Sqn 7.21 - 5.22

H108 PD Ascot; AD Baghdad; 84 Sqn by 10.21 - @11.21; 30 Sqn; 84 Sqn 10.22; Crash landing after raid, Cat W 1.11.22 (F/O HW Hewson OK)

H109 PD Ascot; AD Baghdad; 30 Sqn; Landed in soft ground, Shaibah, Cat W 19.5.21

H110 PD Ascot; AP Baghdad; 8 Sqn, EF, crashed on take-off, Baghdad West, Cat W 1.6.21 (S/Ldr DL Allen AFC); To AP Baghdad

H111 DH rebuilt and renumbered J7013 (c/n 93)

H112 S of AG&B Eastchurch 1.21

H113 No information

H114 PD Ascot; AP Baghdad to 55 Sqn 13.6.21; 30 Sqn; EF, Crashed on landing, Sulaimania, 5.9.22 (F/O CW Attwood OK); Burned on evacuation

H115 AD Hinaidi by 6.22

H116 PD Ascot; AP Baghdad; 8 Sqn, crashed on landing, Mosul, Cat W 14.11.21 (F/O HB Pett MC & another OK); To 55 Sqn for spares

H117 PD Ascot; AD Baghdad; 84 Sqn; Crashed on landing Nasiriyeh, 4.2.21

H118 PD Ascot; AD Baghdad; 55 Sqn 9.22; 84 Sqn 1.25; 45 Sqn 11.28 - 12.28

H119 PD Ascot; AP Baghdad; 30 Sqn by 5.21; Heavy landing, LG.4, Iraq, Cat W 30.7.21 (F/O W Bentley DFC)

H120 PD Ascot; AP Baghdad; 8 Sqn; Crashed landing in sandstorm 2.5.21; 30 Sqn, crashed and caught fire, Cat W 23.11.25 (F/O JA Moore & AC1 AA Rickaby both killed)

H121 PD Ascot; AP Baghdad; 8 Sqn, FL Samarra 12.5.21 (F/O JEH Littlewood); 30 Sqn 5.21 - 7.21

H122 PD Ascot; AP Baghdad; 30 Sqn by 8.21; 30 Sqn 2.23; AD Hinaidi 3.24 - 4.24; 84 Sqn 5.24

H123 to H125 No information

H126 DH rebuilt and renumbered J7014 (c/n 94)

H127 No information

H128 DH rebuilt and renumbered J7015 (c/n 95)

H129 to H137 No information

H138 Arr 6 SD Ascot (via Farnborough) for packing 20.9.20; 207 Sqn 30.10.20 (tested) - @11.23; DH recond (c/n 150); PD Acton; AD Drigh Rd; 84 Sqn 3.26 - 4.26; Swung on take-off, hit wire fence, 31.3.26; 47 Sqn, crashed, Cat W 3.10.27

H139 207 Sqn by 7.22; Grain 10.22; RAE 5.12.22; Grain; RAE 8.9.23; FL Blackdown, Hants, 16.3.27; Last flown 28.2.28

H140 PD Ascot; AD Hinaidi by 1.23; 55 Sqn 8.2.23

H141 DH recond (c/n 69); PD Ascot; AD Hinaidi; to 8 Sqn ('A) 15.8.23 - 9.23; 8 Sqn ('N) 8.24 - 1925; 84 Sqn 2.25 - 7.25

H142 Arr 6 SD Ascot (via Farnborough) for packing 20.9.20; 207 Sqn 30.10.20 (tested) - 8.24; 39 Sqn; AD Hinaidi; 84 Sqn 9.27; Collided with H143 1927; 55 Sqn 5.28; 84 Sqn (DC) 9.31

H143 DH recond (c/n 68); PD Ascot; AD Hinaidi; 55 Sqn

D.H.9As of No.207 Squadron, including H138, J557 and J561, at San Stephano. (via Philip Jarrett)

5.28; 84 Sqn; Collided with H142 1927; Wrecked, 11.6.27

H144 (DC); Hendon; 602 Sqn 7.10.25 - 1.26; PD Ascot; AD Hinaidi; 14 Sqn 8.29 - 9.29

H145 DH recond (c/n 70); PD Ascot; AD Hinaidi; 30 Sqn; EF, FL in bad ground, 24.3.22 (F/O D Maclaren); 8 Sqn 5.24 - 12.24; 55 Sqn ('AIV') 1.25 - 7.25; Smashed main spar landing, Abu Khuweima, Iraq, 9.1.25 (flown back to base and repaired); AOC Iraq 8.26 - 11.26 (personal a/c of Sir John Higgins, painted red overall with white struts)

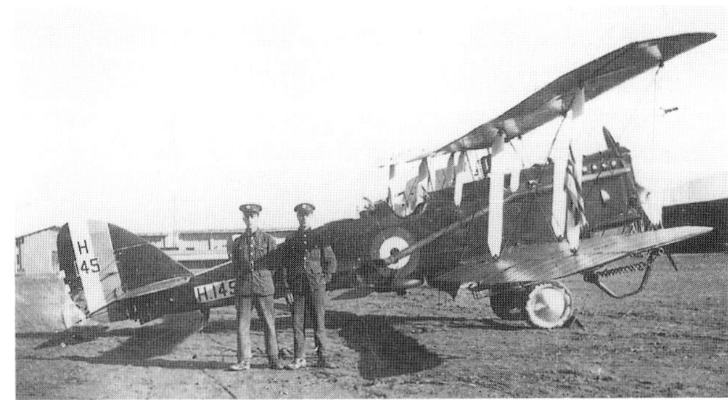

Two airmen posing for the camera in front of Sir John Higgins' red-painted D.H.9A H145. (via R.L. Ward)

H146 No information

H147 DH recond (c/n 67); PD Ascot; AD Hinaidi 4.24; 8 Sqn 5.24; 84 Sqn, armed desert patrol in search of raiding party, FL in desert, S of Jalibah, Southern Iraq, Cat W 24.7.24 (F/L WC Day MC & P/O DR Stewart killed)

H148 & H149 No information

H150 PD Ascot; AP Baghdad; 55 Sqn 30.9.21 - 3.22; 30 Sqn 9.22 - 3.23

H151 PD Ascot; AD Aboukir; 14 Sqn, spun in caught fire, BO, LG 'D', Cat W 26.6.24 (F/O RC Creamer & LAC FC Perrin both killed)

H152 Tested IAAD 19.4.23; 1 FTS Netheravon, landed too close to tarmac, crashed into another aircraft in front of sheds 8.5.23 (Cpl EA Grose unhurt); Struck haystack landing, written off 14.8.24 (Lt M Cursham RN slightly injured)

H153 PD Ascot; AP Baghdad to 55 Sqn 20.6.21; Contact patrol with forces of levies, FL after pilot hit by rebel bullet, Catas, nr Desht-i-Harir, 20m SW of Rowanduz, Iraq, Cat W 12.9.21 (F/O CH Teagle DoI 16.9.21 & AC1 SSB Cox slightly injured); Burnt by crew

H154 PD Ascot; AP Baghdad; 55 Sqn; Engine cut on take-off, 14.6.21 (F/O FK Damant & another OK); Destroyed by crew

H155 PD Ascot; AP Baghdad; 84 Sqn by 10.21; AD Hinaidi by 6.22; 30 Sqn, en route from Baghdad to Kirkuk with spares, crashed after enemy action 6m SW of Kirkuk, Iraq, 6.10.22 BO (F/O EA Locke-Waters killed)

H156 PD Ascot; AD Aboukir; 4 FTS Abu Sueir; Ground collision with J8175 after landing, Cat W 10.10.28

H157 to H160 Sold to Soviet Russian Air Force (RKKVF)

H161 PD Ascot; AP Baghdad; 30 Sqn; Crashed on take-off when sand temporarily blinded pilot, Cat W 29.7.21 (F/O HW Baggs)

H162 PD Ascot; AD Hinaidi; 8 Sqn by 2.20; 8 Sqn by 9.22; 8 Sqn by 5.23 - @9.23

H163 PD Ascot; From Egypt to Mesopotamia with 8 Sqn (ordered 10.1.21); 8 Sqn 6.23 -10.23; 14 Sqn 9.25

H164 PD Ascot; AP Baghdad; 55 Sqn 8.21; FL, crashed on take-off, Desht-i-Harir, Iraq, Cat W 17.12.21 (F/O HSP Walmsley MC)

H165 PD Ascot; AD Hinaidi 3.23; 84 Sqn 3.23 - 9.23; AD Hinaidi 3.24

H166 to H168 No information

H169 PD Ascot; AD Hinaidi; 84 Sqn 11.23

H170 PD Ascot; AD Hinaidi 2.23

H171 & H172 No information

H173 PD Ascot; AD Hinaidi to 55 Sqn 22.5.23; Went into flat spin off turn at low altitude, dived in 4.12.23 (F/O A Ledger killed & Indian officer passenger minor injuries)

H174 PD Ascot; AD Aboukir; 47 Sqn 3.24 - 4.24; AD Aboukir; 47 Sqn; Ground collision with stationary aircraft, Ca W 5.10.27 (F/O CGH Gee OK)

H175 Deld 9.19; PD Ascot; AD Hinaidi to 8 Sqn 21.3.23 - 4.23; FL, crew fought off hostile tribesmen 1923 (F/O JIT Jones & P/O N Vincent who was awarded DFC); Recd UK; 39 Sqn by 7.25; 100 Sqn ('1'); HAD 9.28; RAF (Cadet) College, Cranwell 11.28 - 12.28

H176 to H200 cancelled 12.18

200 D.H.9 ordered c.7.18 from Cubitt Ltd/ National Aircraft Factory No.1 and numbered H3196 to H3395. Order cancelled

150 D.H.9A ordered 17.7.18 on BR.579 under Cont No 35a/2077/C.2410 from Westland Aircraft Works, Yeovil and numbered H3396 to H3545 (400hp Liberty 12A)

H3396 Deld 11.18 (sic); Tested at makers 30.12.18; Convtd to 3-str for Atlantic Fleet needs; To Donibristle 1.3.19; 210 Sqn Gosport by 2.20 - @9.20; PD Ascot; AD Drigh Rd; 60 Sqn, demonstration flight over Waziristan from Arawauli, FL and u/c collapsed on rough ground, Behrang Khel, NWF 1.12.24 (F/O BP Jones & LAC CJ Walsh both unhurt)

H3397 DH rebuilt and renumbered J7011 (c/n 91)

H3398 to H3405 No information

H3406 During delivery, FL en route at Bramham owing to dusk, broke prop 20.12.18 (Lt AS Keep); 5 AAP Bristol 23.12.18; Allotted to EF 28.1.19

H3407 No information

H3408 Tested mkrs 6.1.19; At 5 AAP Bristol 14.2.19 reallotted from SW Area for Store to EF; 110 Sqn by 3.19 - 4.19

H3409 Tested mkrs 30.12.18; At 5 AAP Bristol 14.2.19 reallotted from SW Area for Store to EF;

H3410 Deld 5 AAP Bristol 3.1.19; Reallotted from SW Area for Store to EF 14.2.19; 99 Sqn, on mail flight engine cut out, FL and crashed in ploughed field 24.4.19 (Lt VC Varcoe & Lt PG Addie)

H3411 Tested mkrs 17-28.1.19; At 5 AAP Bristol 19.2.19, allotted to EF

H3412 & H3413 No information

H3414 Fleet Observers School Leysdown by 8.18 - 2.19

H3416 to H3423 No information

H3424 Deld 5 AAP Bristol 4.1.19; PD Ascot; AD Hinaidi; 30 Sqn 10.26

H3425 Deld 5 AAP Bristol 10.1.19

H3426 Tested mkrs 11-16.1.19

H3427 Tested mkrs 10.1.19; Deld 5 AAP Bristol 21.1.19

H3428 & H3429 No information

H3430 DH recond (c/n 52); PD Ascot; AP Hinaidi by 6.23; 55 Sqn 17.7.23 - 1924 (S/L A Coningham's a/c with Mosque silhouette)

H3431 5 FTS Shotwick, EF on take-off, FL 24.8.22 (P/O JAR Stevenson unhurt); Repaired; 24 Sqn, crashed, Farnborough, 21.12.22 (repaired); Tail unit broke pulling out of steep dive from 1,500ft, crashed into house, BO, Kenley, 7.7.23 (F/O MGL Trapagna-Leroy AFC & F/O EW Logsdail both killed)

H3432 PD Ascot; AD Hinaidi; 84 Sqn 10.24; Recd UK; DH recond (c/n 55); 39 Sqn by 1.28; Crashed, Cat W 19.5.28 (Capt Piascolni (Polish)); WOC 5.6.28

H3433 PD Ascot; AD Hinaidi to 30 Sqn 27.5.23; 6 Sqn, struck ridge on edge of aerodrome, Kingerban, 20.4.24 (F/O RL Edward slightly injured & S/Ldr JW Cruickshank unhurt); 30 Sqn 7.24; 8 Sqn 1.25; 30 Sqn ('A') 1926

H3434 Tested mkrs 31.1.19 - 9.2.19; At 5 AAP Bristol 10.2.19 allotted to EF

H3435 Tested mkrs 7.2.19; At 5 AAP Bristol 12.2.19 allotted to EF

H3436 Tested mkrs 24.1.19; At 5 AAP Bristol 5.2.19 allotted to EF

H3437 Tested mkrs 28.1.19; At 5 AAP Bristol 5.2.19 allotted to EF; 110 Sqn; On mail flight crashed nr Aachen 18.4.19 (Lt GA Walker & Lt HS Cook OK); To 8 SS

H3438 Tested mkrs 8.2.19; Deld 5 AAP Bristol 18.2.19 allotted to EF - @21.2.19

H3439 Tested mkrs 9.2.19; At 5 AAP Bristol 12.2.19 allotted to EF

H3440 Tested mkrs 24-26.1.19; Deld 5 AAP Bristol 1.2.19 allotted to EF - @5.2.19; 57 Sqn by 5.19

H3441 PD Ascot; AD Hinaidi; 30 Sqn 4.27

D.H.9A H3510 'L' of No.8 Squadron with a full complement of accessories. (via Philip Jarrett)

H3442 to H3449 No information

H3450 PD Ascot; AD Drigh Rd; AP Lahore 12.4.24; 60 Sqn ('2') 18.11.24 - 6.25; 27 Sqn; Flew under Attock Bridge and crashed in River Indus, 25.4.28 (Sgt D Irving OK & LAC E Turner killed); Repaired; 27 Sqn ('K') 11.27; Caught by downwind while diving to drop mail on column and crashed, Lowari Pass, NWF, Cat W 21.9.28 (F/L AR Prendergast & LAC JA Dwyer)

H3451 HMS *Argus* 11.19; PD Ascot; AD Hinaidi; 8 Sqn 12.22; AD Hinaidi to 8 Sqn 21.7.23; 8 Sqn 5.24; 30 Sqn 7.24 - 3.25

H3452 Tested mkrs 17-26.3.19; Deld 10 AAP Brooklands 9.4.19; Reallotted from Store to EF 30.4.19

H3453 207 Sqn by 5.24; PD Ascot; AD Aboukir; 14 Sqn 11.25 - 10.26; 4 FTS Abu Sueir 8.27 - 7.28

H3454 to H3456 No information

H3457 Sold to Soviet Russian Air Force (RKKVF)

H3458 In France 8.4.19 allotted to EF

H3459 Allocated 5(E) ARD Henlow for Australia by 2-9.1.20; Imperial Gift to Australia, became *A1-18*

H3460 Allocated 5(E) ARD Henlow for Australia by 2-9.1.20; Imperial Gift to Australia, became *A1-19*

H3461 Arr 5(E) ARD Henlow 5.12.19 - @9.1.20 for Australia; Imperial Gift to Australia, became *A1-20*

H3462 Completed 8.2.19; Allocated 5(E) ARD Henlow for Australia by 2-9.1.20; Imperial Gift to Australia, became *A1-21*

H3463 Completed 8.2.19; Allocated 5(E) ARD Henlow for Australia by 2-9.1.20; Imperial Gift to Australia, became *A1-22*

H3464 Allocated 5(E) ARD Henlow for Australia by 2-9.1.20; Imperial Gift to Australia, became *A1-23*

H3465 Allocated 5(E) ARD Henlow for Australia by 2-9.1.20; Imperial Gift to Australia, became *A1-24*

H3466 Tested mkrs 20.2.19; At 5 AAP Bristol 28.3.19 allotted to EF; 57 Sqn by 18.4.19 - @5.19

H3467 Tested mkrs 20.2.19; 5 AAP Bristol 21.2.19; 49 Sqn by 3.19; Crashed 7.4.19 (2/Lt WH Isted & 2/Lt DM Fraser OK)

H3468 Tested mkrs 24-27.2.19; At 5 AAP Bristol 14.3.19 allotted to EF; 6 AI to 57 Sqn 6.5.19

H3469 Tested mkrs 24.2.19; At 5 AAP Bristol 8.3.19 allotted to EF

H3470 At 5 AAP Bristol 3.4.19 allotted to EF; 57 Sqn by 5.19; On mail flight left wheel came off on landing, m/c turned on back 8.6.19 (Lt HS Round OK & 2/Lt PA Savoie injured)

H3471 Tested mkrs 25.2.19; At 5 AAP Bristol 28.3.19 allotted to EF; Overturned, CW [at Risalpur?]

H3472 Tested mkrs 27.2.19; At 5 AAP Bristol 14.3.19 allotted to EF; 110 Sqn by 4.19 - @5.19

H3473 Tested mkrs 17-18.3.19; 57 Sqn by 6.19

H3474 En route from 5 AAP Bristol to EF 1.4.19 allotted to EF; 110 Sqn by 5.19; FL Luje 6.19 (Lt ER Openshaw)

H3475 Tested mkrs 13.3.19; At 5 AAP Bristol 3.4.19 allotted to EF

H3476 No information

H3477 Tested mkrs 21.3.19; At 5 AAP Bristol 7.4.19 allotted to EF; 57 Sqn by 5.19

H3478 Tested mkrs 10-14.3.19; A&AEE 6.26 - 7.26; A&GS Eastchurch 9.29 - 1.30

H3479 Tested mkrs 15.3.19 - 1.4.19; At 10 AAP Brooklands 30.4.19, allotted to EF

H3480 55 Sqn ('C.V') from 5.8.20 - 8.21; Battle casualty 3.11.20 (F/O RJP Grebby, observer, gunshot wound in back); Retd UK; DH rebuilt and renumbered J7008 (c/n 88)

H3481 PD Ascot; AP Baghdad; 30 Sqn; EF on take-off and crashed in to cart, 16.4.20 (squadron repair); Swung landing, u/c collapsed, Diwaniyah, 11.7.20; AP Baghdad to 55 Sqn ('C.V') 5.8.20 - @4.21

H3482 PD Ascot; AP Baghdad; 30 Sqn; Shot through petrol tanks, 30.7.20; 84 Sqn by 9.20

H3483 PD Ascot; AP Baghdad; 30 Sqn 1920 - 1921; Trg Flt, Central Sqn, Shaibah; Unit disbanded 31.3.21; 84 Sqn by 2.22 - @12.22; AD Hinaidi by 5.23 - @10.23; 8 Sqn 5.27; 55 Sqn 1.25

H3484 No information

H3485 Tested mkrs 26.3.19; Deld 10 AAP Brooklands 7.4.19; En route to EF from 10 AAP Brooklands 25.4.18 allotted to EF; 110 Sqn Germany post-war

H3486 Tested mkrs 9 & 22.5.19; Deld 10 AAP Brooklands 31.5.19; PD Ascot; AD Aboukir; 4 FTS Abu Sueir 12.23; Recd UK; DH recond (c/n 53); RAF (Cadet) College, Cranwell

H3487 Tested mkrs 27-29.3.19; Deld 10 AAP Brooklands 1.4.19; En route to EF from 10 AAP Brooklands 25.4.19 allotted to EF; PD Ascot; AD Drigh Rd; 27 Sqn

A D.H.9A three-seater, probably H3536, of No.3 Squadron. (J.M.Bruce/G.S.Leslie collection)

D.H.9A H3586 of No.100 Squadron at Fermoy in 1921. (J.M.Bruce/G.S.Leslie collection)

1920/23; 31 Sqn Patiala

H3488 Tested mkrs 13.3.19; Cranwell by 9.19; RAF (Cadet) College, Cranwell

H3489 Deld 10 AAP Brooklands 29.4.19

H3490 to H3495 No information

H3496 DH rebuilt and renumbered J7010 (c/n 90)

H3497 to H3499 No information

H3500 PD Ascot; Left UK for 55 Sqn 16.2.20; AP Baghdad; 47 Sqn 6.20 - 7.20; 8 Sqn Suez, crashed 14.1.21 (F/O JEH Littlewood & F/O JA Gray OK); AP Baghdad by 6.21; 30 Sqn, port tyre burst landing, Cat W 20.8.21 (S/Ldr M Thomas OK)

H3501 207 Sqn 6.23 - @7.24; Crashed 17.6.24 (repaired); PD Ascot; AD Aboukir; 4 FTS Abu Sueir 5.26 - 6.26; AD Aboukir rebuilt as HR3501; 45 Sqn ('3')

H3502 Allocated 5(E) ARD Henlow for Australia by 2-9.1.20; Imperial Gift to Australia, became *A1-25*

H3503 (DH.4A 3-seater) 24 Sqn by 1.1.20 - @5.21 (DMS)

H3504 PD Ascot; AP Baghdad; 30 Sqn ('C'); U/c collapsed landing, LG.2, Cat W 25.6.21 (F/L LJ Maclean MC & another OK)

H3505 PD Sealand; AD Aboukir; 84 Sqn 9.22

H3506 Cranwell to HMS *Eagle* Trials Flight Gosport 14.4.20 (this flight carried out trials in *Eagle* to 11.20); DH recond (c/n 148)

H3507 Tested mkrs 16.6.19

H3508 Tested mkrs 19.6.19; RAF (Cadet) College, Cranwell until delivered to HMS *Eagle* Trials Flight at Gosport 14.4.20 (this flight carried out trials in *Eagle* to 11.20)

H3509 Mobile Flight 205 Sqn Delny by 6.20

H3510 Grand Fleet SoAF&G Leuchars by 10.19 (at Delny 10.19); Became RAF Base Leuchars 18.3.20 - 5.20; CB Co-op Flt Gosport 6.20; PD Ascot; AD Hinaidi; 8 Sqn ('L') by 2.23 - 1.26; 84 Sqn 11.27 - 12.27; 55 Sqn

H3511 CAAD Leuchars by 5.21; 3 Sqn 1.10.21; Returning from recce flight in conjunction with practice destroyer attack in Moray Firth, struck ridge landing Novar, engine stopped badly damaged 3.10.22 (F/O CG Hancock, F/L JA Macnab & O/O AB Ball all unhurt)

H3512 (Conv three-seater) Mobile Flight Delny by 6.20 - @9.20; Leuchars by 7.21; 3 Sqn 1.10.21 (Leuchars to Delny 25.8.21, retd Leuchars 14.10.21); 30 Sqn by 1.25 - 2.25

H3513 CAAD Leuchars by 4.21 - @9.21; PD Ascot; AD Hinaidi; 55 Sqn 6.25 - 5.26

H3514 Grand Fleet SoAF&G Leuchars by 9.19; Mobile Flt 205 Sqn Delny by 6.20

H3515 (Conv three-seater); CAAD Leuchars 3.21; Mobile Flt 205 Sqn Delny by 9.21; Became 3 Sqn 1.10.21; Upper wing struck by H3533 landing Delny, 8.10.21; 8 Sqn 2.25 - 8.25; 84 Sqn (Club marking, named 'LU-LU') 10.26; Smashed longeron landing Al Jil, Iraq, 2.28; AD Hinaidi repair 2.28

H3516 Delny by 10.19

H3517 No information

H3518 (Conv three-seater); Fleet SoAF&G Leuchars by 12.19; Became RAF Base Leuchars 3.20 - 5.20; 205 Sqn, FL in sea en route Durness (Cape Wrath) to Invergordon 6.10.20 (F/O JM Fairweather, F/O E Smith & F/L JA McNab all OK, landed ashore to Hull 8.10.20)

H3519 PD Ascot; AD Aboukir; 47 Sqn ('BII') 2.25; Landing in formation, collided with E8760, Helwan, Cat W 26.3.26 (Sgt F Walker OK); Rebuilt?; 14 Sqn 1.27 - 7.27; 47 Sqn ('F) 1928

H3520 3 Sqn 1.10.21; Undercarriage collapsed landing 22.2.23 (F/O HLP Lester & P/O JS Newall); DH recond (c/n 80); DH record on Cont No 579165/25 (c/n 252); PD Ascot; AD Aboukir; 47 Sqn; Retd UK?; RAF (Cadet) College, Cranwell 9.27 - 10.27

H3521 CAAD Leuchars by 9.21

H3522 PD Ascot; AD Aboukir 1.25; 47 Sqn ('BIV') 4.26 - 7.26

H3523 3 Sqn 1.10.21 - 1.23; Went on nose, Leuchars; PD Ascot; AD Hinaidi; 30 Sqn 7.25; 55 Sqn ('BIV') 1.26 - 4.26; 8 Sqn ('P') 1926; 84 Sqn; 30 Sqn by 10.26 - @1.27

H3524 3 Sqn 1.10.21 - 10.22; 210 Sqn 10.22 - 4.34; PD Ascot; AD Hinaidi; 30 Sqn 7.25; 84 Sqn 9.26 - 5.27; 55 Sqn 1927 - 1928

H3525 PD Ascot; AD Aboukir; 4 FTS Abu Sueir 3.25 - 4.25; AD Aboukir 6.25; 4 FTS Abu Sueir 6.25 - 10.25; AD Hinaidi; 8 Sqn ('P') 1926; 8 Sqn ('N') 1926; 30 Sqn 10.26; 55 Sqn

H3526 PD Ascot; AD Hinaidi; 8 Sqn 7.25; 55 Sqn 11.25

H3527 RAF Base Leuchars; crashed on nose, Leuchars, 1927

H3528 Donibristle, tested 19.4.21; CAAD Leuchars by 7.21; PD Ascot; AD Drigh Rd; AP Lahore 10.24; 27 Sqn ('L') 10.24; COL Lahore 28.1.25; 60 Sqn ('9') 1925; 27 Sqn 9.25 - 2.26; AHQ India (named 'ALICE'); AP Lahore 1927; 27 Sqn 9.28

H3529 3 Sqn by 8.21; RAF (Cadet) College, Cranwell 11.22; PD Ascot; AD Hinaidi; 55 Sqn; 8 Sqn ('H':'N') 7.25; Hit by E8496 on take-off, Cat W 19.4.26 (P/O BW Knox OK); SOC 26.4.26

H3530 CAAD Leuchars by 7.21; 3 Sqn 1.10.21; Flying from Novar, EF at 4,000ft, FL in Moray Firth, Cat W 6.9.22 (F/O CP Brown DFC injured; O/O LH Stewart & O/O AB Ball both unhurt)

H3531 1 FTS, crashed on nose landing, Netheravon, 7.5.25; HAD 6.26 - 10.26

H3532 2 FTS Duxford 11.22 - 9.23; 207 Sqn 1927

H3533 (Built for ship use); 210 Sqn Gosport by 21.6.21; 3 Sqn 1.10.21; Low approach in low wind conditions, tail skid hit top plane of parked H3515, u/c collapsed Delny 8.10.21 (F/O RM Trevethan MC, O/O WA Thompson & AC1 FR Thornton all unhurt)

H3534 (Built for ship use, DC, three-seater); Tested mkrs 30.5.19; UK 1920; PD Ascot; AD Drigh Rd; 60 Sqn 10.24; Ground collision with E8752, Cat R 14.11.24 (F/L JW Baker MC DFC); AP Lahore 3.25; AD Drigh Rd; 60 Sqn ('S) 1.29 - 7.29; 27 Sqn 1929 - 1930

H3535 (Built for ship use); Tested mkrs 31.5.19; 3 Sqn by 4.22; PD Ascot; AD Hinaidi; 84 Sqn 1.25 - 6.25; W/T generator caught fire in gunner's cockpit joystick but was removed by observer when near ground, aircraft undamaged 2.3.25; 47 Sqn ('C', named 'DARIUS'); 30 Sqn 1.26 - 8.27

D.H.9A H3626 of No.60 Squadron with target towing stripes. The gun ring has been removed from the rear cockpit and a windscreen added. (via Philip Jarrett)

H3536 (Built for ship use - three-seater); CAAD Leuchars by 5.21 - @6.21; 3 Sqn 1.10.21 - 4.22; PD Ascot; AD Drigh Rd; AP Lahore 3.25
H3537 (Built for ship use)
H3538 (Built for ship use); Mobile Flight Delny by 7.20
H3539 (Built for ship use); Tested mkrs 13.6.19; (Conv three-seater) Mobile Flight 205 Sqn Delny by 6.20 - @9.20; 205 Sqn, FL in fog en route Cranwell to Gosport and hit tree, BO, nr.Alton, Hants, 17.12.20 (F/O ECK Kingston seriously injured)
H3540 (Built for ship use - three-seater); Grand Fleet SoAF&G Leuchars by 1.20; Mobile Flight Delny by 6.20; 3 Sqn 1.10.21; Recond; PD Ascot; AD Drigh Rd; AP Lahore to 60 Sqn 18.11.24
H3541 (Built for ship use) Grand Fleet SoAF&G Leuchars by 10.19; RAF (Cadet) College, Cranwell by 1.24 - @1.25; DH recond (c/n 144); HAD 2.28; 1 FTS 7.28; Hendon; HAD 26. 11.28
H3542 (Built for ship use); PD Ascot; AD Aboukir rebuilt as HR3542; 14 Sqn 10.26 - 7.28
H3543 (Built for ship use); 3 Sqn by 7.22; PD Ascot; AD Drigh Rd; 27 Sqn ('H') 1925
H3544 (Built for ship use); CAAD Leuchars by 4.21 - @5.21; 3 Sqn 1.10.21 - 2.22; PD Ascot; AD Drigh Rd; AP Lahore 10.24
H3545 (Built for ship use); Deld 8.19; PD Ascot; AD Aboukir rebuilt as HR3545; 4 FTS Abu Sueir 3.25 - 9.25; 55 Sqn; 45 Sqn 9.28

250 D.H.9A ordered 17.7.18 on BR.580 under Cont No 35a/2084/C.2414 from Vulcan Motor & Engineering Co (1906) Ltd, Southport and numbered H3546 to H3795 (400hp Liberty 12A)

H3546 Deld 1.2.19
H3547 No information
H3548 No information
H3549 PD Ascot; AD Hinaidi 5.23 - 6.23 (special bomb machine)
H3550 1 FTS Netheravon, crashed on take-off 9.2.23; Tested IAAD 11.6.23 (Repair); Retd 1 FTS; FL on one wheel and crashed nr airfield 26.7.23 (Cpl EA Grose unhurt); Tested IAAD 8.11.23 - 3-11.1.24; 7 Sqn by 2.24 - @3.24; 11 Sqn, bounced and overturned landing, Bircham Newton, 3.5.24; DH recond (c/n 145); PD Ascot; AD Drigh Rd; 60 Sqn ('7') 6.25; AP Lahore; 60 Sqn ('X') 9.9.25 - 11.25; 27 Sqn ('D), crashed 1927
H3551 AD Aboukir rebuilt as HR3551; 4 FTS Abu Sueir 8.24; 55 Sqn ('B2') 7.26; AHQ Iraq Cd 7.27 - 9.27
H3552 39 Sqn 6.23 - 7.23; 5 FTS Shotwick 11.23 - 1.24: While landing in sudden thick mist, struck 504K which had already landed, Shotwick, 29.11.23 (P/O JE Doran-Webb unhurt); Repaired; Struck 504K landing in bad visibility, Shotwick, 21.1.24; 39 Sqn
H3553 100 Sqn c.1921
H3554 No information
H3555 PD Ascot; AD Drigh Rd; 27 Sqn 8.23
H3556 100 Sqn 1920 - 1921
H3557 24 Sqn by 2.22
H3558 At 15 AAP Manchester 6.2.19 allotted to EF; 57 Sqn by 5.19
H3559 At 15 AAP Manchester 7.2.19 allotted to EF;
H3560 At 15 AAP Manchester 7.2.19 allotted to EF:
H3561 & H3562 No information
H3563 En route from 15 AAP Manchester to EF 29.4.19 allotted to EF; PD Ascot; AD Hinaidi; 55 Sqn
H3564 & H3565 No information
H3566 Tested IAAD 18.12.23; 1 FTS 5.24 -11.24; DH recond (c/n 165); PD Ascot; AD Hinaidi; 55 Sqn ('Bl') 12.25 - 10.26 .
H3567 AEE Martlesham Heath by 7.22 - 12.22 (tests with oleo type u/c)
H3568 & H3569 No information
H3570 RAF College 3.20 - 4.20; PD Ascot; AD Hinaidi; 8 Sqn 8.24 - 2.25; 39 Sqn ('3') 1.27; PD Ascot; AD Aboukir; 14 Sqn 8.29 - 9.29
H3571 to H3580 No information
H3581 DH rebuilt and renumbered J7303 (c/n 120)
H3582 to H3585 No information
H3586 39 Sqn; 100 Sqn Fermoy 1920 - 1921
H3587 207 Sqn by 2.22
H3588 100 Sqn 4.21; Instrument Design Establishment, Biggin

Hill by 19.8.21; RAE 10.4.22; DH recond; RAE 29.4.26 - 29.10.30; Made flight refuelling test flight, probably with trailing apparatus 6.8.30; RAE (air-cooled Liberty 12 with Fairey Reed metal airscrew), crashed, 13.6.33
H3589 No information
H3590 100 Sqn 12.20 - 5.21
H3591 to H3594 No information
H3595 DH rebuilt and renumbered J7305 (c/n 122)
H3596 Delny by 10.19 (3-seat conversion; 3 Sqn?)
H3597 to H3616 No information
H3617 DH rebuilt and renumbered J7302 (c/n 119)
H3618 & H3619 No information
H3620 PD Ascot; AD Drigh Rd; 60 Sqn ('6') 10.23: EF on take-off, FL on rough ground, Risalpur, 25.2.24 (P/O GH Rawlinson unhurt)
H3621 No information
H3622 PD Ascot; AD Hinaidi; 84 Sqn
H3623 PD Ascot; AD Hinaidi; 84 Sqn
H3624 No information
H3625 PD Ascot; AD Hinaidi 4.23
H3626 55 Sqn 7.22; PD Ascot; AD Drigh Rd; 60 Sqn ('Q') 6.25 - 11.25; AD Drigh Road 1926; 60 Sqn ('X') 3.26; AD Hinaidi by 6.26 - @7.26; 60 Sqn ('X') to AD Drigh Rd 11.8.27; 60 Sqn (comms) (conv DC at some stage) (TT mod at one time)
H3627 PD Ascot; AD Hinaidi; 55 Sqn ('CI':'CII':'CIII') 1922
H3628 PD Ascot; AD Hinaidi by 8.23 - @10.23; AD Hinaidi 9.24; 8 Sqn 10.24; 55 Sqn 5.25 - 8.25; 84 Sqn, air mail duty, FL and over-turned, Diwaniyah, 31.12.25 (P/O JE Tomes unhurt & AC1 JC Turnbull injured); PD Ascot; AD Hinaidi; 8 Sqn 5.27 - 1.28
H3629 AEE Martlesham Heath, erecting W/E 16.3.21 (petrol system tests); Crashed W/E 19.8.21; WO
H3630 RAF (Cadet) College, Cranwell 9.26; DH recond (c/n 159); PD Ascot; AD Hinaidi; 8 Sqn ('E')
H3631 207 Sqn by 5.24 - 11.24; A&GS Eastchurch; HAD 3.29; RAF (Cadet) College, Cranwell 5.29 - 5.30; CFS 1930; 3 FTS Spittlegate 3.31; RAF (Cadet) College, Cranwell 3.31; ASS Hawkinge 27.3.31
H3632 PD Ascot; AD Hinaidi; Rigging tests, EF, FL 23.10.24 (F/L TH McDowell & LAC HW Green both OK); 30 Sqn ('B) 1924 (swastika on fin); Recd UK; PD Ascot; AD Drigh Rd; 60 Sqn ('Y') 1.27 - 3.27; 27 Sqn ('G')
H3633 PD Ascot; AD Hinaidi; 30 Sqn 1924; AD Hinaidi by 5.24; 84 Sqn; 30 Sqn ('30'), mid-air collision at 6,000ft with J7114, spun for 2,000ft but landed safely, Cat W 25.4.27
H3634 PD Ascot; AD Aboukir; 47 Sqn by 8.21 - @10.21; AP Baghdad; 30 Sqn 2.22; 47 Sqn 6.22 - 1.23; Retd UK?; PD Ascot; AD Drigh Rd; 60 Sqn
H3635 Arr 6 SD Ascot (via Farnborough) for packing 20.9.20; To 207 Sqn 11.20, erected 14.11.20; To Farnborough to be packed for Turkey 21.9.22; 207 Sqn Turkey 11.22 - 1.24; PD Ascot; AD Aboukir to 47 Sqn 15.2.26 ('C', named 'DARIUS'); 14 Sqn 11.26 - 7.27
H3636 PD Ascot; AD Aboukir; 4 FTS Abu Sueir 6.1.22 - 2.22
H3637 PD Ascot; AD Hinaidi by 2.23; 84 Sqn 12.3.23; Retd UK; RAF (Cadet) College, Cranwell 9.26 - 9.27
H3638 PD Ascot; AD Hinaidi; 55 Sqn; Engine cut on landing, Cat W 8.3.22 (F/O PW Lingwood OK)
H3639 PD Ascot; AD Hinaidi; 8 Sqn 3.23 - 4.23; 47 Sqn 2.25 - 10.25
H3640 PD Ascot; AD Aboukir; 47 Sqn 8.21 - 10.21
H3641 PD Ascot; AD Aboukir; 47 Sqn 3.22; Retd UK; 39 Sqn 11.24 - 6.25
H3642 Crashed en route Ireland 10.9.20; S of TT Manston 9.21; Tested IAAD 12-16.6.23; 2 FTS Duxford 6.23 - 7.23; 5 FTS, stalled on side-slip landing, TW, Shotwick 31.7.23 (P/O BH Shaw unhurt)
H3643 PD Ascot; AD Hinaidi by 7.23; 84 Sqn 28.8.23; Pilot's cockpit ignited by spark from exhaust on take-off, landed safely 18.8.24; AD Hinaidi; Recd UK; DH recond on Cont No 579165/25 (c/n 179); PD Ascot; AD Drigh Rd; 60 Sqn ('W') 11.26 - 5.27; AD Drigh Rd; FL, 12.12.27; 60 Sqn 8.28; AD Drigh Rd 3.29 (slots fitted); 60 Sqn ('W) 4.29 - 3.30
H3644 & H3645 No information
H3646 DH recond (c/n 24); Waddon 2.2.22; PD Ascot; AD Drigh Rd; AP Lahore; 60 Sqn 7.25
H3647 Sold to Soviet Russian Air Force (RKKVF)
H3648 No information
H3649 Sold to Soviet Russian Air Force (RKKVF)
H3650 DH recond (c/n 20); Waddon 14.12.21
H3651 PD Ascot; AD Drigh Rd; 60 Sqn 7.23; EF at 8,500ft, crashed, nr Duncan's Picquet, Razmak 15.10.23 (F/O LG Nixon injured & WJT Gomm OK?)
H3652 to H3656 No information
H3657 DH recond (c/n 81); Gosport by road; Spittlegate to Martlesham 7.2.22; To Westland to fit oleo u/c for trials
H3658 No information
H3659 1 SoN&BD Stonehenge by 4.19 - @7.19; 100 Sqn 12.20 - 4.21
H3660 to H3669 No information
H3670 Deld 9.19
H3671 to H3795 cancelled 1.19

100 D.H.9 ordered 14.8.18 under Cont No 35a/1030/C.835 (later 35a/1546/C.1648) (BR.521) from Aircraft Manufacturing Co Ltd, Hendon and numbered H4216 to H4315. (230hp Puma)

PM .0"
H4216 & H4217 No information
H4218 6 AI to 211 Sqn 9.12.18; 98 Sqn 24.2.19; 8 AAP Lympne 13.3.19
H4219 At Meteor Flight by 24.2.19 to 21.7.19
H4220 & H4221 No information
H4222 117 Sqn by 10.18 - @1.19; 6 AI to 107 Sqn 16.1.19; 98 Sqn 1.3.19; 8 AAP Lympne 8.3.19
H4223 555/6 Flts 219 Sqn Manston, HACP 10.11.18
H4224 No information
H4225 At 2 AAP Hendon 18.10.18 for 119 Sqn (mob) Wyton; At sqn by 26.10.18; Reallotted by 18.11.18
H4226 No information
H4227 2 ASD to 104 Sqn 7.12.18; SOC 21.1.19
H4228 No information
H4229 1 ASD to 103 Sqn 30.10.18 - @3.19
H4230 No information
H4231 At 2 AAP Hendon 18.10.18 for 119 Sqn (Mob) Wyton; At sqn by 29.10.18; Reallotted by 18.11.18; 59 TDS Scopwick, propeller accident 22.1.19 (3/AM D Edwards seriously injured); Nosed in 5.19
H4232 & H4233 No information
H4233 At 2 AAP Hendon 4.10.18 for 119 Sqn (Mob) Wyton; To sqn 16.10.18; Reallotted by 18.11.18;
H4234 At 2 AAP Hendon 9.10.18 for 119 Sqn (Mob) Wyton; Reallotted to 117 Sqn (Mob) Norwich 18.10.18; At sqn by 31.12.18;
H4235 & H4236 No information
H4237 RAF & Army Co-opn School, Worthy Down by 11.18
H4238 At 2 AAP Hendon 10.10.18 for 119 Sqn (Mob) Wyton; To sqn 23.10.18; Reallotted by 18.11.18
H4239 No information
H4240 At 2 AAP Hendon 14.10.18 for 119 Sqn (Mob) Wyton; At sqn by 29.10.18; Reallotted by 18.11.18
H4241 At 2 AAP Hendon 10.10.18 for 119 Sqn (Mob) Wyton; At sqn by 25.10.18; Reallotted by 18.11.18
H4242 Presentation Aircraft 'The J.M.Dixon No.2'
H4243 At 2 AAP Hendon 25.10.18 for 119 Sqn (Mob) Wyton; At sqn by 29.10.18; Reallotted by 18.11.18
H4244 At 2 AAP Hendon 10.10.18 for 119 Sqn (Mob) Wyton; 119 Sqn by 29.10.18; Reallotted by 18.11.18

D.H.9 H4229 of No.103 Squadron, seen here at Eastbourne, has a roundel under the top wing. (J.M.Bruce/G.S.Leslie collection)

H4245 Recd Rec Pk ex UK for IF 5.11.18; 3 AD 9.11.18; 2 ASD to 211 Sqn 15.11.18; 98 Sqn 23.2.19; 8 AAP Lympne 6.3.19
H4246 No information
H4247 At 2 AAP Hendon 14.10.18 for 119 Sqn (Mob) Wyton; At sqn by 25.10.18; Reallotted by 18.11.18
H4248 No information
H4249 206 Sqn by 12.18; EF, FL Andrimont, E of Verviers 1.1.19 (Lt CL Cumming & 2/Lt HO Brown unhurt); for 8 SS repair
H4250 At 2 AAP Hendon 14.10.18 for 119 Sqn (Mob) Wyton
H4251 At 2 AAP Hendon 14.10.18 for 119 Sqn (Mob) Wyton; Reallotted to 117 Sqn (Mob) Norwich 18.10.18; At sqn by 7.11.18; Seen Gosport
H4252 1 ASD to 98 Sqn 2.11.18; 8 AAP Lympne 7.2.19
H4253 At 2 AAP Hendon 29.10.18 for 117 Sqn (Mob) Norwich
H4254 At 2 AAP Hendon 18.10.18 for 117 Sqn (Mob) Norwich; To sqn 16/17.10.18
H4255 No information
H4256 206 Sqn by 12.18; Hangar collapsed on it during night, Nivelle 20-21.12.18; to 7 SS repair
H4257 At 8 AAP Lympne 23.1.19 allotted to SE Area for Store;
H4258 2 AI to 103 Sqn 7.11.18; 98 Sqn 11.3.19
H4259 Deld Naval Flt 219 Sqn Manston 26.10.18 - @2.12.18; HACPs 5.11.18 & 10.11.18; Allotted Polish Military Purchase Mission on free issue 22.4.20; Desp 19.3.20
H4260 At 2 AAP Hendon 15.10.18 for 119 Sqn (Mob) Wyton; Reallotted to D of T 25.10.18; 6 SD Ascot, allotted Anti-Bolshevik Govt for General Denikin; Re-allotted Polish Military Purchase Mission on free issue 22.4.20; Despatched port for shipment in SS *Neptune* 27.4.20
H4261 No information
H4262 Deld Naval Flt 219 Sqn Manston 31.10.18 - @11.18; Manston to Handley Page, Cricklewood for Polish Military Purchase Mission on free issue 19.3.20
H4263 At 2 AAP Hendon 16.10.18 for 117 Sqn (Mob) Norwich; At sqn by 7.11.18
H4264 At 2 AAP Hendon 16.10.18 for 117 Sqn (Mob) Norwich; At sqn by 7.11.18; Naval Flt 219 Sqn Manston by 21.11.18
H4265 No information
H4266 At 2 AAP Hendon 16.10.18 for 117 Sqn (Mob) Norwich; At sqn 2.11.18
H4267 Deld Naval Flt 219 Sqn Manston 31.10.18 - @7.12.18
H4268 Deld 534 Flt 273 Sqn Covehithe by 4.11.18 @2.12.18; HACP 4.11.18
H4269 No information
H4270 2 AI to 27 Sqn 22.11.18; 98 Sqn 5.3.19; 1 ASD 17.3.19; Meteor Flight (named 'Maud') 6.5.19 to 1.8.19
H4271 No information
H4272 Deld 534 Flt 273 Sqn Covehithe, HACP 10.11.18; At 2 AAP Hendon 28.12.18, reallotted from EF to 120 Sqn (Mob) Bracebridge; To sqn 2.1.19
H4273 1 SoN&BD Stonehenge by 7.1.19; Low flying, lost control, sideslipped in, aileron controls found broken, crashed No.4 Camp, Larkhill killing No.16/113 Pte JB Tairua, Maori, New Zealand Pioneer Regt 13.2.19 (Lt WS Featherstone injured, also 2/Lt WJ Armstead injured [not RAF])
H4274 1 SoN&BD Stonehenge by 29.12.18 - @12.1.19
H4275 At 8 AAP Lympne 20.1.19 reallotted from EF to Midland Area for 120 Sqn (Mob); 120 Sqn, took woollen goods and food to Belgium to relieve scarcity there 1.19; still with 120 Sqn at Hawkinge by 3.19 - 8.19
H4276 1 SoN&BD Stonehenge by 30.12.18 - @6.1.19
H4277 Presentation Aircraft 'Presented by M.W.Oldham Esq of Newsteed, N.S.W'. At 8 AAP Lympne 24.1.19 reallotted from EF to Store
H4278 8 TDS Netheravon by 4.19 - @21.8.19
H4279 Deld 534 Flt 273 Sqn Covehithe by 9.11.18 - @22.11.18; HACPs 9.11.18 & 10.11.18; Manston to Handley Page, Cricklewood for Polish Military Purchase Mission on free issue 19.3.20
H4280 Recd Rec Pk ex UK for IF 7.11.18; 3 AD 9.11.18; TOC EF 9.11.18
H4281 No information
H4282 206 Sqn by 4.19; 49 Sqn, handed in to 1 ASD 14.7.19
H4283 No information
H4284 Deld Mullion by 12.18; Padstow by 12.18
H4285 and H4286 No information
H4287 Deld Padstow by 11.18 - @12.18
H4288 1 ASD to 49 Sqn ('B') 19.6.19; 1 ASD 14.7.19
H4289 At 8 AAP Lympne 24.1.19 reallotted from EF to Store;
H4290 No information
H4291 206 Sqn by 12.18 - @30.1.19; Imperial Gift to Australia; Became *A6-22*
H4292 At 2 AAP Hendon by 30.10.18 for 120 Sqn (Mob) Bracebridge; At sqn by 12.11.18; FL nr Maisoncelle when on postal service 8.3.19; TOC EF 21.3.19 for write-off
H4293 No information
H4294 At 2 AAP Hendon by 30.10.18 for 120 Sqn (Mob) Bracebridge; At sqn by 30.12.18 - 1.19
H4295 No information
H4296 At 8 AAP Lympne 28.1.19 reallotted from EF to SE Area for Store; 120 Sqn by 3.19 - 8.19
H4297 120 Sqn Hawkinge by 5.20
H4298 & H4299No information
H4300 6 AI to 25 Sqn 10.6.19
H4301 (BHP) 4 SoN&BD Thetford, passenger thrown out of a/c 17.12.18 (2/Lt DJ Lewis OK & F/Cdt HStA Davies killed)
H4302 to H4306 No information
H4307 Imperial Gift to India
H4308 No information
H4309 At 8 AAP Lympne 28.1.19 reallotted from EF to Sout Eastern Area for Store; 120 Sqn Hawkinge by 3.19 - 8.19
H4310 to H4312 No information
H4313 Imperial Gift to South Africa
H4314 No information
H4315 6 SD Ascot, allotted Anti-Bolshevik Govt for General Denikin; Re-allotted Polish Military Purchase Mission on

D.H.9 H4272 of No.273 Squadron, Covehithe, with two Parnall Panthers in the background. (via Terry Treadwell)

D.H.9 H4288 ('B') of No.49 Squadron at Bickendorf in 1919. (via Terry Treadwell)

free issue 22.4.20; Despatched port for shipment in SS *Neptune* 28.4.20

1 D.H.9 ordered 13.8.18 under Cont No 35a/166/C.120 from Aircraft Manufacturing Co Ltd, Hendon and numbered H4316. Order cancelled as duplicated E5435

50 D.H.9 ordered 12.6.18 under Cont No 35a/1548/C.1649 from F.W.Berwick & Co Ltd, London and numbered H4320 to H4369. Cancelled 20.8.18, previously duplicated D7331 to D7380

350 D.H.9 ordered 2.9.18 under Cont No 35a/2830/C.3177 (BR.642) from The Alliance Aeroplane Co Ltd, Hammersmith and numbered H5541 to H5890. (230hp Puma)

"H5521" Became *T-DODF* [incorrect serial, out of block]
H5541 Sold to Soviet Russian Air Force (RKKVF)
H5542 At 7 AAP Kenley 3.12.18 reallotted from EF to Midland Area
H5543 No information
H5544 Imperial Gift to South Africa
H5545 Imperial Gift to South Africa
H5546 Imperial Gift to New Zealand; To NZ Flying School
H5547 No information
H5548 'Z' Unit British Somaliland by 1.20 until 5.4.20
H5549 Air Council Inspection Sqn by 8.19; To WEE Biggin Hill 9.19
H5550 At 2 AAP Hendon 2.12.18 reallotted from EF to Midland Area
H5551 At 7 AAP Kenley 30.1.19 reallotted from EF to Store; 206 Sqn 19.1.20; renumbered 47 Sqn 1.2.20; Special Instruction Flt, Almaza by 7.20; 4 FTS Abu Sueir 1.4.21 - 10.21
H5552 To Greek Government
H5553 At 2 AAP Hendon 28.12.18, reallotted from EF to 120 Sqn (Mob) Bracebridge; To sqn 2.1.19; still with 120 Sqn at Hawkinge 5.20
H5554 At 2 AAP Hendon 2.12.18 reallotted from EF to Midland Area
H5555 Arr AD Aboukir ex UK 28.2.20; ASD Aboukir 10.3.20
H5556 1 ASD to 6 AI 17.1.19; 211 Sqn 7.2.19; 98 Sqn 23.2.19
H5557 No information
H5558 To Greek Government
H5559 Cranwell by 4.19
H5560 No information
H5561 'Z' Unit British Somaliland by 1.20 until 5.4.20; Overturned Eil Dar Elan
H5562 Imperial Gift to South Africa as *137*
H5563 At 2 AAP Hendon 11.12.18 reallotted from EF to Midland Area
H5564 to H5566 No information
H5567 Deld 11.18
H5568 No information
H5569 To Greek Government
H5570 Imperial Gift to South Africa
H5571 to H5578No information
H5579 Became *G-EAOP*
H5580 Sold to Russia
H5581 Imperial Gift to South Africa
H5582 Sold to Russia
H5583 Imperial Gift to South Africa
H5584 & H5585 No information
H5586 Imperial Gift to South Africa as *126*
H5587 To Greek Government
H5588 To Greek Government
H5589 to H5591 No information
H5592 Imperial Gift to Australia; Became *A6-23*
H5593 Imperial Gift to South Africa
H5594 No information
H5595 'Z' Unit British Somaliland, crashed God Amod 25.1.20
H5596 & H5597 No information
H5598 3 (T) Group Navigation School, Norwich by 9.19
H5599 4 SoN&BD Thetford to 3 (T) Group Navigation School, Norwich 6.9.19
H5600 No information
H5601 Imperial Gift to South Africa as *132*
H5602 To Greek Government
H5603 to H5606 No information
H5607 Became *G-EAZC* (ferry marks to Belgian AF)
H5608 Imperial Gift to South Africa as *145*
H5609 Imperial Gift to New Zealand; To NZ Aero Transport Ltd
H5610 No information
H5611 Imperial Gift to South Africa as *131*
H5612 'Z' Unit British Somaliland by 1.20 until 5.4.20
H5613 to H5618No information
H5619 Became *G-EAYW* (ferry marks to Belgian AF)
H5620 No information
H5621 Became *G-EBAD* (ferry marks to Belgian AF)
H5622 To Greek Government
H5623 to H5626 No information
H5627 Imperial Gift to New Zealand; Became *G-NZAE* (fitted cabin)
H5628 At Makers 6.2.19 allotted to EF; Arr 206 Sqn Helwan ex France 29.7.19; Special Instruction Flt, Almaza by 7.20
H5629 Special Instruction Flt, Almaza by 10.20 - 11.20; Became *G-EAZA* (ferry marks to Belgian AF)
H5630 No information
H5631 Imperial Gift to South Africa as *122*
H5632 Became *G-EBGQ* (ferry marks to Belgian AF)
H5633 to H5635 No information
H5636 Imperial Gift to New Zealand; Became *G-NZAD* (fitted cabin); To NZPAF as *5636*
H5637 No information
H5638 Free issue to Chile Government
H5639 Imperial Gift to South Africa
H5640 No information
H5641 Imperial Gift to New Zealand; To NZ Flying School
H5642 To Greek Government
H5643 No information
H5644 Imperial Gift to South Africa
H5645 No information
H5646 Sold abroad
H5647 Imperial Gift to South Africa as *129*
H5648 Imperial Gift to South Africa; To SAAF as *121*, named 'Voortrekker'. Made first UK-Cape Town flight
H5649 Imperial Gift to South Africa
H5650 No information
H5651 Imperial Gift to South Africa
H5652 Became *G-EBDF*, later *C-CAEU*
H5653 to H5656 No information
H5657 Imperial Gift to South Africa
H5658 No information
H5659 Imperial Gift to South Africa as *134*
H5660 To Greek Government
H5661 To Greek Government
H5662 Became *G-EBAS* (ferry marks to Belgian AF); To Belgian AF 1.22
H5663 No information
H5664 To Greek Government
H5665 No information
H5666 Became *G-EAZJ* (ferry marks to Belgian AF)
H5667 Imperial Gift to South Africa
H5668 Became *G-EAZZ* (ferry marks to Belgian AF)
H5669 Imperial Gift to South Africa
H5670 Imperial Gift to South Africa
H5671 Sold to Russia
H5672 Imperial Gift to New Zealand; Became *G-NZAQ*
H5673 To Greek Government
H5674 'Z' Unit British Somaliland, crashed east of Ragnala 24.1.20
H5675 to H5677 No information
H5678 Became *G-EBDL* (painted "G-EBDE" in 1922 to cover the accident to the true *G-EBDE*), later *G-CAEU*
H5679 Imperial Gift to Australia; Became *A6-24*
H5680 & H5681 No information
H5682 At Makers 6.2.19 allotted to EF; Arr ASD Almaza ex France 16.9.19; Special Instruction Flt, Almaza 20.1.20; 47 Sqn by 9.20
H5683 To Greek Government
H5684 No information
H5685 Imperial Gift to South Africa
H5686 At Makers 6.2.19 allotted to EF; Arr ASD Almaza ex France 16.9.19; 'H' Unit, Sudan 7.12.19 - @2.20
H5687 Imperial Gift to South Africa
H5688 Became *G-EBEN*
H5689 Imperial Gift to South Africa
H5690 & H5691 No information
H5692 Imperial Gift to South Africa as *139*

H5693 At Makers 6.2.19 allotted to EF but reallotted to Ministry of Munitions Salvage Depot 13.3.19
H5694 At Makers 6.2.19 allotted to EF but reallotted to Ministry of Munitions Salvage Depot 13.3.19
H5694 No information
H5695 Imperial Gift to South Africa
H5696 No information
H5697 Imperial Gift to Australia; Became *A6-25*
H5698 to H5700 No information
H5701 At Makers 6.2.19 allotted to EF; 'X' AD to 206 Sqn Helwan 6.8.19 - @12.19; Special Instruction Flt, Almaza 10.20 - 12.20
H5702 6 SD Ascot, allotted Anti-Bolshevik Govt for General Denikin; Re-allotted Polish Military Purchase Mission on free issue 22.4.20; Despatched port for shipment in SS *Neptune* 27.4.20
H5703 At Makers 6.2.19 allotted to EF but reallotted to Ministry of Munitions Salvage Depot 13.3.19; Sold to Russia
H5704 No information
H5705 Became *G-EAZB* (ferry marks to Belgian AF)
H5706 Became *G-EAZY* (ferry marks to Belgian AF)
H5707 Became *G-EAZN* (ferry marks to Belgian AF)
H5708 No information
H5709 Became *G-EBBB* (ferry marks to Belgian AF)
H5710 Free issue to Chile Government
H5711 Became *G-EBBJ* (ferry marks to Belgian AF)
H5712 Became *G-EBAI* (ferry marks to Belgian AF)
H5713 At Makers 6.2.19 allotted to EF but reallotted to Ministry of Munitions Salvage Depot 13.3.19; Sold to Russia
H5714 No information
H5715 Free issue to Chile Government
H5716 Became *G-EBAO* (ferry marks to Belgian AF)
H5717 No information
H5718 At Makers 6.2.19 allotted to EF; 'X' AD to 206 Sqn 6.8.19; ASD Almaza 24.1.20
H5719 Became *G-EBBK* (ferry marks to Belgian AF)
H5720 Sold to Russia
H5721 6 SD Ascot, allotted Anti-Bolshevik Govt for General Denikin; Re-allotted Polish Military Purchase Mission on free issue 22.4.20; Despatched port for shipment in SS *Neptune* 30.4.20
H5722 Free issue to Chile Government
H5723 At Makers 6.2.19 allotted to EF but reallotted to Ministry of Munitions Salvage Depot 13.3.19
H5724 No information
H5725 Free issue to Chile Government
H5726 Free issue to Chile Government
H5727 & H5728 No information
H5729 Sold to Russia
H5730 Free issue to Chile Government
H5731 to H5734 No information
H5735 Became *G-EBBA* (ferry marks to Belgian AF)
H5736 Became *G-EBAE* (ferry marks to Belgian AF)
H5737 No information
H5738 Became *G-EBDE*; Crashed 28.5.22 (replaced by H5678/*G-EBDL* which was spuriously painted as *G-EBDE*)
H5739 & H5740 No information
H5741 Became *G-EBAP* (ferry marks to Belgian AF)
H5742 Became *G-EBCI* (ferry marks to Belgian AF)
H5743 No information
H5744 to H5746 Sold to Russia
H5747 Became *G-EBAR* (ferry marks to Belgian AF)
H5748 Sold to Russia
H5749 to H5751 No information
H5752 Sold to Russia
H5753 Became *G-EBAQ* (ferry marks to Belgian AF)
H5754 to H5756 No information
H5757 Became *G-EAZE* (ferry marks to Belgian AF)
H5758 Sold to Russia
H5759 to H5762 No information
H5763 120 Sqn Hawkinge by 3.19 - 8.19
H5764 to H5773 No information
H5774 To Irish Air Service as *III* later *DHIII*
H5775 Became *G-EBEF*
H5776 & H5779 No information
H5778 Sold to Russia
H5779 to H5782 No information
H5783 Became *G-EBAA* (ferry marks to Belgian AF)
H5784 & H5785 No information
H5786 Sold to Russia
H5787 & H5788 No information
H5789 (BHP) 11 TDS Old Sarum, spun, dived in, BO 13.12.18 (Lt GT Ritchie killed) [prefix?]
H5790 to H5794 No information
H5795 Sold to Russia
H5796 No information
H5797 To Irish Air Service as *I* later *DHI*
H5798 & H5799 No information
H5800 Sold to Russia
H5801 & H5802 No information
H5803 Sold to Russia
H5804 No information
H5805 Sold to Russia
H5806 & H5807 No information
H5808 Sold to Russia
H5809 to H5810 No information
H5811 to H5813 Sold to Russia
H5814 Sold to Soviet Russian Air Force (RKKVF)
H5815 Sold to Russia
H5816 No information
H5817 Sold to Russia
H5818 No information
H5819 Sold to Russia
H5820 Became *G-EBCJ* (ferry marks to Belgian AF)
H5821 Sold to Russia
H5822 No information
H5823 To Irish Air Service as *V* later *DHV*
H5824 & H5825 No information
H5626 to H5628 Sold to Russia
H5829 No information
H5830 To Irish Air Service as *II* later *DHII*
H5831 No information
H5832 Sold to Russia
H5833 Became *G-EAYY*
H5834 & H5835 No information
H5836 Became *G-EBCH* (ferry marks to Belgian AF); To Belgian AF 4.22 [and others? - check sometime]
H5837 & H5838 No information
H5839 Became *G-EAZH*, later *CH-81*
H5840 No information
H5841 Tested 2 AAP Hendon 11.1.19; Sold to Russia
H5842 & H5843 No information
H5844 Became *G-EBHV* (D.H.9J)
H5845 Became *G-EAZO* (ferry marks to Belgian AF)
H5846 Sold to Russia
H5847 No information
H5848 Became *G-EAYZ*
H5849 & H5850 No information
H5851 Became *G-EBAB* (ferry marks to Belgian AF)
H5852 to H5854 No information
H5855 Sold abroad
H5856 Became *G-EAZD* (ferry marks to Belgian AF)
H5857 to H5859 No information
H5860 Became *G-EAZI*, later *CH-84*
H5861 No information
H5862 To Irish Army Air Corps as *8*
H5863 No information
H5864 Sold abroad
H5865 Became *G-EAZM* (ferry marks to Belgian AF)
H5866 & H5867 No information
H5868 Became *G-EAZP* (ferry marks to Belgian AF)
H5869 To Irish Air Service as *IV* later *DHIV*
H5870 to H5872 No information
H5873 Sold to Netherlands East Indies
H5874 to H5879 No information
H5880 Sold abroad
H5881 to H5885 No information
H5886 Became *G-EBIG*
H5887 & H5888 No information
H5889 (c/n P.32E) Became *G-EAOZ*, later *H-NABF*
H5890 (c/n P.33E) Deld 9.19; Became *G-EAPL*, later *H-NABE*

H6843 to H7342 were allocated for the renumbering of aircraft rebuilt in France. Many such numbers were given to rebuilds which had originally been incorrectly renumbered in the range F6320 onwards. This range included the following D.H.9 and D.H.9A

H7075 (D.H.9) Rebuilt ex F6452 26.8.18; Rep Pk 1 ASD to 1

AI 9.10.18; 108 Sqn 10.10.18; On landing overshot and on taking off again stalled and nose dived into ditch 18.10.18 (Lt HH Cooke OK); Rep Pk 1 ASD 21.10.18
H7076 (D.H.9) Rebuilt ex E657 6.9.18;
H7107 (D.H.9A) Rebuilt from salvage
H7180 (D.H.9) 4 SoN&BD Thetford, stalled landing, dived in 6.1.19
H7201 (D.H.9) Rebuilt ex E8932 27.9.18
H7202 (D.H.9) Rebuilt ex E8938 27.9.18
H7203 (D.H.9) Rebuilt ex E8983 27.9.18
H7204 (D.H.9A) Rebuilt ex F2747 17.12.18

50 D.H.9 ordered 9.8.18 under Cont No 35a/2336/C.2643 (BR.618) from G & J Weir Ltd, Cathcart, Glasgow and numbered H7563 to H7612. Order cancelled 12.18

200 D.H.9 ordered 23.8.18 under Cont No 35a/2687/C.2982 (B.R.639) from Crossley Motors/ National Aircraft Factory No.2, Heaton Chapel and numbered H7913 to H8112. Order cancelled 1.19

Serial numbers H8113 to H8412 reserved for an unidentified order for 300 D.H.9. Not taken up. Numbers reallocated

300 D.H.9 ordered 24.8.18 under Cont No 35a/2686/C.2981 (BR.638) from Aircraft Manufacturing Co Ltd, Hendon and numbered H9113 to H9412. H9372 to H9412 bought back by company. (230hp Puma)

H9113 & H9114 No information
H9115 IAAD; Imperial Gift to India, shipped SS *Hatimura* 8.20
H9116 No information
H9117 Free issue to Chile Government
H9118 Free issue to Chile Government
H9119 Deld 11.18
H9120 to H9124 No information
H9125 Became *G-EAUQ* (D.H.9B)
H9126 & H9127 No information
H9128 Became *G-EAUN*, later *M-AGAG* (D.H.9B)
H9129 Became *G-IAAA*, later *G-IAAP*, later *VT-AAP* (Seaplane)
H9130 to H9132 No information
H9133 Sold to Estonian Government; To Estonian Air Sqn as *No.17*
H9134 No information
H9135 Sold to Estonian Government; To Estonian Air Sqn as *No.16*
H9136 to H9139 No information

D.H.9 H9140 fitted with a Handley Page wing and designated H.P.17. (J.M.Bruce/G.S.Leslie collection)

H9140 Purchased by Handley Page from Aircraft Disposals Board 2.20; Mod with HP slots (retrospectively designated H.P.17); FF 31.3.20; Undercarriage raised 12 inches 5.20; Gosport (for HMS *Argus*); RAE 26.8.20 (HP wing section tests); H-P Cricklewood 30.9.20; Press demonstration Cricklewood 21.10.20; RAE 1.21 (comparative landing trials with standard DH9 D5755)
H9141 to H9146 No information
H9147 Became *G-EBJX*
H9148 to H9151 No information
H9152 Sold to Russia
H9153 to H9156 No information
H9157 Sold to Estonian Government; To Estonian Air Sqn as *No.31*
H9158 to H9164 No information
H9165 Sold to Russia
H9166 to H9175 No information
H9176 Became *G-EAUP* (D.H.9B)
H9177 to H9186 No information
H9187 Became *G-EAUO* (D.H.9B)
H9188 to H9195 No information
H9196 Became *G-EAUH*, later *H-NABP* (D.H.9B)
H9197 Became *G-EAUI* (D.H.9B)
H9198 to H9202 No information
H9203 Became *G-EBHP*
H9204 No information
H9205 Became *G-EBQD*
H9206 to H9208 No information
H9209 Free issue to Chile Government
H9210 & H9211 No information
H9212 Tested 2 AAP Hendon 5-7.4.19; Sold to Belgian Government
H9213 to H9215 No information
H9216 Free issue to Chile Government
H9217 to H9227 No information
H9228 Free issue to Chile Government
H9229 to H9241 No information
H9242 Sold abroad
H9243 Became *G-EAVM*, later *T-DOKL*
H9244 & H9245 No information
H9246 (c/n 3259) Became *T-DOGH*, later *OY-DIC*
H9247 To Irish Army Air Corps as *7*
H9248 Became *G-AACP* (D.H.9B)
H9249 No information
H9250 Sold abroad
H9251 No information
H9252 Sold abroad
H9253 & H9254 No information
H9255 Became *G-EAGX*
H9256 & H9257 No information
H9258 Became *G-EAGY*
H9259 No information
H9260 Sold abroad
H9261 Free issue to Chile Government
H9262 No information
H9263 Free issue to Chile Government
H9264 to H9270 No information
H9271 Became *G-EATA* (D.H.9B)
H9272 Sold abroad
H9273 Allotted *G-EAAD* (NTU)
H9274 Became *T-DOBC*
H9275 Sold abroad
H9276 Became *G-ABYR*, later *G-AUJA* later *VH-UJA*
H9277 Became *K109* (D.H.9B) later *G-EAAC* (D.H.9J)
H9278 Sold abroad
H9279 to H9281 No information
H9282 Became *G-EAUC* (D.H.9B)
H9283 Sold abroad
H9284 No information
H9285 Sold abroad
H9286 to H9288 No information
H9289 Became *G-EBJR* (rebuild c/n 15B)
H9290 Sold to Soviet Russian Air Force (RKKVF)
H9291 to H9293 No information
H9294 Sold to Soviet Russian Air Force (RKKVF)
H9295 & H9296 No information
H9297 Sold abroad
H9298 Sold abroad
H9299 to H9301 No information
H9302 Sold abroad
H9303 to H9308 No information
H9309 Purchased in 1922 by Soviet Russian Air Fleet (RKKVF) [prefix?]
H9310 To Irish Air Service as *IV* later *DHVI*
H9311 Sold abroad
H9312 No information
H9313 Sold abroad
H9314 to H9318 No information
H9319 Became *G-EBKO*
H9320 to H9322 No information
H9323 Purchased in 1922 by Soviet Russian Air Fleet (RKKVF) [prefix?]
H9324 Became *G-AACR* (Puma)

H9325 & H9326 No information
H9327 Allotted *G-AACS* (NTU)
H9328 & H9329 No information
H9330 Sold to Soviet Russian Air Force (RKKVF)
H9331 & H9332 No information
H9333 Became *G-EBJW*
H9334 Sold to Russia
H9335 & H9336 No information
H9337 Became *G-EBKV*; Sold abroad
H9338 & H9339 No information
H9340 Became *G-AUFS* later *VH-UFS*
H9341 Sold abroad
H9342 to H9349 No information
H9350 Sold to Russia
H9351 to H9368 No information
H9369 Became *G-EBTR*
H9370 Became *O-BATA* later *G-EBUM* later *VT-AAK* (D.H.9C)
H9371 No information
H9372 to H9412 bought back by company, of which following reported:
H9375 1 FTS by 10.24
H9378 1 FTS by 11.24
H9412 Deld 9.19; Presented by the City of Birmingham to South Africa as *143*

50 D.H.9A ordered on Cont Nos 35a/3093/C3565 and AS.31684 dated 21.9.18 from Westland Aircraft Works, Yeovil to be numbered J401 to J450. Order cancelled 12.18.

50 D.H.9A ordered on Cont Nos 35a/3092/C3566 and AS.31683 dated 21.9.18 from Mann, Egerton & Co Ltd, Norwich to be numbered J551 to J600. (400hp Liberty 12A)

J551 Deld 3 AAP Norwich 23.11.18
J552 Deld 3 AAP Norwich; PD Ascot; AD Hinaidi; 8 Sqn (DC) 8.22 - 4.23; AD Hinaidi; Rebuilt 10.23 - 12.23; AD Hinaidi 2.24 - 3.24; 84 Sqn; Stalled on take-off, Cat W 12.4.24
J553 Deld 3 AAP Norwich; PD Ascot; AD Aboukir; 47 Sqn 5.22 - 10.22
J554 Deld 3 AAP Norwich; DH recond (c/n 54); PD Ascot; AD Hinaidi; 8 Sqn 15.6.24 - 10.24; 55 Sqn 1927
J555 Deld 3 AAP Norwich; DH recond (c/n 51); Tested IAAD 18.4.23; A&GS Eastchurch 5.23 - 7.23; 39 Sqn 4.24
J556 Deld 3 AAP Norwich; To 4 SD Ascot via Farnborough for packing 20.9.20; Erected 207 Sqn 21.10.20; EF during bombing practice, ditched nr HMS *Iron Duke*, which rescued crew & salved a/c, 16m S of San Stefano, 22.2.23 (F/O SE Storrar & F/O MH Ely picked up unhurt)
J557 Deld 3 AAP Norwich; To 4 SD Ascot via Farnborough for packing 20.9.20; 207 Sqn, tested 3.11.20; Crashed in soft ground after fast landing, San Stefano, 5.2.23 (F/O WE Knowlden & F/O HJ Payne both unhurt)
J558 Deld 3 AAP Norwich; 2 FTS Duxford 11.21 - 6.22
J559 Deld 3 AAP Norwich; 207 Sqn Bircham Newton 7.22; EF at 8000ft, ditched in sea 21m off coast, 1.8.22 (F/L AD Pryor & Sqn Ldr AW Tedder both unhurt)
J560 Deld 3 AAP Norwich; S of AG&B 9.21; Renamed A&GS Eastchurch 1.4.22 - 6.23; 207 Sqn San Stefano 1923; DH recond (c/n 50); PD Ascot; AD Hinaidi; 30 Sqn ('B'); AD Hinaidi 1925; 55 Sqn (B2) 10.26 - 9.28
J561 Deld 3 AAP Norwich; To 4 SD Ascot via Farnborough for packing 20.9.20; 207 Sqn, erected 11.20 - 1.23; DH recond c/n 143); RAF (Cadet) College, Cranwell 8.26 - 7.28
J562 Deld 3 AAP Norwich
J563 Deld 3 AAP Norwich; 2 FTS Duxford 2.22 - 10.22
J564 Deld 3 AAP Norwich; 2 FTS Duxford 2.22 - 7.22; PD Ascot; AD Hinaidi 30 Sqn 6.24
J565 Deld 3 AAP Norwich; 2 FTS Duxford 7.21; Tested IAAD 8-9.11.23; PD Ascot; AD Hinaidi; 55 Sqn ('3') 1929/30
J566 Deld 3 AAP Norwich; 2 FTS Duxford 7.21 4.22; 'A' Flt 207 Sqn ('A') 10.22 - 4.24; Crashed on nose, San Stefano, 24.2.23; HAD Henlow 4.24; AD Drigh Rd; 27 Sqn 8.26 - 11.26; 60 Sqn ('Q'); EF, FL Nemi Chaomoni, India 15.4.27 (F/L JW Baker MC DFC); AD

D.H.9A J565 of No.55 Squadron around 1929/30. (via Philip Jarrett)

D.H.9A J579 'V' of No.57 Squadron in 1919. (RAF Museum P.19735)

Westland-built D.H.9A J6958, fitted with a Napier Lion engine. (via Philip Jarrett)

Drigh Rd; 60 Sqn 1.30; AD Drigh Rd 3.4.30

J567 Deld 3 AAP Norwich; 2 FTS Duxford 5.21 - 7.22; 24 Sqn 1926; PD Ascot; AD Drigh Rd; 27 Sqn 1930

J568 Deld 3 AAP Norwich

J569 Deld 3 AAP Norwich; 2 FTS Duxford 2.21

J570 Deld 3 AAP Norwich

J571 Deld 3 AAP Norwich

J572 Deld 3 AAP Norwich by 12.4.19, reallotted from Midland Area for store to EF; RAE 27.1.20; CB Coop Flt, Gosport 11.2.20; Starting accident, Fort Grange, Gosport, 23.4.20 (F/O DM Cassidy OK & Cpl Mech W Paxton seriously injured); IAAD; RAE 21.12.22; 24 Sqn 23.2.23 - 5.23

J573 Deld 3 AAP Norwich by 12.4.19, reallotted from Midland Area for store to EF

J574 Deld 3 AAP Norwich; 2 FTS Duxford 2.21 - 9.22; RAF (Cadet) College, Cranwell 8.23 - 1.25; RAF (Cadet) College, Cranwell 5.28

J575 Deld 3 AAP Norwich; 2 FTS Duxford 10.22 - 4.23; PD Ascot; AD Aboukir; 4 FTS Abu Sueir 8.25

J576 Deld 3 AAP Norwich

J577 Deld 3 AAP Norwich by 12.4.19, allotted to EF; 57 Sqn 8.19

J578 Deld 3 AAP Norwich by 12.4.19, allotted to EF; Northolt to RAE 12.2.20; CB Coop Flt, Gosport 25.2.20; Ferried Leuchars to Gosport 26.6.20; 24 Sqn 2.23; Lost control and stalled at 900ft, hit tree, wrecked, Taunton Farm, Kenley, 28.1.24 (P/O AW Daly slightly injured); Rebuilt?; 84 Sqn 5.25 - 7.25

J579 Deld 3 AAP Norwich by 12.4.19, allotted to EF; 57 Sqn ('V') 6.19 - 7.19

J580 Deld 3 AAP Norwich by 18.2.19 allotted to EF; Reallotted for Training 5.4.19

J581 Deld 3 AAP Norwich by 18.2.19 allotted to EF; Reallotted for Training 5.4.19

J582 Deld 3 AAP Norwich by 18.2.19, allotted to EF; Reallotted for Training 5.4.19

J583 Deld 3 AAP Norwich by 18.2.19, allotted to EF; Reallotted for Training 5.4.19

J584 Deld 3 AAP Norwich by 18.2.19, allotted to EF; Reallotted for Training 5.4.19

J585 Deld 3 AAP Norwich by 18.2.19, allotted to EF; Reallotted for Training 5.4.19; 99 Sqn, crashed Ambala 4.10.19 (2/Lt J Clarke MC killed)

J586 Deld 3 AAP Norwich by 18.2.19, allotted to EF; Reallotted for Training 5.4.19; 1 AI to 25 Sqn 21.5.19; Wrecked 3.6.19; 6 SS 6.6.19

J587 Deld 3 AAP Norwich by 18.2.19, allotted to EF; Reallotted for Training 5.4.19; 27 Sqn by 12.19; Crashed landing in formation, Risalpur 12.10.20 (F/L JL Vachell MC & O/O JSF Watson both unhurt)

J588 Deld 3 AAP Norwich by 18.2.19, allotted to EF; Reallotted for Training 5.4.19

J589 Deld 3 AAP Norwich by 12.4.19, allotted to EF

J590 Deld 3 AAP Norwich by 12.4.19, allotted to EF

J591 Makers by 6.2.19 for 1 ASD Arques via Richborough in cases; Deld 3 AAP Norwich

J592 Makers by 6.2.19 for 1 ASD Arques via Richborough in cases; Deld 3 AAP Norwich; 15 AAP; Stalled during aerobatics while testing new aircraft before flight to France, Alexandra Park, Manchester 3.5.19 (Sgt RT Parry killed)

J593 Makers by 6.2.19 for 1 ASD Arques via Richborough in cases; Deld 3 AAP Norwich

J594 Makers by 6.2.19 for 1 ASD Arques via Richborough in cases; Deld 3 AAP Norwich

J595 Makers by 6.2.19 for 1 ASD Arques via Richborough in cases; Deld 3 AAP Norwich

J596 Makers by 6.2.19 for 1 ASD Arques via Richborough in cases; Deld 3 AAP Norwich

J597 Makers by 6.2.19 for 1 ASD Arques via Richborough in cases; Still there 17.3.19 reallotted to NW Area for East Retford for squadrons mobilising;; Deld 3 AAP Norwich; Netheravon; RAE 21.10.19 - 17.2.20 (parachute trials); Halton to AEE Martlesham Heath 13.1.21 (parachute tests & tests of additional gravity petrol system); Sent away for repair W/E 23.3.21; 1 SoTT Halton

J598 Makers by 6.2.19 for 1 ASD Arques via Richborough in cases; Still there 17.3.19 reallotted to NW Area for East Retford for sqdns mobilising; Deld 3 AAP Norwich

J599 Makers by 6.2.19 for 1 ASD Arques via Richborough in cases; Still there 17.3.19 reallotted to NW Area for East Retford for sqdns mobilising; Deld 3 AAP Norwich; AD Drigh Rd; HQ RAF India 9.24; 60 Sqn 19.9.24 - 10.24; AD Drigh Rd; 60 Sqn; Crashed on landing, Whad, 24.9.25 (Sgt D Munro)

J600 At Makers 6.2.19 allotted to EF; Still there 17.3.19 reallotted to NW Area for East Retford for sqdns mobilising; Deld 3 AAP Norwich 12.4.19

300 D.H.9A ordered on Cont Nos 35a/3517/C4111 and AS.35449 dated 22.10.18 from Aircraft Manufacturing Co Ltd, Hendon to be numbered J5192 to J5491. Order cancelled 12.18.

6 D.H.9A rebuilds ordered on Cont No 375546/22 dated 14.3.23 from Westland Aircraft Works, Yeovil. To Specification 22/23 to be numbered J6957 to J6962. (465hp Lion II)

J6957 Deld AEE Martlesham Heath 24.4.23; (full performance tests) RAE 7.8.23 (steel airscrew); FL Chiddingfold, Surrey 14.9.23; Brooklands 6.6.24; RAE 24.10.24 - 5.25; Re-engined (400hp Liberty); A&AEE 29.4.26; RAE 23.6.26 (steel wings) (oleo u/c); Passenger killed landing when attached to aircraft by parachute which he had accidentally released while standing up to read an instrument, 30.8.27 (F/L EA Hodgson OK & Mr RJ Lowthian killed); Last flown 6.12.27

J6958 TOC Digby store 1.6.23; RAF Base Gosport 6.24 - 7.25; 55 Sqn 2.27 - 6.27, VIP a/c, AVM Sir JFA Higgins

J6959 TOC Andover store 1.6.23; RAF Base Gosport 6.24; 420 Flt; Collided with Bison N9601 of 421 Flt on take-off, Gosport, Cat R 17.8.25 (F/L HGR Malet OK); Repaired; Re-engined 400hp Liberty; PD Ascot; To Iraq for use of AVM Sir Edward Ellington (AOC) 8.27, painted all-red and based Mosul; Crashed, Hit, Iraq, 28.11.28 (replaced by J8177)

J6960 TOC Andover store 1.6.23; RAF Base Gosport 6.24

J6961 TOC 1.6.23; RAF Base Gosport 6.24 - 6.25; Re-engined

(400hp Liberty); AD Hinaidi; 30 Sqn 11.26 - 12.26; 84 Sqn 3.28; Bombs fell off just after take-off, Cat R 12.9.28 (F/O FW Nuttall OK)

J6962 TOC Andover store 1.6.23; RAF Base Gosport 6.24; Overturned on landing, Cat W 13.10.24 (F/L LC Wynne-Tyson unhurt)

6 D.H.9A rebuilds ordered on Cont No 376225/22 dated 1.3.23 from Handley Page Ltd, Cricklewood and numbered J6963 to J6968. (400hp Liberty 12A) [All allocated 12 Sqn 5.23]

J6963 12 Sqn 8.23 - 2.24; PD Ascot; AD Aboukir; 4 FTS Abu Sueir 8.26

J6964 12 Sqn 8.23 - 2.24; 207 Sqn ('B4') 5.24 - 9.24; EF, FL, crashed, Wormwood Scrubbs, 27.6.24 (F/O LH Weedon & AC Lines both unhurt); RAE 13.8.24 - 9.24; 207 Sqn 12.24; Recond by DH (c/n 226) on Cont No 579165/25

J6965 1 FTS Netheravon, turned to port, stalled and spun in from 60ft avoiding obstruction on airfield when landing, dived into ground, Andover, 20.9.23 (Cpl HSH Meech seriously injured & LAC WE Gray slightly injured); Repaired; PD Ascot; AD Aboukir; 4 FTS Abu Sueir 9.26

J6966 1 FTS 1923; PD Ascot; AD Aboukir; 4 FTS Abu Sueir 11.25 - 12.25; 14 Sqn 9.27 - 10.28

J6967 12 Sqn 9.23; Crashed 15.11.23; Repaired; 12 Sqn 11.23 - 2.24; 207 Sqn ('A3') 3.24 - 1.26; PD Ascot; AD Aboukir; 4 FTS Abu Sueir 4.26 - 11.26; 4 FTS Abu Sueir 7.28

J6968 RAE 26.10.23 (target tower); Last flown 11.7.30

10 D.H.9A rebuilds by de Havilland Aircraft Co.Ltd, Stag Lane numbered J7008 to J7017. To Specification 22/23. C/n's 88 to 97. (400hp Liberty 12A)

J7008 Ex H3480; Tested IAAD 19.12.23 - 11.1.24; 1 FTS Netheravon 8.24; Tyre burst landing, swung on nose 22.9.24 (Lt RN (F/O RAF) FWH Clarke OK); Engine seized when instructor tried to go round again, landed downwind on rough ground, hit tree, overturned 29.8.25 (Instructor & Lt (F/O RAF) FE Judd unhurt)

J7009 Ex E861; Tested IAAD 9.1.24; A&AEE 5.24; A&GS Eastchurch 10.24; Recond by DH (c/n 320) as DC on Cont No 760131/27; 1 FTS Netheravon 10.26; FL in bad weather, overturned in soft ground, Hunger Hill, nr.Pulborough, Sussex, 3.1.29; HAD 1.29

J7010 Ex H3496; Tested IAAD 28-31.1.24; PD Ascot; AD Aboukir; 47 Sqn 12.25 - 2.26

J7011 Ex H3397; Tested IAAD 2-3.1.24; 100 Sqn 1924; A&GS Eastchurch 5.26- 9.27

J7012 Ex E857; PD Ascot; AD Aboukir; 4 FTS Abu Sueir 2.26; 14 Sqn 6.27 - 12.28

J7013 Ex H111; PD Ascot; AD Hinaidi; 55 Sqn ('B3') 7.26; 55 Sqn 4.28

J7014 Ex H126; PD Ascot; AD Hinaidi; 55 Sqn ('B3') 1.25

J7015 Ex H128; PD Ascot; AD Hinaidi; 30 Sqn 1.25; Stalled & crashed, caught fire, Iraq, 11.2.25 (2 injured)

J7016 Ex E859

J7017 Ex E960; PD Ascot; AD Hinaidi; 8 Sqn 31.1.25 - 5.25; 55 Sqn ('CIII') 9.25; Tyre burst after landing, swung into J7344, and u/c collapsed, Cat W 11.1.27 (F/O BN Murgatroyd OK); SOC 15.3.27

15 D.H.9A rebuilds by Handley Page Ltd, Cricklewood numbered J7018 to J7032. (400hp Liberty 12A)

J7018 PD Ascot; AD Hinaidi; 55 Sqn; Crashed, 11.1.27

J7019 PD Ascot; AD Aboukir 10.24; 4 FTS Abu Sueir 3.11.24 - 2.25

J7020 Tested IAAD 1.2.24; 1 FTS 7.24 - 11.24; 602 Sqn 7.27 - 1.28

J7021 24 Sqn; Hit tree landing Kenley, 12.8.24 (P/O JA Mollison unhurt & LAC GH Bunce slightly injured); Repaired; PD Ascot; AD Hinaidi 5.27; 84 Sqn 5.27; AD Hinaidi 10.12.27

J7022 PD Ascot; AD Aboukir; 4 FTS Abu Sueir 9.24; Caught barbed wire landing, bounced, swung 28.10.24 (P/O JJ Fitzgerald unhurt); 14 Sqn 2.26 - 7.26

J7023 1 FTS Netheravon 7.24; Sideslipped in, landed on one wheel which was torn off, crew thrown out due to belt breaking, a/c overturned 28.8.24 (Lt RN (F/O RAF) FWH Clarke and passenger both injured); Repaired; 1 FTS 9.24; Crashed into barbed wire landing, Netheravon, 2.10.24 (repaired); While stationary struck by E9951, Netheravon, Cat R 13.10.25

J7024 PD Ascot; AD Aboukir; 4 FTS Abu Sueir 10.24 - 7.25; AD Aboukir; rebuilt as JR7024; 14 Sqn 4.10.26 - 1.27; 4 FTS Abu Sueir; Crashed on nose, 1927; 14 Sqn 12.33 [this date is too late]; Overturned (swastika on tail) c.1928/9 (F/O PdeC Festing-Smith)

J7025 1 FTS 8.24

J7026 PD Ascot; AD Hinaidi; 84 Sqn, sparking plug blew out in air and gases under cowling caught fire, landed safely 14.1.25

J7027 PD Ascot; AD Hinaidi; 84 Sqn (swastika badge) 8.24

J7028 PD Ascot; AD Aboukir; 47 Sqn 1.25 - 7.25; Retd UK; Recond by DH on Cont No 579165/25 (c/n 253); Makers; Rebuilt by DH as DH.9AJ as STAG (465hp Jupiter VI); FF 15.6.26; A&AEE 6.26; Crashed, 7.26; Makers; A&AEE 2.27; Makers 6.27; A&AEE 10.27 - 6.28; CFS 6.28; Westland 26.6.28; A&AEE 9.28 - 10.28

D.H.9A J7028 rebuilt as the D.H.9AJ Stag, with a Jupiter engine. (J.M.Bruce/G.S.Leslie collection)

J7029 PD Ascot; AD Aboukir; 4 FTS Abu Sueir 27.11.24 - 2.25; Retd UK; Recond; Trg Flt 1 SoTT 6.29 - 4.30

J7030 Recond by DH on Cont No 579165/25 (c/n 180); PD Ascot; AD Drigh Rd 1926; 60 Sqn ('P') 3.26; AD Drigh Rd 16.5.27; 60 Sqn 6.28 - 12.28; 27 Sqn 6.29 - 5.30

J7031 PD Ascot; AD Hinaidi; 55 Sqn 1925

J7032 No information

40 D.H.9A rebuilds by Westland Aircraft Works, Yeovil numbered J7033 to J7072. (400hp Liberty 12A)

J7033 1 FTS 8.24; Caught fire on ground while refuelling, 16.6.25

J7034 207 Sqn ('C2'); Recond by DH (c/n 146); PD Ascot; AD Drigh Rd; AP Lahore 8.25

J7035 PD Ascot; AD Aboukir; 14 Sqn 10.28 - 5.30

J7036 PD Ascot; AD Hinaidi; 55 Sqn 1926

J7037 Tested IAAD 28.12.23 - 9,1.24; 7 Sqn 3.24; 39 Sqn ('1') 4.25 - 6.25; 39 Sqn ('2')

J7038 Tested IAAD 20.12.23; 7 Sqn 3.24; A&AEE 7.24; 207 Sqn ('C2') 8.24; Recond by DH (c/n 164); PD Ascot; AD Aboukir; 8 Sqn 4.28

J7039 Tested IAAD 28-29.1.24; 12 Sqn 4.24; 207 Sqn ('C4') 8.24; 39 Sqn; PD Ascot; AD Drigh Rd; 60 Sqn 6.28; 27 Sqn 5.30

J7040 7 Sqn 4.24; 1 FTS Netheravon 7.24 - 1.25; Swung out of wind landing, crashed, badly damaged 1.8.24 (Lt M Cursham RN OK); PD Ascot; AD Aboukir; 4 FTS Abu Sueir 11.25 - 12.25; 4 FTS Abu Sueir 8.27 - 7.28

J7041 207 Sqn ('C1'); 39 Sqn; PD Ascot; AD Hinaidi; 55 Sqn 1925; 8 Sqn 2.27; 55 Sqn 3.28

J7042 PD Ascot; AD Hinaidi; 55 Sqn, crashed & burnt, Iraq, Cat W 5.8.25 (Sgt JR Gage & LAC F Young both killed)

J7043 Tested IAAD 28-29.1.24; 11 Sqn, stalled on take-off & crashed into J7044, Bircham Newton, 24.3.24 (P/O RAA Cole & AC1 E Burrell unhurt); PD Ascot; AD Hinaidi; 55 Sqn ('B1') 1.26 - 7.27

J7044 Tested IAAD 29.1.24; 11 Sqn, hit by J7043 while parked, Bircham Newton, 24.3.24; Repaired; PD Ascot;

D.H.9A J7067 '10' of No.39 Squadron above the clouds around 1924/5. (via Philip Jarrett)

AD Hinaidi; 55 Sqn ('A') 1925

J7045 PD Ascot; AD Hinaidi; 55 Sqn 1927

J7046 PD Ascot; AD Aboukir; (Conv DC); 4 FTS Abu Sueir 3.28 - 1.29

J7047 39 Sqn 8.24; Recond by DH (c/n 315) as DC on Cont No 726079/26; 1 FTS Netheravon 9.27

J7048 207 Sqn ('C1') 5.24 - 8.24; Recond by DH (c/n 258) on Cont No 579165/25; PD Ascot; AD Hinaidi; 84 Sqn; 55 Sqn 1927

J7049 PD Ascot; AD Aboukir 8.24; 47 Sqn 24.11.24 - 3.25; 55 Sqn; Crashed, 8.25; 4 FTS Abu Sueir 6.26

J7050 PD Ascot; AD Hinaidi; 55 Sqn 11.24 - 7.25; 8 Sqn ('B') 1925; Returned UK; RAF (Cadet) College, Cranwell 10.27 - 5.29

J7051 No information

J7052 PD Ascot; AD Hinaidi; 55 Sqn ('A2'); U/c collapsed on landing

J7053 1 FTS Netheravon 10.24; Lost wings recovering from dive from high altitude, crashed nr Everley, Wilts, 15.5.25 (F/O DB Morgan killed)

J7054 1 FTS Netheravon 9.24; Swung on TO, spun in from 100ft, WO 9.5.25 (Lt RN (F/O RAF) AN Grey injured); Rebuilt; PD Ascot; AD Hinaidi; 84 Sqn 8.27 - 9.27; Crashed, Alum Rahal, Iraq, 29.9.27; Repaired; 30 Sqn 18.10.28 - 4.29; 84 Sqn 8.29; Crashed, 29.9.29

J7055 PD Ascot; AD Drigh Rd; 27 Sqn 1927 - 1928; 60 Sqn 1928; 27 Sqn 10.28 - 1.30

J7056 PD Ascot; AD Hinaidi; 55 Sqn 5.25; 84 Sqn 4.27; 47 Sqn

J7057 AEE 5.24 - 6.24; PD Ascot; AD Drigh Rd; AP Lahore; 60 Sqn 25.1.26; Landing accident, 25.5.26; 27 Sqn (K) 5.27 - 3.28; 60 Sqn ('P') 3.30; 27 Sqn 4.30 - 5. 30

J7058 39 Sqn ('12') 7.24 - 8.24; Recond by DH (c/n 227) on Cont No 579165/25

J7059 RAE 21.4.24 - 17.8.27 (DH oleo u/c, Dunlop wheels, propeller test & flying hood test); Recond by DH (c/n 321) on Cont No 760139/29; DC; 2 FTS Duxford ('6') 6.29 - 4.30

J7060 PD Ascot; AD Aboukir; 4 FTS Abu Sueir 1.26 - 6.26

J7061 39 Sqn ('6') 1924; 1 FTS 7.25; Collided with stationary Snipe E6546 on landing, ridge on a/f contributory factor, Cat W 30.10.25 (F/O (Lt RN) LG Richardson OK)

J7062 PD Ascot; AD Aboukir 10.24; 39 Sqn; 207 Sqn 11.27; Overturned in accident

J7063 PD Ascot; AD Aboukir 11.24; 47 Sqn 20.3.25 - 12.25; AD Aboukir; Rebuilt as DC JR7063; 4 FTS Abu Sueir 1928

J7064 PD Ascot; AD Aboukir; 4 FTS Abu Sueir 17.12.24

J7065 PD Ascot; AD Aboukir 12.24

J7066 39 Sqn ('10') 8.24 - 11.24; 100 Sqn 1.25; 39 Sqn 7.25

J7067 100 Sqn ('2') 1924; 39 Sqn ('10' & '11') 7.24 - 1.25; PD Ascot; AD Aboukir; 4 FTS Abu Sueir 5.25; 14 Sqn 5.28; AD Aboukir to 14 Sqn 5.7.29 - 11.29

J7068 39 Sqn 5.24 - 7.25; PD Ascot; AD Aboukir; 14 Sqn 5.28 - 10.28; AD Aboukir; 14 Sqn 11.11.28 - 6.29

J7069 PD Ascot; AD Aboukir; (Convtd DC); 4 FTS 11.24 - 3.26; 4 FTS Abu Sueir 8.27 - 7.28

J7070 PD Ascot; AD Aboukir 11.24; Rebuilt as JR7070; 47 Sqn; Ground collision with another aircraft, while taxying up slipway, pilot unable to see other a/c on tarmac 5.10.25 (F/O MB MacKay OK); 14 Sqn 6.27 - 9.27

D.H.9A J7059 '6' of No.2 Flying Training School, Digby, in 1930. (RAF Museum P.7321)

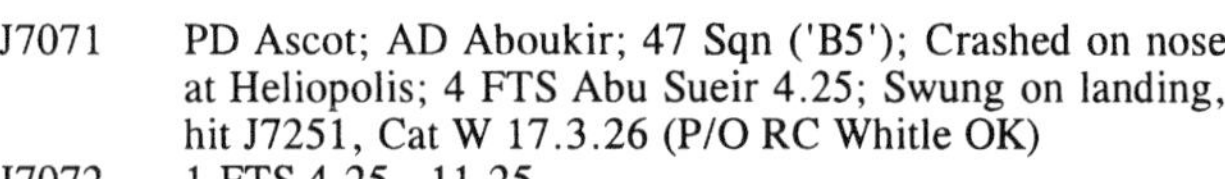
D.H.9A J7086 'BI' and others of No.47 Squadron around 1926/27. (RAF Museum P.21262)

D.H.9A J7124 and others of No.30 Squadron over rough terrain in 1924. (FAA Museum)

J7071 PD Ascot; AD Aboukir; 47 Sqn ('B5'); Crashed on nose at Heliopolis; 4 FTS Abu Sueir 4.25; Swung on landing, hit J7251, Cat W 17.3.26 (P/O RC Whitle OK)

J7072 1 FTS 4.25 - 11.25

15 D.H.9A rebuilds by Gloucestershire Aircraft Co.Ltd, Cheltenham numbered J7073 to J7084. To Specification 45/22 (400hp Liberty 12A)

J7073 39 Sqn ('8') 12.24 - 1927

J7074 100 Sqn (2) 1924; 39 Sqn to 5 FTS Sealand 1.7.25; 39 Sqn ('4'); Crashed, Wykeham, nr Spalding, Lincs, 20.7.27

J7075 RAF (Cadet) College, Cranwell 10.26 - 5.28

J7076 5 FTS Sealand 11.24

J7077 5 FTS 10.24; No wind, struck by J7348 landing in opposite direction, Sealand, Cat W 1.7.25 (P/O DL Evans)

J7078 5 FTS Shotwick, stalled and spun in on turn after take-off, 8.4.24 (F/O RAStG Leeds seriously injured)

J7079 24 Sqn; Starting accident, Kenley, 1.7.24

J7080 Tested IAAD 7-9.1.24; PD Ascot; AD Hinaidi; 84 Sqn 3.27 - 3.28

J7081 39 Sqn; 100 Sqn; RAF (Cadet) College, Cranwell ('D8') 11.24 - 11.26; Recond by DH (c/n 317) on Cont No 760139/27; 1 FTS 5.28; PD Ascot; AD Aboukir; 4 FTS Abu Sueir 8.30 - 11.30

J7082 5 FTS Sealand ('9') , fast landing, ran off 50yds after landing, put on engine to clear 504K H2997 but failed to do so, Cat W 23.1.25 (F/O MABP Storrie and 504 pilot unhurt)

J7083 Recond by DH (c/n 314) on Cont No 726079/26; 600 Sqn ('7'); Spun in off formation turn and caught fire on impact, Mill Hill, London, Cat W 6.5.28 (pilot injured)

J7084 PD Ascot; AD Aboukir; 4 FTS Abu Sueir; AD Aboukir; Rebuilt JR7084; 14 Sqn ('N') 1933

J7085 PD Ascot; AD Drigh Rd; 27 Sqn 4.27 - 8.28; 60 Sqn 1928 - 1929

J7086 5 FTS Shotwick 5.24; PD Ascot; AD Aboukir; 47 Sqn ('BI') 9.12.26 - 3.27; 45 Sqn 11.28 - 2.29; 14 Sqn 10.29; Crashed 11.29

J7087 39 Sqn, mid-air collision with E8654, BO, Cat W 5.6.24 (F/O LG Lucas & AC1 T Coppleston both killed)

15 D.H.9A rebuilds by H.G.Hawker Engineering Co Ltd, Kingston-on-Thames numbered J7088 to J7102 (400hp Liberty 12A)

J7088 1 FTS Netheravon 11.24 - 8.25; Hit ridge landing, tyre burst 19.2.25 (F/L VJ Somerset-Thomas & passenger OK)

J7089 Conv DC at Kenley (VIP hack); 24 Sqn 5.24; Starting accident, Kenley, 1.7.24 (F/L JAW Binnie OK & AC1 DA William seriously injured); 39 Sqn

J7090 1 FTS 12.24

J7091 PD Ascot; AD Drigh Rd; 60 Sqn 12.24; 27 Sqn 6.25 1.27; 60 Sqn ('W') 12.27 - 12.28

J7092 PD Ascot; AD Aboukir 6.25; 14 Sqn 9.26 - 12.26; Rebuilt as JR7092; 4 FTS Abu Sueir

J7093 PD Ascot; AD Aboukir; 47 Sqn 1.26 - 5.26; AD Aboukir; Rebuilt JR7093; 45 Sqn ('2') 11.28

J7094 24 Sqn 7.25; PD Ascot; AD Aboukir; 14 Sqn 4.26; 47 Sqn, while landing to rescue airmen from forced landed Spanish Breguet which was flying from Amman to Baghdad, crashed on bad ground, 5m N of track between LG 'L' and LG 'K', Cat W 16.4.26 (S/Ldr RS Maxwell MC DFC OK); Wreckage salved and carried out by Victoria

J7095 PD Ascot; AD Aboukir; 4 FTS Abu Sueir 5.25 - 10.25; 47 Sqn 3.27 - 3.28

J7096 PD Ascot; AD Aboukir; 47 Sqn 12.25 - 7.28; 4 FTS Abu Sueir

J7097 No information

J7098 PD Ascot; AD Drigh Rd; 27 Sqn 4.26; 60 Sqn ('N') 2.26 - 1.27; AP Lahore 1.27; 60 Sqn 1.27; EF, FL 10.27 (Sgt D Munro); Repaired; AD Drigh Rd 7.28; 60 Sqn ('N') 29.7.28; Crashed, Kohat 11.2.30

J7099 PD Ascot; AD Hinaidi; 84 Sqn; Crashed, 15.9.24; AD Hinaidi; 30 Sqn 11.26; 84 Sqn 11.27 - 2.28

J7100 PD Ascot; AD Hinaidi; 84 Sqn ('N') 9.24 - 10.24; Crashed, Mosul, 16.10.24

J7101 PD Ascot; AD Hinaidi; 47 Sqn; Rebuilt as JR9101; 84 Sqn ('B', named 'NIOBE') 9.24 - 6.25; 14 Sqn 9.25 - 10.25; 55 Sqn 1926

J7102 PD Ascot; AD Hinaidi; 8 Sqn 12.24; Fast landing, swung round, hit boulder, collided J7321 13.3.25 (F/O CHA Farnam OK); AD Hinaidi; 55 Sqn 9.25; 8 Sqn, conrod broke, broke tanks or pipe, a/c caught fire in air, crashed at junction of Lesser Dab and Tigris rivers, Cat W 13.10.25 (Sgt TA Graham killed & AC1 R Stanton slightly injured)

25 D.H.9A rebuilds by RAF Packing Depot, Ascot numbered J7103 to J7127. (400hp Liberty 12A)

J7103 PD Ascot; AD Hinaidi 11.23; Recd UK; PD Ascot; AD Drigh Rd; 27 Sqn 4.29

J7104 PD Ascot; AD Hinaidi 7.24; 55 Sqn ('B3'); 47 Sqn; 30 Sqn; Crashed, 25.4.27; AD Hinaidi; 14 Sqn 5.28 - 4.29

J7105 PD Ascot; AD Aboukir; 4 FTS Abu Sueir 2.28

J7106 PD Ascot; AD Aboukir; 47 Sqn 28.2.24 - 5.24; 14 Sqn; 4 FTS. Abu Sueir 8.25 - 11.25; AD Aboukir 11.25; Rebuilt as JR7106

J7107 PD Ascot; AD Aboukir; Rebuilt as JR7107; 47 Sqn ('B') (Named "NIOBE") 6.26; 47 Sqn ('A1') 10.27

J7108 PD Ascot; AD Aboukir; 47 Sqn 2.25; AD Aboukir (repair) 4.26; 14 Sqn, crashed, Cat W 17.4.26 (S/Ldr HA Tweedie & F/L SH Wallace both killed)

J7109 PD Ascot; AD Hinaidi 6.24; 84 Sqn 6.24; Spark from exhaust set fire to cockpit in flight, landed safely 15.9.24; AD Hinaidi; AD Drigh Rd; 60 Sqn 10.27 - 1 1.28; 27 Sqn 9.29; AP Lahore 11.29; 60 Sqn ('T') 1 1.29

J7110 PD Ascot; AD Hinaidi 5.24; 55 Sqn 30.5.24; AD

D.H.9A J7338 'BII' of No.47 Squadron, Helwan, has springs or coiled wires on the wing skids. (via Dave Birch)

Hinaidi 11.24

J7111 PD Ascot; AD Hinaidi; 8 Sqn 12.24; to UK 2.25; PD Ascot; AD Hinaidi; 30 Sqn 10.26; 30 Sqn 2.28 - 6.28

J7112 207 Sqn; Spun out of formation turn at 1,200ft, CW nr.Eastchurch, 30.4.25 (F/O BG Pool & AC1 WJ Spare both seriously injured)

J7113 PD Ascot; AD Hinaidi 6.24; 8 Sqn 28.7.24 - 9.24; 30 Sqn 1 1.24; 55 Sqn 6.25; Crashed, 20.12.25

J7114 PD Ascot; AD Hinaidi; 30 Sqn 1924; Collided at 6,000ft with H3633, spun from 2,000ft but landed safely, 25.4.27 (F/O JAE Inkster OK); SOC 31.5.27

J7115 PD Ascot; AD Hinaidi; 14 Sqn; 84 Sqn 8.24 - 8.25; Passenger thrown out on bumpy ground, Nasiriyah, Iraq 29.10.24 (F/O GC Shepherd unhurt & AC GLR Collins slightly injured); AHQ Iraq 9.26; 30 Sqn 8.27 - 11.27

J7116 PD Ascot; AD Aboukir; 14 Sqn 7.29 - 11.29; 4 FTS Abu Sueir 2.31

J7117 Recond by DH (c/n 162); PD Ascot; AD Aboukir; 4 FTS Abu Sueir 1928 - 1929

J7118 PD Ascot; AD Hinaidi 5.24

J7119 PD Ascot; AD Hinaidi; 84 Sqn 12.29; 55 Sqn 10.25; 47 Sqn ('BIV') 10.26; Overturned in FL, Baharia oasis, Egypt, Cat W 12.26

J7120 PD Ascot; AD Hinaidi; 84 Sqn 5.25 - 8.25

J7121 PD Ascot; AD Hinaidi; 84 Sqn 10.24 - 1.25; 84 Sqn 10.26; Crashed on landing, Shaibah, 27.1.27

J7122 Recond by DH (c/n 228) Cont No 579165/25; PD Ascot; AD Hinaidi; 55 Sqn 3.25

J7123 PD Ascot; AD Hinaidi; 55 Sqn ('AI') 6.24 - 10.24; Retd UK; A&AEE 31.3.27 - 4.27

J7124 PD Ascot; AD Hinaidi; 30 Sqn 4.24 - 4.29 (star design on fin)

J7125 PD Ascot; AD Drigh Rd; AP Lahore 11.24 - 12.24; 27 Sqn 3.25 - 4.25; 60 Sqn ('O') 3.26 - 1.27; 27 Sqn 2.28 - 6.29

J7126 PD Ascot; AD Hinaidi; 84 Sqn 7.25; 14 Sqn 7.25 - 8.25

J7127 PD Ascot; AD Hinaidi 6.24; 55 Sqn 6.24; U/c collapsed in crash; 84 Sqn 11.24; Air mail duty, part of exhaust pipe fell off in flight, fuselage caught fire, FL, Hillah, Cat W 31.12.24 (Sgt FCJ Fry unhurt & AC1 DF Anderson injured); 84 Sqn 10.25; 84 Sqn 5.27 - 8.27

10 D.H.9A ordered on Cont No 467059/23 dated 21.2.24 from Gloucestershire Aircraft Co Ltd, Cheltenham to Specification 45/22 and numbered J7249 to J7258. (400hp Liberty 12A)

J7249 PD Ascot; AD Hinaidi; 84 Sqn 9.24; Retd UK?; PD Ascot; AD Aboukir; 55 Sqn 11.26; 4 FTS Abu Sueir 3.28

J7250 PD Ascot; AD Aboukir; Rebuilt JR7250; Crashed, Ismailia

J7251 PD Ascot; AD Aboukir; 4 FTS Abu Sueir 5.25; Hit by J7071 on ground, Abu Sueir, Cat R 17.3.26; AD Aboukir; 14 Sqn 4.2.27 - 6.27

J7252 PD Ascot; AD Hinaidi; 55 Sqn 4.25; Coded ('N') at one time; AD Aboukir to 14 Sqn 22.3.28

J7253 PD Ascot; AD Hinaidi; 14 Sqn; 84 Sqn; Flew into ground and overturned, BO, Shaibah, Cat W 11.10.24 (F/O JHG Franklin killed & AC2 T Williams seriously injured)

J7254 PD Ascot; AD Hinaidi; 84 Sqn 12.25; 14 Sqn 8.29; Crashed 2.30

J7255 PD Ascot; AD Hinaidi; 55 Sqn 11.24; 4 FTS Abu Sueir 3.26 - 3.29

J7256 PD Ascot; AD Hinaidi; 55 Sqn ('CIV') 3.25 - 1.27

J7257 PD Ascot; AD Aboukir 9.24; 47 Sqn 1925; 14 Sqn 7.26 - 2.27; AD Aboukir; Convtd DC; 4 FTS Abu Sueir 12.27 - 10.28

J7258 PD Ascot; AD Hinaidi; 84 Sqn 9.24; Retd UK?; PD Ascot; AD Drigh Rd; 27 Sqn ('C') 2.27; FL, Sherpur aerodrome, Kabul, Afghanistan, 18.12.28 (F/O CWL Trusk AFC OK); Repaired on site; Recd Kohat 1.1.29; 27 Sqn 12.29

8 D.H.9A rebuilds on Cont No 495330/24 by de Havilland Aircraft Co.Ltd, Stag Lane numbered J7302 to J7309. C/n's 119 to 124. (400hp Liberty 12A)

J7302 (ex H3617) PD Ascot; AD Hinaidi; 8 Sqn ('X') 1925; 30 Sqn 1927; AD Hinaidi; 30 Sqn 11.1.29 - 4.29

J7303 (ex H3581) PD Ascot; AD Hinaidi; 8 Sqn ('X') 1925; AD Aboukir; 14 Sqn 8.26 - 9.26 & 4.27

J7304 (ex F2828) PD Ascot; AD Aboukir; 4 FTS Abu Sueir 5.25; Overshot landing & hit parked DH.9A H82, Abu Sueir, Cat W 22.5.25 (LAC Rodber injured)

J7305 (ex H3595) PD Ascot; AD Hinaidi; 55 Sqn ('A2') 1924 - 4.26

J7306 (ex E8710) 35 Sqn; PD Ascot; AD Hinaidi; 55 Sqn (A1) 1926

J7307 (ex E8700) A&AEE 7.25; PD Ascot; AD Hinaidi; 55 Sqn; 84 Sqn 10.26; 8 Sqn 1928; 84 Sqn 7.28; 30 Sqn (target towing)

J7308 (ex E8699) PD Ascot; AD Aboukir; 4 FTS Abu Sueir by 10.25 - 5.26; AHQ Iraq Command by 7,27

J7309 (ex E8702) PD Ascot; AD Hinaidi; 84 Sqn ('84'), CO's a/c 1925/7; 30 Sqn 5.27; AHQ Iraq Command by 8.27 - 3.28

12 DE HAVILLAND D.H.9A rebuilds on Cont No 495691/24 by H.G.Hawker Engineering Co Ltd, Kingston-on-Thames numbered J7310 to J7321. (400hp Liberty 12A)

J7310 24 Sqn 2.25; Lost speed in turn after take-off, stalled and crashed behind hangar, Kenley, BO, Cat W 22.11.26 (F/L FStJ Woollard killed & F/O FL Collison seriously injured)

J7311 PD Ascot; AD Hinaidi; 84 Sqn 11.25; AD Hinaidi 7.29

J7312 5 FTS Sealand 12.24

J7313 24 Sqn 1925; 207 Sqn 5.27

J7314 A&GS Eastchurch 10.24 - 10.29

J7315 A&GS Eastchurch 10.26; HAD 11.27 - 12.27; 1 FTS 5.28 - 12.28

J7316 A&GS Eastchurch; RAF (Cadet) College, Cranwell 1925; 39 Sqn; FL West Mersea, Essex 15.8.28 (Sgt Nunneley); 35 Sqn 8.3.29; HAD; A&AEE 10.10.29; 35 Sqn 1930

J7317 Cont DC; RAF (Cadet) College, Cranwell (B11) 11.27 - 10.28

J7318 RAF (Cadet) College, Cranwell 6.26; Hit by Snipe E6310 which was taking off, Cranwell, 8.6.26; Repaired; RAF (Cadet) College, Cranwell 6.26 - 3.28

J7319 605 Sqn 10.26 (2nd of 2 to Sqn); 601 Sqn 12.28 - 23.4.30; 604 Sqn 23.4.30; ASS Hawkinge 30.10.30 WFU

J7320 PD Ascot; AD Hinaidi; 14 Sqn 24.6.25 - 9.25; 55 Sqn 1926

J7321 8 Sqn ('N') 1924; Landed on by J7102 13.3.25; New rear fuselage and tail assembly fitted

20 D.H.9A rebuilds on Cont No 495692/24 by Westland Aircraft Works, Yeovil numbered J7327 to J7346. (400hp Liberty 12A)

J7327 5 FTS Sealand 11.24 - 1.26; PD Ascot; AD Aboukir; 14 Sqn 5.28 - 5.29

J7328 A&AEE 16.2.25 - 12.25; A&GS Eastchurch 11.29 - 4.30

J7329 A&GS Eastchurch 2.26 - 6.26; HAD 5.27 - 6.27

J7330 PD Ascot; Arrived Basrah in badly damaged case 20.1.25; AD Hinaidi (repair); 55 Sqn; Crashed landing, Wasta Khedir, Iraq 10.3.26
J7331 A&GS Eastchurch 4.26; PD Ascot; AD Aboukir; 4 FTS Abu Sueir 10.25; 47 Sqn 4.28
J7332 PD Ascot; AD Hinaidi; 8 Sqn 5.27
J7333 & J7334 No information
J7335 PD Ascot; AD Aboukir 3.25; 4 FTS Abu Sueir 4.25 - 3.26
J7336 PD Ascot; AD Aboukir; 4 FTS Abu Sueir 5.25
J7337 PD Ascot; AD Aboukir 5.25; 47 Sqn 11.25 - 1.26; 14 Sqn; Crashed, Nablus, Palestine 13.3.27; Repaired; 14 Sqn 5.27; AD Aboukir 7.7.28
J7338 PD Ascot; AD Aboukir; 47 Sqn ('BII') 26.4.26 - 12.26
J7339 PD Ascot; AD Aboukir; 47 Sqn 1.26; AD Aboukir rebuilt JR7339; 45 Sqn (B); FL in desert, dismantled 1928
J7340 PD Ascot; AD Drigh Rd; 27 Sqn ('L' in 1927 later 'M') 10.25 - 6.30; Crashed
J7341 PD Ascot; AD Drigh Rd; 60 Sqn ('W') 10.25; Crashed on landing 27.8.26 (Sgt D Munro)
J7342 PD Ascot; AD Drigh Rd; 27 Sqn ('D') 6.25 - 4.26; Crashed, Lowri Pass, NWF; Repaired; 27 Sqn 8.26 - 4.27; 27 Sqn ('D') 12.27 - 5.28; Crashed, Lowri Pass, NWF, c.5.28; AD Drigh Rd; 60 Sqn ('N') 4.29; Crashed on take-off, Kohat, 11.2.30
J7343 PD Ascot; AD Drigh Rd; 60 Sqn 8.25; 27 Sqn ('F') 2.26 - 4.26; 27 Sqn ('J') 2.27; 60 Sqn ('N') 6.28 - 1.29
J7344 PD Ascot; AD Hinaidi; 8 Sqn ('A') 1925; 55 Sqn 11.25 - 10.26; Hit by J7017 landing, Cat W 11.1.27; SOC 15.3.27
J7345 PD Ascot; AL) Drigh Rd; 60 Sqn ('N') 8.25 2.26; 27 Sqn (F)
J7346 PD Ascot; AD Hinaidi; 30 Sqn

10 D.H.9A rebuilds on Cont No 495693/24 by Gloucestershire Aircraft Co Ltd, Cheltenham numbered J7347 to J7356. (400hp Liberty 12A)

J7347 5 FTS Sealand by 12.24; Swung landing and hit by F.2b J6696, Sealand, 31.3.25; Repaired; 5 FTS Sealand 3.25; PD Ascot; AD Drigh Rd; 27 Sqn ('B') 1925; 27 Sqn 1.27 - 10.27; 60 Sqn 12.28 - 2.29; AP Lahore 2.29
J7348 5 FTS 3.25; No wind, failed to see other a/c while landing, hit J7077 landing in opposite direction 1.7.25 (F/L EJA Burke); Makers Recond; PD Ascot; AD Hinaidi; 84 Sqn 6.27; 4 FTS Abu Sueir; 55 Sqn; Stalled and crashed avoiding another aircraft on take-off, Hinaidi, 29.7.29
J7349 5 FTS Sealand 1.26; 2 FTS Duxford 12.26 - 3.27; PD Ascot; AD Aboukir; 4 FTS Abu Sueir 3.28 - 4.28
J7350 5 FTS Sealand 1.26 - 2.26; A&GS Eastchurch 11.27; HAD 5.28 - 6.28
J7351 A&GS Eastchurch 11.25 - 1.27
J7352 207 Sqn 1924; Ground collision with J7354 after formation landing, 21.2.25; PD Ascot; AD Hinaidi; 84 Sqn 5.27 - 12.27
J7353 PD Ascot; AD Drigh Rd; AP Lahore 3.29; 27 Sqn 5.29; AD Drigh Rd 5.29
J7354 207 Sqn by 12.24; Formation landing tuition, ground collision with J7352 after landing, pilot distracted by people standing too close 21.2.25 (F/O HG Rowe OK); Repaired; RAF (Cadet) College, Cranwell, crashed and caught fire, Cat W 12.11.26 (F/Cdt DGH Wood killed)
J7355 207 Sqn ('C3') 1924
J7356 DH recond (c/n 224) Cont No 579165/25

12 D.H.9A rebuilds ordered on Cont No 553694/24 from H.G.Hawker Engineering Co.Ltd, Kingston-on-Thames numbered J7604 to J7615. (400hp Liberty 12A)

J7604 FF 21.2.25; PD Ascot; AD Aboukir; 4 FTS Abu Sueir 5.25; Recd UK; 2 FTS Duxford 1929
J7605 TOC A&AEE (15 Sqn) 16.3.25 - 4.25; PD Ascot; AD Aboukir rebuilt as JR7605; 47 Sqn 15.9.25; Recd UK; Recond by DH (c/n 313) on Cont No 726079/26; A&AEE 7.26; HAD 3.28
J7606 FF 2.3.25; Recond by DH (c/n 232) on Cont No 579165/25
J7607 FF 5.3.25; 15 Sqn, overshot landing, hit another aircraft 26.6.25 (F/O CL Lowe OK); Recond by DH (c/n 222) on Cont No 579165/25; PD Sealand; AD Hinaidi; 30 Sqn 8.28; 55 Sqn ('A1') 1929 - 2.30
J7608 FF 11.3.25; PD Ascot; AD Hinaidi; 84 Sqn 10.26; 55 Sqn ('IV'); Crashed, 1927; 55 Sqn 8.28
J7609 FF 12.3.25; HAD 1.27 - 2.27; 1 SoTT 9.27; PD Ascot; AD Hinaidi; 55 Sqn
J7610 FF 18.3.25; 207 Sqn, crashed, BO, Cat W 11.11.26 (Sgt GF Taylor & AC2 PC Hinton both killed)
J7611 FF 17.3.25; 207 Sqn ('C2') 6.25
J7612 FF 23.3.25; 207 Sqn 5.25; PD Ascot; AD Drigh Rd; 30 Sqn 8.27 - 9.27
J7613 FF 23.3.25; 39 Sqn ('2') 4.25 - 5.26; 39 Sqn ('2') 8.28; HAD; 605 Sqn 30.7.29 - 3.30
J7614 FF 31.3.25; 39 Sqn ('8') 5.5.25 - 8.26; PD Ascot; AD Aboukir; Convtd to DC; 4 FTS Abu Sueir 8.27 - 10.28
J7615 FF 1.4.25; 39 Sqn ('4' & '11') 11.25 - 5.26; PD Ascot; AD Aboukir; 14 Sqn 10.28 - 1.29

1 D.H.9A ordered on Cont No 517176/24 from de Havilland Aircraft Co.Ltd, Stag Lane and numbered J7700. (400hp Liberty 12A)

J7700 PD Ascot; AD Hinaidi; 30 Sqn 10.26; 55 Sqn ('A2') 10.26 - 1.27; Crashed on nose

12 D.H.9A ordered 11.25 on Cont No 623200/25 from de Havilland Aircraft Co.Ltd, Stag Lane and numbered J7787 to J7798. C/n's 202 to 213. (400hp Liberty 12A)

J7787 2 FTS Duxford 1930
J7788 PD Ascot; AD Aboukir; 4 FTS Abu Sueir ('6') 11.28 - 11.30
J7789 1 FTS Netheravon 12.26 - 9.27
J7790 Stn Flt Halton 1929; RAF (Cadet) College, Cranwell 6.29 - 5.30
J7791 1 FTS Netheravon, stalled and spun in, Cat W 23.2.26 (Lt (F/O RAF) HF Baker injured)
J7792 HAD 4.27; 39 Sqn ('10') 8.27 - 5.28
J7793 2 FTS Duxford.25; HAD 8.28; 2 FTS Duxford 11.29 - 6.30
J7794 HQ Wessex Area Comm Flt 28.5.26; 2 Sqn; Crashed, Tilshead LG, 19.7.26; HAD 12.26
J7795 HAD 2.27; 2 FTS Duxford, port wing hit tail of 504N J9016 (P/O AG Cole killed) from behind while landing Digby, Cat W 17.8.28 (F/O AR Feather & P/O BG D'Olier both killed)
J7796 PD Ascot; AD Aboukir; 47 Sqn 11.27; Hit stationary IIIF S1142 on take-off, Khartoum, Cat W 26.3.28 (Sgt WJ Symonds OK); AD Aboukir; Rebuilt as JR7796 47 Sqn
J7797 A&AEE 18.5.25; PD Ascot; AD Hinaidi; 84 Sqn 1927; Crashed on landing, Nugrat Salman, Iraq, 27.1.28
J7798 PD Ascot; AD Hinaidi; 84 Sqn 12.26 - 1.28

21 D.H.9A ordered on Cont No 602586/25 from Westland Aircraft Works, Yeovil and numbered J7799 to J7819. (400hp Liberty 12A)

J7799 84 Sqn 1.28; HAD 8.29; 2 FTS Duxford 12.29 6.30; 35 Sqn 1930
J7800 HAD 11.27
J7801 2 FTS Duxford 12.28 - 1.29; CFS 1.31 - 2.31
J7802 207 Sqn ('CI') c.1926?; Conv DC?; 2 FTS Duxford ('4') 1928; Collided with stationary 504N J9018 on landing, Digby, 4.2.29
J7803 A&GS Eastchurch 1926
J7804 A&GS Eastchurch 9.26 - 10.26
J7805 A&AEE (15 Sqn) 4.26 12.26; A&GS Eastchurch 7.29 - 6.30
J7806 A&GS Eastchurch 9.26 - 9.29; PD Ascot; AD Aboukir; 47 Sqn ('B'); 4 FTS Abu Sueir
J7807 PD Ascot; AD Hinaidi; 55 Sqn 23.10.29
J7808 HAD 1.27; 207 Sqn 1927; PD Ascot; AD Aboukir; 4 FTS Abu Sueir 3.28 - 1.29
J7809 Recond by DH (c/n 312) on Cont No 726079/26; HAD 9.27
J7810 1 SoTT 1.28
J7811 No information
J7812 39 Sqn ('12'), crashed, Manor House, Gosberton, Lincs, 20.9.26
J7813 39 Sqn; A&GS Eastchurch 12.27 - 5.28

J7814 HAD; 605 Sqn 1.11.26; Crashed in FL on south bank of river, nr.Manston, 16.8.28
J7815 PD Ascot; AD Aboukir; 4 FTS Abu Sueir; Wing hit wing of stationary J8138 at 3ft on take-off, Abu Sueir, Cat W 24.1.30 (LAC Chudley OK)
J7816 39 Sqn ('8') 1926
J7817 39 Sqn ('12') 1926
J7818 39 Sqn ('2') 6.26 - 1.27; PD Ascot; AD Aboukir; 4 FTS Abu Sueir 1928; 55 Sqn Trg Flt 1.30 - 11.30
J7819 39 Sqn ('5') 6.26; PD Ascot; AD Hinaidi; 55 Sqn ('A3')

12 D.H.9A ordered on Cont No 623332/25 from Short Bros (Rochester & Bedford) Ltd and numbered J7823 to J7834. C/n's S.671 to S.676 & S.693 to S.698 (400hp Liberty 12A)

J7823 PD Ascot; AD Aboukir; 45 Sqn ('6') c.25; Crashed at some time; 14 Sqn 5.28 - 5.29
J7824 No information
J7825 PD Ascot; AD Aboukir rebuilt as JR7825; 14 Sqn 10.28; Crashed into building while landing Amman c.3.30 (Amman's last D.H.9A)

The result of the last landing of JR7825, Amman's last D.H.9A. (Sq Ldr J.Smith via R.L.Ward)

J7826 Eastchurch 9.26; PD Ascot; AD Hinaidi; 14 Sqn 2.27 - 4.27; 84 Sqn (Heart marking); FL, u/c collapsed landing
J7827 PD Ascot; AD Aboukir; 47 Sqn ('BIV', with white 'H' on dark diamond under lower wings) 12.26 - 3.27; Rebuilt as JR7827; 14 Sqn 5.28 - 5.29;
J7828 PD Ascot; AD Aboukir; 47 Sqn 10.27
J7829 PD Ascot; AD Aboukir; 14 Sqn 3.27 - 10.27; 45 Sqn 8.29 - 9.29; AD Aboukir to 14 Sqn 8.11.29
J7830 No information
J7831 PD Ascot; AD Aboukir; 14 Sqn 5.27 - 1928; 14 Sqn ('O') 12.33; 45 Sqn ('1')
J7832 PD Ascot; AD Aboukir; 45 Sqn ('1') 5.28 - 9.29; AD Aboukir Convtd DC; 84 Sqn 9.31; AD Aboukir 2.32
J7833 PD Ascot; AD Aboukir; 14 Sqn 5.28; Stalled on downwind turn landing, dived in, BO, Cat W 31.8.28 (Sgt VR Saunders OK)
J7834 PD Ascot; AD Aboukir; 14 Sqn 6.27 - 9.27

20 D.H.9A ordered on Cont No 623331/25 from H.G.Hawker Engineering Co Ltd, Kingston-on-Thames and numbered J7835 to J7854. (400hp Liberty 12A)

J7835 RAF Staff College Flt 6.24; 601 Sqn 7.26; Hit landing light on approach, Lympne, Cat W 14.8.29
J7836 OUAS 1.28; 605 Sqn 11.28 1.34; HQ Fighting Area
J7837 600 Sqn 16.10.25; Damaged on landing 6.8.27; 2 FTS Duxford 6.29 - 3.30
J7838 PD Ascot; AD Hinaidi 6.26 7.26; AHQ Iraq Cd 7.27; 55 Sqn 5.28; EF, FL on test flt and overturned, Hinaidi, 2.1.29 BO
J7839 PD Ascot; AD Aboukir; 4 FTS Abu Sueir 8.27 - 3.28; 14 Sqn; 84 Sqn
J7840 1 FTS Netheravon 10.24 - 1.25; PD Ascot; AD Aboukir; 14 Sqn 4.26 - 7.26; 45 Sqn 10.28
J7841 PD Ascot; AD Aboukir; 14 Sqn 4.26 - 9.26; 45 Sqn, crashed, caught fire, Cat W 19.7.27
J7842 PD Ascot; AD Aboukir; 47 Sqn 3.26; AD Aboukir 2.7.26; 47 Sqn ('BIII') 12.26 - 1.27
J7843 PD Ascot; AD Aboukir; 4 FTS Abu Sueir; Crashed nr Station No.6, Suez Canal, while landing Abu Sueir in fog, BO 28.6.26 (P/O NJ Anderson & LAC EE Gregg both killed)
J7844 PD Ascot; AD Aboukir; 14 Sqn 10.27 - 11.27
J7845 & J7846 No information
J7847 PD Ascot; AD Aboukir; 55 Sqn 6.26 - 7.26; 47 Sqn 1927; 84 Sqn 2.27 - 1.28; 30 Sqn 22.3.29
J7848 PD Ascot; AD Hinaidi; 55 Sqn 1.28 - 3.28
J7849 PD Ascot; AD Hinaidi; 8 Sqn 1925
J7850 PD Ascot; AD Hinaidi 6.26 - 10.26; 55 Sqn ('CI') 10.26 - 6.27
J7851 PD Ascot; AD Hinaidi; 55 Sqn 1926 - 1927
J7852 PD Ascot; AD Hinaidi; 84 Sqn ('P') 1927; Crashed & overturned, Samawa, Iraq, 1928
J7853 PD Ascot; AD Hinaidi; 55 Sqn 1927 - 1928
J7854 PD Ascot; AD Hinaidi 7.26; AHQ Iraq 7.26; 84 Sqn; 4 FTS Abu Sueir; 30 Sqn, spun in from 500ft attempting to land near stranded aircraft, caught fire, 2 bombs exploded, Cat W 2.4.28 (P/O JW Wood and AC1 W Waugh both killed)

12 D.H.9A ordered on Cont No 640047/25 from Westland Aircraft Works, Yeovil and numbered J7855 to J7866. (400hp Liberty 12A)

J7855 1 SoTT 7.26 - 1.27
J7856 Convtd to DC; 608 Sqn 1934
J7857 No information
J7858 A&GS Eastchurch 6.27 - 4.30
J7859 207 Sqn; While landing collided with taxying Woodcock J7973 of 3 Sqn, Eastchurch, Cat W 25.10.26
J7860 1 FTS Netheravon 10.26; PD Ascot; AD Aboukir; 45 Sqn 12.28; Undershot in night landing and u/c collapsed, Helwan, 18.1.29
J7861 PD Ascot; AD Aboukir Convtd DC; 4 FTS Abu Sueir 10.30 - 11.30
J7862 A&GS Eastchurch 9.26
J7863 602 Sqn 7.27 - 1.28
J7864 A&AEE (15 Sqn) 11.26 - 9.27; A&GS Eastchurch 11.27; A&AEE (15 Sqn) 1.28 - 11.31 (tested electric stannic chloride smoke release gear 12.29)
J7865 PD Ascot; AD Hinaidi; 55 Sqn 5.28
J7866 PD Ascot; AD Hinaidi; 84 Sqn 16.2.28 - 5.28 (Heart insignia)

10 D.H.9A ordered on Cont No 640048/25 from H.G.Hawker Engineering Co Ltd, Kingston-on-Thames and numbered J7867 to J7876. (400hp Liberty 12A)

J7867 PD Ascot; AD Hinaidi; 55 Sqn 1928 - 1929
J7868 PD Ascot; AD Aboukir; 4 FTS Abu Sueir; Stalled on take-off, spun in and caught fire, Aboukir, Cat W 19.7.27 (Cpl WR Robins DFM killed)
J7869 No information
J7870 PD Ascot; AD Hinaidi; 30 Sqn 1928; 55 Sqn ('A1') 12.28 - 1.29
J7871 PD Ascot; AD Aboukir; 4 FTS Abu Sueir 9.25; 14 Sqn 6.26 - 5.27
J7872 PD Ascot; AD Hinaidi; 55 Sqn ('B') 2.27; AD Hinaidi Convtd comms; 8 Sqn 10.26; 84 Sqn 5.28; Wingtip struck by E963 on take-off Shaibah, Cat M 3.8.28; Starting accident 14.10.30 (LAC HI Wood injured)
J7873 PD Ascot; AD Aboukir rebuilt as JR7873; 14Sqn 4.28 - 6.28
J7874 PD Ascot; AD Aboukir; 14 Sqn 6.27 - 12.27; 45 Sqn 8.29 - 9.29 [also 13 Sqn 9.27; CF Andover 3.31 - 11.31 (Bristol Fighter!)]
J7875 No information
J7876 PD Ascot; AD Hinaidi; 84 Sqn; Burst tyre landing at night, taxied out of flare path to awaiting assistance, then taxied into by E8694, Cat W 27.8.28

7 D.H.9A ordered on Cont No 640049/25 from de Havilland Aircraft Co.Ltd, Stag Lane and numbered J7877 to J7883. C/n's 214 to 220. (400hp Liberty 12A)

D.H.9A J8099 of No.14 Squadron . (via Philip Jarrett)

J7877 PD Ascot; AD Hinaidi; 30 Sqn 11.26
J7878 No information
J7879 PD Ascot; AD Hinaidi; 84 Sqn 5.27 - 6.27; 30 Sqn 7.28 - 1.29
J7880 PD Ascot; AD Hinaidi; 30 Sqn 12.26 - 1.27
J7881 PD Ascot; AD Hinaidi; 30 Sqn ('A') 8.27; overturned on landing in gale
J7882 PD Ascot; AD Hinaidi; 84 Sqn; Struck ridge while landing and u/c collapsed, Nugrat Salman, 13.3.28
J7883 No information

7 D.H.9A ordered on Cont No 640050/25 from Short Bros (Rochester & Bedford) Ltd and numbered J7884 to J7890. c/n's S.699 to S.705. (400hp Liberty 12A)

J7884 No information
J7885 No information
J7886 No information
J7887 PD Ascot; AD Hinaidi; 84 Sqn 3.28 - 5.28; AD Hinaidi 8.29; 55 Sqn Trg Flt 10.29 - 1.31
J7888 PD Ascot; AD Hinaidi; 55 Sqn 2.28 - 5.28
J7889 PD Ascot; AD Aboukir; 14 Sqn 6.27 - 12.27
J7890 PD Ascot; AD Hinaidi; 84 Sqn 3.28

33 D.H.9A ordered on Cont No 682340/26 from Westland Aircraft Works, Yeovil to Specification 13/26 and numbered J8096 to J8128. (400hp Liberty 12A)

J8096 39 Sqn 8.28
J8097 PD Ascot; AD Aboukir; 4 FTS Abu Sueir ('7') 8.27; Hit obstruction landing, went on nose, lower wings and prop broken 6.3.28 (P/O MG Sedorski OK); Struck by J8174 in taxying accident, Cat M 12.4.28; 4 FTS Abu Sueir 5.28 - 8.28
J8098 PD Ascot; AD Aboukir; 45 Sqn 11.28; 14 Sqn 5.29 - 10.29; 4 FTS Abu Sueir 9.30 - 11.30
J8099 PD Ascot; AD Aboukir; 14 Sqn
J8100 PD Ascot; AD Aboukir; DC; 4 FTS Abu Sueir ('3') 8.27 - 9.28
J8101 PD Ascot; AD Aboukir; 14 Sqn 10.28; Crashed 2.30
J8102 PD Ascot; AD Hinaidi; 55 Sqn ('55') 12.27 - 12.28; AD Hinaidi; 30 Sqn 7.1.29 - 2.29; 55 Sqn 12.29 - 2.30
J8103 RAF (Cadet) College, Cranwell; 1 SoTT Halton by 7.27 - 7.28; HAD (CO's a/c) 3.29
J8104 39 Sqn 12.27
J8105 39 Sqn ('12') 10.28; HAD 7.29; 605 Sqn 8.29; Crashed, badly damaged c.4.30
J8106 No information
J8107 605 Sqn 1927; Crashed, on cross-country, caught fire, Great Glen, nr Leicester, Cat W 2.9.28 (P/O GH Aldridge killed)
J8108 504 Sqn; 601 Sqn 1928; EF, FL, u/c collapsed, Greenford, Middx, Cat W 8.6.29
J8109 Assembled by 605 Sqn 9.10.27 - 8.28
J8110 Makers; Rolls-Royce (480hp F.X) FF 11.11.27 (operated for Rolls-Royce by DH at Stag Lane); Completed endurance tests 150 hrs; Flown Netheravon-Farnborough-Brooklands by Capt PWS Bulman 27.6.29, and from Brooklands to Farnborough 8.10.29
J8111 A&GS Eastchurch 9.29 - 1.30
J8112 PD Ascot; AD Aboukir; 14 Sqn 5.28 - 12.29

The wreckage of D.H.9A J8105 of No.605 Squadron after crashing around April 1930. (via J.J.Halley)

J8113 No information
J8114 HAD 4.27; 601 Sqn 8.28
J8115 PD Ascot; AD Aboukir; 4 FTS Abu Sueir 10.27
J8116 600 Sqn ('L':'A':'10') 1929
J8117 PD Ascot; AD Aboukir; 47 Sqn 10.27
J8118 PD Ascot; AD Aboukir; 8 Sqn; 45 Sqn ('2'); Crashed, 30.1.28
J8119 No information
J8120 47 Sqn 11.27; RAF (Cadet) College, Cranwell 1928
J8121 601 Sqn
J8122 PD Ascot; AD Aboukir; 47 Sqn; 4 FTS Abu Sueir 1928 - 1929
J8123 39 Sqn 10.28; HAD 7.29
J8124 HAD 9.28 - 10.28; RAF (Cadet) College, Cranwell 10.28 - 7.29; 2 FTS Duxford 1930
J8125 HAD; 605 Sqn 14.8.28; Crashed on landing, Castle Bromwich, 7.7.29
J8126 PD Ascot; AD Aboukir; 4 FTS Abu Sueir 1928 - 11.30
J8127 HAD 9.28; RAF (Cadet) College, Cranwell; 2 FTS Duxford 10.28 - 2.30; 39 Sqn 1930; 35 Sqn
J8128 PD Ascot; AD Aboukir; 4 FTS Abu Sueir 1928 - 11.30

25 D.H.9A ordered on Cont No 700821/26 from de Havilland Aircraft Co.Ltd, Stag Lane and numbered J8129 to J8153 (last 6 fitted with metal wings). C/n's as listed. (400hp Liberty 12A)

J8129 (221) 603 Sqn; Overshot landing & hit another aircraft attempting to avoid hangar, Turnhouse, Cat W 25.5.28 (PO C Musgrave OK); SOC 30.5.28
J8130 (259) 601 Sqn 8.28; Landing in sun and slight mist, ran into stationary J8165 which was awaiting take-off, Hendon, Cat R 19.1.29 (F/O NH Jones OK)
J8131 (286) No information
J8132 (287) No information
J8133 (288) 39 Sqn 1.28; RAF College; Crashed avoiding another aircraft on landing, Cranwell, Cat W 20.6.29
J8134 (289) RAF (Cadet) College, Cranwell 5.28 - 7.28
J8135 (290) HAD 5.27; PD Ascot; AD Aboukir; 4 FTS Abu Sueir 7.28 - 8.28; Recd UK; HAD 21.3.2 9
J8136 (291) HAD 7.28; 39 Sqn; 603 Sqn
J8137 (292) HAD 5.27; 39 Sqn 8.27 - 8.28
J8138 (293) HAD 6.27; PD Ascot; AD Aboukir; 4 FTS Abu Sueir ('6') 8.28 - 8.30; Wing hit by wing of J7815 taking off, Abu Sueir, Cat M 24.1.30; Crashed, Cat W 14.8.30 (F/O ET Kingsford killed)
J8139 (294) PD Ascot; AD Aboukir; 45 Sqn 4.29 - 7.29; 4 FTS Abu Sueir 1930 - 1.31
J8140 (295) HAD 14.6.27; Attd 12 Sqn 7.27; PD Ascot; AD Aboukir; 14 Sqn 12.28; EF, FL, 15m SE of Ba'ir Wells, 25.3.29 (crew OK); Repaired
J8141 (296) HAD 5.27; PD Ascot; AD Aboukir; 14 Sqn 5.28; Crashed and burnt, Kolundia, Cat W 21.9.29
J8142 (297) PD Ascot; AD Aboukir; 4 FTS Abu Sueir ('4') 7.28 - 10.28; 47 Sqn 8.29 - 9.29
J8143 (288) HAD 5.27 - 6.27; 39 Sqn 4.28 - 11.28; 35 Sqn ('4') 8.3.29 - 6.29; Crashed on *Eagle* during palisade trials
J8144 (299) HAD 5.27; 207 Sqn 11.27; 39 Sqn ('1') 8.28; HAD 6.29

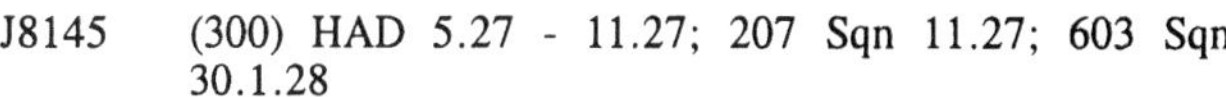

J8145 (300) HAD 5.27 - 11.27; 207 Sqn 11.27; 603 Sqn 30.1.28
J8146 (301) HAD; Makers (fit slots) 8.4.29; HAD 25.4.29; PD Ascot; AD Aboukir; 4 FTS Abu Sueir 11.30
J8147 (302) 39 Sqn 5.28 - 8.28; 55 Sqn ('CI'), crashed, damaged by Arabs, 1927
J8148 (303) No information
J8149 (304) PD Ascot; AD Hinaidi; 84 Sqn (Spade marking) 11.27 - 3.28
J8150 (305) No information
J8151 (306) 39 Sqn; PD Ascot; AD Hinaidi; 30 Sqn; 55 Sqn ('B2') 1927 - 1928; Wrecked after 28 days in desert
J8152 (307) 39 Sqn (10); PD Ascot; AD Hinaidi; 30 Sqn 2.28; 55 Sqn 1930
J8153 (308) HAD 8.29; Makers 26.9.29

18 D.H.9A ordered on Cont No 700822/26 from Short Bros (Rochester & Bedford) Ltd and numbered J8154 to J8171. C/n's S.714 to S.731. (400hp Liberty 12A)

J8154 600 Sqn ('B'); PD Ascot; AD Hinaidi 6.29; 55 Sqn Trg Flt 29.11.29 - 1.30
J8155 PD Ascot; AD Hinaidi; 55 Sqn 1930
J8156 No information
J8157 A&GS Eastchurch 7.29 - 6.30
J8158 No information
J8159 39 Sqn 8.28
J8160 No information
J8161 601 Sqn 8.28; 605 Sqn 4.30 - 7.30
J8162 605 Sqn 14.7.28; Brooklands; 605 Sqn 16.4.29 - 4.30
J8163 605 Sqn 2.8.28 - 6.30
J8164 600 Sqn
J8165 600 Sqn; Hit while stationary awaiting take-off by J8130 landing, Hendon, Cat W 19.1.29 (P/O DBH Coates OK)
J8166 No information
J8167 No information
J8168 No information
J8169 39 Sqn 8.28
J8170 39 Sqn 8.28
J8171 600 Sqn ('B') 1929

18 D.H.9A ordered on Cont No 700823/26 from Geo Parnall & Co.Ltd, Bristol and numbered J8172 to J8189. (400hp Liberty 12A)

J8172 1 FTS Netheravon 1926 - 1927; PD Ascot; AD Aboukir; 47 Sqn 8.29 - 9.29
J8173 39 Sqn
J8174 PD Ascot; AD Aboukir; 47 Sqn; Collided with parked aircraft, 5.10.27; AD Aboukir; Convtd to DC; 4 FTS Abu Sueir 12.27; Taxied into J8097 in strong wind, Abu Sueir, Cat M 12.4.28 (P/O RWM Clark OK); U/c collapsed, Abu Sueir, 25.4.28
J8175 PD Ascot; AD Aboukir; 4 FTS Abu Sueir 10.26; Collided on landing with H156 which was landing at same time, Cat M 10.10.28 (PO SO Bufton OK)
J8176 AW/CN 8.11.26; PD Ascot; AD Aboukir erected and tested 13.4.28; flown to AD Hinaidi 4.28; AD Hinaidi

D.H.9A J8118 at the Aircraft Depot Aboukir. (Dave Birch)

D.H.9A J8143 '4' of No.35 Squadron during palisade trials aboard HMS Eagle in 1929. (via P.W.Porter)

D.H.9A J8184, J8223 and J8116 of No.600 Squadron in formation over the outskirts of London. (RAF Museum)

(overhaul 33hrs 45min) completed 16.10.28; 55 Sqn 10.28 (automatic slots fitted 9.6.29); While low flying hit signpost and crashed, nr.Diyala, 2m SE of Lancaster Bridge, nr.Hinaidi, Cat W 24.10.29

J8177 PD Ascot; AD Hinaidi; AOC Iraq (AVM Sir R Brooke-Popham) 17.1.29 (VIP aircraft painted all-red); 55 Sqn Trg Flt 14.12.29 - 9.30

J8178 PD Ascot; AD Aboukir; 45 Sqn 11.28

J8179 PD Ascot; AD Aboukir; 4 FTS Abu Sueir 10.27

J8180 No information

J8181 39 Sqn; EF, FL in field and hit tree, nr.Thetford, Norfolk 2.4.28

J8182 PD Ascot; AD Aboukir; Convtd to DC; 4 FTS Abu Sueir ('2')

J8183 HAD 9.28; PD Ascot; AD Aboukir; Convtd DC; 4 FTS Abu Sueir ('5')

J8184 600 Sqn ('B') 1926 - 1929

J8185 HAD erected 9.28 and tested 18.10.28; 2 FTS Duxford 12.30 - 11.31

J8186 PD Ascot; AD Aboukir; 45 Sqn 4.29 - 9.29; 4 FTS Abu Sueir; AD Aboukir; Rebuild as JR8186; 4 FTS Abu Sueir ('5') 10.30; FL in desert, wreck set on fire, Cat W 1930

J8187 PD Ascot; AD Aboukir; 4 FTS Abu Sueir ('7') 12.28 - 11.30

J8188 PD Ascot; AD Aboukir; 45 Sqn 12.28 - 9.29; AD Aboukir Rebuild as JR8188; 4 FTS Abu Sueir 8.31 - 4.32

J8189 PD Ascot; AD Aboukir; 45 Sqn ('4') 12.28 - 9.29; AD Aboukir Rebuild as JR8189; 4 FTS Abu Sueir; Crashed & overturned, Abu Sueir, 1.30

18 D.H.9A ordered on Cont No 700824/26 from S.E.Saunders Ltd, East Cowes, Isle of Wight and numbered J8190 to J8207. (400hp Liberty 12A)

J8190 No information

J8191 PD Ascot; AD Aboukir; 47 Sqn 1.28 2.28

J8192 PD Ascot; AD Aboukir; 8 Sqn ('N') 5.27 - 1.28; 30 Sqn 1928; Prop accident on start-up 14.2.29 (LAC J Prunty DoI)

J8193 PD Ascot; AD Aboukir; 8 Sqn ('V') 3.27 - 4.27; Crashed

J8194 PD Ascot; AD Aboukir; 8 Sqn ('L') 5.27 - 1.28

J8195 PD Ascot; AD Aboukir; 8 Sqn ('Y') 5.27 - 2.28; Crashed

J8196 PD Ascot; AD Aboukir; 8 Sqn 5.27 - 10.27

J8197 PD Ascot; AD Aboukir; 8 Sqn 10.27; 14 Sqn 10.19; 4 FTS Abu Sueir 12.30

J8198 PD Ascot; AD Aboukir; 8 Sqn 5.27 - 10.28; 45 Sqn 12.28

J8199 PD Ascot; AD Aboukir; 8 Sqn 3.28; 45 Sqn 1.29

J8200 PD Ascot; AD Aboukir; 8 Sqn 5.27 - 10.27; FL, LG south of Bir Am Makhnuk 12.9.27

J8201 PD Ascot; AD Aboukir; 8 Sqn 8.27 - 12.27

J8202 PD Ascot; AD Aboukir; 8 Sqn 5.27 - 10.27; 45 Sqn 8.29 - 9.29; 4 FTS Abu Sueir, On landing, ran into stationary E914, Abu Sueir, Cat W 17.1.30

J8203 PD Ascot; AD Aboukir; 8 Sqn 12.27 - 3.28; 45 Sqn 6.28 - 7.28; 14 Sqn 8.29 - 9.29

J8204 PD Ascot; AD Aboukir; 8 Sqn 5.27 - 2.28

J8205 PD Ascot; AD Aboukir; 8 Sqn ('P') 5.27 - 10.27

J8206 PD Ascot; AD Aboukir; 45 Sqn 7.28 - 10.28; AD Aboukir Rebuilt as JR8206; 4 FTS Abu Sueir ('8'), crashed on nose 10.30

J8207 No information

18 D.H.9A ordered on Cont No 700825/26 from Blackburn Aeroplane & Motor Co Ltd, Brough and numbered J8208 to J8225. (400hp Liberty 1A)

J8208 A&GS Eastchurch; 605 Sqn 3.2.28 - 6.30

J8209 No information

J8210 RAF (Cadet) College, Cranwell 7.28; FL en route Wittering and crashed, Ancaster, Lincs, Cat W 23.5.29

J8211 603 Sqn 1928 - 1930

J8212 601 Sqn 8.28 - 6.29
J8213 35 Sqn 12.29 - 1.30
J8214 RAF (Cadet) College, Cranwell 9.28 - 7.29; Collided with stationary 504N J8536 taxying, 14.9.28 (repaired)
J8215 No information
J8216 RAF (Cadet) College, Cranwell; While stationary run into by 504N J8575 (Cat M, Sgt LE Speer OK) on ground, Cranwell, Cat W 3.10.28
J8217 RAF (Cadet) College, Cranwell 4.29 - 4.30; A&GS Eastchurch 10.30
J8218 RAF (Cadet) College, Cranwell ('1' in heart design)
J8219 No information
J8220 2 FTS Duxford 12.30
J8221 HAD; 601 Sqn 27.10.28; CFS, overturned landing 25.10.29 (P/O WG Stevenson & P/O GV Carey OK)
J8222 HAD 8.28; 2 FTS Duxford 1.10.28 - 4.30
J8223 600 Sqn ('C':'9') 1926 - 1928; HAD 3.8.28
J8224 601 Sqn 8.28; 2 FTS Duxford 6.29 - 7.29
J8225 HAD 10.27; 605 Sqn 5.1.28 - 6.30

23 D.H.9A (dual control) ordered on Cont No 730775/26 from Westland Aircraft Co Ltd, Yeovil and numbered J8460 to J8482. (400hp Liberty 12A)

J8460 99 Sqn ('3'), ran into watch office while visiting Upper Heyford 20.3.24
J8461 Recond by DH on Cont No 760139/27 (c/n 318)
J8462 1 FTS Netheravon 1.27 - 9.27; Westland conv 2-seat
J8463 1 FTS Netheravon 1.27; Caught fire on ground, Cat W2.5.27
J8464 1 FTS Netheravon 1.27; Collided at 50ft with 504N J8588 (LAC JB Harris injured) on take-off, Netheravon, Cat W 28.1.28 (S/Lt (F/O RAF) OS Stevinson RN injured); SOC 16.3.28
J8465 1 FTS Netheravon 1.27 - 8.27
J8466 1 FTS Netheravon 1.27 - 7.29; 3.30; Recond by DH on Cont No 760139/27 (c/n 322); RAF College 1.30 - 5.30
J8467 1 FTS Netheravon 1.27 - 8.27; HAD 8.29; 2 FTS Duxford 5.30 - 6.30
J8468 No information
J8469 2 FTS Duxford 4.27; 600 Sqn; EF, FL in field, hit wall, lost u/c, nosed up, nr.Lochty Station, Fife, 26.9.30
J8470 CFS 10.27 - 12.27; 5 FTS Sealand
J8471 1 FTS Netheravon 1927; 207 Sqn 5.27; 39 Sqn 5.28; 207 Sqn 9.28 - 5.29; 33 Sqn 10.29; CFS 12.29; 2 FTS Duxford 11.30
J8472 207 Sqn 5.27; 600 Sqn to 2.4.30; 603 Sqn 2.4.30; 6o4 Sqn 8.30; ASS Hawkinge 30.10.30 WFU
J8473 Recond by DH on Cont No 760139/27 (c/n 319); 1 FTS Netheravon 7.28; 2 FTS Duxford 11.29 - 3.30
J8474 CFS 11.28 - 12.29
J8475 CFS 10.27 - 7.29; 601 Sqn 8.30
J8476 2 FTS Duxford; Collided on take-off with 504N J8576 (F/L JR Scarlett OK) which was taxying towards hangar, Cranwell, Cat R 30.11.27 (Sgt C Osmond); 601 Sqn 8.30; PD Ascot; AD Hinaidi; AD Hinaidi CF 1.31
J8477 2 FTS Duxford ('6') 7.28 - 6.30
J8478 TOC 26.4.27 601 Sqn; ASS Hawkinge 10.30 WFU
J8479 No information
J8480 (DC); TOC 22.4.27 605 Sqn - 4.28
J8481 1 FTS Netheravon 5.27 - 8.27
J8482 1 FTS Netheravon 5.27 - 8.27; 601 Sqn; 35 Sqn ('2') 1929; Crashed in sea during palisade trials, *Glorious*, Cat W 1930

12 D.H.9A (dual control) ordered on Cont No 730980/26 from Geo Parnall & Co Ltd, Bristol and numbered J8483 to J8494. (400hp Liberty 12A)

J8483 FF 14.3.27; RAF (Cadet) College, Cranwell 3.27; CFS 4.27 - 5.28; RAF (Cadet) College, Cranwell 7.28; CFS 7.29 - 12.29
J8484 FF 14.3.27
J8485 FF 21.3.27
J8486 FF 21.3.27
J8487 FF 29.3.27; 2 FTS Duxford 10.28 - 1929
J8488 FF 1927; 2 FTS Duxford 7.28 - 2.30
J8489 FF 5.4.27; 2 FTS Duxford, crashed & caught fire, Digby, Cat W 20.6.28 (F/L J Marsden & passenger both injured)
J8490 FF 30.4.27; 2 FTS Duxford ('3') 10.28 - 11.29
J8491 FF 30.4.27; 600 Sqn 10.5.27 - 10.27; 501 Sqn; Ferrying to storage, struck haystack on arrival, landing in mist, overturned, ASS Hawkinge, Cat W 7.11.30 BO
J8492 FF 30.4.27; RAF (Cadet) College, Cranwell 3.28 - 7.28; A&AEE 8.28; RAF (Cadet) College, Cranwell 10.28 - 12.28; 5 FTS Sealand 4.29; RAF College 10.29 - 12.29; CFS 7.30 - 3.31
J8493 FF 17.5.27; RAF (Cadet) College, Cranwell 6.27 - 11.28; 2 FTS Duxford 1930
J8494 FF 17.5.27; 1 FTS Netheravon 5.27 - 8.27

D.H.9A J8211 of No.603 (City of Edinburgh) Squadron flying over the Scottish Lowlands c.1929 (RAF Museum P.15952)

Unidentified D.H.9/D.H.9A incidents etc

17.4.18 (D.H.9) 206 Sqn, hit by ground mg (pilot OK & Sgt JJ Ryan wounded)
17.4.18 (D.H.9) 206 Sqn, in action (2/Lt VFA Rolandi wounded & observer OK)
25.4.18 (D.H.9) "1550" (BHP) 201/2 TDS Cranwell, EF, turned downwind, stalled, dived in (PFO CA Wedekind seriously injured)
14.5.18 (D.H.9) 218 Sqn, accident (2/Lt AG Horneck DoI 15.5.18)
14.5.18 (D.H.9) 218 Sqn (Lt AGH Lane DoW & Lt RJ Chisholm killed)
18.5.18 (D.H.9) 44 TS Waddington, FL, overshot field, crashed into hedge (F/Cdt EM Wilcox slightly injured)
8.6.18 (D.H.9) 104 Sqn Bombing raid on Metz-Sablon Triangle (pilot OK & 2/Lt RK Pollard wounded)
8.6.18 (D.H.9) 103 Sqn, in action (2/Lt SR Payne wounded)
12.6.18 (D.H.9) 206 Sqn, in action (pilot OK & 1/Lt JW Leach USAS wounded/injured)
22.7.18 (D.H.9) 206 Sqn, in action (pilot OK & Lt WH Binnie killed)
31.7.18 (D.H.9) 104 Sqn, in action (2/Lt B Johnson wounded)
31.7.18 (D.H.9) 104 Sqn, accident (2/Lt T Bailey injured)
8.8.18 (D.H.9) "6888" 7 TDS Feltwell, EF on TO, FL in quarry, caught fire (Capt T Hayes seriously injured)
13.8.18 (D.H.9) 206 Sqn, in combat (2/Lt E Calvert DoW 14.8.18)
19.8.18 (D.H.9) 49 TDS Catterick, stalled on diving turn after TO, dived in (Sgt WH Rutter & Sgt A Wright both injured)
22.8.18 (D.H.9) 104 Sqn, in action (observer 2/Lt W Moorhouse killed) [Note - Casualty list has Moorhouse in C6202 BUT also Valentine/Hitchcock FTR in C6202 22.8.18]
30.8.18 (D.H.9) 226 Sqn, FTR raid on Cattaro (2/Lt JE Watkins & 2/Lt HB Hubbard both killed)
30.8.18 (D.H.9) 67 Wing, COL after raid on Cattaro (2/Lt FD Kendall & Pte G/L AH Wynn both killed)
8.9.18 (D.H.9) 206 Sqn, in combat (2/Lt JD Russell wounded & observer OK)
28.9.18 (D.H.9) "580". 10 TS Gosport, stalled on turn, spun in (Capt RE Rumsey DoI 9.10.18)
30.10.18 (D.H.9) 206 Sqn, in combat (pilot OK & 2/Lt WJ Jackson killed)
1.11.18 (D.H.9) 104 Sqn, in action (2/Lt LG Best wounded)
16.6.19 (D.H.9A) 221 Sqdn, FTR raid on Astrakhan, EF, FL Ouvaree (2/Lt AJ Mantle & 2/Lt H Ingram PoWs unhurt)
27.8.19 (D.H.9) 47 Sqn, left arm hit by prop while starting engine (Capt H Elliot DFC)
19.3.20 (D.H.9A) "H4387" 27 Sqn, EF on bombing raid, tried to landing field but crashed in river bed, struck rocks, bombs exploded (F/O ALC Dunn & Sgt WJ Palmer both DoW)
14.10.20 (D.H.9A) "E77", on delivery from Farnborough to Donibristle, FL in thick fog, crashed Hepple, Northants, Cat W
29.7.22 (D.H.9A) 14 Sqn Amman, crashed
4.1.24 (D.H.9A) "9854" 84 Sqn, spun in, crashed in desert S of Nasiriyah, Iraq (F/O RC Harrison & LAC KH Walter both killed)
17.1.24 (D.H.9A), 27 Sqn, carburettor caught fire in air
2.6.24 (D.H.9A), ?? Sqn, spark from exhaust ignited cockpit
22.10.24 (D.H.9A) "J546" 30 Sqn, overturned landing Sulaimania (F/O FS Henderson & AC1 GH Kenny both slightly injured)
27.10.24 (D.H.9A) 47 Sqn, engine trouble, FL nr Rafa, o/t, salved (pilot slightly injured, passenger seriously injured)
5.12.24 (D.H.9A) 27 Sqn, EF on approach, FL, hit bank 7m E of Peshawar (F/O HB Holdway & AC1 TF Mitchell both unhurt)
18.12.24 (D.H.9A) 60 Sqn, engine backfired and caught fire in air
21.6.25 (D.H.9A) 60 Sqn, crashed Peshawar, Cat W (F/O NC Bretherton & Sgt HE Blanche both killed)
26.6.25 (D.H.9A) 4 FTS Abu Sueir, looped at low altitude, port wing broke off, dived in, Cat W (PO DG Wilson & LAC CW Gamage both killed)
8.7.25 (D.H.9A) 30 sqn, crashed on the Qara Dagh above village of Malula, Iraq, Cat W (F/O MG Penny killed)
15.7.25 (D.H.9A) RAE, petrol connection came unscrewed, a/c caught fire in air, fire put out while landing and continued flight
21.10.25 (D.H.9A) 4 FTS Abu Sueir, dived in, Cat W (PO GW Cripps killed)
26.3.26 (D.H.9A) 4 FTS Abu Sueir, spun in after stall (Sgt R Horrocks DoI & PO IR Sweeting killed)
19.9.27 (D.H.9A) 47 Sqn, crashed El Tabbin, River Nile, Cat W (F/O FS Homersham DCM MM OK & AC1 HK Bacon killed)
19.11.27 (D.H.9A) 84 Sqn, spun from low altitude, destroyed by fire and exploding bombs, Cat W (Sgt AA Cole & AC1 P Conlon both killed)
30.1.28 (D.H.9A) 84 Sqn, FL 8m from Hafar after fired on, BO, Cat W (F/O R Kellett rescued)
20.2.28 (D.H.9A) 55 Sqn, pilot hit by bullet while attacking raiders, Busaiyah, Cat W (F/O RBH Jackson killed)
28.3.28 (D.H.9A) 14 Sqn, crashed nr Amman, Cat W (F/Lt G McCormack & LAC J Kimberley OK)
26.6.28 (D.H.9A) 14 Sqn, crashed nr Amman, Cat W (P/O JHL Maund & AC1 JJH Middleton OK)
27.11.28 (D.H.9A) 27 Sqn, EF near enemy lines on vertical photography, crashed Sidkot, salved by AD by road
1.4.30 (D.H.9A) RAF College, crashed Cranwell (F/Cdt WH Hodgkinson killed)

RECONDITIONING

Shorts reconditioned 10 a/c, given c/n's S.732-S.735, S.737-S.743.

D.H.9A J8218 'I' of RAF (Cadet) College, Cranwell. (RAF Museum P.16254)

D.H.9 & D.H.9A - CIVIL AND OVERSEAS USE

UNITED KINGDOM

Quite a number of D.H.9 variants reached the British civil register, as follows:

C6054 D.H.9 ex *C6054* Regd [adopting interim ex military serial] 30.4.19 to Aircraft Transport & Travel Ltd, Hendon; No CofA issued; Took off at 4.30am en route Hendon-Bournemouth on first ever postwar commercial air service flight in England, carrying newspapers, encountered thick mist one hour later and crash landed on Portsdown Hill, north of Portsmouth 1.5.19; Regd *G-EAAA* [CofR 1] 31.7.19 to same owner, but not taken up; Regn cld as pwfu 1.9.19.

H9255 D.H.9B ex *H9255* Regd [adopting interim ex military serial] 14.7.19 to Aircraft Transport & Travel Ltd, Hendon; later named "Ancuba"; Regd *G-EAGX* [CofR 180] 31.7.19 to same owner; CofA [121] issued 7.8.19; Reported as crashed 8.20; Regn cld 9.20.

H9258 D.H.9B ex *H9258* Regd [adopting interim ex military serial] 14.7.19 to Aircraft Transport & Travel Ltd, Hendon; Regd *G-EAGY* [CofR 181] 31.7.19 to same owner; [Also quoted c/n "AE.924"] CofA [145] issued 8.8.19; Sold 1.21 and regn cld 2.21. To KLM, Netherlands, presumably as spares.

H9273 D.H.9 ex *H9273* Regd [adopting interim ex military serial] 30.4.19 to Aircraft Transport & Travel Ltd, Hendon; No CofA issued [although no.34 was allocated, possibly on sale]; Regd *G-EAAD* [CofR 4] 31.7.19 to same owner. Regn cld as sold abroad 9.9.19.

H9277 D.H.9 ex *H9277* Regd [adopting interim ex military serial] 30.4.19 to Aircraft Transport & Travel Ltd, Hendon (possibly named 'Antiopa' here); Rebuilt as D.H.9B and regd *K-109* 5.19 to same owner; CofA [13] issued 6.5.19; Capt H.Shaw made the first British charter flight to Paris on 15.7.19, flying from Hendon to Le Bourget in 2hrs 50min; Reregd *G-EAAC* [CofR 3] 31.7.19 to same owner; Regd [CofR 593] 8.20 to Aircraft Manufacturing Co, Stag Lane; Modified to D.H.9C and regd [CofR 639] 17.3.21 to The De Havilland Aircraft Co Ltd. Came third in 1922 King's Cup Air Race. Later operated by DH School of Flying, Stag Lane, named "Antiopa"; Accident on cross-country test 20.3.24 (F/O Markham OK); Air sickness landing, pilot stalled 4.8.26 (P/O RR Rich OK); Converted by de Havilland to D.H.9J, CofA renewed 2.7.26; Drifted landing, swung, wingtip hit ground, overturned 24.11.26 (P/O W Scott injured); Damaged in cross-wind landing 4.8.27 (P/O JSK Inskip OK); Landed on soft ground, overturned 24.4.28 (F/O WTW Ballantyne injured); Used as a flying workshop for 1929 King's Cup Air Race, following competitors around the course for repairs and spares as needed. Force landed 13.12.29 (F/O LA Lewis OK); Flattened out too high, stalled at 8ft, bounced, damaged u/c, tipped on nose 23.7.32 (P/O HF McCullagh OK); CofA lapsed 28.1.33; Regn cld 12.33 after 14 year service.

K-109 see H9277

K-172 D.H.9R Racer c/n 9R/1 Racing conversion with Napier Lion; Regd 23.7.19 to Aircraft Transport & Travel Ltd, Hendon; Reregd *G-EAHT* [CofR 202] 31.7.19 to same owner; No CofA issued; Scrapped 22; Regn cld 17.1.23.

G-EAAA see C6054

G-EAAC see H9277

G-EAAD see H9273

G-EAGX see H9255

G-EAGY see H9258

G-EAHT see K-172

G-EALJ D.H.9 ex *D2884 [Regd as ex 2884]* Regd [CofR 298] 26.8.19 to Aircraft Transport & Travel Ltd, Hendon; Not overhauled and no CofA issued; Regn cld 10.20.

G-EAMX D.H.9 ex *D5622 [Regd as ex 5622]* Regd [CofR 338] 15.9.19 to Aircraft Transport & Travel Ltd, Hendon; No CofA issued; Regn cld as sold 4.20; Possibly to Major Clayton-Kennedy [Major William Kennedy-Cochran-Patrick?] & F Sydney Cotton and operated in Newfoundland on seal hunting [see G-EAQP]. Believed written off in 1921.

G-EAOF D.H.9A ex *E750* Regd [CofR 372] 9.10.19 to British Government for loan to Aircraft Transport & Travel Ltd, Hendon; CofA [250] issued 28.10.19; Used on Government mail service, Hawkinge to Cologne. Returned to RAF as *E750*; Regn cld as sold 6.20.

G-EAOG D.H.9A ex *E752* Regd [CofR 373] 9.10.19 to British Government for loan to Aircraft Transport & Travel Ltd, Hendon; CofA [251] issued 26.10.19; Used on Government mail service, Hawkinge to Cologne. Returned to RAF as *E752* 6.20; Regn cld as sold 6.20.

G-EAOH D.H.9A ex *E753 [regd as J753]* Regd [CofR 374] 9.10.19 to British Government for loan to Aircraft Transport & Travel Ltd, Hendon; CofA [259] issued 5.11.19; Used on Government mail service, Hawkinge to Cologne. Returned to RAF as *E753 4.20;* Regn cld as sold 4.20.

G-EAOI D.H.9A ex *E754* Regd [CofR 375] 9.10.19 to British Government for loan to Aircraft Transport & Travel Ltd, Hendon; CofA [252] issued 26.10.19; Used on Government mail service, Hawkinge to Cologne. Returned to RAF as *E754*. Regn cld as sold 6.20.

G-EAOJ D.H.9A ex *E756* Regd [CofR 376] 9.10.19 to British Government for loan to Aircraft Transport & Travel Ltd, Hendon; CofA [254] issued 31.10.19; Used on Government mail service, Hawkinge to Cologne. Returned to RAF as *E756;* Regn cld as sold 6.20.

G-EAOK D.H.9A ex *E757* Regd [CofR 377] 9.10.19 to British Government for loan to Aircraft Transport & Travel Ltd, Hendon; CofA [256] issued 2.11.19; Used on Government mail service, Hawkinge to Cologne. Returned to RAF as *E757*. Regn cld as sold 6.20.

G-EAOP D.H.9A ex *H5579 [Regd as ex 5579]* Regd [CofR 381] 20.10.19 to Aircraft Transport & Travel Ltd, Hendon; No CofA issued; Regn cld 9.20 as written off.

G-EAOZ D.H.9B ex *H5889* [remanufactured c/n P.32E] Regd [CofR 392] 29.10.19 to Aircraft Transport & Travel Ltd, Hendon; CofA [262] issued 14.11.19; AT&T ceased operations 17.12.20 and aircraft stored. Sold 27.7.21 and regn cld as sold abroad 11.21; To KLM, Netherlands and regd *H-NABF* 1921

G-EAPL D.H.9B ex *H5890* [remanufactured c/n P.33E] Regd [CofR 405] 13.11.19 to Aircraft Transport & Travel Ltd, Hendon; CofA [265] issued 22.11.19; CofA renewed 22.11.20; AT&T ceased operations 17.12.20 and aircraft stored. Regn cld [undated]; To KLM, Netherlands and regd *H-NABE* 7.21

G-EAPO D.H.9B c/n P.34E Regd [CofR 408] 20.11.19 to Aircraft Transport & Travel Ltd, Hendon; CofA [272] issued 28.11.19; Crashed 9.20. Regn cancelled 27.11.20 as WFU.

G-EAPU D.H.9B c/n P.35E Regd [CofR 414] 25.11.19 to Aircraft Transport & Travel Ltd, Hendon; CofA [282] issued 17.12.19; Regn cld 11.20.

G-EAQA D.H.9B c/n P.36E Regd [CofR 420] 10.12.19 to Aircraft Transport & Travel Ltd, Hendon; CofA [287] issued 4.1.20; AT&T ceased operations 17.12.20 and aircraft stored. Regn cld 2.21.

G-EAQL D.H.9B c/n P.38E Regd [CofR 433] 31.12.19 to Aircraft Transport & Travel Ltd, Hendon; CofA [292] issued 11.1.20; AT&T ceased operations 17.12.20 and aircraft stored. Regn cld as sold to Belgium 27.7.21.

G-EAQM D.H.9 ex *F1278 [Also shown as F1258]* Regd [CofR 434] 31.12.19 to Raymond JP Parer, Hounslow; CofA [285] issued 2.1.20; Departed Hounslow 8.1.20 for Australia flown by Parer and Lt John C McIntosh, carrying a present of Scotch whisky for the Premier of New South Wales. It reached Le Bourget 14.1.20, Toulon 21.1.20 and Rome 23.1.20. It eventually arrived Darwin 2.8.20; first single-engined UK to Australia flight, but damaged on last leg, date unknown; Regn cld 2.21 [but see *G-AUKI*]; Stored until reconditioned 71/72 for display Bathurst.

G-EAQN D.H.9B c/n P.37E Regd [CofR 435] 7.1.20 to Aircraft Transport & Travel Ltd, Hendon; CofA [294] issued 20.1.20; Crashed Le Bourget 9.11.20; Regn cld 12.20 [or 2.21];

G-EAQP D.H.9 c/n P.39E Regd [CofR 437] 12.1.20 to Aircraft Transport & Travel Ltd, Hendon; CofA [296] issued

D.H.9B K-109, a post-war civil conversion of H9277. (via Frank Cheesman)

D.H.9R sesquiplane racer G-EAHT, with a Napier Lion engine. (via Terry Treadwell)

D.H.9A G-EAOG returned to the RAF as E752 after being used on the official mail service to Cologne. (J.M.Bruce/G.S.Leslie)

D.H.9B G-EAUC was operated by Handley Page Transport in 1921. (via Peter Green)

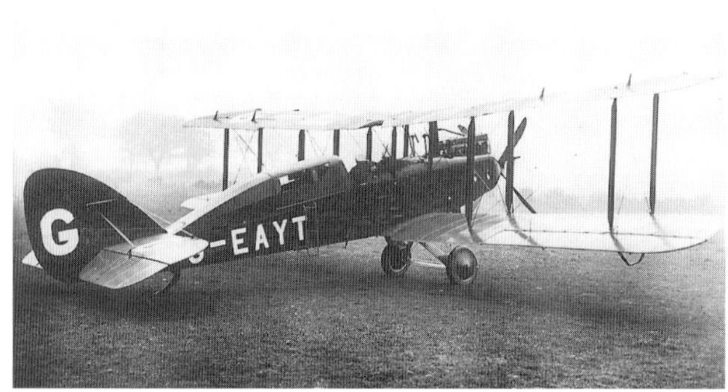

D.H.9C G-EAYT had an enclosed passenger cabin, being operated by the De Havilland Hire Service from Stag Lane. (Philip Jarrett)

D.H.9C G-EBAX was another with an enclosed passenger cabin, operated by the D.H. Hire Service from Stag Lane. (Philip Jarrett)

D.H.9A G-EBCG was fitted with an Eagle engine and used as a demonstrator by Airco. (via Philip Jarrett)

D.H.9C G-EBDD, operated by the D.H.Hire Service, had an open rear cockpit. (MAP)

28.1.20; Wfu 12.20 but CofA renewed 28.1.21 and probably operated by DH Aeroplane Hire Service; CofA lapsed 27.1.22; Regn cld 1.22; *Reported as sold in 1922 to F.S.[Sydney] Cotton for operation by Aerial Survey Co in Newfoundland, but this may have been G-EAMX instead.*

G-EATA D.H.9B ex *H9271 [Regd as 9271]* Regd [CofR 511] 30.4.20 to Handley Page Ltd, operated by Handley Page Transport, Cricklewood; CofA [359] issued 7.5.20; Probably sold abroad; Regn cld 4.21.

G-EAUC D.H.9B ex *H9282 [Regd as 9282]* Regd [CofR 551] 28.6.20 to Handley Page Ltd, operated by Handley Page Transport, Cricklewood; CofA [387] issued 6.7.20; CofA lapsed 5.7.21; Regn cld [undated].

G-EAUH D.H.9B ex *H9196* Regd [CofR 556] 13.7.20 to Handley Page Ltd, operated by Handley Page Transport, Cricklewood; CofA [397] issued 23.7.20; Regn cld 19.3.21, but reinstated; Regn cld as sold abroad 11.21; To KLM, Netherlands and regd *H-NABP*.

G-EAUI D.H.9B ex *H9197* Regd [CofR 557] 13.7.20 to Handley Page Ltd, operated by Handley Page Transport, Cricklewood; CofA [390] issued 11.7.20; CofA lapsed 10.7.21; Regd [CofR 944] 9.3.23 to Surrey Flying Services Ltd, Croydon; CofA renewed 20.3.23; Regn cld as sold 4.6.23; Probably sold to Spain.

G-EAUN D.H.9B ex *H9128* Regd [CofR 563] 17.7.20 to Handley Page Ltd, operated by Handley Page Transport, Cricklewood; CofA [411] issued 18.8.20; CofA lapsed 17.8.21; Regd [CofR 945] 9.3.23 to Surrey Flying Services Ltd, Croydon; CofA renewed 20.3.23; Regn cld as sold 4.6.23; Regd in Spain as *M-AGAG* 6.23 to Cia Espanola del Trafico Aereo; Later became *EC-FFF*

G-EAUO D.H.9B ex *H9187* Regd [CofR 564] 17.7.20 to Handley Page Ltd, operated by Handley Page Transport, Cricklewood; CofA [412] issued 21.8.20; Regn cld as crashed 27.7.21. *[Quoted as later H-NABO - doubtful]*

G-EAUP D.H.9B ex *H9176* Regd [CofR 565] 17.7.20 to Handley Page Ltd, operated by Handley Page Transport, Cricklewood; CofA [419] issued 7.9.20; CofA lapsed 6.9.21; Regn cld [undated].

G-EAUQ D.H.9B ex *H9125* Regd [CofR 566] 17.7.20 to Handley Page Ltd, operated by Handley Page Transport, Cricklewood; CofA [400] issued 30.7.20; Regn cld 19.3.21, but reinstated; Regn cld as sold abroad 11.21; To KLM, Netherlands and regd *H-NABO*.

G-EAVK D.H.9B c/n P.60E Regd [CofR 595] 9.20 to Aircraft Manufacturing Co Ltd, Stag Lane; CofA [423] issued 18.9.20; Regd [CofR 634] 2.3.21 to The De Havilland Aircraft Co Ltd, Stag Lane; CofA lapsed 17.9.21; Regn cld as sold 8.3.22.

G-EAVM D.H.9 ex *H9243* Regd [CofR 598] 13.9.20 to Handley Page Ltd, Cricklewood; CofA [421] issued 14.9.20; Delivered to Copenhagen, Denmark 18.9.20; Regn cld as sold abroad 22.9.21; Regd *T-DOKL* [CofA No.33] 9.2.22 to Det Danske Luftfartselskab, Copenhagen; Broken up for spares Kastrup and regn cld 4.27.

G-EAXC D.H.9A ex *E8791* Regd [CofR 665] 1.6.21 to Aircraft Disposal Co Ltd, Croydon; Used as demonstrator during 1922; No CofA issued; Regn cld 13.11.22 as written off.

G-EAXG D.H.9C *c/n DH9C/16* [reported as ex D516, but this probably a corruption of its c/n]; Regd [CofR 670] 14.6.21 to The De Havilland Aircraft Co Ltd, Stag Lane CofA [514] issued 3.9.21; Deld to DH Aeroplane Hire Service 11.1.22; Flown to *Spain* 26.1.22 by CD Barnard]; Regn cld as sold 15.6.22
[Note: 'Aeroplane' magazine dated 17.4.29 reported this as becoming M-AAGA, but that was c/n 12]

G-EAYT D.H.9C c/n DH9C/14 Regd [CofR 717] 12.10.21 to The De Havilland Aircraft Co Ltd, operated by DH Aeroplane Hire Service, Stag Lane; named "Atlanta"; CofA [538] issued 29.11.21; Used by Alan Cobham for long distance flight to North Africa and the Near East. Crashed in sea in fog off Venice Lido 2.10.22; Regn cld 2.10.22.

G-EAYU D.H.9C c/n DH9C/15 Regd [CofR 718] 12.10.21 to The De Havilland Aircraft Co Ltd, operated by DH Aeroplane Hire Service, Stag Lane; CofA [537] issued 9.12.21; Crashed Woodhouse Moor, nr Leeds 2.10.22; repaired and CofA renewed 22.2.23; CofA lapsed 21.2.24; Crashed 24.6.24 (F/O WE Jaffs OK); Regn cld as sold 3.11.24; To *Hedjaz Government*.

G-EAYW D.H.9 ex *H5619* Regd [CofR 721] 13.10.21 to Aircraft Disposal Co Ltd, Croydon; No CofA issued; Ferried to Belgian Air Force 10.21; Regn cld as sold abroad 28.11.21.

G-EAYY D.H.9 ex *H5833* Regd [CofR 726] 31.10.21 to Aircraft Disposal Co Ltd, Croydon; No CofA issued; To Alfred Comte, Switzerland 12.21; Regn cld as sold 12.1.22; Regd *CH-82*. Regn cld pre.28.

G-EAYZ D.H.9 ex *H5848* Regd [CofR 727] 31.10.21 to Aircraft Disposal Co Ltd, Croydon; No CofA issued; To Alfred Comte, Switzerland 12.21; Regn cld as sold 12.1.22; Regd *CH-83*. Regn cld pre 1928.

G-EAZA D.H.9 ex *H5629* Regd [CofR 729] 8.11.21 to Aircraft Disposal Co Ltd, Croydon; No CofA issued; Ferried to Belgian Air Force 11.21; Regn cld as sold abroad 28.11.21.

G-EAZB D.H.9 ex *H5705* Regd [CofR 730] 8.11.21 to Aircraft Disposal Co Ltd, Croydon; No CofA issued; Ferried to Belgian Air Force 11.21; Regn cld as sold abroad 28.11.21.

G-EAZC D.H.9 ex *H5607* Regd [CofR 731] 8.11.21 to Aircraft Disposal Co Ltd, Croydon; No CofA issued; Ferried to Belgian Air Force 11.21; Regn cld as sold 28.11.21 [also as regn cld 1.22].

G-EAZD D.H.9 ex *H5856* [or H5850] Regd [CofR 732] 8.11.21 to Aircraft Disposal Co Ltd, Croydon; No CofA issued; Ferried to Belgian Air Force 11.21; Regn cld 1.22.

G-EAZE D.H.9 ex *H5757* Regd [CofR 733] 8.11.21 to Aircraft Disposal Co Ltd, Croydon; No CofA issued; Ferried to Belgian Air Force 11.21; Regn cld as sold abroad 28.11.21.

G-EAZH D.H.9 ex *H5839* Regd [CofR 737] 14.11.21 to Aircraft Disposal Co Ltd, Croydon; No CofA issued; To Ad Astra Aero AG, Switzerland 7.2.22; Regn cld as sold 2.3.22; Regd *CH-81* 20.2.22; Regn cld pre 1928.

G-EAZI D.H.9 ex *H5860* Regd [CofR 738] 14.11.21 to Aircraft Disposal Co Ltd, Croydon; No CofA issued; To Ad Astra Aero AG, Switzerland 7.2.22; Regn cld as sold 2.3.22; Deld via Paris and regd *CH-84* 20.2.22 to Ad Astra Aero AG, Zurich; Regn cld? Regd 27.7.26 to same owner; Regd 23.1.31 to K Schroeder, Dubendorf; Regn cld pre-12.33.

G-EAZJ D.H.9 ex *H5666* Regd [CofR 739] 19.11.21 to Aircraft Disposal Co Ltd, Croydon; No CofA issued; Ferried to Belgian Air Force 11.21; Regn cld as sold abroad 28.11.21.

G-EAZM D.H.9 ex *H5865* Regd [CofR 742] 19.11.21 to Aircraft Disposal Co Ltd, Croydon; No CofA issued; Ferried to Belgian Air Force 11.21; Regn cld as sold 12.1.22.

G-EAZN D.H.9 ex *H5707* Regd [CofR 743] 22.11.21 to Aircraft Disposal Co Ltd, Croydon; No CofA issued; Ferried to Belgian Air Force 11.21; Regn cld as sold 12.1.22.

G-EAZO D.H.9 ex *H5845* Regd [CofR 744] 22.11.21 to Aircraft Disposal Co Ltd, Croydon; No CofA issued; Ferried to Belgian Air Force 12.21; Regn cld as sold 12.1.22.

G-EAZP D.H.9 ex *H5868* Regd [CofR 745] 22.11.21 to Aircraft Disposal Co Ltd, Croydon; No CofA issued; Ferried to Belgian Air Force 11.21; Regn cld as sold 12.1.22.

G-EAZY D.H.9 ex *H5706* Regd [CofR 754] 5.12.21 to Aircraft Disposal Co Ltd, Croydon; No CofA issued; Ferried to Belgian Air Force 12.21; Regn cld as sold 12.1.22.

G-EAZZ D.H.9 ex *H5668* Regd [CofR 755] 5.12.21 to Aircraft Disposal Co Ltd, Croydon; No CofA issued; Ferried to Belgian Air Force 12.21; Regn cld as sold 12.1.22.

G-EBAA D.H.9 ex *H5783* Regd [CofR 756] 5.12.21 to Aircraft Disposal Co Ltd, Croydon; No CofA issued; Ferried to Belgian Air Force 12.21; Regn cld as sold 12.1.22.

G-EBAB D.H.9 ex *H5851* Regd [CofR 757] 5.12.21 to Aircraft Disposal Co Ltd, Croydon; No CofA issued; Ferried to Belgian Air Force 12.21; Regn cld as sold 12.1.22.

G-EBAC D.H.9A ex *E8788* Regd [CofR 758] 5.12.21 to Aircraft Disposal Co Ltd, Croydon; Fitted with Liberty; No CofA issued; Ferried to Le Bourget 29.12.21 by FJ Ortweiler; Regn cld as sold 12.1.22.

G-EBAD D.H.9 ex *H5621 [Also reported as H5830]* Regd [CofR 759] 8.12.21 to Aircraft Disposal Co Ltd, Croydon; No CofA issued; Ferried to Belgian Air Force 12.21; Regn cld as sold 4.4.22.

G-EBAE D.H.9 ex *H5736 [Also reported as H5834]* Regd [CofR 760] 8.12.21 to Aircraft Disposal Co Ltd, Croydon; No CofA issued; Ferried to Belgian Air Force 12.21; Regn cld as sold 4.4.22.

G-EBAI D.H.9 ex *H5712* Regd [CofR 764] 12.21 to Aircraft Disposal Co Ltd, Croydon; No CofA issued; Ferried to Belgian Air Force 1.22; Regn cld 2.3.22.

G-EBAN D.H.9A ex *F2867* Regd [CofR 770] 21.12.21 to Aircraft Disposal Co Ltd, Croydon; Fitted with Eagle; No CofA issued; Ferried to Brussels 28.1.22 by EDC Herne; Then on to *Spanish Air Force* for trials, presumed sold locally; Regn cld 2.3.22.

G-EBAO D.H.9 ex *H5716* Regd [CofR 771] 31.12.31 to Aircraft Disposal Co Ltd, Croydon; No CofA issued; Ferried to Belgian Air Force 1.22; Regn cld 2.3.22.

G-EBAP D.H.9 ex *H5741* Regd [CofR 772] 31.12.21 to Aircraft Disposal Co Ltd, Croydon; No CofA issued; Ferried to Belgian Air Force 1.22; Regn cld 2.3.22.

G-EBAQ D.H.9 ex *H5753* Regd [CofR 773] 31.12.21 to Aircraft Disposal Co Ltd, Croydon; No CofA issued; Ferried to Belgian Air Force 1.22; Regn cld 2.3.22.

G-EBAR D.H.9 ex *H5747* Regd [CofR 774] 31.12.21 to Aircraft Disposal Co Ltd, Croydon; No CofA issued; Ferried to Belgian Air Force 1.22; Regn cld 2.3.22.

G-EBAS D.H.9 ex *H5662* Regd [CofR 775] 31.12.21 to Aircraft Disposal Co Ltd, Croydon; No CofA issued; Ferried to Belgian Air Force 1.22; Regn cld 2.3.22.

G-EBAW D.H.9B c/n 25 Regd [CofR 779] 5.1.22 to The De Havilland Aircraft Co Ltd, operated by DH Aeroplane Hire Service/DH School of Flying, Stag Lane; Bounced landing in strong wind, a/c suddenly stopped and brushed the near hedge 6.7.23 (P/O DL Townsend OK); CofA [543] issued 28.2.22; Regn cld 10.9.23 with current CofA.

G-EBAX D.H.9C c/n 26 Regd [CofR 780] 5.1.22 to The De Havilland Aircraft Co Ltd, operated by DH Aeroplane Hire Service/DH School of Flying, Stag Lane; CofA [544] issued 28.2.22; Crashed Lympne 14.8.22; repaired; Struck obstruction after landing 23.11.23 (F/O ADL Carroll OK); CofA lapsed 25.3.24; Regn cld 23.4.24.

G-EBBA D.H.9 ex *H5735* Regd [CofR 783] 9.1.22 to Aircraft Disposal Co Ltd, Croydon; No CofA issued; Ferried to Belgian Air Force 1.22; Regn cld 2.3.22.

G-EBBB D.H.9 ex *H5709* Regd [CofR 784] 9.1.22 to Aircraft Disposal Co Ltd, Croydon; No CofA issued; Ferried to Belgian Air Force 1.22; Regn cld 2.3.22.

G-EBBJ D.H.9 ex *H5711* Regd [CofR 795] 21.2.22 to Aircraft Disposal Co Ltd, Croydon; No CofA issued; Ferried to Belgian Air Force 1.22; Regn cld 4.4.22.

G-EBBK D.H.9 ex *H5719* Regd [CofR 796] 21.2.22 to Aircraft Disposal Co Ltd, Croydon; No CofA issued; Ferried to Belgian Air Force 1.22; Regn cld 4.4.22.

G-EBCG D.H.9A ex *F2868* Regd [CofR 821] 1.4.22 to Aircraft Disposal Co Ltd, Croydon; named "Bellini"; Fitted with RR Eagle VIII and used as demonstrator; CofA [659] issued 11.7.23; CofA lapsed 10.7.24; Regn cld 5.1.27.

G-EBCH D.H.9 ex *H5836* Regd [CofR 822] 1.4.22 to Aircraft Disposal Co Ltd, Croydon; No CofA issued; Ferried to Belgian Air Force 4.22; Regn cld 9.5.22.

G-EBCI D.H.9 ex *H5742* Regd [CofR 823] 1.4.22 to Aircraft Disposal Co Ltd, Croydon; No CofA issued; Ferried to Belgian Air Force 4.22; Regn cld 9.5.22.

G-EBCJ D.H.9 ex *H5820* Regd [CofR 824] 1.4.22 to Aircraft Disposal Co Ltd, Croydon; No CofA issued; Ferried to Belgian Air Force 4.22; Regn cld 9.5.22.

G-EBCZ D.H.9C c/n 38 Regd [CofR 845] 28.4.22 to The De Havilland Aircraft Co Ltd, operated by DH Aeroplane Hire Service, Stag Lane; CofA [561] issued 26.5.22; Crashed Newcastle 4.7.23; Regn cld 7.11.23.

G-EBDD D.H.9C c/n 39 Regd [CofR 853] 18.5.22 to The De Havilland Aircraft Co Ltd, operated by DH Aeroplane Hire Service, Stag Lane; CofA [567] issued 1.6.22; CofA lapsed 31.5.24; Crashed 19.6.24 (F/O AG Lamplugh OK); Accident 3.11.24 (P/O WA Hammerton OK); Ran into concealed fence after good landing at Netheravon 18.6.25 (F/O L Motley OK); Regn cld 6.11.25.

G-EBDE D.H.9 ex *H5738* [Supplied by ADC] Regd [CofR 854] 19.5.22 to Major Wilfred T Blake; No formal CofA issued; Mod to 3-seater by ADC and departed Croydon 24.5.22 on Round the World flight; Forced landed and damaged Parc Borelly, nr Marseilles, France 28.5.22; Taken by lorry to Istres for repairs; reflown 14.6.22 but continuing engine problems resulted in decision to replace; Replacement G-EBDL was shipped out 21.6.22 [see below]; Fully repaired by ADC and then shipped to Vancouver, Canada for [aborted] American sector of Round the World flight; Regn cld 13.11.22; Stored until modified to D.H.9C and regd *G-CAEU* [CofR 263] 12.1.25 to Laurentide Air Service, Ottawa; Badly damaged in forced landing into trees Kekeko Hills 24.1.25, en route Larder Lake, Ont to Rouyn, PQ.

G-EBDF D.H.9 ex *H5652* Regd [CofR 855] 23.5.22 to Aircraft Disposal Co Ltd, Croydon; Intended to be shipped to Canada for use on Major Blake's Round the World flight; but replaced by *G-EBDE*; Reported as operated 7.22 by De Havilland Aeroplane Hire Service, Stag Lane; CofA [651] issued 29.6.23; Regn cld as sold 17.7.24.

G-EBDG D.H.9 ex *"H4890"* Regd [CofR 856] 5.22 to Manchester Aviation Co Ltd, Alexandra Park; Converted to D.H.9C; CofA [666] issued 13.7.23; Regd 3.24 to The Northern Aviation Co, Alexandra Park; Regd [CofR 1102] 7.24 to William Beardmore & Co Ltd, Renfrew and operated by Beardmore Reserve Flying School; CofA lapsed 12.7.26; Rebuilt 10.27 [CofA presumed renewed but not so shown in formal records]; Regd [CofR 2415] 5.2.30 to Northern Air Transport Ltd, Wythenshawe/Barton; Regn cld 12.30.

G-EBDL D.H.9 ex *H5678* Regd [CofR 864] 17.6.22 to Major Wilfred T Blake; No formal CofA issued; Supplied by ADC as replacement for *G-EBDE* [and painted as such; presumably to overcome paperwork problems or filming inconsistencies]; flown to Calcutta; arriving 13.8.22; Auctioned in Calcutta 14.8.22 and sold to Mr Hales for 1,700 rupees; re-auctioned 15.8.22 and sold to Mr Birla, proprietor of [newspaper] Empire Mail, for 2,500 rupees; Donated by him to Hindu University of Benares for preservation; Regn cld 13.11.22.

G-EBEF D.H.9 ex *H5775* Regd [CofR 886] 13.7.22 to Aircraft Disposal Co Ltd, Croydon; No CofA issued; Regn cld as sold 18.9.22.

G-EBEG D.H.9 ex *D1347* Regd [CofR 887] 13.7.22 to Aircraft Disposal Co Ltd, Croydon; No CofA issued; Regn cld as sold 18.9.22.

G-EBEH D.H.9 ex *D5777* Regd [CofR 888] 13.7.22 to Aircraft Disposal Co Ltd, Croydon; No CofA issued; Regn cld as sold 13.11.22.

G-EBEI D.H.9 ex *F1286* Regd [CofR 889] 13.7.22 to Aircraft Disposal Co Ltd, Croydon; No CofA issued; Regn cld as sold 18.9.22.

G-EBEJ D.H.9 ex *F1216* Regd [CofR 890] 13.7.22 to Aircraft Disposal Co Ltd, Croydon; No CofA issued; regn cld as sold 18.9.22.

G-EBEN D.H.9 ex *H5688* Regd [CofR 897] 24.8.22 to Aircraft Disposal Co Ltd, Croydon; Came fourth in 1922 King's Cup Air Race. C of A [713] issued 4.1.24; To British & Egyptian Tea Co Ltd as two-seater; Regn cld as sold 3.12.24.

G-EBEP D.H.9 ex *D5799* Converted by ADC and regd [CofR 903] 8.22 to unknown party [probably The Duke of Sutherland]; CofA [589] issued 21.9.22; Regd [CofR 917] 25.9.22 to Surrey Flying Services Ltd, Croydon; Came 10th in 1922 King's Cup Air Race. Crashed into house in West Hill, Sanderstead, Surrey 17.11.28; Regn cld 1.29.

G-EBEZ D.H.9 c/n 66 Regd [CofR 925] 12.12.22 to The De Havilland Aircraft Co Ltd, Stag Lane; Converted to single-seater and fitted with Napier Lion for 1923 Kings Cup Air Race; named "Eileen"; Reverted to standard and operated by DH Aeroplane Hire Service, later DH School of Flying, Stag Lane; Modified to D.H.9J and CofA [945] issued 17.2.26; later based Hatfield; Came second in 1927 King's Cup Air Race with 540hp Lion, flown by Alan Cobham at 144.7mph. Stalled and crashed on approach, badly damaged 31.7.30 (F/O SR Herringshaw OK); EF at 800ft, FL, ran down slope into hedge, overturned 29.12.30 (P/O RS Gleadow OK); Wfu 4.33 and regn cld 12.33, prior to CofA expiry. Scrapped 1933.

G-EBFQ D.H.9 c/n 76 Regd [CofR 955] 11.4.23 to The De Havilland Aircraft Co Ltd; operated by DH School of Flying, Stag Lane; CofA [613] issued 8.5.23; Accident 30.9.24 (F/O FW Knox OK); Sideslipped in landing, did

D.H.9 G-EBDL (painted as G-EBDE) being escorted by an RAF D.H.9A en route to Bushire 17.7.22. (via R.L.Ward)

D.H.9 G-EBEN came fourth in the 1922 King's Cup Air Race. (via Philip Jarrett)

D.H.9 G-EBEP came tenth in the 1922 King's Cup Air Race. (via Philip Jarrett)

D.H.9 G-EBEZ was fitted with a Lion engine and converted to a single-seater for the 1923 King's Cup Air Race. (via Philip Jarrett)

D.H.9 G-EBJR was fitted with floats before being sold to the British & Egyptian Tea Co Ltd. (MAP)

D.H.9 G-EBPE was flown in Northern Rhodesia, being fitted with floats for operations on the Zambesi River. (Philip Jarrett)

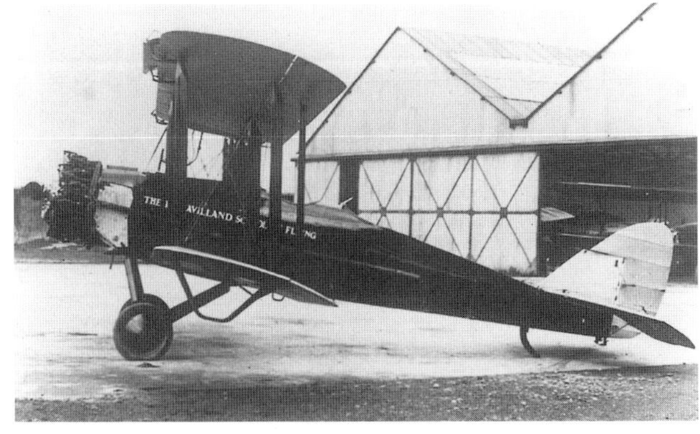

Jaguar-engined D.H.9J G-EBTN was operated by the De Havilland School of Flying at Stag Lane. (via D.M.Hannah)

D.H.9 three-seater G-AACP towed banners with Aerial Sites Ltd, Hanworth in 1937. (RAF Museum P.2233)

not flatten out in time 26.5.25 (F/O SE Taylor OK); U/c collapsed landing 15.7.25 (F/O CDJ Barnard & F/O Bradley OK); Damaged landing 31.8.26 (P/O GW Phillips OK); Converted to D.H.9J Puma Trainer, CofA renewal 11.12.26; later based Hatfield; Lost in fog, force landed, hit goal post, Greenwich 1.1.27 (P/O ER Watson OK); Stalled landing 3.5.27 (F/O DP Jones OK); Caught by wind while taxying for TO, swung into stationary Moth G-AACU, Hendon 20.8.30 (F/P RR Rich OK); CofA lapsed 28.7.32; Regn cld 12.33.

G-EBGQ D.H.9 ex *H5632* Regd [CofR 985] 4.6.23 to William Beardmore & Co Ltd, Renfrew for RAF reserve training; CofA [652] issued 28.6.23; Struck telegraph pole landing 20.12.23 (F/O WH Herd OK); Struck ridge landing 2.6.24 (P/O LE Headley OK); CofA renewed 4.10.24; Swung on TO, banked to left, dived into field adjoining aerodrome 30.10.24 (P/O JB Crawford seriously injured); Regn cld 30.10.24

G-EBGT D.H.9 c/n 82 Regd [CofR 989] 7.6.23 to The De Havilland Aircraft Co Ltd; operated by DH School of Flying, Stag Lane; named "Nulli Secundus"; CofA [647] issued 19.6.23; Accident during cross-country test 20.2.24 (F/O Roberts OK); Converted to D.H.9J Puma Trainer, Cof A renewal 19.8.26; Fast landing, ran into fence, overturned 12.11.26 (P/O LS Webb injured); Later based Hatfield; Cross-country dual ab initio, force landed in darkness at Harrow on return 31.8.28 (F/O J Holma OK & P/O FC Fisher injured); Unable to locate airfield at dusk in bad weather, force landed, overran into trees, badly damaged 4.1.30 (F/O RAC Brie injured); Struck boundary fence landing, badly damaged, Heston 2.8.30 (F/O GW Lavington OK); Undershot landing, prop and lower mainplane hit fence, Lympne 10.7.32 (F/O R Anderson OK); EF, turned back, stalled, engine cut at 600ft, crashed, badly damaged, Hatfield 16.10.32 (F/O FW Marshall slightly injured); Regn cld 12.32.

G-EBGU D.H.9 4-seater c/n 83 Regd [CofR 990] 7.6.23 to The De Havilland Aircraft Co Ltd, operated by DH School of Flying, Stag Lane; CofA [677] issued 13.9.23; Flown from Croydon with Neon advertising signs by Hubert Broad 12.2.24. Crashed 19.8.24 (F/O FGH Ayscough OK); Regn cld as sold 3.11.24.

G-EBGX D.H.9A ex *F2872* Regd [CofR 994] 16.6.23 to Aircraft Disposal Co Ltd, Croydon; named "Aurora"; Fitted with Napier Lion for 1923 Kings Cup Air Race; No CofA issued; WFU c.1924 after regn lapsed.

G-EBHP D.H.9 ex *H9203* Regd [CofR 1020] 29.8.23 to William Beardmore & Co Ltd, Renfrew for Beardmore Reserve Flying School; CofA [695] issued 20.9.23; Struck rough ground landing 21.2.24 (F/O E Humphreys OK); Struck rough ground landing 1.4.24 (F/O H Soulsby OK); Pilot blinded during rainstorm, crashed after stalled on turn 11.6.24 (F/O I Robertson injured); Struck ridge landing 11.12.24 (F/O FG Sinclair); Struck ridge landing 19.3.25 (F/O H Soulsby OK); Landed on high ground, ran down side of hill 1.7.25 (F/O JE Whitehead OK); Crashed landing in snowstorm 18.12.25 (F/O GF Yuill OK); Regn cld 18.1.26, prior to CofA expiry.

G-EBHV D.H.9 ex *H5844* Regd [CofR 1027] 19.9.23 to Sir WG Armstrong Whitworth Aircraft Ltd; operated by Armstrong-Whitworth Reserve School, Whitley; CofA [709] issued 12.11.23; Went on nose landing 2.4.24 (F/O EA Burbridge OK); Converted to D.H.9J Puma Trainer, Cof A renewal 29.9.27; CofA lapsed 28.9.28; Regn cld 24.10.28, scrapped.

G-EBIG D.H.9 ex *H5886* Regd [CofR 1040] 9.23 to William Beardmore & Co Ltd, Renfrew and operated by Beardmore Reserve Flying School; CofA [705] issued 24.10.23; Converted to D.H.9C by Berkshire Aviation Tours Ltd, Shrewsbury; Regd [CofR 1953] 18.4.29 to Northern Air Transport Ltd, Wythenshawe; CofA lapsed 17.4.30; Regn cld 12.31.

G-EBJR D.H.9 ex *H9289* Regd [CofR 1101] 22.7.24 to Aircraft Disposal Co Ltd, Croydon; Rebuilt by DH with floats [and c/n 158] and CofA [833] issued [to De Havilland Aircraft Co Ltd] 1.8.24; To British & Egyptian Tea Co Ltd; Regn cld as sold 3.11.24.

G-EBJW D.H.9 ex *H9333* Three-seater fitted with ADC Nimbus; Regd [CofR 1110] 8.24 to PM Greig & E Higgs, t/a Northern Air Lines, Manchester; CofA [820] issued 30.8.24; Company formed as Northern Air Lines Ltd 1.25; ceased trading 10.25; Regd [5.26] to British Aviation Insurance Group, Stag Lane; Regd [CofR 1409] 13.6.27 to Air Taxis Ltd, Stag Lane; CofA lapsed 5.7.28; Regn cld 1.29.

G-EBJX D.H.9 ex *H9147* Three-seater fitted with ADC Nimbus; Regd [CofR 1111] 8.24 to PM Greig & E Higgs, t/a Northern Air Lines, Manchester; CofA [823] issued 17.9.24; Company formed as Northern Air Lines Ltd 1.25; ceased trading 10.25; Regd 6.26 to Lt GBH Mundy, t/a Air Taxis, Stag Lane; Reformed as company 31.12.26 and regd [CofR 1348] 10.3.27 to Air Taxis Ltd, Stag Lane; CofA lapsed 5.6.27; Regn cld as WFU 5.7.28.

G-EBKO D.H.9 ex *H9319* Regd [CofR 1131] 11.24 to Aircraft Disposal Co Ltd, Croydon; CofA [850] issued 17.4.25; Company renamed ADC Aircraft Ltd 30.7.25; Fitted with ADC Nimbus for 1927 Kings Cup and came fourth at 123.6mph; Regd [CofR 1602] 28.3.28 to The Aircraft Operating Co Ltd, based Hinaidi, Iraq; CofA lapsed 15.2.29; Regn cld 12.30.

G-EBKV D.H.9 ex *H9337* Three-seater fitted with Puma; Regd [CofR 1140] 11.2.25 to The Aircraft Disposal Co Ltd, Croydon; CofA [853] issued 17.4.25; Company renamed ADC Aircraft Ltd 30.7.25; Regn cld as sold 5.1.27; Regd *G-AUFB* 24.9.26 [CofR 143] to DG Brims & Co [quoting c/n "853" - UK CofA No.]; Regd 19.12.26 to Courier Aircraft Ltd, Brisbane; Probably the D.H.9C flown Rabaul-Lae 3.27 by EA Muster for op by Guinea Gold Mining Co; Sold 2.9.27 to Guinea Airways Ltd, Lae, New Guinea; Forced landed 8 ml N of Wau, New Guinea, in Bulolo River area 3.3.28; pilot Alan Cross rescued after 2 days; Regn cld 8.6.28.

G-EBLC D.H.9A ex *E8781* Fitted with Liberty; Regd [CofR 1151] 14.4.25 to The Aircraft Disposal Co Ltd, Croydon; Company renamed ADC Aircraft Ltd 30.7.25; CofA [921] issued 30.12.25; CofA lapsed 6.8.29; Regn cld 12.31.

G-EBLH D.H.9 c/n 181 Regd [CofR 1162] 29.5.25 to The De Havilland Aircraft Co Ltd, operated by DH School of Flying, Stag Lane; CofA [874] issued 27.6.25; Converted to D.H.9J Puma Trainer, Cof A renewal 25.8.26; Hit treetop, crashed Littlewick, nr Maidenhead 12.5.27 (F/O WA Foot killed); Regn cld 1.28.

G-EBOQ D.H.9J c/n 282 Regd [CofR 1281] 5.7.26 to Sir WG Armstrong Whitworth Aircraft Ltd; op by Armstrong-Whitworth Reserve School, Whitley; CofA [1014] issued 17.8.26; Engine failure, force landed 31.7.28 (F/O CHL Needham injured); Stalled at 400ft flat turn on approach, crashed heavily three fields outside airfield 9.7.29 (F/O JD Williamson DoI); Regn cld 10.29.

G-EBOR D.H.9J c/n 283 Regd [CofR 1282] 5.7.26 to Sir WG Armstrong Whitworth Aircraft Ltd; op by Armstrong-Whitworth Reserve School, Whitley; CofA [1053] issued 15.9.26; Engine spluttered at 300ft on approach, hit trees attempting to land in field 27.6.29 (P/O B Apthorpe Webb injured); Regn cld 10.29 with current CofA.

G-EBPE D.H.9 c/n 284 Fitted with ADC Nimbus; Regd [CofR 1300] 2.9.26 to The Aircraft Operating Co Ltd, based N'Changa, Northern Rhodesia and converted to floatplane for operations on Zambesi River; CofA [1074] issued 21.12.26; CofA lapsed 20.12.27; Regn cld 2.29.

G-EBPF D.H.9 c/n 285 Fitted with ADC Nimbus; Regd [CofR 1301] 2.9.26 to The Aircraft Operating Co Ltd, based N'Changa, Northern Rhodesia and converted to floatplane for operations on Zambesi River; CofA [1075] issued 21.12.26; CofA lapsed 20.12.27; Regn cld 12.30.

G-EBQD D.H.9 ex *H9205* Regd [CofR 1336] 1.27 to ADC Aircraft Ltd, Croydon; CofA [1120] issued 21.4.27; Regd [CofR 1645] 24.5.28 to the Aircraft Operating Co Ltd, based Bulawayo, Southern Rhodesia; CofA lapsed 10.5.29; Regn cld 12.30.

G-EBTN D.H.9J c/n 326 Regd [CofR 1464] 29.8.27 to The De Havilland Aircraft Co Ltd, operated by DH School of Flying, Stag Lane; CofA [1210] issued 14.9.27; Hit tree low flying over town, engine and parts of airframe fell out 26.1.29 (F/O AL Monger); EF, FL in hop field, Farnham, badly damaged 8.5.30 (P/O GA Hornblower OK); Failed to clear boundary landing, struck roller, Hendon 8.8.30 (F/O DL Townsend OK); CofA lapsed 1.4.33; Regn cld 12.33.

G-EBTR D.H.9 ex *H9369* Regd [CofR 1468] 26.8.27 to ADC Aircraft Ltd, Croydon; Nimbus engine demonstrator, later converted to 3-seater; CofA [1284] issued 11.1.28; CofA lapsed 23.4.30; renewed 13.9.30; Regn cld as sold abroad 9.30.

G-EBUM see O-BATA

G-EBUN see O-BELG

G-EBXR D.H.9 ex *H9276* Regd [CofR 1619] 24.4.28 to ADC Aircraft Ltd, Croydon; fitted with ADC Nimbus; CofA [1563] issued 13.8.28; Regn cld as sold 1.29; Regd in Australia as *G-AUJA* [CofR 229] 8.11.28 to SJ Taylor, Sydney; named "The Lady Peggy"; To Taylor & Ross Air Transport Co, Lae, New Guinea; Crashed in sea off Salamaua, New Guinea 2.11.29; Regn cld 12.12.29.

G-AACP D.H.9 ex *H9248* Regd [CofR 1806] 7.11.28 to ADC Aircraft Ltd, Croydon; CofA [1861] issued 28.2.29; Regd [CofR 3322] 7.31 to Capt Allen AH Charles, Croydon; operated by his company British Air Transport Ltd; Regd [CofR 3427] 9.31 to British Air Transport Ltd, Croydon; Regd [CofR 3614] 2.32 to Surrey Flying Services Ltd, Croydon; Regd [CofR 4205] 21.2.33 to Sir Alan J Cobham, Ford, for flight refuelling experiments; Advertised for sale 11.34; Regd [CofR 5850] 2.5.35 to Charles Brian Field, Kingswood Knoll, Surrey; Regd [CofR 7157] 30.6.36 to Aerial Sites Ltd, Hanworth; Regn cld as sold 1.38 with CofA current to 29.7.38.
[Also reported leased in 1.34 to Aerial Sites Ltd until regd to them 30.6.36 for banner towing. Bought in 1.38 by Regal Motor Works Ltd, Parkstone, Dorset. Cancelled and broken up at Hanworth in 1938. CofA valid until 29.7.38]

G-AACR D.H.9 ex *H9324* Regd [CofR 1807] 7.11.28 to ADC Aircraft Ltd, Croydon; CofA issued 22.6.32; Regd [CofR 3812] 21.6.32 to National Aviation Day Ltd, Ford and later used [3.33] by Sir Alan Cobham for flight refuelling experiments; CofA lapsed 21.6.33. Regn cld 9.33.

G-AACS D.H.9 ex *H9327* Regd [CofR 1808] 7.11.28 to ADC Aircraft Ltd, Croydon [for Surrey Flying Services but not delivered; possibly completed as G-AADU]; No CofA issued; Regn cld as sold 12.32.

G-AADU D.H.9 [identity unknown] Regd [CofR 1849] 1.29 to Surrey Flying Services Ltd, Croydon; CofA issued 13.7.29; Sold 4.33 and regd [CofR 4590] 9.7.33 to Christopher EB Winch, Halton; Advertised as seized and to be sold 9.34 by Kent Flying Club, Bekesbourne against unpaid hangarage; Regd [CofR 7823] 16.4.37 to Aerial Sites Ltd, Hanworth; Regn cld as sold 1.38.

G-AARR D.H.9J c/n 397 Regd [CofR 2285] 10.29 to Sir WG Armstrong Whitworth Aircraft Ltd; op by Armstrong-Whitworth Reserve School, Whitley; CofA issued 4.10.29; Regd [CofR 3163] 4.5.31 to Air Service Training Ltd, Hamble; WFU upon CofA lapse 25.12.32 and used as Ground Instructional Airframe. Scrapped in 1936. Regn cld 1.37.

G-AARS D.H.9J c/n 398 Regd [CofR 2286] 10.29 to Sir WG Armstrong Whitworth Aircraft Ltd; op by Armstrong-Whitworth Reserve School, Whitley; CofA issued 17.10.29; Crashed 18.12.29 (F/L FEC Benstead OK); Regd [CofR 3164] 4.5.31 to Air Service Training Ltd, Hamble; Crashed nr Hamble after pilot fell out during aerobatics 9.9.34 [he survived by parachute]; Regn cld 10.34 but Cof A valid until 26.4.36.

G-AART D.H.9J c/n 399 Regd [CofR 2287] 10.29 to Sir WG Armstrong Whitworth Aircraft Ltd; op by Armstrong-Whitworth Reserve School, Whitley; CofA issued 5.11.29; Struck small ridge landing wing down and with drift, u/c collapsed, stalled on to ground 9.10.30 (F/O R Radbourne); Used as flying testbed for AS Serval IV engine; Regd [CofR 3165] 4.5.31 to Air Service Training Ltd, Hamble; WFU upon CofA lapse 8.5.33 and used as Ground Instructional Airframe. Scrapped in 1936. Regn cld 1.37.

G-AASC D.H.9J c/n 704 Regd [CofR 2312] 1.11.29 to The De Havilland Aircraft Co Ltd, operated by DH School of Flying, Stag Lane; CofA issued 20.12.29; Cross-wind landing, u/c collapsed, badly damaged 9.5.30 (F/O JMH Hoare OK); Engine trouble, water in petrol filter, FL in sloping field, ran into wire fence, lower mainplanes damaged 2.5.31 (F/O AM Diament OK); Bounced landing, swung, right wing hit ground, Hendon 9.8.31 (F/O HR Turner OK); WFU after accident and Regn cld 12.31. Cof A lapse due 3.2.32.

G-ABPG D.H.9J c/n 1990 Built by DH Technical School, Hatfield; Regd [CofR 3367] 26.8.31 to The De Havilland Aircraft Co Ltd, operated by DH School of Flying, Hatfield; CofA issued 14.10.31; Regn cld 12.33.

NOTE: A D.H.9 of Aircraft Travel & Transport Ltd piloted by Lt McMulen (ex RAF) left Hounslow 26.1.30 for Poland in support of the company's activities in that country. It arrived at Prague on 16.2.20 and was later due to fly to Warsaw and Riga.

Unidentified crashes of Reserve School aircraft

24.5.23 De Havilland, turned near ground with insufficient speed, crashed (F/O DL Stewart OK)
29.8.23 De Havilland, stalled at 20ft landing (P/O CEF Searl OK)
31.10.23 De Havilland, undershot, landed in hedge (F/O AS White & pupil OK)
5.5.24 De Havilland, crashed (F/O WEL Courtney OK)
7.5.24 De Havilland, crashed (F/O AL Monger OK)
20.5.24 De Havilland, crashed (F/O WEL Courtney OK)
26.5.24 Beardmore. u/c smashed landing (F/O J Turpie OK)
18.3.25 De Havilland, ran into soft clay patch landing (F/O JH Huxley injured)
19.6.25 Beardmore, overshot landing (P/O AC Robertson OK)
28.10.25 Beardmore, flattened out too high, crashed (F/O RG Lawson OK)
26.4.26 "G-EBGF". De Havilland, fast landing, crashed into fence (F/O WA Warwick OK)

OTHER BRITISH CofAs ISSUED

To Handley Page Ltd, Cricklewood

H5646 CofA [401] issued 31.7.20.
H9274 CofA [402] issued 31.7.20; [To Denmark as T-DOBC]
Note: One of the above two was possibly the unidentified civil D.H.9 which was wrecked in a crash at Cricklewood Aerodrome 5.8.20; pilot Maurice Helliwell.
H9246 CofA [409] issued 14.8.20; [To Denmark as T-DOGH; although this also reported as H9359]
H9272 CofA [410] issued 14.8.20.

To The Aircraft Disposal Co Ltd, Croydon
Twenty sold to Russia via Arcos Company [also reported as 22]

H5855 CofA [770] issued 1.7.24
H5864 CofA [771] issued 1.7.24
H5880 CofA [772] issued 1.7.24
H9370 CofA [773] issued 1.7.24
H9302 CofA [774] issued 1.7.24
H9313 CofA [776] issued 1.7.24
H9309 CofA [777] issued 1.7.24
H9298 CofA [778] issued 1.7.24
H9341 CofA [779] issued 1.7.24
H9260 CofA [780] issued 1.7.24
H9242 CofA [794] issued 10.7.24
H9311 CofA [795] issued 10.7.24
H9330 CofA [796] issued 10.7.24
H9250 CofA [797] issued 10.7.24
H9252 CofA [798] issued 10.7.24
H9275 CofA [799] issued 10.7.24
H9278 CofA [800] issued 10.7.24
H9283 CofA [801] issued 10.7.24
H9285 CofA [802] issued 10.7.24
H9297 CofA [803] issued 10.7.24

D.H.9As - Issued to ADC Aircraft Ltd, Croydon

E8689 CofA [938] issued 16.2.26
E8787 CofA [939] issued 16.2.26
E8784 CofA [940] issued 16.2.26
E8783 CofA [941] issued 16.2.26
E8779 CofA [942] issued 16.2.26
E8745 CofA [943] issued 16.2.26
E8789 CofA [944] issued 16.2.26

AFGHANISTAN

In December 1924, two D.H.9s arrived at Peshawar, on supply to the Afghan Government by a Mr Murphy, but they were still there four months later. It is not known when (or whether) they finally arrived at Kabul.

In the meantime a Soviet-Afghanistan Treaty had been signed in February 1921, and under this assistance was given in 1924 for the formation of a Military Air Arm as an independent service under the Ministry of War. A Russian mission arrived with pilots and instructors, to set up a flying school and help build airfields. Four (possibly six) R-1s were then supplied, being flown to Sherper, near Kabul in October 1925 after use by the 4th Otdel'nyi razvedivatel'nyi aviaotryad at Tashkent. Intended for bombing and reconnaissance work, they were originally to have been transported overland, but of the only two roads available, one was barred by hostile tribesmen and the other by the difficult terrain. Consequently they were flown via Termez over the Hindu Kush to Kabul, this last sector taking over three and three-quarter hours. It was the first flight ever made over that mountain range, much of it at over 15,000 ft, and the twelve Russian aircrew were decorated with the Order of the Red Banner to mark their safe arrival. By 1927 at least twelve Russian-built D.H.9s or R-1s had been delivered, and possibly sixteen or more.

An Afghan D.H.9

AUSTRALIA

A number of D.H.9 variants were flown in Australia, for both civil and military use.

Civil use

G-AUED D.H.9C c/n 86 [Bought by DH from ADC and UK CofA 671 issued to DH 25.8.23] Sold for £1,719.18s.5d and arrived on SS *Esperance Bay* 23.10.23. Regd [CofR 89] 1.11.23 to QANTAS, Longreach; First used between Longreach and Charleville by Capt G.C.Matthews 5.11.23. Made unscheduled landing of 35min at unknown location, then continued but stalled on approach and crashed on landing Tambo, Qld 24.3.27 (pilot AD Davidson and 2 passengers killed); Regn cld 3.27.

G-AUEF D.H.9C c/n 87 [Bought by DH from ADC and UK CofA 672 issued to DH 31.8.23] Sold for approx £1,715 and arrived on SS *Moreton Bay* 8.11.23. Regd [CofR 90] 1.11.23 to QANTAS, Longreach; Badly damaged on landing Cloncurry 22.9.26 [or 24.9.26]; Regn cld 9.26; Parts, including engine, used to build G-AUFM.

D.H.9C G-AUED was flown by QANTAS until it crashed at Tambo, Qld with the loss of three lives on 24.3.27

G-AUEG D.H.9 ex *A6-5* Regd [CofR 102] 8.8.24 to Civil Aviation Branch, Dept of Defence, Melbourne; op by Larkin Aircraft Supply Co Ltd on Adelaide-Sydney service; Returned to RAAF as *A6-5* and regn cld 18.12.24.

G-AUEH D.H.9 ex *A6-4* Regd 2.9.24 to Civil Aviation Branch, Dept of Defence, Melbourne for use by Australian Aerial Services; Crashed Gunning, NSW 10.24; repaired; Returned to RAAF as *A6-4* and regn cld 18.12.24.

G-AUEU D.H.9 ex unknown. Sold by ADC reported for £1,300 with only 16 flying hours [Converted by HC Miller, Adelaide] Regd [CofR 121] 14.5.25 to HC Miller, c/o Henderson Bros, Melbourne [also reported as Abbot Park Aerodrome, Adelaide]; Cof A 6.8.25. Offered for £950 to Defence Dept when owner then joined RAAF, but NTU. Crashed on landing Port Pirie, SA 16.2.28; Regn cld 17.3.28.

G-AUFB see G-EBKV

G-AUFM D.H.9C ex unknown [Built by Qantas using D.H.9 fuselage, parts from G-AUEF and D.H.50 mainplanes] Ff 5.2.27; Regd [CofR 153] 12.2.27 to Queensland & Northern Territory Aerial Services Ltd, Longbeach; named "Ion"; Crashed Camooweal, Qld 13.1.28; Flown to Longreach to be dismantled. Regn cld 4.1.29; Wings and engine etc used to build D.H.50 G-AUJS.

G-AUFS D.H.9 ex *H9340* [UK CofA 1077 issued 14.1.27 to ADC Aircraft Ltd, Croydon] Regd [CofR 159] 31.3.27 to Matthews Aviation Co Ltd, Essendon; Sold 14.11.27 to Bulolo Goldfields Aeroplane Services Ltd, Sydney; named "The Lachlan"; Sold 6.29 & regd 8.29 to The Morlae Airline, Lae, New Guinea; Regd 28.4.31 to Pacific Aerial Transport Ltd, Lae; Regn cld 11.6.31; Regd *VH-UFS* 16.9.32 to Pacific Aerial Transport Ltd, Lae; Regn cld 15.9.33; regd 26.10.33 to same owner; Regn cld 25.10.34.

G-AUHT D.H.9 [Identity unknown] Regd [CofR 209] 26.7.28 to HC Miller, t/a Commercial Aviation Co, Parafield; CofA issued 14.8.28? Regd *VH-UHT* 1929 to same owner; To MacRobertson Miller Aviation Co Ltd [6.36]; Regd 15.9.36 to Skyways Ltd, Norwood, SA; Crashed Kadina, SA 15.5.37; Regn cld 14.9.37.

G-AUJA see G-EBXR

G-AUKI D.H.9C [Identity unknown; possibly ex G-EAQM?] Regd [CofR 262] 13.2.29 to RJ Parer & PJ McDonald, t/a Morlae Airways, Salamaua, New Guinea; Regd *VH-UKI* 1929 to same owner; Crashed Port Moresby 13.7.29; Regn cld 16.12.29.

VH-UMB D.H.9 ex *D3017, RAAF A6-11* Regd [CofR 324] 17.9.29 to Civil Aviation Branch, Dept of Defence & loaned to Australian Aero Club, Victorian Section, Melbourne; Regn cld 16.9.32.

VH-UMK Marks reserved but replaced by VH-UMT after UMK requested by GE Marni-Kerry.

VH-UML D.H.9 ex *D3220, RAAF A6-21* Regd [CofR 332] 8.10.29 to Australian Aero Club, Queensland Section, Brisbane; named "Albatross"; CofA issued 11.11.29; Regd 12.30 to Queensland Aero Club, Brisbane; Crashed Archerfield 24.7.32; Regn cld 16.8.32.

VH-UMM D.H.9 ex *A6-19* Regd [CofR 353] 15.1.30 to Aero Club of South Australia Ltd, Adelaide; CofA issued 20.6.30; Regn cld 14.1.32; regd 6.9.32 to same owner; Regn cld 5.9.33.

VH-UMT D.H.9 ex *D3189, RAAF A6-9, [VH-UMK]* Regd [CofR 331] 7.10.29 to Australian Aero Club, NSW Section, Sydney; Regd [8.30] to Aero Club of NSW, Sydney; CofA issued 31.10.29; Regn cld 17.5.31.

Military use

The following D.H.9As were held at No.5 (Eastern) ARD, RAF Henlow in December 1919/January 1920 on allotment to the Australian Government as part of the Imperial Gift of 100 aircraft: E793, E794, E795, E900, E901, E903, E904, E905, E906, E907, E908, E909, E910, E916, E8590, E8597, E8616, E9692, E9694, F2776, F2779, H5, H3459, H3460, H3461, H3462, H3463, H3464, H3465 and H3502. Fitted with Liberty engines, they were renumbered in the range A1-1 to A1-29, in the sequence of their original serials minus prefix letters.

The first four aircraft to be received, in 1920, with engines installed were E8590, E8616, F2776 and F2779. They were assembled soon after arriving in Melbourne, then flown by the Central Flying School of the Australian Air Corps at Point Cook (Vic). E8616 went missing in the Bass Strait during a search on 23 September 1920, but the others survived to receive new serials numbers in the A1-1 to A1-29 range, these appearing on aircraft during September 1921. Some details of their Australian careers until that point may be found under their original serial numbers. Later, A1-30 was supplied direct by de Havilland as a replacement for E8616 with new c/n 42, being fitted with a Liberty engine.

Relevant Units:
Central Flying School, Point Cook, Vic.
No.1 Flying Training School, Point Cook, Vic.
No.1 Squadron, Point Cook, Vic. (used by 'C' Flight)
No.3 Squadron, Richmond, NSW. (used by 'C' Flight)
No.1 Aircraft Depot, Point Cook, Vic.

A1-1 (ex H5) LTS at 1 AD to 1924: 1 FTS by 10.24 to at least 7.26; Reconditioned by Pratt Bros 3.28 - 6.28; 1 FTS, left with A1-7 to search for missing Widgeon G-AUKA in northern Australia 12.4.29 (F/L C Eaton & Cpl P Sullivan); Forced landed 8m S of Tennant Creek, NT 21.4.29 (F/Lt C Eaton & Cpl P Sullivan unhurt); SOC

A1-2 (ex E793) LTS at 1 AD to 1926; Reconditioned by Mort's Dock; To 1 FTS 1927; Crashed at Canberra; To Experimental Section Randwick; Approved for conversion to components 20.3.28.

A1-3 (ex E794) LTS at 1 AD to 1927; Reconditioned by Experimental Section 1.3.27; 3 Sqn, crashed Canberra 6.5.27 [12hrs]; Overhauled by 3 Sqn 2.11.27 [23hrs]; To Canberra 14-17.3.28; Escort for Bert Hinkler to Brisbane 28.3.28-5.4.28; Engine failure, forced landed Enoggera, Brisbane 30.3.28 (F/O SdeB Griffith; Approved for conversion to components 2.6.28

A1-4 (ex E795) LTS at 1 AD to 1926; Reconditioned by Mort's Dock 16.2.27; 1 Sqn, to Canberra for Parliament House flypast and engine change 10.5.27; To Adelaide for opening of new aerodrome at Parafield 26.11.27; 106hrs by 14.3.28; Engine failure at 200ft on take-off, hit pile of rocks, Laverton 4.5.28 (P/O LI Ryan & LAC P Sullivan); Approved for conversion to components 17.5.28

A1-5 (ex E900) Recd 12.8.20; LTS at 1 AD to 1925; Reconditioned by Mort's Dock 8.7.26; To 1 FTS; Fitted dual controls 18.10.26; Crashed 8.1.27 [46hrs]; Recommended for reconditioning 19.7.27; U/s at 1 AD 9.3.28 (believed recon'd by Experimental Section); To 1 Sqn 4.29; Left to search for missing Widgeon G-AUKA in N.Australia 17.4.29 (F/O LJ Ryan & Cpl DA Endean); Retd Laverton 12.5.29 (F/O AG Gerrand & Sgt JA Campbell); 1 FTS to 1.30; SOC 4.2.30

A1-6 (ex E901) LTS at 1 AD to 1926; Reconditioned by Experimental Section 19.3.26; 3 Sqn, crashed 23.11.27 at Lake Wallace, NSW 23.11.27; Rebuilt on Sqn 2.28 [167hrs]; Technical inspection 5.12.28; Uneconomic for further repair, approved for conversion to components 12.12.28

A1-7 (ex E903) LTS at 1 AD to 1924; Believed reconditioned by 1 FTS workshops; 1 FTS by 11.24; Damaged landing at Flemington 10.12.24 (F/O LI Balderston); Forced landed at Rochester Vic 13.4.26 (Cdt G Jenkins) [129hrs]; 1 FTS by 7.26; Recommended for reconditioning 19.7.27; Recon'd by Pratt Bros 3.28 to 6.28; 1 Sqn 4.29; Left to search for missing Widgeon G-AUKA in N.Australia 12.4.29 (F/O AG Gerrand & Sgt JA Campbell); Retd Laverton 12.5.29 (F/Lt C Eaton & Sgt E Douglas); Forced landed Kyneton, Vic 5.6.29; Retd store; 1 FTS by 7.29; SOC 4.2.30

A1-8 (ex E904) Recd 12.6.20; LTS at 1 AD to 1926; Reconditioned by Mort's Dock 23.8.28; 1 FTS, damaged 20.9.26; Overhauled 1 FTS 1.4.27; Crashed 16.5.27 [14hrs]; Repaired; To 3 Sqn 28.10.27; Crashed Craigieburn, Vic 11.27; to Mort's Dock for repair; Test flown 8.12.27; To 1 FTS 12.27; Crashed on landing downwind Point Cook 7.2.28 (Lt P Bailhache RAN & Cdt TA Chadwick) [55hrs]; 1 AD for overhaul 3.5.28; Assessed uneconomic for reconditioning 23.1.29; Approved for conversion to components 14.2.29

A1-9 (ex E905) Recd 6.10.20; LTS at 1 AD to 19Z5; Reconditioned by Matthews & Hassell 30.12.25; To 1 FTS 7.3.26; Collided on ground with 504K A3-39 19.5.26; Repaired by 7.26; Condemned 29.7.27; U/s 19.10.27; Overhauled by 1 FTS 6.3.28 [241hrs]; 1 Sqn by 5.29; To 1 FTS 6.29; SOC 4.2.30

A1-10 (ex E906) Recd 12.8.20 LTS at 1 AD to 1925; Reconditioned by Experimental Section 6.10.25; 3 Sqn by 4.26; Fitted with side ladder to enable parachute descents 12.5.26; Rigged for jumps at 1 FTS from 6.26; Crashed at 1 FTS; Assessed as DBR; Being overhauled by 1 FTS 6.3.28 [27hrs]; Approved for conversion to components 20.3.28

A1-11 (ex E907) Recd 12.8.20; LTS at 1 AD to 1926; Was to be reconditioned by Larkin 10.25; To Mort's Dock for reconditioning 11.6.26; To 3 Sqn 4.7.27 for despatch to 1 FTS' Forced landed 19.7.27 (F/O VH Augenson) Forced landed at Harefield, NSW on delivery to 1 FTS 21.7.27 (Sgt GK Rice-Oxley); Again forced landed again Rutherglen, Vic 22.7.27; EF, FL, undercarriage collapsed, nr Violet Town, Vic 28.7.27; Reconditioned by 1 FTS 'C' Flt 15.9.27 [59hrs]; Left for Sydney as Number " 5" for NSW Aerial Derby 30.3.28; Still 1 FTS, hit power lines, lost u/c, crashed nr Bulla Rd, North Essendon, Melbourne during 1928 Victorian Aerial Derby, BO 26.5.28 (F/Lt GA Wells); Approved for conversion to components 20.6.28

A1-12 (ex E908) Recd 9.9.20; LTS at 1 AD to 1926; Reconditioned by Experimental Section 6.12.26; To 3 Sqn for delivery to 1 Sqn; Arr 1 Sqn 23.12.26; To Adelaide for opening of new aerodrome at Parafield 26.11.27; 134hrs by 20.4.28; To Adelaide for 1 Sqn aerial survey 18.10.28; Damaged in forced landing at Yaouk, nr Cooma, NSW 3.12.28 (F/O LJ Ryan); Inspected, uneconomic for reconditioning 12.3.29; Approved for conversion to components 20.3.29

A1-13 (ex E909) Recd 6.10.20; LTS at 1 AD to 1925; Reconditioned at Matthews & Hassell 6.10.25; 1 FTS by 2.26; Forced landed Woodend, Vic, 13.4.26 (F/O WA Holtham & AC1 Allen) [105hrs]; Repaired at 1 FTS; Crashed 1927; Overhauling 1 FTS workshops 6.3.28 [241hrs]; Assessed as uneconomic for further repair, approved for conversion to components 20.3.28

A1-14 (ex E910) Recd 6.10.20; LTS at 1 AD to 1926; Reconditioned by Matthews & Hassell 7.3.26; 1 Sqn by 5.26; Grounded 20.9.27; U/s at 1 FTS 9.3.28 [169hrs]; Reconditioned; 1 FTS by 5.29; EF, FL, Point Cook 1.8.29 (F/Lt Hewitt); SOC 4.2.20, but in use to 5.3.20

A1-15 (ex E916) Recd 6.10.20, LTS at 1 AD to 1924; Reconditioned by 1 FTS Workshops 15.12.24; 1 FTS by 5.25; Being overhauled at 1 FTS 6.3.28 [101hrs]; Flying accident 21.11.29 (Sgt JA Campbell); SOC 4.2.30

A1-16 (ex F2776) Recd 1.5.20; CFS to 1 FTS 31.3.21; Reconditioned in 1 FTS workshops 20.4.22 to 23.8.22; 'E' Flt 1 FTS by 11.22 until overhauled by 1 FTS workshops 27.10.27; To Experimental Section for repair 11.27; 'C' Flt 1 FTS by 6.3.28 [245hrs]; Damaged landing at Point Cook 17.10.28 (P/O AN Evans); Taxied into S.E.5a A2-36 24.10.28 (Cdt RC Jordan); Forced landed Point Cook with broken camshaft 19.12.28; Forced landed Point Cook with broken camshaft 19.2.29 (Flt Lt A Hepburn); Forced landed Point Cook 12.4.29 (Cdt Dalton); Recommended for overhaul 25.7.29; Assessed uneconomic for further repair 5.8.29; Approved for conversion to components 9.8.29

A1-17 (ex F2779) Recd 5.20. 'A' Flt to ARS 17.10.20. CFS to 1 FTS 31.3.21; 'E' Flt 1 FTS 1.7.22 to 1923; Survey, 1 AD 6.3.24; 1 FTS by 1.25; To Matthews & Hassell for reconditioning; Possibly to 1 Sqn 1926; Recommended for further reconditioning 19.7.27; Reconditioned by Pratt Bros 3.28 to 6.28; 1 Sqn by 2.29; Damaged landing Laverton 3.5.29 (F/O Brelaz); EF, on way to Sydney, FL, Keilor, Vic 5.6.29 (P/O Fleming); FL Laverton 7.6.29 (F/O Stevens); 1 FTS, EF, FL Point Cook 31.10.29 (P/O GW Boucher); SOC 4.2.30

A1-18 (ex H3459) LTS at 1 AD to 1925; Believed reconditioned at Experimental Section; 1 FTS by 6.25; Crashed at Cootamundra, NSW 9.12.26 (F/O TW Shortridge); To Experimental Section for repairs 13.12.26; Board of survey 17.8.27; Approved for conversion to components 29.11.27

A1-19 (ex H3460) LTS at 1 AD to 1924; 1 FTS by 5.24;

D.H.9A A1-17 of the RAAF.
(via C.Owers)

D.H.9 A6-16 still bears its wartime RAF colour scheme.
(via Terry Treadwell)

D.H.9A A-22 of the RAAF has the individual number 22 repeated on the rudder.

D.H.9 A6-23 in the post-war RAAF colour scheme.
(J.M.Bruce/G.S.Leslie)

Reconditioned by Matthews & Hassell c.1925; 1 FTS by 2.26; Destroyed in Bessoneau hangar at Point Cook by D.H.9 A6-11 which crashed on take-off 12.3.26 [88hrs]; Approved for conversion to components 31.3.26

A1-20 (ex H3461) LTS at 1 AD to 1927; Reconditioned by Mort's Dock 5.4.27; 1 Sqn, engine change 16.10.27; To Adelaide for opening of Parafield aerodrome 26.11.27; To 1 FTS 3.28 [39hrs by 14.3.28]; To 1 Sqn; To Brisbane for opening of Queensland Aero Club and participate Aerial Services Air Race 20.8.28; Under repair 11.28; 1 FTS by 12.28; Left with A1-5 & A1-28 to search for missing Widgeon G-AUKA in N.Australia 17.4.29 (Sgt E Douglas & LAC WJ Smith); Engine fire on start-up at Wave Hill, NT, 7.5.29; Uneconomic to recover, aircraft destroyed [323hrs]; SOC 15.5.29

A1-21 (ex H3462) Recd 9.9.20; LTS at 1 AD to 1926; Reconditioned by Mort's Dock to 5.1.27; To 1 FTS, engine change 5.1.27; Crashed 11.3.27; To 1 FTS workshops due to rough running 9.4.27; Recommended for reconditioning 19.7.27; U/s at 1 AD 9.3.28 [49hrs]; 1 Sqn by 4.29; To 1 FTS 5.29; SOC 4.2.30

A1-22 (ex H3463) Recd 9.9.20; LTS at 1 AD to 1925; Reconditioned Matthews & Hassell 19.11.25; Crashed 4.12.26; Recommended for reconditioning 19.7.27; U/s, 1 AD 9.3.28 [55hrs]; Technical examination 29.11.28; 1 Sqn by 3.29; To 1 FTS 17.5.29; Landed out of wind, Richmond, NSW 22.6.29 (F/O Fraser); SOC 4.2.30

A1-23 (ex H3464) Stored to 1924; Board of survey at Experimental Section, Randwick 11.8.24; Approved for conversion to components 9.10.24

A1-24 (ex H3465) Recd 9.9.20; LTS at 1 AD to 1927; To Experimental Section for reconditioning 6.5.27; To 3 Sqn 27.7.27; To 1 FTS 24.8.27; 171hrs by 14.3.28; EF, FL, damaged, Point Cook 10.11.28 (LAC CH Scott); Repaired on site; Completed flying time by 8.2.29; Approved for conversion to components 14.2.29

A1-25 (ex H3502) LTS at 1 AD; To 1 Sqn 18.2.26; Overhauled by Experimental Section 2.3.26; To 3 Sqn 9.3.26; Ditched off Bradley's Head, Sydney Harbour 1.8.28 (F/O SdeB Griffith & Mr EB Cremer) [207hrs]; Salvaged, approved for conversion to components 5.9.28

A1-26 (ex E8590) Recd 16.6.20. CFS to 1 FTS 31.3.21; 1 AD storage 1.8.21; To 1 FTS 1.7.22; Crashed Flemington Racecourse, Melbourne 10.12.24 (Flt Lt A Hempel); Board of survey at 1 AD 21.4.25; Reconditioned by 1 FTS workshops 22.2.26; U/s at 1 AD after crash 9.3.28 [251hrs]; 1 Sqn, hit electricity pole landing, Laverton 8.5.29; Approved to components 10.5.29

A1-27 (ex E8597) Recd 1.5.20; LTS at 1 AD to 1926; Reconditioned by Mort's Dock 7.10.26; 1 FTS by 7.27; 3 Sqn, crashed landing at Warwick, Qld 3.7.27; To Mort's Dock for reconditioning 11.27; 1 FTS by 6.3.28 [199hrs]; Completed flying time by 8.2.29; Approved for conversion to components 14.2.29

A1-28 (ex E9692) LTS at 1 AD to 1925; Reconditioned by Experimental Section 25.3.26; 3 Sqn, crashed 30.7.26 [7hrs]; Overhauled by 3 Sqn 1.3.27; 111hrs by 15.2.28; Rigged as single-seater and won 1928 NSW Aerial Derby at Mascot as Number '22" 3.28 (F/O N Mulroney); Under repair 3 Sqn 10.28; To Point Cook 23.10.28; Repaired; 1 Sqn, left in search for Widgeon 17.4.29 (F/O MB Allen & Cpl GW Allen); U/s at Tennant Creek, NT with engine problem 20.4.29 to 8.5.29; Uneconomic to recover [282hrs]; SOC 15.5.29

A1-29 (ex E9694) LTS at 1 AD to 1924; to 1 FTS, acceptance test 5.5.24; Engine trouble in formation, forced landed, engine cut on take-off next morning, Woodford Dale, NSW, . 1924 (P/O Urwin & Mech Mitchell minor injuries); Wreckage shipped to Sydney for possible rebuild; Board of survey approved for conversion to components 9.10.24

A1-30 (c/n 42) Acquired in 1923 to replace E8616; 1 FTS from 7.23; Crashed at Point Cook 16.8.26 (Cdt KM Frewen); To 1 AD for storage 19.8.26; Approved for conversion to components 12.7.27

The RAAF also received 28 D.H.9s as part of the Imperial Gift of 100 aircraft, Their original serials were: C1296, C6241, C6246, C6343, D1115, D1119, D1127, D1129, D1187, D1257, D3000, D3017, D3182, D3186, D3187, D3189, D3191, D3195, D3196,

D3202, D3207, D3220, F1238, F1295, H4291, H5592, H5679, and H5697. Like the D.H.9a's they were renumbered, between September 1921 and February 1922, in the range A6-1 to A6-28, in the sequence of their original serials minus prefix letters.

Relevant Units:
Central Flying School, Point Cook, Vic.
No.1 Flying Training School, Point Cook, Vic.
No.1 Squadron, Point Cook, Vic. (used by 'A' Flight)
No.3 Squadron, Richmond, NSW. (used by 'A' Flight)
No.1 Aircraft Depot, Point Cook, Vic.

A6-1 (ex D1115) LTS at 1 AD to 1925; Reconditioned by Matthews & Hassell; 1 Sqn by 11.25; Western Australia survey 10.3.27 - 8.4.27; Forced landed, Culburra, SA 10.3.27 (F/O TW Shortridge); EF on TO, stalled and crashed from 60ft, BO, Point Cook 20.12.27 (Cdt CC Seach); SOC 20.12.27

A6-2 (ex D1119) LTS at 1 AD to 1926; Reconditioned by Matthews & Hassell; 1 FTS by 12.26; Damaged 12.28; 1 FTS by 1.29; SOC 21.5.29

A6-3 (ex D1127) LTS at 1 AD to 1926; Reconditioned by Matthews & Hassell; 1 FTS by 4.27; FL, crashed, BO, Walry, nr Healesville, Vic 27.10.27 (Cdt CC Seach killed); SOC 20.12.27

A6-4 (ex D1129) LTS at 1 AD to 1924; On loan as *G-AUEH* 2.9.24; Restored as *A6-4* 18.12.24; Believed Pratt Bros, Geelong for reconditioning 1925; 1 FTS by 7.25 - @9.26; 3 Sqn 1927; Ground collision with Moth *G-AUPP*, Mascot, NSW 14.4.28 (P/O FC Elsworth); Damaged taxiing Mascot 11.6.28; SOC 21.5.29

A6-5 (ex D1187); LTS at 1 AD to 1924; On loan as *G-AUEG* 8.8.24: Restored to *A6-5S* 18.12.24; 1 FTS by 4.25: to 1 Sqn 23.7.25; 3 Sqn by 11.25 - 3.27; 1 Sqn, collided with A6-26 and crashed Melbourne whilst on flypast to welcome the Duke & Duchess of York to Australia 21.4.27 (Flt Lt RI Dines & Cpl J Ramsden both killed); SOC 15.6.27

A6-6 (ex F1238) 1 FTS in use 31.3.21; to 1 AD 1.8.21: to 1 FTS by 4.22; Crashed Yass, NSW 21.5.23 (F/O AW Vigers); to 1 AD, boards of survey 30.7.23 & 20.5.24: Approved for conversion to components 10.11.24, action completed 18.9.24

A6-7 (ex D1257) LTS at 1 AD to 1926; Reconditioned by Matthews & Hassell; 1 Sqn by 3.27; Formation take-off at Point Cook, lost control in leader's slipstream crashed 21.1.27 (P/O LJ Robertson & AC1 E Stewart); Approved for conversion to components 25.2.28

A6-8 (ex F1295) 1 FTS in use 31.3.21; Crashed Broadford, Vic 12.6.24; Board of survey 17.6.24; Approved to components 8.8.24.

A6-9 (ex C1296) LTS at 1 AD to 1925; Reconditioned by Pratt Bros, Geelong; 1 Sqn, collided with another a/c landing Essendon 28.11.25 (F/O VH Thornton); Repaired on site; To 3 Sqn 28.4.27; Withdrawn 5.29; Sold 7.10.29 as *VH-UMT*

A6-10 (ex D3000) LTS at 1 AD until 1925: 1 FTS, stalled and spun into sea off Point Cook 24.2.26 (Cdt FR Stott); Salvaged and approved for conversion to components 16.4.26 [50hrs]

A6-11 (ex D3017) LTS at 1 AD to 1925; reconditioned by Pratt Bros, Geelong, fitted dual controls: To 1 FTS 1.3.26; Crashed into Bessoneau hangar on take-off Point Cook, destroying D.H.9A A1-19 12.3.26 (Cdt WS Hamilton): 1 AD 22.3.26; To Pratt Bros, Geelong for reconditioning 3.11.26; Components tested by MSB Maribyrnong 9.27: To 1 Sqn, acceptance test 30.5.28; Forced landed Laverton, 24.6.28; Hit sheep landing Wangaratta North, Vic 24.8.28 (F/O WJ Duncan); 1 FTS, forced landed Point Cook 2.1.29 (P/O AL Walters); Sold as *VH-UMB* 17.9.29

A6-12 (ex D3182) LTS at 1 AD to 1925; Reconditioned by Pratt Bros, Geelong; Retd RAAF 23.11.35; 1 FTS, crashed 3.2.26 (F/O C Eaton); ROS by 15.3.26; 1 FTS, crashed 4.8.26 (F/O CW Lord); To 1 AD for repair 6.8.26, but rescinded 12.8.26, to be repaired by 1 FTS; Night flight from Sydney to Melbourne 2.27; Reconditioned by Pratt Bros, Geelong (components tested by MSB Maribyrnong); To 1 Sqn 11.7.27; Flown around Australia 21.7.27 - 10.9.27 (Sqn Ldr A Hepburn & LAC JA Collopy); Flown with 1 Sqn to Adelaide for opening of new Parafield aerodrome 26.11.27; Hit telegraph post on approach, Point Cook 12.1.28 (P/O LJ Ryan); Approved for conversion to components 25.2.28; To 1 AD for conversion to components 20.3.28

A6-13 (ex D3186) LTS at 1 AD to 1925; Reconditioned by Pratt Bros, Geelong: To 1 FTS 16.4.26; Test flown 19.4.26 (F/O CC Matheson) and 26.4.26 (LAC L Trist); Dual controls fitted 21.5.26 - 21.6.26; Stalled during practice forced landing, dived into ground, BO, Manor Station, nr Werribee, Vic 1.7.26 (F/O WA Holtham & Cdt TSG Watson both killed); SOC 26.8.26 [34hrs]

A6-14 (ex D3187) 1 FTS in use 31.3.21; to 1 AD 1.8.21; 1 FTS, Perth for Western Australia landing ground inspection 6.22 (Flt Lt A Hepburn); Damaged nr Broome, WA 15.8.22 (Flt Lt A Hepburn); Shipped back to Point Cook: Stored 1 AD, board of survey 23.10.22, to be repaired by 1 AD: Further board of survey, extent of damage to airframe would require rebuild from observers seat forward 30.7.23: Approved for conversion to components 21.9.23

A6-15 (ex D3189) Stored 1 AD to 1923; To 1 FTS by 5.23 until 1925: 3 Sqn by 6.26; Carried out air route and landing ground surveys over northern NSW 8.26 (F/O LW Sutherland & F/O V H Augenson); Installed overhauled engine 24.4.27: Forced landed Penrith, NSW 10.3.28 (Sgt RF Somerville); Forced landed Bathurst, NSW 22.3.28; Stalled after take-off at Goulburn, NSW, rigged tail heavy 30.4.28 (F/O CW Lord) ; Approved for conversion to components 2.6.28

A6-16 (ex D3191) 1 FTS in use 31.3.21: To 1 AD 1.8.21; 1 FTS by 6.23 (converted to dual control); Crashed on landing Nhul, Vic 7.10.25 (F/O FRW Scherger & Lt D Ross) [now 489 hours flying time]: To 1 AD 21.10.25 (storage pending overhaul); 1 FTS by 7.26; Hit cow landing, damaged, Geelong, Vic 8.9.26 (Cdt EG Knox-Knight); To 1 AD 21.10.26; To 1 FTS for repairs 28.3.27: 1 FTS by 11.27; Taxied into by S.E.5a A2-31, minor damage, Point Cook 29.11.28; Damaged 3.29; Withdrawn from service 5.29; Authorised for destruction 21.5.29

A6-17 (ex D3195) LTS at 1 AD to 1924; 1 FTS by 7.24; Attempting forced landing to avoid adverse weather, crashed near Geelong, Vic, completely wrecked 5.9.26 (Sgt E B Ebel killed); SOC [567hrs]

A6-18 (ex D3196) LTS at 1 AD to 1924; reconditioned in Melbourne, acceptance test at Essendon 11.5.25 (Flt Lt AW Murphy); To 1 FTS 12.5.25; To 3 Sqn 7.25; Flown to Brisbane 11-16.8.25 (Flt Lt AW Murphy); Crashed Richmond 7.1.26; total flight time 84 hours; approved to components 31.3.26 [84hrs]

A6-19 (ex D3202) LTS 1 AD to 1925; Reconditioned by Larkins, to RAAF 26.7.25; 1 Sqn by 11.25; Hit tree on take-off at Flinders Naval Depot, Vic 16.2.26 (F/O VW Burgess, passenger Governor-General Lord Stonehaven); 1 AD 18.2.26 (storage); To Pratt Bros, Geelong for reconditioning 8.11.26 (components tested by MSB Maribyrnong 9.27); 1 FTS acceptance test 28.3.28; 1 Sqn by 5.28 to at least 8.28; 1 FTS by 12.28; Withdrawn from service 5.29; Sold 15.1.30 becoming *VH-UMM*. *[NB. At one time fitted at Point Cook with 300hp Nimbus engine in a streamlined cowling, reaching a top speed of 150mph]*

A6-20 (ex D3207) 1 FTS in use 3.21; To 1 AD 1.8.21; 1 FTS by 4.24; Flying accident 12.6.24; Board of survey 26.6.24; Approved for conversion to components 8.8.24

A6-21 (ex D3220) 1 FTS in use 3.21; To 1 AD 1.8.21; 1 FTS by 4.22; Participated in NSW Aerial Derby 24.4.22 to 12.5.22 (F/O SG Brearley); To Adelaide 15.6.22; Retd 1 FTS 1.7.22, to at least 5.24; To 3 Sqn 7.25 to 1926; Repaired by Larkins and engine replaced 6.27, returned to 3 Sqn; Withdrawn from service 5.29; Sold 8.10.29, becoming *VH-UML*

A6-22 (ex H4291) LTS at 1 AD to 1926; Reconditioned by Matthews & Hassell; 1 FTS by 4.27, test flown 30.5.27 Technical inspection 22,9.27; Believed reconditioned by Experimental Section 1927/28; After been twice reconditioned, recommended not being worth further repair 16.3.28; Approved for conversion to components 20.3.28

A6-23 (ex H5592) LTS at 1 AD to 1925; Reconditioned by Larkins; To 1 FTS, flight tested 25.5.25; Forced landed

13.9.27 (F/O FRW Scherger); New engine installed 31.1.28, but not flown initially; Forced landed Point Cook, engine failing after only 5 minutes running 23.4.28; Further engine failure 30.5.28; Withdrawn from service 5.29; Authorised for destruction 21.5.29

A6-24 (ex H5679) LTS at 1 AD to 1925; Reconditioned by Larkins; To 1 Sqn 16.7.25; To 1 FTS 1927; Crashed; Bad condition, recommended not worth further repair 16.3.28; Approved for conversion to components 20.3.28

A6-25 (ex H5697) LTS at 1 AD to 1926; Reconditioned by Matthews & Hassell, acceptance test 11.7.27 (Flt Lt AW Murphy); To 1 Sqn 7.27; Around Australia reconnaissance 21.7.27 to 10.9.27 (Flt Lt AW Murphy & Sgt DM Carroll); To Adelaide for opening of new aerodrome at Parafield 26.11.27; Technical inspection 16.7.28 [301hrs]; Approved for conversion to components 8.8.28

A6-26 (ex C6241) LTS at 1 AD to 1924; 1 FTS by 4.24; To 1 Sqn 23.7.25; Participated Western Australia army-coop exercise 11.25; Collided with A6-26 and crashed Melbourne whilst on flypast to welcome the Duke & Duchess of York to Australia 21.4.27 (F/O VH Thornton & Sgt HG Hay both killed); SOC 15.6.27

A6-27 (ex C6246) LTS at 1 AD to 1924; 1 FTS by 7.24; Participated in Western Australia flight 10.3.27 to 8.4.27 (F/O FRW Scherger); Crashed, to 1 AD for storage 11.4.27; In bad condition, recommended not worth further repair 18.3.28; Approved for conversion to components 20.3.28

A6-28 (ex C6323) Stored at 1 AD to 1923; 1 FTS by 7.23; Reconditioned by MSB Maribyrnong 1.6.25 (fitted dual controls); To 3 Sqn 7.25; Crashed Canberra, BO 11.2.26 (F/O P McK Pitt & AC1 WE Callander both killed); SOC 25.6.26 [254hrs]

BELGIUM

A number of D.H.9 variants reached Belgium, being used for both civil and military purposes. [See also under D.H.4]

Civil use

Georges Nélis, director of SNETA, decided to found a Belgian aircraft manufacturing society in order to be independent of foreign builders. SABCA (Société Anonyme Belge de Constructions Aéronautiques) was accordingly established on 16 December 1920 with the intention of becoming operational on 1 August 1921. The Belgian Government gave guarantees of a minimum of orders, as it considered this new company to be strategically necessary for national defence.

The first aircraft to be completed, a Morane-Saulnier MS 35, was rolled out of the workshops on 12 December 1922, followed four days later by the first D.H.9. In 1923, the production capacity reached one aircraft per day. Between December 1923 and March 1924, 29 D.H.9s were built, fitted with 240hp Puma engines. Following this military order, three further D.H.9s were modified for a civil use. The cabin was enlarged and fitted with three sliding windows, these coming from old D.H.4As; a luggage compartment was added in the lower fuselage and special containers were installed under the wings. These modifications were initially made on O-BATA, which was later delivered to the UK re-registered G-EBUM. A second modified D.H.9, O-BELG, also went to the UK, as G-EBUN. Both received their certificates of navigation on 22 December 1927 being later re-sold to India in 1928 as VT-AAK and VT-AAL respectively. A third D.H.9 was modified and registered O-BIEN (later OO-IEN), remaining in use until February 1931.

Civil registered aircraft:

O-BATA D.H.9C c/n "8370" [not ex H9370, as sometimes quoted - see Russian sales] Mod; with cabin for 3 passengers; Regd [CofR 40] 17.3.21 to SNETA, Brussels; Regd [.27] to SABENA; Regn cld 27.12.27; Regd *G-EBUM* [CofR 1494] 29.9.27 to F/O John S Newall & Neville Vincent, Stag Lane; CofA [CofV 5] issued 22.12.27; Flown to India, departing Stag Lane 9.1.28, arriving Karachi 26.4.28; Regn cld 1.29; Regd *VT-AAK* 1.29 to F/O John S Newall and Neville Vincent and flew 5,000 passengers on tour of India to open up Indian air routes

O-BATE D.H.9 [identity unknown] Regd [CofR 44] 12.4.21 to SNETA; Crashed Le Bourget 13.4.21.

O-BEAU D.H.9 ex *F1148* [bought ex ADC] Regd [CofR 5] 19.3.20 to SNETA; Crashed in Switzerland 5.10.25.

O-BELG D.H.9C ex *F1223* [bought ex ADC] *[Regd as 1223]* Mod with cabin for 3 passengers; Regd [CofR 6] 19.3.20 to SNETA; Regd 1927 to SABENA; Regn cld 27.12.27; Regd *G-EBUN* [CofR 1495] 29.9.27 to F/O John S Newall & Neville Vincent, Stag Lane; CofA [CofV 6] issued 22.12.27; Flown to India with G-EBUM [see O-BATA]; Regn cld 1.29; Regd *VT-AAL* 1.29 to F/O John S Newall and Vincent Neville and flew 5,000 passengers on tour of India to open up Indian air routes.

O-BIEN D.H.9 ex *F1293* Regd [CofR 7] 19.3.20 to SNETA; Regd [27] to SABENA; *Regd OO-IEN* 20.6.29; Regn cld 7.2.31.

O-BLAC D.H.9 ex *F1221* Regd [CofR 36] 1.10.20 to SNETA; Regn cld 25.12.21.

Military use

British records show that E8903, E8905, E8910 and E8912 were allocated 1.19 for the Belgian Government; E8903 was apparently retained for use at RAE Farnborough. *[One report says 18 D.H.9s to the Belgian Air Force in 1918, which is unlikely at that date]*

A further 31 were given British civil registrations before being ferried to the Belgian Air Force (Aviation Militaire Belge) between July 1921 and May 1922, as follows:
G-EAQL, G-EAYW, G-EAZA, G-EAZB, G-EAZC, G-EAZD, G-EAZE, G-EAZJ, G-EAZM, G-EAZN, G-AEZO, G-EAZO, G-EAZY, G-EAZZ, G-EBAA, G-EBAB, G-EBAD, G-EBAE, G-EBAI, G-EBAO, G-EBAP, G-EBAQ, G-EBAR, G-EBAS, G-EBBA, G-EBBB, G-EBBJ, G-EBBK, G-EBCH, G-EBCI, G-EBCJ

Belgian records indicate that 29 (possibly 30) D.H.9s were built by SABCA between December 1922 and March 1923, to fill an urgent need to build up the number of reconnaissance units. In addition,

D.H.9 O-BEAU was flown by SNETA until it crashed in Switzerland on 13.4.21. (Brussels Air Museum)

D.H.9 F1201, believed at Bickendorf in 1919, before receiving a Belgian serial number. (via J.M.Bruce)

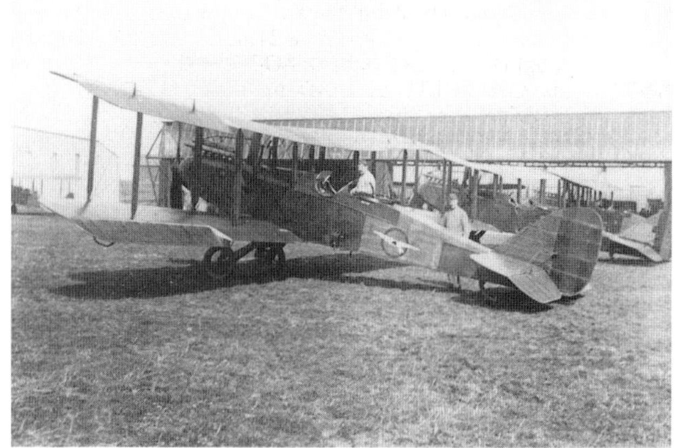

Belgian D.H.9s displaying a variety of unit markings. (M.Willot, J.M.Bruce and Brussels Air Museum)

73 surplus ex-RAF D.H.9s were supplied by the Aircraft Disposal Company, these being for the 1ère, 5ème, 7ème, 3ème and 4ème Escadrilles of I and III Groupes. The first D.H.9s to be delivered were from ADC on 20 April 1921. D.H.9s went to 9/II/3 and 11/II/3 bomber squadrons and also to several reconnaissance squadrons in Escadrille d/Observation 3/II/1. Belgian serial numbers started at *D1* and appear to have ended at *D103*.

Before 1924, D.H.s were flown by 1ère, 2ème, 3ème, 4ème, 5ème, 6ème Escadrilles, which were part of II/1Aé; and also 9ème, 11ème and 12ème which were part of V Groupe.

Belgian D.H.9 units:

1ère Escadrille d'Observation (Mephisto Escadrille)
- at Evère as part of II/1Aé with D.H.4s until 1922, when it moved to Goetsenhoven and re-equipped with D.H.9s. It was renumbered 7ème in 1926.

3ème Escadrille d'Observation (Holly Leaf Escadrille)
- at Goetsenhoven with Bréguet XIVs and Ansaldo from 1922. There is no evidence that either the D.H.4 or the D.H.9 was ever flown, but it would have been quite logical, and therefore the possibility cannot be ruled out.

4ème Escadrille d'Observation (Zebra Escadrille)
- used D.H.9s at Goetsenhoven as part of II/1Aé from 1922 until disbanding in 1924.

5ème Escadrille d'Observation (Swallow Escadrille)
- based at Houthem with SPAD S.11s at the end of the war, it used D.H.9s at Goetsenhoven as part of II/1Aé from 1922, later re-equipping with Ansaldo A.300s and then Bréguet XIXs.

6ème Escadrille d'Observation (Bee Escadrille)
- based at Evère post-war as part of II/1Aé, and had some D.H.9s on strength. In addition to its operational role, it provided transport the Belgian Royal Family with a D.H.4 for His Majesty King Albert and a Bristol F.2b for Her Majesty Queen Elisabeth. It was disbanded during reorganisation in 1926.
Note. The Royal Flight (Escadrille Royale) had a D.H.9 on strength when it formed on 3 November 1919, before being attached to 6ème Escadrille.

9ème Escadrille
- joined 11ème and 12 ème in Vème Groupe to complete its complement.

10ème Escadrille

World record

On Saturday, 2 June 1928, Adjudant L. Crooy and Sergent V. Groenen took off from Gossoncourt in D.H.9 *D32* in order to fly for several days using in-flight refuelling. This aircraft had been specially modified with controls in both cockpits, two additional fuel tanks and a special windscreen. It was refuelled with a long flexible rubber hose from a second D.H.9 flying above, the latter being crewed by Premiers Sergents D.Jordens and G.Creteure. A contemporary photograph shows the refuelling D.H.9 from 5/II/1Aé wearing the usual Swallow insignia in a clear circle but the record attempt D.H.9 from 1/II/1Aé had the Mestipho insignia in a circle.

Adjudant L.Crooy and Sergent V.Groenen's record breaking D.H.9. (Brussels Air Museum)

The record attempt D.H.9 initially carried 650 litres of fuel. There were between 11 and 16 in-flight refuellings (various sources differ), each refuelling giving about 300 to 350 litres. The refuelling was executed with the tanker aircraft less than 10 metres away from the other aircraft. With a 10 metre flexible hose, later reduced to 7.50 metres due to a tear, *D32* was refuelled each time within 5 to 6 minutes.

Having taken off at 06hrs 40min 18sec on 2 June and landing on Monday 4 June at 18hrs 47min 50sec, their total time of 60 hours, 7 minutes and 32 seconds beat the previous record set by the Americans Lowel, Smith and Richter, achieved on 27/28 August 1923 with a Liberty-engined DH-4B.

Goetsenhoven

In December 1921 it was decided to create a military aerodrome at Goetsenhoven. Commandant Avi Desmet took command of the base as well as the Group d'Observation when it arrived. Six hangars were built in line, with two other buildings in the centre housing the HQ, the Officers mess and some rooms for courses. The hangars had been taken over from a German base as compensation for war damage. On 1 May 1922 the 1ère Groupement de Reconnaissance et d'Observation d'Artillerie began to settle in, comprising six Escadrilles d'Observation. These had previously been based at Wilrijk (Antwerpen) and Evère and were then flying SPADs, D.H.4s and D.H.9s. They were numbered 1 to 6 and their aircraft carried the respective insignia Mephisto, Gull, Holly Leaf, Zebra, Swallow and Bee.

École d'Aviation Militaire Belge (Belgian Pilot School)

The Belgian Pilot School had been based in France during the war, but in May 1919 it returned home to be based at As, its aircraft carrying a Penguin insignia. On 25 September it moved to Wevelgem (Wevelghem), but the next course did not begin until the spring of 1925. It comprised three Escadrilles (1, 2 and 3/II/3Aé). Initial training was provided by 3ème Escadrille on Caudron G.IIIs, RSV 32/90s and Avro 504Ks, and at that time candidates were required to have previously gained a pilot's "brevet de tourisme" (licence of tourism) at one of the two civil aviation shcools at Gosselies and Deurne, the lessons there being paid for by the Ministry of Defence. On completion they would return to Wevelgem to gain a "brevet moyen" (intermediate licence) and then a "brevet militaire" (military pilot licence). For these they advanced to 2ème Escadrille where they flew Morane-Saulnier MS 35s and Fokker D VIIs, then finally to 1ère Escadrille with Bristol F.2Bs and D.H.9s. When the Aéronautique Militaire was reorganised into Régiments d'Aéronautique in January 1926, the school comprised 1ère and 3ème Escadrilles of IIème Groupe of 3ème Regiment d'Aéronautique, with 1ère flying D.H.9s, Fokker D VIIs, Bréguet XIVs and Bristol F.2Bs. The D.H.9s were in use until at least 1928, when an accident was recorded to *D101*.

Bolivian Air Arm D.H.9 AM-1, named CORONEL SALAZAR. (G.A.Jenks collection)

BOLIVIA

The Bolivian Air Arm or Cuepo de Aviadores was established in connection with the Centenary celebrations, 40 aircraft participating in a large military review at La Paz, the aircraft being based at Alto La Paz.

In 1926 the Bolivian Government purchased two ex-ADC Puma-engine D.H.9s for survey purposes, these being marked AM-1 and AM-2. AM-1 was named "CORONEL SALAZAR" and was operated by J.R. [Joe] King, who was sent out to demonstrate the aircraft, it being flown on Short floats from Riberalta, Rio Beni, and operated throughout Equatorial South America 1927-1928. He made many notable flights, including one from Riberalta to Maldonado, Peru and back, a total distance of 640 miles, in 5 hours 40 minutes flying time.

D.H.9A G-CYAJ was one of the aircraft which made a trans-Canada flight

CANADA

Military

D.H.9As were flown by No.2 Squadron, Canadian Air Force from its formation (ex 123 Sqn RAF) on 20.11.18 at Upper Heyford. It moved to Shoreham 1.4.19, but was reduced to a Number Plate basis 6.19, being officially disbanded 5.2.20.

Post-war, 11 Imperial Gift D.H.9As supplied and given quasi-civil marks, being commonly painted with just the last two letters of the registration markings.

G-CYAD (ex E1000) TOC 18.6.20 by Canadian Air Board, Civil Operations Dept; Crashed Mordy 23.8.20
G-CYAJ (ex E998) TOC 19.7.20; Made trans-Canada flight; SOC 23.9.27
G-CYAK (ex E994) TOC 19.7.20; WO in Cat B accident 1920; SOC 18.2.29
G-CYAN (ex E996) TOC 19.7.20; Trans-Canada flight 6.9.20; SOC 23.9.27
G-CYAO (ex E1002) TOC 19.7.20; Based Morley, Alberta; SOC 1.2.22
G-CYAZ (ex E997) TOC 10.9.20; Cat A accident at Winnipeg 30.9.20; SOC 1.2.22
G-CYBF (ex E995) TOC 18.9.20; Based at Camp Borden; SOC 18.2.29
G-CYBI (ex E992) TOC 17.9.20; Based at Camp Borden; SOC 18.5.26
G-CYBN (ex E993) TOC 11.10.20; Cat B accident at Camp Borden 22.11.20; SOC 18.2.29
G-CYCG (ex E1001) TOC 16.12.20; Cat B accident at Camp Borden 20.12.20; SOC 23.9.27
G-CYDO (ex E999) TOC 16.3.21; Cat D accident at Arthur, Ontario 17.5.21; SOC 23.9.27

Civil

G-CAEU see G-EBDE

See also G-EAMX/EAQP

CHILE

As compensation to Chile for the wartime takeover of two large warship under construction in England for the Chilean Navy, various other military equipment was offered after the Armistice, including 12 D.H.4s and 8 D.H.9s. In the event the D.H.4s appear to have been substituted by further D.H.9s, of which 20 were supplied in 1919 and numbered *83 to 102*, these being based at Lo Espejo, near Santiago. Previous identities included D1295, D1296, D1307, D1308, D1326, D1327, H5638, H5710, H5715, H5722, H5725, H5726, H5730, H9117, H9118, H9209, H9216, H9228, H9261 and H9263, but no serial number tie-ups are known. D1297 is also noted as being supplied to Chile, although it does not appear in a contemporary official list of aircraft supplied to overseas governments. Individual names known to have been allotted were 89 *Coquimbo*, 91 *Tacna*, 92 *El Ferroviario*, 95 *Linares* and 96 *Talca*. D1307 crashed on 29 December 1920, and H5730 on 14 January 1922.

On 3 March 1921 a midshipman attempted to save a friend from the resulting fire when D1308 crashed at the Military Air School at El Bosque, and Felixstowe F.2A flying boat N4567 was subsequently named *Guardiamarina Zanartu* in his honour.

On 22 May 1921 a new height record was established for a flight over the Andes, when Lieutenant Roberto Herrara made the first crossing to Mendoza with Lieutenant Alfredo Gertner as a passenger, flying D1296.

Between 29 August and 7 September 1922, to celebrate Brazil's independence, a Santiago-based D.H.9 carrying the name *Ferroviario*, piloted by Captain Diego Aracena, the Chilean Director of Civil Aviation, and carrying Arthur Seabrook, made a flight of 1,850 miles to Rio de Janeiro in Brazil, via Argentina and Uruguay. It should have been accompanied by a similar machine, named *Talca* and piloted by Captain Federico Baraona, but this was badly damaged in an accident near Castellanos in Argentina and could not continue.

In 1926 a D.H.9 made the first Chilean non-stop military flight between Santiago and Buenos Aires.

Only three remained with the Army Air Service by 12 February 1927, being used by the Advanced Training Squadron of the Flying School at El Bosque. The type was still in use there in 1928, but was probably withdrawn soon afterwards.

CHINA

Following the signing of a Chinese-Soviet Treaty in May 1924, a Soviet aviation mission was sent to help the Kuomintang led by Dr Sun Yat-sen suppress the assorted war lords in northern China. Instructors, pilots and ground personnel arrived in 1925, together with a number of R-1s, and in June 1926 these carried out bombing and reconnaissance missions for a 'Northern Expedition'. During a 35-day siege of Wuchang (Wuhan) the R-1s dropped 7,054lb of bombs. Aid ceased in 1927 when relations were severed due to Soviet interest in the Chinese Eastern Railway in Manchuria.

Later, the Aircraft Disposal Company was reported in September 1930 to be sending "quite a number" of Puma-engined D.H.9s to China.

A D.H.9/R-1 variant in service in China.
(via Gordon Swanborough)

DENMARK

Four D.H.9s were supplied to Denmark, all for civil use by Det Dankse Luftfartselskab [DDL], Copenhagen:

T-DOBC ex *H9274* [UK CofA 402 issued to Handley Page Ltd 31.7.20; Deld Copenhagen 9.8.20 with CofA No.11 to Det Danske Luftfartselskab A/S [DDL], Copenhagen; Regd 10.8.21 to DDL; Crashed Solbjerg 17.10.21; Regn cld 1.11.21.
T-DODF ex *H5521* [Deld Copenhagen 16.8.20] Regd 16.6.21 to DDL, Copenhagen; Scrapped Kastrup 7.27; Regn cld 13.4.29.
T-DOGH ex *H9246* [UK CofA 409 issued to Handley Page Ltd 14.8.20; Deld Copenhagen 17.8.20] *[also reported as ex*

H9359] Regd 16.6.21 to DDL, Copenhagen; Regd *OY-DIC* 5.29 to same owner; Regd 5.7.30 to Johannes La Cour, Odense; Crashed Dybvad 18.8.30; Regn cld .31.

T-DOKL see *G-EAVM*

EGYPT

Two D.H.9s, ex G-EBEN and G-EBJR, were supplied to the British & Egyptian Tea Co Ltd, but probably continued to Hedjaz (q.v.).

ESTONIA

Eight D.H.9s were supplied by ADC to the Estonia Air Force (Lennuvägi) for observation work, the first two arriving on 2 September 1919, these being serialled *16* and *17*. They were followed on 23 September 1919 by the other six, which were then numbered *27* to *32*. Several flights are recorded during the war of independence, including one from Tallinn to Tartu by *16* and *17* on 2 November 1919, followed three days later by *16* flying from Tartu to Kaubi and *17* from Tartu to Voru. *17* was test flown on 11 and 19 November. The type was not used operationally, however, most reconnaissance flight being made by DFW C.V number *10*.

Overhauled Polish D.H.9s lined up for selection by the Estonian Mission in 1923. (Kazimierz collection via W.Matusiak)

In January 1920 *16* and *17* made a long flight from Tallinn to Riga. During winter the aircraft were operated on skis. The service was restyled Aviation Company (Lennurood) on 1 August 1920, but reverted to its previous tile on 1 June 1921. In the summer of 1922 two D.H.9s and two DFWs of the Landplane Wing (Maalennudivisjon) at Tallinn undertook a flight of around 2,400km from Tallinn to Riga, Vilna, Warsaw and back. One of the D.H.9s was crewed by Lt Haas, OC of the Training School with Col Reek of the General Staff, and the other by 2/Lt Post with Capt Steinberg, OC of the Estonian Flying Service.

By 1923 only half the original strength survived, so on 5 November 1923 five overhauled D.H.9s were purchased from Poland by the Estonian Military Aircraft Mission, these being re-

Estonian D.H.9 number 31 on skis. (Wickenden)

Estonian D.H.9 number 17 with wheeled undercarriage. (via Gordon Swanborough)

serialled *67* to *71*. The service was again restyled on om 15 March 1924 to become the Aviation Regiment (Lennuväe rugement). By 1 January 1927 the service comprised the 1st Eskadrill at Rakvaere with only four D.H.9s (16, 32, 70 and 79), the 2nd Eskadrill at Tartu with 16 aircraft and the Reserve (Tagavara) Eskadrill at Tallinn with Avro 504s. By 1 July 1928 the Aviation Regiment still had six D.H.9s on strength out of a total strength of 41 aircraft.

Individual histories:

16 (ex *H9135)*. At Tallinn 1.2.25 (flight ready); Reported as needing extensive repairs 3.22; With Esk.1 1.1.27 (minor repairs/overhaul); Still in use in 1929.

17 (ex *H9133*). Minor repairs/overhaul 1.1.24; Crashed at Lasnamäe 1924; At Tallinn 1.1.25 (under repair/overhaul); WO 1924.

27 (ex *D1246*). Written off 6.21.

28 (ex *D651*). Crashed 22.3.23. Written off 22.3.23.

29 (ex *D693*). Operational 1.1.24; At Tartu 1.1.25 (minor repairs/overhaul); Still in use 1926

30 (ex *D660*). *30* crashed on landing on return after making a lengthy flight from Helsinki to Tallinn carrying the first load of bank notes for the newly created Estonian Republic 1.20 (Nikolai Veelmann & Juri Lossman survived); Reported needing extensive repairs 15.11.20.

31 (ex *H9157*). Operational 1.1.24; At Tallinn 1.1.25 (under extensive repair); Visited Finland 4-10.3.26*; With Esk.2 1.1.27 (extensive repairs).

32 (ex *D9837*). Operational 1.1.24; Tallinn 1.1.25 (minor repairs/overhaul); Visited Finland 4-10.3.26*; With Esk.1 1.1.27 (operational).

67 Available 1.1.24; At Tallinn 1.1.25 (under minor repair/overhaul); Crashed at Lasnamäe 1924; Needing extensive repairs 1925, also 1927.

68 Available 1.1.24; At Tallinn 1.1.25 (operational); Crashed 13.2.26 (presume repaired); At an air show at Lasnamäe 9.26; With Esk.2 1.1.27 (operational)

69 Available 1.1.24; At Tartu 1.1.25 (operational); Written off 1925 (burned)

70 Available 1.1.24; At Tartu 1.1.25 (operational); Reported a needing extensive repairs 1926; With Esk.1 1.1.27 (minor repair/overhaul)

71 Available 1.1.24; At Tallinn 1.1.25 (under extensive repair); At an air show at Lasnamäe 9.26; With Esk.2 1.1.27 (operational); Crashed 1933 (Lt August Mäe)

* *The crews involved in the visit to Finland were Mjr K Haas/Lt H Kitvel and Lt Döring/Mech Altman.*

FRANCE

One D.H.9 (C6070) was supplied to the French Government in January 1918, but no orders were placed.

GREECE

43 D.H.9s were supplied to the Greek Government for reconnaissance use by the Royal Hellenic Naval Air Service, as follows:

D629, D640, D646, D654, D658, D664, D666, D667, D671, D674, D678, D684, D686, D697, D704, D1152, D2884, D3194, D3199, D3205, D3206, D5795, D5800, D7211, D9838, E8916, E8917, E8991, F1300, H5552, H5558, H5569, H5587, H5588, H5602, H5664, H5673, H5683, H5660, H5661, H5664, H5673 and H5683.

A Greek naval D.H.9. (via Gordon Swanborough)

D.H.9 G-EAYU before being sold to Hejaz. (via Philip Jarrett)

A Royal Navy analysis of overseas Navies in 1922 credited the Greek Navy with 34 D.H.9s, being 7 at Tatoi, 19 at Smyrna and 8 unerected in Central Stores.

The chief naval air station was at Phaleron Bay. A number of D.H.9s were reconditioned by an aircraft factory at Phaleron, near Athens, this being run by the Blackburn Aeroplane & Motor Co Ltd.

HEDJAZ

In the early part of the twentieth century, the two predominant states in the northern part of the Arabian peninsula were the Kingdom of Hedjaz, ruled by Sherif Hussein Ibn Ali and declared independent in 1916, and the rival Nejd, ruled by Sultan Abdal-Aziz III Ibn Saud, which became independent in 1921.

Two D.H.9s arrived at Jeddah from British Disposals Board stocks in Egypt on SS *Tantah* aboard 6.8.21 with two spare engines, having been sold to Schumaker & Lavison and then resold to King Hussein, said to be for patrolling Jeddah-Mecca and Mecca-Medina routes to protect pilgrims. On arrival in Hedjaz a Mr.Brook, an ex-RAF officer, was engaged to organise an Air Force. One was later used for military operations in the Nejd region when the Russian pilot Naidyonoff was twice sent by King Hussein to bomb Taraba, although there were no reports of bombs being dropped in that area. Plans were also reported for the construction of several landing grounds, particularly an airstrip at Taif.

In October Capt Brooke flew to the new landing ground at Taif in 1 hour 10 minutes, but on attempting to take off on his return journey his undercarriage was carried away on a small hillock, and he had to leave the aircraft at Taif, returning by mule.

A report in January 1922 on the distribution of Hashemite air forces, listed one D.H.9 in good condition and another lacking assorted spare parts, none of the pilots being familiar with this type of aircraft. In January 1924 a D.H.9 carrying a pilot and mechanic broke its propeller and undercarriage on the landing ground at Taif, which was described as dangerous.

In 1924 war broke out between Hedjaz and Nejd, and on 22.11.24 three D.H.9s arrived at Jeddah from the UK aboard the P&O vessel SS *Nore*, one being G-EAYU and the others probably G-EBEN and G-EBJR which had ostensibly been sold in Egypt. The first to be assembled had a Puma engine but was not fitted with a machine gun, whilst the other two were three-seater commercial machines reportedly fitted with diesel engines. They were to be used in the defence of Jeddah and to aid King Ali to recapture Mecca. The only D.H.9 pilot available was a Russian refugee named Shirokoff, who went on reconnaissance flights every morning, and refused to fly over enemy territory at less than 9-10,000 feet, and as his observer always wore dark glasses it was considered that their reports were likely to be of little value. Shirokoff refused to bomb the enemy, but in any event there were no proper bombs in the country, so the Army sent him to drop hand grenades, his salary being £60 gold a month plus a bottle of whisky a day!

G-EAYU was destroyed on 18.1.25 when a make-shift bomb, which had been fused incorrectly by the ground crew, exploded at a great height, probably on attempting to throw it out of the aircraft, blowing the aircraft, pilot Shirikoff and three other occupants to pieces. Another D.H.9 was badly damaged at Jeddah around 10.5.25, and by July only one remained capable of flight. All three had been written off by 18.11.25.

On 6.5.25 a further six D.H.9s were shipped from the UK to Hamburg for the East Asiatic Company Ltd of Copenhagen. They were evidently intended for somewhere with a hot climate as they were packed in zinc cases. Their ultimate destination became clear when they arrived at Jeddah on 26.8.25 on board the German ship SS *R.C.Rickmers*, apparently paid for by King Hussein. All traces of their origin had been removed from each airframe and engine. They made a number of raids, including a bombing attack by two D.H.9s on the Wahib camp at Rabigh, Ibn Saud's main supply port on 15 October.

Meanwhile, during 1924-25, Mecca and Medina had been captured, then under the terms of an agreement on 7.12.25 after Ibn Saud had conquered Hussein at Jeddah and forced him to abdicate. All arms, including aeroplanes, had to be handed over, including the six D.H.9s, though one had already crashed and it was doubtful if repairs could be effected.

On 6.4.26 a letter to Lord Trenchard referred to Hedjaz wanting to form an Air Force. It was agreed to send a Sq Ldr J.Noakes AFC MM together with two mechanics from RAF Middle East, and they found that the five D.H.9s and their engines were in good condition.

The Kingdom of Hedjaz and Nejd was created in 1926. Only two of the D.H.9s were listed as serviceable in 1929. The title Kingdom of Saudi Arabia was adopted in 1932, and all five D.H.9s were still listed as being on strength as late as 12.33.

INDIA

A number of D.H.9s were exported to India, as follows:

G-IAAA ex *H9129* Regd 3.26 to The Air Survey Co Ltd, Calcutta [based Rangoon]; Believed rebuilt as *G-IAAP*; Reregd *VT-AAP* 12.28 to The Air Survey Co Ltd, Calcutta; Regn cld 1.8.33.

G-IAAB ex *D3180* Regd 4.27 to F/O JJC Cocks of 60 Squadron, RAF Lahore; It was allegedly built up from two ex-Imperial Gift D.H.9s bought from the Maharajah of Nabha and departed Lahore 11.5.27 for Lympne, England; Lost between Kania & Constantinople, Turkey 25.5.27 [or 26.5.27].

An unmarked D.H.9 seaplane of the Air Survey Co Ltd, Calcutta, at Miri, Sarawak c.1925. (RAF Museum P.1393)

D.H.9 G-IAAU at 2 am on 26 February 1926 at the start of John Oliver's unsuccessful attempt to lower the flying time from Karachi to Croydon. (via Frank Cheesman)

G-IAAG [identity not known] Regd to Raja Mohamed Mumtaz Ali Khan.
G-IAAP see G-IAAA
G-IAAQ ex *E611* Reregd *VT-AAQ* 12.28 to The Air Survey Co Ltd; Regn cld 1.8.33.
G-IAAS ex *D5686* Regd 6.25 to The Air Survey Co Ltd, Calcutta [based Rangoon on River Irrawaddy surveys]; Reregd *VT-AAS* 4.29; Regd to Indian Air Survey & Transport Ltd.
NOTE. A D.H.9 without markings, fitted with floats and piloted by Ronald Kemp, undertook an Irrawaddy Survey during 1923/4, the task being completed in March 1924
G-IAAU [previous identity not known] Used by F/Lt John Oliver and F/O Brooks RAF in an attempt to lower the flying time from Karachi to Croydon to five days. Left Karachi at 2 am on 1.3.26, hoping to reach Bushire, but forced down by thick fog and rear petrol tank problem, came down 7m from Pasni LG. Then delayed by sandstorm, but took off next morning at 6 am, then engine failure, forced landed Surag, about 70m E of Jask on Persian Gulf. Attempt abandoned. Not known whether fresh attempt made.
G-IAAY [identity not known] Regd 1.28 to EA Alton, Bombay; Reregd *VT-AAO* 1.28.
VT-AAK see O-BATA
VT-AAL see O-BELG
VT-AAO see G-IAAY
VT-AAP see G-IAAA

See also G-EBDL

IRISH FREE STATE

Following the acceptance by the Irish delegation of the terms of an Anglo-Irish Treaty, a National Army was formed in early 1922, and in May this occupied the former R.A.F. airfield at Baldonnel, seven miles south-west of Dublin. Within two months an Irish Air Service was formed there, consisting of one flying unit, No. 1 Squadron, comprising "A" Flight, for flying training, and "B" Flight, for operational flying.

In June 1922 a Civil War erupted between the National Army, supporting the Provisional Government, and the Irregulars, supporting the Anti-Treaty faction, the National Army being mainly engaged on combat operations against Republican forces in the south and south-west regions of Ireland. By October the conflict was mainly confined to the south-west of Ireland, comprising Counties Cork and Kerry and a detachment from the Air Service was deployed to the former R.A.F. airfield at Fermoy, Co. Cork in the same month, equipped with Bristol F.2b Fighters and Martinsyde F.4 Buzzards. One aircraft was also deployed to a temporary airfield on the outskirts of Tralee, Co. Kerry during this period. An aircraft was then needed with sufficient range and speed to reach the coastlines in Counties Cork and Kerry, and to fulfil this requirement, six Airco D.H.9s were acquired from ADC stocks early in 1923.

Irish Air Corps D.H.9 DII minus its wings. (Irish Air Corps Photographic Section)

The first two D.H.9s (ex H5797 and H5830) arrived on delivery to Baldonnel on 1 January 1923, followed five days later by H5774. The fourth D.H.9 (ex H5869) was delivered on 12 January, but crashed six days later, killing the pilot, this being the first fatal crash to occur in the Air Service. The fifth aircraft (ex H5823) was delivered on 23 January and the sixth D.H.9 (ex H9310) on 28 February 28. All entered service with 'B' Flight, No.1 Squadron, being initially allotted Roman numeral serial numbers I to VI, later prefixed 'D' (for de Havilland).

A Martinsyde Buzzard and three newly acquired D.H.9s in the hangar at Fermoy in 1923. (via Donald MacCarron)

Operating from the airfields at Fermoy and Tralee until April 1924, the D.H.9s undertook reconnaissance flights, dropping propaganda leaflets and patrolling the railway system in the south-west throughout the Civil War. On 25 June 1923, DI was written-off in a crash near Fermoy, the observer being killed.

In October 1924, following the formation of the Irish Army Air Corps, four D.H.9s (DII, DIII, DV and DVI) remained in service with 'B' Flight, No. 1 Squadron. With other aircraft from this unit they engaged on an aerial survey of the State, a photographic survey of historic sites for the Archaeological Research Commission, advanced flying training and participation in the annual military exercises held by the Irish Defence Forces.

Commencing on February 20, 1926, two D.H.9s and three Bristol F.2b carried out the first Search and Rescue mission by the Air Corps, spending four days searching for a missing trawler off the west coast. On 26 February, during the return flight to Baldonnel, DV crashed near Oughterard, Co. Galway, and was written off.

On April 5, 1929 two further D.H.9s (ex H5862 and H9247), without engines installed, were delivered to Baldonnel as replacements for the crashed aircraft, being supplied by ADC at a cost of £850 each, being serialled 7 and 8 and entering service with 'B' Flight, No. 1 Squadron. By this time the Roman numerals, with prefix letters, had been replaced by Arabic numerals for serial numbers allotted to aircraft in service with the Air Corps.

Commencing in February 1930 with DII, the five D.H.9s were gradually withdrawn from use over the following five years. The last two remaining in service (DIII and 7) were withdrawn in September 1934 following a survey of obsolescent aircraft and aero-engines held in storage by the Air Corps that were to be "valued as scrap and sold or destroyed".

Air Corps D.H.9s were finished overall light grey, with the front section of the nose painted red. The national colours, as green, white and orange stripes, were displayed chordwise on the upper surfaces of the top wings and under surfaces of the bottom wings, and vertically on both sides of the rudder. Each aircraft's serial number, painted black, was displayed on both sides of the rear fuselage section, in front of the tailplane.

Individual Histories:

I Later DI. Ex H5797. Deld Baldonnel 1.1.23. To 'B' Flight, No.1 Sqn. Crashed and written off nr Fermoy, Co, Cork, pilot thrown clear 25.6.23 (Lt W McCulloch OK & Lt K McDonagh killed)

II Later DII. Ex H5830. Deld Baldonnel 1.1.23. To 'B' Flight, No.1 Sqn. Withdrawn from use 2.30

III Later DIII. Ex H5774. Deld Baldonnel 6.1.23. To 'B' Flight, No.1 Sqn. Withdrawn from use 9.30; Scrapped 6.35

IV Later DIV. Ex H5869. Deld Baldonnel 12.1.23. To 'B' Flight, No.1 Sqn. Training flight, crashed and written off 18.1.23 (Lt T Nevin killed)

V Later DV. Ex H5823. Deld Baldonnel 23.1.23. To 'B' Flight, No.1 Sqn. Engine failure while returning from aerial search for missing trawler off west coast of Ireland, crashed and written off, Oughterard, Co. Galway 26.6.26 (Lt O Heron & Sgt J Maher unhurt)

VI Later DVI. Ex H9310. Deld Baldonnel 28.2.23. To 'B' Flight, No.1 Sqn. Withdrawn from use 4.31

7 Ex H9247. Deld Baldonnel 5.4.29. To 'B' Flight, No.1 Sqn. Withdrawn from use 9.34; Scrapped 6.35

8 Ex H5862. Deld Baldonnel 5.4.29. To 'B' Flight, No.1 Sqn. Withdrawn from use 5.32

The British Air Mission at Kasumi-ga-ura with the sole D.H.9 supplied to the Imperial Japanese Navy. (J.M.Bruce/G.S.Leslie collection)

JAPAN

The Imperial Japanese Navy was supplied with one D.H.9.

LATVIA

Order No.38, issued by the Latvian War Ministry's Department of Armaments on 16 February 1926, stated that the Department had accepted the Commission's protocols Nos.6, 7, 9, 13, 14 and 16 on acceptance flights of seven Airco D.H.9As performed in England between 18 & 29 January 1926, by LAF C-in-C Col. Jezups Basko, engineer Vichmanis (now spelt Vihmanis) and virsleitnants (1st Lt) Janis Karklins. The tested aircraft were listed as being numbers 8089 (sic), 8689 (presumably E8689), 8745 (presumably E8745), 8779 (presumably E8779), 8784 (presumably E8784), 8787 (presumably E8787) and 8789 (presumably E8789). Of these, 8089 and 8789 do not appear in other Latvian records, so should be considered suspect.

Order No.022, dated 20 August 1926, assigned Latvian serials to the newly arrived aircraft in the following sequence: Lat. s/n 1 (8779), 3K (8689), 4 (8189), 4K (8785), 5K (8787), 6K (8745), 10 (8784). The letter "K" meant "Kara vajadzibam" (for war needs), being assigned to a certain number of rarely-flown front line aircraft on standby alert. These numbers do not entirely tie in with those originally quoted.

The surviving D.H.9As were given the military designation B1 (scout bombers) in the early 1930s. By 26 August 1931 all seven D.H.9As were in operational service with the Aviation Regiment. By 1 September 1936 the 4th Squadron had Nos.4, 63, 65, 67 and 68, and by 5 May 1937 the 6th Squadron had Nos.1, 4, 67 and 68 of which only No.1 was airworthy. The type was phased out in 1937 in anticipation of delivery of new Stampe et Vertongen SV-5s from Belgium, a somewhat inadquate replacement for future events.

Individual histories:

1 (8779) Liberty engine No.2334. Issued to 1st Kurzeme Division's Reconnaissance Squadron by 1.29; Test flown after overhaul 23.2.32 (Aleksandrs Juzefatovs); Reissued to 4th Recce Squadron; Engine failed over Irlava, FL in meadow, nosed over 25.5.35 (Nikolajs Vults, other crew member unknown); Repaired 2.36 and retd to 4th Recce Squadron; Took off with insufficient speed, tilted to port, ground looped, u/c collapsed 19.5.36 (Sergey Babichev and Eriks Mellups); Repaired; Deld 5th Recce Squadron by 1.9.36; Last recorded with 6th Recce Squadron 5.5.37

3K (8689) With 1st Division's Reconnaissance Squadron 1.29; Nothing further known

4 (8189) Liberty engine No.1246; Repaired 1927; 306 flying hours by 27.3.28; Flight tested, tail assembly damaged on ground 9.1.29 (Janis Putnins and Nikolajs Strukovs); Minor repair, then issued to 1st Division's Reconnaissance Squadron; Overhauled 9.29 - 10.29, then test flown by Nikolajs Jakubovs; During Daugavpils summer camp period, successful forced landing at Daugavpils firing range near the "Zalumi" station while practising bomb dropping 12.8.31 (Arturs Kregers); Retd to sqn; Ran into vegetable garden bushes 11.6.32 (Leons Vaiders & virsleitnants Alberts Tirulis); Repaired, flight tested 27.6.33 (Janis Brunenauvs); Still with 1st Division's Recconnaissance Squadron 6.35; Propeller fell off in mid-air, FL near Vecaki, u/c and propeller smashed on impact against highway embankment 24.10.35 (Nikolajs Vulfs and Davids Timmermanis (now spelt Timermanis)); Repaired and overhauled, test flown 20.11.36 (NCO Karlis Veikins); On 1.12.36 reportedly weighed 2,215 kilograms and was capable of a maximum speed of 201 kph; To 6th Recce Squadron until 6.37; During a repeated start, failed to become airborne from Spilve aerodrome, bounced across the Bolderaja highway and crashed on opposite side, damagaging prop and u/c 8.7.37 (Pauls Kirpitis & (Karlis?/Emils?) Krumins), WOC

4K (8785) No information, possibly reserialled

5K (8787) No information, possibly reserialled

6K (8745) No information, possibly reserialled

10 (8784) Liberty engine No.2100; First repaired 1927; Tested 14.1.30 (Janis Putnins), then to 6th Recce Squadron; Next tested 24.4.30; Bad landing at Spilve, u/c smashed and fuselage deformed 17.2.33 (Voldemars Peculis and Karlis Birznieks); Crashed 16.6.34; EF, FL, nosed over nr Batari (in Daugavpils area) 8.7.34 (Arturs Ieva & virsleitnants Alberts Tirulis both survived); Salvaged engine to reserialled No.65.

An assortment of Latvian D.H.9As. Top right was taken during a visit to Tallinn with the Estonian civil aviation hanger in the background marked 'AERONAUT'. The bottom two are of the 8.7.37 crash of 67. (Top left via Georgijs Jemeljanovs, the remainder via Paul Branke)

Individual histories of reserialled aircraft

63 (circa 1929) Liberty engine No.2335; On landing at Spilve, near Riga, the pilot levelled out too late, the nose hit the Bolderaja highway and the aircraft bounced across the road into a ditch, damaging the engine 17.6.29 (Alfreds Salmins); Repairs were completed 29.2.30, and the aircraft then went to 1st Division's Recce Squadron; It was overhauled, then test-flown 10.11.30 (Arturs Kregers); Transferred to 4th Recce Squadron 6.35; Insufficient take-off speed, crashed, propeller smashed 30.8.35 (Davids Timmermanis); Ferry flight, aircraft began to malfunction, forced down by fog to sea level, wing touched the water surface during a turn, crashed 20.9.36 (Adolfs Vasiljevs (a naturalised Russian) & Leons Vaiders); SOC 1.1.37

65 (1929) Liberty engine No.2100; 7th Squadron, Krustpils, engine failure over Koknese, force landed at the side of the Plavinas-Koknese road, undercarriage, propeller and wing damaged 27.5.31 (Karlis Tenteris and Arturs Kregers); Transported to Riga 27-30.5.31; Repaired and overhauled, then flight tested 1.12.32 & 12.12.32 (Nikolajs Jakubovs); Crashed on landing, undercarriage, fuselage and propeller heavily damaged 13.6.33 (Voldemars Peculis & Karlis Birznieks); Repaired, then to 4th Recce Squadron; Engine failure, nosed over, damaged beyond repair 24.9.36 (Janis Renkulbergs (Rasa) and Arturs Meijerovics); WOC

67 (1930) While taxying too swiftly prior to take-off, throttled up too strongly, ran into a ditch near a hangar 11.9.30 (virsleitnants Janis Rucelis); Repaired and overhauled, then flight tested 29.6.32 (Nikolajs Vulfs); During a bomb dropping exercise, the engine seized over Vecaki, the aircraft force landed, undercarriage ripped off and wing damaged 23.9.32 (Voldemars Peculis); Propeller damaged during take-off 14.6.34 (Arturs Kregers & Kaneps); Repaired and returned to 1st Division's Recce Squadron until at least 6.35; Crashed into Ratsupite brook at Spilve airfield, the undercarriage killing schoolteacher Anna Tillers (now spelled as Tillere) on the river bank 8.7.37 (sergeant (serzants) pilot Edgars Kanailis and Davids Timmermanis); Not worth repair

68 (1930) Liberty engine No.1362. Test flown after repairs 24.4.30; Wing and propeller hit barn, aircraft crashed in a crop field, the wing hitting the ground 27.5.31 (Arnolds Kadikis and Ernests Strauja); Repaired & overhauled, then test flown 7.4.33; Ground collision with a Martinsyde ADC-1 (piloted by Hugo Freimanis) on the ice-covered surface of Lake Tukums 12.4.35; Repaired and transferred to 6th Recce Squadron by 1.9.36 to at least 5.5.37 (this may have been its struck off charge date)

MONGOLIA

In 1925 Mongolia received at least three Russian-built D.H.9s or R-1s, and possibly as many as ten.

NETHERLANDS

Military use in Holland

A number of D.H.9s were interned and flown again after making forced landings in Holland, and on 1 November 1918 the LVA (Luchtvaartafdeeling or aviation service) listed three of these as being in operational condition with five more under repair. Assembly and modification of aircraft was at that time carried out by the LVA's Technical Branch (Technische Dienst). The D.H.9s were given new serials in the Reconnaissance category, which commenced at 400, such serials being preceded by a letter or letters indicating the manufacturer, in this case deH. The serials allocated were *deH433* (ex B7620), *deH434* (ex C1211), *deH437* (ex D5717), *deH438* (ex B7623), *deH439* [not confirmed] (ex D7204), *deH441* (ex C1294), *deH442* [not confirmed] (ex D7336), *deH443* [not confirmed] (ex D1733), *deH444* [not confirmed] (ex D3251) and *deH446* [not confirmed] (ex D3271). Details of the circumstances of internment in each case will be found under the original serials. Other D.H.9s which landed in Holland or in Dutch waters were B7624, C2158, C6348, D1708, D2781, D3107 and D3142.

D.H.9 B7620 'A' of No.211 Squadron after coming down in Holland on 27.6.18. (via Frank Cheesman)

The same machine now bearing the Dutch serial number deH433. (via Bruce Robertson)

deH433 was bought post-war by the Ministry of Colonies to train Netherlands East Indies pilots at Soesterberg, a spare engine also being obtained. The aircraft survived to be sold early in 1925 to KLM together with spares.

deH438 was wrecked in an emergency landing in bad visibility at Laren on 6.2.19, 1/Lt B Stom (NEI Arm) and 1/Lt WP van den Abeelen both being injured. This accident ended the career as a pilot of van den Abeelen. The aircraft was never bought, as quite apart from being written off in the crash, the Ministry of War decided around that time not to purchase any further interned aircraft.

It is uncertain which other D.H.9s were made airworthy, apart from deH433 and deH438, but possibly 434 and 437. They were flown by Lt Plesman, Lt Koppen, Lt Steup, SM van der Drift and Lt Stom.

[Contemporary de Havilland company records, now unfortunately unavailable, supposedly indicated that ten D.H.9s were assembled at the Stag Lane factory in 1922 from unused components, being then supplied to the Netherlands Army Air Service in January 1923, to be numbered 476 to 485 *(the c/n's were quoted as being 56, 57, 62, 59, 60, 61, 58, 63, 64 & 65 in that order). However, this does not agree with surviving Dutch records, which show 476 to 478 and possibly 479 as Rumpler C.VIIIs, 480 to 482 (and possibly 479) as unaccounted for, 483 to 484 as SVA.10s and 485 as Fokker C.Is. The extant Dutch records show no evidence of any D.H.9s having supplied in 1923, nor of any proposals to do so. Perhaps they were actually the final Netherlands East Indies delivery, though it is curious that the quoted serial numbers would appear to have been more appropriate to the Netherlands Army Air Service.]*

D.H.9s of 1e Afdeeling over the ricefields of West Java. (via N.Geldhof)

Military use in the Netherlands East Indies

From 1918 the air branch in the Dutch East Indies was called VliegAfdeeling (VA), and had its headquarters at Soekamiskin (now Sukamiskin), near Bandoeng (now Bandung). It was a completely separate entity from that in Holland. On 1 August 1921 it became known as LA/KNIL, its full title being Luchtvaarttafdeeling/Koninklijk Nederlands Indisch Leger (Aviation unit/Royal Netherlands East Indies Army). Between 1919 and 1922, 36 D.H.9s were supplied to the service, but details are sketchy as most records were lost during the Japanese occupation.

Ir H.A.Vreeburg went to England in 1919 with some NEI pilots to purchase 12 D.H.9 and Avro 504K. The D.H.9s cost *f*26,000 [guilders] each and 4 spare engines cost *f*11,300, the order being placed on 31 May. One D.H.9 was assembled at Croydon and tested for two days, the remainder being inspected and accepted on 10 June at Ascot, where they had been in storage with No.6 Stores Depot. On 15 June the purchasing commission went aboard SS *Insulinde* with 2 Avros, 10 D.H.9s and all the spare engines, the remainder of the order being embarked on SS *Tambora* and SS *Willis* on 5 July and 5 August respectively. The first D.H.9 to at arrive at the Soekamiskin (Java) base was H5873, but no other former RAF serials have come to light, nor any relationships with NEI serials.

Early in 1920, Capt S.L.Manning, the representative of the Disposal Board, offered the MvK (Colonial Office) to take over D.H.9 spares available in Holland, without payment. Then in March a complete aircraft (B7620/*deH433*) was offered for *f*217.50, this being the costs involved in connection with its internment. Although in reasonably good condition, it was not considered sufficiently airworthy as to justify the cost of shipment to the NEI, but it was thought good enough for training NEI pilots in Holland. Spares would also be needed at Soesterberg, and this was agreed to on 30 March 1920. Further orders were placed on 9 March 1921 (6 a/c), 11 April 1921 (8 a/c) and 8 September 1922 (10 a/c) *[perhaps the latter were the ten aircraft referred in the footnote above]*. The type was by now obsolescent, but as a real workhorse it was well suited to the task in NEI and could use normal car fuel, which would be especially advantageous on long-distance flights outside Java. Numbered *H101* to *H136*, the D.H.9s were fitted with Puma engines and had large D.H.50-type radiators.

The first operational D.H.9 unit was 1e Afdeeling, which was established at Soekamiskin in August 1921. "Operational" was something of an overstatement, because there was continual experimentation and difficulty with the armament, which remained unreliable, being prone to jamming and de-synchronisation, until about 1927.

The airfield at Soekamiskin was unsatisfactory, and construction of a new base at Andir (near Bandung) commenced in 1922. The 1e Afdeeling moved there the following year, to be joined on 2 August 1923 by a newly-formed 2e Afdeeling with six D.H.9s. Military D.H.9s flew a regular daily mail service from Batavia (now Jakarta) to Bandung during the annual Trade Fair there in 1923. Andir was more centrally situated for the defence of Java, but due to the general bumpiness of the air in the mountains it was easier to conduct ab initio flight training at Kali Djati on the coastal plains. However, the latter was quite inaccessible at that time by road or rail.

Soekamiskin was finally closed in November 1925, and the LA/KNIL then had only the main base at Andir with all major facilities, and a training base at Kali Djati, near Subang (Soebang), north of Andir.

In June 1926, strength included 18 standard D.H.9s, plus two ambulance conversions (designated HAs) and one photographic D.H.9 (designated HF), with the respective serial suffixes A or F, these being H115A, H117A, H120A, H120F, H124F and H130F. Other aircraft were used for such tasks as air mail, crop dusting, radio, parachute trials etc. The ambulance conversions were inspired by U.S. Army D.H.4 conversions, these having been seen by a LA/KNIL officer who had spent considerable time studying at the USAAC engineering schools as a "reward" for having flown U.S. General Billy Mitchell around in a D.H.9 when he was on his honeymoon to Java and Bali in 1923. They were somewhat similar in appearance to those flown by 'Z' Force in Somaliland in 1919, and were intended primarily for use in the case of a serious

D.H.9s at Soekamiskin, shortly after arrival in 1919, still in their original RAF paint scheme. (via Gerard J.Casius)

The first aircraft to landing at Andir after it opened in 1922. (via Gerard J.Casius)

HL-type D.H.9s under construction at the LA's workshops at Andir. (ML-KNIL 1914 - 1939)

A "home-built" HL-type D.H.9 at Andir with larger vertical rudder. (via Gerard J.Casius)

A Puma-engined ambulance conversion of a NEI D.H.9. (via Gordon Swanborough)

A Wasp-engined HW-type D.H.9 (via Gordon Swanborough)

The front cockpit of HL143 is fitted with a blind flying hood. (NASM)

An LA-built D.H.9 with Wasp Junior engine in use as an advanced trainer. (via Gerard J.Casius)

accident at the remote Kali Djati airfield, so that a casualty could be flown quickly to the central military hospital in Bandung, which had its own airstrip.

New Fokker C.IV and DC.I reconnaissance aircraft were arriving by 1926, but there was a variety of teething troubles with these, so when the 3e Afdeeling was formed early the following year it was equipped with six D.H.9s.

D.H.9s pioneered many long-distance flights in the NEI, including a flight in November 1927 by four aircraft of the 1e Afdeeling from the main base at Andir to Timor, a distance of 2155km (roughly equivalent to London-Casablanca) with four night stops. Another trip was made in June 1928 from Andir to Payakumboh (Sumatra) over 2400km (equivalent to London-Athens). The now elderly D.H.9 was preferred for these very demanding trips, rather than the more modern Fokker C.IV, because of its reliability and also the ability of its Puma engine to run quite well on regular automobile petrol, this being the only fuel available on the barren strips in the outer islands.

The 2e and 3e Afdeelingen re-equipped with the Fokker C.IV, DC.I and C.Ve in 1926-28, but retained some D.H.9s until at least 1929 and probably into 1930, when finally enough Fokker C.Vs and Curtiss P-6s became available to fully equip the 1e and 2e Afdeelingen. The 3e Afdeeling was disbanded in 1932 for economy reasons.

The prototype "home-built" D.H.9 was first flown on 18 Oct. 1925. It had a stressed-plywood fuselage (designed by Laurens Walraven, who later on built several original private aircraft designs in the Indies) but probably still had original D.H.9 wings, because it was counted as the 37th D.H.9. It had a larger vertical stabiliser and the D.H.4/D.H.9a style front radiator.

After completing a series of Avro 504s with a similar plywood fuselage ("ALs"), the Workshops at Andir built a series of twelve plywood-fuselage D.H.9s. Construction started in 1926 and continued until 1928, between three and five being completed each year. These could be produced very cheaply because of the availability of skilled Chinese woodworkers, the cost being *f*8000 (approx. £800-900 sterling then) without the engine. The type was known as "HL", derived from the serial prefix which stood for "Havilland Luchtvaartafdeling", the latter word being the name of the Army Air unit. Initially these were used in the Afdeelingen mixed with standard D.H.9s (as evidenced by Scarff gun mounts and the "cat" insignia of the 1st Afdeeling), but later only as trainers.

The production HLs started life with horn-balanced ailerons and the larger vertical stabiliser, but later on reverted to standard D.H.9 control surfaces. This might have been to make them a bit less docile as advanced trainers, or simply expedient because spares were available. The prototype was reserialled HL137 and the twelve production aircraft HL138 to HL149. HL149 suffered a fatal crash on 7 March 1930, the two crew members both being killed.

In 1931, conversion of surviving aircraft to the 325-hp Pratt & Whitney Wasp Junior engine commenced, the serial prefix being accordingly changed to HW. Three Wasps were received that year and conversions continued until 1934, as money became available to purchase more Wasps and aircraft entered the shops for major overhaul. By 1935 only HWs and two de Havilland Ambulances (it is uncertain whether these had Puma or Wasp) remained in the inventory. In 1937 the remaining HWs were replaced with Koolhoven FK-51s.

Statistics in a 1939 NEI Jubilee book show that 54% of the original NEI D.H.9s were written off after crashes with an average life of 368 hours, whilst the other 46% averaged 790 hours before being struck off charge as being worn out, the overall average life being 590 flying hours. In the case of the HL/HW series, only 34% were written off as a result of crashes at an average of 679 hours, whilst the other 66% averaged 1,465 hours before being SOC as worn out, the overall average being 1,212 flying hours.

The squadron insignia of the 1e Afdeeling was a cat, that of the 2e Afdeeling a flamingo, and that of the 3e Afdeeling a penguin. These emblems were carried for a time on the Fokkers, until being removed around 1930 when they were considered frivolous by the LA leadership. It is uncertain to what extent, if any, they were previously carried on D.H.9s.

Known Individual histories

H104	1st Afdeeling
H106	
H112	1st Afdeeling
H115	Crashed before conversion, no emblem [a photo exists]; Conv HA as H115A
H116	Crashed Soekamiskin 27.10.21 (Cpt O van Houten killed)
H117	Conv HA as H117A
H120	Conv HF as H120F
H121	1st Afdeeling
H124	Conv HF as H124F - 1st Afdeeling
H125	1st Afdeeling
H126	1st Afdeeling
H127	1st Afdeeling
H128	Crashed, no emblem [a photo exists]
H129	1st Afdeeling
H130	Conv HF as H130F - 1st Afdeeling; Crashed Andir 26.11.27 (1/Lt (pupil) C.F.Buysen killed)
H132	1st Afdeeling
H136	1st Afdeeling
HL139	Conv HF as H139F; Reconv HW as HW139F
HL141	Conv HF as H141F; Reconv HW as HW141F
HL143	Conv HW
HL144	Conv HW
HL147	Conv HF; Conv HW as HW147F
HL149	Crashed Kali Djati 7.3.30 (1/Lt J Hoste & sld B.J.Hollebrand both killed)

The method of painting the serial numbers varied. In the first batch, H104 and H106 had quite small serials. Then larger serials were used with a hyphen, probably being introduced with late deliveries, but retrospectively applied to the first batch (H-104, H-155 up to H-136). The HL-series generally had dots but no hyphen (e.g. H.L.145 and H.L.149), an exception being HL 144. The HW series was somewhat similar (e.g. HW.141F and HW.147), but HW.139F. also had a dot after the letter F. The method of painting the conversion letter also varied, one example being HW.141F, but another was H-120 F.

D.H.9B H-NABF was used by KLM for aerial photography. (via Gordon Swanborough)

Civil use

In 1921, four D.H.9Bs were supplied for civil use to Koninklijke Luchtvaart Maatschappij voor Nederland en Koloniën (KLM), 's-Gravenhage and based at Schiphol airport, Amsterdam, as follows:

H-NABE D.H.9B (ex *H5890/G-EAPL)*. Regd 7.21 to CofR No.19, application 12.7.21, expired 1.4.22; WFU 23.5.22; Regn cld 30.5.22 and CofA withdrawn. Airframe then used for a time as an engine test stand.

H-NABF D.H.9B (ex *H5889/G-EAOZ*). CofR No.20, regd 13.8.21. Converted for aerial photography 1922 and operated by KLM Air Survey Division. CofR cancelled 4.2.26 and Cof A withdrawn.

H-NABO D.H.9B (ex *H9125/G-EAUQ*). CofR No.13, applied for 22.11.20. Passed CofA examination 7.5.21. Heavy night landing Schiphol, damaged beyond repair 17.11.22 (pilot R.Hofstra unhurt). CofA suspended 5.12.22. Regn cld 27.2.23 and CofA withdrawn.
[NOTE The unlikely c/n "55889" has been quoted, which looks suspiciously like H5889, the previous identity of G-EAOZ/H-NABF]

H-NABP D.H.9B (ex*H9196/G-EAUH*) Regd 4.21; passed CofA examination 13.4.21. Engine caught fire during a photographic flight, forced landed, damaged beyond repair, Waalhaven 2.9.21 (pilot Hans Wende unhurt); CofA withdrawn 4.10.21; Regn cld 11.4.22.

In addition to these, *H9258/G-EAGY* was also imported, presumably to be used as a source of spares.

NEW ZEALAND

A number of D.H.9s were supplied under the Imperial Gift scheme and were used for civilian purposes prior to formal registration:

G-NZAD (ex *H5636*) [erected and FF c24.3.21] Regd 28.2.22 to Canterbury Aviation Co Ltd, Christchurch; To *NZPAF 5636* 21.6.23; Wfu Wigram 1927 and burnt.
G-NZAE (ex *H5627*) [erected and FF 10.21] Regd 28.2.22 to Canterbury Aviation Co Ltd, Christchurch; To *NZPAF* 21.6.23.
G-NZAH (ex *D3136*) three-seater with cabin, erected and FF 31.8.21. Regd 28.2.22 to Canterbury Aviation Co Ltd, Christchurch; Made first flight from Gisborne to Auckland 4.4.22, retd 7.4.22. Crashed Pahiatua 13.4.22; Rebuilt Wigram; Also reported as wrecked Wairarapua 1922. Later bought by Mr M.W.Buckley and named "Firefly". To *NZPAF 3136* 21.6.23; Wfu Wigram .30 and burnt.
G-NZAM (ex *D3139*) [Deld New Zealand Aero Transport Co Ltd 9.20] Made first flight from Timaru to Auckland 25.10.21. Regd 28.3.22 to New Zealand Aero Transport Co Ltd, Timaru; Made first flight from Invercargill to Auckland 4.4.22. Company ceased ops 27.3.23; To *NZPAF 3139* 14.6.23; Wfu Wigram 1927 and burnt. Propeller reported to be extant in the Auckland Museum
G-NZAQ (ex *H5672*) [Deld New Zealand Aero Transport Co Ltd 9.20] Regd 5.4.22 to New Zealand Aero Transport Co Ltd, Timaru.
F1252 Deld to New Zealand Flying School, Kohimarama 1920 but not used; To New Zealand Government 1.9.24; Dbf North Head Fort, Auckland 1926.
H5546 To New Zealand Flying School 1920
H5609 Deld to New Zealand Aero Transport Co Ltd, Timaru.
H5641 Deld to New Zealand Flying School [with F1252] but not used; History as F1252?

NZPAF D.H.9 5636 was originally H5636 and later G-NZAD, being flown by the Canterbury Aviation Co Ltd. (J.M.Bruce/G.S.Leslie collection)

NICARAGUA

Some D.H.4s or D.H.9s reported supplied to Nicaragua.

PERSIA

In January 1924 four D.H.4 and four D.H.9 were purchased from Russia, as well as four Junkers F-13 from Germany.

In May 1924 six R-1s were flown to Teheran from Russia, but only one of these arrived undamaged. In the summer of that year an Air Office was created as an integral part of the Imperial Iranian Army with Russian, German and French advisers. It originally comprised an Army Co-operation unit with its main base at Galeh-Morghi, Teheran, equipped with miscellaneous types, mostly of French and Russian origin.

By 25 March 1927 the only aircraft still in service were two Junkers and one D.H.9. Two F-13s were supplied in 1929, and also six D.H.9s [R-1s?] from Russia with 400hp Liberty engines, one of which had an accident at Baku-Pahlevi and another at Pahlevi-Teheran. Six more arrived at Pahlevi by ship on 22 June 1930.

In 1932 the service was reorganised as the Imperial Iranian Air Force.

PERU

The Army Aviation Service had a D.H.9A in 1923 and at least three by 15 July 1924 to at least 1927, these being marked with Roman numerals I, II and III. One was donated by the employees of the Central Railroad on 15 July 1924. One was written off on 10 April 1926 and another supposedly the next day.

The Peruvian Naval Air Service operated D.H.9s from its bases at Las Palmas and Arequipa, a close-up photograph of one appearing in 'Janes all the Worlds Aircraft' for 1925. Another report refers to two fitted with floats but without engines at Ancon around 1924.

A Peruvian D.H.9 at Lima in February 1927 (via Dan Hagedorn)

POLAND

In September 1919, Lts Marian Gawel and Henryk Tluchowski went to England to evaluate the D.H.9, which was being offered to the Polish Military Purchasing Mission in Paris by Handley Page. However, they were not very impressed, Kpt Jerzy Boresjza reported that he considered the type inferior to the Bristol Fighter. Nevertheless, 20 D.H.9s were allocated by the British Government on free issue in March-April 1920 to the Polish Military Purchase Mission, these having RAF serials D1081, D1258, D1273, D1275, D1278, D1325, D3242, D5733, E9022, E9031, F1173, F1174, F1217, H4259, H4260, H4262, H4279, H4315, H5702 and H5721. C6277 was also allocated, but not sent.

The first two aircraft (F1173 and H4279) were shipped in SS *Neptun* [also eight others?], which arrived at Gdansk (Danzig) on 24 April 1920, but when these two reached Lwow (now Lvov in the Ukraine) on 19 May they were found to be in a poor state. F1173 had 47 holes; these were repaired but it had crashed by 10 June. H4279 was in an even worse state, being struck off charge before assembly.

In early May a further ten (D1273, D1275, D1278, D1325, D5733, F1217, H4260, H4315, H5702 and H5721) were shipped in SS *Warsawa*. They were accompanied by an English fitter to assist with assembly, though it turned out that he had no experience on the type!

In all, 12 aircraft went to Lwow and 8 to Centralne Warsztaty Lotnicze (Central Aircraft Workshops)/Centralna Skladnica Lotnicza (Central Aircraft Depot) in Warsaw. Of the aircraft which went initially to Lwow, four could not be overhauled due to lack of spares, and were sent back to Warsaw.

D1278 was written off on 26 June 1920 when Plutonowy [platoon commander] Mieczyslaw Botny of No.III Ruchomy Park Lotniczy (Mobile Aircraft Park) crashed during a test flight, he being slightly hurt. The remaining aircraft were test flown by pilots of Nos.5 and 6 Eskadra (squadron) of III Dyon (Wing), who had been recalled from the Polish-Russian front for that purpose. On 4 July they ferried five aircraft to Tarnopol, 5 Eskadra receiving H4315 and H5721, and 6 Eskadra D1325, D5733 and probably D1275 which may have been written off on delivery. They were used against General Budenny's cavalry attacking the city of Lwow.

III Dyon considered the aircraft to have good, sturdy airframes, but with poor engines (Pumas) plagued by fuel pump failures. D5733 flew several combat missions with 6 Eskadra before crashing on 18 July 1920 during a forced landing due to engine failure, whilst D1325 had to be sent back to III Park at Lwow on 25 July for engine repair and fitting of a Benz fuel pump.

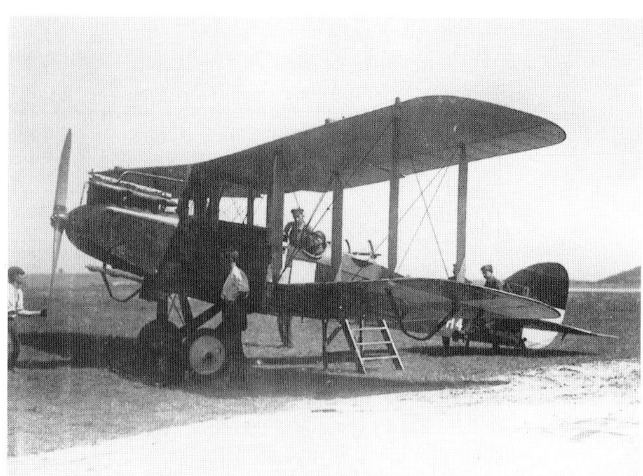

A selection of Polish D.H.9s. (Tomasz Kopanksi collectoon)

In 5 Eskadra the D.H.9s were flown, amongst others, by Porucznik [lieutenant] Wladyslaw Kalkus and Podporucznik [sub-lieutenant] Ludwik Nazimek, H4315 being overturned during a forced landing in July and sent back to III Park and thence to Warsaw.

D1275 emerged from repair at III Park on 1 September to be allocated to 5 Eskadra, only to be transferred to 6 Eskadra on 6 September, then back to III Park on 17 September for further repair. Meanwhile the repaired H4315 was allocated to 6 Eskadra on 8 September, but it too went back to III Park on 22 September after being damaged.

By 14 February 1921 the Polish Air Force had 17 D.H.9s on charge, of which 3 were serviceable and 7 complete but earmarked for overhaul. In addition there were 7 airframes and 10 engines requiring overhaul.

The unserviceable D1325, D1275 and H4315 remained at III Park until 16 March 1921, when they were sent back to Warsaw. That year the surviving aircraft were given Polish type number 26 and individual serials, being numbered *26-1* to *26-17* as they emerged from overhaul; the relationship between these and their respective RAF serials is unknown.

Consideration was given at the end of 1920 to equipping one destroyer (bomber) eskrada with D.H.9s, but this idea was dropped due to insufficient engine power. On 3 August 1920 it was proposed to replace the Siddeley Puma engines with Hispano-Suizas, of which large stocks were held, but this also came to nothing as it would have entailed extensive modifications. There were also plans to convert D.H.9s (amongst other types) for air communication use, but this too failed to materialise.

During the early 1920s D.H.9s were used by 5 Eskadra of 3 Pulk Lotniczy (Air Regiment) at Poznan and by 4 Pulk Lotniczy at Torun.

In August 1923 the Oficerska Szkola Obserwatorow Lotniczch (OSOL or Officers' School of Air Observers) at Torun assembled four D.H.9s which they held in storage, and five more were assembled in late 1923. The OSOL disbanded in May 1924, and its D.H.9s were then reassigned to the newly-formed No.4 Air Regiment at Torun.

Nine surviving D.H.9s were overhauled, and of these at least five were sold to the Estonian Military Aircraft Mission, becoming reserialled *67* to *71*.

In August 1923 a D.H.9 had its Puma engine replaced by a 230hp Austro-Daimler, this requiring filling the tubular fin post with lead, changing the tailplane incidence, and repositioning the upper wing forward by 2.5cm (1-inch) to correct the CoG position, the new engine being 10.9kg heavier with its own CoG being further forward than the Puma. On completion the aircraft went initially for trials at OSOL before going on to No.4 Air Regiment.

The last complete D.H.9 listed in the No.4 Air Regiment inventory was in 1928. On 9 November 1928, Pawel Zolotow, a civilian pilot working under contract, filed a request to purchase this surviving machine, but was turned down, and it was presumably scrapped, being officially struck off charge at Torun in February 1929.

Post-WW2, F1010 (ex German stocks) was stored at Poznan from 1945, until going to a museum at Krakow in 1963. On 15 June 1977 its fuselage was exchanged with the RAF Museum at Hendon for Spitfire LF.XVI SM411.

D.H.9 F1010 and Spitfire SM411 during the exchange in 1977. (Wojtek Matusiak)

Individual histories:
There appears to be some confusion in surviving Polish records as to the correct RAF serials, but the following is as accurate as can be pieced together:

D1081	Shipped in SS *Neptun* 4.20?
D1258	Shipped in SS *Neptun* 4.20?; CSL/CWL 1920; 1.3.21 - 30.5.21 r.[sic]
D1273	Shipped in SS *Warszawa* 5.20; CSL by rail 18.6.20; III RPL, markings applied after assembly 25.6.20; Allocated 5 Eskadra
D1275	Shipped in SS *Warszawa* 5.20; CSL by rail 18.6.20; III RPL, markings applied after assembly 25.6.20; 6 Eskadra 4.7.20?; III RPL 1920; 6 Eskadra 6.9.20; III RPL 17.9.20 (repair); CWL 16.3.21
D1278	Shipped in SS *Warszawa* 5.20; CSL by rail 18.6.20; III RPL, crashed on test flight 26(or 25?).6.20 (Mieczyslaw Blotny slightly hurt)
D1325	Shipped in SS *Warszawa* 5.20; CSL by rail 18.6.20; 6 Eskadra 4.7.20; III RPL 25.7.20 (repair engine and fit Benz fuel pump); 6 Eskadra 4.9.20; III RPL 27.2.21; CWL by rail 16.3.21
D3242	Shipped in SS *Neptun* 4.20?
D5733	Shipped in SS *Warszawa* 5.20; CSL by rail 18.6.20; III RPL, markings applied after assembly 25.6.20; 6 Eskadra 4.7.20; Engine failure, forced landed, crashed 18.7.20; III RPL to 5 Eskadra 30.7.20
E9022	Shipped in SS *Neptun* 4.20?
E9031	Shipped in SS *Neptun* 4.20?
F1173	Shipped in SS *Neptun* 4.20; To Lwow; 5 Eskadra; Crashed by 10.6.20; III RPL, no engine, SOC 1.8.20;
F1174	Shipped in SS *Neptun* 4.20?
F1217	Shipped in SS *Warszawa* 5.20; CSL by rail 18.6.20; III RPL, No engine, SOC 1.8.20
H4259	Shipped in SS *Neptun* 4.20?
H4260	Shipped in SS *Warszawa* 5.20; CSL by rail 18.6.20; III RPL, markings applied after assembly; 5 Eskadra
H4262	Shipped in SS *Neptun* 4.20?
H4279	Shipped in SS *Neptun* 4.20; III RPL 10.6.20; Received in poor condition, no engine; Earmarked for write-off 25.6.20, SOC before assembly
H4315	Shipped in SS *Warszawa* 5.20; III RPL by rail 18.6.20; Assembled 25.6.20; 5 Eskadra 4.7.20; Forced landed, overturned 7.20; III RPL 7.20; 6 Eskadra 8.9.20; Accident 16.9.20; III RPL 22.9.20; CWL 16.3.21; Szkola Pilotow Bydgoszcz [Pilots School], damaged 12.10.21
H5702	Shipped in SS *Warszawa* 5.20; CSL/CWL 5.20; III RPL by rail 18.6.20; Markings applied after assembly 25.6.20; III RPL 1.8.20
H5721	Shipped in SS *Warszawa* 5.20; CSL/CWL 5.20; III RPL by rail 18.6.20; Assembled 25.6.20; 5 Eskadra 4.7.20; OSOL [by?] 31.12.21 [? - listed as H5725]

26-2	CSL to CWL 15.10.20; Overhaul completed 31.3.21
26-3	CSL to CWL 2.12.20 Overhaul completed 1.5.21
26-14	OSOL 1923; to 4 Air Regt 5.24
26-17	OSOL 1923; to 4 Air Regt 5.24

PORTUGAL

One D.H.9A, named 'PATRIA', was bought from the RAF in India in 1924 to continue a long-distance flight to Macao after the original Breguet XIV crashed in India.

The sole Portuguese D.H.9A. (via Philip Jarrett)

ROMANIA

On 22 July 1921 a Mr S.A.Taylor, the Westinghouse Company's representative in Bucharest, signed a contact with the Romanian Government to supply 40 Puma-engined D.H.9 and 20 Rolls-Royce or Puma-engine Bristol F.2B at a price of £1,330 each, plus a quantity of spares valued at £40,904, a total of £120,750, the first instalment of £15,750 to be made by 15 September 1921. The aircraft were to be supplied from surplus RAF stocks, almost certainly those held by Aircraft Disposal Company stocks. It is questionable whether this contract was ever fully completed. [PRO file FO.371/8932 refers]

'Janes All the World Aircraft' for 1923 recorded that the Romanian Flying Corps then comprised a Reconnaissance Group, a Fighter Group and a Bombardment Group, of which the latter was equipped with D.H.9s and Bréguets. There was a flying school at Tecuci and a repair depot at Bucharest.

In 1924 a number of D.H.9s (possibly ten) were converted to carry to two passengers. They appear to have been still in service in 1926, but nothing further is known.

RUSSIA/U.S.S.R.

D.H.9s and D.H.9As were used by the RAF in Russia during the Intervention, and known details of these are given under their individual serials. Some of these and others were supplied to White forces, i.e. the Russian Aviation Corps, or used jointly with the Slavo British Aviation Corps. A number of these were captured when the Soviets won, and were then used by the RKKVF. In addition, others being purchased when normal trade with the USSR resumed in 1924.

By the end of 1920 the Communist forces has 19 captured D.H.9s and D.H.9As, these being mostly flown in Caucasia and the Ukraine. A year later Soviet Russian Air Force (RKKVF) units were flying 43 such aircraft, and these were proving very reliable. A Royal Navy intelligence analysis of overseas Navies in 1922 credited the Russian Navy with ten D.H.9s at Gutuevskii Island, near Petrograd, believed dismantled.

In December 1921, a contract was signed for Russia to be supplied with 40 D.H.9s from Aircraft Disposal Company stocks and fitted with 260hp Mercedes engines, the latter having been smuggled out of Germany and stored in Sweden after the war. The airframes were shipped from London on board the Swedish freighter *Miranda*, arriving at Leningrad on 4 June 1922. They had the former RAF serials F1243, F1285, .2803, H5580, H5582, H5671, H5703, H5713, H5720, H5729, H5744, H5745, H5746, H5748, H5752, H5758, H5778, H5786, H5795, H5800, H5803, H5805, H5808, H5811, H5812, H5813, H5815, H5817, H5819, H5821, H5826, H5827, H5828, H5832, H5841, H5846, H9152, H9165, H9334 and H9350. H5817 was the first to be assembled, being tested on 14 August.

In May 1922 de Havilland supplied D.H.9A c/n 37 (RR Eagle) to Russia for evaluation, this being fitted with a Rolls-Royce Eagle VII, and is shown in VVS record as number 16105. Also supplied was D.H.34 c/n 33.

In 1923 20 D.H.9s with Puma engines and 10 D.H.9As with Liberty engines were bought in England by the Arcos Company from Aircraft Disposal Company stocks. The D.H.9As comprised E8802, F2866, F2870, H157, H158, H159, H160, H3457, H3647 and H3649, whilst the 20 D.H.9s included F1087, F1209, H5541, H5814, H9290, H9294 and H9329 - numbers 138, 168, 206 to 213, 255, 468 and 636 have also been quoted for this batch, but cannot be reconciled.

A Russian D.H.9A
(Alexandrov/Woodman)

An R.2 fitted with a German Hazet-type radiator.
(Alexandrov/Woodman)

The first 17 aircraft were shipped via Antwerp and Reval in the freighter *Saturn*, arriving in Leningrad in October 1923.

These were followed in August 1924 by 4 D.H.9As and 22 D.H.9s. The latter were all given British Certificates of Airworthiness on 1 July 1924, their former RAF serial numbers including H5855, H5864, H5880, H9242, H9250, H9252, H9260, H9275, H9278, H9283, H9285, H9297, H9298, H9302, H9309, H9311, H9313, H9330, H9341 and H9370.

D.H.9s were flown by the following units in varying numbers:
1st Otdel'naya razvedivatel'naya aviaeskadril'ya, Ukhtomskaya.
2nd Otdel'naya razvedivatel'naya aviaeskadril'ya, Vitebsk
5th Otdel'nyi razvedivatel'nyi aviaotryad, Gomel'.
3rd, 6th, 10th and 13th Otdel'nye razvedivatel'nye aviaotryady, Gomel'.
17th and 83rd Aviaotryady.
20th and 24th Aviaeskadrilii.
4th Otdel'nyi razvedivatel'nyi aviaotryad, Tashkent.

D.H.9s and D.H.9As were also used by training units, as follows:
1st Higher School of Military Pilots, Moscow.
2nd School of Military Pilots.
Strel'bom School.
Military School of Special Service.
Military-Technical School.
83rd Training Eskadril'ya.
Akademiya VVS.

In December 1923, 12 D.H.9As arrived at Khar'kov for local assembly. In April 1924 they were issued to the newly-formed Il'ich otryad, this unit being given Lenin's middle name. The aircraft were each given individual names, these including Chervonii vartovik podolii (Red Guard of the Podol'e), Donetskii shakhter (Donets Miner), Krasnyu Kievlyanin (Red Kiev Inhabitant), Nezamoshnik Odesshchiny (Odessa Pauper), Profsoyuzy Ekaterinoslavshchiny (Trade-Unions of Ekaterinoslav Region), Proletarii Odesshchiny (Odessa Protelarian), Samolet Sumshchiny (Aircraft of the Sumy Area), Shakhter Donbassa (Miner of the Donbass), Stalinskii proletarii (Stalin Protelarian), Ukrainskii chekist (Ukrainian Cheka Officer) and Yuzovskii proletarii (Yuzovska Proletarian). By the end of 1924, however, they had been replaced by Russian-built R-1s.

In 1925 the Mercedes-powered D.H.9s were withdrawn from use and handed over to the Dobrolet civil organisation, Of these, 11 were assembled, the remainder being reduced to spares. They were painted with large white individual numbers 1 to 11, the last being prefixed by Russian characters. Previous identities were respectively H9152, H5826, F1285, .2803, H5746, H5778, H5813, H9350, H5821, H5580 and H5817. They were initially tested for crop-dusting work, then re-assigned for photographic work, neither task being performed with a great deal of success. In 1928 the four survivors were given civil registrations CCCP-112 to CCCP-115 (respectively ex 2, 5, 7 and 8), and CCCP-116 was probably allotted to 11, though not taken up. An offer to Dobrolet in 1928 of 28 further D.H.9s was refused.

Double serial numbers were often assigned to Russian aircraft, one being the original s/n or c/n and the other a local number added by a repair shop after major repairs. These included

255/203, 255/204 (in 1924), 4621/204, 256/206, 266/207, 254/208, 258/209, 210, 211, 212, 213, 261/215, none of which can be reconciled with any former RAF D.H.9 or D.H.9A serial numbers.

Others are known to have included 84/1183 (D.H.9 in 10.23 (presumably ex D84), 138, 168, 468 (in 4.22), 619 (D.H.9 in 5.23), 620 (D.H.9 in 11.20, presumably ex D620), 636, 780 (D.H.9A in 2.23, possibly ex E780), 1087 (in 12.21, presumably ex F1087), 1143 (D.H.9 in 12.20, presumably ex D1143), 1209 (in 7.20, presumably ex F1209), 2089 (D.H.9A in 8.20), 5141 (D.H.9 in 5.2), 5415 ("DH9Mc" in 5.23), 5447 (D.H.9A in 10.23), 8982/246/54 (D.H.9 in 2.24) and 9193/5847 (in 10.23, presumably a combination of two aircraft).

R-1

In the meantime, the D.H.4 was superseded on the GAZ No.1 production lines by the D.H.9. The design although externally similar to the original, had been extensively reworked, being designated the R-1 when fitted with the Liberty engine and R-2 with the Puma, the latter designation being changed to R1-SP in 1926. A version fitted with a 400hp Russian M-5 copy of the Liberty engine is referred to as the R1-M5. At least 2,700 R-1 variants were built.

Two initial production R-1s presented to the RKKVF in Moscow on 29 June 1923 were given the names *Moskovskii bol'shevik* and *Izvestiya*. By 1924 production was under way at both GAZ No.1 in Moscow and GAZ No.10 at Taganrog, though well behind schedule. In January 1925 the first R1-M5 (c/n 2654) was test flown after being built in Leningrad by the *Bol'shevik* tractor factory. In June 1925 three aircraft and three reserves were allocated for use in proving flights from Moscow to Peking, these comprising R1-M5s R-RMPA, R-RMPB, R-RMPC (regn unconfirmed) and R-RMPD plus R1-SPs R-RMPE (c/n 2601, fitted with oval radiator) and R-RMPF (serial unconfirmed). In July 1926 RI-M5 R-RINT (c/n 2842) named *Krasnaya zvezda* (Red Star) made a goodwill flight to Ankara in Turkey, whilst RI-M5 R-ROST (c/n 2844) named *Iskra* (Spark) made a similar flight Teheran by way of Baku.

Various experimental modifications were made. The R1-LD was fitted with a 450hp Lorraine Dietrich engine driving a four-bladed propeller, but the performance proved to be inferior to the standard R-1. More successful was the R-1-BMV (R1-B4) built by the GAZ No.10 factory fitted with the 240hp BMW IVa for advanced training units, of which at least 84 were built (c/n's 598 to 610 and 693 to 763). A maritime reconnaissance variant with wooden floats was designated MR-1, at least 102 being built, being c/n's 3017, 3020, 3026 and 3030 by GAZ No.1 and 551 to 566 and 611 to 692 by GAZ No.10. A variation fitted with Muintzel-type floats was referred to as the PM-2.

Numerous aviaeskadrilii were equipped with R-1s, as follows:
Light attack - 50th, 52nd, 54th, 55th, 56th, 58th.
Light bomber - 35th, 38th, 39th, 40th, 42nd, 43rd, 44th, 46th.
Heavy bomber - 51st, 53rd, 55th, 57th, 59th, 61st.
Reconnaissance - 16th, 20th, 22nd, 24th, 26th, 28th, 31st, 32nd, 33rd, 34th, 36th.

Numerous training units received R-1s, most new aircraft being delivered to such units from about 1928.

MR-1 floatplanes began to enter service in 1927, equipping the 55th Aviaotryad at Nikolaev, the 62nd Aviaeskadriil'ya at Vasil'evskii ostrov, Leningrad, the 65th and 66th Aviaotryady at Sevatopol and Leningrad respectively, the 67th and 68th Rechnye aviaotryady (River Patrol Squadrons) at Kiev and Bochkarevo. They were also used for training at the 87th and 88th Training aviaotryay, and also at the School of Naval Pilots at Eisk.

From Jun 1929 numbers of R-1s were purchased from the VVS by Dobrolet for civil use, the first batch being registered CCCP-183 to CCCP-192 (c/n's 303, 308, 348, 350, 352, 360, 2953, 2980 and 3059). They were tested unsuccessfully in Central Asia for locust spraying. Later civil-registered aircraft were used for advanced training, newspaper matrice transport and various other tasks In August 1931 the civil R-1s were assigned the designation P-1.

SOUTH AFRICA

48 Puma-engined de Havilland D.H.9s were presented to the Union of South Africa as part of the Imperial Gift in 1919-1920; one additional aircraft was presented by the City of Birmingham. The aircraft serials were:
D638, D657, D659, D663, D665, D668, D670, D675, D677, D680, D681, D683, D687, D688, D690 D695, D698, D703, D705, H4313, H5544, H5545, H5562, H5570, H5581, H5583, H5586, H5593, H5601, H5608, H5611, H5631, H5639, H5644, [H5647?], H5648, [H5649?], 5651, H5657, H5659, H5667, H5669, H5670, H5685, H5687, H5689, H5692 and H5695; the additional aircraft was H9412. As with the D.H.4s (q.v.), these serial numbers were used until 1924 when the D.H.9s were allotted SAAF serials 101 to 119 (ex D-serialled D.H.9) and 121 to 150 (ex H-serialled D.H.9)

On 4 February 1920, Lt Col P van Ryneveld and Flt Lt Q Brand left Brooklands in a Vickers Vimy in an attempt to fly direct to Cape Town. They force landed in the Sudan on 11 February and had to return to Cairo where they left again in a second Vimy on 22nd. They reached Bulawayo on 5 March, but taking off next morning, the aircraft crashed into low hills. Urgent cables were sent to Pretoria to have one of the D.H.9 aircraft of the Imperial Gift erected for them to continue their flight. H5648 was taken out of its packing case, assembled and test flown on 6 March; it was flown up to Bulawayo on 16th and the following day van Ryneveld and Brand left on the final stages of their historic flight. Aptly named "Voortrekker" the D.H.9 flew via Johannesburg and Bloemfontein, reaching Cape Town on 20 March.

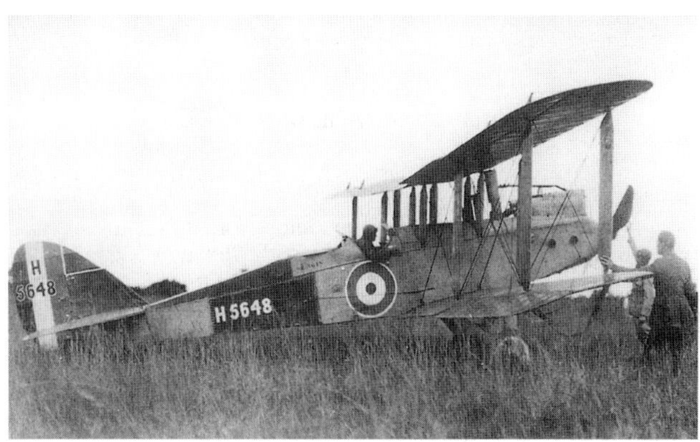

D.H.9 H5648 (later '101'), named 'Voortrekker', at Bulawayo in 1920. (via Ken Smy)

D.H.9 H5648 after becoming '101', with another D.H.9. (via Ken Smy)

By early 1922 only a few aircraft of the Imperial Gift had been erected including seven D.H.9s, with No.1 Squadron at Swartkop aerodrome near Pretoria. In March 1922, an industrial strike broke out in the Transvaal, becoming extremely violent, the strikers taking up arms, destroying property and services. The SAAF were called in to help the Police and Defence Force and carried out bombing and reconnaissance sorties on the "Revolutionaries". One aircraft was written off in an accident during these few days and several damaged by ground fire. Some three more D.H.9s were hastily assembled to replace the losses. Two months later, the SAAF sent three D.H.9 to South West Africa to assist the police in quelling disturbances in the area.

On 5 March 1924, an aircraft piloted by Capt CJ Venter DFC and Capt HC Daniel MC DFC flew from Pretoria to Capt Town, a distance of 1,000 miles, in 9 hours 45 minutes, to become the first aircraft to make this journey during daylight hours in one day.

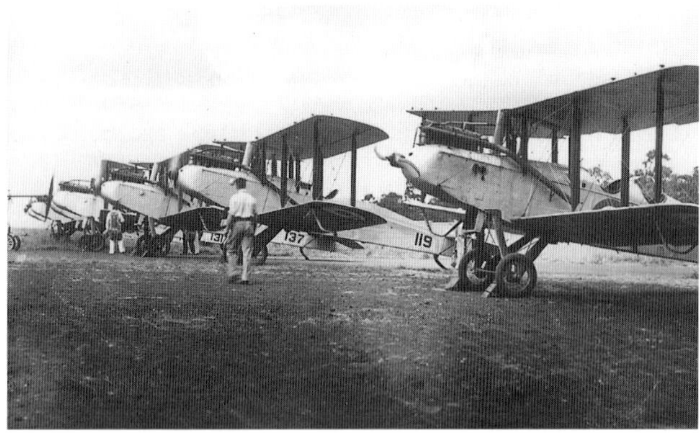

A line-up of Puma-engined South African D.H.9s.
(via Ken Smy)

Puma-engined South African D.H.9 139.
(via Gordon Swanborough)

Puma-engined South African D.H.9 143, marked
'CITY OF BIRMINGHAM - SOUTH AFRICA. (via Ken Smy)

South African D.H.9J 151.
(via Ken Smy)

Radial-engined South African D.H.9 157 with a divided axle.
via Gordon Swanborough)

Unserialled South African D.H.9 still in RAF colours.
(via Gordon Swanborough)

Civil D.H.9 ZS-AOE
(via Norman Franks)

Wingless D.H.9 ZS-AOJ on the street.
(via Ken Smy)

In March 1925, the Government introduced an experimental air mail service between Cape Town and Durban, via Port Elizabeth, timed to connect with the Union Castle mail ship's arrival and departure at Cape Town. This was operated by the SAAF who supplied personnel and ten D.H.9 aircraft for the service, the aircraft involved during the three months operation being 101, 106, 110, 113, 127, 129, 136, 137, 138 and 139.

In May 1925, the D.H.9s again flew up to South West Africa to assist in quelling another uprising in the Rehoboth Ovamboland region, one aircraft being written off in a landing accident. In the same year 139 was converted to take a hopper and used for aerial spraying of cotton and trees to eliminate the snout beetle and locusts. Also in that year, an experimental air mail service was started between Cape Town and Durban, 450lb of mail being carried on each flight.

Trials began in 1927 with a view to improving the performance of the D.H.4 and D.H.9 aircraft due to the high altitude of the Transvaal region. Two ADC Nimbus engines were bought and fitted into D.H.9s 114 and 141, the trials beginning in April 1927. One engine failed completely after a few hours but the other was flown in various D.H.9s until as late as 1936 when it was recorded as fitted in D.H.9 137 at the Central Flying School. D.H.9s 138 and 147 were fitted with the Jupiter VI engine and known as the Mpala in SAAF service, the first of these flying in March 1928. These four Mpala aircraft flew north to Khartoum in May 1928, where they met with an RAF flight and carried out joint operations in Kenya.

This joint co-operational exercise was repeated in 1929, but was not so rewarding. Mpala 153 crashed on taking off at Salisbury, whilst later in the flight, Mpala 153 was hit by a vulture in the Nimule area and then seriously damaged in the ensuing forced landing.

The more powerful Jupiter VIII engine was fitted in several D.H.9s in 1929 for trials to improve performance. Eight aircraft were selected for conversion but only five were completed before the project was terminated in 1930. The aircraft selected are believed to have been 104, 112, 116, 130, 132, 134, 144 and 148 although 127 and 137 are also recorded as having been earmarked for conversion.

The D.H.9 remained in service until August 1937 when seven aircraft were with CFS at Swartkop. In December they were offered for sale to local Flying Clubs for a nominal sum. These aircraft, nos.108, 114, 118, 119, 131 and 141 were allotted civil registrations ZS-AOD to ZS-AOJ, but no record has as yet been found of the serial tie ups. ZS-AOE and ZS-AOI were impressed in 1940 and given new serials 2001 and 2005, but were soon relegated to ground instructional use and allotted serials IS7 and IS8. The latter was transferred in 1943 to the South African War Museum, where it is still on display today.

A number of South African D.H.9s were fitted with a 200hp Wolseley Viper engines, reserialled and unofficially named the D.H. Mantis. The aircraft concerned were *157* to *167*, converted respectively from D.H.9 numbers 104, 112, 116, 130, 144, 132, 134, 148, 202, 205 and 206.

[See also South African D.H.4s]

Known military histories:
101 (ex D683) No.1 Sqn 1920; FTS 6.26; Crashed 19.4.32
102 No.1 Sqn 1920; Crashed Balfour 12.10.23
103 No.1 Sqn 1920; Crashed 13.1.23
104 (ex D668) No.1 Sqn 1923; Converted to Mantis *157*
105 (ex D677) No.1 Sqn 1923; Crashed 21.12.29
106 (ex D675) No.1 Sqn 1923; FTS 12.29; Crashed 12.1.37
107 (ex D690) No.1 Sqn 1923; FTS 3.31; Crashed Bethal 25.6.32
108 (ex D681) No.1 Sqn 1923; FTS 6.31; Sold 12.37
109 (ex D695) No.1 Sqn 1923; FTS 3.31; Crashed
110 (ex D698) No.1 Sqn 1923; Crashed 19.12.32
111 (ex D657) No.1 Sqn 1923; Crashed 19.9.35
112 No.1 Sqn 1925; FTS 3.26; Converted to Mantis *158*
113 No.1 Sqn 1925; FTS 3.29; Mid-air collision with Avro 504, crashed 21.3.31
114 (ex D703) No.1 Sqn 1925; FTS 6.29; Sold 12.37
115 No.1 Sqn 1925; Crashed 18.7.35
116 No.1 Sqn 1925; Converted to Mantis *159*
117 (ex D638) No.1 Sqn 1926; FTS 6.30; Crashed
118 (ex D665) No.1 Sqn 1926; FTS 12.29; Sold 12.37
119 No.1 Sqn 1931; Sold 12.37
121 (ex H5648) No.1 Sqn 1920; Crashed 12.3.22
122 (ex H5631) No.1 Sqn 1920; Crashed SW Africa 10.6.22
123 No.1 Sqn 1920; Crashed 18.4.23
124 No.1 Sqn 1922; FTS 3.31; Crashed Swartkop 15.6.36
125 No.1 Sqn 1923; Crashed 16.3.37
126 (ex H5586) No.1 Sqn 1923
127 No.1 Sqn 1924; FTS 3.26; Crashed Converted to Mantis?
128 No.1 Sqn 1924; Crashed 26.3.25
129 (ex H5647) No.1 Sqn 1924; FTS 9.31; Mid-air collision with Avian 522, crashed 5.8.33
130 No.1 Sqn 1925; Converted to Mantis *160*
131 (ex H5611) No.1 Sqn 1925; FTS 3.31; Sold 12.37
132 (ex H5601) No.1 Sqn 1925; Converted to Mantis *162* (not completed
133 No.1 Sqn 1925; FTS 9.31; Crashed 29.4.36 Hartbeespoorte Dam
134 (ex H5659) No.1 Sqn 1924; FTS 3.29; Converted to Mantis *163* (not completed)
135 No.1 Sqn 1924; Crashed
136 No.1 Sqn 1932; Crashed 8.6.34
137 (ex H5562) No.1 Sqn 6.25; FTS 12.26; Sold 12.37
138 No.1 Sqn 6.25 FTS 3.26; Crashed 24.6.37; Converted to Mpala *155*
139 (ex H5692) No.1 Sqn 6.25; FTS 12.26; Crashed 11.3.27
140 No.1 Sqn 12.28; FTS 3.30; Crashed
141 No.1 Sqn 9.27; FTS 6.29; Sold 12.37
142 No.1 Sqn 6.25; FTS 3.30
143 (ex H9412) No.1 Sqn 6.26; FTS 6.30; Crashed
144 No.1 Sqn 6. 25; Converted to Mantis *161*
145 (ex H5608) Crashed 15.5.25
146 No.1 Sqn 3.26; Crashed 4.6.35?
147 No.1 Sqn 9.26; Converted to Mpala 156
148 No.1 Sqn 9.26; Crashed Parys 25.4.28
149 No.1 Sqn 12.26; FTS 6.30; Crashed Swartkop 13.11.30
150 No.1 Sqn 3.27; Crashed Standerton 21.3.31
151 204 No.1 Sqn 6.27; FTS 6.31; To 68 AS as GI *258* SOC
152 208 No.1 Sqn 6.27; FTS 6.32; Crashed Randjesfontein 3.11.33
153 201 No.1 Sqn 9.28; Crashed Nimule 21.3.29
154 203 No.1 Sqn 9.28; Cape Town 6.30; Crashed Alexander Bay 1929
155 138 No. 1 Sqn 12.28; Cape Town 3.30; Crashed Salisbury 21.3.29: Rebuilt
156 147 No.1 Sqn 12.28; Cape Town 3.30; Forced landed 4.9.30
157 104 No.1 Sqn 12.28; Crashed 16.3.30
158 No.1 Sqn 3.30
159 No.1 Sqn 9.30
160 No.1 Sqn
161 Cape Town 6.30

Sold for civil use in 12.37:
ZS-AOD Pretoria Light Aero Club reg 2.7.38; Reduced to spares 8.5.39
ZS-AOE Rand Flying Club 2.6.38; To SAAF as 2001 1940
ZS-AOF Rand Flying Club; Reg not taken up ?
ZS-AOG Border Flying Club 24.8.38; Wfu and scrapped 4.4.39
ZS-AOH African Flying Services; Reg not taken up?
ZS-AOI African Flying Services 30.6.38; To SAAF as 2005 1940
ZS-AOJ Natal Aviation 18.7.38; Scrapped.

SPAIN

On 13 May 1919 an air exhibition held at Cuatro Vientos (Madrid) involved several types of British military aircraft, these including a D.H.9 (piloted by Mr Hereward de Havilland) and a D.H.4 (piloted by Captain H.H.Square with Lt Anderson as observer). The D.H.9 is believed to be C6078 fitted with the prototype 430hp Lion engine, which arrived at Barcelona by sea and was then transported by rail to Madrid for assembly. The D.H.4 arrived by air.

The Spanish authorities were sufficiently satisfied with these two types to place an order for either 22 or 23 aircraft (the precise number varying in different sources), of which only four or five were D.H.9s. The aircraft received tail numbers and a registration comprising the type code M-MH (Madrid-Militar Havilland), plus two individual letters - e.g. D.H.4 No.1 M-MHAA, No.14 M-MHAN etc. In 1926 the type code was changed from M-MH to '15'.

In July 1921 the Spanish Army suffered a great disaster at Anual in Spanish Morocco at the hand of the Rif tribesmen, leading to a political crisis. As a consequence collections were held throughout Spain for funds to acquire more aircraft. Some 40 were then ordered, of which about 30 were D.H.4s and the remainder D.H.9s, most being named after the provinces or towns which had collected funds for them (e.g. D.H.4 No.47 *Cartagena*, No.48

Avila etc). It appears that in all sixteen D.H.9s were bought between 1919 and 1921. The aircraft acquired from Britain received tail numbers markings Nos.1 to 62. They were provided by the Aircraft Disposal Company, of which Captain Square was their representative in Madrid.

In addition to the imported aircraft, deliveries of licence-built aircraft by Hispano-Suiza began in 1922 with a batch of 8 D.H.9As equipped with 450hp Napier Lion engines, these receiving tail Nos.63 to 70 of which two were presentation aircraft (No.64 *Granada* and No.65 *Badajoz*). Production continued from No.71 onwards, ending in 1929, and totalling some 120 aircraft, with the highest tail number recorded being No.189. They formed six reconnaissance Squadrons (Grupos 21 and 23). When the Breguet XIX entered service as a replacement, they were relegated to the Training School at Cuatro Vientos and the Bombing School at Los Alcazares (Murcia).

Fitted with twin rear guns, D.H.9A G-EBAN was supplied to the Spanish Air Force early in 1922. (via Philip Jarrett)

Civil use

A further four aircraft were acquired for civil use:

M-AAAG D.H.9C c/n DH9C/11. Regd 2.22 to Cia Espanola del Trafico Aereo; Deld ex DH 19.9.21 and ex Croydon 23.9.21.

M-AAGA D.H.9C c/n DH9C/12. Regd 2.22 to Cia Espanola del Trafico Aereo; Deld ex DH 19.9.21 and ex Croydon 23.9.21; Still active with CETA 3.29, being flown by Mr FW Hatchett on Seville-Larache route.

M-AGAA D.H.9C c/n DH9C/13. Regd 10.22 to Cia Espanola del Trafico Aereo; Deld ex DH 7.10.21. Later became *EC-AQA*

M-AGAG see G-EAUN

[See also comments under G-EAUI, G-EAXG, G-EBAN]

D.H.9C M-AAGA was flown by CETA for several years

M-AAAG, M-AAGA and *M-AGAA* were bought by Compania Espanola de Trafico Aereo to cover the air mail service between Sevilla and Larache (Spanish Morocco), which constituted the first Spanish regular airline, and were named *Algeciras*, *Sevilla* and *Larache*, but it is not known in which order. The first flight was made on 15 October 1921 by *Sevilla*, piloted by Jack Hatchett, carrying three passengers. In addition to Hatchett, two other pilots, Wolley Dodd and Sidney St.Barbe, had been hired for one year of service. The latter two were then substituted by Spanish pilots, but Jack Hatchett remained with the line for several years. The D.H.9s, later joined by *M-AGAG*, remained in service until 1926, making an average of 300 flights per year. The open-cockpit D.H.9B was converted to the enclosed-cockpit D.H.9C variant in 1933.

Military service in Africa

The *Grupo de Escuadrillas* No.1 was formed in Spanish Morocco on January 1920, being based at Tetuan (*Escuadrilla* No.1), Zeluan (No.2) and Larache (No.3). The first squadron had a mix of different types, and the other two comprised only D.H.4s. At first they were just used for reconnaissance, but as the situation deteriorated they began bombing and strafing sorties. Five D.H.4s were lost in accidents during 1920, resulting in the death of two airmen and injuries to a further two.

In the summer of 1921, No.2 Squadron from Zeluan (six D.H.4s commanded by Captain Pio Fernandez Mulero) found itself involved in the events leading to the Anual disaster. On 20 June one of its aircraft crashed, the crew, Lieutenant Ramon Ostariz and Corporal Antonio de Cabo, being killed. On 21 June the remaining five aircraft (piloted by Captains Fernandez and Garcia-Munoz and Lieutenants Ruano, Vivanco and Barron) carried out 15 bombing sorties, and 14 more next day, dropping a total of 1,000kg of bombs over the two days. Every morning the crews travelled from Melilla to the airfield carrying with them the bombs for the day's missions.

A D.H.9 in Spanish Morocco, helping to contain Riff uprisings. It has a Lion engine with a large underslung radiator. The rear cockpit mounts an unusually large gun, and the aircraft appears to be fully bombed up. (via J.M.Bruce)

On 23 July all five pilots took off early in the morning to bomb Moorish columns attacking Dar Driux, the leader aircraft receiving eight hits from small-arms. At 14.30hrs they repeated the mission, this time in support of the position at Tuguntz; in the low-level attack all five aircraft received hits, the observer of the leading aircraft (Lieutenant Luis Montalt) being seriously wounded. Despite these efforts, the Moorish forces of Abd-el-Krim advanced swiftly, and in the early morning of 24 July the Zeluan airfield, defended by some 50 infantry under Lieutenant Martinez Vivanco, was surrounded by the enemy. The defenders held their ground for a week, but on 2 August they were overrun and annihilated, all five D.H.4s being burnt at the last moment to avoid capture.

All available aircraft were then rushed to stem the Moorish offensive, and on the same day as the fall of Zeluan a detachment of five D.H.4s commanded by Captain Saenz de Buruaga landed at Melilla, these being Nos.14, 15, 16, 19 and 23. Several air-supply flights were made to the besieged position of Monte Arruit until it fell on 10 August. No.16 (Lts Hidalgo and Gonzalez-Gil) was wrecked when it hit a car during landing, the crew suffering slight injuries. In the autumn of 1921, No.19 (Sgt Campo and Lt Bellod) accidentally hit the cable of a Caquot blimp and crashed inverted, the crew being slightly injured.

A second squadron arrived on 13 October under the command of Captain Moreno Abella, and a third during November (Captain Joaquin Gonzalez Gallarza). All D.H.4s and D.H.9s in Morocco were now integrated into Grupo No.3. Losses to small-arms fire during this period were heavy, three D.H.9s being shot down in a single day on 22 December during an operation to occupy enemy strongholds at Tetuan and Larache; all three were destroyed in crashes or forced landings after being hit, but there were no fatalities among the crews (Capt Buseta/Capt Arizon, Capt Arrion/Capt Ureba and Lt Hidalgo/Lt Bellod).

Early in 1922 the Spanish air forces in Africa were reorganised as follows:

Grupo No.1. Sania Ramel A/F (Tetuan), two squadrons of Breguet XIV

Grupo No.2. Auamara A/F (Larache), two squadrons of Breguet XIV

Grupo No.3. Tauima A/F (Melilla), three squadrons of D.H.4s

Grupo No.4. Tauima A/F (Melilla), one squadron of D.H.9As and two of Bristol F.2bs.

All four Grupos carried out many hundreds of sorties during the next three years of Spanish counter-offensive. Of the five Spanish aircraft shot down by the enemy during 1922, one was a D.H.9. In the following year losses in combat were eight aircraft (including 3 D.H.4s and 1 D.H.9), and losses in accidents a further nine aircraft (including 4 D.H.4s and 2 D.H.9s).

1924 saw the heaviest fighting to date. During February and March fighting centred around the Spanish positions of Issen Lasen and Tizzi Assa. The concentration of enemy machine guns in this area made it impossible to fly below 200 metres without being hit. On 23 March the D.H.4s destroyed on the ground the only aircraft of the insurgents, a two-seater Caudron G.III bought by their leader Abd-el-Krim. During this mission Lieutenant Juan Antonio Ansaldo, in aircraft No.52, won the highest Spanish medal for valour, the Cruz Laureada de San Fernando, for continuing his attack and force-landing at Tafersit despite severe wounds which kept him off flying duties for seven months.

On 7 May, the Air Force made the most concentrated effort of the whole campaign in support of Legion columns which attempted to relieve the surrounded position of Sidi Messaud: the eight squadrons of Eastern Morocco made an average of 6 sorties per aircraft.

On 5 July a D.H.4 was hit several times during a supply sortie to the position of Koba Darsa; pilot Captain Eduardo Gonzalez Gallarza was wounded in the right arm and thigh, force-landing at Uad Lau and saving himself and his observer Captain Mariano Barberan.

Owing to the serious military situation in the sector of Tetuan, Grupo No.3 (Captain Jose Carrillo) arrived on 2 September from Melilla as reinforcements and immediately become heavily engaged. Just two days later Carrillo landed his D.H.4 at Tetuan with his observer (Captain Angel Orduna) killed by enemy ground fire, and in the next three weeks Captains Luengo, Garcia Gracia and Altolaguirre and two air gunners were all killed in operations. Finally on 28 September the Group commander Captain Carrillo lost his life together with Corporal Jose Amat when their D.H.4 was shot down. The Group was then sent to Larache to rest.

The Napier-engined D.H.9As of Grupo No.4 kept covering the bloody retreat from Xauen. On 26 September, three aircraft took off from Auamara to attack positions at Tahar Berda. One of them, No.63 (Captain Gomez-Spencer and Captain Ramon Ochando) was hit, and observer Ochando seriously wounded in the thigh, but he insisted on keeping over the target until all bombs and ammunition were expended. When they force-landed at Sania Ramel, Ochando had already collapsed from loss of blood, dying on 12 October at Tetuan; he was posthumously awarded the Cruz Laureada. On 8 December a D.H.4 on a strafing sortie was hit and set on fire by small arms, crashing in the attempted forced-landing, the pilot, Lieutenant Jose Diaz being killed and his observer, Captain Sanz, injured. In all, 24 Spanish aircraft were shot down by ground fire during 1924, 8 of them being D.H.4s.

In March 1925 the surviving D.H.4s and D.H.9s were sent back to Granada, in Southern Spain, but they returned to Africa in time to take part in the big amphibious operation at Alhucemas. The war in Africa turned decisively against Abd-el-Krim with the landing at Alhucemas which started on 8 September. The operation involved 104 aircraft, including 6 D.H.4s and 4 D.H.9s of Grupo No.3, and in the first day D.H.9 No.68 was shot down over Cala Bonita, the crew (Capt Rodriguez and Sgt Nunez) being picked up form the sea by a French torpedo boat, this being the only total loss of a Napier-engined aircraft. On 20 September 1925, D.H.4 No.69 (Sgt Amoras & Ly Iglesias) was shot down over Malmusi, but fortunately the crew were picked up from the sea by a merchant ship. Total losses in combat during 1925 were 14 aircraft, including two D.H.4s and a D.H.9. 1926 saw only minor operations, no aircraft being lost in action.

With the war in Morocco all but finished, the few surviving D.H.4s were struck off charge in February 1927. One squadron of D.H.9s was still based in Eastern Morocco during the last military action of the campaign, the Senhaya uprising of March to May 1927, but it took no part in the combats.

All in all, during the period 1920-1927 the Spanish Air Force in Africa lost 131 aircraft. Of these, 34 were D.H.4s (13 lost in combat, 16 in accidents, 5 on the ground) and 14 D.H.9s (9 in combat, 5 in accidents). The D.H.4 losses were extremely heavy (34 aircraft destroyed out of 46 acquired), but this type was most appreciated by airmen due to its reliability in the difficult conditions in which they were forced to operate in Africa.

On 4 March 1928, the seven surviving D.H.9As of Grupo No.4 (Captain Felix Martinez) were the first aircraft deployed to the Spanish Sahara (Cabo Juby airfield). They were struck off charge during 1930-31.

Civil War 1936-39

About 40 D.H.9s were still in flying condition in July 1936. At least 21 were based at Los Alcazares (province of Murcia). With the code RH (Reconocimiento Havilland), some Republican D.H.9s saw combat during 1936. On 1 August, three aircraft were transferred to Guadix airfield (province of Granada) and took part in bombing and reconnaissance sorties until 25 August. Two other D.H.9s were reported to have flown with the Alas Rolas squadron in Aragon during 1936, but this is a mis-identification as they were in fact two D.H.87 Hornet Moths used for liaison duties. After 1936 the D.H.9s were used as trainers. Only one Republican D.H.9 was recovered by the Nationalists in a flying condition in April 1939.

During the first weeks of the war, four Republican D.H.9s defected from the airfield of Alcala and landed in Nationalist territory; they received codes 34-10, 34-11, 34-12 and 34-14, so by this time nine aircraft were presumably already under Nationalist control. A total of 18 eventually joined Franco's forces and constituted Grupo 34 (Training) at El Copero (province of Sevilla). They received codes 34-1 to 34-19 (34-13 being omitted as 'unlucky'). In the Summer of 1937, the Flying School at El Copero still had five on charge (34-2, 34-4, 34-6, 34-7 and 34-9). Others were still flying with the Conversion School at Jerez de la Frontera in March 1938. In 1939 34-10 and 34-14 were still available, 34-14 not being struck off charge until late 1940.

Resume of Spanish military D.H.4s/D.H.9s

Nos.1 to 62:	62 aircraft acquired 1919/1921 (46 D.H.4s + 16 D.H.9s).
Nos.63 to 70:	8 D.H.9As (Napier-engined) built (assembled?) by Hispano-Suiza.
Nos.71 to 189?:	About 120 D.H.9s built by Hispano-Suiza.

Three-seater D.H.9 G-EAZH became CH-81 on being sold in Switzerland duriing 1922. (MAP)

SWITZERLAND

Four D.H.9s were supplied to Switzerland for civil use. Two went to Alfred Comte in December 1921, being registered CH-82 (ex G-EAYY) and CH-83 (ex G-EAYZ), and the other two in February 1922 to As Astra Aero AG registered CH-81 (ex G-EAZH) and CH-84 (ex G-EAZI).
[NOTE - One source refers to CH-81 to CH-83 as [becoming?] 709 to 711; Also 706 as a D.H.9A supplied in 1920]

TURKEY

Some D.H.4s or D.H.9s reported as supplied to Turkey, but nothing has been found to support this contention.

URUGUAY

One Puma-engined D.H.9 was supplied to the Uruguayan Army, it being written off on 28 February 1928.

U.S.A.

A number of D.H.9s were supplied for use by the U.S.Marine Corps' Day Wing, Northern Bombing Group in France and numbered E-1 to at least E-22 [see under D.H.4].
The following are known:

E-1 (ex E8465)	Squadron A; Later Squadron C
E-2 (ex E8477)	Squadron A; Later Squadron C 15.11.18
E-3 (ex E8466)	Squadron A; Later Squadron B, crashed Ghistelles 11.18
E-4 (ex E8472)	Squadron A, crashed
E-5 (ex E8475)	Squadron A; Later Squadron B
E-6 (ex E8480)	Squadron A; Later Squadron B
E-7 (ex E8476)	Squadron A; Later Squadron B
E-8 (ex E8469)	Squadron A; Later Squadron B
E-9 (ex E8467)	Squadron A; Later Squadron B
E-10 (ex E8507)	Squadron A; Later Squadron B
E-11 (ex E8502)	Squadron C; Later Squadron B
E-12 (ex E8504)	FTR 17.11.18, retd 23.11.18
E-13 (ex E8506)	Squadron C; Later Squadron B
E-14 (ex E8539)	Squadron C, crashed Knesselare 21.11.18
E-15 (ex E8538)	Squadron C
E-16 (ex E8540)	Squadron C
E-17 (ex E9874)	Squadron C, received after Armistice
E-18 (ex E8478)	Squadron C
E-19 (ex E8501)	Squadron C
E-20 (ex E8542)	Squadron C
E-21 (ex E8541)	Squadron C, wrecked 16.11.18 (Lt Fleer)
E-22 (ex E8540 - but see E.16). Squadron C	

Also supplied were E736 to E741, E8450 to E8455, E8463, E8470, E8503, E8505, E8542 to E8545, E8565 to E8568, E8570, E8571, E8583, E8632 to E8635, E9868 to E9873, E9875, E9876.

The 28th Aero Sqn of the United States Air Service in France had a mixture of D.H.4s and D.H.9s. On 11.6.18, the Headquarters Flight ("18 Misc") was at Alquines with D.H.9s (attd 206 Sqn), 'A' Flt was at Ruisseauville with D.H.9 (attached 98 Sqn RAF), 'B' Flt was at at Serny with D.H.4s (attached 18 Sqn RAF) and 'C' Flt was at Ruisseauville with D.H.4s (attached 25 Sqn RAF). No individual serials are known.

Sample D.H.9 C6058 was marked P-12 at McCook Field. (via D.M.Hannah)

US ARMY SERIAL NUMBERS

USD-9

In the United States before deliveries of the DH-4 began, production of an American version of the D.H.9 was planned as a replacement, with the basic designation USD-9. As the American design progressed and a prototype was under construction, plans were changed to produce the D.H.9A. In early 1918 when a sample D.H.9A was actually needed, D.H.9 C6058 was received from England. Without a sample D.H.9A, the American USD-9 design was developed independently by the Airplane Engineering Division at McCook Field, Dayton, Ohio, and differed from the D.H.9A in many details. A series of 13 prototypes was built in 1918 and 1919 under three designations, and 4,000 production USD-9As were ordered from Curtiss on 1 November 1918, but were cancelled after the Armistice.

The Factory Department at McCook Field delivered the first prototype USD-9 bomber, 40026, in July 1918. The design was almost immediately modified to increase the fuel supply and to more closely match features of the D.H.9A, this version designated the USD-9A. McCook Field completed four of this model, A.S.40060-40063, during the last three months of the war as production samples. Of these, the last two were shipped to France for evaluation by the Air Service of the American Expeditionary Force. Four USD-9As ordered from Dayton-Wright in mid-1918, A.S.40044 and A.S.40066-40068, were delivered in the spring of 1919.

A.S.40060 (P-43) was the first of four USD-9As built at McCook Field. (via Gordon Swanborough)

In June 1918, Dayton-Wright had received an order for an observation version and two were built before the Armistice, these being A.S.40042 and A.S.40043, which were designated USD-9 even though this model number had previously been assigned to the first prototype bomber. However, plans to build the observation model in quantity were cancelled before the Armistice.

Late in 1918, two additional special machines were ordered from McCook Field. To increase the bomber's carrying capacity, A.S.40119 was delivered in early 1919 with additional wing area and was designated the USD-9AB. Lastly, a fuselage used in 1918 in the McCook shop was completed in the summer of 1919 as a flyable machine, A.S.40118, with a modified landing gear.

USD-9A A.S.40118 (P-80) was fitted with an early form of pressure cabin. (via Gordon Swanborough)

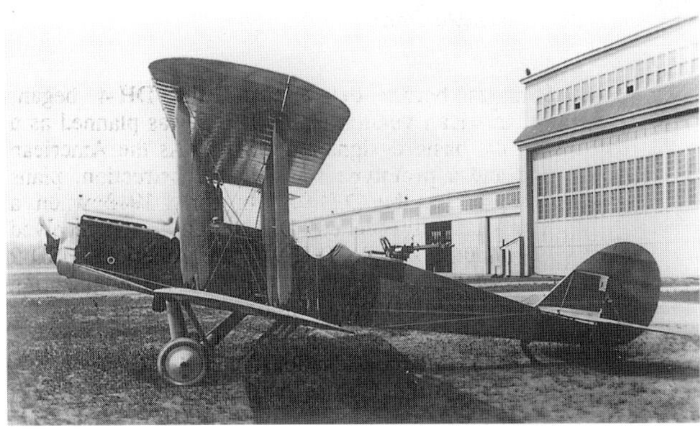

This USD-9A built by the Airplane Engineering Division at McCook Field was fitted with a rounded rudder. (via Gordon Swanborough)

After the Armistice, D.H.9A E.8449 was received from England, apparently for performance comparison with the USD-9A.

In the postwar period, the USD-9A could not meet specifications for the new Type XI Day Bombardment type and most surviving machines were used at McCook Field for general test work. The last was removed from service by 1924.

Known individual details

A.S.40026 USD-9 built by McCook Field 7.18, McCook Field plane P-36; Crashed near McCook 30.7.18

A.S.40042 USD-9 built by Dayton-Wright 8.18, McCook Field plane P-40; Parachute testing at McCook 1919, burned at McCook 30.11.20

A.S.40043 USD-9 built by Dayton-Wright 10.18, McCook Field plane P-45; Engine failure at 1,200ft, forced landed 2m NE of Rochester, Ohio, but the pilot was blinded by smoke from a fire and crashed, completely wrecked 30.12.20 (2/Lt L Wade unhurt)

A.S.40044 USD-9A built by Dayton-Wright 3.19, McCook Field plane P-64; Out of service by 1.2.22

A.S.40060 USD-9A built by McCook Field 8.18, McCook Field plane P-43; Official type performance tests October 1918 at Wilbur Wright Field, Dayton, Ohio; Postwar tests at McCook of a 37mm cannon mounted on rear cockpit; Active 1.2.22; Surveyed 1.8.22

A.S.40061 USD-9A built by McCook Field about 10.18, McCook Field plane P-47; To Curtiss as production sample 29.10.18

A.S.40062 USD-9A built by McCook Field about 10.18, McCook Field plane P-50; Shipped to AEF for evaluation 4.11.18. Returned to U.S. 1919; Stored

A.S.40063 USD-9A built by McCook Field about 10.18. Shipped to AEF for evaluation 4.11.18; Returned to U.S. 1919. Stored

A.S.40066 USD-9A built by Dayton-Wright 4.19; To Bolling Field, DC, 19.4.19

A.S.40067 USD-9A built by Dayton-Wright 4.19, McCook Field plane P-71; Transferred to Bolling Field, DC, 1.6.19; To McCook 12.2.24; To Fairborne Aviation Intermediate Depot 24.5.24

A.S.40068 USD-9A built by Dayton-Wright about 4.19, McCook Field plane
P-74; Active 1.2.22; Wrecked near Selfridge Field, Mich; Awaiting disposition 21.9.23

A.S.40118 USD-9A built by McCook Field about July 1919, McCook Field plane P-80; In Toronto-New York race summer of 1919; Landing gear tested at Wilbur Wright Field, Dayton, Ohio, 10.19; First pressurised cabin installed 1921; Active 1.2.22; In McCook Field Museum 1.1.24

A.S.40119 USD-9AB built by McCook Field about 3.19, McCook Field plane P-60; Wrecked at Toledo, Ohio, 3.7.19

Members of the Army Air Service preparing to jump off the wings of a USD-9A during parachute tests. (via Philip Jarrett)

DH REBUILDS

The following has been extracted from DH Records.

DH Stag Lane D.H.9A conversions/refurbishments for RAF

Batch c/n 17-24, all fitted with Lions:
E8788 c/n 17 deld Waddon 3.12.21
E979 c/n 18 deld Waddon 6.12.21
E8780 c/n 19 deld Waddon 14.12.21
H3650 c/n 20 deld Waddon 14.12.21
E8782 c/n 21 deld Waddon 19.12.21.
E989 c/n 22 deld Waddon 22.12.21.
F2869 c/n 23 deld Waddon 27.12.21.
H3646 c/n 24 deld Waddon 2.2.22

Batch c/n 46-55; engines not fitted:
E8652 c/n 46
E8615 c/n 47
E8622 c/n 48
E8610 c/n 49
J560 c/n 50
J555 c/n 51
H2430 c/n 52
H3486 c/n 53
J554 c/n 54
H3432 c/n 55

H147 c/n 67
H143 c/n 68
H141 c/n 69
H145 c/n 70
E863 c/n 71
E9690 c/n 72
E8592 c/n 78
E925 c/n 79
H3520 c/n 80
H657 c/n 81 Fitted with Liberty and deld Gosport.

Batches reconditioned and given new serials:
J7008 c/n 88 ex "H34B"
J7009 c/n 89 ex E861
J7010 c/n 90 ex H3496
J7011 c/n 91 ex H3397
J7012 c/n 92 ex E857
J7013 c/n 93 ex H111
J7014 c/n 94 ex H126
J7015 c/n 95 ex H128
J7016 c/n 96 ex E859
J7017 c/n 97 ex E960

J7302 c/n 119 ex H3617
J7303 c/n 120 ex H3581
J7304 c/n 121 ex F2828
J7305 c/n 122 ex H3595
J7306 c/n 123 ex E8710
J7307 c/n 124 ex E8700
J7308 c/n 125 ex E8699
J7309 c/n 126 ex E8702

Reconditioning Job No.P414:
E8694 c/n 140
E9951 c/n 141
F2818 c/n 142
J561 c/n 143
H3541 c/n 144
H3550 c/n 145
J7034 c/n 146
F979 c/n 147
H3506 c/n 148
E8725 c/n 149
H138 c/n 150
E828 c/n 153
E8655 c/n 154
E8744 c/n 155
E8805 c/n 156
E8758 c/n 157
H3630 c/n 159
H88 c/n 160
E8761 c/n 161
J7117 c/n 162
E9918 c/n 163
J7038 c/n 164
H3566 c/n 165
E777 c/n 166
E7700 c/n 167

Reconditioning Contract No 579165/25 [DH Job No P886]:
F2842 c/n 170
E805 c/n 171
E911 c/n 172
E8755 c/n 173
E8689 c/n 174
E887 c/n 175
E785 c/n 176
E8637 c/n 177
E8754 c/n 178
E3643 c/n 179
J7030 c/n 180
J7607 c/n 222
E959 c/n 223
J7356 c/n 224
E8728 c/n 225
J6964 c/n 226
J7058 c/n 227
J7122 c/n 228
E969 c/n 229
E789 c/n 230
E9951 c/n 231
J7606 c/n 232
H3520 c/n 252
J7028 c/n 253
E8759 c/n 254
F1023 c/n 255
E9891 c/n 256
E788 c/n 257
J7048 c/n 258

Reconditioning Contract No 623200/25 [First 9 fitted with Liberty, rest without engines] [DH Job No P672]
J7787 to J7798c/n's 202-213

Contract No; 640049/25 [DH Job No P778 - without engines]
J7877 to J7883c/n's 214-220

Contract No.700821/25 [or 700821/26] [DH Job No W830 - without engines]
J8129 c/n 221
J8130 c/n 259
J8131 to J8153c/n 286-308 [J8148/53 fitted metal wings]

Contract No.726079/26
E8596 c/n 309
E8805 c/n 310
F2847 c/n 311
J7809 c/n 312
J7605 c/n 313
J7083 c/n 314
J7047 c/n 315 [fitted dual control]
F1641 c/n 316

Contract 760139/27 [First four all dual-control]
J7081 c/n 317
J8641 c/n 318
J8473 c/n 319
J7009 c/n 320
J7059 c/n 321
J8666 c/n 322

Reconditioned D.H.9s by DH and supposedly supplied to Dutch Government [packed by Cox's]

476 c/n 56 deld 10.1.23
477 c/n 57 deld 17.1.23.
482 c/n 58 deld 17.1.23
479 c/n 59 deld 6.1.23
480 c/n 60 deld 8.1.23
481 c/n 61 deld 8.1.23
478 c/n 62 deld 9.1.23
483 c/n 63 deld 9.1.23
484 c/n 64 deld 10.1.23
485 c/n 65 deld 10.1.23

D.H.4 - INDEX OF RNAS/RFC/RAF NAMES

Note. Where only a date is given, this relates to the list of unidentified incidents.

The pilot's cockpit of a RFC/RAF D.H.4. (via Terry Treadwell)

D.H.9 & D.H.9A - INDEX OF RNAS/RFC/RAF NAMES

Note. Where only a date is given, this relates to the list of unidentified incidents.

An atmospheric shot of a D.H.9A coming in at dusk. (via Mick Davis)

RFC/RNAS/RAF D.H.4, D.H.9 and D.H.9A SQUADRONS AND UNITS

No.3 Squadron

Reformed 1.10.21 from the Mobile Flight of No.202 Squadron as a Naval Air Co-operation unit with D.H.9As and Westland Walruses; to Gosport 4.22 (one flight temp to Leuchars by 9.22, also using Novar); D.H.9As withdrawn 10.22, possibly handed over to No.210 Sqn.

COMMANDING OFFICER
Sqn Ldr DG Donald DFC AFC 1.10.21 - 10.22

No.8 Squadron

Reformed 18.10.20 as Day Bomber squadron at Helwan, Egypt with D.H.9As; In transit to Mesopotamia, disembarked Basrah 23.2.21; Baghdad West 4.3.21; Hinaidi 29.12.21; Khormaksar, Aden 27.4.27; Re-equipped with IIIF 1.28

COMMANDING OFFICERS
Sqn Ldr DL Allen AFC 18.10.20; Sqn Ldr GH Bowman DSO MC DFC 24.2.22; Sqn Ldr WA McClaughrey DSO MC DFC 18.9.24 - 21.1.28

No.11 Squadron

Reformed 15.1.23 as a Bomber squadron at Andover with D.H.9As; Bircham Newton (3 Group) 16.9.23; Netheravon 31.5.24 and re-equipped with Fawn.

COMMANDING OFFICER
Sqn Ldr EAB Rice 15.1.23 - 5.24

No.12 Squadron

Reformed 1.4.23 as a Bomber squadron at Northolt with D.H.9As; Andover 23.3.24 and re-equipped with Fawn.

COMMANDING OFFICER
F/L JR Howett 1.4.23; Sqn Ldr A Gray MC 19.11.23 - 3.24

No.14 Squadron

Reformed 1.2.20 ex No.111 Squadron at Ramleh, Palestine with F.2b; Received five D.H.9 ex No.55 Squadron 25.4.20 (uncertain how long these remained in use); First D.H.9As received 6.24; HQ moved to Amman 15.2.26 and remaining F.2b's discarded (flights periodically detd to Ramleh); First IIIFs arrived 11.29; Last D.H.9A left 3.30.

COMMANDING OFFICERS
Sqn Ldr WL Welsh DSC AFC 9.4.20; Sqn Ldr JST Bradley CBE 21.4.22; Sqn Ldr AN Gallehawk AFC 6.6.24; Sqn Ldr Everidge MC 11.6.26; Sqn Ldr EG Hopcroft 26.9.27; Sqn Ldr FO Soden DFC 22.11.29 - 3.30.

No.15 Squadron

Reformed 20.3.24 as a Bomber squadron with D.H.9As at Martlesham Heath, attached to the Aeroplane and Armament Experimental Establishment there; Re-equipped with Horsley 10.26.

COMMANDING OFFICER
Sqn Ldr PC Sherran MC 20.3.24 - 10.26

No.17 Squadron

Received 12 D.H.9s as partial equipment 26.9.18, the squadron HQ moving to Stojakovo, Serbia that day (various detached flights); Embarked for Turkey 23.1.19; San Stefano 28.1.19 (various detachments); Disbanded 14.11.19.

COMMANDING OFFICER
Mjr SG Hedges MC AFC 2.4.18 - 14.11.19

No.18 Squadron

Re-equipped from F.E.2bs from 26.6.17 at Baizieux (13 Wing 3 Bde); Fitted with RAF.3A engines; la Bellevue 10.7.17 (flt to Auchel 5.10.17); Auchel (Lozinghem) 11.10.17 (transferred to 10 Wing 1 Bde); Treizennes 2.2.18; Serny 9.4.18; Maisoncelle 17.8.18; Re-equipped with D.H.9A 9.18 - 10.18, the first D.H.9A arriving 8.9.18; Le Hameau 13.10.18; La Brayelles 27.10.18 (to 9 Wing 9 Bde); Maubeuge 28.11.18; Bickendorf 24.1.19 (to 11 Wing 2 Bde); Merheim 1.5.19 (9 Wing 9 Bde); Retd to UK 2.9.19 after discarding aircraft.

COMMANDING OFFICERS
Mjr GRM Reid MC by 6.17; Mjr GR Howard DSO 24.11.17; Mjr JB Elliott 1.11.18; Mjr JF Gordon DFC 5.11.18 - 9.19

SQUADRON MARKINGS
White square aft of fuselage roundels on D.H.4s and D.H.9s.

No.24 Squadron

Reformed 1.2.20 as a Communications squadron at Kenley with a variety of aircraft types; Some modified D.H.9As received 6.20; Northolt 1.2.27; D.H.9As withdrawn 6.28.

COMMANDING OFFICERS
Sqn Ldr EH Johnston OBE 1.2.20; Sqn Ldr OT Boyd OBE MC AFC 23.10.22; Sqn Ldr ERL Corballis DS 12.2.23; Sqn Ldr RS Maxwell MC DFC 22.10.23; Sqn Ldr WHL O'Neill MC 27.8.25; Sqn Ldr SN Cole 26.8.27 - 6.28.

No.25 Squadron

Re-equipped from F.E.2ds 6.17 - 7.17 at Auchel (Lozinghem) (10 Wing 1 Bde); Boisdinghem 11.10.17 (transferred to 9 Wing GHQ Bde); Serny 3.2.18; Villers-Bretonneux 6.3.18 (now 9 Wing 9 Bde); Beauvois 24.3.18; Ruisseauville 29.3.18; To 81 Wing 9 Bde 3.6.18; Retd 9 Wing 9 Bde 21.6.18; To 54 Wing GHQ Bde 13.7.18; Retd 9 Wing 9 Bde 4.8.18; La Brayelles 27.10.18; Partially re-equipped with D.H.9A 11.18; Maubeuge 29.11.18; Bickendorf 26.5.19; Merheim 7.7.19; To 11 Wing 2 Bde 21.7.19; South Carlton 6.9.19 and D.H.4s withdrawn; Reduced to cadre 9.10.19.

COMMANDING OFFICERS
Mjr the Hon GM Guest 3.6.17; Mjr CS Duffus MC 5.10.17; Capt JB Fox 26.1.19; Capt S Jones 13.2.19; Capt GM Lawson 2.3.19; Capt CEH Allen 15.3.19; Capt JB Fox 17.3.19; Capt CT Lally 1.4.19; Mjr CS Duffus MC 4.4.19; Capt CT Lally 12.4.19; Mjr GGA Williams 18.4.19 - 1.11.19.

SQUADRON MARKINGS
White horizontal crescent aft of fuselage roundels on D.H.4s.

No.27 Squadron

Re-equipped with D.H.4 (BHP) from Elephant at Clairmarais North from 21.9.17 (9th HQ Wing); Serny 12.10.17; Last Elephant left 12.17; Villers-Bretonneaux 7.3.18; Beauvois 24.3.18; Ruisseauville 29.3.18; Fourneuil 3.6.18; Ruisseauville 21.6.18; Chailly-en-Brie 15.7.18; Mainly re-equipped with D.H.9 7.18 (but a few D.H.4 until 1.3.19); Beauvois 2.8.18; Villers-lès-Cagnicourt 29.10.18; To 51 Wing 9 Bde 23.11.18; Bavai 25.11.18; Retd to 9 Wing by 19.1.19; Last D.H.4s left 1.3.19; Last D.H.9s left 5.3.19 prior to return to UK.

Reformed 1.4.20 ex No.99 Squadron as a Bomber squadron with D.H.9As at Mianwali, India; 14.4.20 Risalpur (3 (Indian Wing, to 1(Indian) Wing late 1920, the 2 (Indian) Wing, joined Razmak Field Force 1.11.22) (detts Tank & Dardoni); Dardoni Fort 14.12.22; Risalpur 20.4.23 (detts Dardoni, Miranshah & Arawali); Peshawar 26.5.25; Risalpur 12.10.25 (Dett Miranshah c.3.25 - 8.25; Flt detd Miranshah 13.10.27 - 1.11.27); Kohat 17.12.28; D.H.9As replaced by Wallaces 3-5.30.

COMMANDING OFFICERS
Mjr WD Beatty 21.9.17; Mjr MG Lee 3.1.18; Mjr GD Hill 18.3.18 - 3.19; Sqn Ldr RJ Mounsey OBE 22.4.20; Sqn Ldr RP Whitehead 15.3.23; Sqn Ldr LM Bailey AFC 27.11.24; Sqn Ldr FW Trott MC 7.3.30 - 5.30.

SQUADRON MARKINGS

Thin white vertical bar aft of fuselage roundels on D.H.4s and D.H.9s.

No.30 Squadron

Began to re-equip from R.E.8 to D.H.9As in 10.20 at Baghdad West ('B' Flt at Kasvin to 9.5.21; Flts at Ramadi 5-18.5.21 & 6-12.6.21); Hinaidi 3.12.22 (forward detts at Kirkuk from time to time); Officially became a Bomber squadron 3.24; Kirkuk 11.4.27 (detts Hinaidi & Sulaimania); Hinaidi 27.10.27; First Wapiti arrived 19.4.29; Last D.H.9A left 9.29.

COMMANDING OFFICERS
Sqn Ldr W Sowrey AFC 10.20; Sqn Ldr R Collishaw DSO OBE DSC DFC 12.11.20; Sqn Ldr EH Johnston OBE DFC 13.12.22; Sqn Ldr JM Robb DFC 19.1.24; Sqn Ldr FH Coleman 3.6.25; Sqn Ldr HP Lale DSO DFC 2.12.27 - 9.29

No.35 Squadron

Reformed 1.3.29 at Bircham Newton as a Bomber squadron, first 5 D.H.9As arrived 8.3.29; Re-equipped with Gordons 6-7.32.

COMMANDING OFFICERS
F/L LM Elworthy 1.3.29; Sqn Ldr GSM Insall VC MC 12.3.29; Sqn Ldr BE Harrison AFC 10.7.29; Sqn Ldr HMK Brown 20.6.31 - 7.32.

No.39 Squadron

Reformed 1.7.19 with 18 D.H.9As ex No.37 Squadron at Biggin Hill; Reduced to cadre 14.10.19

Re-established 12.3.21 at Spittlegate; Bircham Newton 12.1.28; Discarded D.H.9As and sailed for India 29.12.28 to re-equip with Wapiti.

COMMANDING OFFICERS
Sqn Ldr CA Ridley DSO MC 1.7.19;
Sqn Ldr TS Impey 1.4.21; Sqn Ldr AAB Thompson MC AFC 18.1.22; Sqn Ldr JT Whittaker MC 8.2.23; Sqn Ldr HV Champion de Crespigny MC DFC 26.1.25 - 12.28.

No.45 Squadron

Reformed 1.4.21 at Helwan with a few D.H.9As; Almaza 11.7.21 and re-equipped with Vimy to become a Bomber Transport squadron.

Again reformed 25.4.27 with D.H.9As at Heliopolis; Helwan 21.10.27; Began to re-equip with IIIF 15.9.29; Last IIIF left 11.29.

COMMANDING OFFICERS
Wg Cdr EM Murray DSO MC 1.4.21 - 7.21; Sqn Ldr JK Summers MC 25.4.27; Sqn Ldr FJ Vincent 30.10.28 - 11.29

No.47 Squadron

Equipped with a variety of types, one flight receiving D.H.9s at Janes (Yanesh), Macedonia from 2.8.18 (various detachments); Amberkoj 14.2.19; Novorossisk 24.4.19; Ekaterinodar 4.6.19 (various detachments); 1 Flight re-equipped D.H.9As 8.8.19; with Beketovka 7.10.19; Disbanded 20.10.19 to become Nos.11, 12 and 13 Sqns, Russian 7th Division.

Reformed 1.2.20 ex No.206 Sqn at Helwan with D.H.9s; Began to re-equip with D.H.9As 6.20; Last D.H.9 left 9.20; Officially became a Bomber squadron 5.24; Detachment at Khartoum from late 1926; Sqn to Khartoum 21.10.27; Began to re-equip with IIIFs 12.27; Last D.H.9A left 6.28.

COMMANDING OFFICERS
Mjr FA Bates MC 1.8.18; Capt FW Hudson 5.1.19; Mjr R Collishaw DSO OBE DSC DFC 11.7.19 - 20.10.19.
Sqn Ldr GRM Reid DSO MC 1.2.20; Sqn Ldr KC Buss 16.12.20; Flt Lt RC Hardstaff 12.21; Sqn Ldr M Henderson DSO 13.3.22; Sqn Ldr RS Maxwell MC DFC 22.9.25; Sqn Ldr CR Cox AFC 15.9.27 - 6.28.

No.49 Squadron

Received first D.H.4s (RAF.3A) at Swingate Down Dover 4.17 (6 Wing), to gradually replace an assortment of types; In transit to France wholly equipped with D.H.4 8.11.17 (temp accommodated at Rep Pk 1 ASD St.Omer); La Bellevue 12.11.17 (13 Wing 3 Bde); Some Fiat-engined a/c from 2.18 (the only EF sqn to use them); Les Eauvis 27.3.18; Boisdinghem 29.3.18 (overnight, with GHQ Reserve); Petite Synthe 30.3.18 (65 Wing 7 Bde later 9 Wing 9 Bde); Re-equipped with D.H.9 4.18; Conteville 3-4.5.18 (22 Wing 5 Bde); Fourneuil 3.6.18 (to 9 Wing 9 Bde); Beauvois 21.6.18; Rozay-en-Brie 15.7.18; Beauvois 4.8.18; Villers-lès-Cagnicourt 29.10.18 (51 Wing 9 Bde by 23.11.18); Bavai 24.11.18 (to 9 Wing 9 Bde 28.11.18); Re-equipped with D.H.9A 12.18; Bickendorf 29.5.19; Disbanded 18.7.19

COMMANDING OFFICERS
Mjr AS Barratt MC 1.4.17; Mjr BH Turner 9.11.17; Mjr JR Gould 25.2.18; Mjr BS Benning 30.5.18; Mjr JC Quinnell 7.2.19 - 8.7.19.

SQUADRON MARKINGS
Horizontal white dumbbell aft of fuselage roundels on D.H.4s and D.H.9s.

No.55 Squadron

Received D.H.4 1.17 at Lilbourne (21 Wing); in transit 4.3.17; Fienvillers 6.3.17 (9 HQ Wing); Boisdinghem 31.5.17; Ochey 11.10.17 (joined 41 Wing); Tantonville 7.11.17; 41 Wing joined 8 Bde 1.2.18; To HQ 8 Bde 30.3.18; Retd 41 Wing 8 Bde 11.5.18; Azelot 4.6.18; Le Planey 18.11.18; St.André-aux-Bois 2.12.18; Last D.H.4s left to 2 ASD 17.1.19 and squadron reduced to cadre. [Had one D.H.4A to 9.18, nicknamed 'JUMBO']

Reformed 1.2.20 ex No.142 Squadron at Suez becoming a Bomber squadron (dett to Ramleh 4.20), initially with one flight of D.H.9; Began to re-equip with D.H.9As 6.20; Embarked SS *Tambov* at Alexandria for Turkey 8.7.20; Haidar Pasha 12.7.20; Maltepe 24.7.20 (LG at Ismud); HMS *Ark Royal* en route Basrah 1.9.20; Basrah 24.9.20; Baghdad West 30.9.20 (detts Bushire and Mosul); Mosul 20.3.21 and last D.H.9 left (Flight detd Nasiriyah 6.5.21 - 4.6.21); Hinaidi 19.5.24; Began to re-equip with Wapiti 2.30; Last D.H.9A left 11.30.

COMMANDING OFFICERS
Mjr JEA Baldwin DSO by 1.17; Mjr A Gray MC 28.12.17; Mjr BJ Silly MC DFC 20.9.18 - 1.19; Flt Lt CH Elliott-Smith 1.2.20; Sqn Ldr CH Nicholas AFC 25.6.20; Sqn Ldr V Gaskell-Blackburn DSO AFC 19.3.21; Sqn Ldr TF Hazell DSO MC DFC 21.11.22; Sqn Ldr T Coningham DSO MC DFC AFC 7.23; Sqn Ldr ERL Corballis DSO OBE 23.11.23; Sqn Ldr ED Johnson AFC 22.9.25; Flt Lt HA Smith MC (temp) 10.6.27; Sqn Ldr HA Whistler DSO DFC 15.7.27; Sqn Ldr AH Peck DSO DFC 25.4.28; Sqn Ldr JWB Grigson 21.3.29; Sqn Ldr CH Elliot-Smith AFC 8.10.29; Sqn Ldr JW Woodhouse DSO MC 24.1.30 - 11.30.

SQUADRON MARKINGS
Upright white triangle aft of fuselage roundels on D.H.4s and D.H.9s to 11.10.17.

No.57 Squadron

Re-equipped with D.H.4s from F.E.2d 5.17 at Fienvillers (9 Wing GHQ Bde); All with Eagle engines; Droglandt 12.6.17 (to 22 Wing 5 Bde); Boisdinghem 27.6.17; Transferred to 11 Wing 2 Bde 14.11.17; St.Marie-Cappel 23.11.17; Le Quesnoy 29.3.18 (to 13 Wing 3 Bde); Vert Galant 19.9.18; Mory 22.10.18; Béthencourt 9.11.18; To 90 Wing 3 Bde 10.11.18; Vert Galant 23.11.18; Le Casteau 24.11.18 (dett La Bruyères under HQ RAF); Spy 17.12.18 (to 15 Wing 5 Bde) Flt detd La Louveterie, to Franc West 4.1.19); Franc West 5.1.19; Morville 7.1.19 (detts Sart, Maisoncelle, Nivelles (91 Wing), Marquise & Colet); Re-equipped with D.H.9A 2.19; Last D.H.4 left 5.19; D.H.9As withdrawn 7.19 and retd to UK 4.8.19.

COMMANDING OFFICERS
Mjr LA Pattinson MC by 5.17; Mjr CAA Hiatt MC 4.11.17; Mjr GC Bailey DSO 11.9.18.

SQUADRON MARKINGS
White circle aft of fuselage roundels on D.H.4s.

No.60 Squadron

Re-equipped with D.H.9As from D.H.10 4.23 at Risalpur (detts at

Kirkuk (1924), Hassani Abdel, Dardoni, Quetta, Arawali, Delhia & Miranshah (4-5.24)); Peshawar 28.5.25 (detts Quetta & Drigh Road); 'B' Flt detached to Dardoni 5.24 (to begin a policy of detaching one flight from No.27 Sqn or No.60 Sqns there, or when this camp razed, to Miranshah); Kohat 15.10.25 (on the re-organisation of RAF India) (detts Risalpur, Delhi, Miranshah, Quetta, Arawali & Drigh Road; Joined by No.27 Sqn and Kohat then became No.1 (Indian) Wing Station 1.10.28 (detd Rawalpindi for manoeuvres 26.11.28); Re-equipped with Wapiti 4-5.30.

COMMANDING OFFICERS
Sqn Ldr HV Champion de Crespigny MC DFC 27.3.22; Sqn Ldr AWH James MC 14.9.23; Sqn Ldr TF Hazell DSC MC DFC 27.3.25; Sqn Ldr RHG Neville OBE MC 2.9.27 - 5.30.

No.83 Squadron

Received a few D.H.4 as partial equipment from about 10.17 at Wyton (26 Wing); Narborough 12.12.17 (7 Wing) and began to receive F.E.2b as main equipment; St.Omer 6.3.18 with F.E.2b only.

COMMANDING OFFICERS
Mjr VA Albrecht MC by 10.17; Mjr ELML Gower 1.3.18 until 28.7.18.

No.84 Squadron

Reformed 13.8.20 with D.H.9As at Baghdad West, becoming a Bomber squadron; HQ and 'B' Flt to Shaibah 20.9.20 (detts at Baghdad West ('C' Flt formed 9.20), Nasiriyah ('A' Flt 20.9.20 - 14.12.20, also detts by 10.24 and from 6.28) & Bushire); Began to re-equip with Wapiti 6.28; Last D.H.9A left 1.29.

COMMANDING OFFICERS
Sqn Ldr BL Huskisson DSC 13.8.20; Sqn Ldr W Sowrey AFC 1.10.21; Sqn Ldr VS Brown 6.5.22; Sqn Ldr ED Atkinson DFC AFC 14.9.23; Sqn Ldr DE Stodart DSO DFC 18.11.25; Sqn Ldr FJ Vincent DFC 11.2.27; Sqn Ldr JJ Breen 22.10.28 - 1.29.

SQUADRON MARKINGS
Single heart, club, diamond or spade insignia.

No.97 Squadron

Formed 1.12.17 at Waddington initially as a training squadron in Night Training Brigade with Shorthorns and D.H.4s; Stonehenge 21.1.18 (33 Wing, attached to No.1 School of Aerial Navigation and Bomb Dropping); Netheravon 31.3.18 (4 Wing); Began to re-equip with O/400s 5.18; Last D.H.4 left 7.18.

COMMANDING OFFICERS
Capt LW Hall 10.12.17; Mjr VA Albrecht MC 4.4.18 - 4.3.19

No.98 Squadron

Formed 15.8.17 from a nucleus of No.44 Training Squadron at Harlaxton with a miscellany of types including a few D.H.4; Old Sarum 30.8.17 (33 Wing); Began to re-equip with D.H.9 2.18; Wholly equipped by time moved to Lympne for France 1.3.18; St.Omer 1.4.18; Clairmarais 3.4.18 (2 Bde); Alquines 12.4.18; Coudekerque 25.5.18 (5 Group); Ruisseauville 6.6.18 (81 Wing 10 Bde); Drionville 21.6.18 (to 9 Bde 25.6.18); Chailly 13.7.18; Blangemont 3.8.18; Abscon 27.10.18 (51 Wing 9 Bde to 23.11.18 then 10 Wing 1 Bde); Marquain 27.12.18; Alquines 19.1.19 (91 Wing 1 Bde); D.H.9s withdrawn 3.19 and returned to UK.

COMMANDING OFFICERS
Lt DVD Marshall 30.8.17; Mjr ELML Gower 21.9.17; Capt EAB Rice 19.12.17; Mjr HMacD O'Malley 19.2.18; Mjr ET Newton-Clare 5.6.18; Mjr PC Sherren MC 26.8.18 - 3.19.

SQUADRON MARKINGS
White zig-zag aft of fuselage roundels on D.H.9s.

No.99 Squadron

Formed 15.8.17 from a nucleus of No.13 Training Squadron at Yatesbury with a miscellany of types including a few D.H.4s; Old Sarum 30.8.17 (33 Wing); Re-equipped with 18 D.H.9s 3.18; St.Omer 2.5.18; Tantonville 3-4.5.18 (8 Bde, joining 41 Wing in 8 Bde 11.5.18); Azelot 5.6.18; Began to re-equip with D.H.9As 27.8.18; Auxi-le-Chateau 16.11.18 (the last D.H.9 left that day); St.André-aux-Bois 24-29.11.18; Aulnoy 12.12.18 (91 Wing 1 Bde to 1.2.19, then 9 Wing 9 Bde); Entrained for Marseilles en route for India 1.5.19 (18 D.H.9As were packed at 1 ASD); Squadron sailed in SS *Magwa* & SS *Syria* 14-15.5.19; Ambala 15.6.19 (52 Wing) (no a/c initially, these not leaving Marseilles until 24.6.19); Mianwali 26-30.9.19 (dett Ambala); Redesignated No.27 Squadron 1.4.20

COMMANDING OFFICERS
Capt AM Swyny 23.2.18; Mjr LA Pattinson DFC MC 11.3.18; Capt PE Welchman MC DFC 23.9.18 (temp); Capt H Saunders 27.9.18 (temp); Capt WD Thom DFC 28.9.18 (temp); Mjr CR Cox AFC 5.11.18 - 1.4.20.

SQUADRON MARKINGS
Fuselage painted white on top, bottom and sides from leading edge of tailplanes for a distance of 18 inches towards the roundels on D.H.9s.
BUT photographs show white disc on fuselage sides whilst in Independent Force.

No.100 Squadron

Re-established 1.2.20 from cadres of Nos.117 and 141 Squadron as a Bomber squadron with 18 D.H.9As at Baldonnel (Flt detd Castlebar by 5.20 - 12.10) (Special Duty Flight at Oranmore 1.21, to Baldonnel 25.1.22); Spittlegate 29.1.22 - 6.2.22 (11 Wing until 1.5.23, then 3 Group) ('D' Flt formed with Vimy 3.22, these handed over to 7 Sqn 9.7.23); Re-equipped with Fawn 5.24 and moved to Eastchurch.

COMMANDING OFFICERS
Sqn Ldr The Hon JE Twistleton-Wykeham-Fiennes 1.2.20; Sqn Ldr F Sowrey DSO MC AFC 19.2.21; Sqn Ldr NM Martin CBE 10.8.22; Sqn Ldr HFA Gordon 10.9.23 - 5.24.

No.101 Squadron

Reformed 21.3.28 as a Bomber squadron at Bircham Newton, initial equipment unknown; Received 16 D.H.9As ex 39 Sqn 11.28; Began to re-equip with Sidestrand 7.3.29; Last D.H.9A left 6.29.

COMMANDING OFFICER
Sqn Ldr JCP Wood 21.3.28 - 6.29.

No.103 Squadron

Nucleus flight formed 1.9.17 out of 16 TS at Beaulieu (17 Wing) with a few D.H.4s initially for training; Lake Down 8.9.17 (17 Wing); Ford Farm 8.9.17 (renamed Old Sarum 6.10.17) (33 Wing); D.H.9s from 2.18; Marquise 9.5.18; Serny 12.5.18 (1 Bde); Fourneuil 3.6.18 (9 Bde); Serny 21.6.18 (1 Bde until 25.6.18 then 9 Bde until 1.7.18 then 80 Wing 10 Bde); Floringhem 21.10.18; Ronchin 26.10.18; Maisoncelle 25.1.19 (89 Wing); To Shotwick a cadre without a/c 26.3.19.

COMMANDING OFFICERS
Mjr T Maxwell-Scott 21.9.17 to 14.12.17; Mjr WAS Rough 22.2.18; Capt H Turner 22.3.18 (temp); Mjr EN Fuller 26.3.18; Mjr MHB Nethersole 20.9.18 - 3.19

SQUADRON MARKINGS
White bars either side of fuselage roundels, sloping inwards towards the top on D.H.9s.

No.104 Squadron

At Andover (Weyhill) (36 Wing) by 12.17 with D.H.4 as partial equipment; Began to re-equip with D.H.9s 2.18 and fully re-equipped when it went to St.Omer 19.5.18; Le Bourget 20.5.18 (in transit); Azelot 21.5.18 (41 Wing 8 Bde); D.H.10s C4283 & F1867 attached 9.18; Maisoncelle 20.11.18; D.H.10s left 17.12.18; Retd UK and discarded the D.H.9s 1.2.19.

COMMANDING OFFICERS
Capt EA Mackay MC DFC 12.17; Mjr JC Quinnell DFC 1.1.18 to 25.11.18.

SQUADRON MARKINGS
Three vertical white bars aft of fuselage roundels on D.H.9s.

No.105 Squadron

A few D.H.9s received 2.18 for training at Andover (Weyhill) (36 Wing); Re-equipped with R.E.8 4.18.

COMMANDING OFFICERS
Capt HG Bowen 9.9.17; Mjr DG Joy 25.3.18 to 1.19.

No.106 Squadron

At Andover (Weyhill) (36 Wing) by 1.18 with D.H.4s and D.H.9s as partial equipment; Fully re-equipped with R.E.8 4.18.

COMMANDING OFFICER
Mjr EAB Rice by 5.18 to 22.11.18.

No.107 Squadron

At Lake Down (33 Wing) by 2.18 with D.H.4s as partial equipment; Fully re-equipped with D.H.9 5.18; Embarked for France 3.6.18; Le Quesnoy 5.6.18 (13 Wing 3 Bde); Drionville 25.6.18 (51 Wing 9 Bde); In transit 14.7.18; Chailly 15.7.18; Exoivres 3.8.18; Moislains 26.10.18; Bavai 22.11.18; Francwaret, Belgium 15.12.18 (51 Wing 9 Bde); Nivelles 19.12.18; Maubeuge 8.1.19; To UK as cadre and discarded D.H.9s 17.3.19.

COMMANDING OFFICERS
Unknown 2.18; Mjr JR Howett 20.5.18; Mjr H Gordon-Dean 28.9.18 - 17.3.19.

No.108 Squadron

Received some D.H.4 as partial equipment at Lake Down by 2.18 (33 Wing); Kenley 14.6.18 and wholly re-equipped with D.H.9.

Re-equipped 5.18 with D.H.9s at Lake Down (33 Wing); Kenley 14.6.18 (attd 7 AAP); Capelle-le-Grande 22.7.18 (65 Wing 10 Bde); Bisseghem North, Belgium 24.10.18 (11 Wing 2 Bde); Gondecourt, France 16.11.18 (80 Wing 10 Bde); Ronchin 20.12.18; To UK as cadre and discarded D.H.9s 16.2.19.

COMMANDING OFFICERS
Capt M Henderson by 2.18; Mjr SS Halse 6.4.18; Mjr BF Vernon-Harcourt 27.10.18; Mjr EAB Rice 22.11.18 - 10.1.19.

No.109 Squadron

Received some D.H.4s at Lake Down by 3.18 (33 Wing); Kenley 14.6.18 and wholly re-equipped with D.H.9; Earmarked by 12.8.18 for re-equipment with D.H.9As on mobilising, but instead disbanded 19.8.18.

COMMANDING OFFICERS
Unknown

No.110 Squadron

Received some D.H.4s as partial equipment at Sedgeford 1.18 (7 Wing); Re-equipped 2.18 with D.H.9s at Sedgeford (7 Wing); Kenley 15.6.18 (attd 7 AAP where re-equipped with 18 D.H.9As 7-8.18); Bettoncourt 31.8.18 (41 Wing 8 Bde until to 88 Wing 8 Bde 19.10.18); Auxi-le-Chateau 20.11.18 (rejoined 41 Wing 8 Bde); Maisoncelle 30.11.18 (to 89 Wing by 13.2.19) (air mail service to Cologne); Tardinghem 1.2.19; Marquise by 6.5.19 (91 Wing); Some D.H.9s received 7.19; Disbanded 27.8.19.

COMMANDING OFFICER
Mjr HR Nicholl 1.18 - 27.8.19

No.117 Squadron

Formed 1.1.18 at Waddington (27 Wing) and partially equipped with D.H.9s by 2.18; Hucknall 3.4.18; Disbanded 4.7.18.

Reformed 15.7.18 with D.H.9 at Norwich; Disbanded 6.10.18. [Had been intended for Mesopotamia]

Reformed 7.10.18 at Norwich; Wyton 30.11.18; Hooton Park 28.3.19; Tallaght 22.4.19; Gormanston 24.4.19; Disbanded into 141 Sqn 6.10.19 [BUT also recorded as disbanded 31.1.20].

COMMANDING OFFICER
Mjr RH Peck from 3.18; Capt CC Buss 7.12.18 - 24.2.19

No.119 Squadron

Formed 1.1.18 with D.H.9s as main equipment (plus a few training a/c initially) at Andover (Weyhill) (36 Wing); Duxford 1.3.18; Thetford 19.8.18; Wyton 26.9.18; Disbanded 6.12.18.

COMMANDING OFFICER
Capt CC Brill 22.6.18 to 6.12.18

No.120 Squadron

Formed 1.1.18 with D.H.9s as main equipment (plus a few training aircraft initially) at Cramlington (19 Wing); Bracebridge Heath 3.8.18; Wyton 23.11.18; Hawkinge 20.2.19 (as an Aerial Post Squadron for the Army of the Rhine, its aircraft operating across the English Channel to Cologne); Lympne 17.7.19; Disbanded 21.10.19.

COMMANDING OFFICER
Mjr ARS Clarke 1.1.18 - 5.19.

No.121 Squadron

Formed 1.1.18 at Narborough (7 Wing) with D.H.4s and D.H.9s as partial equipment; Filton 10.8.18; Disbanded 17.8.18.

No.122 Squadron

Formed 1.1.18 at Sedgeford (7 Wing) with D.H.9s as main equipment; Disbanded 17.8.18

Reformed 29.10.18 nucleus from 9, 10, 11 & 15 TDS at Upper Heyford with D.H.9 [though one source suggests D.H.10]; Disbanded 20.11.18.

COMMANDING OFFICER
Mjr ASC MacLaren MC 3.18 - 7.18.

No.123 Squadron (later No.2 Squadron, Canadian Air Force)

Formed 1.3.18 at Waddington (27 Wing) with D.H.4s as partial equipment; Duxford 1.3.18; Thetford 21.8.18; Disbanded 14.10.18.

Reformed 20.11.18 at Upper Heyford (27 Wing) with D.H.9As; Shoreham 31.3.19; To number plate basis 6.19 and transferred to Canadian Air Force.

No.124 Squadron

Formed 1.2.18 at Old Sarum (33 Wing) out of a nucleus of No.99 Sqn with D.H.4s and D.H.9s as partial equipment; Fowlmere 1.3.18 (26 Wing); Wyton 10.8.18; Disbanded 17.8.18.

No.125 Squadron

Formed 1.2.18 at Old Sarum (33 Wing) out of a nucleus of No.103 Sqn with D.H.4s and D.H.9s as partial equipment; Fowlmere 1.3.18 (26 Wing); Wyton 10.8.18; Disbanded 17.8.18.

No.126 Squadron

Formed 1.2.18 at Old Sarum (33 Wing) out of a nucleus of No.52 Training Squadron as a day bomber squadron with D.H.4s and D.H.9s; Fowlmere 1.3.18 (26 Wing); Disbanded 17.8.18. [A planned move to Wyton 2.9.18 cancelled]

No.127 Squadron

Formed 1.2.18 at Catterick (19 Wing) out of a nucleus of No.52 Training Squadron as a day bomber squadron with D.H.4s and D.H.9s as partial equipment; Disbanded 4.7.18 into No.49 Training Depot Station.

No.128 Squadron

Formed 1.2.18 at Thetford (26 Wing) out of a nucleus of No.104 Sqn possibly with D.H.4s and D.H.9s as partial equipment; Disbanded 4.7.18.

No.129 Squadron

Nucleus flight formed 1.3.18 at Duxford (26 Wing) as a light bomber squadron with D.H.4s and D.H.9s as partial equipment; Disbanded 4.7.18.

No.130 Squadron

Nucleus flight formed 1.4.18 at Wyton with D.H.4s and D.H.9s; Hucknall 1.4.18; Disbanded 4.7.18.

Was to reform 1.9.18 with 3 D.H.9s at Hucknall, but never materialised.

No.131 Squadron

Formed 1.3.18 at Shawbury with F.E.2b, evidently also some D.H.9. Disbanded 17.8.18

No.135 Squadron

Nucleus flight formed 1.4.18 at Hucknall with D.H.9s as main equipment; Disbanded 4.7.18.

Was to reform 14.9.18 with 3 D.H.9s at Hucknall, but never materialised.

No.136 Squadron

Nucleus flight formed 1.4.18 at Lake Down with D.H.9s as main equipment; Disbanded into 14 TDS 4.7.18.

Was to reform 22.9.18 with 3 D.H.9s at Lake Down, but never materialised.

No.137 Squadron

Nucleus flight formed 1.4.18 at Shawbury as a day bomber squadron with D.H.4s and D.H.9s; Disbanded 4.7.18.

Was to reform 28.9.18 with 3 D.H.9s at Shawbury, but never materialised.

No.142 Squadron

Received D.H.9s as partial equipment 1.19 at Qantara; Suez 17.2.19; D.H.9 the only type in use with 4 a/c 10.19; Redesignated No.55 Squadron 1.2.20.

COMMANDING OFFICER
Mjr RGH Murray 29.9.18 - 20.1.19.

No.144 Squadron

Re-equipped with D.H.9s 7.18 - 10.18 at Port Said (32 Wing); Junction Station, Palestine 14.8.18 (detachment at Haifa; detachment to Mudros, Greece 17.10.18); Mikra Bay 6.11.18 (detachments at Mudros and Amberkoj); Sailed from Salonika to Egypt 25.11.18, thence to UK 4.12.18; Arrived at Ford Junction as a cadre 16.12.18; Disbanded 4.2.19.

COMMANDING OFFICER
Mjr AH Peck DSO MC & Bar 29.4.18 to 29.10.18

SQUADRON MARKINGS
Horizontal thin white bars either side of individual number aft of fuselage roundel.

No.146 Squadron

Was due to form 14.7.18 in Egypt fully equipped with D.H.9s (BHP engines), but the order was cancelled and the aircraft went instead to Nos.555 to 557 Flights, which formed 26.6.18 in the UK (sic).

No.147 Squadron

Due to form 14.8.18 in Egypt fully equipped with D.H.9s (BHP), but never actually formed, and intention dropped 3.19.

No.155 Squadron

Nucleus formed 14.9.18 from Nos.1, 26, 55 and 57 TDS with D.H.9A (Liberty) at Chingford; Disbanded 12.12.18.

No.156 Squadron

Nucleus formed 12.10.18 from Nos.27, 35, 52 & 53 TDS with D.H.9A (Liberty) at Wyton; Disbanded 21.11.18; A/c mostly reallotted to 123 Sqn, some to 155 Sqn.

No.160 Squadron

Nucleus planned to form 1.6.18 at unknown location with D.H.9sA; Disbanded 4.7.18. Probably only existed on paper.

Also planned to form 13.9.18 with D.H.9 (Liberty) but cancelled.

No.161 Squadron

Planned to form 20.9.18 with D.H.9 (Liberty) but cancelled.

No.162 Squadron

Nucleus planned to form 6.18 at unknown location with D.H.9As; Disbanded 4.7.18. Probably only existed on paper.

Also planned to form 20.9.18 with D.H.9 (Liberty) but cancelled.

No.163 Squadron

Nucleus planned to form 1.6.18 at Waddington with D.H.9sA; Disbanded 4.7.18. Probably only existed on paper.

Also planned to form 2.10.18 with D.H.9 (Liberty) but cancelled.

No.164 Squadron

Nucleus formed 25.10.18 out of 'A' Flt 23 TDS and 'B' Flt 25 TDS at Baldonnel/Cookstown with D.H.9 (Liberty) ; Was to re-equip with D.H.9sA and move to Fowlmere 25.12.18, but probably only existed on paper.

No.166 Squadron

At least one D.H.9 on strength in 1.19 at Bircham Newton (86 Wing).

COMMANDING OFFICER
Mjr T Maxwell-Scott 28.12.18 - 7.2.19.

No.167 Squadron

At least one D.H.9 on strength in late 1918 or early 1919 at Bircham Newton (86 Wing).

No.186 Squadron

Formed 30.12.18 on board HMS *Argus* as a composite torpedo and reconnaissance unit partially equipped initially with four D.H.4 for intended service at Baku (Caspian Sea). These to have been replaced by six D.H.9As which arrived at Petrovsk 19.4.19, but in the meantime the deployment had been cancelled and the squadron had re-equipped with Cuckoos aboard HMS *Argus* with the Grand Fleet. The D.H.9As were instead passed to No.221 Squadron after erection.

No.2N/202 Squadron

As No.2 Squadron RNAS, re-equipped with D.H.4s from 1½ Strutters 6.3.17 at St.Pol (1 Wing RNAS); Bergues 26.1.18; Became No.202 Sqn RAF 1.4.18 (61 Wing 5 Group); Partially re-equipped with D.H.9s; D.H.9As from 9.18 and D.H.9s withdrawn; Varsşenaere 20.11.18 (reported detached from Group early 12.18 to work with Grand Fleet); To Dover as cadre 24.3.19.

COMMANDING OFFICERS
S/Cdr DCS Evill by 3.17; S/Cdr PFM Fellowes 1.4.17; S/Cdr FE Sandford 1.11.17; F/Cdr BS Wemp W/E 8.2.18 (became Mjr wef 1.4.18); Mjr RW Gow DSO DFC 7.4.18; Capt J Robinson 1.1.19; Capt RM Bayley 23.3.19.

SQUADRON MARKINGS

Two vertical white bars aft of fuselage roundels? [No evidence of use]

No.5N/205 Squadron

As No.5 Squadron RNAS, re-equipped with D.H.4s from 1½ Strutters 4.17 - 8.17 at Petite Synthe (5 Wing RNAS); Villers-Bretonneux 6.3.18 (to 22 Wing 5 Bde); Mons-en-Chaussee 11.3.18 (shelled out); Champien 21.3.18; Bertangles 23.3.18; Conteville (Bois de Roche) 28.3.18; Became No.205 Sqn RAF 1.4.18; Bovelles 25.8.18; Proyart East 16.9.18; Began to re-equip from D.H.4 with D.H.9As 12.8.18, completed 9.18; Moislains 7.10.18 (to 51 Wing 9 Bde); Maubeuge 27.11.18 (to 9 Wing 5 Bde); La Louveterie 2-5.1.19 (to 15 Wing 5 Bde); Sart 11.2.19; D.H.9As withdrawn then to UK 18.3.19.

COMMANDING OFFICERS
S/Cdr ET Newton-Clare by 4.17; S/Cdr SJ Goble DSO DSC 15.7.17 (became Mjr wef 1.4.18); Mjr JF Gordon DFC 28.8.18; Mjr JB Elliott 2.11.18 - 18.3.19.

No.6N/206 Squadron

Reformed as No.6 Squadron RNAS at Dover 1.1.18 (from personnel of Defence Flight Walmer & 11 Sqn RNAS) with a few D.H.4s to 4.18 for training only (received main equipment of D.H.9s from 2.18); Petite Synthe 14.1.18 (5 Wing); Ste.Marie Cappel 30.3.18 (11 Wing 2 Bde); Became No.206 Sqn RAF 1.4.18 (11 Wing 2 Bde) and D.H.4s soon discarded; Boisdinghem 11.4.18; Alquines 15.4.18; Boisdinghem 29.5.18; Alquines 5.6.18; Ste Marie Cappel 5.10.18 (65 Wing 5 Bde); Linselles East 24.10.18 (11 Wing 2 Bde); Nivelles East 26.11.18 [moved 9.12.18 per Pitt log book entry]; Bickendorf 18-21.12.18; Maubeuge 27.5.19; in transit 7.6.19 via Marseilles; Alexandria 19.6.19; Heliopolis 24.6.19; Helwan 27.6.19 (Training Bde, Middle East); Became No.47 Sqn 1.2.20.

COMMANDING OFFICERS
S/Cdr CT MacLaren 1.1.18 (became Mjr wef 1.4.18); Mjr GRM Reid DSO MC 23.5.19; Disbanded 1.2.20.

No.207 Squadron

At Bircham Newton as a Bomber squadron, re-equipped 4.21 with D.H.9As; Embarked at Liverpool in SS *Eboe*, SS *Montgomeryshire* and SS *Bratton Castle*; San Stefano, Turkey 11.10.22; Shipped home to Southampton 22.9.23; Eastchurch 3.10.23; Re-equipped with Gordon 1.28

COMMANDING OFFICERS
Sqn Ldr AW Tedder 4.21; Sqn Ldr V Gaskell-Blackburn DSO AFC 6.8.23; Sqn Ldr JB Graham MC DFC 28.2.26 - 1.28

No.210 Squadron

Reformed 1.2.20 ex No.186 Squadron as a Torpedo Training squadron at Fort Brocklehurst, Gosport partially equipped initially with D.H.9As of which it had seven in 6.20, these being flown until at least 9.20.

No.11N/211 Squadron

Refd as No.11 Squadron RNAS at Petite Synthe 11.3.18 (5 Wing RNAS) with a few D.H.4 to 4.18 for training only (received main equipment of D.H.9 from 3.18); Became No.211 Sqn RAF 1.4.18 (65 Wing 7 Bde); Wing to 5 Bde 5.18; under SHQ by 8.6.18; to 10 Bde 18.6.18); Clary (Iris Farm) 24.10.18 (22 Wing 5 Bde); Thuillies 3.12.18); D.H.9s withdrawn and retd UK as cadre 15.3.19.

COMMANDING OFFICERS
S/Cdr HG Travers DSC 11.3.18 (became Mjr wef 1.4.18); Mjr R Loraine DSO MC 26.5.18; Mjr GRM Reid DSO MC 25.7.18 - 3.19.

No.12N/212 Squadron

No.12N Squadron (Training) had some D.H.4s by 2.18 at Petite Synthe (5 Wing RNAS); Disbanded 1.4.18.
No.212 Squadron formed 20.8.18 at Yarmouth (73 Wing 4 Group) with D.H.9As as main equipment, also some D.H.4s and D.H.9s initially (comprised Nos.490, 557 and 558 Flights, of which No.558 operated briefly from Holt 8.18); Swingate Down, Dover 7.3.19; Disbanded 9.2.20.

COMMANDING OFFICERS
Mjr E Cadbury DSC DFC 20.8.18 - 15.4.19; Disbanded 9.2.20.

No.17N/217 Squadron

Formed as No.17 Sqn with D.H.4s to replace RNAS Seaplane Base Dunkirk at Dunkirk 14.1.18 (1 Wing RNAS) [also had a few D.H.9 at first]; Bergues 1.2.18; Became No.217 Sqn RAF 1.4.18 (61 Wing 5 Group); Crochte 5.7.18 (61 Wing 5 Group); Varssenaere 23.10.18 (5 Group); Dover 20.2.19; Dunkirk by 3.19 (5 Group); in transit 25-26.3.19; Dover (Guston Road) 27.3.19 (5 Group); To cadre at Driffield 28.3.19.

COMMANDING OFFICER
S/Cdr WL Welsh DSC 14.1.18 - 3.19 (became Mjr wef 1.4.18).

No.218 Squadron

Formed 24.4.18 at Guston Road, Dover (7 Bde) with D.H.9s as main equipment; Petite Synthe 23.5.18 (61 Wing 5 Group); Fréthun 7.7.18 (82 Wing 5 Group); Reumont 23.10.18 8 (9 Wing 5 Bde); Vert Galant 16.11.18 (90 Wing 3 Bde); D.H.9s withdrawn and retd UK as cadre 7.2.19.

COMMANDING OFFICERS
Mjr BS Wemp DFC 24.4.18; Mjr CH Hayward 28.12.18 - 1.19.

No.219 Squadron

Formed 22.7.18 at Westgate (4 Group), operated only from Manston with D.H.9s as partial equipment (in 555 & 556 Flts); D.H.9s withdrawn 6.19.

COMMANDING OFFICER
Mjr GE Livock 22.7.18 - 6.19.

No.220 Squadron

Formed ex C Sqn 2 Wing at Imbros wef 1.4.18 (62 Wing) [ex Recce Sqn Aegean]; Several D.H.4s and D.H.9s on strength from 6.18; mobile 9.18 (62 Wing 15 Group) (included 475, 476 & 477 Flts) (dett San Stephano); Did not actively adopt 220 Sqn number plate until 9.18; Pizzone 11.18 (62 Wing); Mudros 12.18 (62 Wing); Imbros 12.18 (by 14.11.18); Mudros 2.19 (as cadre); Disbanded 21.5.19.

COMMANDING OFFICERS
Mjr FJE Feeney by 7.18 - @18.9.18; Mjr JO Andrews 10.18.

No.221 Squadron

Formed ex D Sqn 2 Wing at Stavros wef 1.4.18 (62 Wing; to 15 Group 9.18) [ex Anti-submarine Sqn (Aegean)] Some D.H.9s by 6.18 and two flights of D.H.4s to 9.18; Did not actively adopt 221 Sqn number plate until 9.18 (included 552, 553 & 554 Flts from 9.18); Absorbed into 222 Sqn Mudros 15.10.18.

Reformed as mobile squadron with some D.H.9s at Lemnos 20.12.18 - @23.12.18; Mudros 12.18; HMS *Riviera* 29.12.18 (first flight embarked for service in South Russia remainder of sqn mobilising; also embarked HMS *Empress*); Batum 5.1.19; Baku 9.1.19 (flt arrived); Petrovsk Kaskar 12.1.19 (D.H.9 flight arrived 14.1.19) (detts Chechen & Lagan) (joined up with "Norperforce" from Persia 3.19); Began evacuating 18.8.19; Disbanded 1.9.19.

COMMANDING OFFICERS
Unknown 1.4.18; Mjr AFF Jacob 8.18; Disbanded 10.18
Mjr JO Andrews 20.12.18; Mjr Baron EAdeL de Ville 4.19; Disbanded 1.9.19.

No.222 Squadron

Formed ex A & Z Sqns 2 Wing at Thasos wef 1.4.18 (63 Wing; 62 Wing 15 Group by 22.9.18) [ex No.1 Fighter Sqn (Aegean)], a few D.H.4s on strength initially; Did not adopt 223 Sqn numberplate until 9.18; Received some D.H.9s 6.18 at Mudros (62/63 Wing) (advanced base Dedeagatch by 27.10.18; dett Amberkoj); San Stefano 14.11.18; Mudros 23.11.18; Disbanded 27.2.19.

COMMANDING OFFICER
W/Cdr REC Peirse DSO 1.4.18; Mjr AB Gaskell DSC by 18.9.18; Mjr HF de la Rue DFC by 10.18.

No.223 Squadron

Formed wef 1.4.18 ex B Sqn 2 Wing RNAS at Mitylene [ex No.2 Fighter Sqn (Aegean)], with a few D.H.4s on strength initially (The No.223 Sqn numberplate as not actuaaly adopted until 9.18) (62/63 Wing); Stavros 21.4.18; Mitylene by 1.5.18; Became a mobile bombing squadron with some D.H.4 and D.H.9s 9.18 (62 Wing 15 Group) (included 559, 560 & 561 Flights from 9.18); To Lemnos Is (Mudros) 11.18 (62 Wing 15 Group); Disbanded 16.5.19.

COMMANDING OFFICERS
Mjr AB Gaskell DSC by 18.9.18; Mjr HF de la Rue DFC by 10.18. [Joint command with No.222 Sqn?]

No.224 Squadron

Formed from the D.H.4 bombing flights of 6 Wing at Alimini (Otranto) wef 1.4.18 (67 Wing) [ex Anti-submarine squadron, Otranto] with twelve D.H.9s from 5.18; Andrano 14.6.18 (included 496, 497 & 498 Flights from 9.18); Pizzone 9.12.18; D.H.4s withdrawn 1.19; Disbanded 15.4.19.

COMMANDING OFFICER
Mjr JSF Morrison 1.4.18 - 27.10.18 & 8.11.18 - 3.12.18

No.225 Squadron

Formed from part of 6 Wing at Alimini (Otranto) wef 1.4.18 (67 Wing Adriatic Group) [ex Fighter sqn, Otranto] with twelve D.H.9s from 5.18; Andrano 14.6.18 (included 481, 482 & 483 Flights from 9.18); D.H.9s replaced by D.H.9As 10.18; Pizzone 9.11.18; Disbanded 19.12.18.

COMMANDING OFFICER
Mjr T Hinshelwood 1.4.18; Mjr JSF Morrison 27.10.18 - 8.11.18; Disbanded 19.12.18.

No.226 Squadron

Formed from the D.H.4 bombing unit [or Bombing Sqn] at Pizzone wef 1.4.18 (67 Wing), with 12 D.H.9s from 5.18; to Otranto 5.18 (67 Wing); to Pizzone 19?.6.18 (67 Wing) (included 472, 473 & 474 Flights from 9.18); Andrano 1.10.18 (detached for operations); Pizzone 3.10.18; Andrano 9.10.18; Marsh (Lemnos) by 14.10.18 [now 62 Wing]; Albania 13.10.18 (en route for Macedonian front); Mudros 10.18; Pizzone 11.11.18 (63 Wing 15 Group); Disbanded 18.12.18. [A few D.H.4s on strength until at least 27.9.18]

COMMANDING OFFICERS
Mjr MS Marsden 1.4.18; Mjr RFS Leslie DSC DFC AFC 19.4.18; Disbanded 18.12.18.

No.227 Squadron

Formed wef 1.4.18 from communication squadron 6 Wing [OR ex Caproni sqn, Taranto] at Pizzone (66 Wing, later 67 Wing Adriatic Group) with some D.H.9s from 6.18, also reported some D.H.4s initially (included 499, 550 & 551 Flts from 9.18); Disbanded 9.12.18. [Squadron never fully established]

No.233 Squadron

Formed 31.8.18 at Guston Road, Dover 31.8.18 (5 Group), included 491 Flt with D.H.9s; Disbanded 15.5.19.

COMMANDING OFFICERS
Capt HV German (temp) 31.8.18 - @27.10.18; Capt AC Reid (temp) by 10.11.18; Mjr R Graham DSO DSC DFC 21.11.18; Disbanded 15.5.19.

No.236 Squadron

Formed 20.8.18 at Mullion 20.8.18, included 493 Flt with D.H.9s; Disbanded 15.5.19.

COMMANDING OFFICERS
Mjr RBB Colmore 20.8.18; Disbanded 15.5.19

No.250 Squadron

Formed 1.5.18 at Padstow (71 Wing 9 Group), included 494 Flt with D.H.9s; Disbanded 15.5.19.

COMMANDING OFFICERS
Mjr RE Orton 31.5.18; Mjr FW Merriam AFC 7.11.18 to 18.2.19; Disbanded 15.5.19.

No.251 Squadron

At Hornsea (79 Wing 18 Group) with some D.H.9s from 11.18; Disbanded 30.6.19.

COMMANDING OFFICER
Mjr JD Maude 23.4.18 to 5.11.18; Disbanded 30.6.19.

No.254 Squadron

Formed 31.5.18 at Prawle Point, included 492 Flt with D.H.9s; Disbanded 22.2.19.

COMMANDING OFFICER
Mjr FG Andreae 31.5.18; Disbanded 22.2.19.

No.260 Squadron

Formed 31.5.18 at Prawle Point (72 Wing 9 Group), included 492 Flt with some D.H.9s; Disbanded 22.2.19.

COMMANDING OFFICER
Mjr FG Andreae 31.5.18; Disbanded 22.2.19.
[Joint command with No.254 Sqn?]

No.269 Squadron

Formed 6.10.18 at Port Said (64 Wing), included 431 & 432 Flts with D.H.9s; Alexandria 15.9.19 (64 Wing); Redesignated 481 Flt 15.11.19.

COMMANDING OFFICERS
Mjr PL Holmes DSC 6.10.18; F/L H Stewart 9.19; Sqn Ldr KC Buss 10.19; Disbanded 15.11.19.

No.273 Squadron

BASES
Formed 20.8.18 at Yarmouth (HQ 4 Wing), included 534 Flight with D.H.9s and a few D.H.4s and D.H.9As (Five D.H.9s at Covehithe and others at Westgate); To cadre and a/c withdrawn 14.3.19.

COMMANDING OFFICERS
Mjr AS Maskell 8.18 - @1.19.

No.501 Squadron

Formed 14.6.29 as (Bomber) (Special Reserve) squadron at Filton; Equipped from 13.3.30 with D.H.9As; Became City of Bristol Squadron 1.5.30; Re-equipped with Wapiti 9-11.30.

COMMANDING OFFICER
Sqn Ldr RS Sugden AFC 26.8.29 - 11.30.

No.600 Squadron

Formed 14.10.25 as (Bomber) (Auxiliary Air Force) (City of London) squadron at Northolt with D.H.9As; Hendon 18.1.27; Began to re-equip with Wapiti 10.29; Last D.H.9A left 10.30.

COMMANDING OFFICERS
Wg Cdr AWH Jones MC 17.11.25; Wg Cdr The Rt Hon FE Guest CBE DSO 19.11.26 - 9.30.

No.601 Squadron

Formed 14.10.25 as (Bomber) (Auxiliary Air Force) (County of London) squadron at Northolt with D.H.9As; Hendon 18.1.27; Began to re-equip with Wapiti 11.29; Last D.H.9A left 10.30.

COMMANDING OFFICERS
Sqn Ldr Lord Edward Grosvenor 14.10.25; Sir Philip Sassoon 18.8.29 - 10.30.

No.602 Squadron

Formed 12.9.25 as (Bomber) (Auxiliary Air Force) (City of Glasgow) squadron at Renfrew with two D.H.9As and some training a/c; Began to re-equip with Fawn 9.27; Last D.H.9As left 1.28.

COMMANDING OFFICER
Sqn Ldr CN Lowe MC DFC 12.9.25; Capt JD Latta MC 1.2.26; Sl Ldr J Fullerton 6.5.27 - 1.28.

No.603 Squadron

Formed 14.10.25 as (Bomber) (Auxiliary Air Force) (City of Edinburgh) squadron at Turnhouse initially with one D.H.9As and some training a/c; Began to re-equip with Wapiti 3.30; Last D.H.9A left 7.30.

COMMANDING OFFICER
Sqn Ldr JA McKelvie 14.10.25 - 7.30

No.604 Squadron

Formed 17.3.30 as (Bomber) (Auxiliary Air Force) (County of Middlesex) squadron at Hendon with two D.H.9As and some training a/c; Began to re-equip with Wapiti 9.30; Last D.H.9A left 10.30.

COMMANDING OFFICERS
Flt Lt FJ Fogarty DFC 17.3.30 (temp); Wg Cdr ASW Dore DSO TD 19.3.30 - 10.30.

No.605 Squadron

Formed 5.10.26 as (Bomber) (Auxiliary Air Force) (County of Warwick) squadron at Castle Bromwich with D.H.9As and some training a/c; Began to re-equip with Wapiti 4.30; Last D.H.9A left 7.30.

COMMANDING OFFICER
Sqn Ldr JAC Wright AFC 5.10.26 - 7.30.

No.2 (Communications) Squadron

Formed 3.19 at Buc (Paris), with D.H.4, D.H.4A and other types; Disbanded 14.10.19.

RNAS TRAINING UNITS

DH4 School Manston - D.H.4
HP Sqn Manston - D.H.4
Observers School Eastchurch - D.H.4
RNASTE Cranwell - D.H.4

RFC/RNAS/RAF TRAINING UNITS

44 RS Harlaxton (became 44 TS 31.5.17) - D.H.4
51 RS Wye/Waddington, became 51 TS 31.5.17) - D.H.4

5 TS Wyton - D.H.9
9 TS Norwich/Sedgeford - D.H.4, D.H.9
10 TS Gosport - D.H.9
12 TS Thetford - D.H.9
15 TS Hucknall - D.H.9
17 TS Yatesbury - D.H.4?, D.H.9
18 TS Montrose - D.H.4
19 TS Hounslow - D.H.4
25 TS Thetford - D.H.4, D.H.9
26 TS Harlaxton/Narborough - D.H.4, D.H.9
28 TS Castle Bromwich - D.H.4
29 TS Croydon - D.H.9
31 TS Wyton - D.H.4, D.H.9
44 TS Harlaxton/Waddington - D.H.4, D.H.9
46 TS Catterick - D.H.4, D.H.9
47 TS Waddington - D.H.9
48 TS Waddington - D.H.9
51 TS Waddington - D.H.4, D.H.9
52 TS Montrose/Catterick (to 49 TDS 15.7.18) - D.H.4, D.H.9
55 TS Narborough - D.H.9
61 TS South Carlton - D.H.4
69 TS Narborough - D.H.9
75 TS Cramlington - D.H.4, D.H.9

1 TDS Wittering - D.H.4, D.H.9
2 TDS Lake Down/Stonehenge - D.H.4
3 TDS Lopcombe Corner - D.H.9
5 TDS Easton-on-the-Hill - D.H.4, D.H.9
6 TDS Boscombe Down - D.H.4, D.H.9
7 TDS Feltwell - D.H.9
8 TDS Netheravon - D.H.9
9 TDS Shawbury - D.H.9
10 TDS Harling Road - D.H.4, D.H.9, D.H.9A
11 TDS Old Sarum - D.H.4, D.H.9
14 TDS Boscombe Down/Lake Down - D.H.9
15 TDS Hucknall - D.H.9
16 TDS Heliopolis - D.H.9
17 TDS El Firdan - D.H.9
18 TDS Ismailia - D.H.9
22 TDS Gormanston - D.H.9
23 TDS Baldonnel - D.H.9
25 TDS Tallaght - D.H.9
31 TDS Fowlmere - D.H.4, D.H.9, D.H.9A
35 TDS Duxford - D.H.4, D.H.9
41 TDS Lopcombe Corner - D.H.9
48 TDS Waddington - D.H.9
49 TDS Catterick - D.H.4, D.H.9, D.H.9A
52 TDS Cramlington - D.H.9
54 TDS Fairlop - D.H.9
55 TDS Manston/Narborough - D.H.4, D.H.9
57 TDS Cranwell - D.H.4, D.H.9
59 TDS Scopwick - D.H.9A
201 TDS Cranwell - D.H.4, D.H.9
202 TDS Cranwell - D.H.4, D.H.9
203 TDS Manston - D.H.4, D.H.9
204 TDS Eastchurch - D.H.4, D.H.9
207 TDS Chingford - D.H.9

1 FTS Netheravon - D.H.9, D.H.9A
2 FTS Duxford - D.H.9A
3 FTS Spittlegate - D.H.9A
4 FTS Abu Sueir - D.H.9, D.H.9A
5 FTS Shotwick/Sealand - D.H.9A
6 FTS Spittlegate - D.H.9A

1 Fighting School Turnberry - D.H.9
2 Fighting School Marske - D.H.4
3 Fighting School Bircham Newton/Sedgeford - D.H.9
1 (O)SoAG New Romney - D.H.4
4 (Aux)SoAG Marske - D.H.4
1 SoN&BD Stonehenge - D.H.4, D.H.9
2 SoN&BD Andover - D.H.9, D.H.9A
Marine Observers School Eastchurch - D.H.9
1 Observers School Eastchurch - D.H.9
Pool of Pilots Joyce Green - D.H.4, D.H.9
RAF (Cadet) College Cranwell - D.H.9A

BOMBING STATISTICS OF INDEPENDENT FORCE D.H.4/9/9A SQUADRONS

55 Squadron - D.H.4

Month	Raids	Bombs (lbs)	Comprised
Oct 1917	3	6,968	4x230lb, 54x112lb
Nov 1917	1	1,362	3x230lb, 6x112lb
Dec 1917	5	8,732	3x230lb, 66x112lb, 26x25lb
Jan 1918	2	4,108	6x230lb, 24x112lb, 1x40lb(phosphorus)
Feb 1918	5	9,400	8x230lb, 60x112lb, 21x40lb(phosphorus)
Mar 1918	10	24,888	14x230lb, 164x112lb, 68x25lb, 40x40lb(phosporus)
Apr 1918	3	7,392	66x112lb
May 1918	13	29,422	5x230lb, 246x112lb, 24x25lb, 3x40lb(phosphorus)
Jun 1918	16	32,792	18x230lb, 211x112lb, 188x25lb, 8x40lb(phosphorus)
Jul 1918	16	35,700	38x230lb, 185x112lb, 184x25lb, 41x40lb(phosphorus)
Aug 1918	14	25,950	13x230lb, 190x112lb, 48x25lb, 12x40lb(phosphorus)
Sep 1918	9	17,600	40x230lb, 75x112lb
Oct 1918	5	8,154	15x230lb, 42x112lb
Nov 1918	4	6,206	4x230lb, 43x112lb, 2x40lb(phosphorus)

99 Squadron - D.H.9

Month	Raids	Bombs (lbs)	Comprised	
May 1918	9	15,792	141x112lb	
Jun 1918	16	30,170	63x230lb, 140x112lb	
Jul 1918	13	21,878	41x230lb, 104x112lb, 32x25lb	
Aug 1918	6	10,743	25x230lb, 39x112lb, 25x25lb	
Sep 1918	14+	29,118	60x230lb, 114x112lb, 102x25lb	+also 28 individual bombing flights
Oct 1918	10+	20,596	54x230lb, 73x112lb	+also 1 individual bombing flight
Nov 1918	3+	7,532	19x230lb, 26x112lb, 5x50lb	+also 3 individual bombing flights

104 Squadron - D.H.9

Month	Raids	Bombs (lbs)	Comprised
Jun 1918	11	19,492	46x230lb, 76x112lb, 16x25lb
Jul 1918	6	8,436	18x230lb, 33x112lb, 24x25lb
Aug 1918	6	15,000	40x230lb, 50x112lb, 8x25lb
Sep 1918	25	25,820	58x230lb, 90x112lb, 96x25lb
Oct 1918	10	26,720	48x230lb, 140x112lb
Nov 1918	5	6,550	17x230lb, 20x112lb, 16x25lb

110 Squadron - D.H.9A

Month	Raids	Bombs (lbs)	Comprised
Sep 1918	4	11,702	9x230lb, 86x112lb
Oct 1918	3	5,872	8x230lb, 36x112lb
Nov 1918	2	4,776	12x230lb, 18x112lb

Westland-built de Havilland D.H.9A H3486 in pristine condition.
(via Philip Jarrett)

Aeroplane De Havilland No. 4.

275 H.P. Rolls Royce.

RAF Wire Lengths

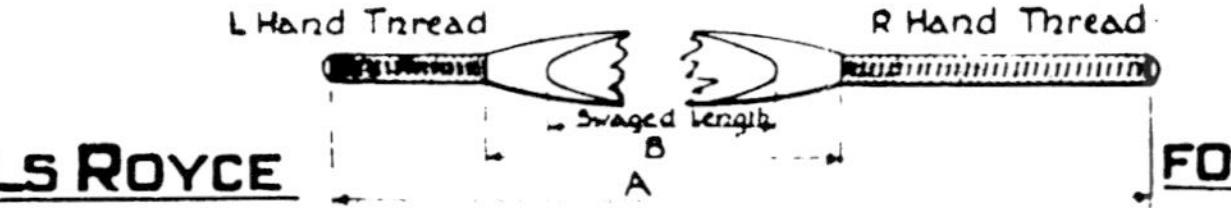

For 275 H.P. Rolls Royce

No. Per Machine	Position on Machine	Size Screw	Overall Length A	Length Between Screws B	Length of LH Screw	Length of RH Screw	Identification Mark	Remarks
2	Incidence Wires	2 BA	5'·5⅛	5·1⅞	1⅛	2⅛	DH4-A	
2	Incidence Wires	2 BA	6·8	6·4½	1⅛	2⅛	DH4-B	
2	Incidence Wires	¼ BSF	5'·5¼	5·1¾	1¼	2¼	DH4-C	
2	Incidence Wires	¼ BSF	6·7½	6·4	1¼	2¼	DH4-D	
2	Landing Wires	2 BA	10'·1⅛	9·10⅛	1⅛	2⅛	DH4-E	
2	Landing Wires	2 BA	10·1½	9·10¼	1⅛	2⅛	DH4-F	
2	Landing Wires	¼ BSF	8·2⅛	7·10⅝	1¼	2¼	DH4-G	
2	Landing Wires	¼ BSF	8·2½	7·11	1¼	2¼	DH4-H	
2	Flying Wires	9/32 BSF	10·7⅛	10·3¼	1⅜	2½	DH4-J	
2	Flying Wires	9/32 BSF	10·7	10·3⅛	1⅜	2½	DH4-K	
2	Flying Wires	⅜ BSF	8·5⅞	8·1½	1¾	2⅝	DH4-L	
2	Flying Wires	⅜ BSF	8·5¼	8·1⅜	1¾	2⅝	DH4-M	
2	Tail Plane Bracing	2 BA	4·6⅞	4·3⅝	1⅛	2⅛	DH4-N	
2	Tail Plane Bracing	2 BA	4·4⅝	4·1⅜	1⅛	2⅛	DH4-P	
2	Tail Plane Bracing	2 BA	4·4½	4·1¼	1⅛	2⅛	DH4-Q	
2	Tail Plane Bracing	2 BA	4·1⅞	3·10⅝	1⅛	2⅛	DH4-R	
2	U/C Bracing Wires	⅜ BSF	3·9¼	3·4⅞	1¾	2⅝	DH4-W	For U/C No. 1
4	Aileron	4 BA	5·8¼	5·5¼	1	2	DH4-X	
2	Centre Section	2 BA	3·2½	2·11¼	1⅛	2⅛	DH4-CCA	
2	Centre Section	¼ BSF	3·7¼	3·3¾	1¼	2¼	DH4-T	
2	Centre Section	¼ BSF	5·6½	5·3	1¼	2¼	DH4-U	
2	U/C Wire (Front)	⅜ BSF	4·0⅜	3·8	1¾	2⅝	DH4-DDA	For U/C No. 2
2	U/C Wire (Rear)	⅜ BSF	4·2⅞	3·10½	1¾	2⅝	DH4-EEA	For U/C No. 2

For 200 H.P. B.H.P. & R.A.F. 3A.

No. Per Machine	Position on Machine	Size Screw	Overall Length A	Length Between Screws B	Length of LH Screw	Length of RH Screw	Identification Mark	Remarks
2	Incidence Wires	2 BA	5·5⅛	5·1⅞	1⅛	2⅛	DH4-A	
2	Incidence Wires	2 BA	6·8	6·4½	1⅛	2⅛	DH4-B	
2	Incidence Wires	¼ BSF	5·5¼	5'·1¾	1¼	2¼	DH4-C	
2	Incidence Wires	¼ BSF	6·7½	6·4	1¼	2¼	DH4-D	
2	Landing Wires	2 BA	10·1⅛	9·10⅛	1⅛	2⅛	DH4-E	
2	Landing Wires	2 BA	10·1½	9·10¼	1⅛	2⅛	DH4-F	
2	Landing Wires	¼ BSF	8·2⅛	7·10⅝	1¼	2¼	DH4-G	
2	Landing Wires	¼ BSF	8·2½	7·11	1¼	2¼	DH4-H	
2	Flying Wires	9/32 BSF	10·7⅛	10·3¼	1⅜	2½	DH4-J	
2	Flying Wires	9/32 BSF	10·7	10·3⅛	1⅜	2½	DH4-K	
2	Flying Wires	⅜ BSF	8·5⅞	8·1½	1¾	2⅝	DH4-L	
2	Flying Wires	⅜ BSF	8·5¼	8·1⅜	1¾	2⅝	DH4-M	
2	Tail Plane Bracing	2 BA	4·6⅞	4·3⅝	1⅛	2⅛	DH4-N	
2	Tail Plane Bracing	2 BA	4·4⅝	4·1⅜	1⅛	2⅛	DH4-P	
2	Tail Plane Bracing	2 BA	4·4½	4·1¼	1⅛	2⅛	DH4-Q	
2	Tail Plane Bracing	2 BA	4·1⅞	3·10⅝	1⅛	2⅛	DH4-R	
2	U/C Bracing Wires	⅜ BSF	3·9¼	3·4⅞	1¾	2⅝	DH4-W	For U/C No. 1
4	Aileron	4 BA	5·8¼	5·5¼	1	2	DH4-X	
2	Front Centre Section Bracing	¼ BSF	4·1⅛	3·9⅜	1¼	2¼	DH4-AAA	
2	Rear Centre Section Bracing	¼ BSF	3·6⅛	3·2⅝	1¼	2¼	DH4-BBA	
2	Rear Centre Section Bracing	2 BA	4·0¼	3·9	1⅛	2⅛	DH4-Z	
2	U/C Wire (Front)	⅜ BSF	4·0⅜	3·8	1¾	2⅝	DH4-DDA	For U/C No. 2
2	U/C Wire (Rear)	⅜ BSF	4·2⅞	3·10½	1¾	2⅝	DH4-EEA	For U/C No. 2

Air Board		
T.D.OTS	584	23'3'17
11'7'17		

D.H.4 wire lengths – one example of an official series of technical tables

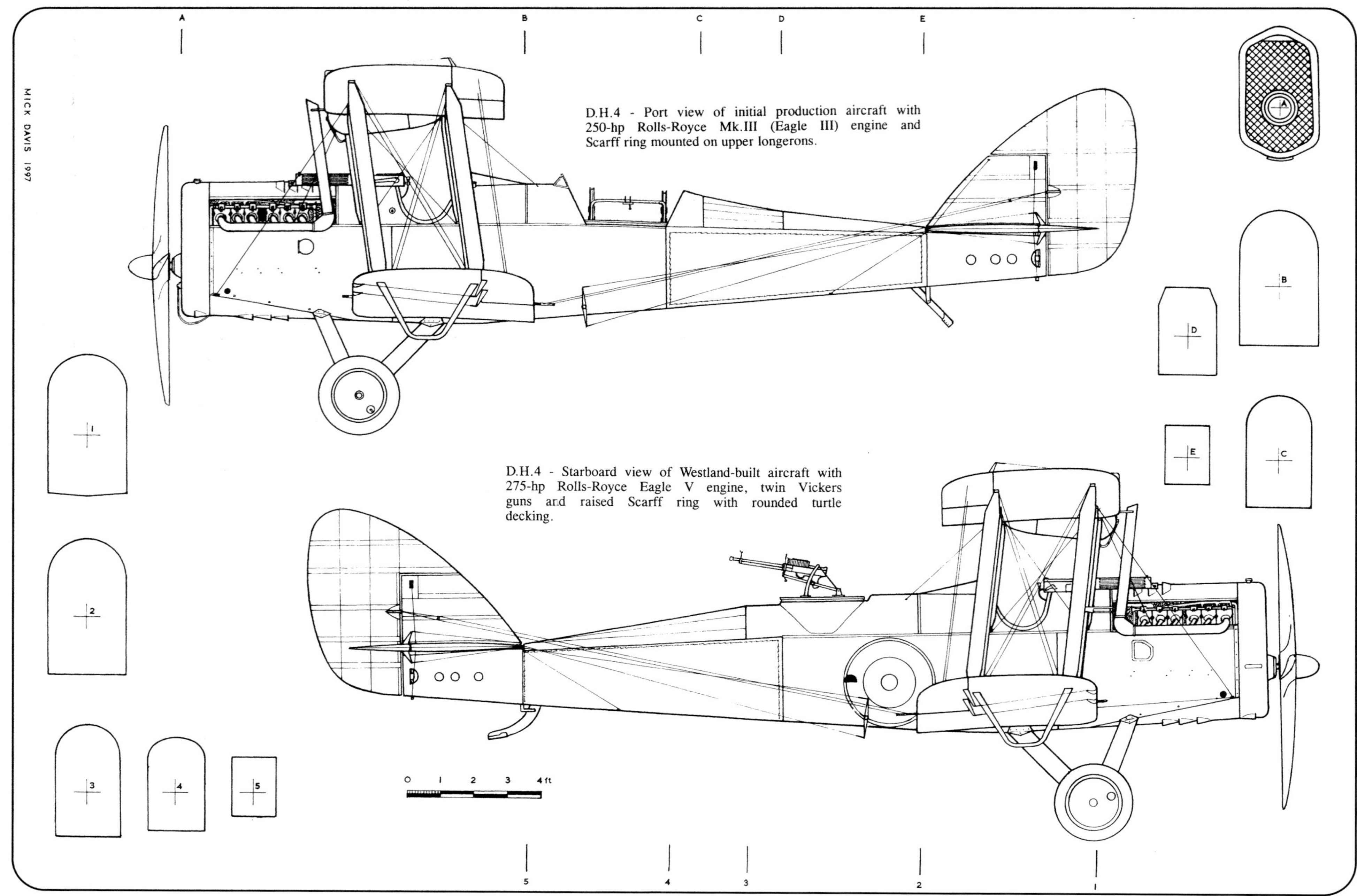

D.H.4 - Port view of initial production aircraft with 250-hp Rolls-Royce Mk.III (Eagle III) engine and Scarff ring mounted on upper longerons.
D.H.4 - Starboard view of Westland-built aircraft with 275-hp Rolls-Royce Eagle V engine, twin Vickers guns and raised Scarff ring with rounded turtle decking.
A
B
C
D
E
1
2
3
4
5
0 1 2 3 4 ft
MICK DAVIS 1997

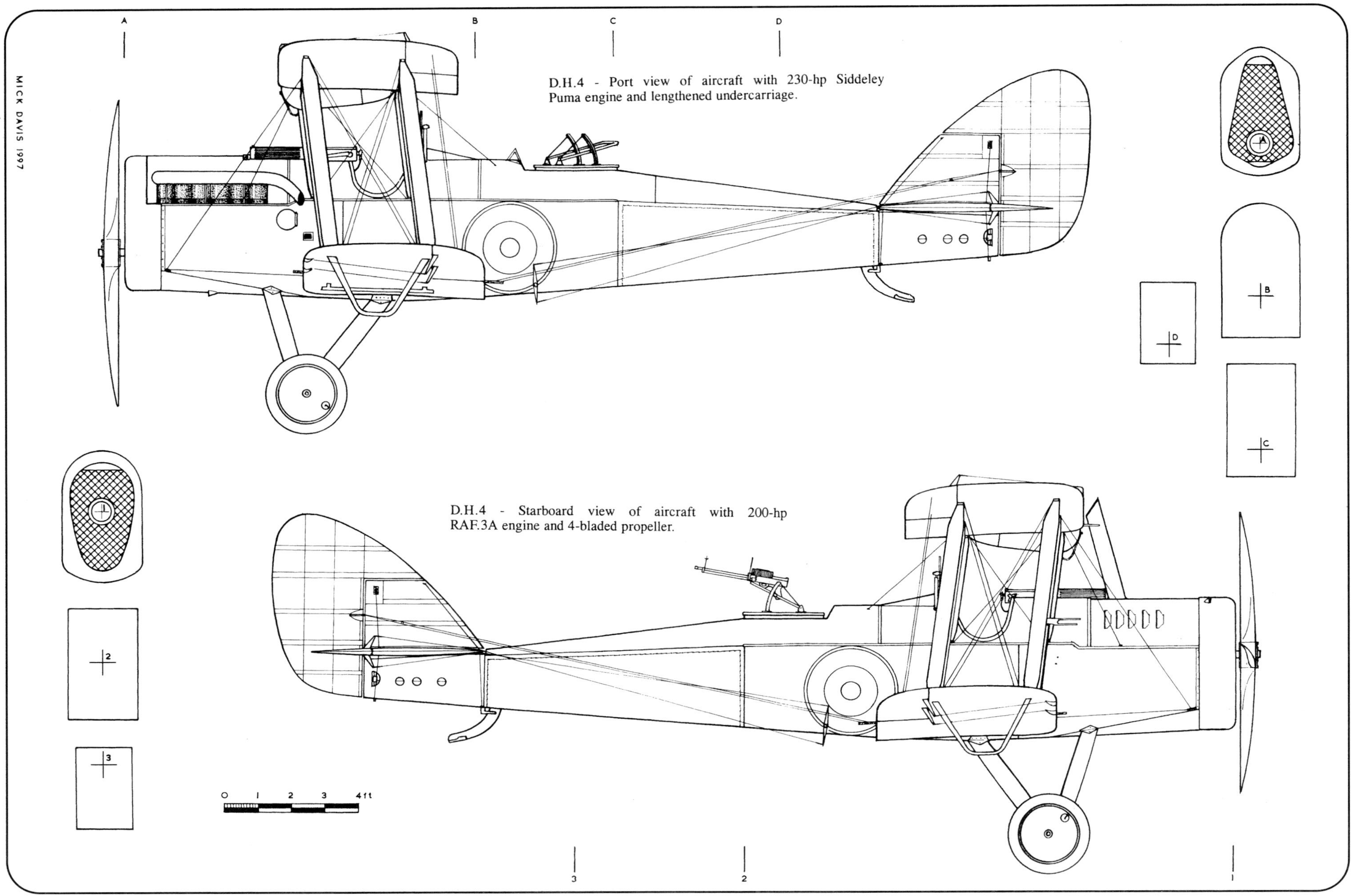

D.H.4 - Port view of aircraft with 230-hp Siddeley Puma engine and lengthened undercarriage.

D.H.4 - Starboard view of aircraft with 200-hp RAF.3A engine and 4-bladed propeller.

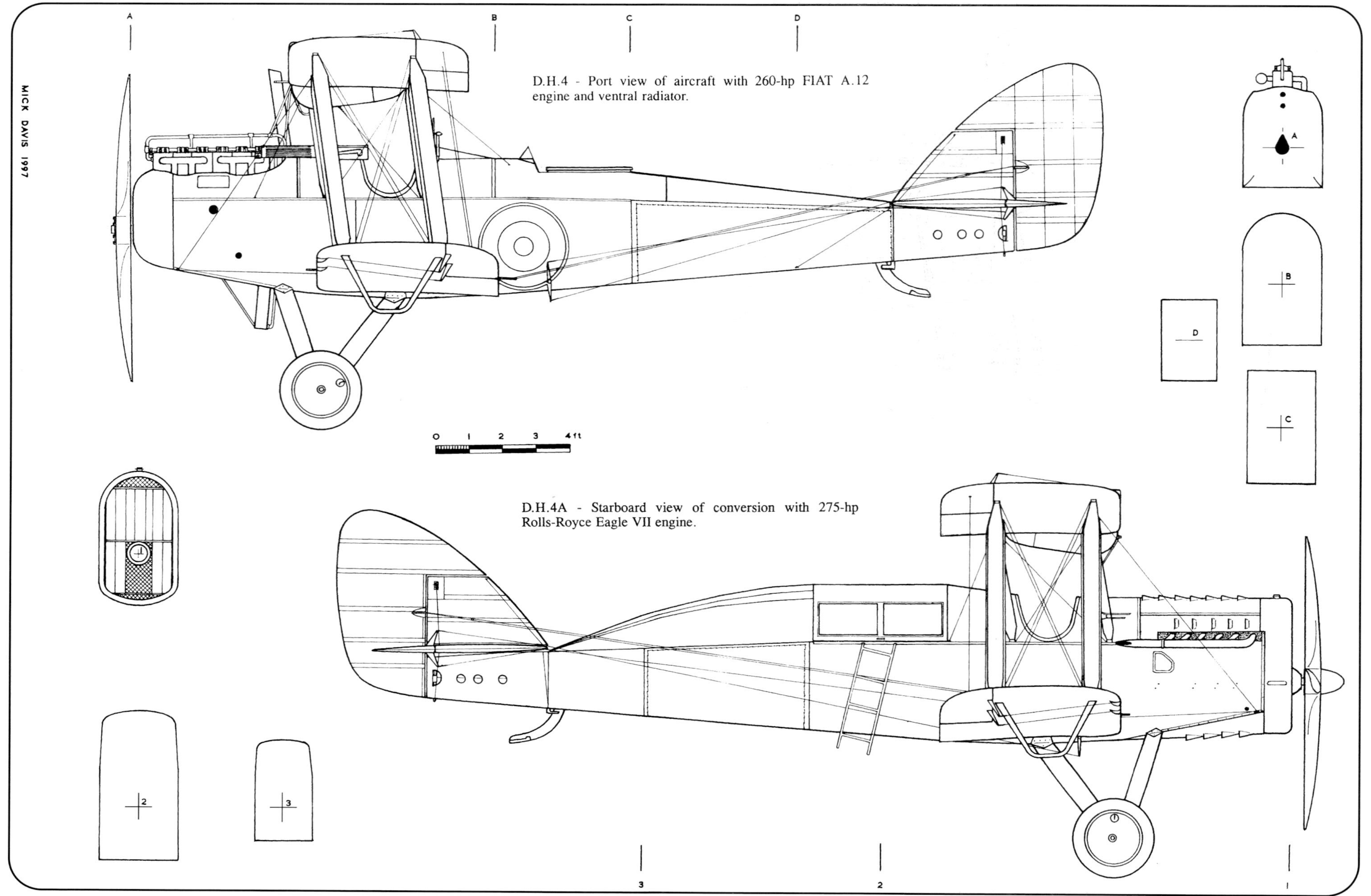

D.H.4 - Port view of aircraft with 260-hp FIAT A.12 engine and ventral radiator.

D.H.4A - Starboard view of conversion with 275-hp Rolls-Royce Eagle VII engine.

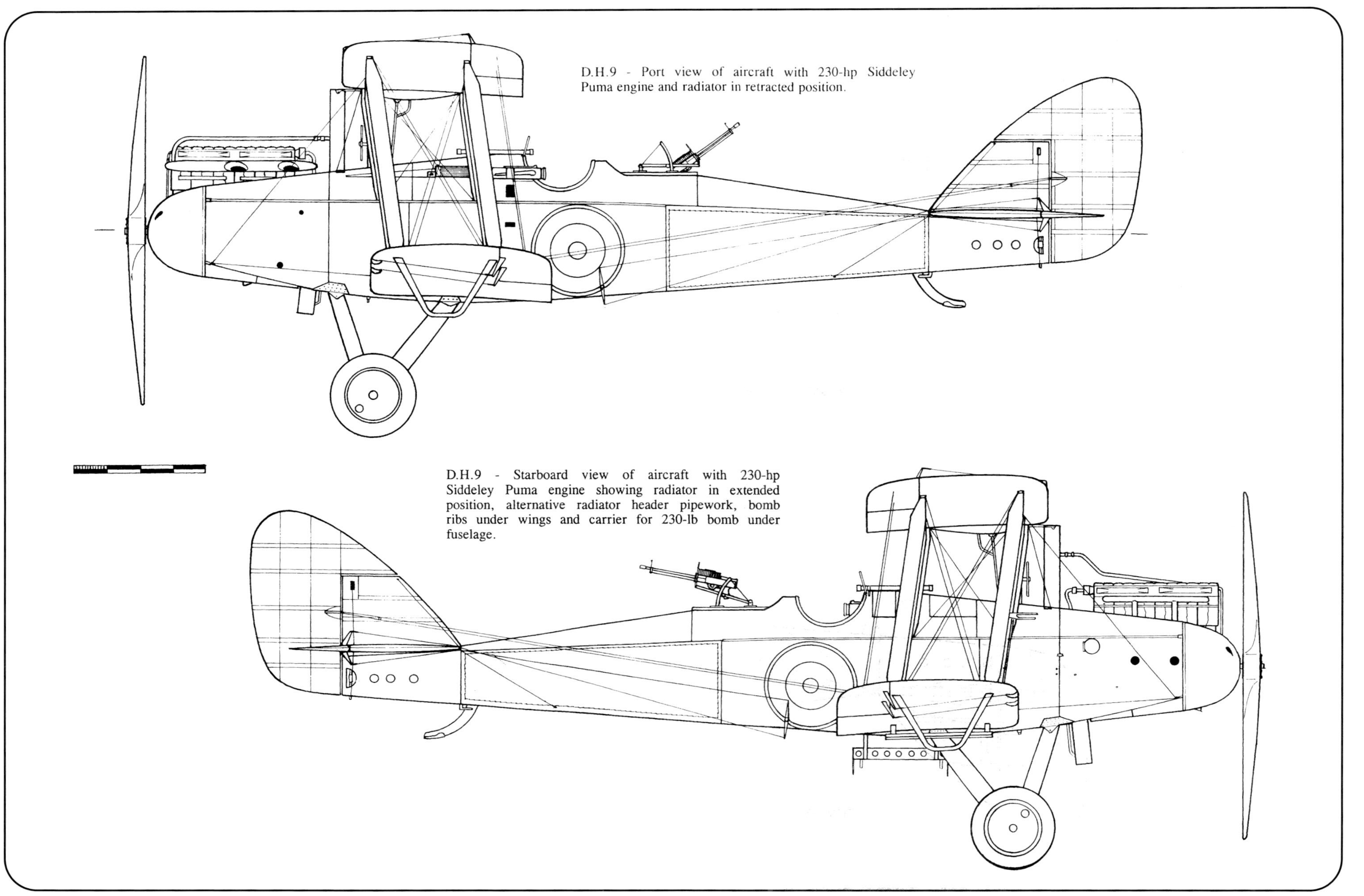

D.H.9 - Port view of aircraft with 230-hp Siddeley Puma engine and radiator in retracted position.

D.H.9 - Starboard view of aircraft with 230-hp Siddeley Puma engine showing radiator in extended position, alternative radiator header pipework, bomb ribs under wings and carrier for 230-lb bomb under fuselage.

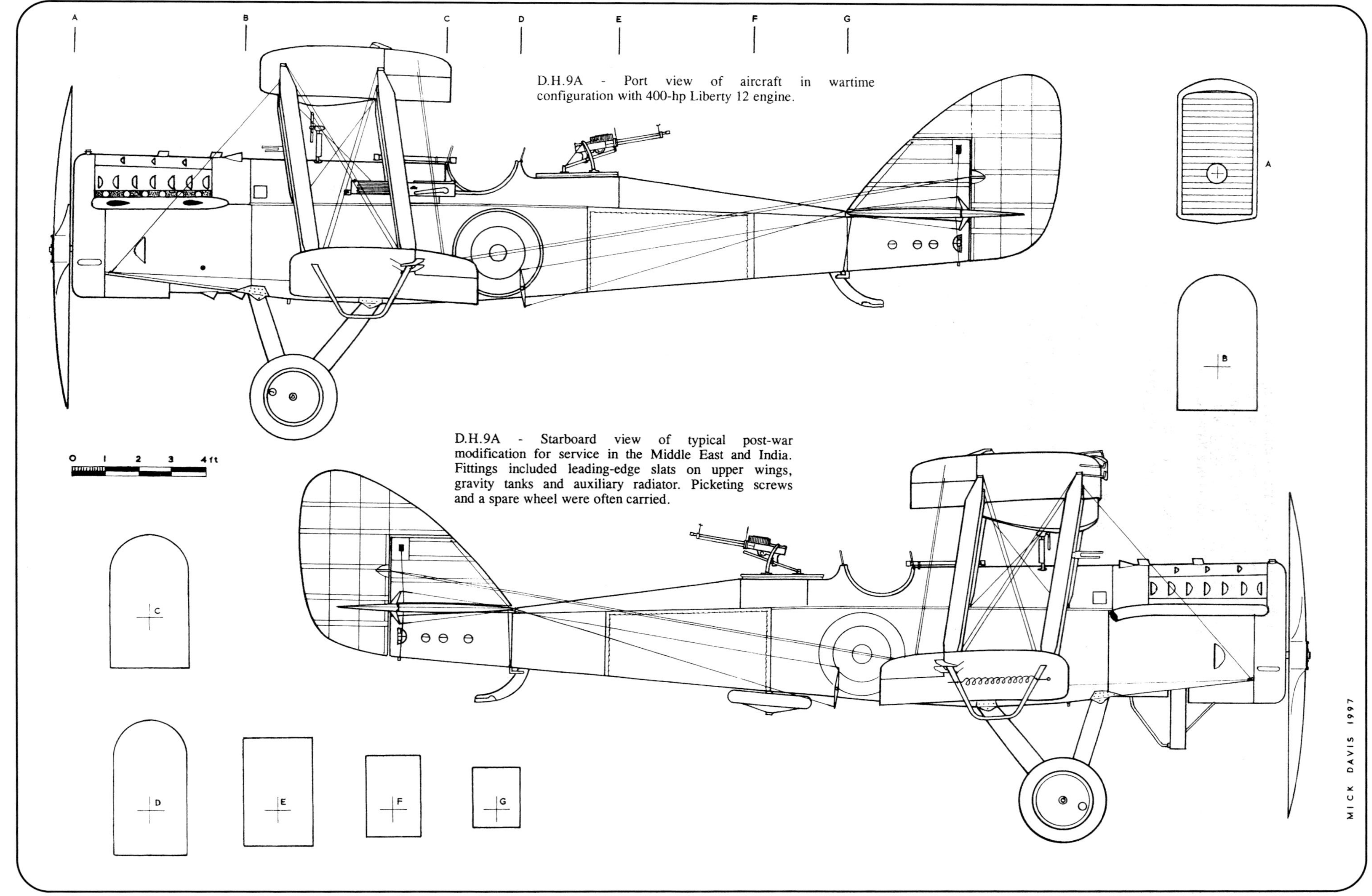

D.H.9A - Port view of aircraft in wartime configuration with 400-hp Liberty 12 engine.

D.H.9A - Starboard view of typical post-war modification for service in the Middle East and India. Fittings included leading-edge slats on upper wings, gravity tanks and auxiliary radiator. Picketing screws and a spare wheel were often carried.

OTHER WORLD WAR ONE BOOKS STILL IN PRINT

THE CAMEL FILE
Ray Sturtivant and Gordon Page

The Sopwith Camel was one of the foremost Allied fighters during the latter part WW1. With hundreds of victories to its credit, it was flown by many famous names of the period. Developed from the Sopwith Pup, it served with 20 front line squadrons on the Western Front and in Italy, and was still in full service at the Armistice. The book lists individual histories of over 6,000 aircraft, including victories and losses. Appendices include comprehensive details of the squadrons and other units with which the Camel served, as well as its use by other air forces, and a detailed index of nearly 3,000 Camel pilots. 272 pages including nearly 200 photographs and 17 pages of general arrangement drawings plus a summary of unit and other markings. Hardback.

THE S.E.5 FILE
by Ray Sturtivant and Gordon Page

The S.E.5 and S.E.5A were produced in large numbers by several aircraft companies and saw extensive service with the Royal Flying Corps and later the Royal Air Force on the Western Front, in the Middle East and in Home Defence and training units. Many were flown by American Aero Squadrons, though planned large-scale production in the USA failed to materialise. Small numbers were supplied overseas post-war, and some converted for commercial use, mainly for 'sky-writing'. Tables of individual histories including the men who flew the type, their victories and losses. Three pages of general arrangement drawings, a cut-away drawing and eight pages of colour drawings. 176 pages with 253 photographs. Hardback.

ROYAL NAVY AIRCRAFT SERIALS AND UNITS 1911 TO 1919
Ray Sturtivant and Gordon Page

Histories of over 15,000 aircraft flown by the RNAS from 1911 and by successor units of the RAF until the end of 1919. It lists their squadrons, units and bases. 16 pages of drawings include plans of over 80 U.K. land and marine bases, as well as location maps of aerodromes and place names in France and Belgium. A comprehensive index with 4,000 individual names. 480 pages with 321 photographs. Hardback.

ROYAL NAVY SHIPBOARD AIRCRAFT DEVELOPMENTS 1912 TO 1931
Dick Cronin

In-depth coverage of early British naval air operations in the North Sea, East Africa, the Eastern Mediterranean and South Russia. Highlights include the destruction of two Zeppelins over the North Sea, and the vital part played in the destruction of the German cruiser Konigsberg lurking up an East African river. 384 pages, nearly 500 illustrations, including maps and side-view drawings of aircraft. Hardback.

THE NORMAN THOMPSON FILE
by Michael H. Goodall

The firm's flying boats were typical of British naval aircraft in WWI, initially as White & Thompson. Based at Bognor, Sussex, it employed sub-contractors in the area, and used the sands as an airfield.Design progressed in cooperation with Glenn Curtiss, under licence, as well as receiving wartime contracts for other company's products. The N.T.2 series saw postwar service in Canada, Peru, Estonia and Japan. 100 pages, 96 photographs. Hardback.

THE MARTINSYDE FILE
by Ray Sanger

Martinsyde was busy developing monoplanes before the outbreak of WW1, but its first operational aircraft were biplane Scouts, followed by the Elephant, a large single-seat aircraft used for fighting, bombing and reconnaissance and built in some quantity, seeing service in France and the Middle East. In 1918, production began of the Buzzard, regarded by many as the best single-seat fighter of World War One, which ended just as the type entered service. Post-war, many were sold abroad and equipped units of the Spanish Navy, as well as the air forces of Russia, Finland and Latvia. Smaller numbers went to other countries as far apart as the Irish Free State and Japan. Martinsyde entered the civil market and sold a number of aircraft to operate in the harsh conditions of Canada and Newfoundland. The company also produced motor-cycles which are still valued by their owners. Handasyde went on to design aircraft for other companies after Martinsyde closed, including ANEC and the Desoutter and British Aircraft companies. 256 pages, 280 photographs. Hardback.

ROYAL AIR FORCE AIRCRAFT J1 - J9999 AND WW1 SURVIVORS
Dennis Thompson and Ray Sturtivant

Comprehensive listing of RAF aircraft of the 1920s, including prototypes. Includes individual post-war histories of WW1 types which continued in service, such as the Avro 504K, D.H.9a, Bristol Fighter, Sopwith Snipe, Vickers Vimy and many others. 208 pages, 270 photographs. Laminated cover.

ROYAL AIR FORCE FLYING TRAINING AND SUPPORT UNITS
by Ray Sturtivant, John Hamlin and James J.Halley

The first complete listing of the many thousands of flying training and support units of the RAF and its predecessor the Royal Flying Corps from 1912 to the present day. Coverage of such units as FTSs, OTUs, CUs, OCUs, WW1 Training Squadrons and numbered flights, as well as MUs, R&SUs, ASP, SPs and numbered Landing Grounds in the UK, 2nd TAF and the Middle East. Cross references to relevant administrative units such as Commands, Groups, Wings, Bases and Brigades, which are also listed. Aircraft types and examples given, and in many cases the periodic strength or establishment. Comprehensive index of bases. 368 pages. 200 photographs. Hardback.

AIR-BRITAIN - THE INTERNATIONAL ASSOCIATION OF AVIATION HISTORIANS - FOUNDED 1948

Since 1948, Air-Britain has recorded aviation events as they have happened, because today's events are tomorrow's history. In addition, considerable research into the past has been undertaken to provide historians with the background to aviation history. Over 15,000 members have contributed to our aims and efforts in that time and many have become accepted authorities in their own fields.

Every month, *AIR-BRITAIN NEWS* covers the current civil and military scene. Quarterly, each member receives *AIR-BRITAIN DIGEST* which is a fully-illustrated journal containing articles on various subjects, both past and present.

For those interested in military aviation history, there is the quarterly *AEROMILITARIA* which is designed to delve more deeply into the background of, mainly, British and Commonwealth military aviation than is possible in commercial publications and whose format permits it to be used as components of a filing system which suits the readers' requirements. This publication is responsible for the production of the present volume and other monographs on military subjects. Also published quarterly is *ARCHIVE*, produced in a similar format but covering civil aviation history in depth on a world-wide basis. Both magazines are well-illustrated by photographs and drawings.

In addition to these regular publications, there are monographs covering type histories, both military and civil, airline fleets, Royal Air Force registers, squadron histories and the civil registers of a large number of countries. Although our publications are available to non-members, prices are considerably lower for Air-Britain members, who have priority over non-members when availability is limited. Normally, the accumulated price discounts for which members qualify when buying monographs far exceed the annual subscription rates.

A large team of aviation experts is available to answer members' queries on most aspects of aviation. If you have made a study of any particular subject, you may be able to expand your knowledge by joining those with similar interests. Also available to members are libraries of colour slides and photographs which supply slides and prints at prices considerably lower than those charged by commercial firms.

There are local branches of the Association in Bournemouth, Central Scotland, Gwent, Heston, London, Luton, Manchester, Merseyside, North-East England, Rugby, Sheffield, Southampton, South-West Essex, Stansted, West Cornwall and West Midlands. There are also overseas branches in France and the Netherlands.

If you would like to receive samples of Air-Britain magazines, please write to the following address enclosing 50p and stating your particular interests. If you would like only a brochure, please send a stamped self-addressed envelope to the same address (preferably 230mm by 160mm or over) - Air-Britain Membership Enquiries (Mil), 1 Rose Cottages, 179 Penn Road, Hazlemere, High Wycombe, Bucks., HP15 7NE.

[More details on Air-Britain website : http://www.air-britain.com]

MILITARY AVIATION PUBLICATIONS

Royal Air Force Aircraft series: (prices in brackets are for members/non-members and are post-free)

J1-J9999	(£8.00/£10.00)	K1000-K9999	see The K-File	L1000-N9999	(£12.00/£15.00)
P1000-R9999	(£11.00/£14.00)	T1000-V9999	(£12.00/£15.00)	W1000-Z9999	(£13.00/£16.50)
AA100-AZ999	(£6.00/£9.00)*	BA100-BZ999	(£6.00/£7.50)	DA100-DZ999	(£5.00/£6.00)
EA100-EZ999	(£5.00/£6.00)	FA100-FZ999	(£5.00/£6.00)	HA100-HZ999	(£6.00/£7.50)
JA100-JZ999	(£6.00/£7.50)	KA100-KZ999	(£6.00/£7.50)	LA100-LZ999	(£7.00/£8.50)
MA199-MZ999	(£8.00/£10.00)	NA100-NZ999	(£8.00/£10.00)	PA100-RZ999	(£10.00/£12.50)
SA100-VZ999	(£6.00/£7.50)	WA100-WZ999	(£5.00/£7.50)*		

Type Histories

The Halifax File	(£6.00/£9.00)*	The Lancaster File	(£8.00/£12.00)*	The Washington File	(£2.00/£3.00)*
The Whitley File	(£4.50/£6.75)*	The Typhoon File	(£4.00/£6.00)*	The Stirling File	(£6.00/£9.00)*
The Anson File	(£10.00/£10.00)*	The Harvard File	(£7.00/£8.50)	The Hampden File	(£11.00/£13.50)
The Hornet File	(£9.00/£11.00)	The Beaufort File	(£10.00/£12.50)	The Camel File	(£13.00/£16.00)
The Norman Thompson File	(£13.50/£17.00)	The S.E.5 File	(£16.00/£20.00)	The Battle File	(£20.00/£25.00)
The Hoverfly File	(£16.50/£19.50)	The Defiant File	(£12.50/£16.00)	The Martinsyde File	(24.00/£30.00)
	The Scimitar File (in preparation)		The Oxford File (in preparation)		

Hardbacks

The Squadrons of the Royal Air Force and Commonwealth (£15.00/£15.00)*
The Squadrons of the Fleet Air Arm (£24.00/£30.00)
Royal Navy Shipboard Aircraft Developments 1912 - 1931 (£10.00/£10.00)
Royal Navy Aircraft Serials and Units 1911 - 1919 (£10.00/£10.00)
Fleet Air Arm Aircraft, Units and Ships 1920 - 1939 (£26.00/£32.50)
Fleet Air Arm Aircraft 1939 - 1945 (£24.00/£30.00)*
Royal Navy Instructional Airframes (£14.00/£17.50)
Central American and Caribbean Air Forces (£12.50/£15.50)*
The British Aircraft Specifications File (£20.00/£25.00)
The K-File (the RAF of the 1930s) (£23.00/£30.00)
Aviation in Cornwall (£14.00/£17.50)
Royal Air Force Flying Training & Support Units (£20.00/£25.00)
Flight Refuelling at Farnborough (£11.00/£14.00)
Broken Wings - Post-War RAF Accidents (in preparation)
Presentation Spitfires and other presentation aircraft (in preparation)

Individual R.A.F. Squadron Histories

With Courage and Faith - No.18 Squadron (£5.00/£7.50)*
United in Effort - No.53 Squadron (£15.00/£19.00)
Scorpions Sting - No.84 Squadron (£11.00/£16.50)
Strike True - No.80 Squadron (£4.00/£6.00)*
Always Prepared - No.207 Squadron (£22.00/£27.50)
The Hornet Strikes - No.213 Squadron (£20.00/£25.00)
Rise from the East - No.247 Squadron (£13.00/£16.50)

Except where out of print (marked *), the above are available from Air-Britain Sales Department, 19 Kent Rd, Grays, Essex RM17 6DE. Visa, Mastercard,Delta/Visa, Switch accepted with number and expiry date, also issue date in the case of Switch.